Security Rights in Movable Property in European Private Law

For every transnational lawyer, it is vital to know the differences between national secured transactions laws. Since the applicable law is determined by the place where the collateral is situated, it may change when movables are brought from one state to another. Introductory essays from comparative lawyers set the scene. The book then presents a survey of the law relating to secured transactions in the member states of the European Union. Following the Common Core approach, the national reports are centred around fifteen hypothetical cases dealing with the most important issues of secured transactions law, such as the creation of security rights in different business situations, the relationship between debtor and secured creditor, the nature of the creditor's rights and their enforcement as against third parties. Each case is followed by a comparative summary. A general report evaluates the possibilities of European harmonisation in the field of secured transactions law.

EVA-MARIA KIENINGER is Professor of German and European Private Law and Private International Law at the University of Würzburg, Germany.

CONTRIBUTORS

Steven Bartels, Michael Bridge, Albina Candian, K. Christodoulou, Frédérique Dahan, Eric Dirix, Georg Graf, Michele Graziadei, George L. Gretton, Torgny Håstad, Jona Israël, Leena Kartio, Eva-Maria Kieninger, Luís Menezes Leitão, Gerard McCormack, Cornelius G. van der Merwe, Hans Viggo Godsk Pedersen, Elisabeth Poulou, Josep Santdiumenge, Harry C. Sigman, John Simpson, Jan Smits, Matthias E. Storme, Jarmo Tuomisto, Willem Zwalve.

The Common Core of European Private Law

General Editors
Mauro Bussani, University of Trieste
Ugo Mattei, University of Turin and University of California, Hastings College of Law

Honorary Editor
Rodolfo Sacco, University of Turin

Late Honorary Editor
Rudolf B. Schlesinger, Cornell University and University of California, Hastings College of Law

Editorial Board
James Gordley, Cecil Turner Professor of Law, University of California, Berkeley; Editor in Chief of the American Journal of Comparative Law
Antonio Gambaro, Professor of Law, University of Milano; President of the Italian Society of Comparative Law
Franz Werro, University of Freiburg and Georgetown University Law Center
Rodolfo Sacco, President of the International Association of Legal Science (UNESCO)

For the transnational lawyer the present European situation is equivalent to that of a traveller compelled to cross legal Europe using a number of different local maps. To assist lawyers in the journey beyond their own locality *The Common Core of European Private Law Project* was launched in 1993 at the University of Trento under the auspices of the late Professor Rudolf B. Schlesinger. This is its fourth completed book.

The aim of this collective scholarly enterprise is to unearth what is already common to the legal systems of European Union member states. Case studies widely circulated and discussed between lawyers of different traditions are employed to draw at least the main lines of a reliable map of the law of Europe.

Books in the Series

Mistake, Fraud and Duties to Inform in European Contract Law
Edited by Ruth Sefton-Green
0 521 84423 1 Hardback

Security Rights in Movable Property in European Private Law
Edited by Eva-Maria Kieninger
0 521 83967 X Hardback

Pure Economic Loss in Europe
Edited by Mauro Bussani and Vernon Valentine Palmer
0 521 82464 8 Hardback

The Enforceability of Promises in European Contract Law
Edited by James Gordley
0 521 79021 2 Hardback

Good Faith in European Contract Law
Edited by Reinhard Zimmermann and Simon Whittaker
0 521 77190 0 Hardback

Security Rights in Movable Property in European Private Law

Edited by
Eva-Maria Kieninger

With the assistance of
Michele Graziadei
George L. Gretton
Cornelius G. van der Merwe
Matthias E. Storme

CAMBRIDGE UNIVERSITY PRESS
Cambridge, New York, Melbourne, Madrid, Cape Town, Singapore, São Paulo

Cambridge University Press
The Edinburgh Building, Cambridge CB2 8RU, UK

Published in the United States of America by Cambridge University Press, New York

www.cambridge.org
Information on this title: www.cambridge.org/9780521839679

© Cambridge University Press 2004

This publication is in copyright. Subject to statutory exception
and to the provisions of relevant collective licensing agreements,
no reproduction of any part may take place without the written
permission of Cambridge University Press.

First published 2004

A catalogue record for this publication is available from the British Library

ISBN 978-0-521-83967-9 hardback

Transferred to digital printing 2007

The publisher has used its best endeavors to ensure that the URLs for external websites referred to in this publication are correct and active at the time of going to press. However, the publisher has no responsibility for the websites and can make no guarantee that a site will remain live or that the content is or will remain appropriate.

Contents

General editors' preface	page xi
Preface	xiii
List of contributors	xv
Table of cases cited by name	xvii
Table of legislation	xxii

Part I Introduction and context

	List of abbreviations	3
1	Introduction: security rights in movable property within the common market and the approach of the study EVA-MARIA KIENINGER	6
2	A labyrinth of creditors: a short introduction to the history of security interests in goods WILLEM J. ZWALVE	38
3	Security in movables in the United States – Uniform Commercial Code Article 9: a basis for comparison HARRY C. SIGMAN	54
4	The English law of security: creditor-friendly but unreformed MICHAEL BRIDGE	81
5	The European Bank for Reconstruction and Development's Secured Transactions Project: a model law and ten core principles for a modern secured transactions law in countries of Central and Eastern Europe (and elsewhere!) FRÉDÉRIQUE DAHAN AND JOHN SIMPSON	98

Part II The case studies

List of abbreviations	117
Bibliographies	128
Glossary	150

Case 1: Furniture for a new office — 171
Transfer of ownership – general effects of insolvency on property – statutory rights of unpaid seller – resolutive clause – goods in transit
- Discussions — 171
- Comparative observations — 222

Case 2: The deceived seller — 230
Transfer of property – effect of fraud – effects of execution on property law questions
- Discussions — 230
- Comparative observations — 243

Case 3: Machinery supplied to be used by the buyer — 246
Simple retention of title
- Discussions — 246
- Comparative observations — 282

Case 4: Jackets for resale — 287
Simple retention of title – entitlement to resell
- Discussions — 287
- Comparative observations — 298

Case 5: Motor cars supplied and resold (I) — 301
Protection of bona fide purchaser – retention of title and resale – consignment – special legislation
- Discussions — 302
- Comparative observations — 343

Case 6: Motor cars supplied and resold (II) — 351
Retention of title and resale – claim arising out of sub-sale still existing
- Discussions — 351
- Comparative observations — 362

Case 7: Supply of material to manufacturer (I) — 365
Retention of title and products clause – property effects of manufacturing

Discussions	366
Comparative observations	394

Case 8: Supply of material to manufacturer (II) — 398
Retention of title – sale of manufactured products – combined products and proceeds clause

Discussions	398
Comparative observations	414

Case 9: Too many toasters — 417
All-monies/sums clause – effects of commingling on retention of title

Discussions	418
Comparative observations	434

Case 10: Bank loan on the basis of a car fleet — 438
Security ownership – sale and lease-back – other non-possessory security rights in individualised movables

Discussions	438
Comparative observations	473

Case 11: Bank loan for a wholesaler — 480
Security right in revolving stock-in-trade – security ownership – enterprise charge – actio Pauliana

Discussions	481
Comparative observations	525

Case 12: Bank loan on the basis of money claims (I) — 531
Security assignment of claims in respect of an identified debtor – distinction between present and future claims – dependence of the secured creditor's rights on communication of the security right to the debitor cessus

Discussions	532
Comparative observations	568

Case 13: Bank loan on the basis of money claims (II) — 573
Security right to a claim against a debtor whose identity is unknown at the time the security right is created – rights of the secured party in execution

Discussions	574
Comparative observations	592

Case 14: Finance leasing of computers	595
Finance leasing – lessor's and lessee's rights in insolvency of the other partner – effects of purchase option	
Discussions	595
Comparative observations	619
Case 15: Indebted businessman sells business to brother	623
Liability of purchaser of a business for pre-existing debts – actio Pauliana	
Discussions	623
Comparative observations	644
Evaluation: a common core? Convergences, subsisting differences and possible ways for harmonisation EVA-MARIA KIENINGER	647
Index by country	674
Index by subject	738

General editors' preface

This is the fourth book in the series *The Common Core of European Private Law*. The *Common Core of European Private Law* Project was launched in 1993 at the University of Trento under the auspices of the late Professor Rudolf B. Schlesinger. The methodology used in the Trento project is novel. By making use of case studies it goes beyond mere description to detailed inquiry into how most European Union legal systems resolve specific legal questions in practice, and to thorough comparison between those systems. It is our hope that these volumes will provide scholars with a valuable tool for research in comparative law and in their own national legal systems. The collection of materials that the Common Core Project is offering to the scholarly community is already quite extensive and will become even more so when more volumes are published. The availability of materials attempting a genuine analysis of how things are is, in our opinion, a prerequisite for an intelligent and critical discussion on how they should be. Perhaps in the future European private law will be authoritatively restated or even codified. The analytical work carried on today by the almost 200 scholars involved in the *Common Core Project* is a precious asset of knowledge and legitimization for any such normative enterprise.

We must thank the editors and contributors to these first published results. With a sense of deep gratitude we also wish to recall our late Honorary Editor, Professor Rudolf B. Schlesinger. We are sad that we have not been able to present him with the results of a project in which he believed so firmly. No scholarly project can survive without committed sponsors. The Dipartimento di Scienze Giuridiche of the University of Trento, its past and present directors and its excellent staff must be thanked. The European Commission has partially sponsored some of our past general meetings, having included them in their High

Level Conferences Program. The Italian Ministry of Scientific Research is now also funding the project, having recognized it as a 'research of national interest'. The Istituto Subalpino per l'Analisi e l'Insegnamento del Diritto delle Attività Transnazionali, the University of Torino, the University of Trieste, the Fromm Chair in International and Comparative Law at the University of California and the Hastings College of Law have all contributed to the funding of this project. Last but not least, we must thank all those involved in our ongoing Trento projects in contract law, property, tort and other areas whose results will be the subject of future published volumes. Our home page on the internet is at http://www.jus.unitn.it/dsg/common-core. There you can follow our progress in mapping the common core of European private law.

General Editors:
MAURO BUSSANI (University of Trieste)
UGO MATTEI (University of Turin and University of California, Hastings College of Law)

Honorary Editor:
RUDOLFO SACCO (University of Turin)

Late Honorary Editor:
RUDOLF B. SCHLESINGER (Cornell University and University of California, Hastings)

Editorial Board
James Gordley, Cecil Turner Professor of Law, University of California, Berkeley; Editor in Chief of the American Journal of Comparative Law
Antonio Gambaro, Professor of Law, University of Milano; President of the Italian Society of Comparative Law
   Franz Werro, University of Freiburg and Georgetown University Law Center
   Rodolfo Sacco, President of the International Association of Legal Science (UNESCO)

Preface

The law relating to security rights in movable property is one of the areas where the diversity of national laws is of special practical importance. As a consequence of the universally accepted rule of private international law, the *lex rei sitae*, two or more different laws have to be applied consecutively to a single transaction, if collateral is moved across borders. Because such movement is at the heart of the idea of a Common Market it comes as no surprise that the first project which emerged from the property law group of the Common Core was dedicated to security rights in movables.

Like all volumes in this series, this book is truly a collective scholarly enterprise. I am grateful to all contributors who prepared their reports and essays and discussed them at various annual meetings in Trento. Three of them, Michele Graziadei, George Gretton and Cornelius van der Merwe, were of special assistance in compiling the reports, drafting the comparative observations and finding a common terminology. Special thanks are due to Matthias Storme, who drafted the first version of the questionnaire and acted as editor in the beginning.

The editor and those contributors who are not native English speakers owe a great debt of gratitude to Alec Brown of the English Bar, who corrected the style of the texts. Without his dedication and diligence, the book might not have seen the light of day. All remaining errors are, however, the respective authors' responsibility. We are also especially grateful to Karin Linhart, Jenny Grimm and Olaf Beller, assistants at the University of Würzburg, who corrected the footnotes and compiled the bibliographies and lists of abbreviations.

Finally, I would like to thank the general editors of the series, Mauro Bussani and Ugo Mattei, for initiating the Common Core project and for providing excellent facilities and an amiable atmosphere at the general meetings in Trento. Thanks are also due to the research network 'Uniform Terminology for European Private Law' co-ordinated by Gianmaria Ajani at the University of Turin for financing part of the research work for this book.

EVA-MARIA KIENINGER
Würzburg, October 2003

Contributors

STEVEN BARTELS, senior lecturer in private law at Nijmegen University (Dutch report)

MICHAEL BRIDGE, Professor of Commercial Law and Dean of the Faculty of Laws at University College London (English report)

ALBINA CANDIAN, Professor of Comparative Private Law at the University of Milan (Italian report for cases 11–15)

K. CHRISTODOULOU, lecturer at the Faculty of Law, University of Athens (Greek report)

FRÉDÉRIQUE DAHAN, lecturer in law, University of Essex, UK, Counsel, European Bank for Reconstruction and Development, Secured Transactions Project (French report)

ERIC DIRIX, Justice in the Supreme Court of Belgium (*Cour de cassation*) and Professor of Insolvency Law at the University of Leuven (Belgian report)

GEORG GRAF, Professor of Private Law at the University of Salzburg (Austrian report)

MICHELE GRAZIADEI, Professor of Comparative Private Law at the Università del Piemonte orientale 'Amedeo Avogadio' (Italian report for cases 1–10)

GEORGE L. GRETTON, Lord President Reid Professor of Law at the University of Edinburgh

TORGNY HÅSTAD, Justice in the Supreme Court of Sweden (Swedish report)

JONA ISRAËL, lecturer in commercial and insolvency law at Maastricht University (Dutch report)

LEENA KARTIO, Professor of Civil Law at the University of Turku (Finnish report)

EVA-MARIA KIENINGER, Professor of German and European Private Law and Private International Law at the University of Würzburg, Germany (German report, Comparative observations)

LUÍS MENEZES LEITÃO, Professor of the Law Faculty, University of Lisbon (Portuguese report)

GERARD McCORMACK, Professor of Law, University of Manchester (Irish report)

CORNELIUS G. VAN DER MERWE, Professor of Civil Law at the University of Aberdeen (South African report)

HANS VIGGO GODSK PEDERSEN, Professor of Law, University of Southern Denmark (Danish report)

ELISABETH POULOU, scientific assistant at the Faculty of Law, University of Athens (Greek report)

JOSEP SANTDIUMENGE, Titular Professor of Civil Law at the University Pompeu Fabra of Barcelona (Spanish report)

HARRY C. SIGMAN, California attorney who has taught at law schools in Europe and California, and was a member of the Drafting Committee that produced Revised UCC Article 9

JOHN SIMPSON, Secured Transactions Project Leader, European Bank for Reconstruction and Development

JAN SMITS, Professor of European Private Law at Maastricht University (Dutch report)

MATTHIAS E. STORME, Professor of Comparative Law and Belgian and European Private Law at the Catholic University of Leuven and the University of Antwerp

JARMO TUOMISTO, Professor of Civil Law at the University of Turku (Finnish report)

WILLEM ZWALVE, Professor at the University of Leiden

Table of cases cited by name

England

Abbey National Building Society v Cann [1990] 1 All ER 1085 270–271
Agnew v Commissioner of Inland Revenue [2001] 2 BCLC 108 89–90
Aluminium Industrie Vaassen BV v Romalpa Aluminium Ltd [1976]
   1 WLR 676 329–330, 347–348, 383–384, 396–397
Re Andrabell Ltd [1984] 3 All ER 407 329
Re Anglo-Moravian Hungarian Junction Railway Co. [1875] 1 Ch 130
   461–462
Appleby v Myers [1867] LR 2 CP 651 382–383
Re Armagh Shoes Ltd [1984] BCLC 405 (NI) 89–90
Re Atlantic Computer Systems plc [1992] Ch 505 89–90
Re Atlantic Medical Ltd [1992] BCC 653 89–90
Re Automatic Bottle Makers Ltd [1926] 1 Ch 412 326
Bank of Baroda v Panessar [1987] Ch 335 94
Bluston & Bramley Ltd v Leigh [1950] 2 KB 548 239–240
Re Bond Worth Ltd [1980] Ch 288 270–271, 326
Borden v Scottish Timber Products Ltd [1981] Ch 25 383–384
Brandt's Sons & Co. v Dunlop Rubber Co. [1905] AC 454 555–556
Re Brightlife Ltd [1987] Ch 200 89–90
British Eagle International Airlines Ltd v Cie National Air France [1975]
   1 WLR 758 84–85
Chaigley Farms Ltd v Crawford Kaye & Grayshire Ltd [1996] BCC 957 382
Re Charge Card Services Ltd 329
Clayton's Case [1816] 1 Mer 572 509
Clough Mill Ltd v Martin [1985] 1 WLR 111 294, 383–384, 427
The Colorado 17
Re a Company (No 005009 of 1987) [1989] BCLC 13 89–90

Re Connolly Bros. Ltd (No 2) [1912] 2 Ch 25 91, 270–271
Re Cosslett (Contractors) Ltd [1998] Ch 495 87
Re Croftbell Ltd 89–90
Re Curtain Dream plc [1990] BCLC 925 460–461
Du Jardin v Beadman Bros. [1952] 2 QB 712 326–327
E Pfeiffer Weinkellerei-Weineinkauf GmbH v Arbuthnot Factors Ltd [1988] 1 WLR 150 329
Re Eastgate [1905] 1 KB 465 239, 508
Evans v Rival Granite Quarries [1910] 2 KB 979 383, 459–460
Forthright Finance Ltd v Carlyle Finance Ltd [1997] 4 All ER 90 611
Re Goldcorp Exchange Ltd [1995] 1 AC 74 329
Gorringe v Irwell India Rubber Works [1886] 34 Ch 128 556–557
Re Hamilton's Windsor Ironworks [1879] 12 Ch 707 326
Helby v Matthews [1895] AC 471 87
Hendy Lennox Ltd v Grahame Puttick Ltd [1984] 2 All ER 152 382–383
Re Highway Foods International Ltd [1995] BCC 271 358–359
Hughes v Pump House Hotel Co. [1902] 2 KB 190 556
Ian Chisholm Textiles Ltd v Griffiths [1994] BCC 96 387–388
Jennings' Trustee v King [1952] 2 All ER 608 610–611
Re Lind [1915] 2 Ch 345 586
Lunn v Thornton [1845] 1 CB 375 458–459
Mace Builders (Glasgow) Ltd v Lunn [1987] Ch 191 92
Re Mace Builders (Glasgow) Ltd [1985] BCLC 154 509
McEntire v Crossley Brothers [1895] AC 457 87, 239, 508
Madell v Thomas [1891] 2 QB 230 239, 508
Manchester, Sheffield & Lincolnshire Railway v North Central Wagon Co. [1988] 13 App Cas 554 461–462
Re MC Bacon Ltd 86–87, 328
Modelboard Ltd v Outer Box Ltd [1993] BCLC 623 332–333, 385–386
National Mercantile Bank v Hampson [1880] 5 QB 177 326
Re New Bullas Trading Ltd [1994] 1 BCLC 485 89–90
Newton's of Wembley Ltd v Williams [1965] 1 QB 560 326–327
Re Opera Ltd [1891] 3 Ch 360 239–240
Pacific Motor Auctions Pty Ltd v Motor Credits Ltd [1965] AC 867 460–461
Re Panama, New Zealand and Australia Royal Mail Co. (1870) 5 Ch App 318 87
Re Peachdart Ltd [1984] Ch 131 85–86, 382, 385–386

Re Permanent Houses (Holdings) Ltd [1988] BCLC 563 89–90
Power v Sharp Investments Ltd [1994] 1 BCLC 111 328, 509
Redgrave v Hurd [1881] 20 Ch D 1 239
Royal Trust Bank v National Westminster Bank plc [1996] BCC 613 89–90
RV Ward Ltd v Bignall [1967] 1 QB 534 207 n.115, 210–211
Shaw v. Commissioner of Police of the Metropolis [1987] 3 All ER 405 358–359
Siebe Gorman v Barclays Bank [1979] 2 Lloyd's Rep 142 89–90
Smith v. Land and House Property Corp'n [1884] 28 Ch D 7 238–239
Spice Girls Ltd v Aprilia World Service BV 238–239
Re Standard Manufacturing Co. [1891] 1 Ch 627 383, 460
Standing v Bowring [1985] 31 Ch 282 239–240, 556–557
Tailby v Official Receiver [1885] 13 App Cas 523 329, 458–459, 555–556, 585–586
Taunton v Sheriff of Warwickshire [1895] 2 Ch 319 239–240
Taylor v M'Keand [1880] 5 CP 358 326
Transag Haulage Ltd v Leyland DAF Finance plc [1994] BCC 356 610–611
Welsh Development Council v Export Finance Guarantee Co. Ltd [1992] BCC 270 87
Re Westover 556
Wheatley v Silkstone and Haigh Moore Colliery Co. (1885) 29 Ch 715 326
Whiteley v Hilt [1918] 2 KB 808 610–611
Wilson v Kelland [1910] 2 Ch 306 92
Re Yeovil Glove Co. Ltd [1965] Ch 148 509

Ireland

Carroll Group Distributors Ltd v Bourke [1990] ILRM 285; [1990] 1 IR 481 330–332
Frigoscandia (Contracting) Ltd v Continental Irish Meat Ltd [1982] ILRM 396 273–274, 428
Re George Inglefield Ltd [1933] Ch 1 332
International Banking Corporation v Ferguson Shaw and Sons [1910] SC 182 385
Re Interview Ltd [1975] IR 382 359–360, 428–429
Kruppstahl AG v Quiltmann Products Ltd [1982] ILRM 551 386, 388

Somers v James Allen (Ireland) Ltd [1985] IR 340   386
Re Stokes & McKiernan Ltd   330–331
Sugar Distributors Ltd v Monaghan Cash and Carry Ltd [1982] ILRM 399   273–274, 330–331
Re WJ Hickey Ltd [1988] IR 126   331–332

Netherlands

Connection Technology BV NJ 1996, 471   554
Stichting Spaarbank Rivierenland/Gispen q.q. NJ 1995, 447   583–584

New Zealand

New Zealand Forest Products v Pogakawa Sawmill Ltd [1991] NZCLC 67   385–386

Scotland

Armour v Thyssen Edelstahlwerke AG 1986 SLT 94, 1989 SLT 182, 1990 SLT 891, [1991] 2 AC 339, [1990] 3 AUER 481   14–15, 385–386, 388, 428–429, 430, 435, 648–649
Carse v Coppen 1951 SC 233, 1951 SLT 145   512
Clark Taylor & Co. v Quality Site Development (Edinburgh) Ltd 1981 SC 111   334, 410
Libertas-Kommer v Johnson 1977 SC 191   559
Sharpe v Thompson 1997 SLT 636   526
Tay Valley Joinery Ltd v C F Financial Services Ltd 1987 SLT 207   560

South Africa

Cullinan v Noordkaaplandse Aantappelkernmoerkwekers Kooperasie Bpk 1972 1 SA 761 (A)   336
Delport v Strydom 1977 3 SA 325 (O)   516
Fernhalls v Ebrahim   640
Konstanz Properties (Pty) Ltd v Wm Spilhaus en Kie (WP) Bpk 1996 SA 362 (A)   390
Lisbon and SA Ltd v The Master 1987 1 SA 276 (A)   560
Macdonald Ltd v Radin NO and the Potchefstroom Dairies & Industries Co. Ltd 1915 AD 454   390

NedcorBank Ltd v Absa Bank Ltd 1998 2 SA 830 (W)   514–515, 516
Quenty's Motors (Pty) Ltd v Standard Credit Corporation Ltd 1994 3 SA 188 (A)   335
Vasco Dry Cleaners v Twycross 1979 1 SA 629 (A)   516, 639

United States of America

Benedict v Ratner [1925] 268 US 353   87

Table of legislation

Austria

Avoidance Act (*Anfechtungsordnung*)

2	487
2(a)	625–626
2(b)	626
3	487

Civil Code (ABGB)

9	418
297a	252–253
366	308
367	307–309
371	308
380	174–175
416	369
423	174–175
426	175–176
427	175–176
428	175–176
429	175–176, 178
452	310
871	178 n.31
874	232
879(1)	486
918	177, 251
1052	176 n.24
1063	176, 252
1090 ff.	597–598

1395	535
1409	625
1409(2)	625
1409(3)	625
1431	232
1811	175

Commercial Code (4 EVHGB)

8/21	177
25	625, 645

Consumer Protection Act 598 n.10
Execution Act (*Exekutionsordnung*) (EO) 37
Insolvency Code (*Konkursordnung*) (KO)

1(1)	177
11	251–252
12	487
21	598
21(1)	177, 251–252
24(1)	598
28(a)	486
28(b)	487
28 N 4	625–626
29	487
30(1) N 1	487–488
30(1) N 3	487
31	487–488
45	178
46(1) N 6	535

Belgium

Act of 25 Oct. 1919 (*nantissement de fonds de commerce*) 493

2	493

Bankruptcy Act

12	494–495
16	187
17(3)	494–495
20	494–495
101	187, 260, 374, 422

xxiv TABLE OF LEGISLATION

	103	602
	104	189
Civil Code (C.civ)		
	570	374
	1138	186–187
	1141	71–72, 186–187
	1167	494–495, 629–630
	1184	188–189
	1321	629–630
	1583	186
	1612	187–188
	1690(2)	346–347
	1690 ff.	542–543, 649–650
	2075	543, 578
	2078	79
	2279	71–72, 186–187, 234–235, 259–260, 315, 374–375, 474, 629
Commercial Code, Title VII, 14		189
Judicial Code, 1514		259–260, 629
Law of 6 July 1994		55, 346 n.150
Mortgage Act		
	7	404
	20, 5°	187–189
	20, 7°	189
Royal Decree of 10 Nov. 1967		601
	1(1)	449
Warrant Act 1862		493

Denmark

Bankruptcy Act		
	61	615
	64	641
	70	518–519
	74	518–519, 641
	85	468–469
	91	469 n.106

Bonds Act, 31   563, 589
Credit Agreements Act
    21   216
    50   217
    Part 10   278–279
Kommisionsloven
    54   337
    57   361
    58   361
Registration of Property Act as amended 1992/1994
    37   468, 517
    42(d) (2)   279, 338, 467
    47(a)   517
    47(b)   517
    47(2)(b)   468
Sale of Goods Act
    28(2)   216
    39–41   217
Tinglysningsloven, 42(d)   337

England

Bankruptcy Act 1914   636 n.31
Bills of Sale Acts 1878 ff.   51–52, 85, 228, 346–347, 508, 556

Companies Act 1985
    196   84–85
    395   92–93, 228, 460–461, 556
    395–396   85–86, 270–271
    396   556
Contracts (Rights of Third Parties) Act 1999   85 n.15
County Courts Act 1984, 98   270
Factors Act 1889, 9   358–359
Hire Purchase Act 1964   610–611
Insolvency Act 1986   327
    8(3)   88
    10–11   88

xxvi   TABLE OF LEGISLATION

15	88
29(2)	88–89
40	84–85, 459, 508
94	91
107	84–85, 508
115	508
127	326–327
156	508
175	84–85, 459, 508
175(2)(a)	508
178	461–462, 611
183(3)(a)	239–240
238	328
240	328
245	328, 509
315	461–462
328	84–85
328(2)	508
339	328, 636
341	328, 636
342	636
344	556
386	84–85, 459–460
423	636
425	636
Schedule 6	84–85, 459–460
Schedule 8, para. 17	508
Schedule 9, para. 22	508
Insolvency Rules	
4.218–20	508
4.95–9	508
6.202	508
6.224	508
12.2	508
Law of Property Act 1925	
94	87 n.22, 328
136	555–556
205	87 n.22
Law of Property (Miscellaneous Provisions) Act 1989	206

Misrepresentation Act 1967, 2(1)	238 n.38
Sale of Goods Act 1979	204–207
17–19	426–427
19	271–272, 648–649
19(1)	272
24	460–461
25	326, 345, 358–359, 610–611
45(3)	207
83 ff.	205
Sale of Goods (Amendment) Act 1995	205 n.112, 208–209
Supreme Court Act 1981	
138(1)	239–240
138B	270

Finland

Aircraft Mortgage Act (*laki aluskiinnityksesta ilma-aluksiin/lag om inteckning i luftfartyg*)	472
Book-entry Accounts Act (*laki arvo-osuustileista/lag om vardeandelskonton*) (ATL) 1991	220
Book-entry System Act (*laki arvo-osuujarjestelmasta/lag om vardeandekssystemet*) (AJL) 1991	220
Commercial Code (*kauppalalki/köplag*)	522
Companies Act (*osakeyhtiölaki/lag om aktiebolag*) (OYL) 1978, chapter 3, s 9	220
Consumer Protection Act (*kuluttajansuojalaki/knosumentskyddslag*)	281
Enterprise Charge Act (*laki takaisinsaannista*	
Enterprise Charge Act (*laki takaisinsaannista konkursipesaan/lag om atervinning till konkursbo*)	522–523
Instalment Sales Act (*laki osamaksukaupasta/lag om avbetalningsköp*)	281, 283, 618
Promissory Notes Act (*velkakirjalaki/lag om skuldebrev*) (VKL) 1947	
22	220
31	220, 567–568

xxviii   TABLE OF LEGISLATION

Rearrangement of Private Person's Debts Act
(laki yksityishenkilön velkajarjestelysta/lag om
skuldsanering för privatpersoner) (VJL) 1993   219–220
Recovery to Bankrupt's Estate Act (laki
takaisinsaannista konkursipesaan/lag om atervinning
till konkursbo)
    3   523–524
    5   524
    14   523–524
Reorganisation of Enterprise Act (laki yrityksen
saneerauksesta/lag om företagssanering) (YrKiinL)
1984   219–220
Sale of Goods Act (kauppalaki/köplag) (KL) 1987
    54   221
    61   221–222
    63   222
Vehicle Mortgage Act (autokiinnityslaki/lag om
inteckning i bil)   472
Vessel Mortgage Act (aluskiinnityslaki/lag om
inteckning i fartyg)   472

France

Code civil 1804
    2017–2072   47
    2076   47
Code civil
    570   373–374
    1116   233
    1117   233
    1129
    1138   181
    1141   313
    1167   627–629
    1183   184, 223
    1184   184
    1583   181, 223, 226–227
    1593   371–372
    1612   182 n.39
    1689 ff.   538–541
    1690   19 n.73, 315,
                                                    538–539, 649

1691	538–539
1804	50
1993	313–314
2102	182 n.39, 185–186, 233
2279	234, 315 n.68, 344–345, 652–653
2279(1)	288–289, 313
2280	234
Commercial Code (C. com)	11, 652–653
L. 521-1 ff.	447
L. 521-3	600–601
L. 611.1-L. 628.3	255
L. 621-1	183, 492–493
L. 621-6	183
L. 621-7	183, 492–493
L. 621-24	186, 209, 355
L. 621-28	184, 448
L. 621-32	256 n.48, 374
L. 621-39	183
L. 621-40	183
L. 621-43	448
L. 621-46	183, 255–257
L. 621-107	492–493, 540
L. 621-107(4)	540
L. 621-107(6)	540
L. 621-108	540
L. 621-115	183, 255–257
L. 621-116	259, 448
L. 621-118	184–185
L. 621-122	255–258
L. 621-122(2)	371–372
L. 621-123	402
L. 621-123(3)	373, 420–421, 436
L. 621-124	402–404, 420–421
Decree No 72-665 of 4 July 1972	
1–7	259
8	600
9	259

Decree No 92-755 of 31 July 1992 (D.)
    81 ff.   233
    126   234
    128   234
    129   234

Decree-Law of 24 June 1939 (warrant over war material)   491

Execution Law (Law No 91-650 of 9 July 1991 (L.))
    3   233
    44   577
    50   234
    50 ff.   233
    52   234

Insolvency Act (Law No 85-98 of 25 Jan. 1985 as amended). See Commercial Code *above*

Law of 17 March 1909 (*fonds de nantissement*)   491
    9   491–492

Law of 21 April 1932 (warrant over oil products)   491

Law No 66-455 as modified by Ordinance No 837 of 28 Sep. 1967   447
    1   447–448, 600

Law No 81-1 (*Loi Dailly*) of 2 Jan. 1981   57, 538–539, 649, 660–661
    1(3)   576–577
    4   541–542
    5   542

Law No 84-46 of 24 Jan. 1984   649

Loi Dubanchet of 12 May 1980. See Commercial Code *above*

Loi Malingre 1934 as amended by decree No 968 of 30 Sep. 1953   314–315, 447, 477–478

Germany

Avoidance Act (*Gesetz, betreffend die Anfechtung von Rechtshandlungen eines Schuldners außerhalb des Konkursverfahrens*) (AnfG)   624–625
    3(1)   485, 624–625

Bankruptcy Act (*Reichskonkursordnung*) (RKO) 1877
    14   47

Civil Code (BGB)
- 93 n.7 — 248
- 142(1) — 212 n.121
- 185 — 291 n.7, 399
- 185(1) — 287–288
- 305 ff. — 593–594
- 307 (pre-2002) — 418, 441–442, 483–484
- 310 n.1 — 418 n.3
- 407(1) — 306, 532
- 419 (pre-1990) — 644–645
- 441 — 174
- 441(3) — 174
- 449 — 246–247
- 455 — 248–249
- 497 ff. — 50
- 812(1) — 230–231
- 816(1) — 302
- 855 — 174
- 868 — 249–250, 439, 481
- 929 — 172, 230–231, 249–250, 285, 399
- 930 — 249–250, 439
- 931 — 174, 475
- 932(2) — 302, 653
- 932 ff. — 344–345
- 933 — 302
- 935 — 653
- 935(1) — 302, 653
- 935(2) — 302
- 946 — 248
- 950 — 366–368
- 951(1) — 366
- 985 — 247
- 1006(1) — 302, 653
- 1204 ff. — 47, 440–441
- 1205 — 11, 47, 476
- 1205 ff. — 440–441
- 1229 — 441, 657
- 1253 — 11, 47
- 1280 — 11

Civil Procedure Code (ZPO)
    727   624
    729(2)   624
    771   231, 247, 368, 399–400, 439–440, 442, 596
    775 n.2   247, 596
    776   247
    805   368 n.13, 399–400

Commercial Code (HGB)
    25   623, 645
    25(2)   623–624
    441 s 3   174

Consumer Credit Act (*Verbraucherkreditgesetz*)
    3(2) n.1   596

Insolvency Code (InsO) 1999   172 n.5
    1(1)   353
    29(1)   352–353
    47   173, 247, 287–288, 442, 596
    48   304, 351–352, 363, 532
    50   173
    50(1)   352, 368, 400, 439–440
    51 n.1   352, 368, 400
    55 n.2   247
    61   247
    80   172–173
    103   247, 442 n.29, 597
    107(2)   247–248, 442 n.29
    108(1)   597
    112 n.1   442 n.28
    129 ff.   484
    130   484
    131(1)   484
    133(1)   484–485
    138   624–625
    159   352–353
    166(1)   368–369

166(2)	352
166 ff.	368, 400, 439–440, 596–597
169	352–353, 368–369
170(1)	352
171	352, 368–369, 596–597
217 ff.	353
223(2)	353
244(1)	353
270 ff.	172 n.6
455(2)	418–419
Insolvency Code (old) (*Konkursordnung*) (KO)	441 n.19
4(2)	352 n.4
41(1)	484–485
44	174 n.11
48	352 n.4
127(2)	352 n.4
Private International Law Act (EGBGB)	
(1999), 43(1)	16 n.57

Greece

Act of 13 December 1878 (insolvency proceedings, limitation to merchants)	179
Civil Code (*Astikos Kodikas*) (A.K.)	
138	626–627
139	626–627
154	232
178	575–576
179	575–576
184	232–233
239	288, 311, 354, 489
281	446, 575–576
383	180–181
390	180–181
409	489
460	537
461	537
479	626
532	180–181, 253, 488

xxxiv TABLE OF LEGISLATION

730	537
903 ff.	232
904	401, 537
936	370–371, 445, 599
936(3)	626–627
939	627
939–946	626–627
941(1)	626–627
942	626–627
946	490
977	444, 488
977a	179
978	181
984	446
987	446
1034	179, 181, 311, 444
1036	179–180, 232–233, 311
1036 ff.	180
1037	311
1043	180
1058	417–436
1059	417–436
1061	370–371
1094	181, 599
1095	446–447, 599–600
1110–1111	180
1211	535–536
1211–1212	312–313
1213	444–445
1215	180
1237	489, 535–536
1239	446
1247.1	535–536
1247.3	535–537
1248	535–537
1252–1254	536–537
1253	537–538
1253–1254	489, 535–536
1256	535–536

Civil Procedure Code (*Kodikas Politikis Dikonomias*)
(KPolD)
936	253–254, 354–355, 445
939	490

Code of Private Maritime Law (*Kodikas Idiotikou Nautikou Dikaiou*) (KIND), 6 — 313

Commercial Law (1987 Draft) (DCC)
10	313
12	313
23	313
280 ff.	313
287	313

Commercial Law (*Emborikos Nomos*) (EmbN)
537	490
538	490
576	599
645	489, 538
670	181

L. 635/37
2	537, 599
2(1)	179
2(4)	179–180

L. 711/1977	312, 445
L. 722/1977	313

L. 1665/1986 (as amended by L. 2367/1995)
1	445 n.42
4(2)	599
4(3)	599

L. 1905/1990 (as amended by L. 2367/1995), 1(1)	536–537
L. 2184/1920	312
L. 2251/1994	254–255
L. 2844/2000	180
10	180, 254–255, 311, 444–445
12	354
16	312, 489, 650–651
L. 5017/1931	313
L.D. 17 July 1923, 35 ff	536
L.D. 21.11/31.12 1925	312

L.D. 1038/1949   312
L.D. 4001/1959   490
L.D. 4208/1961   312

Ireland

Agricultural Credit Act 1978	510–511
Bills of Sale (Ireland) Act 1879-1883	210, 274, 346–347, 387–388
Companies Act 1963	
99	210, 274, 359–360, 386–387, 510–511
99(2)(c)	359–360
285	511
288	511
Sale of Goods Act 1893	207–211, 273
16	208–209
17	274–275, 428–429
18	207
19	275
19(1)	428–429
25	330
44	211
48(3)	210–211
48(4)	210
Supreme Court of Judicature (Ireland) Act 1877,	
28(6)	557–558

Italy

Banking Law (Law Decree 385 of 1 Sep. as amended by Law Decree 342 of 4 Aug. 1999)	
46	498–500, 501, 581–586, 593
46.5	582 n.20
58	453–454, 582–583
Civil Code 1865, 1882	47
Civil Code (*codice civile*) (c.c.)	
294 n.2	552
456 ff.	198
644	582

922	197
939	197–198, 378 n.40
940	197–198, 378
1153	319–320, 582 n.20
1156	319–320
1162	319–320
1173 ff.	198
1260 ff.	406–407, 550, 581
1264	552, 575–576
1344	424
1376	198, 236, 321–322
1378	198
1441 ff.	236
1445	236–237
1454	200
1456	200
1458	607
1519	198–199
1523	267
1523 ff.	423–424
1523–1524	319
1524	268, 283, 319, 499, 581–582, 605, 658
1525	424
1526	266, 606–607
1556–1558	292–293
1557	292–293
1558	292–293
1703 ff.	291 n.7, 321
1704–1707	291 n.7, 321
1705	357
1706(1)	321–322
1707	292–293, 322, 357, 407–408
1731–1736	291 n.7
2038	407–408
2082	503
2189	453–454
2556	633–634
2560	633–634

2704	268
2741	499–500
2744	378–379, 454, 550, 607–608
2751 *bis*	501, 581–582
2752 ff.	501
2762	10, 267–268
2778	267–268
2784 ff.	499–500
2800	499–500
2810(3)	10
2901	501–502, 503, 634
2914	322, 406–407, 633

Civil Procedure Code (*codice di procedura civile*) (c.p.c.)

545	550–551
619	237, 266, 605
621	605–606

Insolvency Act (Royal Decree No 267 of 16 Mar. 1942) (*legge fallimentare*)

1	503
51	199
53–54	199–200, 500–501
64	501–502
65	503
67	501–504
67(3)	503
72	607
72–83	200–201
73	455–456
74	266
75	201
80.2	455–456
103	200, 266

Law 401 of 24 July 1984 (Parma ham)	500 n.54, 663
Law 52 of 21 Feb. 1991 (assignment of claims by enterprises)	321, 551–552, 581
5.1(b)	551–552
5.1(c)	551–552
7	551–552

Law 108 of 7 March 1996 (usury)   501, 582
Royal Decree 436 of 15 March 1927 (registry of
    motor vehicles)   319, 453–454

Netherlands

Civil Code 1838
- 6.231 ff. — 270
- 670 (charges on bills of lading) — 48
- 1198 — 47
- 1555 — 50

Civil Code (*Burgerlijk Wetboek*) (BW) 1992
- 3:7 — 457–458
- 3:11 — 323–324
- 3:44 — 238
- 3:45 — 506
- 3:46 — 507, 635
- 3:53 — 238
- 3:81 — 325
- 3:82 — 457–458
- 3:84 — 201–202, 204, 323–324, 456, 504, 651–652
- 3:84(3) — 58, 203–204, 396–397, 456, 609 n.36
- 3:86 — 238, 323–324
- 3:90 — 201–202
- 3:92(1) — 268
- 3:92(2) — 12, 381, 425
- 3:94 — 324
- 3:95 — 202 n.95
- 3:97 — 381–382, 504
- 3:98 — 201 n.94, 381–382, 456, 504
- 3:115 — 201–202
- 3:236(2) — 324, 553
- 3:237(1) — 456
- 3:237(3) — 505
- 3:239 — 583–584
- 3:239(1) — 324–325, 553

3:246	584–585
3:246(1)	325, 554
3:246(5)	325, 554
3:255	554–555, 584–585
3:276	635
3:278–9	505
3:284	505
3:287	505
3:292	505
3:326(1)	456
3:329(3)	554
5:14	504 n.61
5:16	379–381
6:40	203
6:40(a)	268–269
6:228	238
6:269	203–221
6:271	203–221
7:9	204, 269
7:39	202
7:44	202–203
7:226 (draft) 920.8–16	458
7A:1576h	58, 608, 609–610
7A: 1576l(2)	458

Civil Procedure Code (*Wetboek van Burgerlijke Rechtsvordering*) (RV)

477	408
478h(1)	408

Insolvency Act (*Faillissementswet*) (Fw)

20	505
23	382, 505, 584
35	584
35(2)	382, 505
37	204, 268–269
42	202, 506–507, 635
47	507
52	408
57	505, 584–585
58	505
63a	202, 268–269, 505
182	505

Political Ordonance 1580   44
Revenue Law (*Invorderingswet*) (Rv)
    21   505
    461a   505–506

Portugal

Bankruptcy Code (*Codigo dos Processos Especiais de Recuperçaõ da Empresa e da Falência*) (CPEREF)

46	450
128	190
146	579
147	190
154	235
155(4)	261, 262, 289, 376, 422
156(a)	496
157	579
158(d)	579
164	191
170	450, 603
201	235
201(c)	544–545
209	495–496

Civil Code (*Codigo Civil*) (C.C.)

240	630
241	602–603
274	544
282	496, 579
290	235
291	235
351	261, 375
405	449–450
408	189–190, 261
409	261
409(2)	261–262, 316
435	189–190
577	544, 578–579
583	544–545, 578–579
583(2)	545
584	579

605	630
606	404–405
609	404–405
610	496, 630
612	630
669	495, 544
669(2)	578–579
678	602–603
679	544, 578–579
684	544–545
685(2)	545
686	449
687	449
688	449
694	449–450, 602–603
880	289, 346
886	190
1301	289
1311 n.1	289
1336	375

Civil Procedure Code (*Codigo de Processo Civil*) (CPC)

856	579
865	495–496

Commercial Code (*Codigo Comerciail*) (C. Com.)

398	495
DL No 29,833 of 17 Aug. 1939	495

DL No 149/95

1	602
9(b)	602
18(b)	602

Unfair Contract Terms Act (*Lei das Clausulas Contratuais Gerais*) (LCCG)

5	262
11	262

Scotland

Bankruptcy (Scotland) Act 1985

34	514

36	513
74	514
Companies Act 1985	512
Companies (Floating Charges) (Scotland) Act 1961	512
Consumer Credit Act 1974	613
192(3)(a)	333–334
Hire Purchase Act 1964	333–334
Insolvency Act 1986	512
242	514
243	513
245	514
Leases Act 1449	613
Sale of Goods Act 1893	46
Sale of Goods Act 1979	211–213, 612
17	211, 276
18	211
25	333–334, 345
44 ff.	213
62(4)	463–464
63(1)(a)	333–334
as *corpus alienum*	276

South Africa

Credit Agreements Act 75 1980	466–467
11	294 n.15
Insolvency Act 24 1936	214–215, 360
30(1)	516–517
34	639–640
83	277
84	277, 614
84(2)	294 n.15
95(1)	214–215
Security by Means of Movable Property Act 57 1993, 1	465, 515

Spain

Civil Code (*Codigo civil*) (CC)	191–192

xliv TABLE OF LEGISLATION

325 ff.	289–290
348.2	264–265
383	376
383/II	376
464	263, 317, 344–345, 652–653
908	290
1111	498, 631–633
1123	196–197
1124	264–265
1221/II	194
1227	263–264, 283
1255	263
1266	235–236
1290-1301	235–236
1292	631–632
1295/I	498
1295/II	498
1295/III	498
1297	631–632
1298	498
1299	632
1445	191
1462/2	191–192
1463	191–192
1473/III	194
1505	196–197
1523–1526	263
1524	263
1526–1535	546
1527	546, 548
1532	547, 579–580
1859	452
1863	47
1872	452 n.62
1911	195
1911–1929	193–196
1915	193
1921 ff.	194–195
1922	196

1922.1	196–197, 262–263, 356, 377–378
1922.2	497
1924–1927	196
1924.3	356–357, 580–581
1926.1	497

Civil Laws, Compilation of Catalonian (*Compilacion de Derecho Civil de Cataluña*) (CDCC)

321	633
322	633
326	452–453

Civil Procedure Act (*Ley de Enjuiciamiento Civil*) (LEC)

63.8	193–196
161.3	405
175.1	546–547
177–183	546–547
250.10–11	192–193
250.11	192
517.4–5	192–193, 603
517.4–5–6	376–377
538 ff.	192–193
557	192–193
594.1	236
595	236, 262–263, 376
699 ff.	603
721 ff.	236
727.3	236, 262–263
1156 ff.	193–196
1186	405
1266 ff.	194–195
1400–1401	262–263
Final Provision 7.2	192–193
Final Provision 7.3	192–193

Commercial Code (*Codigo de Comercio*) (CCO)

10	497
85	263, 317, 356
326.1	191

347	546
348	546
833	193
870 ff.	289–290
878	289–290
908	356
913.1	580–581
1113 ff.	194–195
Constitution (EC) 1978, 38	579–580
Law 1/1999 (factoring)	547–548, 579–580
Supplementary Provision 3	547–548
Law 3/1994 (factoring)	545–546
Law of 16 Dec. 1954 (Chattel Mortgage and Pledge without Removal of Possession) (LHMPSD)	192–193, 451
16.1	192
16.2.a	192
52.2	496–497
53.2	377
57	377, 496–497
59–60	496–497
Law of Sale of Chattels in Instalments (*Ley de Ventas de Bienes Muebles a Plazos*) (LVBMP)	
(Law 28/1998)	10, 283, 356, 376, 451
3.1	263–264
5.1	289–290
6.1	263–264
7	196
7.10	263
7.11	263
10	264–265
15.1	263–264
16.2	192–193
16.5	194, 196
Supplementary Provision 1	451–452
Ley Hipotecaria (LH)	
129.2	452 n.62
131	452 n.62
Possessory Guarantees on Chattels Act (Catalan) (LGP), 14	452 n.62

Reglamento Hipotecario (RH)	
225-235	452 n.62
234-236	452 n.62
Decree 1828/1999	265 n.69
Workers' Statute (*Estatuo de los Trabajadores*) (ET), 32	195

Sweden

Bankruptcy Act	
chapter 3, s 3	218
chapter 4, s 5	521–522, 642
chapter 4, s 6	642
chapter 4, s 10	591
chapter 4, s 12	340, 432, 521–522, 565–566
chapter 8, s 10	566
Bills of Sales Act (*lösöreköpslagen*) 1835	219, 286 n.113, 393, 469–471
Code of Execution	
chapter 4, s 17	218
chapter 14, s 1	242–243
Commercial Agents Act (*lagen om handelsagentur*) 1991, 21	280
Commercial Code 1734	471, 617
chapter 10, s 1	469–470, 519
Commission Agency Act (*kommissionslagen*) 1914	
53	392, 616–617
57	340, 361–362, 412–413
Contracts Act (*lagen om avtal*) 1915 (as amended 1976)	470–471
6	280
30	242
36	280
37	469–470, 566
Employment Act (*lagen om ansallningsskydd*), 6b	641
Enterprise Mortgage Act (*lagen om företagsinteckning*) 1984	340, 469, 519–520

xlviii   TABLE OF LEGISLATION

Entrusted Money Act (*lagen om redovisningsmedel*)	
1944	340, 392–393, 412–413, 567, 616–617
Execution Code	469–470
Good Faith Purchase Act (*godtrosförvarvslagen*)	
1986	339
2	242–243, 469
Hire-Purchase Act (*lagen om avbetalningsköp*)	
(as amended 1953)	432
Land Code (*jordabalken*)	
chapter 2, s 4	392
chapter 9, s 35	471
chapter 12, s 36	641
Promissory Notes Act (*skuldebrevslagen*) 1936	
10	340, 564, 566
27	412
31	340, 564, 566, 567, 641
Reconstruction Act, chapter 2, 2	279
Sale of Goods Act (*köplagen*) 1990	
10	218, 564
41	412
54	217–219, 279
62	218
63	279

PART I · INTRODUCTION AND CONTEXT

Abbreviations

AC	Appeal Cases, Law Reports
All ER	All England Law Reports
BCC	British Company Cases
BCLC	Butterworth's Company Law Cases
BGB	*Bürgerliches Gesetzbuch* (German Civil Code)
BGH	*Bundesgerichtshof* (German Federal Supreme Court)
BGHZ	*Entscheidungen des Bundesgerichtshofs für Zivilsachen* (Decisions of the German Federal Supreme Court in Private Law Matters)
BOE	*Boletín Oficial del Estado* (Official Gazette of the Spanish State)
BW	*Burgerlijk Wetboek* (Dutch Civil Code)
C.	Justinian's Code
Cass.	*Cour de Cassation* (French or Belgian Supreme Court)
Cc	*Code civil* (French or Belgian Civil Code)
C.c.	*Codice civile* (Italian Civil Code), *Código civil* (Spanish or Portuguese Civil Code)
Ch	Law Reports, Chancery Division
Ch App	Chancery Appeals
CMLR	Common Market Law Review (law journal)
Cmnd	Command Paper
D.	Digest
Dalloz	*Dalloz, Recueil hebdomadaire de jurisprudence* (1924–1940)
D.H.	*Dalloz Hebdomadaire*
DZWiR	*Deutsche Zeitschrift für Wirtschaftsrecht* (law journal)
EBRD	European Bank for Reconstruction and Development
EC	European Community
ECJ	European Court of Justice

EEC	European Economic Community
EGBGB	*Einführungsgesetz zum Bürgerlichen Gesetzbuch* (German Introductory Act to the Civil Code)
ER	English Reports
ERPL	European Review of Private Law (law journal)
EU	European Union
ICLQ	International and Comparative Law Quarterly (law journal)
IPRax	*Praxis des Internationalen Privat- und Verfahrensrechts* (law journal)
JCP	*Jurisclasseur périodique* (otherwise known as *La Semaine Juridique*), *édition générale* (law journal)
JZ	*Juristenzeitung* (law journal)
Lloyd's Rep	Lloyd's Law Reports
LQR	Law Quarterly Review (law journal)
McGill LJ	McGill Law Journal
MJ	Maastricht Journal of European and Comparative Law
NI	Northern Ireland
NIPR	*Nederlands Internationaal Privaatrecht* (law journal)
NJ	*Neue Justiz* (law journal) or *Nederlandse Jurisprudentie Uitspraken in burgerlijke en strafzaken* (law reports)
NJW	*Neue Juristische Wochenschrift* (law journal)
OJ	Official Journal
QB	Queen's Bench
RabelsZ	*Rabels Zeitschrift für ausländisches und internationales Privatrecht* (law journal)
Rdn.	*Randnummer* (paragraph)
Req.	*Chambre des requêtes* of the *Cour de Cassation*
Rev.crit.d.i.p.	*Revue critique de droit international privé* (law journal)
Rev. int. dr. comp.	*Revue internationale de droit comparé* (law journal)
RG	*Reichsgericht* (German Imperial Court)
RGZ	*Amtliche Sammlung von Entscheidungen des Reichsgerichts in Zivilsachen* (Collection of decisions of the German Imperial Court in Private Matters)
RIW	*Recht der Internationalen Wirtschaft* (law journal)
RKO	*Reichskonkursordnung* (German Bankruptcy Act of 1877)
RP	*Das römische Privatrecht*
SA	South Africa
Ses. Cas.	Session Cases, House of Lords
STS	*Sentencia Tribunal Supremo* (case decided by the Spanish Supreme Court)

tit.	titulus, titre
UCC	Uniform Commercial Code
UNCITRAL	United Nations Commission on International Trade Law
UNIDROIT	International Institute for the Unification of Private Law
Unif. L. Rev./Rev. dr. unif.	Uniform Law Review/*Revue de droit uniforme* (law journal)
U.Pa.J.Int'l Econ.L.	University of Pennsylvania Journal of International and Economical Law (law journal)
US	United States Report
Ves.Sen.	Vesey Senior's Reports, Chancery
WLR	Weekly Law Reports
WM	*Wertpapiermitteilungen, Zeitschrift für Wirtschafts- und Bankrecht* (law journal)
WPNR	*Weekblad voor Privaatrecht, Notariaat en Registratie* (law journal)
ZEuP	*Zeitschrift für Europäisches Privatrecht* (law journal)
ZIP	*Zeitschrift für Wirtschaftsrecht und Insolvenzpraxis* (law journal)
ZVglRWiss	*Zeitschrift für vergleichende Rechtswissenschaft* (law journal)

1 Introduction: security rights in movable property within the common market and the approach of the study

EVA-MARIA KIENINGER

The topic of 'Security Rights in Movable Property' does not need a long introduction. Earlier comparative studies in this field[1] have shown the divergencies with respect to both principle and the practical outcome of cases. Therefore, and because of the pressing need for some measure of harmonisation, it is not surprising that the Common Core Project has chosen the topic as one of its first sub-projects. The task of exploring in greater detail the similarities and differences between the European

---

[1] See foremost the study by Ulrich Drobnig carried out on behalf of UNCITRAL, published as Report of the Secretary-General: study on security interests (A/CN.9/131) Annex, UNCITRAL Yearbook 1977, part two, II. A. Cf. further Ulrich Drobnig, 'Recht der Kreditsicherheiten', in: Europäisches Parlament, Generaldirektion Wissenschaft (ed.), *Arbeitsdokument: Untersuchung der Privatrechtsordnungen der EU im Hinblick auf Diskriminierungen und die Schaffung eines Europäischen Zivilgesetzbuches*, JURI 103 DE (1999) 59 (70 ff.); Ulrich Drobnig, 'Security Rights in Movables', in: Arthur Hartkamp et al. (eds.), *Towards a European Civil Code* (2nd edn, 1998) 511 ff.; Ulrich Drobnig, ERPL 2003, 623 ff.; Karl Kreuzer (ed.), *Mobiliarsicherheiten – Vielfalt oder Einheit?* (1999); Sixto Sánchez Lorenzo, *Garantías reales en el comercio internacional* (1993); Herbert Stumpf, *Eigentumsvorbehalt und Sicherungsübertragung im Ausland* (4th edn, 1980); Anna Veneziano, *Le garanzie mobiliari non possessorie* (2000); and the series *Recht der Kreditsicherheiten in den europäischen Ländern* edited by Walther Hadding and Uwe Schneider (from 1978). Specifically on retention of title: Eva-Maria Kieninger, *Mobiliarsicherheiten im Europäischen Binnenmarkt* (1996) 41 ff.; Stefan Leible, 'Der Eigentumsvorbehalt bei Warenlieferungen in EU-Staaten', in: *Praxis-Handbuch Export*, Gruppe 6/7, 1 ff.; Theophile Margellos, *La protection du vendeur à crédit d'objets mobiliers corporels à travers la clause de réserve de propriété, Étude de droit comparé* (1989); P. L. Nève, *Eigendomsvoorbehoud*, Nederlandse Vereniging voor Rechtsvergelijking no 60 (2000) 1 (19 ff.); Jacobien W. Rutgers, *International Reservation of Title Clauses* (1999) 13 ff. There are also a large number of studies concentrating on one or two jurisdictions, such as, for example, Stefanie Hellmich, *Kreditsicherungsrechte in der spanischen Mehrrechtsordnung* (2000); Martin Menne, *Die Sicherung des Warenlieferanten durch den Eigentumsvorbehalt im französischen Recht* (1998); and Ulrike Seif, *Der Bestandsschutz besitzloser Mobiliarsicherheiten im deutschen und englischen Recht* (1997).

legal systems in the field of security over movables will be undertaken in Part II of this study. The purpose of the following short introduction is to summarise the economic reasons behind the creation of security interests, to give a short overview of the main divergencies and the problems that are created for international and more specifically for intra-community trade through such divergencies combined with the present rules of private international law, and to outline the previous attempts at harmonisation and unification as well as the main arguments usually advanced against their feasibility (part A). Part B will explain the specific approach of the present study which not only differs from the usual type of comparative investigation but also deviates – albeit to a lesser extent – from other studies within the Common Core Project.

A. A short survey of the status quo

I. Economic reasons for the existence of security rights[2]

Security rights enhance the probability that a creditor will receive repayment of his loan, particularly in the event of insolvency. Usually, the creditor will therefore charge a lower interest rate or might extend credit more readily if the debtor is able to give collateral. Thus, a functioning system of security rights is not only beneficial for creditors but also for debtors, since it lowers the price of borrowing. At the macroeconomic level, this means that the amount of low-cost credit and hence the amount of capital that can be used in productive processes will generally be enhanced through a well-designed law on secured transactions. These functions of security rights have been studied both theoretically and empirically.[3] Yet, the basic recognition of the beneficial functions of security rights is not solely due to the advent of economic analysis, nor is it a modern realisation. As the *Corpus Iuris Civilis* said: '*Pignus utriusque gratia datur, et debitoris, quo magis ei pecunia crederetur, et creditoris, quo magius ei in tuto sit creditum.*'[4]

In fact, all projects for a reform or harmonisation of the law on secured transactions invariably start from the proposition that a

---

[2] The critical remarks on the economic usefulness of security rights rest on a contribution to this chapter by George L. Gretton.
[3] Cf. Röver, *Vergleichende Prinzipien dinglicher Sicherheiten* 105 ff. with multiple references, especially to studies carried out by Heywood Fleisig. See also Saunders/Srinivasan/Walter/Wool, U.Pa.J.Int'l Econ.L. 20 (1999) 309 (310 ff.).
[4] *Justiniani Institutiones* 3,14,4. 'A security is given for the benefit of both parties: of the debtor in that he can borrow more readily, and of the creditor in that his loan is safer.'

well-designed, harmonised or uniform law would enlarge the range of available low-cost credit and would therefore be economically beneficial to trade and industry in the individual jurisdiction or in the area where the harmonisation measure would be applicable.[5] This rests not only on the higher probability that a secured creditor will receive repayment of his loan plus interest but also on the ability of security rights to overcome problems of asymmetric information:[6] debtors are usually in a better position than their creditors to know whether they will be willing and able to meet their obligations. The interest rate as such is not able to signal willingness and ability to pay. Creditors do not know whether acceptance of a higher interest rate rests on the profitability of the undertaking or on the fact that the debtor is prepared to take a greater risk. It is likely that a higher interest rate drives the more trustworthy debtors out of the market, a fact that will be anticipated by creditors. Thus, the amount of available credit may decrease as a consequence of a higher interest rate, although usually the amount of goods offered increases with the price. Security rights may overcome this problem by enabling the creditor to inform himself better about the debtor's creditworthiness.

The present study, which concentrates on the search for a common core among the laws of the EU Member States in the area of secured transactions, is certainly not the place to discuss in any depth the economic justifications for the existence of secured transactions in general.[7] However, it should not be overlooked that there exists also a substantial amount of literature which questions the assumption that security rights are economically beneficial.[8] While it can safely be said that a secured transaction either benefits the two contracting parties or at least does not harm their interests, the picture changes once the interests of other, unsecured creditors are taken into consideration. The central purpose of a security right is to confer on the secured creditor a priority as against other creditors or, as Lynn LoPucki has put it: 'Security is an

---

[5] See most recently 'Security Interests', Note by the UNCITRAL secretariat prepared for the thirty-fourth session, A/CN.9/496, paras. 11 ff. Cf. also the preamble of the draft convention on assignment of receivables in international trade, A/CN.9/486 Annex I; Fleisig, Unif. L. Rev./Rev. dr. unif. (1999) 253.
[6] Cf. Röver, *Vergleichende Prinzipien dinglicher Sicherheiten* 116 f. As to the problem of adverse selection in general, see Akerlof, *Quarterly Journal of Economics* 84 (1970) 488.
[7] As to the necessity of harmonisation, see *infra*, IV.
[8] For an overview, including an extensive bibliography, see Bowers, in: Bouckaert/de Geest, *Encyclopedia of Law and Economics*, vol. II.

agreement between A and B that C take nothing.'⁹ Because of this negative externality, other creditors or potential creditors will naturally react so as to minimise the harm. As Alan Schwartz has written: 'Secured creditors will charge lower interest rates because security reduces their risks, but unsecured creditors will raise their rates because security reduces the assets on which they can levy, and so increases their risks.'[10] Hence, in his opinion, debtors will not make an overall net gain from security. Some authors have gone even further, and have argued that security does not merely operate to reallocate value from some creditors to others, but is actually sub-optimal in terms of efficiency. Thus John Hudson has argued that banks which can conveniently lend on a secured basis 'will inevitably be led into making loans that, from the point of view of the economy as a whole, cannot be justified and result in a misallocation of resources'.[11]

As stated earlier, this book and its introduction do not seek to advance this debate. Yet an awareness of the detrimental effects which secured transactions might arguably have on unsecured creditors is helpful for understanding the restrictions that presently exist in Member States' laws. For any future European legislation, it will no doubt be essential to get a clear picture of the economic advantages and possible disadvantages of any suggested regime of security rights.

II. Security rights in movable property: main divergencies

The roots of the present heterogeneity go back to the nineteenth century. As explained in greater detail below by Willem Zwalve,[12] at that time the European jurisdictions came to disapprove of the Roman law hypothec and of practices which allowed the establishment of a pledge with only a theoretical or constructive dispossession on the part of the pledgor. The range of available security rights in movables was thus effectively reduced to the possessory pledge. Yet, at the same time, the industrial revolution brought about an enormous increase in the demand for credit in trade and industry, which could not be met solely through security rights *in personam* and rights in immovable property. It goes without saying that the possessory pledge of movables was ill-equipped to meet

---

[9] LoPucki, *Virginia Law Review* 80 (1994) 1887 (1899).
[10] Schwartz, *Vanderbilt Law Review* 37 (1984) 1051.
[11] Hudson, *International Review of Law and Economics* 15 (1995) 47 (61).
[12] See *infra*, chapter 2, Zwalve, 'A labyrinth of creditors: a short introduction to the history of security interests in goods'.

that need because it immobilises the goods which the debtor needs for carrying on his business, be it machines or other equipment, stock-in-trade, raw materials or semi-finished products. One of the reasons for the present divergencies lies in the fact that the jurisdictions in question responded to the same economic imperative to differing extents and by the adoption of different legal models.

In some jurisdictions the legislature stepped in and created special registered security rights, based on the idea of a pledge but where a registration requirement replaced the need for the pledgor to surrender actual possession of the collateral. This route was followed in France where a wide array of special charges was created over the decades. Some of these charges are designed to support certain branches of trade or industry such as, for example, the various *warrants*[13] or the *gage sur véhicule automobile*[14] (the latter introduced to stimulate car sales, when retention of title was still considered to be invalid in circumstances of the buyer's insolvency), or, to take a last and most peculiar example, the *nantissement des cinématographiques*.[15] Other charges are of a wider application, as, for example, the *nantissement de l'outillage et du matériel d'équipement* or the *nantissement de fonds de commerce* under which all equipment, inventory and intangible rights such as patents and trademarks of an enterprise can be used as collateral.[16] In principle, Belgium, Luxembourg, Italy and Spain followed the French example but their respective range of special security rights remained more modest. In Belgium, the two kinds of charges which are perhaps most important in practice are the statutory preference of the unpaid seller (*privilège du vendeur*)[17] and the *nantissement sur fonds de commerce*.[18] Italian law knows a special hypothec over motor vehicles (*privilegio sull'autoveicolo*)[19] and machinery (*privilegio del venditore di macchine*),[20] whereas the Spanish legislature has opted for a more

---

[13] See *infra*, French report, case 11.
[14] See *infra*, French report, case 5(c) on the *Loi Malingre*.
[15] Law of 22 Feb. 1944. See further Fargeaud, *Le gage sans dépossession comme instrument de crédit et le Marché Commun* 71 ff.
[16] See in greater detail *infra*, French report, case 11.
[17] See *infra*, Belgian report, case 1(a). The preference has been extended to all sellers and the former restriction on sellers of machines and similar professional equipment has been abolished. The requirement of registration which likewise existed until 1 Jan. 1998 (the date on which the new Bankruptcy Act entered into force) has been removed as well.
[18] See *infra*, Belgian report, case 11.
[19] See article 2810(3) C.c. and *decreto legge* 15 Mar. 1927, no 436. See further *infra*, Italian report, case 10(a).
[20] Article 2762 C.c. See further *infra*, Italian report, case 3(c).

comprehensive form of hypothec through the Act on non-possessory pledges and hypothecs in movables (*ley sobre prenda sin desplazamiento y hipoteca mobiliaria*).[21] With the recent exception of the Belgian *privilège du vendeur*,[22] all these rights depend – at least for their enforceability as against third parties – on some form of registration. As a consequence, the courts denied in principle the validity or at least the opposability of security rights which were not contemplated by the legislature but created by practice on the basis of ownership, such as, for example, security transfer of ownership and retention of title. Thus, prior to a change in the respective Insolvency Acts in 1980 (France)[23] and 1998 (Belgium),[24] French and Belgian courts held retention of title to be invalid in the buyer's insolvency.[25] The security transfer of ownership is still viewed as 'inopposable' in both jurisdictions,[26] and in Italy[27] and Spain its admissibility is disputed.[28]

In Germany and to a lesser extent in Greece, Austria and the Netherlands, legal developments took a different course. Apart from special registrable charges on ships, airplanes, agricultural inventory and overseas cables,[29] the German legislature did not introduce any non-possessory security rights. Instead, the courts have since various decisions of the *Reichsgericht* in the 1880s[30] accepted security transfer of ownership as valid and enforceable in conflicts with third parties. This case law was upheld after the BGB entered into force,[31] although §§ 1205, 1253 BGB unambiguously state that the constitution of a pledge requires the transfer of actual possession and that the rights of the pledgee terminate upon the return of the collateral. Security assignments of claims were

---

[21] Act of 16 Dec. 1954, BOE no 352 of 18 Dec. 1954. See further Stefanie Hellmich, *Kreditsicherungsrechte in der spanischen Mehrrechtsordnung* 80 ff.
[22] See *supra*, note 17.
[23] *Loi Dubanchet*, loi 80–335 of 12 May 1980. See French report, case 3(a).
[24] See *supra*, note 17.
[25] See for France Cass. 28 Mar. 1934 and 22 Oct. 1934, published together in Dalloz 1934 Jurisprudence 151 (note Vandamme). See for Belgium Cass. 9.2.1933, Pasicrisie 1933, I, 103.
[26] See *infra*, French and Belgian reports, case 10(a).
[27] See *infra*, Italian report, case 7(a). Cf. further Bussani, ERPL 1998, 23 (45) and Kieninger, *Mobiliarsicherheiten im Europäischen Binnenmarkt* 103.
[28] See Hellmich, *Kreditsicherungsrechte in der spanischen Mehrrechtsordnung* 85 ff.
[29] For details see Drobnig, 'Security over Corporeal Movables in Germany', in: J. G. Sauveplanne (ed.), *Security over Corporeal Movables* (1974) 181 at 187 ff.
[30] Cf. RG 9 Oct. 1880, RGZ 2, 168; RG 17 Mar. 1885, RGZ 13, 298 (on the basis of the French *Code civil*); RG 10 Jan. 1885, RGZ 13, 200; RG 2 June 1890, RGZ 26, 180. See also *infra*, chapter 2, Zwalve, 'A labyrinth of creditors', pp. 50 f.
[31] Cf. RG 8 Nov. 1904, RGZ 59, 146. See also *infra*, German report, case 10(a).

also regarded as valid, following the general rules on assignment which require neither any special contractual form nor any notification of the debtor, again despite § 1280 BGB which, for a charge over a claim to be valid and opposable, clearly requires such notification.[32] Out of a combination of retention of title with security transfer of ownership and security assignment, practice developed so-called 'prolonged' (extended) forms of retention of title through which sellers became able to extend their security rights into proceeds of sale and manufactured goods.[33]

Until the introduction of the new Civil Code in 1992, the Dutch regime of security rights was fairly similar to that prevailing in Germany. In two decisions in 1929, the *Hoge Raad* had accepted security transfer of ownership as effective with respect to third parties.[34] Yet, when, after the Second World War, work was started on the new Civil Code, one of the primary concerns of the drafters was to abolish security transfer of ownership and security assignment (now article 3:84(3) BW) and to replace them with a non-possessory pledge (*stil pandrecht*) which, in order to be effective, must be either registered or evidenced by a notarised deed.[35] Retention of title is still valid *erga omnes*, but is now restricted to its simple form. Article 3:92(2) BW expressly provides that it cannot be used to secure debts other than the purchase price for those goods to which title is retained.[36] Austria mirrors German legal developments only to the extent that no special non-possessory security interests have been introduced on a larger scale, but in contrast to their German counterparts, Austrian courts seem to have taken the provisions of the Civil Code restricting security rights in movables to the possessory pledge more seriously. To this day, Austrian law does not recognise the security transfer of ownership[37] and subjects a security assignment of claims to the same requirements that apply to a charge over claims (notification of the *debitor cessus* or entry of the security assignment into the books of the assignor).[38] However, according to the predominant opinion, such requirements can be satisfied even before the claims have come into

---

[32] See in greater detail *infra*, German report, case 5(c)(ii).
[33] See in greater detail *infra*, German report, cases 5 to 8.
[34] *Hoge Raad* 25 Jan. 1929, NJ 1929, 616; *Hoge Raad* 21 June 1929, NJ 1929, 1096.
[35] See *infra*, Dutch report, cases 5(c) and 12(a).
[36] See *infra*, Dutch report, case 9(a). On products and proceeds clauses see *infra*, Dutch report, cases 7(a) and 6(b).
[37] See *infra*, Austrian report, cases 5(c), 7(a) and 11(a).
[38] See *infra*, Austrian report, cases 5(c) and 12(a) and Posch, IPRax 1992, 51 (52 f.); Koziol, DZWiR 1993, 353 (353 f.).

existence, thus providing for a more practicable possibility to use claims as collateral.[39] Greek law follows German developments more closely than the two jurisdictions just mentioned, although details are still disputed. Following the predominant opinion, Greek law accepts both security transfer of ownership[40] and security assignment[41] without submitting them to any publicity requirements. Yet, surprisingly, it was only in the late 1980s that the courts accepted the validity and enforceability of the (simple) retention of title in the buyer's insolvency.[42]

Because the development and main characteristics of English law are more fully explained by Michael Bridge,[43] a few sentences here will suffice. The most outstanding innovation in the field of security rights under English law is the *floating charge* which can be established over all or part of a company's assets. Where lenders in other jurisdictions must resort to different types of rights for different kinds of assets, English law provides a single security device which manifests the further peculiarity that it attaches to individual assets only at the moment of crystallisation. Other security devices include fixed charges and mortgages. Apart from a requirement of registration if the debtor is a company, the freedom of the parties to tailor security rights that best suit their needs (or those of the party with the stronger bargaining power) is practically unlimited. The only creditors that receive a relatively 'raw deal' are sellers under retention of title – they have very little opportunity to extend their security right into proceeds or manufactured products. It is interesting to note a clear difference in policy between English and German law at this point. In the conflict between a moneylender and a seller, in England, the moneylender usually wins, because the registration of a products or proceeds clause is highly impractical. In Germany, on the other hand, the seller will always win, also with respect to proceeds. According to case law, a security assignment of claims is invalid if the agreement between the bank and the debtor under the loan does not exclude claims that would in the normal course of business become assigned to a seller under a proceeds clause.[44]

---

[39] See in detail *infra*, Austrian report, case 5(c). Of course, a notification can only take place when the *debitor cessus* is known.
[40] See *infra*, Greek report, case 10(a); cf. further Eleftheriadou, in: von Bar (ed.), *Sachenrecht in Europa*, vol. III, 74 ff.
[41] See *infra*, Greek report, case 12(a)(ii).   [42] See *infra*, Greek report, case 3(a).
[43] See *infra*, pp. 81 ff.
[44] See most recently BGH 8 Dec. 1998, JZ 1999, 404 (note Kieninger).

From this short and certainly incomplete *tour d'horizon* the following main dividing lines can be extracted.

First of all, the jurisdictions favour different legal models.[45] In some, the possessory pledge has been extended into non-possessory forms, yet retains the basic principles of the original model, such as the principle that the pledgor remains the owner of the collateral and retains the power to dispose of it, subject to the security right if no special rules on *bona fide* acquisition apply. Another principle is that the right of the secured party is limited to a preferential right in the proceeds of sale of the collateral, be it a forced sale carried out by a court official or an extra judicial market sale. Any surplus not needed to pay off the debt is to be handed over to the former debtor. Also, the secured creditor's right to take possession of the collateral is limited to circumstances where this is necessary, either to ensure that the collateral is not disposed of by the debtor, or for the purposes of enforcing the security right through realisation. Another important principle that has been retained from the original possessory model is the principle of publicity. Most jurisdictions that have been covered in the short overview replace the requirement of dispossession on the part of the pledgor with some other means of publicity, usually a registration requirement. Some, however, are content with mere formal requirements. Dutch law, for example, requires no more for the creation of a *stil pandrecht* than either the use of a public document or the registration of a private one in a register which is not open to the public.[46]

The other basic model is the use of ownership for security purposes, be it in the form of a security transfer of ownership, security assignment, retention of title, hire purchase or a leasing contract. With these types of security interest, the parties are frequently given greater autonomy to shape their legal relationship according to their particular needs. Mostly, they are not subject to publicity.[47] Overall, there is a tendency to accept hire-purchase and leasing agreements and even (simple) retention of title without placing these arrangements under the same restrictive conditions applicable to the possessory, or indeed non-possessory, pledge. In these cases, the ownership of the seller or lessor is regarded as full, 'normal' ownership, not as a disguised security right.[48] A transfer

---

[45] Cf. Drobnig, in: Hartkamp, *Towards a European Civil Code* 511 (516 ff.).
[46] See *infra*, Dutch report, case 10(a).
[47] With respect to leasing contracts, see in greater detail *infra*, case 14. In France and Greece, leasing contracts must be registered.
[48] Cf. House of Lords in *Armour and another v Thyssen Edelstahlwerke AG* [1990] 3 All ER 481 (485) (per Lord Keith).

of ownership purely for security purposes, on the other hand, has met with more resistance, probably because it is too clearly a security transaction, not dressed up as any other type of contract, and thus too closely resembles an (invalid) pledge.

This leads to further fundamental differences: first, the principle of publicity, which is common to most jurisdictions (even to German law so far as the possessory pledge is concerned), is enforced to varying degrees. It has already been stated that non-possessory security rights modelled on the pledge are usually subject to registration whereas the title-based security rights are mostly not publicised. Where registration is required, the rules on the administration of such registers, on their accessibility to interested members of the public and those governing entries made on them also vary greatly, not only from country to country but also within individual jurisdictions depending on the type of security right concerned. Frequently there are different registers existing side by side such as, for example, in Spain, the register set up by the law on hypothecs and non-possessory pledges[49] and the one for instalment sales[50] which covers retention of title;[51] or in France, the different registers created for each type of special non-possessory security interest. Evidently such fragmentation does not assist creditors who wish to make themselves aware of existing security rights granted by the debtor in question. In this respect, there is certainly much to be learnt from the filing system of Article 9 UCC which is set out in greater detail in the contribution by Harry Sigman.[52] Another difference that emerges from the above overview lies between general security rights and those which apply only to a limited category of collateral such as vehicles[53] or cinema films[54] and, or alternatively, those which can only secure specific kinds of debts, such as, for example, a debt arising out of a contract of sale as in the case of the Belgian *privilège du vendeur*.[55]

A further dividing line lies between those jurisdictions which adhere to the principle of specificity – thus not permitting security rights to be created over an entity or *corpus* of assets – and those jurisdictions which allow precisely this, such as England where the floating charge was developed. This distinction touches upon even more deeply rooted preconceptions as to what constitutes a real right (and whether that

---

[49] See *supra*, at note 21.   [50] *Ley* 28/1998 of 13 July 1998, BOE no 167 of 14 July 1998.
[51] There are, however, plans to integrate both registers in a new register on movable property: see Hellmich, *Kreditsicherungsrechte in der spanischen Mehrrechtsordnung* 160.
[52] See *infra*, chapter 3, Sigman, 'Security in movables in the United States – Uniform Commercial Code Article 9: a basis for comparison', pp. 54 ff.
[53] See *supra*, at notes 14 and 19.   [54] See *supra*, at note 15.   [55] See *supra*, at note 17.

question has any merits at all). The difficulties which are created when the floating charge is introduced into (or forced upon) a jurisdiction based on Roman law are exemplified in the Scottish report to case 11. Finally, one can perhaps identify a difference in the overall attitude taken towards security rights: there are jurisdictions, like England, Germany or the United States, where the law seeks to provide creditors with more or less unrestricted freedom to contract for the security they think they need, and others, like France or the Nordic countries, which in the interest of general, unsecured creditors try to limit the range of available security.

III. Private international law

1. Tangible movables: *lex rei sitae* and the limits of the doctrine of transposition

The divergencies which have just been mentioned with respect to the substantive rules would create fewer or perhaps even no difficulties for international trade if the parties could choose the applicable law. Yet, the freedom in choice of law which is the rule for contractual obligations (article 3 Rome Convention[56]) does not apply in the field of property law. In the EU Member States, it is the *lex situs* which determines questions of property law with respect to immovables and movables alike;[57] in the United States, Art. 9 UCC submits proprietary security rights in movables to the law at the place of the debtor.[58] The substantial literature which argues in favour of party autonomy[59] has not found a positive response

---

[56] Convention on the law applicable to contractual obligations of 19 June 1980, OJ EC No L 266/1 of 9 Oct. 1980.

[57] Cf. Venturini, *International Encyclopedia of Comparative Law, Vol. III: Private International Law*, chapter 21, 'Property' 3 ff.; Kieninger, ERPL 1996, 41 (47 n. 33); Kreuzer, *Recueil des Cours* 259 (1996) 9 (44 ff., 53 ff. and 253 ff. each with further references). In Germany, the rule was incorporated in article 43(1) EGBGB by the 1999 reform of the act on private international law (EGBGB).

[58] See revised Articles 9s–301 ff. UCC.

[59] In favour of party autonomy which is not limited to the relationship *inter partes*: Gaudemet-Tallon, note Cass. 8 July 1969, JCP 1970 II, 16182; Khairallah, *Les sûretés mobilières en droit international privé* 181 ff. For freedom as to choice of law with limited effects or limited applicability: Chesterman, ICLQ 22 (1973) 213 (223); Drobnig, RabelsZ 32 (1968) 450 (470 f.); Mayer, JCP 1981 I 3019 (para. 14); Mazzoni, in: *Rapports nationaux italiens au Xe Congrès International de Droit Comparé* 245 (277 ff.); Ritterhoff, *Parteiautonomie im internationalen Sachenrecht*; Staudinger/Stoll, *Internationales Sachenrecht* nos 282 ff. and 292 ff.; Stoll, IPRax 2000, 259 (264); Weber, RabelsZ 44 (1980) 510 (524). Cf. further the summaries in Kaufhold, *Internationales und europäisches Mobiliarsicherungsrecht* 159 ff. and Rott, *Vereinheitlichung des Rechts der Mobiliarsicherheiten* 25 ff.

from courts or legislatures. If freedom as to choice of law is granted, as is the case for example in Switzerland,[60] the effects are confined to the relationship *inter partes*.

Applied to security rights in property that moves across borders, the *lex situs* rule leads to what is known as a '*conflit mobile*'.[61] If, for example, a security right is created while the collateral is in State A and if enforcement is sought after the subject matter has been brought to State B, two different sets of property law rules have to be applied consecutively: the creation of the security right is subject to the laws of A but the rights which the secured party has as against competing creditors are to be determined by the laws of B. Evidently, this will lead to problems where the two sets of rules differ. In some instances, these problems may be overcome through the so-called doctrine of transposition. Perhaps the first case where this doctrine has been applied (although not named as such) is *The Colorado* decided by the English Court of Appeal.[62] *The Colorado* had been charged with a French *hypothèque maritime* to a French bank. Later, a shipyard in Cardiff carried out repairs which were not paid for and therefore also claimed a right in the ship. The question arose as to which of these competing rights had priority. The Court applied English law as the law of the actual *situs*. It held that the French *hypothèque maritime* equated more or less to the English maritime lien and that therefore the priority rules of the maritime lien had to be applied. In the end, this placed the French bank in an even better position than it would have been in under French law. Another good illustration of the doctrine of transposition is a case decided by the German *Bundesgerichtshof* in 1963.[63] A van had been charged in France with a *gage sur véhicule* to a French bank. When in Germany, the vehicle was seized in execution proceedings on behalf of a third-party creditor. The question was whether the *gage sur véhicule* gave the bank a right to preferential treatment under German execution law. The court held that although German law had to be applied after the change of the *situs*, it was nevertheless necessary to take previously established property rights into

---

[60] See article 104 s. 2 Swiss Act on private international law (*Bundesgesetz über das Internationale Privatrecht* of 18 Dec. 1987, in force since 1 Jan. 1989, Bundesblatt 1988 I, 5–60).
[61] See in general Kreuzer, *Recueil des Cours* 259 (1996) 9 (56 ff.).   [62] [1923] All ER 531.
[63] BGH 20 Mar. 1963, BGHZ 39, 173. In that decision the Court did not expressly use the term 'transposition' although the judges did refer to Hans Lewald, who had developed the theory in his *Cours Général* at the Hague Academy: cf. Lewald, *Recueil des Cours* 69 (1939-III) 129 ff. In a later decision, however (BGH 11 Mar. 1991, NJW 1991, 1415), the BGH quoted his earlier judgment as a precedent for the 'predominating doctrine of transposition'.

account for the sake of international trade. Since German law accepted security transfer of ownership, it could not be argued that the principle of publicity was so fundamental to German law as to deprive a registered, non-possessory pledge of its validity. The BGH concluded that the *gage sur véhicule* could be translated into a fiduciary transfer of property, and that the French bank therefore had a right to preferential treatment in the same way as if it had acquired security ownership according to German law.

The doctrine of transposition is, however, unable to solve cases where the collateral is moved from a jurisdiction less strict in attitude to a stricter one. This may be illustrated by the following decision of the French *Cour de cassation*.[64] Security ownership in a car had been transferred to the plaintiff, a German bank, as security for a loan while the car was in Germany. Subsequently, the car was driven to France where the owner of a garage executed against the car because of outstanding debts for repairs. The *Cour de cassation* refused to recognise the security right of the plaintiff. A transposition into a possessory pledge was impossible as was a transposition into a *gage sur véhicule* since the plaintiff's right was not registered. This example clearly shows that 'where the substantive rules differ, private international law can only appeal to try to bridge the gap but it cannot itself provide the necessary material for building that bridge'.[65]

2. Claims: article 12 of the Rome Convention and its various interpretations

As we have seen, in all EU Member States, the *lex situs* is regarded as the connecting factor for proprietary rights in movables. With claims, the position is less clear. Article 12 of the Rome Convention deals explicitly only with two legal relationships. First, the contractual relationship between assignor and assignee is submitted to the proper law of the assignment (article 12(1)). Second, the assignability and the relationship between assignee and *debitor cessus* are both submitted to the law governing the right to which the assignment relates (article 12(2)). In an earlier draft of the Convention, article 16(2), which has now become article 12(2), extended its sphere of application also to the relationship between the parties to the assignment and third parties, such as, for

---

[64] Cass. 8 July 1969 Rev.crit.d.int.p. 60 (1970) 75.
[65] See Drobnig, in: *Festschrift für Kegel* 141 (150): 'Stimmen diese Rechtsordnungen inhaltlich nicht überein, so vermag das Kollisionsrecht nur noch die Parole des Brückenbaus auszugeben, jedoch fehlt in seinem Arsenal das notwendige Baumaterial.'

example, creditors of the assignee. This provision was dropped, first because the drafters thought it fell outside the ambit of the Convention, which focuses on contractual relationships, and secondly because, following the accession of the United Kingdom, Ireland and Denmark to the EEC, there was no longer agreement as to the proper rule for third-party relationships.[66] In the absence of any clear-cut rule, there are at least four possible solutions: the *Hoge Raad*[67] and a substantial literature in the Netherlands[68] and Germany[69] opt for article 12(1) and hence for party autonomy.[70] The BGH[71] and the English Court of Appeal in the *Raiffeisen* case[72] consider article 12(2) Rome Convention as the proper rule. The same solution is favoured by the predominant opinion in German literature[73] despite the problems it evidently presents for bulk assignments in an international context. In France, the law that is applied to the question whether an assignment is 'opposable' is traditionally the law at the place of the *debitor cessus'* residence or business,[74] although there is now also considerable support for applying article 12(2) Rome Convention.[75] A fourth opinion suggests the assignor's place of

---

[66] Cf. further Kieninger, RabelsZ 62 (1998) 677 (689 ff.).
[67] *Hoge Raad* 16 May 1997, Rechtspraak van de Week 1997, no 126 c.
[68] Cf. Bertrams/Verhagen, WPNR 1993, 261; Vlas, 'Goederenrechtelijke aspecten van cessie in het IPR', Ars Aequi 47 (1998) 213; de Ly, NIPR 1995, 329 (335). *Contra* (in favour of article 12(2) Rome Convention): Steffens, *Overgang van vorderingen en schulden in het Nederlandse internationaal privaatrecht* 214 ff.
[69] Cf. Stadler, IPRax 2000, 104; Stadler, *Gestaltungsfreiheit und Verkehrsschutz durch Abstraktion* 707 ff.; Einsele, ZVglRWiss 90 (1991) 1 (17 ff.).
[70] In a piece of legislation relating to reform of control over financial markets (Law of 2 Aug. 2002 concerning surveillance of the financial sector, *Moniteur Belge*, 4 Sep. 2002) the Belgian legislator had introduced a private international law rule supplementing art. 12 Rome Convention. Art. 145 of the law states: 'The enforceability of the agreement of assignment against third parties other than the debtor shall be determined according to the law applicable to the agreement of assignment.' This legislation has recently been repealed.
[71] BGH 20 June 1990, BGHZ 111, 376; BGH 8 Dec. 1998, IPRax 200, 128 (note Stadler at 104 ff.) and JZ 1999, 404 (note Kieninger).
[72] *Raiffeisen Zentralbank Österreich AG v Five Star Trading LLC and others* [2001] 2 WLR 1344. Cf. Stevens/Struycken, LQR 118 (2002) 15 ff.
[73] *Münchener Kommentar*/Martiny, article 33 EGBGB nos. 2, 7; von Bar, RabelsZ 53 (1989) 462 (467–471); von Bar, *Internationales Privatrecht*, vol. II, nos. 565–567; Soergel/von Hoffmann, article 33 EGBGB nos. 7, 12; Basedow, ZEuP 1997, 615 (621).
[74] Sinay-Cytermann, Rev.crit.d.i.p. 81 (1992) 35 (42). See further the references to French court decisions in: Lagarde, Rev.crit.d.i.p. 80 (1991) 287 (336). The French solution can be explained by French substantive law which requires an assignment to be formally notified to the *debitor cessus* or accepted by him: see article 1690 Cc.
[75] Batiffol/Lagarde, *Droit International Privé*, vol. II, 339; Khairallah, *Les sûretés mobilières en droit international privé* 278; Pardoel, *Les conflits de lois en matière de cession de créance* no 385.

residence or business as the most adequate connecting factor.[76] Since this rule is not contemplated by article 12 Rome Convention, it has not yet met with approval in European courts but it is gaining ground on the broader international stage. It is the general private international law rule in the revised Article 9 UCC[77] and in the United Nations Convention on the Assignment of Receivables in International Trade (articles 22 and 30(1)).[78] In the European context, at least a uniform rule could and should indeed be achieved in the future either through the ECJ according to article 68 EC Treaty once the Rome Convention is re-enacted as a regulation or, preferably, through the European legislature itself in the course of such re-enactment.[79] For the time being, it seems safe to conclude that apart from the Dutch courts, the national courts of the Member States will not allow the parties to an assignment to choose the applicable law beyond their relationship *inter partes*.

IV. The need for harmonisation within the EU

The differences with respect to the substantive law which will be outlined in Part II, combined with the rules of private international law that have just been discussed, frequently lead to a discontinuity of security rights once the collateral moves across borders. This may happen in circumstances within the contemplation of the parties, for example in the context of an international sale where the subject matter is

---

[76] Kieninger, RabelsZ 62 (1998) 677 (702 ff.); Lorenz, in: Czernich/Heiss, *EVÜ – Das Europäische Schuldvertragsübereinkommen – Kommentar*, article 12 nos 46 ff.; Struycken, *Lloyd's Maritime and Commercial Law Quarterly* 1998, 345 (357 ff.); von Wilmowsky, *Europäisches Kreditsicherungsrecht* 429 ff. Limited to bulk assignments and/or security assignments: Goode, *Commercial Law* 1128; Staudinger/Stoll, *Internationales Sachenrecht*, nos 349 f.; *Münchener Kommentar*/Kreuzer, nach art. 38 EGBGB Anh. I no 93.

[77] See *infra*, Sigman, p. 68.

[78] The Convention received the approval of the General Assembly on 12 Dec. 2001 (A/RES/56/81). The text is available on UNCITRAL's website: http://www.uncitral.org. See, on the convention, Bazinas, Unif. L. Rev. 2002, 49; Sigman/Smith, *The Business Lawyer* 57 (2002) 727; Kieninger/Schütze, ZIP 2003, 2181 ff.

[79] As to the possibility of transforming the Rome Convention into a regulation on the basis of article 65 lit. b EC Treaty, cf. Basedow, CMLR 2000, 687; Israël, MJ 7 (2000) 81; Leible/Staudinger, *The European Legal Forum* 1 (2000) 225. In response to the Commission's Green Paper on the conversion of the Rome Convention of 1980 on the law applicable to contractual obligations into a Community instrument and its modernisation (COM (2002) 654 final, question 18), the majority of contributions have opted for introducing into art. 12 Rome Convention a new rule which subjects the priority questions to the law at the place of the assignor's place of business or habitual residence.

used as a purchase money security interest, or without such contemplation when the transaction was originally conceived to be a purely domestic one. There are numerous decisions by courts of EU Member States where secured parties suffered a complete or at least partial loss of their security rights due to the fact that the collateral was moved from one Member State to another.[80] It goes without saying that this state of affairs is antipathetic to the concept of an internal market. In fact, it has been frequently stated by academic writers and practitioners alike, that the field of security rights in movables is among those where a European measure of harmonisation is most urgently needed.[81] In a recently published draft report on the approximation of the civil and commercial law of the Member States, the European Parliament Committee on Legal Affairs and the Internal Market identified security rights in movables together with general contract law as one of the areas on which a further development of European private law should focus.[82] It has even been suggested by some authors that the present regime may in certain circumstances violate the principle of free movement of goods and services if it leads to the loss of a security right that had been validly created in the country of origin.[83] Irrespective of whether this proposition is well founded or not, it cannot be doubted that the EU has the competence, on the basis of article 95 EC Treaty, to legislate in this field. Contrary to an argument recently put forward in the European Council of Ministers in the debate on the late payment directive,[84] article 295

---

[80] See the summaries by Graue, *German Yearbook of International Law* 26 (1983) 125; Kaufhold, *Internationales und europäisches Mobiliarsicherungsrecht* 80 ff.; Kreuzer, *Recueil des Cours* 259 (1996) 9 (230 ff.); Schilling, ICLQ 34 (1985) 87; restricted to retention of title: Kieninger, *Mobiliarsicherheiten im Europäischen Binnenmarkt* 41 ff.

[81] Bonomi, in: Franz Werro (ed.), *L'européanisation du droit privé. Vers un Code civil européen?*, 497–515; Drobnig, in: Europäisches Parlament, Generaldirektion Wissenschaft, *Arbeitsdokument: Untersuchung der Privatrechtsordnungen der EU im Hinblick auf Diskriminierungen und die Schaffung eines Europäischen Zivilgesetzbuches*, JURI 103 DE (1999) 173 (175 ff.); Goode, ICLQ 23 (1974) 227 (250 ff.); Hinz, ZEuP 1994, 553 (558); Kreuzer, Rev.crit.d.i.p. 84 (1995) 465 (503).

[82] European Parliament, Committee on Legal Affairs and the Internal Market, *Draft Report on the Approximation of the Civil and Commercial Law of the Member States* 2044/2000 (INI), section IV no 11.

[83] Basedow, RabelsZ 59 (1995) 1 (41 ff.); Kieninger, *Mobiliarsicherheiten im Europäischen Binnenmarkt* 122 ff.; Kieninger, ERPL 1996, 41 ff.; Leible, *Wege zu einem europäischen Privatrecht* (forthcoming) § 4 D. IV. 3. b) cc). Rutgers, *International Reservation of Title Clauses* 167 ff.; von Wilmowsky, *Europäisches Kreditsicherungsrecht*. Contra Kaufhold, *Internationales und Europäisches Mobiliarsicherungsrecht* 281 ff.; Sonnenberger, ZVglRWiss 95 (1996) 3 (27 ff.).

[84] Cf. Schulte-Braucks, NJW 2001, 103 (108). As to article 4 of the late payment directive see *infra*, V.1.

EC Treaty, which provides that the Treaty 'shall in no way prejudice the rules in Member States governing the system of property ownership', does not forbid harmonisation measures in the area of property law in general. It has the much more limited content of leaving decisions on the privatisation or nationalisation of certain sectors in trade and industry to the discretion of the Member States.[85]

V. Attempts at harmonisation or unification: past and present

1. European Union

From 1973 to 1980, the European Economic Community made several attempts at solving at least some of the most pressing problems arising out of the non-recognition of security rights among the Member States. In 1973, a draft directive 'on the recognition of securities over movables without dispossession and of clauses providing for retention of ownership upon sale of movables' was published.[86] The idea was to create an obligation on the part of the Member States to recognise certain security interests validly established in the country of origin and to give the secured party those rights which it would have as a pledgee according to the law at the new *situs*. However, it was planned that such recognition and enforcement would be dependent on prior registration of the security right. Since no agreement could be reached on the system of registration, the project was not carried further forward. In 1979/1980 the EEC Commission made a second attempt, this time limited to the simple retention of title.[87] The draft directive required the Member States to recognise retention of title validly created according to the laws of a Member State provided it was agreed upon in writing not later than at the time of delivery of the goods. The Member States should grant the seller a right to revindicate the goods if the buyer became insolvent or if execution was made against the goods on behalf of a third-party creditor. The work on this project was terminated in 1980 because the

---

[85] Kaufhold, *Internationales und Europäisches Mobiliarsicherungsrecht* 283 f.; Kieninger, *Mobiliarsicherheiten im Europäischen Binnenmarkt* 127 f.; Rutgers, *International Reservation of Title Clauses* 175, each with further references. *Contra*: Sonnenberger, ZVglRWiss 95 (1996) 3 (27); Gambaro, ERPL 1997, 497.

[86] Document XI/466/73-D, printed as 'Appendix' to Drobnig/Goode, in: Simmonds/Goode, *Commercial Operations in Europe* 339 (378).

[87] The documents are not published. As to the content of the draft directive, see Goode, *The Company Lawyer* 1 (1980) 185 and Kieninger, *Mobiliarsicherheiten im Europäischen Binnenmarkt* 223 ff.

European Council had started to launch an international convention on the recognition of retention of title, yet this attempt proved equally unsuccessful.[88]

Security rights have also been the subject matter of various projects for a harmonisation of international insolvency law. But whereas the first drafts presented by the EEC Commission still contained some substantive uniform rules on retention of title and its validity in insolvency,[89] the finally adopted EU Convention on International Insolvency, which was re-enacted on 29 May 2000 as a regulation,[90] is limited to rules according to which insolvency proceedings commenced in one Member State shall not affect creditors' rights *in rem* in movables situated outside the state in which insolvency proceedings were opened (article 5: third parties' rights *in rem* in general, article 6(1): retention of title).

The latest attempt to force the Member States to at least guarantee the validity of a simple title retention in the buyer's insolvency has been made in the context of the late payment directive.[91] The Commission in its second proposal[92] and the European Parliament have tried in vain to achieve a minimum harmonisation according to which retention of title, agreed upon in writing no later than the delivery of the goods, would be enforceable as against the buyer's creditors, in execution and insolvency alike. Our study will show that this would have been a valuable and at the same time an easily attainable measure.[93] Nevertheless, the Council strongly opposed any substantive rules in this field and even resorted to article 295 EC Treaty to prevent it.[94] The Conciliation Committee (see article 251(3)–(6) EC Treaty) proposed the following rule that became the final article 4(1): 'Member States shall provide in conformity with the applicable national provisions designated by private international law that the seller retains title to the goods until they are fully paid for if a retention of title clause has been expressly agreed between the buyer

---

[88] Cf. Kreuzer, in: *Festschrift für von Overbeck* 613 (631).
[89] The 1970 draft is published in RabelsZ 36 (1972) 734, the 1980 draft in Bulletin of the European Communities, Supplement 2/1982, 1 ff. and ZIP 1980, 582 ff.
[90] Council Regulation (EC) No 1346/2000 of 29 May 2000 on insolvency proceedings, OJ No L 160/1 of 30 June 2000.
[91] Directive 2000/35/EC of 29 June 2000 on combating late payment in commercial transactions, OJ No L 200/35 of 8 Aug. 2000.
[92] KOM (1998) 6615 final of 29 Oct. 1998. The first proposal (submitted on 23 April 1998, OJ No C 168/13 of 3 June 1998) did not explicitly deal with the enforcement of the retention of title as against third parties.
[93] See *infra*, Evaluation, C.I.   [94] Cf. Schulte-Braucks, NJW 2001, 103 at 108.

and the seller before the delivery of the goods.' This provision not only lacks any reference to the rights of the buyer as against third parties, it is also deprived of any meaning through the reference to the applicable national provisions designated by private international law.[95] In sum, the EU has not yet been able to adopt any meaningful harmonisation measure with respect to security rights despite more than thirty years of work.

2. UNCITRAL

The United Nations Commission on International Trade Law (UNCITRAL) started in the late 1970s to consider a worldwide attempt at unifying securities law, yet, apart from the thorough comparative report prepared by Ulrich Drobnig[96] and further studies carried out by the UNCITRAL secretariat,[97] nothing happened at the time. At its thirteenth session, the Commission decided to take the topic off its agenda because 'worldwide unification of the law of security interests . . . was in all likelihood unattainable'.[98] More than ten years later the subject was revived, albeit within a more limited framework. In 1993, UNCITRAL started to work on what has now become the UN Convention on the Assignment of Receivables in International Trade.[99] The Convention includes both assignment of international receivables and international assignment of 'national' receivables (article 1(1)(a)) and extends its scope of application to assignments which are made for security purposes (article 2(a)). By expressly allowing bulk assignments and assignments of future receivables, the Convention would probably solve at least some of those problems which

---

[95] See in greater detail, Kieninger, in: Basedow et al., *Aufbruch nach Europa – 75 Jahre Max-Planck-Institut für Privatrecht* 151 ff.; Milo, ERPL 2003, 379 ff. A more favourable interpretation is given by Schulte-Braucks/Ongena, ERPL 2003, 519 ff. (534 ff.).

[96] Study by Ulrich Drobnig on behalf of UNCITRAL, published as Report of the Secretary-General: study on security interests (A/CN.9/131) Annex, UNCITRAL Yearbook 1977, part two, II. A.

[97] Note by the Secretariat on Article 9 of the Uniform Commercial Code of the United States of America (A/CN.9/132), UNCITRAL Yearbook 1977, part two, II. B. 222 ff.; Report of the Secretary-General: security interests; feasibility of uniform rules to be used in the financing of trade (A/CN.9/165), UNCITRAL Yearbook 1979, part two, II. C. 81 ff.; Report of the Secretary-General: security interests; issues to be considered in the preparation of uniform rules (A/CN.9/186), UNCITRAL Yearbook 1980, part two, III. D. 89 ff.

[98] UNCITRAL, thirteenth session, Official Records of the General Assembly, Thirty-fifth Session, Supplement No 17 (A/35/17), para. 26–28, UNCITRAL Yearbook 1980, part one, II. A. 10 ff.

[99] See *supra*, note 78.

in international receivables financing are created by the present divergencies set out below in the context of cases 5, 6, 12 and 13, provided the Convention was signed by the EU Member States.[100] Finally, it should be mentioned that UNCITRAL is presently taking up again the wider subject of security rights over tangible and intangible movables. The Commission has started work on a draft legislative guide on secured transactions which will be directed to assisting states in modernising their secured transactions law, including possible moves towards harmonisation. At its thirty-fourth session held in 2001, the Commission considered an exploratory report[101] and constituted a working group.[102]

3. UNIDROIT

The International Institute for the Unification of Private Law (UNIDROIT)[103] has also been active in the field of security rights.[104] In the late 1980s, it successfully completed two conventions, one on international financial leasing[105] and the other on international factoring.[106] However, both have until now met with only limited interest from EU Member States. The Leasing Convention has been ratified by France and Italy, the Factoring Convention by France, Italy and Germany. Even more relevant to our field of interest is the recently adopted Cape Town Convention on International Interests in Mobile Equipment which is supplemented by a Protocol on Matters Specific to Aircraft Equipment.[107]

---

[100] However, it should not be overlooked that the Convention leaves to national law most questions relating to the relationship between the parties to the assignment and third parties such as creditors of the assignor. Such questions of priority are left to be decided by the law of the State in which the assignor is located (article 22). The Annex of the Convention which provides various alternatives for substantive rules on priority issues only becomes applicable if the Contracting State makes a declaration to that effect (article 42).

[101] Security Interests, Note by the Secretariat, Doc. A/CN.9/496.

[102] UNCITRAL Report on its thirty-fourth session, 25 June–13 July 2001, Doc. A/56/17 paras. 346–359; the present status of the draft legislative guide is published on UNCITRAL's web-site, www.uncitral.org.

[103] All texts referred to in this paragraph are available on the official website of UNIDROIT: http://www.unidroit.org.

[104] See most recently the various contributions delivered on the occasion of the 75th anniversary of UNIDROIT's founding. Unif. L. Rev./Rev.dr.unif. 2003, 321 ff.

[105] UNIDROIT Convention on International Financial Leasing (Ottawa, 28 May 1988).

[106] UNIDROIT Convention on International Factoring (Ottawa, 28 May 1988).

[107] Both signed at Cape Town on 16 Nov. 2001. Draft asset-specific protocols on railway rolling stock and on space property are under consideration. See, on the Draft Convention and the various draft protocols, the contributions in issue 1999-2 of the

The central idea is to provide for uniform rules governing the creation and enforcement of a registered international security interest specifically designed for high-value equipment which by its very nature frequently moves across national borders or even transcends them, such as, for example, airplanes, railway rolling stock and space property. If successful, the convention will be an extremely valuable tool for financing industry which uses such equipment, and it may, in addition, supply proof of the possibility of achieving international unification in the area of security rights, although it cannot be overlooked that creating a uniform regime for security rights in all types of potential collateral is a quite different endeavour.

4. European Bank for Reconstruction and Development

Finally, the Model Law on Secured Transactions which has been prepared by the EBRD, and published in 1994, should be mentioned. Since this volume contains a separate chapter on the Model Law,[108] it is not explored further at this point. It suffices to say that although it is not primarily designed as an instrument of harmonisation or unification but rather as a tool for supporting legal reform in Eastern Europe, it could nevertheless assist the EU in its own search for a way to harmonisation.[109]

B. The approach and purpose of the study

I. The 'Common Core methodology' as applied to secured transactions

This study forms part of a larger project, initiated by Mauro Bussani and Hugo Mattei, under the title 'The Common Core of European Private Law'. Building on the experiences of Rudolf Schlesinger and his team at the Cornell Law School in the 1960s, the project seeks to unearth what is common (or indeed uncommon) among the private law systems of the Member States of the European Union. A specific characteristic of the Common Core project is that the contributors are asked to discuss hypothetical situations instead of presenting their legal systems in an

---

Uniform Law Review/*Revue de droit uniforme*. See further Bollweg/Kreuzer, ZIP 2000, 1362; Kronke, in: *FS Kegel*, 33 f. and the special issue of the ERPL 2004, 3 ff.

[108] See *infra*, chapter 5, Dahan/Simpson, 'The European Bank for Reconstruction and Development's Secured Transactions Project.'

[109] See *infra*, pp. 100 f.

abstract way.[110] Since the project seeks to find out how the law deals with problems raised by factual situations, the editors of the individual questionnaires are asked to use as little legal terminology as possible in selecting and formulating the cases. Applied to the subject of secured transactions, this factual approach proved to be both beneficial and problematic. To start with the beneficial aspects, the dangers that are inherent in comparative studies of the classical sort, focusing on concepts and principles, are especially present in the field of property law. If one concentrates primarily on the important dividing lines between abstract and causal, traditional and consensual systems, or on general principles of property law such as the principles of specificity, publicity and *numerus clausus*, one will certainly be tempted to give much weight to these conceptual differences and perhaps more weight than is justified. The present study shows that these dividing lines and differences in matters of principle have less influence, both on the practical outcome of cases and on the mode of analysis adopted, than one might have thought.[111]

Turning to the more problematic aspects, we found that in contrast to topics such as 'Good Faith in European Contract Law'[112] or 'Pure Economic Loss',[113] it was not possible to formulate cases on secured transactions as mere factual situations. Security rights evidently involve rather complex transactions. Therefore, we could not avoid using legal terminology and descriptions of transactions sometimes even including specific contractual clauses. Secondly, we found that it was often not possible to describe the facts of a case in a conclusive manner, since in different jurisdictions the same economic goal might be achieved through different types of transactions. In such cases, we elected to present only a short set of facts describing a basic business situation and the type of collateral which the parties wish to use.[114] It was then for the national reporters to state the kind of transaction that could be used or that would normally be used in such instances. Where the facts did include a specific secured transaction, for example a contract of sale

---

[110] On the methodology of the Common Core project, see Bussani/Mattei, 'The Common Core Approach to European Private Law', published on the project's website: http://www.jus.unitn.it/dsg/common-core/home.html.
[111] See, for example, comparative observations to case 4.
[112] See Zimmermann/Whittaker, *Good Faith in European Contract Law*.
[113] See Bussani/Palmer, *Pure Economic Loss* (forthcoming).
[114] See particularly cases 10 to 13.

with a retention of title clause, the reporters were requested to state whether that clause was sufficient or whether there was a different or more commonly used form. These latter remarks lead to a third distinct feature of our project. In all but two cases, it was necessary to add to the facts other, more specific questions than just the general 'What rights do the parties have?'. With those three peculiarities we have deviated to a certain extent from the factual 'Common Core' approach, and to that limited extent adopt a more classical type of comparative analysis. Yet, we believe that this deviation from, or adaptation of, the Common Core methodology is inevitable once the studies tackle topics where the transactions which are at the heart of the matter are more complex then just a simple contract.

II. Surveying the legal landscape against the background of a need for harmonisation

The aim of the Common Core project is 'to obtain at least the mainlines of a reliable geographical map of the law of Europe',[115] whereas the use of this map is, according to the General Editors, 'of no concern to the cartographers who are drafting it'. In fact, they 'do not wish to force the actual diverse reality of the law within one single map to attain uniformity'. The project is meant neither as a preservationist activity nor as a move towards a higher degree of private law harmonisation, let alone a step on the way towards a European Civil Code. In contrast to the activities of the so-called *Lando* Commission,[116] the Common Core project is, in the words of its initiators, not engaging in city planning but in agnostic legal cartography.[117]

The editor and the contributors to the present volume share the goal of providing comparative information which is as thorough and reliable as possible without forcing uniformity where it does not exist. Yet, in contrast to the General Editors and other groups within the Trento project, we are also interested in the second step following the process of stock-taking. The reason has been stated in part A of this introduction:

---

[115] Bussani/Mattei, 'The Common Core Approach to European Private Law', part 1 a), published on the project's website: http://www.jus.unitn.it/dsg/common-core/home.html. See further Bussani, ERPL 2000, 85 (87 f.) and Bussani/Mattei, Rev. int. dr. comp. 2000, 29 (31 f.).

[116] See Lando/Beale, *Principles of European Contract Law*, parts I and II, prepared by the Commission on European Contract Law (2000).

[117] See *supra*, note 115.

there is an urgent need for harmonisation in the field of security rights, since the present regime cannot be reconciled with the concept of a common market. Various attempts have failed. The last one which was launched in the context of the late payment directive failed mainly because of a lack of comparative information.[118] Therefore to us it seems necessary not only to emphasise the desirability of harmonisation but also – in the evaluation part – to point to elements of convergence (and of course divergence) and to make tentative suggestions for the next steps to be taken by the European Union should it wish to respond to the needs stated. We are especially interested in the question whether the arguments that are usually put forward against the feasibility of harmonisation prove valid if the divergencies are examined through the specific Common Core methodology. This second step, which extends beyond the goals of the Common Core project in general, has, nevertheless, not blinded us in our survey on the first level. In fact, the cases and questions have been selected to bring out precisely those issues where, judging from our preconceptions, the differences should prevail. Thus, the cases and discussions, including the comparative observations, remain at the level of agnostic legal cartography in the sense of Bussani and Mattei, but in the evaluation the present editor, with the support of the contributors, has taken the liberty to analyse the drafted map through the eyes of a 'city planner'.

III. *The genesis of the book*

1. Narrowing down the topic

The present sub-project was started by Matthias E. Storme as one of the first topics of the Common Core project. The original questionnaire which was presented at the General Meeting in 1995 carried the title 'Movable assets and general creditors. Enforcement of claims by recourse on movable assets actually or formerly detained by a debtor, but on which third persons claim property rights (including the use of trusts)'. It included twenty-two cases, most of them with various sub-cases and questions. The majority of these cases involved secured transactions, including trusts, but the chosen context was broader. The setting was influenced by the Belgian notion of *'concursus creditorum'* (*concours, samenloop*), which can be defined as a situation in which conflicting rights

---

[118] See Kieninger, WM 1998, 2213 (2219 f.); Kieninger, in: Basedow et al., *Aufbruch nach Europa–75 Jahre Max-Planck-Institut* (2001) 151 ff.

of creditors exist with respect to one or more assets of a debtor which the latter has lost his unlimited ability to dispose of. This situation can be created either upon the initiative of a creditor or by operation of law.[119] This special notion of *concours/samenloop* is central to Belgian secured transactions law,[120] yet it does not have an exact counterpart in the other European jurisdictions. Therefore, and because the questionnaire proved to be too large to be manageable, the topic had to be narrowed down. After the 1999 General Meeting, when the present editor stepped in, nearly all cases that were not directly concerned with secured transactions had to be cut out as did the cases on trusts, since that topic had by then been taken up by a separate group.[121] This move reflected not only the relative weight which the national reporters who had already answered the first questionnaire had given to the cases on secured transactions, but also the earlier deliberations of a group consisting of Cornelius van der Merwe, George L. Gretton and Matthias E. Storme that met in Stellenbosch in 1997. At that meeting it must have finally become apparent that the original approach had been too wide. Nevertheless, the present editor could, in respect of those cases that were retained, build upon the comparative observations drafted by that group.

This background explains why the cases concentrate on the relationship between a single secured creditor and general unsecured creditors either in an execution or in an insolvency situation and leave out priority conflicts between different types of secured creditors. The present editor was grateful to the national reporters for their willingness virtually to rewrite their original reports so as to adapt them to the new questionnaire. They were not expected to have to deal with completely new cases. The revised reports and the editor's comparative observations were discussed in detail at the seventh General Meeting in 2000. Amendments in light of these discussions, the linguistic revision of the reports which were written by non-native speakers and the preparation of the present introduction and the evaluation were roughly finished by the time of the eighth General Meeting in July 2001. Unfortunately, the final

---

[119] As to the notion of *concours/samenloop*, see Dirix, *Zekerheidsrechten* 31 ff.; Stranart-Thilly/Hainz, *Recht der Kreditsicherheiten in europäischen Ländern, Teil 3: Belgien* (Walther Hadding, Uwe Schneider, eds., 1979) 207; Renauld/Coppens, *Revue critique de jurisprudence belge* 1965, 101 (105).

[120] For example, before the insolvency law reform of 1998, retention of title was no longer enforceable, once the right of the secured seller 'concurred' with rights of other creditors: see Kieninger/Storme, RIW 1999, 94 (95 f.).

[121] See Graziadei/Mattei/Smith, *Commercial Trusts* (forthcoming in this series).

version of the Spanish report reached the editor only after the eighth General Meeting, so that its language could only be revised superficially. For the same reason, its information could only partly be taken into consideration in the comparative parts.

2. On terminology and the glossary

When the present project was first launched, the question of what terminology the contributors should use was not considered to be a particular problem assuming that everyone was more or less familiar with the relevant terms in English. However, it soon became apparent that the standard English law terminology which most reporters, and indeed the first questionnaire, had relied on would be unsuitable, especially in the field of property law. Examples like 'chattel mortgage', 'floating charge' or the distinction between 'personal property' and 'real property' illustrate the point sufficiently. At a meeting held in Turin in 1997 it was decided that George L. Gretton and the present editor should prepare a list of standardised terms in English, the use of which would be recommended to the contributors. Although not originally intended to be published, the authors finally decided to print the 'glossary', as it was then christened, consisting of the chosen standard terms, selected notes and translations of each term into the contributors' national languages.[122] A short introduction explains the approach and the organisation of the glossary so that no further information seems necessary at this point.

3. Order of the national reports

After a prolonged discussion, our group followed the example of Zimmermann and Whittaker who in the first volume within the present series[123] organised the national answers by legal families instead of alphabetically. The inclusion of South Africa, which is neither a member of the EU nor one of the likely candidates for a future enlargement, rests on two grounds. First, South African law represents a most interesting mixture of Roman–Dutch law and common law and could therefore prove instructive to Europeans seeking to bridge the gap between the continental civil law systems and the common law.[124] Secondly, without

---

[122] See *infra*, pp. 150 ff.   [123] Zimmermann/Whittaker, *Good Faith in European Contract Law*.
[124] On possible lessons of mixed jurisdictions for private law harmonisation in Europe, see Smits, *Europees Privaatrecht in wording. Naar een Ius Commune Europaeum als gemengd rechtsstelsel*.

the commitment of Cornelius van der Merwe, a former Professor at the University of Stellenbosch, this book might not have seen the light of day. He originally prepared his report on South African law merely out of interest, without a view to it being published in this volume. However, the group unanimously decided that it should be published, naturally following the English, Irish and Scottish reports.

After this introduction, the fifteen cases are preceded by four short essays which have already been briefly mentioned at various points. The first one by Willem Zwalve explores in greater detail how the different routes which the national legal systems have taken in order to overcome the restrictions of the possessory pledge have led to the present state of divergency among the EU Member States. As a counterpoint for comparison and a possible model for harmonisation, Harry C. Sigman shows in his presentation of Article 9 UCC how the United States effectively solved its 'labyrinth for creditors' some fifty years ago. He also points out the cornerstones of the recent reform of Article 9 UCC. The American approach is again put into contrast with English common law, characterised by Michael Bridge as 'creditor-friendly but unreformed'. Finally, Frédérique Dahan and John Simpson sketch the solutions of the cases of Part II according to the EBRD Model Law on Secured Transactions, thus suggesting yet another possible model for a harmonised secured transactions law.

Bibliography

George A. Akerlof, 'The Market for "Lemons": Quality Uncertainty and the Market Mechanism', *Quarterly Journal of Economics* 84 (1970) 488 ff.
Christian von Bar, 'Abtretung und Legalzession im neuen deutschen Internationalen Privatrecht', RabelsZ 53 (1989) 462 ff.
  Internationales, Privatrecht, vol. II (1991).
Jürgen Basedow 'Der kollisionsrechtliche Gehalt der Produktfreiheiten im europäischen Binnenmarkt: favor offerentis', RabelsZ 59 (1995) 1 ff.
  'Internationales Factoring zwischen Kollisionsrecht und Unidroit-Konvention', ZEuP 1997, 615 ff.
  'The Communitarization of the Conflict of Laws under the Treaty of Amsterdam', CMLR 2000, 687 ff.
Henri Batiffol, Paul Lagarde, *Droit International Privé*, vol. II (6th edn, 1976).
Spyridon Bazinas, 'UNCITRAL's Contribution to the Unification of Receivables Financing Law: The United Nations Convention on the Assignment of Receivables in International Trade', Unif. L. Rev/Rev.dr.unif. 2002, 49 ff.

R. I. V. F. Bertrams, H. L. E. Verhagen, 'Goederenrechtelijke aspecten van de internationale cessie en verpanding van vorderingen op naam', WPNR 1993, 261 ff.

Hans-Georg Bollweg, Karl Kreuzer, 'Entwürfe einer UNIDROIT/ICAO-Konvention über Internationale Sicherungsrechte an beweglicher Ausrüstung und eines Protokolls über Luftfahrtausrüstung', ZIP 2000, 1362 ff.

A. Bonomi, 'La nécessité d'harmonisation du droit des garanties réelles mobilières dans le Marché unique européen', in: Franz Werro (ed.), *L'européanisation du droit privé. Vers un Code civil européen?* (1998) 497 ff.

James W. Bowers, 'Security Interests', in: Boudewijn Bouckaert, Gerrit de Geest (eds.), *Encyclopedia of Law and Economics*, vol. II (2000).

Mauro Bussani, 'Le droit civil des sûretés rélles. Le modèle Italien des sûretés', ERPL 1998, 23 ff.

'"Integrative" Comparative Law Enterprises and the Inner Stratification of Legal Systems', ERPL 2000, 85 ff.

Mauro Bussani, Ugo Mattei, 'Le fonds commun du droit privé européen', Rev. int. dr. comp. 2000, 29 ff.

'The Common Core Approach to European Private Law', www.jus.unitn.it/dsg/common-core/home.html.

Mauro Bussani, Vernon Palmer, *Pure Economic Loss* (forthcoming).

M. R. Chesterman, 'Choice of Law Aspects of Liens and Similar Claims in International Sale of Goods', ICLQ 22 (1973) 213 ff.

Dietmar Czernich, Helmut Heiss (eds.), *EVÜ – Das Europäische Schuldvertragsübereinkommen – Kommentar* (1999).

Eric Dirix, *Zekerheidsrechten* (1999).

Ulrich Drobnig, 'Eigentumsvorbehalt bei Importlieferungen nach Deutschland', RabelsZ 32 (1968) 450 ff.

'Security over Corporeal Movables in Germany', in: J. G. Sauveplanne (ed.), *Security over Corporeal Movables* (1974) 181 ff.

'Entwicklungstendenzen des deutschen internationalen Sachenrechts', in: *Festschrift für Kegel* (1977) 141 ff.

'Security Rights in Movables', in: Arthur Hartkamp et al. (eds.), *Towards a European Civil Code* (2nd edn, 1998) 511 ff.

'Recht der Kreditsicherheiten', in: Europäisches Parlament, Generaldirektion Wissenschaft (ed.), *Arbeitsdokument: Untersuchung der Privatrechtsordnungen der EU im Hinblick auf Diskriminierungen und die Schaffung eines Europäischen Zivilgesetzbuches*, JURI 103 DE (1999) 59 (70 ff.).

'Present and Future of Real and Personal Security', ERPL 2003, 623 ff.

Ulrich Drobnig, Roy Goode, 'Security for Payment in Export and Import Transactions', in: Simmonds/Goode (eds.), *Commercial Operations in Europe* (1978).

Dorothee Einsele, 'Das Internationale Privatrecht der Forderungszession und der Schuldnerschutz', ZVglRWiss 90 (1991) 1 ff.

Evlalia Eleftheriadou, 'Griechenland' in: Christian von Bar (ed.), *Sachenrecht in Europa*, vol. III (1999) 74 ff.
Philippe Fargeaud, *Le gage sans dépossession comme instrument de crédit et le Marché Commun* (1963).
Heywood Fleisig, 'The Proposed UNIDROIT Convention on Mobile Equipment: Economic Consequences and Issues', Unif. L. Rev./Rev. dr. unif. 1999, 253 ff.
Antonio Gambaro, 'Perspectives on the Codification of the Law of Property', ERPL 1997, 497 ff.
Roy Goode, 'A Credit Law for Europe?', ICLQ 23 (1974) 227 ff.
  'Reservation of Title – The EEC's Faulty Approach', *The Company Lawyer* 1 (1980) 185 ff.
  Commercial Law (2nd edn, 1995).
Eugen D. Graue, 'Recognition and Enforcement of Foreign Security Interests under Domestic Conflict Rules', *German Yearbook of International Law* 26 (1983) 125 ff.
Walther Hadding, Uwe Schneider, *Recht der Kreditsicherheiten in den europäischen Ländern* (from 1978).
Stefanie Hellmich, *Kreditsicherungsrechte in der spanischen Mehrrechtsordnung* (2000).
Hans Werner Hinz, 'Das Interesse der Wirtschaft an einer Europäisierung des Privatrechts', ZEuP 1994, 553 ff.
John Hudson, 'The Case against Secured Lending', *International Review of Law and Economics* 15 (1995) 47 ff.
Jona Israël, 'Conflicts of Law and the EC after Amsterdam – A Change for the Worse?', MJ 7 (2000) 81 ff.
Sylvia Kaufhold, *Internationales und Europäisches Mobiliarsicherungsrecht* (1999).
Georges Khairallah, *Les sûretés mobilières en droit international privé* (1984).
Eva-Maria Kieninger, *Mobiliarsicherheiten im Europäischen Binnenmarkt* (1996).
  'Securities in Movable Property within the Common Market', ERPL 1996, 41 ff.
  'Der Richtlinienvorschlag der Europäischen Kommission zur Bekämpfung des Zahlungsverzugs im Handelsverkehr', WM 1998, 2213 ff.
  'Das Statut der Forderungsabtretung im Verhältnis zu Dritten', RabelsZ 62 (1998) 677 ff.
  'Der Eigentumsvorbehalt in der Verzugsrichtlinie – Chronik einer verpaßten Chance', in: Jürgen Basedow et al., *Aufbruch nach Europa – 75 Jahre Max-Planck-Institut für Privatrecht* (2001) 151 ff.
Eva-Maria Kieninger/Elisabeth Schütze, 'Neue Chancen für internationale Finanzierungsgeschäfte: Die UN-Abtretungs-Konvention, ZIP 2003, 2181 ff.
Eva-Maria Kieninger, Matthias E. Storme, 'Das neue belgische Recht des Eigentumsvorbehalts', RIW 1999, 94 ff.
Helmut Koziol, 'Probleme der Sicherungszession im grenzüberschreitenden Verkehr Deutschland-Österreich', DZWiR 1993, 353 ff.

Karl Kreuzer, 'Europäisches Mobiliarsicherungsrecht oder: Von den Grenzen des Internationalen Privatrechts', in: *Festschrift für von Overbeck* (1990) 613 ff.
 'La reconnaissance des sûretés mobilières conventionnelles étrangères', Rev.crit.d.i.p. 84 (1995) 465 ff.
 'La propriété mobilière en droit international privé', *Recueil des Cours* 259 (1996) 9 ff.
Karl Kreuzer (ed.), *Mobiliarsicherheiten – Vielfalt oder Einheit?* (1999).
Herbert Kronke, 'Parteiautonomie und Prorogationsfreiheit im internationalen Mobiliarsicherungsrecht: Zwei Grundprinzipien der Konvention von Kapstadt', in: *Liber Amicorum Gerhard Kegel* (2002) 33 ff.
Paul Lagarde, 'Le nouveau droit international privé des contrats après l'entrée en vigueur de la Convention de Rome du 19 Juin 1980', Rev.crit.d.i.p. 80 (1991) 287 ff.
Ole Lando, Hugh Beale (eds.), *Principles of European Contract Law*, parts I and II (1995).
Stefan Leible, 'Der Eigentumsvorbehalt bei Warenlieferungen in EU-Staaten', in: *Praxis-Handbuch Export*, Gruppe 6/7, 1 ff.
 Wege zu einem europäischen Privatrecht (forthcoming).
Stefan Leible, Ansgar Staudinger, 'Article 65 EGV im System der EG-Kompetenzen', *The European Legal Forum* 1 (2000) 225 ff.
Hans Lewald, 'Règles générales des conflits de lois – Contribution à la technique du droit international privé', *Recueil des Cours* 69 (1939-III) 129 ff.
Lynn LoPucki, 'The Unsecured Creditor's Bargain', *Virginia Law Review* 80 (1994) 1887 ff.
Philip de Ly, 'Zakelijke zekerheidsvormen in het Nederlandse internationaal privaatrecht', NIPR 1995, 329 ff.
Theophile Margellos, *La protection du vendeur à crédit d'objets mobiliers corporels à travers la clause de réserve de propriété, Étude de droit comparé* (1989).
Pierre Mayer, 'Les conflits de lois en matière de réserve de propriété après la loi du 12 Mai 1980', JCP 1981 I 3019 ff.
Alberto Mazzoni, 'La reconnaissance des sûretés mobilières sans dépossession créées à l'étranger en droit international privé italien', in: *Rapports nationaux italiens au Xe Congrès International de Droit Comparé* (1979) 245 ff.
Martin Menne, *Die Sicherung des Warenlieferanten durch den Eigentumsvorbehalt im französischen Recht* (1998).
John Michael Milo,' Combating Late Payment in Business Transactions', ERPL 2003, 379 ff.
P. L. Nève, *Eigendomsvoorbehoud*, Nederlandse Vereniging voor Rechtsvergelijking no 60 (2000) 1 ff.
D. Pardoel, *Les conflits de lois en matière de cession de créance* (1997).
Willibald Posch, 'Mehrfache Sicherungsabtretung im deutsch-österreichischen Rechtsverkehr: eine Quelle kollisionsrechtlicher Probleme', IPRax 1992, 51 ff.

Kurt Rebmann (ed.), *Münchener Kommentar zum Bürgerlichen Gesetzbuch, Band 7: Einführungsgesetz zum Bürgerlichen Gesetzbuche, Internationales Privatrecht* (2nd edn, 1990).

Jean Renauld, Pierre Coppens, 'La notion de concours entre créanciers, son application au régime des sociétés dissoutes et des successions acceptés sous bénéfice d'inventaire', *Revue critique de jurisprudence belge* 1965, 101 ff.

Ann-Christin Ritterhoff, *Parteiautonomie im internationalen Sachenrecht* (1999).

Thilo Rott, *Vereinheitlichung des Rechts der Mobiliarsicherheiten* (2000).

Jan-Hendrik Röver, *Vergleichende Prinzipien dinglicher Sicherheiten* (1999).

Jacobien W. Rutgers, *International Reservation of Title Clauses* (1999).

Sixto Sánchez Lorenzo, *Garantías reales en el comercio internacional* (1993).

Anthony Saunders, Anand Srinivasan, Ingo Walter, Jeffrey Wool, 'The Economic Implications of International Secured Transactions Law Reform: A Case Study', U.Pa.J.Int'l Econ.L. 20 (1999) 309 ff.

Theodor J. R. Schilling, 'Some European Decisions on Non-possessory Security Rights in Private International Law', ICLQ 34 (1985) 87 ff.

Reinhard Schulte-Braucks, 'Zahlungsverzug in der Europäischen Union', NJW 2001, 103 ff.

Reinhard Schulte-Braucks/Steven Ongena, 'The Late Payment Directive – A Step Towards an Emerging European Private Law', ERPL 2003, 519 ff.

Alan Schwartz, 'The Continuing Puzzle of Secured Debt', *Vanderbilt Law Review* 37 (1984) 1051 ff.

Ulrike Seif, *Der Bestandsschutz besitzloser Mobiliarsicherheiten im deutschen und englischen Recht* (1997).

Harry C. Sigman, Edwin E. Smith, 'Toward Facilitating Cross-Border Secured Financing and Securitization: An Analysis of the United Nations Convention on the Assignment of Receivables in International Trade', *The Business Lawyer* 57 (2002) 727 ff.

Anne Sinay-Cytermann, 'Les conflits de lois concernant l'opposabilité des transferts de créance', Rev.crit.d.i.p. 81 (1992) 35 ff.

Jan Smits, *Europees Privaatrecht in wording. Naar een Ius Commune Europaeum als gemengd rechtsstelsel* (1999).

Hans Theodor Soergel, *Bürgerliches Gesetzbuch, Band 10: Einführungsgesetz* (12th edn, 1996).

Hans Jürgen Sonnenberger, 'Europarecht und Internationales Privatrecht', ZVglRWiss 95 (1996) 3 ff.

Astrid Stadler, *Gestaltungsfreiheit und Verkehrsschutz durch Abstraktion* (1996).
'Der Streit um das Zessionsstatut – eine endlose Geschichte?', IPRax 2000, 104 ff.

Julius von Staudinger, *Kommentar zum Bürgerlichen Gesetzbuch – Internationales Sachenrecht* (13th edn, 1996).

L. F. A. Steffens, *Overgang van vorderingen en schulden in het Nederlandse internationaal privaatrecht* (1997).

Robert H. Stevens, Teun H. D. Struycken, 'Assignment and the Rome Convention', LQR 118 (2002) 15 ff.

Hans Stoll, 'Zur gesetzlichen Regelung des internationalen Sachenrechts in Art. 43-46 EGBGB', IPRax 2000, 259 ff.

Anne-Marie Stranart-Thilly, Hans-Joachim Hainz, *Recht der Kreditsicherheiten in europäischen Ländern, Teil 3: Belgien* (1979).

Teun Struycken, 'The Proprietary Aspects of International Assignment of Debts and the Rome Convention Art. 12', *Lloyd's Maritime and Commercial Law Quarterly* 1998, 345 ff.

Herbert Stumpf, *Eigentumsvorbehalt und Sicherungsübertragung im Ausland* (4th edn, 1980).

Anna Veneziano, *Le garanzie mobiliari non possessorie* (2000).

Gian C. Venturini, *International Encyclopedia of Comparative Law, Vol. III: Private International Law* (1977) chapter 21, 'Property'.

P. Vlas, 'Goederenrechtelijke aspecten van cessie in het IPR', *Ars Aequi* 47 (1998) 213 ff.

Rolf Weber, 'Parteiautonomie im internationalen Sachenrecht?', RabelsZ 44 (1980) 510 ff.

Manfred Wenckstern, 'Die englische Floating Charge im deutschen Internationalen Privatrecht', RabelsZ 56 (1992) 624 ff.

Peter von Wilmowsky, *Europäisches Kreditsicherungsrecht* (1996).

Reinhard Zimmermann, Simon Whittaker, *Good Faith in European Contract Law* (2000) (Common Core Series vol. I).

2 A labyrinth of creditors: a short introduction to the history of security interests in goods

WILLEM J. ZWALVE

1. Introduction

The history of security interests in movables on the European continent begins with the 'reception' of Roman law in the guise of Justinian's *Corpus Iuris Civilis* in the Middle Ages.[1] As with any code, Justinian's codification forms the conclusion of an era in the development of the law. Legal concepts not incorporated into the code, like the ancient *fiducia cum creditore*, were consequently concealed from the legal consciousness for ages, until some of them were drawn from the collective subconscious of the civil law in the course of the nineteenth century. An assessment of the Roman origins of the continental European system of security interests in movables is important, particularly since many aspects of the modern system have been consciously developed as a reaction to the Roman system. The current statutory provisions on the creation of a valid pledge, for example, are only comprehensible if it is appreciated that they were formulated as a response to the deviating provisions of Roman law. It will, therefore, be necessary to glimpse briefly the Roman system of security interests in movables as contained in Justinian's codification.

---

[1] On the reception of Roman law see especially Francesco Calasso, *Medio Aevo del Diritto* (1954), *passim*; Fr. Calasso, *Introduzione al Diritto Commune* (1970), *passim*; Helmut Coing, *Europäisches Privatrecht* I *(Älteres Gemeines Recht)* (1985) ff.; John Dawson, *The Oracles of the Law* (1968) 125 ff., 177 ff. and 263 ff.; Paul Koschaker, *Europa und das römische Recht* (1966), *passim*; and Fr. Wieacker, *Privatrechtsgeschichte der Neuzeit* (1967), *passim*.

2. Justinian Roman law

After the demise of the concept of *fiducia*,[2] Roman law recognised only two proprietary security interests, *pignus* and *hypotheca*. Both interests differed from *fiducia* in the sense that with *pignus* and *hypotheca* the absolute legal title to the object of these security interests remained with the chargor (pledge-debtor), whereas *fiducia* implied a transfer of title by the chargor to the chargee (pledge-creditor).[3] The two remaining proprietary security interests of Roman law were *iura in re aliena*, special proprietary interests in goods belonging to another, mostly (but not necessarily) the debtor. This fundamental fact has some important consequences, dominating the law on this subject to date. One is that the chargor remains entitled to dispose of his property as he sees fit, even though a security interest has been vested in it. He may charge his property again to secure another debt. Furthermore, he may even transfer his title to another person without the permission of the chargee. Any contract to the contrary only has effect as between chargor and chargee[4] and does not affect the rights of third parties, such as supervening chargees and new owners. The original chargee, however, has a security interest, which ranks higher than any security interest subsequently established and which vests in him the right to recover the object of his security interests from any new owner. It would, therefore, be quite wrong to construe the creation of a security interest as a means to separate the objects of security interests from the rest of the assets of the chargor. In spite of the creation of a security interest, they still constitute a part of the assets of the chargor, and are even subject to the rights of his other, non-secured creditors. All the chargee has is a right to satisfy his debt out of the sale of the objects of his security interest

---

[2] On *fiducia* see M. Kaser, *Das römische Privatrecht* (RP) I (1971) 144 f. and 460 ff.; RP II (1975) 275 and 313; and especially G. Noordraven, *De 'Fiducia' in het Romeinse recht* (1988).

[3] Unless otherwise indicated, I will use the term 'charge' throughout in the broad sense, as a 'real' burden attaching to a certain part of the debtor's property as a security interest for the payment of a debt. The words 'chargor' and 'chargee' stand for the grantor and the grantee of a proprietary security interest.

[4] There is one passage in Justinian's Digests (D. 20,5,7,2 (Marcianus)) containing a reference to a contract between chargor and chargee, restricting the chargor's powers of disposition. The passage has been the subject of controversy, as it seems superfluous in view of the fact that the chargee may successfully sue anyone in possession, including a new owner, for recovery. See e.g. Schlichting, *Die Verfügungsbeschränkung des Verpfänders im klassischen römischen Recht* (1973); Wacke, *Rivista Internazionale di Diritto Romano e Antico* 24 (1973) 184 ff.; and Kaser, *Tijdschrift voor Rechtsgeschiedenis* 44 (1976) 283 ff.

with preference over other creditors. That right, however, is a right *in rem*. In order to enforce it, the chargee has an action for recovery of the objects of his security interest against anyone in possession, the *actio Serviana*. It should be stressed, however, that the nature of that action differs from that of the *rei vindicatio*, the proprietary Roman action of the owner for specific restitution of his property. The object of the *actio Serviana* is recovery of the objects of security interests by way of distress, whereas the *rei vindicatio* presupposes an immediate right to possession, irrespective of any particular purpose other than restitution of possession.

Hence there are frequent conflicts of interests between secured creditors on the one hand and the 'trustee in bankruptcy', the *curator bonorum*, on the other in many civil law systems. In Roman law, there was no specific duty of sale on the part of a secured creditor, as there is in modern civil law jurisdictions, but the chargee could be forced to surrender the objects of his security interest to the chargor whenever the latter wanted to dispose of his property.[5] One may, therefore, assume that the *curator bonorum* was able to block an action for recovery by the chargee whenever the latter was not willing to sell. The explanation is, of course, that the equity in the property granted as security that is the surplus value thereof remained with the chargor.

The legal dichotomy between movables and immovables is fundamental to many, if not all, modern continental European legal systems, especially in so far as security interests are concerned. This was not the case in Roman law. There was no rule restricting non-possessory security interests to real (immovable) property and possessory security interests to (movable) goods. On the contrary: pledge (*pignus*), a possessory security interest, could be vested in personal as well as real property, whereas 'hypothec' (*hypotheca*), the non-possessory security interest of Roman law, could also be vested in real, as well as personal, property. It was only as a matter of convenience that pledge (*pignus*) was associated with goods (movables), because they are more suitable for delivery than real property (land).[6] The two security interests of Roman law, accordingly, merely differed in so far as their respective modes of creation were concerned, a pledge being created by delivery of possession (*traditio*) and a *hypotheca* by way of a simple contract:

---

[5] D. 13,7,6 pr. (Pomponius) and see on this passage Noordraven, *Bullettino di Diritto Romano* 83 (1980) 247 ff.
[6] D. 50,16,238,2 (Gaius).

D.13,7,9,2 (Ulpianus): 'Pignus' is properly used when possession has been delivered to the creditor and 'hypotheca', even if possession is not transferred to the creditor.[7]

A Roman pledge (*pignus*) differed radically from a modern European 'pledge'. Some of the problems encountered in modern European law can only be understood if it is kept in mind that this difference can be traced to the origin and development of the Roman concept of *pignus*.

Pignus was created by *traditio*, which is by surrender of *civilis possessio* to the chargee. The latter did not become a mere bailee (detentor), as he is in modern continental European civil law, but a possessor, the pledgor not even retaining constructive possession. A subsequent surrender of possession by the pledgee to the pledgor, however, did not terminate his security interest, as is the case in modern continental European systems. Consequently, the object of a *possessory* security interest was not infrequently leased to the chargor:[8]

D. 13,7,35,1 (Florentinus): 'Pignus' merely confers possession on the creditor, because it remains the property of the debtor: the debtor, however, is allowed to use his own property at the will of the pledgee or as a lessee.[9]

D. 13,7,37 (Paulus): Whenever I have leased a pledge delivered to me to the owner, I retain possession by the lease, because before the debtor took the lease, it was not his possession, all the more so because I have the will to retain possession and a lessee cannot have the will to obtain possession.[10]

Whenever property had been charged by way of pledge and was subsequently bailed (transferred) to the chargor, there was practically no difference between *pignus* and *hypotheca*. This is the apparent reason for the observation by the Roman lawyer Marcianus that 'the difference between *pignus* and *hypotheca* is purely verbal'.[11] The phenomenon also helps to explain why Roman sources use the concept of *pignus* in a rather cavalier way: sometimes it stands for a special security interest, created

---

[7] 'Proprie pignus dicimus, quod ad creditorem transit, hypothecam, cum non transit nec possessio ad creditorem.'

[8] See Tondo, *Labeo* 5 (1959) 157 ff.; and Kaser, *Studia et Documenta Historiae et Iuris* 45 (1979) 1 ff.

[9] 'Pignus manente proprietate debitoris solam possessionem transfert ad creditorem: potest tamen et precario et pro conducto debitor re sua uti.'

[10] 'Si pignus mihi traditum locassem domino, per locationem retineo possessionem, quia antequam conduceret debitor, non fuerit eius possessio, cum et animus mihi retinendi sit et conducenti non sit animus possessionem apiscendi.'

[11] D. 20,1,5,1 (Marcianus): 'Inter pignus autem et hypothecam tantum nominis sonus differt.'

by surrender of possession, sometimes it is synonymous with the concept of 'security interest' in general. On reflection, therefore, the antithesis of *pignus* and *hypotheca* in Roman law does not necessarily correspond to the distinction between possessory and non-possessory security interests of modern civil law systems: a Roman 'pledge' might well have amounted to a non-possessory security interest. It might even have been created by constructive delivery (*constitutum possessorium*), so that the chargor never lost factual possession of the objects securing his debt to the chargee. The famous Roman lawyer Ulpian had already observed that creditors frequently left their debtors in actual possession of property charged by way of pledge (*pignus*).[12]

Roman law found itself in quite a predicament, due to the fact that it was possible in *all* types of security interests to leave the objects of security in the hands of the debtor. The total absence of any system of publicity created serious problems in practice, especially in so far as the ranking of subsequent chargees of the same property was concerned. Ranking has been dominated by a simple rule of thumb – *prior tempore, potior iure*[13] – for most of the history of Roman law. A refinement was introduced only relatively late. In AD 472 the emperor Leo decreed that a security interest, created by 'public instrument', or a written memorandum signed by three witnesses, ranked higher than preceding security interests not created in this way.[14] It should be stressed that the emperor did not invalidate security interests not created in conformity with this provision. On the contrary: even after 472 all security interests, created in accordance with the ancient rules of the Roman common law, were still valid, albeit that security interests created in accordance with Leo's provision had priority over all security interests not complying with his formalities. The significance of the emperor's innovation was that he introduced an additional rule of preference, thus confusing matters even more. After 472 third parties, having acquired title to goods charged by a former owner, continued to be confronted by chargees till then unknown to them with actions for recovery of the property for the execution of a predecessor's debts.

Another factor that considerably complicated the Roman system of security interests was that they could be vested not only in individual parts of the debtor's estate, but in his entire estate as such.[15] The former

---

[12] D. 43,26,6,4 (Ulpianus): 'cottidie enim precario rogantur creditores ab his, qui pignori dederunt'. See also D. 43,26,11 (Celsus).
[13] C. 8,17 (18),3. See also VI°, *De regulis iuris*, reg. 54.   [14] C. 8,17,11,1.
[15] D. 20,1,1 pr. (Papinianus).

were designated as 'special' security interests and the latter as 'general' security interests. There were no fundamental differences between 'general' and 'special' security interests, their relationship being determined by the same ancient rules of preference and by Leo's decree of 472. Consequently it frequently occurred that older general security interests had priority over later special security interests, even if the latter had been created by transfer of possession of the object of security to the chargee.[16]

I will confine this chapter to consensual security interests, namely those created by virtue of an agreement. It should be noted, however, that there were many 'special' as well as 'general' *statutory* security interests in Roman law. They must be distinguished from mere privileges, because the latter are only concerned with priority (preference), whereas the former were a genuine charge on the property of the debtor. Of course, some of these statutory security interests were indeed 'privileged', in that they had priority (preference) over older consensual security interests.

Even disregarding the confusing complexity of 'general' and 'special' pertaining to consensual as well as statutory security interests, the Roman system of security interests had one main deficiency: the absence of an adequate system of publicity, especially in so far as movables were concerned. Without publicity, Roman law could only maintain its system of security interests by calling in the assistance of criminal law by rendering it a crime to transfer property without disclosing to the transferee the charges with which the property was burdened (*stellionatus*).[17]

3. Later developments in the European *ius commune*

At the end of the fifteenth century, the Roman system of security interests had become part of the law of practically all European countries, with the exception of England and Wales. This system drew sharp criticism from the famous Dutch lawyer Johannes Voet (1647–1713), whose *Commentarius ad Pandectas* was regarded as an authoritative restatement of the European *ius commune* all over the European continent and in Scotland up to the nineteenth century. He characterised the system as 'a labyrinth of creditors, where lawyers creep around on winding and tortuous tracks'.[18] The deficiencies of the system were, however, not addressed

---

[16] D. 20,4,2 and 20,5,1 (Papinianus).   [17] D. 47,20,3,1 (Ulpianus).
[18] *Commentarius ad Pandectas*, ed. Geneva 1757, Lib. 20, tit. 4, no 17.

by the introduction of an adequate system of publicity and registration, but by gradually eliminating some, if not all, of the consequences of the Roman non-possessory security interest of *hypotheca*, at least in so far as movables were concerned.

In order to avoid misconceptions, it should be emphasized that the phenomenon known as the 'reception' of Roman law on the European continent and in Scotland did not bring about a European 'common law'. Apart from regional and national differences in customary and statutory law, Roman law only had the status of a subsidiary and never as an exclusive source of law on any subject. Consequently, there were considerable variations in the extent to which the Roman system of security interests had been incorporated into the law of most European countries. This chapter has been written on the basis of 'Roman–Dutch' law, not because it still obtains in the Republic of South Africa, but because it was widely considered an outstanding example of the 'modern application' (*usus modernus*) of Roman law. This changed only after the fame of the Dutch authors of the seventeenth and eighteenth centuries was eclipsed by the celebrated German 'Pandectists' of the nineteenth century. By that time, however, the traditional system had practically ceased to exist everywhere else on the European continent.

In Holland, as in some other European countries, the relationship between 'general' and 'special' security interests was placed on a different footing to Roman law. 'Special' security interests were granted preference over 'general' security interests.[19] This was the first step in the development of the modern continental 'specificity principle' that only allows security interests in specific assets of the debtor and abolishes (at least in theory) the old Roman 'general' security interests. Another new development was that in some, but certainly not all, European 'civil law' jurisdictions all hypothecs, 'general' as well as 'special', were made subject to the ancient customary maxim *mobilia non habent sequelam*, 'meubles n'ont pas de suite' ('movables cannot be traced into the hands of third parties').[20] Whenever personal property subject to a hypothec

---

[19] The so-called 'Political Ordonance' of 1580 is to be found in *Groot Placaet Boek* I, 329.

[20] It has already been emphasised in the text that the 'reception' of Roman law did not provide the European continent and Scotland with uniformity of (private) law: the differences between the various regions and countries could be substantial. This applies especially to the question whether or not the rule *mobilia non habent sequelam* had been adopted in a particular region. In the Saxon territories of the German empire it did not apply to (special or general) non-possessory security interests. The only exception concerned a floating charge on the stock-in-trade of a shop: see Carpzov, *Jurisprudentia forensis Romano-Saxonicus*, Pars II, const. 23, definitio 12 and 13.

was transferred to a third party, that security interest expired.[21] Consequently, hypothecs on movables could only be enforced as long as the chargor was still in possession. The question now was whether this also applied to a non-possessory pledge where the pledgee was not in possession, either because the security interest had been created by constructive delivery (*constitutum possessorium*), or because the pledgee had restored actual possession to the pledgor as his bailee.

Voet held that all non-possessory security interests, be they a hypothec or a non-possessory pledge, were subject to the maxim *mobilia non habent sequelam*.[22] He went even further by suggesting that security interests in movables could only be validly created by transfer of possession to the creditor, thus virtually eliminating the Roman hypothec on movables.[23] His opinion was explicitly rejected by the 'High Council' of Holland, the highest court of judicature in Holland at the time, in an important decision of 13 November 1737.[24] The case concerned a shopkeeper, who had transferred her stock-in-trade to a creditor by way of constructive delivery, obviously in order to avoid the rules applying to hypothecs. The court felt obliged to determine the true nature of the transaction by considering the actual words used by the parties. It found that the parties actually intended to create a security interest by way of constructive delivery. What had actually happened, therefore, was that, despite Voet's contrary opinion, a valid pledge on the stock had been created by constructive delivery. The 'High Council' adhered to this precedent throughout its existence.[25] Consequently, shortly before the introduction of the first Dutch Civil Code (in 1809), the law of Holland recognised no less than four kinds of security interests in movables: possessory pledge (*pignus*, with the pledgee retaining possession), a hybrid 'non-possessory' kind of pledge, hypothec and, of course, the general hypothec on all the movable assets of the debtor.

---

[21] Grotius, *Inleidinge* II, 48, 29. See Pothier, *Traité de l'Hypothèque*, Ch. premier, sect. II, § 1 (*Oeuvres de Pothier* VII, Paris 1818, 315) on similar rules in Normandy and some other French territories.

[22] *Commentarius ad Pandectas* 20,1,12.

[23] *Ibid.*: 'ipsi rei mobilis possessioni incumbere debere creditorem'. See also van der Linden, *Regtsgeleerd Practicaal en Koopmans Handboek* I,12,3.

[24] Van Bynkershoek, *Observationes tumultuariae* IV, no 3051.

[25] See Pauw, *Observationes tumultuariae novae* I, no 187 (23 Sep. 1746). It should be stressed that contemporary legal practitioners were largely unaware of the opinions of the court, because at that time judicial decisions were given without any reasoning. The reports of Bynkershoek and Pauw were not published until the twentieth century. This curious phenomenon helps to explain why the opinion of Voet remained influential, despite the fact that, as we now know, it was explicitly rejected by the 'High Council'.

The situation in Scotland was (and is) less complicated. The Roman hypothec on movables has never been incorporated into Scottish law.[26] Due to the close relationship between Roman–Dutch law and Scottish law,[27] the authority of Voet was sufficient to secure the rejection of pledges created by way of constructive delivery (*constitutum possessorium*) and the introduction of the rule that a pledge is destroyed whenever possession is restored to the pledgor.[28] It hardly needs emphasis that the law of Holland, or that of any other country with similar legal rules, did not accept the concept of a fiduciary transfer of title to movables by way of constructive delivery for the purpose of creating what is essentially a security interest in the movables thus transferred.

The opinion of Voet that transfer of possession was necessary for the creation of a charge prevailed in Scotland and in the 'Roman–Dutch' law of the Republic of South Africa. Attempts to by-pass this strict rule included fiduciary transfer by way of constructive delivery and a sale and lease-back transaction. Both mechanisms failed in Scotland, whenever possession was not transferred *de facto*, i.e. whenever transfer of title was effected by way of a *traditio ficta*. Similar attempts have also been frustrated in South Africa.[29] New possibilities occurred in Scotland after the introduction of the Sale of Goods Act in 1893. In contracts of sale of goods, the Act abolished the ancient Roman rule that title in the goods can only be transferred by *traditio* and introduced the common law rule that title passes on conclusion of the contract of sale.[30] The new system of transfer of title seemed to open an opportunity to create security interests in movables without transfer of possession to the chargee by way of sale and lease-back transactions. These attempts have also failed.[31]

---

[26] Dalrymple of Stair, *Institutions of the Law of Scotland*, ed. Walker IV,25,1 and Bell, *Commentaries on the Law of Scotland* II 25: 'in this country, conventional hypothecs on movables have no force even against personal creditors'. For similar rules in the 'Coûtumes de Paris' and those of Orléans see Pothier, *Traité de l'Hypothèque*, Ch. premier, sect. II, § 1 (*Oeuvres de Pothier* VII, 315).

[27] See *Stewart v LMS* (1943) Ses. Cas. (House of Lords) 19, at pp. 38–39 per Lord MacMillan.

[28] See *North Western Bank v Poynter* (1894) 21 Rettie 513, at 525 and Bell's *Commentaries on the Law of Scotland* II 22. The decision of the Court of Session was reversed on appeal by the House of Lords (*North Western Bank v Poynter* [1895] AC 56), bringing the law of Scotland in line with the common law of England, which adheres less strictly to the dispossession of the pledgor (see *Reeves v Capper* (1838) Bing (NC) 136; 132 ER 1057).

[29] See *Vasco Dry Cleaners v Twycross* (1979) 1 SA 603 A and van der Merwe, *Sakereg* 688 ff.

[30] C. 2,3,20 and Lord Blackburn's dicta in *M'Bain v Wallace & Co.* (1881) 8 Rettie 106 (House of Lords) 111 f.

[31] See the cases cited in Walker, *Principles of Scottish Private Law* II 1582 (7).

4. Security interests in movables in the continental European codes

The French *Code civil* (1804) concluded the process of the demise of the Roman hypothec on movables in France by requiring transfer of possession for the creation of a security interest in movables ('nantissement')[32] and by limiting hypothec to real property (immovables).[33] The creation of pledge ('gage'), by way of constructive delivery, as well as the possibility of allowing the pledgor to hold the movable property on behalf of the pledgee (bailment), were effectively eliminated by article 2076 Cc: 'Dans tous les cas, le privilège ne subsiste sur le gage qu'autant que ce gage *a été mis et est resté* en la possession du créancier, ou d'un tiers convenu entre les parties' (italics added). The old Dutch Civil Code (1838),[34] the old Italian Civil Code (1865),[35] the Spanish Civil Code[36] and even the German Civil Code of 1900[37] contained similar provisions. The German Bankruptcy Act ('Reichskonkursordnung') of 1877 already provided[38] that security interests in movables that had not been created by a permanent transfer of possession to the chargee created no preference, thus finally abolishing the ancient Roman hypothec in movables ('Mobiliarhypothek') in Germany as well.[39] I will leave an analysis of the way in which modern continental European law has been able to cope with these provisions to others and confine myself to general observations on security interests in movables on the European continent during the nineteenth century.

From a modern perspective, it seems strange that the abolition of non-possessory security interests in movables in continental European codes did not meet with stronger resistance from banks and at least a considerable portion of the business community. The statutory provisions forced

---

[32] Articles 2017–2072 Cc. It is usually emphasised in French textbooks (see e.g. Ripert and Boulanger, *Traité de Droit civil* III, Paris 1958, no 52 (19)) that the concepts of 'nantissement' and 'gage' originate from ancient French customary law, rather than from Roman law. True as this may be, one cursory look in Pothier's *Traité du Contrat de Nantissement* suffices to conclude that they were construed and applied on the basis of the Roman concept of *pignus*. A 'nantissement' without 'tradition réelle' by the pledgor to the pledgee was even construed as a Roman *hypotheca*: see Pothier, *Traité de l'Hypothèque*, Ch. IV, article 1, § 1.

[33] Article 2118 Cc. Later statutory provisions have extended 'hypothec' to aeroplanes and ships above a certain tonnage.

[34] Article 1198 O(ud) BW (1838), repealed in 1992.

[35] Article 1882 *Codice civile del Regno d'Italia* (1865).   [36] Article 1863 *Código civil*.

[37] §§ 1204, 1205 and 1253 BGB.   [38] RKO § 14.

[39] On this development see Hromadka, *Die Entwicklung des Faustpfandprinzips im 18. und 19. Jahrhundert*.

the pledge-debtor to part with possession of his movable assets, thus rendering them unproductive, a consequence that may not even have been in the interest of his creditor. The pledge-creditor, on the other hand, was forced to store and maintain goods at a high cost without even being allowed to use the goods himself. In my submission this extraordinarily impractical and ill-considered statutory arrangement can be explained by the following observations.

First, the banking world of the late eighteenth and early nineteenth centuries was, in my opinion, not structured to provide business capital to the industrial community on the basis of security interests in the stock-in-trade and machinery of its clients. Although the banks did indeed finance *trade* on a large scale, this was more often than not done on the basis of personal security (guarantees), rather than on the basis of security of a proprietary nature. An entrepreneur in need of credit to expand his industrial activities was usually dependent on sources other than banks. Hence the proliferation of limited partnerships in the nineteenth century. Presumably banks only explored forms of security other than guarantees after the advent of modern business corporations. This structural change in the financing of industrial activities by banks may well have originated in the oversupply of money on the German market as a result of the reparations made by France after the war of 1870–1871. Was this the economic origin of the German 'Sicherheitsübereignung'?

Secondly, the business community was not severely hampered by the provisions of the new codes. Long before their introduction, the standard procedure in Amsterdam and other important ports was to transfer property stored in warehouses by transfer of the warrants (bills of lading)[40] and to charge such goods by pledging the warrants to a creditor.[41] These practices were even sanctioned in certain codes, for example in the Dutch Code of 1838.[42] It is not surprising that this commercial practice inspired the first French mechanisms to introduce non-possessory security interests in movables after the introduction of the *Code civil*.

---

[40] See the eighteenth-century cases reported in Pauw, *Observationes tumultuariae novae* I, nos 490, 556 and II, no 627.
[41] *Ibid.*, III, no 1490 (a case from 1779).
[42] Article 670 of the Dutch Civil Code of 1838; the provision was repealed in 1934. Of particular interest is van der Lelij, *Levering van roerende zaken door middel van een zakenrechtelijk waardepapier* 3–15.

5. Common law and civil law

English common law also recognises two security interests in goods, one being possessory, namely pledge or pawn, the other being non-possessory, namely the chattel mortgage. The suggestion has even been made that these two common law security interests corresponded to the Roman security interests: pledge being essentially the Roman *pignus*, the nature of the (chattel) mortgage being basically the same as that of the Roman *hypotheca*. This equation, however, was explicitly rejected in the famous case of *Ryall v Rolle* (1749).[43] Burnet J observed correctly that, according to Roman law, delivery of possession was only required for the establishment of a security interest in the case of pledges, as it was – and is – according to common law. However, the learned judge expressly and unequivocally rejected the suggestion that the common law (chattel) mortgage can be identified with the Roman hypothec.

> An hypotheca gave only a lien and no property with a right to be satisfied on failure of the condition and a mortgage with us is an immediate conveyance with a power to redeem and gives a legal property.

It is quite remarkable that Burnet J tried to define a common law mortgage by reference to a text in the *Corpus Iuris*, to wit C.4,54,2:

> If your parents have sold land on condition that it be restored if either they themselves or their heirs have at some time or within a certain period offered to repay the price and the heir of the purchaser is not inclined to keep his part of that agreement, whereas you are prepared to satisfy him, a (personal) action on the basis of that agreement will be given to you.[44]

The Judge remarked that this was the description of an English mortgage in Roman law and also referred to C.4,54,7.[45] These observations provide us with an excellent description of the common law mortgage

---

[43] 1 Atk. 165; 1 Wils. 260; 1 Ves.Sen. 348; 9 Bli.N. S. 377; 26 ER 107; [1558–1774] All ER 82.

[44] 'Si fundum parentes tui ea lege vendiderunt, ut, sive ipsi sive heredes eorum emptori pretium quandoque vel intra certa tempora obtulissent, restitueretur, teque parato satisfacere condicioni dictae heres emptoris non paret, ut contractus fides servetur, actio praescriptis verbis vel ex vendito tibi dabitur.'

[45] 'If the person you have mentioned has bought from you on condition that the thing sold ought to be restituted if a certain amount has been paid within a certain period, you cannot bring an action under our "rescript" that the agreement be annulled. But if he tries to back out of his obligation by retaining that thing on account of his ownership, you can secure your interest by the remedies of signification, deposition and sequestration (i.e. of the money to be paid).' ('Si a te comparavit is cuius meministi et convenit, ut, si intra certum tempus soluta fuerit data quantitas, sit res inempta, remitti hanc conventionem rescripto nostro non iure petis. Sed si se

in terms of Roman law. The texts used by Burnet J have been taken from section 54 of the fourth book of Justinian's Code, inscribed *De pactis inter emptorem et venditorem compositis* ('On the conditions agreed upon between buyer and seller'). The common law mortgage is thus construed as a conditional sale, vesting the general proprietary interest in land or chattels thus mortgaged in the mortgagee. These provisions from Justinian's Code played a crucial role in the development of a new kind of non-possessory security interest in movables in Europe during the nineteenth century.

Most continental European codes, like the French *Code civil*,[46] the Dutch Civil Code of 1838,[47] and even the German Code of 1900,[48] contain provisions derived from this passage in Justinian's Code. These provisions, known as 'faculté de rachat' or 'vente à réméré' in France, concern the stipulation by a seller to redeem his property on tender of the price. Roman law also provided for this kind of contract, not, of course, as an alternative to security interests for which there was no need, but to regulate an option granted to a seller to redeem his property. One possibility was that his option merely conferred a right *in personam*, not a right *in re*. After the introduction of the strict rules on the creation of a pledge in the European codes and the elimination of the Roman hypothec on chattels, these statutory provisions on the right of redemption were relied upon to by-pass the strict statutory provisions on the creation of security interests in movables. Such attempts met with varying degrees of success in Europe, thus causing a genuine divide between the European legal systems. In most jurisdictions, for example in France, these attempts have totally failed. The courts looked beyond the form of these transactions and often found that an apparently valid form concealed an essentially illegal substance.[49] Germany and the Netherlands, however, followed a substantially different approach.

First the German Bankruptcy Act practically abolished the old hypothec on movables by restricting preference (priority) over the general

subtrahat, ut iure dominii eandem rem retineat, denuntiationis et obsignationis depositionisque remedio contra fraudem potes iure tuo consulere.')

[46] Articles 1659 ff. Cc.
[47] Articles 1555 ff. Dutch Civil Code of 1838; the provisions were repealed in 1992.
[48] §§ 497 ff. BGB.
[49] See, for example, the important decision in *Loewenstein, Polak & Co. C. Decaux*, Req. 11 Mar. 1879, D. 79.1.401. The *Cour de cassation* ruled (Req. 21 Mar. 1938, D.H. 1938.2.57) that the decision whether a particular contract is a valid 'vente à réméré' or an illegal security interest is a matter to be decided on the merits of the circumstances of each individual case by the courts taking notice of the facts.

creditors in bankruptcy to pledges created by transfer of possession to the pledgee. Only three years later, the new German *Reichsgericht* was confronted with two cases concerning an attempt to create a security interest in movables by means of sale and lease-back transactions. In one decision, the third civil division of the court decided that this transaction created a security interest in substance under the guise of a contract for the sale of goods with powers of redemption of the seller. It ruled that the contract was void.[50] In the other decision, however, the first civil division of the court held that such a contract was acceptable if it had been the genuine intention of the seller to transfer the true title to his creditor with a stipulation for redemption. The court regarded the fact that the economic purpose of the contract was to create a security interest as immaterial.[51] As long as the form and appearance of a genuine sale and lease-back was retained, a security interest could be created on the basis of a contract of sale and leaseback. The sale was naturally executed by constructive delivery, leaving the seller in possession and converting his powers of redemption into a legal or economic duty to redeem. Ten years later, the 'Reichsgericht' explicitly recognised that the *causa* for the constructive transfer of movable property could be the creation of a security interest in that property.[52] Thus, after a considerable lapse of time, *fiducia* was finally reintroduced in a civil law system. The Dutch 'High Council' followed suit in 1929.[53]

About the same time as continental European lawyers were in the process of reinventing the ancient Roman *fiducia cum creditore* by transforming Justinian's provisions on conveyance of property with a stipulation for redemption to supersede the strict Roman provisions on conveyance, the character of a chattel mortgage – essentially a conveyance

---

[50] RG 24 Sep. 1880, RGZ 2, 173. As the case had to be decided according to Roman law, the court based its decision on D. 18,1,80,3 (*Labeo*) and C. 4,22,3.

[51] RG 9 Oct. 1880, RGZ 2, 168 (170): 'Es ist nicht nur rechtlich zulässig, sondern auch in häufiger Übung, daß einem Gläubiger zu seiner Sicherstellung wegen einer persönlicher Forderung von seinem Schuldner ein Vermögens-Objekt in der durchaus ernstlichen Absicht verkauft und übertragen wird, daß der Gläubiger als Käufer wirklicher Eigentümer und zur Ausübung aller Rechte eines Eigentümers befugt werden soll, der wirtschaftliche Zweck einer bloßen Sicherstellung aber dadurch erreicht wird, daß der Gläubiger sich durch Nebenabreden persönlich verbindlich macht, unter gewissen vereinbarten Bedingungen das Eigentum dem bisherigen Schuldner zurückzuübertragen.' It is a curious but totally accidental coincidence that the formulation of this decision practically matches the important recent decision of the Dutch 'High Council', *In re Sogelease* (19 May 1995 (NJ 1996, 119)), almost verbatim.

[52] RG 2 June 1890, RGZ 26, 180.   [53] *Hoge Raad* 25 Jan. 1929 (NJ 1929, 616).

of property with a stipulation for redemption[54] – was fundamentally changed in England. The legislative act which triggered this change was the introduction of Bills of Sale Acts (since 1878) and the requirement of registration. After then, 'chattel mortgages' were only allowed if the grantor had actually transferred possession to the grantee. Only then did the mortgagee enjoy preference over the general creditors upon his debtor's bankruptcy. Creditors have naturally tried to by-pass these provisions by returning to the archetype of non-possessory security in chattels of the common law, the conditional sale (the sale and lease-back or a hire-purchase contract). Insufficient attention has been paid on the continent, especially in the Netherlands, to the way in which English courts enforce the Sale of Goods Act. 'The court is to look through and behind the documents, and to get at the reality.'[55] More often than not, the court finds a sham or simulated security transaction behind an apparently valid transaction and refuses to allow a creditor to avail himself of a proprietary security interest created in this way.[56]

Bibliography

G. J. Bell, *Commentaries on the Law of Scotland* II (7th edn, 1870).
Cornelis van Bynkershoek, *Observationes tumultuariae* IV (1962).
Fr. Calasso, *Medio Aevo del Diritto* (1954).
  Introduzione al Diritto Commune (1970).
B. Carpzov, *Jurisprudentia forensis Romano-Saxonicus* (1650).
Helmut Coing, *Europäisches Privatrecht* I (*Älteres Gemeines Recht*) (1985).
J. Dalrymple of Stair, *Institutions of the Law of Scotland*, ed. Walker (1981).
John Dawson, *The Oracles of the Law* (1968).
Hugo Grotius, *Inleidinge tot de Hollandsche rechtsgeleerdheid* (1895).
Wolfgang Hromadka, *Die Entwicklung des Faustpfandprinzips im 18. und 19. Jahrhundert* (1971).
M. Kaser, *Das römische Privatrecht* (RP) I (1971); II (1975).
  'Studien zum römischen Pfandrecht', *Tijdschrift voor Rechtsgeschiedenis* 44 (1976) 283 ff.
  'Besitzpfand und "besitzloses" Pfand', *Studia et Documenta Historiae et Iuris* 45 (1979) 1 ff.
Paul Koschaker, *Europa und das römische Recht* (1966).

---

[54] There is, however, a fundamental difference between a mortgage and a civil law transfer of title with a power (or duty) to redeem. English equity has transformed the common law right to redeem, a right *in personam*, into a proprietary interest *sui generis*, the 'equity of redemption'.
[55] *Maddel v Thomas & Co.* [1891] QB 230, at 234 per Lord Esher.
[56] See *Polsky v S & A Services* [1951] 1 All ER 185.

A. J. van der Lelij, *Levering van roerende zaken door middel van een zakenrechtelijk waardepapier* (1996).
J. van der Linden, *Regtsgeleerd Practicaal en Koopmans Handboek* (1806).
C. G. van der Merwe, *Sakereg* (2nd edn, 1989).
G. Noordraven, 'D. 13,7,6 pr: un caso di pignus', *Bullettino di Diritto Romano* 83 (1980) 247 ff.
 De 'Fiducia' in het Romeinse recht (1988).
Willem Pauw, *Observationes tumultuariae novae* I (1964).
R. J. Pothier, *Traité de l'Hypothèque* (1818).
G. Schlichting, *Die Verfügungsbeschränkung des Verpfänders im klassischen römischen Recht* (1973).
S. Tondo, '"Pignus" e "Precarium"', *Labeo* 5 (1959) 157 ff.
Andreas Wacke, 'Ein Verfügungsverbot des römischen Verpfänders?', *Rivista Internazionale di Diritto Romano e Antico* 24 (1973) 184 ff.
D. Walker, *Principles of Scottish Private Law* II (1975).
Fr. Wieacker, *Privatrechtsgeschichte der Neuzeit* (1967).

3 Security in movables in the United States – Uniform Commercial Code Article 9: a basis for comparison

HARRY C. SIGMAN

The purpose of this chapter is to provide the reader with an opportunity to compare movables security law in Europe, particularly this volume's discussion of its common core, with the corresponding body of law in the United States. This chapter will describe the approach taken in the US, an approach that has already had significant influence beyond the borders, ranging from a substantially complete adoption in virtually all of the provinces of Canada, to visible impact in the formulation of the EBRD Model Law on Secured Transactions (1994), the United Nations Convention on Assignment of Receivables in International Trade (approved by the General Assembly in 2001), the UNIDROIT Convention on International Interests in Mobile Equipment (recently approved at the diplomatic conference in Cape Town), and the OAS Model Inter-American Law on Secured Transactions (recently approved at the sixth Inter-American Specialized Conference on Private International Law) and to direct or indirect influence on contemporary reform legislation in New Zealand, Eastern Europe, Mexico and elsewhere.

Article 9, part of the Uniform Commercial Code ("UCC"), is a substantial piece of legislation, first enacted in the early 1950s, that seeks to facilitate financing secured by "personal property" (i.e., movables, whether tangible or intangible, as distinct from "real property", i.e., land and buildings) by making such financing more efficient, economical and widely available. Facilitative rather than regulatory, Article 9 seeks to

---

Harry C. Sigman was a member of the Drafting Committee that revised Article 9 UCC; the views in this chapter, however, are his own.

attain this goal by providing as much certainty and predictability as possible, by providing a comprehensive set of flexible market-oriented rules for the creation and enforcement of security interests and for the determination of priority among competing claims to the collateral, minimizing the need for and likelihood of litigation. The legislation, of course, stands over a base of property and contract law, but the rules are based on practicality rather than theory, formulated with a view to the needs of the marketplace.

While the US is a common law jurisdiction, the movables security field is governed in comprehensive and detailed fashion by Article 9, with, quite deliberately, little left to judicial development. This approach is significantly different from movables security law in Europe, where the law is either almost entirely developed by the courts, based on very few Civil Code provisions, as for example in Germany; or where there is a combination of general Civil Code provisions supplemented by specific legislation dealing with particular transactions, such as the various *nantissements* and *warrants*, as in France, in instances where the legislator was persuaded by practical necessity to depart from either, or both, the rule or the logic of general Civil Code principles, but did so only on a limited basis; or, more recently, where there has been broad legislation directly modifying the otherwise applicable general rules, as illustrated by the Belgian Law of 6 July 1994 concerning transfer of claims (*cession et mise en gage de créances*).

In this chapter, terms defined in the UCC are shown in bold italics the first time they appear. Calling attention to the fact that a term is defined serves to stress the importance of the definitions in the methodology of Article 9, to assist the reader who desires to go further in depth into Article 9, and to warn the reader that a term may not have its simple vernacular meaning. In the UCC, many substantive elements are built into the definitions. Thus, the definitions are key to the understanding and application of the substantive rules, particularly those concerning perfection and priority. This chapter is not a comprehensive treatise and space does not allow quotation of the definitions. They are, however, easy to find in the statute. Although some definitions are found in section 1-201, most are found in section 9-102, in alphabetical order. When a term is defined elsewhere than in one of these two sections, the section providing the definition is identified. Concepts or terms that are significant but which are not defined in the statute are shown in single quotation marks the first time they appear.

Brief description of key features of Article 9

Article 9 provides for a unitary security device applicable to virtually all forms of personal property, tangible and intangible (including intellectual property and rights to payment or other claims against third parties), applicable to the use of future as well as present property as collateral, applicable without regard to the nature of the obligation secured, applicable to all types of creditors (i.e., not limited to banks or specific types of lenders and including sellers on secured credit, such as title-retaining vendors), and applicable to all types of *debtors* (i.e., not limited to commercial enterprise debtors and including individuals whether they be professionals, sole traders or consumers).

Rather than total categorical exclusion, when appropriate, distinctions with respect to types of debtors, *secured parties* and *collateral* are made, and special, precisely drawn, rules are provided; these are based not on abstract concepts but rather on the basis of policy in the context of the realities of the marketplace. Thus, for example, rather than complete exclusion of consumer transactions, which would have the effect of depriving consumers of the benefit of efficient less costly financing, specific protective rules applicable to *consumer debtors* or to *consumer transactions* or to *consumer-goods transactions* are provided within the framework of Article 9.

Further, the comprehensive scope of Article 9 brings together in a single regime coverage with respect to both tangibles and rights to payment, which are frequently encumbered together. This differs from the structure typically found in Europe, where separate regimes cover these two types of assets.

The unitary device, denominated a *security interest*, is an interest in property – a real rather than a personal right. Indeed, guaranties embodied in the promises of third parties, which are personal rights rather than real rights, are not, as such, directly viewed as collateral under Article 9, are distinct from security interests and are governed by a separate, largely non-statutory, body of law (very usefully systematized recently by the Restatement of the Law of Suretyship and Guaranty). Thus, B's obligation to L to repay a loan, accompanied only by G's guaranty, would not be a secured obligation and Article 9 would not be applicable to the transaction. In a transaction otherwise subject to Article 9 (e.g., because the obligation is secured by personal property collateral), however, where the collateral is a right to payment (e.g., B's obligation to L to repay a loan is secured by B's right to payment of a debt owed to B by X), if B's right to payment from X is accompanied by a guaranty given by G, that guaranty relating to the collateral would be treated as additional collateral for the benefit of L, as a *supporting obligation* (discussed below).

Coverage of both present and future collateral (facilitated by the acceptability of general collateral "descriptions") and permitting the collateral to secure both present and future obligations, without limitation as to nature or amount, together may be referred to as the "floating lien" concept. The floating lien facilitates modern financing transactions such as revolving credit and bulk assignments of receivables. Some or all of the elements of the floating lien are found in some of the European systems, although they often (i) are limited to a particular class of debtor (for example, in England, the "floating charge," although not necessarily conceptually limited to corporate debtors, has been embodied in the Companies Act and has been developed judicially in the context of corporate debtors and is not used with respect to other debtors such as sole traders and partnerships); (ii) are limited to a particular class of secured party (for example, the Belgian *gage sur fonds de commerce/pand op de handelszaak* and the advantaged mode of assignment of receivables under the French *Loi Dailly* (2 Jan. 1981) may be made only in favor of a bank or other financial institution); and/or (iii) cover much but not all of the debtor's assets (for example, the French *nantissement sur fonds de commerce* does not cover inventory and the Belgian analog covers inventory only up to 50 percent of its value). See also the special laws on enterprise mortgages enacted in Sweden and Finland in 1984, and compare the EBRD Model Law provisions on an "enterprise charge."

The Article 9 security interest is based on a functional approach, rather than on theoretical distinctions, and the location of title to the property that serves as collateral is, for this purpose, irrelevant. This contrasts with those European systems where ownership (even, in some cases, an ownership created for security purposes) is outcome-determinative. Article 9 is applicable to all transactions in movables which serve the purpose or have the effect of providing security for an obligation. Thus, there is not a body of specialized *nantissements* or *warrants* having different rules and producing different consequences than the general principle, and there is not a general distinction made between the seller of goods who retains title to secure deferred payment of the purchase price and the third-party lender who (by paying the seller or lending money to the buyer who uses that money to pay the seller) has performed the identical economic function of providing the purchase-money credit to the debtor-buyer.

The apparent form of the transaction and the language of the documentation are, for this purpose, disregarded; it is the economic substance that governs. Form and language may, of course, continue to have impact for other purposes, e.g., tax consequences, balance sheet presentation, etc. The debtor receives the same protection of his equity in the goods regardless of the nature of the credit or the creditor, and all types of creditors that have "purchase-money security interests" (this term is not, strictly speaking, defined but is given substantive meaning by the very extensive provisions of section 9-103) in those goods are provided with the same priority rules and remedies. Denomination of a transaction as a "lease" does not control; for Article 9 purposes, the transaction is treated as a secured transaction if its actual economic effects are identical to a secured deferred payment sale of the **equipment**. While the concept of ignoring the nomenclature used by the parties to a transaction is not unknown in Europe (see, e.g., the Dutch provision on sale with payment by installments: "All contracts, that have the same tenor, entered into in whichever form or under whichever name, are treated as purchase and sale on installments." 7A:1576 lid 3 BW, and the analogous provision in the hire-purchase law, 7A:1576h lid 3 BW, both dating back to 1936), judicial re-characterization of a transaction appears to be rare. The German system recognizes a category of ownership for security purposes; this category has been explicitly rejected in the Netherlands (3:84 lid 3 BW) and Belgium (assignment of claim rejected in insolvency because made with an obligation to re-assign upon payment of debt, Cass. 17 Oct. 1996).

Under Article 9, the functional approach is explicit and is a key element of the law. Moreover, as there is but a single device, Article 9 presents no issue of distinctions between simultaneously co-existing types of security rights and no issue of the inability of parties to create new types of property rights not specified in the Civil Code (*numerus clausus*). Further, Article 9 avoids dependence on judicial ingenuity to fashion arrangements that modernize the law or are otherwise responsive to business needs (consider, for example, the recent German case law on "over-security").

To maximize certainty and to allow secured parties effectively to assess their exposure to claims of others against the collateral, Article 9 provides a detailed, carefully nuanced priority scheme, specifying outcomes in the statute (rather than leaving them to be developed over time and unpredictably by the courts). These rules are carefully drawn to support the UCC's overall policy goals in the context of the marketplace. See, for example, the discussions below of the distinctions made by the special purchase-money super-priority rules or the *buyer in ordinary course of business* rules.

A crucial part of the priority scheme is the "filing" system. The filing of a *financing statement* establishes an objective marker, a date certainly not subject to private manipulation, which can be, and in most cases is, used as a priority determinant. These important functions are served without the need for public disclosure of private financial details, and without the need for imposition of requirements, such as notarization, that entail significant costs and/or delays. As discussed in detail below, the filing system provides a database of information that suffices to warn that a creditor may, presently or thereafter, claim a security interest in property in which the identified debtor may, presently or thereafter, have rights, with the collateral being indicated in either specific or general terms, while at the same time the information provided in the financing statement is not so extensive as to either disclose confidential data or overburden the filing office. The financing statement provides only minimal identifying data sufficient to enable a searcher to protect its interests. Original security agreements or other documents need not be filed. Indeed, a financing statement is not limited to a particular transaction (it may serve with respect to post-filing transactions as well, whether or not foreseen at the time of filing or of the initial transaction) and may be filed before a security agreement exists. The database is publicly and inexpensively accessible.

The existence of this filing system makes possible efficient financing secured by nonpossessory interests in tangibles and by assignments of intangibles, present and future, and individually or in bulk. The notion of publicity with respect to security rights in movables has had varying acceptance in Europe, being generally rejected in Germany and playing a limited but significant role in Belgium and France and a substantial role in Norway (Hungary, Poland, Bulgaria and Albania also have created registries for nonpossessory rights in movables). The Cape Town Convention contemplates an international registry. That, however, will be an asset-based registry, as contrasted with the debtor-based Article 9 filing system; asset-based registries with respect to aircraft already exist in many countries.

Finally, Article 9 introduced an efficient market-based remedial scheme, permitting the parties to go to court to obtain such assistance or protection as they may deem necessary, but only if one of the parties chooses to do so. Otherwise, the secured party may realize upon the collateral by disposing of it without judicial or administrative involvement, albeit subject to the obligations to act in good faith and in a commercially reasonable manner. Availability of efficient and speedy remedies makes the legal regime effective, and resort to judicial involvement in the realization process is relatively rare.

This discussion is not intended to assert that Article 9 offers the only effective movables security typology. There can be no doubt that the *Eigentumsvorbehalt* (especially when *verlängerter Eigentumsvorbehalt* and *erweiterter Eigentumsvorbehalt*), as judicially developed in Germany during the twentieth century, is a very powerful device for sellers, highly successful in the prevailing economic and social conditions and legal structure. Indeed, that device is far more powerful than its counterparts in other European countries, although in France and Belgium title retention has been made more effective during the last two decades. Efforts during that period toward unification of law on title retention on the European level have, however, thus far not been successful. Likewise, especially in tandem with the current insolvency law and practice in England, fixed and floating charges are highly potent and flexible, if somewhat technical, tools for the extension of secured credit in England.

History and context

A discussion of the history and context of Article 9 may be informative to the European reader, to explain how Article 9 came to be what it is, to provide a contrast in the lawmaking process, and to facilitate further research into Article 9.

Under the US federal system, generally speaking, property and contract law are matters left to the states. Certain specified subjects are allocated by the US Constitution to federal law, including (relevant to our subject) bankruptcy law, patent and copyright law and, to the extent determined by Congress, certain matters affecting interstate commerce. Under this structure, movables security law is determined by the states, but, in some contexts, federal law may interact with or, to the extent determined by Congress, supersede state law. The UCC is not a single federal law, but rather a law separately enacted by each state; Article 9 is currently in force in all states in essentially identical form.

The UCC was developed by a cooperative effort of the National Conference of Commissioners on Uniform State Laws and the American Law Institute. The former, over 100 years old and composed of persons designated by officials of each state, drafts model acts but has no legislative power. The latter is a national membership organization, over seventy-five years old and composed of respected judges, academics and practitioners, dedicated to the task of organizing and reforming law. In addition to its participation in the formulation of the UCC, the Institute engages in other projects, the best known of which is the production of the highly influential Restatements of the Law (e.g., Contracts, Torts, Conflict of Laws and, more recently, Suretyship and Guaranty) that broadly synthesize the law in various subjects as it has developed over time throughout the country. For over a century, the Conference has drafted and presented to the states for consideration uniform laws on many subjects; these proposals have met with varying degrees of success. Shortly before World War II, while the Conference was drafting an updated version of the Uniform Sales Act, it was determined to broaden the scope of the project; it was also determined to collaborate on this project with the Institute. These decisions ultimately led to the UCC, first enacted in 1953, in Pennsylvania.

The UCC is not a systematic statement of general principles. Rather, it is drafted in more standard legislative format and deals with several subjects in varying degrees of comprehensiveness and detail. Initially, it was comprised of nine articles, each containing numerous, often lengthy and complex, sections. Article 1 consists of general principles and definitions applicable throughout the rest of the UCC. Article 2 deals with transactions in goods and is the successor to the earlier Uniform Sales Act (which itself was based on the English Sale of Goods Act 1893). Article 3 deals with negotiable instruments; it also was the successor to an earlier uniform law, the Uniform Negotiable Instruments Law. Article 4 deals with the check collection process. Article 5 deals with letters of credit. Article 6, subsequently repealed in most states, deals with bulk transfers, essentially the uniform law successor to statutes adopted by many states in the late nineteenth century which were intended to thwart bulk sales of inventory designed to defraud the seller's creditors. Article 7 deals with documents of title (warehouse receipts, bills of lading and the like). Article 8 deals with investment property, primarily concerned with rights and obligations among issuers, issuees and transferees of securities (substantive investor protection and trading regulation are dealt with in federal and other state laws). Finally, Article 9 covers secured transactions involving personal property collateral.

During the 1950s and 1960s, the UCC was enacted in virtually all states. Enactment in Louisiana came somewhat later, although the deferment of adoption of Article 9 was due to local politics concerning the management of the filing system and had nothing to do with Louisiana movables security law having originated in the civil law tradition.

Since the late 1980s, the UCC has undergone several changes. Repeal of Article 6 was recommended; Articles 3 and 4 were significantly revised; Article 8 underwent two revisions, the latter (1994) making it a very modern flexible tool in an age of dematerialized and indirectly held securities (European recognition of the need for modernization of the law in this area is seen in the current preparation of a Directive on the cross-border use of such collateral and in the Hague Conference on Private International Law draft Convention on "the law applicable to certain rights in respect of securities held with an intermediary"); Article 5 was revised to coordinate more clearly with the International Chamber of Commerce's Uniform Customs and Practices and to take into account the substantial growth of the use of standby letters of credit; and Article 2A, dealing with "true" leases of goods, and Article 4A, dealing with electronic funds transfers, were added. A revised version of Article 1 was approved by the sponsors recently, and the enactment effort will begin shortly. References in this chapter to Article 1 are to the original version.

Article 9 was recently substantially revised (there had been rather modest amendments in 1972). The substantive discussion of Article 9 in this chapter is based on the 2000 Official Text of Revised Article 9 (it was initially approved by the sponsors in 1998 and was slightly amended in 2000), which is currently in effect in all fifty states.

It is worthwhile to elaborate on both the nature of the revisions to Article 9 and the revision process. The process had a profound impact on the substance. The Drafting Committee consisted of practitioners (one of whom was a bankruptcy court judge) of great experience and expertise in the subject, as well as several academics, all of whom were designated by the UCC's two sponsors, the Conference and the Institute. All of its proceedings were public, the drafts were posted on the internet and were the subject of programs for practicing lawyers, paralegals, bankers, filing officers and others. Interested groups were invited to attend meetings and send comments, although anyone could attend without invitation. Funding was provided to enable representatives of consumer interests to attend and participate in the drafting process. Drafts were reviewed by the membership of the sponsor organizations and finally approved by them at their respective annual meetings. The openness of the process, and the participation by those reflecting affected interests, on both the debtor and the creditor sides, served to assure not only acceptance and support but also balance in the adoption of practical solutions desired by affected interests.

In the short time since its promulgation by the sponsoring organizations, Revised Article 9 has already been adopted by every state and the District of Columbia. In an effort to minimize transition issues and conflict of laws problems, the sponsors suggested a nationwide uniform effective date of 1 July 2001. Revised Article 9 became effective simultaneously on 1 July 2001 in forty-six states, and since 1 January 2002, has been in effect in all states.

This is remarkable in at least three respects: (1) Article 9 has been enacted with almost perfect uniformity (such local tinkering as has occurred has been minor and at the margins, generally adding some narrow exclusions from the scope of Article 9's coverage); thus, national uniformity has essentially been achieved despite this body of law being enacted by the states rather than by Congress; (2) in the past, several years passed before all the states had enacted the various revised articles or other uniform laws, while in this case, the entire enactment process has been accomplished within three legislative sessions; and (3) an agreed deferred uniform effective date has been successfully used for the first time in the history of uniform laws in the US, thereby dramatically lessening the cost of change in the law.

It is noteworthy that despite the risks of nonuniformity inherent in the fact that Article 9 is state rather than federal law – to wit, it might be enacted with significant local variations and it might be interpreted differently by the courts of different states – neither of these risks has materialized to any significant extent, and the risks are even smaller under Revised Article 9, based on the success in the enactment process and the conscious effort to leave even less for judicial development.

Substantively, Revised Article 9 left intact all of the fundamental principles and policies found in the prior version. It did expand the scope, reorganize the statutory structure somewhat, introduce some new terminology, and modernize and make the filing system more efficient, uniform and transparent, by, inter alia, further limiting the role of the filing office to a more clearly ministerial function. The revisions also rendered Article 9 more responsive to technological developments, reflecting the greatly increased economic importance of intangibles such as intellectual property rights, and recognizing that transactions were now being achieved without writings, that rights were increasingly being reflected in non-material forms, and that the communications revolution was enabling parties to act in electronic or other forms heretofore unknown. Article 9's provisions also were modified to make them more responsive to new high-speed and more sophisticated transactions, in direct response to the needs of the economy. The revisions expanded the override of contractual and statutory provisions prohibiting or limiting assignability of rights. Finally, the default provisions were refined to reflect experience and to provide more guidance, making certain provisions more debtor-protective and making some remedies more flexible.

Revised Article 9 is organized in seven parts and comprises 135 sections.

Article 9 in depth

Creation, attachment and enforceability of a security interest

An Article 9 security interest is "created" by simple contract. Indeed, **security agreement** means any agreement that "creates or provides for" a security interest. There are no language requirements, no magic words that must be used. A security agreement need not be denominated as such or found in a separate document or special form. Indeed, a single sentence such as follows will more than suffice: Debtor grants a security interest to Secured Party in all of Debtor's inventory, wherever located, whenever acquired, to secure all of Debtor's present and future obligations, of whatever nature, whenever and however arising, in favor of Secured Party. This will create a security interest not only in Debtor's present and future **inventory**, but also, automatically (unless excluded), in all **proceeds** of whatever nature (including checks and rights to payment on open account) or evidenced by an **instrument** (e.g., a promissory note) or **chattel paper** (a term coined by Article 9 to denote a lease of goods or the combination of the buyer's obligation to pay and an interest in the goods securing that promise, such as title retention, which in the US is more commonly called a conditional sale contract). The illustrative language also demonstrates the relaxed collateral description rules of section 9-108. This provision expressly makes sufficient a description using terms defined in the UCC. Vernacular usage is, of course, also permissible; for example, one might describe the inventory as "all computers held by Debtor for sale or lease."

Thus, creation of a security interest is simple and inexpensive. Of course, typical loan documentation will include far more than the simple phrase sufficient to create the security interest, e.g., borrower's covenants and warranties, but these are not legally essential elements of a security agreement, are not required in order to create a security interest and are not governed by Article 9.

Although a security interest is created by agreement, three elements are required in order for the security interest to "attach" (section 9-203) to a particular item of collateral – attachment is the moment when the security interest becomes "enforceable" against the debtor and third parties with respect to particular collateral.

The three elements of attachment and enforceability are: (1) **value** has been given (this requires no more than simple consideration; it includes the existence of previously extended credit as well as a promise to extend credit); (2) the debtor has rights in the collateral (the debtor's interest need not be full ownership, nor need it necessarily have been paid for, and it might even be a voidable title); and (3) either (i) the debtor has authenticated a security agreement that provides a description of the collateral, or (ii) with respect to specified types of collateral, the collateral is, pursuant to a security agreement, in the secured party's "possession" (although not a defined term, the concept is given meaning in section 9-313) or **control** (a term defined, with respect to particular types of property, in sections 9-104–9-107 and 8-106). The third element – an authenticated agreement – is evidentiary; it is the only formality requirement, in the nature of a statute of frauds. It is easily satisfied and rarely a hurdle. **Authenticate** is a defined term reflecting Article 9's embrace of modern technology – it includes **signing** (which, under the definition in section 1-201, has long not been limited to a manually applied name in cursive script) and encompasses any adoption of a symbol or encryption or similar processing of a record with the intent to identify the person and adopt or accept the record. **Record** means "information that is inscribed on a tangible medium or which is stored in an electronic or other medium and is retrievable in perceivable form." Thus, a security agreement may be in electronic form.

It is useful to examine briefly the element of "description" of the collateral, as it contrasts with the concept of specificity under, for example, Dutch law. The general meaning is reasonable identification, but this is supplemented by specific provisions that permit description by category, by type (using any term defined in the UCC), quantity or allocational formula. The statute expressly renders insufficient, however, use of a supergeneric description such as "all the debtor's assets" (although section 9-504 provides that use of a supergeneric description is sufficient for purposes of the "indication" of collateral provided by a financing statement). This rule concerning supergeneric description is not a rule limiting the extent of collateral that may be taken; it relates only to the manner of its description in the security agreement.

The three elements of attachment need not occur in any particular sequence, but a security interest does not attach to a particular item of collateral until all three have occurred.

Attachment of a security interest to collateral not only automatically gives the secured party rights in the proceeds of the collateral but also, under section 9-203, constitutes attachment of a security interest in any supporting obligation (e.g., a *letter-of-credit right* or a guaranty), and in any security interest or mortgage or other lien on personal or real property which supports or secures collateral that is a right to payment or performance (e.g., an instrument or an account). Also, under section 9-203, attachment of a security interest in a *securities account* (defined in section 8-501) constitutes attachment of a security interest in all *security entitlements* (defined in section 8-102) carried in the securities account. This latter provision is an element of the methodology, and illustrates the terminology, used to facilitate financing secured by "indirectly held" *securities* (defined in section 8-102). See, generally, part 5 of Article 8.

Section 9-204 confirms the effectiveness of provisions in a security agreement which provide for a security interest in after-acquired collateral (except for consumer goods) and which provide that collateral may secure future advances or other value, whether or not the same are given *pursuant to commitment*. Section 9-205 validates (declares not fraudulent against creditors) secured transactions despite freedom given to the debtor to use, commingle or dispose of the collateral without accounting for the proceeds or replacing the collateral. These provisions, in the context of the permissiveness as to form and language, serve to validate and facilitate the floating lien.

The provisions discussed above reflect the basic Article 9 structure concerning the creation and attachment of a security interest that is a property right enforceable against the debtor and third parties. This structure is accompanied by a detailed priority scheme, discussed below, that specifies when, and the extent to which, the security interest will have priority over the claims, rights and interests of particular third parties under particular circumstances.

Scope of Article 9's coverage

Article 9 applies to "a transaction, regardless of its form, that creates [(1)] a security interest in personal property or **fixtures** by contract; . . . [(2)] a sale of **accounts**, chattel paper, **payment intangibles**, or **promissory notes**; [(3)] a **consignment**; . . ." (section 9-109). The first of these three categories is extremely broad, and its articulation implements the functional approach described above. This category encompasses, for example, transactions that are denominated as leases but which, when their terms are examined (under a set of carefully articulated statutory provisions found in section 1-201(37), the definition of security interest), are economically indistinguishable from conditional sales. The second category encompasses transfers of rights to payment which are not made for security purposes. For essentially practical reasons, these transfers are treated in some respects, by making Article 9 applicable to them, as if they were made for security purposes. In some instances, these transactions are very difficult to distinguish from transfers made for security purposes; inclusion under Article 9 renders them subject to filing requirements and obviates the need to make such a distinction until after default. In other instances, they were included in Article 9 (at the request of the industry) to give such transactions, often the subject of securitizations, the benefit of the clear rules, certainty and uniformity provided by Article 9. Likewise, consignments are included so as to provide creditors of consignees with the benefit of the publicity requirements of Article 9, again obviating the need to inquire into the true nature of transactions labeled as consignments (i.e., whether made for security purposes or not) until after default.

This broad scope is narrowed slightly by a list, in section 9-109, of exclusions – particular transactions to which it was deemed inadvisable to apply Article 9. Also, while not an exclusion from scope, section 9-201 subordinates Article 9 to any rule of law that establishes a different rule for consumers.

Other provisions spell out the rights and duties of the parties when the secured party is in possession or control of the collateral (e.g., the power of a secured party who is a pledgee of securities to re-pledge those securities) and the obligation of the secured party to respond to a debtor who requests an **accounting** or a list of collateral.

While virtually all of the foregoing provisions may be modified by agreement between the parties, the careful articulation in the statute does away with the need to elaborate them in the agreement when no modification is desired.

Choice of Law (including, importantly, where to file)

Because of the federal nature of the United States, rules concerning determination of the applicable law in the context of transactions having contacts with more than one state are provided, although not discussed here. Of course, to the extent that the substantive laws of the implicated states are identical, there is no conflict. Nevertheless, even in that situation, there is a need for a pointer as to where to file, i.e., rules that determine which state's filing system governs.

For this purpose, the primary rule, found in section 9-301, is the "location" of the debtor (whether the collateral is tangible or intangible), which is specified as the "principal residence" when the debtor is an "individual" (even with respect to business-related debts), and the "place of business" (or the "chief executive office", if the debtor has more than one place of business), if the debtor is an **organization**. The concept of location is developed in section 9-307.

Importantly, the meaning of the general debtor location rule is modified in the case of a debtor that is a **registered organization** (most commonly typified by a domestic corporation), in which case the debtor's location is the jurisdiction of the organization rather than the place of the chief executive office. This pointer provides an objectively determinable location that is verifiable from the public records. Section 9-307 also provides special location rules for registered organizations organized under federal law, foreign bank branches and agencies and selected other classes of debtors.

The general debtor location rule, however, is not applicable in the case of a debtor whose location is not in a jurisdiction "whose law generally requires information concerning the existence of a nonpossessory security interest to be made generally available in a filing, recording, or registration system as a condition or result of the security interest's obtaining priority over the rights of a lien creditor with respect to the collateral." In that case, the debtor is deemed located in the District of Columbia. This rule will not come into play if the debtor is located in the US, but may well become applicable if the debtor is located elsewhere.

An important exception to the general debtor location rule is found in section 9-305(a)(3), which refers instead to the local law of the "securities intermediary's jurisdiction" (as specified in section 8-110(e)) for determination of the law governing perfection, and also priority, with respect to security interests in security entitlements and securities accounts. (Compare the draft provisions of the Hague Convention.)

Section 9-316 provides rules concerning the effect on perfection of a change in the governing law (e.g., a change in the facts which results in a different state's filing system becoming the one that governs). Special four-month and one-year rules may require a filing in a different jurisdiction when the debtor location changes from one jurisdiction to another or the collateral is transferred to a transferee located in a different jurisdiction. (NB: a transferee of collateral becomes a debtor even when, because it does not undertake to pay or perform the secured obligation, the transferee does not become an *obligor*.)

Perfection

The concept of "perfection" (see sections 9-308–9-316) is used by Article 9 as an element of the priority scheme. The term is somewhat misleading in that it suggests an absolute that is not the case. A perfected security interest generally but not always prevails over a competing interest, and an unperfected security interest does not always lose. Rather, it is necessary to examine the specific priority rule applicable to a particular contest to ascertain whether perfection determines which party will prevail. Perfection is irrelevant *vis-à-vis* the debtor.

How is perfection achieved?

In certain instances, perfection is *automatic*, that is, no special steps need be taken beyond those needed for the attachment of a security interest to the collateral. See section 9-309. Examples of security interests that are perfected automatically include: a purchase-money security interest in consumer goods; a security interest in investment property created by a *broker* or a *securities intermediary* (both defined in section 8-102); and a sale of a payment intangible or a promissory note. This last rule has the effect of continuing the practice under former (pre-revision) Article 9 – filing was not required because former Article 9 did not cover these transactions. Inclusion within Article 9 but with automatic perfection offers Article 9 coverage of loan participations (with the resulting certainty and uniformity of applicable law) without requiring a useless filing against the transferor lead bank. In addition, under section 9-308, perfection of a security interest in collateral also perfects a security interest in a supporting obligation for the collateral; perfection of a security interest in a right to payment also perfects a security interest in security interests and other liens on property which secure that right to payment; and perfection of a security interest in a securities account automatically perfects a security interest in the security entitlements carried in that account.

When perfection is not automatic, one of three perfection techniques is required: *filing* of a financing statement, *possession* or *control*. See sections 9-310–9-314. The key variable is the nature of the collateral. As to some types of collateral, one of these methods is the exclusive method; as to others, that method may be permissible or may be unavailable. Filing is almost always a permissible method. Note that choice of the method of perfection may have an impact on priority. Also, when a particular type of property is governed by an applicable state or federal law that designates a particular method of perfection or a particular place of filing, that rule, rather than Article 9, controls the method of perfection. See section 9-311. The most common instance of application of this rule is the state law in most jurisdictions which provides for perfection with respect to a motor vehicle (other than while it is inventory in the hands of a dealer), which is commonly achieved by notation on a title certificate. Thus, while Article 9 governs the substantive elements relating to security interests in motor vehicles, perfection is typically not achieved by filing in an Article 9 filing office. Note that this is not the case in the Canadian provinces, where filings against motor vehicles constitute a major fraction of all PPSA (Personal Property Security Act) filings.

Control as a perfection method is available only with respect to investment property, deposit accounts, letter-of-credit rights and **electronic chattel paper**, with the manner of achieving control being defined separately for each of these four types of collateral. Control is defined in a way that allows a secured party to perfect the security interest while allowing the debtor to trade in the items carried in its securities account and write checks against its deposit account. Thus, control does not necessarily entail dispossession (or, more precisely, disempowerment) of the debtor, but it is a technique that both definitively fixes a time for priority purposes and also facilitates post-default enforcement.

Possession, of course, can be used as a method of perfection only with respect to tangible collateral. Possession has its traditional meaning, with the secured party able to hold possession itself or through its agent (or through a bailee who has attorned to the secured party), but the debtor, of course, cannot serve as the secured party's agent for this purpose. This perfection method means actual, not constructive or other fictitious, possession.

With respect to most types of collateral, the most common technique, by far, is filing. The filing system is discussed in some detail below.

The perfection step may occur before or after attachment (see section 9-308(a)) (perfection, however, is not attained until attachment occurs). For example, in the typical floating lien context, filing will, of course, always occur prior to the debtor's obtaining rights in the after-acquired collateral. It is not uncommon for the filing of the financing statement to occur before all of the elements of attachment have occurred. See section 9-502(d).

When a debtor disposes of collateral, generally, the security interest continues in the collateral even in the hands of the transferee, except as otherwise expressly provided in the statute (as described below, in the context of inventory collateral sold to a buyer in ordinary course of business, the exception swallows the rule), and also continues in identifiable proceeds of the collateral. See section 9-315.

Priority rules

The Article 9 priority scheme is found in sections 9-317–9-339. These very extensive provisions set out not general principles but rather detailed rules that specify outcomes for particular competitions. The key rules are summarized briefly as follows.

Secured party v **lien creditor** (this term refers to a creditor who has obtained, by a judicial procedure rather than by contract, a lien on particular property of the debtor (e.g., garnishment of a claim), as contrasted with a creditor who has only a personal right against the debtor but no right in the debtor's property; the term includes a trustee in bankruptcy): A secured party prevails over a lien creditor unless the person becomes a lien creditor prior to the earlier of (i) the time the security interest is perfected, or (ii) the time a financing statement covering the collateral is filed and a security agreement has been made. See section 9-317(a).

Secured party v buyer of collateral: This competition is subject to several rules. A buyer in ordinary course of business (as noted above, this is a defined term) of goods from "a person in the business of selling goods of that kind" takes free of a security interest in the goods, even if the security interest in the goods is perfected and even if the buyer knows of its existence (although not if the buyer knows that the sale would violate the secured party's rights). See section 9-320. This is a rule based on efficiency that enables goods to move freely from inventory, fully in accord with the expectations of the secured party, who intends (indeed, desires) the inventory to be sold and whose security interest continues in the proceeds. The rule places the risk of the debtor's dealing with the proceeds of the inventory on the secured party, not the buyer. It raises relatively few fact questions. In some circumstances the rule will produce a different result than would obtain under a generalized "good faith" acquirer rule based on acquisition from someone in possession (e.g., art. 2279 of the Belgian Civil Code). For example, a buyer of equipment from a debtor does not come within this rule, because the debtor is not in the business of selling its equipment; therefore, the buyer of equipment takes the equipment subject to a perfected security interest. Section 9-321 provides an analogous lessee in ordinary course of business provision with respect to leased goods, and a licensee in ordinary course of business rule protecting a nonexclusive licensee of a **general intangible** (e.g., a copyright).

With respect to unperfected security interests (see section 9-317), the (non-ordinary course of business) buyer or lessee takes free of the security interest only if the buyer or lessee gives value, and, in the case of tangible collateral, receives delivery of the collateral, without knowledge of the security interest and before it is perfected. Licensees of general intangibles take free only if they give value without knowledge of the security interest and before it is perfected.

A special rule (section 9-317(e)) provides a twenty-day grace period; this gives, to a secured party with a purchase-money security interest which files a financing statement before or within twenty days after the debtor receives delivery of the collateral, priority over the rights of a lien creditor, buyer or lessee which arise between the time the security interest attaches and the time of filing. Again, this is a rule based on efficiency, allowing a seller on credit to deliver goods promptly, without being forced to delay delivery until after having filed.

Note that buyer and **purchaser** are not interchangeable terms. Buyer is used in essentially the vernacular sense of one who acquires in a sale transaction. Purchaser, in contrast, is anyone who takes in a voluntary transfer – this includes, importantly, a secured party. This distinction must be borne in mind as some priority rules apply to buyers while others apply to all purchasers (which, of course, includes buyers).

Secured party v secured party – general (see section 9-322): Under Article 9, several security interests in the same collateral may exist simultaneously. In fact, section 9-401 expressly empowers a debtor to further encumber collateral even in the teeth of a prohibition in the security agreement, although that provision does not preclude the secured party from exercising default remedies if the violation of such a prohibition is made an event of default.

Article 9 attachment and priority rules reject the conceptual premise that, having granted a security interest in collateral, the debtor has nothing left to convey to another. Moreover, section 9-318 provides that, for purposes of determining the rights of creditors of, and purchasers for value of an account or chattel paper from, a debtor that has sold the account or chattel paper, while the buyer's security interest (recall that the scope of Article 9 encompasses an outright sale of an account or chattel paper as well as a transfer for security purposes) is unperfected, the debtor is deemed to have right and title thereto identical to those sold to the buyer, and so the debtor has the power, if not the right, again to sell or to transfer for security purposes the same account or chattel paper.

The general rule in the competition between conflicting security interests in the same collateral is that priority goes to the secured party who is the 'first to file or perfect.' This rule is based on time, but the relevant determinant is not the sequence of the creation of the competing security interests. It is not even the sequence of perfection, as the rule gives priority to a secured party who filed before the competitor perfected, even if the first to file is the second to perfect. Moreover, the element of knowledge is irrelevant; i.e., the first to file prevails even if it knows of the existence of the competing security interest at the time it files or later perfects. This rule gives effectiveness to the public record, gives an incentive to file promptly and eliminates the need to litigate the fact-intensive and less objective question of knowledge. And, of course, a perfected security interest has priority over an unperfected one, and the first to attach prevails when both security interests are unperfected.

This rule is elaborated and refined with respect to proceeds (section 9-322), and as it relates to future advances (section 9-323). While these refinements add complexity, they are essential for efficient flexible secured finance.

Secured party v secured party – purchase-money security interests (section 9-324): Cutting across the above-described general rules of priority among competing secured parties are special rules for purchase-money security interests. Again, Article 9 provides a detailed set of rules. These rules are based on efficiency, not on the notion of favoring sellers. Indeed, as noted above, a purchase-money security interest may exist in favor of a third-party financier who makes possible the acquisition of the collateral by the debtor, so its availability is not confined to sellers. Because of the validation of the floating lien concept and the award of priority to the first to file, a secured party, in the absence of these super-priority provisions, would be in a position to preclude or monopolize the financing of the subsequent acquisition of new inventory or equipment by a debtor on a secured basis. Since the policy of Article 9 is to promote the availability and efficiency of secured financing, in this context supplemented by a policy to facilitate acquisition of new goods, a super-priority is given to enable a purchase-money security interest in goods to gain priority over an earlier filed secured party whose filing covers the after-acquired goods. In the case of non-inventory collateral, the super-priority is conditioned on the purchase-money security interest being perfected no later than twenty days after the debtor receives possession of the collateral.

A similar rule is provided with respect to inventory collateral, but in this case there are additional conditions that must be satisfied in order to gain the super-priority. In the inventory situation, the purchase-money financier must, before the debtor receives possession of the inventory, both achieve perfection and notify the earlier-filed competitor that it has acquired or expects to acquire a purchase-money security interest in the described inventory. A single notice is effective for a five-year period. The reason for these additional requirements is due to the nature of inventory financing. Here, absent the notification, an earlier in time financier, relying on the priority that its earlier filing gives it (obviating any need to re-check the record before making additional advances), would give additional credit based on either presentation of the invoices showing that the debtor was acquiring new inventory or an inspection showing newly delivered inventory. This efficient arrangement (which does not normally exist in the context of goods other than inventory) must be protected, and, therefore, the burden is on the purchase-money financier seeking super-priority to notify the prior-filed secured party as a condition to attaining super-priority with respect to inventory collateral.

The foregoing discussion, while far from exhaustive, is intended to illustrate the complex highly refined approach of Article 9's priority regime and the market-based reasons for the rules.

Other priority rules: Additional priority provisions include: rules governing the relative positions of a secured party whose interest continues in collateral transferred by a debtor *vis-à-vis* a secured party of the transferee who has a security interest in the transferred collateral by virtue of an after-acquired property provision (section 9-325); a rule specifying the effect on the perfection and priority of a secured party when its debtor merges with a successor entity (section 9-326); special rules for those having control over deposit accounts (section 9-327), investment property (section 9-328), or letter-of-credit rights (section 9-329); special rules for conflicting interests in instruments and chattel paper which reflect the negotiable nature of the former and the established financing techniques in existence with respect to the latter (sections 9-330 and 9-331); a special rule for priority *vis-à-vis* holders of statutory possessory liens that are provided under other law to those supplying services and materials with respect to collateral, e.g., repairer's liens (section 9-333), a lien somewhat analogous to the *droit de retention/retentierecht*; rules for priority with respect to fixtures, reflecting the interplay between Article 9 and rights arising in fixtures under real property law (section 9-334); and rules with respect to collateral that becomes an **accession** to other property (section 9-335) or becomes 'commingled' with other property (section 9-336).

While this detailed priority regime makes for a complicated statute, it provides pre-transaction guidance to parties, it obviates the need that would otherwise exist for judicial development, over time and in an uncertain manner, of rules to cover all these situations, and it provides rules that were generated by those with expertise and access to data typically not found in the context of judicial development of such rules. This also substantially diminishes the need otherwise sometimes encountered for courts to distort rules in order to avoid unjust, inefficient or otherwise inappropriate results.

Third-party rights

Article 9 also contains an array of provisions with respect to third-party rights other than priority issues.

Article 9 validates, on specified conditions, the enforceability, by an assignee of an account, chattel paper or a general intangible, of an agreement by an *account debtor* (the person obligated on the assigned right, i.e., the *debitor cessus*) with the assignor that the account debtor will not assert against an assignee any claim or defense that it might have against the assignor. See section 9-403. This provision serves to make these payment rights more valuable as collateral; presumably, account debtors thereby benefit. Similarly, Article 9 provides for the override of both contractual and statutory anti-assignment clauses (albeit with protections, in the context of the assignment of rights other than rights to payment, for a third party who is otherwise entitled to such protection against having to deal with, as contrasted with simply paying money to, a party other than its original counter-party). See sections 9-406 and 9-408. Section 9-406 also contains provisions that elaborate on how an account debtor on an assigned payment right obtains discharge of its obligation. The provisions here described were influential in the development of the United Nations Convention on the Assignment of Receivables.

The filing system

Article 9 provides for a "notice filing" scheme – a minimum amount of information (provided on a simple one-page form when filed on paper) is put on the public record. A financing statement is sufficient, under section 9-502, if it identifies the debtor and the secured party and provides an "indication" of the collateral (which may, under section 9-504, be specific or in very general terms or even in supergeneric language). The filing systems in the US are in the process of changing from paper-based to electronic filing (almost half of the states already accept electronic filings). In Canada, electronic filing is the norm; indeed, in New Brunswick, a province that recently adopted its Personal Property Security Act, only electronic filings are accepted. Any jurisdiction adopting a notice filing regime today no doubt would be fully computerized and likely would function solely on an electronic filing basis. Such a system not only is virtually error-free, but also is not expensive to establish, is extremely efficient, and is financially self-sustaining. Even in the paper-based US systems, filing is quite speedy, and in many states filings may be presented by fax. Filing fees generally range from $5 to $20. Searching can be done electronically via remote access on the internet in more than half of the states (and in half of these, searching the index can be done free of charge).

Even the existing Article 9 filing system is inexpensive to operate, efficient and does not require a vast bureaucracy. It is not a repository of underlying documents and does not create, or even necessarily reflect, property rights. It simply provides to a searcher a method of discovering that there *may* be a secured party who *may at some time* claim real rights (created by a security agreement the terms of which are not put on the public record) which *may* have priority based on the date of filing of the financing statement. It is up to the searcher – typically a prospective creditor – to act on the information received from the public record (along with information received from the debtor and from marketplace sources) in whatever way it deems prudent to protect its interests. What is filed, whether on paper or electronically, is barebones information – no details concerning a present or future credit extension are required and there is no requirement that a maximum amount secured be specified.

Under this system, for a nominal fee and the few minutes it takes to provide minimal data, a secured party can gain with certainty the priority accorded to a filed security interest that may cover millions of dollars of credit secured by millions of dollars worth of present and/or future collateral over a long period of time.

In most situations, under section 9-515, the effectiveness of the financing statement must be continued every five years – again, by the filing of a simple continuation statement – to retain priority over competing purchasers for value. The fixed duration makes calendaring and fee-calculation simple and efficient for both filer and filing office and enables the records to be automatically self-purging.

As noted above, a financing statement may be filed before attachment of the security interest, indeed, even before a security agreement is made. See section 9-502(d). A filed financing statement, however, is not effective unless the filing is authorized by the debtor. See section 9-509. Although authorization need not be evidenced by a signature on the financing statement, it must be reflected in an authenticated record (the authenticated security agreement will suffice). Evidence of authorization need not be placed in the public record. No information concerning the nature or amount of the secured obligations need be provided.

Because the debtor's name is the key to discovery of the financing statement in the public record, Article 9 provides elaboration concerning the sufficiency of the name provided. See sections 9-503 and 9-506. On the other hand, the actual provider of credit need not be identified, as the financing statement may provide the name of a representative of the secured party and the representative capacity need not be indicated. (For example, a title-retaining supplier or its customer might wish, for perfectly legitimate business reasons, to keep their relationship confidential.)

Revised Article 9 added several provisions to make even more clear the ministerial nature of the role of the filing office, and to make operation of filing offices more efficient, more transparent and more uniform. Article 9 specifies a limited number of grounds on which a filing may be rejected by the filing office – a short list, susceptible of objective application, of items necessary for the functioning of the system, but not based on formalities. Likewise, the revisions express the filing provisions in language that is neutral as to medium, to encourage the use of electronic filing or still more efficient techniques that might be developed in the future.

The Article 9 filing system should be distinguished from registries familiar to virtually all legal systems such as those covering real property. Those are, in many cases, the source of real rights (rather than simply a form of publicity for actual or potential rights otherwise created). In those registries, original substantive documents, usually manually executed with great formality (e.g., notaries, witnesses, seals), are placed in full on the record. Not infrequently, in such registries, the record is accessible only to those who have satisfied the registry officials of their legitimate interest in examining the record. Also, in such registries, the registry officials commonly scrutinize the documents before permitting their recordation. Thus, registering is often a slow, expensive and highly technical process.

The Article 9 filing system should also be distinguished from registration such as exists, for example, in the Netherlands for the private (non-notarized) deed for a *bezitloos pand* or a *stil pand*; that registration is designed to establish a certain date for the effectiveness of the transaction, but is not searchable by the public and is not intended to serve a notice function.

Post-default rights and remedies

Finally, Article 9 provides efficient flexible market-oriented enforcement remedies. While providing debtor protection in several key provisions (which mostly may not be waived, although some may be waived by an agreement authenticated after default), it recognizes that in most instances creditors are not abusive and that debtors benefit by the maximization of the net proceeds realized as a result of enforcement.

The key remedy added by Article 9, which supplements otherwise available judicial remedies (e.g., the familiar sale by a court officer), is the authorization to the secured party to dispose of the collateral at a nonjudicial sale. Inclusion of this remedy recognizes that a far better price is likely to be realized when the collateral is sold, in a public or private sale, by the secured party on a businesslike basis than would be obtained at a sale by a court officer, and likely also more rapidly and at a lower cost. The secured party's obligation is to carry out the disposition in good faith and in a 'commercially reasonable' manner. Although much of the case law under former Article 9 involved the issue of commercial reasonableness, the vast majority of enforcement of security interests in the US is carried out without judicial involvement. Of course, either party may invoke judicial intervention at any stage of the enforcement process. Nonjudicial disposition is typically carried out after the secured party has peacefully obtained possession of the collateral without the involvement of a court officer (often referred to in the literature as "self help"). Article 9 authorizes the secured party to take possession of the collateral "without judicial process, if it proceeds without breach of the peace." Debtor cooperation is commonplace because of the existence of effective enforcement remedies.

Orderly creditor action is made more likely because of the existence of the definitive priorities regime. Of course, if a federal bankruptcy proceeding has been commenced prior to disposition of the collateral, the secured party must obtain "relief" from the "automatic stay" before proceeding with enforcement remedies; in the interim, the secured party is entitled to "adequate protection" (these are terms of art in US bankruptcy practice).

Article 9's nonjudicial enforcement scheme contrasts sharply with that typically found in Europe. In Belgium, for example, even a pledgee in possession may not dispose of the collateral without judicial involvement (see Civil Code article 2078).

Finally, an alternative, highly efficient, remedy, significantly enhanced under Revised Article 9, is also available to the secured party – acceptance of the collateral in full or partial satisfaction of the secured obligation. See sections 9-620–9-622. The secured party, upon notification to the debtor and others having subordinate interests in the collateral, may propose such retention in lieu of disposition, but may not retain the collateral as proposed over timely objection.

Conclusion

Article 9 has effectively facilitated the efficient extension of secured credit in the United States. Despite its complexity, unfamiliar language and foreign style, it is likely to play an important role as a source of ideas, if not also as a model for their implementation, in the context of European domestic, regional and international reform of movables security law.

4 The English law of security: creditor-friendly but unreformed

MICHAEL BRIDGE

A. Article 9 through the eyes of an English lawyer

To understand the character of English law in general, it is always helpful to compare it with United States law, which is both similar and different. English law and US law may both be common law systems, the latter developing out of the former, but the differences between them are highly significant. It is increasingly difficult for lawyers as practitioners or academics to migrate between the two systems.

If one descends to the particular and looks at the structure of the rules dealing with secured transactions, fundamental differences between English law and US law appear to surface. Yet a close examination of the two laws reveals that both are at root alike in the friendly response they give to secured credit. Furthermore, the differences between the two laws are, to a significant extent, differences of legislative style. If one were to take the existing body of English rules on personal property security and restate them in US legal terminology, the result would probably be not greatly different from US Article 9 UCC. The basic values of the two systems of law are very similar.

The dominant feature of US law in the area of secured transactions is its commitment to the guiding principles of the jurisprudential movement known as American realism. This philosophy manifests itself in an impatient attitude to conceptual differences that conceal an identity of function. If two concepts do the same thing, they should be labelled and treated in the same way. It is not enough to say that they evolved at different times and in different ways, or that one represented the contribution of common law courts and the other the contribution of the

---

I should like to record my thanks to Harry Sigman for his helpful comments.

courts of equity. What matters above all is whether they do the same thing.

Article 9 of the Uniform Commercial Code represents the supreme achievement of American realist philosophy. First of all, it draws no distinction between equitable and legal ownership or security rights, which distinction persists in English law. Furthermore, the division between the reservation of property (or title as the Americans call it) by an unpaid seller and the taking of a charge by a creditor over assets of the debtor is discarded completely. Approaching the matter with the values of an American lawyer, suppose I go to a bank to seek an advance that will permit me to buy a car. The bank takes a charge over that car. Alternatively, I go to the seller and ask for credit. The seller transfers possession of the car to me and undertakes to transfer title only when payment in full is made. In the one case, the creditor bank's security is a charge; in the other case, the creditor seller's security is the reservation of title. That seller may in turn transfer its right to be paid and its title to the car to a bank for present value. Why distinguish between the various protective devices adopted by creditors? If they do the same thing, should they not be treated in the same way? And why should one be concerned about the label given to the creditor's security, whether it is called a charge or a reservation of title? If the creditor's remedies are the same – and Article 9 lays down a code of remedies based upon the rights of a mortgagee[1] – there is no practical advantage to be gained by attaching any particular label to the creditor's protective device.

This approach permits functionally identical devices to be dealt with in the same way in the same statute. It allows also for a basic rule of priority, which is a proprietary one, namely that the first security to be filed or otherwise perfected prevails over all others. Yet principled exceptions are introduced. These do not turn upon simple propositions, such as, for example, a subsequent reservation of title always prevails over an earlier charge of all present and future assets of the debtor, on the ground that the charge cannot attach to things not yet owned by the debtor. This is the approach of English law and is rejected in the United States. By this line of reasoning, and contrary to immediate impressions, the first in time is the unpaid seller and not the chargee bank because the starting point is not the agreement between debtor and creditor but the date when the debtor acquires rights in the collateral (or secured assets). This attaches too much importance to the abstract

---

[1] See now Part 6 ('Default') of UCC (2000) Article 9.

notion of title and is too mechanical to be acceptable to an American realist.

Instead, a special priority is accorded by Article 9 to the later creditor supplying funds for the acquisition of particular assets (as well as the unpaid seller). It is called a purchase money security interest[2] and its unstated statutory justification can be put in various ways. One way, for example, is to say that it permits debtors to go elsewhere for fresh finance and thus helps to break a situational monopoly exercised by that debtor's general financier.[3] Another way is to say that it encourages additional profit-making assets to be brought into the business, part of whose yield goes in payment of the price to the supplier. Payment is not made out of the debtor's already encumbered assets. Both the existing general creditor and the purchase money creditor therefore gain from an adjustment of the basic priority rule. The great bulk of a voluminous literature deals with the economics and bargaining features of this and other aspects of Article 9 and the bankruptcy laws.[4] Its unifying characteristic, apart from the polemical tone of the debate, is its resolute concentration upon matters theoretical and a refusal or at least a marked disinclination to look at the empirical evidence that lies behind credit practices. What is entirely absent from the scene is any principled commitment to ownership. Goods and other items of personal property are for the most part wasting assets with a limited life.

The above philosophy runs throughout the Uniform Commercial Code. Article 2, dealing with contracts for the sale of goods, is similar in its approach towards ownership. The contractual rights of seller and buyer are severed from the passing of title between them, though Article 2 does lay out a transfer rule that may be needed for fiscal, licensing and other reasons falling outside the performance of the contract.[5] It can be argued that the UCC pays insufficient regard to the deep sentimental roots of ownership[6] and that the formal character of law cannot be eradicated simply by a functionalist insight.[7] Article 9 is successful in integrating the treatment of various devices that serve in fact to secure

---

[2] Often abbreviated to pmsi. See UCC (2000), sections 9-103 (definition) and 9-324 (super-priority rules).
[3] A pmsi would also defeat an earlier security that was not a blanket security over the debtor's assets.
[4] See for example Kronman/Jackson, *Yale Law Journal* 88 (1979) 1143; Schwartz, *Journal of Legal Studies* 10 (1981) 1; Schwartz, *Journal of Legal Studies* 18 (1989) 209; Buckley, *Virginia Law Review* 72 (1986) 1393.
[5] Article 2-401.   [6] See UCC (2000), section 9-202 (title immaterial).
[7] See Bridge/Macdonald/Simmonds/Walsh, McGill LJ 44 (1999) 567.

payment promises, but it is not quite so successful in establishing the initial test of functionalism, which should serve as a litmus test for determining what transactions are subject to Article 9. In particular, it is by no means clear that the payment of monies subject to a trust that they be applied to a required purpose amounts to a form of security.[8] Again, Article 9 systems in Canada and the United States have been far from uniform in the way that they subject types of financial lease[9] to their various provisions.

Article 9 is a regulatory statute in this sense. It pays no regard to how the parties themselves structure their transaction, and is indifferent to whether they borrow the trappings of pre-code transactions, though its success has over time ensured the abandonment by parties of old transaction types. What Article 9 does is to regulate the effect of the parties' transactions. It does not overtly set out its distributional goals, though these are certainly the subject of speculation and informed comment. English law, on the other hand, appears to be driven by one basic idea and to be oblivious to distributional considerations. Those considerations are certainly to the fore in the basic rule of insolvency distribution, which is that the assets of the insolvent are distributed on a *pari passu* basis amongst all ordinary creditors of the insolvent.[10] But it is important to understand how marginal this rule is and how little real assistance it gives to ordinary unsecured creditors. First, there are limited categories of preference creditors, who have no security but who rank *pari passu* amongst themselves and ahead of ordinary creditors.[11] Secondly, secured creditors are allowed to encumber all assets of the debtor so as to leave nothing for distribution to ordinary creditors. Ordinary creditors are then citizens of a democracy in a destitute world: they are free to starve equally. There is no fund of assets that must be left free for insolvency distribution.[12] Secured creditors can evacuate

---

[8] See Bridge, *Oxford Journal of Legal Studies* 12 (1992) 333.
[9] An accountancy term, rather than a legal term, that corresponds to those leases that are functionally identical to a conditional sale.
[10] See, e.g., Insolvency Act 1986 ss. 107, 328; Insolvency Rules, r. 4.181; *British Eagle International Airlines Ltd v Cie Nationale Air France* [1975] 1 WLR 758.
[11] Insolvency Act 1986 s. 386 and Schedule 6.
[12] A proposal to ringfence for unsecured creditors a guaranteed 10 per cent of the debtor's net assets (by the *Report on Insolvency Law and Practice* (the Cork Report 1982, Cmnd 8558)) was never implemented. Recently, the Government in a White Paper, *Insolvency – A Second Chance* (Cmnd 5234, July 2001), has signalled its intention to surrender Crown preference rights (which rank ahead of a secured creditor with a floating charge) in favour of unsecured creditors.

the insolvent's estate and leave nothing. To this proposition there is one exception: certain types of security (floating charges) are postponed by statute to preference creditors.[13]

B. The values of English law

The basic idea that drives forward the English law of security is that of freedom of contract. This value is most strikingly seen in the ability of a financing creditor to take one single security over all of the assets of a debtor company. When this is accomplished, the security is a floating charge. It may not be desirable for priority reasons to rely upon just the one security but, in contrast with German and French law, for example, English law does not create difficulties for secured creditors by requiring a multiplicity of different forms of security if all or most of the debtor's assets are to be encumbered. Furthermore, there are no assets of the debtor that may not be encumbered by a floating charge in this way.

Two further points deserve particular emphasis. First, there are very few practical limitations placed upon the extent to which creditors can help themselves to security, even though the standard bank debenture is presented to the debtor on a take it or leave it basis. There is hardly any room at all for negotiation. In the case of individuals and partnerships, there are some limited controls by way of debtor protection in the Bills of Sale Acts 1878–1891. These were created as a reaction to certain forms of oppressive behaviour in the Victorian era and in practical terms are little more than an historical footnote. The Acts do not apply to company debtors,[14] for whom there is no equivalent form of debtor protection.

Secondly, contract is a bilateral relationship, particularly so in English law given its commitment to the doctrine of privity, which is indifferent to the interests of third parties.[15] Distributional considerations are foreign to contract law.[16] Admittedly, in the case of most but by

---

[13] Insolvency Act 1986 ss. 40, 175; Companies Act 1985 s. 196.
[14] See Bills of Sale Act (1878) Amendment Act 1882 s. 17 (inapplicability of Act to debentures issued by incorporated companies).
[15] A major reform, permitting contracting parties to create enforceable third-party rights, was proposed by the Law Commission (*Privity of Contract: Contracts for the Benefit of Third Parties* (Law Commission No 242, 1996)) and enacted in substantially that form by the Contracts (Rights of Third Parties) Act 1999.
[16] And especially restitution, which is threatening the borders of contract law.

no means all security granted by company debtors, it is a condition of the secured creditor's right to repel the competing claims of third-party creditors that the charge be publicly registered.[17] That does nothing for pre-existing unsecured creditors and it does not do much for future trade creditors. Individually, they may not challenge an unregistered charge. It is only upon liquidation that a liquidator, acting on the collective behalf of the unsecured creditors, can do so. When competing with registered charges, trade creditors supplying goods also come up against the limits of title reservation in English law, in that their reservation of title clauses only work as such for the original goods supplied and not for new goods manufactured out of them.[18] Trade creditors commonly have no real alternative to supplying goods on credit to the debtor buyer. Their status as purchase money financiers is recognised but only to a limited degree,[19] such recognition taking the form of a refusal to see them as taking security in the first place over the original goods supplied. They are therefore not obliged to register their title reservation.

The recognition of freedom of contract in the taking of security is complemented by the absence of any organised collocation or comprehensive legislative statement of the ranking of various creditors of the debtor. A table of rankings could no doubt be informally drawn up but only with some difficulty after synthesising a range of bilateral priority comparisons drawn from the case law and from statutory provisions.[20] In its commitment to freedom of contract, English law condones a type of individualistic free-for-all creditor mentality that might be regarded in some quarters as more American than US law itself. It could benefit from some of the efficiencies that are characteristic of Article 9. The introduction of notice filing of security interests would be an improvement on the current practice of filing particulars of charge which are checked by Companies House staff against the instrument of charge itself. Although the legislation permits brief particulars of the charge to be given, it is common practice for details running to scores of pages to be filed. Furthermore, the right of secured creditors to make future advances that can draw upon an existing priority position has not been taken as far in

---

[17] Companies Act 1985 ss. 395–396.
[18] See for example *Re Peachdart Ltd* [1984] Ch 131. A purported reservation of title interest in new goods will be treated as tantamount to a charge that must be registered for perfection under ss. 395–396 Companies Act 1985.
[19] See Bridge, *Oxford Journal of Legal Studies* 12 (1992) 333–361.
[20] See the difficulties posed by expenses of the liquidation in *Re MC Bacon Ltd* [1991] Ch 127.

English law as it has in Article 9.[21] On the other hand, English law was receptive to the taking of security over fluctuating future assets long before Article 9 swept away restrictions[22] on this type of security. This is exemplified by the invention in Equity in the middle to late nineteenth century of the floating charge.[23] It therefore did not have the same compelling need as US law for major reform of the law of security to satisfy business's thirst for credit.

English law recognises only three types of consensual security device, namely, pledge, charge and mortgage.[24] Charges may be floating or fixed (sometimes called specific). Within these limited types, however, English law permits a significant degree of freedom so that few creditors with the contractual power to bargain for a security are frustrated in their desire to extract an effective security. In the law of secured transactions, there is quite a close similarity to that body of law that distinguishes between tax evasion and tax avoidance. In a similar way, the law tolerates artificial transactions. It will, however, strike down sham transactions, but a sham transaction is one that misrepresents the legal steps taken by the parties. It is not enough that the transaction is an implausible one designed for legal rather than economic effect. The rather far-fetched transaction called hire purchase would never have been invented had it not been for constraints imposed by bills of sale, title transfer and moneylender legislation.[25] English law attached a substantial premium to legal ingenuity in the service of major institutional lenders. The following example of this approach at work is instructive.[26] Numerous other examples could be provided.[27]

This example concerns the lightweight floating charge.[28] To understand this creation, it must first be appreciated that administration was introduced in the mid-1980s as an insolvency procedure, to confer upon a designated office-holder, the administrator, powers of management of

---

[21] There are restrictions on the so-called 'tacking' of later advances on to an earlier mortgage: Law of Property Act 1925 s. 94. This section applies to all types of property, not just land, and 'mortgage' is defined so as to include 'charge': ibid., s. 205(1)(xvi).
[22] As exemplified by *Benedict v Ratner* (1925) 268 US 353.
[23] *Re Panama, New Zealand and Australia Royal Mail Co.* (1870) 5 Ch App 318.
[24] *Re Cosslett (Contractors) Ltd* [1998] Ch 495.
[25] See *Helby v Matthews* [1895] AC 471; *McEntire v Crossley Bros.* [1895] AC 457.
[26] For others, see Bridge, *Canadian Business Law Journal* 27 (1996) 196 ff.; Bridge/Macdonald/Simmonds/Walsh, McGill LJ 44 (1999) 567.
[27] See for example *Welsh Development Council v Export Finance Guarantee Co. Ltd* [1992] BCC 270.
[28] Oditah, *Journal of Business Law* 1991, 49.

the company in excess of those possessed by liquidators, in order to achieve one or more stated statutory purposes. These include the better realisation of the assets of the company than could be achieved by a liquidator and the survival of the company as a going concern.[29] The essential idea was to provide for the appointment of an administrator in those cases where a bank debenture did not exist under which there could be appointed a private receiver with extensive powers. This receivership procedure had in the past, besides benefiting the bank, been credited with having beneficial effects on the position of creditors and shareholders of the company. In order to achieve the statutory purpose or purposes, the administrator was given rights of interference with security and title reservation rights.[30] Since the administrator, while respecting security and title reservation rights, had a duty to act in the interests of all creditors, and the private receiver was bound only to act in the interest of the appointing bank, it meant that banks with the power to appoint a receiver would normally wish to prevent the appointment of an administrator. The Insolvency Act 1986 permitted them to do this in stated conditions.[31]

In brief, a bank appointing a receiver classed as an administrative receiver could block the appointment of an administrator.[32] But the extensive powers of an administrative receiver were associated with an appointment under the terms of a debenture containing a floating charge. On the face of it, the bank was faced with an invidious choice: it could either avail itself of a floating charge, and thus block the appointment of an administrator who would not serve exclusively its interests, or it could protect itself by a series of fixed, not floating, charges over as many of the assets of the company as it could, thus ranking ahead of preference creditors, who in turn ranked ahead of creditors with a floating charge. It did not appear that it could protect itself from preference creditors and from the appointment of an administrator at the same time.

Nevertheless, a closer examination of the definition of an administrative receiver is instructive. Section 29(2) of the Insolvency Act 1986 states that an administrative receiver is one who is 'a receiver or manager of the whole (or substantially the whole) of a company's property appointed by or on behalf of the holders of any debentures of the company secured

---

[29] Insolvency Act 1986 s. 8(3).   [30] Insolvency Act 1986 s. 15.   [31] See ss. 10–11.
[32] Ibid. The Government has recently signalled an intention to remove the powers of secured creditors outside the capital markets to block the appointment of administrators in this way: *Insolvency – A Second Chance* (Cmnd 5234, July 2001).

by a charge which, as created, was a floating charge, *or by such a charge and one or other securities*' (emphasis added). It means that, provided the receiver controlled almost all of the company's property, which could be done by a combination of fixed and floating charges, that receiver qualified as an administrative receiver and the debenture-holder with the power of appointment could thereby block the appointment of an administrator. A floating charge was, however, a *sine qua non* if this was to be achieved.

In *Re Croftbell Ltd*,[33] it was demonstrated just how insubstantial this floating charge could be. The company was a special corporate vehicle, not engaged in trading, whose only substantial asset was its ownership of the share capital of another company which owned a valuable plot of land. The bank took a fixed charge over the debtor company's shareholding and a floating charge over any residual assets the company might have, which were, and were expected to be, negligible. Although the only true purpose of the floating charge was to put the bank in a position to block the appointment of an administrator upon the petition of other creditors of the company or of one or more directors, the floating charge was recognised. This was a triumph of form over substance.[34]

Re Croftbell Ltd reveals in collateral terms what has happened to the floating charge. From being the all-encompassing instrument, the English equivalent of the floating lien, that resembles the blanket security interest under Article 9, it has now become a sort of final flourish in an instrument of charge catching only those items that are not susceptible to a fixed charge. English law, in a series of cases decided over the last thirty years or so,[35] has permitted fixed charges over book debts (accounts receivable) to be taken by banks, always provided that the proceeds are paid into an account controlled by the bank.[36] This means

---

[33] [1990] BCLC 844.   [34] See also Bridge, *Journal of Business Law* 1992, 1.
[35] *Siebe Gorman v Barclays Bank* [1979] 2 Lloyd's Rep 142; *Re Armagh Shoes Ltd* [1984] BCLC 405 (NI); *Re Brightlife Ltd* [1987] Ch 200; *Re Permanent Houses (Holdings) Ltd* [1988] BCLC 563; *Re a Company (No 005009 of 1987)* [1989] BCLC 13; *Royal Trust Bank v National Westminster Bank plc* [1996] BCC 613. See generally, Ferran, *Company Law and Corporate Finance* 517–29.
[36] But see the extraordinary decisions of *Re New Bullas Trading Ltd* [1994] 1 BCLC 485; *Re Atlantic Computer Systems plc* [1992] Ch 505; *Re Atlantic Medical Ltd* [1992] BCC 653. The first of these, at least, which recognised a distinction between a debt and its money proceeds, permitting a fixed charge over the former even if no controls at all were exercised over the proceeds, must now be regarded as unsound and unsafe in the aftermath of the Privy Council decision in *Agnew v Commissioner of Inland Revenue* [2001] 2 BCLC 108.

that the only substantial category of assets for which the bank can take only a floating charge will be raw materials, work-in-progress and stock-in-trade (inventory), in view of the impracticability of banks controlling the use and consumption of such assets.

C. The future of English law

On a number of occasions, official reports have called for a reform of the English law of security along the lines of Article 9.[37] Nevertheless, the Department of Trade and Industry has in the past, after canvassing practitioner and commercial opinion, demonstrated a clear preference for the existing approach to security. This was the case after the law on company charges was reformed in 1989 along lines that were consistent with a movement in the direction of an Article 9 type of security.[38] The legislation providing for this, however, never came into force as certain features of it were adamantly opposed by user groups.

A new consultation process has recently taken place[39] and has led to proposals to effect significant changes to existing law.[40] Since only company charges were on the agenda, and not bills of sale granted by individuals and partnerships, the adoption of a general statute along the lines of Article 9 is not an active prospect. Nevertheless, while it is always difficult to predict with any accuracy future legislative developments, the current signs are that notice filing, instead of the filing of particulars coupled with the instrument of charge, is a likely prospect for future law reform. Carried to its logical conclusion, a system of notice filing would permit filing to take place ahead of the grant of a charge and would permit one single filing to cover all future advances, whether or not pursuant to prior commitment. This would certainly facilitate the registration of reservation of title clauses[41] in those cases where trade

---

[37] *Report of the Committee on Consumer Credit* (the Crowther Report 1971, Cmnd 4596 (Part V)); Department of Trade and Industry, *A Review of Security Interests in Property* (the Diamond Report 1989); *Report on Insolvency Law and Practice* (the Cork Report 1982, Cmnd 8558).
[38] See Bridge, *Journal of Business Law* 1992, 1.
[39] See the Consultation Document of the Company Law Steering Group of the Department of Trade and Industry, 'Registration of Company Charges' (9 Oct. 2000) (accessible at http://www.dti.gov.uk/consultations/closed.htm).
[40] *Modern Company Law for a Competitive Economy* (June 2001). (http://www.dti.gov.uk/cld/review.htm) (chapter 12).
[41] If registration were to be extended to reservation of title in general, it would be relatively simple to impose a registration requirement for financial leases.

suppliers deliver goods to the debtor on credit terms on repeated occasions. Nevertheless, if reservation of title clauses were without more ado made registrable, the current rules on tacking[42] would prevent trade suppliers from protecting themselves by means of one single filing for all future supplies. These rules grant priority to a secured creditor (SC1) for future advances, over another secured creditor (SC2) intervening between the grant of the first security and the future advance, in limited circumstances only. Specifically, discretionary advances made after notice[43] of an intervening security of SC2 are subordinated to SC2's security. The problem here for suppliers of goods is that individual supplies, commonly made on a small scale, are rarely made pursuant to earlier and long-standing commitment. To give full effect to future advances financing, SC1's priority position should extend to discretionary future advances.

As and when notice filing is introduced, English law will move some way in the direction of Article 9. For a really substantial movement to take place, there would also have to be a requirement that all reservation of title clauses be registrable, coupled with a change to the tacking rules to encourage future advances financing. Neither of these latter developments is likely to occur in the short to medium term. Nevertheless, if these developments did occur, what else would be needed to complete the transition to Article 9? There would have to be a commitment to the concept of purchase money security ranking ahead of a prior registered charge. This would not be a difficult pill to swallow, echoing title and tending to favour smaller classes of secured creditor. The concept certainly exists already in embryo;[44] moreover, the rule that reservation of title ranks ahead of mortgages and charges granted by the debtor buyer[45] provides mute support for the existence in English law of a concept of purchase money security.

If reservation of title clauses were made registrable, then, provided they were not statutorily deemed to be charges, there would be no necessity to create a special rule of statutory priority in their favour, so as to rank them ahead of even prior registered charges. Nevertheless,

---

[42] See s. 94 Law of Property Act 1925.
[43] See note 49 below for the rule on constructive notice arising out of registration of a charge.
[44] See *Re Connolly Bros. Ltd (No 2)* [1912] 2 Ch 25.
[45] Because the prior charge can only attach assets to the extent that the debtor buyer has a property interest in them. For the same reason, (genuine) reservation of title clauses are peculiarly powerful in insolvency cases.

if it were felt that all priority rules (including title reservation versus charge) should be contained in one statute, it would aid clear thinking to embrace charge and reservation of title under the general umbrella of security interest. The incremental convergence of English law to Article 9 would thus become even more apparent.

There is a further major consideration. At present, filing under Article 9 is a priority point. In English law, registration of a charge on the company charges register is a perfection point in that, unless registration takes place, the charge is liable to be defeated at the hands of stated individuals such as company liquidators, administrators and competing secured creditors.[46] It remains perfectly valid as between chargor and chargee[47] and as against purchasers (including factors). A charge that has been registered and is therefore not liable to defeasance depends for its priority, not upon any rules in the Companies Act, but upon uncodified rules of common law and equity. One of these rules is that registration under section 395 of the Companies Act 1985 amounts to constructive notice of the charge.[48] At present, it is hard to be precise about the scope of constructive notice. Plainly, not everyone dealing with the company has constructive notice. One such exception should be the outright buyer of property subject to a fixed charge imposing restrictions on the manner and circumstances of the sale of that property. The informality and dispatch of outright sales ought not to be compromised by a practical requirement to search the register of security interests. Another exception should be the bank that has taken a security for an overdraft facility granted under a current account.[49] If this rule of constructive notice were to be adequately defined and rendered in statutory form, then English law would indeed be a close cousin of Article 9. An Article 9 purist would, however, say that if all property contests, involving liquidator, purchaser, unpaid seller and chargee, were embraced within one statute, there would be no need to speak of constructive notice. It would simply be a matter of comprehensively ordering priority conflicts

---

[46] S. 395 Companies Act 1985.
[47] See *Mace Builders (Glasgow) Ltd v Lunn* [1987] Ch 191.
[48] *Wilson v Kelland* [1910] 2 Ch 306.
[49] Where the normal rule concerning current accounts is in operation, each drawing on an overdrawn account constitutes a fresh advance by the bank. Because banks do not make such advances pursuant to commitment, they may not freely tack such advances to their earlier security so as to rank ahead of other chargees intervening between the grant of security to the bank and the fresh advance made by the bank. If the bank had to scrutinise the register each time it honoured a cheque on an overdrawn account, the business of banking would become intolerable.

according to the fact of registration (along with other methods of perfection, namely taking possession or control of certain assets). Proposed changes to the registration of company charges, shifting from registration being a perfection point to a priority point, are a clear step in this direction.[50]

D. Summary

In this short study, I have tried not to present a general summary of the English law of security but rather to capture its flavour. English law, as might be expected, shows on the surface its historical antecedents. Despite all the twists and turns of statutory innovation and commercial ingenuity, the law today is fundamentally the law as it was laid down more than a century ago. If the resistance to modernisation seems to some English lawyers irksome, it may be explained in part by the fact that the common law of England has always been sympathetic to commercial needs and expectations so that there is no perceived need for a major reform going to the legal roots of the credit system. The floating charge has long encouraged credit to be advanced to companies. It may now have shrunk in the company of various fixed charges over defined types of asset but its existence demonstrates that business and credit in England have not suffered at the hands of an obstructive property law. Concern has long been expressed in England about the shortage of credit available for small and medium enterprises. Whatever the reasons for this, they do not include the inadequacy of legal protection afforded to banks seeking security for their advances. The absence of statutory modernisation is by no means confined in English law to security. It affects numerous areas of commercial law such as sale of goods and bills of exchange. One of the great obstacles to modernisation is the absence of Parliamentary time for the reform of private law, which is hardly likely to engage the passions of partisan groupings in the House of Commons. In the absence of Parliamentary reform, it is difficult to see a way of dealing with this problem.

Finally, no reference to English law would be complete if mention were not made of the powerful remedies it affords to secured creditors in the event of the debtor's default. The law does not inhibit the contractual freedom of debtor and creditor to provide, without having to go

---

[50] *Modern Company Law for a Competitive Economy* (June 2001) (http://www.dti.gov.uk/cld/review.htm) (chapter 12).

to court, for the freedom to appoint a receiver to manage the debtor's business and pay down the loan. The technique by which this is done is that the creditor is given by the debtor a power of attorney to act as the debtor's agent in appointing a receiver, whose mandate it is to act in the interests of the creditor. Although owing fiduciary duties to the debtor company, and superseding the board of directors, the receiver's fundamental duty is to act for the creditor. Such freedom is not granted to American secured creditors. English law, furthermore, grants a wide freedom to the creditor in the case of a demand loan to accelerate its repayment on very short notice. This has been defined as the time a debtor needs to obtain funds for repayment from a convenient place, as opposed to the time needed to apply elsewhere for alternative financing.[51] Yet already the signs are that the high tide of secured creditors' rights may have begun to ebb. The Insolvency Act 2000 allows for the grant to company directors, seeking a corporate voluntary arrangement, of a moratorium on the enforcement of secured creditors' rights. As seen above, the Government has announced its intention to seek legislation preventing secured creditors, outside the capital markets, from appointing administrative receivers so as to block the more evenly balanced procedure of company administration.[52] It is not unlikely that further erosion will follow.

Postscript

The law set out in this chapter has been modified in important respects by a statute, the Enterprise Act 2002, that has recently come into force as a result of a series of commencement orders. Briefly, it accomplishes three things.

First, with certain very important exceptions in the capital and private finance initiative markets,[53] it prevents the chargee from acquiring by contract with the debtor the right to procure the appointment of an administrative receiver, who, as seen above, responds only to the needs of the chargee. This right, however, is substituted by a new, entrenched power to appoint out of court an adminstrator, an office holder who could previously only be appointed by a court order. This measure

---

[51] See for example *Bank of Baroda v Panessar* [1987] Ch 335.
[52] *Modern Company Law for a Competitive Economy* (June 2001).
[53] See ss. 72B–G of the Insolvency Act 1986 as added by s. 250 Enterprise Act 2002. There is also a saving for powers of appointment under existing debentures: s. 72A(4)(a) of the Insolvency Act 1986 as added by s. 250 Enterprise Act 2002.

places the chargee with the existing power to appoint an administrative receiver in the driving seat when it comes to the appointment of an administrator. As with the present regime of administrative receivership, there is no requirement that the debtor be insolvent within the meaning of the Insolvency Act 1986 for an appointment to be made by the chargee. The chargee, under the new provisions, must be the holder of a 'qualifying floating charge'.[54] Furthermore, the chargee with such a power, while not the only person with an out-of-court power of appointment, has the preferential right to make the appointment.[55] It is only by the barest thread that the appointment of an administrator by the chargee can be called a collective procedure at all.

In contrast with the former statutory purposes of administration, the new system presents three compulsory purposes in descending order of choice. First, there is the rescue of the 'company'. It is almost impossible to contemplate that the 'company', as opposed to the business, can be saved by the time that informal processes and rescues have been exhausted and the process of administration has begun. After so much talk of the rescue culture in the last twenty years or so, the stark truth is that corporate break-up and not salvation lies at the heart of the corporate insolvency regime in England.

The second statutory purpose, which comes into play when the first is 'not reasonably practicable', is that the administrator must strive for 'a better result for the company's creditors as a whole' than would be likely on a liquidation. This points to an administrator exercising management powers that a liquidator does not have and to dealing with the company's assets, encumbered and unencumbered alike, as a block in order to maximise their value. No doubt case law will clarify what is meant by 'reasonably practicable'. How the administrator takes account of the welfare of the company's creditors as a whole is not obvious, in that there is no true community of interest between secured and unsecured creditors, especially where in the majority of cases the secured creditor fails to recover in full from the enforcement process, the effect of which is that nothing is left to pass on to the preference and unsecured creditors. The length of the management process will be a key issue here. It is however unlikely that the administrator will have to deal with creditors in their various classes. Only in the event of this second purpose proving not to be reasonably practicable will the

---

[54] Schedule B1 Insolvency Act 1986 (as added by Enterprise Act 2002), para. 14.
[55] *Ibid*. para. 26(1).

administrator turn to the third purpose of making a distribution to one or more secured or preferential creditors. In a clear break from the past, the administrator is now firmly located in the business of making distributions, and chargee creditors making the appointment will hope and expect that the administrator will move quickly and smoothly to the execution of this third statutory purpose.

The second main feature of the Enterprise Act 2002 is that it abolishes Crown preference, a matter of particular importance in respect of unpaid VAT and PAYE deductions from the payroll.[56] Thirdly, it creates a fund drawn from the assets of the insolvent party to be distributed among its unsecured general creditors.[57] The amounts available for distribution are limited and will be drawn from assets of the company that would formerly have gone to the Crown as a preference creditor. The unsecured creditors will therefore, in respect of this fund, rank ahead of any floating chargee.

There is also the prospect of a major legislative change that goes to the very heart of the English law of security. The Law Commission's recent Consultative Document on the Registration of Security Interests[58] puts forward for consideration a reform of the law of secured credit that would largely remodel the law along the lines of Article 9 of the American Uniform Commercial Code. There is a very real prospect that these proposals will take effect as secondary legislation under the Companies Act, applicable in the first instance only to company borrowers, with the possibility of extension to individual and partnership borrowers at a later date by means of primary legislation.

Bibliography

Michael Bridge, 'Form, Function and Innovation in Personal Property Security Law', *Journal of Business Law* 1992, 1 ff.
  'The Quistclose Trust in a World of Secured Transactions', *Oxford Journal of Legal Studies* 12 (1992) 333 ff.
  'Is Article 9 Exportable? The English View', *Canadian Business Law Journal* 27 (1996) 196 ff.
Michael Bridge, Roderick A. Macdonald, Ralph L. Simmonds and Catharine Walsh, 'Formalism, Functionalism, and Understanding the Law of Secured Transactions', *McGill LJ* 44 (1999) 567 ff.

---

[56] S. 251 Enterprise Act 2002.
[57] S. 176A Insolvency Act 1986 as added by s. 252 Enterprise Act 2002.
[58] *Registration of Security Interests: Company Charges and Property other than Land* (No 164, 2002).

F. H. Buckley, 'The Bankruptcy Priority Puzzle', *Virginia Law Review* 72 (1986) 1393 ff.

E. Ferran, *Company Law and Corporate Finance* (1999).

A. Kronman and T. Jackson, 'Secured Financing and Priorities Among Creditors', *Yale Law Journal* 88 (1979) 1143 ff.

F. Oditah, 'Lightweight Floating Charges', *Journal of Business Law* 1991, 49 ff.

Alan Schwartz, 'Security Interests and Bankruptcy Priorities: A Review of Current Theories', *Journal of Legal Studies* 10 (1981) 1 ff.

'A Theory of Loan Priorities', *Journal of Legal Studies* 18 (1989) 209 ff.

5   The European Bank for Reconstruction and Development's Secured Transactions Project: a model law and ten core principles for a modern secured transactions law in countries of Central and Eastern Europe (and elsewhere!)

FREDERIQUE DAHAN AND JOHN SIMPSON

Introduction

It is noteworthy that the Project on the Common Core of European Private Law has chosen, among the many subjects it endeavours to cover, the question of security over movable property. Indeed, movable property may be a subject that is neglected during the years of studying law at university, especially it seems in the UK where it falls somewhere between the courses on land law and commercial law. However, in practice, movable property is of the utmost importance; this is particularly visible in the realm of credit where the diversity and versatility of movable property will make it of prime appeal to creditors as a means of guaranteeing their claims. Moreover, since transactions involving movables are far more numerous, this multiplies further the number of occasions when elaborate legal constructions over these assets can be imagined. The fifteen cases drawn as part of the questionnaire for this volume give a good, if small, sample.

In economies in transition such as the economies of Central and Eastern Europe and the former Soviet Union Republics – now the Commonwealth of Independent States – movable property as a tool to enhance credit facilities and conditions is a new concept. To some extent, secured credit is also a new concept. Until the 1990s, there was hardly any legal provision allowing movable property to be used to guarantee a loan without losing the ability to use the assets. Basically, the possessory pledge, often referred to as a pawn, was the only means available. The alternative was the *hypothec* or mortgage over immovable property. This, however, when it was possible at all, only concerned debtors who owned land or buildings.

As Central and Eastern European states started moving towards a market economy, it became clear that business development was closely dependent on the availability of credit. In Poland, for example, in the few years following 1989 and the radical economic and political changes in the country, new businesses managed to flourish without recourse to bank finance, thanks to the nature of their activities (mainly services, requiring little initial capital) and funds provided by relatives and friends. However, as the years passed, it became clear that external finance was necessary and that creditors would require some sort of security to guarantee their loans and overdraft facilities. If foreign investment was to pour into the countries, as hoped, foreign investors had to be confident that they could secure their loans efficiently, using at least some of the legal techniques commonly found in the West.

The EBRD Model Law on Secured Transactions: four objectives

In this context, the European Bank for Reconstruction and Development decided in 1992 to make secured transactions law reform a priority. Specifically, discussion of the problem at a roundtable held in Budapest that year led to three eminent lawyers from Central Europe[1] requesting that the EBRD propose a basis for uniform or similar regulation of secured transactions across the region. The outcome was the EBRD Model Law on Secured Transactions, which was published in April 1994.[2] It was stressed from the outset that the Model Law is *not* intended as detailed legislation for direct incorporation into local legal systems of the region. The Model Law was prepared in order to fulfil four distinct objectives.

First, the Model Law can be used as an *illustration* of the principal components of a set of rules for secured transactions and of the way in which these rules can be incorporated into legislation. Although a national law could play this role, it is more practical to have all components listed in one single document in a rational and progressive fashion. It also avoids the issue of national pride when it comes to deciding which foreign legal system is to be looked at in the context of legal reform.

---

[1] Professor Dr Atilla Harmathy of Hungary, Professor Petar Sarcevic of Croatia and Professor Stanislaw Soltysinski of Poland.
[2] *The Model Law on Secured Transactions*, EBRD, 1994; see also http://www.ebrd.com/english/st.htm.

Second, the Model Law acts as a *reference point and checklist* for the law reformer. Since each country has to take into account its own legal background and the existing legal and institutional framework, it is important to provide a list of points that have to be covered in order to establish a comprehensive system. The Model Law puts particular emphasis on a number of issues where the existing legal provisions are likely to be the weakest, for example, the type of assets that can be offered as collateral and the registration of security interests. The Model Law is intended to form a basis from which national legislation for transition countries can be developed, to act as a starting point, indicating through a detailed legal text how the principal components of a secured transactions law can be drafted but allowing for a high degree of flexibility to enable adaptation to local circumstances. Although the issues are complex, the Model Law had to be kept simple in order to be of use for market economies in transition. From this basic system, more sophisticated rules can be developed.

Third, the Model Law provides guidance as to the *expectations of international investors and lenders*. Clearly, the Model Law was drafted by an international financial organisation which is also a commercial bank that applies sound banking and investment principles in all its operations. When signing a deal, the Bank pays particular attention to the security package and seeks to take security over property according to modern financial practice. The Model, for example, permits security over all types of movable and intangible assets without the need to take possession of the collateral. It also proposes solutions to enable rapid and effective enforcement and to facilitate the situation where a number of lenders (a banking syndicate) want to share the same security.

Fourth and finally, the Model Law is also intended to promote some *harmonisation* in the approach to secured transactions legislation across the region. Harmonisation is an attractive but very complex concept. Confined to the European Union, it has shown its limits in many areas. The Common Core of European Private Law's objective is not harmonisation but, in our understanding, the identification of the main differences between the legal systems. Once the differences are highlighted – or possibly the lack of real differences – it is only a short step towards proposing ways of eliminating them completely. The Model Law was itself the result of a comparative study and has been influenced by a number of legal systems, thanks to the support of an international advisory board (comprising twenty members from fifteen different jurisdictions). One principle which has guided the drafting of the Model has been to produce a text which is compatible with the civil law concepts which underlie many Central and Eastern European legal systems and, at the same time, to draw on common law systems which have developed many useful solutions to accommodate modern financing techniques.[3] The drafters drew on a broad range of legal and practical sources both in Central, Eastern and Western European countries and elsewhere in the world, in particular in the United States. For countries which already have well-established legal provisions on secured transactions, any change to the system requires an overwhelming desire for change on the part of all stakeholders and an agreement as to the contents of the new rules. In Central and Eastern Europe, at least, the impetus for change was (more or less) already there. There was thus an opportunity for trying to introduce some sort of uniformity into legal regimes for secured transactions throughout the region, if only to facilitate intra-regional commercial transactions. Yet, this was not the primary objective of the Model Law and its success should not be measured accordingly.

The EBRD Ten Core Principles

Another important contribution of the EBRD to the reform process on secured transactions in the region is the Ten Core Principles, which followed the publication of the Model Law. In effect, during the country-specific work of the Bank's Legal Transition Team, it became evident that the Model Law was an important and helpful instrument for local reformers. However, it also became clear that *a more general formulation* of the goals and principles of successful reform to foster economic development was needed. This has led to the EBRD defining a set of ten core principles for a modern secured transactions legislation. These principles form the basis for assessing a country's secured transactions law and for identifying the need for reform. The principles draw on the assumption that the role of a secured transactions law is economic. It is not needed as part of the essential legal infrastructure of a country: its only use is to provide the legal framework which enables a market for secured credit to operate. To some extent, the Core Principles serve to remind law-makers that they would be making a mistake if they took the Model Law as immediately available material that they can 'cut and paste' into their own legal system. To put it in even more blunt terms, translating the Model Law into the local language cannot provide the

---

[3] Although it is acknowledged that the division of civil law and common law in this area of the law may not be as fundamental as in other areas. This volume brings detailed and compulsive evidence of that.

country with an up-and-running new pledge law. There is no substitute for the long and pains taking process of legal reform, which implies designing a law that really suits the local circumstances and interfaces efficiently with existing laws.

The Core Principles do not seek to impose any particular solution on a country – there may be many ways of arriving at a particular result – but they do seek to indicate the result that should be achieved. As with any set of general principles of this nature, they must be read within the context of the law and practice of any particular country and they do not aim to be absolute; exceptions inevitably have to be made.

The Principles read as follows:

1 *Security should reduce the risk of giving credit, leading to an increased availability of credit on improved terms.* This goes to the basic assumption made by the EBRD in all its work on secured transactions law reform.
2 *The law should enable the quick, cheap and simple creation of a proprietary security right without depriving the person giving the security of the use of his assets.* In most market economy scenarios depriving the debtor of the use of his assets is self-defeating; non-possessory security which gives a remedy attached to the charged asset is an essential element of a modern secured transactions law. Any delay, cost or complexity in the creation process reduces the economic efficiency of security.
3 *If the secured debt is not paid, the holder of security should be able to have the charged assets realised and to have the proceeds applied towards satisfaction of his claim prior to other creditors.* The exact nature of the proprietary right that arises when security is granted has to be defined in the context of the relevant laws. If it is to be effective it must link to the creditor's claim the remedy of recovering from the assets given as security in priority to other creditors.
4 *Enforcement procedures should enable prompt realisation at market value of the assets given as security.* A remedy is only as good as the procedures and practice for exercising it allow it to be. If the value received on realisation is expected to be only half the market value, then the provider of credit will require more assets to be given as security. If it is expected that enforcement will take two years, then the creditor will give less favourable credit terms to the debtor.
5 *The security right should continue to be effective and enforceable after the bankruptcy or insolvency of the person who has given it.* The position against which the creditor most wants protection is the insolvency of the debtor. Any reduction of rights or dilution of priority upon insolvency will reduce the value of security. A limited exception to this principle may be necessary to make it compatible with rules which permit a moratorium at the commencement of insolvency.

6   *The costs of taking, maintaining and enforcing security should be low.* A person granting credit will usually ensure that all costs connected with the credit are passed on to the debtor. High costs of security will be reflected in the price for credit and will diminish the efficiency of the credit market.

7   *Security should be available (a) over all types of assets, (b) to secure all types of debts, and (c) between all types of person.* This principle covers a multitude of issues that may arise between the way law is applied and commercial reality. Such issues may appear technical but can be of critical importance when seeking to implement a commercial agreement. With very limited exceptions (e.g. personal clothing), a person should be able to give security over any of his assets, including assets he may acquire in the future. Similarly, a charge should be capable of securing any type of present or future debt or claim that can be expressed in money terms. The charged assets and the secured debt should be capable of general description (e.g., all machines in a factory, all debts arising under a sales contract). It should also be possible to charge constantly changing 'pools' of assets such as inventory, debts receivable and stocks of equipment and to secure fluctuating debts such as the amount due under a bank overdraft facility. Any physical or legal person (whether in the public or private sector) who is permitted by law to transfer property should be able to grant or receive security.

8   *There should be an effective means of publicising the existence of security rights.* Where security is possessory the mere fact that the assets are held by the creditor is enough to alert third parties that the debtor has charged them. Where security is non-possessory some other means (normally a public registry or notification system) is needed to ensure that third parties do not acquire charged assets without being made aware of the existence of the charge.

9   *The law should establish rules governing competing rights of persons holding security and other persons claiming rights in the assets given as security.* Even when an effective means of publicity is in place there remain some cases for which the law has to provide, for example, sales of charged assets in the ordinary course of the owner's business (where the purchaser cannot be expected to inspect a register before purchasing).

10 *As far as possible the parties should be able to adapt security to the needs of their particular transaction.* The law is there to facilitate the operation of the secured credit market and to ensure that necessary protections are in place to prevent debtor, creditor or third parties being unfairly prejudiced by secured transactions. It should not be the purpose of the law to create rules and restrictions for the operation of secured credit which are aimed principally at directing the manner in which parties to secured credit should structure their transaction.

Although these principles seem to make perfect sense to commercial and business people, it is far from easy to fit them into a legal system, where the traditional interpretation of legal concepts may clash with practical needs. The International Financial Law Reform Sub-Committee of the International Bar Association (IBA) held a conference in May 2000 on the legal framework for secured credit at which IBA members from eleven countries (Argentina, Australia, Canada, Finland, France, Hungary, Italy, Netherlands, Poland, South Africa and Switzerland) presented papers. These papers examined the extent to which the laws of these countries correspond to the EBRD Core Principles on Secured Transactions. Publication is now envisaged, enlarging the number of countries covered to all those in the European Union. It will be very interesting to see how, and to what extent, countries incorporate these principles in their laws.

How does the Model Law score? Answers to the questionnaire

The purpose of this contribution, however, is to examine how the cases which were designed for this volume and considered extensively by the European Union countries' reports could be dealt with under a legal system which drew its legal provisions from the EBRD Model Law and Core Principles. This exercise is clearly an academic one since the Model Law, as we explained above, is *not* an actual and 'living' law and does not aim to provide a complete legislative text. Yet, we hope that this will give a flavour of what the Model Law and the Core Principles can provide in terms of simplicity and certainty to the countries which seek to reform or improve their secured transactions law. Also we believe that the exercise demonstrates the unsatisfactory and complex position that has developed in European legal systems as a result of fragmented and limited changes being made over the years in response (often belated) to market needs. If it were possible to quantify the economic benefits that are lost as a result of legal inefficiencies and restrictions affecting secured credit markets, it would be likely that the case would be amply made for comprehensive reform in a number of jurisdictions of the legal rules on pledge, assignment and retention of title.

Cases 1 and 2

Case 1 deals with issues which are beyond the scope of legal provisions on secured transactions. The jurisdiction's general rules on transfer of ownership and the impact of the debtor's bankruptcy apply. Therefore, the answer to the question whether A, a producer of furniture, who sold to B desks and chairs without taking security or retaining title, has any right with respect to the furniture in the event that B becomes bankrupt after delivery but before payment to A, will depend on the country's legal rules on movable property and bankruptcy.[4] Case 2 is also outside the scope of the Model Law, as it deals with the effect of fraud on a contract and the enforcement procedure.

However, in many jurisdictions the unpaid seller can obtain protection, especially by retaining or reserving title in the goods sold. The case of the unpaid seller deserves attention because credit in trade transactions is a common feature in a market economy that needs to be encouraged. The Model Law makes special provision by introducing an innovative feature called 'the unpaid vendor's charge' (article 9). This is an example of the Model providing an illustrative solution for an issue which often causes much legal complexity and uncertainty to the general disadvantage of the market and those who operate in it. For an unpaid vendor's charge to come into existence, an agreement is required between seller and buyer and it is therefore explained under case 3. If the legal system in question organises a statutory lien in favour of the unpaid vendor on the sold asset or over the proceeds of sale without any specific agreement of the parties (as case 1 provides), in principle the Model Law does not interfere with it. However, the unpaid vendor's charge that the Model Law provides should encourage the law-makers to repeal additional security interests in favour of the vendor to streamline such privileges.

Case 3

Case 3 covers the case where title is reserved to the seller by contract and it is this that is addressed by the Model Law in the section on the unpaid vendor's charge. As the commentary to article 9 of the Model explains, this charge is meant to replace the forms of retention of title that many jurisdictions recognise. Pursuant to the Model Law, when seller and buyer agree that the seller will retain title in the thing sold until payment of the purchase price, title *actually* passes automatically to the buyer and simultaneously a charge is given back automatically

---

[4] Similarly, the answer to question (b) would be dealt with under the domestic contract law and the answer to question (c) under the rules applicable to carriers (such as a specific lien protecting the carrier when still in possession of the freight).

in favour of the seller. The agreement must be in writing at or before the time of the transfer of title but no further formalities are required. It should be noted that the parties' will is in fact disregarded. What is created is a charge just as if that is what was agreed between the parties: title does pass to the buyer in any case. However, this charge does not need to be registered, and therefore the parties do not even need to be aware of the provisions of article 9. The unpaid vendor's charge is the one area where the Model provides a solution which looks at the broader intention of the parties (to give the seller security for the unpaid price) and not the specific form (retention of title).[5] It does so because of the inherently complex and unsatisfactory nature of retention of title rules which have developed in several European jurisdictions (England and France are only two, but compelling, examples of this complexity). The system becomes clearly unworkable in sales across national boundaries. A seller cannot be expected to be acquainted with the rules on retention of title as they apply to each individual sale he makes in various countries where he is operating. In practice, he is likely to include a form of retention of title wording in his general sale conditions in the hope that this may give some protection. The intention of the unpaid vendor's charge under the Model Law was to encourage trade with countries in Central and Eastern Europe by giving uniform protection by way of security in all cases where the parties have agreed to retention of title or security, even where the sale contract is not under the law of the buyer's jurisdiction. The Model provisions are intended to cover sales on normal credit terms: this is why the unpaid vendor's charge terminates automatically after six months unless it has been converted into a registered charge by registration (see below).

The Model Law provisions on execution are particularly noteworthy. Execution cannot start without the charge becoming enforceable. A charge becomes immediately enforceable if there is a failure to pay the secured debt (article 22.1). Execution requires the chargeholder to deliver an enforcement notice to the debtor. The chargeholder obtains an immediate right to possession of the charged property or otherwise to ensure that it is protected (article 23) and after sixty days he has the right to transfer title to the charged property by way of sale in order to have the proceeds of sale applied towards satisfaction of the secured debt (article 24.1). The objective here is to provide simple, quick and efficient rules. Naturally, appeal by the chargor is possible and is provided in article 29.

---

[5] On this aspect, the Model adopts the approach of the US UCC, Article 9.

The chargeholder's duty to realise a fair price is spelt out (articles 24.3 and 24.5) and the chargor can claim damages for any breach.

Case 4

In case 4 the parties (a manufacturer of menswear and a retailer) agree on a sale contract of winter jackets where payment is to be made sixty days after delivery, but subject to retention of title, and the buyer is allowed to resell the jackets to customers.

Under the Model Law the unpaid seller benefits from an automatic charge without registration when he and the buyer have agreed that the title will remain with the seller until full payment. As no jackets have yet been sold, there is no problem of third parties becoming involved. Where B becomes bankrupt without having paid the full price, A still has a proprietary right over the jackets which will be enforced in accordance with the law on bankruptcy in question. The Model Law does not cover questions related to insolvency but is based on the assumption that the bankruptcy provisions should allow the right of the chargeholder to be respected and effective in insolvency (see Core Principles No 5 and Model Law, article 31).

If there is a risk of the six-month validity period of the unpaid vendor's charge expiring, A should convert his automatic charge into a registered charge by registering the charge (article 8.2). In either case A would have an enforceable security right over the jackets.

Cases 5 and 6

In these cases the situation becomes more complicated as the goods (cars) have been sold on by the buyer. In one case the buyer has been paid, in the other he has not, but that does not affect the position under the Model Law. The unpaid vendor's charge under the Model Law only gives protection while the buyer still owns the goods (except in cases of bad faith: see article 21.2.7). It does not extend to the proceeds of sale of the goods and thereby avoids the potential conflicts and complexities that can arise from tracing proceeds. The problem here is also one of balance: the case for continuing security in the goods in favour of the seller becomes harder to justify when the goods have been sold on. The Model Law allows the chargor (buyer) to sell the goods by giving him a licence (article 19) to sell the charged assets in the ordinary course of his trading activity. So in these cases the subsequent purchasers of the cars would have acquired good title and the seller would have no claim against the buyer for unauthorised sale (even in the absence of a contractual provision permitting it). Thus A would only have a claim as an unsecured creditor in B's bankruptcy and would not have any special rights in the proceeds of the cars sold by B.

The position of the seller could be improved by taking additional security, for example a charge over the buyer's bank account into which payments from customers are deposited and over the buyer's claims on purchasers for the price of cars sold. Such security under the Model would be by way of registered charge which would be created by agreement and registration.

Cases 7 and 8

A similar answer must be given to cases 7 and 8, which deal with the effect of the charged assets being used in a manufacturing process. Here cloth is turned into curtains – the question is whether the seller of the cloth, A, still has any proprietary right, by virtue of a retention of title clause, in the curtains that are made out of the cloth. Pursuant to article 32.1.4 of the Model Law, a charge terminates when the charged property is changed or incorporated with another thing or right in such manner that it ceases to exist in identifiable or separable form. The Model intentionally avoids a situation where the pledge on a raw material continues once the material has been incorporated into a manufactured product, with the related problems of 'measuring' the part of the raw material in the final value of the product and of resolving competing claims from persons claiming title to different components. This is the case here, so A can have no title over the curtains. Again, the seller of the cloth could improve his position by taking, in addition to his unpaid vendor's charge over the raw materials, a registered charge over the work in progress and/or the finished products of the manufacturer or over his bank account and/or his claims against purchasers. Such additional security would require agreement between the seller and buyer and be by way of registration.

Cases 9 and 11

Case 9 introduces the problem of identifying the goods to which the retention of title relates. The case envisages a wholesaler of electrical household goods, B, who has a stock of identical toasters purchased from A, some paid for, some not. The Model does not seek to provide a solution for this case as it is part of the broader issue of identification of property which does not properly fall for special treatment under the law on secured transactions. If A is unable or unwilling to set up a system of date stamps, batch marks or other similar method of identification, he could take a 'class' charge under the Model covering all toasters and other electrical goods sold by him to B. Pursuant to article 5.5, charged property may be identified specifically (in which case the charge is a specific charge) or generally (in which case the charge is a class charge). The objective of the class charge, as stated in the commentary, is to allow *a permanently changing pool of present and future assets* to be charged, such as inventory. Thus, in this case, the class charge would cover the whole inventory of goods (coffee-makers and toasters) supplied by A at any time and held by B. Upon each new supply by A the new goods will automatically be added to the pool of charged assets and upon sales being made by B to his customers goods sold will automatically leave the pool.

Case 11 also deals with security over stock-in-trade as A, a financial institution, wishes to guarantee a loan to B, with a security right over the stock-in-trade, present and future. As seen above, this can be covered under the Model Law by a class charge. Pursuant to articles 5.8 and 5.9, a charge can cover property which is not yet owned by the chargor; once the property is owned, the charge is deemed to have been created at the time of registration. It is also useful to note at this stage that article 5.6 allows a class charge to cover all the things and rights used in an enterprise which is capable of operating as a going concern or such part of the things and rights of an enterprise which would need to be transferred to enable an acquirer to continue the enterprise as a going concern. This class charge can be registered as an *enterprise charge*, which results in specific provisions becoming applicable in the case of enforcement (article 25), enabling a sale of the business as a going concern. This is an option that A and B could consider adopting, although the circumstances of the case do not require it. It should be noted that the enterprise charge is not the same as the device known in English law as the floating charge. The particular feature of an enterprise charge is that it entitles the chargeholder to the remedy of selling the enterprise as a going concern, but in other respects it is the same as any other charge, having immediate effect and not involving any concept of 'crystallisation'. Although it is recognised that an enterprise charge is an instrument that can be of practical use in countries in transition, it raises complex and delicate issues such as the rights of the chargeholder to manage the enterprise pending sale. It is thus considered preferable for countries in transition to introduce the enterprise charge concept once the basic secured transactions law is operative.

The Model Law does not cover the issue of security being granted for earlier debts within a certain period prior to bankruptcy as this belongs in the insolvency law.

Cases 10 and 14

Both these cases involve situations which are often covered by financial leasing arrangements. In case 10, B wants to use his fleet of vehicles as security; in case 14, B wants to obtain financing for the purchase of a computer. Financial leasing is outside the scope of the Model Law. It is a commonly used device which has a similar effect to a grant of security but it is structured differently and consequently gives rise to a different legal relationship. The Model Law does not adopt the approach of Article 9 UCC which looks at the intent of the transaction, and therefore treats a lease as a security interest if 'the consideration the lessee is to pay the lessor for the right to possession and use of the goods is an obligation for the term of the lease not subject to termination by the lessee' (Article 1-201(37) UCC). The only case in which the Model provides for the recharacterisation of the transaction is the unpaid vendor's charge referred to above.

Both situations could be covered under the Model Law by a registered charge over the car fleet or the computer. Such a charge would allow the owner, B, to remain in possession of the cars or computer and to use them for his business. It gives the lender a proprietary right in the cars or computer which is effective against third parties as long it has been registered. Registration ensures the creditor's ranking: first registered is first paid, and it should be easy for any prospective chargeholder, including the lender in these cases, to check with the central registry whether any previous charge has been granted over the cars or the computer. An unsecured creditor would not be able to take priority over the lender's right in the assets. A sale by B of any cars from the fleet or the computer would only be free from the charge if it was made (a) with the lender's consent (article 20), or (b) as a sale of B's trading stock in the ordinary course of B's business (article 19.2), or (c) where B habitually transfers cars or computers in the ordinary course of his business, as a sale in the ordinary course of B's business (article 19.3). These exceptions are not likely to be relevant to these cases.

If the lender becomes bankrupt the position would depend on the relevant bankruptcy law but it is likely that (a) the lender's administrator would continue to have rights under the charge, and (b) the charge given by B could not be enforced unless he failed to pay under the terms of the loan.

In these cases the parties have a choice whether to provide for security by way of a registered charge or to use a financial lease. The preferred solution would inevitably depend on the particular circumstances of the relevant jurisdiction (not least upon the fiscal treatment of the transaction). The intention of the Model Law is to provide for a simple and effective means of giving security which can easily be adapted to the commercial context of the transaction. If it achieves that purpose it is likely that a registered charge would most often be the better choice.

Cases 12 and 13

Cases 12 and 13 deal with the very important question of security over claims or receivables. In case 12, the claims are already known and identified in terms of amount and debtor: B has a contract with a firm, Happyplay Ltd, which provides him with monthly earnings. He wants to obtain a loan from A, a bank, secured on these earnings. Pursuant to the Model Law, A and B can agree to create a charge over the claims (or rights) as identified. There is no need to notify the claim's debtor in advance in order for the charge to be valid, but registration of the charge is required in the charges registry. The Model Law provides that the person owing the charged debt may satisfy it in a manner agreed with the chargor, unless the chargeholder notifies that person. The Model Law leaves it to the chargeholder to give the notice and it would be possible for chargor and chargeholder to agree when this could, or could not, take place. The manner in which the notice is given is a matter for each jurisdiction to define but the basic requirements are that it must be in writing, identify the chargor, describe the claim and give clear instructions as to the person to whom the claim is to be paid (article 12.3). Once notified, the debtor must pay the chargeholder or as the chargeholder directs and can be pursued directly by the chargeholder if he fails to do so. There is flexibility for the parties to agree that the claims are paid into an escrow account or a joint account or an account of the chargor which is charged to the chargeholder. Thus, in this case, there is considerable scope for the parties to structure the transaction in a manner which suits them and to agree on an arrangement which may avoid the need to notify Happyplay.

The position in the case of B's insolvency depends on relevant insolvency rules but, provided – as the Model envisages in article 31 – that the charge remains valid, B's bank would continue to have the same rights against Happyplay as it had prior to insolvency. It would have no right to sums paid by Happyplay to B or B's administrator unless they were charged separately (e.g. by a charge over the bank account into which the payments were made). However, if B had given notice to Happyplay and Happyplay had failed to make payment as required by the notice, then B's bank would have a claim against Happyplay.

In case 13, the facts are similar except that the claims that B wants to charge are future claims against unidentified future customers. In principle the Model Law allows a class charge over future claims generally described as long as the description is, or will be, adequate to identify the claims. The rights of B's bank under the charge will be similar to those in the previous case and its right to collect the claims will depend on it giving notice to the debtor customers, once known, in the manner described above. Even prior to notice, the bank has a charge in the claims and therefore has priority against any unsecured creditor seeking to establish a right in the claims.

A charge of a claim under the Model is distinct from an assignment of claims, although it may share many features. Security over claims is often given by way of assignment and the Model does not prevent this continuing. However, a charge will reflect better the parties' intention where the objective is to give security and should in many cases provide a preferable alternative.

The Model does not impose any limit on the amount of security that can be given for a claim; that is a matter for the parties to agree. However, article 33.2 provides a mechanism whereby a chargor or another chargeholder with a charge in the same asset can have the charge replaced by a charge over a deposit equal to 130 per cent of the secured debt.

Case 15 and a conclusion

Clearly case 15 is beyond the scope of a law on secured transactions, although insolvency law and general civil law should provide the right provisions to determine the rights of the parties in what is an obvious case of fraud. This is a good occasion to remind transition countries' law-makers that secured transactions legislation cannot and should not cover each and every issue which is somehow related to the subject. Law should be harmoniously built and organised – and a new single piece of legislation should fit within the existing framework. Over-ambitious enthusiasm to cover all cases can lead to a law which is ill-adapted and over-restrictive for modern market practice.

As can be seen from this short presentation, the EBRD Model Law and Core Principles are designed to illustrate how complex and advanced legal transactions can take place in a rather simple and straightforward fashion, which departs from the sometimes convoluted or restricted ways that European legal systems have adopted. A secured transactions law has to start by facilitating transactions and only then to put in place the necessary protections for the different parties involved. If it starts with impractical restrictions, the transactions will never take place and the whole law becomes pointless. The Model is designed to allow security over the broadest range of assets to secure the broadest range of debt in a manner which is relatively simple but at the same time allows practical remedies if a party is in breach of his obligations or abuses his position. The unpaid vendor's charge is put forward as an alternative to retention of title, giving a similar degree of protection but with less uncertainty. It cannot pretend to put forward the best solution for every case but the fact that it can provide the basis for straightforward solutions to cases that cause great legal angst in many Western European jurisdictions indicates the need for law-makers of Europe in a pan-European dimension to take a closer and critical look at their own laws on secured transactions. The laws in Central and Eastern Europe are changing and this could lead to a reversal of position with their countries having an economic advantage over their Western neighbours in the market for secured credit.

PART II · THE CASE STUDIES

Abbreviations

Germany

AcP	*Archiv für die civilistische Praxis* (law journal)
AGBG	*Gesetz zur Regelung des Rechts der Allgemeinen Geschäftsbedingungen* (Act on Unfair Contract Terms)
AnfG	*Gesetz, betreffend die Anfechtung von Rechtshandlungen eines Schuldners außerhalb des Konkursverfahrens* (Avoidance Act)
BAG	*Bundesarbeitsgericht* (Federal Labour Court)
BB	*Betriebs-Berater, Zeitschrift für Recht und Wirtschaft* (law journal)
BGB	*Bürgerliches Gesetzbuch* (Civil Code)
BGBl	*Bundesgesetzblatt* (Government Gazette)
BGH	*Bundesgerichtshof* (Federal Supreme Court)
BGHZ	*Entscheidungen des Bundesgerichtshofs in Zivilsachen* (Decisions of the Federal Supreme Court in Private Law Matters)
DB	*Der Betrieb* (law journal)
HGB	*Handelsgesetzbuch* (Commercial Code)
InsO	*Insolvenzordnung* (Insolvency Code)
IPRax	*Praxis des Internationalen Privat- und Verfahrensrechts* (law journal)
JR	*Juristische Rundschau* (law journal)
JuS	*Juristische Schulung* (law journal)
JZ	*Juristenzeitung* (law journal)
KO	*Konkursordnung* (old Insolvency Code)
LM	*Lindenmaier/Möhring, Nachschlagewerk des Bundesgerichtshofs in Zivilsachen* (reference work for decisions of the Federal Supreme Court)
NJW	*Neue Juristische Wochenschrift* (law journal)

118   THE CASE STUDIES

NJW-RR	*Neue Juristische Wochenschrift Rechtsprechungs-Report*
O.J.	Official Journal of the European Communities
OLG	*Oberlandesgericht* (Regional Appeal Court)
RG	*Reichsgericht* (Imperial Court)
RGZ	*Amtliche Sammlung von Entscheidungen des Reichsgerichts in Zivilsachen* (Decisions of the Imperial Court in Private Law Matters)
sent.	sentence
VersR	*Zeitschrift für Versicherungsrecht* (law journal)
WM	*Wertpapiermitteilungen* (law journal)
ZEuP	*Zeitschrift für Europäisches Privatrecht* (law journal)
ZIP	*Zeitschrift für Wirtschaftsrecht und Insolvenzpraxis* (law journal)
ZPO	*Zivilprozeßordnung* (Civil Procedure Code)
ZZP	*Zeitschrift für Zivilprozeß* (law journal)

Austria

ABGB	*Allgemeines Bürgerliches Gesetzbuch* (Civil Code)
AnfO	*Anfechtungsordnung* (Avoidance Act)
EO	*Exekutionsordnung* (Execution Act)
EvBl	*Evidenzblatt der Rechtsmittelentscheidungen*
EVHGB	*Einführungsverordnung zum Handelsgezetzbuch*
GlU	*Glaser-Unger* (collection of decisions of the OGH in the nineteenth century)
HGB	*Handelsgesetzbuch* (Commercial Code)
HS	*Sammlung handelsrechtlicher Entscheidungen* (collection of commercial law decisions)
JB	*Judikatenbuch* (collection of important decisions of the OGH edited by the court itself)
JBl	*Juristische Blätter* (law journal)
KO	*Konkursordnung* (Insolvency Act)
KSchG	*Konsumentenschutzgesetz* (Consumer Protection Act)
MietSlg	*Mietrechtliche Entscheidungssammlung* (annually published collection of court decisions with relevance for rent matters)
NZ	*Notariatszeitung* (law journal)
ÖBA	*Österreichisches Bank Archiv* (law journal)
OGH	*Oberster Gerichtshof* (Supreme Court in private law matters)
ÖJZ	*Österreichische Juristen Zeitung* (law journal)
RdW	*Recht der Wirtschaft* (law journal)
Rspr	*Die Rechtsprechung* (law journal)

SZ	*Entscheidungen des österreichischen Obersten Gerichtshofes in Zivilsachen* (official publication of the decisions of the OGH in Private Law Matters, edited by the court itself)
WBl	*Wirtschaftsrechtliche Blätter* (law journal)

Greece

A.K.	*Astikos Kodikas* (Civil Code)
AP	*Areios Pagos* (Supreme Court in civil and criminal matters)
ArchN	*Archeion Nomologias* [Archive of Court Rulings] (law journal)
Arm	*Armenopoulos* (law journal)
DCC	Draft Commercial Code
DEE	*Dikaion Etaireion kai Epichiriseon* [Business and Company Law] (law journal)
EEmbD	*Epitheorisis Emborikou Dikaiou* [Review of Commercial Law] (law journal)
EEN	*Ephimeris Hellinon Nomikon* [Greek Lawyer's Journal] (law journal)
Ef	*Efetio* (Court of Appeal)
EllDni	*Helliniki Dikaiosyni* [Greek Justice] (law journal)
EmbN	*Emborikos Nomos* [Commercial Law] (law journal)
ErmAK	*Ermineia tou Astikou Kodika* [Interpretation of the Civil Code] (collective work)
KIND	*Kodikas Idiotikou Nautikou Dikaiou* [Code of Private Maritime Law]
KPolD	*Kodikas Politikis Dikonomias* [Code of Civil Procedure]
L.	Law
L.D.	Law Decree
NoV	*Nomikon Vima* [Law Tribune] (law journal)
Them	*Themis* (law journal)

France

Ass plén	Decision of the *Assemblée plénière* of the *Cour de cassation*
BRDA	*Bulletin rapide de droit des affaires*
Bull civ I	*Bulletin des arrêts des Chambres civiles de la Cour de cassation* (Decisions of the 1st Civil Chamber of the *Cour de cassation*, as published in the official Bulletin)

Bull civ II	*Bulletin des arrêts des Chambres civiles de la Cour de cassation* (Decision of the 2nd Civil Chamber of the *Cour de cassation*, as published in the official Bulletin)
Bull civ III	*Bulletin des arrêts des Chambres civiles de la Cour de cassation* (Decision of the 3rd Civil Chamber of the *Cour de cassation*, as published in the official Bulletin)
Bull civ IV	*Bulletin des arrêts des Chambres civiles de la Cour de cassation* (Decision of the Commercial Civil Chamber of the *Cour de cassation*, as published in the official Bulletin)
Cah dr entr	*Cahiers de droit de l'entreprise* (law journal)
C. civ	*Code civil* (Civil Code)
C. com	*Code de commerce* (Commercial Code)
Chr	*Chroniques*
Civ. (1)	First civil chamber of the *Cour de cassation*
Civ. (2)	Second civil chamber of the *Cour de cassation*
Civ. (3)	Third civil chamber of the *Cour de cassation*
Com	Commercial chamber of the *Cour de cassation*
Conc	*conclusions*
D	*Recueil Dalloz* or *Dalloz Sirey* (law journal)
D.	Decree No 92–755 of 31 july 1992
D affaires	*Dalloz Affaires* (law journal)
DH	*Recueil Dalloz hebdomadaire de jurisprudence* (law journal)
DP	*Recueil Dalloz périodique et critique* (prior to its amalgamation with *Sirey* in 1965 to form *Dalloz Sirey*, 'D') (law journal)
ÉdE	*Edition Entreprise*
Gaz Pal	*La Gazette du Palais*
IA 85	Insolvency Act, Law No 85-98 of 25 Jan. 1985 as amended
IR	*Informations rapides*
J.	Justice
JCP	*Jurisclasseur Périodique* (otherwise known as *La Semaine Juridique*) (law journal)
JCPédE	*Jurisclasseur Périodique (La Semaine Juridique), édition Entreprise* (law journal)
JDI	*Journal de Droit International (Clunet)* (law journal)
JEX	*juge de l'exécution*
JO	*Journal officiel*
L.	Law No 91-650 of 9 July 1991
obs.	*Observations*
Pan	*Panorama*

Rapp	*Rapport*
Req	decision of the *Chambre des Requêtes* of the *Cour de cassation*
Rev huiss	*Revue des huissiers* (law journal)
Rev jur com	*Revue de jurisprudence commerciale* (law journal)
Rev proc coll	*Revue des procédures collectives* (law journal)
RJDA	*Revue de jurisprudence de droit des affaires* (law journal)
RTDC	*Revue trimestrielle de droit civil* (law journal)
RTDCom	*Revue trimestrielle de droit commercial* (law journal)
S	*Recueil Sirey* (prior to its amalgamation with *Recueil Dalloz* in 1965 to form *Dalloz Sirey*, 'D') (law journal)
Som	*Sommaire*
TGI	*Tribunal de grande instance*

Belgium

Cass.	*Hof van Cassatie/Cour de cassation* (Supreme Court)
C.civ.	*Code civil* (Civil Code)
concl. proc. gen.	*conclusions du procureur général*
JT	*Journal des Tribunaux* (law journal)
Pas	*Pasicrisie belge* (law journal)
RCJB	*Revue critique de jurisprudence belge* (law journal)
RevBanque	*Revue de la Banque* (law journal)
RIW	*Recht der Internationalen Wirtschaft* (law journal)
RW	*Rechtskundig Weekblad* (law review)
TPR	*Tijdschrift voor Privaatrecht* (law review)

Portugal

BMJ	*Boletim do Ministério da Justiça*
C.C.	*Código Civil* (Civil Code)
C.Com.	*Código Comerciail* (Commercial Code)
CPC	*Código de Processo Civil* (Civil Procedure Code)
CPEREF	*Código dos Processos Especiais de Recuperação da Empresa e da Falência* (Bankruptcy Code)
DL	*Decreto-Lei*
LCCG	*Lei das Cláusulas Contratuais Gerais* (Unfair Contract Terms Act)
RDE	*Revista de direio e economia* (law journal)
ROA	*Revista da Ordem dos Advogados* (law journal)
STJ	*Supremo Tribunal de Justiça* (Supreme Court)

Spain

ADC	*Anuario de Derecho Civil* (law journal)
BCRE	*Boletín del Colegio de Registradores de España*
BIMJ	*Boletín de Información del Ministerio de Justicia* (Ministry of Justice Information Bulletin)
BOE	*Boletín Oficial del Estado* (Official Gazette of the Spanish State)
CC	*Código Civil* (Civil Code)
CCO	*Código de Comercio* (Commercial Code)
CDCC	*Compilación de Derecho Civil de Cataluña* (Compilation of Catalonia Civil Laws)
CDCFN	*Compilación de Derecho Civil Foral de Navarra* (Compilation of Navarre Historical Civil Laws)
CE	*Constitución Española* (Constitution of 1978)
CGPJ	*Consejo General del Poder Judicial*
CRPME	*Colegio de Registradores de la Propiedad y Mercantiles de España*
EFC	*Establecimientos Financieros de Crédito* (Credit Institutions)
ET	*Estatuto de los Trabajadores*
La Ley	*Revista jurídica española La Ley* (law journal)
LEC	*Ley de Enjuiciamiento Civil* (Civil Procedure Act)
LGP	*Ley de Garantías Posesorias sobre Cosa Mueble* (Catalan Possessory Guarantees on Chattels Act)
LH	*Ley Hipotecaria*
LHMPSD	*Ley de 16 Dec. 1954 sobre Hipoteca Mobiliaria y Prenda sin Desplazamiento* (Law of Chattel Mortgage and Pledge without Removal of Possession)
LVBMP	*Ley de Ventas de Bienes Muebles a Plazos* (Law of Sale of Chattels in Instalments)
PALC	*Propuesta de Anteproyecto de Ley Concursal* (Bankruptcy Law Draft)
PYME	*Pequeña y Mediana Empresa* (small or medium-size company)
RCDI	*Revista Crítica de Derecho Inmobiliario* (law journal)
RD	*Real Decreto* (Royal Decree)
RH	*Reglamento Hipotecario*
SAT	*Sentencia de la Audiencia Territorial* (Regional Court of Appeal decision)
STS	*Sentencia del Tribunal Supremo* (Supreme Court decision)

Italy

App.	*Corte d'appello* (Appeal Court)
Arch. civ.	*Archivo Civile* (law journal)
Cass.	*Corte di cassazione* (Supreme Court)
c.c.	*codice civile* (Civil Code)
Contr. e impr.	*Contratto e impresa* (law journal)
Corr. giur.	*Corriere giuridico* (law journal)
c.p.	*codice penale* (Criminal Code)
c.p.c.	*codice di procedura civile* (Code of Civil Procedure)
d. lgs.	*decreto legislativo* (legislative enactment)
decr.	*decreto*
Digesto sez. civ.	*Digesto delle discipline privatistiche – sezione civile* (legal encyclopedia)
Digesto sez. comm.	*Digesto delle discipline privatistiche – sezione commerciale* (legal encyclopedia)
Digesto sez. pub.	*Digesto discipline pubblicistiche* (law journal)
Dir. comm. internaz.	*Diritto del commercio internazionale* (law journal)
Dir. fall.	*Diritto fallimentore e delle società commercial* (law journal)
Enc. dir.	*Enciclopedia del diritto*
ERPL	European Review of Private Law (law journal)
Foro it.	*Il Foro italiano* (law journal)
Giur. comm.	*Giurisprudenza commerciale* (law journal)
Giur. it.	*Giurisprudenza italiana* (law journal)
Giust. civ.	*Giustizia civile* (law journal)
l.	*legge* (law)
L. Fall.	*legge fallimentare* (Insolvency Act)
NLCC	*Nuove leggi civili commentate* (law journal)
obs.	observations
O.J.	Official Journal of the European Communities
P.R.A.	*Pubblico Registro Automobilistico*
r.d.L.	*regio decreto legge* (royal decree)
Riv. dir. civ.	*Rivista del diritto civile* (law journal)
Riv. dir. priv.	*Rivista di diritto privato* (law journal)
Riv. it. leasing	*Rivista italiana del leasing* (law journal)
Riv. not.	*Rivista del notariato* (law journal)
Riv. trim. dir. proc. civ.	*Rivista trimestiale di diritto e procedura civile* (law journal)
s.u.	*sezioni unite*
Trib.	*Tribunale* (Court of First Instance)
vita not.	*Vita notarile* (law journal)

The Netherlands

AA	*Ars Aequi* (law journal)
BW	*Burgerlijk Wetboek* (Civil Code)
ECR	European Court Reports
Fw	*Faillissementswet* (Insolvency Act)
HR	*Hoge Raad* (Supreme Court)
Inv.	*Invoeringswet* (Implementation Act)
NJ	*Nederlandse Jurisprudentie* (law reports)
NJB	*Nederlands Juristenblad* (law journal)
NTBR	*Nederlands tijdschrift voor Burgerlijk Recht* (law journal)
Parl. Gesch.	*Parlamentaire Geschiedenis*
Rv	*Wetboek van Burgerlijke Rechtsvordering* (Code of Civil Procedure)
WPNR	*Weekblad voor privaatrecht, notariaat en registratie* (law journal)

England

AC	Appeal Cases, Law Reports
All ER	All England Law Reports
All ER (D)	All England Reports Digest
App Cas	Law Reports, Appeal Cases, House of Lords
BCC	British Company Cases
BCLC	Butterworth's Company Law Cases
CA	Court of Appeal
CB	Common Bench
Ch	Law Reports, Chancery Division
Ch App	Law Reports, Chancery Appeals
Cmnd	Command Paper
CP	Law Reports, Common Pleas Division
JIBFL	Butterworth's Journal of International Banking and Financial Law
KB	Law Reports, King's Bench Division
Lloyd's Rep	Lloyd's Law Reports
LQR	Law Quarterly Review
LR	Law Reports
Mer	Merivale's Reports
QB	Law Reports, Queen's Bench Division
WLR	Weekly Law Reports

Ireland

AC	Appeal Cases, Law Reports
BCC	British Company Cases
BCLC	Butterworth's Company Law Cases

Ch	Law Reports, Chancery Division
CP	Common Pleas
ILRM	Irish Law Reports Monthly
IR	Irish Reports
JBL	Journal of Business Law
LR	Law Reports
NZCLC	New Zealand Company Law Cases
QB	Law Reports, Queen's Bench Division
SC	Session Cases (Scotland)
WLR	Weekly Law Reports

Scotland

AC	Appeal Cases, Law Reports
JR	Juridical Review
JLSS	Journal of the Law Society of Scotland
SC	Session Cases
SLT	Scots Law Times

South Africa

StellLR	Stellenbosch Law Review
TSAR	Tydskrif vir die Suid Afrikaanse Reg

Denmark

B	section for legal literature in the weekly law reports
CISG	United Nations Convention on Contracts for the International Sale of Goods
DKK	Danish krone
H	*Højesteret* (Supreme Court); after a case in the weekly law reports, indicating that the case was decided by the *Højesteret*
TfR	*Tidsskrift for Rettsvitenskap* (law journal)
U	*Ugeskrift for Retsvæsen* (weekly law reports)

Sweden

BGB	*Bürgerliches Gesetzbuch* (German Civil Code)
CISG	United Nations Convention on Contracts for the International Sale of Goods
NJA I	*Nytt Juridiskt Arkiv* I (cases from the Supreme Court)
NJA II	*Nytt Juridiskt Arkiv* II (legislative preparatory works)
SOU	*Statens Offentliga Utredningar* (committee reports)
SPV	Special Purpose Vehicle
SvJT	*Svensk Juristtidning* (law journal)

126   THE CASE STUDIES

Finland

AJL	*laki arvo-osuusjärjestelmästä/lag om värdeandelssystemet* (17 May 1991/826) (Act on Book-entry System)
AlusKiinL	*aluskiinnityslaki/lag om inteckning i fartyg* (29 July 1927/211) (Vessel Mortgage Act)
ATL	*laki arvo-osuustileistä/lag om värdeandelskonton* (17 May 1991/827) (Act on Book-entry Accounts)
AutoKiinL	*autokiinnityslaki/lag om inteckning i bil* (15 Dec. 1972/810) (Vehicle Mortgage Act)
Ilma-alusKiinL	*laki kiinnityksestä ilma-aluksiin/lag om inteckning i luftfartyg* (15 June 1928/211) (Aircraft Mortgage Act)
KK	*kauppakaari/handelsbalk* (Commercial Code)
KKO	*korkein oikeus* (Supreme Court)
KL	*kauppalaki/köplag* (27 Mar. 1987/355) (Sale of Goods Act)
KSL	*kuluttajansuojalaki/konsumentskyddslag* (20 Jan. 1978/38) (Consumer Protection Act)
OsamKL	*laki osamaksukaupasta/lag om avbetalningsköp* (18 Feb. 1966/91) (Instalment Sales Act)
OYL	*osakeyhtiölaki/lag om aktiebolag* (29 Sep. 1978/734) (Companies Act)
TakSL	*laki takaisinsaannista konkurssipesään/lag om återvinning till konkursbo* (26 Apr. 1991/758) (Act on Recovery to Bankrupt's Estate)
VJL	*laki yksityishenkilön velkajärjestelystä/lag om skuldsanering för privatpersoner* (25 Jan. 1993/57) (Act on Rearrangement of Private Person's Debts)
VKL	*velkakirjalaki/lag om skuldebrev* (31 July 1947/622) (Act on Promissory Notes)
YrKiinL	*yrityskiinnityslaki/företagsinteckningslag* (24 Aug. 1984/634) (Act on Enterprise Charge)
YSL	*laki yrityksen saneerauksesta/lag om företagssanering* (25 Jan. 1993/47) (Act on Reorganization of Enterprise)

Evaluation/Comparative observations

AGBG	*Gesetz zur Regelung des Rechts der Allgemeinen Geschäftsbedingungen* (German Act on Unfair Contract Terms)
A.K.	*Astikos Kodikas* (Greek Civil Code)
All ER	All England Law Reports
Aranzadi	*Aranzadi, Repertorio de Jurisprudencia* (law journal)

BGB	*Bürgerliches Gesetzbuch* (German Civil Code)
BGH	*Bundesgerichtshof* (German Federal Supreme Court)
BGHZ	*Entscheidungen des Bundesgerichtshofs für Zivilsachen* (Decisions of the German Federal Supreme Court in Private Law Matters)
BOE	*Boletín Oficial del Estado* (Official Gazette of the Spanish State)
BW	*Burgerlijk Wetboek* (Dutch Civil Code)
Cass.	*Cour de cassation* (French or Belgian Supreme Court)
C.c.	*Codice civile* (Italian Civil Code) *Código civil* (Spanish or Portuguese Civil Code)
C.civ.	*Code civil* (French or Belgian Civil Code)
C.com.	*Code de commerce* (French Code of Commerce)
CISG	United Nations Convention on Contracts for the International Sale of Goods
EBRD	European Bank for Reconstruction and Development
ERPL	European Review of Private Law (law journal)
EU	European Union
HGB	*Handelsgesetzbuch* (German or Austrian Commercial Code)
InsO	*Insolvenzordnung* (German Insolvency Act)
JBl	*Juristische Blätter* (law journal)
JCP	*Jurisclasseur périodique* (otherwise known as *La Semaine Juridique*), *édition générale* (law journal)
JZ	*Juristenzeitung* (law journal)
OGH	*Oberster Gerichtshof* (Austrian Supreme Court)
RabelsZ	*Rabels Zeitschrift für ausländisches und internationales Privatrecht* (law journal)
Rev.crit.d.i.p.	*Revue critique de droit international privé* (law journal)
SLT	Scots Law Times
STS	*Sentencia Tribunal Supremo* (decision of the Spanish Supreme Court)
UCC	Uniform Commercial Code
UNCITRAL	United Nations Commission on International Trade Law
UNIDROIT	International Institute for the Unification of Private Law
Unif. L. Rev./Rev. dr. unif.	Uniform Law Review/*Revue de droit uniforme* (law journal)
WG	*Wechselgesetz* (Act on Bills of Exchange)
ZEuP	*Zeitschrift für Europäisches Privatrecht* (law journal)
ZIP	*Zeitschrift für Wirtschaftsrecht und Insolvenzpraxis* (law journal)

Bibliographies

Germany

Manfred Balz, Hans-Georg Landfermann (eds.), *Die neuen Insolvenzgesetze* (1995).
Adolf Baumbach, Klaus J. Hopt, *Handelsgesetzbuch* (30th edn, 2000).
Adolf Baumbach, Wolfgang Lauterbach, Jan Albers, Peter Hartmann, *Zivilprozeßordnung* (60th edn, 2002).
Fritz Baur, Rolf Stürner, *Zwangsvollstreckungs-, Konkurs- und Vergleichsrecht, Band I: Einzelzwangsvollstreckungsrecht* (12th edn, 1995), *Band II: Insolvenzrecht* (12th edn, 1990).
Jürgen Baur, Rolf Stürner, *Sachenrecht* (17th edn, 1999).
Reinhard Bork, *Einführung in das neue Insolvenzrecht* (3rd edn, 2002).
Hans Brox, 'Das Anwartschaftsrecht des Vorbehaltskäufers', JuS 1984, 657 ff.
Peter Bülow, 'Der erweiterte Eigentumsvorbehalt nach der Insolvenzrechtsreform', DB 1999, 2196 ff.
  Recht der Kreditsicherheiten (5th edn, 1999).
Bundesministerium der Justiz (ed.), *Erster Bericht der Kommission für Insolvenzrecht* (1985).
Claus-Wilhelm Canaris, *Die Vertrauenshaftung im deutschen Privatrecht* (1971).
Eberhard Dorndorf, Jürgen Frank, 'Reform des Rechts der Mobiliarsicherheiten – unter besonderer Berücksichtigung der ökonomischen Analyse der Sicherungsrechte', ZIP 1985, 65 ff.
Ulrich Drobnig, 'Empfehlen sich gesetzliche Maßnahmen zur Reform der Mobiliarsicherheiten?', *Gutachten F zum 51. Deutschen Juristentag* (1976).
Diederich Eckardt, 'Die Ausübung von Mobiliarsicherheiten in der Unternehmenskrise', ZIP 1999, 1734 ff.
Erman, *Handkommentar zum Bürgerlichen Gesetzbuch in zwei Bänden* (10th edn, 2000).
Josef Esser, Eike Schmidt, *Schuldrecht Band I: Allgemeiner Teil, Teilband 2* (7th edn, 1993).
Werner Flume, 'Der verlängerte und erweiterte Eigentumsvorbehalt', NJW 1950, 841 ff.

Allgemeiner Teil des Bürgerlichen Rechts, Band 2: Das Rechtsgeschäft (3rd edn, 1979).
H. Franke, 'Eigentumsvorbehalt und Verarbeitung', BB 1955, 717 ff.
Hans Friedhelm Gaul, '*Lex commissoria* und Sicherungsübereignung', AcP 168 (1968) 351 ff.
Joachim Gernhuber, 'Die fiduziarische Treuhand', JuS 1988, 355 ff.
Peter Gottwald, Jens Adolphsen, 'Die Rechtsstellung dinglich gesicherter Gläubiger in der Insolvenzordnung', in: Arbeitskreis für Insolvenz- und Schiedsgerichtswesen e.V. (ed.), *Kölner Schrift zur Insolvenzordnung: Das neue Insolvenzrecht in der Praxis* (2nd edn, 2000) 1043 ff.
Jörg Stefan Greving, *Der Treuhandgedanke bei Sicherungsübertragungen im italienischen und deutschen Recht* (2002).
Ludwig Häsemeyer, *Insolvenzrecht* (2nd edn, 1998).
Michael Hoffmann-Becking, Helmut Schippel (eds.), *Beck'sches Formularbuch zum Bürgerlichen, Handels- und Wirtschaftsrecht* (7th edn, 1998).
Paul Hofmann, 'Verarbeitungsklausel und § 950 BGB', NJW 1962, 1798 ff.
Heinrich Honsell, 'Aktuelle Probleme des Eigentumsvorbehalts', JuS 1981, 705 ff.
International Chamber of Commerce (ed.), *Retention of Title. A Practical Guide to Legislation in 35 Countries* (2nd edn, 1993).
Othmar Jauernig, *Zwangsvollstreckungs- und Insolvenzrecht* (21st edn, 1999).
Georg Kuhn, Wilhelm Uhlenbruck, *Konkursordnung* (11th edn, 1994).
Karl Larenz, *Lehrbuch des Schuldrechts, Band I: Allgemeiner Teil* (14th edn, 1987).
Allgemeiner Teil des deutschen Bürgerlichen Rechts (7th edn, 1989).
Karl Larenz, Manfred Wolf, *Allgemeiner Teil des deutschen Bürgerlichen Rechts* (8th edn, 1997).
Franz Laufke, 'Zum Eigentumserwerb nach § 950 BGB', in: Rolf Dietz, Hans Carl Nipperdey, Eugen Ulmer (eds.), *Festschrift für Alfred Hueck* (1959) 69 ff.
Stefan Leible, *Finanzierungsleasing und 'arrendamiento financiero'* (1996).
Manfred Lieb, 'Eigentumsvorbehalt und Abwehrklausel', in: Hanns Prütting (ed.), *Festschrift für Gottfried Baumgärtel* (1990) 311 ff.
Hans-Jürgen Lwowski, *Das Recht der Kreditsicherung* (7th edn, 1994).
Wolfgang Marotzke, 'Die Behandlung der schwebenden Rechtsgeschäfte', in: Dieter Leipold (ed.), *Insolvenzrecht im Umbruch* (1991) 183 ff.
'Der Eigentumsvorbehalt im neuen Insolvenzrecht', JZ 1995, 803 ff.
'Die dinglichen Sicherheiten im neuen Insolvenzrecht', ZZP 109 (1996) 429 ff.
Michael Martinek, *Moderne Vertragstypen Band I: Leasing und Factoring* (1991).
Münchener Kommentar zum Bürgerlichen Gesetzbuch, Band 1, Allgemeiner Teil (§§ 1–240) (3rd edn, 1993), *Band 2, Schuldrecht Allgemeiner Teil (§§ 241–432)* (3rd edn, 1994).
Münchener Kommentar zur Zivilprozeßordnung, Band 2 §§ 355–802 ZPO (2nd edn, 2002)
Jörg Nerlich, Volker Römermann (eds.), *Insolvenzordnung* (looseleaf, January 1999).

Gerd Nobbe, 'Aktuelle Entwicklungen zu Sicherungsübereignung und
    Globalzession im Lichte des AGB-Gesetzes', ZIP 1996, 657 ff.
Palandt, *Bürgerliches Gesetzbuch* (61st edn, 2002).
Christoph Paulus, 'The New German Insolvency Code', *Texas International Law
    Journal* 33 (1998) 141 ff.
Ludwig Raiser, *Anmerkung zu BGH 2.10.1952*, NJW 1953, 217 ff.
Dietrich Reinicke, Klaus Tiedtke, *Kreditsicherung* (4th edn, 2000).
Franz Jürgen Säcker, 'Zum Begriff des Herstellers in § 950 BGB', JR 1966, 51 ff.
Karsten Schmidt, *Handelsrecht* (5th edn, 1999).
Klaus Schurig, 'Schiffbruch beim Eigentumsvorbehalt – Sachenrechtsstatut,
    Vertragsstatut, Sprachenrisiko', IPRax 1994, 27 ff.
Rolf Serick, *Eigentumsvorbehalt und Sicherungsübertragung, Monographie in 6
    Bänden: Band III: Die einfache Sicherungsübertragung – Zweiter Teil* (1970); *Band
    IV: Verlängerungs- und Erweiterungsformen des Eigentumsvorbehalts und der
    Sicherungsübertragung – Erster Teil: Verlängerungsformen und Kollisionen* (1976);
    *Band V: Verlängerungs- und Erweiterungsformen des Eigentumsvorbehalts und der
    Sicherungsübertragung – Zweiter Teil: Erweiterungsformen – Dritter Teil: Sonstiges:
    Insolvenzrecht (Konkurs)* (1982); *Band VI: Verlängerungs- und Erweiterungsformen
    des Eigentumsvorbehalts und der Sicherungsübertragung – Dritter Teil: Sonstiges:
    Insolvenzrecht (Vergleich); Insolvenzrechtsreform* (1986). Cited as: Serick,
    Eigentumsvorbehalt und Sicherungsübertragung III–VI.
    'Die Mobiliarsicherheiten im Referentenentwurf zur Insolvenzrechtsreform',
    BB 1990, 861 ff.
    Eigentumsvorbehalt und Sicherungsübertragung (2nd edn, 1993).
Stefan Smid (ed.), *Insolvenzordnung* (1st edn, 1999; 2nd edn, 2001).
Soergel, *Bürgerliches Gesetzbuch, Band 3: Schuldrecht II §§ 433–853* (12th edn, 1991);
    Band 6: Sachenrecht §§ 854–1296 (12th edn, 1989).
Staudinger, *Kommentar zum Bürgerlichen Gesetzbuch, §§ 925–984, Anhang zu §§ 929 ff*
    (13th edn, 1995); *§§ 397–432* (13th edn, 1999); *§§ 433–534 BGB* (13th edn,
    1995).
Friedrich Stein, Martin Jonas, *Kommentar zur Zivilprozeßordnung, Band 6
    §§ 704–863* (21st edn, 1995).
Charles E. Stewart, *Insolvency Code, Act Introducing the Insolvency Code* (1998).
Lars Peter Wunibald Van Vliet, *Transfer of Movables* (2000).
Andreas Wacke, 'Eigentumserwerb des Käufers durch schlichten Konsens oder
    erst mit Übergabe? Unterschiede im Rezeptionsprozeß und ihre mögliche
    Überwindung', ZEuP 2000, 254 ff.
Elmar Wadle, 'Das Problem der fremdwirkenden Verarbeitung', JuS 1982, 477 ff.
Jobst Wellensiek, 'Ein Jahr Insolvenzordnung – Erste Praxiserfahrungen mit
    dem neuen Recht', BB 2000, 1 ff.
Harm-Peter Westermann, Karl-Heinz Gursky, Dieter Eickmann, *Sachenrecht*
    (7th edn, 1998).
Friedrich Graf von Westphalen, *Der Leasingvertrag* (5th edn, 1998).

Jan Wilhelm, *Sachenrecht* (2nd edn, 2002).
Manfred Wolf, Norbert Horn, Walter Lindacher, *AGB-Gesetz Kommentar* (4th edn, 1999).
Reinhard Zimmermann, *The Law of Obligations* (1996).
Reinhard Zimmermann, Simon Whittaker (eds.), *Good Faith in European Contract Law* (2000).

Austria

Peter Apathy, *Der Verwendungsanspruch* (1988).
Peter Avancini/Gert Iro/Helmut Koziol, *Österreichisches Bankvertragsrecht*, vol. I (1987), vol. II (1993).
Raimund Bollenberger, *Irrtum über die Zahlungsunfähigkeit* (1995).
  'Veräußerung von Vorbehaltsgut', ÖJZ 1995, 641 ff.
  'Gutglaubenserwerb nach Maßgabe der Zahlung – Anhaltspunkte in der Rechtsordnung', ÖJZ 1996, 851 ff.
Franz Bydlinski, 'Probleme des Quantitätseigentums', JBl 1974, 32 ff.
Peter Bydlinski, 'Eigentumsvorbehalt und Rücktrittsrecht', RdW 1984, 98 ff.
Constanze Czermak, 'Das Besitzkonstitut beim Sale and Lease-back-Verfahren', ÖBA 1987, 232 ff.
Armin Ehrenzweig, *System des österreichischen allgemeinen Privatrechts*, vol. II/1 (2nd edn, 1928).
Constanze Fischer-Czermak, *Mobilienleasing, Rechtsnatur, Gewährleistung und Gefahrtragung* (1995).
Hanns Fitz, 'Globalzession als Kreditsicherung im österreichischen Recht', ÖJZ 1973, 595 ff.
Gerhard Frotz, *Aktuelle Probleme des Kreditsicherungsrechts* (1970).
Georg Graf, 'Übermäßige Inanspruchnahme der Garantie: Voraussetzungen der Rückforderung durch den Garanten', *ecolex* 1998, 15 ff.
Christian Holzner, 'Gutglaubenserwerb nur nach Maßgabe der Zahlung?', ÖJZ 1996, 372 ff.
Hans Hoyer, 'Einseitig erklärter Eigentumsvorbehalt?', WBl 1995, 181 ff.
Gert Iro, 'Sicherungsglobalzession und Drittschuldnerverständigung', RdW 1989, 357 ff.
Peter Jabornegg (ed.), *Kommentar zum HGB* (1997).
Heinrich Klang (ed.), *Kommentar zum ABGB* (2nd edn, 1950).
Bernhard König, 'Buchvermerk und EDV-Buchhaltung', RdW 1993, 34 ff.
Helmut Koziol, *Grundlagen und Streitfragen der Gläubigeranfechtung* (1991).
  'Abtretung künftiger Forderungen und Konkurs des Zedenten', ÖBA 1998, 745.
  'Sicherungszession und andere Mobiliarsicherheiten aus rechtsvergleichender Sicht', in: Wolfgang Wiegand, *Mobiliarsicherheiten* (1998) 19 ff.

Helmut Koziol, Rudolf Welser, *Grundriß des bürgerlichen Rechts*, vol. I (11th edn, 2000) and vol. II (10th edn, 1996).
Peter Rummel (ed.), *Kommentar zum ABGB*, vol. I (3rd edn, 2000) and vol. II (2nd edn, 1992).
Michael Schwimann (ed.), *Praxiskommentar zum ABGB*, 8 vols. (2nd edn, 1997).
Karl Spielbüchler, 'Eigentumsvorbehalt und Verarbeitung', JBl 1968, 589.
  Der Dritte im Schuldverhältnis (1973).
Manfred Straube (ed.), *Kommentar zum HGB*, vol. I (2nd edn, 1995).
Georg Wilhelm, 'Unrechtmäßig gezogene Garantie – Rückforderungsanspruch der Garantin', *ecolex* 1998, 612 ff.
Christian Zepke, 'Zur Abtretung künftiger Forderungen', ÖBA 1997, 984 ff.

Greece

G. Balis, *Enochikon Dikaion, Genikon Meros* [*Law of Obligations General Part*] (1954).
  Empragmaton Dikaion [*Real Law*] (4th edn, 1961).
  Genikai Archai tou Astikou Dikaiou [*General Principles of Civil Law*] (8th edn, 1961).
E. Banakas, in: *Georgiadis–Stathopoulos AK* 939.
D. Bosdas, 'Di atirisis tis kyriotitos ypo tou politou' ['Reservation of Title by the Vendor'], EEN 46, 5.
  'I metavivasis kyriotitos pros asphaleian apaitiseos' ['Transfer of Ownership for Securing of a Claim'], ArchN 26, 313.
I. Brinias, *Anagastiki ektelesis* [*Compulsive Execution*] (1971).
P. Deliyiannis-Kornilakis, *Eidiko Enochiko Dikaio I* [*Law of Obligations Special Part I*] (1992).
Ph. Doris, in: *Georgiadis–Stathopoulos AK* 211 vol. I (1978).
  Empragmati Asphaleia [*Real Security*] (1986).
P. Filios, *Empragmato Dikaio tomos 2* [*Real Law II*] (2000).
A Gazis, ErmAK 532.
L. Georgakopoulos, *Egchiridio Emborikou Dikaiou Geniko Meros tomos I* [*Manual of Commercial Law vol. I General Part*] (1995).
Ap. Georgiadis, *Symphonon proaireseos kai dikaioma proaireseos* [*Option Contract and Option Right*] (1970).
  'I katapeustiki metavivasis kyriotitos pros exasphalisin apaitiseos' ['The Security Transfer of Ownership on Movables for Securing of a Claim'], EEmbD 1973, 301.
  Kyriotis [*Ownership*] (1975).
  Empragmato Dikaio II [*Real Law II*] (1993).
  Nees morphes symvaseon tis sygchronis oikonomias [*New Contractual Forms of Modern Economy*] (Leasing – Factoring – Franchising – Forfeiting) (4th edn, 2000).
  I exasphalisi ton pistoseon [*Credit and Security*] (2001).
  'Scholia' [*Comments*], NoV 22, 87 and NoV 31, 517.

Ap. Georgiadis, M. Stathopoulos, *Astikos Kodix [Civil Code]* (collective work) (vol. I 1978, vol. II 1979).
I. Karakatsanis, in: *Georgiadis-Stathopoulos AK 138-139* vol. I (1978).
P. Kornilakis, *I katapisteutiki ekchorisi ton apaitiseon [The Security Assignment of Claims]* (1987).
Kotsiris, *Nees morphes symvaseon tis sygchronis oikonomias* 353.
L. Kotsiris, *Ptocheutiko Dikaio [Bankruptcy Law]* (6th edn, 1998).
A. Kritikos, in: *Georgiadis-Stathopoulos AK 455* vol. II (1979).
N. Livanis, *Diathesi mellondikou dikaiomatos [Disposition of Future Rights]* (1990).
G. Mantzoufas, *Enochikon Dikaion [Law of Obligations]* (1971).
P. Mazis, *To plasmatikon enechyron [The Non-possessory Pledge]* (1977).
  Empragmati exasphalisi trapezon kai anonymon etairion [Real Securing of Banks and Corporations] (2nd edn, 1993).
  I chrimatodotiki misthosi – Leasing [Leasing] (2nd edn, 1999).
  'I katapisteutiki metavivasi tis kyriotitas pragmatos me skopo tin exasphalisi apaitiseos, symphona me to helliniko dikaio kai tin praktiki' ['The Security Transfer of Ownership on Purpose to Secure a Claim according to the Greek Law and Practice'], NoV 27, 311.
K. Pamboukis, 'I polisis me epiphylaxin kyriotitos mechris apopliromis tou timimatos en periptosei ptocheuseos tou agorastou' ['Sale of Goods under a Retention of Title until Payment in Full of the Purchase Price in Case of the Purchaser's Bankruptcy'], Arm 27, 874.
N. Papantoniou, *Genikes Arches tou Astikou Dikaiou [General Principles of Civil Law]* (3rd edn, 1983).
P. Paparseniou, *I symvasi chrimatodotikis misthosis [The Contract of Leasing]* (1994).
K. Rokas, *Ptocheutikon Dikaion [Bankruptcy Law]* (12th edn, 1978).
N. Rokas, *Emborikes Etairies [Business Associations]* (4th edn, 1996).
  Stoicheia ptocheutikou dikaiou [Elements of Bankruptcy Law] (1997).
K. Roussos, 'I epekteinomeni epiphylaxi kyriotitas' ['The Extended Retention of Title'] in: *Miscellany in Honour of Michailidis – Nouaros* (1987) 397 ff.
N. Simantiras, *Genikes Arches tou Astikou dikaiou [General Principles of Civil Law]* (4th edn, 1988).
G. Simitis, *I di emboreumaton isphalismeni trapeziki pistosis [The Secured by Goods Banking Credit]* (1933).
K. Simitis, *I anamorphosis tou plasmatikou enechyrou [The Reformation of the Non-possessory Pledge]* (1968).
Sourlas, ErmAK 455 ff.
I. Spyridakis, *Empragmato Dikaio [Real Law]* (1983).
  Genikes Arches [General Principles] (1987).
  'Scholia' ['Comments'], NoV 24, 639 and NoV 33, 242.
M. Stathopoulos, *Contract Law in Hellas* (in English) (1995).
  Enochiko Dikaio [Law of Obligations] (3rd edn, 1998).
A. Toussis, *Empragmato Dikaio [Real Law]* (4th edn, 1988).

B. Vathis, *I symvasi Factoring* [*The Contract of Factoring*] (1995).
Em. Vouzikas, 'I metavivasis kyriotitos pros exasphalisin apaitiseos kata ton AK' ['Transfer of Ownership for Securing of a Claim by the Civil Code'], EEN 18, 657 ff.

France

Michel Cabrillac, Christian Mouly, *Les sûretés* (5th edn, 1999).
Michel Cabrillac, Philippe Petel, 'Juin 1994, le printemps des sûretés réelles?', D 1994, 243 ff.
Jean Carbonnier, *Les biens* (18th edn, 1998).
Eric Charlery, 'L'efficacité de la réserve de propriété en cas de redressement judiciaire de l'acquéreur', JCP 1997 I 4013 ff.
François Collart-Dutilleul, Philippe Delebecque, *Contrats civils at commerciaux* (4th edn, 1998).
John H. Crabb, *The French Civil Code Revised Edition (as amended to 1 July 1994)* (1995) (cited as: Crabb, *The French Civil Code*).
Pierre Crocq, *Propriété et garantie* (1995).
    'Propriété-garantie. Reserve de propriété. Feu l'accord des volontés ou un nouvel et malheureux épisode de "La jurisprudence combattue par la loi"!', RTDC 1996, 675.
Frédérique Dahan, 'La floating charge: Reconnaissance en France d'une sûreté anglaise', JDI 1996, 381 ff.
Patrice De Lapasse, 'Le moment du transfert de propriété lors de la vente des valeurs mobilières et d'autres droits incorporels', JCPédE 1995, Supplément 5, 18 ff.
F. Debruyne, 'Le point de vue de l'acheteur', JCPédE 1995, Supplément 5, 40 ff.
Jean-Pierre Dumas, Réné Roblot, 'Cession et nantissement de créances professionnelles', *Encyclopédie Dalloz, vol. Commercial*, April 1998.
Guy Duranton, 'Crédit-bail (Leasing)', *Encyclopédie Dalloz, vol. Commercial*, 1999.
M. Gardner de Béville, 'Les pratiques contractuelles', JCPédE 1995, Supplément 5, 8 ff.
Jacques Ghestin, Bernard Desché, *Traité des contrats – La vente* (1990).
Jacques Ghestin, Christophe Jamin, Marc Billiau, *Traité de droit civil – Les effets du contrat* (2nd edn, 1994).
Rémy Libchaber, 'Les biens', *Encyclopédie Dalloz, vol. Civil*, 1997.
Philippe Malaurie, Laurent Aynès, *Cours de droit civil, les sûretés – La publicité foncière* (9th edn, 1998).
Philippe Malaurie, Laurent Aynès, P. Y. Gauthier, *Cours de droit civil, les contrats spéciaux* (13th edn, 1999).
Christian Mouly, 'Résumé', JCPédE 1995, Supplément 5, 1 ff.

G. Parléani, 'Le contrat de lease-back', RTDCom 1973, 699 ff.
Françoise Pérochon, 'La revendication des biens fongibles par le vendeur', *Les Petites Affiches* 1994, No 110.
  'La réforme 1994 de la réserve de propriété', JCPédE 1995, Supplément 5, 25 ff.
Françoise Pérochon, Daniel Mainguy, 'Réserve de propriété – Revendication', D affaires 2000, No 9, 65 ff.
G. Ripert, 'Le nantissement de l'outillage et du matériel d'équipement', D 1951, Chr, 41 ff.
E. Robine, 'Le point de vue du vendeur', JCPédE 1995, Supplément 5, 42 ff.
Alain Sayag, 'The Distribution of Cars: French Report', in: Donald Harris, Denis Tallon (eds.), *Contract Law Today – Anglo-French Comparisons* (1989) 335 ff.
P. Scholder, 'Le régime juridique du warrant', Rev jur com 1980, 121 ff.
Philippe Simler, Philippe Delebecque, *Droit civil – Les sûretés – La publicité foncière* (2nd edn, 1995).
Michel Storck, 'Revendication des marchandises et sort d'un contrat de vente conclu avec une clause de réserve de propriété', D 1988, 131.
P. Thery, *Sûretés et publicité foncière* (2nd edn, 1998).
Jean Thréard, 'Les concessionnaires et les agents dans l'automobile après la loi du 25 juin 1991', Gaz Pal 1992, I, Doc, 74.

Belgium

Henri De Page, *Traité élémentaire de droit civil belge*, vols. VI and VII (1952).
Eric Dirix, 'De vormvrije cessie', RW 1994–95, 137 ff.
  'Eigendomsvoorbehoud', RW 1997–98, 481 ff.
Eric Dirix, Karen Broeckx, *Beslag* (1992).
Eric Dirix, Rogier De Corte, *Zekerheidsrechten* (4th edn, 1999).
Louis Fredericq, *Traité de droit commercial belge*, vol. VIII (1949).
Michèle Grégoire, *Théorie générale du concours des créanciers en droit belge*, Brussels, 1992.
  'Chronique de jurisprudence. Le gage', RevBanque 1998, 447 ff.
Eva-Maria Kieninger, Matthias Storme, 'Das neue belgische Recht des Eigentumsvorbehalts', RIW 1999, 94 ff.
Pierre Van Ommeslaghe, 'Le nouveau régime de la cession et la dation en gage de créances', JT 1995, 529 ff.
Jean Van Ryn, Jean Heenen, *Principes de droit commercial*, vol. III (1981).
Guido Schrans, 'Het beding van eigendomsvoorbehoud en zijn externe werking', TPR 1982, 145 ff.
Anne-Marie Stranart, *Les sûretés* (1992).
François T'Kint, *Les sûretés* (3rd edn, 2000).
Michel Waelbroeck, *Le transfert de la propriété dans la vente d'objets mobiliers corporels en droit comparé* (1961).

Portugal

José de Oliveira Ascensão, *Direito Civil. Teoria Geral*, vol. II – *Acções e Factos Jurídicos* (1999).
Diogo Leite de Campos, 'A locação financeira na perspectiva do utente', ROA 43 (1983) 319 ff.
António Menezes Cordeiro, *Manual de Direito Bancário* (1st edn, 1998, 2nd edn vol. I, 2001).
Luís Carvalho Fernandes, *Teoria Geral do Direito Civil*, vol. II (2nd edn, 1996).
Luís Carvalho Fernandes, João Labareda, *Código dos Processos Especiais de Recuperação da Empresa e de Falência Anotado* (1994).
Heinrich Ewald Hörster, 'Sobre a formação do contrato segundo os arts. 217° e 218°, 224° a 226° e 228° a 235° do Código Civil', RDE 9 (1983) 121 ff.
Luís Menezes Leitão, *O enriquecimento sem causa no direito civil* (1996).
Pires de Lima, João Antunes Varela, *Código Civil Anotado*, vol. I (1987).
Pedro Romano Martinez, *Contratos em especial* (1998).
Pedro Romano Martinez, Luís Fuzeta da Ponte, *Garantias de Cumprimento* (2nd edn, 1998).
João de Castro Mendes, *Teoria Geral do Direito Civil*, vol. II (1979).
Ana Maria Peralta, *A posição jurídica do comprador na compra e venda com reserva de propriedade* (1990).
Luís Lima Pinheiro, *A cláusula de reserva de propriedade* (1988).
Carlos da Mota Pinto, *Teoria Geral do Direito Civil* (3rd edn, 1999).
Miguel Teixeira de Sousa, *Acção executiva singular* (1998).
Raul Ventura, 'O contrato de compra e venda no código civil. Efeitos essenciais: A transmissão da propriedade da coisa ou da titularidade do direito', ROA 43 (1983) 581 ff.

Spain

Guillermo Alcover Garau, *Factoring y quiebra* (2000).
Joaquín Ataz López, *Ejercicio por los acreedores de los derechos y acciones del deudor* (1988).
Emilio Beltrán Sánchez, 'El derecho de separación en la quiebra', in: Ubaldo Nieto Carol/José Ignacio Bonet Sánchez (coord.), *Tratado de garantías en la contratación mercantil*, vol. I, *Parte general y garantías personales* (1996) 253 ff.
Rodrigo Bercovitz, Rodríguez-Cano, 'El pacto de reserva de dominio y la función de garantía del leasing financiero', in: Ubaldo Nieto Carol/Miguel Muñoz Cervera (coord.), *Tratado de garantías en la contratación mercantil*, vol. II-1, *Garantías reales – Garantías mobiliarias* (1996) 377 ff.
José-Ramón Cano Rico, *Manual Práctico de Contratación Mercantil* (4th edn, 1994).
Angel Cristóbal Montes, *La vía subrogatoria* (1995).
Luis Díez-Picazo, *Dictámenes Jurídicos* (1987).

Fundamentos de derecho civil patrimonial, vol. I, *Introducción. Teoría del contrato* (1993).
  Fundamentos de derecho civil patrimonial, vol. II, *Las relaciones obligatorias* (1993).
  Fundamentos de derecho civil patrimonial, vol. III, *Las relaciones jurídico-reales. El Registro de la propiedad. La posesión* (1995).
Eduardo Estrada Alonso, *Las garantías abstractas en el tráfico civil y mercantil* (2000).
Juan-Manuel Fernández López, 'La hipoteca mobiliaria y la prenda sin desplazamiento', in: Consejo General del Poder Judicial (ed.), *Garantías reales mobiliarias* (1998) 367 ff.
Javier García de Enterría, *Contrato de factoring y cesión de créditos* (1995).
José-Antonio García-Cruces González, *El contrato de factoring* (1990).
José Luis García-Pita y Lastres, 'La hipoteca mobiliaria y la prenda sin desplazamiento', in: Ubaldo Nieto Carol/Miguel Muñoz Cervera (coord.), *Tratado de garantías en la contratación mercantil*, vol. II-1, *Garantías reales – Garantías mobiliarias* (1996) 149 ff.
Fernando García Solé, *Comentarios a la Ley de Ventas a Plazos de Bienes Muebles* (1999).
  'El factoring en la práctica. Aspectos generales', in: Rafael García Villaverde (coord.), *El contrato de factoring* (1999) 231 ff.
  'Reciente normativa en materia de cesión empresarial de crédito', in: Rafael García Villaverde (coord.), *El contrato de factoring* (1999) 595 ff.
  'Venta a plazos y leasing tras la nueva Ley de Enjuiciamiento Civil', *Revista Jurídica La Ley*, No 5044, from 5 May 2000.
Rafael García Villaverde, 'Una forma especial de garantía: los efectos de la declaración de la quiebra y la suspensión de pagos sobre las relaciones jurídicas bilaterales preexistentes y pendientes de ejecución', in: Ubaldo Nieto Carol/José Ignacio Bonet Sánchez (coord.), *Tratado de garantías en la contratación mercantil*, vol. I, *Parte general y garantías personales* (1996) 301 ff.
Víctor Garrido de Palma (dir.), 'Acción pauliana', in: Fundación Tomás Moro, *Diccionario Jurídico Espasa* (1993).
Julio-Vicente Gavidia Sánchez, *La cesión de créditos* (1993).
Carlos-J. González-Bueno, *Comentarios a la Ley de Hipoteca Mobiliaria y Prenda sin Desplazamiento* (1996).
Margarita Jiménez-Horwitz, 'La reintegración de la masa de la quiebra: régimen de ineficacia de los actos de enajenación perjudiciales para los intereses concursales', *Revista Crítica de Derecho Inmobiliario*, 76, No 658, 1257 ff.
Miquel Martín Casals, 'Comentario al artículo 321', in: Manuel Albaladejo (dir.), *Comentarios al Código Civil y Compilaciones Forales*, vol. XXX (1987).
Carlos Martínez de Aguirre, *Las ventas a plazos de bienes muebles* (1988).
José-María Miquel González, 'Comentario al artículo 464', in: Cándido Paz-Ares/Luis Díez-Picazo Ponce de León/Rodrigo Bercovitz/Pablo Salvador Coderch, *Comentario del Código Civil*, vol. I (1991), vol. II (1991).

José-Luis Navarro Pérez, *La cesión de créditos en el derecho civil español* (1988).
Fernando Pantaleón Prieto, 'Cesión de créditos', ADC 41, fasc. 4 (1988) 1033 ff.
   'Prenda de créditos: Nueva jurisprudencia y tarea para el legislador concursal', in: Consejo General del Poder Judicial (ed.), *Garantías reales mobiliarias* (1998) 175 ff.
Pere del Pozo Carrascosa, *La venda a carta de gràcia en el dret civil de Catalunya* (1993).
Pascual V. Raga Blanch, *Subrogación por pago y juicio ejesutivo basado en pólizas de contratos mercantiles y escrituras públicas* (2000).
T. Ramón Fernández, 'La nueva Ley de venta a plazos de bienes muebles', BCRE 43 (1998) 3008 ff.
L.-Fernando Reglero Campos, 'Ejecución de las garantías reales mobiliarias e interdicción del pacto comisorio', in: Ubaldo Nieto Carol/Miguel Muñoz Cervera (coord.), *Tratado de garantías en la contratación mercantil*, vol. II-1, *Garantías reales – Garantías mobiliarias* (1996) 417 ff.
Manuel Rivera Fernández, *La posición del comprador en la venta a plazos con reserva de dominio* (1994).
Almudena Rodríguez Herrero, *La hipoteca de bienes muebles registrables* (1996).
Luis Rodríguez Vela, 'Garantías del acreedor frente a las mutaciones patrimoniales convencionales del deudor tendentes a impedir o menoscabar la ejecución (la acción pauliana)', in: Consejo General del Poder Judicial (ed.), *Protección registral de los derechos reales y tutela judicial efectiva* (1999) 59 ff.
Luis Rojo Ajuria, *'Leasing' mobiliario* (1987).
Adolfo Sequeira Martín, 'Derechos y obligaciones del cliente', in: Rafael García Villaverde (coord.), *El contrato de factoring* (1999) 304 ff.
Nemesio Vara de Paz, 'Extinción del contrato. La quiebra en particular', in: Rafael García Villaverde (coord.), *El contrato de factoring* (1999) 331 ff.
Francisco Vicent Chuliá, *Compendio Crítico de Derecho Mercantil*, vol. II, *Contratos, títulos valores, derecho concursal* (3rd edn, 1990).
María Ysàs Solanes, 'Comentario al artículo 326', in: Manuel Albaladejo (ed.), *Comentarios al Código Civil y Compilaciones Forales*, vol. XXX (1987) 592 ff.

Italy

Guido Alpa, Michele Dassio, 'La dissolution du lien contractuel dans le code civil italien', in: Marcel Fontaine, Geneviève Viney (eds.), *Les sanctions de l'inexécution des obligations contractuelles. Études de droit comparé* (2001) 871 ff.
Stefano Ambrosini, *La revocatoria fallimentare delle garanzie* (2000).
Franco Anelli, *L'alienazione in funzione di garanzia* (1996).
Umberto Apice, *Il contratto di leasing nelle procedure concorsuali* (1991).
Carlo Argiroffi, 'La rivendica del venditore. Prospettive storiche e soluzioni attuali', in: Letizia Vacca (ed.), *Vendita e trasferimento della proprietà nella*

prospettiva storico-comparatistica. Atti del Congresso Internazionale Pisa-Viareggio-Lucca 17-21 aprile 1990 (1991) 501 ff.
Alberto Auricchio, 'Autorizzazione', in: Enc. dir. IV (1959) 502.
Augusto Baldassarri, 'I contratti di distribuzione, agenzia, mediazione, concessione di vendita, franchising', in: Francesco Galgano (ed.), *I contratti del commercio, dell'industria e del mercato finanziario* III (1995) 1999 ff.
Lelio Barbiera, 'Responsabilità patrimoniale. Disposizioni generali (Art. 2740-2744)', in: Pietro Schlesinger (ed.), *Commentario al Codice Civile* (1991).
Stefano Bastianon, *Il leasing nel fallimento* (1999).
Mario Beltramo (ed.), *The Italian Civil Code and Complementary Legislation*, trans. by Mario Beltramo, Giovanni E. Longo, John H. Merryman (1991).
Cesare Massimo Bianca, *Il divieto del patto commissorio* (1957).
   'La vendita e la permuta', in: *Trattato di diritto civile italiano* VII.1 (2nd edn, 1993).
   'Il principio del consenso traslativo', *Diritto privato*, 1995, 5 ff.
   Diritto civile – VI La proprietà (1999).
   Il contratto (2nd edn, 2000).
Fernando Bocchini, 'Vendita con riserva della proprietà', *Trattato di diritto privato diretto da Rescigno* XI, 3 (2nd edn, 2000), 708 ff.
Guido Bonfante, *I rapporti pendenti nel fallimento e la locazione finanziaria* (1989).
Sido Bonfatti, 'L'accertamento del passivo e dei diritti mobiliari', in: Giuseppe Ragusa Maggiore, Concetto Costa (eds.), *Le procedure concorsuali – Il fallimento* III (1997) 1 ff.
Andrea Bonomi, *Der Eigentumsvorbehalt in Österreich und Italien unter Berücksichtigung anderer europäischer Systeme* (1993).
Franco Bricola, Francesco Galgano, Gerardo Santini (eds.), *Legge Fallimentare – Commentario Scialoja-Branca* (1974 to date).
Mauro Bussani, 'Il contratto di lease-back', Contr. e impr. 1986, 558 ff.
   Proprietà-garanzia e contratto. Formule e regole nel leasing finanziario (1992).
   'Le droit civil des sûretés réelles. Le modèle italien', ERPL 6 (1998) 23 ff.
   Il problema del patto commissorio (2000).
Mauro Bussani/Paolo Cendon, *I contratti nuovi: Leasing, factoring e franchising* (1998).
Oreste Cagnasso, 'Concessione di vendita', in: Gastone Cottino (ed.), *Trattato di diritto commerciale e di diritto pubblico dell'economia. Contratti commerciali* XVI (1991) 382 ff.
   'Contratto di appalto e trasferimento della proprietà', *Diritto privato*, 1995, 35 ff.
Oreste Cagnasso, Maurizio Irrera, *Concessione di vendita, merchandising, catering* (1993).
Albina Candian, *Le garanzie mobiliari. Modelli e problemi nella prospettiva europea* (2001).

'Transmission des créances dans le monde des finances modernes', in: VV. AA., *Rapports nationaux italiens au XVème Congrès International de Droit Comparé - Bristol 1998* (1998) 380 ff.

Francesco Capriglione (ed.), *Commentario al testo unico delle leggi in materia bancaria e creditizia* (2001).

Ugo Carnevali, 'Patto commissorio', in: Enc. dir. XXXII (1982) 499 ff.

Brunetto Carpino, 'Real Security over Corporeal Movables in Italian Law', in: J. G. Sauveplanne (ed.), *Security over Corporeal Movables - Studies in Comparative Law under the Auspices of the Netherlands Association of Comparative Law* (1974) 136 ff.

'La vendita', in: *Trattato di diritto privato diretto da Rescigno* XI, 3 (1984).

Luigi Carraro, *Il mandato ad alienare* (1947).

'Autorizzazione', in: *Novissimo digesto italiano* I, 2 (1958) 1577 ff.

Bianca Cassandro Sulpasso, 'La vendita con riserva di proprietà in diritto comparato', in: Letizia Vacca (ed.), *Vendita e trasferimento della proprietà nella prospettiva storico-comparatistica. Atti del Congresso Internazionale Pisa-Viareggio-Lucca 17-21 aprile 1990* (1991) 781 ff.

Angelo Castagnola, *Le rivendiche mobiliari nel fallimento* (1996).

Carlo Castronovo, 'La risoluzione del contratto nel diritto italiano', in: Letizia Vacca (ed.), *Il contratto inadempiuto. Realtà e tradizione del diritto contrattuale europeo. III Congresso Internazionale ARISTEC, Ginevra, 24-27 settembre 1997* (1999) 205 ff.

Angelo Chianale, *Obbligazione di dare e trasferimento della proprietà* (1990).

Sebastiano Ciccarello, 'Privilegio (Diritto Privato)', in: Enc. dir. XXXV (1986) 723 ff.

Fabio Cintioli, 'Il fallimento del concedente di beni in *leasing*', Banca borsa 1997 I, 475 ff.

Giorgio Costantino, Antonio Jannarelli, 'Norme sulla costituzione di pegno su prosciutti a denominazione d'origine tutelata', NLCC 1986, 540 ff.

'La realizzazione dei crediti assistiti da privilegio industriale', Riv. trim. dir. proc. civ. 1995, 1313 ff.

Maria Costanza, 'Commissione (contratto di)', in: Digesto sez. comm. III (1988) 167 ff.

Stefano D'Ercole, 'L'azione revocatoria', in: *Trattato di diritto privato diretto da Rescigno* XX 2 (1998) 161 ff.

Stefan Dangel, 'Die Entwicklung der Mobiliarkreditsicherheiten im italienischen Recht', in: *Jahrbuch für italienisches Recht Bd. 12* (1999) 20 ff.

Giorgio De Nova, 'Appunti sul sale and lease back e il divieto del patto commissorio', Riv. it. leasing 1985, 307 ff.

'Il lease back', Riv. it. leasing 1987, 517 ff.

'Leasing', in: Digesto sez. civ. X (1993) 463 ff.

Il contratto di leasing (3rd edn, 1995).

Aldo Angelo Dolmetta, *La data certa* (1986).
  'Sui più recenti sviluppi in materia di data certa e fallimento, con particolare riguardo al tema dell'ammissione al passivo', Vita not. 1996, 11 ff.
Aldo Angelo Dolmetta, Giuseppe P. Portale, 'Cessione del credito e cessione in garanzia nell'ordinamento italiano', *Banca borsa* 1999 I, 105.
  'Wirksamkeitsvoraussetzungen für Forderungsabtretungen, insbesondere zu Kreditsicherungszwecken in Italien', in: Walter Hadding, Uwe H. Schneider (eds.), *Die Forderungsabtretung, insbesondere zur Kreditsicherung in ausländischen Rechtsordnungen* (1999) 342 ff. (same contribution, German version).
Ulrich Drobnig, 'Legal Principles Governing Security Interests', in: *United Nations Commission on International Trade Law Yearbook VIII: 1977* (1978).
Guido Ferrarini, Paola Barucco, 'La locazione finanziaria (leasing)', in: *Trattato di diritto privato diretto da Rescigno* XI, 3 (2nd edn, 2000) 3 ff.
Paolo Ferro-Luzzi, Giovanni Castaldi (eds.), *La nuova legge bancaria – Commentario*, with supplements (1996–2000).
Francesca Fiorentini, 'Garanzie reali atipiche', Riv. dir. civ. 2000 II, 253 ff.
Marcel Fontaine, Geneviève Viney (eds.), *Les sanctions de l'inexécution des obligations contractuelles. Etudes de droit comparé* (2001).
Aldo Frignani, Giuseppe Rossi, 'Il factoring', in: *Trattato di diritto privato diretto da Rescigno* XI, 3 (2nd edn, 2000) 51 ff.
Enrico Gabrielli, 'Pegno', in: Digesto sez. civ. XIII (1995) 329 ff.
  'Rotatività della garanzia', in: Digesto sez. civ. XVIII (1998) 102 ff.
Francesco Galgano, *Trattato di diritto civile e commerciale* II, *Le obbligazioni e i contratti* (1993).
Paolo Gallo, *L'arricchimento senza causa* (1990).
Antonio Gambaro, 'Le transfert de la propriété par actes entre vifs dans le système italien', in: *Rapports nationaux italiens au Xe Congrès International de Droit Comparé* (1978) 199 ff.
  'Il diritto di proprietà', in: Antonio Cicu, Francesco Messineo, Luigi Mengoni (eds.), *Trattato di diritto civile e commerciale* VIII.2 (1995) 840 ff.
  Il diritto di proprietà (1995).
Serafino Gatti, *I crediti su pegno* (1997).
Carlo Giannattasio, 'L'appalto', in: Antonio Cicu, Francesco Messineo, Luigi Mengoni (eds.), *Trattato di diritto civile e commerciale*, XXIV.2 (1977).
Michele Graziadei, 'Agire senza spendita del nome, con effetti sul patrimonio altrui', Resp. civ. prev. 1985, 23.
  'Contratto estimatorio', Digesto sez. comm. IV, 1989, 103.
  'Mandato', in: Digesto sez. civ. XI (1994) 154 ff.
Michele Graziadei/Ugo Mattei/Lionel Smith (eds.), *Commercial Trusts*, forthcoming in this series.
Jörg Stefan Greving, *Der Treuhandgedanke bei Sicherungsübertragungen im italienischen und deutschen Recht* (2002).

Lino Guglielmucci, 'Gli effetti del fallimento sui rapporti giuridici preesistenti',
in: Giuseppe Ragusa Maggiore, Concetto Costa (eds.), *Le procedure
concorsuali – Il fallimento* II (1997) 238 ff.
Bruno Inzitari, 'Effetti del fallimento per i creditori', in: Giuseppe Ragusa
Maggiore, Concetto Costa (eds.), *Le procedure concorsuali – Il fallimento*
(1997).
 'La cessione del credito a scopo di garanzia: inefficacia ed inopponibilità ai
creditori dell'incasso del cessionario nel fallimento, nel concordato e
nell'amministrazione controllata', *Banca borsa* 1997 I, 153 ff.
 'Besondere Probleme der Sicherungsabtretung in Italien', in: Walter
Hadding, Uwe H. Schneider (eds.), *Die Forderungsabtretung, insbesondere zur
Kreditsicherung in ausländischen Rechtsordnungen* (1999) 404 ff. (same
contribution, German version).
Pier Giusto Jaeger, *La separazione del patrimonio fiduciario nel fallimento* (1968).
 'Sull'intestazione fiduciaria di quote di società a responsabilità limitata',
Giur. comm. 1979 I, 181 ff.
Massimo Lascialfari, 'Le alienazioni in funzione di garanzia', in: Cuffaro (ed.),
Le garanzie rafforzate del credito (2000).
Marco Lipari, 'Vendita con riserva di proprietà', in Enc. dir. XLVI (1993) 526 ff.
Emanuele Lucchini Guastalla, *Danno e frode nella revocatoria ordinaria* (1995).
Angelo Luminoso, 'Mandato, commissione, spedizione', in: Antonio Cicu,
Francesco Messineo, Luigi Mengoni (eds.), *Trattato di diritto civile e
commerciale* XXXII (1984).
 'Lease back, mercato e divieto del patto commissorio', Giur. comm. 2000 II,
489.
Francesco Macario, 'Trasferimento del credito futuro ed efficacia verso i terzi:
lo "stato dell'arte" (di giudicare)', Riv. dir. priv. 2000, 437 ff.
Alberto Maffei Alberti (ed.), *Commentario breve alla legge fallimentare* (2000).
Crisanto Mandrioli, *Corso di diritto processuale civile* III (12th edn, 1998).
Ugo Mattei, 'Il diritto di proprietà,' in: Rodolfo Sacco (ed.), *Trattato di diritto
civile* (2001).
Luigi Mengoni, *Gli acquisti 'a non domino'* (3rd edn, 1975).
Maurizio Miglietta, Francesco Prandi, 'I privilegi', in: Walter Bigiavi (ed.),
Giurisprudenza sistematica di diritto civile e commerciale (1995).
Pier Giuseppe Monateri, *La sineddoche – Formule e regole nel diritto delle
obbligazioni e dei contratti* (1984).
Paolo Montalenti, 'Il contratto di commissione', in: Gastone Cottino (ed.),
*Trattato di diritto commerciale e di diritto pubblico dell'economia. Contratti
commerciali* XVI (1991) 633 ff.
Luca Nanni, 'Dell'estinzione del mandato. Art. 1722–1730', in: *Commentario del
codice civile Scialoja-Branca. Libro quarto – Delle obbligazioni* (1994).
Pietro Perlingieri, 'Della cessione dei crediti. Art. 1260–1267', in: *Commentario
del codice civile Scialoja-Branca. Libro quarto – Delle obbligazioni* (1982).

Gaetano Presti, 'Il privilegio per i finanziamenti bancari a medio e lungo termine delle imprese', *Banca borsa* 1995 I, 594.

Carmine Punzi, *La tutela del terzo nel processo esecutivo* (1971).

Giuseppe Ragusa Maggiore, Concetto Costa (eds.), *Le procedure concorsuali – Il fallimento* (1997).

Alberto Ravazzoni, 'Privilegi', in: Digesto sez. civ. XIV (1996) 371 ff.
  'Privilegi (parte speciale)', in: Digesto sez. civ. XIV (1996) 380 ff.

Matteo Rescigno, 'Il privilegio per i finanziamenti bancari a medio e lungo termine a favore delle imprese con particolare riguardo alla rotatività del suo oggetto', *Banca borsa* 1999 I, 583 ff.

Vito Rizzo, 'Data, data certa', in: Digesto sez. civ. V (1989) 107 ff.

Vincenzo Roppo, 'Il contratto', in: Giovanni Iudica, Paolo Zatti (eds.), *Trattato di diritto privato* (2001).

Domenico Rubino, 'L'appalto', in: *Trattato di diritto civile italiano* VII.3 (4th edn, 1980).

Domenico Rubino, Giovanni Iudica, 'Dell'appalto. Art. 1655–1677', in: *Commentario del codice civile Scialoja-Branca. Libro quarto – Delle obbligazioni* (3rd edn, 1992).

Rodolfo Sacco, Giorgio De Nova, 'Le transfert de la propriété des choses mobilières determinées par acte entre vifs en droit comparé', Riv. dir. civ. 1979 I, 442 ff.
  'Il contratto', in: Rodolfo Sacco (ed.), *Trattato di diritto civile* (2nd edn, 1993).
  'Pubblico registro automobilistico', Digesto sez. pub. XII (1997) 327 ff.

Carlo Santagata, 'Del mandato. Disposizioni generali. Art. 1703–1709', in: *Commentario del codice civile Scialoja-Branca. Libro quarto – Delle obbligazioni* (1985).

Marcella Sarale, 'Il contratto estimatorio', in: Gastone Cottino (ed.), *Trattato di diritto commerciale e di diritto pubblico dell'economia. Contratti commerciali* XVI (1991) 161 ff.

Bianca Cassandro Sulpasso, 'La vendita con riserva di proprietà in diritto comparato', in Letizia Vacca (ed.), *Vendita e trasferimento della proprietà nella prospettiva storico-comparatistica* II (1991) 781 ff.

Davide Supino, *La rivendicazione nel fallimento* (1881).

Giovanni Tatarano, 'Retroattività', in: Enc. dir. XL (1989) 83 ff.

Giuseppe Terranova, 'Effetti del fallimento sugli atti pregiudizievoli ai creditori', in: *Commentario Scialoja-Branca alla legge fallimentare (arts 68–71)* I (2000).

Stefano Troiano, *La cessione di crediti futuri* (1999).

Giuseppe Tucci, 'I privilegi', in: *Trattato di diritto privato diretto da Rescigno* XIX, 1 (1985) 449 ff.
  'Il legislatore italiano degli anni novanta e il paradosso dei privilegi dall'art. 46 del testo unico in materia bancaria al nuovo articolo 37 nonies, introdotto della Merloni ter', Giur. it. 1999, 1985 ff.

Letizia Vacca (ed.), *Vendita e trasferimento della proprietà nella prospettiva storico-comparatistica. Atti del Congresso Internazionale Pisa-Viareggio-Lucca 17–21 aprile 1990* (1991).
   Il contratto inadempiuto. Realtà e tradizione del diritto contrattuale europeo. III Congresso Internazionale ARISTEC, Ginevra, 24–27 settembre 1997 (1999).
Filippo Vassalli, 'Sulla revoca della vendita a giusto prezzo', Giur. comm. 1974 I, 289 ff.
Anna Veneziano, 'La garanzia sull'intero patrimonio dell'imprenditore della nuova legge bancaria italiana al confronto con i modelli stranieri: una riforma a metà?', Dir. comm. internaz. 1996, 921 ff.
   Le garanzie mobiliari non possessorie. Profili di diritto comparato e di diritto del commercio internazionale (2000).
Mirella Viale, 'Le garanzie bancarie', in *Trattato di diritto commerciale e di diritto pubblico dell'economia*, diretto da Galgano, XVIII (1994).
Ruggero Vigo, *I contratti pendenti non disciplinati nella legge fallimentare* (1989).
VV. AA., *Rapports nationaux italiens au XVème Congrès International de Droit Comparé – Bristol 1998* (1998).
Reinhard Zimmermann, Simon Whittaker (eds.), *Good Faith in European Contract Law* (2000).

The Netherlands

J. Beuving, R. P. J. L. Tjittes, 'Het tegengaan van een overmaat aan zekerheden', NJB 1998, 1547 ff.
J. E. Fesevur, *Goederenrechtelijke colleges* (1997).
H. A. G. Fikkers, 'Varkens zonder verlengd eigendomsvoorbehoud', WPNR 6321 (1998) 465 ff.
   Natrekking, vermenging en zaaksvorming (1999).
P. C. C. Haanappel, Ejan Mackaay, *New Netherlands Civil Code; Patrimonial Law* (1990).
Jacobus Johannes van Hees, *Leasing* (1997).
Jac. Hijma, M. M. Olthof, *Compendium Nederlands vermogensrecht* (1999).
Kortmann/Faber, WPNR 1998, 6324 ff.
A. Pitlo, W. H. M. Reehuis, A. H. T. Heisterkamp et al., *Het Nederlands burgerlijk recht (Deel 3), Goederenrecht* (2001).
E. B. Rank-Berenschot, 'Art. 3:84 verbiedt alleen overdracht ten titel van verhaal', NTBR 1995, 207 ff.
W. H. M. Reehuis, *Eigendomsvoorbehoud* (1998).
H. J. Snijders, E. B. Rank-Berenschot, *Goederenrecht* (2001).
Lars Peter Wunibald Van Vliet, *Transfer of Movables* (2000).
R. D. Vriesendorp, 'Sogelease', AA 1995, 872 ff.

England

M. G. Bridge, *The Sale of Goods* (1997).
　Personal Property Law (1993).
R. J. Calnan, 'Property, Security and Possession in Insolvency Law', JIBFL 11 (1998) 530 ff.
N. Furey, 'Goods Leasing and Insolvency', in: N. E. Palmer, E. McKendrick (eds.), *Interests in Goods* (2nd edn, 1998) 787 ff.
Sir Peter Millett, 'Equity's Place in the Law of Commerce', LQR 114 (1998) 214 ff.
G. K. Morse et al. (eds.), *Palmer's Company Law* (1992, looseleaf).
G. Spencer Bower, A. K. Turner, *The Law of Actionable Misrepresentation* (3rd edn, 1974).
W. Swadling, 'The Proprietary Effect of a Hire of Goods', in N. E. Palmer, E. McKendrick (eds.), *Interests in Goods* (2nd edn, 1998) 491 ff.

Scotland

Douglas J. Cusine (ed.), *A Scots Conveyancing Miscellany: Essays in Honour of Professor J. M. Halliday* (1987).
James Dalrymple (Lord Stair), *Institutions of the Law of Scotland* (Edinburgh 1681 and many subsequent editions) (cited as: Stair, *Institutions*).
J. J. Gow, *The Mercantile and Industrial Law of Scotland* (1964).
J. H. Greene, I. M. Fletcher, *The Law and Practice of Receivership in Scotland* (2nd edn, 1992).
G. L. Gretton, 'Using Trusts as Commercial Securities', JLSS 1988, 53 ff.
　'Assignation of Contingent Rights', JR 1993, 23 ff.
G. L. Gretton, K. G. C. Reid, 1985 SLT (News) 329 and 1989 SLT (News) 185.
D. J. Hayton, S. C. J. J. Kortmann, H. L. E. Verhagen, *Principles of European Trust Law* (1999).
David Johnston, Reinhard Zimmermann, *Unjustified Enrichment* (2002).
William W. McBryde, *Bankruptcy* (2nd edn, 1995).
　The Law of Contract in Scotland (2nd edn, 2001).
D. L. Carey Miller, *Corporeal Moveables in Scots Law* (1991).
J. B. Miller, *Law of Partnership in Scotland* (2nd edn by G. Brough, 1994).
Kenneth G. C. Reid, 'Trusts and Floating Charges', 1987 SLT (News) 113 ff.
　The Law of Property in Scotland (1996).
　'National Report for Scotland', in: D. J. Hayton/S. C. J. J. Kortmann/H. L. E. Verhagen (eds.), *Principles of European Trust Law*, 67 ff.
Donna W. Mackenzie Skene, *Insolvency Law in Scotland* (1999).

South Africa

David L. Carey Miller, *The Acquisition and Protection of Ownership* (1986).

Johannes C. De Wet, Abraham G. Du Plessis, 'Agency and Representation', in: Willem A. Joubert (ed.), *The Law of South Africa*, vol. I (1993) paras. 100–59.

Johannes C. De Wet, Andreas H. Van Wyk, *De Wet en Yeats; Die Suid-Afrikaanse Kontraktereg en Handelsreg* (4th edn, 1978).

George R. J. Hackwill, *Mackeurtan's Sale of Goods in South Africa* (5th edn, 1984).

Duard G. Kleyn, Andre Boraine, *Silberberg and Schoeman's The Law of Property* (3rd edn, 1992).

Gerhard F. Lubbe, 'Mortgage and Pledge', in: Willem A. Joubert (ed.), *The Law of South Africa*, vol. XVII (1983) paras. 392–520.

Petrus M. Nienaber, 'Cession', in: Willem A. Joubert (ed.), *The Law of South Africa*, vol. II (first reissue, 1993) paras. 223–74.

Johan M. Otto, *Credit Law Service* (1990–6, looseleaf).

Pieter J. Rabie, *The Law of Estoppel in South Africa* (1992).

Johan Scott, Susan Scott, *Wille's Law of Mortgage and Pledge in South Africa* (3rd edn, 1987).

Susan Scott, *The Law of Cession* (2nd edn, 1991).

Catherine Smith, *The Law of Insolvency* (3rd edn, 1988).

Catherine Smith, Robert Sharrock, 'Insolvency', in: Willem A. Joubert (ed.), *The Law of South Africa*, vol. XI (first reissue, 1998) paras. 112–301.

Sonnekus, 'Vloerplanooreenkomste en 'n Sober Klank van die Regbank daarteen' TSAR 1999, 776 ff.

Cornelius G. van der Merwe, *Sakereg* (2nd edn, 1989).

Cornelius G. van der Merwe, Catherine Smith, 'Financing the Purchase of Stock by the Transfer of Ownership: A Simulated Transaction?', StellLR 1999, 303 ff.

Cornelius G. van der Merwe, W. J. Schalk, Louis F. van Huyssteen et al. *Contract General Principles* (1993).

Cornelius G. van der Merwe, Marius J. de Waal, *The Law of Things and Servitudes* (1993).

Denmark

Lennart Lynge Andersen, Palle Bo Madsen, Jørgen Nørgaard, *Aftaler og mellemmænd* (3rd edn, 1997).

Lennart Lynge Andersen, Peter Møgelvang-Hanse, Niels Ørgaard, *Gældsbrevsloven* (1997).

Lennart Lynge Andersen, Erik Werlauff, *Kreditretten* (3rd edn, 2000).

Vagn Carstensen, *Ting og Sager*, vol. I (1981), vol. II (1984).

Nis Jul Clausen, *Sikkerhed i fordringer* (3rd edn, 2000).

Michael Elmer, Lise Skovby, *Ejendomsretten*, vol. I (3rd edn, 1995).

W. E. von Eyben, *Formuerettigheder* (7th edn, 1983).

  Panterettigheder (8th edn by Henning Skovgaard, 1987).

Bernhard Gomard, *Hovedpunkter af selskabsretten* (4th edn, 1994).
  Fogedret (4th edn, 1997).
Hans Verner Højrup, *Ejendomsret* (1976).
Knud Illum, *Ejendomsforbehold* (1946).
Bent Iversen, Jørgen Nørgaard, Morten Wegener, Niels Ørgaard, *Danish Business Law* (1998).
Mogens Munch, *Konkursloven* (9th edn by Lars Lindencrone Petersen and Anders Ørgaard, 2001).
Noe Munck, Lars Hedegaard Kristensen, Jørgen Nørgaard, *Selskabsformerne* (3rd edn, 1997).
Niels Ørgaard, *Sikkerhed i løsøre* (3rd edn, 1998).
  Konkursret (7th edn by Anders Ørgaard, 1999).
Lars Lindencrone Petersen, Niels Ørgaard, *Danish Insolvency Law – A Survey* (1996).
Thomas Rørdam, Vagn Carstensen, *Pant* (6th edn, 1998).

Sweden

Tore Almén, 'Om äganderättsförbehåll till föremål som införlivats med fast egendom', SvJT 1918, 5 ff.
Tore Almén, Rudolf Eklund, *Lagen om köp och byte av lös egendom* (4th edn, 1960).
Sjur Braekhus, *Omsetning og kreditt, Pant og annen realsikkerhet* (2nd edn, 1994) (Norwegian).
Ulf Göranson, *Traditionsprincipen* (1985).
Kurt Grönfors, *Sjölagens bestämmelser om godsbefordran* (1982).
  Torgny Håstad, *Studier i sakrätt* (1980).
  'Reform av de nordiska avtalslagarna', 32 *Nordiska Juristmötet* 1990, 247 ff.
  Sakrätt rörande lös egendom (6th edn, 1996).
  Den nya köprätten (4th edn, 1997).
Bo Helander, *Kreditsäkerhet i lös egendom* (1984).
Jan Hellner, 'Standardavtal vid avtals slutande', *Juridiska Föreningen i Finland Tidskrift* 1979, 298 ff.
Henrik Hessler, *Allmän sakrätt* (1973).
  Mikael Möller, *Civilrätten vid finansiell leasing* (1996).
  Tiberg, 'Stoppningsrätt', SvJT 1993, 548 ff.
Östen Unden, *Svensk sakrätt. I. Lös egendom* (9th edn, 1974).

Finland

Erkki Havansi, *Esinevakuusoikeudet* [Security Rights in Property] (2nd edn, 1992).
Janne Kaisto, *Tiesi tai olisi pitänyt tietää* [Knew or Should Have Known] (1997) (with a summary in English).
Leena Kartio, *Esineoikeuden perusteet* [Foundations of Property Law] (1991).

Risto Koulu, 'Irtaimen esineen omistuksen kirjaamisesta' ['Registration of Ownership of Chattels'], *Oikeustiede – Jurisprudentia* 1987, 183 ff. (with a summary in English).
Ilmari Ojanen, Juhani Sutinen, *Yrityskiinnitys [Enterprise Charge]* (2nd edn, 1991).
Tapio Takki, *Factoring* (1994).
Jarno Tepora, *Omistuksenpidätyksestä [On Retention of Title]* (1984) (with a summary in German).
  'Leasing-rahoitus ja vastuun toteuttaminen eräissä sivullissuhteissa' ['Financial Leasing and Realization of Responsibility in Certain Third Party Relations'] *Oikeustiede – Jurisprudentia* 1988, 245 ff. (with a summary in German).
  Jarno Tepora, 'Komissiosta vaihtoehtoisena vakuusmuotona' ['On Commission as an Alternative Security Right'], *Defensor Legis* 1991, 623 ff.
  'Konsignaatiosta itsenäisenä vakuusmuotona' ['Consignment as Independent Form of Security'], *Lakimies* 1992, 1043 ff.
  'Luottokauppa omistuksenpidätysehdoin jälleenmyyntiä varten' ['Credit Sale for Retail with Retention of Title'], *Lakimies* 1992, 328 ff.
Jarmo Tuomisto, *Omistuksenpidätys ja leasing [Retention of Title and Leasing Agreements]* (1988) (with a summary in German).
  Vuokranantaja ja vuokralaisen konkurssi (1991).
  Takaisinsaannista [On Recovery in Bankrupt's Estate] (1997).
Asko Välimaa, 'Omistuksenpidätysehdon sitovuus ostajan erityisseuraajia kohtaan autokaupassa' ['Effectiveness of Retention of Title in Relation to the Transferee of the Buyer of a Car'] *Oikeustiede – Jurisprudentia* 1992, 345 (with a summary in German).
Thomas Wilhelmsson, *Suomen kuluttajansuojajärjestelmä [Finnish System of Consumer Protection]* (1987).

Comparative observations

Peter Bülow, *Recht der Kreditsicherheiten* (4th edn, 1997).
Ulrich Drobnig, 'Transfer of Property', in: Arthur Hartkamp et al. (eds.), *Towards a European Civil Code* (2nd edn, 1998) 495 ff. (cited as: Drobnig, in: Hartkamp et al.).
Anja Fenge, 'Probleme der floating charge im schottischen Sachenrecht', ZEuP 2000, 342 ff.
Axel Flessner, 'Befreiung vom Vertrag wegen Nichterfüllung', ZEuP 1997, 255 ff.
Leopold von Gerlach, *Der Einfluß des deutschen und französischen Rechts auf den Eigentumserwerbsschutz beweglicher Sachen im spanischen Recht* (1995).
George L. Gretton, 'Scots Law in Shock: Real Rights and Equitable Interests', ERPL 1998, 403 ff.
Stefanie Hellmich, *Kreditsicherungsrechte in der spanischen Mehrrechtsordnung* (2000).

Eva-Maria Kieninger, *Mobiliarsicherheiten im Europäischen Binnenmarkt* (1996).
Karl Kreuzer, 'La proprieté mobilière en droit international privé', *Recueil des Cours* 259 (1996) 92 ff.
Ole Lando/Hugh Beale (eds.), *Principles of European Contract Law*, Part I (1995).
Ralf Michaels, 'Short Distinctions and Floating Transitions − A German View of *Sharp v. Thomson*', ERPL 1998, 407 ff.
A. V. M. Struycken, 'The Proprietary Aspects of International Assignment of Debts and the Rome Convention Art. 12', *Lloyd's Maritime and Commercial Law Quarterly* 1998, 345 ff.
Karsten Thorn, *Der Mobiliarerwerb vom Nichtberechtigten* (1996).
Lars Peter Wunibald van Vliet, *Transfer of Movables in German, French, English and Dutch Law* (2000).
Andreas Wacke, 'Eigentumserwerb des Käufers durch schlichten Konsens oder erst mit Übergabe?', ZEuP 2000, 254 ff.
Philip R. Wood, *Principles of International Insolvency* (1997).

Glossary

EVA-MARIA KIENINGER AND GEORGE L. GRETTON

I. Introduction

The glossary originated from the necessity to establish some degree of terminological uniformity in the national discussions of the cases. It was felt by all contributors that for a number of key terms such as 'security right', 'ownership', 'execution', 'insolvency proceedings', etc. a standardised term (in English) should be used. Given that the approach of English law is quite different from that of the civil law systems – a general statement which is especially true in property law – it was thought advisable not to use standard English law terminology but to choose neutral expressions where available, such as, for example, 'enterprise charge' instead of 'floating charge'. As a consequence of this approach, terms of art in English law which have not at the same time been chosen as overall standard terms appear *italicised* in the discussions of the cases, just as do national terms of art in languages other than English.

The glossary which emerged from the work on the reports was first meant to be addressed only to the contributors. However, as we went along, it became apparent not only that the glossary would be useful to the reader, but also that knowledge of our terminological decisions would indeed be necessary for a proper understanding of the reports.

The glossary is divided into three parts. In the first column the reader will find the standardised terms used in the reports. Sometimes, related terms (which are not translated) are added in square brackets. For some terms it was felt that a note or definition might be helpful. These can be found in the third column. The second and more important column contains translations of the standard terms into the various languages of the legal systems under consideration. It must be noted, however, that the use of the word 'translation' in this context is to be understood to be taken with a pinch of salt. The purpose was to state terms of art in each of the contributors' languages rather than give explanatory translations. Where the concept referred to by the chosen standard term exists in the given country, it was possible to provide a translation of the standard term using a national term of art. Yet, where legal concepts are more diverse, we still decided to indicate the national terms of art denoting legal institutions which are the closest approximations, rather than to attempt a descriptive translation. This caveat applies especially to the translations given for the term 'enterprise charge'. It is evident that, for example, the English floating charge and the French *nantissement du fonds de commerce* are in fact widely different. Finally, where no national standard term existed, not even in comparative legal writing, the contributors were asked to fill in 'no standard term' rather than invent terms. Nevertheless, it must be made clear that the fact that a contributor stated a national term of art, e.g. for 'security ownership', does not necessarily mean that the concept of security ownership exists and is regarded as valid in that specific jurisdiction. In sum, the glossary should be seen in the context of the cases and should not be understood as a separate attempt to produce a dictionary.

It follows from the use of standardised terms in English rather than English terms of art that the standard terms are not necessarily valid or appropriate in the context of English, Irish, Scottish or South African law. This is why the second column also contains a 'translation' of the standard terms into terms used in the English, Irish, Scottish and South African legal systems. It should also be noted that the standard terminology was followed only in Part II of this volume, and in the Introduction and Evaluation. In all other contributions to Part I of this book, the authors used their own terminology.

Standard term	Terms in other languages[1] in the same order as the cases, always separated by ';' (Order: Germany, Austria; Greece; France; Belgium; Portugal; Spain; Italy; the Netherlands; England; Ireland; Scotland; South Africa; Denmark; Sweden; Finland)	Selected notes
Accession	Verbindung; Verbindung; enosi, synafeia; incorporation; accession/natrekking; acessão; accesión; accessione; natrekking; accession; accession; *accessio*/accession; accession; accession; accession; aksessio, liittäminen/ accession, förbindelse	
Action in court	Klage; Klage; agogi; action en justice, demande en justice; action en justice, demande en justice/vordering in rechte; acção; demanda judicial; azione, azione in giudizio; rechtsvordering; action in court; action in court; action; action; søgsmål; talan; kanne/talan	
Assignment	Forderungsabtretung, Zession; Forderungsabtretung, Zession; ekchorisi; cession de créance; transfert de créance, cession de créance/overdracht van schuldvordering; cessão de créditos; cesión de crédito; cessione del credito; cessie; assignment; assignment; assignation; cession, assignment; overdragelse; överlåtelse; siirto, luovutus/överlåtelse	Transfer of movable intangible property, such as claims. See also security assignment.

[1] Terms in different languages which are used in one jurisdiction are separated by a solidus (/). Different terms within one language and jurisdiction are separated by a comma (,).

Standard term	Terms in other languages in the same order as the cases, always separated by ';' (Order: Germany; Austria; Greece; France; Belgium; Portugal; Spain; Italy; the Netherlands; England; Ireland; Scotland; South Africa; Denmark; Sweden; Finland)	Selected notes
Avoidance	Anfechtung; Anfechtung; akyrosi; la nullité (relative) du contrat; annullation/vernietiging; anulação; impugnación/anulabilidad; annullamento;[2] vernietiging; rescission; rescission; avoidance, rescission; avoidance, rescission; ugyldighed, omstødelse; ogiltighet, återvinning;[3] moite/klander	Avoidance of a contract because of fraud, misrepresentation, mistake, threat, irrespective of whether the effects are *ex tunc* or *ex nunc*. The terms *ex tunc* and *ex nunc* are used to specify the effects of an avoidance. The term 'rescission' is not used as a standard term. The term avoidance is also used in the context of *actio pauliana*.
Bailiff	Gerichtsvollzieher; Vollstreckungsorgan, Gerichtsvollzieher; dikastikos epimelitis; huissier de justice; huissier de justice/gerechtsdeurwaarder; oficial de justiça, funcionário judicial; funcionario judicial; ufficiale giudiziario; gerechtsdeurwaarder; sheriff; sheriff; officer of court; bailiff, messenger of the court; fogde; utmätningsman; ulosottomies/ utmätningsman	Public official charged with the duties of civil execution.

(*cont.*)

---

[2] But in the context of *actio pauliana*: *impugnazione*.
[3] This is the term used in the context of insolvency proceedings.

(cont.)

Standard term	Terms in other languages in the same order as the cases, always separated by ';'. (Order: Germany; Austria; Greece; France; Belgium; Portugal; Spain; Italy; the Netherlands; England; Ireland; Scotland; South Africa; Denmark; Sweden; Finland)	Selected notes
Bona fide acquisition	Gutgläubiger Erwerb; gutgläubiger Erwerb; kalopisti ktisi; acquisition de bonne foi;[4] verkrijging te goeder trouw/acquisition de bonne foi; aquisição de boa fé; adquisición de buena fe; acquisto di buona fede; verkrijging te goeder trouw; *bona fide* acquisition; *bona fide* acquisition; *bona fide* acquisition; *bona fide* acquisition; godtroserhvervelse; godtrosförvärv; vilpittömän mielen saanto/godtrosförvärv	
Charge	Pfandrecht; Pfandrecht; plasmatiko enechyro; droit de sûreté; zekerheidsrecht/droit de sûreté; penhor sem entrega;[5] hipoteca mobiliária;[6] derecho pignoraticio, derecho prediario; privilegio; (stil) pandrecht; charge; charge; no standard term; no standard term; underpant, panteret; inteckning, registerpant, hypotek; hallinnaton panttioikeus, hypoteeki/hypotek	General term used for all security rights in movables or in claims which are neither a security transfer of ownership nor a possessory pledge. Term may be supplemented by specifications such as e.g. 'registered charge' or 'charge over a claim'. The term 'pledge' is reserved for the possessory pledge of movables, except where it is qualified by supplements such as 'registered', etc.

[4] Although in French law, what matters is the possession not the acquisition.
[5] For property that is not subject to registration.
[6] For property that is subject to registration.

Standard term	Terms in other languages in the same order as the cases, always separated by ';' (Order: Germany; Austria; Greece; France; Belgium; Portugal; Spain; Italy; the Netherlands; England; Ireland; Scotland; South Africa; Denmark; Sweden; Finland)	Selected notes
– Enterprise charge	Unternehmenspfandrecht; Unternehmenspfandrecht; enechyro epichirisis; nantissement du fonds de commerce; pand op de handelszaak/gage sur fonds de commerce; penhor de establecimento comercial; hipoteca de establecimiento mercantil; privilegio; no standard term; floating charge; floating charge; floating charge; pledge of stock in trade, security right in stock in trade (inventory); flydende pant; företagsinteckning, företagshypotek; yrityskiinnitys/ företagsinteckning	Charge over the enterprise or undertaking as a whole or over significant parts of it.
Claim	Forderung; Forderung; apaitisi; créance; créance/schuldvordering; crédito; crédito; credito; vorderingsrecht; claim; claim; debt; claim, debt; fordring, fordran; (enkel) fordran; saaminen/(enkel) fordran	In general the use of 'claim' is preferred to that of 'receivable' or 'book debt'.

(cont.)

(*cont.*)

Standard term	Terms in other languages in the same order as the cases, always separated by ';' (Order: Germany; Austria; Greece; France; Belgium; Portugal; Spain; Italy; the Netherlands; England; Ireland; Scotland; South Africa; Denmark; Sweden; Finland)	Selected notes
Commingling	Vermischung; Vermischung; symmeixi, syghisi; transformation; confusion/vermenging; confusão; confusión; commistione,[7] confusione;[8] commixtio/vermenging, confusio/oneigenlijke vermenging; commingling; commingling; *commixtio*/commixtion, *confusio*/confusion; mingling/confusio, mixing/commixtio; sammenblanding; sammanblandning; sekoittuminen/sammanblandning	Mixing in such a way as to destroy the individualisation of the original components
Condition	Bedingung; Bedingung; airesi; condition; condition/voorwaarde; condição; condición; condizione; voorwaarde; condition; condition; condition; condition; betingelse, vilkår, villkor, förbehåll; ehto/villkor, förbehåll	

[7] This term refers to the commingling of solid things.
[8] This term refers to the commingling of liquid things.

Standard term	Terms in other languages in the same order as the cases, always separated by ';'. (Order: Germany; Austria; Greece; France; Belgium; Portugal; Spain; Italy; the Netherlands; England; Ireland; Scotland; South Africa; Denmark; Sweden; Finland)	Selected notes
– Resolutive condition	Auflösende Bedingung; auflösende Bedingung; dialytiki airesi; condition resolutoire; condition resolutoire/ontbindende voorwaarde; condição resolutiva; condición resolutoria; condizione risolutiva; ontbindende voorwaarde; condition subsequent; condition subsequent; resolutive condition; resolutive condition; resulativ betingelse; resolutivt villkor; purkava ehto/resolutivt villkor	
– Suspensive condition	Aufschiebende Bedingung; aufschiebende Bedingung; anavlitiki airesi; condition suspensive; condition suspensive/opschortende voorwaarde; condição suspensiva; condición suspensiva; condizione ssospensiva; opschortende voorwaarde; condition precedent; condition precedent; suspensive condition; suspensive condition; suspensiv betingelse; suspensivt villkor; lykkäävä ehto/suspensivt villkor	

(cont.)

(cont.)

Standard term	Terms in other languages in the same order as the cases, always separated by ';' (Order: Germany; Austria; Greece; France; Belgium; Portugal; Spain; Italy; the Netherlands; England; Ireland; Scotland; South Africa; Denmark; Sweden; Finland)	Selected notes
Debitor cessus	Drittschuldner; Drittschuldner; opheiletis; débiteur de la créance cédée; derde-schuldenaar/débiteur de la créance cédée; debitor cessus; deudor cedido; debitore ceduto; debitor cessus; account debtor; account debtor; debtor; debtor; skyldner, debitor; debitor cessus, sekundogäldenär; debitor cessus, siirtovelallinen/debitor cessus, sekundogäldenär	The debtor of an assigned claim. The term 'debtor' is also used where this does not lead to confusion.
Delivery	Besitzübertragung, Übergabe; Besitzübertragung, Übergabe; paradosi; délivrance, livraison; délivrance/levering; tradição, entrega, délivrance/levering; tradición; consegna/traditio; bezitsverschaffing, levering; delivery; delivery; delivery; delivery; overgivelse; avlämnande, besittningsövergång, tradition; hallinnan siirto, traditio/besittningsövergång, tradition	The *traditio* of the *ius commune*. Refers to passing of possession, not to passing of ownership (though ownership may pass as a result of delivery). The expression 'actual delivery' is used where direct possession is given.

Standard term	Terms in other languages in the same order as the cases, always separated by ';'. (Order: Germany; Austria; Greece; France; Belgium; Portugal; Spain; Italy; the Netherlands; England; Ireland; Scotland; South Africa; Denmark; Sweden; Finland)	Selected notes
Execution	Zwangvollstreckung; Zwangvollstreckung; anagastiki ektelesi; exécution forcée; exécution forcée/gedwongen uitvoering; execução; acção executiva, processo executivo; ejecución forzosa, esecuzione forzata, processo esecutivo; executie, verhaal; execution; execution; diligence; execution; tvangsfuldbyrdelse; utmätning; ulosmittaus/utmätning	Judicial steps leading up to and culminating in the forced sale (normally by a bailiff) of an asset belonging to the debtor on behalf of a single (normally unsecured) creditor. Other terms such as to 'levy', to 'seize' and to 'attach' are only used as terms of art in English-speaking jurisdictions. The questionnaire uses 'to execute against' not to mean self-help by a creditor, but to mean an execution that is performed by a bailiff on behalf of a creditor who has obtained a judgment against his debtor or otherwise has a title that can be executed. Some cases expressly say that a bailiff is executing. By this, no distinction is intended.

(*cont.*)

(cont.)

Standard term	Terms in other languages in the same order as the cases, always separated by ';' (Order: Germany; Austria; Greece; France; Belgium; Portugal; Spain; Italy; the Netherlands; England; Ireland; Scotland; South Africa; Denmark; Sweden; Finland)	Selected notes
Immovable (property)	Unbewegliche Sache, Grundstück; unbewegliche Sache, Liegenschaft; akinito; immeuble; immeuble/onroerend; imóvel; bien inmueble; cosa immobile; onroerend; real property, realty;[9] real property, heritable property, immoveable property; immovable property; fast ejendom; fast egendom; kiinteä esine/fast sak	
Insolvency administrator	Insolvenzverwalter; Masseverwalter; syndikos ptocheuseos; l'administrateur judiciaire, le mandataire liquidateur; curator/curateur; administrador judicial, liquidatário; síndico de la quiebra; curatore fallimentare; curator, bewindvoerder; trustee-in-bankruptcy, liquidator; trustee-in-bankruptcy, liquidator; trustee in sequestration, liquidator; trustee in insolvency; kurator; konkursförvaltare, rekonstruktör;[10] pesänhoitaja, selvittäjä/ konkursförvaltare, utredare	General term in the context of the insolvency both of natural and of juristic persons. The terms 'receiver' and 'trustee-in-bankruptcy' are used only as terms of art (in brackets and italics) in English-speaking jurisdictions.

[9] Note, however, that 'realty' does not exactly correspond to 'immovables'. For historical reasons, leasehold interests in land have always been treated as personal property.
[10] In case of reconstruction outside bankruptcy.

Standard term	Terms in other languages in the same order as the cases, always separated by ';' (Order: Germany; Austria; Greece; France; Belgium; Portugal; Spain; Italy; the Netherlands; England; Ireland; Scotland; South Africa; Denmark; Sweden; Finland)	Selected notes
Insolvency proceedings [insolvency creditors] [the insolvency estate]	Insolvenzverfahren; Konkursverfahren; ptocheutiki diadikasia; redressement judiciaire, faillite; faillissement/faillite; processo de falência; procedimiento concursal; procedura concorsuale; faillissement, surseance van betaling, schuldsanering natuurlijke personen; bankruptcy and winding-up; bankruptcy and winding-up; sequestration or liquidation; insolvency (liquidation) proceedings; tvangsakkord, konkurs, insolvensförfarande, konkurs, företagsrekonstruktion; maksukyvyttömyysmenettely, konkurssi, yrityssaneeraus, yksityishenkilön velkajärjestely/insolvensförfarande, konkurs, företagssanering, skuldsanering för privata personer	Collective judicial or administrative proceeding, in which the assets and affairs of the debtor are subject to control or supervision by a court for the purpose of reorganisation or liquidation.[11] The term may also be used to signify extrajudicial winding-up of a company as long as there are supervisory powers of a court; the term 'receivership' is only used as a term of art (in brackets and italics) in English-language jurisdictions.

[11] See definition of 'insolvency proceeding' in art. 5 lit. f of the UNCITRAL Convention on Assignment of Receivables in International Trade, A/RES/56/81. Council Regulation (EC) no 1346/2000 of 29 May 2000 on insolvency proceedings (OJ L 160 of 30 June 2000) does not provide a definition of 'insolvency proceedings' in a strict sense but lists translations into all official languages in Annex A.

(cont.)

(*cont.*)

Standard term	Terms in other languages in the same order as the cases, always separated by ';' (Order: Germany; Austria; Greece; France; Belgium; Portugal; Spain; Italy; the Netherlands; England; Ireland; Scotland; South Africa; Denmark; Sweden; Finland)	Selected notes
Leasing	Leasing; Leasing; chrimatodotiki misthosi; crédit-bail; leasing/crédit-bail; locação financeira, leasing; arrendamiento financiero/leasing; leasing, locazione finanziaria; no standard term; leasing; leasing; leasing; leasing; leasing; leasing;[12] leasing, vuokrausluotto/leasing.	Includes both operating leases and finance leases.
Movable (property)	Bewegliche Sache; bewegliche Sache; kinito; meuble; meuble/roerend; móvel, bem móbel; bien mueble; cosa mobile; roerend; personal property; personal property; movable property; movable; løsøre; lösöre, lössak; irtain esine/lösöre, lös sak	
Ownership (of), title (to)	Eigentum; Eigentum; kyriotita; droit de propriété; propriété/eigendom; propriedade; propriedad, dominio; proprietà, titolarità; eigendom; ownership; ownership; ownership, title; ownership, title; ejendomsret; äganderätt; omistusoikeus/äganderätt	Both terms are used, though some contributors may prefer to use 'ownership' for corporeal things (tangible movables) and 'title' as the broader term. The term 'property' is not used in the sense of ownership, but only as a general, non-technical expression, in the sense of someone's assets, whatever legal form they have.

[12] Operating leasing may be called 'hyra'.

Standard term	Terms in other languages in the same order as the cases, always separated by ';'; (Order: Germany; Austria; Greece; France; Belgium; Portugal; Spain; Italy; the Netherlands; England; Ireland; Scotland; South Africa; Denmark; Sweden; Finland)	Selected notes
Pledge	Faustpfand; Faustpfand; kino enechyro; gage; gage avec dépossession/vuistpand; penhor; prenda; pegno, diritto di pegno; vuistpand; pledge; pledge; pledge; pledge; hândpant; handpant; käteispantti/handpant	Possessory security right in movable property created by actual delivery of the collateral to the creditor. For non-possessory security rights or security rights in claims, the use of 'charge' instead of 'pledge' is preferred: see the note on *charge* above.
Possession	Besitz; Besitz; nomi, katochi; possession; bezit/possession; posse; posesión; possesso, detenzione;[13] feitelijke macht, bezit, houderschap; possession; possession; possession; besiddelse; besittning; hallinta/besittning	The term does not distinguish whether A possesses for himself or for another person. It is left to the contributors to make such distinctions and to choose appropriate terms. The term 'direct possession' is used to stress that someone (e.g. the creditor) has to have actual control of the thing; in other words, that a *constitutum possessorium* is not sufficient.

(*cont.*)

[13] These two terms are not synonyms under Italian law: the first is used to denote the exercise of a real right, the second the exercise of a personal right.

(cont.)

Standard term	Terms in other languages in the same order as the cases, always separated by ';' (Order: Germany; Austria; Greece; France; Belgium; Portugal; Spain; Italy; the Netherlands; England; Ireland; Scotland; South Africa; Denmark; Sweden; Finland)	Selected notes
– *Constitutum possessorium*	Besitzkonstitut; Besitzkonstitut; antifonisi nomis; détention; *constitutum possessorium*; constituto possessório; constituto posesorio; costituto possessorio; *constitutum possessorium*; attornment;[14] possessory agreement; *constitutum possessorium*; *constitutum possessorium*; *constitutum possessorium*; *constitutum possessorium*, avtal om besittning; *constitutum possessorium*, avtal om besittning hallintasopimus/*constitutum possessorium*	Possessory agreement: X retains immediate possession but agrees that he now possesses on behalf of Y.
real	Dinglich; dinglich; empragmatos; réel; zakelijk/réel; real; real; reale; zakelijk; real; real; real; real; tingsretlig; sakrättslig; esineoikeudellinen/sakrättslig	
– real right	Dingliches Recht, Sachenrecht; dingliches Recht, Sachenrecht; empragmato dikaioma; droit réel; droit réel/zakelijk recht; direito real; derecho real; diritto reale; zakelijk recht; right *in rem*, real right; real right; real right; tinglig ret; sakrätt; esineoikeus/sakrätt	
– limited real right	Beschränktes dingliches Recht; beschränktes dingliches Recht; periorismeno empragmato dikaioma; no standard term; droit réel limité/beperkt zakelijk recht; direito real menor; derecho real limitado; diritto reale minore, diritto reale limitato; beperkt zakelijk recht; encumbrance; encumbrance; subordinate real right; limited real right; begrænset tinglig ret; begränsad sakrätt; rajoitettu esineoikeus/begränsad sakrätt	

[14] Nearest expression. 'Attornment' gives constructive possession to the person to whom the bailee attorns.

Standard term	Terms in other languages in the same order as the cases, always separated by ';'. (Order: Germany; Austria; Greece; France; Belgium; Portugal; Spain; Italy; the Netherlands; England; Ireland; Scotland; South Africa; Denmark; Sweden; Finland)	Selected notes
Rei vindicatio [*rei vindicatio* outside insolvency] [to vindicate]	Vindikation; Eigentumsklage; diekdikisi; action en restitution, revindication; revindication/revindicatie; reivindicação; reivindicación, acción reivindicatoria; revindica, azione di rivendicazione; revindicatie; claim *in rem*; claim *in rem*; vindication/*rei vindicatio*; vindication/*rei vindicatio*; vindikation; vindikation; vindikaatio/vindikation	Latin term used for all instances where the owner claims repossession, including the case of insolvency.
– *Rei vindicatio* inside insolvency	Aussonderung; Aussonderung; diekdikisi stin ptocheusi; no standard term; revindication/revindicatie; reclamação da restituição de bens; acción de restitución de bienes; azione di rivendicazione, azione di restituzione, azione di separazione;[15] revindicatie; claim *in rem*; claim *in rem*; vindication/*rei vindicatio*; vindication/*rei vindicatio*; separatist ret; separation; separaatio/separation	
Retention (or reservation) of title	Eigentumsvorbehalt; Eigentumsvorbehalt; epifylaxi kyriotitas; clause de réserve de propriété; réserve de propriété/ eigendomsvoorbehoud; reserva de propriedade; reserva de dominio; riserva di proprietà; eigendomsvoorbehoud; retention of title; retention of title; retention of title; reservation/retention of title; ejendomsforbehold; äganderättsförbehåll, återtagandeförbehåll; omistuksenpidätys, omistuksenpidätysehto/äganderättsförbehåll	The term 'simple retention of title' can be used to stress that there are no special clauses such as proceeds or products clauses. The term 'sale under retention (or reservation) of title' is used rather than 'conditional sale'.

(*cont.*)

---

[15] These terms are not synonyms.

(cont.)

Standard term	Terms in other languages in the same order as the cases, always separated by ';' (Order: Germany; Austria; Greece; France; Belgium; Portugal; Spain; Italy; the Netherlands; England; Ireland; Scotland; South Africa; Denmark; Sweden; Finland)	Selected notes
– all sums (or, all monies) retention of title	Erweiterter Eigentumsvorbehalt; erweiterter Eigentumsvorbehalt; epekteinomeni epifylaxi kyriotitas;[16] no standard term; réserve de propriété pour toute somme/eigendomsvoorbehoud voor alle sommen; reserva de propriedade até ao pagamento de todas as dívidas; reserva de dominio prolongada; riserva di proprietà a garanzia di tutti i crediti;[17] verlengd eigendomsvoorbehoud; all monies retention of title; all monies retention of title; all-sums retention of title; reservation of title covering all debts; no standard term; kopplingsförbehåll; kytkentäehto/kopplingsförbehåll	Ownership is retained by the seller until the buyer has paid all debts, i.e. not only the price of the particular subject matter of the sale.
– proceeds clause	Verlängerter Eigentumsvorbehalt mit Vorausabtretungsklausel; verlängerter Eigentumsvorbehalt; epekteinomeni epifylaxi kyriotitas;[18] no standard term; no standard term; no standard term; no standard term; verlengd eigendomsvoorbehoud; proceeds clause; proceeds clause; no standard term; no standard term; no standard term	Clause extending the seller's rights to the proceeds of a subsale. This may happen by assignment or otherwise.

[16] For this form of retention of title and the following two, Greek law uses the same technical term; its exact meaning is explained by the context.
[17] This terminology does not reflect current Italian practice, but it is employed to denote foreign use.
[18] See note 16.

Standard term	Terms in other languages in the same order as the cases, always separated by ';' (Order: Germany; Austria; Greece; France; Belgium; Portugal; Spain; Italy; the Netherlands; England; Ireland; Scotland; South Africa; Denmark; Sweden; Finland)	Selected notes
– products clause	Verlängerter Eigentumsvorbehalt mit Verarbeitungsklausel; verlängerter Eigentumsvorbehalt mit Verarbeitungsklausel; epekteinomeni epifylaxi kyriotitas;[19] no standard term; no standard term; no standard term; no standard term; no standard term; no standard term; products clause; no standard term; no standard term; no standard term; no standard term; no standard term	Clause extending the seller's rights to goods created out of the goods sold.
Security assignment	Sicherungsabtretung, Sicherungszession; Sicherungsabtretung, Sicherungszession; exasfalistiki ekchorisi; cession de créance à titre de garantie; cession de créance à titre de garantie/zekerheidscessie; cessão de creditos em garantia; cesión de créditos en garantía; cessione del credito in garanzia; cessie tot zekerheid; security assignment, assignment by way of security; security assignment; assignation in security; cession *in securitatem debiti*; overdragelse til sikkerhed; säkerhetsöverlåtelse; vakuusluovutus/säkerhetsöverlåtelse	Assignment for security purposes.

(*cont.*)

[19] See note 16.

(cont.)

Standard term	Terms in other languages in the same order as the cases, always separated by ';' (Order: Germany; Austria; Greece; France; Belgium; Portugal; Spain; Italy; the Netherlands; England; Ireland; Scotland; South Africa; Denmark; Sweden; Finland)	Selected notes
Security ownership	Sicherungseigentum; Sicherungseigentum; exasfalistiki kyriotita; propriété fiduciaire; propriété fiduciaire à titre de sûreté/zekerheidseigendom; propriedade fiduciária; propiedad fiduciaria; proprietà a scopo di garanzia; zekerheidseigendom; security ownership; security ownership; no standard term; transfer of ownership as security/*fiducia cum creditore*; fiduciarisk ejendomsret; fiduciarisk äganderätt; fidusiaarinnen omistusoikeus/fidusiarisk äganderätt	This term is used in preference to 'fiduciary ownership' or *fiducia cum creditore*. The term 'security transfer of ownership' is used for the action of creating security ownership.
Security right	Sicherungsrecht; Sicherungsrecht; dikaioma empragmatis asfalias; sûreté réelle; sûreté réelle/zakelijk zekerheidsrecht; direito real de garantia, garantia real; garantía real; garanzia reale, diritto reale di garanzia; zekerheidsrecht; security interest; security interest; right in security; real security; sikkerhedsret; säkerhetsrätt; vakuusoikeus/säkerhetsrätt	To be used as a general term for a real right which serves the purpose of securing the creditor against the debtor's default.
Specificatio	Verarbeitung; Verarbeitung; eidopoiia; individualisation; spécification/zaaksforming; especificação; especificación; specificazione; zaaksvorming; specification; specification; specification/*specificatio*; specification; specification; specifikation, bearbetning; spesifikaatio, valmistaminen/specifikation, bearbetning	

168

Standard term	Terms in other languages in the same order as the cases, always separated by ';'; (Order: Germany; Austria; Greece; France; Belgium; Portugal; Spain; Italy; the Netherlands; England; Ireland; Scotland; South Africa; Denmark; Sweden; Finland)	Selected notes
Statutory preference	*National terms not stated since the variety of statutory preferences is too wide*	Term indicating a non-consensual right to preferential payment out of the proceeds of sale of an asset in execution or insolvency. Preferences are given to certain classes of creditors and may be general (relating to all assets) or special (relating to a specific asset or a specific class of assets).
Termination	Rücktritt; Rücktritt; ypanachorisi; résolution; résolution/ontbinding; resolução; resolución; risoluzione; ontbinding; termination, discharge for breach;[20] termination, discharge for breach; rescission, termination; rescission, termination; ophævelse; hävning, uppsägning utan uppsägningstid;[21] purku, purkaminen, irtisanominen/hävning, uppsägning	Termination of a contract on the ground of breach by the other party. Termination may or may not have real/retroactive effect. The term 'rescission' is not used except as a term of art in English-speaking jurisdictions. 'Termination' is also used in the context of the right of the insolvency administrator to put an end to a contract.

[20] Not rescission, because rescission works *ex tunc*.
[21] With no notice period/with immediate effect.

(cont.)

(cont.)

Standard term	Terms in other languages in the same order as the cases, always separated by ';'. (Order: Germany; Austria; Greece; France; Belgium; Portugal; Spain; Italy; the Netherlands; England; Ireland; Scotland; South Africa; Denmark; Sweden; Finland)	Selected notes
Title	*See* Ownership	Title is used as a general term, which includes ownership. Title should not be used in the sense of *titulus* in the *ius commune* (*causa*).
Transfer of ownership	Übereignung; Übereignung; metavivasi kyriotitas; transfert de propriété; transfert de propriété/overdracht van eigendom; transmissão da propriedade, transferência da propriedade; transmisión, transferencia de la propiedad; trasferimento della proprietà; eigendomsoverdracht; transfer of ownership; transfer of ownership; transfer of ownership, transfer of title, conveyance; transfer of ownership, transfer of title, conveyance; overdragelse; överlåtelse (av äganderätt); luovutus/överlåtelse (av äganderätt)	Used to signify all ways of transfer of ownership in, or title to, an asset. The term only covers derivative acquisition, not original acquisition.

Case 1: Furniture for a new office

(Transfer of ownership – general effects of insolvency on property – statutory rights of unpaid seller – resolutive clause – goods in transit)

A is a producer of office furniture. B buys from A desks and chairs for his newly opened call centre. Since B cannot pay immediately, they agree that payment will be made in three monthly instalments. The contract does not contain any additional clauses of relevance. Without having paid a single Euro, B goes bankrupt two months after delivery of the furniture.

Questions

(a) Does A have any rights in respect of the furniture? In this context, describe also the general effects of insolvency on the property law aspects of the case.
(b) Would the answer change if the parties had agreed that the seller would be entitled to terminate the contract in the event of the buyer's failure to pay? What action would A have to take in that event?
(c) What would the position be if the furniture was not delivered to B, but was in transit, in the hands of a carrier, when B went bankrupt?

Discussions

GERMANY

(a) A will not have any rights in respect of the furniture, if ownership of the desks and chairs has passed to the buyer (B).

German law distinguishes between the contract of sale, which creates only an obligation to transfer ownership, and the transfer of ownership itself. According to § 929 sent. 1 BGB, ownership of movable property passes from the transferor to the transferee upon the conclusion of (1) the agreement that title should pass (hereinafter referred to as 'the real agreement', *Einigung*), and (2) the delivery of the movable.[1] Although in practice the real agreement will usually coincide with the contract of sale (often the parties will be ignorant even of the need to conclude a second agreement), both agreements are regarded as strictly separate in law. Moreover, the validity of the real agreement is independent of the validity of the contract of sale or other obligation to transfer ownership.[2] Finally, the passing of ownership does not depend on the payment of the purchase price, except when the contract of sale provides for retention of title.[3]

In the present case, ownership of the chairs and desks will have passed to B upon delivery. It can be assumed that at the time of delivery, the parties will have agreed, at least implicitly, that ownership should pass.

German law does not have a general theory on the effects of insolvency on property law, such as, for example, the Belgian concept of *samenloop/concours*.[4] All the property belonging to the debtor when insolvency proceedings are commenced simply comes under the administration of the insolvency administrator (see § 80 InsO[5]).[6] Whilst the debtor does not cease to be owner of his assets, he does lose his entitlement to dispose of or otherwise administer them. 'Property that belongs to the debtor', in this context, means all legal rights to which the debtor is entitled, with the exception of strictly personal rights such as his name or a copyright. Such legal rights may be absolute (ownership of movables

---

[1] See further Van Vliet, *Transfer of Movables* 31 f., 34 ff.
[2] This is the famous 'principle of abstraction' (*Abstraktionsprinzip*). For a more detailed explanation see Van Vliet, *Transfer of Movables* 32 ff.; for its development see also Zimmermann, *The Law of Obligations* 867, n. 200, and Wacke, ZEuP 2000, 254 (255 ff.). For a practical application see *infra* (b) and German report, case 2.
[3] See *infra*, German report, case 3.
[4] For a discussion of this concept, see *infra*, Belgian report, case 1(a).
[5] The new Insolvency Code (*Insolvenzordnung* of 5 Oct. 1994, Bundesgesetzblatt I 2866, hereinafter cited as InsO) came into force in its entirety on 1 Jan. 1999. Texts and materials are reproduced together with an introduction in: Balz/Landfermann, *Die neuen Insolvenzgesetze*. See also the German–English edition by Stewart, *Insolvency Code, Act Introducing the Insolvency Code*. For an overview of the Insolvency Code in English see Paulus, *Texas International Law Journal* 33 (1998) 141.
[6] Provided that the court administering the insolvency proceedings has not approved so-called 'self-administration' (*Eigenverwaltung*) by the debtor. This procedure was first introduced by §§ 270 ff. InsO.

or immovables) or relative (claims). They may also consist of a share or shares in a partnership or company.

If the debtor (X) is merely in possession of a movable which is in fact the property of another (Y), the latter (Y) is entitled to vindicate it (§ 47 InsO, so-called *Aussonderung*). Evidently, that movable does not form part of the insolvent debtor's assets. If Y has only a security right (pledge, security transfer of ownership, security assignment) in the movable, the latter will form part of the insolvent debtor's assets. Y would, however, be entitled to preferential payment out of the proceeds of the sale of the collateral or other realisation of its value (§ 50 InsO, so-called *Absonderung*). Whether the holder of a specific security right has a right to vindicate the collateral or whether he is only entitled to preferential payment will be discussed in detail during the course of the following cases. The basic rule is, however, that retention of title gives a right to *rei vindicatio*,[7] whilst security ownership or security assignment only entitles the creditor to preferential payment.[8]

In this case, A has no right to the furniture, since ownership has passed to B prior to the commencement of insolvency proceedings. Also, unpaid sellers do not benefit from any statutory preferences (statutory privileges or pledges) in the event of their buyers' insolvency. A is merely an insolvency creditor.

(b) Because the real agreement exists independently of the underlying contract (the principle of abstraction), termination or avoidance of the contract of sale alone has no effect on the real agreement, even if such termination, etc., rendered the contract void *ab initio*.[9] Additionally, a right to terminate the contract, whether it be a statutory right based on a breach of contract or a contractual right, has effect only *ex nunc*. The contract is not retroactively extinguished but instead is transformed into a new legal relationship under which the parties are obliged to return what they have received.

For both reasons, any entitlement of the seller to terminate the contract because of the default of the buyer would not alter the answer to part (a). Only a retransfer of ownership (e.g. pursuant to an obligation based on unjust enrichment) prior to the commencement of insolvency proceedings, or retention of title,[10] would assist A.

---

[7] See *infra*, German report, case 3.
[8] See *infra*, German report, case 6(b) – security assignment – and case 7(d) – security transfer of ownership.
[9] See also *infra*, German report, case 2.   [10] See *infra*, German report, case 3.

(c) Under the new Insolvency Code (InsO), there is no longer a special statutory provision governing this situation.[11] The solution therefore depends on whether ownership of the movables had already passed from A to B when the furniture was in the hands of the carrier. The real agreement may be concluded anticipatorily; for example, together with the contract of sale. It will remain valid until the moment of delivery, provided the parties still want to be bound by it. The crucial point is the time of delivery of the furniture. Usually, delivery takes place when the buyer or his employees (see § 855 BGB[12]) take direct possession.[13] In the present case this would be the moment at which the goods arrive at B's premises. However, actual delivery can be replaced by an assignment of the claim for recovery of the property to which the transfer relates (§ 931 BGB).[14] This would require A to assign to B his contractual claim for recovery of the furniture against the carrier. Without such an assignment, the goods remain the property of A whilst in transit.[15] A's rights may however be subject to the carrier's statutory preference (under § 441 HGB). This preference secures the carrier against non-payment of the freight and subsists for as long as the goods are in the possession of the carrier. It ends three days after delivery unless the carrier has, during this time, brought an action in court to enforce his rights (§ 441 s. 3 HGB).

AUSTRIA

(a) A does not have any real rights in respect of the furniture. B became the owner of the furniture when it was handed over to him.

This is due to the rules of Austrian law dealing with the transfer of property (and the creation of any right *ad rem*[16]), which require a title

---

[11] Under the old Insolvency Code (*Konkursordnung*), § 44 KO, the seller had a right to stop goods in transit, when the goods had not been fully paid for, provided that insolvency proceedings were commenced in respect of the buyer before the goods had reached him. No provision to this effect is to be found in the new Code. Obviously, it proved to be irrelevant in practice.

[12] § 855 BGB provides that if someone exercises physical power over a thing on behalf of someone else within the latter's household or business, only the latter person has possession. The former person is called the *Besitzdiener*. This provision must be strictly distinguished from that of an agency. It is generally agreed that the transfer of possession is not a legal act, but a factual one. Therefore, representation by an agent is not possible. See further Van Vliet, *Transfer of Movables* 49 f.

[13] BGH 5 Dec. 1950, BGHZ 1, 4.   [14] See further Van Vliet, *Transfer of Movables* 55 ff.

[15] Although the contractual risk may nevertheless have passed to B according to § 447 BGB.

[16] Austrian legal scientific writing and the practice of the courts distinguish between absolute and relative rights. Absolute rights must be respected by everybody, whereas

and the observance of a *modus* (*titulus* and *modus* cf. § 380 ABGB). The title for a transfer of property can be a contract, a last will, and sometimes even a legal provision (cf. § 423 ABGB).

The *modus* consists of two parts; a real agreement (*Einigung*) and, generally, the delivery of the goods. The real agreement is a creation of legal scientific writing which was influenced by German doctrine after the enactment of the German BGB; the ABGB of 1811 does not know it. In the real agreement the parties declare that ownership of the object shall pass to the buyer.

There are two theories about when the real agreement is concluded. The first (majority) theory[17] holds that it is part of the contract, for example the contract of sale. According to the second theory,[18] however, it is concluded at the moment when the goods are handed over to the buyer. Originally the OGH followed the second opinion;[19] but since the decision ÖBA 1987, 51 the court has followed the first opinion.[20]

Nevertheless, the transfer of ownership does not take place upon entering into a contract but only when the object is handed over to the buyer (§ 426 ABGB). When the object cannot physically be handed over, the transfer may take place symbolically (§ 427 ABGB). It is also possible to make use of a *constitutum possessorium* (constructive possession, *Besitzkonstitut*), under which the former owner agrees to hold the goods for the transferee (§ 428 ABGB).[21] If the purchaser is already in possession of the object bought, the transfer of property is done by way of a *traditio brevi manu* (§ 428 ABGB). If the object is held by a third party, this person can be instructed to hold it on behalf of the transferee (instruction

---

relative rights impose obligations on certain persons only. Rights arising from a contract, for example, are relative rights, as they can be enforced only against the other party. A subclass of absolute rights are '*dingliche Rechte*', rights *ad rem*. These are rights to property, which must be respected by everybody. Absolute rights which are not rights *ad rem* are the rights relating to the person, the right to live, etc. The ABGB operates with a slightly different conceptual apparatus. It does not recognise absolute rights, but only rights *ad rem* (cf. § 307 ABGB). It furthermore classifies certain rights as rights *ad rem*, which – according to modern doctrine – are not rights *ad rem*, such as *possessio* and the right of inheritance.

[17] Spielbüchler, *Der Dritte im Schuldverhältnis* 101 ff.; Klang/Bydlinski IV/2 370 ff.
[18] Koziol/Welser, *Grundriß des bürgerlichen Rechts II* 75; Bollenberger, *Irrtum über die Zahlungsunfähigkeit* 90 ff.
[19] EvBl 1955/200, HS 7345 and 10.746, JBl 1984, 671 = RdW 1984, 310.
[20] See also RdW 1987, 157 and 11 Feb. 1997, 5 Ob 18/97a *ecolex* 1997, 424 = NZ 1998, 136.
[21] It is not necessary for the seller and the buyer to make a contract of deposit, thereby creating a new *causa*; cf. OGH 10 June 1981, 3 Ob 52/81, JBl 1982, 311. In general it is a matter of interpretation whether the parties genuinely agreed to a *constitutum possessorium*; the parties must articulate their will in order to transfer ownership of the goods sold.

on possession, *Besitzanweisung*).[22] If the seller has to send the goods to the buyer, the buyer becomes the owner of the goods as soon as they are handed over to the carrier by the seller, provided that the buyer has accepted the form of transportation chosen by the seller (cf. § 429 ABGB). If the seller chooses a common form of transportation, the consent of the buyer is presumed by law.

If the seller credits the sale price (and the contract of the parties does not contain a retention of title clause), ownership of the sold goods is transferred when the goods are handed over to the buyer. This is the result of § 1063 ABGB. Without, therefore, such an agreement,[23] there is no reservation of property, even when the sale price is credited.[24]

This rule does not apply, however, if, according to the contract, the buyer is obliged to pay the sale price *at the time of the delivery of the goods*. If the seller delivers the goods without receiving payment for them, it is presumed[25] that transfer of title will be subject to the suspensive condition of payment of the sale price (*kurzfristiger Eigentumsvorbehalt*, that is short-term retention of title).

In the present case, B became the owner of the furniture because the requirements of title and *modus* were fulfilled. As A credited the sale price to B, § 1063 ABGB applies and ownership of the furniture passed to B.

Effects of bankruptcy

The commencement of insolvency proceedings does not, of itself, terminate the contract. Nor, unless otherwise agreed, does the commencement

---

[22] Ownership of immovable property can only be transferred by registration in the land register (§ 431 ABGB).

[23] An exception is made when the contract of sale is part of an ongoing business relationship between the seller and the buyer. If the contracts of such parties usually contain reservation of title clauses, such a clause will be incorporated into the present contract by implication: Schwimann/Binder § 1063 ABGB n. 38.

[24] In the legal scientific writing, Hoyer has argued that, even in such a case, the seller has the right to stipulate for reservation of title unilaterally if the financial situation of the buyer deteriorates after the conclusion of the contract and prior to the handing over of the goods. Hoyer bases this argument on § 1052 ABGB, which gives a seller the right to terminate a credit agreement with the buyer if the financial situation of the buyer deteriorates in the period of time between the conclusion of the contract and the handing over of the goods (Hoyer, WBl 1995, 181). The OGH (11 Feb. 1997, 5 Ob 18/97a *ecolex* 1997, 424) expressed sympathy for this view.

[25] Cf. Klang/Bydlinski IV/2 376 f.; Rummel/Aicher I § 1063 ABGB n. 9; Bollenberger, *Irrtum über die Zahlungsunfähigkeit* 77 f.

of such proceedings (in respect of the buyer) give the seller the right to terminate the contract. If the insolvency administrator (*Masseverwalter*) fails, however, to pay the sale price, the seller has the right to terminate the contract because of the administrator's default.

He cannot, however, terminate the contract if he has credited the sale price. This is due to a special provision of the Commercial Code. In general, if the buyer fails to pay the price when required the seller is entitled to terminate[26] the contract. Such a right does not, however, exist if the seller credits the sale price to the buyer. This is due to article 8/21 of the fourth EVHGB.[27] Although this rule[28] was enacted in respect of those commercial transactions regulated by the Commercial Code, it is also applied, by way of analogy,[29] to other transactions.[30] The seller can only, therefore, demand payment of the sale price, a claim for which he will receive only the quota payable to insolvency creditors.

According to § 21(1) of the Bankruptcy Code (*Konkursordnung*, KO), the insolvency administrator is entitled to cancel contracts, provided that both parties have not yet discharged their obligations when insolvency proceedings commence. In this case, this rule does not apply, as A had already completely fulfilled his contractual obligations.

The commencement of insolvency proceedings does not, as such, affect the property rights of the bankrupt person. He does, however, lose the capacity to conclude any agreement in respect of his property (cf. § 1(1) KO).

The assets of the bankrupt are sold in order to pay his creditors. Property which the bankrupt possesses, but does not own, does not form part of his assets. The insolvency administrator is not, therefore, entitled to sell such property; rather he must hand it over to the owners.

Applied to the present case, these rules mean that A is not entitled to terminate the contract.

---

[26] If he wishes to terminate the contract the seller has to grant the buyer a period of grace (cf. § 918 ABGB) by declaring that the contract will be terminated unless the debtor fulfils his obligation within this period.

[27] This is the fourth of a number of directives which enacted the German Commercial Code (HGB) in Austria in 1938 after Austria was occupied by Nazi Germany.

[28] Until 1 Jan. 2002, a similar rule was contained in § 454 of the German BGB.

[29] OGH JBl 1988, 107; cf. Klang/Bydlinski IV/2 137 f. and Koziol/Welser, *Grundriß des bürgerlichen Rechts II* 240.

[30] It is not applied, however, if the goods are sold subject to reservation of title. In such a case it is presumed that this rule is excluded by implied agreement (cf. Koziol/Welser, *Grundriß des bürgerlichen Rechts II* 327). Some argue, however, that article 8/21 of the fourth EVHGB does not apply by operation of law: cf. P. Bydlinski, RdW 1984, 98.

(b) Such a termination would not have any effect in respect of the ownership of the furniture. B would remain owner, although he would be obliged to return it to A.

The termination would not have what Austrian legal doctrine calls '*ex tunc* effect' (retroactive effect). By way of contrast, the position when a contract is avoided for error[31] or fraud, for example, is, in respect of ownership of the goods, as if the contract was never made.[32] Ownership in such a case reverts with effect *ex tunc* to the seller. If the goods remain in the possession of the buyer, the seller is entitled to vindicate them. If A was able successfully to avoid the contract because of mistake, he would gain priority over the other creditors of B.[33]

(c) According to § 429 ABGB, B became the owner of the furniture when it was handed over by A to the carrier, provided that B accepted the form of transportation chosen by A. A is, however, entitled to vindicate the furniture (§ 45 KO), provided that insolvency proceedings were commenced before the furniture was handed over to B or to a person acting for B (the right of stoppage). Ownership of the furniture reverts to A as soon as the carrier returns the furniture to him.[34]

GREECE

(a) As the furniture was delivered to B, it is presumed that ownership was transferred to B. When B goes bankrupt, A will not be able to claim ownership of the furniture. He has neither a statutory preference nor a pledge and so cannot claim any preferential treatment. He is simply an insolvency creditor. The fact that the purchase price has not yet

---

[31] If a mistake (*Irrtum*) has occurred when entering into the contract, a party only has the right to avoid the contract if the mistake does not relate merely to the motive for entering into the contract but also relates to the subject matter of the transaction itself or results from a mistake in the contractual declaration of intent. The precondition for such avoidance by one party is that the mistake was either caused by the other party or should have been obvious to the other party or was corrected in due time (§ 871 ABGB). If the mistake was a material one, then the entire contract may be avoided. If, however, it relates only to a minor point, then the contract will be adjusted accordingly. The right to avoid a contract on the basis of mistake expires after three years.

[32] See also *infra*, Austrian report, case 2.

[33] Bollenberger argues that a mistake as to the liquidity of the buyer entitles a seller to avoid the contract (Bollenberger, *Irrtum über die Zahlungsunfähigkeit* 9 ff.).

[34] *Rummel*/Spielbüchler I § 429 ABGB n. 7.

been paid does not affect the validity of the transfer of ownership. The question of whether the purchase price is paid relates only to the contract of sale,[35] unless title is retained.

The Greek Civil Code, following the German legal system, distinguishes between contracts which create only an obligation and real agreements, by which the disposal (i.e. the transfer, charge, abolition or alteration) of a right is effected. By way of contrast, under the French legal system (the system of consent), the agreement of the parties alone is sufficient to effect a transfer of ownership (*vendre c'est aliener*).

Sale is a promissory contract. Therefore, the transfer of ownership of a movable requires a real agreement between the owner and the transferee (article 1034 A.K.). The effectiveness of the transfer depends, in addition to the agreement of the parties, on delivery of the movable to the transferee. This transfer of possession fulfils the aim of publicity. However, actual delivery may be replaced with a *constitutum possessorium* (article 977a A.K.). Neither registration of the transfer in the public transcription registers, nor the use of a notarial deed, both of which are conditions for the valid transfer of ownership of immovable property, are required in the case of a movable.

So far as the effects of insolvency are concerned, under Greek law,[36] insolvency proceedings are only applicable to merchants. After the juridical pronouncement of insolvency, the bankrupt is deprived of the right to manage and administer his property, which passes to an insolvency administrator, appointed by the court (article 2 § 1 L. 635/37). As a consequence of the above, every transaction of the bankrupt, whether real or giving rise only to an obligation (after the pronouncement of insolvency), which relates to assets acquired by the bankrupt before the pronouncement is null and void (article 2 § 4 L. 635/37). If, for example, the bankrupt transfers ownership of a thing to a third party, the insolvency administrator will be able to vindicate the asset. Article 1036 A.K. (*bona fide* acquisition of a movable) is inapplicable, as the special provision of article 2 § 4 L. 635/37 prevails. The policy of the provision therefore favours protection of the creditors over the security of transactions. According to the same provision, any transaction in favour of the bankrupt (including monetary payments or payments of bills of

---

[35] The contract of sale is separate from the real agreement, which operates to transfer ownership of the movable: the principle of abstraction.
[36] Act of 13 Dec. 1878 which replaced the third book of the Commercial Code.

exchange, promissory notes and cheques) is null and void. Consequently, a payment to the bankrupt by a debtor in good faith does not release the debt. The debtor continues to be liable in respect of the debt to the insolvency administrator. Clearly, the debtor may claim back the sum from the bankrupt, in accordance with the provisions on unjust enrichment. A new Bankruptcy Code is under preparation to modernise the existing provisions and to make them compatible with the law of the European Union.

Excepting specific legislation providing for the registration of dispositions of ships, aircraft, etc. and the recently introduced statute on 'Contracts concerning movables or claims subject to publicity and other contracts providing security' ('Symvaseis epi kiniton i apaitiseon ypokeimenes se dimosiotita kai alles symvaseis parochis asphaleias', L. 2844/2000),[37] there is no scheme of registration for the creation of real rights in movables. The transfer of possession fulfils the aim of publicity, as it demonstrates to third parties the disposition of the thing. Direct possession of movables may be decisive in some cases of conflict between the transferor and transferee of a movable. According to the rebuttable presumptions of articles 1110–1111 A.K., the possessor of a movable is presumed to be its owner. Also the *bona fide* acquisition of real rights in a movable by a non-owner requires that the transferor passes direct possession of it to the transferee (articles 1036 ff., 1043, 1215 A.K.). This protects third parties acting in good faith and upholds the security of transactions.

(b) If the seller is entitled to terminate the contract in the event of default by the purchaser, it is obvious that the transfer of ownership has been agreed on the resolutive condition of the purchaser's default or the seller's termination (article 532 A.K.). However, even if a special agreement granting A a right to terminate the contract in the event of B's failure to pay has not been stipulated, A may rescind the contract seeking reasonable compensation (article 383 A.K.). He must, however, first set a reasonable time-limit for performance to B, declaring that if the time-limit passes without action being taken, he rejects the performance. If the parties have agreed that there is no need for a time-limit to be set, A may exercise his right to terminate the contract immediately. A's right

---

[37] The statute has been in force since 13 Oct. 2001. For the modifications which L. 2844/2000 has brought to the Greek legal system of real security see Georgiadis, *I exasphalisi ton pistoseon* 547.

is exercised by a simple unilateral declaration of will addressed to B (article 390 A.K.).

(c) If the furniture has been delivered to a carrier, and B goes bankrupt before the arrival of the furniture, A has a right of stoppage *in transitu* (article 670 EmbN). A may claim retransfer of the furniture, if the price has not been paid and the goods not been sold to a third person. This action has only obligatory effects. The right of stoppage *in transitu* may be exercised by A independently of whether the ownership of the furniture has been transferred to B, for example by the issue of a warehouse warrant (articles 1034, 978 A.K.). If ownership has not yet been transferred to B, the right of stoppage is an additional protection of the owner, A, who may also claim revindication (article 1094 A.K.).

FRANCE

(a) The first point to establish is who *owns* the goods at the time of the commencement of insolvency proceedings. Under French law, the transfer of ownership (or title) by sale is completed and perfected by the execution of the contract alone (C. civ, article 1583). It does not, therefore, depend on delivery of the asset, the object of the contract or the payment of the price. According to C. civ, article 1138:

The obligation of delivering a thing is perfected by the consent alone of the contracting parties.
It makes the creditor the owner and places the thing at his risk from the moment when it should have been delivered, although the transfer has not been made, unless the debtor is in delay in delivering it, in which case the thing remains at the risk of the latter.[38]

However, another provision to consider is C. civ, article 1129, which provides that

an obligation must have for its object a thing determined at least as to its kind. The amount of the thing may be uncertain, provided that it can be determined.

In other words, the parties must have, by their contract, determined what the object of the sale is. If the sale has as its object generic goods, such as wheat, as opposed to specific goods, these assets will have to be individualised for title to them to pass to the buyer. Without such

---

[38] Translation taken from Crabb, *The French Civil Code*.

individualisation, the contract of sale is valid, but the transfer of title is postponed until individualisation takes place. At the latest, individualisation occurs with delivery. It could, however, also take place if the assets were somehow designated as being the object of the sale, for example, if the assets were packed and tagged with the name of the buyer in the seller's warehouse. In the present case, if the chairs were generic goods (that is, not individualised by *the contract of sale*), ownership will not pass before delivery. If the chairs were individualised by the contract of sale, however, title would have passed as soon as the contract was agreed.

Yet, even in the second case, where A would have lost ownership before delivery, he is not left without rights in respect of the furniture. The French Civil Code grants to the seller of movable assets a number of statutory rights to guarantee the payment of the sale price, which vary according to whether payment or delivery is to be immediate.[39] In the present case, because credit facilities were granted and delivery occurred two months ago, A would have a statutory preference. He would be able to bring an action, entitling him to preferential payment out of the proceeds of sale of the furniture. This must be ordered by the court and subsists only for as long as the assets remain in B's possession (C. civ, article 2102, 4°, para. 1). There is no need for registration or any other prerequisite.

However, B has become bankrupt and insolvency proceedings have commenced. The procedure used to be governed by the French Insolvency Act, the Law No 85-98 of 25 January 1985 as amended (hereafter IA 85).[40] Following the consolidation in 2001 of various laws into a new, renumbered Commercial Code, the IA 85 has now become articles

---

[39] C. civ, article 1612 provides the seller with the right to retain the assets if the sale price was to have been paid immediately and has not been so paid. This means that, although the sale was concluded, delivery of the asset can be suspended for as long as the sale price remains unpaid. Also, pursuant to C. civ, article 2102, 4°, para. 2, the seller has an action for the return of an asset that has been delivered when the payment should have been immediate, which he must initiate within eight days of delivery. In practice, these statutory rights are almost never used.

[40] The Act governs the insolvency proceedings of all traders (*commerçants*), artisans, farmers and all legal private persons (as opposed to public or state-owned entities). Pursuant to C. com, article L. 621-1, the debtor must apply for the commencement of insolvency proceedings within two weeks of the point at which he was unable to honour due debts with the available assets (the suspension of payments). A creditor can also form an action for the commencement of proceedings, but this is very rare.

L. 611-1 to L. 628-3 of the new Commercial Code. The substance, however, remains unchanged.

From the commencement of proceedings, an 'observation period' begins.[41] The court appoints an insolvency administrator,[42] a creditors' trustee[43] and a *juge-commissaire*.[44] The court will also determine the date of the suspension of payments, that is, the point at which the debtor found itself incapable of paying due debts from available assets (C. com, article L. 621-1). This date can be fixed many months prior to the commencement of the insolvency proceedings. It determines the beginning of the so-called 'suspect period', a period during which the activities of the debtor may be declared void (see cases 11 and 15). At the end of the observation period, a decision will be made as to which insolvency procedure should be adopted: the implementation of a rescue plan for the continuation of the business, the sale of all or part of the business, or liquidation. During insolvency proceedings, a moratorium is imposed on all individual payments. Executions pending at the time of the commencement of proceedings are suspended (C. com, article L. 621-40). Once insolvency proceedings have been commenced, A's statutory preference (under C. civ, article 2102, 4°, para. 1) loses much of its force, as it cannot in such circumstances be enforced. In order to keep his claim alive, A must inform the creditors' trustee of it within two months of being notified of the commencement of proceedings (C. com, article L. 621-46).[45] Once a rescue plan is approved or liquidation is ordered, creditors will be paid according to their ranking. A would be an unsecured creditor, and as such would be paid last.

---

[41] Until 1994, IA 85, article 8 (now C. com, article L. 621-6) required a compulsory observation period, lasting a minimum of three months from the commencement of insolvency proceedings. It was felt that the period was not in all cases justifiable given that further debts would inevitably accrue, whilst the actual survival of the business might be very doubtful. Since 1994 and the amendments made to the IA 85, liquidation can follow immediately after the commencement of insolvency proceedings 'when the company has ceased all activities or when reorganisation is manifestly impossible' (C. com, article L. 621-1, formerly IA 85, article 1).

[42] The administrator must undertake all actions necessary to preserve the debtor's property and is responsible for making proposals for its reorganisation.

[43] The creditors' trustee acts as an agent of the creditors and may in particular undertake actions to recover sums of money, but such sums will form part of the insolvency estate and will be distributed in accordance with creditors' ranking (C. com, article L. 621-39).

[44] The *juge-commissaire* is a magistrate who supervises the procedure and arbitrates in any disputes.

[45] Creditors with a registered charge, or leasing contract, are personally informed of the start of the proceedings (C. com, article L. 621-43).

(b) The contract of sale can include a resolutive clause which will terminate the contract if B defaults on the obligation to pay the instalments. Resolutive conditions are governed by C. civ, article 1183, which specifies:

> A resolutory condition is one which, when it is fulfilled, works the revocation of the obligation and which returns matters to the same state as if the obligation had never existed. It does not suspend execution of the obligation; it only obliges the creditor to restore what he has received, in the case where the event envisaged by the condition happens.[46]

In fact, such a condition is deemed to exist in all bilateral contracts, when one of the parties fails to perform an obligation, such as the obligation of payment. The contract is not terminated automatically: the contracting party not in default may elect between forced execution or the termination of the contract and payment of damages (C. civ, article 1184, para. 2).[47] The option of forced execution remains even if the contract includes an express resolutive clause.[48] Finally, termination is at the discretion of the court. This is so even if the contract includes an express resolutive clause, unless the terms of the clause are unambiguous as to the circumstances triggering its operation.

In principle, the contract is terminated on the date when the contracting party failed to perform the obligation,[49] in this case when B failed to pay the first monthly instalment for the office furniture.

B's insolvency complicates matters. First, pursuant to C. com, article L. 621-28, the suspension of payments caused by the commencement of insolvency proceedings is not permitted to be a ground for the termination of a contract, even if the parties expressly so provided. Secondly, an action for *rei vindicatio* of assets remaining in the hands of the bankrupt is possible only when the sale was terminated *before* the order which commenced insolvency proceedings. This is so regardless of whether the termination arises by court order or through the operation of a resolutive condition clause (C. com, article L. 621-118).[50] In the present case,

---

[46] Translation taken from Crabb, *The French Civil Code*.
[47] The court could grant the defendant a stay in which to perform his obligations (C. civ, article 1184, para. 3).
[48] Civ. (1), 11 Jan. 1967, Bull civ I, No 15.   [49] Civ. (1), 1 July 1963, Gaz Pal 1963, 2, 388.
[50] Moreover, the *rei vindicatio* action would still be admissible in spite of the fact that the resolution of the sale was pronounced or ordered by court *after* the commencement of insolvency proceedings when the action for the termination of the contract or the *rei vindicatio* action was presented before courts *before* the order providing for the commencement of insolvency proceedings by the seller and for a motive other than the non-payment of the sale price (C. com, article L. 621-118).

although in any event implicit in bilateral contracts, A and B have provided for a resolutive condition, which came to be fulfilled. Termination should therefore be more or less automatic and, in particular, would avoid the need for an action in court. Courts are reluctant, however, to give up their control. Case law has developed a requirement that, for termination to be effective without an action in court, the contract must expressly state that no court action is required. Moreover, the term 'automatic termination' would be insufficient. The creditor must send to the defaulting debtor a registered letter requiring him to perform and reminding him of the existence of the clause, its terms, and the grace period during which he can still perform.[51] On the facts, it does not appear that A brought any action in court prior to the commencement of insolvency proceedings or indeed notified B of the termination of the contract. A is unlikely, therefore, to be able to have the contract terminated and will find himself in the same position as in part (a).

(c) Since B is not in possession of the goods, the statutory preference of A does not apply. Additionally, the preference would not be enforceable in the event of B's insolvency. A is thus in the position of an unsecured creditor. Moreover, the carrier may be entitled to be paid in priority to A. Indeed, French law grants to carriers statutory rights over the transported assets to guarantee payment for carriage and ancillary expenses such as storage, customs duties, etc. (C. civ, article 2102, 6°). Most importantly, the carrier benefits from a right of retention (which is not to be confused with retention of title); that is, the right to retain an asset in order to secure performance of the contracting party's obligations such as payment for carriage.[52] For as long as the obligation remains

---

[51] Civ. (3), 28 Nov. 1968, Bull civ III, No 498, 382; Com 17 Mar. 1992, Bull civ IV, No 122, 88; JCP 1992 I 3608, obs. Virassamy.
[52] This right is complex and takes various forms. First, in several instances, the law provides for a statutory right of retention. In particular, the seller of movable assets can keep the object of the sale for as long as the price remains unpaid, provided that it was to have been paid immediately (C. civ, article 1612: see case 1(a)). The courts have also recognised the existence of a right of retention in instances where the Civil Code does not. The debt on which the creditor bases his claim must be certain, liquid and enforceable. Payment by instalments in principle excludes the seller's right of retention. There must also be a link between the claim and the retained asset. For example, the garage that services a car is entitled to keep it until the service charges have been paid, the debt and the detention of the car arising from the same contractual relationship. There could be cases where no previous relationship existed between the parties: an example would be someone who takes care of someone else's property in his absence on his own initiative, who would then expect payment for his services (*gestion d'affaires*). It is the retention of the thing that created the claim.

unperformed, the carrier is entitled to retain the asset. He would be granted also a preferential right over the proceeds, should a sale of the asset be ordered by the court.

In the case of insolvency, the *juge-commissaire* could authorise the insolvency administrator to pay the claim of a creditor exercising his right of retention, if the return of the asset is necessary for the activities of the insolvent (C. com, article L. 621-24).[53] In other words, the carrier who benefits from a right of retention supersedes all other creditors, whether unsecured, secured or preferential. As a result, being in possession of the office furniture, the carrier will exercise his right of retention against A, even if he was aware that A had not been paid.[54] If the insolvency administrator forms the view that the furniture is necessary for B's activities, he will ask the *juge-commissaire* to allow him to pay the claim of the carrier ahead of A.

BELGIUM

(a) The transfer of ownership pursuant to a contract of sale of goods takes effect according to the agreement between the parties (articles 1138 and 1583 C.civ.). In the case of generic goods, ownership will pass at the moment of their identification. The delivery of the goods is not a condition for the transfer of ownership to the buyer. The contracting parties are free to postpone the point at which ownership is transferred or subject the transfer to certain conditions (for example, payment of the price or delivery of the goods). In relation, however, to third parties who claim certain rights in goods, delivery remains important. This follows from the general principle of article 2279 C.civ., which states that possession of movable property gives rise to a presumption of ownership. When, for instance, the same movable asset is sold successively to different buyers, priority is granted to the purchaser, if acting in good faith, to whom the goods were delivered (article 1141 C.civ.). Other third parties, acting in good faith, with conflicting rights may equally claim protection under this principle. The security interest of a pledgee, who obtains in good faith the collateral from his debtor, who turns out not to be the owner, cannot be attacked.[55] Accordingly, creditors who have

---

[53] Com 31 May 1994, Bull civ IV, No 196; JCPédE 1995 I 417, No 18, obs. Cabrillac.
[54] Com 8 July 1981, Bull civ IV, No 311. This would be the case even if the asset still belonged to the seller under a retention of title clause.
[55] De Page, *Traité élémentaire de droit civil belge* VI 1011, n. 1023.

executed against goods in the possession of their debtor, can, under certain conditions, challenge the rights of those who pretend to have real rights in the goods. The courts will therefore protect creditors (or the insolvency administrator) of the seller when the sale cannot be considered to be a normal business transaction.[56]

The insolvency estate includes both the existing assets of the debtor and assets that come into existence during the proceedings themselves (article 16 Bankruptcy Act). The declaration of insolvency by the court effects a 'collective seizure' of all these assets on behalf of the creditors as a whole. According to the principle of article 1138 C.civ., movable property sold to the debtor will fall into the estate regardless of whether the price has been paid or whether the goods have been delivered (unless title to the goods has been retained).

The new Bankruptcy Act of 8 August 1997 has drastically strengthened the position of the unpaid seller of movable property under Belgian law. Reservation of title has been introduced by article 101 Bankruptcy Act (see case 3). Furthermore, an existing statutory preference, for the unpaid balance of the price, has been enhanced (article 20, 5° Mortgage Act). This preference entitles the unpaid seller to preferential payment out of the proceeds, when the goods are realised by the insolvency administrator. This statutory protection is granted to the seller in all cases of *concursus creditorum*. The notion of *concursus* (*samenloop/concours*) covers every situation when different creditors of the same debtor are exercising their rights of recourse to the estate (or to a particular asset) of the debtor. When such a situation occurs, the *paritas creditorum* rule applies. Furthermore, the position of each creditor is 'fixed'. According to this principle, security rights, or other devices designed to strengthen the position of a particular creditor, which come into existence or are perfected after the *concursus* occurs, are not binding upon the other creditors.[57]

In contrast to the previous position, the statutory preference is conferred automatically on any seller (the restriction to equipment was abolished). It is not necessary to comply with any formalities. This right must be exercised within five years of the sale. In the event of a sub-sale, the seller may claim priority over the proceeds of such a sale, on the basis of 'real subrogation'.

---

[56] Dirix/Broeckx, *Beslag* 304–305.
[57] Gregoire, *Théorie générale du concours des créanciers en droit belge*; Dirix/De Corte, *Zekerheidsrechten* 31–74.

In addition to the protections introduced by the 1997 Act, the traditional means of protection of the unpaid seller remain in place. The seller can therefore retain sold property, for as long as he remains unpaid, if he is not obliged to deliver the goods before payment (article 1612 C.civ.). This 'right of retention' is considered a general principle and can be enforced against the buyer, the creditors of the latter and the insolvency administrator.[58]

A relic of ancient customary law means that the seller who was not under the obligation to deliver the goods before payment is entitled to a so-called 'improper' *rei vindicatio* (article 20, 5° Mortgage Act). This right enables him, notwithstanding the transfer of ownership to the buyer, to vindicate the goods within a period of eight days following delivery, to prevent a sub-sale in order to protect his statutory preference. Under these conditions, the right to recover possession of the goods can be exercised against both the creditors of the buyer who have executed against the goods and the insolvency administrator. The importance of this right in business practice is however very limited.

Finally, it may be possible for the seller to terminate the contract on the ground of breach by the buyer (article 1184 C.civ.), in a way that is binding upon third parties. This is linked to the above-mentioned improper *rei vindicatio*. When, however, the period for the *vindicatio* (eight days) has expired, or if the seller did not have this right in the first place, a termination of the contract will no longer be possible *vis-à-vis* creditors of the buyer or the insolvency administrator.[59]

The position of the unpaid seller in the event of the buyer's insolvency can therefore be summarised as follows: the statutory preference, reservation of title, the right of the seller to refuse to deliver the goods and the *rei vindicatio* are all upheld in the insolvency of the buyer. By contrast, the right of the seller to terminate the contract (article 1184 C.civ.), and consequently to recover the goods, is in principle no longer effective after the commencement of the insolvency proceedings (unless the goods remain undelivered or the seller is entitled to *rei vindicatio*). Termination of the contract will only be binding on other creditors if the termination was either declared by the court or if the seller filed for the termination of the contract, regardless of the date of the court's verdict, *before* the commencement of insolvency proceedings. If the contract

---

[58] Cass. 7 Nov. 1935, Pas 1936 I 38; Cass. 7 Oct. 1976, RCJB 1979, 5 note Fagnart.
[59] Cass. 23 May 1946, Pas 1946 I 204; Cass. 27 Mar. 1952, Pas 1952 I 475 concl. proc. gen. Hayoit de Termicourt.

provides for a resolutive clause, which allows the seller to terminate the contract unilaterally in the event of the buyer's default, the principle is the same. The clause will only have effect *vis-à-vis* other creditors if the seller has expressly declared his intention to terminate the contract to the buyer prior to the commencement of the insolvency proceedings.

The statutory preference and retention of title can be transferred to a third party by either assignment or subrogation.

(b) A clause in the contract of sale enabling the seller to terminate the contract, if the buyer does not meet certain obligations under the contract, is valid. Following the termination of the contract, ownership of the goods returns to the seller. Such a clause does not operate automatically on the breach of contract by the buyer. The clause must be invoked expressly by the seller and the buyer must be notified. No formalities are necessary; a letter, fax, or even an oral statement (the problem of proof aside) are all sufficient. Furthermore, this statement must be made before any *concursus creditorum*. As pointed out above, the right of the seller to terminate the contract of sale in a way that is binding upon third parties is limited under article 20, 5° Mortgage Act. It is vital therefore that the seller makes clear his intention to terminate the contract before the commencement of insolvency proceedings or execution against the goods. It is not necessary, however, for the goods to have been returned to the seller before the execution or the insolvency.

(c) If the goods have not been delivered to B, the seller can reclaim them from the hands of a carrier or an agent (article 104 Bankruptcy Act). Carriers and forwarders are protected in respect of their own claims relating to the goods by a statutory preference and a right of retention (article 20, 7° Mortgage Act and article 14 of Title VII, Commercial Code) which supersede the rights of the seller.

PORTUGAL

(a) A does not have any rights in respect of the furniture, as B has become its owner. A has the status of an insolvency creditor.

According to article 408° C.C., the transfer of ownership of individualised things depends merely on the contract; that is to say, there is no need for any other act such as, for instance, delivery or registration, to transfer ownership. The transferee immediately becomes the owner of the things bought by virtue of the contract, regardless of whether they have been delivered or paid for.

This rule has led legal writers to state that the Portuguese system for the transfer of ownership is based upon the system of title (i.e., the transmission of ownership depends only on the formation of the contract). This system is governed by two principles: first, the principle of consensuality, which holds that no special formalities, above and beyond the contract, are necessary to transfer ownership; secondly, the principle of causality, which holds that any flaws in the agreement (such as, for example, mistake, fraud, incapacity) may prevent the transfer of title.[60]

In the present case, therefore, the fact that B has not paid any part of the purchase price does not prevent him from acquiring ownership of the furniture. A would be left with a claim to the price in insolvency proceedings, as the furniture will form part of the insolvency estate.

In fact, according to article 128° CPEREF (*Código dos Processos Especiais de Recuperação da Empresa e da Falência*, Portuguese code of the proceedings of recuperations of enterprises and bankruptcy[61]), a judicial declaration of insolvency effects a seizure of all the insolvent's assets, even if some have already been executed against by creditors. These assets will fall under the control of the insolvency administrator, whose duty it is to sell the assets for the benefit of all creditors. As a result of this, the bankrupt ceases to be entitled to administrate and to dispose of his present or future assets (article 147° CPEREF).[62]

(b) Under Portuguese law, the seller is not entitled to terminate the contract following delivery, on the ground of the buyer's failure to pay, unless both parties agreed to a clause authorising such termination or unless title has been reserved (article 886° C.C.). The contract can, therefore, provide for a resolutive clause. According, however, to article 435° C.C., the termination of a contract cannot affect rights already acquired by a third party, and according to article 147° CPEREF, the declaration of insolvency transfers control of the bankrupt's assets to the insolvency administrator. So, the termination of the contract of sale does not prevent the furniture from forming part of the insolvency estate.

---

[60] See Hörster, RDE 9 (1983) 121 (124, n. (3)); Ventura, ROA 43 (1983) 581, and Menezes Leitão, *O enriquecimento sem causa no direito civil* 473 n. 32.
[61] Approved by *Decreto-Lei* 132/93 of 23 Apr. 1993.
[62] See Carvalho Fernandes/João Labareda, *Código dos Processos Especiais de Recuperação da Empresa e de Falência Anotado* 353 ff.

(c) If the seller has not delivered the goods when insolvency proceedings commence, he may elect either to fulfil his obligation by delivering the goods or to suspend his performance by refusing to deliver. In the former case, he will receive no preferential treatment and will share rateably with the other insolvency creditors of the bankrupt. In the latter case, the insolvency administrator may choose either to maintain the sales contract, in which case he is obliged to fulfil the obligations of the buyer, or to set it aside, in which case the seller ceases to be obliged to deliver the furniture. This rule is contained in article 161° CPEREF.

The same rule is also applied if the furniture remains in the hands of a carrier when B goes bankrupt. In this case, article 164° CPEREF allows A to recover the furniture from the carrier, provided that he pays the costs of transit.

SPAIN

(a) A has no real rights in respect of the furniture, but merely the right to claim payment from B as an insolvency creditor. Given the facts, this transaction would be a purchase contract; hence subject to article 1445 CC, not article 326.1 CCO. According to the Civil Code, ownership of the desks and chairs has been transferred to B. B acquires ownership on taking possession of the goods. Spanish law follows the doctrine of *título y modo*, which requires both a legal title and the transfer of possession of the movable. Therefore ownership is not transferred until the purchaser has effective possession of the furniture. The Civil Code, which so often follows the Napoleonic Code, adopts a different position with regard to the conclusion of the contract of sale and its efficacy to transfer real rights. Ownership is not transferred until the purchaser has both legal title (*título*) and effective possession of the tangible movable (*modo*). The purchaser who has legal title but has not taken possession of the asset will not fulfil the requirements necessary to become owner.

In practice, real transfer of possession is the most usual way of transferring ownership in movables. In some cases, however, the transfer of possession may take place fictitiously. In such cases the following will be effective to transfer ownership: (1) the execution of the sales contract in a public deed; or (2) the use of a transfer agreement which does not require the transfer of possession to take place simultaneously.[63]

---

[63] See García Cantero, in: Paz-Ares/Díez-Picazo/Bercovitz/Salvador 913 f.

In the first case, the drawing up of a public deed by a notary (article 1462/2 CC) will be considered to have the same effect as the delivery of the thing which is the object of the contract. In the second case, the transfer agreement between the parties may take place either by *traditio brevi manu* (article 1463 CC) or by *constitutum possessorium* (article 277/I CDCC).

These contracts fall under either the general system regulated by the Civil Code, or a specific system regulated by Law 28/1998.[64] The Civil Code does not impose formal requirements upon the parties in respect of the transfer of ownership. The parties, however, will have to produce evidence of their respective rights, and the action in court (*juicio declarativo*) will usually be both long and costly. Under Law 28/1998 contracts of sale of tangible movables on hire purchase have to be in writing. This Law provides procedural advantages, such as direct access to executory proceedings[65] or access to summary oral trial,[66] irrespective of whether: (1) the contract was executed in a public deed (*escritura pública* or *póliza mercantil*); or (2) the contract was recorded in the official fill-in form; or (3) the contract was registered on the Chattels Registry. Article 517.4–5 LEC states that if the contract has been legalised as a public deed, then A can take advantage of a procedure called an executive suit.[67] This procedure is shorter because the grounds of opposition are limited[68] and because there is no evidential phase with regard to the nature of the debt upon which the suit is based.[69] If, however, the contract was recorded in accordance with the official printed form, which is available at the Chattels Registry, then A will have a direct claim against the goods acquired in instalments, provided that the applicable legal prerequisites are followed (article 16.2 LVBMP). In such a case, the debtor is required by the public notary to pay his creditor within three days or to return the goods. If he fails to pay, but returns the goods, then a public auction is carried out by the notary. If the highest amount bid does not cover the amount of the debt, then the creditor may still sue

---

[64] The LVBMP applies to sales on hire-purchase instalments if the purchaser agrees to pay the price to the seller over a period no shorter than three months. The purchase price must exceed 1,800 Euros. The law only applies to: (1) tangible movables (goods); (2) goods which are not consumable in use; (3) goods which are identifiable. To be identified, the brand and serial number must appear on one or more of the main components in such a way that they cannot be erased or detached; or, alternatively, they must have some distinctive feature which prevents them from being confused with other similar goods (article 1.2 LVBMP).
[65] See article 16.1 LVBMP.   [66] See article 16.2.a LVBMP and article 250.11 LEC.
[67] See articles 538 ff. LEC.   [68] See article 557 LEC.   [69] See Final Provision 7.2 LEC.

the debtor for the outstanding amount. If he fails to return the goods, then the creditor may initiate a summary oral suit.[70]

The basic rules of the Spanish legal system on the effects of insolvency on property-related issues are provided in articles 1911–1929 CC and also in articles 63.8 and 1156 ff. LEC.[71] If the debtor cannot pay the claims owed to all creditors, an insolvency situation will arise. According to civil procedure provisions, all individual measures to collect the claims are displaced by a single collective measure, namely insolvency proceedings, against the insolvent. Types of insolvency proceedings include: (1) if the insolvent person is an individual who is not a businessman, the declaration of insolvency (*concurso de acreedores*);[72] (2) if the insolvent is a businessman or a firm, either (i) a temporary receivership with suspension of payments (*suspensión de pagos*) or (ii) general insolvency proceedings (*quiebra*).[73] The judicial declaration of insolvency disentitles the insolvent from managing his own property and any other property the management of which is accorded to him by law. The practical consequence of all these proceedings is the eventual sale of the debtor's assets and the distribution of the proceeds amongst his creditors. In case of the debtor's insolvency, article 1915 CC and article 833 CCO have the effect that B's unpaid debts become due as of the date of insolvency. Any existing claims are stopped, and the claim will fall within the insolvency proceedings.[74] In the same way, any assets which the debtor might own, as of the date of his insolvency, will fall into the insolvency estate, which henceforth will be controlled by the insolvency administrator. The insolvency administrator can be commissioned by the court for the purpose of preserving the assets of the debtor's insolvency estate while they are liquidated in pursuance of the insolvency proceedings. The insolvent is represented by the insolvency administrator who will perform the acts necessary for the preservation of the insolvency estate. Creditors' interests are also protected by the insolvency administrator, whose duty it is to act on the behalf of creditors in trying to preserve the assets of the insolvent debtor, so as to make them available to pay the outstanding debts.

---

[70] See article 250.10°–11° LEC, and Final Provision 7.3 LEC.
[71] On 8 Jan. 2001, Law 1/2000 on Civil Procedure came into force. The new LEC completely amends the Civil Procedure Act of 3 Feb. 1881. Henceforth, references to articles from the LEC are to the new statutory provisions, but article 63.8–9 and articles 1156 ff. remain applicable (Derogatory Provision 1/I).
[72] See Díez-Picazo, *Fundamentos de derecho civil patrimonial* II 778.
[73] See Vicent Chuliá, *Compendio Crítico de Derecho Mercantil* II 845, 875, 907.
[74] See Vicent Chuliá, *Compendio Crítico de Derecho Mercantil* II 842.

Available mechanisms to protect creditors' rights are the publicity of attachments or the entry of a preventive note in a public register about the insolvency proceedings in respect of a specific good of the debtor. The problem is that not all contracts are capable of being recorded in public registers for publicity purposes. In some cases, an entry in a registry will not be feasible. The Civil Code, for example, does not provide for ordinary sales of movables to be recorded. The only exception to this rule is in the case of sales subject to Law 28/1998, which may be recorded in the *ad hoc* Registry. Recording such a transaction has the effect of publicising the agreement and of binding third-party purchasers who may subsequently acquire the goods. If the parties agreed on a reservation of title clause in their contract of sale on hire purchase, then the creditor would retain ownership of the chattel, so long as both the guaranteed price has not been paid and the specific agreement has been recorded in the Registry (article 16.5 LVBMP). In default of a registry record or of a secured possessory right, priority conflicts in respect of the same movable are resolved in favour of the person who presents the older title (articles 1221/II and 1473/III CC). Restraints of sale are often used as a mechanism to protect creditors' interests by trying to keep debtors' assets available to pay the debts. However that may be, Spanish law prohibits the parties from concluding contractual agreements that restrict the alienation of goods that have been transferred on an onerous (i.e. non-gratuitous) basis. The only exception is the sale of tangible movables subject to Law 28/1998, as long as this specific agreement has been recorded in the Registry. Additionally, contracts can be avoided so as to restore goods to the insolvency estate which have been fraudulently conveyed to third parties by the debtor. To further protect creditors' interests, a suspect period will be determined by the court to commence at a point prior to the date of the filing of the insolvency petition.[75] This procedure, called *retroacción de la quiebra*, is essentially a retroactive mechanism provided for by insolvency law, which causes the retrospective avoidance of fraudulent dealings with assets of the debtor's estate. Under this provision (article 878 CC), therefore, the validity of transactions which were undertaken in the period leading up to the declaration of insolvency, when the debtor may have begun to experience the economic difficulties that led to that state of insolvency, may be affected.

---

[75] The duration of the suspect period will be determined by the judge and will vary according to the specific circumstances of each case.

A creditor with an unpaid claim against the insolvent cannot pursue an individual action to recover once insolvency proceedings have been initiated. Consequently, the creditor's entitlement to be paid will depend on the kind of right he possesses.[76] The system of preferences clearly demonstrates the difference between the rights of unsecured and secured creditors in the circumstances of their debtor's insolvency. The rights of secured creditors in insolvency may fall into three different categories: (1) privileged rights; (2) rights that give rise to separate execution; (3) rights that enable the secured party to separate the collateral from the insolvency estate.[77] The different legal positions of creditors are set out in articles 1921 ff. CC, articles 1113 ff. CCO, and articles 1266 ff. LEC. Once the public administration, creditors who enjoy a general privilege and those who enjoy a privilege with respect to specific movables within the insolvency estate.[78] have been paid, the insolvency administrator will distribute the insolvent's remaining assets pro rata amongst the insolvency creditors to satisfy their claims.[79] There is no legal restriction that could adversely affect privileged creditors if the assets of the insolvency estate are insufficient to satisfy the claims of both secured and unsecured creditors.[80] Ultimately, if the claims are not paid in full, privileged creditors retain their right, after termination of insolvency proceedings, to subject any assets which the debtor may subsequently acquire to the satisfaction of their debts (article 1911 CC).

An example of a right giving rise to separate execution is provided by the charge (hipoteca mobiliaria). The right to separate execution in insolvency proceedings places secured creditors in a better position so far as the ultimate sale and distribution of the insolvent's assets are concerned in comparison to other creditors whose rights were not secured by either pledge or charge. Goods subject to rights of severance, though in the possession of the insolvent, may not form part of the insolvency estate. Thus, if the parties included a resolutive clause in the contract of sale, the creditor could vindicate the movable sold from the insolvency estate if the debtor failed to make payment. Finally, if the parties

---

[76] See García Villaverde, in: *Tratado de garantías en la contratación mercantil* I 306.
[77] See Díez-Picazo *Fundamentos de derecho civil patrimonial* III 750; Beltrán Sánchez, in: *Tratado de garantías en la contratación mercantil* I 258.
[78] Such creditors are those who either claim payment of workers' salaries and other rights (article 32 ET), or have the benefit of tangible movable securities and real estate guarantees.
[79] See Vicent Chuliá, *Compendio Crítico de Derecho Mercantil* II 842.
[80] See Díez-Picazo, *Fundamentos de derecho civil patrimonial* III 751.

have not agreed to any form of security, the claim will be subject to the general rule of *par conditio creditorum*.

The priority order of privileged debts is provided for by articles 1924–1927 CC. Rights that accord priority to a creditor over other insolvency creditors are those whereby the creditor *ex ante* has agreed a contract with the debtor to set up: (1) a reservation of title clause; or (2) an express resolutive clause; or (3) a charge over movables (*hipoteca mobiliaria*) affecting the goods up to the total amount of the debt, recorded in the *ad hoc* Registry;[81] or (4) a non-possessory pledge (*prenda sin desplazamiento*), recorded in the *ad hoc* Registry. According to Law 28/1998, a creditor would have priority if the parties agreed to pay the price in instalments and if such agreement was recorded in the Registry which publicises the transaction (article 16.5 LVBMP). Nonetheless, even if the agreement is not so recorded, the seller is still protected by the priority established by article 1922 CC.[82] Should the parties to the contract have agreed upon some sort of security, the creditor will accordingly have the preferential right established by the civil and insolvency legislation. For the contract to be effective as against third parties, it is necessary for it to be executed in a public document. As a result, this document will determine the creditor's priority through an indisputable date of purchase.[83] Legal priority is a public affair and cannot be modified by the creditor and the debtor contractually. Therefore, if the debtor agrees with a single creditor or with a small group of creditors a different regime in the case of future insolvency, such an agreement will be ineffective *vis-à-vis* third parties.

(b) The use of a resolutive condition as a security in the case of the purchaser's failure to pay is practically non-existent in Spain. Indeed, article 7 LVBMP does not incorporate a resolutive condition as a typical guarantee clause.[84] The use of resolutive conditions in respect of

---

[81] Such a security can only be created on businesses; on cars, trams and trains; on aircraft; on industrial machines; on patents, trademarks and copyrights (article 12 LHMPSD).

[82] The following claims have preference with regard to certain personal property of the debtor: (1) claims that are secured by a possessory pledge, in respect of the thing pledged and to the extent of its value; and (2) claims that are guaranteed by the deposit of goods or securities at a public or commercial establishment, in respect of the security and to the extent of its value (article 1922.2–3 CC).

[83] In insolvency proceedings, the creditor's priority relative to other creditors will depend on the security agreed upon with the debtor, not on the mere 'official date' of the contract. See Vicent Chuliá, *Compendio Crítico de Derecho Mercantil II* 842.

[84] See, Martínez de Aguirre, *Las ventas a plazos de bienes muebles* 85, 89.

movables is governed by article 1123 CC, and provides the seller with a personal right to claim the recovery of the movable sold. Article 1505 CC, which also refers to resolutive conditions in the sale of movables, does not offer A a real right or security. According to this latter article, if the parties have agreed to postpone payment and B fails to pay, A will have only a personal right or claim against B. Nevertheless, in the case of B's insolvency, article 1922 1 CC awards A priority of payment out of the sale proceeds of the goods. The priority subsists only as long as the goods remain in the debtor's possession and the creditor's claim remains unpaid, and only to the extent necessary to satisfy the claim.

If the parties have agreed that the contract will be terminated in the event of non-payment, one of the following clauses must be added: the parties may agree on a reservation of title clause, a statutory restriction of transfer clause, or on the resolutive condition clause which has just been discussed. The most commonly used clauses in commercial practice are reservation of title clauses and clauses restricting the transfer of the object sold to third parties.

(c) If the goods have not been delivered to the purchaser, the seller remains the owner. The carrier should return the goods to the seller, but if he delivers the goods to the purchaser, then they will not form part of the insolvency estate.

ITALY*

(a) The answer to part (a) is obvious. The seller has no rights in the furniture nor is he entitled to preferential payment of the purchase price. He will be treated by the insolvency administrator as an insolvency creditor of the buyer.

The questions raised by this case are best addressed by considering the basic rules concerning transfer of ownership under, and insolvency proceedings in, Italian law. Chapter III of the third book of the Italian Civil Code ('On ownership') deals with the modes of acquisition of ownership. In particular, article 922 lists the modes by which ownership is acquired.[85] Modes of acquisition of ownership are traditionally divided into those which are 'original' and those which are 'derivative'. An original acquisition takes place whenever ownership is acquired without the

---

* Albina Candian and Michele Graziadei are the joint authors of the Italian report. Michele Graziadei answered questions 1–10; Albina Canolian answered questions 11–15.
[85] Scholars do not regard this list as exhaustive but as merely illustrative. For general coverage: Gambaro, *La proprietà* 671 ff.; Mattei, *Il diritto di proprietà* 166 ff.

co-operation of a transferor. This may happen, for example, through *commixtio* (article 939 c.c.) or *specificatio* (article 940 c.c.). Derivative acquisition involves a transfer of ownership from one person to another, either by way of succession on death, or by an act *inter vivos* (for example, a contract), and it is regulated by the corresponding Code provisions covering succession on death (second book, articles 456 ff. c.c.) and the law of obligations (fourth book, articles 1173 ff. c.c.).

In respect of the present case, it is crucial to know when ownership of the furniture was transferred from the seller to the buyer.

Under Italian law, when ownership is transferred under a contract of sale, that transfer takes effect in accordance with the intent of the parties, provided that the goods sold are either specific (for example, a particular painting) or have been unequivocally allocated to the contract.[86] This solution replicates the general rule of article 1376 c.c.:

> In contracts having as their object the transfer of ownership of a specified thing, the constitution or transfer of a real right or the transfer of another right, such ownership or right is transferred and acquired by virtue of the lawfully expressed agreement of the parties.

Hence, in principle, transfer of ownership (i.e. title) under Italian law does not require delivery of the thing sold or payment of the contract price. The sale in the present case had the effect of transferring ownership of the furniture to the buyer before the commencement of insolvency proceedings. The insolvency administrator was entitled to regard the furniture as forming part of the insolvency estate. Yet, the sweeping generalisation of article 1376 c.c. concerning the transfer of ownership by consent, which the *codice civile* inherited from the French codification, must be taken with a pinch of salt. It does not give the whole picture. In Italy the operative content of this principle is attenuated by a number of rules, which will be examined in the Italian report to subsequent cases. Suffice it to say here that the principle must be measured against other rules which, at best, do not sit easily with it and, at worst, contradict it.[87]

---

[86] Article 1378 c.c.: 'In contracts having as their object the transfer of things specified only as to kind, ownership is transferred on identification by agreement between the parties or in the manner established by them. In the case of things which must be carried from one place to another, identification also takes place by delivery to the carrier or to the forwarding agent.' (Beltramo, Longo, Merryman translation; except as otherwise indicated citations to the Civil Code are to this translation).

[87] There are a number of works covering this point: Sacco, Riv. dir. civ. 1979 I 442 (a ground-breaking contribution); Sacco, De Nova, *Il contratto I*, 718 ff.; Gambaro, in:

One clear example of such a rule, which may be mentioned here, despite its minimal practical impact, is the unpaid vendor's lien provided for by article 1519 c.c.[88] This article allows the seller to recover goods sold and delivered to the buyer if: (1) the contract price was due on the day of the sale; (2) the buyer did not pay it within fifteen days of the date of delivery; and (3) the goods in possession of the buyer are in the same condition as they were when delivered. This right is enforced through an action in court. It protects the seller against even a creditor who is executing against the buyer, if that creditor was aware that the price remained outstanding. This special remedy does not revest property in the seller, but enables him to withhold performance against the buyer and his creditors.

The basic text dealing with insolvency proceedings is Royal Decree n° 267, of 16 March 1942, as amended ('*legge fallimentare*').[89] Insolvency proceedings are available only to certain categories of subjects defined by the law. According to the Insolvency Act, following the declaration of insolvency by the court, the insolvent's patrimony will be administered by the court-appointed insolvency administrator, who will also carry out the insolvency proceedings under court supervision. The insolvency administrator acts as an independent third party, whose duty it is to satisfy the claims of the creditors and then to turn over any residue to the bankrupt. He will prepare an inventory of the assets and liabilities of the insolvent. To promote equality of treatment between creditors, some transactions entered into by the bankrupt during the suspect period (established by the insolvency legislation) are automatically set aside. Other transactions may be vulnerable to attack by the administrator by means of an *actio Pauliana*. In due course, the assets recovered by the administrator will be made available to pay the creditors.

Pending the insolvency proceedings, creditors cannot initiate or continue individual execution on the insolvent's assets (article 51 l. fall.). Instead, executing creditors are entitled to claim *pari passu* payments in respect of debts owed to them by the insolvent (*concorso dei creditori*). Certain creditors are accorded statutory rights. Included amongst these

---

Rapports nationaux italiens au Xe Congrès International de Droit Comparé, 206 ff.; Monateri, La sineddoche 347 ff.; Chianale, Obbligazione di dare e trasferimento della proprietà; Gambaro, La proprietà 671 ff.; Vacca, Vendita e trasferimento della proprietà nella prospettiva storico-comparatistica (with reports on many legal systems); Bianca, Diritto privato 1995, 5.

[88] Bianca, in: Trattato di diritto civile italiano 1088 ff.; Argiroffi, in: Vacca, Vendita e trasferimento della proprietà II 501 ff.

[89] For in-depth commentary: Bricola/Galgano/Santini, Legge Fallimentare – Commentario Scialoja-Branca; Ragusa Maggiore/Costa, Le procedure concorsuali – Il fallimento.

are pledgees and those who hold certain other rights specified by the law (articles 53–54 l. fall.). They may sell the collateral, even before the closure of insolvency proceedings, provided that they obtain the authorisation of the court, in order to obtain preferential payment of their claims. The property available to creditors does not include claims or things which the insolvent does not own, such as things sold to him under a retention of title clause, or things that are kept by him for safe custody, etc. Such assets are restored to the true owners, according to article 103 l. fall.[90]

The Insolvency Act does not contain an organic body of rules concerning contractual obligations generally. It contains some provisions applicable to certain types of contracts (articles 72–83 l. fall.).[91] The interpretation of these articles forms the basis of the following general principles:

(1) Contracts where one party has fully performed its obligations are valid. If the party that has fully performed is the creditor and not the bankrupt, its sole remedy is participation in the insolvency proceedings, where it will share *pari passu* with the other insolvency creditors.
(2) Contracts not yet performed can be deemed to be valid or can be terminated, depending on the nature of the obligation, at the election of the insolvency administrator.

(b) In general terms, the termination of the contract may be obtained by a court action or by extrajudicial means. Thus, one party can serve on the party in default a written declaration that the contract is terminated unless performance follows within a given number of days (usually fifteen) (article 1454 c.c.). The contract itself can provide expressly for termination if one party breaches an obligation he agreed to perform (article 1456 c.c.). For such a clause to operate, the decision to enforce it must be communicated to the party in default. If timely performance was essential, the contract may also be terminated in the case of delay (article 1457 c.c.). Termination of the contract has retroactive effect as between the parties, entitling the seller to vindicate the goods from the buyer.[92] The action in question will not, however, necessarily be a real

---

[90] For in-depth treatment: Castagnola, *Le rivendiche mobiliari nel fallimento*; Bonfatti, in: Ragusa Maggiore/Costa, III 407–438.
[91] Guglielmucci, in: Ragusa Maggiore/Costa, II 238 ff.
[92] Castronovo, in: Vacca, *Il contratto inadempiuto* 206 ff.; Alpa/Dassio, in: Fontaine/Viney 871 ff., *ibid*. On the relationship between the action to terminate the contract and the action to obtain restitution of the goods delivered to the buyer, see Gallo, *L'arricchimento senza causa* 279 ff.

action, because title to the goods will not automatically revert in the seller if the goods sold are not found *in specie*. Hence, termination of the contract before the declaration of insolvency does not necessarily mean that the seller will be better off. He will still rank as an insolvency creditor if he is unable to demonstrate which goods, out of the general assets of the buyer, were the subject of the sale.[93] Having said this, a clause providing for termination of a contract in the event of the non-payment of an instalment may well be effective, provided that the seller communicated to the buyer his intention to regard the contract as terminated in accordance with such a clause before the beginning of the insolvency proceedings. The same restriction applies to a court action instituted by the seller to obtain termination of the sale.

(c) A special statutory provision governs this situation. Article 75 of the Insolvency Act states that if movables have been dispatched to the purchaser prior to the declaration of insolvency, but remain in the hands of the carrier at that time, the seller is entitled to get the goods back by paying the carrier's fee. Of course, the seller may also allow delivery to be made to the buyer, in which case he will be able to claim the price of the goods, as an insolvency creditor, in the insolvency proceedings. Should the insolvency administrator decide to enforce the contract of sale, he will be entitled to obtain delivery, but will then be obliged to pay the full price owed under the contract.

THE NETHERLANDS

(a) The Dutch Civil Code (BW) adopts a uniform system for the transfer of ownership, quite irrespective of the nature of the property in question. Thus the requirements for transfer are in principle the same for all goods, movable or immovable, as well as for the assignment of debts and other rights.[94] The general requirements of a valid transfer of ownership are provided by article 3:84 BW. A transfer requires a delivery (*traditio*) by someone with the power to dispose (following the principle of *nemo plus*) and a valid *causa traditionis* (called *titel* in Dutch). The form of the *traditio*

---

[93] Cass. 20 Feb. 1984, n. 1200, Fallimento, 1984, 809; Trib. Milano, 29 Sept. 1983, Fallimento, 1983, 1452; Trib. Genova, 17 June 1988, Fallimento, 1988, 1265; Trib. Vicenza, 29 Sept. 1988, Fallimento, 1989, 341; Trib. Genova, 20 July 1991, Fallimento, 1991, 1304. Castagnola, *Le rivendiche mobiliari nel fallimento* 317–342.
[94] The requirements of article 3:84 BW apply also to the establishment of limited rights (*beperkte rechten*): see article 3:98 BW.

depends on the nature of the rights to be transferred. In respect of movables, the delivery required may take place either by actual delivery (i.e. the handing over of the goods) or by bilateral declaration, without further material acts (delivery by way of *constitutum possessorium*, *brevi manu* or *longa manu*).[95] Although not mentioned by the Civil Code, the majority of commentators subscribe to the view that delivery requires, in addition to these formalities, a 'real agreement'.[96]

A had, as producer, the power to dispose; the contract of sale constituted a valid *causa traditionis*. As delivery of the furniture has taken place also, ownership of the furniture has passed to B, leaving A without any real rights in respect of the goods.

The commencement of insolvency proceedings does not in principle affect the property relationships existing at the time of the insolvency adjudication. Pre-insolvency entitlements in respect of goods are usually respected, subject to possible challenge on grounds of fraudulent or preferential transfer,[97] or to a temporary moratorium, which may affect the rights of third parties.[98]

A may of course submit a proof for the sale price in the insolvency proceedings, but will have no real rights in the furniture.

Dutch law makes an exception, however, in respect of the unpaid seller of movables. The Dutch Civil Code grants to an unpaid seller a statutory right to terminate the contract and claim back the goods sold (*recht van reclame*).[99] This statutory right is subject to a number of conditions and limits. First, it applies only to movables; secondly, the seller must be entitled to terminate the contract of sale under the law of contract; thirdly, the goods must still be in the same state as they were in when delivered; and, finally, the right must be exercised by means of a written declaration within a period of time specified by article 7:44 BW.[100] This period consists of two elements: the seller's right is lost only when both elements have elapsed. The right lapses when both six weeks have passed since the debt became due and sixty days have passed since the goods came into the hands of the buyer or the buyer's agent.

The right to reclaim goods which have not been paid for has real effect and thus remains effective in the event of the buyer's insolvency. The

---

[95] Article 3:90 in conjunction with article 3:115 BW. In some cases, when the transferor is not in possession of the object, delivery is possible by deed: see article 3:95 BW.
[96] The requirement of a 'real agreement' remains controversial in doctrine: see further Van Vliet, *Transfer of Movables* 133 ff.
[97] Article 42 Fw.   [98] Article 63a Fw.   [99] Articles 7:39 ff. BW.
[100] Third party acquirers in good faith are protected by virtue of article 7:42 BW.

seller must, however, give reasonable notice, by written declaration, to the insolvency administrator, who may then pay the price (or provide security for payment) in order to retain the goods within the estate.[101]

Is A entitled to claim back the goods in the present case? First A must be entitled to terminate the contract in accordance with the law of contract. The last instalment is not yet due, hence A would not normally be entitled to do so. The commencement of insolvency proceedings means, however, that the final instalment is regarded as being due, thus A is entitled to terminate the contract.[102]

B went bankrupt two months after the delivery of the furniture. The problem is that 'two calendar months' may, or may not, depending on the months in question, exceed the statutory period of sixty days contained in the Civil Code. Assuming that two months means at least sixty days, A's right to claim back the goods depends on whether more than six weeks have passed since the debts became due. As the purchase price was to be paid in three monthly instalments, the first instalment has been due for more than the six weeks allowed, whilst the other two instalments are still within the limits of article 7:44 BW. Consequently, the seller may claim back only the proportion of the delivered goods for which payment has not been due for more than six weeks. In the present case, because the first instalment has been outstanding for more than six weeks, A may only claim back the proportion of goods attributable to the second and third instalments, namely two-thirds.[103]

(b) A right to terminate the contract of sale, other than when pursuant to the statutory right of the unpaid seller, does not of itself have real effect and does not automatically revest ownership in the seller. Instead, the buyer comes under a duty to retransfer the goods.[104] This is a right *in personam* and does not, therefore, guarantee the retransfer of the goods to the seller in the event of the buyer's insolvency.

In principle it is possible for parties to agree that the initial *transfer* is to be made subject to a resolutive condition. Such a condition, when triggered, would automatically retransfer ownership to the seller. Although parties are free to agree on a transfer subject to the

---

[101] Article 7:40 BW.   [102] Article 6:40 BW.
[103] The statutory right operates in respect of each individual item sold and delivered. Or, when partial payment has been made for the goods, the seller can claim back only a proportionate part of the goods. By analogy, the same principle would apply to the time-limits of article 7:44 BW.
[104] Articles 6:269 and 271 BW.

resolutive condition of payment of the purchase price, the availability of such a condition is nevertheless restricted by the closed system of real rights, and the prohibition of security transfers, obtaining under Dutch law.[105]

(c) At the time of insolvency, A remained the owner of the goods because no delivery had taken place.[106] However, in principle he or she remains under the obligation to deliver the goods under the contract of sale.[107] On A giving reasonable notice, the administrator must decide whether or not to perform the contract (and pay the price or provide security).[108] If the administrator elects not to perform, A will be entitled to terminate the contract of sale and retain the goods.

ENGLAND

(a) The real rights of A, the unpaid seller, are governed by the Sale of Goods Act 1979, which largely restates the provisions of the former Sale of Goods Act 1893. The first issue to be considered is what happens to the so-called 'property' of the seller after the conclusion of the contract of sale. Property means the general property and can be regarded as tantamount to ownership. The common law has no conception of absolute ownership of personalty[109] and lacks remedies of a revindication character. Real rights in tangible personalty[110] are protected by actions in tort which directly safeguard the right of possession and the right to immediate possession, so that ownership is only indirectly in issue in such proceedings. The nature of such proceedings is that a claimant succeeds who is able to show that his right is superior to that of the defendant. In consequence, the common law rules governing disputes over goods favour the idea of relativity of right.

In the Sale of Goods Act, the passing of title between seller and buyer is treated as an aspect of contract. The dominant rule is that title in goods

---

[105] See Pitlo/Reehuis/Heisterkamp, *Het Nederlands burgerlijk recht* III n. 123. On the prohibition on fiduciary transfers, article 3:84(3) BW, see *infra*, Dutch report, cases 10 and 14.
[106] 'Delivery', in the context of this question, is understood to mean *traditio*. Of course, the handing over of the goods to a carrier may in fact constitute a *traditio*, in the sense of article 3:84 BW.
[107] Article 7:9 BW.   [108] Article 37 Fw.
[109] This corresponds closely but is not identical to movable property.
[110] Referred to below as goods.

passes when the parties intend it to pass.[111] These rules do not formally apply to other types of contract for the transfer of proprietary interests in goods but it is likely that an English court would apply them by analogy to such contracts. The parties may therefore stipulate that title shall pass at any time after the contract date. There is no requirement that the goods first be delivered, whether actually or constructively, and no need for the parties to fulfil any writing or other formal requirement to effectuate their intention. It is common for parties not to state when title passes. In dealing with this omission, the Sale of Goods Act lays down a series of rules of presumptive intention. These depend upon whether the goods are 'specific', so that the very goods that are the subject matter of the contract are identified at the contract date, or 'unascertained'. Unascertained goods include goods not yet produced or manufactured, generic goods and goods that have not been separated in an identifiable way from other goods of the same type.

In the case of specific goods, the presumptive rule is that, apart from exceptional cases, title passes at the contract date. It is unlikely that the present case concerns specific goods unless B has gone to A's business premises and handpicked the furniture that is needed. In the case of unascertained goods, the starting point is that the goods must first be ascertained before it is legally possible for title to pass. Ascertainment connotes a process of earmarking or selection of goods that the seller is minded to use in performance of the obligation to deliver. It could include the packaging of goods as well as the separation from a larger mass of goods of those intended for the buyer.[112] The rule for unascertained goods is that the goods must be unconditionally appropriated to the contract by one party (usually, the seller) with the assent, express or implied, of the other. It is as though the parties by a further contract designated the goods that were to be used in fulfilment of the seller's duties under the contract of sale. Where delivery takes place at the seller's premises, this probably means that title passes when the seller notifies the buyer that the goods are ready for collection. Where the seller employs an independent carrier to transport the goods to the

---

[111] There is one case, however, where the parties cannot stipulate that title will pass: see below.
[112] Particular difficulties have been caused in the case of commodities sold in bulk. To avoid problems posed by the insolvency of the seller, English law since 1995 has permitted a buyer to acquire a common ownership right, along with other interested parties, in a larger bulk from which that buyer's share has not yet been separated. See Bridge, *The Sale of Goods* 83 ff.

buyer, title will pass on delivery to that carrier. Where the seller personally transports the goods to the buyer's premises, title will pass when possession of the goods is surrendered to the buyer.

The present case almost certainly concerns unascertained goods. Title will thus pass to B when delivery, however defined, occurs.

Under the common law rules applicable outside the sphere of application of the Sale of Goods Act (e.g. in the case of a gift), delivery is principally still a prerequisite for the transfer of ownership. Yet in English law, a deed (the requirements for which are laid down in the Law of Property (Miscellaneous Provisions) Act 1989) would be as effective as delivery. For transactions that are not sale and are *not* gratuitous, there is a real dearth of authority. If a real problem were ever to arise in the modern law, one should expect an English court to apply the rules in the Sale of Goods Act 1979 by analogy.

If B is an individual, his assets upon insolvency (*bankruptcy*) will vest in the insolvency administrator (*trustee-in-bankruptcy*). The *trustee* distributes the proceeds of B's assets among those creditors putting in a proof on a *pari passu*, or rateable, basis. The unpaid seller with no retained real rights in the goods is not entitled to special treatment. In particular, that seller does not in English law have any special right of recovery of the goods in the case of *bankruptcy* occurring within a stated period after delivery. Similar principles apply in the case of corporate insolvency proceedings (*liquidation*), except that the assets of the company do not usually vest in the insolvency administrator (*liquidator*), whose powers in any case are broad enough to encompass the distribution of the insolvent company's estate without a vesting.

(b) If the parties were to agree that the contract would be resolved or set aside in the event of the buyer's failure to pay, this would not be sufficiently clear to evince an intention that title would not pass until payment was made. In so far as it evinced an intention that title would be passed back to the buyer, which again is unlikely, it would be treated as an attempt by the seller to take a charge over the goods.[113] The conventional view[114] is that, when a contract of sale is terminated by the seller because the buyer has committed a discharging breach of the contract, any real rights in the goods that have passed to the buyer will revert to the seller provided that the seller remains in possession of the

---

[113] The issue of registration that this raises is dealt with under cases 6–8.
[114] *RV Ward Ltd v Bignall* [1967] 1 QB 534; but the authority for this is slight.

goods, which is not the position in case 1. This is because the seller by terminating the contract has put it out of his power to perform his primary duty of delivery under the contract. For reasons that remain unarticulated, such a revesting of title is not permitted if the buyer is in possession of the goods. The probable reason is that this would represent an extension of the seller's right of stoppage not permitted by the terms in which that right may be exercised under the Sale of Goods Act.

(c) Even if the carrier is an independent carrier engaged on the buyer's behalf by the seller, the presumptive rule at common law is that the carrier is the agent of the buyer so that the goods are constructively delivered to the buyer when they are handed over by the seller to the carrier. The seller's statutory right of stoppage in transit is therefore exceptional in that it permits the seller to recapture goods owned by the buyer and already in the buyer's possession. In the event of the buyer's insolvency, the seller may issue a stop notice to the carrier who then must make the goods available to the seller, provided the goods have not been delivered, either actually or constructively,[115] to the buyer. By this means, the unpaid seller's lien, or possessory right to retain the buyer's goods until payment, is revived. The buyer's insolvency does not, unless the contract otherwise provides, permit the seller to terminate the contract and resell the goods. The buyer's insolvency administrator may elect to affirm the contract if it is profitable, which would then compel him to find the resources to pay the seller, or he may disclaim it or (more likely) suffer the contract to remain unperformed so that the seller may terminate it for this reason so as to revest title in himself.

IRELAND

(a) The simple answer is 'no'. A does not have any rights in respect of the furniture. Ownership has been transferred to B.

In so far as the transfer of title to movables is concerned, the basic statute is still the Sale of Goods Act 1893. 'Goods' are defined in the Act to include all personal movables other than things in action and money. For the purpose of the passing of title, a basic distinction is

---

[115] This would happen if the transit had been completed and the carrier indicated to the buyer that the goods were being held on behalf of the buyer: Sale of Goods Act, s. 45(3). Merely informing the buyer that the goods had arrived would not of itself suffice to bring to an end the right of stoppage: *Bolton v Lancashire and Yorkshire Railway Co.* (1866) LR 1 CP 431.

drawn between specific goods and unascertained goods. Specific goods are defined as goods which are identified and agreed upon at the time a contract of sale is made. If there is a contract for the sale of specific goods the title to them is transferred to the buyer at such time as the parties to the contract intend it to be transferred – as evidenced by the terms of the contract, the conduct of the parties and the circumstances of the case. It is specifically provided in the Act that a seller may retain or reserve title even though physical possession of the goods has been handed over to the buyer. Such reservation of title clauses are very common in sale of goods contracts and are principally designed to provide an unpaid seller with some security for payment of the purchase price. The general presumption however is that the parties intend title to pass whenever the contract of sale is made and it is immaterial whether the transfer of possession and/or payment of the purchase price have been postponed. Section 18 goes on to set out a series of presumptions to assist in ascertaining the intention of the parties, but such presumptions can always be ousted by any express indication of intention.

There is no definition in the Act of unascertained goods but it would appear that two basic categories are included within this term. The first category is purely generic goods. Here the seller has complete freedom to decide where he will obtain goods that answer the contractual description. An example would be a contract for the sale of '200 boxes of canned fruit'. The second category refers to goods sold 'ex-bulk'. In other words, the goods to be supplied are an unidentified part of a larger quantity. A standard example relates to a contract for the sale of '50 tonnes of wheat out of the consignment of 200 tonnes now on board a certain ship'. With unascertained goods the rule is that title passes once the goods have been ascertained and when the parties intend it to pass. Section 16 makes it clear that title cannot pass until the goods are ascertained. This is a commonsensical view based on the principle that a buyer cannot acquire title until it is known to which goods the title relates. Whether the title then passes will depend upon the intention of the parties and in particular on whether there has been a consensual appropriation of particular goods to the contract.

This rule about ascertainment has generated some practical problems in the case of goods sold 'ex-bulk'. If the buyer has paid the purchase price for goods which are to come out of a larger consignment and the seller becomes insolvent before the goods have become ascertained, then the buyer gets no title to the goods and ranks as a mere unsecured creditor in the seller's insolvency. All he has is a simple unsecured claim for the return of the purchase price. In England it may be noted that the relevant law was amended by the Sale of Goods (Amendment) Act 1995. This new legislation applies to contracts for the sale of a specified quantity of unascertained goods where the goods form part of an identified bulk. Basically the buyer becomes a co-owner of the bulk in the proportion that the goods paid for by him bear to the total amount of goods in the bulk.

With respect to the effect of insolvency on property law aspects, the general rule is that real rights survive insolvency. If a person or company has become insolvent and their affairs are being administered by a court-appointed official and the insolvent is in possession of some property in which another person has an ownership claim, the principle is that this ownership claim will trump or outrank the creditors, both unsecured and secured, of the insolvent.

In the context of insolvency, the difference between merely personal rights and real rights is of huge significance. If one has a breach of contract or tort claim against a company that has become insolvent then one has little hope of recovering anything. When a company becomes insolvent the order of distribution of the assets of the company is roughly as follows:

(1) expenses of realisation;
(2) fixed charge holders;
(3) preferential debts;
(4) enterprise charge (*floating charge*) holders;
(5) unsecured debts.

The bulk of business is of course transacted through the corporate form so that the above-mentioned state of affairs is the order of the day. Even if the insolvent is an individual or a partnership, the general regime applicable in the event of insolvency is largely the same. The main difference lies in the fact that it is not possible for individuals or partnerships to create *floating charges* over their assets.

Suppliers of goods under a valid retention of title clause have what might be described as 'super-priority' status in the buyer's insolvency. They are not to be treated as unsecured creditors but rather have a real claim for the return of the goods in question or alternatively money representing the same. In Irish law there is no system of registration of ownership of chattels. The general rule concerning transfer of movables is the *nemo plus* principle. If A makes a contract of sale with B and title to goods passes on foot of that contract, and A then makes a contract with C relating to the same goods purporting to pass title to C, B has a better title to the goods than C. A has divested himself of any real interest by virtue of the first contract and there is nothing left which he can transfer to C.

For the sake of completeness though, one should note that certain types of security interest executed by companies require registration under the Companies Act 1963, section 99, as amended. The section contains an exhaustive list of registrable security interests and if a particular type of security interest is not on the list then it does not require registration. The penalty for non-registration is quite severe in that if a registrable security interest is not registered it is invalid in the event of the company granting it becoming insolvent. Security interests over goods executed by individuals or partnerships require registration under the Bills of Sale (Ireland) Acts 1879–1883. Bills of Sale must be in a certain statutory form and the prescribed form is so technical and cumbersome that chattel financing in favour of individuals seldom takes the appearance of a security interest strictly so-called. Instead a hire-purchase transaction is normally employed. A person hires rather than agrees to buy goods, but his period of hire may extend for the useful life of the asset in question. At the end of the period the hirer has an option, but no obligation, to purchase the goods.

(b) The answer to this question depends on whether the seller has rescinded the contract prior to the buyer's insolvency. If the seller has done so, the effect of this is to revest title to the goods in the seller. The seller then has a title to the goods which outranks any countervailing claim by the buyer's insolvency administrator. Where a seller validly exercises a right of resale the effect of this is to revest the seller with title to the goods prior to passing to the new buyer. Section 48(4) Sale of Goods Act states:

Where the seller expressly reserves the right of re-sale in case the buyer should make default, and on the buyer making default re-sells the goods, the original contract of sale is rescinded, but without prejudice to any claim the seller may have for damages.

Section 48(3) Sale of Goods Act provides:

Where the goods are of a perishable nature, or where the unpaid seller gives notice to the buyer of his intention to re-sell, and the buyer does not within a reasonable time pay or tender the price, the unpaid seller may re-sell the goods and recover from the original buyer damages for any loss occasioned by his breach of contract.

While s. 48(3) Sale of Goods Act does not explicitly state that a resale under that provision has the effect of terminating the original contract of sale and revesting title in the seller, the subsection has been judicially held to have that effect.[116] Apart from the specific circumstances delineated in the subsections, there has not been a precise delineation of the events necessary to constitute an effective termination. It seems clear however that the seller must manifest his decision to rescind by some overt means, whether by communication to the buyer or by whatever else is reasonable in the circumstances.

(c) A is in the position of an unpaid seller and consequently has a right to stop the goods in transit under section 44 of the Sale of Goods Act. The section provides that when the buyer of goods becomes insolvent an unpaid seller who has parted with the possession of the goods has the right of stopping them in transit. In other words, he may resume possession of the goods as long as they are in course of transit and may retain them until payment or tender of the price. Goods are deemed to be in course of transit from the time when they are delivered to a carrier until the buyer or his agent in that behalf takes delivery of them. The unpaid seller may exercise his right of stoppage in transit either by taking actual possession of the goods or by giving notice of his claim to the carrier.

SCOTLAND

(a) A has no rights with respect to the furniture.

The Sale of Goods Act 1979 applies in Scotland. It should, however, be mentioned that it does not always produce the same effects in Scotland as in England, because of differences in property law. The Act provides that when movables are sold, ownership passes when the parties intend it to pass.[117] If the parties do not make their intentions apparent, certain presumptions apply.[118] The effect of those presumptions, in this case, will be that B is the owner. It should be noted that under the 1979 Act ownership can pass to the buyer without delivery, even notional delivery.[119] The law does not imply a clause of retention of title.

---

[116] *RV Ward Ltd v Bignall* [1967] 1 QB 534.
[117] S. 17 Sale of Goods Act 1979.   [118] S. 18 Sale of Goods Act 1979.
[119] Thus the 1979 Act does not make use of the concept of *constitutum possessorium*.

Scots property law adheres, on the whole, to the 'principle of abstraction'.[120] In other words, not only does Scots law distinguish between contract and conveyance but it also recognises that the validity of the transfer does not depend on the validity of the *causa*.[121] The Sale of Goods Act 1979 derogates to some extent from this principle, but the principle has full effect except in so far as the Act applies. Thus, once ownership has passed from seller to buyer, it cannot pass back to the seller without a juridical act by the buyer, plus some form of delivery.[122] Therefore, even if A could and did rescind the sale contract, that would have personal effect, but not real effect. In that case, he might be said to have a 'right with respect to the furniture' but it would be merely a personal right.

However, where a buyer knows that he will be unable to pay for goods he is under a duty to refuse to accept delivery of them. If he breaches that duty then the seller can take the goods back, despite the claims of the buyer's creditors. Although this doctrine is part of the law, it is in practice seldom applied, and its details and juridical basis are unclear. But it is accepted that an asset acquired by fraud is not available to the creditors of the fraudster, even though he is the owner.[123]

For clarity, it should be repeated that delivery by X to Y is not required for ownership of corporeal movables[124] to pass, provided that the transfer is by way of sale by X to Y. But if the transfer is not by way of sale, delivery is necessary for ownership to pass. The reason for this is that the common law makes delivery (*traditio*) a requirement, and it is only in the case of sale that statute has altered the common law.[125] Hence if the *causa* of the transfer is not sale, delivery is required. It should also be explained that Scots law has never fully decided whether or not to accept the competency of delivery by *constitutum possessorium*. Although legal writers tend to accept it,[126] it is generally ignored by practitioners

---

[120] Reid, *Law of Property in Scotland* paras. 608–612; Miller, *Corporeal Moveables in Scots Law* chapter 8.
[121] Generally speaking, the principle of abstraction in Scots law is similar to the German one, but there are some differences. For example, the rule contained in § 142 s. 1 BGB probably does not apply in Scots law.
[122] Delivery is necessary to pass ownership of movables *except* in sale. Since the passing-back of ownership from B to A would not be a sale, delivery would be required.
[123] See further McBryde, *The Law of Contract in Scotland* paras. 10–45 ff. and paras. 24–31.
[124] That is, 'movables' in the sense of the present work.
[125] The bulk of Scots private law remains unenacted, i.e. common law.
[126] See e.g. Miller, *Corporeal Moveables in Scots Law*.

and judges have been reluctant to accept it. Probably the best summary of the law about *constitutum possessorium* is that it is recognised, but only if the *causa detentionis* is of a legitimate kind. In practice the law will seldom regard the *causa detentionis* as legitimate.

(b) No: see above. The termination of a contract has only personal and not real effect. An exception to this would be if the goods were still in A's possession. The law in that case is probably that rescission of the contract, assuming that it is a justified rescission, would reverse the transfer of ownership.

(c) The law confers on the seller a right of 'stoppage in transit'.[127] This is virtually unknown in practice.

The law of stoppage in transit is obscure. If the seller still holds indirect possession (i.e. the carrier has direct possession on behalf of the seller) the right of stoppage is, it seems, unnecessary, while if the buyer has indirect possession (i.e. the carrier has direct possession on behalf of the buyer) stoppage is, it seems, incompetent. Yet it is not easy to see how indirect possession can be vested in neither the seller nor the buyer. The carrier must hold on behalf of someone.

SOUTH AFRICA

(a) The answer to this question depends on who owns the desks and chairs. One of the prerequisites for the passing of ownership in terms of a contract of sale under South African law, based on Roman and Roman–Dutch principles, is that (1) the price must have been paid in cash; (2) security for payment must have been given by the buyer; or (3) credit must have been given by the seller.[128] Whether a particular sale is a cash sale or a credit sale depends on the agreement as to payment reached by the parties. Since it has been agreed that the price is to be paid in instalments, this is a credit sale and not a cash sale. A further requirement for the passing of ownership is that there must be some sort of delivery. Ownership does not pass under South African law on conclusion of the contract but only on delivery.[129] South African courts have furthermore adopted the abstract as opposed to the causal system

---

[127] Sale of Goods Act 1979 ss. 44 ff. For discussion see Gow, *The Mercantile and Industrial Law of Scotland* 193 ff.
[128] See Van der Merwe, *Sakereg* 304–305.   [129] *Ibid.*, 300–301.

of transfer of ownership. The validity of the transfer of property is wholly 'abstracted' from the validity of any underlying (contractual) basis. The causal system is only adhered to in cases where fraudulent contractual agreements vitiate both the preceding agreement as well as the passing of ownership in terms of such agreement.[130] On the facts, delivery has taken place and thus ownership of the furniture passed to B on the contract followed by delivery.

If B goes bankrupt, his position is governed by the Insolvency Act 24 of 1936. The main object of the Act is to provide for the *liquidation* (i.e., insolvency proceedings) of the insolvency estate and to secure an even distribution of the assets of the bankrupt amongst his creditors in accordance with the ranking provided for by the Act. The insolvency administrator (*trustee-in-insolvency*) must fulfil this object by gathering the bankrupt's assets, realising them and distributing the proceeds amongst the creditors. In order to render this possible, and to ensure that the assets are preserved, insolvency proceedings against the estate of the bankrupt divests the bankrupt of his ownership of his assets and vests title to the estate in the master of the court and thereafter in the insolvency administrator on the latter's appointment. The bankrupt, however, retains a vital reversionary interest in the insolvency estate.[131]

Under the South African Insolvency Act, claims rank in a specific order. The proceeds of the insolvency estate must first be applied for the payment of certain costs (e.g. the cost of maintaining and realising the asset in question and the remuneration of the insolvency administrator). After the payment of initial costs, the balance must be applied for the payment of all claims (plus interest) secured by the movable in question in proper order of preference, namely enrichment liens, pledges, special notarial bonds of movables, debtor and creditor liens, an instalment sale *hypothec* (a form of charge) and a landlord's lien for unpaid rent.[132] The so-called free residue (proceeds from unsecured assets) must thereafter be applied to defray certain statutory preferences (so-called preferential claims), e.g. funeral expenses, the cost of insolvency proceedings and income tax. Any balance of the free residue remaining, after all the above have been paid, is distributed proportionally amongst the insolvency creditors (*concurrent creditors*). In ordinary circumstances A would not qualify as a secured creditor in respect of his claim for the price of

---

[130] See *Commissioner of Customs and Excise v Randles Bros. and Hudson Ltd* 1941 AD 369; *Trust Bank van Afrika Bpk v Western Bank Bpk* 1978 40 SA 281(A); *Air-Kel (Edms) Bpk h/a Merkel Motors v Bodenstein* 1980 3 SA 917 (A). See also Van der Merwe, *Sakereg* 304–314.
[131] See Smith/Sharrock, in: *The Law of South Africa* XI para. 112.
[132] See s. 95(1) of the Insolvency Act 24 of 1936.

the furniture and thus would be last in line together with other insolvency creditors of B.[133]

(b) The answer would not change if the parties had agreed that the seller would be entitled to terminate the contract in the event of the buyer's (B's) failure to pay. A would not have acquired a real right in respect of the furniture but only a personal right on account of the contract of sale. On insolvency he would still rank as an insolvency creditor.

(c) Where the furniture is handed to a carrier for delivery to B, title to the furniture will depend on whether the carrier is the agent of A or B. If, as in the present case, the carrier is acting as the agent of A, ownership of the furniture will only pass to B once the carrier has delivered the furniture to B. If B becomes insolvent or is unable to pay his debts while the furniture is still *in transitu*, the unpaid seller (A) has the right to stop the goods *in transitu* and therefore to prevent the goods falling into B's insolvency estate. This is in accordance with the English doctrine of stoppage *in transitu*, which, though not part of Roman–Dutch law, has been received into South African law. Stoppage *in transitu* is the act by which the unpaid seller stops the progress of the goods and resumes possession of them, whilst they are in the course of transit from him to the purchaser, but not yet actually delivered to the latter, who has gone bankrupt. However, the South African doctrine is restricted to the case where the carrier is the agent of the *seller*. It does not apply to the case where the carrier is the agent of the buyer.[134] Note that if the carrier is the agent of the seller, the stoppage prevents the goods from being delivered to the bankrupt buyer. If, by contrast, the carrier is the agent of the purchaser, delivery of the goods to the carrier would amount to delivery to the purchaser and the resultant transfer of ownership cannot be undone by this doctrine.

DENMARK

(a) According to Danish law, there is not a specific phase in the process of sale which can be described as the moment at which ownership of the property passes from the seller to the buyer in all respects. It is necessary to examine the context in order to determine whether or not the transfer of ownership has occurred.

---

[133] See, on the ranking of claims, Smith, *The Law of Insolvency* 230-241; Smith/Sharrock, in: *The Law of South Africa* XI paras. 236-241.
[134] See Hackwill, *Sale of Goods* 67-69.

In the context of the relationship between the buyer of an asset and the creditors of the seller, it is a general rule that, in order for any person to claim a right in an asset, the specific asset must be identified in the contract or identifiable on the basis of the contract. (This is not only so in respect of a contract of sale, but also in respect of other contracts: such as contracts of charge or those providing for retention of title.) Because of this, the buyer is not protected so long as the seller has a right to choose which specific asset within the limits of the description of the contract he will use to fulfil the contract. Therefore, the buyer is not protected against the seller's creditors (or assignees) in a sale of generic goods. The buyer will only be protected against creditors if the seller, in relation to the buyer, has chosen a specific asset to fulfil the contract, in such a way that he is bound not to change it.

In the case of the sale of specific goods, because the seller has no such choice, the buyer obtains protection against the seller's creditors from the moment of the conclusion of the contract.[135]

The general rule in respect of the relationship between the seller and the buyer's creditors is that, after delivery, the seller cannot terminate the sale nor claim any rights in the sold goods, unless he has reserved such a right prior to delivery. This is stated in section 28(2) of the Sale of Goods Act. After the goods have been handed over to the buyer, the reservation of a right to them is primarily by reservation of title. If the goods have been handed over by mistake a real right may arise. The seller has another opportunity to get a real right to the goods, i.e. a sort of charge. This last-mentioned right will not arise, however, if the buyer is a consumer (cf. section 21 of the Credit Agreements Act).[136]

If the debtor is declared bankrupt, the insolvency estate includes all the property of the debtor except assets which cannot be executed against. On the other hand, rights which are protected against the creditors are not included in the estate.[137] As the seller cannot cancel the sale, nor reserve a right to the goods, when they have been handed over to the buyer, the seller has no right to the goods which is protected against the creditors of the buyer, nor can the seller claim preferential payment from the proceeds of the realisation of the furniture.

---

[135] Cf. Carstensen, *Ting og Sager* I 69 ff.; Elmer/Skovby, *Ejendomsretten* I chapter 2 and Eyben, *Formuerettigheder* § 10.
[136] Cf. Rørdam/Carstensen, *Pant* 361 ff. and Ørgaard, *Sikkerhed i løsøre* 53 ff.
[137] Cf. Munch, *Konkursloven*; Petersen/Ørgaard, *Danish Insolvency Law – A Survey* 269 ff.; and Ørgaard, *Konkursret* 41 ff.

These rules are mandatory. If the seller has handed over the furniture, he cannot claim ownership of the furniture or preferential payment from the proceeds of the sale from the furniture unless either the contract stipulated for a reservation of title clause or a charge of the furniture has been registered.

(b) If it was agreed that the seller would be entitled to terminate the contract in the event of the buyer's default, this does not give the seller a right to reclaim the furniture unless the contract stipulates a reservation of title clause. Such a clause must be part of the agreement between the seller and the buyer. It is important to note that the seller cannot unilaterally provide for retention of title. It should also be noted that this agreement has to be concluded before the goods are handed over to the buyer. The Credit Agreements Act Part 10 contains the conditions for reservation of title not only in consumer sales but also in other sales according to section 50.

If the contract contained a reservation of title clause, the seller would have a right to terminate the sale if the purchase price was not paid and to reclaim the furniture. Such a right is protected against the buyer's creditors even if the buyer is declared bankrupt.

(c) So long as the furniture has not been delivered to B, and remains in the hands of a carrier, the seller has a right of stoppage. The precise conditions for the right to stop the goods are stated under sections 39–41 of the Sale of Goods Act. If, after conclusion of the sale, it appears that the buyer is insolvent, the seller may retain the goods or prevent them being handed over, even if they have passed into the hands of the carrier. If the buyer is declared bankrupt, or negotiations for a compulsory composition are commenced against him, the estate may get possession of the goods by providing adequate security for the payment of the purchase price in due course.

If the goods are handed over to the estate by mistake after the buyer is declared bankrupt, the seller has a right to get the goods back unless the estate pays the purchase price or provides adequate security for payment in due course.

SWEDEN

(a) Pursuant to the Sale of Goods Act (*köplagen*, 1990), section 54, the seller may rescind the contract in the event of a serious delay in payment by the buyer. If, however, the goods have come into the possession of the buyer, the seller is not even entitled to reclaim the goods from the buyer, unless the seller has reserved such a right. Consequently, he has no better right in relation to the creditors of the buyer.

(b) If the seller has reserved a right to rescind the contract, should the buyer fail to pay, the seller may reclaim the goods when the delay in payment is 'not insignificant': section 54 Sale of Goods Act. Such a reservation is effective as against the buyer's creditors, i.e. the seller has a *ius separationis* in insolvency and execution. At one time it was disputed whether the seller must have reserved the title (i.e. ownership), but pursuant to a Supreme Court decision in 1975, it is clear that the seller need not reserve the title. It is sufficient, in respect of the buyer and third parties alike, that the seller has reserved a right to rescind the contract, since that is the desired remedy. The use of the term ownership is thus mere surplusage.[138]

(c) If the buyer becomes insolvent following the conclusion of the contract, the seller may prevent the goods from being delivered to the buyer, even when he agreed to a credit sale (sections 10 and 62 of the Sale of Goods Act). This right does not cease until the buyer comes into direct possession of the goods.[139] Whether the seller can take advantage of this rule when the goods are in the hands of a carrier, depends also on the legislation concerning carriage. It is disputed whether, for instance, the seller must have retained a copy of the bill of lading, so as to be able to prevent the carrier from discharging his obligations by delivery to the buyer, even though the seller has informed the carrier that he wants to exercise his right of stoppage in transit.[140]

General remarks on transfer of ownership

According to the Code of Execution (chapter 4, section 17) and the Bankruptcy Act (chapter 3, section 3), only property 'belonging' to the debtor may be taken by execution or form part of an insolvency estate. In so far as title or ownership is a concept pursuant to Swedish law, the question of whether property belongs to the debtor or someone else is decided by other statutes or by precedents. When a buyer becomes

---

[138] NJA 1975, 222. Hessler, *Allmän sakrätt* 191 ff.   [139] NJA 1985, 879.
[140] NJA II 1936, 512 f., Grönfors, *Sjölagens bestämmelser om godsbefordran* 296; Håstad, *Den nya köprätten* 174 ff.; and Tiberg, SvJT 1993, 548 ff.

insolvent, the answers are provided by section 54 of the Sale of Goods Act, as mentioned above. Hence, the unpaid seller is, for the purposes of the Code of Execution and the Bankruptcy Act, *regarded* as the owner (i.e. has a right of separation). This is so until the buyer has taken possession of the goods, unless the contract reserves a right of rescission, in which case the right of separation will continue to subsist after the buyer has taken possession. Should the seller go bankrupt, the buyer would be *regarded* as the owner (i.e. have a right of separation) not only when he has taken possession of the goods (a *constitutum possessorium* is not accepted), but also if he has registered a purchase of individualised goods, pursuant to certain acts (principally the Bills of Sales Act from 1835: see case 10 below). Thus, either the seller or the buyer may be regarded as owner, irrespective of whether the goods are in the seller's or the buyer's possession, depending on whose insolvency is in issue. Alternatively, one can say that both the seller and the buyer can be the owner at the same time (i.e., that their ownership may overlap). In Swedish (and Scandinavian) doctrine, it is therefore generally accepted that the concepts of title or ownership normally can, and should, be dispensed with, as they only complicate matters and may lead to false conceptual conclusions. Instead, the issues should be discussed on the basis of real facts and remedies. Modern statutes are tailored accordingly. Furthermore, in Swedish law (and other Scandinavian legal regimes) there is no need for the parties to conclude, or for the courts to imply, a real agreement, in addition to the contractual one, in order to transfer (or retransfer) ownership. The sale of goods involves only one contract (the one that the parties are aware of), which is potentially sufficient to transfer all powers to the buyer. The protection of the buyer from the seller's creditors is dependent on possession or registration; a joint intent that the buyer should become the 'owner' on conclusion of the contract has no effect.[141] However, as demonstrated above, the intent of the seller, accepted by the buyer, may be of importance in determining the rights of the seller in the buyer's insolvency, namely when the seller has reserved the ownership or merely a right to rescind should the buyer not pay the price.

FINLAND

(a) Insolvency proceedings, according to Finnish law, can be applied to private persons as well as to companies. The goal of such proceedings

[141] NJA 1945, 400.

is to sell the property of the debtor in order to satisfy all his or her creditors at the same time. In order to avoid unnecessary insolvencies, an alternative procedure exists, involving the reorganisation of enterprises.[142] There also remains a procedure aimed at the rearrangement of the debts of a private person.[143]

The property which forms the insolvency estate roughly corresponds to the property that can be used for the satisfaction of the bankrupt's creditors by the reorganisation and rearrangement procedures. The main purpose of a reorganisation, however, is not to sell the debtor's property. Special efforts will be made to allow a private person to retain ownership of his home. Save for these special features of reorganisations and rearrangements, the rules concerning the effects of insolvency proceedings, described below, apply equally to reorganisation and rearrangement. As a matter of fact, the same rules apply also, in most cases, to executions.

Movable tangible goods sold by the bankrupt before insolvency are not included in the estate, even if left in the possession of the debtor, provided that the goods are specific or properly ascertained (individualised). Shares, bonds and other securities sold before insolvency are not included in the estate if the share certificates or similar documents are delivered to the buyer or a book-entry registration is made.[144] In the case of an assignment of claims, a notice to the *debitor cessus* is required.[145] Because protection from creditors in the insolvency of the seller is usually regarded as the most relevant criterion for the transfer of ownership to the buyer mentioned above, one could say that the prerequisites described represent at the same time the prerequisites of the transfer of ownership. Having said that, the buyer, after those prerequisites are fulfilled, would not be in an identical position to that of a typical owner. Above all, one must appreciate that the seller, having the sold goods or the share certificates or similar documents still in his or her possession, can, for example, sell or pledge them to some third

---

[142] See the Act on Reorganisation of Enterprise (*laki yrityksen saneerauksesta/lag om företagssanering*).
[143] See the Act on Rearrangement of Private Persons' Debts (*laki yksityishenkilön velkajärjestelystä/lag om skuldsanering för privatpersoner*).
[144] See s. 22 of the Act on Promissory Notes (*velkakirjalaki/lag om skuldebrev*), chapter 3 s. 9 of the Companies Act (*osakeyhtiölaki/lag om aktiebolag*), the Act on Book-entry System (*laki arvo-osuusjärjestelmästä/lag om värdeandelssystemet*) and the Act on Book-entry Accounts (*laki arvo-osuustileistä/lag om värdeandelskonton*).
[145] See s. 31 of the Act on Promissory Notes (*velkakirjalaki/lag om skuldebrev*).

person. This third party will be protected against the first buyer if he or she gains possession of the goods or documents and is acting *bona fide*.[146]

On the facts of case 1, the seller (A) cannot terminate the contract of sale. The seller loses that right when the item sold is delivered to the buyer, irrespective of whether the buyer goes bankrupt.[147] Nor does A have any preferential status as a creditor in the bankruptcy of the buyer. If the furniture had been delivered after the commencement of insolvency proceedings, the seller would be in a much better position.[148]

(b) According to a precedent[149] of the Finnish Supreme Court, a resolutive clause, giving the seller only the right to terminate the sale if the buyer does not fulfil his or her obligations, does not protect the seller against other creditors, even if the clause is, unquestionably, binding *inter partes*. A retention of title clause, in contrast, normally provides full protection against a buyer's creditors. This difference between suspensive clauses and resolutive clauses has often been criticised in the doctrine.[150]

(c) The seller has always the right of stoppage in transit, if B becomes bankrupt whilst the furniture remains in the hands of a carrier.[151] The seller can, therefore, stop fulfilling his or her obligations and refrain from performance. The seller can, in particular, prevent the delivery of the goods. It does not, in this respect, make any difference whether a retention of title clause, or any similar clause, has been

---

[146] Book-entry registration or, in the case of the assignment of claims, notification to the *debitor cessus*, has a similar function of protecting the buyer against the insolvency creditors of the seller, but also as against later *bona fide* buyers or pledgees of the goods. The vulnerability of the buyer in relation to subsequent buyers or pledgees of seller is regarded as acceptable, primarily due to the fact that every owner who has entrusted his or her goods to the possession of someone else is similarly at risk of losing his or her goods to some third person who has obtained the goods acting *in bona fide*. In any event, because the transfer of property usually occurs as a gradual process, Finnish lawyers often evade taking any stand whatsoever on the question at what point ownership is transferred from the seller to the buyer. Rather they try to describe the process of transfer of ownership by reference to different legal relations and factual situations.
[147] See s. 54 of the Sale of Goods Act *(kauppalak/köplag)*.
[148] See *infra*, part (c).   [149] See KKO 1983 II 132.
[150] See e.g. Havansi, *Esinevakuusoikeudet* 523–524 and 536–538.
[151] See s. 61 of the Sale of Goods Act and e.g. Tuomisto, *Omistuksenpidätys ja leasing* 196–197.

included in the contract of sale.[152] The right of the seller exists *ipso iure*.

The insolvency administrator is always entitled, however, to make use of the contractual rights of the buyer. The administrator can, therefore, prevent the seller from terminating the contract, if the insolvency administrator agrees to fulfil the contract and either pays the purchase price or, if the price is not yet due, gives guarantees that the price will be paid promptly.[153]

Also, if the furniture was delivered to the buyer after the commencement of his or her insolvency proceedings, the furniture would have to be returned to the seller.[154]

Comparative observations

part (a)

Passing of ownership

On the facts of a common business contract for the sale of goods, where the goods have been delivered to the buyer, all systems under consideration arrive at the same solution with respect to the passing of ownership, i.e. the buyer has become the owner of the goods. This is not astonishing. The different doctrines as to the transfer of ownership in movable property (consensual and *traditio* systems, causal and abstract systems) only matter in cases where the underlying contract or the real agreement are missing, or suffering from some defect, or where delivery has not yet taken place. It was, however, not the purpose of this case closely to examine the different regimes on the transfer of ownership, which

---

[152] The right of stoppage in transit is not regarded as inconsistent with the fact that the buyer may be regarded as the owner of the goods. According to the general rules described above, in the answer to part (a), the buyer of the furniture would probably be protected against the insolvency creditors of the seller and he or she could, therefore, be regarded as the owner of these goods. Part (c) does not, however, concern the buyer's protection against the creditors of the seller but the seller's protection against the creditors of the buyer. As mentioned above, the question of the general prerequisites for the transfer of property is, generally, seen as less important by Finnish lawyers.

[153] See s. 63 of the Sale of Goods Act and e.g. Tuomisto, *Vuokranantaja ja vuokralaisen konkurssi* 81 ff.

[154] The insolvency administrator could, however, even in this case, make use of the contractual rights of the buyer, in the way described above.

is a complex issue that has given rise to an extensive debate.¹⁵⁵ In so far as this first case touches upon these questions, it is merely intended to provide an opportunity briefly to set out the different regimes and thus to serve as a reference point for the following discussions. As we continue, we will see whether the differences in respect of the rules on the passing of ownership will in fact influence a legal system's approach to the issue of security rights.

As to the general rules on the passing of ownership, there are three main dividing lines:

(i) The question of whether delivery is necessary separates the consensual systems from the *traditio* systems. The principle that ownership passes upon the mere conclusion of the contract of sale was first introduced in the French *Code civil* (articles 1138, 1583 C. civ.) and was subsequently adopted by Belgian, Italian and Portuguese law. In respect of contracts for the sale of goods, England, Ireland and Scotland may also be said to adhere to the consensus principle, since ownership passes when the parties intend it to pass. However, under the common law rules applicable outside the sphere of application of the Sale of Goods Act delivery usually¹⁵⁶ remains a prerequisite for the transfer of ownership.

The necessity of delivery – applicable also to the sale of goods – subsists in German, Greek, Austrian, Spanish, Dutch and South African law. It is interesting to note that the Spanish *Código civil*, which was otherwise heavily influenced by the *Code Napoléon*, did not adopt the consensus principle but instead adhered to the requirements of *titulus* and *modus*.

Swedish, Finnish and Danish law may also be said to belong to this group although, as the Swedish and Danish reporters pointedly remark, their jurisdictions are less interested in the question of how the passing of ownership is to be construed than in the question what remedies are to be granted in specific situations. Accordingly, the Nordic systems distinguish between two perspectives. For the seller's protection against the creditors of the buyer (in the latter's insolvency) it is necessary that the seller has either retained possession of the movables or that he has reserved the right to terminate the contract (Sweden) or reserved title (Denmark, Finland). For the buyer's protection against the creditors of

---

¹⁵⁵ See recently Drobnig, in: *Towards a European Civil Code* 495 ff.; Kreuzer, *Recueil des Cours* 259 (1996) 92 ff.; Van Vliet, *Transfer of Movables*; Wacke, ZEuP 2000, 254.

¹⁵⁶ For exceptions see English report, *supra* (a).

the seller delivery of the goods or registration of the contract of sale is decisive in Sweden. In Denmark and Finland, the mere conclusion of the contract will secure the buyer if the sale relates to specific goods. If it relates to generic goods the seller must also have selected the goods with which he intends to fulfil the contract.

It should however be borne in mind that, for practical purposes, the gap between consensual and *traditio* systems is not as wide as it may seem since – with the exception of Sweden – all *traditio* systems under consideration allow actual delivery to be replaced with a *constitutum possessorium*.[157]

(ii) A second dividing line is drawn by the necessity to conclude a real agreement in addition to the contract of sale. Turning first to those jurisdictions which demand delivery, the real agreement is necessary for the transfer of ownership and is strictly separated from the contract of sale in German, Greek and South African law. In Austria and the Netherlands, the same approach is favoured by the doctrine although it is not found in the text of the respective Civil Codes. In Spain and Sweden, on the other hand, there is no need for a real agreement or for a special demonstration of the parties' intent to pass ownership. In Sweden, the issue of specification is taken care of by the requirement of actual delivery or registration, for which the goods must also be individualised.

Turning towards the consensual systems, neither French nor English law (and the systems influenced by these two jurisdictions) know of a real agreement. However, the necessity for the parties to specify the objects of the transfer and to express their intent to pass ownership in *these* objects is present in the consensual systems as well.[158]

(iii) The third dividing line lies between causal and abstract systems. This will be discussed below, in the context of case 2.

Except for South African law, the passing of ownership in no jurisdiction depends on the payment of the purchase price, leaving aside for the moment the possibility of retention of title and the statutory rights of the unpaid seller. Even in South Africa, however, the rule that the transfer of ownership depends on payment can be set aside by a credit agreement as has happened in our case.

---

[157] See also Van Vliet, *Transfer of Movables* 200 f.; Wacke, ZEuP 2000, 254 (259 f.).
[158] See further Van Vliet, *Transfer of Movables* 202 ff. The rules respecting unascertained goods (see s. 18 Rule 5 of the Sale of Goods Act) are modelled on a contract so that, *in a sense*, there is a contract within a contract.

Unpaid seller's statutory rights in the goods after delivery

A seller whose claim for the purchase price remains outstanding will usually have a personal claim against the buyer for payment or – after having terminated the contract – for the return of the goods. Of greater interest in our context, however, are the unpaid seller's rights in respect of the goods themselves. They alone may provide a security with respect to other creditors of the buyer.

The majority of the jurisdictions do not grant to the unpaid seller any special rights if he delivers the goods and does not secure himself (e.g. through a retention of title clause). These countries are: Germany, England, Ireland, Scotland, Denmark, Sweden, Finland, Greece and Portugal. Austria also belongs to this group, but if no credit has been granted, a retention of title clause is implied into the contract. Similarly, in South Africa, if no credit has been granted, ownership does not pass without payment.

France, Belgium, Italy, Spain and the Netherlands, on the other hand, confer upon the unpaid seller certain statutory rights. With the exception of the Netherlands, however, they appear to be rarely invoked in practice. It is difficult to see any common denominator in these different statutory rights.

One criterion that determines the availability of certain statutory rights is the granting of credit. Italian law takes the view that a seller who has extended credit and did not secure himself against non-payment, e.g. by a retention of title, does not deserve a statutory protection. Only when no credit was agreed upon does the unpaid seller have a statutory lien, whose value is, however, greatly diminished by the fact that it is only enforceable as against third-party creditors who know that the purchase price has not yet been paid. Therefore, in the buyer's insolvency, the statutory lien will generally be useless.

French, Belgian and Dutch law, on the other hand, grant statutory rights to both the seller who provided credit and the seller who delivered the goods prior to payment even though he could have made use of his right to withhold performance.[159] French and Belgian law, however, confer the special right of *rei vindicatio* (*droit de revendication*) and termination with third-party effect (*droit de résolution*)[160] only to the second

---

[159] As to the right to withhold performance, see article 9.201 Principles of European Contract Law (July 1998) and the comparative commentaries to ex article 4.201 in Lando/Beale, *Principles of European Contract Law I* 165 ff.
[160] This right only exists in Belgium.

category of sellers. Both rights have to be invoked within eight days of delivery and may be understood as a continuation of the seller's original right to withhold performance. Because of the narrow time-span they are hardly ever used in practice.

Rights of the unpaid seller that do not depend on this question of whether credit was granted are the Belgian statutory preference of the unpaid vendor and the Dutch statutory right to termination with real effect (*recht van reclame*). The Belgian preference was enlarged and strengthened by the reform of the Insolvency Act 1998. It now extends to all movables, it no longer requires registration and – perhaps most importantly – it is now valid in the buyer's insolvency. The preference's importance in practice cannot yet be fully estimated but it may well acquire the same relevance as has retention of title in other European jurisdictions. The Dutch *recht van reclame* rests on a totally different legal ground since it is construed as giving real effect to a right to terminate the sales contract (see also *infra*, part (b)). The time frame applicable is not as restrictive as the eight days which apply to the French and Belgian *droit de revendication* and *droit de résolution*, but as can be seen from the solution of our case, the statutory right can only be relied on in respect of transactions providing short-term credit.

French law provides a special statutory preference to the seller who did enter into a credit agreement with the buyer. The seller can bring an action in court claiming preferential payment out of the proceeds of the goods' realisation as long as the goods are in the possession of the buyer. However the right loses its validity as soon as insolvency proceedings are commenced in respect of the buyer's assets.

One possible explanation for why France, Belgium, Spain, Italy and the Netherlands grant statutory rights to the unpaid seller at all could lie in the fact that, in these systems, retention of title (the typical sellers' security) was accorded third-party effect only at a relatively late stage.[161] Yet, this explanation is unconvincing, because in the Netherlands, for instance, (simple) retention of title has long been considered as valid as against third parties, and in Belgium, the vendor's preference was only accorded effectiveness in insolvency at the same time as retention of title, in 1998. Another explanation, which has been advanced in respect of French law,[162] could lie in the rules governing the transfer of ownership. It could be said that there is a greater need to protect the vendor in

---

[161] For further details, see case 3.   [162] Cf. Wacke, ZEuP 2000, 254 (260).

a consensual system since he parts with his property the moment that the contract of sale is concluded, thus well before receiving payment. Yet, this explanation is also not fully convincing. Under the systems which require delivery or even a separate real agreement, the transfer of ownership does no more depend on the payment of the price, at least in the absence of additional contract provisions. Such additional terms may likewise be used under French law, where the parties to the sales contract are at liberty to set aside article 1583 C. civ. Finally, statutory rights of the unpaid seller are not only known in consensual systems (France, Belgium, Italy) but also in Dutch law, which adheres to the necessity of delivery. On the other hand, there are consensual systems (e.g. Portugal) which do not grant the seller a special statutory protection.

The survival of the seller's statutory rights which, as the national discussions have pointed out, are of limited practical value (with the exception of the Belgian *privilège du vendeur*) can perhaps best be explained by tradition or, in economic terms, by path dependency.

part (b)

Today, all European legal systems provide a mechanism for a contract to be terminated in the event of a material breach.[163] One of the main differences between the systems under consideration, reflected in the answers to part (b), is the way in which such termination can be effectuated.[164] French and Belgian law still principally require a court judgment whereas Italian law has adopted a more liberal attitude: the party who remained faithful to the contract is entitled to terminate the contract by a mere informal declaration. In France and Belgium, the necessity to obtain a judicial declaration can only be derogated from by inserting a duly framed 'resolutive clause' into the contract.

In the context of security rights, the termination of a sales contract on the ground of a material failure of performance, i.e. non-payment, is interesting in so far as ownership may automatically revert to the seller at the moment at which the contract comes to an end. One would expect that the solution which a legal system adopts in respect of this issue should – *inter alia* – depend on the general rules on transfer of property. Systems which are both consensual and causal[165] can be expected to

---

[163] For a detailed comparative survey see Flessner, ZEuP 1997, 255.
[164] *Ibid.*, 270 ff.
[165] As to the difference between abstract and causal systems, see also case 2.

conclude that ownership will *ipso iure* revert to the seller.[166] The French, Belgian, Italian and Irish solutions conform with the assumption: ownership is automatically and retroactively revested in the seller. Finnish and English law,[167] however, are out on a limb. Under the English Sale of Goods Act, ownership passes only with a valid contract and at the time when the parties intend it to pass. Hence, the English system may be termed both consensual and causal,[168] at least in so far as sales contracts are concerned. Nevertheless, ownership would only automatically be revested in the seller if he was still in possession of the goods. A clause providing for the contract's termination with real effect contravening this rule would be regarded as a charge and therefore be subject to the registration requirements under the Bills of Sale Acts, if the buyer were an individual, or under the Companies Act, if the buyer were a company.

Within an abstract system, ownership cannot be revested in the seller. Since the breach of contract can only affect the obligation, the real agreement remains intact. This is the solution adopted by German, Greek, Scottish and South African law.

In between the two are the *traditio* systems. On the one hand, the termination of the contract may destroy the basis of the transfer, taking effect at least from the moment of such termination. On the other hand, if delivery has taken place, one might take the view that redelivery is necessary for ownership to revert to the seller. Austrian, Spanish and Dutch law take the second view: termination of a contract on the ground of a breach is not accorded real effect. Swedish law, which as we have seen may be counted among the *traditio* systems, takes a different stand: if the seller has reserved the right to rescind the contract this has the same effect which under other jurisdictions is attributed to retention of title. For that reason it is also the only jurisdiction which confers real effect on a termination that is declared after the buyer has gone bankrupt, always provided that this right was reserved by the seller.

---

[166] The Italian report especially mentions the requirement that the goods have to still be present in the buyer's hands. Although the French and Belgian reports do not say so specifically, it can be assumed that this requirement applies in France and Belgium alike.

[167] The solution of Scots law, applying the Sale of Goods Act, is similar to that of English law, although the starting point of Scots common law is distinct ('principle of abstraction').

[168] See Van Vliet, *Transfer of Movables* 111 ff.

With the exception of Swedish law,[169] all systems that provide for a termination with real effect do not recognise its efficacy in the event of the buyer's insolvency. Therefore, a resolutive clause which, in principle, is effective as against third parties cannot be termed a security right in a true sense. In practice, it played a (limited) role as a security right only in Belgium prior to the introduction of the validity in insolvency of reservation of title and the sellers' preference.

part (c)

Since, on the facts of case 1(c), there is no special agreement between the buyer and the carrier, nearly all systems that require delivery for the transfer of ownership conclude that the seller is still the owner of those goods which are in the hands of the carrier.[170] *Vice versa*, the consensual systems reach the conclusion that ownership has already passed to B when he goes bankrupt. If it is thought necessary to protect the seller in a situation such as that described in part (c), the need primarily arises within the consensual systems. Belgian, Italian, English, Irish and Finnish law seem to follow this line of thought. All five confer the right of stoppage in transit upon the seller who has already lost ownership when the goods are in the hands of a carrier. French law, on the other hand, seems to have no sympathy for the seller.

Of those systems that require delivery to the buyer in order for ownership to be transferred, and which do not let delivery to the carrier suffice, German, Dutch and Spanish law do not give the seller a special right to stop the goods in addition to his ownership. Greek and South African law, on the other hand, do grant the seller this additional protection. The existence of this right in South African law may be a legacy of English law, even though the underlying rationale for this right in England is not so clearly discernible in South Africa.

---

[169] And the Dutch *recht van reclame* which is, however, not to be equated with a resolutive clause.

[170] See for example the German report. Contrast the Austrian report which identifies an exception to this principle in certain circumstances.

Case 2: The deceived seller

(Transfer of property – effect of fraud – effects of execution on property law questions)

B persuades A to sell him a painting. Although B knows that it is an early and unusual work of William Turner, he induces A to believe that the painting was by an unknown artist. The purchase price is fixed at 500 Euros. On 1 March, A delivers the painting to B. B immediately pays the purchase price. On 15 March, C, a creditor of B, executes against B's property, including the painting. On 20 March, A discovers the truth. He avoids the sale on the ground of fraud and demands the return of the painting.

Question

Can A claim the painting free of any rights of B or of the creditor of B?

Discussions

GERMANY

Ownership of the painting passed to B with the conclusion of the real agreement (*Einigung*) and delivery (§ 929 BGB).[1] As stated *supra*,[2] the transfer of ownership is independent of the contract of sale. Since in the present case only the contract of sale has been avoided,[3] the transfer

---

[1] German report, case 1(a).   [2] German report, case 1(a).
[3] Since the questionnaire is concerned with property law, and not the law relating to the avoidance of contracts on the basis of fraud or misrepresentation, the question whether A is in fact entitled to avoid the contract is not discussed.

of ownership remains valid.[4] A cannot vindicate the painting. He has only a claim against B based on unjust enrichment (§ 812 s. 1 sent. 1, alternative 1 BGB, *condictio indebiti*).

Generally, only someone who has a real right in property can resist an execution against it. According to § 771 ZPO, a third party, who claims to have a right in property against which a bailiff is executing, can bring an action in court resisting the execution, provided that his right is one 'that prevents the transfer of ownership'. Evidently, not even ownership by a third party will prevent a 'transfer of ownership' because of the rules on *bona fide* acquisition.[5] The wording of § 771 ZPO is thus misleading. It is generally interpreted as meaning all rights of third parties that prevent an asset from forming part of the pool of assets belonging to the debtor that are available to insolvency creditors.[6] Such rights include full ownership and security ownership.[7] Claims *in personam* for the recovery of an asset only fall within § 771 ZPO if they result from a contract which provides for the grant of possession, for example, a leasing contract. Claims in unjust enrichment do not fall within that category. Since A's claim is only in unjust enrichment, it ranks behind C's claim.

The solution would differ if A was able to, and did, avoid the real agreement. This avoidance would render the agreement invalid from the beginning, in respect of B and third parties alike.[8] Thus, the transferor would never have lost ownership.[9] Third parties who acquire a real right in goods in between transfer and avoidance are protected only by the rules on *bona fide* acquisition (§§ 932–936 BGB).[10] Yet, since attachment in an execution or in insolvency proceedings is not an acquisition by way of a transaction, §§ 932–936 BGB do not apply. Therefore, A could vindicate the painting from B or C, as applicable, if he was entitled to, and did, avoid not only the contract of sale but also the real agreement. In general, an error or other fault concerning the contract of sale does not extend to the real agreement.[11] An exception, however, is made for

---

[4] Cf. Mayer-Maly, *Münchener Kommentar*/Mayer-Maly § 142 BGB n. 10; Larenz/Wolf, *Allgemeiner Teil des deutschen Bürgerlichen Rechts* § 23 n. 78.
[5] See further *infra*, German report, case 5(a).
[6] Cf. Jauernig, *Zwangsvollstreckungs- und Insolvenzrecht* 59.
[7] See further *infra*, German report, case 10(a).
[8] *Münchener Kommentar*/Mayer-Maly § 142 BGB n. 13; Palandt/Heinrichs § 142 BGB n. 2.
[9] Larenz, *Allgemeiner Teil des deutschen Bürgerlichen Rechts* 482.
[10] See further *infra*, German report, case 5(a).
[11] Palandt/Heinrichs Überblick vor § 104 BGB n. 23; *Münchener Kommentar*/Mayer-Maly § 142 BGB n. 10; see also Van Vliet, *Transfer of Movables* 35 f.

fraudulent misrepresentation which usually entitles the defrauded party to avoid the contract and the real agreement alike.[12]

AUSTRIA

A is entitled to demand that the painting be returned to him. If a sale is invalidated because of fraud (§ 874 ABGB), such an avoidance has effect *ex tunc*.[13] This means that the parties are treated as if the contract had never been made; B is treated as if he never became the owner of the painting. Ownership in such a case reverts with effect *ex tunc* to the seller. A can vindicate the painting and he has a claim against B based on unjust enrichment (§ 1431 ABGB). As the painting does not therefore form part of B's assets, his creditors are not entitled to execute against it.

An execution does not amount to *bona fide* acquisition, therefore B's creditors cannot, under this principle, acquire any rights in the painting.

GREECE

If the contract of sale only has been avoided (article 154 A.K.),[14] the real agreement remains valid because of the principle of abstraction. The transfer of ownership of movables is not invalidated by the absence of a legal cause. A has simply a claim against B to return his enrichment, that is to say the transferred painting (articles 903 A.K. ff.).[15] As a claim in unjust enrichment is an obligation *in personam*, A cannot resist the execution.

If both the contract of sale and the real agreement are avoided by court order, the effects of the juridical act are retroactive (article 184 A.K.). This means that the ownership transferred to B by the avoided real agreement will revert *ipso iure* to the transferor, A. In the case of movables, provision is made for the protection of a third party who, in

---

[12] Palandt/Heinrichs Überblick vor § 104 BGB n. 23; RG 24 Nov. 1908, RGZ 70, 55 at 57; BGH 22 Dec. 1965, DB 66, 818; OLG Hamm 2 July 1973, VersR 1975, 814; see also Van Vliet, *Transfer of Movables* 36; Zimmermann/Verse, in: Zimmermann/Whittaker 209 f.

[13] Koziol/Welser, *Grundriß des bürgerlichen Rechts I* 139; Schwimann/Apathy N 18/§ 870 ABGB; OGH SZ 32/14, SZ 61/26.

[14] The law requires a declaration of avoidance by the court. The requirement of a court judgment favours the security of transactions.

[15] Ef. Thr. 6/70 EEN 38, 834.

the meantime, has acquired ownership in good faith (article 1036 A.K.). Execution is not a transaction to which the rules on *bona fide* acquisition apply. A can, therefore, resist the execution and claim the goods in B's insolvency.

FRANCE

In order for A to avoid the sale, A must prove that his consent was obtained by fraud – this is referred to as a *dol*.[16] Fraudulent conduct must have been used by the contracting party in such a way that, without it, the counterparty would not have entered into the contract (C. civ, article 1116). The burden of proof lies on A. In the present case, as B was aware of the identity of the artist and induced A to believe it was worthless, it can be assumed that the requirement of fraudulent conduct is satisfied. Even if fraud is established, a party may not avoid the contract himself: a court order is always necessary.[17] The avoidance of the contract has retroactive effect *vis-à-vis* the transferor and also third parties. A can, therefore, once the contract of sale has been avoided, vindicate the painting from B on the basis of his right of ownership. The court could also order the payment of damages.

The case is complicated by the fact that C has started an execution procedure against B's property. In French law, execution procedures have been extensively modified by Law No 91-650 of 9 July 1991 (hereafter L.) and Decree No 92-755 of 31 July 1992 (hereafter D.). At present, a creditor wishing to execute against the tangible property of his debtor will use the procedure of *saisie-vente* (L. articles 50 ff., D. articles 81 ff.). In principle, pursuant to article 2102 C.civ, the debtor's entire estate can be the object of an execution by creditors. In order to execute, the creditor must obtain an execution title. An execution title is, generally, a final court decision, that is, a decision that cannot be appealed. It could also be (L. article 3) a notary deed bearing a writ of execution, a document issued by a bailiff to certify the non-payment of a cheque by a bank or certain categories of decisions having the same legal effect as a judgment. Once the creditor has obtained an execution title, execution can be effectuated simply by the use of a bailiff, who will seal the assets. After one month, the sale of the assets by auction is permitted

---

[16] The *fraude* under French law is a separate term that has different consequences so far as avoidance is concerned.
[17] See C. civ, article 1117. A court order would not be required if both parties agreed to avoid the contract, but this exception clearly is not relevant to this case.

(L. article 52). If the procedure is contested, the execution judge (*juge de l'exécution*, JEX) is competent.[18] The creditor may execute against only those assets which belong to the debtor (L. article 50). If assets belonging to third parties are executed against, the true owner may, while the execution procedure is ongoing, bring before the JEX a *rei vindicatio* action in respect of those assets (*action en distraction de biens saisis*). This action suspends the execution procedure (D. article 126). A case has upheld a *rei vindicatio* action by the purchaser of a lot of wood which had been sold by the debtor before the execution procedure started, but remained on his premises.[19] The plaintiff must specify all the elements on which his title to the asset is founded (D. article 128). If the asset has been sold, however, a *rei vindicatio* action is no longer possible (D. article 129). Indeed, article 2279 C.civ would assist the new buyer, unless he acted in bad faith (even if the asset had been stolen or lost, since the sale took place as an auction sale: article 2280 C.civ).[20] If the proceeds of the asset sold have not been distributed to creditors, however, the true owner of the asset could lay claim to them. If the proceeds have been distributed, his only remedy would be a *rei vindicatio* against the debtor himself, which is usually worthless, as the latter will almost always be bankrupt. In exceptional cases, the owner may have an action against the executing creditor, if the latter knew that the former was the true owner of the assets.

BELGIUM

The invalidity of the contract of sale results in a retransfer of property rights to the seller. Third parties who have acquired rights in the goods are protected, however, under article 2279 C.civ.[21] Hence, in case of a subsequent sale by the buyer, the purchaser will be protected.[22] The same protection is granted to a pledgee. However, in contrast to the

---

[18] The JEX has exclusive competence to hear disputes arising out of execution procedures. He is usually a judge from the *Tribunal de grande instance*, but may also be the President of the Commercial Court if requested prior to the filing of a claim that falls within this court's jurisdiction. In both cases, the competent judge is the judge of the court of the district in which the debtor lives or in which the asset is located.

[19] Civ. 14 Jan. 1959, D 1959, Som, 100.

[20] On articles 2279 and 2280, see French report, case 5(a).

[21] See Belgian report, case 1.

[22] De Page, *Traité élémentaire de droit civil belge* II 753, nr. 829, C; Waelbroeck, *Le transfert de la propriété dans la vente d'objets mobiliers corporels en droit comparé* 77, n. 71.

termination of the contract,[23] the principle of article 2279 C.civ. does not extend its protection to the creditors of the buyer if the contract is avoided on the grounds of fraud or mistake.

PORTUGAL

As stated above,[24] Portuguese law is based on the principle of causality, which means that any flaw in the contract of sale also affects the transfer of ownership. The consequence of this approach is that the invalidity of the sale can affect the position of third parties who acquire in good faith. Such parties are only protected when, in respect of things subject to registration, their acquisition was registered prior to the registration of the invalidity action (article 291° C.C.). In all other cases, if the court holds the contract of sale to be invalid, the law regards the position to be as if the transfer of ownership never occurred. A can therefore vindicate the painting, provided that, at the same time, he gives up the price received in respect of it (article 290° C.C.).[25]

The insolvency of B makes it more difficult to obtain a favourable court order. When A establishes his claim, he will be entitled to vindicate the painting. A's claim must, however, be made in the insolvency proceedings, at the same time as all other actions concerning the assets of the debtor (article 154° CPEREF), which may result in considerable delay (article 201° CPEREF).

SPAIN

If the parties are experts on the subject matter, the contract may not be avoided. If, however, the parties are not experts, then the contract may be avoided on the basis of a mistake related to the object (article 1266 CC). In such cases the price is the key element.[26] Contracts may be avoided when there is defect of form, from the retrospective avoidance of dealings with assets of the debtor's estate within the suspect period,[27] and from the lack of consent of the contracting parties (articles 1290–1301 CC). Any contract entered into under these circumstances can be

---

[23] See Belgian report, case 1.   [24] Portuguese report, case 1(a).
[25] See Mota Pinto, *Teoria Geral do Direito Civil* 616 ff.; Castro Mendes, *Teoria Geral do Direito Civil II*, 294 ff.; Ascensão, *Direito Civil. Teoria Geral II* 332 ff.; Carvalho Fernandes, *Teoria Geral do Direito Civil II*, 396 ff.
[26] See Morales Moreno, in: *Comentario del Código Civil II* 461.
[27] See Spanish report, case 1(a).

declared null and void by the judge, and once he gives such a ruling the seller can claim *rei vindicatio*.

Execution against the painting by C is valid (article 594.1 LEC). A may not challenge the sale of the painting if it has been acquired in good faith by a third party. However, once the judge has declared the contract of sale to be void, A can claim *rei vindicatio* against B's creditors (in this case, a third-party claim to ownership) (article 595 LEC). A, in order to vindicate, must submit some evidence of his claim in writing to the judge.

Before the sale is avoided, A may request that the judge grant a precautionary measure (articles 721 ff. LEC) in order to prevent third parties from acquiring the painting in good faith (for example, by ordering the chattel, formerly in the defendant's possession, to be deposited with a trustee or to be placed in judicial custody: article 727.3 LEC).

ITALY

Will A recover the painting from B? The answer to the question is probably yes, although it cannot be regarded as entirely free from doubt, especially if the action to recover the painting is contemplated after the commencement of insolvency proceedings.[28]

The effect of the sale is to transfer ownership of the picture to the buyer under the principle of article 1376 of the Civil Code.[29] The contract between A and B *can* be avoided, however, because it appears to be vitiated by fraud (*dolo*).[30] Indeed, the contract *must* be avoided if A intends to recover the picture from B. For this purpose, A will have to start an action in court, according to articles 1441 ff. c.c. According to article 1445 c.c., avoidance of the contract for fraud, mistake or coercion does not affect the rights acquired by third parties in good faith pursuant to a non-gratuitous transaction (article 1445 c.c.).[31] Hence, if B had sold the picture to Z – *ex hypothesi* a good faith purchaser under a genuine sale – Z's ownership of the picture would stand even if A's contract with B was avoided. The crucial issue, therefore, is whether

---

[28] Cf. Cass. 17 Jan. 1998, n. 376, Fallimento, 1999, 39; Dir. fall., II, 83 (contract terminated for facts antedating the opening of insolvency proceedings; action to recover the goods sold and delivered initiated after the opening of insolvency proceedings is rejected by the court).
[29] See Italian report, case 1.
[30] See on this point Graziadei, in: Zimmermann/Whittaker 224 ff.
[31] The contract vitiated by incapacity is subject to the opposite rule (article 1445 c.c.).

B's executing creditor, C, stands in the same position as that of a third party who acquired rights for value in good faith from B over movable assets transferred to him. In this case, A's claim to recover the painting would be defeated. There are, however, some reasons to think that the executing creditor cannot be regarded as a good faith purchaser of the painting. Hence, A should be able to recover the painting, though, as I have anticipated, opinions on the point may not be unanimous.

To argue in favour of A's claim, one need only mention that article 1445 c.c. is usually considered to be an exceptional provision. The exception is to the principle that the avoidance of the contract has retroactive effect inasmuch as it aims to restore the parties to the same positions as they held before entering into the contract. Under Italian law, the retroactive effect of avoidance is not written large in the Code. It is rather taken for granted by the Code and illustrated by commentators and court decisions.[32] Under Italian rules on transfer of property, judicial avoidance of the contract results in title to the picture automatically revesting in the seller because the passing of title to the buyer is undone the moment the contract is avoided. This interpretation of the Code explains why the provision of article 1445 c.c. is exceptional: it derogates in favour of an innocent third party.[33] But there are no reasons to stretch this exceptional rule to cover the case of an executing creditor. Hence, A will recover the picture by proposing an action in court pursuant to article 619 c.p.c. This provision governs opposition to execution by third parties (*opposizione del terzo assoggettato all'esecuzione*). According to the letter of this article, only a third party who claims to be an owner, or to have another real right to the assets against which the executing creditor is proceeding, can oppose execution. The interpretation of article 619 c.p.c., however, extends the rules to claims for avoidance of the contract in cases like the one under consideration as well as to other claims.[34] To recover the picture from the defendant, the claim to avoid the contract must be joined with a claim for delivery of the picture. This will usually be a personal claim, but it can also be a *rei vindicatio*.

---

[32] Sacco/De Nova, in: *Trattato di diritto civile* 544–545; Bianca, *Il contratto* 634–675.
[33] Mengoni, *Gli acquisti 'a non domino'* 33, n. 45; Tatarano, 'Retroattività', in: Enc. dir., XL, 90 (the principle which is derogated is *resoluto jure dantis resolvitur et jure accipientis*). For the opposite opinion: Roppo, *Il contratto* 873–875.
[34] Mandrioli, *Corso di diritto processuale civile III*, 162, n. 12; Punzi, *La tutela del terzo nel processo esecutivo* 197 (the point is not disputed). Cf. Cass. 4 Nov. 1982, n. 5789.

The above remarks must be read in the light of an important caveat. The answer to our case rests more on first principles than on clear authority. In Italy, those principles could be questioned by assuming that executing creditors should be put on the same footing as good faith purchasers for value. If such an argument were to prevail, case 2 would generate an opposite answer. There is presently little chance of making an accurate prediction about the actual outcome of our hypothetical case.

THE NETHERLANDS

According to article 3:44 para. 1 BW, a contract can be avoided on the ground that it was entered into as a result of 'fraud'.[35] The avoidance of a contract has retroactive effect; the contract is regarded as if it never existed.[36] Consequently, when the contract constituted the *causa traditionis* of a transfer of ownership, the retroactive nature of annulment results in the transfer losing its validity. In other words, ownership of the painting is deemed never to have been transferred, even though the painting was paid for and delivered.

In the present case therefore, A may exercise the right of *rei vindicatio* and claim back his or her painting free of any rights of B or of B's creditors, since the latter may execute only against B's property. Third parties who acquire property in good faith are protected under Dutch law.[37] However, execution against property is not regarded as an acquisition in this sense, hence the protection does not extend to B's creditors.

ENGLAND

In a normal case involving the sale of art, the buyer is not bound to disclose to the seller his belief or knowledge that the painting is more valuable than the seller thinks or should be attributed to a painter other than the one believed by the seller to be its creator. In this case, there has been a misrepresentation inducing the seller to enter into the contract, the effect of which, even in the absence of fraud, is to permit the seller to have the contract avoided (*rescinded*).[38] Fraud, too, gives

---

[35] Aside from fraud, misrepresentation and mistake are also grounds for the avoidance of the contract: article 6:228 BW.
[36] Article 3:53 BW.   [37] Article 3:86 BW: see *infra*, Dutch report, case 5.
[38] A statutory right to damages exists in the case of negligent misrepresentations, namely, those where the maker of a misrepresentation is unable to rebut the presumption of fault: Misrepresentation Act 1967, s. 2(1).

rise to a right of avoidance (*rescission*), though the incidents of *rescission* may be slightly different in this case. A misrepresentation for present purposes is a false statement of material fact that at least in part induces entry into the contract. Even a statement of opinion may be regarded as a statement of fact if it rests upon an implied factual substratum that the maker of the statement has knowledge that supports the opinion.[39] A misrepresentation need not be verbal to give rise to relief: it can take the form of conduct leading up to the sale.[40]

Rescission means that the parties are returned to their precontractual position. The effect of *rescission*, therefore, is that ownership will revest in the seller if it has already passed to the buyer. This will be so even if possession of the subject matter of the contract has been acquired by the buyer. In the meantime, the buyer is said to have a voidable title so that any disposition for value to a *bona fide* purchaser acquiring from the buyer a legal[41] real interest in the painting will pass to that purchaser a real interest that overrides the seller's *equity of rescission*. Apart from this case, the seller's right persists even as against the buyer's insolvency administrator,[42] including a *trustee-in-bankruptcy* in whom the buyer's assets vest.[43] The reason is that the insolvency administrator is considered to stand in the shoes of the insolvent[44] and to have his conscience burdened in the same way as the insolvent.[45] That insolvency administrator cannot claim to be treated as though he were a *bona fide* purchaser.

In the case of goods, once a judgment has been handed down in favour of the claimant it may be enforced by means of a writ of *fieri facias*. The writ is delivered to the bailiff (*sheriff*) and at that point it binds the goods.[46] The *sheriff* does not yet acquire a real right in the goods but has the right to execute against (*seize*) the goods so long as they can be found in his administrative district. The *sheriff* does acquire a real interest at the time of *seizure* but, just as that interest is liable to be overridden by a secured creditor whose enterprise charge (*floating charge*) becomes fixed while the goods remain in the hands of the *sheriff*,[47] so it should also be

---

[39] *Smith v Land and House Property Corp'n* [1884] 28 Ch D 7.
[40] *Spice Girls Ltd v Aprilia World Service BV* (unreported, 24 Feb. 2000).
[41] As opposed to equitable.   [42] *Re Eastgate* [1905] 1 KB 465.   [43] See *supra*, case 1.
[44] *Madell v Thomas* [1891] 2 QB 230, 238; *McEntire v Crossley Brothers* [1895] AC 457, 461.
[45] Relief against misrepresentation originated in equity, the principle being that even the wholly innocent maker of a misrepresentation was not entitled to retain the benefit of a contract once on notice that the misrepresentation had deceived the person to whom it was made: *Redgrave v Hurd* [1881] 20 Ch D 1.
[46] Supreme Court Act 1981, s. 138(1).
[47] *Re Opera Ltd* [1891] 3 Ch 360; *Taunton v Sheriff of Warwickshire* [1895] 2 Ch 319.

overridden by the revesting on *rescission* of the buyer's real interest in the seller. Again, just as the executing creditor, acting through the *sheriff*, must complete the execution before a secured creditor's *floating charge* becomes a fixed charge on crystallisation, so too should that execution creditor be defeated by the seller if the property in the painting revests in the seller before completion of the execution. The reason is that the *sheriff* takes subject to existing equities.[48] Execution is completed in the case of insolvency when the goods are *seized* and sold and the proceeds remitted to the judgment creditor.[49] In non-insolvency cases, where the law is unclear, it may be that execution is completed when the goods are *seized* and sold.[50] Certainly, if the painting remained in the hands of the *sheriff*, a seller *rescinding* the contract would be entitled to demand its return.

IRELAND

There is no right in Irish law to avoid a contract on grounds of fraud, etc., and so revest title in the seller once third parties have acquired rights against the property which forms the subject matter of the contract. Therefore, in this case A cannot claim the painting free of any rights of B, or of B's creditor. A merely has a contractual claim against B.

SCOTLAND

A can claim the painting back, free of the rights of B or of B's creditor. Although ownership of the painting will by now have vested in B, and although in general a termination/avoidance of a sale contract has only personal effect, not real effect, the present circumstances constitute an exception to the general rule. If a transfer (by A) is induced by the fraud of the transferee (B), A can avoid the contract, and the avoidance will be effective against B's creditors (though not against a person who buys

---

[48] *Re Standard Manufacturing Co.* [1891] 1 Ch 627, 641.
[49] Insolvency Act 1986, s. 183(3)(a); *Bluston & Bramley Ltd v Leigh* [1950] 2 KB 548. Where the judgment debt is for more than £500, the *sheriff* must retain the proceeds of sale for fourteen days and, in the case of a corporate *winding-up* within that period, must pay the proceeds to the company *liquidator*: Insolvency Act 1986, s. 183(3).
[50] In the case of receivership and secured creditors, the point was left open by Lindley LJ in *Taunton v Sheriff of Warwickshire* [1895] 2 Ch 319, 322, and in *Re Opera Ltd* [1891] 3 Ch 360.

from B in good faith[51]). The effect is much as if B were not the owner, or as if the avoidance of the contract transferred ownership back to A. But actually this is not the accepted analysis. B is the owner, and the avoidance of the contract does not, of itself, transfer ownership back to A. But the rule is that an asset acquired by fraud is not available to the creditors of the fraudster, even though he is the owner.

Scots law requires delivery to transfer ownership of movables, except where the Sale of Goods Act 1979 applies. Thus if ownership has passed to a buyer, ownership cannot pass back from the buyer to the seller without delivery, because that transfer is not a sale.[52] Perhaps a judicial 'reduction' of the transfer could also have real effect, but that is unclear. If it did have real effect, it would be *ex nunc* and not *ex tunc*.[53]

SOUTH AFRICA

In order to reclaim the painting, A must have not only the contract of sale declared void, but also the real agreement for the transfer of ownership. This is because South African law follows the abstract (as opposed to a causal) system for the passing of ownership.[54] Circumstances which render the contract of sale which forms the basis of the transfer of ownership void do not normally affect the validity of the (real) agreement to transfer ownership. However, in the case of fraudulent misrepresentation, South African case law has, on the basis of Roman–Dutch law, accepted that fraud does not only affect the contractual (obligatory) agreement, which gives rise to the transfer, but also the real agreement to transfer ownership.[55] If this particular case can be construed as a case of fraudulent misrepresentation, the real agreement would be declared void. Consequently, ownership of the painting would not have passed to B and A would be entitled to revindicate the painting. A further consequence would be that C, even though entitled to execute against B's property, would not be entitled to execute against the painting, since ownership therein never passed to B. If the misrepresentation is not considered serious enough to affect the real agreement, ownership would have passed to B and C would have been entitled to include the painting

---

[51] Even if the third party has purchased after the *rescission*. *Rescission* of a contract cannot, in most cases at least, have real effect.
[52] This is the general opinion, but there exists no reported decision which clearly so holds.
[53] Scots law probably does not accept the principle set forth in s. 142 of the BGB.
[54] See van der Merwe, *Sakereg* 305–314.   [55] *Ibid.*, 311–314.

in the execution. In such a case, A would only have an unsecured claim (a *concurrent claim*) based on unjustified enrichment against B's insolvency estate.

DENMARK

According to Danish law, B's creditors normally enjoy no better position than B. There are some exceptions to this principle, but, if B is in possession of movables and this possession is based on an agreement which is invalid, A will be able to reclaim ownership of the asset not only against B but also against the creditors of B.[56] In the present case, where B has used fraud against A, A can reclaim the painting free of any rights of B and B's creditors.

SWEDEN

A transfer may be declared void according to, for instance, the rules on fraud in section 30 of the Contracts Act (*lagen om avtal*, 1915). These rules seem to be applicable to case 2, in which case the transferor becomes entitled to have the property separated from the assets of the bankrupt available to insolvency creditors or to the execution creditors of the transferee (a *ius separationis*). The transferor will thus be entitled to the return of the painting free of any rights of the transferee or his creditors.[57]

The *ius separationis* may arise even if the invalidity of the transfer is caused in part by events which occurred after the conclusion of the contract, as exceptionally may be the case when the transferor's presumptions are frustrated.[58]

When the contract thus is voidable also in relation to the buyer's creditors, the transferor has a right of separation even if he had permitted the buyer to dispose of the goods prior to payment (cf. cases 4–8).[59]

If the invalidity gives the transferor a right of separation in the transferee's insolvency, the transferor may also vindicate the goods from a third party who has bought the goods from the transferee, unless the third party has taken possession of the goods (chattels) in good faith.

---

[56] Cf. Elmer/Skovby, *Ejendomsretten* I 157 ff. and Ørgaard, *Sikkerhed i løsøre* 71.
[57] NJA 1995, 162.
[58] NJA 1985, 178, where the seller delivered raw materials in the false belief, supported by the buyer, that the government would support a shipyard.
[59] NJA 1985, 178.

This applies irrespective of whether the third party bought the goods directly from the transferee, from his insolvency administrator or at an execution auction (section 2 of Good Faith Purchase Act 1986 and chapter 14 section 1 of the Code of Execution).[60]

There may exist cases of invalidity, however, where the invalidity has effect only against a transferee and not against the latter's creditors or third parties (in some cases, provided that the third party did not have actual knowledge of the invalidity[61]). These cases are grounded in arguments of legal policy, without using the concept of the real agreement, but with the same effect.

FINLAND

The seller, A, can claim the painting, if the contract of sale is avoidable, for instance, on grounds of fraud. Neither execution nor insolvency affect the transferor's right to avoid the contract.

Comparative observations

Abstract and causal systems

Case 2 illustrates the difference between abstract and causal systems of the transfer of ownership. German, Greek, Scots and South African law not only require a separate real agreement for the transfer of ownership, but they also regard the real agreement as valid independent of the validity of the underlying obligation (principle of abstraction). All other jurisdictions[62] consider the passing of ownership as necessarily bound up with the validity of the obligation. This is so irrespective of whether delivery, or the conclusion of a real agreement, is required in addition to the conclusion of the contract.[63]

In an abstract system, avoidance of the underlying contract of sale, even if it has retroactive effect, does not suffice to revest ownership in the seller. This is so only in limited circumstances, in Germany, Greece and South Africa, *viz.* where the real agreement suffers from the same

---

[60] In the near future, most probably, *bona fide* acquisition by a transferee will be excluded if the transferor obtained the goods by coercion (or theft): SOU 2000:56.
[61] NJA 1997, 418 concerning impermissible dividends from a share company.
[62] Swedish law, again, does not fit into such general categories. It is possible that invalidity will have effect only between the parties, although such cases are rare, without using the concept of a real agreement.
[63] As to that question, see *supra*, case 1(a).

fault as the contract and where it also is avoided. Fraud constitutes one such exception. In Scotland, the principle of abstraction seems to be followed even more strictly than in the other three abstract systems. As the Scottish report identifies, even in the case of fraud, ownership is not regarded as being revested in the seller. Instead, the same solution is reached by the rule that an asset acquired by fraud is not available to the fraudulent party, nor to his creditors.

In the causal systems (Austria, France, Belgium, Portugal, Spain, the Netherlands, England,[64] Ireland, Denmark, Sweden, Finland) avoidance of the contract is sufficient to revest ownership in the seller.[65] This result does not depend on whether the transfer of ownership also requires a separate real agreement. Austrian law, for example, requires a real agreement, at least according to its predominant legal literature, but nevertheless avoidance of the contract automatically reverts ownership to the seller.

If the facts did not involve fraudulent misrepresentation but, for instance, a mere error, the causal systems would still conclude that ownership is revested in the seller upon avoidance of the contract whereas in the abstract systems the seller would only have a claim in unjust enrichment.

It is interesting to note the difference between avoidance and termination (which was discussed *supra*, case 1(b)). Termination on the ground of a breach of contract, although it is also held to put an end to the contract *ex tunc*, does not revest ownership in the seller according to English law and the tradition systems (Austria, Spain and the Netherlands).

Protection of third parties

All jurisdictions except Ireland draw a distinction between a *bona fide* purchaser and third-party creditors. Had the painting been sold to a third party before the avoidance of the sale, the second buyer would have been protected under the rules on *bona fide* acquisition, provided that their requirements were met. Third-party creditors, however, do not enjoy the same protection. As some reporters point out, execution is not seen as an acquisition of a real right to which the rules on *bona fide* acquisition could be applied.

---

[64] See Van Vliet, *Transfer of Movables* 111 ff.
[65] For Spain see von Gerlach, *Der Einfluß des deutschen und französischen Rechts auf den Eigentumserwerbsschutz beweglicher Sachen im spanischen Recht* 122 f.

In this respect Irish law seems to form an exception. However, it does not apply the rules on *bona fide* purchase but states that avoidance cannot have the effect of revesting ownership to A once a third party, including an executing creditor, has acquired a right in the goods. It is surprising to see that the solution which favours the buyer's creditors, which one might have expected from an abstract system, is, on the facts of the case, adopted only in a jurisdiction which is both consensual and causal, thus requiring nothing more than a valid contract to effectuate the passing of ownership.

The solution would again be different in the abstract systems if the case had not involved fraud but, for example, a mere error on the part of A. In that case A would merely have a personal claim against B for the retransfer of ownership. Such a claim would not enable A to resist the execution. On slightly different facts the principle of abstraction would therefore come to the aid of B's creditors.

Case 3: Machinery supplied to be used by the buyer

(Simple retention of title)

A sells a machine to B. The contract contains the following clause: 'Title to the machine is reserved until the seller has received full payment.' Before the price has been paid, C, who is an unsecured creditor of B, executes against the machine. In the alternative, B goes bankrupt. In either case, the machine is on B's premises.

Questions

(a) What is A's legal position?
(b) Is the clause stated above sufficient to be effective? Is there a more suitable or common wording?
(c) Do the parties have to agree on the insertion of a retention of title clause? Or could the seller stipulate one unilaterally?
(d) Is the point in time at which the parties agree that title should be reserved relevant?
(e) Do A's rights in respect of the machine depend on anything other than the inclusion of a reservation of title clause in the agreement: for example, compliance with certain formalities (e.g. agreement in writing, agreement having a 'certain date') or registration? Are such clauses efficacious if they are simply contained in the seller's general conditions of sale?

Discussions

GERMANY

(a) The reservation of title clause subjects the real agreement[1] to a suspensive condition, usually one of full payment of the purchase price

---

[1] See *supra*, German report, case 1(a).

(unless the parties have agreed on a different meaning) (§ 449 BGB). If the parties agree on a reservation of title within the meaning of § 449 BGB, the seller remains the owner of the goods, for as long as the purchase price remains unpaid. Upon fulfilment of the condition of full payment, ownership will automatically pass to the buyer, who is already in possession of the goods. It will be noted that the separation of the contract of sale from the transfer of ownership[2] simplifies the legal operation of retention of title, since this principle means it is possible to subject only the real agreement to the suspensive condition. The contract of sale is affected only in so far as the seller is not obliged to pass full title at the time of delivery.

Because the contract between A and B contains a retention of title clause, A remains the owner of the machine and is thus entitled to vindicate it (§ 985 BGB). If another creditor, C, executes against the machine, A may resist the execution (§ 771 ZPO[3]). The court will order the execution to be stopped and set aside (§§ 775 n. 2, 776 ZPO), in order to enable A to recover his property.

In the event of B's insolvency, the machine does not form part of the insolvency estate and may be vindicated (§ 47 InsO), provided that B's right to possess the machine has been determined. If A has not terminated the contract before the commencement of insolvency proceedings, it is for the administrator to decide whether or not to continue the contract (§§ 103, 107 s. 2 InsO). If he opts for continuation, the outstanding obligations under the contract will enjoy priority in the insolvency estate (§ 55 s. 1 n. 2 InsO). The administrator must ensure that they are satisfied out of the estate, otherwise he will incur personal liability (§ 61 InsO). If the administrator opts for termination, B's right to possess the machine ends and A may take possession of it.

Early in the debate on the reform of German insolvency law which led to the new Insolvency Code,[4] it was suggested that simple title retention should be treated like security ownership,[5] thereby giving the seller a right only to preferential payment out of the sale or other realisation of the goods.[6] In the end, however, this proposal was not adopted. Some argued that it would have amounted to an unconstitutional restriction

---

[2] See *supra*, German report, case 1(a).   [3] See also *supra*, German report, case 2.
[4] See *supra*, German report, case 1(a).
[5] Cf. Bundesministerium der Justiz, *Erster Bericht der Kommission für Insolvenzrecht* proposition n. 1.1.4.(1) lit (b) and the explanatory notes thereto (93 ff.); Marotzke, in: *Insolvenzrecht im Umbruch* 183 (187).
[6] See *infra*, German report, case 7(d).

of owners' rights.⁷ Others took the view that retained property, having never belonged to the insolvent buyer, can and should be treated differently from property that originally belonged to the debtor and was transferred by way of a security agreement.⁸ In any case, the debate is closed for the time being.⁹ The new Code has improved the insolvency administrator's rights in respect of retention of title only in so far as he can now postpone the decision, to terminate or continue the contract, until the creditors' meeting has decided on the realisation of the insolvency estate generally (§ 107 s. 2 InsO).¹⁰ This was intended to put an end to the widespread practice of withdrawing goods subject to title retention at the very moment that insolvency was declared.¹¹ However, the question of whether the administrator has the right to use the goods during this time is still open.¹²

(b) The clause in the present case is effective. It is commonly used in circumstances, such as the present, where the buyer does not intend to resell, mix or alter the movables. Simply by bringing the machine on to his premises, and possibly fixing it to them, B does not acquire ownership of it. § 946 BGB limits the acquisition of ownership by accession to those situations where the movable becomes an *essential* part of the immovable. Usually machines do not form an essential part of the premises of a business.¹³ If however the machine did form an essential part of the premises, then the contracting parties would not be able to derogate from § 946 BGB,¹⁴ nor could the seller acquire security ownership of the machine.¹⁵

(c) One has to distinguish between the contractual and the property law aspects of the transaction. Obviously, in order for retention of title to form part of the contract, the parties must agree on such a clause. If, for

---

[7] See namely Serick, *Eigentumsvorbehalt und Sicherungsübertragung* VI § 82 IV 5.
[8] See e.g. Bülow, *Recht der Kreditsicherheiten*, 4th edn, 1997, n. 729; *contra*: Häsemeyer, *Insolvenzrecht* n. 11.10.
[9] Marotzke, ZZP 109 (1996) 429 (430).
[10] The so-called *Berichtstermin* (report meeting), § 156 InsO, which must be held in the period six weeks to three months after the commencement of insolvency proceedings: see § 29 (1) n. 1 InsO.
[11] Gottwald/Adolphsen, in: *Kölner Schrift zur Insolvenzordnung* n. 111 ff.; Marotzke, JZ 1995, 803 (812 f.).
[12] See Wellensiek, BB 2000, 1 (4) with further references.
[13] Cf. *Palandt*/Heinrichs § 93 BGB n. 7.   [14] *Palandt*/Bassenge § 946 BGB n. 1.
[15] According to § 93 BGB, essential parts of another thing cannot be the object of separate real rights.

example, the retention of title clause is contained in the seller's general conditions, which the buyer fails to accept, the retention will not form part of the agreement. However, even if retention of title is not incorporated into the contract of sale, the seller may still declare subsequently that he is only willing to agree to the passing of ownership (that is, the real agreement) on the suspensive condition of full payment. Buyers are well advised not to oppose this declaration, because otherwise they will not receive even the so-called *Anwartschaftsrecht*.[16] In this sense, retention of title can in fact be provided for by the seller alone. There is a doctrinal dispute as to whether such unilateral conduct amounts to a breach of the contract of sale. The better view is that it does not amount to a breach.[17] If the contract of sale does not contain any special provisions, a party is obliged only to perform its obligations thereunder simultaneously with performance by the other party. Thus, a seller is only obliged to deliver the object of the sale, and agree to the passing of ownership, when he receives payment. A buyer who fails to pay immediately still receives more than that to which he is entitled if the seller nevertheless agrees to transfer ownership to him on the condition of full payment.

(d) Retention of title can be agreed upon or be declared unilaterally, as described in part (b) *supra*, at any time prior to delivery. If ownership has already passed to the buyer unconditionally, there remain several possible ways of creating security rights in the goods through mutual agreement. First,[18] ownership can be retransferred to the seller by a further real agreement (agreement that ownership should pass) and by an agreement that the buyer will possess the goods on behalf of the seller (*constitutum possessorium*, § 868 BGB),[19] rendering physical redelivery of

---

[16] The *Anwartschaftsrecht* (the term may be translated as expectancy) is a real right of a buyer under a retention of title agreement, subsisting during the period when the suspensive condition has not yet been fulfilled. It refers to the buyer's increasing legal interest in the goods, which, as it were, slowly pass into his ownership as he pays the instalments of the purchase price. The *Anwartschaftsrecht* has been invented by the courts and legal scholars to enable the buyer under retention of title (or his creditors) to make use of his emerging property right even before it has grown into full ownership: see generally Baur/Stürner, *Sachenrecht* § 59 nn. 32 ff. See also *infra*, case 11(a).

[17] Cf. Schurig, IPRax 1994, 27 (31); Flume, *Allgemeiner Teil des Bürgerlichen Rechts II* 675; Lieb, in: *Festschrift Baumgärtel* 311–324; *contra*: Soergel/Mühl § 929 BGB n. 52 and § 455 BGB n. 17.

[18] This is the solution favoured by the courts: see BGH 2 Oct. 1952, NJW 1953, 217.

[19] As to the *constitutum possessorium* as a substitute for delivery, see Van Vliet, *Transfer of Movables* 53 f.

the goods unnecessary (§ 930 BGB). Afterwards, the parties can agree on a conditional transfer of ownership to the buyer. Again, no actual delivery will be necessary since the buyer will already be in direct possession (§ 929 sent. 2 BGB).[20] There is considerable doctrinal support for a second method:[21] the buyer is said to be able to retransfer to the seller full ownership less that which belongs to the buyer under a conditional transfer of ownership (*Anwartschaftsrecht*[22]). The BGH, however, does not consider such a transaction possible.[23] Thirdly, the buyer can transfer security ownership to the seller.[24] In that case, however, the rights of the seller in the buyer's insolvency would only be those of a security owner.[25] In sum, because of the liberal attitude of German law towards non-possessory security interests in general, the delivery of the goods does not preclude the parties from subsequently creating a security right in the goods in favour of the seller.

(e) There is no need to register either a retention of title agreement nor the fact that the purchase price is unpaid. There are no formal requirements for such a clause. Even an oral agreement would be valid. It is sufficient that the clause was stipulated in the general conditions of either party.[26]

AUSTRIA

(a) Retention of title (reservation of property) means that the parties have agreed that ownership of the delivered goods will be transferred from seller to buyer only upon full payment of the purchase price.[27] In such a case, the real agreement is concluded subject to the suspensive condition that the price is paid in full.[28] Usually the parties agree that the buyer shall be entitled to process[29] or resell the goods. Without such

---

[20] The so-called *traditio brevi manu*: see further Van Vliet, *Transfer of Movables* 52.
[21] See Raiser, note BGH 2 Oct. 1952, NJW 1953, 217; Honsell, JuS 1981, 705; Brox, JuS 1984, 657 (658); Bülow, *Recht der Kreditsicherheiten* n. 647.
[22] See *supra*, German report, case 3(b).   [23] BGH 2 Oct. 1952, NJW 1953, 217.
[24] For details see *infra*, German report, case 10(a).
[25] See *infra*, German report, cases 7(d) and 10(a).
[26] As to the necessity of consent see *supra*, German report, case 3(b).
[27] The first decision of the OGH to accept the validity of a retention of title clause was 23 May 1916, JB 246.
[28] Such an agreement can be made only prior to the handing over of the goods to the buyer: cf. OGH 5 Sep. 1963, HS 4323; Klang/Klang II 308 f. This view is criticised by Frotz, *Aktuelle Probleme des Kreditsicherungsrechts* 136 ff.
[29] See *infra*, case 7 for the effects of processing of the goods.

a provision the buyer does not have the right to do so, as he must respect the seller's ownership.

If the buyer fails to pay the price for the objects sold under retention of title, the seller has two options. First, he may terminate the contract in accordance with § 918 ABGB. If he wishes so to do, he must grant the buyer a period of grace (cf. § 918 ABGB) declaring that the contract will be terminated unless the debtor fulfils his obligation within a specified period. If the contract is terminated, the buyer must hand back the property in question to the seller. The parties to a contract of sale providing for retention of title usually agree that the seller has the right to demand that the goods sold are handed over to him if the buyer defaults without having to terminate the contract. In such a case, the seller can demand the return of the goods without terminating the contract. The contract remains valid and the buyer will receive the goods only if he makes full payment.[30]

The second option open to the seller is to enforce his claim arising from the contract of sale. In order to do this, he must first bring an action in court against the debtor. After he has obtained a judgment in his favour, he can execute against the goods of this debtor, in particular the goods sold under reservation of title. Other creditors of the buyer are prevented from executing against these goods, therefore the seller will rank, in respect of these goods, above the other creditors of the buyer.

As the seller remains, until full payment of the purchase price, the owner of the goods sold, no other creditor of the buyer can execute against these goods. If another creditor attempts to execute against the goods, the seller can resist the execution.[31] The court would then declare the execution invalid.

The commencement of insolvency proceedings does not, of itself, terminate the contract. If the administrator fails, however, to pay the purchase price, the seller may terminate the contract because of the administrator's default.

§ 21 (1) KO gives the administrator the right to cancel the contract of sale. According to § 21 (1) KO, the administrator has the right to cancel contracts provided that both parties had not discharged their obligations when insolvency proceedings were commenced. In the present case both

---

[30] It is possible that the contract may give the seller the right to sell the goods he has taken from the buyer. Such a clause is valid provided that the buyer is credited at least with the market value of the goods, i.e. his debt is reduced by this amount.

[31] Cf. § 37 EO.

parties have not yet discharged their obligations, as the buyer still has to pay the price and the seller still has to transfer ownership of the goods. The administrator has, therefore, the right to cancel the contract.[32] If the administrator cancels the contract, he must hand over the goods to the seller. The seller must return any payments he has received from the buyer. The seller has, therefore, the 'right of separation': an entitlement to have the goods sold under reservation of title separated from the assets of the buyer generally (*Aussonderungsrecht*).[33]

(b) The wording of the clause is sufficient.

(c) The parties have to agree to the insertion of a retention of title clause. If they fail to agree on such a clause, § 1063 ABGB applies. According to this provision, if the seller credits the purchase price, ownership of the sold goods is transferred when the goods are handed over to the buyer.

(d) The point in time at which the parties agree on the clause is relevant. The retention of title clause must be agreed upon before the goods are handed over to the buyer.[34] This can, however, occur after the conclusion of the contract.

(e) A's rights to the machine do not depend on anything other than the reservation of title clause. There are no formalities. There is no publicity requirement for retention of title, provided that the goods sold secure only the claim arising from the contract of sale. It is not necessary to register the reservation of title agreement, nor is it necessary to affix signs to the goods to inform other creditors that they have been sold under retention of title. Retention of title is the only type of security interest in Austrian law to which the publicity requirement does not apply. Furthermore, it is the only non-possessory type of security interest. This makes it the most popular security instrument in Austrian law. In all other cases, the publicity requirement applies; its purpose is to inform other creditors that the goods are used as security. It has been argued[35] that, in the case of retention of title, there is no need for the protection of the debtor's creditors because the property in question is

---

[32] Cf. *Schwimann*/Binder N 111/§ 1063 ABGB.   [33] Cf. § 11 KO.
[34] OGH 5 Sep. 1963, HS 4323; *Klang*/Klang II 308 f.; *Rummel*/Spielbüchler I §§ 357–360 n. 5. This view has been criticised by Frotz, *Aktuelle Probleme des Kreditsicherungsrechts* 136 ff.
[35] Cf. Koziol/Welser, *Grundriß des bürgerlichen Rechts I* 368; Bydlinski, in *Klang*/Bydlinski IV/2 459 ff.

not property that is taken away from the assets of the debtor but, on the contrary, is property that is added to his assets. The assets of the debtor are not, therefore, diminished.

An exception to the general rule that it is not necessary to register reservation of title agreements, or the fact that the price is unpaid, is made in respect of machines (cf. § 297a ABGB). It is advisable to register reservation of title to a machine on the land register. If such an entry is not made, there is a danger that a charge granted by the buyer over the immovable property on which the machine is located will include the machine. This can be the case if the creditor to whom the charge is granted *bona fide* believes that the machine belongs to the owner of the immovable property.

It is sufficient that the clause is contained in the seller's general conditions of sale, provided they became part of the agreement.

GREECE

(a) If a retention of title clause is included in the contract, the vendor will remain owner of the thing sold, even after delivery, until the purchaser pays the price in full.[36] The condition may be a suspensive or a resolutive one. According to the interpretative rule of article 532 A.K., if the nature of the condition is in doubt, the transfer of ownership will be regarded as having been agreed on the *suspensive* condition of the payment of the purchase price.

In the event of the default of the purchaser, A is entitled to terminate the contract and exercise his rights of ownership (article 532 A.K.). If another creditor of B executes against the machine, A, as owner, is entitled to resist the execution (article 936 KPolD).[37] In the event of B's insolvency, the rights of the vendor are disputed. Greek courts,[38] having changed their previous position, take the view that the vendor can vindicate the thing sold under retention of title, if (1) the purchaser was in

---

[36] For retention of title clauses see in general Gazis, ErmAK 532; Georgiadis, NoV 22, 87 and 31, 517; Georgiadis, *Empragmato Dikaio II* 212 ff.; see also Bosdas, EEN 46, 5.
[37] Brinias, *Anagastiki ektelesis* § 178, 499 and § 679, 2313; Georgiadis, *Empragmato Dikaio II* 219.
[38] AP 1027/74 (all the members) EEmbD 1775, 144 and NoV 23, 612. Before 1987 *Areios Pagos*, the Greek supreme civil court, favoured the view that the contract must be terminated before insolvency had been pronounced by the court. AP 22/87 (all the members) NoV 36, 87 and EEmbD 1988, 334; AP 1581/88 EEmbD 1989, 641; AP 1039/91 EEmbD 1993, 631.

default in respect of his obligations of payment arising under the contract and (2) the vendor exercised the right of termination either before or after the commencement of insolvency proceedings.

Different views have been supported by legal scholars.[39] According to the prevailing view,[40] if B was in default of payment before insolvency proceedings were commenced A can terminate the contract and vindicate the machine. The contrary view holds that the insolvency administrator is entitled to pay the price due. If he does not, A can terminate the contract and vindicate the thing sold.[41]

(b) The above-stated clause is sufficient.

(c) The parties must agree on the insertion of the clause. If the seller unilaterally declares his intention to insert a retention of title clause in the contract and the other party does not agree, there is no meeting of minds (consensus) of the contracting parties and thus the contract is not concluded.

(d) A retention of title clause should be agreed, at the latest, on the conclusion of the real agreement. After the conclusion of the real agreement, a purported agreement between the parties for retention of title would have the effect of granting security ownership to the seller[42] under a *constitutum possessorium* (articles 532, 977 A.K.). In any event, retention of title should be agreed before execution or insolvency.

(e) No formality requirements are imposed. Public registers record only transfers of, and other acts which involve a change in real rights to, immovable property. According however to article 10 of the recently introduced L. 2844/2000 on 'Contracts concerning movables or claims subject to publicity and other contracts providing security' ('Symvaseis epi kiniton i apaitiseon ypokeimenes se dimosiotita kai alles symvaseis parochis asphaleias'),[43] it is possible to register a contract of sale and

---

[39] See in general Kotsiris, *Ptocheutiko Dikaio* 333 ff.
[40] Georgiadis, *Empragmato Dikaio II* 220; Kotsiris, *Ptocheutiko Dikaio* 337–338; Pamboukis, Arm 27, 874. See also Deliyiannis/Kornilakis, *Eidiko Enochiko Dikaio* I 279–280; Georgakopoulos, *Egchiridio Emborikou Dikaiou Geniko Meros tomos* I/3 155.
[41] Prevailing view, Kotsiris, *Ptocheutiko Dikaio* 336; Georgiadis, *Empragmato Dikaio II* 220–221; Pamboukis, Arm 27, 874; Deliyiannis/Kornilakis, *Eidiko Enochiko Dikaio* 280.
[42] As to security ownership see further *infra*, Greek report, case 10.
[43] See *supra*, Greek report, case 1(a).

a transfer of ownership under a retention of title clause on a public register. If the retention of title agreement is registered, third parties will be able to acquire title to the goods only exceptionally[44] by way of a *bona fide* acquisition.

Such a clause will be valid, notwithstanding that it is merely contained in the general conditions of sale, unless the particular term is judged to be contrary to the provisions of article 2 of L. 2251/1994 on consumer protection ('Prostasia ton katanaloton') and thus abusive.

FRANCE

(a) Based on the freedom of contract principle, a clause providing for retention of title can be agreed in respect of the sale of any asset, entitling the seller to retain ownership until he receives full payment of the price. Yet, until the Law of 12 May 1980, such clauses could not be enforced in the event of the buyer's insolvency. Since 1980, as confirmed in the Insolvency Act 1985 (which has now become C. com, articles L. 611.1 to L. 628.3, the current insolvency law), retention of title clauses remain effective in insolvency proceedings.

The *Cour de cassation* established some time ago that 'the payment of the sale price in a retention of title clause is analysed as a suspensive condition for the transfer of title'.[45] Thus, the contract of sale exists and is valid, but title will not pass until the price has been fully paid.

The validity of retention of title clauses depends on general contract and property law. Both parties must have agreed to include the clause and the property must remain identifiable (see cases 7 and 8 on this point). If C, a creditor of B, executes against property sold under a retention of title agreement, but in the possession of B, A may assert his title to the machine by producing the contract (see case 2 for the problems arising in the context of the execution procedure).[46] A remains the owner of the machine, therefore *rei vindicatio* is possible. Specific rules apply when the debtor is bankrupt. C. com, article L. 621-122 provides

---

[44] See Georgiadis, *I exasphalisi ton pistoseon* 586; Mazis, *To plasmatikon enechyron* 151: for instance, title in the goods will be transferred in case the goods sold under retention of title have been brought to another place where they have been sold.

[45] Com 20 Nov. 1979, Bull civ IV, 237, No 300 (Mécarex) where the Court expressly rejected the characterisation of the clause as a resolutive clause; see also Versailles, 20 May 1987, D 1988, 72, No 4, obs. Derrida.

[46] On the question of the effect of *rei vindicatio* on the sale contract, see Storck, D 1988, 131. See also Charlery, JCP 1997 I 4013.

that the return of assets sold under retention of title is permitted, so long as the assets can physically be identified in the debtor's estate at the time of the commencement of the insolvency proceedings.[47] The insolvency administrator could avoid the need to return the assets by paying immediately the sale price (C. com, article L. 621-122). The *juge-commissaire* could also, with the agreement of the seller, permit payment to be delayed. If so, the debt would then qualify as an 'article 40 debt', which has a very high priority ranking.[48] Creditors who have retained title must declare this to the insolvency administrator within three months, undeclared claims being extinguished (C. com, article L. 621-46).[49] Similarly, the return of the assets is possible only for three months after the commencement of insolvency proceedings (C. com, article L. 621-115). Once the seller-creditor has submitted a claim for the return of the asset, provided the claim is submitted within the permitted period, the insolvency administrator cannot, without being held liable, sell the assets in question. Recent cases have linked the right of *rei vindicatio* with the preparation by the insolvency administrator of an inventory of the insolvency estate (which in principle is not compulsory).

---

[47] Return is also possible if the asset has been incorporated into another asset, if the return of the former would not damage the latter (C. com, article L. 621-122). A claim is also permissible in respect of generic assets (assets in bulk, fungible, C. com, article L. 621-122). See the later cases.

[48] The insolvency provisions in the C. com accord special treatment to debts incurred after the commencement of insolvency proceedings, which has only recently been curtailed. These debts used to be granted a super-preference: they were paid ahead of any other debt if the sale of the business or liquidation was finally ordered. If the court opted for the rescue of the business and these debts were not paid on time, their enforcement would again supersede all other payments (formerly IA 85, article 40). Thus, the ranking of 'article 40 creditors' superseded secured creditors and even other creditors benefiting from a statutory preference. Only the last three months of employees' wages and social security contributions had a higher ranking. The policy was to encourage creditors to take part in the process of corporate rescue. It proved to be counterproductive, encouraging transactions where there was in fact no real chance of recovery. The 1994 reform shifted the balance in favour of secured creditors: C. com, article L. 621-32 (formerly IA 85, article 40 para. 2) provides that, in liquidation, creditors secured on immovable assets, or movable assets coupled with a right of retention of title, or pursuant to the Law of 18 Jan. 1951 (charge on industrial equipment), will be paid in priority to the article 40 creditors. Again, the highest ranking is accorded to employees and legal costs. This change, however, does not have the major practical consequences one might expect. Indeed, the secured creditors with a right of retention were actually already well protected, since this right entitles them to an interest in the proceeds of any sale ordered by the insolvency administrator (C. com, article L. 621-21). See Cabrillac/Pétel, D 1994, 243.

[49] Com 9 Jan. 1996, Bull civ IV, No 9; JCP 1996 I 3935, No 19.

Consequently, when inventories were not prepared, sellers were allowed to claim ownership of the asset, and its return, based solely on the evidence of delivery receipts[50] or order forms.[51] Moreover, if the asset had been sold, the insolvency administrator could be held liable on the basis of not having established that inventory as ordered by the *juge-commissaire*, despite the fact that the seller had not declared his claim earlier.[52]

(b) The wording of this clause is valid and sufficient. Difficulties relating to the form of the clause arise in connection with the question of parties' consent (see part (c), below).

(c) The question of the parties' consent to a retention of title clause gives rise to many difficulties. This is due to a reform introduced in 1996 by IA 85 article 121 which has now become C. com, article L. 621-122. It is also due to case law, which laid down extremely refined requirements. As discussed in part (e) below, the clause must be contained in a written document relating to the sale (or the seller's general conditions of sale, or in a previous set of contracts between the same parties). The courts have always acknowledged that the buyer's acceptance did not need to be in writing *as long as his adhesion to the clause was certain and unequivocal.*[53] The key point is that, as is to be expected in contractual matters, the parties reached agreement.

Agreement can be inferred from the performance of the contract by the buyer, but depends also on the extent to which it could be said that the buyer had knowledge of the existence of the clause – ultimately a question of form. For example, in one case a supplier produced a quotation which mentioned the clause on the front and back of the document. The buyer was regarded as having consented to the clause, because he had performed part of the contract. The clause was held to be valid in insolvency proceedings.[54] In another case, the clause was found on the back of the seller's ordering forms, and here also the court decided that there was no evidence that the buyer was ignorant of the clause.[55] In contrast, a clause contained in the small print of an

---

[50] Com 13 Apr. 1999, D affaires 1999, 833; RTDC 1999, 885, obs. Crocq.
[51] Versailles, 17 Sep. 1998, D affaires 1998, 1781, RTDC 1999, 885.
[52] Com 6 July 1999, D affaires 1999, 1366.   [53] Paris, 18 Dec. 1990, D 1991, IR, 18.
[54] Com 6 June 1989, Bull civ IV, No 175.   [55] Com 13 Oct. 1998, RJDA 1998, No 1391.

agreement, to which the buyer did not react, was held to be invalid due to lack of consent.[56]

The question of consent used to be particularly acute when the seller's general conditions of sale included the standard clause of retention of title whereas the buyer's general conditions of purchase specifically excluded them. In such cases, the courts took the view that the inconsistency precluded any agreement for retention of title, the clause being held to be ineffective.[57] However, the new article 121, para. 3 (as modified by the Law of 1 July 1996, article 19) provides that

> notwithstanding any contrary clause, the retention of title clause is binding upon the buyer and can validly be invoked against him and third parties unless the parties have agreed in writing to exclude the clause or to modify it.

It means that parties' agreement is no longer required: the seller could unilaterally stipulate for retention of title. It would be excluded only by an express agreement of the parties. The intention of the legislature was to favour the suppliers of goods, as against the large retailers who occupy a position of strength such as invariably to provide for the exclusion of title retention in their general purchase conditions.

The problem is that this rule does not have general application: its operation is confined to insolvency proceedings.[58] Therefore, in the present case, the validity and efficacy of the clause will depend on the exact nature of the agreement between A and B. The clause will definitely be held to be valid in the event of B's insolvency. In such circumstances it may be invoked against the insolvency administrator.

(d) The latest point at which such a clause can be provided for is the delivery of the asset (C. com, article L. 621-122). The delivery in question is the one which relates to the contract of sale, and not any earlier delivery, such one relating to an earlier leasing contract.[59]

---

[56] Rennes, 2 Nov. 1988, Rev proc coll 1989, 215, obs. Soinne; also Com 14 June 1994, Rev huiss 1994, 1287. Here the clause was buried in the middle of other general conditions of sale, appearing only on the back of the ordering forms and invoices. It did not appear on the face of the documents, nor in bold type. In Paris, 12 Sep. 1997, D affaires 1997, 1260, the clause was referred to on the front of the documents but was also difficult to read.

[57] Com 13 June 1989, Bull civ IV, No 186; Com 10 Dec. 1991, JCPédE 1991, I, 201, No 11; Com 11 May 1993, D 1993, Som, 287, obs. Pérochon, Rev proc coll 1993, 555, obs. Soinne.

[58] See, for example, Com 12 July 1994, Bull civ IV, No 268; D 1996, Som, 212, obs. Pérochon. See also Crocq, RTDC 1996, 675.

[59] Versailles, 8 Nov. 1990, Cah dr entr 1991, 6, No 3, note Pérochon.

(e) The clause providing for retention of title cannot be agreed orally – it must be contained in a document relating to the sale. Otherwise, there are no formal requirements for the creation of a retention of title clause. Registration or publicity is not required under French law.[60] If the buyer is a company, the annual balance should be mentioned, but this requirement is rarely respected in practice. This makes retention of title the most effective and the least publicised security right – sometimes called the 'Queen of Security'. Since 1994, however, publicity in respect of retention of title is encouraged: C. com, article L. 621-116 exempts the owner from the requirement to establish title to the asset, if the relevant contract was previously published (for example, the contract of sale containing a retention of title clause). Pursuant to article 85-5 of the 1985 Decree, publication takes the same form as that provided for leasing contracts (articles 1-7 and 9 of Decree No 72-665 of 4 July 1972). That is, the contract must identify the parties and the assets concerned. The seller registers the agreement on the registry held at the Commercial Court of the place where the buyer is itself registered (as a company, a partnership or a merchant). There is no deadline for publication. As the registry is open for public inspection, third parties are able to discover whether any of the buyer's assets are subject to reservation of title agreements. This is an incentive for the seller to publish, since publication means he will not have to establish his title if the buyer becomes bankrupt and insolvency proceedings commence. He may simply assert his *rei vindicatio* claim against the insolvency administrator. His rights, however, remain the same as described in part (a).

BELGIUM

(a) Reservation of title was recognised only recently, in 1997, by the new Bankruptcy Act (article 101). Before this change in the law, the *Cour de cassation* had held that the recognition of property rights of the seller, in conflict with other creditors of the buyer, was irreconcilable with the principle of article 2279 C.civ.[61] Although the new provision is contained in the Bankruptcy Act, one must assume that the new rule applies to all situations of *concursus creditorum*. The new provision was to a large extent inspired by the French example. Reservation of

---

[60] As confirmed in Com 11 May 1993, D 1993, IR, 145; JCPédE 1993, I, 277, No 15, obs. Cabrillac and Petel.
[61] Cass. 9 Feb. 1933, Pas 1933, I, 103 concl. proc. gen. Leclercq; Cass. 22 Sep. 1994, RW 1994–95, 1264 note Dirix.

title must be agreed upon by the parties and be formalised in a written document prior to the moment of delivery. The law requires no other formalities or publicity. The property rights of the seller remain intact after the insolvency of the buyer, or execution by other creditors, providing that the goods are still capable of identification in the estate of the buyer. If the goods are executed against by other creditors, the seller may challenge this execution by means of a *rei vindicatio* (article 1514 *Code Judiciaire/Gerechtelijk Wetboek*). In the event of the buyer's insolvency, the seller may recover the goods from the insolvency administrator on the condition that he declares his title before a certain stage of the insolvency proceedings is reached. The only way for the insolvency administrator to resist the *rei vindicatio* is to pay the outstanding balance (article 107).

(b) The formulation as mentioned is sufficient.

(c) The insertion of a retention of title clause requires the consent of both parties. The agreement between the parties can come into existence after the conclusion of the contract, but it must be concluded before the point at which the goods are delivered. The acceptance by the buyer of the clause may be explicit or implicit. This consent can be implicit in his behaviour following the delivery of the goods. In accordance with French case law, it is sufficient that the clause is inserted in a document (letter, invoice) which is sent to the buyer before, or simultaneously with, delivery and that the goods are accepted without protest.

(d) There must be an agreement concluded not later than the moment of the delivery of the goods. An agreement providing for reservation of title concluded after delivery would be regarded as invalid *vis-à-vis* third parties.

(e) The only formal requirement of article 101 Bankruptcy Act is that the agreement must be in writing. There are no particular formalities or publicity requirements to be observed. Furthermore, the acceptance by the buyer of the clause does not need to be established through the document itself (e.g. by his signature). His acceptance, as in all commercial matters, can be proven by any means (including presumptions). The clause can therefore be inserted by the seller in his 'General Conditions of Sale'. It is sufficient that the buyer has knowledge of the clause prior to delivery and makes no protest.

PORTUGAL

(a) According to Portuguese law, as already stated in case 1(a), the buyer becomes owner of the equipment supplied, so long as it is individualised, as soon as the contract is concluded (article 408°, n°1 C.C.). As a result of this, the seller is not entitled to preferential payment from the proceeds of the sale of the machine, if another creditor executes against the equipment or if the buyer goes bankrupt. Portuguese law does not provide a specific statutory preference, nor any other special right, for the unpaid seller.

However, in the present case, reservation of title is provided for in the contract of sale. Use of a reservation of title clause is permitted in all alienation contracts by article 409° C.C. which states that the transferor may stipulate that the transfer of ownership will only take effect after the full payment of the price due.[62] Reservation of title is always opposable to (i.e. effective against) third parties (creditors or subsequent acquirers), although it must be registered in case of immovables and those movables subject to registration (see article 409°, n°2 C.C.). These movables are cars, ships, planes and shares in companies. Since machines are not subject to registration, the reservation of title clause in this case does not need to be registered. If the machine is executed against by another creditor, the seller can resist the execution by *embargos de terceiro* (article 351° *Código de Processo Civil*, CPC, Civil Procedure Code).[63] In the event of the insolvency of the buyer, however, the reservation of title clause is only effective against the insolvency administrator if it was agreed by an act under private signature before the delivery of the machine (article 155°, n° 4 CPEREF).

The effect of reservation of title is that the buyer becomes owner of the thing only after full payment; this means that he cannot sell it and his creditors cannot execute against it because it still belongs to the seller. Should the buyer fail to pay, the seller has a right immediately to recover the thing. As a result of the system of title, this type of clause is very common in commercial practice, because it provides the best security for sellers. As they remain the owners of the things sold, they do not even need a right of priority in payment, because the thing cannot be executed against by creditors of the buyer.

---

[62] See Lima Pinheiro, *A claúsula de reserva de propriedade* and Peralta, *A posição jurídica do comprador na compra e venda com reserva de propriedade*.
[63] See Teixeira de Sousa, *Acção executiva singular* 308.

(b) The reservation of title clause is sufficient and there is not a more suitable or common form of wording.

(c) According to article 232° C.C., a contract is not concluded until both parties agree to all clauses of it. The reservation of title clause is no exception, thus both parties must agree to its insertion in the contract.

(d) The law does not prohibit reservation of title from being agreed upon after delivery, with effect against third-party creditors of the buyer. However, if such reservation of title is agreed as a modification to the contract of sale, the creditors would be entitled to bring an *actio Pauliana* claim.[64] In the event of the insolvency of the buyer, article 155 n. 4 CPEREF states that a reservation of title clause is only effective against the insolvency administrator if it was provided for in an act under private signature before the delivery of the subject matter of the sale.

(e) In general, the rights of A depend only on the terms of the reservation of title clause. As stated, reservation of title needs to be registered only in case of immovables and movables subject to registration (article 409°, n°2 C.C.), which is not the case here.

It is sufficient therefore that the clause was contained in the seller's general conditions of sale. However, according to articles 5° and 11° *Lei das Cláusulas Contratuais Gerais* (LCCG),[65] all general conditions must previously be communicated to the other party, otherwise they are considered invalid.

In case of the insolvency of the buyer, the reservation of title clause must comply with certain formalities in order to be valid in the insolvency proceedings. As has been noted above, article 155°, n° 4 CPEREF states that, in the event of the insolvency of the buyer, the reservation of title clause is only effective against the insolvency administrator if it was provided for in an act under private signature before the delivery of the machine.

SPAIN

(a) If the contract falls under the CC, A is the owner, and he may assert *rei vindicatio* (article 348/II). A may terminate the contract if B does not

---

[64] See *infra*, Portuguese report, case 11 (Variation) and case 15.
[65] Act on General Conditions, DL 446/85, of 25 Oct., reviewed by DL 220/95, of 31 Aug.

CASE 3: MACHINERY SUPPLIED TO BE USED BY THE BUYER   263

perform his obligation of payment (this is a personal action, namely, an action brought to enforce the obligation owed by B). A has a right of *rei vindicatio* as against C, if C has executed against the machine (article 595 LEC). A may also request the judge to grant a precautionary measure in respect of the goods in B's possession (article 727.3^a LEC).[66] A's rights in B's insolvency are, in accordance with article 1922.1 CC, that A has a preferential right to the price of the machine which is on B's premises, this preference being limited, however, to the machine's value.

(b) The clause is sufficient as stated. Clauses frequently stipulate that the buyer is merely a trustee of the movable until the last instalment has been paid.

(c) Yes, the parties should expressly agree on the clause. A reservation of title clause cannot be unilaterally inserted by the seller into the contract (article 7.10 LVBMP), while the prohibition of disposal may be so inserted.[67]

Reservation of title is not expressly contemplated by the Civil Code. However, the courts acknowledge that reservation of title clauses are lawful under article 1255 CC in so far as they are not contrary to statutory provisions, morals or public order.[68] In this way, the seller who includes a reservation of title clause in the contract can vindicate the goods of the purchaser if subjected to execution or insolvency proceedings. Reservation of title affects the buyer's creditors, since it interferes with execution by creditors. However, with respect to movables, as a general rule reservation of title by the seller will not survive a transfer to subsequent acquirers who have acted in good faith. Such acquirers are protected by the specific legal rules of commerce such as article 464 CC and article 85 CCO. Exceptionally, in the case of contracts of sale of movables or hire purchase, a reservation of title clause recorded in the Chattels Registry can be successfully opposed to the claims of later purchasers.

(d) Reservation of title must be agreed by the parties in the contract itself and always before the machine has been delivered. If the sale

---

[66] See articles 1400–1401 LEC, which include: precautionary measures; recording of a prohibition to make free use of his goods; preventive attachment of goods; sequestration of goods.
[67] See article 7.11 LVBMP and article 4, c), 3° of Bylaw of 19 July 1999.
[68] See Díez-Picazo, *Fundamentos de derecho civil patrimonial* III 783.

and the delivery of the movable have already been effected, reservation of title is no longer possible, since B at that point owns the movable. Once delivery has been carried out, it is no longer possible for the seller to insist on inserting a reservation of title clause in the original sales contract, except in the improbable case of the purchaser agreeing to draw up a similar guarantee in the seller's favour, which could not be characterised as reservation of title in any event.

There is no such thing as a statutory reservation of title. For the date of the reservation of title clause to be opposable to third parties, the contract must either be drawn up as a public deed (article 1227 CC) or be recorded duly on the Chattels Registry (article 15.1 LVBMP). Thus, if the contract is governed not by the CC but by the LVBMP, the date of entry on the Registry is essential to its validity *vis-à-vis* third parties.

(e) Under the CC, only an express agreement is required to make reservation of title valid. If the contract has been formalised in a public deed, then the date on which the deed has been submitted to the notary will be considered as the official date for all practical purposes with regard to third parties. It is sufficient that the clause is contained in the General Conditions of Sale, because the purchaser is aware of the reservation of title clause, and therefore its inclusion is not to be considered unfair.

Under the LVBMP, there are further requirements that must be fulfilled: contracts have to be set out in writing and recorded on the Registry. Specifically, for the sales contract of the machine to be recorded in the Chattels Registry, and for it to be considered as a legitimate sale under the LVBMP, the machine must be identified by the serial number, or must have some distinguishing feature that prevents any possible confusion with other similar movables. Furthermore, the period for payment must be greater than three months (article 3.1 LVBMP). This contract must be formalised in writing for it to be valid (article 6.1 LVBMP). With regard to its content, the contract must indicate the following particulars: place, time, the identity of the parties, identification of the object being sold, and also whether there are any conditions pertaining to finance, reservation of title, and restraint on resale. Additionally, it is necessary to include the addresses at which the parties may be notified, and an estimate of the value of the movable for auction purposes (article 7 LVBMP).

If a reservation of title clause has been agreed, the creditor may vindicate the sold goods (article 348.2 CC) and, additionally, claim compensation for damages caused. In accordance with article 10 LVBMP, the creditor may further claim either payment or the termination of the contract. If the contract is terminated, the creditor may either claim the fulfilment of his obligation and compensation for damages caused or *rei vindicatio*; additionally, he may claim interest for delayed payment (article 1124 CC). The unpaid creditor has the right to initiate an action in court, and the parties involved have to produce evidence to support their claims. In the case of insolvency, the assets subject to reservation of title will not form part of the insolvency estate, provided that the reservation of title clause has been recorded in the Chattels Register.[69]

ITALY

(a) Sale with retention of title is regulated by articles 1523–1526 of the Civil Code.[70] Article 1524 provides that reservation of ownership by the seller is effective *vis-à-vis* the purchaser's creditors only if it is contained in a written document bearing a *data certa* (certain date)[71] prior to the date of the attachment (cf. article 2914 n. 4 c.c.). Pursuant to article 1524 c.c., if the sale concerns machinery and the price exceeds 15.49 Euros, the clause will be effective even against a third-party purchaser of the machinery, provided that: (1) the reservation of title clause was recorded on the special register kept in the office of the clerk of the court having jurisdiction over the place where the machinery is located; and that (2) when the machinery was acquired by the third party, it remained in the same place as that where registration took place. In addition to these requirements, another law, of 18 November 1965, n. 1329, applies to machine tools that have a price exceeding 258.23 Euros. It provides

---

[69] Royal Decree 1828/1999 established a Central Registry of Chattels which is made up of the Central Registry of Sales of Chattels on Hire-Purchase Instalments, and the Central Registry of General Conditions of Sale. Henceforth any reference to the Chattels Registry is to the Central Registry of Chattels.

[70] For a general treatment of the topic: Bianca, *La vendita e la permuta* 580 ff.; Lipari, Enc. dir., XLVI, 526 ff.

[71] The term '*data certa*' (certain date) is a term of art that refers to an evidentiary rule regarding the date of private writings. Article 2704 c.c. provides that: 'The date of a private writing in which the signature has not been authenticated is not certain and cannot be asserted against third persons, except from the day on which the writing was registered or from the date of death or supervening physical incapacity to sign of the person or persons who signed it, or from the date when the contents of such writing are reproduced in public acts, or from the date when other circumstances occur which establish with equal certainty that the writing was drawn up previously.' On this rule see: Dolmetta, Vita not., 1996, 11; Rizzo, *Digesto sez. civ.* V, 107 ff.; Dolmetta, *La data certa*.

that the retention of title clause will be effective against a sub-purchaser only if the machines bear a plate recording the seller's name and the fact that he is the owner, together with other information identifying the machine.

These rules apply both to insolvency and to individual execution.

If B is declared bankrupt, the contract is not terminated automatically. According to article 73 of the Insolvency Act, the insolvency administrator can adopt the buyer's contract, with the permission of the court. In this case, the seller is entitled to receive a bond, which will secure payment of the price. The insolvency administrator may also decide immediately to pay the entire sum that is outstanding under the contract. Such a sum will be lower than the outstanding price, because it will be discounted at the official rate of interest. If the insolvency administrator does not adopt the contract, A may bring an action against the insolvency administrator to recover the machine sold (article 103 l. fall.).[72] The retention of title clause is as effective against the insolvency administrator as it would have been against the bankrupt, B, that is effective to the extent that ownership has not yet passed from A to B. Therefore A, who remains owner of the equipment, may recover it by means of a *rei vindicatio* action, provided for by article 948 of the Civil Code.

If a civil execution is levied against machinery sold subject to retention of title, the seller may bring an action in court to enforce his right according to article 619 of the Code of Civil Procedure, in order to prevent the sale of the thing against which the execution was levied.

If the buyer defaults the seller may, of course, terminate the contract of sale and recover the thing sold by means of a *rei vindicatio* action against B. In that case the seller will have to return the instalments he has received subject to his right to fair compensation for the use of the thing and for damages. If it was agreed that the instalments paid should be retained by the seller as indemnity, the court, according to the circumstances, can grant a reduction of the agreed indemnity (article 1526 c.c.).[73]

Court decisions take a restrictive approach to the application of the statutory rules concerning the effectiveness of title retention in insolvency proceedings. The plaintiff who brings a *rei vindicatio* action against

---

[72] Castagnola, *Le rivendiche mobiliari nel fallimento* 291 ff.; see e.g. Cass. 14 Apr. 1988, Giust. civ., 1989, I, 166; Cass. 6 Feb. 1986, n. 723, Fallimento, 1986, 1183; Cass. 4 June 1983, n. 3803, Fallimento, 1983, 1178.

[73] See, e.g., Cass. 28 June 1995, n. 7266, Vita not., 1995, 1424.

the insolvency administrator must prove that the contract of sale contains an express retention of title clause and that the document containing the clause has a certain date, a date which must be prior to the declaration of the insolvency of B. If the retention of title clause is contained in a different document, which does not satisfy the certain date requirement, it is considered ineffective as against the insolvency administrator. This would be so if the title retention clause was contained in general conditions of sale, regulating a series of future transactions.[74]

(b) The clause stated above is sufficient and commonly used in cases such as the present.

B does not acquire ownership over the machine simply by bringing it onto his premises. Article 1523 c.c. expressly provides that, where a retention of title clause is inserted in the contract, the purchaser acquires ownership by the payment of the last instalment of the price.

(c) Both parties must agree on the insertion of the retention of title clause when the contract is formed. Nevertheless, the parties may agree upon the clause orally, when the contract is formed, and later sign a document that will provide for reservation of title.[75] Indeed, the clause need only be reduced to writing in order to make it effective against the creditors of the purchaser. Note, however, that article 2762 of the Civil Code provides the seller of machinery with a *privilegio*, i.e. a non-possessory security interest, for the amount of the unpaid purchase price.[76] This charge is established by law, therefore operating even though it is not agreed upon by the parties or mentioned in the contract of sale. The statutory charge in respect of machinery becomes effective on the registration of the document witnessing the sale and the claim. Registration must take place in the register that is kept in the office of the clerk of the court having jurisdiction over the place where the machinery is located. It lasts for three years from the date of the sale. It remains

---

[74] See Cass. 17 Dec. 1990, n. 11960, Giust. civ., 1991, I, 1214; Giur. it., 1991, I, 1, 773; Cass. 20 May 1994, n. 4976, Foro it., 1995, I, 893; Trib. Catania, 10 Nov. 1992, Giur. comm., 1993, II, 394.

[75] Cass. 24 Feb. 1998, n. 1999, Fallimento, 1998, 604 (note, however, that the transaction in question, inasmuch as is evidenced after it was concluded, could be attacked under the rules on the revocatory action, article 64 l. fall.); Cass. 20 May 1994, n. 4976, Foro. it., 1995, I, 893 (the document must be signed by both parties; it cannot be a unilateral act). Cf. Bocchini, in: *Trattato di diritto privato* 717 ff.

[76] For a general view of *privilegi*: Tucci, in: *Trattato di diritto privato* 449 ff.; Ravazzoni, in: *Digesto sez. civ.* XIV, 371 ff.; *id.*, in: *Digesto sez. civ.* XIV 380 ff.

effective for as long as the machine is in the possession of the buyer, in the place where the registration was made, unless it has been taken away fraudulently. This charge gives the seller a right to be paid in priority to the insolvency creditors of the buyer. Its ranking is established by article 2778 of the Civil Code, which postpones it to many other security rights and statutory preferences.

(d) Under Italian law retention of title cannot be agreed upon after the contract is concluded.[77] Of course, sometimes delivery takes place before a contract is concluded, e.g. pending negotiations between the parties. In that case, the parties can still agree upon a retention of title clause when the contract is formed, though delivery has already taken place.

(e) It is important to distinguish the effect of the agreement as between the parties and the enforceability of the agreement against creditors. Although retention of title is effective between the parties even if agreed orally, the enforceability of the agreement against creditors of the buyer requires a written document having *data certa* prior to the date of insolvency or execution (articles 1524, 2704 c.c.). Compliance with the formalities, mentioned above in part (a), for the sale with reservation of title of machinery exceeding the price of 15.49 Euros or of 258.23 Euros, will render the clause effective against even a third-party purchaser of the machinery.

THE NETHERLANDS

(a) Retention of title is fully recognised under Dutch law as a means for the seller to secure payment of the purchase price. Retention of title is a species of transfer under a suspensive condition, by which the seller remains the owner until the price has been paid.[78] The machines sold to B did not therefore become part of B's estate and the seller, A, remained the owner.

---

[77] Accordingly, reservation of title contained in an invoice is ineffective, inasmuch as it was not agreed upon when the contract was concluded: Cass. 30 Aug. 1991, n. 928, Arch. civ. 1992, 431. This rule will probably be changed when the decree of 20 Sep. 2002, implementing the directive 2000/35/EC of 29 June 2000 on combating late payment in commercial transactions, enters into force. Art. 11 of the decree enacts that the reservation of title clause shall have a certain date if the clause is mentioned in the invoice sent with the goods. The scope of the new rule appears to be limited to the case of individual execution against the debtor (cf. Art. 2(1) of the decree).

[78] Article 3:92(1) BW.

A retention of title clause is also effective if the buyer is adjudicated bankrupt. A, as owner, may bring a *rei vindicatio* action in respect of the goods sold, although the insolvency administrator may of course choose to pay the price and thus consolidate the estate.[79]

In order to be able to rely on the *rei vindicatio* action in respect of the goods sold and delivered under a retention of title clause, it is necessary first to terminate the contract of sale. So long as the purchase price is not due, a right to terminate does not normally exist. Insolvency proceedings mean, however, that the purchase price becomes due by operation of law.[80] The contract would, however, still be classified as executory for the purposes of the insolvency proceedings. This means that the insolvency administrator may opt to perform the contract. If so, he or she will have to provide security. The creditor must allow the administrator a reasonable period in which to make this choice. If the administrator chooses not to perform, or does not do so in time, the seller may terminate the contract and claim back the goods sold.[81]

(b) There are no specific requirements as to the wording of an effective retention of title clause. Such a clause depends above all on the agreement, the meeting of minds, between parties. It is usual that the clause will be contained in a written document, but the use of writing is not required.

(c) As both parties must agree upon the clause, a unilateral stipulation for retention of title will not have the desired effect. Under the contract of sale, the seller would be obliged to transfer the property.[82] Retaining title would therefore place the seller in breach of contract.

(d) In principle, parties are entirely free to agree upon retention of title at any time prior to the transfer of ownership. Once ownership has passed, however, retention of title by the seller is impossible.

---

[79] Goods sold under a retention of title clause are potentially subject to a temporary moratorium under Dutch insolvency law, article 63a Fw. Furthermore, movables on the debtor's premises, even though they belong to third parties, may be vulnerable to execution by the Dutch Revenue. See for an example of German machine sellers to a Dutch buyer: European Court of Justice, Case 96/88, ECR 1990, I-583 (Krantz).
[80] Article 6:40(a) BW.
[81] Article 37 Fw. The commencement of insolvency proceedings (or execution) does not of itself terminate a contract nor entitle the seller to rescind.
[82] Article 7:9 BW.

(e) All that is required for a valid retention of title clause is the agreement of the parties. There are no further requirements, such as writing, registration or the use of a date. It is, therefore, also possible, indeed very common, to include the clause in the general conditions of the seller.[83]

ENGLAND

(a) Reservation of title clauses are fully effective in English law. Since the passing of ownership turns on the intention of the parties, and the Sale of Goods Act lays down only presumptive rules with respect to the intention of the parties, the seller may insist that his ownership be reserved until certain conditions, usually payment, are fulfilled. This right of the seller persists even after delivery has been made to the buyer. A reservation of title clause like the present one will fully protect the seller against the buyer's insolvency administrator for reasons stated above. It will also protect the seller against an executing creditor[84] subject to the following point.

It is perfectly possible that goods in the possession of a buyer are sold notwithstanding the seller's reservation of title. The executing bailiff (*sheriff*) may not be aware of the reservation of title and the execution may be completed before the seller's rights are appreciated. The position is that the *sheriff* is protected from liability unless it is proved that he had notice or by reasonable inquiry could have ascertained that the goods sold did not belong to the judgment debtor. Furthermore, anyone purchasing the goods from the *sheriff* will acquire a good title to the goods as against the unpaid seller with the reservation of title clause.[85]

(b) The above wording would be adequate to express the intention that ownership would not pass until payment in full had occurred even though, technically, it would be more apt to say that the 'property' does not pass until payment in full. A seller reserving title must also avoid a minor pitfall. He must take care to avoid reserving only the 'beneficial' or 'equitable' ownership. For dogmatic (and not entirely uncontroversial)

---

[83] For general conditions to be effective, it is necessary that the other party is given a 'reasonable' opportunity to take cognisance of them and that they are not unreasonably onerous. See articles 6:231 ff. BW.
[84] Again, for reasons stated above.
[85] Supreme Court Act 1981, s. 138B; County Courts Act 1984, s. 98.

reasons, the bare legal ownership cannot be transferred to the buyer in one step while the seller reserves the equitable (or beneficial) ownership.[86] A two-stage process occurs consisting of, first, the transfer of ownership in the goods to the buyer, followed instantaneously by, secondly, the grant back by the buyer to the seller of an equitable real interest. The second stage of the process is treated as a charge over the goods which must, if the buyer is a company, be registered as a company charge (which it never is in these cases) or be void against unsecured and secured creditors of the company.[87]

(c) This has not proven to be a controversial issue in English law but the answer can be discovered from basic principle. First of all, the passing of ownership is a joint consensual act. If either party, buyer or seller, declines to participate in the process, the passing of ownership cannot take place. It should not matter, as far as this consequence goes, that one or the other party is acting in breach of contract in refusing to participate. That is a separate matter. So far, this points to the conclusion that the seller can take action to show an intention on his part that ownership should not pass according to the presumptive rules contained in the Sale of Goods Act even if his action is not supported by the terms of the contract with the buyer. Furthermore, section 19 of the Sale of Goods Act deals with a reservation of the right of disposal by the seller until certain conditions are fulfilled. This provision reinforces other provisions of the Act underlining the dominance of the parties' intention in the passing of ownership. But the striking feature of section 19 is the emphasis that it places on the seller and not on the seller and buyer jointly. The section states that the seller may by the terms of the contract or the appropriation reserve the right of disposal.

Appropriation, undefined, would certainly take place at the point of delivery so that a seller, making it clear no later than delivery, for example when handing the goods over to a carrier, that the buyer was not yet to have ownership of the goods would effectively protect himself by reserving ownership until the occurrence of the stated condition. Delivery is the critical moment, because it is at that time when ownership of goods originally unascertained will pass to the buyer. The seller's

---

[86] *Re Bond Worth Ltd* [1980] Ch 228. This reasoning is difficult to reconcile with the reasoning in *Abbey National Building Society v Cann* [1990] 1 All ER 1085 and *Re Connolly Bros. Ltd* [1912] 2 Ch 25.
[87] Companies Act 1985, ss. 395–396.

reservation prevents this from happening. If ownership has already passed to the buyer, the seller's unilateral action could not alone revest ownership of the goods in him.

(d) The clause should not have to be incorporated in the contractual agreement given that the passing of property is a consensual act and the seller's refusal to co-operate will therefore prevent the property from passing. Furthermore, the Sale of Goods Act 1979,[88] in granting recognition to the seller's reservation of the right of disposal – in other words, the seller's reservation of title – states that the right of disposal may be reserved 'by the terms of the contract *or appropriation*'.[89] Appropriation is a notoriously ambiguous word but it can be treated here as signifying the seller's act in earmarking the goods for the contract. Putting the goods into the hands of a carrier, together with a delivery note containing the seller's reservation of title, should therefore prevent ownership of the goods from passing to the buyer. The incorporation of the seller's reservation in the delivery note ought not in principle to have to satisfy the usual contractual test of incorporation of terms, since by definition the type of appropriation is not a term of the contract. There is no law on this.

(e) As stated above, there is no requirement that the reservation of title form part of the agreement. A seller's reservation need satisfy no formal or publicity requirement. Any words, if they clearly enough evidence the seller's intention that ownership does not pass to the buyer according to the usual presumptive rules in the Sale of Goods Act 1979, will suffice. As a matter of evidence, it is better that the seller's reservation be in writing though there is no requirement that it has to be. Unlike charges granted by corporate buyers, or bills of sale executed by sole traders and other individuals, the seller's reservation of title does not have to be registered or filed in order to be opposable against the buyer's other creditors or the insolvency administrator of the buyer. Although the American Uniform Commercial Code, in Article 9, adopts a functional definition of security, English law declines to treat title reservation as a charge even though in fact it serves to secure the buyer's obligation to pay the price.[90]

---

[88] S. 19(1).   [89] Emphasis added.
[90] *Armour and another v Thyssen Edelstahlwerke AG* (House of Lords) [1990] 3 All ER 481 at 485 (Lord Keith).

IRELAND

(a) A's legal position essentially turns on the answer to a simple question – who has ownership of the equipment? If ownership has passed to the buyer, B, then A is not entitled to reclaim the machine irrespective of whether any part of the purchase price has been paid. A is simply an unsecured creditor for the unpaid purchase price in B's insolvency.

If, on the contrary, A still has title to the equipment, then the analysis is fundamentally different. He can recover possession of it notwithstanding whether some or all of the purchase price has been paid or whether the purchase price was payable only by instalments. If, in this eventuality, A recovers possession of the machinery, then B should be entitled to the return of whatever he has paid on the basis of failure of consideration. It seems, however, that B would merely be an unsecured creditor in respect of this claim.

Prima facie, ownership passes at the time of the making of the contract of the sale and it does not matter whether either the price will be paid at a later date or possession will be transferred at a later date. Ultimately, however, the Sale of Goods legislation makes it clear that passing of ownership depends on the intention of the parties. The seller is perfectly at liberty to 'reserve' or postpone the passing of ownership until the purchase price has been paid in full or some other event occurs.

(b) There is no particular form of words necessarily to be employed before a reservation of title clause is held to be effective. Wording which has been successful in decided cases includes the following:

The ownership of the sugar . . . shall only be transferred to the purchaser when the full amount of the purchase price has been discharged.
(*Sugar Distributors Ltd v Monaghan Cash and Carry Ltd*)[91]

Until all sums due to the seller shall have been fully paid to it, the plant, machinery and materials supplied by the seller herein shall remain the seller's personal property.
(*Frigoscandia*)[92]

The seller, however, should avoid the use of terminology which purports to reserve only 'equitable and beneficial ownership'. That wording has been construed as passing full legal and beneficial ownership to the buyer and then after a split second of time (*scintilla temporis*) has elapsed, transferring back equitable ownership to the seller by way of charge.

---

[91] [1982] ILRM 399.
[92] *Frigoscandia (Contracting) Ltd v Continental Irish Meat Ltd* [1982] ILRM 396.

While this reasoning may be criticised as highly artificial, it has been judicially endorsed in both Ireland and England.[93] There are however, Irish cases which go the other way and suggest that such wording does not create a charge. In this climate of judicial uncertainty, clearly the safest course for the drafter of a retention of title clause is to avoid the expression 'equitable and beneficial ownership'.

Generally speaking, there is no requirement that reservation of title clauses are publicly registered. If, however, a reservation of title clause is held to create a charge, then it must be registered and in that case it will invariably fail for want of registration. If the charge construction is upheld, then the buyer is viewed as granting the seller a limited real interest in the goods by way of security. If the buyer is a company, then the charge will be registrable as a charge under the Companies Act 1963, s. 99 as either a charge over goods or an enterprise charge (*floating charge*). Likewise, if the buyer is an individual or a partnership, then the charge will be registrable as a bill of sale under the Bills of Sale legislation. Registration is in practice not effected by suppliers of goods largely because it adds factors of delay and expense to the transaction that may be disproportionate to the cost of the goods involved. The practical difficulties in going through the process of registration are compounded where there is a long-term relationship between seller and buyer involving multiple supply contracts that extend over a period of time.

It would seem that the wording of the clause in the example is sufficient to retain title. Examples of wording which has received the stamp of judicial approval are supplied above.

(c) Generally speaking, for a retention of title clause to be effective it must form part of the contract between the parties. Section 17 of the Sale of Goods Act recognises the primacy of the parties' intentions and states that where there is a contract for the sale of specific or ascertained goods ownership of them is transferred to the buyer at such time as the parties to the contract intend it to be transferred. The section goes on to provide that for the purpose of ascertaining the intention of the parties, regard shall be had to the terms of the contract, the conduct of the parties and the circumstances of the case. In the case of a contract for the sale of unascertained goods, no title passes unless and until

---

[93] See *Re Bond Worth Ltd* [1980] Ch 228 in England and *Frigoscandia (Contracting) Ltd v Continental Irish Meat Ltd* [1982] ILRM 396 in Ireland.

the goods are ascertained. Once ascertainment occurs, ownership passes when the parties intend this to happen.

One commentator has argued on the basis of the equivalent English statutory provisions that post-contractual reservation of title may be effective in certain circumstances.[94] The argument is based on s. 19 of the Sale of Goods Act which states:

> Where there is a contract for the sale of specific goods or where goods are subsequently appropriated to the contract, the seller may, by the terms of the contract or appropriation, reserve the right of disposal of the goods, until certain conditions are fulfilled . . .

The proposition is advanced that the section permits a seller in a contract for the sale of non-specific goods to reserve a 'right of disposal' when goods are subsequently appropriated to the contract. This conclusion, however, is by no means obvious on the wording of the relevant provision. Perhaps a more plausible interpretation is that post-contractual reservation of title is permitted only where this is contemplated in the terms of the original contract.

(d) The retention of title clause should be agreed upon at the time of the making of the contract. If title has already passed to the buyer it cannot be 'retained' by the seller. In a contract for the sale of specific goods title passes upon the making of the contract and it is irrelevant that the time of payment and/or delivery is postponed.

(e) Basically 'simple' retention of title clauses like the one used in this case are not subject to any requirement of registration – the only exception being for clauses which purport to reserve only 'equitable and beneficial ownership' which arguably must be registered.

A clause contained in the seller's general conditions of sale must be incorporated into the contract between the parties before it is effective.

SCOTLAND

(a) Scots law has always recognised the validity of retention of title.[95] For ownership to pass, it is necessary that both parties so agree: there must be an intention to transfer ownership (*animus transferendi dominii*)

---

[94] See Bradgate [1988] JBL 477.
[95] For instance, it is recognised as effective in Stair's *Institutions* (Book 1, Title 14, para. 4). Stair is regarded as the 'father' of modern Scots law.

on the part of the transferor and an intention to acquire ownership (*animus accipiendi dominii*) on the part of the transferee.[96] In the absence of such intention on either side, ownership will not pass, notwithstanding delivery.

The law on the passing of ownership in sale is currently contained in s. 17 of the Sale of Goods Act 1979. This provides that ownership passes when the parties intend it to pass. Delivery is not a requirement. Therefore if the parties state in the contract that ownership is to pass when payment is made, that is when ownership will pass, regardless of when delivery takes place. Therefore at the time of the execution by C, the owner of the machine is A. C can execute only against the assets of B. Hence the execution against the machine is ineffective. That is true even though the machine is on B's premises. The same would be true if B were to become bankrupt.

(b) In practice there is some variation in the wording of such clauses. But the wording in the instant case is sufficient in law. Usually one would expect to see further provisions providing that if payment is not made by a certain time then A can *rescind* the contract, and that, if that happens, B must hand back the machine.

(c) The parties must agree to the clause. The seller cannot insert it unilaterally. If the contract has a provision as to when ownership passes, that provision will apply. If the contract is silent as to when ownership passes, then ownership will pass according to the rules laid down in s. 18 of the Sale of Goods Act 1979. Whether a seller might, before ownership has passed, and in breach of the terms of the contract, retain ownership, is a possibility that has not been discussed in Scotland. The answer under Scottish common law is affirmative, but the position under the Sale of Goods Act, which is a *corpus alienum* within Scots property law, is unclear. In the view of the writer it should be possible.

(d) See the last answer. After making the contract, the parties could alter it (*novatio*) with a different provision about passing of ownership. But if ownership has *already* passed, such a *novatio* will generally be ineffective. For example, A and B contract that ownership will pass on delivery. The goods are then delivered. A and B now novate the contract, and under

---

[96] At common law there also had to be delivery. But this is only now necessary for non-sale transfers, such as gift.

the novated contract ownership will pass only when the goods are paid for. That will be ineffective, for the parties are attempting to transfer ownership back from B to A. That can be done only by delivery. Delivery is unnecessary in a sale, but B is not selling the goods to A!

(e) There are no special requirements. Registration is not required. There is no requirement for a 'certain date'. Writing is not required. However, as a matter of practice a clause of retention of title in an oral contract would be likely to be ineffective. For the buyer is in possession, and possession raises a presumption of ownership. The *onus probandi* therefore lies on the seller to show that he, not the buyer, is the owner. He may be able to prove this on the basis of an oral contract. But it will be difficult.

A clause of retention of title may be contained in the seller's general conditions of sale. The clause will be effective if the seller can show that the conditions became part of the contract. That is a matter of general contract law.

SOUTH AFRICA

(a) If the seller, A, has retained title to the machinery until the purchase price has been paid in full, then title to the property will remain with A until he has been fully paid. Although the buyer's rights under the contract are capable of being executed against, the property itself (the machinery) does not form part of the estate of B. However, once insolvency proceedings have been commenced in respect of the buyer's estate, the legal situation changes radically. According to section 84 of the Insolvency Act,[97] the seller loses ownership of the machinery on the insolvency of the buyer. His title in the asset is replaced by a security right (a *tacit hypothec*) in his (the seller's) favour. Ownership henceforth rests with the insolvency administrator (*trustee-in-insolvency*) of the insolvency estate. The security right (*tacit hypothec*) serves to secure the seller's claim for the amount outstanding under the agreement.[98]

(b) The formulation as mentioned is sufficient. Reservation of 'ownership', rather than 'title', is more commonplace.

---

[97] Act 24 of 1936.
[98] See further s. 83 of the Insolvency Act 24 of 1936; Smith, *The Law of Insolvency* 166–168; van der Merwe, *Sakereg* 695–698; Lubbe, *Mortgage and Pledge* para. 513.

(c) The parties must agree on the insertion of a retention of title clause. Although it could be inserted unilaterally by the seller, it would not be valid unless explicitly or implicitly accepted by the buyer.

(d) Reservation of title must be agreed prior to the moment of delivery of the machinery. An agreement providing for reservation of title after delivery would not be enforceable *vis-à-vis* third parties.

(e) No particular formalities or publicity requirements need to be observed. In practice the contract is invariably reduced to writing. Acceptance by the buyer can be either explicit or implicit. Insertion of the clause in the 'general conditions of sale' is predominant in practice.

DENMARK

(a) If the contract contained a reservation of title clause the seller would be entitled to terminate the contract and to vindicate the machinery in the event of the buyer's failure to pay the purchase price. This right is protected as against the buyer's creditors. If the buyer is declared bankrupt, the insolvency administrator has a right to choose between full payment of the remaining purchase price and termination of the contract, the latter giving rise to the seller's right to vindicate the machine.

(b) The clause 'Title to the machinery is reserved until the seller has received full payment' should be effective under Danish law. Other wordings might be used, but the above-mentioned formulation, or clauses similar to it, is suitable and in all probability common.

(c) In Denmark a reservation of title clause must be part of the agreement between the seller and the buyer. It is important to note that the seller cannot unilaterally provide for retention of title. It must be accepted by the buyer. The Credit Agreements Act Part 10 contains the conditions for reservation of title not only in consumer sales but, according to section 50, also in other sales. These conditions are: (1) that the reservation of a title clause was agreed on before the assets were handed over to the buyer; (2) that the purchase price exceeds a specified amount (2,000 DKK/2,300 Euros); and (3) that the sale has not taken place pursuant to an agreement in which the sum secured is variable.

(d) According to the Credit Agreements Act, the reservation of title clause has to be concluded before the goods are handed over to the buyer.

(e) A reservation of title clause cannot be stipulated by the seller unilaterally. It must be accepted by the buyer. It should also be mentioned that reservation of title can only take place in respect of specific goods which are specified in such a way as to leave no doubt about what has been sold under reservation of title. Such clauses are not subject to registration or any similar requirement. Reservation of title to movables cannot be registered; any attempt to register such a clause would be refused. However, an exception is made in respect of motor vehicles. A reservation of title clause to a motor vehicle must be registered in the Car Register, cf. section 42 d(2) of the Registration of Property Act. Reservation of title clauses to vessels and aircraft also have to be registered.

SWEDEN

(a) Reservation of title, as well as any reservation to the effect that the seller is entitled to terminate the contract if the price is not paid, is valid not only against the buyer (section 54 of the Sale of Goods Act) but also against the creditors of the buyer. The goods are not regarded as the property of the debtor by the execution and insolvency legislation. Thus, the seller has a right of separation, but with an obligation to give up the value exceeding his claim. This demonstrates that in reality reservation of title is a security right. However, if the seller has not terminated the contract before insolvency proceedings are commenced, either the insolvency estate or a buyer under reconstruction (pursuant to the Reconstruction Act) may avoid termination by paying the price, if it is due, or by providing security (chapter 2 section 20 of the Reconstruction Act and section 63 of the Sale of Goods Act). This rule is mandatory under the Reconstruction Act, but it is disputed whether a condition that insolvency as such (*ipso facto*) terminates the contract, or that the estate may not adopt the contract, is valid.[99] The seller's right of separation is extinguished if the goods become fixed to other goods, e.g. when an engine is mounted on a boat or tyres are fitted on a car.[100]

---

[99] See references in Håstad, *Sakrätt rörande lös egendom* 403 f.
[100] NJA 1942, 195 and 1960, 9.

(b) As stated in case 1, it is not necessary to reserve the title, a simple reservation of a right of termination will do. A power of the buyer to dispose of goods prior to payment may be fatal (see further case 4), however, and a reservation of title clause has the advantage of normally being interpreted as prohibiting the buyer from doing so. In any event, a reservation is normally drafted as a reservation of title.

(c) In principle the parties must agree to a reservation (whether of title or termination), but it may be inserted unilaterally by the seller to the extent that such an insertion forms part of the contract, according to ordinary contractual principles. For instance, a blank acceptance of an offer, with a reference to general conditions including reservation of title, will make the reservation valid.[101] An attempt to insert a reservation of title clause after the conclusion of the contract in an invoice, however, normally is too late and does not need explicitly to be rejected by the buyer. Inclusion of a reservation of title clause in an acceptance is valid, provided that the offeror realised that the seller-offeree believed that title retention was to form part of the agreement.[102]

(d) The courts normally hold that the reservation must be made prior to delivery.[103] However, if the goods are delivered prior to the conclusion of the contract, and the seller is not able to avoid the contract, should the parties not agree on the outstanding questions, an agreement after delivery that the seller may reclaim the goods in case of non-payment will probably be effective against creditors of the buyer and sub-purchasers.[104] A resale of the goods to the seller, with registration pursuant to the Bills of Sales Act (but not merely a *constitutum possessorium* or a temporary transfer of possession[105]), combined with a

---

[101] Earlier it was assumed that onerous conditions must be presented in an obvious manner in order to be incorporated (NJA 1949, 609), but this requirement seems to have been replaced today by an increased possibility that unreasonable contractual conditions will be set aside pursuant to s. 36 of the Contracts Act (as amended in 1976) (NJA 1980, 46).

[102] See s. 6 of the Contracts Act and cf. NJA 1962, 276 and 1977, 92. It is open to argument whether insertion in an acceptance or a confirmation would otherwise (i.e. strictly) require an objection, cf. article 18 of the CISG. An insertion in a confirmation made after the agreement is in principle too late, cf. s. 21 of the Commercial Agents Act *(lagen om handelsagentur 1991)*. See further Hellner, *Juridiska Föreningens i Finland Tidskrift* 1979, 298 ff. and Håstad, 32 *Nordiske juristmöde* (1990), 247 ff.

[103] Cf. NJA 1932, 755.   [104] See Håstad, *Sakrätt rörande lös egendom* 186.

[105] NJA 1925, 535 and 1934, 193.

CASE 3: MACHINERY SUPPLIED TO BE USED BY THE BUYER 281

new transfer to the buyer with a reservation of title or a lease, will also provide the seller with security.

(e) No requirements of form (writing, registration, etc.) apply to tangible movables in general. The clause may be included in the seller's general conditions of sale. As to the question of incorporation, see part (c).

FINLAND

(a) In the case of an execution against the buyer's assets, the rules determining the seller's legal position would depend on the details of the case. If the price was to be paid in instalments, the Instalment Sales Act (*laki osamaksukaupasta/lag om avbetalningsköp*) would be applicable. In this case, B's creditors could execute against the machine notwithstanding the existence of a valid retention of title clause in the contract of sale. The rights of the seller would, however, be protected by the so-called 'rule of the lowest acceptable price'. This rule means that the goods could be sold only if it would be possible to pay the purchase price out of the income. If the Instalment Sales Act was not applicable, the goods could not be sold. In this case, execution could take place against only the buyer's rights under the contract. In other words, only the contractual right of the buyer to become the owner of the goods by paying the price could be the subject of execution and sale.

In the event of B's insolvency, the seller, A, would be entitled to separate the machine if the buyer, or the insolvency administrator, failed to fulfil the contract. However, the seller has to account for any surplus exceeding the secured claim. If neither the Instalment Sales Act nor the Consumer Protection Act (*kuluttajansuojalaki/konsumentskyddslag*) applied, the seller would also be able to separate the machine if the insolvency administrator decided not to adopt the contract or was prepared to adopt the contract but was not prepared to pay the price or offer adequate security for the price not yet due.

(b) The clause described in the question is sufficient and commonplace. The seller, A, would be protected according to the general rules concerning retention of title in the way described above.

(c) The parties must agree to the insertion of a retention of title clause. A clause inserted unilaterally by the seller, e.g. in the bill sent to the buyer, is neither valid nor does it normally oblige the buyer to inform the seller that he does not agree to the clause.[106]

(d) The parties agreed upon the clause prior to the delivery of the goods to the buyer and the seller has, therefore, lost his or her right of stoppage in transit. If the agreement is made after delivery, it is valid as between the parties, but it does not protect the seller against the creditors of the buyer.[107]

(e) There are no essential formalities required for a retention of title clause to be valid. The clause can be contained in the seller's general conditions. The parties can even agree upon the clause orally, although this may, of course, give rise to difficulties of proof.

Parties are not obliged, nor able, to register retention of title clauses. Even if a duty or option to register existed, registration would not be a prerequisite for the validity of the clause.[108] A title retention clause can be valid, therefore, even if the buyer was, incorrectly, registered as the owner. In such cases, *bona fide* third parties can, however, often claim protection against the seller.

Comparative observations

Case 3 involves what is known as simple retention of title, excluding all possible difficulties arising from resale, manufacturing, commingling, etc. Considering the difficulties which the European Union has faced up to now in its attempts to harmonise this area of the law,[109] the similarities revealed by the national reports are in fact striking. One must note, however, that this harmony is of a relatively recent date.

Parts (a) and (e)

All jurisdictions conclude that it is possible to reserve title until full payment of the purchase price. There is no longer a difference between

---

[106] See e.g. Tepora, *Omistuksenpidätyksestä* 209–210 and Tuomisto, *Omistuksenpidätys ja leasing* 160 ff.
[107] See e.g. Tuomisto, *Omistuksenpidätys ja leasing* 181 ff.
[108] See e.g. Koulu, *Oikeustiede – Jurisprudentia* 1987, 183 ff. Title retention to cars, buses, trucks-aircraft, aircraft under construction, vessels, vessels under construction, etc., may be registered, but registration is never a prerequisite for the validity of title retention.
[109] See Introduction, pp. 22 ff.

those systems which require a separate real agreement and those which do not.[110] The dogmatic difficulties which retention of title poses in a consensual system have been overcome even in French law and the jurisdictions influenced by French legal thinking. The translative effect (*effet translatif*) of the contract is considered to remain under the suspensive condition of full payment whereas the rest of the contract, especially the duty of the buyer to pay the price, is regarded as fully operative.

With the exception of Swedish and Finnish law, all jurisdictions regard the seller who has reserved title as the owner of the goods. In an execution carried out on behalf of a third-party (unsecured) creditor of the buyer, the seller is given the right to enforce his ownership through *rei vindicatio* as against any opposing rights of such creditors. Swedish and Finnish law take a slightly different view, influenced by their general mistrust of the suitability of legal concepts such as ownership. In both jurisdictions, the seller under retention of title may terminate the contract and claim separation of the goods. However, in the (unlikely) event that the value of the goods exceeds the value of the seller's claim, the seller must account for this surplus. Also in Finnish law, the seller has only a right to preferential payment out of the proceeds of sale of the goods when the Act on Instalment Sales applies. In both systems, the seller has therefore merely a security right that is, in theory but perhaps not in practice, less than full ownership.

With the exception of Belgian, Italian and Spanish law, the enforceability of the seller's title as against an executing creditor is not subject to any formal prerequisites or any requirements as to publicity. In Belgium, the clause merely needs to be in writing, in Italy and Spain the agreement also has to carry a 'certain date' (*data certa*, article 1524 C.c.; *fecha cierta*, article 1227 C.c.). In Spain, the usual method of satisfying the requirement of a 'certain date' is through the use of a public deed. If the contract is subject to the Spanish *Ley de Ventas de Bienes Muebles a Plazos*, the effectiveness of the retention of title will also depend on registration.[111]

In the buyer's insolvency, all systems under consideration have come to accept the effectiveness of retention of title. France introduced this rule in 1980, Belgium in 1998 and Greece in 1987 by a change in case law. In addition to the formal requirements of Belgian, Italian and Spanish law already mentioned, French and Portuguese law also require a written

---

[110] See *supra*, comparative observations, case 1(a)(ii).
[111] See Hellmich, *Kreditsicherungsrechte in der spanischen Mehrrechtsordnung*, 164.

document for the seller's ownership to be enforceable. Subject to these qualifications, all Member States bar Sweden and Finland give the seller the right to vindicate the goods so long as they remain in the hands of the buyer or of his insolvency administrator, as applicable. In the two Nordic countries, the seller only has a right of separation which also means that he has to account for any surplus of the goods' value. In South Africa, the insolvency of the buyer leads to a change in the seller's legal position. He is no longer regarded as the owner but is instead granted a *hypothec* as security for his claim.

Some reports specifically describe a right of the insolvency administrator to elect between continuation or termination of the contract. If the administrator elects for termination, the systems in question require the administrator to make payment (or provide security for payment) or accord to the seller a priority above that of insolvency creditors for their claim. In the event of an election for termination, the seller may exercise the right of *rei vindicatio*.

It is interesting to note the following difference between German and French law in respect of temporal considerations arising in respect of retention of title. Since the reform of German insolvency law, the seller may have to wait up to three months before the administrator is obliged to elect between termination or continuation of the contract, whereas French insolvency law requires the seller to realise his rights within the first three months following the commencement of insolvency proceedings. Both rules are thought to benefit the administration of the insolvency procedure and thus to work to the advantage of the insolvency creditors: the French rule by speeding up the proceedings and the German rule by giving the administrator the chance to continue the bankrupt's business for a certain time.

Only Spanish law insists on registration as a prerequisite for retention of title, and only then if the contract falls under the *Ley de Ventas de Bienes Muebles a Plazos*.[112] If the sold goods are subject to registration for other purposes, mainly of administrative law, retention of title may also need registration. This is the case with motor vehicles (Portugal, Denmark), vessels (Portugal) and aircraft (Portugal). While registration is possible under Italian law in respect of certain types of machine, it is not required in order for retention of title to be enforceable as against third-party creditors. Instead, registration provides the seller with better protection *vis-à-vis* third-party purchasers. Likewise in Finland, the possibility, or

---

[112] *Ibid.*, 164 f.

even the requirement, of registration of retention of title in respect of certain equipment does not concern the effectiveness of the security right.

Part (b)

Although some reporters suggested a more common wording, or some additional clauses, the terms used in case 3 were generally considered to be sufficient.

Part (c)

According to German and English law, the seller can withhold ownership also by means of a unilateral declaration to the effect that he only wants ownership to pass at the moment of full payment. This declaration must be made prior to delivery since otherwise § 929 BGB and section 18 of the Sale of Goods Act, respectively, dictate that ownership will pass. The same is also possible under French law since the 1996 amendment of the Insolvency Act. In fact, a retention of title clause is automatically implied into every sales contract under French law unless the parties explicitly exclude it by mutual agreement. This was a reaction against court decisions, which took an unduly narrow view of the requirement of agreement. Whether the reaction is to be regarded as excessive is for French commentators to decide. From the comparative perspective it is unique.

All systems, excepting the three just mentioned, require an agreement between seller and buyer for retention of title to be effective. It is again interesting to note that this rule, as well as its exceptions, cuts across the differences in respect of the general rules on transfer of ownership.

Part (d)

In the majority of the EU Member States and in South Africa, retention of title must be established prior to the delivery of the goods. It is important to note that (with the exception of Ireland) the crucial point in time is not the conclusion of the contract but delivery, although this is only logical for the tradition systems, not for those which adhere to the principle of *solo consensu*. That delivery brings to an end the possibility of providing for retention of title seems to stem from the prohibition of the security transfer of ownership and the mistrust of non-possessory security rights in general. Correspondingly, it is unsurprising that England and Germany are the only jurisdictions where retention of title may be established even after delivery without a need to meet any publicity requirements.[113] This finding accords with the liberal attitude that both systems take with regard to security rights in general and – related to this – with their view that factual possession is virtually immaterial.

[113] Swedish law also allows a retention of title or a reservation of the right to rescission to be established after delivery. This, however, requires first a resale to the former seller which has to be registered under the Bills of Sales Act.

Case 4: Jackets for resale

(Simple retention of title – entitlement to resell)

A produces men's clothing and sells it to retailers. B, who runs a chain of fashion shops, buys 1,000 winter jackets for the coming season. The contract grants to B a period of sixty days before payment has to be made. It also contains a clause whereby A reserves title to the jackets until payment in full, but also permits B to resell the jackets in the ordinary course of business.

Before B has paid for the jackets in full, he goes bankrupt. As the winter season has not yet started, no jacket has yet been sold.

Question

What are A's rights in respect of the jackets?

Discussions

GERMANY

The solution to case 4 is the same as the solution to case 3. A can vindicate the jackets as his property (§ 47 InsO). They do not form part of the insolvency estate. The entitlement to resell the jackets does not in any way affect the validity of the retention of title clause. On the contrary, such a right is usually provided for because it enables B to transfer ownership to his customers without having to rely upon the rules of *bona fide* acquisition. In German law (see § 185 s. 1 BGB), an entitlement to dispose of property[1] may be separated from ownership and be conferred upon a different person, in this case on B.

AUSTRIA

A's rights are the same as in case 3: the clause permitting B to resell the jackets does not affect these rights. Indeed, it is usual for the parties to agree that the buyer shall be entitled to resell the goods. If the buyer has such an entitlement to dispose of the goods, ownership of the goods is transferred by such a sale from the first seller to the second buyer. Such an authority does not diminish A's rights to the jackets, so long as they remain in B's possession.

GREECE

B's entitlement to resell the jackets (article 239 A.K.) does not by itself change A's legal position. The solution is the same as in case 3. Such an entitlement is common business practice. It enables the sub-purchasers to acquire ownership of the thing sold independently of whether they acted in good or bad faith.

FRANCE

In principle, a party who buys goods under a retention of title clause receives them in consignment. He has no title to them. Under the *nemo plus* principle, he cannot dispose of them before payment of the full sale price. If the parties were to agree that the initial buyer has the right to resell the goods, the clause would provide that the sub-sale is undertaken on the seller's behalf, and, presumably, the proceeds would be transferred to him. Yet, in practice, many goods sold under retention of title are indeed meant to be resold,[2] which means that, although in theory the transaction should be made by way of consignment, in practice it is not, so that sub-purchasers can only acquire ownership under the rules on *bona fide* acquisition.

The seller would not be entitled to trace into the goods, following sale to the sub-buyer, because of the principle of C. civ, article 2279 (see

---

[1] The German term is *Verfügungsbefugnis*. Its true meaning is difficult to translate: see further Van Vliet, *Transfer of Movables* 60 ff., who uses the term 'privilege to dispose'.
[2] See Debruyne, JCPédE 1995, Supplément 5, 40.

case 5(a)). Here, however, the jackets remain in B's fashion shops when B goes bankrupt. A is thus entitled to assert his title to them and claim *rei vindicatio*.

BELGIUM

A clause which reserves ownership of the goods to the seller until payment does not prevent the buyer from selling the goods in the ordinary course of business. An express authorisation to sell does not undermine either the validity or the effectiveness of reservation of title. A is therefore entitled to a *rei vindicatio* of the goods out of the insolvency estate.

PORTUGAL

As under Portuguese law the transfer of ownership occurs by the contract, the buyer normally is entitled to resell things bought prior to payment. If, however, reservation of title is stipulated, the goods would still be regarded as belonging to the seller until full payment of the price. In such a case, if the contract permits the buyer to resell, this would mean that the resale would be a sale of future things (article 880º C.C.). In such circumstances the transfer of ownership to the sub-purchasers is conditional on the payment of the price to the original seller.

Portuguese law does not provide for the acquisition of ownership from a non-owner on the basis of the transferee's good faith. The owner can always vindicate his property, but must prove that his is the better right (article 1311 nº 1 C.C.). This applies also if the *bona fide* purchaser bought the movable from a businessman, but in that case the purchaser has a claim for the monies paid against the owner (article 1301 C.C.).

As, therefore, A remains the owner of the jackets, he has the right to recover them in the event of non-payment. As, however, B went bankrupt, the reservation of title clause is only effective against the insolvency administrator if it was stipulated in an act under private signature before the delivery of the jackets (article 155º, nº 4 CPEREF).

SPAIN

This is a contract of sale, which falls under articles 325 ff. CCO. The Civil Code is not applicable because the transaction is between businessmen. Law 28/1998 also does not apply (article 5.1 LVBMP). Additionally, since this case deals with insolvency, articles 870 ff. CCO are applicable. A's rights depend on when the suspect period is determined to commence (article 878 CCO). The suspect period begins on the date specified by the judge and will necessarily fall before the date on which insolvency is declared. All voluntary acts of the insolvent within the suspect period are null and void. The purpose of the suspect period is to avoid the sale of assets to benefit third parties.[3] If A's debt arises before both the declaration of insolvency and the beginning of the suspect period, he may vindicate the jackets. They would not, in those circumstances, form part of the insolvency estate. A's debt arises on the date on which the contract was signed, not on the date agreed upon for payment. However, if the debt arises after the declaration of insolvency or within the suspect period, A's debt will be considered in B's insolvency proceedings, and consequently, A will not be able to vindicate the jackets.[4] A's position with regard to the other creditors of B depends on whether A is a privileged creditor or a common insolvency creditor (a distinction dependent on the nature of his debt). If privileged creditors exist, A will only receive payment after such creditors; if, however, all creditors are common insolvency creditors, A will receive payment according to the principle *par conditio creditorum*. In neither case will A be able to vindicate the jackets, which will go into public liquidation, in order that the proceeds can go to the satisfaction of the insolvency creditors. A will receive a *pro rata* share of the insolvency estate, a proportion of the debt owed to him by the insolvent.[5]

The solution to the case is the following: since A reserved title and since ownership has not been transferred to B, A can vindicate the jackets that B might have on his premises (article 908 CCO), provided that his right has been recognised by the Board of Creditors or confirmed by a judge's final decision.

ITALY

The solution to case 4 is the same as the solution to case 3. The power to resell the jackets does not *per se* affect the validity of the retention of title clause, which protects the seller's rights, as explained above in case 3, provided that the clause is incorporated in a document that has a certain date prior to insolvency. Of course, the seller will have to prove

---

[3] See Jiménez-Horwitz, RCDI 76, 1257 (1263).
[4] See Vicent Chuliá, *Compendio Crítico de Derecho Mercantil* II 880.
[5] See Díez-Picazo, *Fundamentos de derecho civil patrimonial* II 749.

that the jackets found in the possession of the buyer are the same jackets that were sold under reservation of title. This may be problematical if no sign identifies them as such.

The power of sale could be held to be invalid if coupled with a reservation of title clause which extended to the new thing produced out of, for example, raw materials, even if the raw materials are still found *in specie* in the buyer's possession. A reservation of title clause over raw materials that are sold and transformed into new things has indeed been held to be inconsistent with the intention to sell, and therefore null and void, by an old Court of Appeal case.[6] Some commentators have criticised this as being a dogmatic approach, because the inconsistency of the parties' will, which is assumed by the Court, is far from being crystal clear. No case so far has, however, established that the power to resell the goods is *by itself* inconsistent with a title retention clause in respect of goods that the buyer is not going to transform into new things. Such a power to sell the goods may spring from a mandate without representation to sell, or from an authorisation to sell. Neither are expressly regulated by the Italian Civil Code, but this does not mean they are invalid (although, especially in the past, some commentators have argued against the validity of such an authorisation).[7] This means

---

[6] App. Napoli 5 July 1955, Foro it., 1956, I, 101.

[7] The contract of mandate is regulated by articles 1703–1730 c.c. (mandate), articles 1731–1736 c.c. (contract of commission, which is also considered a mandate). Under Italian law, the contract of mandate can be coupled with a power of representation, or may be concluded without conferring that power to the intermediary (cf. articles 1704–1707, 1731 c.c.). The Code does mention the *commissione a vendere* (article 1731 c.c.), thereby implicitly affirming its validity. But the validity of contracts of mandate to sell has never been seriously questioned anyhow. The doubts raised with respect to them were mainly doctrinal. The question was whether or not the intermediary could transfer title to the goods sold directly, without acquiring it for a *scintilla temporis* (Luminoso, in: *Trattato di diritto civile e commerciale* XXXII 241 ff., 295 ff.; Costanza, *Digesto sez. comm.* III 167, 169–171; Montalenti, in: *Contratti commerciali* 633, 638 ff.). On the other hand, the issue of whether an authorisation to sell, like the German *Ermächtigung* (cf. § 185 BGB), was admissible in Italian law has been lively debated. On this academic controversy: see Carraro, *Novissimo digesto italiano*, I, 2, 1577; Auricchio, Enc. dir. IV 502; Mengoni, *Gli acquisti 'a non domino'* 3–5; Santagata, in: *Commentario del Codice Civile Scialoja-Branca* 232 ff.; Luminoso, *Il mandato* 81 ff. The controversy arose because the Italian Civil Code does not contain any provision matching that of § 185 BGB. Nevertheless, despite the silence of the Italian Code on the point, there are no strong reasons to hold that Italian law should turn its back on the operative solution enacted by § 185 BGB (cf. Graziadei, Resp. civ. prev. 1985, 23). There are opinions to the effect that the law of mandate in Italy plays the same function which in Germany is performed by the notion of *Ermächtigung*: Jaeger, *La separazione del patrimonio fiduciario nel fallimento* 266 ff.; Jaeger, Giur. comm. 1979, I, 181, 199 ff.; Graziadei, *Digesto sez. civ.* XI, 154 ff. For an instructive presentation of this debate in German see: Greving, *Der Treuhandgedanke bei Sicherungsübertragungen im italienischen und deutschen Recht* 46–47.

that a clause such as that mentioned in case 4 will be valid and the buyer will be able to transfer title to a sub-purchaser.

The combination of the power to resell the jackets with the stipulation that ownership of the jackets shall not pass to the buyer before the price is paid to the seller makes the sale resemble, to some extent, a consignment contract (*contratto estimatorio*), regulated by articles 1556–1558 c.c.[8] Under these provisions goods delivered to a consignee are held at his risk (article 1557 c.c.). Dispositions of the goods by the consignee to third parties are valid, but the consignee's creditors cannot execute against the goods until the price has been paid to the consignor (article 1558 c.c.). The main differences between the consignment contract and a sale under reservation of title coupled with a power to resell the goods are as follows. The buyer under retention of title cannot return the goods to the seller and is obliged to pay the purchase price. The consignee of goods may return them to the consignor at will, and is obliged to pay the price only if he does not return them to the consignor within a stipulated time. Consignment contracts are fairly common in certain trades, such as those concerning magazines and newspapers. On the other hand, reservation of title clauses granting the buyer the power to resell, such as that in the present case, are unknown in Italian commercial practice, despite their theoretical validity. The difficulty is that they are no more effective than simple reservation of title clauses, unless the owner of the goods can gain priority to the proceeds arising from the sale to the third party. How to secure such priority is a difficult point in Italy. The Civil Code rules on assignment of claims are not very helpful in this respect (for a discussion of these rules, see case 10). Nor is it likely that a sale transaction will be interpreted as a mandate just to let the owner under reservation of title get priority over other creditors. True, the principal's rights will be protected *vis-à-vis* the intermediary's executing creditors, or his insolvency administrator, even when the mandate was undisclosed, provided that it had a certain date prior to the execution or the agent's insolvency (article 1707 c.c.).[9] But if the contract between the parties was a genuine sale, it is unlikely that it will be treated like a mandate,

---

[8] Sarale, in: *Contratti commerciali* 161 ff.; Graziadei, *Digesto sez. comm.* IV, 1989, 103.

[9] Article 1707 c.c.: 'The creditors of a mandatory cannot enforce their rights on property which the mandatory has acquired in his own name in carrying out the mandate, provided that in the purchase of movable property or claims, the mandate be evidenced by a writing bearing a certain date prior to the attachment of the property or, in the case of immovable property or movable property inscribed in public registers, the transcription of the transaction effecting the transfer of ownership or of the judicial petition for the purpose of obtaining said transfer be prior to such attachment.'

even though the buyer was granted the power to resell the goods. Note also that under a consignment contract, the consignor does not obtain priority to the claims that the third party owes to the consignee, or over the monies the third party paid to the consignee.

THE NETHERLANDS

Parties are free to agree that the buyer will have a power to resell the goods.[10] Such a contractual entitlement to resell the goods does not invalidate the reservation of title clause but leads to what is called 'conditional retention of title'.[11] Where the contract of sale itself is silent, an entitlement to resell may be implied. It is important to note, however, that the mere fact that it is evident that the goods are intended to be resold is not of itself sufficient reason to conclude the existence of 'conditional retention of title'.[12]

The general view appears to be that a power to resell should be regarded as a resolutive condition of the ownership of the seller, in addition to payment of the purchase price. In other words, when the first buyer makes use of his or her power to resell, the condition is fulfilled with the effect of transferring ownership to B a logical second before ownership is then transferred to the second buyer.[13]

As B has not paid the price, nor made use of the power to resell, A has remained the owner and may, after the termination of the contract, rely on *rei vindicatio* and claim the jackets.

ENGLAND

This is no different from any other reservation of title where the buyer retains possession for personal use. The seller's reservation of title remains effective for reasons stated in case 3. There is no principle of

---

[10] This is acknowledged by the Dutch Supreme Court (see *Hoge Raad* 8 June 1973, NJ 1974, 346 (*Nationaal Grondbezit/Kamphuis*) 14 Feb. 1992, NJ 1993, 623) and fully accepted in the literature. It should be noted that the power to resell is to be understood to be a power to dispose; a mere selling of someone else's property (car) does not invalidate the contract of sale.

[11] *Geclausuleerd eigendomsvoorbehoud*.

[12] *Hoge Raad* 14 Feb. 1992, NJ 1993, 623 (*Hinck/Van der Werf*).

[13] This is why it leads to what in Germany is called *Durchgangserwerb*. See Reehuis, *Eigendomsvoorbehoud* n. 38 and literature there cited as well as Fesevur, *Goederenrechtelijke colleges* 107. Sometimes *Direkterwerb* is argued by which the reseller is entitled to dispose 'directly' of the original seller's right, Pitlo/Reehuis/Heisterkamp, *Het Nederlands burgerlijk recht III* nr. 968. The key issue is whether ownership passes to B at all.

reputed ownership in English insolvency law which would subordinate A's reservation of title to the claims of B's creditors enforced on their behalf by B's insolvency administrator (either the *liquidator* or the *trustee-in-bankruptcy*).

IRELAND

In this case we have a 'simple' retention of title clause coupled with an express entitlement on the part of the buyer to resell the goods. The entitlement to resell does not affect the validity of the retention of title clause. There is a decision of the Court of Appeal – *Clough Mill Ltd v Martin*[14] – to that effect in England and it is virtually certain that the same view would prevail in Ireland.

SCOTLAND

The fact that B is authorised by the contract to resell the jackets makes no difference. Nor does it make any difference that B has been allowed a credit period. The jackets still belong to A. Therefore if B becomes bankrupt, the jackets do not form part of the insolvency estate.

SOUTH AFRICA

The fact that the buyer is entitled to resell the jackets does not affect the validity or enforceability of the reservation of title clause. If the buyer resells the jackets and then defaults on payment, the original seller (A) will still be able to reclaim his property.[15] South African law does not recognise the *bona fide* acquisition of ownership by *bona fide* third parties. The only limitation in this respect on the *rei vindicatio* of the original owner is the English doctrine of estoppel, which has been adopted in

---

[14] [1985] 1 WLR 111.
[15] Note that most sales by instalments fall under a consumer protection statute, the Credit Agreements Act 75 of 1980. Under s. 11 of this Act the hire-purchase seller (A) must notify the hire-purchaser (B) of his breach of contract and must grant him thirty days to remedy his breach. Thereafter he can recover his property (the jackets) from B. The notification must be by letter either personally delivered or sent by registered post. However, if the property is returned to the creditor within a month before the sequestration of the purchaser's (B's) estate, s. 84 (2) of the Insolvency Act 24 of 1936 applies. Pursuant to this section, the insolvency administrator may demand that the seller deliver to him the property or the value thereof, taking into account the part payments already made.

South African law.[16] Since no jackets have been sold, no impression has been created vis-à-vis third parties and the doctrine of estoppel would not apply to this case. A can therefore reclaim his property wherever he finds it.

Since B has not become the owner of the jackets, A can reclaim possession of the jackets from the insolvency estate of B.

DENMARK

According to Danish law, an arrangement which allows the buyer to resell the goods, even if bought under a contract providing for reservation of title, is regarded as a credit consignment agreement. There is an air of artifice about an agreement which provides for reservation of title but also provides the buyer with a right to resell the goods. In order to conclude a valid credit consignment agreement some further conditions must be fulfilled. Case law has established the main conditions as being (1) that the consignee must pay the consignor when the goods are resold; and (2) that the consignor must make sure that the consignee acts in accordance with the agreement. The precise conditions for payment and control may vary according to the type of goods sold under consignment. If the assets are relatively expensive each resale should be paid for at once; in contrast, if the unit cost of the goods is relatively low, payment might be over a period of time.

As the buyer has been granted a fixed period of sixty days before payment falls due, the contract fails to meet the condition of payment to the consignor on resale. Because this condition is the most important condition, the reservation of title clause is invalid, which means that the seller, A, cannot reclaim the jackets or claim preferential payment from the proceeds of the sale of the jackets.

SWEDEN

The entitlement of the buyer to resell the goods prior to payment invalidates the seller's reservation of title or right of rescission in relation to the buyer's creditors.[17] An exception is made if the buyer is obliged to pass on the seller's reservation of title to the next buyer.[18]

---

[16] On the limitations imposed on the *rei vindicatio* by the doctrine of estoppel, see van der Merwe, *Sakereg* 368–373.
[17] See for instance NJA 1932, 292 and 1959, 590. [18] NJA 1980, 219.

Initially, the reason for this invalidity was that such reservations of title were not intended seriously, but were only made *in fraudem creditorum*, since the buyer was entitled himself to dispose of the goods as an owner.[19] Today, this argument has been discarded. Instead, the question put is whether the law should allow securities of this unreliable kind. The goods will often have been sold (or transformed in the manufacturing process) when the buyer goes bankrupt, without the seller having security in any substitute. Recognition of such a security would not, therefore, say the defenders of the present position, lead to an expansion of low-cost credit. The cost of credit from other sources, especially the banks, would increase by a comparable amount, since they normally, at present, have priority over the assets by virtue of an enterprise charge. Hence debtors' aggregate credit bills would not be lowered. A reform, giving sellers the option of reserving a right also to the proceeds (claims and new products), would provide them with a more effective security. It would, however, cause technical problems and it would undermine the registered enterprise charge. Despite the arguments for reform, for example, that producers and wholesalers are usually unable to compete with the banks for the enterprise charge, and that their risks are less diversified, the legislature has not so far been convinced that security in sold goods should be extended. An alternative proposal is that the enterprise charge should extend to all assets, but be restricted to 50 per cent of their value.[20]

To the extent that the reservation of title clause is invalid, a sub-purchaser will become owner without any need to rely on the rules governing *bona fide* acquisitions.

The limitations on reservation of title may to some degree be circumvented if the goods are handed over to the retailer, B, on a commission (undisclosed agency, *kommission*) basis, i.e. without transferring ownership to B but providing B with the right to sell the goods on A's behalf; or as a consignment, i.e. which would provide B with an option to become the owner and sell on his own behalf, when he has found a third party willing to buy. In both cases A would have in principle a right of separation in respect of the unsold goods. However, agreements are not regarded as being concluded on a commission or consignment

---

[19] Almén/Eklund, *Lagen om köp och byte av lös egendom* § 28 fn. 129 and Almén, SvJT 1918, 5 (21).
[20] See e.g. Helander, *Kreditsäkerhet i lös egendom* 649 ff. and 723 ff.; Håstad, *Sakrätt rörande lös egendom* 189 ff.; SOU 1988:63 and 1999:1.

basis unless the agent/consignee has a right to return the goods, without excessive penalties or charges, should he not find a buyer. Without such a right, the transaction would be, in reality, by way of sale. However, it seems to be permissible for A to charge a fixed price from B (instead of a percentage). In some judgments, courts have made mention of the fact that the principal (consignor) had ensured that a fast settlement took place, but that seems not to have been the *ratio decidendi*.[21]

FINLAND

According to the settled case law, a retention of title clause is invalid as against the creditors of the buyer if the buyer has the right to resell the goods before full payment of the purchase price to the seller.[22] The position may be different if the buyer's right to resell the goods has been so restricted that it does not jeopardise the security interest of the seller.[23] It is unlikely that this requirement would be met in the present case, however, as the buyer had the right to sell the jackets in the ordinary course of business.

The rules concerning commission or consignments can sometimes protect the seller.[24] The description of case 4 does not, however, indicate that these rules would apply.

---

[21] See s. 53 of the Commission Agency (Undisclosed Agency) Act (*Kommissionslagen*, 1914), Håstad, *Sakrätt rörande lös egendom* 147 ff. and SOU 1988:63. It appears that, from preparatory material to the Commission Agency Act, the legislature assumed that commission agency contracts would have commission fixed as a percentage for the agent (NJA II 1914, 272 ff.). This is not observed in practice, however, and the courts would now find it difficult to impose such a requirement.

[22] See e.g. KKO 1986 I 2 and KKO 1995:128.

[23] See e.g. Tuomisto, *Omistuksenpidätys ja leasing* 331 ff.

[24] The term 'consignment' signifies a type of agreement different from the 'commission'. In both cases the goods are delivered to the 'middleman' who is under no obligation to buy them. It is, however, typical in the case of a consignment that the 'middleman' has an option to buy the goods. In such a case, the intention of the parties is that goods are bought by the 'middleman' and resold on his own account. On the other hand, it is typical under the commission that the goods are sold on the account of the principal and that the principal receives money from the proceeds that the agent has collected from his own customers. See e.g. Tepora, *Defensor Legis* 1991, 623 ff. and Tepora, *Lakimies* 1992, 1043 ff. However, the borderline between commissions and consignments is unclear. Even under a commission, the 'middleman' sometimes has an option to buy the goods for himself, and it is not easy to decide whether the goods are sold on the account of the 'middleman' or the principal.

Comparative observations

On the rather simple facts of case 4, the jurisdictions under consideration produce no less than seven different approaches. The last two, pursued by the Nordic systems, also produce a difference in result.

Pursuant to German, Greek, Austrian, Italian, English, Irish and Scots law, the buyer's entitlement to resell the jackets gives him the power to transfer ownership directly from the seller to the sub-purchasers. The sub-purchasers receive title to the goods without having to rely on the rules of *bona fide* acquisition. So long as the goods remain in the hands of the first buyer, retention of title remains unaffected and thus enables the seller to vindicate the goods irrespective of whether the buyer is insolvent. One minor difference emerges between German, Greek and Austrian law on the one hand, and Italian, English, Irish and Scots law on the other hand, at the academic level. Within the first three systems the entitlement is construed as a power of disposal (a limited real right, separable from ownership), whereas under the latter jurisdictions the entitlement follows the rules on mandate.

As in case 2, it will be noted that the dividing lines do not correspond to the differences in the regimes relating to the transfer of ownership. In this first group we find abstract, tradition and consensual systems side by side, not only reaching the same result but also adopting the same method of analysis.

Dutch law, although it reaches the same result as the systems just mentioned, differs from the above analysis in so far as the resale is regarded as fulfilment of a suspensive condition for the transfer of ownership between the seller and the first buyer. Therefore the buyer transfers title in the goods as owner, not merely as someone with an entitlement to dispose. So long as the goods remain in the hands of the first buyer, the title retained by the seller remains unaffected also under Dutch law.

Portuguese law presents yet another solution: the sub-purchasers merely receive what may be called an expectancy. They will acquire full title only when the first buyer pays the price to the seller. This is so, irrespective of whether the sub-purchasers acted on a good faith belief in the buyer's ownership, since Portuguese law has not adopted the principle of *bona fide* acquisition from non-owners. However, on the facts of case 4, where no sub-sale has yet taken place, the result is the same as under the aforementioned jurisdictions: A's retention of title remains unaffected, thus enabling him to vindicate the jackets from the insolvency estate.

A fourth way to resolve the case is adopted by French and Belgian law. The buyer's authorisation to resell is regarded as legally irrelevant, so long as it does not form part of a consignment agreement in the strict sense. Thus, the sub-purchasers will only acquire ownership according to the rules on *bona fide* acquisition. Yet, since the goods are still in the hands of the buyers, the result does not differ from that reached by the systems mentioned so far.

A fifth solution is adopted by South African law, according to which the entitlement to resell the jackets is legally irrelevant. It does not confer upon B the power to transfer good title to his customers, nor does it estop A from vindicating the resold jackets. Nevertheless, upon the facts of case 4, where the jackets are not yet resold, the result does not differ from the previous solutions: A can vindicate the goods from B's insolvency administrator.

A sixth solution, and a slightly different result, is reached in Danish law. A reservation of title may be accepted if the goods are sold and transferred to the buyer with an entitlement to resell them before payment. But such an arrangement is valid only if framed as a credit consignment, which means that the buyer (consignee) must be under an obligation to make ready settlement and the seller (consignor) must closely supervise the process of settlement. A right for the buyer (consignee) to return unsold goods might help to uphold the reservation but it is certainly not indispensable. If a contract takes the form of a sale with retention of title and entitlement to resell but the contract does not conform to the relatively strict requirements of a consignment contract, the reservation of title will be void.

A seventh solution, and a materially different result, is adopted by Swedish and Finnish law. Here a retention of title is invalid when coupled with a power for the buyer to resell on his own account prior to payment, i.e. when the buyer bears the risk that the goods cannot be resold. A retains a right of separation in the remaining stock only if the retailer is entitled to return goods for which he cannot find a customer. A transaction such as the one contemplated in case 4 can only take one of the following two forms: (1) it can be a commission agreement, which means that B sells the goods as an undisclosed agent on the producer's (A's) account, or (2) the parties may agree that B buys the goods when he has found a customer whereafter he resells the goods on his own account (often called consignment, although this term sometimes is used also for commission).

The rationale of this approach, set out by the Swedish report, is shared by the other two Nordic jurisdictions. So far as the possibility to take a security right in the proceeds is concerned, their point of view resembles that of other European jurisdictions which do not allow such security rights except if they are registered or publicised (see e.g. English report, cases 5 and 6). In respect of proceeds clauses there is in fact a danger of conflict between the seller's security and those of banks, either under an enterprise charge or a security assignment of claims. The flood of German court decisions on conflicts between sellers' proceeds clauses and banks' rights under security assignments illustrates this danger.[25] However, the striking feature of the Danish, Swedish and Finnish solutions lies in the strict stance which these systems adopt in respect of unsold goods that are still in the possession of the buyer under retention of title. The transaction cannot, at this point, be regarded as a fraud against the third-party creditors of the buyer in any additional way than a normal retention of title, as the Swedish report also identifies, nor does it appear convincing, at least from the point of view of a German observer, to deprive the seller of the simple title retention if he cannot also get a security right in the claims arising out of sub-sales.

---

[25] See most recently BGH 8 Dec. 1998, JZ 1998, 404 (note Kieninger).

Case 5: Motor cars supplied and resold (I)

(Protection of bona fide purchaser – retention of title and resale – consignment – special legislation)

A is a producer (or importer) of cars. He sells five cars to B, a licensed distributor. The contract allows B a period of forty-five days before payment has to be made. It also contains the following clause: 'The seller hereby retains title to the cars delivered under this contract. The buyer, however, is entitled to resell the cars in the ordinary course of business.' Two weeks after delivery of the cars, B has managed to sell all of them to various customers (C1–C5) who have paid for them and taken them away immediately. Before paying A, B goes bankrupt.

Questions

(a) Can A still claim ownership of, or any other real right in, the cars? To what extent, if at all, does the answer depend on B's entitlement to resell the cars?

(b) Who is entitled to the monies that have been paid by the customers (C1–C5) to B? Is it A? Or is it B's insolvency administrator/insolvency creditors?

(c) Could A improve his position in some way? If so, on what further circumstances would such an improved position depend? Are such arrangements commonly used? Is there a typical arrangement (perhaps for specific goods, whether cars or otherwise), the use of which would grant to A a security that would survive resale?

Discussions

GERMANY

(a) A can no longer claim ownership of the cars. B's entitlement to resell the cars meant that the customers (C1–C5) became owners without reliance on the rules governing *bona fide* acquisition.

Bona fide acquisition of ownership from a non-owner

If B had not been entitled to resell the cars, the customers would still have acquired ownership if the prerequisites for *bona fide* acquisition had been fulfilled. § 1006 s. 1 sent. 1 BGB states that a person in possession of a movable is presumed to be the owner. Thus, the seller's (B's) possession of the goods is the basis for the good faith of the purchaser.[1] The latter generally is entitled to believe that a seller who is in possession of the movable is the owner. Good faith is presumed and is only rebutted if the transferee positively knew that the transferor was not the owner or if his ignorance was grossly negligent: see § 932 s. 2 BGB. A *bona fide* purchase must be for value. If the transfer is gratuitous, the transferee will still become owner, but he will be under the obligation to retransfer ownership to the original owner according to the rules on unjust enrichment (§ 816 s. 1 sent. 2 BGB). Furthermore, a *bona fide* acquisition is not possible if the owner has been deprived of his possession involuntarily: § 935 s. 1 BGB. This provision does not apply to money and negotiable instruments issued to bearer (§ 935 s. 2 BGB).

The remaining requirements for the *bona fide* acquisition of ownership from a non-owner depend on the way in which ownership is transferred:

(1) If the transfer is carried out by actual delivery, the transferee will acquire ownership provided that, at the time of delivery, he is in good faith.
(2) If, instead of actual delivery, the parties agree that the transferor will possess the movable on behalf of the transferee (*constitutum possessorium*), a *bona fide* acquisition of ownership is only possible if and when the transferee comes into direct possession, provided that at that moment he is still in good faith (§ 933 BGB).[2]

---

[1] *Staudinger*/Wiegand, Vorbemerkung zu §§ 932 ff. BGB nn. 7–11.
[2] This rule resolves the conflict between a seller under retention of title and a creditor of the buyer to whom security title in the goods is transferred (see Baur/Stürner, *Sachenrecht* § 52 n. 20). The seller will not entitle the buyer to transfer for security

(3) If, instead of actual delivery, the parties agree to an assignment of the claim for the recovery of the property,[3] good faith at the time of the assignment suffices (§ 934 BGB). In contrast to the rule in § 933 BGB, it is not necessary for the transferee to come into direct possession of the movable. It is remarkable that in this case indirect possession on the side of both parties is thought sufficient, whereas in case (2) indirect possession of the transferee is not. This inconsistency could be resolved if the decisive factor is regarded as being the complete loss of any possession on the part of the transferor.[4]

Today, a major problem arising in respect of the good faith of purchasers is the increasing use of non-possessory security interests based on ownership (retention of title with various extensions,[5] security transfer of ownership[6]). One may ask whether purchasers (or creditors) nowadays can still believe that the movables they find in the possession of a seller (or debtor) are really owned by him. The BGH has decided that, in those business sectors where practically all goods are sold under retention of title, purchasers can no longer assume that the seller owns the goods in his possession. The Court said (translation by author):[7]

In the course of economic development, the decisiveness of factual possession, which is the basis for the statutory provisions on *bona fide* acquisition, has lost its meaning to a considerable extent. This applies to all movables that are normally purchased on credit and therefore delivered under retention of title. In this area, possession points to ownership only to a very limited extent.

However, the BGH has not yet concluded generally that possession has lost all relevance to the resolution of conflicts as to ownership, rather it views each case on its facts.[8] In a second decision the Court said:[9]

Although one has to acknowledge the eminent importance of retention of title in today's business, the statutory principle laid down in §§ 932, 935 BGB should not be lost sight of. This principle says that whoever voluntarily gives up possession of his property takes the risk that another acquires title to it.

---

purposes the goods to which he has retained title. The creditor cannot acquire title from the buyer as non-owner because the goods are not actually handed over to him. Retention of title thus prevails over security transfer.

[3] As to this substitute for delivery, see further Van Vliet, *Transfer of Movables* 55 ff.
[4] Cf. Baur/Stürner, *Sachenrecht* § 52 n. 20 with further references.
[5] Products and all-monies clauses: see *infra*, German report, cases 7 and 9.
[6] See *infra*, German report, case 10.   [7] BGH 18 June 1980, BGHZ 77, 274.
[8] For an overview of the court practice see *Staudinger*/Wiegand § 932 BGB nn. 171–187.
[9] BGH 9 July 1990, ZIP 1991, 176 (178).

(b) The monies that have been paid to B form part of his assets and will be apportioned between his creditors in the insolvency proceedings.

(c) There are two principal ways in which A may improve his position. However, neither are applicable to this case.

(i) The first way is *not* to permit B to resell the cars.[10] The customers would still become owners, provided they were in good faith when taking possession of the cars (see *supra*). A may, however, in certain circumstances, be able to claim the proceeds that B received, even after the commencement of insolvency proceedings. § 48 InsO protects a creditor whose right to vindicate goods in insolvency (e.g. on the basis of retention of title) has been unlawfully frustrated either by the debtor prior to the commencement of insolvency proceedings or by the administrator after commencement. Such a creditor can claim the consideration that the debtor or the administrator has received, provided that it remains in the insolvency estate in an identifiable manner (§ 48 sent. 2 InsO). Here, the resale of the cars by B would have been unlawful, in the sense meant by § 48 InsO, if the contract between A and B did not contain an entitlement to resell. The problem lies, however, in the second requirement. If the claim arising out of the sub-sale has already been satisfied, A's rights pursuant to § 48 InsO could only subsist if the monies had been paid into a separate account. According to the predominant opinion, monies paid into the buyer's normal business account are no longer distinguishable for the purposes of § 48 sent. 2 InsO.[11]

(ii) Usually, contracts for the sale of goods which are intended to be resold contain a retention of title clause that extends the seller's rights to the proceeds of sale (a proceeds clause). In addition to simple retention of title and the entitlement of the first buyer (B) to resell the cars, such a clause will contain an anticipatory assignment of the claims arising out of such sub-sales. A typical proceeds clause reads as follows:

The goods remain our property until the purchase price has been paid. The buyer is entitled to resell the goods in the ordinary course of business. The buyer, however, already assigns to the seller all claims arising out of the resale of the goods to third parties. The buyer is authorised to collect these claims even

---

[10] According to Serick, *Eigentumsvorbehalt und Sicherungsübertragung* V 361, an entitlement to resell will come to an end even without an explicit revocation at the moment at which the debtor stops all payments (*Zahlungseinstellung*) or applies for the commencement of insolvency proceedings.

[11] Cf. *Nerlich/Römermann/Andres* § 48 InsO nn. 11 f.; *Smid/Gundlach* 1st edn, 1999, § 48 InsO n. 61.

after their assignment so long as he observes the terms of the contract and is not insolvent.[12]

The following features of German (judge-made) law make proceeds clauses legally possible and practically workable:

(1) German law allows the assignment of future claims. An agreement by which the buyer (B) assigns claims to the seller (A) arising out of sub-sales is valid even if these sub-sales have not yet been concluded.[13] Of course, A cannot claim anything until the contract with C has been concluded, but as soon as that contract is entered into, B's claim against C will automatically vest in A.[14] This does not depend on B's continuing willingness to assign the claim.[15] The principle of specificity[16] only requires (1) that the claims to which the assignment relates are clearly identifiable when they come into existence and (2) that they are determinable at the time of the assignment.[17] In contrast to the decisions of the *Reichsgericht*,[18] the BGH does not apply these prerequisites rigorously.[19] It does not consider it necessary for the agreement to provide in advance for all eventualities and for it to specify without any possible doubt the claims that will later be covered by the assignment.[20] It is thus possible, for example, to assign all future claims arising out of sub-sales concluded within the business of the assignor,[21] or all future claims arising out of contracts

---

[12] Cf. International Chamber of Commerce, *Retention of Title. A Practical Guide to Legislation in 35 Countries* 55.
[13] General opinion, cf. BGH 15 Oct. 1952, BGHZ 7, 365; BGH 16 Dec. 1957, BGHZ 26, 185 (188); BGH 22 Sep. 1965, NJW 1965, 2197; BGH 9 July 1960, BGHZ 32, 367; Reinicke/Tiedtke, *Kreditsicherung* n. 602; Staudinger/Busche § 398 BGB nn. 63 f.; Bülow, *Recht der Kreditsicherheiten* nn. 1221 f.; Serick, *Eigentumsvorbehalt und Sicherungsübertragung* IV 270–273.
[14] It is disputed whether for a logical second the claim vests in the first buyer before being transferred to the seller (*Durchgangserwerb*) or whether the seller acquires the claim directly (*Direkterwerb*): see *infra*, German report, case 12(b).
[15] Reinicke/Tiedtke, *Kreditsicherung* n. 603.
[16] The principle that real rights must relate to a specific piece of property: see generally Van Vliet, *Transfer of Movables* 27 f.
[17] BGH 25 Oct.1952, BGHZ 7, 365 (369); BGH 16 Dec. 1957, BGHZ 26, 185 (189); BGH 24 Apr. 1968, NJW 1968, 1516 (1518 f.); BGH 7 Dec. 1977, BGHZ 70, 86 (89); BGH 20 Nov. 1980, BGHZ 79, 16 (20 f.); Bülow, *Recht der Kreditsicherheiten* n. 1190; Münchener Kommentar/Roth § 398 BGB n. 49; Staudinger/Honsell § 455 BGB n. 54; Lwowski, *Das Recht der Kreditsicherung* n. 705; Reinicke/Tiedtke, *Kreditsicherung* n. 607.
[18] RGZ 149, 96 (101 f.); RGZ 155, 26 (29).
[19] Cf. BGH 25 Oct. 1952, BGHZ 7, 365 (369); BGH 4 Oct. 1965, WM 1966, 13; BGH 24 Apr. 1968, NJW 1968, 1516 (1518 f.).
[20] See note 19.
[21] BGH 9 June 1960, WM 60, 838; Lwowksi, *Das Recht der Kreditsicherung* n. 759; Reinicke/Tiedtke, *Kreditsicherung* n. 608.

with customers whose names begin with the letters 'A' through to 'K',[22] or who reside in a specific area,[23] or all claims arising out of contracts concluded within a specified period of time.[24] The BGH has even accepted as determinable an assignment of a future claim 'equal to the value of the goods delivered'.[25] There is, moreover, no need to impose a time-limit.[26]

(2) German law acknowledges the validity of an assignment for the purpose of securing a debt (security assignment).[27]

(3) An assignment does not require any specific form or publicity. In particular, there is no need to communicate it to *debitores cessi* (C1–C5) in order for it to become effective *erga omnes*. This is also so in respect of security assignment, although a notification requirement exists for the pledge of a claim (§ 1280).[28] As in the case of the security transfer of ownership, the courts have always treated the security assignment as a 'normal' assignment and have refrained from applying the rules on the pledge of rights.

In this case, however, a proceeds clause would not have improved A's position since the monies have already been paid to B. This conforms with usual business practice. In cases such as the present, A will usually permit B to collect the monies for him. B will be under a contractual obligation to use the money to pay off the debt owed to A. If C pays B, the monies will belong to B.[29] He will be under an obligation to transfer the money to A but this is only a claim *in personam*. Usually, if A realises that B is getting into financial difficulties, he will terminate B's entitlement to collect the claims for him[30] and will notify B's customers of the assignment. Notification prevents the customers from making valid payment to B.[31] The termination of B's entitlement to collect the money can, in certain circumstances, provide A with an additional remedy in

---

[22] Reinicke/Tiedtke, *Kreditsicherung* n. 608; Lwowksi, *Das Recht der Kreditsicherung* n. 759.
[23] Lwowksi, *Das Recht der Kreditsicherung* n. 759. [24] BGH 4 Oct. 1965, WM 1966, 13.
[25] BGH 24 Apr. 1968, NJW 1968, 1516 (1519). The BGH, however, does not accept a security assignment of claims equalling the value of the secured claim if the latter is constantly fluctuating: see BGH 5 July 1965, NJW 1965, 2196.
[26] OLG Oldenburg 21 Jan. 1997, WM 1997, 1383; Lwowski, *Das Recht der Kreditsicherung* n. 707.
[27] Cf. Bülow, *Recht der Kreditsicherheiten* nn. 930 ff. See also *infra*, German report, case 10(a).
[28] Cf. Reinicke/Tiedtke, *Kreditsicherung* n. 591. [29] *Ibid.*, n. 742.
[30] This entitlement is also regarded as automatically terminated at the moment at which the debtor (B) stops all payments or applies for the commencement of insolvency proceedings: see *Smid*/Gundlach 1st edn, 1999, § 48 InsO n. 47.
[31] See § 407 s. 1 BGB: payment by the *debitor cessus* to the assignor is invalid as against the assignee if the *debitor cessus* knows of the assignment.

B's insolvency. This remedy is by way of analogy with the aforementioned § 48 InsO. The application would not be direct but analogous[32] because a security assignment or transfer of ownership gives the creditor only a right to preferential payment out of the proceeds of the realisation of the collateral.[33] Here, the wrongful transfer by the debtor (B) would lie in the collection of the claims from the customers after A has terminated B's entitlement. Yet, in this case, A's right to the monies paid would fail for two reasons. First, A did not revoke the entitlement to collect before B received the money from C1–C5, and, secondly, the monies are no longer identifiable, because they were not paid into a separate bank account.[34]

In conclusion, the monies paid by C1–C5 to B belong to B or – in the case of insolvency – to B's insolvency creditors.

AUSTRIA

(a) A has lost ownership of the cars to the buyers (C1–C5). B was entitled to resell the cars, therefore he was able to transfer ownership (*qua* derivative acquisition of ownership) of these cars, notwithstanding the fact that he was not their owner. In Austrian (and German) legal terminology he had a *Verfügungsermächtigung*.

Without such an entitlement to resell the cars he would not have been able to transfer ownership of the cars. There would have been, however, the possibility of a *bona fide* purchase.

If the seller is not the owner of the object of the sale, and has not been authorised by the owner to sell the object in question, the buyer can become the owner only by way of a *bona fide* transfer. There are four cases of *bona fide* transfer. According to § 367 ABGB, the buyer of an object becomes the owner notwithstanding the fact that it did not belong to the seller if (1) he purchases it at a public auction; (2) the seller is a businessman and the object is sold in the course of that business; or (3) if the true owner had handed it over to the seller (not necessarily

---

[32] Predominant doctrinal opinion, see *Smid/Gundlach* 1st edn, 1999, § 48 InsO nn. 19 ff.; Baur/Stürner, *Zwangsvollstreckungs-, Konkurs- und Vergleichsrecht II* n. 15.6; Bork, *Einführung in das neue Insolvenzrecht* n. 260. The question whether the rule in § 48 InsO (formerly § 46 KO) may be applied by way of analogy has hitherto been left open by the BGH: see BGH 10 Mar. 1967, BGHZ 47, 181 (182).
[33] See *infra*, German report, case 6(b).
[34] Cf. *Nerlich/Römermann*/Andres § 48 InsO nn. 11 f.; *Smid/Gundlach* 1st edn, 1999, § 48 InsO n. 61.

for the purpose of selling it). In the third case, the seller is described as a *Vertrauensmann* (man of confidence).

§ 367 ABGB does not apply to gratuitous transactions. In such cases, a *bona fide* transfer can take place according to another provision of the code, § 371 ABGB, if the property in question consists of monies or securities.

It is necessary for the buyer to be entitled to believe that the seller is the owner of the object. According to one opinion,[35] it is sufficient that he believes that the seller is entitled to sell it. If his belief is, however, based on slight negligence, § 367 ABGB does not apply.

Legal scientific writers disagree as to whether it is necessary for the goods to be handed over to the buyer. Some[36] think that a *bona fide* transfer can be completed by means of a *constitutum possessorium*. This is also the position of the OGH (SZ 11/12). Others,[37] however, argue that this is not possible. Furthermore, there is disagreement as to whether the acquisition of ownership depends on full payment for the object sold. The majority opinion[38] holds that this is not necessary, a minority opinion[39] holds that it is.

If the seller is a businessman, § 366 HGB applies in addition to § 367 ABGB. By virtue of this provision, it is sufficient that the buyer believes that the seller is entitled to sell the object. § 366 HGB does not apply if the object was stolen or lost by the original owner, unless the subject matter of the transfer consists of monies or securities or of goods sold in a public auction.

If the seller did not authorise the buyer to resell the goods, or if the second sale is not in accordance with any authorisation, a second buyer can become owner only by means of a *bona fide* purchase, which depends on whether he was entitled to believe that the seller was the owner of the object sold or was authorised to sell it. There is at least partial disagreement about the conditions under which the buyer is entitled to hold such belief, especially as to whether the buyer is obliged to check whether an authorisation does in fact exist. Several cases must be distinguished:

---

[35] Rummel/Spielbüchler § 367 n. 6. Koziol/Welser, *Grundriß des bürgerlichen Rechts II* 82, follow Spielbüchler only when the object is sold by a businessman.
[36] Rummel/Spielbüchler § 367 n. 3.
[37] Frotz, *Aktuelle Probleme des Kreditsicherungsrechts* 154.
[38] Rummel/Spielbüchler § 367 n. 6.
[39] Bollenberger, ÖJZ 1995, 641; *contra* Holzner, ÖJZ 1996, 372; reply by Bollenberger, ÖJZ 1996, 851.

(1) If the goods are bought by way of a cash purchase, the purchaser (e.g. C1) does not have to make any further inquiries, even if the goods in question are normally sold under retention of title. This rule[40] applies only if the purchaser is entitled to assume that the goods were handed over to the first buyer for the purpose of resale and if they are sold by the first buyer in the usual course of his business. The rule does not, therefore, apply to goods which are part of the permanent capital of the first buyer. The rationale proffered for this rule is that the purchaser is entitled to believe that his seller will transfer the money paid to the first seller.

(2) If the second buyer purchases the goods on credit, some authors[41] argue that he has to make further inquiries, as he is not entitled to assume that the first seller authorised the buyer to sell the goods on credit. This view was expressed by the OGH in the decision SZ 60/13.[42] In this case, the second buyer was a businessman, a car dealer, who bought a car for the purpose of resale. A recent decision of the OGH[43] concerned a case where the object – a car – was bought by a person for private purposes on credit. In this case, the OGH held that the buyer was under no obligation to make further inquiries. The buyer was entitled to believe that the first seller had authorised the first buyer to sell the car on credit and to transfer ownership of the car on full payment.

(b) If A and B do not agree any special provision as to payment, then the monies will form part of B's estate and will therefore be taken by B's insolvency administrator.

(c) To avoid this problem, A and B usually agree on reservation of title with a proceeds clause, which will provide that B's claim against C is to be assigned to A. This is known in Austrian law as extended reservation of title (*verlängerter Eigentumsvorbehalt*). Such an agreement has the effect that C must pay A.

---

[40] Cf. OGH 16 Apr. 1987, 7 Ob 551/87 JBl 1988, 313; OGH 7 July 1992, 4 Ob 536/92 ÖBA 1993, 156 (Bollenberger). In earlier decisions the OGH applied stricter criteria: cf. OGH 11 July 1985, 8 Ob 534/85 JBl 1986, 235 (Czermak). Here it argues that the second buyer must make further inquiries if he purchases goods which are usually sold under retention of title. In this case, however, the second buyer bought the goods *on credit*. In OGH 24 June 1987, 1 Ob 614/87 JBl 1988, 314 (Czermak) = SZ 60/120, the OGH held that there is a duty to make further inquiries if the second buyer is a businessman who buys the goods for the purpose of resale. This view has now been abandoned. The legal scientific writers share the view of the OGH: cf. Koziol/Welser, *Grundriß des bürgerlichen Rechts II* 157; Bollenberger, ÖBA 1993, 159 (162).

[41] Cf. Koziol/Welser, *Grundriß des bürgerlichen Rechts II* 157; Bollenberger, ÖBA 1993, 159 (161).

[42] 28 Jan. 1987, 1 Ob 713/86 JBl 1988, 311.   [43] 19 May 1993, 8 Ob 606/92 RdW 1993, 331.

As the purpose of an assignment of a claim arising from a resale is to provide security, a publicity requirement is imposed. According to Austrian law, all security interests except retention of title are subject to a publicity requirement. This means that the security interest must manifest itself externally in some respect, in order to signal to third parties that such an interest exists. A charge over land, for example, must be registered on the land register. Movable objects that are pledged, or are the subject of security ownership, must be handed over to the creditor.[44] If a claim is charged (or assigned) it is also necessary to comply with the publicity requirement (§ 452 ABGB). This is done either by notifying the *debitor cessus*[45] or by making an entry in the books[46] of the creditor, B, whose claim is charged.[47] Notification[48] and entry into creditors' books can be carried out even in respect of claims that have not yet come into existence. Notification is, of course, only possible if the identity of the future *debitor cessus* is already known. According, however, to the majority view in legal doctrine, the book-entry procedure is possible even if the identity of the future *debitor cessus* is unknown at the time the entry is made.[49] The assigned claims would, however, have to be specified in a sufficiently precise way.[50]

As long as the *debitor cessus* has not been informed about the assignment, he can make payment to the assignor. A and B could conclude

---

[44] A pledge cannot be created by means of a *constitutum possessorium*, as such an act does not fulfil the publicity requirement: cf. *Rummel/Petrasch* § 451 n. 3; OGH SZ 27/18 and 46/50.

[45] In a recent decision, the OGH (26 Oct. 1997, 5 Ob 2155/96i; *ecolex* 1998, 22) articulated doubts about whether notification to the *debitor cessus* really suffices to fulfil the publicity requirement. The court argued that such a notification does not guarantee that the assignment is made obvious to the creditors of the assignor, as there is no duty on the part of the assignor to tell such a creditor whether the claim was assigned or not. A similar argument was put forward by *Schwimann/Honsell/Heidinger* § 1392 n. 22. In an even more recent decision, however, the court ruled that notification of the *debitor cessus* is sufficient (cf. OGH 29 Sep. 1998, 1 Ob 406/97f RdW 1999, 21).

[46] According to the decision mentioned in note 45, it is necessary that the entry is made in such a way that it appears in any list of unliquidated claims.

[47] The priority of charges over land *inter se* is determined by the chronological order in which they were registered.

[48] Graf, *ecolex* 1998, 16; Wilhelm, *ecolex* 1998, 614; Koziol, in: *Mobiliarsicherheiten* 19, 32; Zepke, ÖBA 1997, 984; Karollus, ÖBA 1998, 397; OGH 29 Sep. 1998, RdW 1999, 20; *contra* Iro, RdW 1989, 357.

[49] See Fitz, ÖJZ 1973, 598; *Schwimann/Honsell/Heidinger* § 1392 n. 53; Karollus, ÖBA 1999, 332; against this view *Klang/F. Bydlinski* IV/2 690 Fn 895a; Iro, RdW 1989, 357 and Koziol, ÖBA 1998, 745. There is no decision of the OGH on this point, but in RdW 1999, 20 the OGH evinced a certain sympathy for the first view.

[50] E.g.: 'All claims from sales of a certain product within a certain period are assigned.'

an agreement under which B would be obliged to keep the payments from the *debitores cessi* separate from his other assets, in the name of A.[51] This type of transaction[52] is called *antizipiertes Besitzkonstitut* (anticipated *constitutum possessorium*). As there are some problems in respect of the construction of such an agreement, it is debatable to what extent it offers A real protection.[53] After notification, C could only make valid payment to A.[54]

GREECE

(a) A cannot claim ownership of the cars. C1–C5 have become the owners of the cars, according to articles 1034, 239 A.K., since B was empowered by A to resell (and obviously to transfer ownership of) the cars.

Even if B was not entitled to resell the cars, C1–C5 would have become the owners if the requirements of article 1036 A.K. (*bona fide* acquisition of ownership of a movable) were met. According to the most persuasive,[55] but not the prevailing view, the possibility of *bona fide* acquisition is excluded if a *constitutum possessorium* is substituted for actual delivery. Where actual delivery takes place title passes to the transferee when the latter acquires direct possession of the movable, if, at that time, the transferee is acting in good faith. Good faith is presumed and is only excluded either if the transferee positively knew that the transferor was not the owner or if his ignorance was grossly negligent (article 1037 A.K.). According to article 10 of L. 2844/2000,[56] contracts including a retention of title clause may be recorded in special public registers which are kept at the so-called 'pledge registry'. It is obvious that in this case, the possibility of *bona fide* acquisition is very limited, since registration will exclude good faith in most cases.

(b) If B goes bankrupt, the monies that have been paid by the customers form part of the insolvency estate and will be taken by the insolvency administrator.

---

[51] A is therefore owner of the money!
[52] Cf. *Klang*/F. Bydlinski IV/2 694 ff.; *Rummel*/Spielbüchler § 429 n. 6 and Aicher, *ibid.* § 1063 n. 116.
[53] Cf. *Rummel*/Aicher § 1063 n. 116.
[54] A can, however, authorise B to receive C's payment.
[55] See Georgiades, *Empragmato Dikaio II* 230 ff. with further references; Stathopoulos, *Contract Law in Hellas*, 49; *contra*: Balis, *Empragmaton Dikaion* para. 56; Spyridakis, *Empragmato Dikaio* 164; Toussis, *Empragmato Dikaio* para. 100 n. 3 a.
[56] See *supra*, Greek report, case 1(a).

(c) A proceeds clause would entitle A to the claims arising from the subsales. If the buyer is a retailer, it is common business practice to combine retention of title with an assignment of future claims arising from sub-sales of the goods (proceeds clause).[57]

A would also be able to gain priority over B's creditors by the use of an enterprise charge, even though it would not confer on A any additional real rights to the particular asset sold. The enterprise charge has been recently introduced to the Greek legal system by article 16 of the above-mentioned L. 2844/2000 (in force since 13 October 2001).[58] However, if A wished to have a real right in the particular asset sold, he would have to take a specific security over that asset (by way of a pledge or a non-possessory charge, called a 'fictitious pledge') or would have to reserve title to the asset without empowering B to resell it.[59]

In respect of certain categories of movable property, legislation specifies the requirements for creating a pledge. Though the delivery of the thing to the creditor or to a third party (the *pledge-custodian*) is required to constitute a pledge (articles 1211–1212 A.K.), the law allows the registration of a contract on special public registers to replace such delivery for certain types of movables. The most important types of fictitious pledges recognised by Greek legislation are:

(1) pledges on the machinery of enterprises for the purpose of securing banks' claims arising from loans granted (L.D. 1038/1949);
(2) pledges on film machinery for the production of films and claims arising from the exploitation of such films (L.D. 4208/1961);
(3) pledges on cars (L. 711/1977) for the purpose of securing the claims of any creditor;
(4) pledges on technical equipment, products and animals belonging to farmers, cattle-breeders and agricultural associations (L. 2184/1920);
(5) pledges on tobacco for the purpose of securing banks' claims arising from loans granted to tobacco producers (L.D. 21.11/31.12 1925).

Since they are real (absolute) rights, these fictitious pledges are effective against the world. The holder has the right of pursuit in spite of any transfer of ownership. Following a compulsory sale of the collateral, the pledgee enjoys priority over the proceeds. Yet, these special pledges cannot reasonably be used in cases such as this, where the goods are

---

[57] See also *infra*, Greek report, case 6. [58] See *supra*, Greek report, case 1(a).
[59] However, if B nevertheless resold the cars to customers acting in good faith, A would still lose his title if the other prerequisites of articles 1036–1039 Draft Commercial Code were fulfilled.

intended to be resold, since no-one would be prepared to buy something encumbered with a limited real right.

The new Commercial Code, which is currently under preparation, provides for the constitution of a pledge without the delivery of the subject matter for the purpose of securing commercial claims (articles 280 ff. Draft Commercial Code, 1987). The same Code provides for the recognition of enterprise charges and for the taking of a charge over the contents of a warehouse: articles 10, 12, 23 and 287 Draft Commercial Code, 1987.

Specific legislation also exists for the transfer of special categories of movables such as cars (L. 722/1977), ships (KIND article 6) and aircraft (L. 5017/1931).

FRANCE

(a) B did not, by virtue of the contract of sale, become the owner of the cars and could not, therefore, sell them to a sub-buyer, C. He could only sell them on behalf of A (applying the *nemo plus* principle). However, the customers, C1–C5, bought the cars and took direct possession of them (they took them away). Possession of assets, even when the assets were sold subject to reservation of title, gives a third party in good faith a good title to the assets. Pursuant to C. civ, article 2279, para. 1, 'with regard to movable property possession equals title'.[60] This principle is completed by C. civ, article 1141, which grants the *bona fide* possessor title to the chattels. Thus, if the sub-buyer knew that the asset remained the property of the initial seller, he would have to return it, for he would not be in good faith.[61]

Whether B was entitled to sell the cars or not is irrelevant. It is clear that customers C1–C5 would be regarded as *bona fide* possessors and would thus be entitled to retain the cars.

(b) C1–C5 paid B immediately. A could have claimed, prior to B's insolvency, the monies paid by C1–C5. He would have had to prove that there was a tacit contract of agency between himself and B (*mandat*). The contract gave B a mandate to sell the cars on behalf of A and to receive payment. Pursuant to C. civ, article 1993, the agent must pass to the

---

[60] Generally, see Libchaber, 'Les Biens', *Encyclopédie Dalloz, vol. Civil.*
[61] Rennes, 13 Nov. 1991, Rev proc coll 1993, 125, obs. Soinne.

principal all sums that the agent receives on his behalf. Whether the sums were kept in a separate account or not is irrelevant.

Once insolvency proceedings have commenced, the seller cannot claim a right over any proceeds in the hands of the debtor or of the insolvency administrator,[62] unless he can prove that the price was paid to the debtor after the commencement of insolvency proceedings.[63] A would only be entitled to lodge his claim for payment of the sale price with the insolvency administrator.

(c) The distribution of cars is usually arranged through a contract of *concession* between the supplier and the dealer.[64] The contract provides a framework, which requires the dealer to deal exclusively in the cars produced by the supplier and includes a quota clause under which the dealer undertakes to buy a specified number of vehicles within a given period of time. It is separate from the contract of sale: the supplier must authorise the display of his trademark and provide the dealer with technical and commercial support. In return the dealer must display the trademark, undertake sale promotion, etc. Most concession contracts take the precaution of stating that dealers do not work as agents of the supplier.[65] The dealer acts independently, buying and selling for his own profit.[66] Usually, the vehicles are bought by the dealer only when a customer has ordered a car. Therefore, the supplier does not need to take a security right in the particular asset in question in order to guarantee payment for the cars, as the case suggests.

If A wished to sell several cars to B at the outset, he could have taken a specific pledge over them, as governed by a 1934 Law (called '*Loi Malingre*' after the name of its initiator), as amended by Decree No 968 of 30 September 1953. This security right aims to protect car manufacturers and their subsidiaries. The pledge is available only to protect the seller (or the agent of the seller) who sells on credit, or the credit institution that finances the purchase of the car.[67] It deems the creditor to be in

---

[62] Com 3 Jan. 1995, Bull civ IV, No 3; JCPédE 1995, 1, 457, No 13, obs. Cabrillac and Petel. This is a consequence of the moratorium over payments.
[63] Com 11 July 1995, JCP 1995, Pan, 1141.
[64] Sayag, in: *Harris/Tallon* 335. See also Thréard, Gaz Pal 1992, I, Doc, 74.
[65] The contract of agency (*mandat*) would imply that the dealer-agent is to be paid on commission on sales and is not free to fix the sale price; moreover he does not purchase the stock and does not bear the risk of the customer's insolvency (see Com 22 Apr. 1976, D 1976, IR 199).
[66] Com 13 May 1970, JCP 1971, II, 16891, note Sayag.
[67] The constitution of a pledge on a motor vehicle requires a notarised deed or a signed written agreement subsequently registered (in accordance with C. civ, article 2074)

possession of the car – a sort of *constitutum possessorium* – with an associated right of retention (see case 1(c)). As a result, the creditor can claim *rei vindicatio* over the car at any time against anyone.[68] Moreover, the buyer-debtor must look after the car and return it to the seller-pledgee in the event of his default. The courts have held that the buyer-debtor can resell the car since the pledgee's interest is not endangered thereby, provided that he has registered the pledge. It is however advisable for the buyer first to obtain the pledgee's consent to such resale.

So it would be open to A to sell the cars to B and take a pledge over each, which would secure payment of the sale price.

Finally, B could agree to assign the claims that will arise from C1–C5 to A. Such an assignment will have to comply with the requirements of C. civ, article 1690 (see case 12), in particular notification of the assignment would have to be made to C1–C5. This is very cumbersome and therefore not used in practice.

BELGIUM

(a) A does not have any real rights in the cars. The customers are protected against such claims by the principle of article 2279 C.civ., by which third parties who in good faith acquire movable property from a person who had the goods in his possession obtain property rights. An express authorisation entitling B to sell the cars in the ordinary course of business is irrelevant.

(b) According to the principle of 'real subrogation', the claims are subject to the same rights and privileges as were attached to the cars.[69] A *concursus creditorum*[70] will occur on the insolvency of the buyer, B,

   specifying the vehicle and the price (article 1 *Loi Malingre*). In order to be effective against third parties, the pledge must be registered by the creditor, within three months of delivery of the car, at the town hall (*Préfecture*) where the administrative documents of the car are also held (article 2, para. 3 *Loi Malingre*). A receipt is issued to the creditor that deems him to have remained in possession of the vehicle (article 3 *Loi Malingre*). Registration of the pledge is not possible after the commencement of insolvency proceedings against the buyer. Registration is valid for five years and can be renewed once. Striking off the pledge requires the presentation of a payment receipt.

[68] C. civ, article 2279 does not have its usual effect since the condition of possession is by hypothesis unfulfilled. See for example Civ. (1), 20 May 1990, Bull civ I, No 70; JCP 92, II, 27787, note Amlon; Com 12 Dec. 1995, Bull civ IV, No 295.

[69] Dirix, RW 1997–98, 481 (491–493); T'Kint, *Les sûretés* 255. The same principle applies in case of the statutory preference of the unpaid seller: De Page, *Traité élémentaire de droit civil belge* VII 180, n° 217.

[70] For an explanation of the concept of *concursus creditorum*, see Belgian report, case 1.

or on execution against goods in the hands of one of B's customers.[71] In such circumstances, the seller can exercise his rights over those money claims. Before such an occurrence, the buyer (B) is entitled to collect those claims. In that event, the monies will normally have been mixed in the buyer's estate and the seller (A) will lose his right when the proceeds can no longer be traced. The outcome would be different if no mixing of funds took place, e.g. if the proceeds were kept in a separate account. The situation is different after *concursus*. The insolvency administrator will be entitled to collect the monies, but the seller can claim that he is due those proceeds on the grounds of 'real subrogation'.[72]

(c) The parties could stipulate that the seller obtains a security interest in the claims that arise from the sub-sale of the goods. Notification of the charge to the sub-buyers (C1–C5) prevents them from making valid payment to the buyer (B) and entitles the seller (A) to collect the proceeds, thus avoiding the danger of the funds becoming mixed into the estate of the buyer. Such agreements are not common in ordinary business transactions. The reason probably lies in the fact that 'reservation of title' is a new concept and that (presumably) the business community has not yet discovered all its aspects.

PORTUGAL

(a) If there is a reservation of title clause, A can still claim ownership of the cars. However, as cars are movable things subject to registration, the claim must be registered in order to be effective as against third parties (article 409°, n°2 of the Civil Code). Once registered, this clause is effective against anyone who buys the cars, irrespective of the fact that B is entitled to resell them. Normally, in these cases, the resale is only registered after the reservation of title has been cancelled, which happens only after the seller receives the payment. If the resale is registered, and the registration of the reservation of title remains effective, the producer will have registration priority.

(b) In this case, the monies will be collected by the insolvency administrator.

---

[71] That is, C1–C5.   [72] See *infra*, Belgian report, case 6.

(c) The position of A is already sufficiently protected. It is not usual to improve on it, irrespective of whether the transaction concerns specific or general goods.

SPAIN

(a) A has no real rights with regard to the cars; he only has a personal claim against B. A cannot assert any real right against the purchasers. Whether or not B is authorised to resell the cars is of no importance. This solution is based on article 85 CCO and is fully applicable to this case. This article is basically a legal safeguard in commerce, and is not a rule which depends on the good faith of the purchaser, but on the legal framework which surrounds the commercial transaction.[73] Its parallel is article 464 CC, which establishes the principle *possession vaut titre* and which, on the contrary, does depend on the good faith of the purchaser; however, this applies only to contracts governed by the Civil Code.[74]

(b) The amount paid will fall into B's insolvency estate, managed by the insolvency administrator. A is simply an insolvency creditor and has no entitlement to the proceeds of sale of the bankrupt's assets in preference to other creditors. The reservation of title clause does not accord priority to A's claim *vis-à-vis* that of other creditors.

(c) A can only improve his position if he demands additional securities from B, such as a banker's reference, or a charge (*hipoteca*, whether over immovable or movable property). If the claim has been embodied in a public deed (requiring registration before a public notary), the creditor will receive preference in insolvency proceedings and will also have an enforceable right if B does not pay within forty-five days.

Reservation of title is not a very common type of security in this area of commerce. The car salesperson usually requires an immediate cash payment. Therefore, the purchaser has to acquire the necessary credit from a finance company (a contract which is commonly facilitated by the seller). It is indeed true that such reservation of title is often used in leasing contracts, whereas in other commercial branches, transactions are often secured by means of bankers' references or banks' promissory notes. In general, however, the most common ways of guaranteeing

---

[73] See Vicent Chuliá, *Compendio Crítico de Derecho Mercantil II* 151.
[74] See Miquel González, in: Paz-Ares/Díez-Picazo/Bercovitz/Salvador, *Commentario del Código Civil I* 1241.

the payment of a debt in commercial practice are, in order of importance: drafts, policies supervised by an authorised broker and charges. The pledge is the most commonly used device in the field of real security rights, be it either in the form of a endorsement of a bond conveying an enforceable right or in the form of endorsement of capital stock. Sales of motor vehicles in hire-purchase instalments are often used as a kind of security device, in so far as such vehicle is sold by the seller (in combination with a finance company), who will reserve title to the movable until the purchaser has paid the whole amount due. At that point, the purchaser, who prior to completion of the payments will only have had beneficial ownership of the vehicle, will become the legal owner as well. A type of charge (*hipoteca mobiliaria*) can be taken over certain classes of movable property, such as industrial property, as on trademark rights and patents. Likewise, lease contracts are entered into which include a right of transfer that in practice is used as if it were a form of charge (*hipoteca mobiliaria*) over the leased asset. On the other hand, in the field of personal securities, the most commonly used are bankers' references, voluntary bonds and 'joint and several' notes.[75]

ITALY

(a) A does not own, or have any other real right in, the cars which the dealer B sold in the regular course of business to customers C1–C5. In this case B transferred ownership of the cars to C1–C5 pursuant to the contractual term that granted the car dealer the power to sell them. The dogmatic nature of such term could be discussed – is it a mandate to sell, an authorisation to sell, or something else? – but its effect seems to be clear.

The use of retention of title clauses by the producers or importers (hereafter 'producers') of cars sold to dealers is neither a rare, nor a universal, practice in Italy. The clauses with which the writer is familiar, however, do not grant the dealer the power to resell the cars. Such clauses do not seem to be employed in Italian business practice. In the opinion of the writer, they are not in use because they are sensible – from the point of view of the seller – only if the seller is able to obtain priority over the purchase money which the ultimate buyer will eventually owe, or pay, to the initial buyer under retention of title. Yet in Italy such

---

[75] See Estrada Alonso, *Las garantías abstractas en el tráfico civil y mercantil* 187, 213.

priority is difficult to obtain, for reasons that will be apparent from the discussion below, under part (c).

Retention of title in respect of the cars pursuant to article 1523 c.c., on instalment sales, as amended by the d. lgs. of 9 October 2002, n. 231, art. 11, will be effective *vis-à-vis* the buyer's creditors as long as the cars are unregistered movables if (1) the clause is agreed upon in writing in the main contract governing the relationship between the producer and the dealer; and (2) it is confirmed in each invoice duly registered in the business books with *data certa* prior to execution on the cars by the buyer's creditors. Under current business practice, a producer does not register the new vehicles that will eventually be sold to the final customers C1–C5 in the public register of vehicles (*pubblico registro automobilistico*: P.R.A.), established by Royal Decree n. 436 of 15 March 1927.[76] He will not register the cars in order to save money and to avoid depreciation of the cars (which, if on the register, will be dated). The cars remain unregistered even when the producer or importer sells them to the dealer, because registration of transfer in the P.R.A. is not compulsory. Nor do the cars need a licence plate until they are to be used on a public road. Hence, first registration of the cars will occur when these are sold to the dealer's customers, C1–C5. Registration will be in the names of the customers. Up to that point, the car sold by the producer to the dealer is considered an unregistered movable, which is not subject to the rule that makes reservation of title over a registered movable effective only upon its registration in the public register (article 1524 c.c.).

Because the cars sold to the customers were previously unregistered, such customers could acquire title to them in accordance with article 1153 c.c., which enacts the Italian rule concerning good faith acquisition of movables through possession. According to article 1153 c.c., a person may acquire ownership of movable things, when they are alienated from him by someone who is not the owner, if he is in good faith at the moment of actual delivery and if there was a transaction capable of transferring ownership. After registration of the car in the P.R.A., however, such a mode of acquisition is barred because the car is now a registered movable, to which the rule of article 1153 c.c. on *bona fide* acquisition does not apply (article 1156 c.c.). From the moment the car is registered, a *bona fide* acquisition of the vehicle from a non-owner is subject to the different rule enacted by article 1162 c.c. That article provides that when a person acquires a movable thing which is registered

---

[76] For an overview of this register: Saracco, Digesto sez. pub. XII 327 ff.

in public registers from one who is not the owner, he will acquire ownership of it if the following criteria are met: (1) he acquired it in good faith; (2) it was transferred under a transaction that is capable of transferring ownership; (3) he has had possession of it for three years from the date of the registration of the transaction in the public register. If any of these requirements are lacking, acquisition of ownership by possession of a registered movable will take effect after the passage of ten years.

(b) The monies paid to B belong to him. His insolvency creditors and his insolvency administrator may take it to satisfy their claims. The contract between A and B does not provide for a different solution. Hence there is no reason why the monies in question should not be regarded as property belonging to the debtor, to which his creditors can have recourse to satisfy their claims.

(c) How can the producer or importer obtain a security that can survive resale?

There are a number of possibilities that can be explored in this respect and they will be addressed below. Before discussing them, however, it should be noted that they are mainly of theoretical interest, because the writer is not aware of any significant usage in business practice.

Therefore, before discussing these theoretical possibilities, it is more sensible to try to understand the main features of current business practice in this context, in order to realise how the producer obtains security from the dealer.

Producers of cars need to establish long-term contractual relationships with car dealers.[77] Long-term relationships justify investment in the car industry that would not otherwise be commercially feasible. Hence, for car producers it is vital to find reliable and trustworthy business partners. The selection of such business partners involves full assessment of their financial standing, business skills and reputation. Furthermore, even after commercial relations with such business partners are successfully established, the producer or importer is well aware that the best way to avoid problems with payments for car sales is to let someone else bear the risk of dealers' breach of contract, or, more specifically,

---

[77] This is one of the reasons why such agreements are exempt from compliance with article 85, s. 1 of the EC Treaty. See Regulation n. 1475/95 of 28 June 1995, O.J. 1995, L. 145/25.

of their inability to pay. Hence, the producer will require the dealer to obtain bank guarantees (like performance bonds) to cover the risks which relate to that phase of performance. Personal guarantees of this kind are also made in favour of the producer by such persons as have a stake in the dealer's business. If the dealership is a family business, as is quite common in Italy, these guarantees may be made not only by the persons occupying senior positions in that business, but also by other persons, such as those who belong to the family or are connected to it, whether they are involved in managing the business or not. Having obtained such guarantees, the producer or importer will be careful not to extend credit to the dealer for amounts in excess of the sum covered by the above-mentioned guarantees. In addition to personal guarantees, producers may contract for part payment of the price of the vehicle before delivery to the dealer. Current business practice between dealers and producers therefore de-emphasises recourse to real securities over cars, although retention of title clauses in respect of cars upon sales to dealers are far from unknown in Italy. The widespread recourse to personal securities is the key to understanding why producers successfully manage to minimise the risk of non-payment in respect of credit sales to car dealers. On the other hand, if the final buyer of the car is unable to pay cash, he will be financed by a finance company which will take a charge over the registered vehicle, which is registered in the P.R.A. These companies will be able to raise monies by assigning their claims to factoring companies through a global assignment, as provided by Law n. 52 of 21 February 1991.

As mentioned above, one could think of ways by which A could obtain priority over the sums that B will receive on sales to its customers.

In order to obtain such priority it would be necessary to: (1) prove that such monies belong to A; and (2) ensure that the money in question is kept separate from other assets belonging to the dealer (B).

The first requirement could be met by recourse to several different contractual techniques.

The producer's relationship with the dealer, which is normally governed by a contract of *concessione di vendita*,[78] could be set up as a commission contract under articles 1703 ff. c.c. This contract is a variety of mandate.[79] The parties to such contract would agree that any monies

---

[78] For the features of this contract see the French report to case 5(c).
[79] The point is not disputed. See, e.g., Montalenti, in: *Contratti commerciali* XVI 633 (634); Costanza, Digesto sez. comm. III 167.

paid by the dealer's customers are to be received by the dealer on behalf of the producer. Such an agreement would be sufficient to vest ownership of the monies in the producer under the general provision of article 1376 c.c. (see above, case 1) and the specific rule of article 1706(1) c.c., which allows the party granting the mandate to claim *rei vindicatio* of movables that a third party owes to the agent.[80] In order to ensure that the agreement proves efficacious *vis-à-vis* the commission agent's creditors and the insolvency administrator, the commission contract should have a certain date prior to execution or the commencement of insolvency proceedings (article 1707 c.c.).[81] Yet, the agreement in question hardly reflects commercial reality, that is to say the independent position of the car dealer *vis-à-vis* the producer. Producers will wish to pass onto car dealers the commercial risk of selling cars to the public. On the other hand, for the same reason, car dealers are free to dispose of their cash flow. Car dealers will act, if at all, as commission agents in the sale of used cars belonging to private customers. Even then, the price will normally be received by the commission agent in his own capacity, rather than for the private owner of the used car.[82] Hence, courts will probably be reluctant to adopt such a construction of the relationship between the producer and the dealer, unless there is strong evidence that the parties entered into a commission contract. A mere sham would not be enough.

Instead of entering into a commission contract, A and B could agree that the future claims owed to B by his customers will be assigned to A, as payment for the cars.[83] Such an assignment could be coupled with a power of attorney, or a mandate, authorising B to receive the sums payable by the third-party customers as A's agent. The assignment in question will not be effective *vis-à-vis* B's creditors, or his insolvency administrator, unless the customers (being the *debitores cessi*) are notified of it, or it is accepted by them, by an instrument that has a *data certa* (cf. article 2914, n. 2 c.c.).[84] Furthermore, according to scholarly

---

[80] Cass. 6 Mar. 1999, n. 1925, Giur. comm. 2000, II, 174, obs. Abriani; Foro it., 2000, I, 2299.
[81] For commentary see Luminoso, in: *Trattato di diritto civile e commerciale* 280 ff.; Santagata, Art. 1655–1677, in: *Commentario del Codice Civile Scialoja-Branca* 466 ff.
[82] Cass. 22 Feb. 1999, n. 1469, Giur. it., 1999, 1653, obs. Cagnasso; Cagnasso/Irrera, *Concessione di vendita, merchandising, catering* 35 ff.; Cagnasso, in: *Contratti commerciali* XVI, 382 ff.; Baldassarri, in: *I contratti del commercio, dell'industria, e del mercato finanziario* III 2142 ff. See Cass. 7 Dec. 1994, n. 10522, Giust. civ., 1995, I, 2165, obs. by Battaglia.
[83] On assignment of claims see *infra*, Italian report, case 12.
[84] Recent decisions on the application of this provision include: Cass. 29 Sep. 1999, n. 10788, Foro it., 2000, I, 825; Cass. 27 Sep. 1999, n. 10668; Cass. 14 Nov. 1996,

opinions and court decisions, the assignment will be valid only if it identifies with sufficient precision the claims to which it relates.[85] For all these reasons, the assignment of future claims in favour of producers of goods (registered or unregistered) is practically unknown in Italy, though it is impossible to rule it out as a theoretical possibility if the customers of B could be identified in advance.[86]

In any case, even supposing that monies were paid by C1–C5 to B as agent for A, they will still be available to B's creditors or insolvency administrator if they are not kept separate from the rest of B's assets. Monies deposited in a bank account in A's name will probably not be regarded as belonging to B if such monies have not been mixed with other sums. This should be so even if the account is opened in B's name, in order to deposit monies which he has collected for A under a commission contract, or as debts owed to A under the assignment.[87]

THE NETHERLANDS

(a) B was granted the power to resell. By selling the cars in the ordinary course of business, B exercised the power to dispose. He or she could therefore effectively transfer ownership to C1–C5. B would acquire ownership of the cars for only a logical second in time; C1–C5 will be recognised as the owners of the cars.

The result would not necessarily differ if B did not have a power to resell. B would lack the power to dispose and the transfers to C1–C5 would therefore be defective in light of the requirements of article 3:84 BW. Ownership would not have been transferred. However, third-party customers, if in good faith, may be protected from the consequences of B's lack of power to dispose by article 3:86 BW, which reads:

---

n. 9997; Cass. 22 Feb. 1996, n. 1413, Fallimento, 1996, n. 759. On this point see: Dolmetta/Portale, *Banca borsa* 1999, I, 84–88. See also *infra*, Italian report, case 12 (a), (b).

[85] Cf. Dolmetta/Portale, *Banca borsa* 1999, I, 89–90. This requirement no longer means that the future claims that are transferred must refer to an existing relationship: Cass. 8 May 1990, n. 4040, Foro it., 1991, I, 2489; Trib. Bari, 27 July 1996, 6 Nov. 1996, *Banca borsa* 1998, II, 701.

[86] Note, however, that factoring companies and banking institutions are not subject to these stringent requirements (cf. *infra*, Italian report, case 12(a), (b)).

[87] Jaeger, *La separazione del patrimonio fiduciario nel fallimento* 397; App. Milano, 15 Feb. 1985, Fallimento, 1985, 793. This case was reversed by Cass. 16 May 1990, n. 4262, Giur. comm., 1991, II, 608; Fallimento, 1990, 1113, but the reasoning of the decision rendered by the Court of Cassation is not wholly convincing.

Although an alienator lacks the right to dispose of the property, a transfer . . . of a moveable thing, unregistered property . . . is valid, if the transfer is not by gratuitous title and if the acquirer is in good faith.[88]

The requirement of good faith, *bona fides*, defined in article 3:11 BW, is not fulfilled when the person relying on it either knew, or in the given circumstances should have known, of the relevant facts. Moreover, the impossibility of making conclusive inquiries is no defence if there were good grounds for reasonable doubt.

(b) B's insolvency administrator will take the monies paid by C1–C5.

(c) Assuming there is a right to resell, the retention of title, or for that matter any other security right *in rem*, would come to an end. All would be subject to the same resolutive clause of a resale in the ordinary course of business. Furthermore, there is no general rule of substitution that would grant A as of right an interest in the monies or claims replacing the sold cars. Consequently, the only way for A to improve his or her position in these circumstances would be to create some claim against either the monies paid or the claims of B against C1–C5.

It is possible for A to oblige B, by the original contract of sale, to grant A a charge over the claims B will have against his or her buyers, C1–C5, when the cars are sold.

Dutch law recognises two kinds of charges on claims: (1) those with notification of the debtor (*openbaar pandrecht*), and (2) those without such notification (a 'silent charge', *stil pandrecht*). Article 3:236 para. 2 BW provides that a charge of a right *in personam* must be created in the manner prescribed for the 'delivery' of such a right. Thus, as with an assignment of a debt, the creation of a charge requires that a deed be used and that the debtor be notified.[89] To create a charge without notifying the debtor, article 3:239 para. 1 BW requires a notarised or registered deed.[90] This latter type of charge is preferred in practice.

The potential to create charges on future debts is limited, irrespective of the type of charge selected. A charge requiring notification will often be unfeasible, as the identity of the future debtor, who is to be notified,

---

[88] Translation from Haanappel/Mackaay, *New Netherlands Civil Code; Patrimonial Law* 50.
[89] Article 3:94 BW.
[90] This is not a 'public' registration as such. Its primary aim is the prevention of antedating.

will be unknown. The creation of a 'silent' charge, on the other hand, requires that the debt exists at the time of creation, or that the debt will arise directly from a legal relationship existing at that time, such as lease or contract of employment.[91] A will not therefore be able to secure a charge over B's claim against C at the point at which the contract providing for retention of title was agreed, but only when that claim comes into existence.

A crucial distinction between a charge with notification and a charge without notification arises in the risk that the debtor will discharge the claim, thereby extinguishing it and bringing the charge to an end.[92] This risk is particularly acute when the debtor has not been notified of the existence of the charge. Without notification the debtor cannot but pay his or her creditor, B.[93] In contrast, the holder of a charge that the debtor has received notification of is entitled to collect the debt personally.[94] The consequence of such collection would still be that the original charge is extinguished. However, although the holder of the original charge does not become directly entitled to the monies, he or she is granted a statutory charge over the monies collected (substitution).[95]

In practice, the original seller will regularly require his or her buyer to include a retention of title clause in the contract of resale.[96] The effectiveness of such an arrangement is doubtful, as it still extinguishes A's ownership and accords him no preferential claim against either the goods resold or the monies paid in respect of them.

---

[91] Article 3:239(1) BW. As to the creation of charges on future debts, see *infra*, Dutch report, case 12.

[92] Article 3:81 BW provides that 'derived rights are extinguished by the extinction of the right from which they derived'. The *Hoge Raad* explicitly rejected the possibility of substitution in those cases. However, if the debt is collected by the insolvency administrator (*trustee-in-bankruptcy*), the holder of the charge retains his or her right of priority in distribution. See *Hoge Raad* 17 Feb. 1995, NJ 1996, 471 (*Mulder q.q./CLBN Connection Technology BV*).

[93] See also article 3:246(1) BW.

[94] Article 3:246(1) BW. The holder of the charge can notify the *debitor cessus* also during insolvency proceedings against the person who granted the charge. By virtue of the notification he or she becomes entitled to collect the claim. *Hoge Raad*, 17 Feb. 1995, NJ 1996, 471.

[95] Article 3:246(5) BW. The holder of the charge is under a duty to take care that the collected claim does not become mixed with his or her own monies. For instance, a payment by giro obliges him or her to receive the money on a separate account or in any event in such a manner that would enable sufficient separation. See *Hoge Raad*, 3 Feb. 1984, 752 (*Slis-Stroom*).

[96] Snijders/Rank-Berenschot, *Goederenrecht* 390.

ENGLAND

(a) B cannot claim ownership of the cars at the expense of the various customers (C1–C5) in the unlikely event that A should seek to make a claim against them. There are two principal ways in which C1–C5 will succeed. First of all, as a matter of ordinary agency law, A has authorised B to dispose of the cars in the ordinary course of business. In the ordinary course of the car retailing business, C1–C5 will not reasonably expect to acquire from B a vulnerable title when they pay the price in full to B. If A's mandate to B can fairly be interpreted as one to dispose of the cars in an unfettered way, A will be unable to assert any real rights in the cars sold to C1–C5.

The law relating to enterprise charges (*floating charges*) presents a useful analogy. The company chargor is authorised to dispose of the assets in the ordinary course of business, the chargee's real interest being broad enough to catch assets coming into the business to replace assets sold on. It is recognised here that assets sold on are free of the charge.[97] The title reserving seller has no such right over other assets of the buyer, but the principle of the sub-purchasers' unencumbered title remains the same.

Even if B is not expressly or apparently authorised to dispose of the goods unencumbered to C1–C5, they will be protected by an important exception to the rule of *nemo dat quod non habet*. Although English law has not acceded to any doctrine that possession is tantamount to title, it does have at common law a doctrine of apparent ownership that, in view of its limitations in protecting good faith purchasers, has served as the inspiration for a number of broader statutory exceptions, mainly stemming from the late nineteenth century, in favour of good faith purchasers. One of these exceptions concerns the buyer in possession of goods. According to section 25 of the Sale of Goods Act 1979,[98] where someone who has bought or agreed to buy goods is in possession of them with the consent of the seller, then a delivery to a good faith purchaser taking the goods under any sale, pledge or other disposition is deemed to have been authorised by the seller/owner.

---

[97] *Re Hamilton's Windsor Ironworks* [1879] 12 Ch 707; *Wheatley v Silkstone and Haigh Moore Colliery Co.* (1885) 29 Ch 715; *Re Automatic Bottle Makers Ltd* [1926] 1 Ch 412; *Re Bond Worth Ltd* [1980] Ch 228. See also *National Mercantile Bank v Hampson* [1880] 5 QB 177; *Taylor v M'Keand* [1880] 5 CP 358.
[98] Almost identical to the earlier provision, s. 9 of the Factors Act 1889, which remains in force.

In the present case, the cars have been sold on by B to C1–C5 in circumstances falling within section 25. The fact of B's insolvency is irrelevant to the transaction between B and C1–C5, except that a disposition of B's property after the commencement of B's insolvency proceedings (the filing of a petition for *bankruptcy* or a *winding-up* by the court) is void unless it is saved by the discretion of the court.[99] Where A reserves title, then the cars are not B's property, unless for a *scintilla temporis* they vest in B immediately before they then vest in C1–C5. This is not a real problem: a court would certainly exercise its discretion to uphold the transaction since it is in no way prejudicial to B's other creditors.

The transactions between B and C1–C5 are effective to transfer a good title to the purchasers even if B is acting fraudulently.[100] Once B is in possession of the cars with A's consent, that consent remains effective even if A revokes it, provided A does not recover actual possession of the goods or C1–C5 are not in fact notified of the revocation of consent.[101]

(b) A has no claim to the money which, as an asset of B, is gathered in by the insolvency administrator (*liquidator* or *trustee-in-bankruptcy*)[102] for distribution according to the statutory scheme laid down in the Insolvency Act 1986.[103] Even if B could be said to sell on the goods as agent for A, that of itself would not impress the proceeds of the sale in B's hands with a trust or security in favour of A.

(c) A is at liberty in English law to secure himself by taking a charge over the proceeds of sale generated by the cars or, indeed, over any other assets of B. English law has long been receptive to the taking of non-possessory security though, nevertheless, the security will have to be registered to be effective against parties other than the buyer. There is now a very modest fee exacted for the registration of charges, but time and legal costs in preparing documents for registration may be

---

[99] S. 127 of the Insolvency Act 1986.
[100] *Du Jardin v Beadman Bros.* [1952] 2 QB 712.
[101] *Newton's of Wembley Ltd v Williams* [1965] 1 QB 560.
[102] Unless it is caught by a charge granted by B to one of B's creditors, in which case a *receiver* will commonly step in to ensure that that creditor is paid.
[103] Briefly, the monies would be paid out in the following order: (a) the expenses of the *liquidation* (or *bankruptcy*) according to a lengthy priority protocol (Insolvency Rules 4.218–20, 6.224; Insolvency Act 1986, s. 156); (b) statutory preference creditors (a very limited group) who rank together equally (Insolvency Act 1986, ss. 328(2) and 386 and Schedule 6); (c) unsecured creditors on a *pari passu* basis (Insolvency Act 1986, ss. 107 and 328(3) and Insolvency Rules 4.181); (d) contributaries (Insolvency Act 1986, s. 107).

significant. In the case of complex modern bank debentures, an extensive document (the instrument of charge) is prepared and particulars of registration, which need not be set out in long form but very commonly are, are sent with the instrument to Companies House in Cardiff. There, civil servants conduct a careful monitoring of the instrument of charge itself alongside the particulars, the details of the latter appearing on the register. There will consequently be substantial transaction costs that will be passed on by the chargee to the chargor.

The registration process is not suitable for informal and rapid dealings between seller and buyer. In this respect, the English system is probably more expensive to operate than American and Canadian Article 9 systems. Moreover, assuming that reservation of title clauses have to be registered, it cannot practicably be done by sellers on a multiple basis for all future supplies. Restrictive rules on 'tacking', which is the attachment of future advances to the security taken for an earlier advance,[104] mean that a registration would be required for each and every supply contract. Moreover, there are problems to be overcome if the seller supplies the goods before taking an enterprise charge (*floating charge*) and the company within twelve months goes into *liquidation* (corporate insolvency proceedings) in that the charge is invalid to the extent that it exceeds in value any advance given 'at the same time as, or after, the creation of the charge'.[105] This, along with the need to comply with the rules on unlawful preferences and undervalue transactions,[106] is not an insuperable problem but it casts a shadow over any further provision of secured credit in the twilight period before insolvency. As regards unlawful preferences, the preference must leave the creditor better off than before. Furthermore, the debtor would have to be influenced by a subjective desire to improve the creditor's position relative to the debtor's other creditors, which is not an easy thing to demonstrate.[107] A debtor who pays under pressure and without a subjective intention to prefer will therefore not be regarded as having given a preference.

If the seller takes a charge over proceeds but the buyer receives the proceeds and commingles them so that they are not clearly identifiable, the seller has an equitable real right which allows him to trace (i.e., follow) the proceeds into the commingled account. The seller is liable to be defeated if the proceeds are exhausted or are acquired by a *bona fide*

---

[104] Law of Property Act 1925, s. 94.
[105] Insolvency Act 1986, s. 245; *Power v Sharp Investments Ltd* [1994] 1 BCLC 111.
[106] Insolvency Act 1986, ss. 238, 240, 339, 341.
[107] See *Re MC Bacon Ltd* [1990] BCLC 324.

purchaser for value without notice of the legal estate (e.g., a bank which receives the proceeds and applies them against the buyer's indebtedness to it). The subject is vast and is covered in texts on trusts and restitution.

In English law, there is no difficulty at all in agreeing to create a charge over future debts (*book debts*) even though at the time those debts are not in existence and even though the contracts that will give rise to the debts have not yet been concluded. This is a commonplace observation which, since case law rarely states the obvious, receives general support from decisions like *Tailby v Official Receiver*[108] and *Re Charge Card Services Ltd*.[109]

It is common for sellers to set out extended reservation of title clauses that purport to attach automatically to the money proceeds of sales by the buyer. These clauses take various forms. One version, for example, requires the buyer to 'pass on' to the seller the buyer's proceeds rights against sub-buyers. Although in principle English law imposes few prohibitions on transactions and adheres to the principle of freedom of contract, it has given short shrift to such clauses in so far as these clauses purport to confer on the seller an outright, rather than security, right to the proceeds.[110] These clauses will be treated as conferring a charge on the seller to the extent that the seller's interest in the money proceeds is defeasible upon the payment of the price by the buyer.[111] There is, for reasons stated above, no objection to the grant of a charge over the proceeds in favour of the seller, but this imposes a registration requirement.

Apart from extended reservation of title clauses, attempts have been made in the past to advance the seller's case in another way. In the immediate aftermath of the decision of the Court of Appeal in *Aluminium Industrie Vaassen BV v Romalpa Aluminium Ltd*,[112] it appeared that the seller could, by careful drafting, claim the proceeds of sale of goods supplied (in this case, aluminium foil) by way of equitable tracing rights. The clause in *Romalpa* did not say explicitly what was to happen to the proceeds of sale of the aluminium foil but it did state that the buyer was the 'fiduciary owner' of new goods made with the foil supplied and that the buyer was to 'hand over' to the seller claims concerning the sale of these new goods against the sub-buyers. Now the buyer conceded that it

---

[108] [1888] 13 App Cas 523.   [109] [1987] Ch 150.
[110] See, e.g., *E Pfeiffer Weinkellerei-Weineinkauf GmbH v Arbuthnot Factors Ltd* [1988] 1 WLR 150.
[111] *Tatung (UK) Ltd v Galex Telesure Ltd* [1989] 5 BCC 325; *Compaq Computer Ltd v Abercorn Group Ltd* [1991] BCC 484.
[112] [1976] 1 WLR 676.

held the foil as bailee; the court therefore concluded that this made the buyer a fiduciary. The consequence of this, in the opinion of the court, was that the seller was entitled in equity to trace the proceeds of sale of the foil and its right to do so was not in the nature of a registrable charge. Subsequent cases have distinguished *Romalpa* out of existence. It is most doubtful that the buyer would now be seen as a fiduciary; moreover, whether a buyer could be seen as a fiduciary would depend upon an objective characterisation of the relationship and not upon self-serving statements by the parties.[113] Finally, it is now recognised that a fiduciary relationship is not an absolute notion; rather, fiduciary relations of different sorts have variable incidents.[114]

The position stated above is not sensitive to the particular goods that are the subject to the security, except that there are special registers dealing with ships and aircraft.

IRELAND

(a) If A has sold goods to B with ownership passing and B has in turn sold the goods to C with ownership also passing, then C's title to the goods is immune to any claim by the creditors of either B or C. *Prima facie*, ownership of the goods will pass from B to C on the making of the contract of sale though this can be postponed until the price is paid or some other condition fulfilled. A, therefore, cannot claim ownership or any other real right in the cars. If B has no entitlement to sell the cars the analysis is slightly different. Irish law adheres to the principle of *nemo plus* but there are exceptions. One of the exceptions is the buyer in possession exception embodied in section 25 of the Sale of Goods Act. If a person has agreed to buy goods and is in possession of the goods – B in our example – then he can pass a good title to a third party – C – notwithstanding the fact that he has not got a good title himself. The third party must have acted in good faith and without notice of any right of the original seller. It may also be the case that B has the implied authority of A to resell even though B has not yet acquired title.

(b) This case raises the question of the validity of claims to resale proceeds by original sellers who have supplied goods subject to a reservation of title clause. I would suggest that B's insolvency administrator has a

---

[113] See *Re Andrabell Ltd* [1984] 3 All ER 407; *Re Goldcorp Exchange Ltd* [1995] 1 AC 74; *Compaq Computer Ltd v Abercorn Group Ltd* [1991] BCC 484.
[114] Sir Peter Millett, 'Equity's Place in the Law of Commerce' LQR 114 (1998) 214.

better claim than A. It seems reasonably clear now from a series of decisions that the mere fact that there is a retention of title clause in a sale of goods contract does not give the seller an automatic claim against resale proceeds. In the immediate wake of the English *Romalpa* decision there was some support for the contrary view in Ireland in cases like *Re Stokes & McKiernan Ltd*[115] and *Sugar Distributors Ltd v Monaghan Cash and Carry Ltd*.[116] That view is no longer in the ascendancy in Ireland and this is evidenced by the decision of Murphy J in *Carroll Group Distributors Ltd v Bourke*.[117] The case mirrors contemporaneous developments in England.

In this case the plaintiff supplied goods to the defendants on four weeks' credit. The conditions of sale provided that the ownership of the goods should remain with the plaintiff until the defendants had discharged all sums due but the defendants were given an express right to resell the goods. It was further stated that, if the defendants did resell the goods, they did so on their own account and not as agent for the plaintiff and that in the event of a sale, the defendants undertook to hold all monies so received 'in trust' for the plaintiff and to maintain an independent account of all sums so received. The defendants became insolvent and the question of the plaintiff's entitlement to resale proceeds became an important issue. According to the judge, the source of the plaintiff's rights was the contract between the parties. Had the resales been wrongful then the plaintiff would have been entitled to trace resale proceeds. Carroll J said that where a trustee or other person in a fiduciary position disposes of property the proceeds of sale are impressed with a trust which entitles the beneficiary or other person standing in the fiduciary relationship to trace such proceeds into any other property acquired therewith by the trustee. In this case however, resales were positively anticipated by the conditions of sale and therefore no fiduciary duties were imposed by law on the buyers in relation to the resale proceeds.

(c) One way of A trying to improve his position is by inserting a clause in the original contract of sale conferring an entitlement to resale proceeds. In certain cases such clauses have been upheld in Ireland. A case in point is *Re WJ Hickey Ltd*,[118] where the clause stipulated that the proceeds shall 'be held in trust for the seller' in a 'manner which enables such proceeds to be identified as such'. The court held that by virtue of the clause the seller had property in, and not just a charge over, the proceeds. It

---

[115] High Court, unreported, 12 Dec. 1978.   [116] [1982] ILRM 399.
[117] [1990] ILRM 285; [1990] IR 481.   [118] [1988] IR 126.

is submitted, however, that nowadays a claim over resale proceeds is unlikely to be successful. The courts are likely to hold that the clause constitutes a registrable security interest. The aforementioned *Carroll Group Distributors Ltd v Bourke*[119] is a case in point. In this case the sellers, Carrolls, included such a clause in the conditions of sale. The buyers were required to bank resale proceeds separately from other monies. The judge said:[120]

> If one ignores the particular facts of the case and simply analyses the bargain made between the parties it is clear that such an arrangement properly implemented would result in a bank account with sums of money credited thereto which would probably be in excess of the amounts due by Bourkes to Carrolls. This would arise partly from the fact that the goods would be resold at a marked up price and partly from the fact that the proceeds of sale would include some goods the cost price of which had been discharged and some had not. In other words, the bank account would be a fund to which Carrolls could have recourse to ensure the discharge of the monies due to them even though they would not be entitled to the entire of that fund. Accordingly, the fund agreed to be credited would possess all the characteristics of a mortgage or charge.

The judge referred to the three essential ingredients of a charge identified by Romer LJ in *Re George Inglefield Ltd.*[121] In that case it was said that in a sale transaction the vendor is not entitled to get the property back merely by returning the purchase price. With a charge, the borrower could get the property back free from encumbrances by repaying the principal borrowed plus interest. Secondly, if a lender realised the charged property for an amount that was more than sufficient to repay the loan plus interest, he had to account to the borrower for the surplus. With a sale, on the other hand, if the buyer resold at a profit he was entitled to keep that profit. Thirdly, if the lender realised the charged property for an amount that was insufficient to repay the loan, he could sue the borrower for the deficit. With a sale, however, if the buyer resold at a loss there was no way in which this loss could be made good from the original seller. It must be said, however, that while the difference between a sale and a charge is relatively clear-cut in theory, there may be considerable blurring between the two transactions in practice. For example, options to repurchase are not uncommon in sale transactions.

In the English cases perhaps there has been more extensive discussion of the issues surrounding an original seller's claim to resale proceeds. One such case is *Modelboard Ltd v Outer Box Ltd*,[122] where a supplier of

---

[119] [1990] ILRM 285; [1990] 1 IR 481.   [120] [1990] ILRM 285 at 289.
[121] [1933] Ch 1 at 27-28.   [122] [1993] BCLC 623.

cardboard sheets made such a claim on the basis of a reservation of title clause which provided that the buyers were entitled to resell only as 'agents and bailees and on terms that the proceeds are held in trust for the [seller]'. The court held that the interest of the suppliers in the proceeds of sale was by way of charge and a hypothetical example was given in support of that conclusion. Assuming the buyer resold at a profit, in the court's opinion, the supplier could have recourse to the full resale price, so far as necessary to discharge the outstanding obligation of the buyer, subject to which the supplier must account to the buyer for the balance. This was in accordance with commercial reality and meant that the suppliers' interest in resale proceeds was properly designated a charge.

On the other hand, no charge was involved if the supplier was entitled to keep the whole resale price but with an obligation to refund the resale profit element if the buyer subsequently paid the purchase price. The court rejected the latter interpretation for it entailed devising an elaborate system of implied contractual obligations and this was felt to be beyond the bounds of judicial capabilities. Leaving aside implied contractual terms, one might argue that there is a law of restitution in place to prevent unjust enrichment. The courts have affirmed that unjust enrichment exists as an independent principle of both English and Irish law and imaginative use could be made of the principles of unjust enrichment in a reservation of title context.

To conclude, on the facts as given, short of a registrable charge there is not a typical arrangement through which the parties could grant a security to A that could survive the resale. A registrable charge could certainly be created over assets which do not yet exist but which may come into existence in the future, so there is no problem about charging the claims against B's customers even though these customers are not even known.

SCOTLAND

(a) Assuming that the customers have acted in good faith, A is no longer the owner of the cars and has no rights in relation to the cars. The fact that B authorised A to sell means that the sales by A will transfer to C all rights in the cars held by A and B. So C will become owner.

The result would be the same even if B was not authorised to sell.

Unlike some countries, Scots law does not have any general principle that a buyer who is in good faith acquires ownership. The general principle is *nemo plus iuris ad alium transferre potest quam ipse haberet*. Certain exceptions to this principle are, however, recognised, and the present situation is one of them. Section 25 of the Sale of Goods Act provides that if X sells and delivers movables to Y, but ownership is retained, and if Y then sells and delivers to Z, and Z is in good faith, then Z becomes owner.[123] To this exception there is an exception for motor vehicles. Thus if what is sold is a car, Z will not be the owner, even though he acted in good faith. But there is also an exception to the exception to the exception. If Z is a private buyer of a motor vehicle, he is protected and will be the owner.[124] It cannot be pretended that this area of law is rational.

We do not know whether the customers were in good faith. But almost certainly they were. There was nothing to suggest to them that B was not the owner. The fact that retention of title clauses are common is not enough to prevent sub-purchasers from being in good faith.

(b) The money paid by C is simply part of B's patrimony (estate[125]). It thus passes to B's insolvency administrator for the benefit of all creditors. A is one of those creditors, but he has no special rights to this money. That remains true even if the money is identifiable in some way.

(c) Attempts have been made to improve B's position by inserting into the A–B contract a clause saying that the proceeds of any resale must be held by B in trust for A. In general, the trust is 'insolvency proof'. That is to say, if X holds assets in trust for Y, and X becomes bankrupt, the assets do not form part of X's insolvency estate. Y is protected. Y's right is thus similar to a real right.[126] However, such attempts are ineffective.[127]

---

[123] The actual wording of the section is complex and obscure. But the approximate meaning is as given here.

[124] Hire Purchase Act 1964 ss. 27–29, Consumer Credit Act 1974 s. 192(3)(a), Sale of Goods Act 1979 s. 63(1)(a). See Miller, *Corporeal Moveables in Scots Law* para. 10–22.

[125] The word 'estate' is used in Scots law to mean patrimony, and also to mean patrimony in a particular context, such as the estate of a bankrupt or of a person who has died. 'Estate' is also used to mean a special patrimony, especially a trust.

[126] In fact, however, Scots law does not regard the right of a beneficiary in a trust as being real. Scots law considers the trustee as having two patrimonies (estates), his general or private patrimony and his special or trust patrimony. The right of the beneficiary is regarded as being a personal right in respect of the trust estate (patrimony). For a valuable account see the chapter on Scots Law by Reid, in: Hayton/Kortmann/Verhagen, *Principles of European Trust Law*.

[127] *Clark Taylor & Co. v Quality Site Development (Edinburgh) Ltd* 1981 SC 111.

SOUTH AFRICA

(a) The fact that the buyer is entitled to resell the cars in the ordinary course of business does not necessarily invalidate A's retention of ownership in terms of the reservation of title clause. Unlike most European systems, South African law does not *per se* protect the buyer in good faith who acquires movable property from a person who had the goods in his possession. The only possible remedy C1–C5 may have would be a defence against A's *rei vindicatio* based on the doctrine of estoppel.[128]

The requirements for estoppel are that: (1) there must have been a representation by the owner, by conduct or otherwise, that the person who disposed of the property was the owner of it or was entitled to dispose of it; (2) the representation must have been relied on by the person raising the estoppel and such reliance must have been the proximate cause of his detriment; (3) the person raising the estoppel must have acted to his detriment; and (4) there must have been fault on the part of the person making the representation. An obvious example of estoppel is where an owner leaves his secondhand motor car in the showroom of a dealer in secondhand cars. By buying the car the purchaser is taken to have acted to his detriment in relying on the impression created by the owner that the dealer has the right to dispose of the car and this representation was the proximate cause of the detriment.

The fact that B is entitled to sell the cars in the ordinary course of business is not *per se* sufficient to found a claim on estoppel. A must by his conduct have created the impression that B was the owner of the cars or that B had authority from the owner to sell the cars. This impression could be created by A allowing B to display the cars together with his other stock in the showroom and without there being any outward manifestation that A has retained title to the cars. If the other requirements for estoppel are met, C1–C5 could raise a defence of estoppel against A's claim of ownership.[129] Since estoppel is legally regarded as a shield (defence) and not a sword (right of action), A is not divested of his ownership, but he is paralysed from enforcing it. This *inter alia* has the consequence that C1–C5 would not acquire ownership of the cars and could not give valid transfer thereof.

---

[128] On the limitation on institution of the *rei vindicatio* in terms of the doctrine of estoppel, see van der Merwe, *Sakereg* 368–373.
[129] For a good illustration, see *Quenty's Motors (Pty) Ltd v Standard Credit Corporation Ltd* 1994 3 SA 188 (A). For the requirements for estoppel, see van der Merwe, *Sakereg* 368–372.

(b) Once B has been declared bankrupt, ownership of the cars held under reservation of title by A passes from A to the insolvency administrator of B, while A retains a security right (a *tacit hypothec*) in the cars. The proceeds of the sale will thus go to B's insolvency administrator, subject to A's security right.

(c) In view of the above, A should exercise reasonable care not to create the impression that B is the owner of the cars or has the power to sell them. On the basis of his retention of title, he can still reclaim the cars from C1–C5 and, if unsuccessful on account of the doctrine of estoppel, can rely on his security right to claim the proceeds of a sale from the insolvency estate of B.

If A has consigned the cars to B, or if B had been appointed A's 'undisclosed agent', A would be taken to have authorised the sale of the cars and would not therefore be entitled to vindicate the cars from a *bona fide* purchaser. This is because the English doctrine of the undisclosed principal is recognised in South African case law.[130]

DENMARK

(a) If the buyer has a right to resell the cars the agreement will be regarded as a credit consignment agreement according to Danish law. Under case law it is stated that a retention of title clause is not valid unless the buyer has to settle with the seller as soon as the cars are resold. In the present case, the buyer has been granted a fixed period of forty-five days for payment. This does not fulfil this requirement of immediate settlement. Because of this, A cannot claim a right to the cars sold to B and, as a consequence of this, he can claim no right to the cars when they have been resold.

Even if the agreement provided for a valid retention of title clause, A would not have a right to the cars after resale. This is in fact an exception to the general rule. According to Danish law, a person who has a right to an asset can in most cases reclaim the asset from a *bona fide* buyer. There are exceptions to this rule, but an ordinary retention of title clause must be respected by a sub-buyer. If, for example, a distributor sells an asset to his customer under a contract stipulating a valid reservation of title clause, and the customer then resells the asset, the distributor

---

[130] See *Cullinan v Noordkaaplandse Aartappelkernmoerkwekers Kooperasie Bpk* 1972 1 SA 761 (A). See further De Wet/Du Plessis, in: *The Law of South Africa I* paras. 146–159.

can still reclaim the asset, even if the sub-buyer was in good faith. This rule means that buyers cannot be completely sure that they get a valid right to the asset purchased. A number of buyers of secondhand cars were disadvantaged by the operation of this rule, hence the Car Register (*Bilbogen*) was established in 1992. Under section 42(d) in *Tinglysningsloven* a reservation of title clause to a motor vehicle must be registered on the Car Register in order to be effective in the case of a *bona fide* acquisition. The buyer of a secondhand car is, therefore, able to check the register before buying the car. A reservation of title clause to a vessel or an aircraft must also be registered. However, reservation of title clauses in respect of other assets cannot be registered. An exception to the rule that a retention of title clause to a car is to be registered is made in the case of a reservation of title clause in a credit consignment agreement for a new car. But of course registration would be required in respect of a secondhand car.

If the buyer had permission to resell the asset, the seller cannot reclaim the asset, nor assert any real right in it, when it has been resold. This might be seen as a rule requiring the seller to assume the risk of the retailer's insolvency in contracts which provide for resale. In fact, even if the buyer did not have permission to resell the asset, if the seller ought to have realised that the buyer was dealing in the assets, the seller may lose his right to the asset if the sub-buyer has bought the asset in good faith and the asset has been handed over to him.

Additionally, it should be mentioned that the result would be similar if the distributor had handed the assets over to an agent to sell the assets on the distributor's behalf (commission of undisclosed agency), cf. *Kommisionsloven* section 54.

(b) The monies that have been paid by the customers C1–C5 to B are regarded as part of the insolvency estate. This means that A cannot claim preferential payment. Even if a valid retention of title clause had been provided for in the contract, the monies paid to B by his customers would be taken by B's insolvency administrator on behalf of B's creditors.

(c) The importer or producer of cars could improve his position if the contract was a valid credit consignment agreement. Under case law some conditions – which are said to make the retention of title clause a reality between the parties – must be fulfilled in order to make the retention of title clause valid. The main conditions established by the case law in this respect are that (1) the consignee must settle with the consignor when the goods are resold; and (2) the consignor must make sure that the consignee acts in accordance with the agreement. The precise conditions for settlement and control may vary depending on the type of goods that are sold in consignments. If the assets are relatively expensive, each resale should be settled at once, whereas settlement might take place over a period if the goods have a lower unit cost.

A consignment agreement does not need to be registered. Since a consignment is regarded as a sort of reservation of title, it should only be registered if the assets concerned are motor vehicles. In fact, when an amendment to the Registration of Property Act concerning the Car Register was passed in 1992, consignment agreements concerning cars were to be registered not generally, but in respect of each car. Since consignments are generally used by importers when they sell cars to car dealers, it proved to be a virtually unworkable system. Therefore another amendment to the Act was passed in 1994, stating that a consignment agreement in respect of new cars need not be registered. But if a secondhand car was sold pursuant to a credit consignment, the reservation of title clause must be registered. Registration is also necessary in respect of vessels and aircraft.

When credit consignments are used, the consignor's right to the goods is protected against the consignee's creditors until the goods are resold. As soon as the goods are resold the consignor cannot claim a right to the goods. According to Danish law, this is a consequence of the buyer's right to resell.

If there had been a valid credit consignment agreement it would have been possible to stipulate in the contract that the claims arising out of sub-sales belonged to the importer, A. If such a clause was stipulated in the contract it would also be possible to stipulate that monies paid by the customers of the distributor, B, would belong to the importer, A. Such a clause has no effect unless the contract also stipulates that B is obliged to keep the monies separated from his own monies. Furthermore, A can only claim the monies if B has in fact kept the monies separated from his own monies, for example in a special bank account.

As discussed, it is common that cars are sold to distributors under credit consignment agreements. It is probably uncommon, however, that such contracts stipulate that the claims arising out of the sub-sales belong to the importer.

It would also be possible to register a charge in the assets. The question of whether such a charge would be protected against the sub-purchase when the buyer had a right to resell the goods has been debated.

However, the Supreme Court has recently held, in a case reported in *Ugeskrift for Retsvæsen* (weekly law reports) 2000 at 1117, that such a charge is protected against sub-purchasers if it is stipulated to continue until the seller has received the purchase price. When, however, it comes to the attention of the seller that the goods have been resold, he must claim his right within a reasonable time. It has been discussed above whether the seller in such cases must ensure that the buyer settles with him when the goods are resold. This question has not been finally settled by the last-mentioned judgment. This form of security is uncommon in respect of stock-in-trade, because a charge can have effect only in respect of the precise assets mentioned, which is not easy to achieve in practice. It would, for example, be necessary to re-register the charge regularly when some goods have been resold and replaced with new goods of the same type. But the security is used from time to time, e.g. for stocks of secondhand cars.

SWEDEN

(a) The fact that the reservation of title or rescission is void in relation to A's creditors (see case 4) does not in itself mean that the reservation is void also in relation to B or B's purchasers. However, since A has entitled B to resell the cars prior to payment without any remaining liens in favour of A, A has no right to claim ownership of the cars as against B's customers, irrespective of whether they have paid for and taken possession of the cars.

Consequently, B's customers need not rely on the rules governing *bona fide* acquisition. However, if B had sold the cars without such an entitlement to resell, B's customers could, pursuant to an act on good faith acquisition of chattels (Good Faith Purchase Act 1986), have become the owners, provided that: (1) B had the cars in his possession; (2) B's customers took possession of the cars; and (3) B's customers were in good faith. It is often necessary for the purchaser to investigate the transferor's right to sell or pledge the assets, but such requirements do not exist when the goods were purchased from a regular retailer. Today, even stolen goods and goods that the transferor acquired by coercion may be acquired *bona fide*, but a change is expected to be made to this position.[131] If B's customers did not make a *bona fide* acquisition, A would have a right to vindicate the goods or a clearly defined surrogate.[132]

---

[131] SOU 2000:56.   [132] NJA 1941, 711.

(b) The distributor, B, has, with the consent of the producer, A, sold the cars on his own behalf. He did not act as an undisclosed agent for A. Accordingly, B has received the monies from the customers on his own behalf and, therefore, the monies form part of the insolvency estate. If B had acted as an agent for A, A would have had a right to separate not only unsold cars that could be identified as having been supplied by him, and outstanding claims,[133] but also the monies received from B's customers, if B had, without delay, held those monies separately from his own.[134]

Even if B has sold the cars on his own behalf, A may acquire a right in the claims that has priority over the creditors of B, if the claims (which may be future identifiable claims) are assigned or charged to A. However, such protection presupposes that the customer is notified,[135] which cannot be done until the car is sold. Another prerequisite is that A must not be permitted to collect the monies for his own use.[136] An alternative method would be for A to be granted a form of registered enterprise charge (*registered mortgage*), according to the Enterprise Mortgage Act (*lagen om företagsinteckning*, 1984), under which the security comprises stock and outstanding claims.

(c) If B was not permitted to resell the goods without reserving A's title in the goods for A's claim on B, A's reservation of title (or of rescission) could validly be incorporated in B's contract with his customer. In such circumstances, B's customer pledges the goods for B's debt to A. Such a pledge is, under these special circumstances, valid notwithstanding that the subject matter of the pledge remains in the possession of the pledgor. Such forwarded reservations are not common, but occasionally they occur.[137] Another method is for B to hold a revolving *a-conto* account with unspecified payments in advance at A's bank, large enough to cover

---

[133] S. 57 Commission Agency Act.
[134] Entrusted Money Act (*lagen om redovisningsmedel*, 1944). Pursuant to this act, the monies must be received on the principal's behalf and the agent must not have been entitled to jeopardise the value of the principal's claim. It is not a requirement that the agent (being solvent) should be obliged to hold the money separately. However, when the agent has been declared bankrupt or execution is levied against the money, the principal is regarded as owner only of such monies as have been separated without delay or at least have been separated while the agent was solvent.
[135] Ss. 10 and 31 Promissory Notes Act (*skuldebrevslagen*, 1936). If notification, or the sale, occurs less than three months prior to the application for the commencement of insolvency proceedings, avoidance is possible pursuant to chapter 4 s. 12 Bankruptcy Act.
[136] NJA 1949, 164 and 1995, 367.   [137] NJA 1980, 219.

B's resales (or manufacture) for the near future, with permission to resell only to the extent payment is covered by the *a-conto* account. Then the reservation of title or rescission is valid in respect of the remaining stock. The usual method, however, is to work with some sort of commission agency or consignment agreement.[138]

FINLAND

(a) The distributor, B, was entitled to sell the cars in the ordinary course of business even if the price of the cars was not paid to A. Moreover, it seems that B was not obliged to reserve A's rights to the cars when he was reselling them. Under these circumstances, the customers, C1–C5, have acquired full ownership to their cars and neither A nor B or his creditors have any real rights in the cars. As a matter of fact, A could not have taken the cars back even if they had been unsold when B became bankrupt. This is because B had the right to resell the cars in the ordinary course of business, even if the price was not paid to A.[139]

If B had not been entitled to resell the unpaid cars, A could have claimed the cars back from C1–C5, unless they had acquired the cars *bona fide*.[140] A *bona fide* acquisition usually presupposes that (1) the seller had the goods in his or her possession; (2) the buyer took possession of the goods; and (3) the buyer was still in *bona fides* at the moment of delivery. B's entitlement to resell the cars in the present case means the question of *bona fide* acquisition is unlikely to be relevant. It may arise, however, if B has breached the terms of the agreement with A, *viz.* sub-sales to be in the ordinary course of business. The Supreme Court of Finland has held, in such circumstances, the retention of title to be valid against a sub-purchaser *in mala fide*, although the Court has consistently regarded the clause as invalid against creditors in similar situations.[141] The prerequisites of a *bona fide* acquisition are, however, in this kind of situation, somewhat unclear.[142]

(b) The monies would belong to the insolvency estate of B and not to A. This is primarily so due to the fact that A did not have any real rights in the cars, which B was entitled to sell quite freely.

---

[138] See Swedish report, case 4.   [139] See above, Finnish report, case 4.
[140] See e.g. Kaisto, *Tiesi tai olisi pitänyt tietää* and Välimaa, *Oikeustiede – Jurisprudentia*.
[141] See KKO 1990:104.   [142] See further, e.g., Välimaa, *Oikeustiede – Jurisprudentia*.

(c) A's situation would have been better if A and B had agreed that the cars would remain A's property and that the cars would not be delivered to B's customers before B had paid the purchase price. The distributor, B, would, in other words, only make a 'preliminary' contract with his or her own customer before the payment of the purchase price to A. If A had, moreover, ensured that these restrictions were followed, the retention of title clause would have been effective as against other creditors. This kind of arrangement makes it possible for the distributor to sell, against cash payment, cars which he or she cannot, or will not, pay for in advance. On the other hand, such arrangements cause some inconvenience, because the distributor must rapidly deliver the cash payment of his own customer to the importer or manufacturer, in order to secure his or her acceptance to the sale and the delivery.

Also, the rules concerning commission, i.e. undisclosed agency, or consignment could, under certain circumstances, have protected A.[143] These rules can only, however, protect A if B is permitted to return to A cars which he cannot resell. Therefore a central economic risk of reselling activities must be borne by A. If B is obliged to pay the price of the cars, regardless of whether he or she manages to resell them or not, the rules concerning commission or consignment cannot protect A. Even if A chooses to assume the economic risk inherent to commission or consignment arrangements, in the way described above, his protection would probably depend on certain other prerequisites. B would have been liable to forward to A, without any major delay, the proceeds arising from the cars sold by him. As principal, A would also have to control, to some extent, the activities of B in order to ensure that the proceeds were appropriately forwarded to him and that the other provisions of the commission or consignment agreement were observed by B. If all the necessary prerequisites were met, A would, however, be treated as the owner of the cars and A would be entitled to claim the cars out of the insolvency estate of B. Furthermore, if there was a commission agreement, that is, an undisclosed agency, neither the purchase-money claims against the sub-purchasers nor the purchase monies (which B would have collected acting as undisclosed agent of A) which B had kept separated from his own monies would belong to the insolvency estate of B.

---

[143] See e.g. Tepora, *Defensor Legis* 1991, 623 ff. and Tuomisto, *Omistuksenpidätys ja leasing* 333 ff. Regarding the differences between commission and consignment, see above, Finnish report, case 4.

The dominant type of distribution arrangement, especially in the motor vehicle trade, has the features described above. These arrangements often, however, include features of consignment or commission agreements and retention of title, with the consequence that it is not always easy to say whether the agreement is one or the other.[144]

If the goods sold by A had been lorries, buses or similar kinds of equipment, it would also have been possible to use a form of charge (*registered mortgage*). This charge would have protected A against B's creditors, as well as against the sub-purchasers. The use of this kind of charge is, however, rather inconvenient in distribution arrangements and it is rare for it to be used in such a context.

Cars, as well as other motor vehicles, are also potentially subject to an enterprise charge. The same applies to claims against B's customers and monies paid by the customers of B. The main problem in using an enterprise charge is that it secures priority over only half the value of the personal property, i.e. other than immovables, belonging to the enterprise. Enterprise charges are, however, fairly commonly used as a part of the security arrangements in distribution contracts between a producer or importer and a distributor, in addition to being used to secure long-term bank loans. Nevertheless, the enterprise charge is usually regarded as a secondary form of security.

There is also always the possibility of establishing a charge over the claims. The main difficulties are that the sub-purchasers must be informed of this agreement and that the distributor, most probably, must not be permitted to collect the monies. An assignment of the proceeds of sale to C1–C5 would give rise to the same kind of problems. Such arrangements would offer protection to A, however, in that, if the sub-purchasers had paid B after notification, they would be obliged to pay the monies once again to A.

Comparative observations

Part (a)

In contrast to the previous case, the goods have now been sold to the customers. Except for Portuguese and South African law, all systems under consideration conclude that C1–C5 have acquired ownership in the cars free of any rights of the first seller (A). According to German,

---

[144] See KKO 1994:145.

Austrian, Greek, Dutch, English, Irish and Scots law, a buyer who is entitled to resell the goods can validly transfer ownership to his customers irrespective of the rules on *bona fide* acquisition. However, if the contract between A and B lacked such an entitlement, the customers could still receive unencumbered ownership if they were in *bona fides*. In France, Belgium and Spain, *bona fide* acquisition would be the only way by which the customers could receive title since the entitlement to resell the goods is regarded as irrelevant. In Italy, an entitlement to resell would probably not be irrelevant but it is not usually included in the contract of sale between A and B since the parties are not able to grant A a security right in the proceeds. Under Danish law, it is not necessary to rely upon *bona fide* acquisition nor an entitlement to resell. Since the entitlement to resell the goods invalidates the reservation of title (see case 4), B disposes of the cars as owner. Under Finnish law, however, only a sale in the ordinary course of business would pass ownership to the sub-buyer irrespective of his good faith. The entitlement to resell the goods merely invalidates the retention of title as against B's insolvency creditors but not as against B's purchasers in *mala fide*.

In Portugal, the seller under retention of title can only transfer an expectancy with the consequence that the second buyer can only become owner when the first buyer pays the purchase price. Therefore, the solution in Portugal to part (a) is different from the majority: the seller's ownership survives the resale. It should be noted, however, that in the special case of cars reservation of title must be registered in order to be effective *vis-à-vis* third parties.

The questionnaire did not seek to analyse the differences in respect of *bona fide* acquisition in any greater detail. So a few words on this topic should suffice.[145] With the exception of South Africa and Denmark, all jurisdictions protect the purchaser who in good faith and for value buys goods in a normal commercial situation not giving rise to doubts about the seller's ownership. However, the theoretical foundations are quite different. In German and Greek law, the decisive aspect is the transferor's possession of the goods; this forms the basis of the acquirer's belief that the transferor is the owner of the goods. In contrast, the French rule that possession equals ownership (article 2279 C.civ.) emphasises the acquirer's possession: someone who has in good faith received possession of a movable is protected against the *rei vindicatio*

---

[145] For a comparative overview see Thorn, *Der Mobiliarerwerb vom Nichtberechtigten* 45 ff.

of the former owner.¹⁴⁶ Italian law follows the same line of thinking. The Spanish *Código civil* has taken over article 2279 C.civ. almost literally (see article 464 section 1 C.c.). In recent years, however, legal literature as well as the courts have reinterpreted article 464 section 1 C.c. in a way that moves the present law on *bona fide* acquisition into close vicinity to the German §§ 932 ff. BGB.¹⁴⁷ Swedish and Finnish law require both possession on the side of the transferor prior to the transfer and actual delivery leading to possession on the side of the transferee. In England, Ireland and especially in Scotland, the old Roman rule that nobody can transfer a better right than he has himself, still survives as a basic principle, although the English common law has developed a principle of apparent ownership. Today, there are a considerable number of statutory exceptions to the '*nemo-dat*' rule as it is called, among them section 25 of the Sale of Goods Act 1979 which basically applies if goods sold under retention of title are resold to a *bona fide* purchaser. Austrian law resembles English law in so far as it does not seem to work with one general principle but rather regulates certain typical situations where the acquirer in good faith is regarded as deserving of protection.

Part (b)

On the facts of case 5, the ultimate buyers have paid for the cars before B's bankruptcy and the contract provides for no more than simple reservation of title coupled with an entitlement to resell. In such circumstances, all jurisdictions conclude that the money paid belongs to B's insolvency estate. A number of jurisdictions draw a distinction between the case where the money has been paid to B before he has been declared bankrupt and the case where the money is still due or has been paid to the insolvency estate. The second situation, and the possible distinctions between the two, will be explored in case 6.

Part (c)

This part was deliberately drafted in an open-ended way, in order to allow every contributor to set out the ways in which a seller might

---

[146] Cf. von Gerlach, *Der Einfluß des deutschen und französischen Rechts auf den Eigentumserwerbsschutz beweglicher Sachen im spanischen Recht* 23 ff. with further references.
[147] See further *ibid.*, 90–139.

obtain better protection, irrespective of the construction or the wording of specific clauses.

(i) Solutions which do not require additional clauses or transactions

Obviously, a seller in Portugal does not need greater protection than that provided by a simple retention of title clause under article 880º C.c.:[148] his ownership simply survives the resale. In South Africa, the best way for the seller to secure himself is not to include a power of resale into his contract with the buyer, as this will preserve his ownership of the goods, the reason being that South African law does not protect *bona fide* purchasers except by the doctrine of estoppel which is of rather limited application. Equally in German law, the seller might achieve a better position by not providing for a power of resale. Yet, this rests on a totally different ground, namely the right to claim proceeds arising from an unlawful transaction by the debtor (who later becomes insolvent), if that transaction has invalidated the creditor's retention of title. However, this improves A's position only if B has kept the monies paid by the sub-purchasers in a separate account. In France and Belgium, the seller may benefit from a real subrogation into the proceeds. In order to be effective, however, the claims against the sub-purchasers must still be subsisting at the point at which insolvency proceedings commence.[149]

(ii) Charge over the proceeds

A charge over the proceeds is possible principally in Belgium, the Netherlands, England, Ireland and Finland. However, with the exception of Belgium, where the relevant provision (article 1690 C.civ.) was changed in 1994,[150] a charge over proceeds would only accord to A priority over B's insolvency creditors if further requirements were met. In Finland, the third-party debtors (in this case, C1–C5) must be notified of the charge in order for it to be opposable towards third parties, a requirement which renders the charge impractical in all situations where the identities of

---

[148] See *supra*, Portuguese report case 4.   [149] See *infra*, French report case 6.
[150] Before the Act of 6 July 1994 (*Moniteur Belge* 15 July 1994, 18625), Belgian law was the same as French law in requiring a formal notification of the assignment or its formal acceptance by the third-party debtor ('*signification*') in order for the assignment or the charge over claims to be valid as against third parties in general. According to the new article 1690 s. 2 (Belgian) C.civ (informal) notification is only necessary to prevent the *debitor cessus* validly from paying the assignor.

the third-party debtors (sub-purchasers) are not yet known. In the Netherlands, a charge over claims must be registered or the third-party debtors must be notified of its existence. Again, this is not feasible in respect of future claims where even the framework under which the claims will arise has not been created. In England and Ireland charges over book debts of a company have to be entered on the Companies Register. If the chargor is a private person, a duty to register exists under the Bills of Sale Acts. Although the mere fact that the claims will arise only in the future does not seem to be an obstacle to registration, this procedure appears to be too time-consuming and costly to be practicable for sellers granting short-term trade credit.

(iii) Assignment of the proceeds

In Germany, Austria and Greece, sellers usually employ an anticipated security assignment of the proceeds. In German and Greek law, this requires no more than an adequately drafted retention of title clause, whereas in Austria, security assignment is subject to the same requirements as the charge of a claim. Therefore, in order to be effective as against third parties, the assignment must either be entered into the books of the debtor (B), or the *debitor cessus* (in this case, C1–C5) must be notified of it. Notification can only take place when the identity of *debitor cessus* is known but, according to a view in legal doctrine that is not undisputed, the book entry method may be used in respect of claims where the legal foundation is not yet laid.

Yet, even in Germany, Austria and Greece, a proceeds clause framed as a security assignment cannot protect a seller who permits his buyer to collect the claims and mix the proceeds of realisation with his other funds. Although notification of the assignment is not a requirement for its effectiveness *vis-à-vis* third parties, it is a way for the seller to protect himself as soon as he realises that his customer is getting into financial difficulties.

In Belgium, the Netherlands, England, Ireland and Finland, a security assignment of the claims against the sub-purchasers would be held ineffective or, at best, be regarded as a charge (see (ii)).

(iv) Employing the law of trusts to gain a right over the proceeds

In the famous *Romalpa* case of 1978, the English Court of Appeal for the first and the last time held that a fiduciary relationship existed between a seller and a buyer under what may be termed an extended retention of title clause. In that case, the extension, however, did not relate to proceeds resulting from sub-sales but to new products made using the purchased material. In *Romalpa*, the Court of Appeal, basing its decision on principles of trust law, allowed the seller to trace his rights into the newly formed products. Subsequently, sellers tried to use the same concept in relation not only to products but also to proceeds of sale. Yet, no English court ever again applied the solution adopted in *Romalpa*. As the English report states, the subsequent cases 'have distinguished *Romalpa* out of existence'. The same development took place in Ireland, where today, *Romalpa*-clauses are treated as charges requiring registration. Likewise, in Scotland, attempts to apply trust law to the relationship between a seller and a buyer under retention of title have been fruitless.

(v) Contracts other than sale under retention of title
(consignment and commission)

As explained in case 4, retention of title is not a suitable device in Denmark, Sweden and Finland if the goods are to be resold. Instead, other types of contract are used. In Denmark, the typical contract to be used in such cases is consignment. Since it requires that the buyer (B) accounts to the seller (A) for each sub-sale practically immediately, a situation like the one described in case 5 will usually not arise. An additional clause stipulating that the proceeds vest directly in A is possible although uncommon. On the facts of case 5, however, such a clause would not be able to protect A if the money has not been kept in a separate account. Similar solutions are adopted in Sweden and Finland. Here, the typical contract is a commission agreement. Again, the problem described in case 5 would not arise since the claims generated by the sub-sales would belong directly to A. But as the Finnish report points out, if B (obviously in breach of the commission agreement) collected the money himself without separating it from his own funds, A's rights to the money would still be extinguished.

In Italy, a commission agreement is also a theoretical way by which A could obtain a right in the proceeds, provided B keeps separate the money he receives from his customers. In practice, however, such contracts are hardly ever used because Italian courts (like Swedish and Finnish courts[151]) would probably require the principal (A) effectively

---

[151] See *supra*, Swedish and Finnish reports and Comparative Observations, case 4.

to assume B's business risk. Instead, commercial practice in Italy uses personal guarantees.

(vi) Rights in the sold goods other than retention of title

Retention of title has the advantages of simplicity and low transaction costs: in nearly all jurisdictions it needs simply to be inserted into the contract and does not need to be registered. The rights of the seller are vulnerable, however, for example in the event of a sub-sale. A registered charge in the sold goods is an alternative, but it must be registered in such a way that it enables third parties to inform themselves of its existence, thus destroying the possibility of *bona fide* acquisition. French, Italian, Spanish and Danish law for instance provide for such a registered charge. In Spain, it takes the form of a *hypothec* in movables (*hipoteca mobiliaria*) which seems to be available in respect of all categories of movable property. The same is true of Danish law. In France, the registered charge only exists for certain well-defined categories of movables, the most important being vehicles (*gage sur véhicule*). A registered charge in cars and other vehicles also exists in Italy (*privilegio sull'autoveicolo*),[152] but for the practical reasons set out in the Italian report (lack of registration) it is not used in respect of new cars. If A and B had established such a *gage*, *privilegio* or *hipoteca*, and complied with the registration formalities, A's rights based on the registered charge (right to preferential payment out of its realisation) would be enforceable in B's insolvency. Registration would have prevented B's customers from acquiring rights in the cars that could take priority over A's rights. In Denmark, the exact scope of the chargee's rights are still disputed.

(vii) Summary

The safest protection for the seller is a right over the goods themselves which is able to survive resale. This is exemplified by Portuguese, South African and Danish law, which places the seller's retained ownership above the interests of *bona fide* purchasers. It is further illustrated by the possibility of taking a registered charge under French, Italian and Spanish law over cars.

In contrast, the potential for the seller to take an effective right in the proceeds of sub-sale is limited. Although most jurisdictions as a matter of principle allow the taking of a security right in claims, be it in the

---

[152] See *infra*, Italian report, case 6.

form of a security assignment or by way of a charge, many require a form of publicity that is either too costly (England, Ireland) or makes it near to impossible to take a security in truly future claims[153] (France, Italy, the Netherlands, Finland). Consequently, proceeds clauses are not commonly used in practice in these countries.

Germany and Greece are the jurisdictions that stand out in respect of the use and effectiveness of proceeds clauses. The so-called *verlängerter Eigentumsvorbehalt* can also be used with truly future claims and is not subject to any registration or notification requirements. The same applies in Belgium with the sole difference that the proceeds clause would have to be framed as a charge; yet, as the Belgian report points out, this way for sellers to extend their security rights into proceeds of sub-sales has not yet been fully exploited by Belgian practice, presumably because simple retention of title only recently became effective in insolvency. Austrian law may be said to be similar to German law, although the OGH still has yet clearly to approve of the view that the book entry of assignments is possible even before the legal foundation of the future claim has been laid. However, even German and Austrian law (or the contractual arrangements used in Denmark, Sweden and Finland) cannot provide the seller with any right that would give him priority over B's insolvency creditors in a situation like the one in case 5: money paid to the first buyer that has been mixed with other funds is always lost irretrievably.

---

[153] Claims where the legal foundation out of which they will arise does not yet exist.

Case 6: Motor cars supplied and resold (II)

(Retention of title and resale – claim arising out of sub-sale still existing)

A is a producer (or importer) of cars. As in case 5, he sells five cars to B, a licensed distributor. The contract allows B a period of forty-five days before payment has to be made. It also contains the following clause: 'The seller hereby retains title to the cars delivered under this contract. The buyer, however, is entitled to resell the cars in the ordinary course of business.' Two weeks after delivery of the cars, B has already managed to sell them to various customers (C1–C5), who have taken them away immediately. Before anyone has paid anything, B goes bankrupt.

Questions

(a) Who can claim payment from C1–C5? Is it A or is it B's insolvency administrator?
(b) Could A get a better right in respect of the claims arising out of the sub-sales (for example, by adopting a differently worded clause, or by using a different type of retention of title clause)? What would be the precise prerequisites? Are such clauses commonly used?

Discussions

GERMANY

(a) Since the contract does not contain an anticipatory assignment of the claims arising out of the sub-sales (see *infra*, part (b)), it is the administrator who is entitled to claim payment from the customers. A's position would be better if the contract provided only for simple retention of title, without granting B permission to resell the cars. In that case, § 48 InsO would apply:[1] due to the unlawful sub-sale, A would have been deprived of his right to vindicate the cars. As B's claims against the customers would not yet have been satisfied, A could then require the insolvency administrator to assign the outstanding claims to him.

(b) As explained previously,[2] a proceeds clause would be the appropriate and most commonly used way to provide a seller with security when it is intended that the goods are to be resold. In pursuance of such a clause, the buyer anticipatorily assigns to the seller the claims against his sub-purchasers. All that is required is the inclusion in the contract of a properly worded clause. It should be noted, however, that the seller's position is that of the holder of a security right, not that of a 'normal' assignee; in other words, his relationship with the buyer/assignor is a fiduciary one. This *inter alia* determines the nature of the seller's rights in the buyer's insolvency,[3] especially after the new Insolvency Code[4] entered into force: it is the insolvency administrator, and not A himself, who can claim payment from C1–C5 (§§ 50 s. 1, 51 n. 1, 166 s. 2 InsO). However, the insolvency administrator is obliged to satisfy A's claim out of the monies he receives from C1–C5, after deducting the costs incurred in assessing and realising the security right (§ 170 s. 1 InsO).[5] The new Insolvency Code (§ 171 InsO) fixes these costs at 9 per cent of the amount received by the administrator from the third-party debtor (C1–C5). So long as the value of the collateral is equal to or greater than the aggregate of the secured claim and the costs of assessment and realisation of the security right, the secured creditor will be paid in full.

An important point to note in this respect is the time-span within which the administrator has to realise the value of the collateral. After

---

[1] See *supra*, German report, case 5(b).   [2] German report, case 5(c).

[3] In an execution against B's assets, A's rights in respect of the claims against C1–C5 would not differ from the rights of a 'normal' assignee. The creditors of B could not execute against the claims, simply because the claims do not belong to B.

[4] See the summary by Eckardt, ZIP 1999, 1734 f. Under the old Insolvency Code (§ 48 Konkursordnung), the realisation of the collateral was administered primarily by the creditor himself and did not form part of the insolvency proceedings (§§ 4 s. 2, 127 s. 2 KO). Moreover, secured creditors did not have to contribute to the costs of the assessment of their rights and the realisation thereof.

[5] This right to preferential payment out of the proceeds of the realisation is called *Absonderung*. Before the new Insolvency Code came into force, this right existed under judge-made law: see RG 9 Apr. 1929, RGZ 124, 73 (75); BGH 9 Dec. 1970, LM (from 1971 on) § 157 (Ga) Nr. 18; BGH 1 July 1985, BGHZ 95, 149 (152); BGH 17 Apr. 1986, ZIP 1986, 720 (722). It was also generally accepted in the doctrine: see Kuhn/Uhlenbruck, Konkursordnung § 48 KO n. 24 a; *Münchener Kommentar*/Roth § 398 BGB n. 85.

the commencement of insolvency proceedings, the court will fix a date for a general meeting of all creditors, at which the administrator will outline how he intends to take the procedure forward (the so-called report meeting: see §§ 156 ff. InsO).[6] This meeting should take place within six weeks, and must take place within three months, of the commencement of insolvency proceedings (§ 29 s. 1 n. 1 InsO). After the meeting, the administrator is obliged to realise the bankrupt's assets as soon as possible, including those subject to security interests (§ 159 InsO). If the administrator does not fulfil this obligation in a timely manner, the secured creditor is entitled to be paid interest (§ 169 sent. 1 InsO).

Apart from the contribution to the costs and the waiting period just mentioned, the new Insolvency Code has introduced another novel measure which may severely curtail the rights of creditors who do not have a right to vindicate, but only a right to preferential payment (for reasons of simplicity, hereinafter called secured creditors). According to § 217 ff. InsO, the creditors' general meeting can decide to set aside all the rules governing the satisfaction of creditors' claims and opt for an individually negotiated insolvency plan. This procedure is especially designed for cases where a reorganisation appears to be feasible (see § 1 s.1 sent. 1 InsO). At this point, it is not necessary to describe in detail the procedure by which an insolvency plan may be set up.[7] It is sufficient to note that the plan must expressly specify the percentage by which the rights of secured creditors will be curtailed and, or alternatively, a timetable for the realisation of the collateral (§ 223 s. 2 InsO). Also, the insolvency creditors cannot approve an insolvency plan contrary to the wishes of the majority of the secured creditors. § 244 s.1 n. 1 InsO provides that, in order to approve the plan, a majority of each group of creditors, including the secured creditors (see § 222 s. 1 n. 1 InsO), is required.

AUSTRIA

(a) As no anticipatory assignment of the claims arising out of the sub-sales took place, B's insolvency administrator is entitled to claim payment from C1–C5.

---

[6] See further Paulus, *Texas International Law Journal* 33 (1998) 141 (148).
[7] See further Bork, *Einführung in das neue Insolvenzrecht* nn. 310 ff.; Wellensiek, BB 2000, 1 (5 f.). Until recently, the insolvency plan procedure was not particularly well received by practitioners: see Wellensiek, BB 2000, 1 (6).

(b) As discussed previously, A and B could provide for extended reservation of title: reservation of title coupled with a security assignment of claims arising from resales (*verlängerter Eigentumsvorbehalt*).[8]

GREECE

(a) If B goes bankrupt, the claims against C1–C5 belong to the insolvency estate. Thus, it is the insolvency administrator who is entitled to claim payment.

(b) Only an extended retention of title clause (i.e. a proceeds clause) would entitle A to recover the claims arising from the sub-sales. In business practice, when the purchaser is a retailer, the retention of title agreement usually provides for an assignment to the vendor of the future claims of the purchaser arising from the resale of the product (a proceeds clause).[9] This form of assignment is in reality a fiduciary one, because it provides security for the satisfaction of the vendor's (A's) claims as against the assignor (B). The latter will often be authorised by the assignee (article 239 A.K.) to collect the monies. No special prerequisites are required for such a security assignment. A can, however, register the assignment (article 12 L. 2844/2000) if he wishes to gain priority over possible future assignees of the same claim.

If A and B agreed such an extended reservation of title agreement, and B went bankrupt, the assigned claim would not form part of the insolvency estate, as, by virtue of the assignment, the claim would have been separated from the assignor's property.[10] According to the prevailing view, this is so irrespective of whether the assignment has been notified to the *debitor cessus*. If the assigned claim falls due, the assignee is entitled to collect the money, unless the administrator pays the secured debt.

A differing view, as supported by N. Rokas,[11] contends that the provisions governing pledge are applicable by way of analogy to an insolvent

---

[8] For details, see above, Austrian report, case 5(c).
[9] For extended retention of title, see Roussos, 'I epekteinomeni epiphylaxi kyriotitas' 397.
[10] The prevailing view is supported by Georgiadis, *Empragmato Dikaio II* 267; Kornilakis, *I katapisteutiki ekchorisi ton apaitiseon* 126.
[11] N. Rokas, *Stoicheia ptocheutikou dikaiou* 29. According to this opinion, if the notification of the assignment has not occurred before the commencement of insolvency proceedings, the claim forms part of the insolvency estate.

debtor who assigned his claims in a fiduciary way.¹² The assignee-initial creditor, though holder of the claim, cannot claim payment directly from the *debitor cessus*, but will be entitled to preferential payment from the proceeds of sale. This seems the better view, as the assignor is not the typical but the substantial holder of the right. The fiduciary assignment of a claim resembles a pledge, as both ensure the satisfaction of the assignee's claims. If B's creditors seek to execute against the assigned claim, A, after having notified the *debitor cessus* of the assignment,¹³ can resist the execution (article 936 KPolD).

FRANCE

(a) C. com, article L. 621-124 enables the seller to claim from the sub-buyer the sale price, or part of the price, of the assets sold under a retention of title agreement, so long as the price was not paid to or settled in kind with the debtor, or set off as between debtor and sub-buyer, at the date of the commencement of the insolvency proceedings. In order for A to be able to claim real subrogation into the proceeds arising from the resale of the cars, it is necessary that the assets supplied to the sub-purchasers remained in their original state. A, apparently, will be able to claim payment from C1–C5 for the cars, limited in quantum to the amount of his own claim.

(b) A's right under C. com, article L. 621-124 is good (see part (a), *supra*), so long as the assets have not been transformed in nature (as considered in cases 7 and 8, *infra*).

BELGIUM

(a) The insolvency administrator is entitled to claim payment from the different customers, but A will be entitled to preferential payment out of the proceeds.

(b) According to the principle of 'real subrogation', the seller can require that the proceeds are to be handed over to him. The proceeds of each

---

[12] *Ibid.*, 35–36; see also Mantzoufas, *Enochikon Dikaion* 193 and AP 1669/95 DEE 1996, 375.
[13] AP 42/1969 NoV 17, 550; Balis, *Enochikon Dikaion, Genikon Meros* § 157, 4; Kritikos, in: Georgiadis – Stathopoulos AK 455 II n. 71. For the opposite view, i.e. that the notification of the assignment is unnecessary to resist the execution, see Georgiadis, *Empragmato Dikaio II* 266; Kornilakis, *I katapisteutiki ekchorisi ton apaitiseon* 71.

sub-sale are regarded as the substitute for the car to which the seller reserved title. Therefore, neither the buyer nor his creditors can claim to have a stronger right to these proceeds than to the car itself.

PORTUGAL

(a) The solution to case 6 is the same as that to case 5. The fact that the customers have not yet paid for the cars makes no difference. In both cases, if A has registered a reservation of title agreement, then the customers would not be able to register their ownership unless A receives his full payment and cancels the registration in his favour.

(b) Identical to case 5(c).

SPAIN

(a) Only B's insolvency administrator can claim payment from C1–C5. A is simply an insolvency creditor. In this case, the retention of title clause cannot accord to A any priority if B goes bankrupt.[14]

The purchasers are protected by article 85 CCO, according to which their acquisition is protected by virtue of having been obtained in a shop open to the public. The insolvency administrator can claim payment from C1–C5. A's reservation of title clause accords to him no greater guarantee, since in this case ownership of the goods has passed to third parties who are protected by law. In such a case, the good faith of the purchaser is of no importance. If, however, the sale was governed by the LVBMP, and if the reservation of title clause had been recorded in the Chattels Registry, A would not be affected by B's insolvency (article 908 CCO) and any rights of third parties such as C1–C5 would evaporate, entitling A to vindicate the cars from B's insolvency estate.

(b) A could not obtain a better right to the subsale claims, unless the creditor took a special security (e.g. the contract had been included in a public deed conferred by a notary, article 1924.3 CC). In this case, the parties have to comply with specific formal requirements in the presence of the notary, who will ensure that the goods that are the object of the contract of sale are properly identified, which in this case would

---

[14] See article 1922.1 CC and article 908 CCO. See Díez-Picazo, *Fundamentos de derecho civil patrimonial* I 761.

mean recording the trademark of the car, the model, the chassis number and the licence number, if there is one. Finally, a copy of the vehicle registration document for each car would also need to be attached to the public deed. If the debt was defined in this way, A would have, in B's insolvency, a preferential right of payment, in priority to other debts which are embodied neither in a public deed nor in a judge's final decision (article 1924.3 CC).

ITALY

(a) Considering the contractual term in question, B's administrator is entitled to the sums that are still due from C1–C5. A will rank as an insolvency creditor in B's insolvency proceedings.

(b) For general remarks on how the risk of the car dealers' insolvency is addressed by current Italian business practice see above, case 5(c).

In principle, A would be better off if he had entered into a commission contract with B. In such a case, article 1705 c.c. expressly entitles A to sue B's customers for the sums they owe B.[15] This entitlement is not curtailed by B's insolvency, provided that the contract in question has a certain date prior to the commencement of insolvency proceedings (article 1707 c.c.). For the reasons explained previously, in case 5(c), it is, however, unlikely that A and B will opt to enter into such a contract.

As an alternative, A and B could provide that the future claims, arising between B and his customers, should be assigned in favour of A. It is highly unlikely that such an assignment will be used in practice, however, for the reasons explained above, in case 5(c).

In either case, the fact that the customers have not yet paid B would prevent problems concerning the identification of the monies due to A under the commission contract, or the assignment provision, from arising.

---

[15] Article 1705 c.c.: 'A mandatory acting in his own name acquires the rights and assumes the duties arising from transactions made with third persons, even if the latter had knowledge of the mandate. Third persons have no relationship with the principal. However, the principal can, by substituting himself for the mandatory, exercise claims arising from the performance, except when in doing so he impairs the rights attributed to the mandatory by the provisions of the following articles.' The origins of this provision go back to the epoch of the *ius commune*: Supino, *La rivendicazione nel fallimento*. Several decisions hold that the proper application of article 1705 c.c. is still limited to claims for fixed sums of money. Accordingly, a claim for damages would not be covered by that provision: Cass. 5 Nov. 1998, n. 11118, Foro it., 1999, I, 94.

Finally, A could sell the cars to B and take a charge for the purchase price under the special rules applicable to cars and other vehicles.[16] This charge would entitle A to collect the monies that C1–C5 still owe to B, in priority to the insolvency creditors. Yet even this solution is very unlikely, because the charge is not valid unless it is registered in the public registry established for transactions concerning vehicles (P.R.A.). But new vehicles that are sold by producers to dealers are not subject to such registration, as has been explained previously. Hence no charge can be taken on them.

THE NETHERLANDS

(a) The claims arising from the subsales are owed by C1–C5 to B. A has no claim against C1–C5. This does not change with the commencement of insolvency proceedings against B.

(b) Dutch law does not provide for a form of retention of title that would provide A with a better right to the proceeds of the sub-sales. Nor would it be possible to create a charge over the *future* claims arising from the sub-sales. As in case 5(c), the only way would be for A to oblige B by their contract of sale to grant him or her a charge at the time the claims come into existence.[17]

ENGLAND

(a) It makes in principle no difference in such a case whether the sub-buyers have paid the buyer, as in case 5, or not. The mere fact that payment has not been made is irrelevant. A obtains no direct right to payment on the ground that C1–C5 have not yet paid.

Nevertheless, the above simple approach needs to take account of the terms on which the goods have been sold. Suppose the contracts between B and C1–C5 provide for ownership to pass only when B is paid and B has not been paid at the date when B's insolvency proceedings commence (whether they be *bankruptcy* or *liquidation*). Under s. 25 of the Sale of

---

[16] R.d.l. 15 Mar. 1927, n. 436, articles 2–6, converted into law 19 Feb. 1928, n. 510; article 2810 c.c. For a commentary: Miglietta/Prandi, in: *Giurisprudenza sistematica di diritto civile e commerciale* 312–317.

[17] NB one should be aware that, in practice, B would often already have charged or, rather, would be under an obligation to charge, these claims in favour of his or her bank.

Goods Act,[18] C1–C5 will obtain against A only such rights as they would obtain against B, which is possession under sub-sale contracts where title to the cars has not yet passed.[19] If C1–C5 obtain notice before the statutory exception to the rule of *nemo dat* is completed, they cannot acquire good title as against A.

(b) As stated above, it is not difficult for A to acquire rights in the money proceeds of the sub-sales by way of charge. The difficulty is for A to register his rights in an effective way.

IRELAND

(a) Basically the analysis is the same as for case 5. It is submitted that B's insolvency administrator has a better claim than A to payment from C.

(b) Moreover, with respect to part (b) it is difficult if not impossible to conceive of circumstances whereby A could get a better right to the claims arising out of the sub-sales. If there is a provision in the original contract of sale under which the seller may sue the sub-buyer for resale claims, the courts are likely to hold that the provision constitutes a registrable charge. A registrable, but unregistered, charge will be void for want of registration. Among the categories of registrable charge specifically enumerated in s. 99 Companies Act 1963 is a charge on 'book debts', i.e. ordinary trade claims. Claims by the seller to claims owing from resale buyers may be held to fall squarely within this provision.

Re Interview Ltd[20] illustrates this proposition. In this case, an Irish company imported electrical goods from a German supplier with the sales contract providing *inter alia*:

With respect to a case of resale of the goods . . . in any condition whatsoever . . . the purchaser agrees to assign and assigns to the supplier, at the conclusion of the supply contract and effective up to the time of payment of all debts owing by the purchaser to the supplier, any claims against the purchaser's customers which may have arisen or arise in future from the resale, by way of security, and undertakes to notify the supplier at his request of the names of third-party debtors and of the amount of the debts owing by these to the purchaser.

---

[18] As amplified by its companion provision, s. 9 of the Factors Act 1889.
[19] *Re Highway Foods International Ltd* [1995] BCC 271. Cf. *Shaw v Commissioner of Police of the Metropolis* [1987] 3 All ER 405.
[20] [1975] IR 382.

The judge held that the provision represented a charge on the buyer's book debts requiring registration under s. 99(2)(c) of the Companies Act 1963. He reached this conclusion on the basis that there was an assignment of claims 'by way of security', the contract itself using that expression. There was no absolute assignment, for, if the purchaser had paid for the goods immediately, there would have been no assignment of the claim created by the resale.

SCOTLAND

(a) C1–C5 must pay the price to B's insolvency administrator and not to A.

(b) For the trust device, see case 5(c). The trust device does not work.

No attempt has in practice been made to include in the A–B contract an anticipatory assignment by B to A of the future proceeds of sale. There has been some theoretical discussion of this possibility. The arrangement would probably fail, since *assignation*[21] must be completed by notification,[22] and in the case of a future claim notification is not yet possible.

SOUTH AFRICA

(a) The insolvency administrator is entitled to claim payment from C1–C5. A will, however, have a security right (*tacit hypothec*) over the proceeds of the sale according to the provisions of the Insolvency Act.[23]

(b) In view of A's security right (*tacit hypothec*), his position would be satisfactory.

DENMARK

(a) According to Danish law, the retention of title clause used in this case is not valid because it is not stipulated that the distributor, B, has to settle with the importer, A, when the cars are resold. (This is described in detail in case 5.) As a consequence of this, B's insolvency administrator can claim payment from B's customers, C1–C5. Even if a valid retention of title clause had been included within the contract, B's

---

[21] 'Assignation' is the Scottish term for assignment.
[22] Notification of assignation is called 'intimation'.   [23] No 24 of 1936.

insolvency administrator could claim payment from C1–C5 unless the contract stipulated that the claims from the sub-sales belonged to A.

(b) In a credit consignment agreement, a valid retention of title clause could be stipulated if the buyer is obliged to settle with the seller within a short period of time after the resale and if the seller checked that the buyer was acting in accordance with this condition. If a consignment agreement was provided for, the contract could also stipulate that the claims against B's customers belonged to A, the importer. In such circumstances, A could claim payment from B's customers C1–C5. If the customers pay B, A will have no special right to the monies if they have been mixed with B's own monies. However, the contract could stipulate that the monies paid by the customers also belonged to A and were to be kept separate from B's own monies. If the contract provided so, and B had kept the monies separate from his own in such a way that there was no doubt what monies belonged to A, A would be entitled to those monies. Such clauses are not in all probability very common. It is not practical for B to keep the monies separate from his own: if B settles with A within a short time after the resale, it would be onerous for B to be obliged to keep the monies separated from his own for this short period. After all, B may seek to obtain his stock from a supplier who did not insist upon such a restriction. Furthermore, if the sub-purchasers cannot pay cash, the purchase is usually financed not by A or B but by a third party (e.g. a bank or a leasing company), so that B (and A) will be paid after B has sold the goods.

If the arrangement was a sort of undisclosed agency (commission) the claims against B's customers would belong to A, who could obtain payment from the customers if B was declared bankrupt: cf. *Kommissionsloven* ss. 57 and 58.

In reality the security over claims is a silent charge, which comes very close to the German prolonged reservation of title. If one may assume that it is common for German sellers to demand payment within a certain time from resale, or on a day when the goods are assumed to be resold, the difference between German and Danish law is only that the Danish seller must control when sales are made.

SWEDEN

(a) The producer, A, has permitted the distributor, B, to resell the cars prior to payment. As a consequence of this, A has no right to the cars in relation to B's creditors. Consequently, A does not have any right to the outstanding claims against B's customers. The claims belong to the insolvency estate and can be executed against.

(b) The first way by which A might have a right to the claims owed by C1–C5 to B, is to transfer the cars to B on a commission (undisclosed) agency basis. If so, the claims vest directly in A, and A may separate the claims in B's insolvency: s. 57 of the Commission Agency Act (*Kommissionslagen*, 1914). However, it must be a true commission agency, which presupposes that the agent, B, has a right to return unsold goods.[24] Such constructions are commonly used in Sweden to overcome the restrictions imposed on reservations of title. The claims could also be assigned or charged to A (see case 5).

FINLAND

(a) The retention of title clause is invalid as against the creditors of B, if B had the right to resell the cars in the ordinary course of business, before he or she has paid the price to A. Therefore, the unsold cars would belong to the insolvency estate of B and the same would be true of the claims owed by the customers of B. It would, therefore, be the insolvency administrator who would be entitled to claim the price from C1–C5.

(b) The situation of A would have been improved if the prerequisites of commission, i.e. undisclosed agency, were met. Then A, as the principal, would have been entitled to collect the claims which would have been regarded as the result of his or her agent's activities in selling his or her principal's property.[25]

Comparative observations

Case 6 supplements case 5 by examining the situation where the claims against the sub-purchasers still exist. For a number of jurisdictions, namely Germany, Austria, France and Belgium, this can make a material difference; whereas for the others, the analysis remains the same.

---

[24] Håstad, *Sakrätt rörande lös egendom* 147 ff. and SOU 1988:63 with NJA 1945, 406 and other cases.

[25] The prerequisites have been discussed above: see Finnish report, case 5(c).

Part (a)

According to German, French and Belgian law, A's simple retention of title is extended to the claims arising out of the sub-sales by way of a statutory provision, not by private agreement. The dogmatic foundations are, however, different. In French and Belgian law, A's right to the claims against B's customers rests on the principle of real subrogation, whereas in German law, § 48 InsO is a special remedy for a creditor whose rights have been frustrated by an unlawful transaction. There is also a difference in respect of the prerequisites: in German law, the buyer's entitlement to resell the goods renders § 48 InsO inapplicable whereas the same entitlement would be irrelevant under French and Belgian law.

If we compare the situation in case 5 to that in case 6, the crucial event for sellers under French and Belgian law is the payment of the price by the sub-purchasers. If payment is made before the commencement of insolvency proceedings, the money irretrievably belongs to B's insolvency estate. Under German law, the crucial event is the mixing of the funds. If the seller has not entitled the buyer to resell the goods, he can claim the money paid by the sub-purchasers pursuant to § 48 InsO even if it has been paid to B before insolvency, as long as the money is still distinguishable from B's other assets. In practice however, the result will often be the same, as buyers under retention of title do not normally separate the money they receive from sub-purchasers of those goods to which title is retained.

With the exception of Portuguese and South African law which, as we have seen in case 5, protect the seller who has reserved ownership even as against good faith purchasers, all other systems under consideration conclude that A has no more rights than those of an insolvency creditor. He can claim no right in the cars nor to the claims that B's insolvency estate still has against C1–C5.

Part (b)

Case 6 is the typical situation where, under German, Greek and Austrian law, proceeds clauses confer upon the seller an effective and at the same time practical security right against non-payment. German and Greek law both allow the security assignment of future claims without requiring any publicity; Austrian law requires no more than an entry into the books of the creditor which, according to a predominant but not undisputed opinion,[26] may be performed even before the identity of the *debitor cessus* is known. Also Denmark gives effect to proceeds clauses without notification provided that the requirements of credit consignment are adhered to.

The security assignment of claims or the taking of a charge over the proceeds of sale is also possible, in principle, in a number of other European jurisdictions. However, the requirements as to formalities and publicity (notification, registration) render it impossible to assign or charge future claims where the legal foundation has not yet been laid (see Italian, Dutch and Scots law), or such requirements render the transaction too costly to be practical (England, Ireland). As a result, reservation of title which extends to the proceeds of sub-sale is only practised in Germany, Austria and Greece. In Belgium, although a charge over future claims is possible, it is not practised in connection with a retention of title.[27] Likewise, the new Spanish legislation of 1999 which provides for the assignment of future debts does not seem to be of use in cases like the present. In Sweden and Finland, the requirement of notification of charges over claims renders it impossible to have a perfected charge before the customers are known. The registered enterprise charge comprises future claims, and the registration fee for the enterprise charge is not regarded to be deterrent. However, sellers can only rarely take advantage of an enterprise charge, since the first priority will usually already be in the hands of the buyer's bank.

In Sweden and Finland, goods are often transferred to a retailer with an entitlement for the retailer to sell the goods 'on the producer's account', which means that the retailer shall be entitled to return unsold goods and be obliged to pay a fixed price after the sale to the third party has been completed. In such cases, the producer may be regarded as the principal under an undisclosed commission agency arrangement; he is therefore entitled to the claims against the retailer's customers without any publicity. Such an arrangement may be possible in other jurisdictions, as for example the Italian report to case 5 points out, but it will rarely be used where other solutions exist since sellers usually do not want to carry their buyers' economic risks.

---

[26] See *supra*, Austrian report, case 5(c).
[27] For the possible reasons see *supra*, case 5, comparative observations, part (c)(vii).

Case 7: Supply of material to manufacturer (I)

(Retention of title and products clause – property effects of manufacturing)

B is a producer of curtains and other decorative items. A sells 500 rolls of cloth to him. The contract contains the following clause: 'The seller reserves title to the goods sold under this contract until he has received full payment.' In the two weeks following delivery, B transforms the cloth into curtains. Of the final value of the curtains, 60 per cent can be attributed to the cloth, the remaining 40 per cent to the manufacturing process. Before the curtains are sold and delivered to B's customers, a bailiff, acting on behalf of an unsecured creditor, C, attempts to execute against B's property, including the curtains.

Questions

(a) Who owns the curtains? Does the ratio of the value of the material supplied and the value added by the manufacturing process matter? Does it matter who bears the risk of the manufacturing process, A or B?
(b) May the newly produced items be subjected to execution on behalf of C?
(c) Could A obtain a better right to the products (for example, by adopting a differently worded clause, or by using a different type of retention of title clause, or through a legal transaction other than pure sale)? What would be the precise prerequisites? Are such arrangements commonly used?
(d) Instead of an unsecured creditor attempting to execute against B's property, B goes bankrupt. What are the answers to parts (b) and (c) in that situation?

Discussions

GERMANY

(a) Since the contract contains only a simple retention of title clause, the statutory rules on the effects of a manufacturing process (*specificatio*) must be applied. According to § 950 BGB, ownership of a newly produced movable vests in the manufacturer, not in the owner(s) of the material, unless the value of the manufacturer's work is considerably lower than that of the material(s). The BGH has decided that up to a ratio of 100:60 (value of the material: value of the work), the manufacturer will become owner pursuant to § 950 BGB.[1] § 950 BGB does not define who should be regarded as manufacturer. Generally,[2] this is to be decided objectively, according to the general view of the business community.[3] The question of who bears the risk of manufacturing will be one of the criteria used in this assessment.

In the present case, B is undoubtedly to be regarded as the manufacturer for the purposes of § 950 BGB. Since the value-ratio between the material and the work is 3:2 (about 100:66), B becomes sole owner of the curtains. The supplier (A) can claim remuneration only according to the rules on unjust enrichment (§§ 951 s. 1, 812 ff. BGB).

(b) The products are owned by B, therefore they may be subjected to execution on behalf of C.

(c) In cases such as the present, it is general business practice to add a products clause to the retention of title agreement. Usually, the seller (A) stipulates that if the buyer (B) produces new goods out of the material supplied, then this will take place for the seller as manufacturer, but the seller will not be obliged to buy the goods nor incur any obligations arising from the process of manufacture.[4] By virtue of such a clause, which has been held clearly to be valid by a long line of cases,[5] A will

---

[1] BGH 12 Jan. 1972, JZ 1972, 165 (166); BGH 22 May 1995, NJW 1995, 2633.
[2] But see *infra*, German report, case 7(c).   [3] BGH 20 Jan. 1988, BGHZ 103, 101 (108).
[4] See the model retention of title clause in: Hoffmann-Becking/Schippel, *Beck'sches Formularbuch zum Bürgerlichen, Handels- und Wirtschaftsrecht* 101.
[5] BGH 3 Mar. 1956, BGHZ 20, 159; BGH 23 Oct. 1963, BB 1963, 1354 (1355); BGH 15 Oct. 1966, BGHZ 46, 117 (118): 'It is to be regarded as undisputed that a supplier who delivers raw materials to a manufacturer under retention of title may extend such retention of title into the products through the insertion of a so-called products clause despite § 950 BGB.' (Translation by the author.) See also BGH 12 Jan. 1972, BB 1972, 197 (198); BGH 9 Dec. 1970, BB 1971, 17.

acquire security ownership[6] in the products. This acquisition takes place not only *inter partes* but also *erga omnes*.

There remains, however, a question as to how the products clause should be construed. There are three broad positions. The first regards § 950 BGB as non-mandatory.[7] Therefore, the parties can derogate from it and simply stipulate that ownership of the products shall vest in the seller. The other two positions regard § 950 BGB as mandatory, for the simple reason that rules of property law generally have a mandatory character. However, these two positions differ as to the way in which the identity of the manufacturer should be determined. According to a number of scholars, this question has to be decided on a purely objective basis, disregarding entirely the agreement between seller and buyer.[8] By way of contrast, the BGH and other academic writers hold that parties' agreements should be taken into account.[9] This third opinion, which predominates in practice, produces practical results very similar to the first one (non-mandatory character of § 950 BGB).

The most significant difference between the second opinion (determination of manufacturer on a purely objective basis) and the other two is this: if one denies to the parties the right to define who is the manufacturer, the seller cannot *directly* acquire title to the products. Instead, title will necessarily vest in the buyer. But as German law accepts the security transfer of ownership,[10] it would also be possible to draft a products clause as an anticipatory security transfer of ownership of the future products.[11] This would transfer ownership in the products to the seller the very second that the buyer acquired ownership through the manufacturing process. Nevertheless, in practice, it is not necessary to word a products clause this way,[12] because German courts consistently

---

[6] See also *infra*, German report, case 10(a).
[7] Flume, NJW 1950, 841 at 843 f.; Laufke, in: *Festschrift für Alfred Hueck* 69 (74 f.); Franke, BB 1955, 717 (718); Baur/Stürner, *Sachenrecht* § 53 n. 20; Soergel/Mühl § 950 BGB n. 3; the jurisdiction of the *Reichsgericht*: RG 14 June 1932, *Juristische Wochenschrift* 1932, 2634; RG 21 Dec. 1938, *Juristische Wochenschrift* 1939, 563; RG 17 Aug. 1939, RGZ 161, 109 (113).
[8] Palandt/Bassenge § 950 BGB n. 8; Westermann/Gursky/Eickmann, *Sachenrecht* § 53 III 2 e; Erman/Hefermehl § 950 BGB n. 7; Säcker, JR 1966, 51; Wadle, JuS 1982, 477 (482 f.); Staudinger/Wiegand § 950 BGB nn. 27–30; Wilhelm, *Sachenrecht* nn. 974 f.
[9] BGH 3 Mar. 1956, BGHZ 20, 159 (163)f.; BGH 28 June 1954, BGHZ 14, 114 (117); Serick, *Eigentumsvorbehalt und Sicherungsübertragung* IV § 44 III 6 b; Hofmann, NJW 1962, 1798 (1802).
[10] See *infra*, German report, case 10(a).
[11] As to the anticipatory security transfer of ownership, see *infra*, German report, case 11(a).
[12] Serick, *Eigentumsvorbehalt und Sicherungsübertragung* IV 162.

accept the above-mentioned clause, whereby the seller is to be regarded as manufacturer for the purposes of § 950 BGB.

If, in the present case, the parties had agreed on a retention of title agreement including a products clause, A would have acquired security ownership of the curtains. There are no other prerequisites for such a clause to be effective, other than its inclusion as a term in the contract. In particular, there are no formal requirements nor is there a need to publicise the rights of the seller in any way. As security owner, A can bring an action in court to resist an execution against the products initiated on behalf of another creditor (§ 771 ZPO).[13] Upon such an action, the execution will be stopped and set aside.[14]

(d) Without a products clause, A will be an insolvency creditor if B goes bankrupt.

If a products clause as described under part (c) was used, A would have security ownership of the products. Therefore, he would be able to claim preferential payment out of the sale or other realisation of the value of the products: see §§ 50 s. 1, 51 n. 1 and 166 ff. InsO. What has been said about the rights of a security assignee and their limits[15] applies *mutatis mutandis* to security ownership. The realisation of property that was in the possession of the debtor and comes subsequently to be possessed by the insolvency administrator lies in the hands of the latter (§ 166 s. 1 InsO). As stated previously,[16] the administrator can postpone the realisation until after the report meeting. This represents an important change to the old *Konkursordnung*, under which the security owner was able to take and sell the collateral immediately. The new Code seeks to enhance the prospect of a reorganisation by putting an end to what was previously a widespread practice.[17] Under the new Code, the interests of the secured creditors are protected in two ways. First, from the report

---

[13] See BGH 4 Feb. 1954, BGHZ 12, 232 (234); BGH 28 June 1978, BGHZ 72, 141 (143); BGH 13 May 1981, BGHZ 80, 296 (299); BGH 25 Feb. 1987, WM 1987, 539 (541); BGH 12 May 1992, BGHZ 118, 201 (207); Jauernig, *Zwangsvollstreckungs- und Insolvenzrecht* § 13 IV 1 a; Stein/Jonas/Münzberg VI § 771 ZPO n. 26; Bülow, *Recht der Kreditsicherheiten* n. 1085. Some authors contend, however, that the security owner can only exercise the rights of a pledgee (§ 805 ZPO), which, if accepted, would mean that he could not resist the execution but only claim preferential payment out of the proceeds: see Baumbach/Lauterbach/Hartmann § 771 ZPO n. 26; *Münchener Kommentar*/Schmidt § 771 ZPO n. 29. As to § 771 ZPO in general, see *supra*, German report, case 2.

[14] As to the methods by which the security owner may realise the collateral's value, see *infra*, German report, case 10(a).

[15] See *supra*, German report, case 6(b).

[16] German report, case 6(b).   [17] Cf. Smid/Smid § 166 InsO n. 1.

meeting onwards, the creditor receives interest for the period during which the administrator fails to sell or otherwise realise the value of the collateral (§ 169 sent. 1 InsO). Secondly, the administrator must notify the secured creditor if he decides to sell the collateral. The secured creditor may, within a week of such notification, bring to the attention of the administrator any potential for sale at a higher price. In such a case, the administrator is obliged to make use of the opportunity presented by the creditor or – alternatively – to indemnify him against any losses. After the sale or other realisation has taken place, the administrator will deduct the costs (9 per cent of the proceeds: see § 171 InsO) and will use the rest to pay off the secured claim. As to the possibility of setting up an insolvency plan, see the German report, case 6(b).

AUSTRIA

(a) As A's contract with B contains a reservation of title clause,[18] A and B become co-owners of the curtains. This was first acknowledged by the OGH in SZ 49/138.[19] This decision (which bears similarities to the present case, involving clothes produced from fabrics) represented a shift in the jurisprudence of the OGH, which previously had held that retention of title became invalid if the goods sold were changed into something different by the manufacturing process.[20] The court changed its position after heavy criticism by legal scientific writers.[21] These writers argued that the position of the OGH was contrary to the rule of § 416 ABGB.[22] The new practice of the courts was, of course, applauded by those businessmen who sell goods to manufacturers. The size of the shares of A and B depend on their respective contributions (i.e. materials and labour, in the present case 60 per cent and 40 per cent respectively).

If the agreement between A and B purported to accord to A a share larger than that represented by his contribution, then a problem would arise due to the publicity principle. According to Austrian law, only the goods sold under a retention of title clause secure the seller's claim arising from the contract of sale in respect of these goods. It is only to

---

[18] The result would be the same if a short-term reservation of title was used.
[19] Cf. *Rummel*/Spielbüchler § 415 n. 7.   [20] SZ 18/92, 12 Apr. 1961, EvBl 1961/246.
[21] See Spielbüchler, JBl 1968, 589; Frotz, *Aktuelle Probleme des Kreditsicherungsrechts* 91 and *Klang*/Bydlinski IV/2 624.
[22] According to this rule, a new product, produced by the use of materials and labour, is co-owned by the owner of the material and the producer. The size of each share depends on their respective contributions.

this extent that Austrian law accepts a non-possessory security right. If other goods are intended to secure the claim, then they must be handed over to the seller. Therefore, an agreement which purports to grant A a security right more extensive than the proportion of the value of the curtains represented by his contribution of the cloth would be invalid, because of a conflict with the publicity principle.

It *does* matter who bears the risk of the manufacturing process. If A, and not B, bears the risk (i.e. if B manufactures *for* A), then A will be owner of the curtains.[23] In such a case it is not necessary for the contract between A and B to contain a reservation of title clause.

(b) The newly produced items may be subjected to execution on the behalf of C, to the extent that they belong to B.

(c) A cannot obtain more than 60 per cent of the final value of the curtains, unless A and B make use of an arrangement which respects the publicity requirement. This could, for example, be done by handing over the curtains to A.

(d) The same answers apply.

GREECE

(a) If a retention of title clause is included in the contract, the vendor will remain the owner of the thing sold, even after delivery, until the purchaser pays the price in full. In this case, A is the owner of the curtains. Article 1061 A.K., which regulates specification, establishes that a person who, using material owned by another, produces a new movable, will only acquire ownership of it if the value of the work done is obviously greater than the value of the material. As in the present case the value of the work, i.e. the manufacturing process, is not greater than the value of the material, the question of who bears the risk of the manufacturing process is irrelevant.

(b) If C, the creditor of B, executes against the curtains, A, as owner, is entitled to resist the execution (article 936 KPolD).[24]

---

[23] Cf. Koziol/Welser, *Grundriß des bürgerlichen Rechts II* 70.
[24] Brinias, *Anagastiki ektelesis* § 178, 499 and § 679, 2313; Georgiadis, *Empragmato Dikaio II* 219.

(c) Only the fiduciary (re)transfer of full ownership of the curtains to A would accord to him a superior right (i.e. full ownership) over the products. Of course, should A lose ownership of the cloth because of the manufacturing process, B will become owner and the solution will differ. In this case, it is usually stipulated that, until the purchaser pays the price in full, ownership of the new products will rest with the supplier (extended retention of title or retention of title with a products clause).[25] The validity of this clause is disputed, because it presupposes that article 1061 A.K. is not a mandatory rule, that is to say it can be displaced by the agreement of the parties.[26] According to the most persuasive view,[27] article 1061 is mandatory, thus a products clause can only be drafted as a security transfer of ownership of the future products with a resolutive condition of the full payment of the purchase price. Delivery is substituted by an anticipated *constitutum possessorium*, which is generally accepted as valid under Greek law. No further prerequisites are required. In the case of an extended retention of title, A can claim ownership of the clothing against which execution is made, which has been transferred to him (article 936 KPolD).[28] If the curtains had been sold, he would simply be entitled to preferential payment from the proceeds of the sale.[29]

Products clauses are not used in practice.

(d) It is evident that B's creditors may not execute against the assets of a third party, i.e. A. Nor do such assets form part of the insolvency estate. A is, in any case, fully protected against them (see part (c), *supra*).

FRANCE

(a) A retention of title clause can be used for any type of asset, in so far as the assets are individualised by delivery. The present case differs from the previous cases because of the nature of the assets, *viz.* rolls of cloth. Textile fabrics are raw materials, intended to be used in the

---

[25] See Gazis, ErmAK 532 n. 71; Georgiadis, *Kyriotis* 277; Livanis, *Diathesi mellondikou dikaiomatos* 16; Roussos, in: *Miscellany in Honour of Michailidis – Nouaros* 397 ff.
[26] For the different views which have been advanced, see Georgiadis, *Kyriotis* 278.
[27] Georgiadis, *Kyriotis* 278. Different views are suggested by Gazis, ErmAK 532 n. 74 and Roussos, in: *Miscellany in Honour of Michailidis – Nouaros* 397 (410).
[28] Georgiadis, *Kyriotis* 222; Kornilakis, *I katapisteutiki ekchorisi ton apaitiseon* 126; Mazis, *Empragmati exasphalisi trapezon kai anonymon etairion* para. 450.
[29] For the rights of the vendor, when the purchaser who transferred security ownership goes bankrupt, see in detail *infra*, case 8.

manufacturing process, and therefore will not remain in the condition in which they were supplied. The problem that confronts A concerns the individualisation and the transformation of the fabrics. The question is whether retention of title can survive the transformation by means of the manufacturing process of the cloth into curtains. French law again demonstrates the very narrow scope it accords to reservation of title. Pursuant to C. com, article L. 621-122, para. 2, *rei vindicatio* of assets sold under reservation of title is possible only *when they can be found in kind*. This rule applies in the event of the buyer's insolvency, but also outside insolvency proceedings, according to general property law.[30] The question of whether the assets remain in kind (*specificatio*) has been widely discussed.

Case law takes the view that once the goods have reached their 'final stage of transformation', they cannot be claimed by a seller pursuant to a retention of title clause. It was decided that cattle, once slaughtered, could not be found in kind on the buyer's premises.[31] With regard to fabrics, the *Cour d'appel* of Paris decided that, once fabrics were cut into clothing, they could not be claimed back by the seller.[32] The same applied to wool knitted into jumpers.[33] On the other hand, it was decided that yarn bought by a tapestry manufacturer, which had been dyed but had not yet been woven into fabric (and where the dyeing process had not transformed the thread), was perfectly identifiable and could be returned to the owner. All that was required was to roll the yarn back into balls.[34] In fact, one could argue that it may very often be possible to reverse the transformation of the assets, especially when the seller is prepared to accept the return of his property as such, that is, deknitted wool or cut and tailored fabrics. The real argument, which underpins the court decisions, lies not in the analysis of the transformation but in the value added by the manufacturing process. Allowing the return of the assets would mean that the added value would benefit the seller only (or, if the transformation is reversed, then the added value

---

[30] See C. civ, article 1593, as confirmed in Com 20 June 1989, D 1989, 431, note Pérochon; RTDC 1990, 121, obs. Brandac, which states that: 'Goods sold under retention of title are affected by the guarantee of the seller. The seller can claim the return of the goods for as long as the goods exist in kind within the buyer's hands, and, after their resale in the same state, the seller can claim a right on the proceeds of the sale.'

[31] Com 22 Mar 1994, Bull civ IV, No 121; D 1996, Som, 219.

[32] Paris, 28 Nov. 1984, Juris-Data No 026 561.

[33] Toulouse, 27 Nov. 1984, D 1985, J., 185, note Mestre; Com 27 May 1986, Rev jur com 1986, No 1158, note Gallet.

[34] Com 6 Mar. 1990, D 1991, Som, 46.

is lost to other creditors, especially the unsecured).[35] Therefore, given that, in the present case, the fabric has been transformed into curtains and only 60 per cent of the final value is attributable to the cloth, it is unlikely that the court will recognise A's title to the curtains. As a result of the transformation, B has become the owner of the curtains, in spite of the retention of title clause.

If the case had involved the incorporation of the assets sold into another asset (i.e. commingling), rather than their transformation, C. com, article L. 621-122 (previously IA 85, article 121 para. 3 as amended in 1994) would apply. It provides that, where the assets have been incorporated into other movable assets, *rei vindicatio* is possible if it can be done without damaging either asset.[36]

(b) As B is regarded as the owner of the fabric once it has been cut into curtains, the curtains may be subjected to the execution procedure initiated by C, under the same procedure of *saisievente*, as described in case 2.

(c) If A wishes to retain ownership of the fabrics, and not to be deprived of it by the manufacturing process, he can conclude a contract with B (*contrat d'entreprise*) under which B is paid a fixed and agreed price for manufacturing the curtains. In such circumstances, A will remain the owner of the cloth. Then, pursuant to C. civ, article 570:

if a crafts man or anyone used some material which did not belong to him to make a thing of a new form, whether or not the material is able to revert to its initial form, the owner has the right to claim the return of the transformed things, paying back the price of the work at the date of the reimbursement.

---

[35] See Ghestin/Desché, *La Vente* n. 648.
[36] It is still too early to assess how strictly this requirement will be applied by the courts. The previous decisions looked to the extent to which the assets retained their individuality and the ease with which they could be returned to the owner. For example, in a case involving the affixation of tyres to vehicles, the *Cour de cassation* confirmed the decision of the *Cour d'appel* that the affixation did not affect the identity or the autonomy of the goods and therefore the tyres could be returned (see Com 18 July 1989, D 1991, Som, 45). In a case, however, involving an aluminium ceiling structure used to support concrete plates of the ceiling, the court held that, although it was physically possible to remove the structure from the plates, the consequence of that would be to destroy the ceiling, since together they constituted a single item. The ceiling structure had, therefore, lost individuality and autonomy (Paris, 30 Apr. 1993, D 1993, Som, 291). Clearly, the 1994 amendment to the former IA 85, article 121, now C. com, article L. 621-122, has eliminated the concepts of autonomy and individuality, retaining only the criterion of whether disassociation would damage the final product.

A, having remained owner, could thus claim ownership of the curtains, on the condition that he paid to B the price for the manufacturing (as agreed in the contract). It is unclear whether this type of arrangement is used in practice, however.

(d) In the event of the debtor's insolvency, whether the assets remain in kind or not is to be assessed at the time of the commencement of insolvency proceedings. Should the assets subsequently be transformed or disappear, then the owner will still have title to them or will be entitled to receive compensation for their loss. He will be, as it were, a creditor guaranteed by C. com, article L. 621-32.[37]

BELGIUM

(a) According to article 565 C.civ., questions about *specificatio* and *accessio* must be answered in a way that accords with the principles of natural justice. Certain cases are dealt with by specific provisions. When, for example, a manufacturer creates a new movable out of material that did not belong to him, the owner of the material becomes the owner of the newly created good, except to the extent that the manufacturer becomes entitled to compensation (article 570 C.civ.). These rules are however of little practical use in case of reservation of title.

Article 101 Bankruptcy Act requires that the goods are still *in natura* in the estate of the buyer and have not been mixed with other goods. This means that they should remain identifiable. The ownership of the seller will not therefore survive the transformation of the goods or their use in the creation of a new product. The legislature has not defined the criteria of identification. Whether the object of a preferential right can be identified must be determined according to common sense. In this case, the courts will consider the curtains to be a different asset and the security right of the seller will therefore be extinguished.[38] Under these circumstances, and for the same reasons, the seller will also lose his statutory preference in respect of the goods (see Belgian report, case 1).

(b) The newly produced items can be subjected to execution on the behalf of C. According to the principle of article 2279 C.civ., a creditor may

---

[37] Com 9 June 1987, Bull civ IV, No 142, RTDCom 1988, 120, obs. Hémard and Bouloc; Com 9 June 1992, D 1992, IR, 211. See case 3.
[38] Fredericq, *Traité de droit commercial belge* VIII 679 n. 477.

assume that movable property in the possession of his debtor is the property of that debtor. This right cannot, in the given circumstances, be challenged by the seller.

(c) It is not possible to confer a stronger right to the seller. Belgian law does not recognise a products clause which would extend the security interest to the transformed or newly created goods.[39]

(d) The insolvency of the buyer would not alter the position of the seller.

PORTUGAL

(a) In this situation, A would be regarded as the owner of the curtains. As reservation of title to the goods was stipulated and cloth is not a movable thing subject to registration, this clause would be effective against any third party. As the cloth was transformed into curtains by the buyer, the issue of *specificatio* arises. In this case, because the value of the manufacturing process was less than the value of the cloth, A would be regarded as the owner of the curtains (article 1336° C.C.). He would, however, have to pay to the buyer an amount representing the value added by the manufacturing process.

The ratio between the value of the curtains attributable to the materials and that attributable to the manufacturing process is crucial to the question of who owns the curtains. If the value added by the manufacturing process is greater than the value of the materials, A would lose his ownership by *specificatio* (article 1336° C.C.), in which case the reservation of title clause would lose its effect.

It does not matter who bears the risk of the manufacturing process.

(b) If A owns the curtains, he can resist an execution over them by the *embargos de terceiro* proceeding (article 351° CPC).

(c) The position of A is sufficiently protected. It is not usual to attempt to improve it.

If the value ratio was different so that A would not acquire ownership in the products, A could only ask for different securities from B. A better right over the products would not be possible, because no right can survive *specificatio*. However, instead of concluding a contract of sale,

---

[39] Dirix/De Corte, *Zekerheidsrechten* 392; Kieninger/Storme, RIW 1999, 102.

A and B could stipulate that B manufactures and sells the products for A (mandate) but this kind of agreement is not common in practice.

(d) In the event of the buyer's insolvency, the reservation of title clause would be effective against the insolvency administrator, if it was stipulated in an act under private signature before the delivery of the goods (article 155° n° 4 CPEREF). If this requirement as to form was met in the present case, the answers to parts (a) and (b) would be identical.

SPAIN

(a) A can elect to claim either the payment of the debt or the recovery of the manufactured items. According to article 383/II CC, A is the owner of the curtains, since the value of the raw materials represents a greater proportion of the value of the finished product than that attributable to the manufacturing process. If the converse were so, the owner would be B, the producer of the curtains. Nevertheless, B should compensate A, the seller of the material, to the extent of its value. In this case, the value is the nominal price uprated to reflect inflation.

Reservation of title clauses are not enforceable in respect of manufactured goods, since the material transformation of the object means that the original title to the raw materials has been extinguished and replaced by a new species of property, namely the curtains. There exists a specific solution to this case, found in article 383 CC. The issue of the identifiability of the cloth is so difficult that it seems unlikely that the reservation of title clause would be effective to secure payment for the material, and still less if the transaction falls within the scope of Law 28/1998.

(b) If the bailiff tries to execute against B (on behalf of C), A may claim *rei vindicatio* (article 595 LEC). A could bring an action in court against B to enforce his debt, called a declaratory suit, which is both lengthy and hedged around with more procedural guarantees.

(c) A could obtain a better right in respect of the products, but only if the contract has been formalised through the use of an executive public deed or as a bill of exchange (article 517.4°–5°–6° LEC). The issue arising in respect of the sale of the material and its subsequent transformation is that of its identifiability. It is very difficult to establish real securities when the manufacturing process transforms the raw material into a new product. The particulars that the seller would need to specify in the public deed include: the quantity (in metres) of the cloth concerned, its quality and its price. However, this would not ensure that a real security is taken over the curtains, if their value exceeds that of the cloth.

Theoretically, A could also obtain a better right in respect of the goods if the contract was secured by means of a real right, i.e. a charge over movables (*hipoteca mobiliaria*) or a non-possessory pledge (*prenda sin desplazamiento*). However, in this case, A could not take a charge over the products, since they are no longer capable of being identified separately. A charge over movables is only possible in certain circumstances, which are not present in this case. The same is true of a non-possessory pledge. Although Spanish law admits a pledge on commodities and on stored raw materials (article 53.2 LHMPSD), such a pledge could not be granted in the circumstances of this case, since the cloth sold is not, strictly speaking, a commodity (unlike the manufactured curtains themselves), and because the cloth ceased to be a raw material on being transformed into the curtains.

Nevertheless, a non-possessory pledge could be granted over the curtains once they have been manufactured to secure B's claim. In such cases, the security should be executed in a public deed. In accordance with article 57 LHMPSD, the following requirements must be satisfied. First, certain particulars must be recorded: (1) a description of the pledged goods specifying their nature, quantity, quality, condition and other circumstances which might help to distinguish or identify them; (2) the location of the building in which the goods are stored (together with an indication of their provenance, use, storage and whereabouts in the depot where they are held); (3) the insurance contracts, which must bear a number referring to the corresponding policy. Secondly, the owner is obliged to take care of the pledged goods and to make them freely available to the creditor so that the latter can, at any moment, inspect them and verify their existence and condition.

(d) As to part (b): If B goes bankrupt, A has the following choice. If he chooses to recover the curtains, they will be excluded from the insolvency estate. If, on the other hand, A chooses to claim the payment of the debt, the curtains will form part of the insolvency estate and A's rights will be subject to the insolvency procedural rules (article 1922.1° LEC).

As to part (c): A's position in B's insolvency proceedings depends on whether or not he has chosen to recover the curtains. In such a situation, it is advisable for A to elect to recover the manufactured items by means of a *rei vindicatio* because this would exclude them from the insolvency estate.

ITALY

(a) According to the rule on *specificatio* (article 940 c.c.), as soon as the cloth supplied by A is manufactured by B into curtains, it becomes the property of B. Article 940 c.c. provides an exception for situations where the value of the textile significantly exceeds the cost of its transformation into clothing. In such a case, the owner of the textile may claim ownership of the clothing, on the condition that he pays for the cost of its manufacture.

Whether it is possible to derogate from this rule by way of contract is a matter of controversy. Some authors argue that the parties should be able to do so,[40] but there are also opinions to the contrary.[41] The latter view is adopted by the only case in point on this issue.[42] Such doubts are intelligible in the light of the hostile stance prevailing in the Italian legal system towards the transfer of property for security purposes, which lies at the root of the current, expansive interpretation of the Civil Code rule banishing *pactum commissorium* (article 2744 c.c.).[43] In different contexts, there is little doubt that the rule on *specificatio* can be derogated by way of contract (see below, part (c)). As a matter of fact, 'prolonged' title reservation clauses, in the mould of the German *verlängerter Eigentumsvorbehalt mit Verarbeitungsklausel* or the English *Romalpa* clauses, must be a rarity in practice because they are not litigated in Italian courts, though Italian authors are aware of foreign

---

[40] Bianca, *La vendita e la permuta* 602, is rather cautious on this point: reservation of title to the new product is valid (for the amount of the value of the original *res*) to the extent it is possible to derogate from article 939 c.c.; Gambaro, in: Cicu/Messineo/ Mengoni, *Trattato di diritto civile e commerciale* 840 ff., supports the rule which is more favourable to party autonomy.

[41] Carpino, in: *Trattato di diritto privato* 324, note 32.

[42] App. Napoli, 5 July 1955, Foro it., 1956, I, 101, affirms Trib. Salerno, 30 July 1954, Foro it., 1955, I, 618. According to these decisions, any reservation of title clause that would put the debtor under excessive pressure should be avoided. For their critique see Bonomi, *Der Eigentumsvorbehalt in Österreich und Italien*.

[43] Article 2744 c.c.: 'Any agreement establishing that, upon failure to pay the claim within the fixed time limit, ownership of property subject to *hypothec* or given in pledge shall pass to the creditor, is void. Such an agreement is void even if subsequent to the establishment of the *hypothec* or the pledge.' (Translation by the author.) On article 2744 c.c. see *infra*, Italian report, case 9(b), (c); case 12(a), (b).

developments concerning them.⁴⁴ On the relevance of the distribution of risk in the manufacturing process, see part (c).

(b) If it is not possible to derogate from the rule described above, the newly produced items would be susceptible to execution on behalf of C, on the assumption that they are owned by B.

(c) A could probably get a better right to the product if the contract with B was regarded as a *contratto d'appalto*. This is the contract by which an independent contractor undertakes to perform a piece of work (or render a service) by organising the necessary means and operating at his own risk (articles 1655–1677 c.c.). If the raw materials to be used in the manufacturing process are provided to the independent contractor by the party who wants to acquire title to the new product, ownership will pass to the independent contractor simply because they are delivered to him, inasmuch as they are considered as fungibles.⁴⁵ On the contrary, if the parties agree that the materials are to be treated as infungibles, commentators hold that the owner of the materials will acquire ownership of the new thing as soon as it is produced.⁴⁶ Proof of the relevant intention, however, may be difficult to establish if the parties did not express their intention to regard the raw materials as infungibles.⁴⁷

(d) The answers to parts (b) and (c) do not change in the event of B's insolvency.

THE NETHERLANDS

(a) B became the owner of the curtains by virtue of *specificatio*. *Specificatio* is governed by article 5:16 BW, which lays down who is to be regarded as

---

⁴⁴ Candian, *Le garanzie mobiliari* 1 ff.; Veneziano, *Le garanzie mobiliari non possessorie* 16 ff. Chianale, *Obbligazione di dare e trasferimento della proprietà* 215 ff.; Sulpasso, in: Vacca II 782 ff.
⁴⁵ Cass. 20 Feb. 1984, n. 1200, Fallimento, 1163; Dir. fall., II, 424 (use of silver to manufacture new objects).
⁴⁶ Rubino/Iudica, in: *Commentario del codice civile Scialoja-Branca* 340–341; Rubino, in: *Trattato di diritto civile italiano* 808–809 (see also 241–242); Giannattasio, *L'appalto*, in *Trattato di diritto civile e commerciale* 282–283. App. Messina, 5 Oct. 1956, Foro it., Repertorio 1957, sub 'Appalto' n. 18. Cass. 21 June 1974, n. 1823, Giust. civ, 1974, I, 1740, cannot be cited to the contrary, because the materials in questions were provided by the manufacturer. On these cases: Cagnasso, *Diritto privato*, 1995, 35.
⁴⁷ Cf. Cass. 20 Feb. 1984, n. 1200, Fallimento, 1163; Dir. fall, II, 424.

owner of a *newly created thing*. A thing is considered *new* when, according to general opinion, it has its own, separate and new identity. The curtains will be regarded as a *newly created thing*.[48]

The rule provided by the Dutch Code is complex and perhaps rather unfortunately drafted. The main rule, which is stated almost as an exception in the second paragraph of article 5:16 BW, is that, if somebody creates a *new thing*, or has it made for him- or herself, out of one or more movable goods which do not belong to him- or herself, he or she will become the owner of the newly created thing. In other words, one may become owner through *specificatio* by either creating a thing for oneself or having a thing created for oneself by somebody else.

Occasionally it will be difficult to determine whether the actual 'creator' created the thing for him- or herself *or* whether somebody else *had the thing created* by the actual 'creator'. Nevertheless, the question of ownership depends on this distinction. The judgment of the Supreme Court in *Breda/St Antonius* provides a necessary illustration of the Dutch law on this matter.[49]

Breda/St Antonius concerned the manufacturing of machine parts by St Antonius according to the order of Breda. Breda gave detailed instructions as to the productive process and provided the raw materials for the parts to be produced, namely steel plates. Breda was not, however, the owner of the steel plates, which in fact belonged to a third party (the bank was fiduciary owner). Following production, the machine parts were handed over to Breda, who shortly thereafter experienced financial difficulties. Subsequently, both Breda and St Antonius claimed to have become the owner of the machine parts by reason of *specificatio*. St Antonius claimed to have created the parts for itself, while Breda claimed it had had the parts created for itself *by* St Antonius.

The lower courts found in favour of St Antonius. The Supreme Court, however, reversed these decisions. It held that the answer depended on the relationship between Breda and St Antonius. It continued by saying that, in case of industrial production processes, relevant factors are who bears the economic risk of the manufacturing process and, also, which party decides on the production methods and the distribution of the products.

By far the majority of cases decided on the basis of *specificatio* will turn on the second paragraph of article 5:16 BW. There are only a few

---

[48] See e.g. the case law mentioned by Fikkers, *Natrekking, vermenging en zaaksvorming* 65.
[49] Hoge Raad 5 Oct. 1990, NJ 1992, 226 (*Breda/St Antonius*).

situations where the main rule does not apply and where recourse is necessary to the rule contained in the first paragraph.[50] First, when somebody creates a new thing (or has it created for him- or herself) out of his or her own goods, the main rule does not apply because it requires the use of one or more goods belonging to somebody else. In this case, the first paragraph provides the basis for the manufacturer's new ownership. Secondly, and this is perhaps the most important exception to the main rule, when the costs of manufacturing are too marginal to justify the operation of the main rule, the newly created thing will belong to the owners of the original goods.[51]

Consequently, because B manufactured the curtains for himself, they have become his property. This result does not change because the materials were sold subject to a retention of title agreement. Dutch law does not recognise extended retention of title (*verlängter Eigentumsvorbehalt*) as such.[52] A remains the owner only until the *specificatio*.[53]

(b) As the curtains have become the property of B, B's creditors may execute against them.

(c) As noted above in part (a), Dutch law does not recognise extended retention of title as such. A products clause (purporting to extend retention of title to the newly created thing) is a legal impossibility. As the putative subject matter of such a clause is a new thing, and consequently a 'new' title, there is nothing for A to retain.

The alternative offered by the Civil Code is the creation 'in advance' of a pledge over future movables.[54] It is possible to meet all the requirements necessary to create a pledge, except for the requirement that the pledgor possesses the power to dispose.[55] The pledge will come into

---

[50] See Pitlo/Reehuis/Heisterkamp, *Het Nederlands burgerlijk recht III* nn. 522–525, who also include the situation of somebody mistakenly thinking he or she is creating a thing for somebody else (putative order).

[51] If the original goods belonged to different owners, the rules of accession apply, which may indicate either that only one of the original owners will become the owner of the newly created thing or that there will be co-ownership of it.

[52] This is not entirely true, but the *verlengd eigendomsvoorbehoud* is very limited in scope (cf. article 3:92 para. 2 BW). See Fikkers, *Natrekking, vermenging en zaaksvorming* 59 and, specifically on the issue in the present case, Fesevur, *Goederenrechtelijke colleges* 214.

[53] Hoge Raad 5 Dec. 1986, NJ 1987, 745 (*gescheurde orchideeën*).

[54] For instance, Fesevur, *Goederenrechtelijke colleges* 214; Fikkers, WPNR 6321 (1998) 465 (466); Pitlo/Reehuis/Heisterkamp, *Het Nederlands burgerlijk recht III* 560.

[55] Article 3:98 in conjunction with article 3:97 BW.

existence without more when the new thing is created and B acquires, as the owner, the power to dispose.

Sometimes a different approach is encountered, where parties agree that the buyer (B) will create the new thing not for him- or herself, but on behalf of the seller (A). As described above, according to the Dutch rule on *specificatio*, the seller and not the buyer becomes the owner of the newly created thing in such circumstances. A would therefore be the owner at all times – though the old ownership is still being replaced by a new one – and would not run the risk of B going bankrupt. Although such a clause would appear to be valid in principle, it may have a more limited application than might, at first sight, appear. It would usually imply that the manufacturing takes place on behalf of A, who would therefore bear the economic risk. This would obviously reduce the practicability of this type of clause for many categories of creditors, e.g. credit institutions or suppliers of raw materials.[56]

(d) As a rule, insolvency proceedings would make no difference to the position, except when a pledge on future movables was involved. In insolvency proceedings the debtor/creator loses the power to dispose. The pledge will therefore not come into existence when the debtor first acquires the movables after the commencement of insolvency proceedings.[57]

ENGLAND

(a) The answer to this question is perfectly clear: new goods have been manufactured by the buyer who becomes the owner of those goods.[58] This is a case of specification, where a new product is manufactured out of raw materials and labour, rather than accession. It will not matter how much of the value of the new product is attributed to the raw materials or to the manufacturing process (labour). Nor will it matter who bears the risk of the manufacturing process, where the buyer genuinely is a buyer and not someone manufacturing goods as agent for the seller, which is an unlikely way to characterise the relationship.

For the sake of completeness, though this question concerns goods that are altered to produce something new, the same type of problem

---

[56] Fikkers, *Natrekking, vermenging en zaaksvorming* 77–78. Although the risk may be allocated by contract, it would bring the clause dangerously close to the prohibition on fiduciary transfers, article 3:84(3) BW. Parl. Gesch. Boek 5 Inv. 1023.
[57] See articles 23 and 35(2) Fw.
[58] *Appleby v Myers* [1867] LR 2 CP 651; *Re Peachdart Ltd* [1984] Ch 131; *Chaigley Farms Ltd v Crawford Kaye & Grayshire Ltd* [1996] BCC 957.

might arise where goods are supplied and then are irrevocably attached by the buyer to other goods. The question is who owns the new goods that arise upon the attachment. To the extent that this property rule favours the buyer, any attempt on the seller's part to draft out of the rule will be characterised as a charge. The basic rule concerning attachment, or accession, is that the owner of the greater part retains ownership of the whole in the case of an irrevocable attachment[59] but that the separate ownerships remain distinct if the attachment can be reversed without damaging the greater thing.[60]

(b) To the extent that the goods are owned by the buyer, then execution may be levied against them in the normal way. The position of the bailiff (*sheriff*) who executes against goods that only appear to be owned by the buyer but in fact are not has been considered above. If the seller has taken a charge over the goods or over new goods manufactured with the goods supplied, then, in the case of an enterprise charge (*floating charge*), the position is as follows. When a *floating charge* crystallises, the chargee will prevail against the execution creditor if crystallisation takes place before the *sheriff* sells the assets subjected to execution.[61] It is likely (the point has not been settled) that the latter will also prevail if crystallisation occurs before the *sheriff* distributes to the execution creditor.[62]

(c) The debate in English law has not centred on the specification and attachment rules as such, which is perhaps why there is so little case law in this area. Rather, the focus has been upon attempts by sellers to draft reservation of title clauses that purport to vest in the seller the new goods as soon as they come into existence. The idea is that, if such clauses are successful in reservation terms, then they will not be characterised as charges with all of the systemic disadvantages suffered by trade creditors when seeking to register their charges.

Just as equitable tracing and artificial fiduciary relationships have not found favour in the years following the *Romalpa* decision,[63] so too the courts have declined to recognise as title *reservation* clauses those clauses that purport to make the seller the original owner of new goods made

---

[59] *Appleby v Myers* [1867] LR 2 CP 651.
[60] *Hendy Lennox Ltd v Grahame Puttick Ltd* [1984] 2 All ER 152.
[61] *Evans v Rival Granite Quarries* [1910] 2 KB 979; *Re Standard Manufacturing Co.* [1891] 1 Ch 627.
[62] Morse, *Palmer's Company Law* § 13.138.
[63] *Aluminium Industrie Vaassen BV v Romalpa Aluminium Ltd* [1976] 1 WLR 676: see case 5(c), *supra*.

384   SECURITY RIGHTS IN MOVABLE PROPERTY

by the buyer, whether by adding just labour to the seller's raw materials or by adding both labour and another supplier's raw materials. In *Clough Mill Ltd v Martin*,[64] however, Robert Goff LJ was sympathetic in principle to such extended reservation clauses, but was insistent that they should be very clearly drafted because of their tendency to expropriate the buyer where value was added to the goods supplied by the seller. Nevertheless, this is an area of law where, above all, it is important to look at what courts in fact do rather than at what they say they might do. The view of Robert Goff LJ should be contrasted with that of Buckley LJ in the (equal-ranking) Court of Appeal decision in *Borden v Scottish Timber Products Ltd*[65] that the property in new goods could not vest in the seller at the outset without a proprietary grant from the buyer.

Technically, it might be possible to stipulate for extended title reservation rights with the aid of the pledge and an overseas sales transaction known as a trust receipt, used in connection with bills of lading. It is certainly possible to draft such a clause. But, in view of the hostility shown in recent years by our courts to extended *Romalpa* clauses, it is highly doubtful that such a clause would escape characterisation as a charge. Another possibility in view of recent developments would be to create express tenancy in common rights of seller and buyer in new goods manufactured by the buyer. Again, it is highly doubtful that such a clause would be effective without registration.

(d) If insolvency proceedings are commenced against B, then the position of A will depend upon whether A has reserved title in the way discussed above or has registered a charge in the way provided for by legislation. There is no principle of reputed ownership or expropriation that would expand the assets of B available for distribution to B's creditors.

IRELAND

(a) Where goods supplied subject to a retention of title clause have been used as raw materials in a process of manufacture it is not clear if and when the title of the original supplier is lost. There are very few authorities on this question in Ireland and none that closely correspond to the facts of the problem. So one must argue by analogy, from first principles and by reference to cases in comparable common law jurisdictions.

---

[64] [1985] 1 WLR 111.   [65] [1981] Ch 25.

One might plausibly contend that B, the manufacturer, becomes the owner of the entirety of the finished article, i.e. the curtains. The courts have often held that title to goods is lost once the manufacturing process is embarked upon. A *prima facie* retains title to the fabrics but they form the raw materials for a manufacturing process undertaken by B on A's authorisation. If the clothing is manufactured for the account of A, then A clearly has title to the article. The position is less clear where B bears the economic risk of the manufacturing operation. There is a view that the creator of a new thing (*nova species*) becomes the owner of the same. The writer is not aware of any Irish case law but there is a Scottish case – *International Banking Corp. v Ferguson Shaw and Sons*[66] – which may be taken as lending some support to this view albeit that the facts are completely different. In this case, A purchased *bona fide* from B oil which in fact belonged to C and, with the oil and other materials, A manufactured lard. An action was brought by C against A for delivery of the oil and the court held that A, by creating in the process of manufacture a new *species* which could not be resolved into its original elements, became proprietor of the substance manufactured under the Roman law doctrine of *specificatio*.

A well-known English case is *Re Peachdart Ltd*,[67] where leather was supplied to a company which used it to manufacture handbags. The court held that the parties must have intended that, at least after a piece of leather had been appropriated to be manufactured into a handbag and work had started on it (when the leather would cease to have any significant value as raw material), the leather would cease to be the exclusive property of the sellers. Thereafter, the sellers would have a charge on handbags in the course of manufacture and on the distinctive products which would come into existence at the end of the process of manufacture. The value of these products would be derived for the most part from the buyer's reputation and skill in design and the skill of its workforce.

Re Peachdart might be distinguished from the facts of the present case where 60 per cent of the value of the finished article still derives from the value of the raw material, but it is not clear that this is a sufficient grounds of distinction.

Certainly, the English courts have not been hesitant to hold that the title of an original supplier is lost. Another case is *Modelboard Ltd v Outer Box Ltd*,[68] which concerned cardboard sheets that were subjected to a

---

[66] [1910] SC 182.   [67] [1984] Ch 131.   [68] [1993] BCLC 623.

'process' by the buyer at the end of which 'process' they lost any significant value as raw material. The court concluded that the suppliers' interest in the goods was lost and their interest in the processed goods was in the nature of a charge. On the other hand, there are cases which hold that minor manufacturing operations do not prejudice the title of the original supplier. An example is *Armour v Thyssen Edelstahlwerke AG*,[69] where it was held that the supplier's title remained unaffected by the cutting of the raw material, steel. The New Zealand case – *New Zealand Forest Products v Pongakawa Sawmill Ltd*[70] – also merits attention in this context. There it was held that title to timber supplied on reservation of title terms did not disappear when the timber had been converted by a process of sawmilling into a different form.

While the Irish courts have not specifically addressed the precise points at issue in this problem, the basic message seems to be that any attempt to extend retention of title clauses into manufactured products is doomed to failure. In *Somers v Allen*,[71] Carroll J held that if a contract deals with the future title of the buyer in the goods to be manufactured from the goods supplied, then, as regards that future title, the contract would be in the nature of a charge. *Kruppstahl AG v Quitmann Products Ltd*[72] involved a detailed retention of title clause which dealt with, *inter alia*, handling, processing, blending and mixing the goods supplied (steel). While the contract was stated to be governed by German law, Gannon J held, as a matter of Irish law, that regarding the steel used in the manufacturing process, the interest of the suppliers was in the nature of an enterprise charge (*floating charge*).

Reverting to the facts of the problem, B probably has the best claim to the curtains and in this context the relationship between the value of the raw materials and the value created by the manufacturing process probably does not matter. If, however, A bears the risk of the manufacturing process, then it is submitted that he is entitled to the finished article.

(b) The answers are the same as to the previous question. In other words, the newly produced items will be subject to execution on behalf of C.

(c) A's reservation of title clause will in all probability be ineffective. It is likely to be held to constitute a charge granted by the buyer, B. Assume

---

[69] [1991] 2 AC 339.   [70] [1991] NZCLC 67.
[71] *Somers v James Allen (Ireland) Ltd* [1985] IR 340.   [72] [1982] ILRM 551.

that B is a corporate body. In that eventuality the charge requires registration. There is an argument based on the wording of the Companies Act 1963, s. 99, that a charge constituted by a reservation of title clause dealing with manufactured products does not require registration. It is submitted, however, that the argument is not well founded. Section 99 does not refer specifically to charges over goods but instead refers to charges which if executed by an individual would require registration as a bill of sale.

The Bills of Sale (Ireland) Acts 1879–1883 are quite complex and deal with non-possessory securities over chattels granted by individuals. The legislation is best described as a primitive form of consumer protection measure. Bills of sale are required to be in a certain form on pain of invalidity. The definition of a 'bill of sale' contained in section 4 of the 1879 Act is again complex, stating:

> The expression 'bill of sale' shall include bills of sale, assignments, transfers, declarations of trust without transfer, inventories of goods with receipt thereto attached, or receipts for purchase monies of goods, and other assurances of personal chattels, and also powers of attorney, authorities or licences to take possession of personal chattels as security for any debt, and also any agreement, whether intended or not to be followed by the execution of any other instrument, by which a right in equity to any personal chattels, or to any charge or security thereon, shall be conferred.

There are various exemptions from the category of bills, including a transfer of goods made in 'the ordinary course of any trade or calling'. Reliance was placed unsuccessfully on this exception in one English case – *Ian Chisholm Textiles Ltd v Griffiths*.[73] The judge held that the onus of proof was on the seller to show that what was in effect a charge, created by an 'extended' reservation of title clause, was created in the ordinary course of business of the buyer's trade. The seller contended that the sheer volume of cases on retention of title was enough to discharge the onus of proof, but the judge disagreed. In his view, it would require a very exceptional case before the court was prepared to conclude, merely on the volume of reported cases on a particular topic, that something was in the ordinary course of business of any trade. Moreover, the seller did not normally deal with its customers, who were mostly in the same sort of business as the buyer, on the basis of retention of title arrangements. Furthermore, it only entered into a retention of title with the

---

[73] [1994] BCC 96.

buyer in this particular case when the financial condition of the latter became parlous.

In a number of Irish cases, the retention of title provision has addressed the products issue. *Kruppstahl AG v Quitmann Products Ltd*[74] concerned a contract to supply steel between a German supplier and an Irish manufacturer. The contract stated:

> In the case of processing, blending and mixing of the reserved goods with other goods by the buyer, we acquire a joint title to the new goods in accordance with the ratio of the invoice value of the reserved goods to the invoice value of the other goods used. If our title lapses due to blending or mixing, the buyer assigns to us already at this stage his title to the new goods in accordance with the invoice value of the reserved goods, and holds them in trust for us, without charge.

Gannon J held that the supplier's interest in the manufactured steel was by way of security for the discharge of a potential indebtedness. Consequently, it was in the nature of a charge which required registration under the Companies Act 1963. The judge expressly concluded that the goods supplied fell within the definition of a bill of sale in s. 4 of the Bills of Sale (Ireland) Act 1879.

(d) The analysis is not affected if B has become bankrupt instead of unsecured creditors trying to make execution against B's property.

SCOTLAND

(a) If the fabric has passed through a manufacturing process sufficient to destroy its identity, so as to create a *nova species*, there has been *specificatio*, and the product is owned by B, who carried out the work. What amounts to the creation of a *nova species* will vary from case to case. Probably, manufacture into curtains would amount to *specificatio*.[75]

The relative value of (1) the material and (2) the work is of no relevance. Nor is it relevant who was to bear the risk.

The law on *specificatio* remains substantially as it was left by the *Corpus Iuris Civilis*.

---

[74] [1982] ILRM 551.
[75] In *Armour v Thyssen Edelstahlwerke AG* 1986 SLT 94, 1989 SLT 182, 1990 SLT 891, [1991] 2 AC 339 steel strip coils were cut into shapes. The judges took different views as to whether this amounted to *specificatio*. But the case for *specificatio* here (curtains out of cloth) is stronger.

(b) Since the curtains are owned by B, B's creditors can execute against them.

(c) Although the law is not certain, it is probably true that change of ownership by *specificatio* can be excluded by agreement.[76] Therefore, if the retention of title clause in the contract between A and B provided that ownership would remain with A notwithstanding *specificatio*, that would probably be effective. Such clauses are occasionally seen in practice.

(d) The same would be true.

SOUTH AFRICA

(a) Despite A's reservation of title to the 500 rolls of cloth, B will become owner of the finished curtains because of specification. The supplier (A) who loses his ownership of the material because of specification has a right of recourse against B on the ground of unjustified enrichment. If the production of the curtains amounts to a delict (highly unlikely because production of curtains was contemplated by the parties), the supplier (A) can claim delictual damages from B.

The pertinent requirements for specification under South African law are that a new species (*nova species*) must have been created (curtains from cloth) and that the new product (curtains) must be incapable of being reduced to their previous state (cloth). In establishing whether a new species has been created, the relative value of the cloth and workmanship does not play a role. Even if the final product is of an inferior value, the rules of specification are still considered applicable.

In specification, the person on whose behalf the work is done becomes the owner of the finished product. Thus the manufacturer and not the artisans who transformed the cloth into curtains becomes the owner of the curtains. By analogy, the person who bears the risk of the manufacturing process might be considered the owner of the finished product.

(b) Since the curtains have become the property of B by specification, B's creditors (thus also C) can execute against them.

---

[76] Miller, *Corporeal Moveables in Scots Law* para. 4-01.

(c) There is no authority in South African case law that change of ownership can be excluded by agreement between the parties. There is, however, authority that reservation of title in a contract of sale of a movable (e.g. parts of an irrigation system) can prevent the movable from becoming a part of the land on attachment because it was never the intention of the owner to relinquish ownership until the full purchase price has been paid.[77] Analogous application of this dogmatically unsound case law may result in the exclusion of the rules of specification on account of a reservation of ownership in an agreement between the parties.

(d) The insolvency of the buyer would not alter the position of the seller. If B has become the owner by specification, the curtains will fall into his insolvency estate. If the effect of the reservation of title is to exclude the consequences of specification, the curtains will not fall into B's insolvency estate.

DENMARK

(a) According to Danish law, it is possible to stipulate a reservation of title clause in a sort of credit consignment agreement if goods are sold to be manufactured. However, this clause will only be effective up to the point at which the goods are manufactured.

When the buyer uses the cloth to make curtains, the contract should stipulate that the buyer has to settle with the seller when the cloth is manufactured. Like other credit consignment agreements, the contract should allow A to check that B settles as agreed and A should do so. Furthermore, it is necessary that the cloth is kept apart from cloth of the same type supplied by other suppliers and from cloth which B has paid for already.

Even if the contract stipulates a valid reservation of title clause, this will only mean that the seller, A, can reclaim the cloth in the event of B's non-payment up to the point at which the cloth is used for manufacturing. When the cloth is manufactured into curtains, A cannot claim any right to the curtains. The curtains belong to B, the manufacturer.

(b) As the curtains belong to B, they can be executed against by B's creditor, C. This is a consequence of the fact that A cannot claim a right to the curtains.

---

[77] See e.g. *Macdonald Ltd v Radin NO and the Potchefstroom Dairies & Industries Co. Ltd* 1915 AD 454; *Konstanz Properties (Pty) Ltd v Wm Spilhaus en Kie (WP) Bpk* 1996 SA 362 (A).

(c) According to Danish law, it is not possible for the seller to reserve a right to the produced curtains. In the case law only one attempt to preserve such a right has been seen. A purported not to sell the cloth to B, but rather simply to send the cloth to B in order for B to undertake manufacturing on behalf of A. But in the case it was also agreed in the contract that B should sell the items on behalf of A, that B's salary was a percentage of the earnings of the products and that B was to bear the risks arising in respect of payments from the customers. The Supreme Court ruled that, since A had not really run the business, A could not claim any right to the items.[78]

(d) According to Danish law, the insolvency estate includes all the debtor's property except assets which cannot be executed against. On the other hand, rights which are protected against creditors are not included in the estate.[79] This means that, with very few exemptions, the assets included within the insolvency estate are the same as the assets which can be executed against by creditors. Therefore, the answers are the same as in parts (b) and (c) in the event of B's insolvency.

SWEDEN

(a) The seller of the cloth, A, has reserved title until full payment is made. According to the wording of the clause, he has not permitted the producer, B, to manufacture curtains prior to payment. It is then a question of interpretation as to whether he impliedly consented to manufacture prior to that date. If he has reserved a right in the proceeds, it is obvious that he has accepted a resale prior to payment.[80] In another Supreme Court case, the seller had realised that the buyer intended to dispose of the property (pigs) prior to payment, but he had not consented, and, therefore, the reservation was valid (the Court also had regard to the fact that the identity of the property had not been changed by breeding).[81] In a subsequent case, the seller had delivered doors to a builder with reservation of title and a condition of immediate payment. Nevertheless, the reservation was regarded as invalid as the seller knew that the buyer was erecting a building.[82] In a third case, where doors were to be incorporated in a building, the reservation of title clause was upheld,

---

[78] The case is reported in *Ugeskrift for Retsvæsen* (weekly law reports) 1978, 880.
[79] Cf. Munch, *Konkursloven* 269 ff. and Ørgaard, *Konkursret* 41 ff.
[80] NJA 1932, 292.   [81] NJA 1959, 590. Cf. § 950 BGB.   [82] NJA 1960, 221.

presumably because the seller was supposed to assist in the mounting of the doors.[83] There may be a presumption that the seller has consented to resale or manufacture prior to payment when he sells to a retailer or manufacturer, respectively, but all the details of the rule are not entirely clear. In the present case, it would seem likely that the seller, A, will be presumed to have accepted manufacture prior to payment, and, therefore, the reservation of title will be invalid in relation to the creditors of the buyer, B. Otherwise, the change of identity from cloth to curtains (rather than the value ratio) would presumably render the reservation of title ineffective.[84] The fact that the manufacturing process in this case might have been unauthorised (and otherwise the specification problem does not arise) does not seem to justify co-ownership having regard to the value ratio.[85]

(b) See part (a) above.

(c) A might enjoy an improved position if he contracts with B that the manufacture shall be on his behalf.[86] This would require, however, that A assumes the business risk of manufacture (i.e. undertakes to compensate B for his costs if the goods are not sold), which he probably will not want to do, unless the seller and buyer belong to the same group of companies. If the business risk is placed on A, an analogy can be drawn with section 53 of the Commission Agency Act, which would suggest that A would be the owner.

In practice, sellers like A sometimes deposit raw materials with buyers like B without selling them but with an option, but not an obligation, for B to buy the raw materials on credit as and when he needs them for manufacture. The idea is that A will have a right to separate that part of the stock which B has not bought when insolvency or execution occurs. It is unclear whether such an arrangement is valid. On the one hand, according to section 53 of the Commission Agency Act, the principal has a right of separation even if the commission agent may buy the goods for himself, perhaps with deferred payment, but has not yet

---

[83] NJA 1974, 660.
[84] Cf. NJA 1959, 590; Unden, *Svensk sakrätt I* § 15; Håstad, *Sakrätt* 43 ff. and SOU 1988:63, 204 f.
[85] Cf. chapter 2 s. 4 of the Land Code, where a reservation of title or rescission is deemed to be invalid when the goods have become a fixture to immovable property.
[86] See further Almén/Eklund, *Lagen om köp och byte av lös egendom* § 2 (notes 10 and 16); Håstad, *Studier i sakrätt* 9 ff.

done so; there is no requirement that the agent must be solvent. On the other hand, according to the 1944 Entrusted Money Act (*lagen om redovisningsmedel*), which is applicable to fungible goods by analogy, a principal has a right of separation even if the agent (often a commission agent) is entitled to dispose of the entrusted monies for his own purposes. Such a permission, however, must be restricted to situations where the agent is solvent; should the principal have taken a credit risk, the right of separation is excluded from the beginning even if the monies have been kept separately at all times. Thus, the law seems to be contradictory. A legislative proposal has sought to resolve this issue,[87] but no legislation has thus far been enacted.

A could have been granted security in the manufactured products under the registered enterprise charge. A (security) assignment or a pledge would not work, however, since actual delivery is required (a *constitutum possessorium* is not sufficient) and future goods cannot be registered under the Bills of Sales Act.

(d) See parts (a)–(c).

FINLAND

(a) The retention of title clause could, perhaps, bind the buyer, B, personally. The problem in this respect is, primarily, whether the retention of title clause is regarded as unreasonable or not. If the clause is binding between A and B, one could perhaps say that the curtains are owned by A. In Finnish doctrine, the question of ownership is, however, usually regarded as far too indefinite.[88] It is not usual primarily to ask who owns an item, but who should be regarded as owner in certain specific relationships. So even if A was regarded as the owner *inter partes*, i.e. as between A and B, the answer may very well differ when it is asked who is to be regarded as the owner when B goes bankrupt or when a bailiff tries to execute against the item in question on behalf of B's creditors.

(b) The seller can, in general, obtain protection against other creditors of the buyer by using a retention of title clause. If the subject matter of the purchase is, however, a raw material, and the buyer is entitled to use the material in question before full payment of the purchase price, the

---

[87] SOU 1988:63 *Kommission och dylikt*.
[88] See further e.g. Kartio, *Esineoikeuden perusteet* 160 ff.

retention of title clause is not effective as against other creditors. The same is probably so in cases where the seller must have been taken to understand that the buyer will use the raw material, whether he or she is entitled to do so or not. The curtains would, therefore, be regarded as belonging to B and the creditors of B could execute against the curtains.

The relationship between the value of the material and the value added would certainly be of some relevance in deciding whether a 'new item' was made out of the raw material. The value ratio would not, however, be the only relevant factor. On the contrary, the 'common view of the trade and business' would probably count for more. In the present case, it seems tolerably clear that the curtains would be regarded as new items in this sense.

(c) If an essential economic risk in the manufacturing activities was borne by A, the rules concerning commission could possibly apply. This would mean that, first of all, B would not be obliged to pay for the raw material. This kind of arrangement would be conceivable if the curtains produced using the cloth were meant to be sold on behalf of A. In that case, the new products could be regarded as belonging to A, and B would be entitled only to some kind of reward for undertaking the manufacturing process. This kind of arrangement is not very common.

(d) The rules applied in the event of insolvency would be the same as the rules applied to executions against B's property on behalf of an unsecured creditor.

Comparative observations

Part (a)

If raw material is sold under retention of title and subsequently transformed into new products, the first issue that has to be dealt with is the question of ownership, or, in terms that may sound more adequate to Swedish and Finnish lawyers: how does the jurisdiction resolve the conflict between the owner of the material and the manufacturer? This issue is a general one and is not necessarily tied to the law on retention of title, although today, retention of title may be the most practical application of these rules.

Surprisingly, a majority of twelve out of sixteen jurisdictions conclude that B will own the curtains even though the value of B's work is less than that of the material. Greek, Spanish and Portuguese law reach the opposite conclusion. Austrian law is the only system which grants shares to the manufacturer and the owner of the material: they become co-owners according to their respective contributions.

If we look at the criteria that decide the question of ownership, we can distinguish two main factors: the creation of a new thing and the value ratio between material and work.

In English, Irish, Scots, South African and Belgian law, the only, or at least main, question that matters is whether a new thing has been created. That being the case, English, Scots and South African law conclude that ownership in the product is vested in the manufacturer – irrespective of the ratio between the value of the material and that of the manufacturing process and no matter who has borne the risk of the manufacturing. The position seems to be less clear in Ireland, where the burden of risk may be a factor in deciding the question of ownership. In Belgium, the position is largely the same as in England and Scotland except when the value of the manufacturing process is only marginal. In that event, Belgian law would accord ownership of the products to the owner of the material, while the manufacturer will only have a personal claim for compensation. Dutch law comes close to Belgian law, as it also focuses on the question whether a new thing has been created and provides a separate rule in favour of the owner of the material if the value of the manufacturing process is only marginal. However, there is a major difference between Dutch law and the other jurisdictions mentioned in this paragraph, in so far as the Dutch Supreme Court considers the question of risk-bearing as essential in deciding for whom a new thing has been created.

In German, Greek, Spanish, Portuguese and Italian law, the value ratio is either the only factor that decides the question of ownership or it is at least one important factor, but whereas in Germany and Italy preference is given to the manufacturer unless the value of the material is materially higher than that of the work, Greek law takes the opposite position. In Spain and Portugal, neither the owner of the material nor the manufacturer is generally preferred. Leaving aside the question of good faith which is another factor in Spanish and Portuguese law, ownership is granted to that person whose contribution has been more valuable.

Sweden and Finland cannot be said clearly to belong to either of the two groups. Both criteria, the value ratio and the creation of a new thing, are taken into consideration with perhaps the latter carrying more weight.

A second question concerns the effect that an express or implied entitlement to use the goods in a manufacturing process would have on (simple) retention of title. As with the entitlement to resell (see cases 4 and 5), Swedish and Finnish law take the rather strict position that the entitlement renders the reservation of ownership invalid *ab initio* and not only from the beginning of the manufacturing process. This last position also appears to be taken by Danish law.

Part (b)

The question of ownership also decides part (b). To the extent that the buyer has become owner, B's creditors can execute against the newly produced items. If A is granted ownership over the products the opposite is so.

Part (c)

Only German and Greek law give effect to a retention of title clause that extends to the newly produced goods. There is a slight dogmatic difference between the jurisdictions in so far as the predominant opinion in Germany, especially of the courts, allows the parties to derogate from the rules on *specificatio*, whereas in Greece, the products clause is regarded as a security transfer of ownership of the new products. In Germany, this last solution represents only the view of a minority in legal literature.

Derogation from the rules on *specificatio* is also considered possible in Scotland and – with reservations – in Italy and South Africa, but there is no established business practice.

An extension of retention of title into products or a derogation from the rules on *specificatio* would in most jurisdictions be regarded as a charge over goods otherwise not belonging to the seller. This is clearly the view taken by English and Irish courts in the aftermath of *Romalpa*. The same analysis applies according to Dutch law, which in its new Civil Code has completely abolished security transfer of ownership (article 3:84 (3) BW). In all three jurisdictions, a registered charge over future movables would be the only method by which the seller could take a real right in the products. Spanish law, on the other hand, although it also knows a registered charge, does not permit the future products to be charged in advance since it strictly requires the charged goods to be capable of identification at the moment in which the transaction is concluded.

Within French and Belgian law, the same reason, i.e. that the seller is attempting to gain a non-possessory security right in goods belonging to the buyer, may be put forward as an explanation of why the insolvency legislation of these countries puts an end to retention of title as soon as the goods are no longer present 'in nature'. Any right of the seller in the products would amount to a non-possessory security right and therefore violate general principles of French and Belgian property law. This position is also advanced by Austrian doctrine which likewise considers any rights of the seller as ineffective if they go beyond those given to him pursuant to the rules on *specificatio*.

In a number of countries (Austria, France, Italy, Denmark, Sweden and Finland), in an attempt to meet the obvious economic need to grant the seller of raw materials a right in the end products, use is made of a contractual agreement which purports to make the seller the *manufacturer* of such products. However, the commercial practicability of such arrangements is severely limited by the basic requirement that the seller must effectively bear the risks of the manufacturing process and the sub-sale. In none of the countries named have such arrangements become a common feature in business practice.

Part (d)

In none of the jurisdictions under consideration do the answers to parts (a) to (c) change in the event of B's insolvency.

Case 8: Supply of material to manufacturer (II)

(Retention of title – sale of manufactured products – combined products and proceeds clause)

As in case 7, B has manufactured curtains from cloth supplied by A under retention of title. This time however, B has sold all the curtains produced to two customers, D and E. By the time a bailiff, acting on behalf of an unsecured creditor, C, tries to execute against B's property, D has paid the purchase price in full by transferring the monies to B's bank account. Neither E nor B has paid anything.

Questions

(a) Who is entitled to the monies paid to B by D? Can the bailiff execute against those monies (that is to say, B's bank account as a whole)?

(b) Who can claim payment from E? Can the bailiff execute against the claim arising out of the sub-sale?

(c) Could A get a better right to the claims arising out of sub-sales (for example, by using a differently worded clause or a different type of retention of title clause)? What would be the precise prerequisites? Are such arrangements commonly used?

(d) Instead of an unsecured creditor trying to execute against B's property, B becomes bankrupt. What are the answers to parts (a), (b) and (c) in that situation?

Discussions

GERMANY

(a) Under a simple retention of title clause, the monies paid by the sub-purchaser (D) belong to the buyer (B). Thus, the bailiff may execute against the monies deposited in B's bank account free of any rights of A.

(b) Without any extension of retention of title through further provisions (see *infra*, part (c)), the claim arising out of the sub-sale clearly belongs to B and may therefore be executed against on behalf of B's creditors.

(c) In cases such as the present, sellers generally use a combination of products[1] and proceeds[2] clauses. The parties stipulate that the seller (A) is the manufacturer of the new products and that the buyer (B) is entitled to sell the products to his customers (D and E). The claims arising out of the sub-sales are anticipatorily assigned to the seller (A), so that at the very moment the sub-sale is concluded the claims will automatically vest in him. This widely used type of clause provides sellers with comprehensive protection against non-payment. They can either recover the original goods or claim preferential payment out of the manufactured products or out of the claims resulting from sub-sales, depending on the stage reached when execution or insolvency occurs. The validity of a combined products/proceeds clause, including as against third parties, does not depend on anything other than the use of adequate wording in the contract, which may even be concluded orally.

If, in the present case, the contract between A and B contained such a combined products and proceeds clause, the newly produced curtains would be owned by A, but the customers of B would acquire ownership of them by virtue of B's entitlement to transfer title (§§ 185, 929 BGB). The monies that have been paid into B's general bank account are lost to A.[3]

However, in respect of the claim subsisting against E, A will take priority over other creditors (such as C). The result is undisputed, but there are different opinions as to how the secured creditor (A) can realise his priority. The courts and the predominant view in the doctrine hold that the security assignment entitles the assignee (A) to resist and thus stop any execution against the assigned rights (§ 771 ZPO).[4] Others think that the assignee, like a pledgee, can only claim preferential payment out of

---

[1] See *supra*, German report, case 6(c). [2] See *supra*, German report, cases 5(c) and 6(b).
[3] See *supra*, German report, case 5(c).
[4] Cf. RG 9 Apr. 1929, RGZ 124, 73; BGH 4 Feb. 1954, BGHZ 12, 232 (234); Reinicke/Tiedtke, *Kreditsicherung* n. 649; Baur/Stürner, *Zwangsvollstreckungs-, Konkurs- und Vergleichsrecht I* 525 and 527; Baur/Stürner, *Sachenrecht* § 58 n. 2; Staudinger/Busche Einleitung zu §§ 398 ff. n. 96.

the proceeds of the claim's realisation according to § 805 ZPO.[5] Serick[6] states that an action pursuant to § 771 ZPO is unnecessary, because the assigned claim is held by the assignee. Any attempt by the assignor's (B's) creditors to execute against it will be in vain. The only action that the assignee might bring would be an action for a declaratory judgment.

(d) If the parties have not included a combined products and proceeds clause as described under part (c), the monies already paid to B as well as the claim against E will be the property of B and thus subject to distribution amongst his insolvency creditors. A would not have any rights to the money or the claim.

If the contract contains a combined products and proceeds clause, A can claim preferential payment out of the claim against E (see §§ 50 s. 1, 51 n. 1, 166 ff. InsO).[7] However, the monies paid by D to B are still lost to A.[8]

AUSTRIA

(a) As the contract contains only a simple retention of title clause, the monies paid by D belong to B. A does not, therefore, have any real rights to the monies deposited in B's bank account. The bailiff can, therefore, execute against the monies.

(b) As the contract contains only a simple retention of title clause, B's claim against E belongs to B; the bailiff can therefore execute against this claim.

(c) Only an extended retention of title clause would afford A adequate protection.[9]

(d) This makes no difference; the answers to parts (a) and (b) are the same, as the monies or the claims are assets belonging to B.

---

[5] *Baumbach/Lauterbach/Hartmann* § 771 ZPO n. 26; *Münchener Kommentar/Roth* § 398 BGB n. 86.
[6] Serick, *Eigentumsvorbehalt und Sicherungsübertragung* III § 34 III 1.
[7] See further *supra*, German report, case 6(b).
[8] Cf. Reinicke/Tiedtke, *Kreditsicherung* n. 742 and *supra*, German report, case 5(c).
[9] For details see *supra*, Austrian report, case 5(c).

GREECE

(a) C may execute against the monies deposited in B's bank account, since the claim against D, and hence the proceeds of its realisation, belongs to B, so long as this does not infringe bank secrecy. Only an extended retention of title clause would grant to A rights in the claims arising from the sub-sales. When the purchaser is a retailer, common business practice is to combine the retention of title agreement with an assignment to the vendor of the future claims of the purchaser arising from the resales (extended retention of title, a proceeds clause).[10] In such a case, since D must be notified of the assignment, D would be obliged to make payment to A, not to B. Thus, if he had nevertheless paid B, A's claim against D would remain undischarged. D would be able to claim back the money paid to B on the basis of unjust enrichment (article 904 A.K.).

(b) The claim arising from the sub-sale belongs to B. Since, in the present case, the parties have not included a proceeds clause (see below, part (c)), it is clear that the claim may be subjected to execution by the bailiff.

(c) Only an extended title clause would grant to A rights in the claims arising from the sub-sales. If the purchaser is a retailer, it is common business practice to combine the retention of title agreement with an assignment to the vendor of the future claims of the purchaser arising from the resales (a proceeds clause). This form of assignment is, in reality, a fiduciary one because it ensures that the vendor's claims against the assignor are satisfied. No further prerequisites are imposed, except that the *debitor cessus*, E, must be notified of the assignment.

(d) The claim arising from the sub-sale belongs to B, as do the collected monies; they therefore form part of the insolvency estate. Hence, the answers to parts (b) and (c) do not change. It should be mentioned that, according to the prevailing view, in case of extended retention of title, if B went bankrupt after the assignment, the assigned claim does not form part of the insolvency estate, irrespective of whether the *debitor cessus*

---

[10] For a treatment of extended retention of title, see Roussos, in: *Miscellany in Honour of Michailidis – Nouaros* 397.

(i.e. E) has been notified of the assignment. The claim has been separated from the assignor's property.[11]

FRANCE

(a) In principle, the seller's (A's) claim to the proceeds would be as good as his claim over the goods sold under retention of title, because his interest in the goods is, by means of real subrogation, transferred to the proceeds.[12] C. com, article L. 621-124 expressly refers to the proceeds of the assets as defined in C. com, article L. 621-123.[13] Yet, two cases have upheld a court action by the seller against the sub-buyer to the sale proceeds despite the transformation of the assets.[14] In 1984, the Court of Appeal of Toulouse held that the unpaid seller of wool could not require the return of the wool, which had since been knitted into pullovers; but could claim the proceeds of the sale to the sub-buyer.[15] Yet, the decision was repealed by the *Cour de cassation*.[16] Since then, various decisions have refused to accept the claims of sellers to the proceeds of sub-sales, when the assets have been transformed.[17]

Assuming that the court would adopt a liberal approach to this question, it is necessary to consider whether A will have any claim over the price *already* paid by D to B for the curtains. Although the writer is

---

[11] The prevailing view is supported by Georgiadis, *Empragmato Dikaio II* 267; Kornilakis, *I katapisteutiki ekchorisi ton apaitiseon* 126.

[12] Com 27 May 1986, Bull civ IV, No 102; D 1988, Som, 63, obs. Derrida; Com. 15 Dec. 1992, Bull civ IV, No 412; D 1993, Som, 293, obs. Pérochon.

[13] Com 3 Jan 1995, Bull civ IV, No 3; RTDC 1997, 166, obs. Zénati; D 1996, Som, 121: A machine sold under reservation of title had been resold by the buyer to a sub-buyer and installed on a production line. The Court held that, since the installation documents noted that the machine would be able to work even if disconnected from the chain, the machine was still to be found in kind according to C. com, article L. 621-124, and thus the claim to the sale proceeds was successful.

[14] Lyon, 29 Apr. 1983, Juris-Data No 041 412; Toulouse, 27 Nov. 1984, D 1985, J. 185, note Mestre.

[15] See obs. Pérochon, D 1993, Som, 293, note (1). The return of the transformed assets that remain in the possession of the buyer is impossible because then only the initial seller would reap the benefits of the manufacturing process, at the expense of the creditors as a whole. However, because the interest of the seller in the sale proceeds (owed to the buyer by the sub-buyer) would be limited to the amount of the outstanding debt, no creditors would suffer by this. It would simply be a case of real subrogation.

[16] Com 27 May 1986, Bull civ IV, No 102; D 1988, Som, 63, obs. Derrida.

[17] Com 15 Dec. 1992, Bull civ IV, No 412; D 1993, Som, 293, obs. Pérochon; Com 17 Mar. 1998, Bull civ IV, No 108; D 1999, Som, 72, obs. Honorat; JCPédE 1998, No 37, 1398, obs. Pétel.

unaware of any cases dealing with this question, A will probably not be able to claim the money, for the simple reason that as the claim had already been paid, the real subrogation provided by C. com, article L. 621-124 will be inapplicable. The money, a fungible asset, has now been mixed in B's bank account with other monies, thus extinguishing the title of A.

(b) Here again, the question of transformation arises, with the same consequences as explained in part (a). In contrast with (a), when claims arising from sub-sales remain outstanding, the courts have taken the view that, based on real subrogation, the proceeds of sale are assigned to the seller as soon as the original buyer and sub-buyer have concluded the subsale. It is, therefore, irrelevant whether either the assets are then sold again[18] or the claim to the proceeds is charged by the original buyer.[19] In fact, the sub-buyer would not be able to refuse to pay the seller because of default in the sold assets.[20] The fiction is that the claim to the sale proceeds never passes into the estate of the original buyer.

So A will certainly be entitled to claim payment from E. As the claim against E is unlikely to equal the amount outstanding between A and B, A will continue to be a creditor of B for the remainder.[21]

(c) The existence of A's right depends on the asset subject to retention of title remaining untransformed. Fabrics are meant to be transformed during the course of manufacturing, hence the use of a retention of title clause is inherently inapposite. French law has not, however, adopted a more suitable approach.

(d) The claim will only be admissible if the sum owing between B and E has not been paid prior to the commencement of insolvency proceedings, i.e. it was paid *after* they commenced. It is up to the first seller to bring evidence of this.[22] The sub-buyer who pays the price with

---

[18] Com 8 Mar. 1988, Bull civ IV, No 99; RTDC 1989, 348.
[19] See Com 20 June 1989 (D 1989, 431, note Pérochon; RTDC 1990, 121, obs. Brandac), where the creditor-seller's claim prevailed over the claim of a bank, to which the claim over the sale proceeds had been charged.
[20] Com 3 Jan. 1995, Bull civ IV, No 3; RTDC 1997, 166, obs. Zénati; D 1996, Som, 121.
[21] According to Com. 15 Jan. 1991, Bull civ IV, No 31; JCPédE 1991, I, 102, No 10, if the sale proceeds exceed the outstanding debt between the original seller and buyer, the claim is limited to the quantum of the outstanding debt.
[22] Com 2 Nov. 1993, Bull civ IV, No 375, D 1994, IR, 7. Confirmed for the new wording of article 122 in Com 11 July 1995, JCPédE 1995, Pan, 1141.

knowledge both of the fact that insolvency proceedings have commenced against his creditor, and of the claim of the initial seller, can be required to pay the sale price again, to the latter, according to the provisions of C. com, article L. 621-124.[23]

BELGIUM

(a) All the assets owned by a debtor can be subjected to execution by his creditors (article 7 Mortgage Act). Since the real rights of the seller have been extinguished, no real subrogation can occur. The bailiff can execute against the bank accounts of B on behalf of creditor C.

(b) Only B is entitled to claim payment from his customers. The debt of E is also an asset of the estate of B and is therefore potentially subject to attachment by his creditors.

(c) In addition to reservation of title, the parties can agree that the seller takes a charge over the claims arising from subsequent sales. A security interest can be created in the proceeds of the sub-sales by the use of a charge over future claims. Such a charge will grant to the seller priority over subsequent creditors who execute against the claims, even without prior notification of the charge to the customers (see Belgian report, case 12). As stated above, in case 5(c), such arrangements have not frequently been used, at least until today, presumably because the business community has yet to appreciate the full potential of the recent reform of Belgian insolvency law.

(d) The positions of the seller and the insolvency creditors will be similar, in the event of the insolvency of the buyer.

PORTUGAL

(a) The proceeds of sale, paid by D to B, belong to B, because they were delivered to him, and, in case of money, delivery always implies the transfer of ownership. Therefore, the bailiff can execute against the money.

(b) As the contract of sale was agreed between B and E, it is B who is entitled to claim payment from E. However, A can, as creditor of B, also

---

[23] Com 5 Mar. 1996, RJDA 1996, No 837.

exercise his rights. In fact, according to Portuguese law, it is possible for any creditor to claim payment from anyone indebted to the debtor in question, by virtue of a subrogation action (*acção subrogatória* – article 606º C.C.). This action does not, however, grant any priority in payment, as it is made available for the benefit of creditors generally (article 609º C.C.).

Claims are assets subject to execution, so the claim arising from the sub-sale may be executed against by a creditor of B. The execution is performed by informing the debtor in question that the claim should be paid to the court.

(c) The only way for A to acquire a superior right to the claims arising from the sub-sales would be to execute against them.

(d) If B becomes bankrupt, the insolvency administrator would be entitled to the money paid by D and to claim the payment owing from E. A subrogation action brought by A would be ineffective, because it has no preferential status.

SPAIN

(a) The bailiff may execute against the monies paid by D to B.

(b) B may claim payment from E. The bailiff may execute against the claim arising out of the sub-sale.

(c) Legally, A has neither a real right to the money paid by D, nor any claim against E. Nevertheless, in the contract for the sale of the cloth, it would be possible for B, in order to provide security for A's claim, to assign to A any claims that he (B) might acquire in the future against his customers. The wording of such a contract clause might be as follows: 'B assigns to A as a guarantee of payment of the hire purchase price all credits which may accrue to B from future purchasers of the curtains.' The assignment of future debts as a security is only admissible if their provenance can be identified as to their amount and origin, and if they result from the resale of the curtains.

(d) As to part (a): B's goods fall into the insolvency estate and the bailiff may no longer execute against them.

As to part (b): Only the insolvency administrator may demand payment from E. Insolvency proceedings have the effect of consolidating all individual executions into a single insolvency suit.[24]

As to part (c): An assignment of B's claims against his customers would not be feasible, as they now form part of B's insolvency estate. In spite of the fact that A has a reservation of ownership right over the curtains, this right does not extend to the proceeds that may arise from the resale of those curtains. A cannot recover directly from the insolvency estate, because A is merely an insolvency creditor. Eventually, A will collect what is due to him in accordance to the provisions governing insolvency proceedings. Since the commencement of insolvency proceedings stays all individual claims, A cannot claim payment from E.

ITALY

(a) and (b) Since the curtains belong to the manufacturer, the price paid by D in respect of them belongs also to B. Therefore, the monies deposited in his bank account are subject to execution by the bailiff. The same is true of the claim B has against purchaser E.

(c) Let it be assumed, as required by our case, that the contract between the parties is a genuine sale, and not something else. That being so, A and B may still agree that A is to have an assignment of future claims owed to B by his customers. The situation would be the following: B owns the curtains, if we assume that the retention of title clause in favour of A cannot extend to the products produced with the cloth. Yet, A would still secure his claim for the purchase price by obtaining priority to the value of the product, by virtue of an assignment of future claims agreement relating to the claims arising from the sale of the curtains owned by B. The difficulty with this approach stems from the fact that A is neither a bank nor a factoring company (see below, case 12(a) and (b)). Hence the Civil Code rules on the assignment of claims apply to the facts of the present case (articles 1260 ff. c.c.). These rules allow for the assignment of future claims only in so far as it is possible to ascertain which claims are subject to the assignment.[25] Therefore, the assignment of future claims agreement will not operate effectively if B's customers

---

[24] See articles 161.3 and 1186 LEC.
[25] For a recent treatment of the topic: Troiano, *La cessione di crediti futuri*.

are persons who cannot be identified at the time of the assignment. But commercial partners may be identifiable in advance, in a number of circumstances. In any case, to prevail in a conflict with B's insolvency creditors, A must comply with the rather burdensome requirements of the Civil Code governing how the assignment is made effective against them. According to article 2914, n. 2 c.c., the assignee will prevail against a creditor of the assignor who has attached to the claim, whenever the *debitor cessus* accepted the assignment or received adequate notice of it prior to attachment. Legal authors and case law hold that acceptance or notification only render the assignment effective as against the individual creditors (or the insolvency administrator of the assignor) if evidenced by documents that have a certain date prior to the execution or insolvency.[26] According to some decisions assignment should be effective even if each of the assigned claims came into existence following execution against the assignor's assets,[27] or if the assigned claim came into existence following his insolvency, though the majority view favours the opposite conclusion.[28]

On the other hand, if the relationship between A and B was not one of sale, but rather an *appalto* (see case 7(c)), whereby the curtains are owned by A, it would be possible to maintain that payments received by B, or claims owed to him by third parties who bought the curtains, were received (or were to be received) by B in a ministerial capacity, as agent for A. B could be considered as *mandatario senza rappresentanza* for A, in the sale of the curtains to D and E, and A could claim the unpaid price directly from E under article 1705 c.c.[29] In that case, if the contract between A and B had a certain date prior to the bailiff's act of execution against B, the claim in question would not be considered as an asset available to C's creditors (article 1707 c.c.).[30] Alternatively, if those sales were not authorised, B may be entitled to collect the sums

---

[26] The matter is not disputed. See Bianca, *La vendita e la permuta* I 592, note 6. On the need to comply with the above-mentioned evidentiary requirement, see: Cass. 22 Feb. 1996, n. 1413, Fallimento, 1996, 759. The assignee must satisfy this requirement for every assignment, despite the fact that a master contract with a certain date exists, which obliges the assignor to assign all the claims that originate from a certain source to the assignee: cf. Cass. 14 Nov. 1996, n. 9997. Perlingieri, in *Commentario del codice civile Scialoja-Branca* 227 ff.
[27] See e.g. Trib. Bari, 1 Apr. 1998, Foro it., 2000, I, 1992, obs. Macario.
[28] Cass. 29 Jan. 1999, n. 785, Foro it., 2000, I, 1991, obs. Macario; Cass. 12 Oct. 1999, n. 1132; Cass. 14 Nov. 1996, n. 9997; Giust. civ., 1997, I, 1879; Giur. it., 1997, I, 1, 1558; Fallimento, 1997, 787, obs. Badini Confalonieri. Cf. Macario, Riv. dir. priv. 2000, 437.
[29] See above, Italian report, case 6(a), (b).
[30] For commentary on article 1707 c.c. see above, Italian report, case 4.

still owed by E by analogy with the rule that allows the owner to claim the price of the wrongful sale of goods, which remain unpaid for by the buyer (article 2038 c.c.). In such a case, A would be entitled to those claims.

If, however, the proceeds were paid by D to B and were mixed with other monies in B's bank account, this would defeat any claim of A to priority in respect of the proceeds of the wrongful sale, though the unauthorised mixing of the monies would be considered wrongful.[31]

In any case, the arrangements discussed under this part are uncommon in Italy and their litigation would raise fresh issues.

(d) The general rules on insolvency apply to this situation.

THE NETHERLANDS

(a) The bailiff can execute against the monies paid, as they belong to B.

(b) As a rule, only B may demand payment from E. However, it is possible to execute against unpaid claims. Monies due to the debtor can be attached by the executing creditor. In that case, the *debitor cessus* must pay the bailiff. Payments made to any other party would generally fail to discharge the claim.[32]

(c) The answer to this question is the same as in case 5(c), concerning the power to resell. The only difference between the two cases is that the supplier's retention of title does not end because of a resolutive clause for resales in the ordinary course of business, but because of the manufacturing process, leading to *specificatio*. A's position could likewise be improved by the creation of a charge on the claims.

(d) If insolvency proceedings are commenced, only the insolvency administrator may demand payment from E. Following publication of the insolvency adjudication, E would not be able to release himself by making payment to anybody other than the administrator.[33] The sum paid by D to B before the insolvency forms part of the insolvency estate.

---

[31] Cf. Cass. 6 Mar. 1999, n. 1925, Giur. comm., 2000, II, 174, obs. Abriani; Foro it., 2000, I, 2299.
[32] See articles 478h(1) and 477 Rv.   [33] Article 52 Fw.

ENGLAND

(a) In so far as the seller, A, does not have a real interest in the money proceeds coming from D, then execution may be levied against those proceeds or against any other assets of B. Execution may take the form of a garnishee order against the bank so that the bank is ordered to pay the garnishing creditor instead and that creditor is able to give the bank a good discharge for the sums it owes to B.

(b) An unpaid seller has no rights, whether in law or equity, to the money proceeds of the goods supplied. A claim due from E can be the subject of garnishee proceedings issued by a creditor of B.

(c) Any attempt of the seller to bargain for rights in these proceeds will be treated as the taking of a charge.[34]

(d) The availability for insolvency distribution of money proceeds of goods sold on and of money claims against sub-buyers depends upon the real rights of B, the insolvent.

IRELAND

(a) Since B is selling his own property, the money already paid by D belongs to B and is subject to execution by B's creditors.

(b) It follows from the answer to the previous question that, since B is selling his own property, it is B who can claim payment from E and this claim, like the rest of B's property, is subject to execution by B's creditors.

(c) Any attempt by A to gain a better right with respect to the claims arising out of sub-sales is likely to be doomed. The courts will probably hold that such an attempt constitutes a charge over B's property, which is void for want of registration. The discussion in cases 5 and 6 explained how judicial thinking in Ireland has moved against recognising 'proceeds of sale' retention of title. In this particular example we have a 'products' claim coupled with a 'proceeds' claim. The case is *a fortiori*.

[34] Under case 5.

(d) B's insolvency would not affect the analysis in relation to parts (b) and (c).

SCOTLAND

(a) The money paid by D is simply part of B's patrimony (estate) and is thus susceptible to execution by B's creditors. Because D will never get the goods, he will have a right to get his money back. But this will be an ordinary claim and if B is insolvent D will lose money.

(b) The claim by B against E is also part of B's patrimony (estate) and is thus susceptible to execution by B's creditors. However, if E does not get the goods he can refuse to pay. His right to refuse to pay is effective not only against B but also against B's creditors.

(c) Attempts have been made for the contract between A and B to provide that the proceeds of sub-sales shall be held in trust by B for A. Such attempts have not succeeded.[35]

(d) This would make no difference.

SOUTH AFRICA

(a) The money paid by D into B's bank account has become B's, as it has been mixed with his own money. All the assets of the debtor (B), whether corporeal or incorporeal, are susceptible to execution by B's creditors, including C. C can execute against B's bank account as a whole. Since D will never receive the curtains, he will have a contractual claim against B for breach of contract. If he does not execute against B's property himself, his claim will rank lower than that of C.

(b) Only B has a contractual right to claim payment from E. The bailiff (*messenger of the court*) can execute against all assets of B, whether corporeal or incorporeal, thus including contractual rights. E can however refuse to pay the price on the ground that B has not fulfilled his part of the contract. This would have the effect of avoiding B's claim.

---

[35] *Clark Taylor & Co. v Quality Site Development (Edinburgh) Ltd* 1981 SC 111. See above, Scots report, case 5(c).

(c) The parties could agree that the proceeds of any sub-sales would be subject to a charge in favour of A. Such a clause is not very common in South African commercial practice.

(d) The legal position of the seller (A) and the unsecured creditors will be the same as above on B's insolvency.

DENMARK

(a) According to Danish law, the monies paid to B's bank account can be executed against by B's creditors.

(b) A cannot preserve any right to the cloth after it has been manufactured into curtains. After the manufacturing he has only an unsecured claim against B. On the other hand, according to Danish law, B should settle with A when the cloth is used in the manufacturing process. Therefore, it is not possible for A to have a right which reaches B's customers. In other words, the claim against E belongs to B and can be executed against by his creditor, C.

(c) A cannot get a better right in respect of the claims arising from the sub-sales through the use of a reservation of title clause. A might have some security for his claim if it has not been paid. B could assign the claims which arise from the sub-sale to A as payment of A's claim against B or assign them as security for A's claim. This approach will not fully protect A against a loss because there is a lack of security from the point at which the cloth is used for manufacturing to the point when the curtains are sold, and thus a claim has arisen. If there is a continuing relationship between the supplier and manufacturer, a credit consignment agreement may improve the position of the supplier. Under such an agreement B should settle with A when the cloth is used in the manufacturing. It might also be agreed, at the same time, that B could settle by assigning the claims against his customers to A as payment of A's claim or as security for it. In order to protect A's right against B's creditors, the *debitor cessus* of each claim must be notified that the claim has been assigned to A.

In an arrangement like this it is important to note two facts. It is important that B settles with A when the cloth is used for manufacturing; if not, the court might rule that A has no right to the cloth remaining with B. It is also important that each settlement is of a sufficient value. If A had an unsecured claim which was paid or secured by assignment of a claim, the assignment might be invalidated if B is declared bankrupt.

It is probably very rare for a model like this to be used.

(d) The answers to parts (b) and (c) would not change if B was declared bankrupt.

SWEDEN

(a) Since a products and proceeds clause has been stipulated, A obviously has permitted B to manufacture the cloth before A has been paid. The reservation of title is invalid (see cases 4–7), and the curtains sold belonged to B. Hence, the monies paid by D have not been received on behalf of A to be held in trust under the Entrusted Money Act (*lagen om redovisningsmedel*, 1944). The monies can be subjected to execution for C's claim, even if they have been held separately.

(b) Since the goods sold belonged to B, B is the owner of the claim against E. His creditors may execute against the claim. Alternatively, they may prefer to execute against the curtains that E certainly has bought, but has neither taken into his possession nor registered pursuant to the Bills of Sales Act (a *constitutum possessorium* will not suffice). If the creditors of A prefer to execute against the curtains, with the consequence that these are not delivered, E is not obliged to pay B,[36] and B's creditors will not enjoy a better right to payment from E than B.[37]

(c) Should B manufacture the cloth on A's behalf, and at A's risk (i.e. receiving compensation for the costs and with a right to return the curtains to A should B not find a buyer), then B is acting as a commission (undisclosed) agent. In such circumstances, the principal has a right to separate claims against the agent's customers, such as E, pursuant to section 57 of the Commission Agency Act (see case 6). Furthermore, the monies will be received on behalf of the principal, and, if the monies without delay have been held separately, the principal will be able to separate the money pursuant to the Entrusted Money Act. Manufacture on behalf of someone else is uncommon, since producers of the raw

---

[36] S. 41 of the Sale of Goods Act.   [37] S. 27 of the Promissory Notes Act.

materials or semi-manufactured products usually do not wish to bear the business risk. Such clauses exist, but the question would arise of whether they are a correct reflection of the agreement between the parties.[38]

(d) The answers are the same.

FINLAND

(a) The creditors of B can execute against the monies paid by D to B. This is partly due to the fact that the retention of title clause would be invalid against those creditors, because it appears that B was entitled to use the cloth in the manufacturing process, and to sell the products resulting therefrom, before B had paid the price to A. Because of this, the creditors of B are also entitled to the monies paid in respect of the goods by B's customers. Even if, however, the retention of title clause was, as such, binding as against B's creditors, they would be entitled to execute against the money paid by D to B, because retention of title does not, as such, grant the seller any right to purchase monies paid to the buyer's bank account.

(b) The bailiff could normally execute against a claim arising out of the sub-sale. The reason is the same as that mentioned above.

(c) A would enjoy a better right to the claims arising out of the sub-sales, if B had been acting on the basis of a commission agreement. In such a case, B would manufacture the cloth and sell the products on the account of A. Acting on the account of A would mean, primarily, that A, as the principal, would have to bear the commercial risk of the activity. This would require, above all, an entitlement on the part of B to return to A those products which he or she has not been able to sell, and to receive compensation for the costs of the manufacturing from A. If these requirements were fulfilled, A would be treated as the owner not only of the raw material and the products, but also of the claims and the monies paid by B's customers and kept separately from B's own monies. Arrangements of this type are, however, not commonly used.

---

[38] As to the possibilities of assignment, charge, pledge and enterprise charge, see case 6.

Another possibility would be, of course, to charge or assign the claims arising from the sub-sales. Such a course is, however, in many cases, too burdensome because the sub-purchasers must be informed of that kind of agreement.[39]

One last possibility would be the use of an enterprise charge, which would include within its ambit both the claims and the monies paid by the sub-purchaser. However, an enterprise charge can only extend to half the value of the movable property of the enterprise. Furthermore, it ranks below any charge or security assignment of claims.

(d) The rules in the event of the insolvency of B would be the same.

Comparative observations

Parts (a) and (b)

On the basis of a pure sale with a simple retention of title, all reports conclude that the money paid by D to B as well as B's claim against E are part of B's estate. The money paid and the claim can therefore be executed against on behalf of B's creditors. In the event of B's insolvency, they form part of his insolvency estate; A does not have any right in preference to B's insolvency creditors.

Part (c)

Germany is the only jurisdiction that has developed a comprehensive security right for A which survives the transformation of the raw material as well as the sub-sale of the new products. However, even the use of a combined products and proceeds clause cannot provide the seller with a watertight security right. This can be seen from the position in respect of the money already paid before execution or the commencement of insolvency proceedings. Greek law has followed the German example and – at least theoretically – allows the same type of security right. In Belgium and South Africa, it seems to be possible for the seller to take a charge over the claims against the sub-seller without having to comply with any formalities. Nevertheless, in practice, this does not

---

[39] As to the charge, security assignment and enterprise charge, see also Finnish report, case 6.

appear to be widely used. In Austria, the publicity requirement for security assignments may be met by a simple entry onto the books of the creditor. According to a predominant but not undisputed opinion, this is also feasible before the identity of the *debitor cessus* is even known. Through such a transaction, the parties in case 8 could extend reservation of title into the proceeds of sub-sale, although A has partly lost his title to B through the transformation of the cloth into curtains. This type of security assignment is widely practised.

In case 6, where the goods sold by B are still in their original state, French and Belgian law vest the claim arising out of the sub-sales in the seller if the contract contained a retention of title clause (real subrogation). In the present case, B does not sell the original goods but instead products made from them. As pointed out by the French report, this – at least according to the point of view of the *Cour de cassation* – puts an end to the possibility of real subrogation. The same is true for Belgian law.

In the remaining jurisdictions, the possibility for A to gain a right in the proceeds of sub-sale is undermined by the following rules, which have already been discussed in cases 5 and 6 and are hence only set out by way of summary. An assignment or charge is required to be accepted by the *debitor cessus* or formally notified to him (France, Italy, Finland, Scotland). This prerequisite cannot be met before the identity of the *debitor cessus* is at least known. Charges have to be registered, which again either means that it is not possible to charge future claims[40] (Dutch law), or renders the whole transaction impracticable (England, Ireland). The position of Spanish law does not yet seem to be finally settled as is demonstrated by the answers to part (c) and to case 6, part (b).

The possibility in Sweden and Finland to reserve a real right in the raw materials and the manufactured goods and in claims on third parties by agreeing that the manufacture and sale will be performed for A and at his risk, i.e. with an obligation to compensate B should B not obtain compensation from payments by a customer, does not seem to be commonly used, at least not outside groups of companies. By way of contrast, a consignor under a Danish credit consignment agreement need not carry the consignee's business risk; instead, the parties are

---

[40] That is, claims where the legal relationship out of which they will arise does not yet exist.

only obliged to settle each transaction immediately. Nevertheless, the requirement of immediate settlement seems to render credit consignment impractical in cases like the present.

Part (d)

In no jurisdiction is there a material distinction between an execution on behalf of an individual creditor and insolvency.

Case 9: Too many toasters

(All-monies/sums clause – effects of commingling on retention of title)

B is a wholesaler, dealing in electrical household items. He regularly buys large numbers of toasters and coffee machines from A, a manufacturer, and sells them to retailers. A and B have concluded a contract which serves as a framework agreement for all orders from B. This contract contains the following provision: 'Each delivery has to be paid for within thirty days. In any event, the seller (A) retains title to the goods until the customer (B) has paid all sums that are due to the seller (A) under this contract.' On 1 June, A delivers 500 toasters to B. They are stored on B's premises, together with 1,000 identical toasters previously delivered by A, of which only 500 have been paid for. B manages to sell 500 of the 1,500 toasters before he becomes bankrupt on 1 August. He has made no payments to A since 1 June. There are still 1,000 toasters on B's premises. It is impossible to discover to which delivery the toasters sold and the remaining toasters relate.

Questions

(a) Does A have any real right in the remaining toasters? Or any right to preferential payment out of the proceeds of sale? Do the toasters form part of the insolvency estate?

(b) Could A acquire a better right (for example, by adopting a differently worded clause or through the use of a different kind of retention of title clause)? What would be the exact prerequisites?

(c) Are clauses such as that described in the case, or under part (b), commonly used?

Discussions

GERMANY

(a) Under German law, an all-monies clause, such as the one used in the present case, is valid. This is another reflection of the liberal attitude of German law towards non-possessory security interests in general. After the buyer has paid for the goods to which the specific contract relates, retention of title is simply transformed into security ownership. A has, therefore, security ownership of the 1,000 toasters that remain on B's premises. The toasters form part of the insolvency estate, in the sense that the administrator is entitled to realise their value. A is, however, entitled to preferential payment out of the proceeds of such realisation.[1]

If contained in general conditions, all-monies clauses may be invalid pursuant to § 307 BGB.[2] Yet, there is a general presumption of invalidity only in contracts between consumers and businesses; in contracts between non-consumers, all-monies clauses of the type used in case 9 are generally considered valid.[3] The problem of the collateral's value exceeding that of the secured claim, which used to be given as a reason for invalidating all-monies clauses, is now avoided through the use of an implied waiver of the creditor's rights.[4]

(b) As stated under part (a), the wording of the clause used in this case will secure the seller to a sufficient extent.

(c) All-monies clauses are extremely common. Usually, the parties use a so-called *Kontokorrentvorbehalt*, by which the goods delivered under retention of title (often with a combined products and proceeds clause) secure all claims of the seller resulting from the business relationship with the buyer. Another kind of all-monies clause is the so-called *Konzernvorbehalt*. The term *Konzern* signifies a group of companies. Through this type of retention of title clause, the seller seeks not only to secure the claims against his immediate contract partner (company X), but also claims against other contract partners who are members of the same group

---

[1] As to the procedural rules, see *supra*, German report, case 7(d).
[2] § 307 BGB (prior to 1 Jan. 2002: § 9 AGBG) transposes article 3 n. 1 of the Directive 93/13/EEC of 5 Apr. 1993 on unfair contract terms in consumer contracts (O.J. No L 95/29 of 21 Apr. 1993) into German law.
[3] Cf. *Wolf/Horn/Lindacher*/Wolf § 9 AGBG nn. E 33 and E 36. Note that, in contrast to the above-mentioned directive, the German rules on unfair contract terms in general also apply to non-consumer contracts (§ 310 n. 1 BGB).
[4] See *infra*, German report, case 11(d).

of companies as X. This type of clause is now void, according to the new section 2 of § 455 BGB, introduced in 1999 together with the new Insolvency Code (InsO).[5]

AUSTRIA

(a) According to Austrian law, goods sold under a retention of title clause secure only the seller's claim arising from the contract of sale of those goods. Only to this extent does Austrian law accept a non-possessory security right. An agreement according to which ownership of the goods should pass to the buyer only if the other claims of the seller are discharged (*erweiterter Eigentumsvorbehalt*, an all-sums clause) is therefore ineffective under Austrian law. In so far as it purports to extend retention of title to other claims, the clause in the contract of A and B is therefore invalid.

It is not clear, however, how these rules apply to case 9. The author would analyse the situation in the following way. Of the 1,000 'old' toasters, 50 per cent did belong to A due to retention of title. As they are a homogeneous set of items, it does not matter whether or not it can be ascertained which particular toasters were paid for by B. The 500 toasters delivered on 1 June must be added to this, meaning that A owned 1,000, or two-thirds, of the total amount of toasters delivered to B (1,500). Of this set, 500 were sold by B. Of the toasters sold, some, all or none could have belonged to A. A could thus own any amount between 500 and 1,000 of the remaining toasters. The question is thus who should bear the risk arising from the fact that the ownership of the remaining toasters is indeterminate? Here the writer would argue that A must bear the risk. The extent of real rights must be definite (*Bestimmtheitsgrundsatz*, the principle of specificity). A's security rights can only exist, therefore, to the extent that they are clearly identifiable. A can therefore vindicate 500 toasters.

(b) A's problems arise as a result of a poorly drafted retention of title clause. They lie in the fact that it is not clear which toasters were sold, those which B had acquired ownership of through payment or those which remained the property of A. To remedy this problem, it would be necessary to find a mechanism that would have ensured that B would first sell the toasters for which he had paid, e.g. separate storage.

---

[5] See further Bülow, DB 1999, 2196.

(c) Such clauses are commonly used, although they do not have any legal effect.

GREECE

(a)–(c) If the ownership of the remaining 1,000 toasters cannot be ascertained, then A and B become co-owners of the goods. Their respective shares are determined by the value of the toasters belonging to each party at the time of commingling: *viz.* 33.3 per cent for B and 66.6 per cent for A (articles 1059, 1058 para. 1 A.K.). Only 33.3 per cent of the remaining toasters fall into the insolvency estate. This solution does not depend on any other clauses, just simple retention of title. All-sums clauses have not been discussed by Greek authors; they are not commonly used in Greece.

FRANCE

(a) The question is whether A will to be able to claim title to the 1,000 remaining toasters, or assert a claim to the proceeds of the sale of the 500 toasters. He will be competing with the insolvency administrator, who will want all that property to form part of the insolvency estate. The toasters are fungible goods, because they are identical. Until the reform to the law in 1994, the seller could only vindicate those goods which he could clearly establish remained unpaid for. In a decision of 5 October 1993, the Commercial Chamber of the *Cour de cassation* held that, in the context of successive sales between the seller and the buyer (as part of an exclusive distribution contract), should the buyer become insolvent without having paid all sums due to the seller, the return of the goods could not be allowed unless it was established that the supplies still in the hands of the buyer were those which had not been paid for.[6] The company's books did not provide enough evidence that the goods remaining in stock corresponded to the unpaid goods, and thus the supplier was unable to claim their return.

Since the 1994 reform, article 121 para. 3 IA 1985 (now: C. com, article L. 621-122, para. 3)[7] provides that the creditor can claim *rei vindicatio* of fungible assets, when assets of the same quality and nature as those he delivered to the debtor can be found on the buyer's premises. The seller

---

[6] Bull civ IV, No 316, D 1993, IR, 234.
[7] It should be noted that following consolidation in 2001 of various laws into a new renumbered Commercial Code, the IA 1985 has been transposed into C. com, articles L. 611-1 to L. 628-3. The substance, however, remains unchanged.

does not need to establish that these particular assets were the ones he delivered.[8] In sum, in so far as fungible goods are concerned, there is no need to establish that the goods remaining are exactly those goods which are still unpaid for. Two recent cases illustrate the operation of the new rules. Both concerned pharmaceutical products found in the stock of an insolvent company. They were classified as fungible goods as they appeared to be interchangeable in their type, nature, origins, packaging and trademarks. A *rei vindicatio* brought by the unpaid seller was upheld by the court, despite the fact that he was not the company's only supplier of pharmaceutical products. The other supplier had been paid and was not claiming the goods.[9] Another case, where the fungible character of the goods (again, medicines and pharmaceutical products) was not contested, rejected the argument of the defendant that rapid turnover meant it was unlikely that the present goods would actually be the ones unpaid for.[10] On this basis, A can claim *rei vindicatio* of the 1,000 unpaid-for toasters remaining on B's premises. If the 1,000 toasters could no longer be vindicated because they had been resold, A would have a preferential claim to the outstanding proceeds of such sub-sales (C. com, article L. 621-124: see cases 7 and 8). The fact that the sold toasters were only of the same species as, but not necessarily identical to, the unpaid-for ones does not prevent real subrogation into the proceeds.[11]

(b) Despite the preceding analysis, it should be noted that this type of retention of title clause, the 'all-monies clause', is unusual in France, and was, until 1994, inefficacious.[12] Now, so long as the supplied goods are fungible, title can be retained over those found on the buyer's premises. It must be noted, however, that there is to date no decision of the *Cour de cassation* confirming this position.

(c) Although there is no evidence, it is to be assumed that these clauses are fairly uncommon in France. When used, there remains the risk that the test of fungibility will fail.

---

[8] Pérochon, *Les Petites Affiches* 1994, No 110.
[9] Rouen, 4 Apr. 1996, RJDA 1996, No 1543; Paris, 26 June 1998, D affaires 1998, 1401, obs. A.L.
[10] Paris, 3 Apr. 1998, D affaires 1998, 845, obs. A.L.; RJDA 1998, No 1017; RTDC 1998, 709, obs. Bandrac and Crocq. See also Paris, 22 Jan. 1999, D affaires 1999, 340, obs. A.L.
[11] Com 14 Jan. 1997, D 1997, IR, 52.
[12] The *Cour de cassation* (*Chambre commerciale*) declared invalid a clause according to which identity between unpaid-for goods and goods still in possession of the buyer would be presumed (Com 9 January 1990, D 1991, 130, note Virassamy; Bull civ IV, No 8).

BELGIUM

(a) First of all, the effectiveness of a framework agreement covering all future purchases is questionable. Article 101 Bankruptcy Act is interpreted to mean that reservation of title must be established in a document relating to each sale. A framework agreement may however be useful in proving that the clause was accepted in the documents relating to the subsequent sales. Furthermore, reservation of title is only effective to secure the unpaid balance of a particular sale. It cannot be extended in order to provide a security interest for unpaid balances relating to other sales, or for other sums owed by the buyer to the seller. Finally, the rights of the unpaid seller will be lost when the goods have been mixed with goods of the same species. Most authors accept, however, that, when all the goods have been sold by the same person, the seller can vindicate those goods sold under reservation of title notwithstanding the mixing.[13]

(b) Article 101 Bankruptcy Act marks the boundaries of the security interests available to the seller. Any extension beyond those limits will be regarded as a fiduciary transfer for security reasons, which does not bind third parties.

(c) Clauses of this type are not commonly used.

PORTUGAL

(a) Under Portuguese law, it is possible to provide that reservation of title will subsist not only until the payment of the purchase price, but also until the occurrence of any other event (article 409° C.C.). It would, therefore, be possible to provide for reservation of title until the payment of all sums owed by the buyer to the seller. In this case, as B has not yet paid all the sums he owes to the seller, he would not acquire ownership of the toasters delivered to him. So A would be considered the owner of the 1,000 toasters in question. As the clause was stipulated in an act under private signature before the delivery of the goods, it is effective as against the insolvency administrator (article 155°, n° 4 CPEREF). Therefore, the toasters do not form part of the insolvency estate.

---

[13] Dirix, RW 1997–98, 481 (499–500) n. 31.

(b) No.

(c) In Portugal, reservation of title clauses such as the one described are not common.

SPAIN

(a) A may claim reservation of title in respect of 1,000 toasters. A can vindicate the 1,000 toasters on the basis of the all-sums clause. Such an all-sums clause might be set out as follows: 'The current framework contract binds both parties to the reservation of ownership clause in favour of the seller with regard to the goods sold, as well as to those which may be sold in the future and which are of the same make and model.' A may vindicate the toasters if B becomes bankrupt, preventing them from forming part of the insolvency estate. Thus, since the toasters would not form part of the insolvency estate, A does not have a preferential right of payment from the proceeds of sale.

(b) A cannot obtain a better right. Given these circumstances, it is in A's best interests to maintain a *rei vindicatio* against the toasters.

(c) Such clauses are frequently used in commercial practice.

ITALY

(a) A will have no real rights in the remaining toasters, nor will he obtain a preferential entitlement to the proceeds of their sale. The toasters will form part of the insolvency estate.

(b) and (c) The retention of title clause in question is seldom seen in Italy. In any case, on the facts of case 9, it will be ineffective, since it is contained in a framework agreement, rather than in each contract of sale concluded between A and B. Under the current interpretation of articles 1523 ff. c.c., concerning reservation of title in instalment sales, such clauses are effective only if they form part of each contract of sale between the same parties.[14] The framework agreement between A and B does not purport to be a sale. In Italy, A's acceptance of B's order will

---

[14] See Italian report, case 5.

constitute a sale. Hence, that is the agreement which should contain the relevant clause.

Assuming that the clause had been inserted in each sale, and that the formal requirements for its validity *vis-à-vis* B's creditors were satisfied,[15] it remains unlikely that such clause would provide effective protection of the seller's claim to the purchase price in circumstances such as those of the present case.

Under Italian law, an 'all-monies' contractual clause, purporting to retain title to all the goods that the vendor sells to the same purchaser through a number of discrete transactions, will probably be held to be oppressive and therefore void and of no effect. Article 1525 c.c. provides that, in instalment sales, the buyer's failure to pay a sum which is equal to or less than one-eighth of the entire contract price does not entitle the seller to terminate the contract. There is no doubt that article 1525 c.c., which bars an action by a seller to claim the goods sold whenever the outstanding debt is 10 per cent or less of the contract price, applies to sales under reservation of title. In case 9, it is certain that one-third of the goods that A sold to B have been paid for. Yet, according to the agreement between A and B, all the remaining goods are still to be owned by the seller, as a security for what the buyer owes him.[16] In this respect, the 'all-monies' clause seems to circumvent the mandatory provision of article 1525 c.c.; as such it may be held void under article 1344 c.c., which attacks fraudulent evasions of mandatory rules of law.

Finally, several judgments and some scholars hold that there cannot be a successful *rei vindicatio* of fungible goods unless the plaintiff asserting title to them proves that the goods claimed are the very goods he owns.[17] Although this argument has no direct bearing on the present case, given that the relevant contractual clause purports to reserve title

---

[15] See Italian report, case 5.

[16] Note that the current, expansive, interpretation of article 2744 c.c. (dealing on its face only with forfeiture clauses in pledges and *hypothecs!*), dating from the cases which established the invalidity of sales for security purposes (Cass. 3 Apr. 1989, n. 1611, Foro it., 1989, I, 1427, obs. Mariconda, Realmonte; Corr. giur., 1989, 522, obs. Mariconda; Giust. civ., 1989, I, 1569, obs. Canessa; Giur. it., 1990, I, 1, 104, obs. Pellegrini; Cass. 21 April 1989, n. 1907, Giust. civ., 1989, I, 1821, obs. Costanza; Foro it., 1990, I, 205, obs. Valcavi), holds that the transfer of ownership of movables (and immovables) for security purposes is void (on this issue, in a critical vein, see Bussani, *Il problema del patto commissorio* 203 ff.; Anelli, *L'alienazione in funzione di garanzia* 420 ff.). Hence it would be useless to try to construe the all-monies clause as an alienation for security purposes to the seller of the goods that the buyer has acquired.

[17] Italian report, case 1(b).

to all goods until B pays to A the outstanding sums owed, it demonstrates the hostility of most Italian judicial decisions, and of many scholars, towards the idea of using a reservation of title clause as a means of obtaining security over a changing mass of goods. This hostility is traditionally grounded in the following dogma, i.e. an argument that real rights have a determinate object, or that a *vindicatio* of movables requires their precise identification. However, it is fair to say that none of the objections to such wider use of the concept of retention of title rest purely on logical premises.[18] In the field of financial instruments law, for example, these dogmatic statements have been challenged successfully, to enhance the level of protection for investors.[19] There is little sign, however, that similar developments will take place in the commercial context, where reservation of title clauses such as that mentioned in the present case are still unknown in Italy.

THE NETHERLANDS

(a) In all probability, A would still be the owner of all the remaining toasters. None of the toasters would form part of B's insolvency estate.[20]

As to the validity of the 'all-sums' clause, retention of title may not be extended so as to serve as a security for all debts owed to the supplier. A retention of title for 'all sums owed *for whatever reason* to the seller' would be invalid.[21] It must serve in principle as a security for credit given for the purchase. However, the Code does not restrict retention of title to claims arising from simultaneous contracts of sale. Suppliers may agree on a retention of title clause not only for claims arising from the delivery of the goods sold at that time, but also for those arising from deliveries already made and from deliveries yet to be made.[22]

---

[18] Hence, in related subjects, such as revolving pledges, there are significant concessions to the idea that a real right can be created over changing assets by party autonomy: Gabrielli, *Rotatività della garanzia*, Digesto sez. civ., XVIII, 102; Cass. 27 Sep. 1999, n. 10685, Foro it., 2000, I, 528; Giust. civ., 2000, I, 1459, obs. Carozzi; Corr. giur., 2000, 1226, obs. Dabormida; Fallimento, 2000, 775, Finardi.

[19] Cass. 14 Oct. 1997, n. 10031, Foro it., 1998, I, 851, obs. Crisostomo and Macario; Giur. comm., 1998, II, 299, obs. Di Maio; Fallimento, 1998, 391; Dir. fall., 1998, II, 459. See now: *Regolamento recante norme di attuazione del decreto legislativo 24 febbraio 1998, n. 58 e del decreto legislativo 24 giugno 1998, n. 213, in materia di mercati*, arts. 46, 54 (adopted by the *Commissione nazionale per le società e la borsa*).

[20] It may be noted that the risk that the Dutch revenue services may attach third-party property found on the premises of the debtor, as discussed in case 3, does not exist with respect to stock-in-trade.

[21] Article 3:92(2) BW.   [22] *Ibid*.

Where, as in this case, a framework agreement exists between parties, on the basis of which several separate sales and deliveries are to be made, a retention of title clause can validly be extended to cover them all.

Stipulating an 'all-sums' clause of this kind provides the supplier with important advantages. First, retention of title normally ends when the goods are either processed (*specificatio*) or resold. An 'all-sums' clause, however, enables the supplier to invoke his or her retention of title clause to goods delivered *and* paid for, if the buyer uses goods for resale or manufacturing that have not been paid for. Secondly, as a procedural matter, the supplier is protected against the commingling (*confusio*) of paid-for and unpaid-for goods. If the retention of title clause only related to the purchase price owed from separate deliveries, he or she would often be hard pressed to show which of the goods delivered were not yet paid for and thus still his or her property, and which were paid for. Under Dutch law, the inability to do so would necessarily result in the buyer (*detentor*) becoming the owner of the goods by reason of *confusio*.[23]

(b) In so far as A seeks to secure claims arising from past and future deliveries under the framework agreement, a retention of title clause would provide effective security for the seller.

(c) The use of retention of title clauses extending to multiple deliveries is very common in practice. In fact, the draft provision of the Civil Code governing retention of title did not allow for this type of clause at all. The omission was heavily criticised by practising lawyers, who argued that, because of the difficulties that would be encountered by traders in showing exactly which delivery had not been paid for, traders would become very reluctant to continue extending credit on the same conditions or at the same price.[24] It was in the interest of the business community that the relevant clause was included in the final draft.

ENGLAND

(a) 'All-monies' clauses are effective in English law. Where the seller's goods are mingled with other fungible stock supplied by the seller and in the buyer's possession, it is as a practical matter very difficult for the seller to enforce his claim against an insolvency administrator or against a *receiver* acting for a secured creditor of the buyer. ('Show me the

---

[23] See generally, Reehuis, *Eigendomsvoorbehoud* 14.   [24] *Ibid.*, 13.

goods you supplied. Prove that they have not already been consumed.') In the case of the seller who supplies the same kind of goods regularly, the seller's difficulty in proving that the particular goods in the buyer's possession have not yet been paid for can be avoided by the expedient of an 'all-monies' clause. According to this clause, which is not treated as a registrable charge,[25] the seller retains title to *all* goods supplied until *all* outstanding bills have been paid. It would therefore not matter if the buyer has already consumed goods for which payment has not yet been made and is still in possession of goods for which the seller has already been paid. The seller can transfer the obligation to pay for the consumed goods to the unconsumed goods still in the buyer's possession. The Sale of Goods Act permits the seller to stipulate for the passing of property to take place on any event:[26] the payment of all sums owed to the seller can be just such an event.

To the extent that the seller exercises its rights under the all-monies clause and recovers in full the amounts owed, leaving a surplus, then it is likely that the buyer, or the buyer's insolvency administrator (*liquidator* or *trustee-in-bankruptcy*), would have a restitutionary claim for the balance.[27] In the case of a seller who repossesses and resells the goods without terminating the contract (surely a very rare case indeed), an implied term of the contract of sale would oblige that seller to account to the buyer for any surplus over the amount owed.[28]

An all-monies clause adds nothing to the discussion in case 8 above on the seller's rights in respect of the money proceeds of goods sold on by the buyer.

(b) The all-monies clause is effective in respect of the goods covered. The seller's rights in respect of money proceeds, in the light of specially drafted clauses, is dealt with in the same way as the seller's rights under any other type of extended reservation of title clause.

(c) All-monies clauses are commonly used.

IRELAND

(a) 'All-monies' retention of title clauses are used in Ireland to get around the particular factual difficulties highlighted in this problem – in other

---

[25] *Armour v Thyssen Edelstahlwerke AG* [1991] 2 AC 339 (Scotland). [26] Ss. 17–19.
[27] *Clough Mill Ltd v Martin* [1985] 1 WLR 111 (Robert Goff LJ). [28] *Ibid.*

words, so as to overcome identification difficulties. With an 'all-monies' clause a supplier retains title not only until the goods which form the subject matter of the particular contract of sale have been paid for but until all indebtedness arising between seller and buyer has been discharged. All-monies clauses have been upheld both in Ireland and in the United Kingdom.

Nevertheless, there is a degree of ambiguity in the case law. In many cases the expression 'all sums due' is used and it is not clear whether this refers only to indebtedness arising under the contract of sale or, alternatively, encompasses extraneous indebtedness. An example of such ambiguity occurred in *Frigoscandia (Contracting) Ltd v Continental Irish Meat Ltd*,[29] where the relevant clause provided: 'Until all sums due to the seller have been fully paid to it, the plant, machinery and materials supplied by the seller herein shall remain the seller's personal property . . .' The provision was held to be effective, with the judge saying:[30]

A difficulty which arises with regard to clauses of this nature is that they are included in the contracts to secure the payment to the vendor of the price of the goods and therefore it may be said . . . that the goods once delivered, are intended to be held by the purchaser as security for such payment and that the transaction is in the category of a mortgage in that the vendor, although retaining ownership or an interest in the goods, cannot take possession of them provided that the specified instalments are paid, and that this leads to the conclusion that such a clause must be treated as creating a mortgage or a charge over the goods. In my opinion such a conclusion can have no general application to these clauses and each case must depend on its own facts. The parties to a contract can agree to any terms they wish and, amongst others, they can agree that the property in the goods shall not pass to the purchaser until all the instalments of the purchase price have been paid.

In other Irish cases what is unmistakably an 'all-monies' retention of title clause has been judicially validated. A leading case is *Re Interview Ltd*,[31] where an Irish firm agreed to import electrical goods from a German company subject to a clause which stated: 'The product supplied shall . . . remain the property of the supplier until all debts owing to the supplier or to be created in the future and arising from the business connection with the purchaser have been paid in full.' The clause was upheld. It should be noted that while the contract was explicitly stated to be governed by German law there was no suggestion that Irish law on the point was any different. While the issues have not been dealt with at

---

[29] [1982] ILRM 396. [30] *Ibid.*, at 398. [31] [1975] IR 382.

any length in the Irish case law, there is statutory support for 'all-monies' clauses in the Sale of Goods Act. Section 19(1) of the Act provides that a seller may reserve ownership in the goods supplied until the conditions specified in the contract of sale as to the time of passing of ownership are fulfilled. Section 17 states that parties to a contract are free to agree when ownership of the goods supplied is to pass and consequently can agree that it will not pass until the buyer pays the seller all sums due. It should perhaps be noted that similar arguments based on equivalent UK wording found favour with the House of Lords in *Armour v Thyssen Edelstahlwerke AG*.[32]

In this particular example, if the 'all-monies' clause is effective, A will acquire real rights in the remaining toasters and the toasters will not form part of the insolvency estate. There is however some ambiguity about the facts of the example. The 'all-monies' clause forms part of a general framework agreement but it is not expressly stated whether each delivery is the subject of a separate contract of sale and whether the retention of title clause has been incorporated into these individual contracts. If it has not been incorporated and there are separate contracts of sale, then title to the goods supplied thereunder will, *prima facie*, pass on delivery.

(b) Further to the answer to the previous question, A could get a 'better right' by endeavouring to ensure that the 'all-monies' clause is incorporated in each separate contract of sale.

(c) 'All-monies' clauses are used in Ireland quite commonly to get around identification difficulties that spring from the use of 'simple' clauses. Take the situation where generic goods are supplied subject to a simple retention of title clause and there have been many different deliveries – all subject to a separate contract containing the same simple clause. Some consignments have been paid for but others have not. If the buyer becomes bankrupt with some of the goods supplied still in its possession it may be difficult, if not impossible, for the seller to link these goods with a particular unpaid invoice. If, however, 'all-monies' clauses have been used the seller can say to the buyer: 'The goods remaining are mine and I will take them back. You have acquired title to none of the goods because all of the claims have not been paid.'

---

[32] [1991] 2 AC 339.

SCOTLAND

(a) Retention of title for all claims owed by the buyer to the seller is lawful. It is based on the fact that ownership can pass only if both parties so consent. If the agreement is that ownership will not pass before all claims have been paid, it follows that, until all claims have been paid, the requirements for the passing of ownership have not been met. This view of matters was, indeed, a matter of some controversy at one time, but is now settled.[33] In the present case, therefore, A is owner of all the toasters that are in B's possession.

Since the toasters belong to A, they do not form part of the insolvency estate of B. B's contractual right to the toasters, however, does form part of the insolvency estate. But that is a point of limited importance.

(b) A could not get a better right than retained ownership.

(c) Such clauses are commonly used in practice.

SOUTH AFRICA

(a) So-called floor plans (master or framework agreements) are known to South African commercial practice in the motor industry. In the case of the sale of other stock (for example, the toasters and coffee machines of the present case), there would have to be a clear reference to or incorporation of the framework agreement in each sale before it would be acceptable to South African courts. If this was done, the manufacturer would retain ownership of each shipment of toasters until the purchase price for the batch was paid. The difficulty here is that the new batch of toasters has been mixed with 1,000 other toasters, some of which have been paid for. This means that at least some of the remaining toasters have become the property of B. The fact that these toasters have been mixed with the 500 (identical) new toasters will have resulted in B having acquired ownership (of the 500 and perhaps of all the remaining toasters) by commingling. There is no evidence in South African law that a reservation of title would exclude the effects of commingling. A has, therefore, neither a real nor a preferential right to the remaining toasters. The toasters form part of B's insolvency estate.

---

[33] *Armour v Thyssen Edelstahlwerke AG* 1990 SLT 981 ([1991] 2 AC 339 (Scotland)). For the controversy see Gretton and Reid at 1985 SLT (News) 329 and at 1989 SLT (News) 185.

(b) A could try to obtain a stronger legal position by including a clause in the framework agreement excluding the consequences of commingling. This has, however, not been tested by the courts.

(c) Not in the context of toasters and such like items.

DENMARK

(a) When the buyer has a right to resell the goods a retention of title clause is not valid unless the buyer has to settle with the seller when the goods have been resold. The clause in this case does not fulfil this condition. (For a fuller discussion, see case 4.) Therefore, A has no right to the remaining toasters.

Even if a valid retention of title clause was stipulated in a credit consignment contract, A could claim no right to the toasters. In Danish law it is a general rule that a person who claims a right to an asset must be able to identify the specific asset on the basis of the contract. Because the toasters which have not been paid for are stored together with toasters which have been paid for it is impossible to point out the precise toasters to which A would assert a right. The toasters will form part of the insolvency estate and A cannot claim any right to the toasters nor claim preferential payment from the proceeds of their sale.

(b) If the contract contained a valid retention of title clause, the contract should also state that B had to keep those toasters in which A could claim a right separated from those toasters already paid for. If A checked that B acted according to that contract, A could claim a right to the toasters remaining on B's premises which had not been paid for. It is important that the process of separation is conducted in such a way that no doubt arises as to which toasters A can claim a right to.

(c) It is probable that almost all credit consignment agreements contain a clause which states that the goods delivered under the contract shall be stored separately from other assets of the same or similar sort.

SWEDEN

(a) The retention of title clause is void, because the buyer has been entitled to dispose of the goods prior to full payment (see case 4). Below, this restriction is disregarded and attention is devoted to the other problems, especially commingling.

Pursuant to sales law, more precisely the Hire Purchase Act (*lagen om avbetalningsköp*) amended in 1953 and its successors, a seller may not in relation to the buyer make a valid reservation of title to goods X for the payment of goods Y under some other contract of sale.[34] Since such reservation is already void as between the parties, it cannot have any effect against the creditors of the buyer. In the instant case, it appears that there are two different sale agreements, although they are governed by the same framework agreement, and therefore the reservation of title by A to the toasters delivered on 1 June is valid only in respect of the toasters delivered on that day, for the claim arising from that purchase. Leaving aside the hurdle presented by the hire-purchase restrictions, a clause giving A security in goods X for claims arising from contract Y would sit uneasily with the denial of non-possessory and unregistered securities in movables in Swedish law.[35]

Thus, A may vindicate the 500 toasters delivered on 1 June to satisfy only those claims relating to those toasters. However, these toasters cannot be identified in the remaining stock of 1,000 toasters. If the sold toasters are apportioned in proportion to the quantity of toasters owned by A and B, B remains the owner of 250 toasters. It is a general principle of, or at least a point of departure in, property law that real rights can exist only in specified objects[36] and that it must be possible to identify these objects, especially in relation to objects belonging to the debtor,[37] when it comes to insolvency and execution. Hence, in principle, there could be no right of separation for the seller, A, because of both the hire-purchase legislation and the general requirement of identification in property law. However, one might argue that an exception should be made when commingling has taken place in respect of fungible goods (i.e. goods of the same character), when creditors would not be harmed irrespective of whether object X or object Y was separated, provided that the commingled quantity has never dropped below the quantity claimed

---

[34] The seller is entitled to reserve a right of rescission only for the payment of purchase monies for the actual goods (and for their repair).

[35] A security (X) perfected within three months prior to the application to commence insolvency proceedings, but with delay in relation to the extension of the credit (for Y), would also be avoidable pursuant to chapter 4 s. 12 of the Bankruptcy Act.

[36] NJA 1910, 216.

[37] If one seller's goods were commingled with goods belonging to another seller, they would become co-owners of the whole and would have a right of separation in proportion to their contributions, NJA 1959, 590 and Entrusted Money Act.

for in separation in insolvency (the lowest balance principle). That question has arisen in a couple of cases. In NJA 1976, 251, containers had been delivered under different hire-purchase contracts each with reservations of title (although not linked to the other contracts). Some instalments had been paid. Protection from execution against the containers still in place was denied, because the parties had not separated the different sales in their payments for delivery, with the effect that the balance for each contract could not be established,[38] and because the remaining containers were not referable to specific contracts. In a subsequent case, NJA 1994, 506, A had deposited corn (possibly for grinding and return of flour) with a miller, who commingled the corn with corn of the same kind owned by himself. It was assumed that the miller had not been entitled to let the total quantity of corn fall below the quantity A had deposited and that the total quantity had not, in fact, fallen below that quantity. Therefore, it was held that A was co-owner, with a right to separate the quantity[39] that he had deposited. The latter case demonstrates that the requirement of identification is subject to (wide) exemptions and that the 'principle of lowest balance' debated in the literature, at least in some situations, applies to fungible goods.[40] This principle, however, has not so far been applied to commingled money.[41]

(b) It follows from the answer to part (a) that the seller must prescribe that all deliveries fall under the same purchase agreement and that the relevant goods can be identified in the buyer's possession. However, it seems difficult to treat all deliveries as made under one agreement of sale, if both parties are not prepared prospectively to agree on the total quantity and the total price.

(c) All-monies clauses appear sporadically, but they are probably not common.

---

[38] Pursuant to other cases (e.g. NJA 1958, 117), the creditor would, in this situation, be entitled to decide from which debts the deductions should be made.
[39] If the total quantity decreased because of a cause extraneous to withdrawals by B (e.g., if it had been eaten by rats in circumstances that B could not have prevented) and not only by withdrawals by the miller B, it is open to question whether A would have been entitled to separate all the deposited quantity.
[40] See Håstad, *Sakrätt rörande lös egendom* 173 ff. and 333 ff.
[41] In NJA 1995, 367 II the Supreme Court found instead that minor commingling (a few deposits and withdrawals) could be overlooked. In NJA 1998, 275 the principle simply was not applied to money, without any discussion.

FINLAND

(a) The retention of title clause would be invalid as against the creditors of the buyer, because the buyer was entitled to resell the toasters before they were paid for. Two other features of the case would also result in the invalidity of the clause.[42] First, retention of title may be used as a security for the purchase price of the transaction to which it relates and other claims of the seller closely connected to that particular sale. A clause binding several independent sales together, however, in the manner described in this case, is not valid against the creditors of the buyer.[43] Secondly, a retention of title clause is valid against the creditors of the buyer only if the unpaid items can be individualised and reliably distinguished from items belonging to the buyer.[44] This requirement applies also to circumstances where all the items in question are delivered by the same seller. If the unpaid-for toasters cannot reliably be distinguished from the toasters that have been paid for, then the seller, A, has no real right in the remaining toasters. The toasters belong to the insolvency estate and the seller, A, has no right to preferential payment out of the proceeds of their realisation.

(b) There does not seem to be any practicable means of general application by which A could obtain a better right.

(c) This kind of retention of title clause is not commonly used. This is because, first, the clause does not protect the seller against the other creditors of the buyer. Secondly, this kind of a clause is not valid even *inter partes* when used in either an instalment sales contract or a consumer credit sales contract.

Comparative observations

Part (a)

(i) Validity of all-sums clauses

All-sums clauses are principally regarded as valid in Germany, Spain, Portugal, England, Scotland and Ireland. The legal basis, however, differs.

---

[42] See Finnish report, case 4.
[43] In instalment sales, and in all consumer credit sales, this type of clause is invalid also as between the parties. See further e.g. Tuomisto, *Omistuksenpidätys ja leasing* 376 ff.
[44] See e.g. ibid., 316.

In Germany, retention of title is transformed into security ownership the moment at which the particular goods are paid for. In other words, these goods are transformed into collateral under a security agreement. In B's insolvency, A consequently has a right to preferential payment out of the collateral's realisation instead of a right to vindicate the goods. Pursuant to Portuguese, English, Scots and Irish law, on the other hand, the seller's rights in respect of already paid for goods under an all-sums clause do not differ from his rights under simple reservation of title. The parties are simply at liberty to choose the event upon which ownership will pass to the buyer. In *Armour v Thyssen*, the House of Lords explicitly rejected the position of the Scottish Court of Session which had considered the extension of title retention to goods already paid for as a charge (*hypothec*) over goods owned by the buyer.

Under English, Irish and Scots law, the seller can after termination of the contract (e.g. on the basis of breach of contract) vindicate all goods delivered, no matter to what extent they have already been paid for. In case 9, the number of unpaid-for items equals the number of items which are found on B's premises when he becomes bankrupt. But even if the buyer under an all-sums clause had for instance paid 80 per cent of the total purchase price, the seller could still after termination of the contract vindicate 100 per cent of the goods delivered, subject to a claim in unjust enrichment. Portuguese law, on the other hand, would consider this an abuse of the seller's rights and grant vindication only in so far as there are still goods that have not yet been paid for.

(ii) Invalidity of all-sums clauses

The majority of jurisdictions under consideration, however, regard all-sums clauses as invalid. Unlike the House of Lords in *Armour v Thyssen*, courts and legal doctrine analyse this kind of retention of title as granting the seller a non-possessory security right. The buyer has received ownership through payment, consequently the seller's right can no longer exist as title retention but merely as a non-possessory security right, which is either invalid in principle or can at least not be enforced as against third parties. This view is spelled out explicitly in Austria, the Netherlands[45] and Belgium, yet it would also meet with approval in France, South Africa and the Nordic countries.

---

[45] With the exception of framework contracts covering multiple deliveries.

(iii) All-sums clauses and commingling

All-sums clauses are not only designed to provide the seller with additional collateral and hence with additional security, they also aim to avoid the kind of practical and probative difficulties that are illustrated by case 9. The 500 toasters that have been delivered on 1 June have been commingled with toasters of the same kind and from the same supplier. In such a case, an all-sums clause has the additional function that the parties can derogate from the legal effects of commingling. If such clauses are held invalid, we are faced in case 9 with a problem: namely, that 1,000 toasters remain unpaid for and 1,000 toasters of the same kind and from the same supplier are found in B's storage rooms, yet no-one knows whether B has resold the paid-for or the unpaid-for toasters. As the Austrian report points out, the question can be regarded as one of risk allocation: who is to bear the risk that the goods are not identifiable?

As to this question, the jurisdictions take different approaches. Austrian, South African, Swedish[46] and Finnish law on the one hand allocate the risk to the seller. If A does not avoid commingling by putting the buyer under an obligation to store the goods separately, B will acquire ownership in all the goods irrespective of payment. Commingling, in other words, ends all rights of the seller under retention of title.

French law, on the other hand, lets the buyer – or rather his creditors – bear this risk. According to the 1994 amendment of article 121 Insolvency Act 1985 (now C. com, article L. 621-122), the seller can vindicate his unpaid-for goods so long as he finds either these or goods of the same kind and nature in the hands of the buyer irrespective of whether they might already have been paid for or might even have been supplied by another seller. This may rather be seen as more of a statutory exemption to the rules on commingling, rather than as a statutory extension of the retention of title into goods already paid for.

A midway solution is adopted by Dutch, Belgian and Greek law. Since practical problems are most likely to occur with contracts covering multiple deliveries of goods of the same kind, Dutch law, pragmatic as it generally is, simply makes a statutory exception from the general invalidity of all-sums clauses for such kinds of transactions. In Belgium, the predominant opinion advocates the same solution: if all goods are

---

[46] Although recent Swedish cases demonstrate that co-ownership may arise when the total quantity has never been lower than the quantity deposited by A and, further, that a commingling of minor importance may be disregarded.

supplied by one seller, an amount of goods equal to the unpaid-for ones may be vindicated notwithstanding the commingling.

(iv) Invalidity of simple retention of title

The strictest view is taken by Danish, Swedish and Finnish law. B, as a retailer, will – at least implicitly – be entitled to resell the goods within the thirty days of credit that has been granted to him. As has already been pointed out in the context of case 4, such an entitlement renders the retention of title void from the beginning. Hence, the question of whether an extension of title retention is valid does not arise.

Part (b)

The alternative methods for achieving the same result as an all-monies clause are limited in scope. The Austrian report points out that a simple retention of title coupled with an obligation for the buyer to store the goods separately might help, but there are no remedies in the way of real rights available to the seller if the buyer does not comply. In Denmark, parties may use a credit consignment contract which should again be supplemented by an obligation to keep the goods separate. Swedish and Finnish law would only accept continuing rights of A in the goods if A carried the economic risk of the sub-sales concluded by B.

Part (c)

Evidently, this question was thought to be answerable only by those contributors who could set out a way for sellers to reserve some sort of real right in the already paid-for and/or commingled goods. However, part (c) has been answered positively by the contributors from Austria and Sweden who denied the validity of all-sums clauses in their systems. On the other hand, the Greek and Portuguese contributors point out that all-sums clauses are not commonly used, although they are said to be clearly valid. These answers interestingly shed light on the well-known discrepancy between theory and practice.

Case 10: Bank loan on the basis of a car fleet

(Security ownership – sale and lease-back – other non-possessory security rights in individualised movables)

B owns a car fleet, which he wants to use as collateral for a bank loan without the need to transfer direct possession of the cars to the bank. B does not deal in cars and will not sell the cars in the fleet in the ordinary course of trade. He approaches A, a financial institution. A would like to have a real right in the cars in the event of B's insolvency. Moreover, A does not wish an unsecured creditor to be able to obtain priority over its own rights in situations other than insolvency.

Questions

(a) How could this be done? How is it usually done? Please state the precise prerequisites.
(b) Can such a security be achieved through a sale and lease-back arrangement? Is that common?
(c) Is your answer confined to cars, or does it apply to different kinds of collateral?
(d) The parties have adopted your proposals, either to create a security right in the cars, or to provide for sale and lease-back. A becomes bankrupt (though that may be unusual in practice). What would B's position be?

Discussions

GERMANY

(a) For cases such as the present (and the following case 11), German law has developed *praeter legem* (security transfer of ownership), which has already been mentioned in the context of products¹ and all-money clauses.² Here, the foundations will be more fully explained.³

§ 930 BGB allows the parties to transfer ownership without actual delivery. A contract by which the transferor agrees to possess the collateral on behalf of the transferee (*constitutum possessorium*, § 868 BGB)⁴ is substituted for actual delivery. It is contained in the so-called *Sicherungsvertrag* (security agreement) which also represents the contractual basis of the transfer.⁵ The contract will usually also specify the conditions under which the transferee (A) may realise the security, by taking possession of the collateral and selling it. In general, the statutory rules on the realisation of a pledge do not apply.⁶ Security transfer of ownership and the underlying agreement contain elements of a fiduciary relationship.⁷ The transfer gives the creditor more rights than are justified for the purpose of obtaining security in case of non-payment. The rights which extend beyond what is necessary for this purpose are held by the creditor in a fiduciary capacity. One consequence is that the creditor, although formally the owner, can only take possession of the collateral if the debtor is in default of payment. If, however, the debtor fails to pay, the security owner is entitled to take possession of and to sell the collateral to realise its value.⁸ Usually, the amount of the debt will be higher than the value of the collateral. If, however, it turns out that the value of the collateral taken by the creditor exceeds the outstanding debt, the creditor is obliged to return to the debtor those goods which are not needed to cover the debt. A creditor who fails to do so becomes liable for damages.⁹

If the parties have concluded an agreement for security transfer of ownership and if, subsequently, a creditor of B executes against the cars, A can bring an action in court resisting the execution (§ 771 ZPO).¹⁰ Upon such an action, the execution will be stopped and set aside. In the event

---

[1] *Supra*, German report, case 7(c). [2] *Supra*, German report, case 9.
[3] See generally Baur/Stürner, *Sachenrecht* § 57; Reinicke/Tiedtke, *Kreditsicherung* nn. 447 ff.
[4] See *supra*, German report, case 3(c) and Van Vliet, *Transfer of Movables* 53 ff.
[5] This document, however, is not the same as the contract of loan.
[6] Bülow, *Recht der Kreditsicherheiten* n. 1038.
[7] Reinicke/Tiedtke, *Kreditsicherung* nn. 449 f.; Bülow, *Recht der Kreditsicherheiten* n. 932; see further Gernhuber, JuS 1988, 355.
[8] Bülow, *Recht der Kreditsicherheiten* n. 1048. [9] *Ibid.*, n. 1049.
[10] See BGH 4 Feb. 1954, BGHZ 12, 232 (234); BGH 28 Feb. 1978, BGHZ 72, 141 (143); BGH 13 Feb. 1981, BGHZ 80, 296 (299); BGH 25 Feb. 1987, WM 1987, 539 (541); BGH 12 May 1992, BGHZ 118, 201 (207); Jauernig, *Zwangsvollstreckungs- und Insolvenzrecht* § 13 IV 1 a; Stein/Jonas/Münzberg § 771 ZPO n. 26; Bülow, *Recht der Kreditsicherheiten* n. 1085. Some authors contend, however, that the security owner can only exercise the rights of a

of B's insolvency, A has the same rights as a pledgee, which means that he can claim preferential payment out of the realisation of the collateral (§§ 50 s. 1, 51 n. 1, 166 ff. InsO[11]). In both situations, A thus takes priority over B's general creditors.

It is necessary to consider some of the general principles of property law that might be invoked against the validity of the security transfer of ownership:

(i) Principle of publicity

The only security right in movable property that the BGB explicitly provides for is the possessory pledge (§§ 1204 ff. BGB). Yet, prior to the introduction of the BGB, the *Reichsgericht* had already accepted as valid the transfer of ownership for the sole purpose of creating a security right for the transferor. In a decision of 2 June 1890,[12] the *Reichsgericht* spoke of security transfer of ownership as being an established institution according to 'predominant opinion and long-standing jurisdiction'. This did not change on the entering into force of the BGB[13] although, in essence, security transfer of ownership amounts to a non-possessory pledge, and thus circumvents § 1205 BGB, which requires, for the creation of a pledge in movables, the pledgee to take possession of the collateral. From the *travaux préparatoires* it is apparent that §§ 1205 ff. BGB were not intended to put an end to previously established practice.[14] The reason why the courts and the legislature accepted the *praeter legem* lies in the acute economic need for secured credit and hence, for the use of movables as collateral, in circumstances where it would not be practicable for them to be handed over to the creditor.[15] Today, the validity of security ownership and security assignment is completely without doubt and is sometimes even referred to as customary law (*Gewohnheitsrecht*).[16]

---

pledgee (§ 805 ZPO), which means he cannot resist the execution, but only claim preferential payment out of the proceeds, see: *Baumbach/Lauterbach/Hartmann* § 771 ZPO n. 26; *Münchener Kommentar/Schmidt* § 771 ZPO n. 29. As to § 771 ZPO in general, see *supra*, German report, case 2.

[11] This is now expressly stated in § 51 n. 1 InsO. Under the old Insolvency Code (KO), this was judge-made law: see RG 9 Apr. 1929, RGZ 124, 73 (75); BGH 24 Oct. 1979, ZIP 1980, 40 (42). As to the procedure, see also *supra*, German report, case 7(d).

[12] RG 2 June 1890, RGZ 26, 180. [13] RG 8 Nov. 1904, RGZ 59, 146.

[14] Cf. Gaul, AcP 168 (1968) 351 (357 ff. with further references).

[15] *Ibid.* (359 with further references).

[16] Baur/Stürner, *Sachenrecht* § 57 n. 1; Serick, *Eigentumsvorbehalt und Sicherungsübertragung* 25–26.

However, the Commission for the Reform of Insolvency Law suggested in its first report that the rights of creditors with non-possessory security rights such as security ownership should be curtailed.[17] Some scholars have also expressed concerns about the fact that the security transfer is in no way apparent to other creditors.[18] Yet, these proposals and criticisms have led only to marginal alterations[19] and it seems unlikely that any significant changes will be made in the near future.

(ii) Prohibition of forfeiture clauses (*pactum commissorium*)

According to the rules governing the pledge of movables, the parties cannot agree prior to the debtor's default that the secured creditor should obtain unrestricted ownership of the movable (see § 1229 BGB). This rule is not regarded as a statutory prohibition of security ownership, which *nota bene* restricts the rights of secured parties through its fiduciary character. However, clauses which derogate from the fiduciary constraints imposed and provide that the secured creditor should obtain unrestricted ownership of the collateral are widely regarded as invalid, at least if they are contained in the general conditions of the seller.[20]

(iii) Unconscionability

Until recently, the courts have frequently considered security ownership (especially of stock-in-trade), or global security assignments, as invalid if the security agreement did not contain a properly framed waiver when the realisable value of the collateral exceeded the outstanding debt, or the credit line, to a considerable extent.[21] The decisions were based

---

[17] Bundesministerium der Justiz, *Erster Bericht der Kommission für Insolvenzrecht* 298. These suggestions were heavily criticised: see Serick, *Eigentumsvorbehalt und Sicherungsübertragung: Band IV*, 846 ff.; Serick, BB 1990, 861 ff.; Dorndorf/Frank, ZIP 1985, 65 (79).

[18] Drobnig, *Gutachten F zum 51. Deutschen Juristentag* F 35; see also Baur/Stürner, *Sachenrecht* § 57 n. 35.

[19] Under the old Insolvency Code (*Konkursordnung*), security owners were able to realise their rights outside of the insolvency proceedings. Now, such creditors must at least wait until the report meeting. Also, under the new law, secured creditors must bear the costs of assessing and realising their rights: see *supra*, German report, case 6(b).

[20] Cf. Reinicke/Tiedtke, *Kreditsicherung* nn. 530 ff. Others regard such clauses to be invalid by an analogous application of § 1229 BGB: see *Staudinger*/Wiegand, Anhang zu §§ 929–931 BGB n. 234.

[21] See further *infra*, German report, case 11(d); cf. from a German–Italian comparative perspective, also Greving, *Der Treuhandgedanke bei Sicherungsübertragungen im italienischen und deutschen Recht* 83 ff.

on § 307 BGB[22] and the principle that the court will not restrict the operation of an unconscionable clause to its valid extent (§ 306 BGB[23]). In 1997, this jurisdiction was changed fundamentally by a decision of the BGH.[24] Today, an appropriate waiver is implied into the security agreement.[25]

(b) Under a sale and lease-back agreement, A would have the rights of a full owner. In B's insolvency, A would be entitled to vindicate the cars (§ 47 InsO).[26] This right presupposes that the leasing contract has been terminated, in order to put an end to B's entitlement to possess the cars.[27] Prior to the commencement of insolvency proceedings, A would be entitled to terminate the contract if B defaulted in the payment of the leasing rates;[28] after the commencement, this right rests with the insolvency administrator.[29] If the cars are executed against on behalf of B's creditors, A can resist the execution (§ 771 ZPO).[30]

Although a sale and lease-back agreement would provide A with a better right in B's insolvency (a *rei vindicatio* instead of a right to preferential payment), security transfer of ownership is much more commonly used in circumstances where the provision of security is the sole purpose of the transaction.

(c) Security transfer of ownership can be used in respect of any corporeal movables. For special rules as to revolving stock-in-trade, see *infra*, case 11.

---

[22] § 307 BGB (prior to 1 Jan. 2002: § 9 AGBG) transposes article 3 n. 1 of the Directive 93/13/EEC of 5 Apr. 1993 on unfair contract terms in consumer contracts (O.J. No L 95/29 of 21 Apr. 1993) into German law.
[23] Prior to 1 Jan. 2002: § 6 AGBG.
[24] BGH (*Großer Zivilsenat*) 27 Nov. 1997, NJW 1998, 671 = BGHZ 137, 212.
[25] See *infra*, German report, case 11(d).
[26] Martinek, *Moderne Vertragstypen I* 215 f.; Leible, *Finanzierungsleasing und 'ar rendamiento financiero'* 195 with further references.
[27] BGH 5 Apr. 1978, WM 1978, 510; BGH 24 Nov. 1993, BB 1994, 239.
[28] If an application for the commencement of insolvency proceedings has already been made, the lessor can only terminate the contract if the lessee has not been in default of payment prior to this application (§ 112 n. 1 InsO).
[29] See § 103 InsO. Other than in the case of retention of title (see § 107 InsO and *supra*, German report, case 3), the administrator is not entitled to postpone his decision until after the report meeting: see von Westphalen, *Der Leasingvertrag* n. 1533.
[30] General opinion, cf. Leible, *Finanzierungsleasing und 'ar rendamiento financiero'* 193; Martinek, *Moderne Vertragstypen* 215; von Westphalen, *Der Leasingvertrag* n. 1451.

(d) If the parties have agreed upon a security transfer of ownership, B will still have a right to vindicate the cars if A becomes insolvent,[31] provided that B pays back the loan.[32] This is one of the consequences of the fiduciary nature of A's position.[33] Rather than being the full owner, he has only a security right.

AUSTRIA

(a) B's car fleet, which he already owns, cannot be used as collateral for a bank loan. Due to the publicity requirement, the cars would have to be handed over to A. This, however, is impracticable, because B would be unable to make use of them.

The only way for A to obtain a *ius ad rem* in the cars would be to grant B a loan, which would be used by B to purchase the cars. If the contract between a third-party seller and the buyer (B) contained a reservation of title clause, and A paid the seller the credit sum as payment for the cars, then the seller's claim arising from the contract of sale could be assigned to A. In such a case, it would be open to A and the seller to agree that title to the cars would pass to A, provided that B is instructed by the seller to hold the cars on behalf of A. This type of transaction is very common in Austria, because retention of title is the only security in respect of which the publicity requirement does not apply.

(b) A sale and lease-back arrangement is not a feasible alternative, because, in such a situation, it would be classified as being a credit transaction and the publicity requirement would thus apply.

Note, however, that there are no decisions of the OGH[34] where the Court lays down criteria as to the classification of sale and lease-back contracts. In a paper on this problem, Czermak[35] proposes a solution to

---

[31] RG 5 Nov. 1918, RGZ 94, 305 (307); Reinicke/Tiedtke, *Kreditsicherung* n. 588; Baur/Stürner, *Sachenrecht* § 57 n. 39; Serick, *Eigentumsvorbehalt und Sicherungsübertragung* III § 35 II 2 a; Bülow, *Recht der Kreditsicherheiten* n. 1067.
[32] If B does not pay, he can claim only the difference between the proceeds and the remaining debt: see Reinicke/Tiedtke, *Kreditsicherung* nn. 588 f.
[33] Bülow, *Recht der Kreditsicherheiten* n. 1067.
[34] There is one decision, however (22 Mar. 1988, 6 Ob 575/86; MietSlg 40.105), in which the OGH holds that the publicity requirement does not apply to sale and lease-back contracts. Given the fact that the Court was obviously unaware of Czermak's paper, it is doubtful whether the decision, which does not consider the classification problem, will be upheld if the OGH is asked to decide a similar case.
[35] ÖBA 1987, 232–249; cf. *Schwimann/Binder* § 1090 n. 60.

it. She distinguishes between two situations, depending on whether the total amount the lessee has to pay corresponds to the price paid for the cars plus the financing cost plus the net profit of the lessor (situation (a)) or not (situation (b)). In situation (a), she argues that the contract should be classified as a credit transaction if ownership of the goods reverts to the lessee at the end of the contract or if he has a right to buy at a price which does not reflect adequately the value of the goods at that time. In situation (b), she argues that the contract should be classified as a credit transaction if ownership of the goods reverts to the lessee at the end of the contract or if he has a right to buy them back from the lessor at all. If the lessor has the option of reselling the cars to the lessee if he wishes, Czermak does not classify the contract as a credit transaction.

(c) The answer is limited to objects that can be handed over *in corpore* to the creditor. For other objects, see case 11.

(d) As a consequence of what has been said under parts (a) and (b), this question cannot be answered.

GREECE

(a) The following possibilities might be considered by the parties.

> (i) The parties could stipulate a security transfer of ownership of the cars to A. Security ownership is not regulated by law. It has developed in practice to serve commercial needs. In view of the disadvantages of the possessory pledge, which, in order to be validly constituted, requires corporeal delivery of the movable by the owner, B would, under security ownership, be able to transfer ownership of the cars to A under a *constitutum possessorium* (articles 1034, 977 A.K.).
> The validity of security ownership has been disputed in Greek law.[36] As to the question whether security ownership circumvents article 1213 A.K., which prohibits the constitution of a pledge through a *constitutum possessorium*, the prevailing view[37] suggests that the

---

[36] See in general Georgiadis, EEmbD 1973, 301; Mazis, NoV 27, 311; Bosdas, ArchN 1975, 313; Spyridakis, Comments, NoV 24, 639 and NoV 33, 242; Vouzikas, EEN 18, 657.
[37] Ef of Aegean Sea 113/1974 Arm 28, 550; Ef of Athens 6395/1976 NoV 25, 406; Ef of Athens 236/1976 NoV 24, 638; Georgiadis, *Empragmato Dikaio II* 231; Balis, *Empragmaton Dikaion* para. 200; Kornilakis, *I katapisteutiki ekchorisi ton apaitiseon* 73. *Contra* Ef of Patras 76/1949 Them 61, 310; Ef of Patras 74/1950 Them 61, 995; K. Simitis, *I anamorphosis tou plasmatikou enechyrou* 44. See also Doris, in: *Empragmati Asphaleia* 114 ff.

principle of the freedom of contract supports the validity of security ownership. Greek scholars have also considered the problem of whether the securing of a claim is a valid cause for the transfer of ownership. According to the prevailing view[38] it is not, consequently security ownership of an immovable is invalid. However, according to this view,[39] security ownership of a movable should be considered as valid, because of its abstract character. A third opinion[40] suggests that the agreement creating an obligation to transfer ownership for security purposes should be considered a *iusta causa* of the transfer, therefore security transfer of ownership of a movable is valid. For the valid constitution of security ownership no form or publicity is required. However, the parties have the option to register the security transfer of ownership of the cars pursuant to article 10 of L. 2844/2000.

If B's creditors execute against the cars, the ownership of which has been transferred to A, A can resist the execution (article 936 KPolD). In B's insolvency A has the rights of a pledgee.[41]

(ii) If the cars were tour coaches, the parties could create a registrable charge over them according to article 11 of L. 711/1977. This charge secures any claims of any creditor.

(b) The parties could also stipulate a sale and lease-back agreement.[42] The lessee sells the assets and transfers their ownership to the leasing company, which cedes the use of the things to the lessee for a rent. A right of the lessee to take back the things against a purchase price is agreed. In contrast to security transfer of ownership, the leasing contract, the duration of which in respect of movables must be at least three years, must also be concluded in writing and registered on a special register which is kept at the Athens Court of First Instance. As a consequence of the registration, the rights of the lessee deriving from the contract are opposable to any third party. The leasing company must be an anonymous society specialising in this form of business. In reality a sale and lease-back agreement is a statutory form of security ownership.[43] This form of financing is not very common.

---

[38] AP 369/1978 NoV 27, 173; AP 733/1975 NoV 24, 138; Balis, *Empragmaton Dikaion* para. 61; Toussis, *Empragmato Dikaio* 945 ff.
[39] Toussis, *Empragmato Dikaio* 944.
[40] Ef of Athens 1142/1957 NoV 6, 557; Georgiadis, *Empragmato Dikaio II* 232; Kornilakis, *I katapisteutiki ekchorisi ton apaitiseon* 58 ff. and others.
[41] See further Greek report, case 11(b).
[42] For this form of leasing (which is provided by article 1 L. 1665/1986) see Georgiadis, *Nees morphes symvaseon tis sygchronis oikonomias* 45 ff.; Paparseniou, *I symvasi chrimatodotikis misthosis* 40 ff.
[43] Mazis, *I chrimatodotiki misthosi – Leasing* 57 ff.

(c) Security ownership can apply to any kind of movable. Lease-back, in contrast to finance leasing, applies only to movables. Any kind of movable may be used as the subject of a lease-back transaction, e.g. aircraft (although the duration of a lease-back agreement for aircraft must be at least *five* years).

(d) When security transfer of ownership is stipulated and A becomes insolvent,[44] B has the right to pay the debt in full, even before it becomes due. If ownership of the cars was transferred to A under the resolutive condition of full payment, B would acquire ownership automatically on payment. If the security agreement did not contain a resolutive condition of full payment, B has a right to claim the retransfer of ownership back to him. Consequently, if the insolvency administrator claims ownership and possession of the cars, B will oppose his right (*dolo facit, qui petit, quod statim redditurus est*) and thus ensure that the administrator's claim is rejected pursuant to article 281 A.K. (prohibition of the abuse of a right). Before the debt becomes due, if B chooses not to pay the debt in full, he may refuse to return the cars, as he is entitled, as owner, to possess the cars (articles 1095, 987, 984 A.K.).

After the debt has matured, if B defaults in payment during A's insolvency,[45] the administrator, acting for the creditors, may claim ownership of the cars and sell them according to the provisions of pledge (article 1237 A.K.), which are by analogy applicable. The insolvency administrator is obliged to follow the procedure of compulsory sale (e.g. by public auction) even if an agreement has been stipulated between the parties that, in case of B's default, A can keep the collateral permanently. Such an agreement would be contrary to article 1239 A.K. which prohibits *lex commissoria* and is applicable, according to the prevailing view, by analogy to security agreements.[46] B will receive the difference between the proceeds of the sale and the outstanding debt.

In the case of lease-back, if A goes bankrupt, the insolvency administrator may not terminate the contract.[47]

---

[44] See Georgiadis, *Empragmato Dikaio II* 241.
[45] *Ibid.*; also N. Rokas, *Stoicheia ptocheutikou dikaiou* 45.
[46] AP 448/1964 NoV 12, 1078; Georgiadis, *Empragmato Dikaio II* 238; Kornilakis, *I katapisteutiki ekchorisi ton apaitiseon* 102; Stathopoulos, *Enochiko Dikaio* 615; *contra* Simitis, *I anamorphosis tou plasmatikou enechyrou* 34.
[47] Georgiadis, *Nees morphes symvaseon tis sygchronis oikonomias* 96; Kotsiris, *Nees morphes symvaseon tis sygchronis oikonomias* 353; N. Rokas, *Stoicheia ptocheutikou dikaiou* 52; Mazis, *I chrimatodotiki misthosi – Leasing* 159.

CASE 10: BANK LOAN ON THE BASIS OF A CAR FLEET   447

Therefore, if A's creditors claim the cars before the expiration of the lease, B can resist the claim based on his own right of possession (article 1095 A.K.). The insolvency administrator has the right to terminate the contract only if B defaults in payment.

FRANCE

(a) B would find it difficult to use his car fleet as the collateral for any loan from the bank, A, because presumably B would wish to remain able to use the cars in the course of his business. In consequence, any security interest which requires the debtor to surrender possession of the collateral is excluded (as required in respect of the ordinary pledge governed by C. com, articles L. 521-1 ff.). Nor can the special pledge of vehicles be used (*Loi Malingre*), as the credit is not advanced for the purpose of the purchase of the cars (see case 5(c)). Therefore, the best means available for A to secure a real right in the cars would be to use a contract of lease-back.

(b) The contract of leasing *credit-bail* was introduced into French law by Law No 455 of 2 July 1966, modified by Ordinance No 837 of 28 September 1967. The provisions are applicable only to equipment used in professional activities (e.g., machinery) and the lessors must be commercial enterprises or individual traders. This type of contract is commonly used in respect of vehicles, as the numerous cases involving cars attest.[48] The particular contract applicable to this case would be a lease-back *cession back*, because the lessee first sells the assets to the lessor and then buys them back progressively, based on a lending agreement coupled with an option to repurchase – in fact a leasing agreement.[49]

To qualify as a leasing agreement, the agreement must (article 1) provide the lessee with an option to acquire all or part of the leased assets at the end of the letting term, for a price that must, at least to some significant extent, take into account the amount previously paid in rent.

---

[48] E.g., Com 11 May 1993, Rev huiss 1993, 982, 3rd case, note Vidal.
[49] The *arrêté* of 29 Nov. 1973 defined this variation of the leasing contract (JO of 3 Jan. 1994, JCP 1974, III, No 41218). See Parléani, RTDCom 1973, 699. It seems in practice that the distinction between leasing and lease-back is not always clear, as is apparent in a decision of the *Cour de cassation* of 19 May 1999 (BRDA 1999, No 11, 7). The Court rejected the classification of a contract by the parties as being one of lease-back. A bank bought the premises of a craftsman, and then rented them back to him with an option to purchase. The court viewed this as a leasing contract.

It is this unilateral promise to sell that distinguishes the leasing contract from a pure letting agreement.[50] The leasing contract must also be registered on a registry held by the Commercial Court which has jurisdiction over the lessor. Registration must be renewed every five years. In the absence of registration, the lessor will not be able to enforce his title against third parties, unless he can prove that these third parties had actual knowledge of his title (article 8 of the decree). As a result, if A has not registered the leasing contract, he will not be able successfully to assert his title to the cars *vis-à-vis* B's creditors. As B has an apparent title to them, B's creditors would be able to execute against them. Registration also has consequences in the event of B's insolvency. Pursuant to C. com, article L. 621-116: 'the owner of an asset is relieved from declaring his title over it when the contract concerning this asset has been published'. Moreover, pursuant to C. com, article L. 621-43, para. 1, he is entitled to be personally informed of the commencement of insolvency proceedings against his debtor. Finally, if the insolvency administrator decides to continue the leasing contract, he must immediately make the payments due (C. com, article L. 621-28) – unless the creditor agrees to defer payment.

(c) Leasing and lease-back can apply to any type of asset, whether movable or immovable.

(d) The question is whether the commencement of insolvency proceedings against A affects the leasing contract. Since A is the owner of the assets, the insolvency administrator could, pursuant to C. com, article L. 621-28, decide to suspend the leasing agreement and sell the assets. In fact, the lessee's title does not depend on the payment of the rent, but is independent of this. Should the lessee fail to pay the rent when it falls due, the lessor would be entitled to claim the return of the assets and would retain a claim for the unpaid rent and additionally any penalty stipulated by the contract in the case of default. Thus, if A went bankrupt, there is no question that A's insolvency administrator would be entitled to suspend the leasing contract, perhaps paying B an indemnity for the early termination of the contract. The cars would then be sold; B would be unable to claim ownership of them.

---

[50] Com 14 Apr. 1972, Bull civ IV, No 105; JCP 1972, II, 17269, note Alfandari; Com 30 May 1989, Bull civ IV, No 167; RTDCom 1990, 93, obs. Bouloc.

CASE 10: BANK LOAN ON THE BASIS OF A CAR FLEET   449

BELGIUM

(a) Belgian law does not recognise a fiduciary transfer of property for security purposes. Such a transfer is valid as between the parties, but will have no external effects *vis-à-vis* the creditors of B.

(b) In respect of a finance lease, the ownership of the lessor in the event of the insolvency of the lessee was expressly recognised by the Supreme Court (see Belgian report, case 14). It is generally assumed that the position of the lessor in a sale and lease-back operation will be the same.

(c) Leasing is limited to financing equipment used exclusively for business purposes (article 1, 1° Royal Decree of 10 November 1967[51]). It cannot be used for collateral of a different kind.

(d) The position of the lessee will not be altered in event of the insolvency of the lessor.

PORTUGAL

(a) Cars are movable things subject to registration. So, in this case, it would be possible to establish a charge (*hipoteca*) over them (articles 688° f. C.C.). The charge provides a real right in immovables, or in movables that are subject to registration, that accords to the holder of the charge priority in payment over those creditors without priority arising from registration (article 686° n°1 C.C.). In a case such as the present, the bank would ask for a charge over the cars. The charge would have to be registered, otherwise it would be ineffective (article 687° C.C.).

(b) Portuguese law recognises the possibility of creating leasing contracts by DL 149/95 of 24 June 1995. However, this legislation contains no rules concerning lease-back. Only legal writers have referred to it.[52] They support the creation of this kind of contract, on grounds of freedom of contract (article 405° C.C.). Therefore, the lease-back contract is available under Portuguese law and it has been used by several financial

---

[51] Art. 1, 1° reads as follows: '... *bedrijfsmateriaal uitsluitend gebruikt voor beroepsdoeleinden*'.
[52] See Leite de Campos, ROA 43 (1983) 319 (342); Menezes Cordeiro, *Manual de Direito Bancário* 554; and Martinez, *Contratos em especial* 311.

institutions. However, it must be considered that there is a risk that this contract will be regarded as a sham charge. If so, the transaction will be illegal: it is forbidden for the creditor under a charge to become owner of the things charged without a judicial sale (*pacto comissório*, article 694° C.C.).

(c) Besides cars, the only movable assets that can be charged are ships and aircraft. The answer would apply equally to them.

(d) The insolvency of A would be a very unusual occurrence indeed, because the supervising authorities would not let a bank collapse. In this situation, however, if B had granted a charge over the cars, his position would not be affected, because the charge would be extinguished with the payment of the loan to the insolvency administrator (article 146° CPEREF). If the parties have agreed a contract of sale and lease-back, by analogy with the rule applicable to leasing contracts (article 170° CPEREF), the insolvency of the lessor does not affect the rights of the lessee, so he will be able to require that the insolvency administrator fulfils the contract.

SPAIN

(a) A lease-back contract is the transaction most likely to be employed.[53] Other securities prove ineffective or have other disadvantages. For example, a charge over movables (*hipoteca mobiliaria*) is impractical because the goods must be carefully identified, and also because it requires a public deed. A lease-back contract can be concluded by means of a more expeditious public deed. The financial institution, usually a bank, draws up four copies of a document using standard clauses, many of which incorporate general contractual terms. Once the contract has been drawn up, it is delivered to a notary who checks its legality and the identity and legal capacity of the parties to the document. Moreover, the notary explains to B the financial conditions that the bank has offered to the latter. The contract establishes the leasing instalments, and once it has been signed, this contract gives rise to a swift executive procedure. A's rights will be recognised in the event of B's insolvency. Furthermore, as

[53] Spanish law admits of both leasing of immovables and leasing of movables. See Vicent Chuliá, *Compendio Crítico de Derecho Mercantil II* 273.

it appears in a *póliza mercantil*, it has priority over and above other debts (e.g. those deriving from private contracts, bills, delivery notes, etc.).[54]

On the other hand, a much slower procedure applies to charges over movables (*hipotecas mobiliarias*).[55] Both contracts have to be drawn up by a notary using a public document, in order to acquire legal status and thus have access to executory proceedings. Transaction costs are increased by the fact that the charge has to be drawn up by a notary (as distinct from a financial institution) and also has to be recorded in the Registry. Another potential disadvantage of using a charge over movables is that the relevant Law (LHMPSD) was enacted half a century ago and is nowadays obsolete. On the other hand, a leasing contract can be recorded in the Chattels Registry. In sum, although all these forms of security have similar effects in business practice, a lease-back contract formalised on a *póliza mercantil* is more common.

In Spain, leasing of movables is closely connected but not identical to hire-purchase sales. The principal differences are as follows. First, unlike hire-purchase sales, leasing involves a third party, a financial institution. Secondly, the purchaser enjoys ownership of the movable so financed, without the need for any reservation of title agreement. It is a contract by virtue of which possession of the movable is awarded in exchange for a price, with a clause added by virtue of which the lessee is allowed permanently to acquire the movable on the expiry of the agreed period.[56] Such leasing is not subject to the formal and substantive requirements of Law 28/1998.

For leasing to be opposable to third parties, it must apply to physical goods which must be identifiable yet not consumable.[57] The possibility of registering the leasing contract on the Chattels Registry provides the parties with an expedient security.[58] If the leasing contract is not drawn up in a public deed it is still perfectly valid, but has no executive character, and hence the corresponding action in court will be more protracted. If the contract has not been recorded in the Chattels Registry it will not be opposable to third parties.[59]

---

[54] See Raga Blanch, *Subrogación por pago y juicio ejesutivo basado en pólizas de contratos mercantiles y escrituras públicas* 111.
[55] See García-Pita, Lastres, in: *Tratado de garantías en la contratación mercantil II-1* 197.
[56] See Rojo Ajuria, '*Leasing*' *mobiliario* 33.
[57] See Vicent Chuliá, *Compendio Crítico de Derecho Mercantil II* 272.
[58] The lessor may proceed by way of a summary oral trial if the contract was legalised in a public deed or was drawn up in the fill-in form (article 250.10-11 LEC).
[59] See Bercovitz/Rodríguez-Cano, in: *Tratado de garantías en la contratación mercantil II-1* 379.

The security transfer of ownership (*venta en garantía*) is not expressly regulated by the Civil Code; however, it has been accepted under case law.[60] Nonetheless, in financial practice, the use of lease-back is preferred. Supplementary Provision 1 LVBMP enables lease-backs to be recorded in the Chattels Registry, which offers an important advantage not offered by fiduciary sale.

The reason why security transfer of ownership does not exist explicitly in Spanish law arises from article 1859 CC, which prohibits the creditor from appropriating to himself goods subject to a pledge or charge. According to this, an agreement that allows the creditor to appropriate goods charged or pledged in the event that the debtor defaults in payment would run up against the prohibition of forfeiture rule (*pacto comisorio*).[61] Hence the sale of the debtor's assets is organised either by a court or a public notary by means of a public auction.[62] This notwithstanding, security transfer of ownership has evolved to such an extent in commercial transactions that Supreme Court decisions have stated on several occasions that the agreement between assignor and assignee, by virtue of which the assignee will become holder of the debt as security up to the point when the debt has been liquidated, is lawful and does not run contrary to the legal nature of the non-binding agreement.[63] Moreover, this agreement is unaffected by the insolvency of the assignor.[64]

On the other hand, in certain regions of Spain, which have particular civil laws (*derechos forales*), explicit regulations governing security transfer of ownership do exist. The sale with a repurchase agreement (*venta a carta de gracia* or *empenyorament*) is a peculiarity of Catalan civil law, applicable both to movable and immovable property, and is of fiduciary character.[65] The fiduciary debtor passes ownership to the fiduciary creditor, but reserves the right to recover the thing sold within a maximum period of thirty years with respect to immovable property, and six years with regard to movables (article 326 CDCC). The price of reacquisition is

---

[60] See Díez-Picazo, *Dictámenes Jurídicos* 25.
[61] See Reglero Campos, in: *Tratado de garantías en la contratación mercantil* II-1 421.
[62] If the debt was secured with a charge, the court usually organises a foreclosure proceeding to sell the charged property in order to satisfy the debt (articles 131 LH and 225–235 RH). Still, the charge deed may validly include a covenant on non-judicial foreclosure proceedings, in which case the sale would be organised by a notary (articles 129,2 LH and 234–236 RH). If the debt was secured with a pledge, the sale is organised by a notary (articles 1872 CC and 14 LGP).
[63] See STS of 19 Apr. 1997 and 7 Oct. 1997.
[64] See Pantaleón Prieto, in: *Garantías reales mobiliarias* 191.
[65] See Pozo Carrascosa, *La venda a carta de gràcia en el dret civil de Catalunya* 43.

repayment of the principal debt with interest. This price for the recovery of the goods may be paid in instalments.[66] This is in fact a money loan from the buyer to the seller with a real security on the 'sold' object, disguised as a contract of sale. In business reality, however, for immovables, financial institutions prefer the use of lease-back to the sale under *carta de gracia*. A similar instrument exists under the law of Navarre (*pacto de retro en garantía*). Basically, both these 'sales under guarantee' carry out a function which is similar to that of lease-back. In financial practice, the latter is used more often, as far as movables are concerned, than other contractual forms.

(b) Yes, it can be achieved and it is frequently used in the automobile business.

(c) The lease-back contract also applies to other goods, specifically machinery, railway carriages and immovable property. In principle, practically any form of movable property can form the subject matter of a lease. Nevertheless, for a leasing contract to be registrable in the Chattels Registry, it has to apply to physical goods which are identifiable but not consumable. Goods would be regarded as identifiable if, for example, the factory number appears indelibly on, or is inseparable from, one or more of the movable's basic components. The most important thing is that the goods must be distinguishable from other, similar types of goods.

(d) A is a financial institution subject to insolvency law under the CCO. Accordingly, B's cars would form part of the insolvency estate. Nevertheless, B would remain entitled to possession of the cars as long as he paid the instalments due under the lease. At the end of the contract, he would be entitled to exercise the option to purchase and, by paying the residual value, obtain full ownership of the cars. This option to purchase is binding on the insolvency administrator and other creditors.

ITALY

(a) It is possible to create a non-possessory security right in the cars, by registering a type of charge (*ipoteca*) over them, pursuant to the Civil Code rules applicable to registrable movables (article 2810 c.c.). This

---

[66] See Ysàs Solanes, in: *Comentarios al Código Civil y Compilaciones Forales* 583, 643; Pozo Carrascosa, *La venda a carta de gràcia en el dret civil de Catalunya* 250.

regime was established for cars and other vehicles that are registered in the *pubblico registro automobilistico* (on the P.R.A., see the Italian report to case 5(a)). Any vehicle that has an Italian licence plate is registered on the P.R.A. The formalities that must be observed in order to create the charge (*ipoteca*) are set out in detail by Royal Decree n. 436 of 1927. They basically consist of registration of the notarised document, which witnesses the agreement of the parties to the creation of the *ipoteca*, on the *pubblico registro automobilistico*, which is held by the Italian Automobile Club. The costs of creating this security are not prohibitive, but the market for securities rights in used cars in Italy has not flourished, possibly because used cars rapidly lose their value. Refinancing operations, whereby used cars are offered as collateral, are not advertised in Italy, nor do they seem to be widespread. Of course, if the car fleet in the present case is a going concern, the same facts could be analysed as amounting to the transfer of an entire business undertaking. Such a transaction could fall under the provision of article 58 of the Italian banking law, which is discussed in cases 11 and 13(d). On the basis of the facts given above, this appears a remote possibility.

(b) Alternatively, the parties could establish a sale and lease-back contract. According to most commentators,[67] and to a number of recent decisions of the *Corte di cassazione*[68] and of lower courts,[69] the contract is valid in principle, on the basis of the autonomy of the parties. It may, however, be null and void, if it is not concluded in the ordinary course of business.[70] In such a case, it would be considered as contrary to current interpretation of the Civil Code provision against *pactum commissorium* (article 2744 c.c.), that invalidates any alienation of movables or immovables for security purposes only. In Italy, the transfer of ownership of the cars from the lessee to the lessor must be registered in the P.R.A. in order to be effective *vis-à-vis* the lessee's executing creditors, or his insolvency administrator.

---

[67] Ferrarini/Barucco, in: *Trattato di diritto privato diretto da Rescigno* 24–27; Bussani, *Proprietà-garanzia e contratto* 147 ff.; Luminoso, Giur. comm. 2000 II, 489 ff. For an instructive overview, see Fiorentini, Riv. dir. civ. 2000 II, 253, 281 ff.
[68] Cass. 15 Apr. 1998, n. 4095, Foro it., 1998, I, 1820, obs. Simone; Cass. 19 July 1997, n. 6663, Foro it., 1997, I, 3586; Cass. 16 Oct. 1995, n. 10805, Foro it., 1996, I, 3492, obs. Monti; Giust. civ., 1996 I, 1739, obs. Schermi; Giur. it., 1996 I, 1, 382, obs. Cinquemani.
[69] E.g., Trib. Roma, 22 May 1996, Arch. civ. 1997, 44, obs. Santarsierre.
[70] This is the opinion of most commentators and of leading decisions such as Cass. 16 Oct. 1995, n. 10805, cited above. The opinion was first advanced by Bussani, Contr. e impr. 1986, 558; De Nova, Riv. it. leasing 1985, 307; 1987, 517.

Sale and lease-back contracts are only rarely used in practice, with respect to cars. Leasing companies and bank departments that operate in this economic sector usually acquire title to new vehicles, not to used ones. Nevertheless, the writer has been informed by practitioners that some sale and lease-back transactions have been carried out in respect of durable vehicles of a certain value, such as big trucks, or imported luxury cars. This last example requires some explanation. The importation of cars into Italy is subject to a certain number of administrative formalities. Banking and financial institutions are not prepared to attend to these formalities. Hence, they are not able to acquire title to and finance the purchase by means of sale and lease-back of new, imported cars as readily as they would like. This is the reason why some importers buy cars from foreign manufacturers, acquire title to them, import them into Italy, and then immediately obtain financing for their deal by arranging a sale and lease-back transaction in respect of the new cars they own.

(c) The answer would be the same for other registrable movables or immovables. The sale and lease-back of immovables and of ships is not unknown in Italy, despite the fact that our Codes allow for the registration of charges (*ipotecas*) over both such assets.[71]

(d) If the transaction is a sale and lease-back, and the lessor becomes bankrupt, most commentators hold that the contract shall continue with the insolvency administrator, either by analogy to the rule on ordinary leases (article 80.2 l. fall.), or by analogy to the rule on sale under retention of title (article 73 l. fall.).[72] There are, however, court decisions to the contrary, and some commentators support them.[73] These decisions hold that the insolvency administrator should be free to decide whether to terminate the contract, or to maintain it in being, especially if the value of the lessee's redemption right is substantial. Furthermore, one decision rendered by the *Corte di cassazione* held that the insolvency

---

[71] For a lease-back operation concerning an immovable, see Cass. 18 Oct. 1995, n. 10805, cited above.
[72] Ferrarini/Barucco, in: *Trattato di diritto privato* 31 ff.; Bussani, *Proprietà-garanzia e contratto* 93 ff.; Vigo, *I contratti pendenti non disciplinati nella legge fallimentare* 149 ff.; Bonfante, *I rapporti pendenti nel fallimento e la locazione finanziaria* 86 ff. For a different opinion, Apice, *Il contratto di leasing nelle procedure concorsuali* 342–343. App. Torino, 23 Nov. 1984, Giur. comm. 1986, I, 76.
[73] Decr. Trib. Napoli, 22 Jan. 1992, Fallimento, 1992, 1040; Decr. Trib. Roma, 29 Oct. 1990, 21 Nov. 1990 (both cited in Apice, *Il contratto di leasing nelle procedure concorsuali* 53); Cintioli, Banca borsa 1997 I, 475.

administrator is not bound by the lessee's redemption right.[74] The reasoning supporting this conclusion is that the lessee's right against the insolvency administrator is a personal right. The soundness of this conclusion is questionable, inasmuch as this solution is contrary to the initial allocation of the benefits and burdens of the contract.[75]

THE NETHERLANDS

(a) In order to provide A with the desired security, B could create a pledge over the cars in favour of A. As in the case of charges over claims (see case 5), the Code provides for two types of pledge over movables: those with and those without 'publicity'. The former, *vuistpand*, requires that the movables over which the pledge is to be created are brought into the hands of A or a third party (article 3:236(1) BW). The main drawback of this type of pledge is that B would therefore no longer be able to use the cars. The latter type of pledge, known as the 'silent' pledge, is essentially non-possessory. This type of pledge is the most suitable one, assuming that B wishes to continue to use the cars. The 'silent' pledge was first introduced by the new Civil Code of 1992 and was to replace the customary practice of fiduciary transfers, although it was not intended materially to affect credit practice. A fiduciary transfer *cum creditore* is now prohibited in the Code, which provides that such a transfer does not constitute a valid *causa traditionis* (article 3:84(3) BW).

In order to create a 'silent' pledge, the Code requires, as it does for the transfer of all property interests, a valid *causa*, the power to dispose, and a 'delivery' or, more appropriately in this case, an 'act of creation'. The formalities required for this latter act consist of a notarised or registered deed (article 3:98 in conjunction with articles 3:84 and 3:237(1) BW). This requirement fixes the moment at which the pledge comes into existence, which above all prevents antedating. If a notarised deed is not used, the deed must be registered in a non-public register. As it is a non-public register, third parties, more particularly creditors of the pledgor, have no access to this register.

(b) The use of ownership as security within a sale and lease-back transaction is problematic because the Dutch Civil Code expressly prohibits security (or fiduciary) ownership (Art. 3:84(3) BW) under which

---

[74] Cass. 12 Dec. 1990, n. 11792, Fallimento, 1991, 457 (a case of ordinary leasing).
[75] Ferrarini/Barucco, in: *Trattato di diritto privato* 32–33; Bussani, *Proprietà-garanzia e contratto* 110–112; Bussani/Cendon, *I contratti nuovi: Leasing, factoring e franchising* 98.

circumstances exactly judges would consider a leasing arrangement to amount to a (prohibited) security transfer of ownership is unclear.

Sale and lease-back arrangements are used in various ways. They may serve as a means of obtaining both purchase-money credit and cash for collateral already owned. The latter arrangement, in particular, would appear to be inconsistent with, if not the letter, then at least the spirit of the Code's prohibition on fiduciary transfers.[76] Essentially it allocates all the risk, that is the economic and legal liability, to the seller/lessee (B in the above case).

The Dutch Supreme Court, however, endorsed exactly this type of credit arrangement, holding that it did not come within the ambit of the prohibition on fiduciary transfers.[77] The Court held that the prohibition forms no bar when parties intend a 'genuine transfer', that is a transfer where the buyer is to obtain ownership without restrictions, such as a right only to the proceeds rather than to the thing itself. The Court continued by stating that this would also apply if the transaction involved the provision of some kind of credit to the transferor/seller/lessee.

On the other hand, sale and lease-back will not in all circumstances avoid the prohibition of fiduciary transfers. The Court indicated that there might exist additional facts from which it could be inferred that the parties merely intended to evade the Code's prohibition. In such a case, the transfer would be void.

In the present case, it would, therefore, also be possible for B to sell the cars to A, who would then lease them back to B. The fact that B was to obtain credit, or that B already owned the cars, would not, of itself, be sufficient to conclude the transaction amounted to a prohibited fiduciary transfer.

(c) Though cars are in fact a popular example, the above analysis also holds true for different types of collateral. There has been some debate as to the validity of the so-called 'techno-lease', which involves the sale and lease of 'know-how'. The problem would appear to lie in the question of whether, and if so to what extent, 'know-how' qualifies as 'goods' for the purposes of property law.

(d) The effects of the commencement of insolvency proceedings against the credit institution, A, differ according to whether the parties agreed on a pledge or on a sale and lease-back arrangement.

---

[76] Cf. conclusion of Hartkamp in *Hoge Raad* 19 May 1995, NJ 1996, 119.
[77] *Hoge Raad* 19 May 1995, NJ 1996, 119 (*Sogelease*).

If A had taken a pledge over B's cars, the security interest and A's claim against B would form part of the insolvency estate. The insolvency administrator would be entitled to sell the claim of A against B to a third party. With the assignment, not only the claim itself would pass, but also the security interest, *viz.* the pledge (due to the accessory principle, article 3:7 in conjunction with article 3:82 BW). The insolvency administrator would not be entitled to sell the cars, as B is the owner. Consequently, a possible insolvency of A does not substantially affect B's position. B remains owner of the cars, and cannot be forced to repay the loan at any point earlier than that which was agreed in the original contract.

If A and B had agreed on sale and lease-back, however, the cars would become part of A's insolvency estate. B's position would, on the whole, appear to be more troublesome. A contract of lease is not regulated as such by the Code. But in classifying the lease arrangement, some support may be found in known types of specific contract, such as rental (*huur*) and hire purchase (*huurkoop*).[78] In both cases the lessee is protected against the sale of the goods subject to the lease by the lessor or, as the case may be, by the lessor's insolvency administrator. The transfer does not operate to the detriment of the lessee.[79]

ENGLAND

(a) The first thing to ascertain is the nature of the security. It cannot be a pledge, which confers a legal (as opposed to equitable) interest in A, for that requires A to be in possession. The American system of field warehousing never gained a hold in England. It is possible that the interest described would be a fixed charge (or *fixed mortgage*), but more likely that it would be an enterprise charge (*floating mortgage* or *charge*). Whether fixed or floating, the charge would have to be registered if it is to be asserted against B's insolvency administrator (*trustee-in-bankruptcy* or *liquidator*). A charge gives rise to a limited real right (an *equitable property interest*) and not a legal one. The common law does not permit *mortgages* of future assets: there would have to be a separate conveyance

---

[78] The essential difference between these types of contract is that the latter implies that the intention of parties is that, at the end of the lease agreement, the goods, B's cars, are to become the property of B again.

[79] Article 7A:1576l(2) BW (hire purchase) and article 7A:1612; see also article 7:226 (draft) BW (rental). Currently, in case of hire-purchase agreements, a separate assignment by the lessor, or the lessor's trustee, is necessary, Hoge Raad 25 May 1962, NJ 1962, 256.

of those assets as and when they came into existence (i.e., were acquired by B).[80] This is wholly impracticable in the case of stock-in-trade or equipment. But equity permits a *mortgage* or charge of future property so that future assets automatically fall into the charge as soon as they come into existence.[81] Furthermore, there is no such thing as a legal charge. (The distinction between a *mortgage* and a charge is a subtle one that need not be brought out here.)

If the car fleet represents equipment (for example, the cars that B supplies to its employee sales representatives) then A should take a fixed charge which puts it in a strong position against executing creditors of B and also against creditors of B benefiting from a statutory privilege (*preference creditors*).[82] In the case of equipment, A is in a better position than a bank taking a charge over a dealer's stock which is to be sold in the ordinary course of trade. In such a case, A would have to take a *floating charge* since it would be impracticable to obtain permission from A every time a car was sold on by B: freedom to deal with charged assets in the ordinary course of trade is the badge not of a fixed but of a *floating charge*. A *floating charge* would put A at a disadvantage against B's *preference creditors*[83] and would also put A at risk against B's execution creditors in the period leading up to crystallisation of the charge. In the case of a *floating charge*, B's freedom to deal in the ordinary course will be to do so in such a way as to embrace the normal consequences of being sued to judgment.[84] Hence, the courts will not permit *selective* intervention by a debenture holder with a *floating charge* in order to defeat a particular execution creditor.[85] But a crystallisation of a *floating charge*, determining the debtor's authority to continue dealing with the stock, is a different matter and can be brought about, as a matter of contract, by any event stipulated in the debenture. The stipulated event will often be a matter of implication, such as *liquidation* (the commencement

---

[80] *Lunn v Thornton* [1845] 1 CB 375.
[81] See *Tailby v Official Receiver* [1888] 13 App Cas 523.
[82] See ss. 40 and 175 of the Insolvency Act 1986; s. 196 of the Companies Act 1985. *Preference creditors* are listed in Schedule 6 of the Insolvency Act 1986.
[83] These are the following – see Insolvency Act 1986, s. 386 and Schedule 6 to the Act (statutory *numerus clausus*): 1, debts due to the Inland Revenue (as deductions made by the insolvent under the Pay As You Earn (PAYE) scheme); (2) debts due to Customs and Excise (previous six months, mainly VAT and alcohol); (3) social security contributions that an insolvent employer ought to have made; (4) contributions to occupational pension schemes; (5) remuneration of employees (previous four months up to £800 (trivial)); (6) European Coal and Steel Production levies.
[84] See Morse, *Palmer's Company Law* § 13.138.
[85] *Evans v Rival Granite Quarries* [1910] 2 KB 979, a very important case.

of insolvency proceedings against a company) or the appointment of a *receiver*.

When a *floating charge* crystallises, this has an effect on the priority position between execution creditor and debenture holder. The latter will certainly prevail if the charge crystallises before the bailiff (*sheriff*) sells the assets seized.[86] It is likely (the point has not been settled) that the latter will also prevail if crystallisation occurs before the *sheriff* distributes to the execution creditor.[87]

(b) Sale and lease-back is a common transaction in English law, particularly in the fields of aviation and railway rolling stock financing. It is an example of off-balance-sheet activity. The key question in English private law is whether it will be regarded as a disguised charge. If so, it will have to be registered under section 395 of the Companies Act if it is to be opposed to third parties (including for present purposes the seller's insolvency administrator, that is their *liquidator* or *trustee-in-bankruptcy*). There is little case law.[88] In one case,[89] a sale and resale arrangement was characterised as a charge, largely because of errors in drafting. The document, for example, referred to 'interest' and to a line of credit. Since English law in this area is preoccupied with freedom of contract, and routinely underestimates the importance of distributional considerations, a well-drafted document will probably be recognised as a sale and lease-back. It should not be assumed that courts, in giving effect to the substance as opposed to the form of the transaction, will draw the line between those two things in the same way as an accountant applying financial reporting standards or statements of standard accountancy practice.

It is impossible to be confident in predicting the attitude of courts in matters of construction. It may be relevant that, objectively, the seller is paying a finance price rather than a genuine rental sum. It should not matter much in such a case that, at the end of the lease term, title to the cars revests automatically in B. But, in matters of construction, little things can add up and tip the balance. If the arrangement is seen as a charge, then it will have to be registered on the Companies Register

---

[86] *Evans v Rival Granite Quarries*; *Re Standard Manufacturing Co.* [1891] 1 Ch 627; Morse, *Palmer's Company Law* § 13.138.

[87] Morse, *Palmer's Company Law* § 13.138.

[88] *Re Curtain Dream plc* [1990] BCLC 925; cf. *Welsh Development Agency v Export Finance Co. Ltd* [1992] BCC 270.

[89] *Re Curtain Dream plc* [1990] BCLC 925.

at Cardiff. Incidentally, although the question does not raise issues of title transfer, the seller will be regarded as a seller in possession for the purpose of section 24 of the Sale of Goods Act (providing that possession is unbroken).[90] Despite holding the goods as a lessee, the seller has the *power* (even if he does not have the right) to transfer title to a *bona fide* purchaser for value without notice of A's interest. The marking of the goods, as a matter of fact, could affect purchasers with notice.

(c) The above discussion is not confined to cars.

(d) English law gives no clear answer to the question whether the possessory interest of a lessee may be asserted against third parties and against the owner's insolvency administrator. One commentator takes the view that a lease creates only a personal interest and that no more than any other contract does it bind third parties who are strangers to the contract that created it.[91] The same commentator is not persuaded to the contrary by the right of a person in possession to sue in the tort of conversion for the full value of the chattel those who interfere directly with possession (a right subjected to certain limitations in the Torts (Interference with Goods) Act 1977). Other writers have opined that the lessee has a real interest that may be asserted in insolvency.[92] If the matter came up for full discussion and determination, it is submitted that a court would find that the lessee obtained a real interest that was good in the lessor's insolvency. Equipment leases have become far too important as financing devices to be jeopardised by a hole in the development of English personal property law. If, however, the former view is correct, it is worth examining the legislative and general insolvency position. A's insolvency administrator is immune from personal liability on contracts that he concludes on behalf of the insolvent.[93] *A fortiori* he will not be liable on contracts concluded between A and B prior to A's insolvency. Any other result would outflank the statutory prohibition on bringing actions against companies in *liquidation* without the leave of the court.[94] But does it follow from this that the *liquidator* may lawfully repossess A's chattel from B, the lessee? Sections 178 (*liquidators*) and 315 (*trustees-in-bankruptcy*) of the Insolvency Act 1986 allow for the disclaimer of onerous

---

[90] *Pacific Motor Auctions Pty Ltd v Motor Credits Ltd* [1965] AC 867.
[91] See Swadling, in: Palmer/McKendrick, *Interests in Goods* 491 ff.
[92] Calnan, JIBFL 11 (1998) 530; Furey, in: *Interests in Goods* 787 ff.
[93] *Re Anglo-Moravian Hungarian Junction Railway Co.* (1875) 1 Ch 130, 133.
[94] Insolvency Act 1986, s. 130(2).

property (which includes disadvantageous contracts). A contract of this sort may not be onerous if it is profitable, though the result would be different if a new financier could not be found to take the benefit of the contract by way of assignment. The practical result in many cases would indeed be for the *liquidator/trustee*, seeking a quick settlement of the insolvency estate, to assign the benefit of the contract with B to another financier. B might even wish to take active steps to bring about new financing. An example of a financier assigning a hire-purchase contract is *Manchester, Sheffield & Lincolnshire Railway v North Central Wagon Co.*[95]

IRELAND

(a) On these facts A may gain 'real rights' in the case of B's insolvency in at least two ways. One of these ways involves sale and lease-back. The second is by way of charge. If there is held to be a genuine sale and lease-back, then it will not have to be registered. The courts may however construe the transaction as creating a charge, in which case it would have to be registered under the Companies Act 1963, s. 99, if B was a company and as a bill of sale if B was a sole trader. The actual registration process itself is not particularly costly but it adds considerable complexity to the transaction in terms of delay and preparing additional documents. A will get ownership of the cars if there is a genuine sale and lease-back. It is very difficult to be dogmatic on what points the courts consider will tip the scales one way or the other. Any reference to 'credit line', 'finance price', etc. will make it difficult to uphold a sale and lease-back construction. How the lease payments are calculated, it is suggested, may have some impact on the attitude of the courts but is unlikely to be decisive. The fact that at the end of the lease term B has an option to repurchase the goods is not in itself decisive but could suggest that the transaction is really a disguised advance of money on the security of goods.

(b) It is possible that 'security' can be achieved through a sale and lease-back arrangement and these transactions are not uncommon. There is usually a clause in the lease stating that if the lessee becomes subject to any form of insolvency procedure, then the lessor is entitled to forfeit the lease. The court has jurisdiction, however, to grant relief against forfeiture and it is likely to exercise this jurisdiction if the effect of

---

[95] [1888] 13 App Cas 554.

forfeiture would be to confer a substantial windfall benefit on the lessor over and above the payments which the original agreement stipulated that the lessor should receive. The court would grant relief on terms that confined the benefits to the lessor to those provided for in the leasing agreement.

(c) The answer applies also to collateral of a different kind.

(d) If A obtains a charge over the cars and then becomes bankrupt, it is submitted that B's position is not significantly worsened. B can obtain the cars back free from 'encumbrances', i.e. the charge, on repaying the loan. It may be that there is an acceleration clause in the loan agreement obliging B to repay the loan earlier than expected on the occurrence of certain stated events, including A's insolvency. In the case of a sale and lease-back, the same analysis generally holds good – pre-insolvency entitlements are respected. Express provision may have been made in the lease agreement to cover the contingency, such as by an accelerated payment or forfeiture clause. Since, however, the lessor's insolvency is not a likely scenario it may be that the lease is silent on this point. If there is a forfeiture clause, then the courts have jurisdiction to relieve against forfeiture so as to prevent the lessee from being unduly disadvantaged by this eventuality.

SCOTLAND

(a) This cannot normally be done by sale and lease-back (see below). It could be done only by means of a *floating charge* (enterprise charge): see case 11 below.

(b) Sale and lease-back transactions are lawful. But the law looks at the underlying motive. If the underlying motive is to give security for a debt, the initial 'sale' will not normally be regarded as a contract of sale, with the consequences outlined below.

Thus if B sells the vehicle fleet to A for a fair market value, and if B rents the fleet back from A at a rental level which accords with market rents, and the contract is in other respects the sort of contract one would expect to find in vehicle leasing contracts, then the transaction is valid.

But if it appears that the motive was to create security for a debt, the law will conclude that the contract is not in truth a contract of sale.[96] It

---

[96] The Sale of Goods Act 1979 states this expressly at s. 62(4).

will be regarded not as the nominate contract of sale but as an innominate contract. Innominate contracts are, of course, lawful, in accordance with the principle of private autonomy. However, the problem is this. It is only in contracts of sale that it is possible for ownership to pass without delivery. If parties wish to transfer ownership in cases where there is no contract of sale, delivery is necessary. It is not necessary for the validity of the contract, but it is necessary to pass ownership. Scots law is reluctant to recognise *constitutum possessorium*. Therefore a sale and lease-back transaction which is intended to operate as a security will have to be completed by actual delivery. But actual delivery is problematic. B wishes to keep possession. Possibly it would be enough for B to deliver the fleet to A and for A to keep the fleet for an hour or a day and then deliver the fleet back. But even this is inconvenient and is not attempted in practice. Moreover, there is some authority that a temporary delivery of this sort is insufficient.

Hence it is not possible to create a security by transferring ownership of goods but retaining possession.[97]

(c) What has been said above does not apply only to cars. It is true of other movables also.

(d) If a *floating charge* has been used, the insolvency of the *floating chargeholder* cannot prejudice the debtor, since the creditor does not acquire ownership. The issue posed by case 10(d) therefore does not arise in this context. See, however, the answer to case 14(d).

SOUTH AFRICA

(a) South African law has up to now failed to reach a satisfactory solution for case 10 (and also case 11), which involves a transfer of ownership without actual delivery. Commercial practice, especially in the motor industry, has endeavoured to legitimise a security transfer of ownership construction based on the Roman *fiducia cum creditore*. This is done by a security transfer of ownership in the car fleet, for security purposes, structured as a 'sale and resale with retention of title' transaction. The car fleet is sold and transferred by means of *constitutum possessorium* to A, but then resold to B with retention of title in favour of A. B thus become the hire-purchaser of the car fleet and owner once the price

[97] For discussion of this complex area of law, see Gretton, in: *Cusine*.

has been (re)paid in full. However, South African courts have up to now been unwilling to accept transfer by means of *constitutum possessorium* in this case. The courts treat these agreements as simulated transactions, disguising what is in effect a non-possessory pledge, a type of secret charge not allowed in South African law. There are, however, indications that our courts would accept security transfer of ownership as a valid *causa* for the transfer of ownership by *constitutum possessorium*, as long as the transaction is couched in the correct form, indicating that it was the intention of the parties to resort to this form rather than to create a pledge. Lack of *bona fides*, in the form of there being no real intention to transfer ownership to A, would render the transaction void as being an attempt to create a non-possessory pledge of a movable.[98] Security transfer of ownership is, however, still awaiting recognition by South African courts and there is a distinct possibility that the motor industry will confront the Supreme Court of Appeal with a test case to settle the matter.

Legislative reform in South Africa has in the meantime endeavoured to tackle this problem in the guise of the Security by Means of Movable Property Act.[99] This Act expands the scope of the pledge device by contemplating a non-possessory pledge. Movables furnished as security can be 'specified and described' in a special notarial bond, and this bond may be registered. If this is done, the particular movable is deemed to have been pledged and delivered to the pledgee. Although this system has been welcomed by at least one academic writer,[100] it is submitted that it is not suitable for commercial practice, especially not for the automobile industry. The main objection is that the Security by Means of Movable Property Act[101] requires the goods to be *specified* as well as described, 'in a manner which renders it readily recognisable'. However, in the present case, this clumsy method can be used as long as each car in the fleet is clearly identified as subject to a notarial bond in favour of the bank.

(b) This question would only be relevant once the South African courts have recognised the security transfer of ownership construction. In such a case, B would presumably like to be in a position to sell the cars in the fleet even before he has paid back the loan. This he could do as hire-purchaser, but not as lessee, of the motor cars. The sale and resale with

---

[98] See van der Merwe/Smith, StellLR 1999, 303 ff.   [99] Act 57 of 1993 s. 1.
[100] See Sonnekus, TSAR 776 ff.   [101] Act 57 of 1993.

retention of title construction is therefore more appropriate. The other problem with the lease-back construction is that the contract might have to contain a fairly artificial clause whereby A undertakes to abandon ownership in the fleet once the purchase price has been paid in order for B to regain ownership of the fleet.

(c) The commercial need for such a construction seems to be most urgent in the sphere of the motor industry.

(d) Under South African law, the seller's insolvency does not by itself terminate the lease or hire-purchase contract. If the insolvency administrator decides to abide by the contract, he must perform all the duties that the insolvent himself would have performed. The effect of insolvency is to put the insolvency administrator in the shoes of the insolvent. In practice the administrator would in the majority of cases elect to abide by the lease or hire purchase provided the lessee or hire-purchaser pays the instalments regularly. There is no point in an administrator compelling a sound and punctilious purchaser to surrender a secondhand article and thereafter selling it, probably at a loss and simultaneously involving the estate in a claim for damages. Ownership of the articles remains with the seller (lessor) in the case of hire purchase, even though it is whittled away by payment of instalments, until the last payment is made. Because of this real right, the lessee (with an option to buy) or the hire-purchaser cannot compel the insolvency administrator to pass full ownership even if he tenders the full price. On the seller's insolvency the purchaser is in the same position as any other person who is involved in a contractual relationship not yet fully implemented. The insolvency administrator can only alienate assets to the advantage of the general body of creditors and cannot perform any obligation which vested in the insolvent to the disadvantage of the general body of creditors, unless a preferential right has been created. Should the administrator decide that it would be to the advantage of the general body of creditors to repossess the hire-purchased or leased articles, there is little doubt in South African law that he may do so with impunity, leaving the hire-purchaser or lessee with a mere claim for damages for breach of contract as an insolvency creditor. Though the South African Credit Agreements Act[102] (regulating hire purchase) changed the traditional law in many respects,

---

[102] Act 75 of 1980.

it did not expressly or by inference clothe the hire-purchaser with a real interest.[103]

DENMARK

(a) If A wishes to obtain a real right to the cars which is protected against B's creditors, A can take a sort of charge over the cars. A charge over a car has to be registered in a public register called the Car Register, cf. section 42(d) of the Registration of Property Act. The registration cannot as such be made in respect of the car fleet as a whole because this charge can only be registered in respect of specific assets. Therefore, a charge has to be registered for each car.

In Denmark it is debated whether A in a sale and lease-back agreement can claim a right to the asset when B's creditors execute against the asset. The usual way for A to obtain a right in an asset which is already in B's possession is by way of charge.

(b) In Denmark the question arises of whether A, as a lessor in a sale and lease-back agreement, can claim ownership of the asset when B's (the lessee's) creditors execute against the asset. The background to the discussion surrounding this question is that a security on movables can only be created as a charge or as a pledge. One contention is that the sale and lease-back agreement is a financial transaction in which A lends money to B and attempts to get a security right (through ownership) in the cars in the event that B fails to repay the outstanding debt. Since a security right can only be created as a charge or a pledge, such a transaction is, under this analysis, regarded as an evasion which should not be effective as against B's creditors.[104]

A differing interpretation is that sale and lease-back is an ordinary transaction, which should be recognised as valid if the asset has been sold at a fair price and the conditions stipulated in the contract are in line with normal conditions in such a contract. Ownership should probably not automatically pass to B at the end of the contract period as this would be indicative of a credit sale.[105]

However, in a case reported in the Danish weekly law reports 1983 p. 783, the High Court ruled that a sale and lease-back agreement

---

[103] See Smith, *The Law of Insolvency* 169.   [104] Cf. Ørgaard, *Sikkerhed i løsøre* 69 f.
[105] Cf. Andersen/Werlauff, *Kreditretten* 186 ff. and Elmer/Skovby, *Ejendomsretten I* 75 ff.

permitted the lessor to claim ownership of the assets as against B's creditors. The decision notes that there was no strong indication that the lessee had a right to have ownership of the assets retransferred to him.

This case did not bring the debate to an end. Unless a case is brought to the Supreme Court, the discussion may continue indefinitely. Therefore, sale and lease-back agreements are not very common.

(c) The answers to parts (a) and (b) also apply to other assets. However, some difficulties arise when the assets are not cars. If B owns the immovable property from which he is running his business and the property has been charged, then the charge will include machinery and technical plant used in the enterprise, cf. section 37 of the Registration of Property Act. These rules include all machinery and technical plant and nothing else. Claims against third parties or goods in stock cannot be used as security under these sections. Under section 37 machinery and technical plant will be included in the charge as equipment when it becomes a part of the enterprise, unless a special right (charge, retention of title or leasing) has been established in respect of such machinery and plant before that. In this case the machinery and technical plant has already been used in the enterprise at the point at which the bank wished to obtain security. Therefore, the bank cannot get a right without respecting any charge over the immovable property.

If B does not own the land and buildings from which he is running his business he may have charged the machinery and technical plant. Under these circumstances he might have charged all the machinery and technical plant of the enterprise under section 47(2) (b) of the Registration of Property Act. Such a charge is very common and will have an effect similar to that of section 37 of the same act.

(d) If A has a registered charge over the car he is entitled to the proceeds from the sale of the car. But he has to wait for the estate to sell the car. The main rule governing the position in respect of registered security rights when the owner of the asset has been declared bankrupt is section 85 of the Bankruptcy Act. Under this section a compulsory sale of the debtor's assets may only be made upon the request of the estate or with the consent of the estate. This mainly comprises a charge on immovable property and a charge on chattels. If the estate has not requested a compulsory sale within six months of the day on which the insolvency was declared, a chargee who has a due claim can demand that the estate realises the charged property.[106]

SWEDEN

(a) Under the Enterprise Mortgage Act 1984 (*lagen om företagsinteckning*), a debtor may charge all his personal property, subject to a few exceptions (property that can be charged under other legislation, shares, promissory notes and debentures intended for the public, cash and claims on banks). In other words, it is an enterprise charge on most of the debtor's personal property. However, the debtor may freely dispose of the property (even pledge it with transfer of possession), so long as he does not sell the whole business. Consequently, a purchaser can take priority over the chargee in the property. If A wishes to ensure that no third party will take priority over his right in the car fleet, he must buy the cars and either take possession of the cars (which is not a practical solution; a *constitutum possessorium* is not permitted) or register his purchase under the Bills of Sales Act, applicable to chattels (*lösoreköpslagen*, from 1835 and later amended). Then he is entitled to a *ius separationis*. In order to extinguish A's right, a later purchaser must have acted in good faith and taken the cars in his possession (the 1986 Good Faith Purchase Act, *lagen om godtrosförvärv av lösöre*), also applicable to chattels. A's right in the purchased goods is not invalidated by the fact that A might have granted the seller, B, a lease of the goods. If the buyer has permitted the seller to substitute new goods for the individually registered goods, the buyer is protected as owner in respect of the original goods, but has no right to the substitutes (NJA 1927, 369).

Up to 1835, there was no doubt that a purchaser acquired title and became protected against the creditors of the seller by the conclusion of the agreement of sale. In that year, the first Bills of Sales Act was enacted, however. According to this legislation (later amended), a purchaser who leaves chattels in the possession of the seller is protected against the creditors of the seller only if he has registered his purchase at a court (specifying the goods affected) and thirty days have elapsed

---

[106] However, some security rights may be enforced independently of insolvency. S. 91 of the Bankruptcy Act states that a pledge of chattels, the charge of a claim and the charge over registered securities are not affected by insolvency proceedings and hence the creditor may realise the collateral irrespective of them. Cf. Munch, *Konkursloven* 529 ff. and Ørgaard, *Konkursret* 201 ff.

since registration before insolvency or execution supervene. The purpose was to prevent debtors, when faced with an execution, from pretending that the property had been sold to someone else, who would confirm the statement, which had been all too easy to do in the past. According to case law, it is quite clear that a purchaser who leaves the goods in the possession of the seller without registration has no protection against the seller's creditors, no matter whether it was in fact a genuine sale (see e.g. NJA 1925, 130). It does not help the buyer that the goods have been individually specified in the agreement and can be identified in the execution. For many years it was debated whether registration pursuant to the Bills of Sales Act could be effective also when the purchase was for security purposes, notwithstanding that a pledged chattel must be handed over to the pledgee (chapter 10 section 1 of the Commercial Code from 1734). In NJA 1912, 156 it was decided that the Bills of Sales Act registration applied and gave protection also to security transactions. In such a case, the purchaser has a right of separation in insolvency and execution, but must account for any proceeds of realisation in excess of the secured claim (see the mandatory section 37 of the Contracts Act 1915). The Bills of Sales Act is not widely used, since the purchaser does not take priority over enterprise charges granted prior to or within thirty days of the registration of the purchase. Many authors argue that genuine sales (but not sales for security purposes) should also be effective against the seller's creditors simply by the fact of their agreement; and that frauds should be tackled by the existing presumption in the Execution Code that chattels in the possession of the debtor belong to the debtor.[107] A reform has recently been proposed regarding sales to consumers by a committee whose terms of reference were limited to this issue (SOU 1995:11).

(b) Sale and lease-back arrangements with registration of the buyer's right under the Bills of Sales Act are practised (but hardly common), for instance when a private person wants to borrow money using individually specified chattels, such as a sailing boat, as collateral which the seller shall retain. Otherwise, the enterprise charge is the *remedium*. A *constitutum possessorium*, or a time-limited transfer of possession, will not suffice (NJA 1925, 535). A lessor has a right of separation when the lessee

---

[107] See e.g. Göranson, *Traditionsprincipen*. In NJA 1997, 660 the Supreme Court declared that the requirement of tradition or registration cannot be changed by a precedent.

CASE 10: BANK LOAN ON THE BASIS OF A CAR FLEET   471

defaults, but forfeiture and damage clauses may be modified pursuant to the Contracts Act.

(c) The answer is applicable to all chattels, except ships and aircraft, to which special rules apply in certain respects. There is also special legislation applicable to livestock and to agricultural equipment which a landlord leases to his tenant (chapter 9 section 35 Land Code, *jordabalken*). Here the requirement of individualisation of the leased chattels is deserted; the cows and hay-forks may float within a fixed value.

(d) Should the finance company, A, become bankrupt, the insolvency estate will step into A's shoes. For instance, B may separate goods that he may have assigned and transferred into A's possession for security purposes, just as if A had been a pledgee. Things may differ in respect of leases, however. The starting point, based on principles contained in the Commercial Code of 1734, is that a lessee does not have protection against the creditors of the lessor. This would imply that the insolvency administrator could elect between the continuation or termination of the lease, termination giving rise to a claim for damages by the lessee that lacks priority. It has been much discussed in the literature whether this principle should be restricted when the lease is of the financial kind, especially if the lessee has, on the expiration of the lease, an option to buy at a price that does reflect the value of the goods. Patent and trademark leases (i.e. licences) have recently been afforded third-party protection, because of their economic importance. No precedents exist concerning finance leases, but it presumably would be possible for the Supreme Court to provide the lessee with protection.[108]

FINLAND

(a) The safest way for A to acquire a real right in the cars would be by the registration of a vehicle charge. This type of charge may be used if the motor vehicle in question is a bus, lorry, truck or similar, but not if it is a car. The problem with this kind of charge is that it must be registered separately for each vehicle; the vehicle fleet cannot, as such, be registered as a whole. On the other hand, the vehicle charge gives a

---

[108] See Håstad, *Sakrätt rörande lös egendom* 431 ff. Leases of real property have long been protected against the landlord's insolvency through legislation.

preferential right of first class and it cannot be extinguished by a *bona fide* purchaser.

Any type of motor vehicle can be used as collateral for the purposes of an enterprise charge.[109] An enterprise charge comprises practically all the movable property used in the business concerned and there is no need to individualise that property in more detail. The weaknesses of the enterprise charge include, however, a relatively inferior preferential status and the possibility that the charge may be extinguished by a sale in the ordinary course of business or by a *bona fide* purchase.

Both arrangements are used on a relatively large scale. No exact statistics are, however, available.

(b) The rules concerning sale and lease-back arrangements are unclear.[110] There is no clear precedent of the Supreme Court and some lower courts have given inconsistent rulings in the few reported cases. Obviously, such agreements have certain attractions to financiers, some of whom have already made use of them. The negative attitude of the doctrine is, on the other hand, mainly based on the argument that this kind of contract has essential similarities with a typical transfer for security purposes and, as such, it must be regarded as an effort to evade the rules concerning pledge.

(c) The rules described above generally apply also to items other than motor vehicles. The registration of a charge relating to specific items of property is, however, possible only in special cases. This regime covers, in addition to lorries, trucks and similar vehicles, also: (1) vessels; (2) vessels under construction; (3) aircraft; (4) aircraft under construction; (5) patents and other industrial property rights; and (6) publicly traded shares, bonds and other securities.[111]

(d) The insolvency of A does not affect B's position, if the parties have used a charge. The insolvency administrator cannot require the debt to be paid prematurely. After payment, B's property is freed from any

---

[109] See further e.g. Havansi, *Esinevakuusoikeudet* 286 ff. and Ojanen/Sutinen, *Yrityskiinnitys* 47 f.

[110] See e.g. Tepora, *Oikeustiede – Jurisprudentia* 1988, 245 ff. and Tuomisto, *Omistuksenpidätyksestä* 224 ff.

[111] See the Vehicle Mortgage Act (*autokiinnityslaki/lag om inteckning i bil*), the Vessel Mortgage Act (*aluskiinnityslaki/lag om inteckning i fartyg*) and the Aircraft Mortgage Act (*laki kiinnityksestä ilma-aluksiin/lag om inteckning i luftfartyg*). Vessels do not fall within the ambit of an enterprise charge.

encumbrances. If the parties have used a sale and lease-back arrangement, B's situation is somewhat unclear. Most probably, however, the insolvency of A would not affect B's position.

Comparative observations

Parts (a)–(c)

Case 10 presents a factual situation where a security for a bank credit is sought, as opposed to a purchase-money security. The collateral consists of equipment, that is identifiable objects, which the debtor does not want to hand over to the creditor and which are not intended to be resold in the normal course of business. In order to satisfy the need for a security right in this specific situation, different constructions can be used and are in fact adopted in the EU Member States and South Africa.

The following summary starts from the basic distinction between security rights based on ownership (group (i)) and non-possessory security rights which are based on the idea of a pledge but where other means of publicity are substituted for the delivery of the collateral, i.e. registration (group (ii)). According to this distinction, the use of sale and lease-back arrangements (part (b)) belongs to group (i) and is therefore discussed together with security transfer of ownership. In case 10, cars have been selected as the potential collateral because they provide an extremely practical example of individually distinguishable equipment (i.e. property that is not meant to be continuously sold and replaced) used as the subject matter of a security right. Nevertheless, the discussions are not limited to cars (part (c)). The following observations, too, seek to address all kinds of specific goods which will remain in the possession of the debtor, to be used in his business.

(i) Use of ownership for security purposes

Germany and Greece are the only jurisdictions that consider the transfer of ownership for the purpose of creating a security right as valid and opposable without requiring any specific form or publicity. All other jurisdictions regard such a transaction either as completely invalid, including as between the parties, or as at least ineffective *vis-à-vis* third parties. Swedish law permits a registered sale that can also be used for security purposes and which would protect the seller (A) against the buyer's (B's) creditors; however, for the reasons pointed out in the

Swedish report, the registered sale is not much used in practice. In Spain,[112] the admissibility of security transfer of ownership and its validity as against third parties is still disputed.[113]

Retention of title which – as we have seen – meets with more approval, may also be used in the present context, yet only within certain limits. The Austrian and South African reports describe such practices whereby either the retained title is transferred by a third party to the bank (Austria), or the cars are sold to the bank and then sold back under retention of title to the loan debtor (South Africa). Only the second method would be possible in the circumstances of case 10. It is interesting to note that the same kind of sale and resale transaction which today seems acceptable in South African law was also in use in Germany and the Netherlands at an early stage in the evolution of security transfer of ownership and was sanctioned by the courts at the end of the nineteenth and the beginning of the twentieth century.[114]

Sale and lease-back transactions are a third and more widely accepted way to use ownership as a security right. As to the degree of admissibility, we can roughly distinguish four groups of jurisdictions:

(1) In Germany, Belgium, Spain and the Netherlands sale and lease-back transactions are valid without the need to avoid giving the appearance of a security transfer of ownership. This is not surprising for German law. As the Dutch reporters have pointed out, however, it is in fact astonishing that the *Hoge Raad* has adopted this stance only three years after the general prohibition of security transfer of ownership and security assignment entered into force (even though the *Hoge Raad* has left the door open for exceptions). It is also surprising for Belgian law to allow sale and lease-back, since until recently it strictly adhered to the doctrine of apparent credit (*crédit apparent*).[115]

(2) The second group consists of Austria, Portugal, Italy, England, Ireland, Scotland, Denmark and Finland. The contributors emphasise, albeit to varying degrees, the danger that a sale and lease-back transaction may be characterised, with differing consequences, as a security transfer of

---

[112] This means according to the Spanish *Código civil*. Some of the Autonomous Communities have adopted special legislation: see Spanish report, *supra* and Hellmich, *Kreditsicherungsrechte in der spanischen Mehrrechtsordnung* 130 ff. and 145 ff.

[113] See on the one hand Spanish report, *supra* (security transfer of ownership valid but not used), and on the other hand Hellmich, *Kreditsicherungsrechte in der spanischen Mehrrechtsordnung* 82 ff.

[114] Germany: RG 9 Oct. 1880, RGZ 2, 168; RG 17 Mar. 1885, RGZ 13, 298 (on the basis of the *Code civil!*); RG 10 Jan. 1885, RGZ 13, 200. Netherlands: *Hoge Raad* 25 Jan. 1929, NJ 1929, 616.

[115] See *supra*, Belgian report, case 3(a).

ownership, or – more generally speaking – as a non-possessory security right, if the contract did not appear to be a true lease.
(3) A third group is formed by France and Sweden. Both escape the problem of distinguishing between a leasing contract and a security right which would be subject to registration by simply requiring the same publicity also for leasing transactions.[116] Without registration, the lessor's right in the goods is not opposable as against third parties.
(4) Greek law presents an anomaly compared to the other jurisdictions as it submits leasing contracts to stricter requirements (written form, registration) than security ownership.

The most striking difference in respect of the use of ownership as a security right lies evidently between German and Greek law on the one hand and the other European jurisdictions on the other hand. The reasons that have been advanced in the national reports to explain this fundamental difference in approach merit some further consideration.

The necessity of delivery for the transfer of ownership may be said to present an obstacle for establishing security ownership, as is pointed out especially in the Scots report. Yet, in German law, too, delivery is necessary for ownership to pass to the buyer. It is true, as has been emphasised in the German report, that actual delivery may be replaced with a *constitutum possessorium* (§ 931 BGB), yet this possibility also exists in a number of jurisdictions which regard security ownership as invalid, e.g. Austria[117] and the Netherlands.[118] Moreover, there is no requirement of delivery in those systems which, with respect to the transfer of ownership, adhere to the *solo consensu* principle, such as France, Belgium and Italy, but which nevertheless do not recognise the validity of security transfer of ownership.

Another reason frequently referred to is the prohibition of the so-called *pactum commissorium*. This reason is explicitly advanced in the Italian and Portuguese reports, but it can also be found in a decision of the French *Cour de cassation* on the question of whether a German security ownership agreement could be upheld, when the collateral subject to it crossed the Franco-German border.[119] Again, this prohibition is also part of German law on possessory pledge: see § 1229 BGB. But since the fiduciary character of the security ownership effectively limits the

---

[116] In Sweden, the need to register the lease only applies to sale and lease-back transactions, such as in the present case, and not if the movables were bought by the lessor from a third party.
[117] See *supra*, Austrian report, case 1(a).   [118] See *supra*, Dutch report, case 1(a).
[119] Cass. 8 July 1969, Rev.crit.d.i.p. 60 (1970) 75 ff.

owner's powers, § 1229 BGB does not invalidate the transaction. One may be able to think of similar solutions in order also to overcome the prohibition of the *pactum commissorium* in other jurisdictions.

Thirdly one may argue that the purpose of creating a security right is not a valid or sufficient *causa* for the transfer of ownership, thus either preventing a valid transfer or subjecting it to a claim in unjust enrichment. This reason is referred to for instance in the South African report,[120] albeit with respect to sale and resale under retention of title. However, the argument seems to be a *petitio principii*. If the security transfer is regarded as valid, one may well construe the underlying security agreement as a valid *causa*, otherwise the opposite solution applies. In contrast to views expressed in Greek and Spanish legal literature,[121] the principle of abstraction cannot be seen as the decisive reason for the admissibility of security ownership. Although under the principle of abstraction the transfer of ownership remains valid even without a just cause, the transfer still needs a valid obligation to support it. Otherwise ownership has to be retransferred on the basis of unjust enrichment. South African law, which adheres to the principle of abstraction,[122] provides an example.

The fourth and probably most persuasive reason that has been put forward for the prohibition of security ownership is its lack of publicity. Yet, in so far as this consideration is based on an application of the rules on possessory pledge, German law, which starts from the same *lex scripta* as the other jurisdictions, again provides an example of a construction which supports the validity of security ownership. The difference lies in the fact that the German courts have simply not applied the requirement of actual delivery (§ 1205 BGB) to the security transfer of ownership. It is perhaps more due to the introduction of special or general non-possessory security rights which require registration that the principle of publicity has been reinforced in those jurisdictions which do not recognise security ownership. With the exception of Austria and South Africa, all those jurisdictions provide a specific way to create a non-possessory security right in movable property, be it in the form of a fixed or enterprise charge, a *mortgage*, a *hypothec* or a pledge.

---

[120] It is also advanced by the predominant opinion in Spanish legal literature that argues against the validity of security transfer of ownership: see Hellmich, *Kreditsicherungsrechte in der spanischen Mehrrechtsordnung* 85 ff.

[121] For Spain, see Hellmich, *Kreditsicherungsrechte in der spanischen Mehrrechtsordnung* 86.

[122] See *supra*, South African report, case 2.

To conclude this brief discussion, it is submitted that the difference between German and Greek law and the other jurisdictions under consideration cannot satisfactorily be explained through differences as to the general rules on the transfer of ownership or statutory rules relating to the possessory pledge. The reason rather seems to lie in the development of this area of the law around the end of the nineteenth century and the beginning of the twentieth century.[123] At this time the expanding European economies faced an enormous increase in the demand for credit and security which could not be satisfied only through the use of the possessory pledge or charges over immovable property. In a number of jurisdictions, e.g. in France, Belgium and Italy, the legislature intervened and created specific security rights under which the need for delivery was replaced by a registration requirement. Nothing of this sort happened in Germany where the courts and ultimately the legislature sanctioned what the practice had created for itself.

(ii) Security rights based on the idea of a pledge without dispossession

There are three main criteria according to which one may analyse the various non-possessory security rights that are mentioned in the reports: (1) the question of whether the right attaches only to specified movables or may attach to a corpus of movables where the individual ingredients may change (fixed and enterprise charges); (2) the question of whether a specific security right may apply to all kinds of movable property and to all kinds of claims or whether it is limited to specific categories such as registrable movables (cars, vessels, aircraft) or to specific kinds of claims, such as the claim arising out of a sale; and (3) the question of how the lack of actual delivery is addressed.

In respect of the first question, the *floating charge* (enterprise charge) is a child of English common law and has also taken root in Ireland and Scotland. It has likewise taken hold in Sweden and Finland and is about to be transplanted into Greek law. All other jurisdictions know only what may be termed a fixed charge, meaning a security right that attaches to specified property. This distinction will be considered in detail in case 11 which, dealing with security rights in floating stock, is more in point.

As to the second question, Spanish, Dutch, English and Irish law recognise types of registrable pledges or fixed charges that apply to all categories of movables. The majority of jurisdictions, on the other

---

[123] See in more detail Kieninger, *Mobiliarsicherheiten im Europäischen Binnenmarkt* 24 ff.

hand, offer the statutory framework to create registrable charges only in respect of specific kinds of movables, such as, for example, cars, trucks, aircraft, vessels, etc. France, Belgium, Portugal, Italy, Denmark, Sweden and Finland belong to this group, but also England and Germany which recognise, in respect of certain equipment of high value such as aircraft and vessels, a special registrable pledge.[124] In France, the statutory possibility to establish a charge may even be confined to specific kinds of debts. The French report points out that, for instance, the *gage sur véhicule* can only be used by the seller to secure the payment of the purchase price of the vehicles in question.

Finally, the lack of publicity arising from the absence of actual delivery is most commonly (more than) compensated by a requirement of registration in publicly accessible registers. Such registration may be tied to the person giving the security or to the collateral. The first option is adopted by English, Irish and Scots law; the second is followed by most jurisdictions which provide charges only for specific kinds of assets: such as, for example, the French *gage sur véhicule* or the Italian *privilegio sull' autoveicolo*.

However, there are also jurisdictions which require the observance of a certain form without rendering the security right public. The most prominent example is the Dutch 'silent pledge' which has been introduced to replace security ownership, on its invalidation. The pledge is in fact silent. Even if the parties opt for registration instead of setting up a notarised deed, third parties remain unable to inform themselves about the existence of such pledges because the register is not publicly accessible. If the reason for the prohibition of security ownership was the uncertainty that is created by hidden, non-possessory security interests, one may well ask what the advantage of such a 'silent' pledge may be. This tension might be one of the reasons why the *Hoge Raad* itself does not seem to take the prohibition of security ownership[125] and security assignment[126] too seriously.

Part (d)

B's situation, in the unlikely event of A's insolvency, depends on the nature of secured transaction entered into. As a general rule, B enjoys

---

[124] See, for German law, *ibid.*, 26 note 38 with further references.
[125] See Dutch report, *supra* at note 77.
[126] See *Hoge Raad* 16 May 1997, *Rechtspraak van de Week* 126 (*Brandsma q.q. v Hansa Chemie AG*); Struycken, *Lloyd's Maritime and Commercial Law Quarterly* 1998, 345 (352 f.).

a better position if the parties have agreed on a security right in the strict sense, including security ownership, than if they have utilised a sale and lease-back contract.

Those jurisdictions which recognise the charge (England, Ireland, Scotland, Portugal) or a non-possessory pledge (the Netherlands) draw the obvious conclusion that B has remained the owner of the cars and is therefore entitled to vindicate his unencumbered property provided he pays back the loan. The same solution applies under German and Greek law when B has transferred security ownership to A. This result, which is less obvious, is a consequence of the fiduciary character of the transaction.

If the parties have concluded a contract of sale and lease-back, the answers to part (d) are more diverse. They will be discussed in the comparative observations to case 14(d).

Case 11: Bank loan for a wholesaler

(Security right in revolving stock-in-trade – security ownership – enterprise charge – actio Pauliana)

A, a financial institution, intends to make a loan to B, who is starting a business as a wholesaler of motorcar accessories. To avoid personal liability, B sets up a private limited company (C). A wishes to take a security right over the stock that will be present on C's premises. The nature of the business is such that the stock will continuously be sold and replaced. A does not, therefore, wish its security right to be confined to present stock; rather it wishes it to include the stock that will be purchased by C in the future.

Questions

(a) Is such an arrangement possible? Describe its main features and prerequisites, including any requirements that may exist as to form, registration, separate storage, etc.
(b) What rights would such an arrangement confer on the secured party (A) in the event of C's insolvency? Or if another (unsecured) creditor tried to execute against the stock?
(c) How common are arrangements of this kind in business practice?
(d) Are there any limits in respect of the value the collateral may have in relation to the amount of the secured loan?

Variation

The position is as described above, except that the security right was created many months after the loan was made, at a time when C was already beginning to be in financial difficulties.

Does this affect A's legal position? If so, in what way?

Discussions

GERMANY

(a) As in case 10, the parties may use security transfer of ownership. In case 10, the security right related to specific property which was easily capable of identification. In such a context, the principle of specificity (the principle that real rights must always relate to a specific piece of property)[1] did not present any problems. In respect of stock-in-trade, however, two questions must be considered: (1) How can stock that will be acquired in the future be included within the ambit of the security right? (2) How can the principle of specificity be complied with?

In respect of the first question, in German law, a transfer of security ownership of movables may extend to stock that will be acquired by the debtor in the future. Both the agreements necessary to transfer ownership, the real agreement (*Einigung*)[2] and the *constitutum possessorium* (§ 868 BGB) as a substitute for delivery,[3] may be concluded in advance.[4] They become operative as soon as the debtor acquires ownership of the new stock.

So far as the second question is concerned, the test for compliance with the principle of specificity is whether a third party, who was aware of the contents of the agreement between the parties, would be able to point to the specific goods subjected to the security transfer of ownership, without having to refer to other documents, books, etc.[5] Security transfer of ownership in stock-in-trade is usually undertaken in one of the following ways, both of which meet this requirement:[6] (1) it is stipulated that the transfer relates to all stock stored in a specific room, or (2) the stock in question is stored separately and either marked or described by individual characteristics such as serial number, etc. By

---

[1] See generally Van Vliet, *Transfer of Movables* 27 f.
[2] See *supra*, German report, case 1(a).
[3] See *supra*, German report, case 3(c) and Van Vliet, *Transfer of Movables* 53 ff.
[4] See Staudinger/Wiegand, *Kommentar zum Bürgerlichen Gesetzbuch* Anhang zu §§ 929–931 BGB n. 128; Baur/Stürner, *Sachenrecht* § 51 n. 31.
[5] Cf. BGH 31 Jan. 1979, BGHZ 73, 253 (254), with further references; BGH 3 Dec. 1987, JZ 1988, 471; BHG 4 Oct. 1993, NJW 1994, 133 (134); Reinicke/Tiedtke, *Kreditsicherung* n. 460; Baur/Stürner, *Sachenrecht* § 57 n. 13; Staudinger/Wiegand Anhang zu §§ 929–931 BGB nn. 97–102.
[6] BGH 27 Sep. 1960, WM 1960, 1223 (1226); BGH 13 Jan. 1992, NJW 1992, 1161; BGH 18 Apr. 1991, NJW 1991, 2144 (2146); Reinicke/Tiedtke, *Kreditsicherung* n. 460; Baur/Stürner, *Sachenrecht* § 57 n. 13; Staudinger/Wiegand Anhang zu §§ 929–931 BGB n. 108; Palandt/Bassenge § 930 BGB nn. 3–5; Bülow, *Recht der Kreditsicherheiten* nn. 1109–1111.

way of contrast, a security transfer is not valid if it relates to a certain percentage of stock or to stock equalling the value of the remaining debt.[7] In the case of a security transfer of ownership of future stock, the newly acquired goods must be stored in the same separate room as the remaining collateral or must be marked and stored separately.[8] It is only at this point that security ownership will pass from the debtor to the creditor.[9]

If these requirements are met, there is no need for any further publicity (registration or suchlike).

Stock-in-trade containing goods sold under retention of title

Security transfer of ownership of stock-in-trade gives rise to a special problem,[10] due to the widespread use of retention of title clauses in simple or extended form.[11] Often, goods acquired by C will be subject to a retention of title agreement and therefore will not (yet) be owned by C. C's supplier will usually only have entitled C to transfer ownership in these goods in the normal course of C's business, not for security purposes, as this would contravene the seller's own security interest. A *bona fide* acquisition of ownership cannot take place, because that would require the transferee (A) to take direct possession of the goods (see § 933 BGB).[12] The problem cannot be solved through an agreement to transfer title only to those goods (out of the pool of goods as a whole) which are owned by the debtor, since the BGH considers such an arrangement to be in conflict with the principle of specificity.[13] Usually, therefore, the parties agree to transfer all goods marked or stored separately irrespective of whether they are already owned by the debtor or not.[14] So far as such a transfer includes goods delivered under retention of title, A will only get a security right in the expectancy (*Anwartschaftsrecht*)[15]

---

[7] BGH 13 June 1956, BGHZ 21, 52 (55); Baur/Stürner, *Sachenrecht* § 57 n. 13.
[8] Reinicke/Tiedtke, *Kreditsicherung* n. 466. For a thorough analysis of this requirement, see Staudinger/Wiegand Anhang zu §§ 929–931 BGB nn. 129–138.
[9] Reinicke/Tiedtke, *Kreditsicherung* n. 466; Baur/Stürner, *Sachenrecht* § 51 n. 32; Bülow, *Recht der Kreditsicherheiten* n. 1116.
[10] See generally Staudinger/Wiegand Anhang zu §§ 929–931 BGB nn. 109–122.
[11] See *supra*, German report, cases 3 to 6.   [12] See *supra*, German report, case 5(a).
[13] BGH 13 June 1956, BGHZ 21, 52 (56); BGH 24 June 1958, BGHZ 28, 16 (20); BGH 20 Mar. 1986, WM 1986, 594 (595); BGH 12 Oct. 1989, NJW–RR 1990, 94 (95); *contra*: Staudinger/Wiegand Anhang zu §§ 929–931 BGB n. 110.
[14] BGH WM 20 Mar. 1986, 594 (595); Staudinger/Wiegand Anhang zu §§ 929–931 BGB nn. 112 f. (general opinion).
[15] See *supra*, German report, case 3(c).

that C has under the retention of title.[16] The rights of the seller thus take priority over those of the security owner, irrespective of the point in time when the agreements were concluded.

(b) A has the status of a security owner.[17]

(c) Security ownership of stock-in-trade is extremely common.

(d) According to property law principles, the existence and validity of security ownership does not depend on the existence of the secured claim,[18] yet the secured creditor should not obtain more than the value of his claim. During the existence of a security agreement, a situation may arise where the value of the collateral exceeds that of the secured claim. This is especially prevalent where security ownership of revolving stock-in-trade is concerned, which, according to German law, may even extend into the proceeds of sale of such stock (security assignment of claims[19]). Such a situation is detrimental to the debtor, since he will no longer be able to use his property as collateral for other loans. The law could react in one of two ways: it could either consider an agreement void, if it does not adequately protect the debtor; or it may itself imply into the agreement the appropriate protection. Prior to a landmark decision of the BGH in 1997, the courts adopted the first solution. They held that a security transfer of ownership contained in general contract terms was invalid *as a whole* according to § 307 BGB,[20] if the contract did not include a properly worded waiver of the transferee's rights, in so far as their realisable value exceeded the outstanding debts by more than 20 per cent.[21] This jurisdiction was widely criticised, since in practically all cases it was the insolvency administrator who invoked the invalidity of the security transfer in question for the benefit of the insolvency creditors, and thus for third parties, whom the rules on unfair contract terms do not aim to protect. Due to this criticism, the jurisprudence

---

[16] See Baur/Stürner, *Sachenrecht* § 57 n. 11.   [17] See *supra*, German report, case 7(c), (d).
[18] Bülow, *Recht der Kreditsicherheiten* nn. 944 f.
[19] See *supra*, German report, case 6(b) and *infra*, German report, cases 12 and 13.
[20] § 307 BGB (prior to 1 Jan. 2002: § 9 AGBG) transposes article 3 n. 1 of the Directive 93/13/EEC of 5 Apr. 1993 on unfair contract terms in consumer contracts (O.J. No L 95/29 of 21 Apr. 1993) into German law.
[21] BGH 20 Mar. 1985, BGHZ 94, 105 (113/114); BGH 2 Dec. 1992, BGHZ 120, 300 (= NJW 1993, 533); BGH 9 Feb. 1994, NJW 1994, 1154; Bülow, *Recht der Kreditsicherheiten* nn. 1262 and 1297; Nobbe, ZIP 1996, 657.

was changed and now the second solution has been adopted.[22] Generally speaking, the creditor has to retransfer collateral if its value exceeds the secured claim. The difficulty evidently lies in fixing the value of the collateral. Principally, the BGH assumes that the realisable value of movables and claims is about two-thirds of their market price or nominal value. Therefore, the duty to retransfer collateral to the debtor only arises if the secured claim exceeds the collateral's nominal or market value by more than 150 per cent. As mentioned earlier, the parties no longer have to include in the security agreement an express provision imposing such an obligation: this is now implied by law.

Variation

Under such circumstances, the insolvency administrator may be able to avoid the security transfer of ownership by virtue of §§ 129 ff. InsO. The law distinguishes between two situations. If the favoured creditor (A) had a right to claim the security granted, for example, because C had by contract promised to provide it, the security in question is called *congruous*. If, however, A had no such previous right, or if he did not have the right to claim a security at that point in time, such security is called *incongruous*. According to § 130 InsO, the granting of a congruent security can be avoided if (1) the security was granted within the three-month period prior to the application for the commencement of insolvency proceedings; (2) the debtor was unable to pay his debts at the time at which the security was granted; and (3) the favoured creditor (A) knew this or knew of circumstances which necessarily pointed to insolvency. The granting of an incongruous security can be avoided if it took place within one month prior to the application for the commencement of insolvency proceedings; there are no further requirements as to knowledge on the part of the favoured creditor (§ 131 s. 1 Nr. 1 InsO). If the grant took place in the second or third month prior to the application, there are two alternative requirements, one of which must be met. Either the debtor must have been insolvent at the time of grant or the favoured creditor must have known that the act was detrimental to other creditors (§ 131 s. 1 Nr. 2 and 3 InsO).

Furthermore, the new Insolvency Code (InsO) maintains avoidance provisions in respect of agreements that have been entered into by the debtor with the intention of prejudicing other creditors, if that

---

[22] See BGH (*Großer Zivilsenat*) 27 Nov. 1997, NJW 1998, 671 = BGHZ 137, 212.

intention was known to the other party to the transaction (§ 133 s. 1 InsO). The right of avoidance is now limited to transactions within ten years (instead of the former period of thirty years: see § 41 s. 1 sent. 3 KO) prior to the application for the commencement of insolvency proceedings. Knowledge by the other party is presumed if that party knew that the debtor would no longer be able to pay his debts as they fell due *and* that the transfer prejudiced other creditors.

Powers of avoidance also exist in the context of execution.[23] According to § 3 s. 1 AnfG, a third-party creditor (on behalf of whom the execution is initiated and who does not get full satisfaction) can avoid a legal act performed by the debtor if (1) that act was performed within the last ten years; (2) the debtor acted with the intention of prejudicing third-party creditors; and (3) the favoured creditor knew of the intention at the time the act took place. Such knowledge is assumed if the favoured creditor knew that the debtor was close to being unable to pay his debts and that the act was detrimental to other creditors.

AUSTRIA

(a) According to Austrian law, it is possible to pledge a stock of goods. If it is not possible to hand the stock over to the pledgee,[24] it is necessary that *control* over the stock is handed over to the pledgee in some other way[25] *and* that signs are attached to the stock, making it evident to third persons that the stock has been pledged. In order to give the pledgee control over the stock, it is necessary to appoint a person of confidence on behalf of the pledgee, who is able to control whether items of the stock are taken away.[26] If the signs are taken away, the pledgee will lose his

---

[23] See also *infra*, German report, case 15.
[24] The same rules (and especially, the publicity requirement) apply to security ownership.
[25] OGH 30 Jan. 1991, 8 Ob 678/89 ÖBA 1991, 594. A transfer of control over the stock to the pledgee means that the pledgee can decide whether goods are taken out of the stock or not. This was first decided in GlU 8592. In Rspr 1926/166, the OGH looked at the problem in a different way. In this case a wine cellar was pledged. The pledgor had the right to remove wine, but was obliged to replace the quantity taken out. The OGH held that this was sufficient for the pledge to be effective. In the legal scientific writing, some writers argue that an entitlement of the pledgor to remove goods does not affect the validity of the pledge; cf. *Rummel*/Spielbüchler § 303 ABGB n. 3. His argument, however, is conceptual: he argues that the stock is a *universitas rerum*, to which the strict rules for other objects do not apply.
[26] OGH 27 Apr. 1994, 3 Ob 45/94 ÖBA 1994, 992; OGH 18 Dec. 1996, 3 Ob 2442/96f ÖBA 1998, 216.

rights in the stock.[27] These rules apply not only to the present stock, but also to stock purchased in the future.

(b) If these requirements are met, A will have a valid pledge over the stock. In the event of C's insolvency, he has the right to preferential satisfaction (*Absonderungsrecht*): the proceeds of sale of the pledged objects are primarily used to satisfy his claim. If another creditor of C executes against the stock, A's rights have priority over the rights of this creditor: again, the proceeds of sale will be used primarily to satisfy A's claim; the second creditor would receive only any eventual surplus.

(c) They are quite common.

(d) No court decisions exist on this issue. It has to be pointed out, however, that an arrangement where the value of the collateral greatly exceeds the value of the secured loan could be against the *bonos mores* (*gute Sitten*, § 879 (1) ABGB.)

Variation

A pledge that is granted after the pledgor has begun to experience financial difficulties can, in certain circumstances, be set aside by C's insolvency administrator.

The Austrian Bankruptcy Act contains provisions detailing which transactions disadvantageous to the bankrupt's creditors can be avoided by the administrator of C's assets. There are the following categories:

(1) § 28 (a) KO: Transactions based on the debtor's intention to defraud his creditors. If the other party knew of this intention, the transaction can be avoided by the administrator if it took place within ten years prior to the commencement of insolvency proceedings. If the other party did not know of this intention but could have known it, the transaction can be avoided by the administrator if it took place within two years prior to the commencement of insolvency proceedings. If the other party did not know the intention and could not have known of it, the transaction cannot be avoided. It is for the administrator to prove that the requirements for avoidance are met, unless the other party is a near relative of the bankrupt.

---

[27] OGH 27 Apr. 1994, 3 Ob 45/94 ÖBA 1994, 992; OGH 18 June 1997, 3 Ob 2403/96w ÖBA 1998, 123.

(2) § 28 (b) KO: Transactions by which the debtor sold goods at dumping prices. The buyer must know that the transaction at a dumping price was to the disadvantage of the seller's creditors. Such a transaction can be avoided if it took place within the last year prior to the commencement of insolvency proceedings.

(3) § 29 KO: Gratuitous transfers within two years prior to the commencement of insolvency proceedings.

(4) § 30 (1) N 1 KO: The payment or grant of an incongruous security right (such as a pledge, etc.) in respect of a debt when the creditor in question was not entitled[28] to claim payment or security at that time, provided that the payment or grant took place after the debtor became unable to pay his debts. The transaction can be avoided by the administrator if it took place within the year prior to the commencement of insolvency proceedings.

(5) § 30 (1) N 3 KO: The payment or grant of an incongruous security right (such as a pledge, etc.) in respect of a debt by which the debtor prefers one creditor over others, provided that the creditor knew of the debtor's intention to prefer him and that the payment or grant took place after the debtor became unable to pay his debts. The transaction can be avoided by the administrator if it took place within the year prior to the commencement of insolvency proceedings. It is for the administrator to prove that the requirements for avoidance have been met, unless the other party is a near relative of the bankrupt.[29]

(6) § 31 KO: The payment or grant of an incongruous security right (such as a pledge, etc.) in respect of a debt, or any other legal act by the bankrupt that is to the detriment of the creditors; provided that the transaction was carried out for the benefit of a creditor who either knew or should have known of the incapability of the debtor to pay his debts. The transaction can be avoided by the administrator if it took place within the six months prior to the commencement of insolvency proceedings. It is for the administrator to prove that the requirements for avoidance have been met, unless the other party is a near relative of the bankrupt.

The avoidance of a transaction on grounds (1) to (3), *supra*, can also take place outside of insolvency (cf. §§ 2 and 3 Avoidance Act (*Anfechtungsordnung*)).

---

[28] This could be because either the original agreement did not provide for such a right or the creditor gave credit without exercising his right!

[29] § 30 n. 1 and n. 3 KO are based on the principle that the debtor, once he is unable to pay his debts, must treat all his creditors alike – he is not allowed to prefer one above the others: see Koziol, *Grundlagen und Streitfragen der Gläubigeranfechtung* 15 ff.

A right to seize (*exekutives Pfandrecht*) established within the sixty-day period prior to the commencement of insolvency proceedings becomes ineffective on commencement (§ 12 KO).

A security which is granted near to the date of the debtor's insolvency can be avoided on the basis of either ground (4) or ground (5), *supra*. The security can be avoided on ground (4), § 30 (1) N 1 KO, if the creditor was not entitled to be granted such a security. If he had a right to the grant of a security, then it could be avoided on ground (5), § 30 (1) N 3 KO, if the debtor, when granting the security, had the intention to prefer the creditor and the creditor had to know about the debtor's intention to prefer him. In both cases, it is necessary that the grant took place *after* the debtor became unable to pay his debts. If the creditor knew, or should have known, of the debtor's inability to pay his debts (*Zahlungsunfähigkeit*), the grant of the security could be avoided on ground (6), § 31 KO.

GREECE

(a) A may obtain a security right over the replaced stock. This can be achieved in one of the following ways:

(1) Security transfer of ownership of the future stock. Ownership of future movables can be transferred by an anticipated *constitutum possessorium* (article 977 para. 1 A.K.). At the moment the debtor acquires ownership of the new stock, it is *ipso iure* transferred to A. Security transfer of ownership of a replaced stock presents the following problems:
   (i) According to the principle of specificity, the object of the real transaction must be specifically identified. In respect of the circulating stock of a shop, it is suggested[30] that the principle of specificity is satisfied in the following cases: (a) when a detailed catalogue of the things transferred is attached to the contract; (b) when the whole of the merchandise stored in a clearly identifiable warehouse is transferred; or (c) when each item to be transferred is clearly marked and the contract makes reference to these markings. Generally, it is not regarded as sufficient to identify the goods by reference to information not specified in the contract itself. Further publicity is not required.
   (ii) If the new stock is delivered to C under retention of title (article 532 A.K.), a common practice in transactions, A acquires only C's

---

[30] Georgiadis, *Empragmato Dikaio* II 234.

right of expectancy. When C pays the price in full to the seller, A acquires full ownership of the new stock.
  (iii) Under a security transfer of a circulating stock, the creditor usually empowers the debtor further to transfer the goods (article 239 para. 1 A.K.). This solution serves the interests of the creditor and corresponds to the destination of the merchandise.
(2) According to article 16 of L. 2844/2000 on 'Contracts concerning movables or claims subject to publicity, and other contracts providing security'[31] (*Symvaseis epi kiniton i apaitiseon ypokeimenes se dimosiotita kai alles symvaseis parochis asphaleias*), A is able to obtain an enterprise charge over C's new stock, without a security transfer of ownership being necessary. The enterprise charge, in contrast to security ownership, must be registered in special books kept at the so-called 'pledge registry'. The debtor will be obliged to inform the creditor periodically about the status of the stock.

(b) In the event of C's insolvency, it is disputed whether A can claim the goods as owner,[32] or whether he is simply entitled to preferential payment out of the proceeds of the sale.[33] The latter view prevails. Accordingly, A has the rights of a secured creditor (application by analogy of the provisions on pledge, article 1237 A.K.) unless the insolvency administrator pays the debt in full (article 645 EmbN).

(c) Security transfer of ownership is the method usually adopted.

(d) A general clause regulating this case does not exist in Greek law. It is obvious that the problem has proved to be increasingly interesting in the case of security transfer of ownership of replaced stock. Neither Greek courts nor Greek literature have dealt with the problem.

It could be suggested that in this case it may be possible for the debtor to ask for the judicial reduction of the collateral, when its value is disproportionately higher than that of the secured claim (article 409 A.K. by analogy). According to article 409 A.K., which regulates excessive penalties, 'if the agreed penalty is disproportionately high, the court, at the petition of the debtor, may reduce it to the due measure'. This clause stems from the principle of good faith (article 288 A.K.).

---

[31] See *supra*, Greek report, case 1(a).
[32] See G. Simitis, *I di emboreumaton isphalismeni trapeziki pistosis* 72; K. Simitis, *I anamorphosis tou plasmatikou enechyrou* 34.
[33] AP 1307/1994, DEE 1995, 407. This view is followed by Georgiadis, *Kyriotis* 223 and the authors mentioned there. See also Kotsiris, *Nees morphes symvaseon tis sygchronis oikonomias* 340; N. Rokas, *Stoicheia ptocheutikou dikaiou* 35.

Variation

The fact that the security transfer took place many months after the credit was granted does not affect its validity. But if the transfer, which caused the insolvency of C, was made with an intention of prejudicing the other creditors of C, and this was known to A, then C's creditors have the right to contest the alienation within the following five years (articles 939, 946 A.K.). In C's insolvency the administrator may *ipso iure* revoke the subsequent security transfer. According to article 537 EmbN, the grant of a real security for a pre-existing debt during the suspect period, or ten days before it, is revocable, irrespective of the good or bad faith of the creditor. It has also been suggested[34] that a security transfer of ownership which is granted to reinforce a previous claim, rather than a present or a future claim, is revocable, according to an expansive interpretation of the above rule.

It should also be mentioned that the above provision is not applicable if the real security is granted to secure the pre-existing claim of a bank (L.D. 4001/1959). If A is a bank, the insolvency administrator cannot revoke a security transfer of ownership, even if made many months after the loan was made. There is a contention, however, that such security ownership could be annulled by the court (article 538 EmbN).

FRANCE

(a) French law does not provide for a security interest akin to the English *floating charge*.[35] The main problem about creating a security right over stock-in-trade stems from the invalidity under French law of security rights over future and/or non-individualised assets. Yet, due to the needs of commerce, French law has created specific instruments by which fungible or revolving assets may be charged. These instruments are based on the legal concept of the *warrant*.[36] This is a form of security available to professionals, which takes the form of a promissory note handed to the creditor, as a guarantee for credit, that can subsequently be assigned. Publicity is arranged. The debtor must retain and look after the collateral or, where the assets are fungible, he must maintain the stock in

---

[34] N. Rokas, *Stoicheia ptocheutikou dikaiou* 41; see also K. Rokas, *Ptocheutikon Dikaion* 243 who suggests that article 537 EmbN is applicable also in the case of a security transfer of ownership over a ship.
[35] For general information on the *floating charge* and French law, see Dahan, JDI 1996, 381.
[36] From the English term *warranty*. See Scholder, Rev jur com 1980, 121.

the same quantity or value. The nature of the assets concerned is such that the creditor has no right to trace into the hands of third parties, but the creditor is granted fictitious possession and a right of retention, which means that he has a right to the proceeds of a sale ordered by an insolvency administrator.[37]

The warrants available in respect of fungible assets are:

(1) the agricultural warrant over fungible assets;[38]
(2) the warrant over a stock of products derived from petrol;[39]
(3) the warrant over a stock of war material;[40]
(4) the warrant over industrial assets.[41]

In practice, only the first warrant is used. In the instant case, C cannot grant a security right by way of warrant over his revolving stock-in-trade, because there is no warrant applicable to motorcar accessories.

Of more relevance to the present case would be a security right over C's trading activity. The Law of 17 March 1909 allows the charge of an undertaking's *fonds de commerce*. Basically, a *fonds de commerce* is made up of the property of the business (equipment, rental agreement of the premises, patents and trademarks, etc.) and the attributes of the business (name, commercial appellation, clients, location of the business that contributes to commercial activities, etc.). In order for a valid charge to be constituted over the *fonds de commerce*, the business must possess a clientele and the said clientele must be included within it. The *fonds de commerce* represents wealth that can be traded: either sold or used as collateral for a security right.

(b) It is possible to create a security right over a *fonds de commerce*. The charge (*nantissement*) is equivalent to a pledge, although of course it does not require the surrender of possession, since the very value of the *fonds de commerce* depends on its continued exploitation as a going concern. The parties are free to specify what is included as collateral, but it should be noted that immovable assets (e.g., title to buildings and materials

---

[37] TGI Douai, 17 Sep. 1992, Rev proc coll 1993, 424, obs. Dureuil.
[38] Rural Code, articles L. 342.1 ff.; Wine Code. This warrant may be used only by farmers and producers, in order to charge crops, animals or farming equipment.
[39] Law of 21 Apr. 1932. The warrant is available only to oil companies.
[40] Decree-Law of 24 June 1939.
[41] Law of 12 Sep. 1940. This was created during wartime and required manufacturers to have been granted a letter of agreement which invited them to undertake the production of goods for the war effort.

incorporated into immovable assets) *cannot* form part of a *fonds de commerce*. Moreover, the charge (as opposed to the sale) *cannot* include stock-in-trade (Law of 17 March 1909, article 9).[42] Publicity is arranged in order to inform third parties. Registration on a special register is required within fifteen days following the execution of the charging agreement.[43] The chargee does not have a direct interest in the particular assets, his interest lies in the undertaking as a whole. Thus, enforcement must be ordered by a court, which will arrange the sale of the undertaking by auction and pay the chargee out of the proceeds of sale.

An important drawback of the instrument is that the chargee does not enjoy a very high level of priority (all taxes are paid ahead of him). Also, the very value of the *fonds de commerce* depends upon the ability of the trader to manage it and to generate profits. Enforcement of the charge is likely to occur at a time when it has failed.

(c) The *nantissement de fonds de commerce* is well known to the retail sector and is very commonly used in practice, despite its limitations. So in the present case, A will certainly wish to take such a charge over C's undertaking, as this will provide security over many elements of C's business, but *not* the stock.

(d) No limitation is imposed on the value of the *fonds de commerce* that may be charged referable to the amount of the secured loan.

Variation

Pursuant to C. com, article L. 621-107, a number of transactions concluded by the debtor before the commencement of insolvency proceedings but after the date for the suspension of payments (as defined by C. com, article L. 621-1 and 621-7) are deemed to be void. This period is called the suspect period. Paragraph 6 refers to security rights (contractual, statutory or judicial) on immovable and movable property to secure pre-existing debts. There are exceptions to this rule, in particular when the new security interest was created only to replace another one already in existence.[44] So if A was granted a charge over a *fonds*

---

[42] But materials could be included: Req, 21 June 1933, DH 1933, 426.
[43] As confirmed in Civ. (1), 18 Feb. 1997, JCP 1997, Som, 252, obs. Piedelièvre; D affaires 1997, 406.
[44] Com 20 January 1998, Bull civ IV, No 28; JCP 1998, I, 141, obs. Cabrillac; RTDC 1998, 707, obs. Bandrac/Crocq.

de commerce, or a warrant, and after that grant C went into financial difficulties, such a security right could be declared void by the court.

BELGIUM

(a) Financial institutions will generally ask for a *pand op de handelszaak/gage sur fonds de commerce*. This is a form of enterprise charge and was created by the Act of 25 October 1919. It is only available to banks and financial institutions. Other creditors are not entitled to use this form of security. The introduction of this non-possessory security right explains why the business community did not forcefully lobby for the introduction of security transfer of ownership. The chargor remains in possession of the assets and is, as under an English *floating charge*, entitled to dispose of them in the ordinary course of his business. The security right covers not only existing but also future assets. The security interest is perfected by registration of the charging agreement on a public register. The charge must include the essential classes of assets of the business (equipment, goodwill, trademarks). The parties may also include other classes of movable assets (e.g. claims against customers). So far as stock is concerned, article 2 restricts the security interest to 50 per cent of the value of the assets of the enterprise. The parties may not limit the collateral to a particular class of assets (e.g. only stock).

In other cases, the principle that the pledgee must take possession of the assets can be circumvented by the use of constructive possession on the part of a third party. Under the Warrant Act of 1862, stock may be stored in a warehouse, whereupon the warehouse-holder may then prepare a document which represents the goods, which will be a negotiable instrument. This instrument may be transferred to a creditor for security purposes. It is also possible for pledged goods to be stored on the premises of the pledgor, if certain conditions are met in order to prevent him from having free access to the stock. In either case, only the equivalent of an English-model *fixed charge* may be obtained.

(b) A financial institution with a charge of the *pand op de handelszaak/gage sur fonds de commerce* obtains the right to realise the whole of the assets and obtain preferential payment out of the proceeds. However, the security on stock is limited to 50 per cent of its value. In so far as the creditor's claim exceeds an amount that equals 50 per cent of the value of the stock, the creditor will be unsecured. When the debtor is declared bankrupt, the courts will appoint an insolvency administrator (*curator*) to liquidate the assets on the behalf of the chargee and the other creditors. The security rights of the chargee are not jeopardised in the event of insolvency or of execution by other creditors.

(c) The enterprise charge is one of the most important security devices in Belgian commercial practice.

(d) There is no limitation on the value of assets that may be used as collateral referable to the quantum of the debt to be secured. The pledge is valid for existing and future debts.

Variation

Transactions undertaken by the debtor which are intended to infringe the right of recourse of his creditors to his estate can be challenged by those creditors by means of the *actio Pauliana* (article 1167 C.civ.). Such an action is brought directly against the third party. If successful, the transaction in question will be avoided, in order to restore the rights of recourse of the plaintiff. When this is not possible, the third party will be required to pay compensation. In order to be successful, the plaintiff must prove: (1) a personal prejudice that resulted from the transaction (e.g. a reduction of his right of recourse); (2) the intention of the debtor; and (3) the knowledge of the third party. In the case of a gratuitous act, no complicity or knowledge on the part of the third party is required. An important feature of the *actio Pauliana* is that its effects benefit only the creditor who undertook the action. When, for example, a contract of sale is declared void, the plaintiff may have recourse to the object of the sale as if it still formed part of the estate of his debtor, but the contract remains valid in relation to all other parties.

After the commencement of insolvency proceedings it is no longer possible for individual creditors to have recourse to the *actio Pauliana*. From that moment on only the insolvency administrator can bring a claim to have transactions set aside, for the benefit of the creditors generally. The general principle of article 1167 C.civ. is restated in article 20 Bankruptcy Act, according to which all transactions or payments made with the fraudulent intention of prejudicing creditors may be set aside, without any time limit. In addition, the Bankruptcy Act provides for more specific rules of avoidance. According to article 12, the commercial court can fix a period, up to a maximum of six months before the commencement of insolvency proceedings, in which the debtor is assumed to have been insolvent. All transactions during this so-called 'suspect period' are subjected to special scrutiny. In particular, certain types of transactions are void *per se*. According to article 17, 3° Bankruptcy Act, security rights created during this period in respect of pre-existing debt are void. There is no need to establish a fraudulent intent on behalf of the third party, nor that the third party had knowledge of the financial difficulties of the debtor. As a general rule, article 18 furthermore declares void all dealings with the debtor in the 'suspect period' by those with knowledge of his insolvency position.

PORTUGAL

(a) Portuguese law does not recognise a security which allows the debtor (B) continuously to replace stock, provided that a certain quantity of goods remain present at his place of business. It is possible to establish a pledge (article 669° C.C.), but this will require the pledged goods to be identified and, normally, to be delivered to the pledgee. However, the latter requirement does not apply to banks: things can be pledged to banks without delivery. The things must be individualised and the pledge must be created by a written document specifying what things are to be pledged (article 2° DL n° 29833, of 17 August 1939 and DL n° 32.032, of 22 May 1942). Should such a pledge be used in the present case, C would not be entitled to sell the things without the consent of A. If he did so, he would be subject to criminal liability (DL n° 29.833, of 17 August 1939). The bank can therefore permit a sale of some of the goods pledged, but new stock will not be brought within the ambit of the security unless a further pledge is created.

It is also possible to establish a charge over the enterprise as a whole (and not only the stock). This kind of enterprise charge is called '*penhor de estabelecimento comercial*'. It is admitted if a symbolic delivery of the enterprise to the creditor is performed pursuant to article 398° C.Com.[45]

(b) In the present case, A will be entitled to preferential payment, but only in respect of the goods pledged. He can therefore claim the payment in the event of the insolvency of C (article 209° CPEREF), or in the event

---

[45] See Menezes Cordeiro, *Manual de Direito Comercial* I 234.

that another creditor should try to execute against the stock (article 865° CPC).

(c) Arrangements of this kind are not very common in business practice. Instead of a security over the stock, a bank would normally ask for a pledge over the shares of the private limited company, or an enterprise charge (*penhor de estabelecimento comercial*). This is a security that creates real rights in the whole of the enterprise, but not the stock alone. Such a security, in the case of non-payment, allows for the enterprise to be judicially sold to enforce the creditor's rights.

(d) There is no limit on the value of collateral, in relation to the amount of the secured loan. In Portuguese law, no restrictions are imposed as to the amount of security a creditor can obtain. It is only possible that, in certain circumstances, a debtor may be able to have declared null and void a contract under which he granted excessive security when he was in a state of weakness (usury, article 282° C.C.).

Variation

The fact that the pledge was created months after the loan was made, and that at that time C was already beginning to experience financial difficulties, could affect A's legal position. In this case, the pledge would be regarded as being gratuitous in nature, thus entitling the unsecured creditors to have it set aside by bringing a revocation action, on the ground of *fraus creditorum* (article 610° C.C.). In the event of insolvency, the pledge, in addition to all other acts of a gratuitous nature performed by the debtor in the previous two years, would be dissolved by the insolvency administrator (article 156° (a) CPEREF).

SPAIN

(a) An arrangement of this kind is possible by means of a real security interest, such as a charge (*hipoteca mobiliaria* or *prenda sin desplazamiento*) under article 52.2 LHMPSD. The following requirements have to be fulfilled with regard to the contract: (1) it must be formalised as a public deed, which should describe the charged goods; (2) it must be recorded in a special register of non-possessory securities. The LHMPSD is flexible with regard to the identification of the goods. It does not require any serial or registration numbers to be stated. Prescribed particulars under the law are: the nature and features, the quantity and the quality of the goods as well as the building where they are located. The owner is obliged to take good care of the movables so charged.[46] B is liable for their safekeeping. The law also requires that they should not be removed to another place without the creditor's consent.[47] In spite of statutory safeguards applicable to such charges, this type of security tends, in practice, only to be resorted to by financial institutions when there is no other way to secure the credit advanced.

(b) In the event of B's insolvency, A has a preferential right to receive payment from the stock.[48] The charged goods will not be included in the insolvency estate as long as A's debt has not been paid by B. In other words, the chargee enjoys priority over other insolvency creditors.

(c) Business practice does not resort frequently to this type of security. The charged goods may disappear, the actions in court are long and the transaction costs of establishing such a charge, observing the formalities of the use of a public deed and registration, are high. Such considerations may act as deterrents. Additionally, all security interests, both of movables and immovables, require the collateral to be identified in the security instrument in order to facilitate a later recovery. If it is not possible to identify movables, as is usually the case with stock-in-trade, consumables and other classes of circulating goods, it is not possible to draw up a security instrument which will be both efficient and efficacious, especially with regard to third-party purchasers.

(d) There are no such limits.

Variation

In principle, the fact that the security right was created after the loan was made and at a time when B was experiencing financial difficulties does not affect A's legal position. However, in business reality, if a financial institution anticipates its debtor's economic difficulties, then it will request as many securities from him as possible (e.g. pledge, charge over

---

[46] See Fernández López, in: *Consejo General del Poder Judicial* 393.
[47] See articles 57, 59–60 LHMPSD. See González-Bueno, *Comentarios a la Ley de Hipoteca Mobiliaria y Prenda sin Desplazamiento* 58.
[48] See article 10 LHMSDP, articles 1922.2° and 1926.1° CC.

movables, charge over immovables, charge of a deposit of funds, either pension funds or current accounts).

An agreement establishing a security right at a time when the debtor is already experiencing financial difficulties may give rise to a revocatory action (article 1111 CC) by any creditor who considers that the agreement was made in order to defraud his collecting rights by conferring on another a preferential right. The *actio Pauliana* is an action of last resort which means that the creditor must first exhaust any other possibilities to enforce payment of the debt (such as filing an *acción subrogatoria*).[49] Only when it is not possible to bring any further claim can the creditor rescind the contracts validly entered into by his debtor with third parties, if creditors have been defrauded.[50] The process of rescission involves, between the respective parties to the contract, the return of the goods and the refund of the price paid (article 1295/I CC). Nevertheless, if goods that were the object of the contract are found legally in the possession of third parties who acted in good faith, rescission would not be permitted (article 1295/II CC). In a such case, however, the injured party would be entitled to claim damages from the party who had injured him (article 1295/III CC).

Rescission in pursuance of the *actio Pauliana* will only be barred in circumstances where the third party has acted in good faith. Accordingly, if the purchasing third party knew that the transaction had a fraudulent end, he will also be held liable for any damages and losses caused to the creditors of the transferor. Article 1298 CC stipulates that whoever acquires in bad faith the goods sold to defraud creditors and cannot return them must compensate the latter for any losses caused.

ITALY

(a) Under certain conditions, the arrangement described in the instant case is possible under Italian law, if carried out in accordance with a provision of the new Italian Banking Law. Article 46 of Italian Banking Law (d. lgs. 1 September 1993, n. 385, as amended by d. lgs. 4 August 1999, n. 342)[51] introduced a charge (*privilegio speciale*) that secures

---

[49] See Cristóbal Montes, *La vía subrogatoria* 118 and Ataz López, *Ejercicio por los acreedores de los derechos y acciones del deudor* 82.
[50] See García Amigó, in: Paz-Ares/Díez-Picazo/Bercovitz/Salvador 70; Moreno Quesada, in: Paz-Ares/Díez-Picazo/Bercovitz/Salvador, 525.
[51] D. lgs. 4 Aug. 1999, n. 342, article 8.

long- to medium-term bank loans to enterprises.[52] According to article 46 of this decree, the charge attaches to assets which are not registered in a public register, provided that they fall within one of the following categories: (1) existing or future manufacturing plant, tools of any kind, and any asset that is instrumental to the enterprise business; (2) raw materials, semi-manufactured products, stock, finished products, fruit, livestock and merchandise; (3) any asset bought with the loan secured by the charge; (4) present or future claims arising from the sale of any asset specified in the preceding categories.

The charge introduced by article 46 of Decree n. 385/1993 will be void unless it is created by a written instrument. The document in question must specify:

(1) exactly what collateral is included within the ambit of the charge;
(2) the names of the lender, the debtor and the subject who created the charge, if that subject is a third person;
(3) the amount of the loan and its terms; and
(4) the sum secured by the charge.

The charge is effective *vis-à-vis* creditors and third parties after registration of the said document in the register of article 1524 section 2 c.c. Such a register is kept at every *Tribunale*. The charge shall be registered at the court having jurisdiction over the territory where the enterprise has its seat and at the court of the place where the chargee is resident, or has its seat.

If all the formalities established by article 46 of the Italian Banking Law are met, the lender obtains security over a changing mass of assets, such as stock-in-trade.[53] Apart from the article 46 Banking Law charge, one would have to rely on some other legislative provision to secure a debt, if recourse was not to be had to the rules which accord priority over movable things solely to pledgees who part with actual possession of the thing, which is either handed over to the pledgor, or to a third party (articles 2784 ff. c.c.), or with documents of title thereof. To a great extent, the system of charges (*privilegi*) established by the Civil Code and

---

[52] For commentary see: Capriglione/Tucci 341 ff.; Sepe, in: Ferro-Luzzi/Castaldi 706 ff.; *id.*, Seconda appendice di aggiornamento 113–155; Rescigno, *Banca borsa* 1999 I, 583 ff.; Tucci, Giur. it. 1999, 1985; Veneziano, Dir. comm. internaz. 1996, 921; Costantino, Riv. trim. dir. proc. civ. 1995 I, 1313 (1321).

[53] Rescigno, *Banca borsa* 1999 I, 583. Note, however, that Presti, *Banca borsa* 1995 I, 594, 612–614, holds that a changing mass of assets cannot be covered by the new statutory charge, inasmuch as it is impossible to know what is the precise object of the charge in the case of fungibles.

by a long list of legislative provisions aimed at enhancing the position of various categories of creditors[54] does perform the function of providing non-possessory securities for creditors.[55] Furthermore, some of these charges do provide security over a changing mass of things, though in respect of activities not directly connected with the example mentioned in the present case. Nevertheless, this system is far from rational in nature.[56] Since the enactment of the Civil Code, in 1942, it has grown into a jungle, because exceptions have eaten up the rule which proclaims: 'creditors have equal rights to be paid out of the property of the debtor, subject to lawful causes for preferences' (article 2741 c.c.). Lawful causes for preferences are now a maze where private autonomy has little or no place. Furthermore, the fact that most of these charges spring directly from a great number of legislative provisions has the consequence that the whole system signals in a rather weak way those forms of credit that are secured and those which are not. Finally, one may wonder whether the system is fair, or whether it is unduly tilted in favour of certain categories of creditors. The fact that the categories of claims and the order of preferences that are protected through the system of charges are established by the legislature, no longer provides an easy answer to this question. One does not have to be an expert on the capture theory of regulation to draw the conclusion that certain charges must have been put on legislative agenda because of the efforts of lobbyists, or to placate certain economic sectors. Even the article 46 Banking Law charge could be examined from this point of view. Why should only banks, rather than other entrepreneurs, have the opportunity to secure their claims over such a wide array of assets as is possible under this provision? One commentator[57] posed this question in the context of examining the constitutionality of the said provision in the light of article 3 of the Italian Constitution, dedicated to the principle of equality before the law. Quite surprisingly, he ended up by explaining that banks perform the important function of supplying credit to the economy!

(Postscript: The amendments to the Italian Civil Code articles on company law that will enter into force in 2004 will add to the solution described above a new instrument of secured credit, i.e. the creation of

---

[54] Such as producers of Parma ham! (Law of 24 July 1985, no 401). Costantino/Jannarelli, NLCC 1986, 540.
[55] Cf. Drobnig, UNCITRAL Yearbook 1977 (A/CN.9/131) Annex, part II, II. A.
[56] On this point: Candian, Le garanzie mobiliari, passim; Bussani, ERPL, 1998, 23, with citations to a number of authors who share the same diagnosis.
[57] Sepe, in: Ferro-Luzzi/Castaldi, La nuova legge bancaria I 709.

patrimonies dedicated to a specific affair (*patrimoni dedicati ad uno specifico affare*, cf. new Civil Code articles 2247 bis–2247 decies c.c.). This is a form of asset segregation available only to *società per azioni*. It creates a security in favour of creditors who are willing to finance a specific affair of the company by taking a non-possessory security over floating company assets related to the affair in question. Even under the new regime, the company cannot create this kind of security over all its assets, however.)

(b) In the event of B's insolvency, A has a preferential claim in respect of the monies that B owes to him. The procedural aspects of this claim are governed by articles 53 and 54 of the Italian Insolvency Act. These provisions provide that the preference of secured creditors may be satisfied, pending insolvency proceedings, through the sale of the collateral which secures the credit. The sale is authorised by the judge, who is in charge of supervising insolvency administration.

The preference ranking of the secured creditor's debt is fixed by article 46 of the Banking Law itself. The article 46 charge ranks behind certain other charges and statutory preferences listed by the Civil Code, which secure claims such as employees' salaries, commercial agents' commissions, etc. (see article 2751 *bis* c.c.). It also ranks behind a pledgee's preferential claim. On the other hand, it is preferred to the claims of insolvency creditors and to a number of other charges (articles 2752 ff. c.c.).

Individual creditors may execute against any asset that is subject to the charge. Contrary to the position with respect to pledges and *ipotecas*, the chargee cannot resist the execution.

(c) At the moment, I cannot answer question (c) because I am not aware of any literature covering the actual practice under the new banking legislation. There are no clear indications that a substantial number of financing operations have been carried out on the basis of article 46 of the new banking legislation.

(d) The Banking Law does not place a limit on the value of the collateral to which the charge discussed under part (a) may attach. Such limits may, however, result from the Law of 7 March 1996, n. 108, *disposizioni in materia di usura*. This enactment reformed the law on usurious loans, which are void and punished with criminal sanctions. The rate of interest that is considered to be usurious is now fixed by decrees of the Ministry of the Treasury, with reference to the interest rates of markets for different kinds of operations. The law's definition of usurious loans includes any operation that, having regard to the circumstances, accords to the lender advantages that are disproportionate to the loan, if the person who applied for it was experiencing economic or financial difficulties.

Variation

B's other creditors may be able to have the transaction creating the charge set aside either through the revocatory action (*actio Pauliana*) of article 2901 c.c., or by the revocatory action that the insolvency administrator may bring under articles 64, 67 ff. of the Italian Insolvency Act. It is impossible to overestimate the importance of these provisions, which should also be considered in relation to any case where the transaction of a debtor endangers creditors' rights.[58]

(a) According to article 2901 c.c., even if the claim is not ripe, a creditor can demand that acts whereby the debtor disposed of assets to the prejudice of his rights be declared ineffective in respect of himself. The action is allowed under the following circumstances:

(1) the debtor was aware of the prejudice which the act would cause to the rights of the creditor, or, if the act antedates the claim, it was fraudulently accomplished in order to prejudice the future creditor's rights;
(2) in the case of a non-gratuitous act, the third person involved was aware of said prejudice or, if the act antedates the claim, the third person shared the fraudulent intention of the debtor.

The same article provides that personal or real securities, even though created for the benefit of a third party, are not considered gratuitous if they were perfected at the time when the secured claim came into being. The limitation period for this action is five years. If the revocatory action of article 2901 c.c. is successful, the transaction, though effective as between the parties, is without effect in respect of the creditor, who may then proceed with execution against the asset which the debtor alienated to the third party, and therefore owns no more. The creditor who brought the action under article 2901 c.c. will have no priority to

---

[58] For a quick overview of the Insolvency Act provisions: Maffei Alberti, *Commentario breve alla legge fallimentare* 228 ff., 237 ff.; for complete coverage: Terranova, in: *Commentario Scialoja-Branca alla legge fallimentare (articles 64–71)*. With specific regard to security rights: Ambrosini, *La revocatoria fallimentare delle garanzie*. On the *actio Pauliana* as regulated by article 2901 c.c.: D'Ercole, in: *Trattato di diritto privato* XX 2 (1998) 161 ff.

the asset in question simply because he brought this action (or started execution!), though the creditors who did not join in the action do not benefit from it.

Assuming that the transaction to secure the loan in the present case was carried out several months after B obtained the loan, it is certain that A's position as a secured creditor will be endangered. The transaction establishing the charge will be treated as gratuitous, and it will, therefore, be declared of no effect in respect of the creditor who can prove damage. The plaintiff in this case will not have to prove that the financial institution knew that the debtor was suffering financial difficulties.

(b) In the case of insolvency proceedings (*fallimento*), which in Italy are open only to 'commercial' entrepreneurs, as defined by articles 2082 and 2195 c.c.,[59] the insolvency administrator can bring a revocatory action pursuant to article 2901 c.c., with the effects described above in part (a) of the Variation (article 65 l. fall.). Nevertheless, in most cases, he will invoke the special provisions of law contained in the Italian Insolvency Act to avoid a number of transactions, embracing, for sure, the transaction described in the Variation. The Insolvency Act automatically avoids certain categories of gratuitous transactions (article 64 l. fall.) and renders of no effect payments of claims made within the two years preceding insolvency if the claims in question were not yet due (article 65 l. fall.). It also gives the insolvency administrator the power to avoid a number of other transactions through the *azione revocatoria fallimentare*, which is based on article 67 l. fall., unless the third party against whom the action is initiated proves that he entered into the transaction without knowing that the debtor was insolvent.

In most cases, the insolvency administrator does not have to prove that all these transactions were aimed at defrauding creditors, or that they damaged creditors. The purpose of the revocatory action of article 67 of the *legge fallimentare* is, first and foremost, to provide equal treatment of the bankrupt's creditors, in accordance with the ranking of their claims.

Leaving gifts and other gratuitous transactions aside – although the giving of security after the loan would fall within the concept of a gratuitous transaction, if the debtor did not benefit from it – the main categories of acts mentioned in article 67 l. fall. are: (1) transactions at an

---

[59] Italian Insolvency Act, article 1. Exceptions apart, an entrepreneur is a person or entity undertaking the production or exchange of property or services on a professional basis (article 2082 c.c.). Article 2195 c.c. lists the activities which are considered 'commercial' for this purpose.

undervalue, entered into during the two years preceding the commencement of insolvency proceedings; (2) payments of money claims, which are satisfied through abnormal means of payment, if done during the two years preceding the commencement of insolvency proceedings; (3) pledges and charges (specifically: *ipoteche*) which were created by an act of the debtor, to secure pre-existing claims, before maturity, if perfected during the two years preceding the commencement of insolvency proceedings; and (4) the transactions mentioned under (3), if the security was perfected in order to secure a debt that had expired in the year before the commencement of insolvency proceedings.

Finally, if the insolvency administrator can prove that the third party knew that the debtor was insolvent, he can also avoid payments of claims that were due, transactions at market price and securities perfected during the year preceding the commencement of insolvency proceedings (article 67 sec. 3).

THE NETHERLANDS

(a) Although Dutch law does not provide for an enterprise charge *strictu sensu*, it is possible for a creditor to take a broad non-possessory security interest, the 'silent' pledge, in both the present and future trading stock of a debtor. The only limitation is that the pledged goods must be sufficiently identifiable at the time at which the secured creditor wishes to exercise his or her right.

Because the trader/debtor, C, does not yet own the future stock, he lacks the power to dispose that is necessary for the creation of a pledge (article 3:98 in conjunction with article 3:84 BW). However, the Code allows all other requirements (*causa* and the 'act of creation') to be fulfilled in advance, so that the pledge will come into existence at the time C acquires the future stock and thereby gains the power to dispose.[60]

Should *all* C's future stock be pledged, no further steps appear necessary in order to ensure that the goods are sufficiently identifiable at the time of exercise. If the pledge only concerns part of the future stock, care should be taken to have the goods stored separately.

Such arrangements normally involve trading stock, the goods that are continuously sold and acquired in the course of C's business. This raises the following issue: a pledge is a (limited) real right and thus has *droit de suite*. This would hamper the ability of the pledgor to use the stock in

---

[60] Article 3:97 BW.

the course of his business. Admittedly, buyers in good faith may well take free of A's pledge, but C would still be liable as against A.[61] It is therefore more common to include a (resolutive) clause in the credit agreement allowing C to sell the goods in the 'ordinary course of business', similar to the situation described in cases 4 and 5 in relation to retention of title.

(b) The pledgee enjoys a superior position to that of insolvency creditors in the event of the debtor's insolvency. He or she may exercise his or her rights 'as if there were no insolvency'.[62] This rule is subject to two qualifications. First, if the insolvency administrator gives reasonable notice to the secured creditor, requiring him or her to exercise his or her right within a reasonable period, and he or she fails to do so, then the administrator may claim the collateral as part of the estate and execute against it.[63] This does not affect the secured creditor's priority to the proceeds, but he or she will have to contribute to the administrative costs of insolvency.[64] Secondly, the administrator may petition the court for a temporary general moratorium suspending execution against the collateral.[65]

A pledge also gives the secured creditor a priority claim to the proceeds. The secured creditor generally takes priority over all other creditors.[66] However, in some instances, the revenue takes priority over the 'silent' pledge, though not the public pledge.[67] It may, in this context, be noted that a creditor who secures a claim by a 'silent', non-possessory pledge has the power to convert the pledge into a public one. He or she may demand that the goods are handed over either to him or her or to a third party.[68]

In respect of security interests in *future* stock, it should also be noted that a pledge will not arise in respect of stock acquired by the debtor after the commencement of insolvency proceedings. Insolvency prevents the debtor from acquiring the power to dispose of the new stock, hence one of the requirements for the creation of a pledge remains

---

[61] Aside from being defeated by *bona fide* purchase, the security right may also be lost through accession of the goods. After being sold, the motorcar accessories may very well be installed in a car. If so, the accessory will cease to be an independent 'thing': article 5:14 BW.
[62] Article 57 Fw.   [63] Article 58 Fw.   [64] Article 182 Fw.
[65] Article 63a Fw.   [66] Articles 3:278–279 BW.
[67] Article 21 *Invorderingswet*. Further exceptions are, for example, to be found in Articles 3:292, 3:284 and 3:287 BW.
[68] Article 3:237 (3) BW.

unfulfilled.[69] This rule does reintroduce a certain risk of commingling (*confusio*). If the goods acquired in insolvency are stored with the goods acquired before the commencement of proceedings and burdened with a pledge, then the debtor will be regarded as owner of the whole of the stock, free of any security rights, hence it will all form part of the insolvency estate.

Outside insolvency proceedings, it is possible that an unsecured creditor will seek execution against stock in which the bank has acquired a security interest. This is in principle possible. However, the secured creditor is allowed, when his or her claim becomes due, to take over the execution.[70] Furthermore, the secured creditor's priority over the unsecured creditor is fully respected. The unsecured creditor will be entitled to no more than is left after the secured creditor has been paid.

(c) The use of non-possessory, silent pledges on future stock is very common in practice.[71]

(d) There appears to be no case law, at least not of general application, and doctrine has also been largely silent on the issue.

In one case it was held that a creditor may be liable as against the other creditors of the debtor for taking 'too much collateral without taking the interests of the other creditors sufficiently into account'.[72] The case is, however, special. In particular, the outcome was probably affected by the fact that it concerned a parent–subsidiary corporate relationship. The parent company, Osby-Sweden, had taken a security interest in essentially all of the subsidiary's (Osby-Holland's) assets in order to secure a credit facility. Even though it must have been evident to Osby-Sweden that its daughter company would go bankrupt in the foreseeable future, it held the credit available. By continuing to extend credit to Osby-Holland, other creditors were given an impression of solvency and, at the same time, were left without recourse to any assets. Although the case did not concern the issue of the proportionality of the debt–collateral ratio directly, it indicated that under certain circumstances secured creditors may be under a duty to take into account the interests of other creditors.

It can also be argued that a secured creditor is bound by principles of fairness and equity *vis-à-vis* the debtor. Arguably the exercise of the

---

[69] Articles 20, 23 and 35(2) Fw.   [70] Article 461a Rv.
[71] Fesevur, *Goederenrechtelijke colleges* 197; Beuving/Tjittes, NJB 1998, 1547.
[72] Hoge Raad 25 Sep. 1981, NJ 1982, 443.

secured creditor's rights will, in certain circumstances, be contrary to such principles. Although fairness is of limited importance in property law, the principle applies in any event to the parties on the basis of their contract of credit.[73]

Variation

The granting of security for antecedent debt can in further circumstances be set aside as a fraudulent or preferential transfer reducing the assets available to C's other creditors: the *actio Pauliana*.[74]

Creditors are protected against detrimental acts of their debtor by the *actio Pauliana*. The protection is similar in and out of insolvency proceedings. Fraudulent or preferential transfers may be avoided under specific circumstances. The avoidance operates only to the extent the individual creditor outside insolvency proceedings or the debtor's estate in insolvency proceedings has been detrimentally affected.

The general requirements to avoid a transfer are:

> a juridical act (transaction);
> without an obligation out of law or contract;
> causing detriment to one or more creditors;
> while the debtor knew or should have known that the transaction would result in detriment to his or her creditors;
> and, if the transaction was for value, also the other party knew or should have known that the act would result in detriment to the creditors.

In principle the burden of proof is with the creditor or, during insolvency proceedings, the insolvency administrator. Even though no intent to defraud is required, in practice the showing of knowledge is considered to be the main obstacle for a successful action for avoidance. However, if the transaction took place within a year of the action of avoidance or the opening of insolvency proceedings, a statutory presumption that knowledge is present on both sides may arise in specific situations. In particular, the burden of proof is shifted where the transaction was at (manifest) undervalue; where it concerned payment of debts not due or the granting of a security interest for those debts; or the transaction was with parties having family or corporate ties with the debtor.[75]

---

[73] Cf. Beuving/Tjittes, NJB 1998, 1547 ff. [74] Article 3:45 BW and article 42 Fw.
[75] Article 3:46 BW and article 43 Fw.

If in the above case the grant of security in the stock was included in the original credit agreement, the pledge would not have been without a legal obligation, placing the transfer in principle beyond a challenge on grounds of the *actio Pauliana*.[76] If it was not, because the pledge was granted for antecedent debt, the transfer is non-obligatory. Security for antecedent debt is not necessarily gratuitous: granting a deferment for payment would be valid consideration. If the security was gratuitous, avoidance would require that only the debtor knew that the pledge would be detrimental to his or her other creditors. If it was for value, the pledgee must have the same knowledge.

ENGLAND

(a) A security over stock-in-trade is perfectly possible in English law. The nature and incidents of a fixed charge and of a *floating charge* (enterprise charge) have been discussed in previous cases, as have the means of perfecting a charge by registration. There is no requirement that the charged stock be isolated.[77]

(b) Once again, the executing creditor takes subject to A's real interests so long as, in the case of the *floating charge*, that charge crystallises before the execution is completed, as discussed previously.

As for C's *liquidation* or *bankruptcy* (insolvency proceedings against companies and individuals, respectively), again as discussed previously, A's real rights may be asserted in the event of C's insolvency. In this respect, C's insolvency administrator (whether *liquidator* or *trustee-in-bankruptcy*) is bound to respect equities and equitable proprietary interests (forms of limited real rights) in favour of A (and not just legal proprietary interests). The reason is that the insolvency administrator is considered to stand in the shoes of the insolvent.[78] A's interest may be in the nature of a *floating charge* at the date of its creation. It was stated previously that this placed A at a disadvantage as regards C's statutory preference creditors. The reason is that an administrative receiver acting on behalf of A, and a *liquidator* winding up C's estate, are bound to distribute to preference creditors before distributing to A.[79] This further relegates A

---

[76] In bankruptcy, avoidance may still be possible if both parties had the intention to defraud the other creditors, article 47 Fw.
[77] See the reference to field warehousing, English report, case 10.
[78] *McEntire v Crossley Bros.* [1895] AC 457, 461; *Madell v Thomas* [1891] 2 QB 230, 238; *Re Eastgate* [1905] 1 KB 465; Bower/Turner, *The Law of Actionable Misrepresentation* § 278.
[79] Insolvency Act 1986, ss. 40 and 175.

behind the expenses of the insolvency proceedings since these expenses rank ahead of preference creditors.[80] It should also be added that A's security does not prevent A from proving as an unsecured creditor in the event of C's insolvency to the extent that the security is insufficient to satisfy A's claim in full.[81]

(c) The taking of security over stock-in-trade is very common indeed, particularly when the trader is a company. Difficulties concerning the Bills of Sale Acts 1878–91 and future property – an important matter since stock turns over from time to time – make it impracticable for a sole trader to grant security over present and future stock.

(d) Unlike German law, English law places no limits on the amount of security that may be taken, either as to total amount or as to ratio of security to the amount owed. In particular, there are no penalties attaching to a creditor who is over-secured. Conventional wisdom has it, anyway, that no matter how extensive the security, the creditor is only rarely over-secured.

Variation

According to section 245 of the Insolvency Act 1986, *floating* (but not fixed) charges granted by a company in the twelve months[82] preceding the onset of insolvency are valid[83] only to the extent of the value given by the secured creditor in return for the charge[84] 'at the same time as, or after, the creation of the charge'. The purpose of the section is to protect the position of unsecured creditors on the occasion of the future insolvency distribution. Within the limits of the section, no individual unsecured creditor can break ranks by obtaining a security in return for value previously given. Departing from an earlier, more relaxed view of the matter, the current position is that even a minimal time gap between the giving of value and the grant of the charge, will be fatal.[85] In the case of current accounts, where the rule in *Clayton's Case*[86] applies, value

---

[80] For *liquidation* see Insolvency Act 1986, s. 175(2)(a); also ss. 107, 115 and 156, Schedule 8 para. 17 and rules 4.218–20 and 12.2. For *bankruptcy*, see Insolvency Act 1986, s. 328(2) and Schedule 9 para. 22 and rules 6.202, 6.224 and 12.2.
[81] Insolvency Rules 4.95-99.
[82] Two years for those connected with the company.
[83] S. 245 invalidates only the charge: see *Re Mace Builders (Glasgow) Ltd* [1985] BCLC 154.
[84] The phrase 'in consideration for' means 'as a result of', so that a bank's later factual forbearance from calling in a loan will suffice: *Re Yeovil Glove Co. Ltd* [1965] Ch 148.
[85] *Power v Sharp Instruments Ltd (Re Shoe Lace Ltd)* [1994] 1 BCLC 111.
[86] [1816] 1 Mer 572.

given later than the charge can be found despite its apparent absence. If, for example, an overdraft limit of £50,000 before the charge remains £50,000 afterwards, the bank will still be able to rely upon the charge in so far as any sum outstanding represents new debt created as a result of payments out of the account.[87]

IRELAND

(a) It is possible to have a security arrangement of the kind described in this problem through the vehicle of the enterprise charge (*floating charge*). The essence of a *floating charge* is that it is over a class of assets and permits the company granting the charge to carry on business in the ordinary way until some event occurs which causes the chargeholder to intervene. Such an event is referred to as a crystallising event. Crystallisation occurs as a matter of law when the company ceases to carry on business in the ordinary way, when insolvency proceedings are commenced against the company (*liquidation*) and when the chargeholder appoints a person called a receiver to take control of the charged assets and ultimately to sell off the same so as to satisfy the debt. The instrument creating the charge – the debenture – may specify other crystallising events. The central characteristic of a *floating charge* is this management autonomy on the part of the company creating the charge, but typically a charge is a *floating charge* if it has the following three ingredients:

(1) if it is a charge on a class of assets of a company present and future;
(2) if that class is one which, in the ordinary course of the business of the company, would be changing from time to time; and
(3) if it is found that, by the charge, it is contemplated that, until some future step is taken by or on behalf of those interested in the charge, the company may carry on business in the ordinary way as far as concerns the particular class of assets.

Even though the chargor can deal with the assets which are subject to the charge without the chargeholder's permission until crystallisation occurs, it is now clear that a *floating charge* creates a presently subsisting equitable interest (a form of limited real right) although the interest is not attached to specific assets.

So, to address the facts of the problem, A may take a *floating charge* over C's stock-in-trade. Such a *floating charge* would be effective in the

---

[87] *Re Yeovil Glove Co. Ltd* [1965] Ch 148.

various given fact situations. It does not matter that the stock-in-trade is mixed with other goods of the same type nor that the stocks are regularly substituted by other stocks of the same kind or a different kind provided that the coverage of the charge is sufficiently extensive. It has been held that a *floating charge* on a company's undertaking will cover its entire business operations.

Section 99 Companies Act 1963 requires a *floating charge* granted by a company to be registered. Generally speaking, it is not possible for individuals or partnerships to create floating charges but the Agricultural Credit Act 1978 brings into existence a specific statutory creation – the floating agricultural chattel mortgage. Such mortgages must be registered with the local Circuit Court. The purpose of this legislation is to facilitate lending to the farming sector. A floating chattel mortgage is over the stock from time to time of the borrower given to secure money owing to the Agricultural Credit Corporation or a recognised bank. Registration of such a mortgage is effective to create an ambulatory and shifting charge on all stock described in the charge which from time to time is on the mortgagor's land. A mortgagor is not allowed to sell any stock other than in the ordinary course of business and is required to maintain his stock on his lands at the same level of value as they were when the charge was granted.

(b) As explained above, a *floating charge* will crystallise, i.e. become fixed, in the event of C's insolvency. In that scenario A then has a fixed charge on assets that are still in the possession of B and that come within the subject matter covered by the charge. According to the relevant insolvency legislation, A is entitled to be paid out of such assets in priority to the claims of unsecured creditors, though his entitlement ranks after that of statutory preference creditors. The categories of statutory preference are set out in s. 285 Companies Act 1963 as amended and basically encompass unpaid taxes and certain employee claims. It should be noted that if an unsecured creditor completes the execution process prior to the completion of the *floating charge*, then the creditor can keep the proceeds of the execution, but if the process is incomplete at the time of crystallisation, then the creditor's claim comes after that of the *floating chargeholder*.

(c) *Floating charges* are a standard feature of bank lending practice.

(d) There are no limits with respect to the value the collateral might have in relation to the amount of the secured loan.

Variation

Under Companies Act 1963, s. 288 as amended, a *floating charge* created within twelve months prior to the commencement of *liquidation* becomes invalid by the fact of the company going into *liquidation* to the extent that the charge secures past indebtedness. The relevant period is two years if the *floating charge* is granted to a person connected with the company. For the invalidating rule to operate, the company must have been insolvent at the time of the creation of the *floating charge*.

SCOTLAND

The *floating charge* in England and Ireland is not a creation of statute, but of the courts of equity. By contrast the *floating charge* does not exist in Scots common law but is purely statutory, having been introduced by legislation in 1961.[88] It is currently regulated by the Companies Act 1985 and the Insolvency Act 1986. Before 1961, a leading judge observed that 'it is clear in principle and amply supported by authority that a *floating charge* is utterly repugnant to the principles of Scots law'[89] and many similar remarks have been made since that time. Although the legislation introduced an institution modelled on the English institution, there are differences in detail, and also conceptual differences caused by the fact that the institution is embedded into a civilian system of property law. However, for the purposes of the present question there appear to be no important differences.

A *floating charge* is competent only if the debtor is a company.[90] It affects either (1) the whole patrimony of the debtor, movable and immovable, corporeal and incorporeal, real and personal, present and future, or (2) a defined part of the patrimony. The charge must be publicly registered.[91] While the company continues to be solvent, the effect of the charge is suspended. At this stage, it is not a real right. When the company becomes insolvent, the change may 'attach' (or, a synonymous term, 'crystallise'). By attachment it becomes a real right. Attachment takes place by either (1) receivership or (2) *liquidation*.

'Receivership' is purely a means for enforcing a *floating charge*. It can be, and in practice always is, extrajudicial, and is triggered by a 'deed of appointment' by the holder of the *floating charge*. The receiver takes

---

[88] Companies (Floating Charges) (Scotland) Act 1961.
[89] Lord President Cooper in *Carse v Coppen* 1951 SC 233, 1951 SLT 145.
[90] The creditor need not be a company.   [91] In the Companies Register in Edinburgh.

control of all the assets which are subject to the charge, and has power to do juridical acts in the name of the company. He can thus sell individual assets or – and this is common – the whole active side of the patrimony. 'Liquidation' in Scotland means two things: (1) the winding up of a solvent company and (2) formal insolvency proceedings in respect of an insolvent company. *Liquidation* can be (in either case) either judicial or extrajudicial.

The *floating charge* is unlike ordinary security rights in many ways. One difference is that, once the charge has been created, any assets acquired by the debtor become subject to the charge without the need for any new juridical act by the debtor. Another difference is that as soon as an asset is alienated by the company it ceases to be subject to the charge, without the need for any juridical act by the creditor.

Whereas ordinary rights in security have a ranking which is prior to statutory preferences (*preferential claims*) such as tax claims, the *floating charge* is ranked *posterior* to such preferences. But it will rank in priority to ordinary unsecured claims. On the question of whether there is priority over creditors who execute against assets of the debtor company before the charge attaches, there has been considerable controversy.[92]

Whether a *floating charge* is (1) over the whole of C's patrimony or (2) over some defined part of the patrimony, such as all movable property, is a matter for the parties to agree. In practice most *floating charges* are over the whole patrimony.

The law does not place any limits on the value of the collateral in relation to the amount of the debt. It would be lawful to have a *floating charge* over the whole patrimony of a debtor company to secure a debt of £1. The same is true of other security rights.

Variation

If a debtor grants a security for a pre-existing debt, and later becomes insolvent, the security may be voidable. Scots law has received the *actio Pauliana*, though there are many complexities and specialities.

The general principle, which is applicable not only to *floating charges* but to any security, is that if (1) the security was granted for a pre-existing debt, and (2) the debtor was at that time already factually insolvent, in the sense that the total value of his patrimony was negative,[93] and (3) the

---

[92] For a summary see Skene, *Insolvency Law in Scotland* 256–260.
[93] That is to say, the value of the assets was less than the value of the liabilities.

debtor becomes insolvent within six months[94] thereafter, then (4) the security can be *reduced*, which means declared by the court to be invalid. Fraudulent intent is not relevant. The action can be by any creditor, but in practice the action is almost always by the insolvency administrator. This area of law is known as that of 'unfair preferences'.[95]

Reduction (judicial avoidance) is not the only possible remedy. Other remedies are also possible, depending on the circumstances of the case. Thus, in the example, if, a few weeks after the creation of the security A enforced it and sold to X, and X was in good faith, then X's position could not be attacked. In that case the creditor who has received the unfair preference could be required to restore, by a money payment, the benefit which he has received.

Curiously, there is, in addition to the general law which has just been outlined, a special rule for *floating charges*, whereby the suspect period is not six months but one year or (if the creditor is connected with the debtor company in certain defined ways) two years.[96] Since this suspect period is longer, actions to avoid *floating charges* are in practice raised under this special rule rather than under the general rules.

Scots law divides the *actio Pauliana* into two parts. One is the law of 'unfair preferences', which has just been outlined. The other is the law of 'gratuitous alienations'. An unfair preference does not diminish the net patrimony (estate) of the debtor, for any diminution in the value of the assets is balanced by an equal diminution in the value of the liabilities. A gratuitous alienation, by contrast, is a juridical act which diminishes the net value of the estate.[97] A donation is an example, but other examples are sales at overvalue, purchases at undervalue, and gratuitous discharges of debts. The remedies available are the same as for unfair preferences. However, the time-limits are more generous. A gratuitous alienation within two years before insolvency can be attacked, and if the beneficiary was an 'associate' the period is extended to five

---

[94] In some cases (namely where the action is a 'common law' one) a longer period may be applicable.
[95] The law about unfair preferences rules is contained mainly in the Bankruptcy (Scotland) Act 1985 s. 36. The 1985 Act does not apply to registered companies, but s. 243 of the Insolvency Act 1986 extends s. 36 of the 1985 Act to registered companies. For analysis of the law see McBryde, *Bankruptcy* and Skene, *Insolvency Law in Scotland*.
[96] Insolvency Act 1986 s. 245.
[97] The law is contained mainly in the Bankruptcy (Scotland) Act 1985 s. 34 and the Insolvency Act 1986 s. 242, the latter applying to companies and the former to all other persons. The provisions are effectively identical.

years. This term includes spouses, near relations and certain business associates.[98] A company can be an 'associate'.

The question of whether 'reduction' (judicial avoidance) operates *ex tunc* or *ex nunc* is one which cannot be answered simply, partly because there are certain complexities and partly because aspects of the law are unsettled.

SOUTH AFRICA

(a) The two mechanisms described under case 10, namely security transfer of ownership and the registration of a notarial bond creating a non-possessory pledge in terms of the Security by Means of Movable Property Act, are the only mechanisms available to obtain such an arrangement. However, both of these mechanisms have serious flaws. It has already been indicated that the South African courts consider attempts to create a security transfer of ownership as a disguised non-possessory pledge.[99] But even if this mechanism is in future accepted by our courts,[100] it would still require a good deal of pressure from the motor industry for our courts (or more probably the legislature) to recognise, like the German system, that the security transfer of ownership by means of *constitutum possessorium* may be concluded in advance with the result that the security becomes operative as soon as the debtor acquires ownership of the new stock. As the law stands, A can therefore claim neither ownership (nor possession) of the stock, nor preferential treatment in respect of the proceeds of the sale of the stock. The difficulty with registering a notarial bond over the stock-in-trade, as provided for by the Security by Means of Movable Property Act,[101] is that the goods subject to the notarial bond must be specified and described 'in a manner which renders them readily recognisable'. This seems to exclude a registration with a general description, such as 'automobiles held as stock'. This also implies that new stock must be separately registered and thus that a blanket registration for all stock held by the wholesaler would not suffice.[102] Nevertheless, if stock was stored on a specified part of the premises, or if a clear notice was attached to each item indicating that it was pledged in favour of A, it would fit the description of

---

[98] Bankruptcy (Scotland) Act 1985 s. 74.
[99] *NedcorBank Ltd v Absa Bank Ltd* 1998 2 SA 830 (W). See Van der Merwe, *Sakereg* 688–695; Van der Merwe/Smith, Stell LR 1999, 303 ff.
[100] See Van der Merwe/Smith, Stell LR 1999, 303 (324–327).
[101] Act 57 of 1993 s. 1.   [102] See Van der Merwe/Smith, Stell LR 1999, 303 (325).

specified, readily recognisable movable property. Every replacement would, however, require a new notarial bond to be registered and a new notice to be fixed. This evokes memories of the clumsy phenomenon of the 'field warehousing' construction formerly employed in the United States to overcome this problem.[103]

(b) If the parties could convince the court that the structure of their agreement achieved a security transfer of ownership, then A would retain his ownership, which would mean that the stock would not fall into C's insolvency estate nor be subject to execution by C's creditors. If the cumbersome method of registering notarial bonds over existing stocks and keeping registering bonds over future stocks and clearly identifying them was followed, the secured party (A) would be in the position of a pledgee with a preferential right to the proceeds of the sale of a particular motor vehicle in the event of C's insolvency. If another (unsecured) creditor executes against the stock, A's position as a secured creditor would rank higher.

(c) Framework agreements (floorplan agreements) embodying a security transfer of ownership are frequently used in practice, especially by the motor industry.[104] It is expected that the question of their validity will come before the Supreme Court of Appeal of South Africa in the near future for clarification.

(d) If a security transfer of ownership to the financial institution (A) is attempted and the purchase price in the contract of sale is either fictitious or not serious in that it is not proportionate to the market value of the vehicle, it would suggest that the sale and resale transaction was a 'simulated' pledge rather than a serious attempt to create a security right by means of transfer of ownership.[105]

Variation

If created within the six months preceding the commencement of insolvency proceedings in respect of C, the security right (if recognised) could,

---

[103] Under this system, goods were held on the site of the trader, but in a physically cordoned-off area. In this way, they were possessed not by the trader, but by a warehouseman who held them for the financier. This allowed the use of the pledge construction, but it was hardly a model of modern commercial efficiency.
[104] See e.g. *NedcorBank Ltd v Absa Bank Ltd* 1998 2 SA 830 (W).
[105] See e.g. *Delport v Strydom* 1977 3 SA 325 (O); *Vasco Dry Cleaners v Twycross* 1979 1 SA 620 (A).

in appropriate circumstances, be treated as an undue preference under the Insolvency Act.[106]

In order to succeed in having the security right set aside as an undue preference, the insolvency administrator (*trustee-in-insolvency*) must prove the following:

(1) that there was a disposition of his property by C (the creation of the security right);
(2) that at the time the disposition was made, C's liabilities exceeded his assets;
(3) that the disposition was made to the creditor in such a way that the creditor would benefit from the disposition;
(4) that C intended to prefer one of the creditors above another; and
(5) that thereafter the estate of C was sequestrated.

DENMARK

(a) According to Danish law, a security right to movables can only be created as a charge or as a pledge (see also the general remarks in case 1).

A *charge* must be registered in a public register called the Personal Registry. The contract of charge must describe the asset in such a way as to leave no doubt as to which asset has been charged. In other words, a charge can only be registered in respect of specified assets, cf. section 47(a), (b) of the Registration of Property Act. An exception is made in respect of the equipment and plant (machinery and technical plant) of an enterprise: cf. sections 37 and 47(2) of the Registration of Property Act. No such exception is made for the enterprise's stock. As a result, it is almost impossible to charge stock, since it would be necessary to register both each individual item comprising the stock and every subsequent substitute.

To create a *pledge*, the subject of the pledge must be removed from the owner's possession. A pledge is only valid if C cannot take possession of the asset on his own. On the other hand, replacement of the stock may be allowed but only if it is checked by A or on behalf of A by a third party, who is completely independent of C. Under these circumstances, the assets might be stored on C's premises, if the assets were locked up in a separate room. But it is important to note that measures must be taken to ensure that C cannot take possession of the assets on his own.

---

[106] Act 24 of 1936 s. 30(1). See Smith/Sharrock, in: *The Law of South Africa* XI para. 187.

(New locks should be fitted to the room and A should regularly check that C has not been able to gain possession of the assets in some way.)

Since the charge and pledge are the only ways by which a security may be taken in stock, it might be said that security cannot be taken in circulating stock in Denmark. One might have a charge in an asset which is to be stored for a long period. If C was permitted to sell the asset, the contract should stipulate that C had to settle with A when the asset was sold and A had to make sure (on the premises) that the asset has not been sold in the same way as in a credit consignment agreement (see general remarks under cases 1 and 2). This is not stated in legislation but is discussed by most authors.

It may also be possible to pledge such a stock. The requirement that C should not be able to take possession of the pledged assets would however confine its operation to special circumstances.

If A had a valid charge or pledge, A would be entitled to preferential payment from the proceeds of the sale of the goods. If not, A is just an unsecured creditor.[107]

(b) If the assets are subject to a valid charge or pledge, the right will be protected against creditors who execute against the debtor. The right must also be respected if the debtor is declared bankrupt.

(c) In Denmark, it is rather difficult to take security in a stock. The common way to have a security right in a stock is by means of a pledge where the assets are stored by a third party (who has to be notified of the pledge), or by having reserved title to the goods under a credit consignment agreement. The charge or pledge are ill-suited to the creation of security over goods stored on the debtor's premises. Such arrangements are uncommon.

(d) According to Danish law, there are no limits with respect to the value of collateral in relation to the amount of the secured loan. On the other hand, in Denmark the secured creditor can only claim payment of the amount of the loan, and the interest on it, from proceeds of the sale of the collateral. It is also perhaps worthy of mention that the debtor can give secondary rights to another person who will give a loan.

---

[107] Cf. for more details Andersen/Werlauff, *Kreditretten* 108 ff. and 137 ff.; Rørdam/Carstensen, *Pant* 340; and Ørgaard, *Sikkerhed i løsøre* 16 f. and 27 f.

Variation

If a (valid) security was created after the credit had been advanced and C was declared bankrupt, the security might be invalidated. Under section 70 of the Bankruptcy Act, a charge or other security, which was not granted to the creditor when the debt arose, is invalidated if it was created within the period of three months before the date of notice. (The date of notice will normally be the date on which the bankruptcy court received a notice of the suspension of payments.) If the charge or security was created more than three months before the date of notice, it might still be invalidated under section 74 of the Bankruptcy Act, if the estate can prove (1) that the debtor (B) was insolvent at that time; and (2) that the creditor (A) was in bad faith as regards the debtor's insolvency. In practice, the estate will find it very difficult to establish the latter requirement. Another provision in section 74 is that the transaction in an inappropriate way favoured one creditor and that this creditor was in bad faith about these circumstances. If a security right was created after the credit had been advanced, it is usually not difficult for the estate to prove that requirement.

SWEDEN

(a) A fiduciary transfer will not work, since the assignor, C, then has to either give up possession of the goods or register individually specified goods at a relevant court. Nor can the stock be pledged to the financial institution, A: the pledgee must take possession of the pledged chattels (chapter 10 section 1 Code of Commerce, *handelsbalken*, from 1734). However, both a transfer and a pledge would be possible, if the debtor placed his stock in the possession of a third party who is instructed to hold the stock for the assignee or the pledgee. A proviso is that the assignor or the pledgor must not be entitled to retract any goods without the assent of the assignee or pledgee. A general assent to such retraction will make the transaction void in relation to C's creditors.[108] If the stock is deposited with a notified third party, for instance, the pledge may comprise future goods that can be identified in some way, e.g. 'all goods in the possession of X'. In principle, only ascertainable objects can be comprised within a pledge (NJA 1910, 216), but this rule is questioned in the literature when the pledged stock is fungible. It is argued that in this case it should be possible to pledge a quantity; cf. the case where

[108] NJA 1949, 164 and 1996, 52.

10 Euros out of a claim of 100 Euros against a bank is charged.[109] It is also argued that a value-defined pledge should be accepted at least when the pledgor may retain all objects before the debt becomes due (in execution, a pledge is always limited to the value of the debt), but also otherwise, provided that the value which the pledgor did not dispose of, although it exceeded the pledged value and was permissible for disposition, can be avoided as a favour to the pledgee as if it had been inserted on the same date (see further variation, below[110]).

The practical solution in the present case would be for the wholesaler, C, to charge his revolving stock pursuant to the Enterprise Mortgage Act (*lagen om företagsinteckning*, from 1984). Under this Act, all the debtor's property, actual or future, is encompassed by the enterprise charge, with the exception of goods that may otherwise be charged (such as immovable property or airplanes; shares; promissory notes; debentures intended for the public; claims against banks; and cash). Technically, the debtor takes out a letter (certificate) of charge from a court and transfers the letter to the chargee as a security for his debt. The chargee has a priority in insolvency (and, if necessary, in execution) superior to taxes and wages but subordinate to pledges. The chargor may be, and normally is, entitled freely to dispose of the goods, and the buyer need not concern himself with the charge, as long as the chargor does not sell his whole business or a part of it. The chargee's right in the goods is replaced by a right in the claim on the buyer. If the chargor sells the whole or part of his business, however, the charge remains valid, for a specified period, in the sold goods in the possession of the buyer, enjoying priority over any enterprise charge granted by the buyer. In insolvency the charge crystallises on the insolvency day. This would suggest that any subsequent increase in the values of raw material or claims, etc., vests in the insolvency creditors.[111]

(b) See part (a) above.

(c) Enterprise charges are very frequently encountered in practice. Why should banks forgo such a security, even if they would have been prepared to extend credit on an unsecured basis, when the debtor need only pay an initial fee of 1 per cent and when other creditors seem to

---

[109] Quantity-defined pledges of money are accepted, NJA 1987, 105 and 1989, 705.
[110] Håstad, *Sakrätt rörande lös egendom* 333 ff. Disputes in major insolvencies have been settled accordingly, without litigation in the courts.
[111] NJA 1982, 900.

be prepared to continue to deal with debtors on an unsecured basis? Such charges are less common, however, in two particular cases. The first of these is in respect of fledgling enterprises, with no employees and limited or non-existent collateral. In such circumstances, banks typically take a personal guarantee against the directors of the enterprise. Secondly, in respect of large enterprises, financial institutions often rely upon contractual covenants (i.e., to not grant security to others, to maintain certain financial ratios, etc.).[112]

(d) The collateral may have any value in relation to the secured loan. However, if the security is given for future credit and the lender controls whether the credit will be extended, the lender must give up the security in favour of other creditors that seek execution in the security. Thus, when a revolving credit facility within a certain limit is granted with the proviso that there will be security, the collateral subject to that security may be executed against when no debt is outstanding (since the bank then has a right to terminate the credit agreement). This would not be so of a security for a bank guarantee that may be called upon beyond the control of the bank. A special rule governs the enterprise charge, which could be granted all too readily, as it permits the chargor to remain in possession of the charged assets. If another creditor seeks to execute against an asset subjected to an enterprise charge, the enterprise chargee can successfully resist the execution only if he does not have adequate security in other assets. In insolvency a pledgee must immediately surrender his pledge on full payment. In principle, the borrower himself would be able to ask for modification under section 36 of the Contracts Act if an excessive security is unconscionable, but no such cases are reported. Normally he has to rely on borrowing against security with secondary priority.[113]

---

[112] The enterprise charge has recently been thoroughly discussed in SOU 1999:1. The legislation committee proposed that the charge should be able to encompass all the debtor's property, but would be valid only to 50 per cent of its value. This would very much simplify the administration of the charge prior to and in insolvency, and also increase the amount remaining for unsecured creditors. The committee report, controversial in respect of its proposal to confine the enterprise charge to 50 per cent of the estate, analyses the advantages and disadvantages of secured credit in the context of the supply of credit and the behaviour of creditors prior to and in insolvency.
[113] If the borrower is entitled to expand the credit with primary security in spite of the existence of a secondary pledge, the secondary pledge ought to be void, since the secondary pledgee then has no control over the available collateral; the *situation* is

Variation

In the Bankruptcy Act (*konkurslagen*, 1987) there are two means of recovery (avoidance) which apply to security rights (pledges, charges and fiduciary transfers) that have been granted after a loan was made. Pursuant to chapter 4 section 12, a security may always be recovered (avoided) if it was perfected (by transfer of possession, registration, etc.) less than three months prior to the application for insolvency, provided that it was perfected with delay and after the actual transfer of credit, or that the security was not required when the debt arose. There is one exception to this rule in a special statute concerning financial instruments, according to which an additional security may not be recovered if required from the outset and later perfected without delay after either the original security (collateral) decreased in value or the debt increased in value, further provided that the transfer of the additional security was ordinary. Should the security have been perfected more than three months prior to the application to commence insolvency proceedings, chapter 4 section 5 may apply (*actio Pauliana*). Here the time limit is five years, unless the transaction was made in favour of a closely related person (legal or natural); in such case there is no time limit. The application of this rule requires that: (1) the transaction has in some way been to the disadvantage of all creditors or to some particular creditor; (2) the debtor was insolvent or became insolvent; (3) the creditor was inappropriately favoured; and (4) the creditor realised or ought to have realised these circumstances.

Avoidance is possible subject to the same requirements if a composition is confirmed by a court.

FINLAND

(a) A pledge is ineffective as against other creditors of the pledgor, if the pledged property remains at his disposal.[114] The same applies when, while the debtor formally transfers ownership of the goods, the parties are in reality trying to arrange a security for the creditor. The stock can, however, in both cases be left on the premises of the debtor if the debtor

---

the same as if the secondary pledgee had accepted sale to a third party, which no doubt would have invalidated the pledge. In Sweden, everyone accepts this in principle but almost everybody, and especially the banks, denies any practical application! Håstad, *Sakrätt rörande lös egendom* 330 ff.

[114] See chapter 10 s. 1 Commercial Code (*kauppalaki/köplag*) and e.g. Kartio, *Esineoikeuden perusteet* 134–135.

has access to the stock only with the co-operation of the creditor, e.g. the keys are delivered to the creditor or to a third party acting on behalf of the creditor. If these prerequisites are fulfilled, the stock can even be substituted, provided, of course, that it happens under the control of the creditor. If the security subsequently increases in value due to the activities of the parties, the security may be *pro tanto* voidable according to the rules of recovery relating to the insolvency estate.[115]

It is not possible to register either of the two types of contract discussed above. It is, however, also possible to make use of an enterprise charge.[116] The enterprise charge must be registered and a negotiable promissory note with an attached certificate of the registration must be delivered to the creditor. The enterprise is, according to the law, entitled to dispose of the charged property in the ordinary course of business. Even if a disposition has taken place outwith the ordinary course of business, the purchaser is protected as against the enterprise chargee if he or she has been acting *in bona fide*.

(b) The enterprise charge does not accord to the creditor a preferential status as strong as, for example, that of a pledge. For example, on insolvency (unlike in execution) the rights of an enterprise chargee are limited to only half the value of the charged property.

(c) Enterprise charges are quite commonly used, even if often only as a secondary security. Exact, recent figures are not available.

(d) There are no direct restrictions that affect the right of creditors to take securities. The fact that the preferential rights of an enterprise chargee are limited to half of the value of the charged property on insolvency, restricts, however, in its own way, the use of security rights.

Contractual clauses, according to the creditor an arbitrary right to claim new or additional securities, are, however, often considered to be unreasonable. Of course, the security agreement may, in principle, become unreasonable even because the value of the collateral rises due to, for example, the expansion of stock-in-trade, etc. In practice, this does not prove problematical because the security used by the parties is normally an enterprise charge, which does not prevent the debtor from disposing of the property in the ordinary course of business, and the same property can be charged several times.

---

[115] See 'Variation' below. [116] See the Act on Enterprise Charge.

Variation

The security right must be established without any unnecessary delay. A delay of many months is not acceptable. Therefore, the security right would be voidable according to the rules of recovery relating to insolvency estates, if C later became bankrupt and the application for insolvency was filed less than three months or, in certain circumstances, less than two years after the security was granted.[117] The longer time-limit applies if the parties are connected to each other in the way more precisely defined in the law, e.g. near relatives or enterprises belonging to the same owner.[118]

The security right could also be voided on grounds of the general rule of recovery relating to insolvency estates (*actio Pauliana*).[119] The legal consequences of any act or omission of the debtor can be voided, if (1) that act or omission has been to the prejudice of the creditors; (2) the debtor was insolvent or has become insolvent, wholly or partially, because of that act or omission;[120] (3) the other person has known or should have known of these facts; and (4) the act or omission occurred within the period of five years before the insolvency petition was filed.[121]

The rules concerning avoidance, described above, are applicable both in insolvency and to execution.[122] The basic legal consequence of recovery is that the disposition made by the debtor or another person concerned is declared by the court to be of no legal effect. Therefore, the payments or other performances, which are made on the basis of this legal disposition, are to be returned by both sides. When the disposition to be avoided is, for instance, the grant of a security to the creditor, there is, of course, nothing to be returned to the creditor.

---

[117] See s. 14 of the Act on Recovery to Bankrupt's Estate *(laki takaisinsaannista konkurssipesään/lag om återvinning till konkursbo)* and e.g. Tuomisto, *Takaisinsaannista* 255 ff.

[118] See s. 3 of the Act on Recovery to Bankrupt's Estate *(laki takaisinsaannista konkurssipesään/lag om återvinning till konkursbo)* and e.g. Tuomisto, *Takaisinsaannista* 14 ff.

[119] See s. 5 of the Act on Recovery to Bankrupt's Estate *(laki takaisinsaannista konkurssipesään/lag om återvinning till konkursbo)* and e.g. Tuomisto, *Takaisinsaannista* 38 ff.

[120] If the act or omission has been beneficial, the relevant factor is whether the debtor was excessively indebted or became excessively indebted.

[121] When the debtor and the other person are natural or legal persons connected to each other there is, in principle, no time-limit.

[122] They are, as a matter of fact, applicable even to the reconstruction of enterprise and the adjustment of a natural person's debts.

Comparative observations

Parts (a)–(c)

If we consider the ways in which the stock-in-trade of an enterprise, or the enterprise as a whole, may be offered as collateral, the jurisdictions can be roughly divided into three groups:

(1) Systems which recognise an enterprise charge which covers the business as a whole or at least significant parts of it: England, Ireland, Scotland, Sweden, Finland, France, Belgium and Portugal.
(2) Systems where it is practicable[123] to create a security in revolving stock-in-trade other than by the use of a *floating charge* or a security right in the enterprise as a whole. This group consists of Germany, Greece and the Netherlands.
(3) Systems where it is neither practicable to take a security right in revolving stock nor possible to charge the enterprise as a whole. This group consists of Austria, Italy, Spain, South Africa and Denmark. In France, the enterprise charge (*nantissement de fonds de commerce*) cannot include stock.

With respect to the parties' freedom to draft a charge which best meets their individual needs, the enterprise charge developed by English law, and received in Ireland and Scotland (*floating charge*), is probably the most advanced security device. From a comparative point of view, its most striking features are its floating character prior to crystallisation, which makes it possible to include the whole patrimony of the debtor irrespective of its legal status during the life-time of the charge; the parties' liberty to choose the event upon which crystallisation will take place; and the existence of the procedure of receivership as an extrajudicially administered liquidation.[124] *Floating charges* put the secured creditor in a fairly strong position, hence it is self-evident that they need to be registered. The *floating charge* is tied to the procedure of receivership, hence it is impossible for individuals to grant *floating charges*.

The Swedish and Finnish enterprise charge comes very close to the common law *floating charge*. There are, however, some material differences. First, the two Scandinavian jurisdictions do not know of an extrajudicial liquidation procedure such as receivership. Secondly, the

---

[123] In some jurisdictions, e.g. the Scandinavian ones, it is theoretically possible to grant security in revolving stock by means of a possessory pledge. This approach cannot be regarded as practicable, however.

[124] For the most recent development in English law see Bridge, *supra*, p. 94.

property to which the charge may extend is limited: in Sweden, a considerable part of the debtor's patrimony cannot be included (for example, real property or claims against banks). In Finland, only half of the patrimony included within the ambit of the charge can be used for the satisfaction of the secured debt in the debtor's insolvency. On the other hand, Swedish and Finnish enterprise charges rank in front, and not behind, statutory preferences such as claims for unpaid taxes and wages.

The French and Belgian enterprise charge (*nantissement de fonds de commerce*) is further removed from the English *floating charge*. First, one can hardly regard it as possessing a floating character since the French *nantissement* attaches only to specific assets such as equipment or patents and trademarks. Only in so far as the charge also attaches to intangible property that is subject to change, such as the enterprise's goodwill, might one speak of a floating character. Also, the *nantissement* is regarded as attaching to such assets as there are at any given moment. The *nantissement* could always be regarded as a real right in specified assets; this could not be said of a *floating charge* prior to crystallisation (see especially the Scots report). As to the practical solution of case 11, there is a notable difference between French and Belgian law: according to Belgian law, half of the stock may be included within the *nantissement* whereas in France, an enterprise's stock-in-trade cannot be charged as a matter of principle.

The German and Greek security transfer of ownership and the Dutch silent pledge may, in English legal terminology, be regarded as a 'fixed' security right. In contrast to the *nantissement* or the Swedish and Finnish enterprise charges, security transfer of ownership and the silent pledge cannot as such relate to a shifting fund, nor to an enterprise as a whole. These securities must be granted over specific movables. It is the principle of specificity in relation to real rights which precludes the possibility both of recognising a *floating charge* and of charging a shifting mass of assets or an entity such as an enterprise. As the Scots report points out, the *floating charge* is not considered to be a real right before crystallisation, yet in the civil law systems it does not seem possible to conceptualise of a right relating to property in a way that can be termed neither personal nor real.[125]

---

[125] The fact that the transplant of the floating charge into the Roman law-based Scots system has given rise to fundamental difficulties is illustrated by the decision of the House of Lords in *Sharp v Thomson* 1997 SLT 636. See Gretton, ERPL 1998, 403; Michaels, ERPL 1998, 407; Fenge, ZEuP 2000, 342.

Despite the principle of specificity, German and Dutch law have found ways to grant a security right in revolving stock-in-trade and in other collateral that is continuously alienated and replaced. The courts take a rather liberal attitude to the application of the said principle. Thus it is sufficient that the goods are identifiable at any given moment (German law) or at the moment at which the secured party wishes to take hold of the collateral (Dutch law). The necessity of separate storage when not all property is to be transferred or pledged is the only practical limit which stems from the principle of specificity. Furthermore, the necessary agreements, including (in Germany) the real agreement, may under both systems be concluded in advance and may relate to property which the debtor will acquire in the future. With respect to the creation of the security right, the main practical difference between German and Dutch law would appear to be the Dutch requirement of registration or the use of a notarial deed. Apart from the latter, the prohibition of fiduciary transfers in the new Dutch Civil Code seems to be of limited importance. In fact, the silent pledge places the creditor in an even stronger position than that of a security owner under German law. In the debtor's insolvency, the holder of a Dutch silent pledge may realise his security right outside the insolvency proceedings, at least up to a certain date set by the insolvency administrator. It is only after that date that the creditor has to contribute to the costs of the proceedings. In Germany, the position of the security owner was roughly the same under the old *Konkursordnung*. However, since the new Insolvency Code has entered into force, the creditor is always required to take part in the insolvency proceedings from the beginning and must always contribute towards the costs of the realisation of his security right.

Leaving aside for the moment the enterprise charge mentioned under (1), above, German and Dutch law are the only systems under which it is feasible to take a security right in revolving stock. Under all other jurisdictions, a pledge or fixed charge of stock fails for one or both of the following reasons:

(1) The principle of publicity. A pledge would require the debtor to surrender possession of the stock. Whilst it would not be strictly necessary for the creditor to take actual possession of it, the stock would have to be stored in such a way that would prevent the debtor from having access to it (see Austrian, Belgian, Danish, Swedish and Finnish reports). It is evident that on the facts of case 11, this is not a viable solution.

(2) The principle of specificity. In a number of countries a rather strict view is taken on the issue of the determinability of those assets which are to be the subject of a security right. Therefore, future stock cannot be included. This is the case in France, Portugal and South Africa.

As compared to the previous cases, case 11 has probably brought out the most significant differences, especially as between the common law jurisdictions, which have developed or adopted the *floating charge*,[126] and the civil law systems. However, the introduction of enterprise charges which closely approximate the *floating charge* in Sweden and Finland, the anticipated introduction of the *floating charge* in Greek law and the ways in which German and Dutch law have watered down the principle of specificity may provide useful examples of how rapprochement and midway solutions might be achieved.

Part (d)

The question of whether there are any limits as to the value of the collateral in relation to the amount of the secured claim can arise in any regime of security rights. It is, however, more relevant in connection with security rights in assets which are subject to change. Where the collateral remains fixed, one can apply the principle of party autonomy: if the debtor accepts that his property is being charged even though its value significantly exceeds the secured claim, it is his bargain. The only possible reason for legal intervention would lie either in the possible detriment to unsecured creditors of the same debtor or in the protection of parties who are in a weaker bargaining position, such as, for instance, consumers. By way of contrast, there is a special risk of 'oversecurity' in relation to security rights in constantly changing collateral.

The English report points out that oversecurity is a rare event, if the term is confined to the situation where the proceeds of the collateral's realisation in the insolvency of the debtor exceed the amount of the secured debt. Obviously, this is the perspective of English, Irish and Scots law. But 'oversecurity' may also be used in a wider sense; such as, for example, in the meaning attributed to the term under German law. There, a state of 'oversecurity' can exist when the debtor is still solvent. Oversecurity occurs when the value of the collateral, assessed by reference to the value of the debtor's business as a going concern, exceeds that of the secured debt by more than a specified percentage.

---

[126] In this sense, Scotland is regarded as a common law jurisdiction.

This view of oversecurity looks less to the interests of the insolvency creditors and more to the debtor's freedom to enter into new security agreements, although obviously, the doctrine can also benefit unsecured creditors. 'Oversecurity' in this sense presents a problem especially in systems which resort largely or exclusively to security devices based on ownership. Where the debtor has given away full ownership to the secured creditor one should assume that the former has no possibility to grant a junior security right to a subsequent lender. However, under German law, this assumption is not entirely correct. Because German courts have classified as a real right the expectancy of a buyer under retention of title to eventually receive ownership upon full payment (*Anwartschaftsrecht*),[127] this real right can itself be made the subject of a security right, for example, a security transfer of ownership.[128] Therefore, even this explanation is less than entirely satisfactory.

The general restrictions imposed by Belgian law (only 50 per cent of the stock can be charged under a *pand op de handelszaak/gage sur fonds de commerce*) and Finnish law (only 50 per cent of the collateral can be realised for the benefit of the creditor)[129] can also be seen as a means of avoiding oversecurity, but rather with a view to protecting unsecured creditors.

Variation

Any survey of the law relating to security rights would be incomplete if it did not mention the possibility of avoiding or setting aside transactions entered into either with a fraudulent intent, or gratuitously, or in a defined period prior to the commencement of insolvency proceedings. These three elements (fraud, gifts, suspect period) are in fact the main grounds on which avoidance can be sought in the various jurisdictions under consideration.[130] However, apart from this commonality, the reports reveal a large degree of variety, which is impossible fully to reflect in any short summary.

The most striking difference is perhaps the variation in the time periods during which avoidance can be sought. As a general rule, however, fraudulent transactions are subjected to the threat of avoidance for a

---

[127] See *supra*, German report, cases 3(c) and 11(a).
[128] See Bülow, *Recht der Kreditsicherheiten* n. 1099.
[129] The possibility of introducing a similar requirement to that obtaining in Finland has also been mooted in Sweden: see Swedish report, *supra*.
[130] See also Wood, *Principles of International Insolvency* paras. 4–5.

much longer time than gratuitous transactions or the grant of an incongruous security. For example, the time-limit relating to the avoidance of a preference intentionally given to a particular creditor varies from six months under South African law to an unlimited period under Belgian law.

The complexity of this area of the law is also reflected in the fact that most reporters were unable to give a definite answer as to the outcome of the case. In most jurisdictions, additional information would be needed to reach such a determination.

Returning to the subject of security rights and their possible harmonisation, it is evident that any attempt to harmonise the law on the *actio Pauliana* in this context would prove to be impossible. However, it is submitted that there is no necessary link. For a uniform regime of security rights, the simple statement of their enforceability in insolvency or execution, together with rules on the secured party's principal remedies, would be sufficient. There is no reason why the treatment of fraudulent transactions or contracts made within a suspect period could not be left to the national laws of the Member States or to harmonisation at a later stage. This is also the approach of the Cape Town Convention on International Interests in Mobile Equipment of 16 November 2001.[131] Under 'Effects of Insolvency', article 30(3) states: 'Nothing in this Article affects (a) any rules of law applicable in insolvency proceedings relating to the avoidance of a transaction as a preference or a transfer in fraud of creditors or (b) any rules of insolvency procedure relating to the enforcement of rights to property which is under the control or supervision of the insolvency administrator.'

---

[131] See *supra*, 'Introduction', at p. 25.

Case 12: Bank loan on the basis of money claims (I)

(Security assignment of claims in respect of an identified debtor – distinction between present and future claims – dependence of the secured creditor's rights on communication of the security right to the debitor cessus)

B, a software developer, has concluded a three-year contract with Happyplay Ltd (H) under which he is obliged to develop one new computer game every two months, against a regular monthly payment of 3,000 Euros. His bank (A) is prepared to grant him a loan amounting to 50,000 Euros but would like to take a security over B's monthly earnings. If necessary, B is prepared to accept that H be notified of the security right. Otherwise he would prefer that A's security right is not made known to H, so that he (B) would remain entitled to collect the money.

Questions

(a) Is it possible to conclude an agreement by which B gives A a security over the monthly claims against H? Are these claims regarded as present or future/conditional? Describe the main features and prerequisites of such an agreement, including any requirements as to form, registration, communication of the assignment to the *debitor cessus* (H), etc. How common are agreements of this kind in business practice?

(b) Suppose that A's right was not communicated to H before B became bankrupt. What rights would A have in B's insolvency in respect of (i) money already earned by B but not yet paid to him and (ii) money already earned and paid to B's bank account before insolvency?

(c) Suppose that A's right was communicated to H before B became bankrupt. What rights would A have in B's insolvency in respect of (i) money already earned by B but not yet paid to him and (ii) money already earned by B and paid by H to B's bank account before B's insolvency?

Discussions

GERMANY

(a) The parties can agree on a security assignment of B's monthly earnings. Such arrangements are extremely common in practice. The principal rules governing such arrangements are set out *supra*, in the context of proceeds clauses.[1] Note that the validity of the assignment does not depend on it being communicated to the *debitor cessus*. In the present case, B's claims against H are not future claims in a strict sense, since the obligation out of which they will arise already exists. This may have consequences for the rights of the security assignee: see *infra* (b).

(b) The secured creditor's (A's) rights in relation to B's insolvency creditors do not depend on the assignment being communicated to the *debitor cessus* (H). As soon as the claim comes into existence, it is automatically transferred to the assignee. In situation (i), A has a right to preferential payment out of the realisation of the claim against H.[2] In situation (ii) however, the claim has already ceased to exist. Since H was unaware of the assignment he could still extinguish the debt by paying B (see § 407 s. 1 BGB). A might have a right to the money paid if B's entitlement to collect the claims had already been revoked at the time of payment. As explained *supra*,[3] A will, in principle, have a right to the money paid pursuant to § 48 InsO (application by way of analogy), if the following requirements are met. First, the collection of the claims from H by B must have been wrongful. This depends on B's entitlement. If B had already stopped making all payments under the loan, his entitlement to collect claims that are assigned to the creditor in question would determine without express termination.[4] Secondly, the money paid by H must still be present in the insolvency estate in a distinguishable manner. Money paid into the debtor's general business account is no longer distinguishable in this sense.[5] Therefore, A would only have a preferential right to the money paid by H, if payment was made to a separate account and if those funds remain identifiable.

The questionnaire only deals with the question of A's rights in respect of money already earned by B prior to his insolvency. However, A would

---

[1] German report, case 5(c). [2] As to the procedure see *supra*, German report, case 6(b).
[3] German report, case 5(c). [4] Cf. *Smid*/Gundlach § 48 InsO n. 47.
[5] See *supra*, German report, case 5(c).

also be able to acquire a right in B's future earnings, since the foundation of such future claims has already been laid in the contract between B and H. The BGH[6] and the predominant scholarly opinion[7] distinguish between a claim where the obligation from which it will arise already exists (here: the contract between B and H), and claims which are future claims in the full sense. In the first case, the commencement of insolvency proceedings prior to the inception of the individual claim does not affect the assignment; whereas, in the second case, the claim will fall into the insolvency estate. The distinction is often explained by a difference in the legal construction: if the obligation already exists, the claim is thought to vest directly in the assignee (*Direkterwerb*). If however the obligation does not yet exist at the time of the assignment, the claim is thought to belong to the assignor for a 'logical second' before it is transferred to the assignee (*Durchgangserwerb*).[8] Others criticise this explanation; a 'construction' should not decide a practical question.[9] These authors reach the same conclusion but through an analysis of the different interests involved. They argue that insolvency creditors (unlike execution creditors) are unable to seek satisfaction in other property. As the global assignment of future claims is a widespread practice, unsecured creditors are in danger of being deprived completely of all assets, even those which come into existence after the commencement of the insolvency procedure. Such a solution would economically be unsound. Therefore, at least those claims which are future claims in the full sense should form part of the insolvency estate.

A similar question is whether the future claim can be the subject of an execution by the assignor's (B's) creditors, thus preventing A from acquiring it. Here, the answer is different: so long as the claim does not yet exist, execution has no legal consequences. As soon as the receivable comes into existence, it immediately vests in the assignee (B). Therefore, an intermediate execution cannot give the executing creditor priority

---

[6] BGH 5 Jan. 1955, NJW 1955, 544.
[7] *Palandt*/Heinrichs § 398 BGB n. 12; *Staudinger*/Busche § 398 BGB nn. 72–75; *Münchener Kommentar*/Roth § 398 BGB n. 65; Larenz, *Lehrbuch des Schuldrechts I* § 34 III; Serick, *Eigentumsvorbehalt und Sicherungsübertragung* IV § 47 IV; Reinicke/Tiedtke, *Kreditsicherung* n. 614; Baur/Stürner, *Sachenrecht* § 58 n. 21. *Contra*, and for the priority of the assignee in both cases, Bülow, *Recht der Kreditsicherheiten* nn. 1123 f.; Esser/Schmidt, *Schuldrecht I/2* 310.
[8] Cf. *Palandt*/Heinrichs § 398 BGB n. 12; Larenz, *Lehrbuch des Schuldrechts I* § 34 III; Serick, *Eigentumsvorbehalt und Sicherungsübertragung* IV § 47 IV; *Staudinger*/Busche § 398 BGB nn. 72–75.
[9] Reinicke/Tiedtke, *Kreditsicherung* n. 614; *Münchener Kommentar*/Roth § 398 BGB n. 64.

over the assignee irrespective of whether the receivable is a future claim in the full sense or not.[10]

(c) (i) Since A's rights do not depend on the communication of the assignment, the solution is the same as under (b) (i): A has a right to preferential payment out of B's claims against H.

(ii) Since the assignment had been communicated to H, the latter's payment to B was invalid. H has to pay again, this time to A. He will have only a personal claim against B, as an insolvency creditor, on the basis of unjust enrichment.

AUSTRIA

(a) Such an agreement is possible. B can either charge his claims against H to A or he can assign these claims to A for security purposes. There are no fundamental differences between the two, but A may prefer a security assignment. If B defaults, A would be entitled to collect B's claim against H. In the case of a charge, he would first need to obtain a court order against B, which would then allow him to have recourse to B's claim against H.[11] (Other creditors may also execute against the claim but they would rank after A.) In both cases it is necessary to comply with the publicity requirement.[12] This is done either by notifying the *debitor cessus*[13] or by making an entry in the books of the chargor. Such agreements are very common. B's claims against H are not future claims, as the obligation out of which they will arise already existed at the time of the assignment.

(b) (i) If an entry was made in B's books, the charge or assignment thereby became effective. In the case of a charge, A is entitled to preferential payment out of the realisation of the claim against H. If the claim was assigned, A is entitled to collect it. Realisations in excess of the secured debt must be remitted to the insolvency administrator. If no entry was made in B's books, the money goes to B's insolvency administrator.

---

[10] BAG 24 Oct. 1979, WM 1980, 661 (662); Reinicke/Tiedtke, *Kreditsicherung* n. 605; Palandt/Heinrichs § 398 BGB n. 13; *Münchener Kommentar*/Roth § 398 BGB n. 66.
[11] When creating a charge, the parties can agree on a different mode of realisation.
[12] Compliance with the publicity requirement is necessary for the validity of the charge against third parties, but not for its validity *inter partes*.
[13] See above, Austrian report, case 5.

(ii) As H did not know of the charge (assignment), he was entitled[14] to pay B; his debt was thereby discharged. A's rights then depend on whether an entry was made in B's books. If such an entry was made, A has the right of preferential payment as against B's insolvency administrator, provided that the money was kept separate from B's other assets. If the payment was made after the commencement of insolvency proceedings, A would have priority over the other creditors of B, regardless of whether the money was kept separate from the other assets.[15]

(c) (i) H has to pay A, as the charge (assignment) is valid. In the case of an assignment, A is entitled to collect B's claim against H. In case of a charge, he has the right to claim preferential payment out of the proceeds of the claim against H.

(ii) If H knew that the claim was assigned to A, payment to B could not discharge the debt; he must therefore make a second payment to A.

GREECE

(a) An agreement to provide security in future claims, in the circumstances of this case, can take any of the following forms:

(1) A can take a charge over B's claims against H. According to article 1247.1 A.K., 'a pledge [sic][16] may also be constituted in regard to a right to the extent that such right is transmissible'. Following the constitution of the charge, the holder of the right remains the same, but the power to alienate the right (articles 1256, 1237 A.K.) and the power to collect the claim (articles 1253–1254 A.K.) are transferred to the chargee. Though real rights are meant to exist in respect of things, the Greek Civil Code recognises 'real rights' in rights. These rights have simply the main characteristics of real rights, i.e. an absolute and direct power on the charged right. In order to constitute a charge over claims validly, the following requirements must be met: (1) a notarial deed, or a private deed bearing an officially certified date, must be used (article 1247.3 A.K.) and (2) the *debitor cessus* (i.e. H) must be notified of the charge (article 1248 A.K.). The notification

---

[14] § 1395 ABGB; cf. Koziol/Welser, *Grundriß des bürgerlichen Rechts I* 293.
[15] In such a case, his claim is regarded as a privileged claim because of an unjust enrichment of the insolvency estate: cf. § 46 (1) N 6 Insolvency Code.
[16] The Civil Code provision concerns pledges. The term 'charge' has been used in the context of claims, however, as the intangible nature of such property renders the surrender of actual possession on the part of the pledgee impossible: see the Glossary.

requirement to charge claims corresponds to the delivery requirement for the pledge of a tangible movable (article 1211 A.K.). Agreements of this type are rare.

(2) The parties could also agree on a special sort of charge, pursuant to articles 35 ff. of L.D. of 17 July 1923 on 'special provisions concerning corporations'. The distinctive features of this charge are: (1) the chargee must be a bank or a company of a type recognised by the decree; (2) the charge may be constituted by a private document; and (3) the requirement to notify the *debitor cessus* may be performed by the chargee.

(3) The difficulties inherent in the charge of claims (principally the notification requirement, article 1248 A.K.; the formalities, article 1247.3 A.K.; and the complex rules applicable to the determination of the rights of the chargee, articles 1252–1254 A.K.) have been responded to in practice by developing the institution of security assignment. The validity of security assignment is disputed. According to the prevailing view of the courts[17] and legal writers,[18] it is valid. Assignment of future claims for security purposes is commonly encountered in transactions, mainly in cases when the businessman/debtor assigns future claims against clients to a bank. Jurisprudence and theory accept the validity of the assignment of future claims even when they are only determinable. Thus it is accepted[19] that assignment may be valid even if the identity of the future debtor is not known at the moment of the assignment, or the legal relationship from which the assigned claim will arise has not yet been constituted. It is clear that B can assign his claims against H to A. Such agreements are quite common.

(4) Undisclosed or confidential factoring[20] is the fourth possibility open to the parties. As one of the purposes of factoring is the provision of finance, A and B can agree on a factoring contract. Under this contract, A will pay to B, on signature, a sum representing the discounted value of the assigned claims. B will assign his future claims against H to the factor, who will be responsible for their collection. A may act as a factor: Law 1905/1990 (as modified by L. 2367/1995), which governs the factoring relationship, stipulates that factoring may only be undertaken by banks or corporations specialising in this form of business (article 4). The factoring contract must be concluded

---

[17] AP 649/1968 NoV 17, 412; Ef of Athens 7843/1986 Arm 41, 670; Ef of Athens 1541/1985 EllDni 26, 702.

[18] Georgiadis, *Empragmato Dikaio II* 257; Kornilakis, *I katapisteutiki ekchorisi ton apaitiseon* 63; Papantoniou, *Genikes Arches tou Astikou Dikaiou* 35; Stathopoulos, *Enochiko Dikaio* 615.

[19] Kornilakis, *I katapisteutiki ekchorisi ton apaitiseon* 47.

[20] See Georgiadis, *Nees morphes symvaseon tis sygchronis oikonomias* 126; Vathis, *I symvasi Factoring* 28; for a treatment of factoring and future claims, see Livanis, *Diathesi mellondikou dikaiomatos* 13 ff.

in writing (article 1 para. 1). Tax relief is provided for factoring, in order to promote the development of Greek enterprise.

(5) The parties could also combine the loan with a maturity factoring of B's future claims concluded between B and a factor. B would assign to A his rights under the factoring contract and would order the factor, which usually is a subsidiary company of a bank, to deposit the collected claims in his financing account at the bank, A.

(6) Finally, A and B are able to stipulate an enterprise charge over B's claims against H (article 16 of L. 2844/2000 on '*Symvaseis epi kiniton i apaitiseon ypokeimenes se dimosiotita kai alles symvaseis parochis asphaleias*' ('Contracts concerning movables or claims subject to publicity and other contracts providing security'). Enterprise charges need to be registered.

(b) A valid charge cannot be constituted unless H is notified of it prior to B's insolvency. Real rights cannot be constituted over property belonging to an insolvency estate: article 2 of L. 635/1937. Thus, in situations (i) and (ii), A will rank only as a normal insolvency creditor.

Claims which are the subject of a security assignment will not, in circumstances of insolvency, form part of the insolvency estate, irrespective of whether the *debitor cessus* has been notified or not.[21] Thus, in situation (i) A is entitled to collect the claim, after notification has been made to H (article 460 A.K.). A is obliged to return any surplus realisation to the insolvency estate.[22] If the debt has been paid to the assignor (as in situation (ii)), or in any other way extinguished (article 461 A.K.[23]), before the *debitor cessus* has been notified of the assignment, the *debitor cessus* will be released from his obligation of payment. A is entitled to announce his claim, and participate in the insolvency procedure as an insolvency creditor of B, either because B has been unjustly enriched to the detriment of A (article 904 A.K.), or because B has wrongfully collected the assigned claim (article 730 A.K.).

Should the parties, in the future, make use of an enterprise charge, A would be entitled to the monies after the registration requirement is satisfied, irrespective of whether the charge was communicated to H or not.

(c) (i) Charge: When B's claims against H have been charged and the debt which forms the collateral has not yet become due, A and B's insolvency

---

[21] Georgiadis, *Empragmato Dikaio II* 267.
[22] Georgiadis, *Empragmato Dikaio II* 268; Livanis, *Diathesi mellondikou dikaiomatos* 125.
[23] Ef of Athens 6370/1982 Arm 37, 107.

administrator will be jointly entitled to collect the monies from H. Furthermore, either A or B's insolvency administrator may require the monies to be deposited in an interest-bearing account, the right of charge being reserved (article 1253 A.K.). The kind of deposit shall be determined by the chargor.

Security assignment: It is disputed, in the circumstances of the assignor's insolvency, whether the assignee under a security assignment is entitled to claim payment from the *debitor cessus* as the holder of the claim,[24] or whether he is simply entitled to preferential payment out of the proceeds of collection.[25] The latter view prevails. According to it, A has the rights of a chargee of claims (application by analogy of the provisions of charge) unless the insolvency administrator pays the debt in full (article 645 EmbN).

Undisclosed factoring: According to the prevailing view,[26] insolvency terminates *ipso iure* the contract of factoring.

(ii) Since A's rights were communicated to H, any payment to B is invalid and A maintains his rights against B and H. H will have to make payment again, this time to A. B will be obliged to return the payment received from H on the basis of unjust enrichment.

FRANCE

(a) The 'traditional' assignment of claims is provided for by C. civ, articles 1689 ff. This is a contract between the assignor and the assignee, by which the assignor transfers a claim that he has against a debtor to the assignee. Pursuant to C. civ, article 1690, the assignee can enforce the assignment against third parties only if the *debitor cessus* has been formally notified, by means of an official letter delivered by a bailiff, or has formally accepted the assignment by deed (that is a document having a certain date). Before notification, the assignment will be effective only as between the parties: the debtor can pay the assignor and is free from any further obligation (C. civ, article 1691).[27] Notification has

---

[24] G. Simitis, *I di emboreumaton isphalismeni trapeziki pistosis* 72; K. Simitis, *I anamorphosis tou plasmatikou enechyrou* 34.
[25] AP 1307/94, DEE 1995, 407: this view is followed by Georgiadis, *Kyriotis* 223 and the authors mentioned there. See also Kotsiris, *Nees morphes symvaseon tis sygchronis oikonomias* 340; N. Rokas, *Stoicheia ptocheutikou dikaiou* 35.
[26] N. Rokas, *Stoicheia ptocheutikou dikaiou* 52.
[27] There has been some discussion, however, of the situation where the *debitor cessus* has been informed of the assignment, but in a manner not complying with the formal

to be made in respect of each claim, which is highly impracticable in the present case, where B wishes to assign his monthly claim against H. Because the requirements of C. civ, article 1690 proved highly impracticable for parties who very often will be assigned claims, such as banks and financial institutions, a specific regime was created. Law No 81-2 of 2 January 1981, the so-called '*Loi Dailly*' (after the senator who initiated the new regime), provides a new method for the 'professional' assignment of debts.[28] A person, legal or natural, may assign a bulk of claims, present or future, that he has over one or several debtors, so long as the assignment is part of his professional activity and the assignee is a financial institution. The assignment can be perfect (sale) or made for security purposes, for example, to guarantee the repayment of a loan.[29] It is also possible to charge the claims (*nantissement*), but this has not been used in practice since assignment accords to the creditor a better ranking (he owns the claims) than that conferred by a charge. The procedure is very simple. B delivers to A, his bank, a document *bordereau* where specific particulars must be listed. These particulars are: (1) whether the transaction is an assignment or a charge; (2) the names of the parties and their signatures; and (3) the list of the assigned claims identified by, for example, the name of the *debitor cessus*, the place of payment, the amount and the terms.[30] The debts can be due and liquid, but also may arise from a transaction that has just occurred or will occur (for details, see French report, case 13). Here, the claims owed by H are future claims, but the term is known (monthly payment) and so is the amount. Most importantly, the assignment is deemed perfect from the date of the document *and* is effective against third parties from that very day (article 4). This is the *Dailly* regime, which will be used in this case. As B would prefer not to inform H of the assignment, he may persuade A to allow him to collect the payments on A's behalf, consequently H will be ignorant

---

requirements provided in article 1690. The question would be whether the *debitor cessus* would be able to pay the assignee in such circumstances, in such a way as to discharge the assigned debt.

[28] See Dumas/Roblot, *Encyclopédie Dalloz, vol. Commercial*, Apr. 1998.

[29] As confirmed by the *Cour de cassation* in Com 24 Apr. 1990, Bull civ IV, No 118; D 1990, IR, 118; RTDCom 1990, 442, obs. Cabrillac/Teyssié. This is a rare example in French law of security ownership, the *fiducia* concept. A draft law was presented a few years ago to introduce the concept into French law generally (Doc Ass. Nat. 1991–92, No 2583) but it was never adopted.

[30] 1981 *Dailly Law*, article 1. If the assignment is done by computerised means that permit the identification of the claims, it is enough to mention these means in the document, the number of assigned debts and the total amount.

of the assignment. This will be problematical when B becomes bankrupt (see part (b)).

A problem may arise concerning the validity of the assignment if it took place in the suspect period. In principle, once someone has been declared bankrupt by court order, they cannot make assignments. *Before* the commencement of insolvency proceedings and *after* the date of the suspension of payments (the period of time forming the suspect period), no payment can be made for debts not yet due (C. com, article L. 621-107°). Article L. 621-107, 4° also forbids the payment of debts due, when such payment is to be by means other than cash, letter of credit, bank transfer, *Dailly* assignment or any other mode of payment commonly used in the trade business. This provision is ambiguous, as C. com, article L. 621-107, 6° provides that no security interest (charge or pledge) can be agreed then upon the debtor's estate to guarantee debts already in existence. A recent decision considered the position where a *Dailly* assignment was granted by a company to a bank to guarantee the balance of its bank account. The company went bankrupt and it was established that the suspension of payments had taken place before the assignment. The insolvency administrator thus attempted to have the assignment declared void on the basis of article 107, 6°. The *Cour de cassation* rejected his demand, on the basis that a *Dailly* assignment transfers to the assignee ownership of the debt (even if the assignment is made to guarantee an already existing debt), so that it is not a security interest and therefore C. com, article L. 621-107, 6° is not applicable.[31] Finally, the payment of due debts, and any transactions for consideration with the debtor, after the suspension of payments, can be held to be void if those who paid or contracted knew of the suspension of payments (C. com, article L. 621-108). C. com, article L. 621-108 is inapplicable to assignments because they are not regarded as payment.[32]

(b) It is most likely, in practice, that the *debitor cessus* will be ignorant of the assignment. The assignor will collect the sums on behalf of the assignee, acting as an agent, and must transfer the sums to the assignee. The difficulty arises if the assignor becomes bankrupt.

(i) The money had not yet been paid by H to B, before B became bankrupt. Under the general regime governing the assignment of claims (C. civ,

---

[31] Com 28 May 1996, Bull civ IV, No 151; RTDC 1996, 671, obs. Crocq.
[32] Although this is more open to criticism: see Crocq, *ibid*.

articles 1689 ff.), an assignment is not effective as against third parties unless formal notification has been made. Third parties in this sense means those who were not parties to the assignment and have an interest in the assignor remaining the creditor.[33] For example, if B goes bankrupt, the insolvency administrator would have such an interest: the claims against H would form part of B's insolvency estate. In such circumstances, the insolvency administrator would be entitled to claim payment from H of the monthly sums, as formal notification was not made prior to the commencement of insolvency proceedings. A would not be entitled to the claims,[34] nor to the money already earned but unpaid before insolvency. In contrast, under the 1981 *Dailly* Law, article 4, the assignment is effective *vis-à-vis* the debtor and third parties from the date of the assignment. Where the assignor becomes bankrupt, the assignee may declare his claim to the insolvency administrator, but most importantly he is also entitled to claim payment directly from the *debitor cessus*. Thus, A can require H to pay him directly.

(ii) If the money was paid to B, does A have a right to the sums? If it was paid directly, in cash, to B, he does not. The only option left to the assignee is to declare his claim in the insolvency proceedings. If payment was made by a transfer of funds into the assignor's bank account, the answer is less straightforward, as a conflict arises between the bank-assignee and the bank-recipient. In a criticised decision of 1986, the *Cour de cassation* held that, when payment had been made into the assignor's bank account, the recipient bank ought to transfer the money back to the assignee bank even though the assignor had become bankrupt and, therefore, the recipient bank had no recourse against him.[35] However, in 1995, the Court changed its position: it refused to order that three claims, which had been assigned but paid into the bank account of the assignor, should be transferred to the assignee.[36] Payment had been made in the name and on the account of the assignor. The bank is not a third party in the sense of the 1981 Law, but only one receiving funds

---

[33] Civ. (3), 12 June 1985, Bull civ III, No 95; RTDC 1986, 350, obs. Mestre.
[34] However, the lack of notification does not prevent the assignee from requiring the *debitor cessus* to pay him when such payment would not cause prejudice to others: see Civ. (3), 26 Feb. 1985, JCP 1986, II, 2060, note Petit.
[35] Com 28 Oct. 1986, D 1986, 592, note Vasseur; JCP 1987, II, 20735, obs. Stoufflet; RTDCom 1987, 89, obs. Cabrillac/Teyssié. Also Com 12 Oct. 1993, Bull civ IV, No 328, D 1993, IR, 237.
[36] Com 4 July 1995, Bull civ IV, No 203; D 1996, Som, 208, obs. Piedelièvre; JCP 1995, II, 22553, note Legeais; RTDC 1996, 192, obs. Gauthier.

by deposit and who, thus, can return funds only to the holder of the account. So, on the basis of the most recent decision, A has no legal right to require B's bank to transfer the payments already made by H into B's account to him.

(c) (i) Here, A's right was communicated to H before B became bankrupt. Article 5, 1981 Law, provides that the assignee can at any time inform the *debitor cessus* of the change of creditor and such information can be given by any means (article 2 Decree of 9 September 1981 that accompanies the law). Formal notification is not required. The purpose here is not so much to inform the *debitor cessus* of the assignment, but rather to forbid him from making further payment. As such, while formal notification is not required, there are nevertheless formal conditions which must be complied with, in particular those provided in Annex 1 of the decree.[37] Once informed, the *debitor cessus* is not allowed to pay the assignor, or he will run the risk of having to pay twice. Therefore, A will be able to claim the monthly payments directly from H. If B goes bankrupt, pursuant to the 1981 *Dailly* Law, article 4, A may declare his claim to B's insolvency administrator but is also entitled to claim payment directly from H, the debtor of B. The solution would also apply in the case of a traditional assignment since formal notification was made to H.

(ii) Because H knew of the assignment, he must make payment again, to A. His claim against B for restitution is only a personal claim.

BELGIUM

(a) Before the change of the law in 1994, the charge of claims was subjected to the same formalities that existed for the assignment of claims under the system of the old articles 1690 ff. C.civ. Those formalities were drastically simplified under the new article 1690. Belgian law shifted from the French solution towards the German approach. According to the new provisions, the transfer is effective between assignor and

---

[37] See Com 7 Jan. 1997, Bull civ IV, No 2; RTDC 1997, 474. In this case, the assignee sent the *debitor cessus* a request that he should agree to the assignment. The *debitor cessus* did not reply and paid the assignor directly. The *Cour de cassation* held that, so long as the *debitor cessus* had not received an order not to pay the assignor, he could validly pay him directly, regardless of whether or not he knew of the existence of the assignment.

assignee and binding upon third parties as from the moment at which assignment is agreed.[38] The notification of the *debitor cessus*, which is now form-free, remains necessary only in relation to the position of the *debitor cessus* and in respect of conflicts with third parties who have vested rights in the claims which are in conflict with those of the assignee. The abolition of the formal requirements for assignment made a change in the law regarding the charge of claims inevitable. The new article 2075 s. 1 C.civ. provides that the creditor obtains the security interest at the point at which the charging agreement is concluded. As from that moment, the charge is valid between the parties and binding upon third parties. The charge is only binding upon the *debitor cessus* after notification to him or after his acceptance. As under article 1690 C.civ., neither notification nor acceptance are submitted to specific formalities. Conflicts between the chargee and third parties who have vested rights in the claim (e.g. a subsequent chargee or assignee) are also dealt with according to the moment of notification (or acceptance). The chargee is entitled to notify the *debitor cessus* as from the moment the charging agreement is concluded. The parties may however make explicit provision for the point in time and conditions under which notification may take place.

Belgian law is generally hostile towards fiduciary transfers for security purposes. A security assignment is only valid *inter partes*, having no legal effect *vis-à-vis* third parties.[39] In case 12, B can charge his claims against H to A, but is unable to assign them as a security.

(b) Conflicts with third parties with vested rights in the claim are, as mentioned previously, dealt with according to the time of notification (or acceptance). The majority of legal authors hold the view that executing creditors of the chargor who have attached the claim, or the creditors in the insolvency of the chargor, cannot be considered to be 'protected' third parties. According to this view, the absence of notification will not endanger the position of the chargee in the case of the insolvency of the chargor. The monies paid after the commencement of insolvency proceedings will therefore be allocated to the chargee. The payments before the proceedings made in good faith by the *debitor cessus*, who had not been notified by the chargee, are valid. Since the monies

---

[38] Dirix, RW 1994–95, 137; Van Ommeslaghe, JT 1995, 529.
[39] Cass. 17 Oct. 1996, Pas 1996 I 992 concl. proc. gen. Piret, RW 1996–97, 1395, note Storme.

will have been mixed in the estate of the chargor, the chargee will lose his security right.

(c) (i) A notification before the insolvency proceedings will secure the position of the chargee by preventing any payment by the *debitor cessus* and by strengthening the position of the chargee in the priority contest with third parties.

(ii) A payment by the *debitor cessus* after notification will be invalid in respect of the chargee.

PORTUGAL

(a) B is able to give A a security over the monthly claims against H by assignment (article 577° C.C.) or by charging the claims (article 679° C.C.). These claims would be regarded as future claims because, under the agreement, they are to arise monthly. Portuguese law does not prohibit future or conditional debts from being assigned or charged.[40] However, in this case, the effects of the assignment or the charge would remain dependent on the existence of the claim (article 274°, n°2 C.C.). If the claim never arises, the agreement would be considered void. If the claim does arise, the agreement would be considered retroactively valid.

There are no special requirements of form or registration to assign or charge a claim. It is only necessary to communicate it to the *debitor cessus*, in order to make it effective against him. In fact, according to articles 583° and 669°, n°2 C.C., the assignment or charge of claims is only effective after it is communicated to the *debitor cessus* or after he accepts it.

Assignments of future claims are common in business practice, especially in factoring.[41] The assignment of claims for security purposes is neither established by statute nor common in commercial practice. A charge of claims is established by the statute and so would probably be more common, although there are better and much more commonly used securities for creditors.

(b) (i) As stated in part (a), the assignment or charge of claims takes effect only after it is communicated to the *debitor cessus* or after he accepts it, but the assignee or chargee may notify the *debitor cessus* of its existence

---

[40] See de Lima/Varela, *Código Civil Anotado* I 594.
[41] See Menezes Cordeiro, *Manual de Direito Bancário* 573.

at any time prior to payment. Therefore, if H has not yet paid B, A can still notify H of the assignment or charge and collect the monies from him. The insolvency of B makes no difference because the assignment was agreed before its occurrence. If payment of claim is called for by the insolvency administrator, A would be entitled to ask that the proceeds be separated from the insolvency estate (article 201° (c) CPEREF). Separation means that A can claim payment directly from H. There is no difference between assignment and charge in these circumstances, because the charge and the assignment are subject to the same statutory rules in this respect (article 684° C.C.).

(ii) If the monies were paid to B before the communication of the assignment or charge and B goes bankrupt, either would be considered to be ineffective in respect of the *debitor cessus*. A has no real right in the monies that have been paid to the now insolvent assignor or chargor. He will only have a claim based on unjust enrichment, which grants no right to preferential payment. Should the assignee be able to prove that the *debitor cessus* had prior knowledge of the assignment or charge, he could then force the *debitor cessus* to pay the debt again, to him (article 583°, n°2 C.C.).

(c) (i) If the assignment or charge had already been communicated to the *debitor cessus*, it would be effective in relation to him. Therefore, A alone would be considered the creditor of H and would be entitled to require a separation of the claim from the insolvency estate, in the case of subsequent seizure of the claim by the insolvency administrator.

(ii) After the communication of the assignment or charge, H must no longer pay the monies to B. In the case of an assignment, the money must be paid to A only (article 583° C.C.). In the case of a charge, the monies must be paid to A and B jointly at the same time or deposited in favour of both (article 685°, n°2 C.C.). If, therefore, H deposits the monies in B's bank account, such payment would not extinguish the debt and A could require H to pay the debt a second time. In consequence of this, A would not have any right to the monies received by B.

SPAIN

(a) Such an agreement would take the form of a factoring contract between a financial institution (*factor*) and a business person (*cliente*) whereby the former receives the latter's rights to collect the payment from his customers.

In Spain, factoring contracts rest on the mechanism of assignment (*cesión de créditos*).[42] More specifically, the factoring transaction falls under Law 3/1994 and Law 1/1999. By means of factoring, the customer (*cliente*) assigns debts owed to him by his customers, to the financing institution. The financial institution then assumes responsibility for subsequent debt collection. The factoring company may decide to undertake the risk of the *debitores cessi* becoming insolvent or not.[43] Factoring also constitutes a mechanism for administering the accounts of the factor's customers. The financing institution can be a bank, a savings bank, a savings and loan association or a credit institution, which must be authorised by Spain's Central Bank to carry out factoring. The customer is usually a businessman, who may need cash to carry out his business activities.

The case under consideration involves 'future claims', namely those which arise from a commercial activity between B and his customers. The main features and requirements of a factoring agreement are as follows: (1) the factoring contract must be in written form, although it does not have to be legalised as a public deed (such contracts are usually based on a commercial public deed, called *póliza de contrato bancario de facturación*); (2) there is no need for registration, in fact a public registry for factoring transactions does not exist; (3) there is no need to inform the *debitor cessus* of the assignment. Nevertheless, in practice, financial institutions, in order to avoid the application of article 1527 CC,[44] require the business person to notify the *debitores cessi* of the assignment. This notification can take place either by means of an explicit communication to the *debitores cessi* or tacitly by means of a notation within the contract (bill, delivery note, etc.) which is sent to the *debitor cessus* to inform him of the date of collection of the assigned debt.

Indeed, factoring contracts are commonly used in business reality, although probably not as much as the discounting of bills as regulated by article 175.1° CCO and by articles 177–183 CCO.[45] In commercial

---

[42] See articles 1526–1535 CC and articles 347, 348 CCO. See Sequeira Martín, in: García Villaverde 307.

[43] See Vicent Chuliá, *Compendio Crítico de Derecho Mercantil II* 267. See also García Solé, in: García Villaverde 602.

[44] According to article 1527 CC, if the *debitor cessus* pays the assignor, in ignorance of the prior assignment of this debt to the financial institution, then the *debitor cessus* will be released from his obligation to pay the debt to the financial institution.

[45] Discounting of bills receivable refers to commercial securities, such as bills of exchange, receipts, invoices, delivery notes, bank drafts and promissory notes.

discounting, the financial institution buys a debt from a businessman (usually a bill of exchange or a promissory note from one of his debtors), paying a price which it deposits in the businessman's bank account after deducting a certain amount as commission for its part in the process. The financial institution, however, does not assume any liability for non-payment on the part of the *debitores cessi*.[46] Although there are no formal requirements for the discounting of bills, a public deed called *póliza de afianzamiento* is usually signed by the parties to facilitate subsequent judicial execution. Another commonly used method of securing the creditor's right is by requiring the client and his bankers personally to guarantee the fulfilment of the discounted bills.

The assignment of future debts in exchange for a lump sum (*venta alzada* or *en globo*) is not explicitly covered in the CC, although some authors hold that article 1532 CC indirectly allows for the sale of rights to debt recovery in exchange for a lump sum. In recent years, legal literature has upheld the lawfulness of the assignment of future debts in exchange for a lump sum in spite of the difficulty of identifying the debts to which such an assignment relates.[47]

This issue has been resolved by the legislature by means of Supplementary Provision 3 of Law 1/1999, which recognises: (1) the assignment of future debts *en masse* and in exchange for a lump sum in respect of unidentified future debtors of the assignor, providing that such debts arise within one year from the date of agreeing the contract; and (2) the assignment of future debts in exchange for a lump sum with respect to *debitores cessi* who are identified and specified in the contract, in which case the debts may arise after the expiry of the one-year limit applicable under (1).[48] For this regulation to apply, the debts must exist at the moment of conclusion of the contract. If they do not yet exist, any future debts (whoever the *debitor cessus* may be) must result from the business or professional activities of the assignor and must arise within one year from the date of conclusion of the contract. This period can be renewed or extended by the parties year by year.[49] This regulation is also applied to future debts arising from *debitores cessi* who have already been duly identified in the factoring contract, in which case the assignment of debts will be valid without any time-limit other than the period

---

[46] See García Solé, in: García Villaverde 245.
[47] See Pantaleón Prieto, ADC (1988) 1094; García-Cruces González, *El contrato de factoring* 124; Gavidia Sánchez, *La cesión de créditos* 207; García de Enterría, *Contrato de factoring y cesión de créditos* 90.
[48] See García Solé, in: García Villaverde 601.
[49] See García Solé, in: García Villaverde 603.

envisaged in the contract. In both cases, when the debts arise, they will be owed to the financial institution.

The assignment of future debts *en masse*, in advance and for a lump sum, has not been adopted in practice. Nevertheless, the new regulation might well contribute to its wider acceptance.

(b) In both situations, A is affected by B's insolvency.
(i) In the first situation, if H has not paid B, A will be a normal insolvency creditor. However, if A and B have set up a factoring contract and if this contract and the assignment of B's debt to A have been legalised as a public deed, A will have a preferential right in B's insolvency.

(ii) In the second situation, if H, unaware of the assignment of his debt to A, has paid B, the monies received will fall into the insolvency estate and will be subject to the insolvency proceedings. In accordance with article 1527 CC, H will have legally fulfilled his obligation to pay the creditor only if he (H) has paid the person who may be considered the current creditor. In other words, in so far as H is ignorant of the fact that B has transferred his claim to another person, H's payment to B is valid. Contrariwise, if A can produce evidence that H already knew, by any means other than notification, about the assignment, then A (as the real creditor) is entitled to claim payment from H. On the other hand, if the contracting parties have explicitly agreed that the transfer of B's claim to A is to be governed by Supplementary Provision 3 of Law 1/1999, A would still be able to collect from H the money already earned by B but not yet paid to him. On the contrary, A would not be allowed to collect from H with regard to the money earned by B which H has already paid to B before insolvency. In the second case, B's claim falls into the insolvency estate and A will have the status of an insolvency creditor to be satisfied from the proceeds of the sale of B's insolvency assets according to the *par conditio creditorum* rule. A would acquire a preferential right only if he provides evidence of having legalised the assignment as a public deed.

(c) (i) If B has already earned the money, his creditor A will be entitled to collect the money from H. B's future debt against H will arise in A's estate after B has complied with his obligation with regard to H (i.e. to develop another new computer game). In the case of a factoring contract under Law 1/1999, A can claim payment from H. Insolvency proceedings do not affect A's right to collect what is due to him. In the case of a common assignment of debts under the CC, if A has not received payment from H before B's insolvency declaration (or prior to the commencement of the suspect period, i.e. the period fixed by the judge to which B's insolvency is retroactively extended), A will only be paid by the insolvency administrator from the proceeds of B's insolvency estate. In the current case, however, A can assert that B's debt against his customer H does not belong to B's insolvency estate any more, since B has already performed the obligation he owed to H. Consequently, what originally was a future debt has become an asset of A, and he is entitled to claim payment from H as long as he can produce evidence that the assignment of B's debt was agreed on a date beyond the reach of B's insolvency proceedings.

(ii) If H knew of the assignment of B's debt to A, H should have made payment directly to A. Any payment by H to B will be invalid and consequently A can still claim payment of the debt. If B falls into insolvency, A can claim payment from H in pursuance of either a factoring contract or an assignment agreement. With regard to factoring contracts, Law 1/1999 states that if the assignor is declared bankrupt, the factoring institution (A) will still hold the debts which have been assigned to him by the debtor (B). This would also be the case if those debts fell within the suspect period. In such cases, A can claim payment from H. Since H made a wrongful payment to B (who was no longer his creditor), H can claim back the amount paid to B. The insolvency administrator cannot keep this amount as if it was an asset of the insolvency estate. With regard to the assignment of debts, article 1527 CC implicitly states that H's payment by means of a deposit in B's bank account does not liberate the *debitor cessus* of his obligation and consequently of his duty to pay the transferred debt to his current creditor, A. Accordingly, A can claim the payment from H before B is declared bankrupt at any time and even afterwards. Since H paid his former creditor instead of the current one, he can claim back the amount paid to B. Neither B nor the insolvency administrator are entitled to keep this money; it does not form part of the insolvency estate.[50]

---

[50] See Alcover Garau, *Factoring y quiebra* 78. The courts have not addressed the insolvency issue with regard to factoring contracts. Firms involved in insolvency proceedings usually try to reach compromise settlements with insolvency administrators before any actions in court have been able to run their course.

ITALY

(a) and (b) There are several ways to accomplish most of what the parties wish to do, either under the general Civil Code rules on the assignment (articles 1260–1267 c.c.) and charge of claims (articles 2800–2807 c.c.) or under special laws. The delicate point, however, is whether the parties, i.e. the software developer and the bank, should inform the *debitor cessus* of the agreement they reached or not.

Such notification would be necessary under the Civil Code rules governing the assignment of claims, in order to prevent the insolvency creditors of the software developer from having recourse to the claims owed to him by Happyplay. Pursuant to the Civil Code rules concerning the assignment of claims, future or (conditional) claims may be assigned or charged for a valuable consideration.[51] They may even be assigned for security purposes only, though the Code is silent on the point, because according to commentators and court decisions the Civil Code ban on *pactum commissiorium* (article 2744 c.c.) cannot be applied to the assignment of pecuniary claims for security purposes only (*cessione del credito a scopo di garanzia*).[52]

Yet, article 2800 c.c. provides that a charge of claims is effective *vis-à-vis* executing creditors only if the will of the chargor and the chargee was expressed in writing and the assignment was notified to (or accepted by) the *debitor cessus* in an act in writing bearing a certain date (cf. article 2704 c.c.). Furthermore, according to the current interpretation of article 2914 n. 2 c.c., the requirements are the same for normal assignments and assignments for security purposes. Hence, under these rules, the software developer and the bank can assign for security purposes the claims in question, even though they are future claims, or may charge them. But if they do not communicate the assignment or the charge to the *debitor cessus*, it will be ineffective in respect of creditors of the assignor (article 2914 n. 2 c.c.). This communication is subject to formal requirements, i.e. it must be in writing and have a certain date. Before such communication, the *debitor cessus* who pays the assignor is discharged unless the assignee proves that the debtor paid the debt with knowledge that the assignment had taken place (article 1264 c.c.). Nevertheless, in practice, if there is little risk of insolvency, banks

---

[51] See Italian report, case 8(c).
[52] Dolmetta/Portale, *Banca borsa* 1999 I, 76; Inzitari, *Banca borsa* 1997 I, 153, 172–175; Anelli, *L'alienazione in funzione di garanzia* 189 ff.; Viale, in: *Trattato di diritto commerciale diretto da Galgano* 109 ff.; Perlingieri, *Della cessione dei crediti – art. 1260–1267* 37 ff.

sometimes will not trouble to give notice of an assignment or charge of claims, which will then be effective only *inter partes*. In that case, the assignor shall not disclose the assignment to the *debitor cessus*. The consequence of such practice is that if insolvency occurs the bank will not be considered owner of the claim, despite the *inter partes* validity of the assignment, and consequently will rank *pari passu* with the rest of the assignee's insolvency creditors.[53] It should be noted, in any event, that if the claims generated by the contract between Happyplay Ltd and the software developer are considered to be a salary or analogous thereto, they may not be charged nor will they be liable to execution for a value exceeding one-fifth of the salary (article 545 c.p.c.). The monies paid by Happyplay to the software developer will probably be regarded as being a salary, or analogous thereto, thus they will probably belong to the software developer in the event of his insolvency. Hence, in such circumstances, the bank will probably rank as an insolvency creditor. A different solution is not unthinkable, though would be difficult to establish, if a clear agreement between the assignor and the assignee provides for the separation of these monies from the rest of the assignor's assets, on the basis that the sums would be received by B as an undisclosed agent of the assignee.[54]

The problems posed by the communication requirement mentioned in the preceding paragraph are difficult to overcome in the present case. If the software developer could be regarded as an entrepreneur for the purposes of article 2082 c.c. (although this is most unlikely in the present case), an out and out assignment (i.e. an assignment not for security purposes) would be subject to rules more facilitative of the agreement of the parties. Entrepreneurs may assign their claims to specialised institutions (factoring companies) according to the provisions of the Law of 21 February 1991, n. 52, *Disciplina della cessione dei crediti d'impresa*.[55] Factoring companies in Italy are subject to the supervision of the Bank of Italy and their activities are by no means marginal. They are normally owned by banks. An assignment of claims arising in the business of the

---

[53] This practice led to abundant litigation. See Graziadei, in: Digesto sez. civ., XI 183–185; Nanni, in: *Commentario del Codice Civile Scialoja-Branca* 139 ff.

[54] Cf. Cass. 6 Mar. 1999, n. 1925, Giur. comm., 2000, II, 174, obs. Abriani; Foro it., 2000, I, 2299.

[55] See Candian, in: VV. AA. 380 ff., 391 ff.; Frignani/Rossi, *Il factoring* in: *Trattato di diritto privato*, XI, 51 ff.; Italy has ratified the UNIDROIT Convention on International Factoring of 28 May 1988 (14 July 1993, n. 260), which entered into force on 1 May 1995. The discussion in the text does not consider the application of the Convention to the case.

assignor, under l. 52/1991, will be effective *vis-à-vis* his creditors, even if the assignment is not communicated to or accepted by the *debitor cessus*, provided that the consideration for the assignment was wholly or partly paid by the assignee to the assignor with certain date prior to the date on which the assignor's creditor levied execution against the claim, or the opening of insolvency proceedings (article 5.1 (b), (c), l. 52/1991). If the assignment complies with these requirements, the assignee's rights will be protected *vis-à-vis* the assignor's creditors, subject to the good faith limitations established by article 7 of the same law in the event of the assignor's insolvency. This law does not, however, apply to assignment for security purposes only.

In sum, without notification to or acceptance by the *debitor cessus* (Happyplay), A would not be able to obtain a right in the claims that still subsisted between B and H when B became bankrupt: (b)(i). Moreover, if H has paid B in good faith, his debt will have been extinguished: (b)(ii).

(c) (i) The bank, A, will be entitled to the amount which is owed by the third party to B, the software developer, because the *debitor cessus*, Happyplay Ltd, was notified of or accepted the assignment or the charge of the claims, according to the rules explained under parts (a) and (b), *supra*.

(ii) Since H knew that B had no right to collect the monies with preference over A, he will have to pay the claim again to A, if requested. H will then rank as an insolvency creditor in B's insolvency proceedings for restitution of the monies wrongly paid to him.

THE NETHERLANDS

(a) It is certainly possible to grant A a security interest in B's monthly payments from H. Such security interests are in fact quite common in practice. On the other hand, a security assignment of claims is not possible due to the Code's prohibition on fiduciary transfers.[56]

It is common draftsmanship to use the phrase 'creating a charge over future claims'. However, strictly speaking, the charge is not actually created by the charging instrument. The Code only allows the *traditio* (act of creation) to be performed 'in advance'. But since B by definition lacks the power to dispose in respect of non-existent claims, the charge cannot

---

[56] See Dutch report, case 10 above.

be created immediately. The charge comes into existence, though without more, only when the claim arises and B acquires the right to dispose.[57]

Two types of charges are available under the Code that can in principle be created over future claims, as has been discussed in the report to case 5(c). In respect of both types, there are restrictions as to the circumstances in which future claims can be charged in advance. In respect of the charge with notification to the debtor, notification implies that the identity of the debtor must be known and that there must be a relationship which justifies regarding him as a future debtor.[58] In respect of the charge over future claims without notification, the Code requires the claim to arise directly from a legal relationship that exists at the time the charge is created 'in advance'.[59]

For the purposes of creating a charge, B's monthly claims are future and not present claims.[60] In this context, it should also be noted that the Dutch Supreme Court distinguishes between 'future' claims and 'conditional' claims. The latter are considered to be *existing* claims under a suspensive condition.[61] Consequently, a charge over a conditional claim can be created immediately, which implies that a possible insolvency of B will not affect its validity. It is not always easy to draw a sharp distinction between future and conditional claims. The decisive factor appears to be whether or not all the requirements for the claim to come into existence, and in particular whether one or both parties still have to perform, have been met.[62] For instance, salary payments would be regarded as future claims, as would the monthly payments which in the present case B *hopes* to receive, because the employee must still work, and B must still develop the games, for the claims actually to arise.

(b) Without communication to H, the security right must by definition be a 'silent' charge.[63] Such a charge, as already noted, is perfectly valid. The main consequence of not having notified the debtor of the charge lies in the fact that it is B, the creditor of the claim, and not A, the chargee, who is entitled to demand and receive payment from H. Normally, payment

---

[57] See Dutch report, case 7(d) above.
[58] Article 3:236(2) in conjunction with articles 3:94 and 3:97. See Pitlo/Reehuis/Heisterkamp, *Goederenrecht* n. 813.
[59] Article 3:239(1). [60] Article 3:239 in conjunction with articles 3:97, 3:94 and 3:98.
[61] Hoge Raad 26 Mar. 1982, NJ 1982, 615 (*Visserijfonds/ABN*).
[62] Hoge Raad 30 Jan. 1987, NJ 1987, 530 (*WUH/Emmerig q.q.*).
[63] Articles 3:236 and 3:239 BW.

by H extinguishes the claim and, as a consequence, the charge. Consequently, the charge no longer exists in respect of the money earned *and* paid to B prior to B's insolvency (situation (ii)).[64]

As a general rule of Dutch insolvency law, secured creditors can exercise their right as if there were no insolvency. In respect of the rights of the holder of a 'silent' charge, this means above all that he or she is entitled to inform the debtor, H, of the existence of the charge. By so doing, A acquires the exclusive right to demand and receive payment.[65] This right of conversion exists generally whenever the debtor of the secured creditor stops fulfilling his or her obligations as they become due or when there are good grounds to assume that he or she will not be able to fulfil them.[66] The commencement of insolvency proceedings does not affect this right. Although A does not actually become entitled to the money, he or she may, as soon as his or her claim on B becomes due, satisfy the debt by using that money (situation (i)).[67]

If A 'chooses' not to exercise his or her right, and does not communicate the charge to H, before H pays B, or rather the insolvency administrator, he or she would at first sight appear to be vulnerable to the general rule that payment brings the charge to an end. However, the Dutch Supreme Court has held that, in such instances, the holder of a 'silent' charge retains his or her right of priority to the monies paid. However, he or she will have to contribute to the administrative costs of the proceedings and will have to prove his or her claim. In the case before the Supreme Court, *Connection Technology*, a payment was made into the bankrupt's bank account, which was held at the same bank that held a silent charge. The Court decided that, although the bank had lost its right of separation and could not execute against the monies, the bank could avail itself of set-off.[68]

(c) (i) If the charge is communicated to the debtor, the holder of the charge gains the exclusive right to receive payment. A would not, strictly, become entitled to the funds, but execution against money would simply consist of deducting the debt.[69] Should the debtor pay the insolvency administrator, this would not extinguish the debt and he or she would still be obliged to pay on the debt to A. The general rule is that, after the charge has been communicated to the debtor, H, he or she can no

---

[64] See *supra*, Dutch report, case 5.   [65] Article 3:246(1) BW.   [66] Article 3:239(3) BW.
[67] Article 3:246(5) BW, granting a charge over the monies as of right, in conjunction with article 3:255 BW.
[68] *Hoge Raad* 17 Feb. 1995, NJ 1996, 471 (*Connection Technology BV*).   [69] Article 3:255 BW.

longer release him- or herself by paying his or her creditor, B. Payment to B after communication of the charge would be no defence against A. Conversely, H is under a duty of care to verify whether or not A is in fact the holder of the charge.

(ii) After A's charge has been communicated to H, H would only be able to gain release from the debt by payment to B if he or she could show that he or she could 'on reasonable grounds' have assumed that his or her creditor B was still entitled to receive payment. This, however, would only very rarely be the case. The creditor, B, would only be allowed to demand and receive payment when authorised by the court or by the holder of the charge. In both instances, it must be assumed that the debtor should exercise due care in ascertaining whether this is the case.

ENGLAND

(a) B wishes to use an income stream, due from H, as security for a bank loan from A. English law readily permits such arrangements, which are in very common use. In English law, B may grant a security assignment (assignment by way of *mortgage*) or charge H's present and future indebtedness to B. It is no objection that the future indebtedness is wholly contingent at the date of the assignment.

The assignment of future indebtedness is recognised in equity provided that the assignee has given value. This means that, as soon as the item (i.e., the debt) comes into existence, it is automatically attached in equity by the assignment.[70] There is no need for a fresh assignment to be executed with each new debt. Since we are concerned with intangible rights, pledge is not a possibility in English law. The assignment of intangible rights is a matter for equity and not the common law. There is such a thing as statutory assignment (under section 136 of the Law of Property Act 1925), but this does not affect the nature of the right assigned. Rather, it concerns the machinery by which the right can be vindicated. In equity, an assignment of present assets takes effect as soon as the assignor executes the assignment. Execution is informal (though statute sometimes imposes formalities for certain types of intangible right, such as shares in a company). This means that, so long as the

---

[70] *Tailby v Official Receiver* [1888] 13 App Cas 523.

intention of the assignor is made plain, any form of words, written or oral, will suffice.[71]

In order to enforce payment by H, A would have to join B in an action in court as co-claimant, or as co-defendant if B was not willing to have his name used in this way.[72] If the assignment complies with the requirements of section 136 of the Law of Property Act 1925, there is no need for this joinder process. Section 136, however, requires the assignment to be in writing. Moreover, the assignment must be absolute. This means that it cannot be by way of charge (though it can take the form of a *mortgage*[73] and certainly it can be absolute by way of discount). Finally, the *debitor cessus (account debtor)*, H, must be notified if the assignment is to be a statutory one. An assignment that fails to meet the test of a statutory assignment may nevertheless be a perfectly valid equitable assignment.

Although an equitable assignment takes effect as soon as the assignee is notified and regardless of whether the *debitor cessus* is notified, it may be prudent for the assignee to inform the *debitor cessus* of the assignment. Unless and until the assignee does so, it means that the *debitor cessus* can continue to pay the assignor who may give the *debitor cessus* a good discharge. If the assignee does not trust the honesty or solvency of the assignor, then the assignee takes a risk in not notifying the *debitor cessus*. After notification, the assignor is no longer able to give a discharge.

If B were a company, the assignment would have to be registered under section 395 of the Companies Act 1985 to be opposable against B's insolvency administrator (*liquidator*). This is because a charge of book debts is on the list of registrable charges.[74] If B is a sole trader, there is no registration requirement since the Bills of Sale Act's registration requirement extends only to general assignments of book debts and not to assignments of single debts or of debts from a single source.[75]

(b) As stated above, there is no need in equity for the *debitor cessus* to be notified in order for the assignment to be a valid one. In *Gorringe v Irwell India Rubber Works*,[76] the assignor became insolvent before the *debitor cessus* was notified of the assignment. The assignor's *liquidator* argued unsuccessfully that the assignment was perfected after the insolvency

---

[71] *Brandt's Sons & Co. v Dunlop Rubber Co.* [1905] AC 454.   [72] *Re Westover* [1919] 2 Ch 104.
[73] *Hughes v Pump House Hotel Co.* [1902] 2 KB 190.
[74] In s. 396 of the Companies Act 1985.   [75] See s. 344 of the Insolvency Act 1986.
[76] [1886] 34 Ch 128.

and therefore too late, but the court held that the assignment was perfected as soon as the assignee was notified. There is no difference in this respect to be drawn between monies paid and unpaid before the insolvency event. The consent of the assignee is necessary if an assignment is to be valid.[77]

(c) As stated above, equitable assignment is effective without notification. A's security always was effective. In taking steps to enforce the security, A may direct H to make payment directly to A. A well-drawn charge will certainly make express provision for this, though, technically, it is not one of the remedies otherwise available as a matter of law to a chargee.[78]

IRELAND

(a) To answer this question properly, it is necessary to look at the extent to which it is possible to create security rights over debts in Irish law. Such security is quite common and for this purpose it does not matter whether the debts are regarded as present or future/conditional. It is possible to grant a security assignment of debts (*mortgage*), to charge them, or even to sell them outright. B may create a charge in favour of A over existing or future indebtedness owed to him by H. Such a charge normally takes the form of an enterprise charge (*floating charge*) but it is also possible to create a fixed charge in these circumstances. Before a fixed charge is recognised, however, B must be restricted in some way in the manner he can deal with the debts or the proceeds thereof. Normally such restrictions will take the characteristic of an obligation to pay debt collections into a special bank account.

B may also sell outright existing or future debts to A. Such a transaction is referred to as factoring and may take various forms. In all cases, the price paid by A for the debts will be less than their face value given the fact that B is receiving accelerated payment. Sometimes A assumes the risk of non-payment of the debts, in which case the transaction is said to be without recourse. Recourse factoring is also quite common and in this scenario B agrees to indemnify A if the account debtors do not honour their debts.

Assignment of debts is possible both at law and in equity. For an assignment to be legal, the conditions specified in s. 28(6) of the Supreme

---

[77] *Standing v Bowring* [1885] 31 Ch 282. [78] See Bridge, *Personal Property Law* 155–157.

Court of Judicature (Ireland) Act 1877 must be satisfied. Basically, the assignment must be of the whole debt, i.e. not by way of charge. The assignment must also be in writing and notice must be given to the *debitor cessus*. Equitable assignments can be completely informal and take effect if the intention on the part of the assignor to assign is clear and the assignee is notified. There is no requirement to notify the *debitor cessus*. Equitable assignments are somewhat risky however, because, until notice of assignment has been received, the *debitor cessus*, H, can continue to pay the assignor, B, and will get a good discharge for the debt.

It should be noted that while an assignment by way of charge needs to be registered if the assignor is a company, this requirement does not apply to factoring transactions whether or not such transactions take the form of legal or equitable assignment.

(b) A will have superior rights to B's other creditors if the debt owed by H has been assigned to him irrespective of whether the assignment is legal or equitable or whether notice of the assignment has been communicated to H. The same analysis holds good if a fixed charge over the debt has been created in favour of A, but B's preferential but not unsecured creditors (i.e. those creditors entitled to a statutory preference) will prevail if A merely has an enterprise charge *(floating charge)*.

In principle, the analysis does not differ with respect to (i) money already earned by B but not yet paid to him, and (ii) money already earned and paid to B before insolvency. It is possible to assign in equity future or conditional debts. The assignment takes effect in equity as soon as the debt comes into existence, with it being immediately attached in favour of the assignee. If there has been a non-notification factoring arrangement, then B will continue to collect the debts as A's agent and remit the proceeds at regular intervals, having segregated them in the meantime from his own assets. Likewise, with a fixed charge over debts the person creating the charge, B in our example, must be subject to restrictions in the way he can deal with the debts. In both of these scenarios A may try to trace the debt proceeds if they have been misapplied by B. If, however, A has merely the benefit of a *floating charge* over the debts, then B may do what he wishes with the debt collections. There is a substantial risk that such proceeds will have been dissipated prior to B's insolvency.

(c) (i) and (ii) If the assignment has been communicated to H, then the latter will only get a good discharge for the debt if he pays A rather than B. In other words, if he disregards the notice and insists on paying B, A can still obtain payment from him. In effect, H has to pay the debt twice over.

SCOTLAND

(a) The assignment (or *cession*) of incorporeals is called assignation. Assignation requires 'intimation' (notification). This is an essential part of the transfer. The assignor (usually called the *cedent*) remains creditor until the intimation has happened. Therefore, if the creditors of the assignor attach the claim before there has been intimation, the creditors will prevail.

How intimation should be correctly done is a matter of some uncertainty. As one scholar has written, 'one of the long, slow burning questions . . . is whether a debtor's mere knowledge of an assignation is sufficient intimation to him'.[79] The older rule was that intimation must be made either by a court officer or by a notary, or accepted by the debtor. This rule has been eroded in the case law,[80] and it might be argued that the modern position may now be that *de facto* knowledge by the *debitor cessus* is all that is necessary. But the predominant view remains that the law still requires formal intimation, or acceptance by the debtor.[81]

The assignment of debts which do not yet exist is an area of law of some difficulty. The law seems to be that if it is already possible to identify the person to whom intimation must be made, and intimation is made to that person, then the assignment is effective. Thus, in the present case, if the assignment by B to A is intimated to H, that will probably give rise to a valid assignment of future debts.[82]

If B had been a company, it is probable that the arrangement would have had to be registered in the Companies Register,[83] on pain of nullity. The statutory provisions state that securities over 'book debts' must be so registered if the debtor is a company.[84]

Arrangements of this sort are unusual except in one economic sector, namely factoring. Factoring is where a company sells its invoices for

---

[79] McBryde, *Law of Contract in Scotland* para. 12.113.
[80] E.g. *Libertas-Kommerz v Johnson* 1977 SC 191.
[81] McBryde, *Law of Contract in Scotland* para. 12.114.
[82] For discussion see Gretton, JR 1993, 23.   [83] In Edinburgh.
[84] Companies Act 1985 s. 410. The meaning of 'book debts' is not wholly clear but it probably extends to the present example.

goods or services to a finance company. The example under consideration could be regarded as factoring in a legal sense, but in a business sense this would not be regarded as factoring. In factoring the main motivation is improved cash-flow.

(b) An unintimated assignment does not transfer the claim in question. Thus if B becomes bankrupt, the claims against H will form part of the insolvency estate, and A will be merely an ordinary insolvency creditor. If H has paid B, unaware of the assignment, that makes no difference. Until intimation has been made to H, B is still the creditor, and so B is the person to whom payment should be made.

Attempts have been made, in cases of this sort, to establish a trust. The idea is that B will hold the claims in trust for A. If B becomes bankrupt, the trust estates can be separated from his insolvency estate. In one case[85] a device of this type was upheld, but the general view is probably that such arrangements are invalid.[86]

(c) (i) Such monies would be payable to A.

(ii) If the assignment has been intimated, and H has nevertheless paid B, then H has paid the wrong person. H will have to pay B again.

SOUTH AFRICA

(a) An agreement by which B (the software developer) gives A (his bank) a security over his monthly claims against H (Happyplay Ltd) is possible in South African law. However, the legal construction of such an agreement poses difficulties. As the law currently stands, there is authority for the view that a security assignment (*security cession*) may be either in the nature of a charge or in the nature of an out-and-out assignment. This means that the entire claim is transferred to the transferee (assignee, *cessionary*) without leaving a real right in the transferor.[87] Since the requirements for these forms are not clearly defined, parties to assignments *in securitatem debiti* couch their agreements in such wide terms that it is almost impossible to determine which construction was contemplated.[88]

The distinction between the two forms of security lies in the fact that the position of the parties in the case of charge is governed by

---

[85] *Tay Valley Joinery Ltd v C F Financial Services Ltd* 1987 SLT 207.
[86] For discussion see Reid, SLT (News) 1987, 113 and Gretton, JLSS 1988, 53.
[87] See in general van der Merwe, *Sakereg* 673–688; Scott, *The Law of Cession* 233–252.
[88] See e.g. *Lisbon and SA Ltd v The Master* 1987 1 SA 276 (A).

the law of property whereas in the case of out-and-out assignment it is governed by the general principles of the law of assignment. In respect of the charge, the right remains part of the chargor's (*cedent*) estate; in an out-and-out assignment it becomes part of the assignee's estate. In contrast to the *Sicherungszession* in German law, the right in the case of an out-and-out assignment is not regarded as forming part of the assignor's estate in the event of insolvency and attachment. In South African law, the chargor and his creditors therefore enjoy better protection than that accorded to an assignor and his creditors. First, in the event of an out-and-out assignment, the insolvency administrator of the bankrupt assignor's estate has only an unsecured (*concurrent*) claim against the assignee for the remainder, unless the assignment may be set aside in terms of the Insolvency Act. The assignor (B) or his insolvency administrator has only a personal right against the assignee or his insolvency administrator and thus enjoys no preference. In the case of charge, the right remains part of the chargor's estate and on his insolvency the chargee is a secured creditor. Secondly, in an out-and-out security assignment, the assignee may negotiate with the debtor and may, for instance, reach a settlement with the debtor. By contrast, the chargee has no such right. Thirdly, after the debt has been discharged, the assignee is obliged to recede the right in terms of the *pactum fiduciae* incorporated in the agreement. In the case of charge, the right reverts automatically on account of the accessory nature of charge. Fourthly, if the assignee becomes insolvent after the assignor has paid his debt but before the assignee has receded the right, the assignor has only a personal right to recession against the insolvency estate of the assignee. The chargor is thus in this regard also in a better position than the assignor in the case of an out-and-out assignment.[89]

This example involves the security assignment (*cession in securitatem debiti*) of a future right, namely the monthly remuneration of B. This could be construed as an undertaking to cede his rights to remuneration if and when they arise (cf. the German *Mantelzession*) or as an outright assignment of future rights (cf. the German *Globalzession*). Although certain academic criticisms have been levelled at the assignment of future rights,[90] there is no doubt that the assignment of future rights is accepted by the South African courts.[91] The courts argue that the transfer agreement involved in an assignment can be concluded *in anticipando*, that

---

[89] See Scott, *The Law of Cession* 232–233.
[90] See De Wet/Van Wyk, *Die Suid-Afrikaanse Kontraktereg en Handelsreg* 228.
[91] See Scott, *The Law of Cession* 50 and the case law cited there.

is, before the right has materialised. Since this agreement is the sole requirement for assignment, it is regarded as a completed juristic act which cannot be dissolved unilaterally by the parties concerned.[92]

There are no formalities for a security assignment in South African law, either for the obligatory agreement or for the real agreement. The parties may themselves come to an agreement that the assignment of a particular right has to comply with certain formalities: e.g. that it will only be valid if reduced to writing, that the consent of the debtor is to be obtained, that the assignment will be void unless registered in the books of the debtor company and that the document of title must first be delivered. Subject to the operation of the doctrine of estoppel, an assignment undertaken in defiance of these agreed formalities is legally ineffectual.[93] Therefore, assignment is a juristic act between the assignor (B) and the assignee (A) and the co-operation of the *debitor cessus* (H) is not required. Moreover, the validity of the assignment does not depend on it being intimated (that is, notified) to the *debitor cessus*,[94] unless required by the agreement between the assignor and the *debitor cessus*.[95] A wise assignee would, however, inform the *debitor cessus* of the assignment to avoid discharge of the *debitor cessus*'s obligation by payment in ignorance of the assignee. Notice is therefore a precaution, not a precondition.

(b) The main consequence of the non-communication to H of the assignment of B's right to A before B became bankrupt is that the *debitor cessus* (H) could validly discharge his debt by payment to the assignor (B). In respect of situation (i), i.e. money already earned by B but not yet paid to him, A would, on B's insolvency, on the out-and-out assignment construction (whether construed as either a *Mantel* or a *Global* assignment), have a direct claim against H for the money, since the claim would (on having arisen already on the date of assignment) have been transferred from B's estate to A. On the charge construction, A would have acquired a mere security interest in the insolvency estate of B. In respect of situation (ii), i.e. money already earned and paid to B before insolvency, the payment to B discharged H's debt to B and therefore also A's claim against him on account of the assignment. In such a case, A would merely have an unsecured claim against B's insolvency estate.

---

[92] See *Muller NO v Trust Bank of Africa Ltd* 1981 2 SA 117 (N).
[93] See Nienaber, in: *The Law of South Africa II* para. 246.   [94] *Ibid.*, para. 251.
[95] See De Wet/Van Wyk, *Die Suid-Afrikaanse Kontraktereg en Handelsreg* 226–227.

(c) (i) If A's right was communicated to H before B became bankrupt, H would no more be in a position validly to discharge his debt by payment to B. On the out-and-out assignment construction, A would therefore have a direct claim against H for the money. On the charge construction, he would be able to realise his security right to the claim.

(ii) If A's right was communicated to H and H nevertheless paid the money into B's bank account, H will have paid the wrong person and his debt will not have been discharged. If he knowingly paid the money into the bank account, A can still claim the money from him on the out-and-out assignment construction.

DENMARK

(a) According to Danish law, it is possible to grant a security right over claims. However, if the assignor (i.e., B) does not fulfil his obligations according to the contract, then the other party has no obligation to pay the amount. The assignee will not have a better right than the assignor. Ordinary claims are mainly governed by part 3 of the Bonds Act.[96] (Part 2 governs negotiable instruments.)

Section 31 of the Bonds Act states that the transfer of an ordinary claim is only protected against the assignor's creditors if the *debitor cessus* has received notification of the assignment from the assignor or the assignee. This applies not only to a transfer to ownership but also to a transfer by way of charge. The notification must state that an assignment has taken place. If a notification just states that the *debitor cessus* has to pay a third person, it will not be effective to protect the assignee from the assignor's creditors. In the present case, if H, the *debitor cessus*, has been notified that B's claim against him has been assigned to A, A will get priority.

In Denmark, claims are commonly used as collateral.

According to Danish law, it might be agreed that B can collect the debt in spite of the assignment to A. But in that case the agreement should stipulate that B has to settle with A when the debt is paid and A should ensure that B acts in accordance with the agreement.

(b) If A's right was not communicated to H before B was declared bankrupt, A would not have any right to the claims which were protected

---

[96] Cf. Andersen/Møgelvang-Hanseo/rgaard, *Gældsbrevsloven* 163 ff. and Clausen, *Sikkerhed i fordringer* chapter 3.

against B's creditors. This means that A could not claim the monies, which had not yet been paid, from H. The insolvency estate of B would be entitled to these monies. A would also be unable to claim the monies which had already been paid to the estate. A would be an insolvency creditor.

(c) If A's right was notified to H before B was declared bankrupt, A's right would be protected as against B's creditors.

(i) A could claim the monies from H at the time when the claim fell due.

(ii) If H had paid the money into B's bank account, the bank, A, could keep the money. But if H had already paid the money to B's insolvent estate, A could claim the money from the estate. A would not be an unsecured creditor and the estate would have to pay the whole amount.

SWEDEN

(a) The software developer, B, may give his bank, A, a security over the monthly claims that he has against his customer, H. B may either charge or make a fiduciary assignment of the claims; no requirements as to form apply. In both cases, in order for the assignee or chargee to be protected against the creditors of B, it is necessary that H is informed of the security by B or A in some way; it is not sufficient that H in some other way has received knowledge of the assignment or charge.[97] The requirement of notification serves the same purpose as the requirement that possession of assigned or pledged movables must be transferred to the assignee or the pledgee, with no independent access for the assignor or pledgor, to be binding in insolvency or execution: the transaction is to be public and the assignor or chargor is to be deprived of his authority to dispose of[98] the claim, in order to counteract false statements when insolvency proceedings have started and fraudulent constructions prior to such proceedings.[99] Pursuant to the case NJA 1949,

---

[97] Ss. 10 and 31 of the 1936 Promissory Notes Act (*skuldebrevslagen*), which is a piece of joint Nordic legislation and applies not only to negotiable and non-negotiable promissory notes but also to contract claims, whether written or oral.
[98] In Swedish: '*förfoga över*'. There has been much discussion of whether this comprises not only the authority to assign but also the authority to receive and collect.
[99] See the preparatory works in NJA II 1936, 112 f.

164, the assignor or chargor may not reserve a right to collect the collateral, i.e. the claims, for his own use. In such a case, the transaction is invalid in relation to his creditors.[100] In NJA 1995, 367, the assignor of rights under a contract of lease was permitted to receive payments and goods from the lessee on behalf of the assignee, possibly with the intention to set off the monies received against his purchase claim, or to hold it for the assignee, or to forward it to him. It was held that such a permission did not invalidate the assignment in relation to the assignor's creditors. This ruling is somewhat surprising, as a *constitutum possessorium* is not permitted when chattels are assigned, but it was assumed that notification, which gave publicity and deprived the assignor of his authority to re-assign prior to discharge, served the purposes sufficiently.

If B goes bankrupt, or if the claim is taken in execution, the secured creditor has a privilege only in respect of the monies at that date earned by the performances of the assignor/chargor.[101] The explanation of this rule seems to be that an insolvency administrator would not perform the bankrupt debtor's obligations under the contract in order to earn monies for the secured creditor, unless this party agreed to pay at least the costs of future performance to the insolvency estate, and thus the future or conditional security would be of practically no value. One may compare the position where a pledge is granted comprising all present and future goods in a certain warehouse; in such circumstances the pledgee would not enjoy a privilege over goods that the insolvency estate deposits in the warehouse.[102] Furthermore, it should be observed that the security in monies earned less than three months prior to the application to commence insolvency proceedings can be recovered (avoided) according to chapter 4 section 12 of the Bankruptcy Act, if the security

---

[100] In this case, a boat in the possession of a third party was assigned, possibly by way of security. It was assumed that the Promissory Notes Act was applicable by analogy. Here, one may also compare the invalidation of reservation of title clauses when the buyer is entitled to dispose of the goods prior to payment (as in case 4).

[101] NJA 1973, 635.

[102] A problem is that a claim earned on the insolvency day must be evaluated, which, in certain situations, may cause theoretical and practical difficulties. Two approaches to valuation might be adopted. The first would value the claim on the basis that the estate would have defaulted in performance, leading H to terminate the contract and claim damages. The second would calculate the value by apportioning the total value of the claim to the performance prior to and after the insolvency day. The latter seems preferable when performance is continued, since it would be applied when the estate performs obligations under contractual rights that are comprised by an enterprise charge. See NJA 1982, 900.

was granted after the secured debt arose (a delay of more than a few days is sufficient). It is of no significance whether the monies were earned in the ordinary course of business.[103] These assignments or charges of future claims are common in business life; the transaction and the notification can be done once and for all.[104] It should be noted, however, that a creditor may have a security in these money claims also through the use of an enterprise charge, providing the chargor with a right to collect the monies. Such a security will rank in priority after security assignments and ordinary charges, however. No special legislation applies to factoring; such agreements are subject to the ordinary rules described above.

(b) If the assignment or charge in favour of A was not communicated before B became bankrupt, A has no superior rights to those of the other creditors to money earned by B, no matter whether such money is outstanding[105] or has been paid to B and held separately by him.[106]

(c) (i) As stated under part (a), A would, after communication, have a real right in or priority to monies earned by B but not yet paid by H, provided that B has not been authorised to receive the monies for his own use. No matter whether A is a fiduciary assignee or a chargee, he is entitled to collect from H but must account for any excess value. He must also surrender his security interest against full payment from the estate.[107]

---

[103] NJA 1973, 635. Also, security in new claims for credit provided earlier, such as in factoring relations, may be recovered under the same rule, NJA 1987, 320. See case 11 (Variation). An exception to this rule has been proposed recently (Ds 1998:40), since a corresponding exemption exists to the recovery rules applicable when debts are paid in the ordinary way and time (s. 10). As of yet, the legislature has not decided whether to adopt it.

[104] Another possibility would be for B to set up a Special Purpose Vehicle, i.e. a special company, which would conduct the business and earn the money. A would then grant credit to this SPV (possibly requiring the SPV to grant it an enterprise mortgage, which will rank over, for example, the statutory preference accorded to tax creditors). The costs would be borne by B and B would subordinate his compensatory claim against the SPV to the claims of A. In such circumstances, A would not need to become involved in the collection of the claims and any insolvency proceedings in respect of the SPV would be conducted solely for the benefit of A and the tax creditor.

[105] Ss. 10 and 31 Promissory Notes Act.

[106] In NJA 1995, 367 it was assumed that A must have had a real right to the claim in order to be able to separate monies paid under the claim.

[107] S. 37 Contracts Act, chapter 8 s. 10 Bankruptcy Act and NJA 2000, 78.

(ii) Since H was notified of A's security right, and provided that B was not authorised to collect the payments for his own use,[108] B has received the payments from H with a duty to account for them to A. If insolvency then occurs before B is regarded to be 'in delay' in separating the money from his own, in a separate account,[109] A has a right to vindicate the amount (should it still be there) pursuant to the 1944 Entrusted Money Act (lagen om redovisningsmedel). If insolvency occurs later, A would have a real right or a preference as chargee only if B separated the monies from his own assets while he was still solvent or, although insolvent, separated the monies from his own assets without delay. This means that if the monies are commingled with B's own monies for more than a period of around three days when B was insolvent, A has in principle no real or preferential claim, notwithstanding that the money was legally received on A's behalf. This rule may be somewhat inconsistent with NJA 1994, 506, where other fungible property (corn) was commingled and it was held that co-ownership arose, but it seems that co-ownership will not as readily be extended to commingled money (see Swedish report, case 9).

If A cannot be satisfied in B's insolvency due to commingling, even though he had a real right to the claim,[110] he may force H to pay again, since H by way of the notification knew or at least should have suspected that B had no right to receive payment.[111] (If B was authorised to receive the payments solely for A, then H is discharged, although A had a right to the claim that would be protected as against the other creditors.)

FINLAND

(a) The monthly claims of B based on future software development would be regarded as 'unearned' and, in that sense, conditional claims. That does not, as such, prevent the parties from using those claims as the object of a charge or a security assignment.[112] The principal problem,

---

[108] The Entrusted Money Act does not exclude a real claim in insolvency because an agent is entitled to use the principal's money for his own purposes while being solvent (at least not if such use was not the main purpose), provided that the amount was held separately prior to the occurrence of insolvency. In the present case, however, if B is permitted by A to use the monies for his own purposes, this would invalidate the acquisition pursuant to s. 31 of the Promissory Notes Act.

[109] A period of three days is not to be regarded as a delay for these purposes, NJA 1999, 812.

[110] Should he raise a claim on H, notwithstanding that he had a real right or a preference in B's insolvency, H would probably be forced to pay again but would be able to subrogate to A's right.

[111] See s. 29 of the Promissory Notes Act concerning good discharge.

[112] See e.g. Tepora/Takki, Factoring 47 ff. and Tuomisto, Takaisinsaannista 261 ff.

however, is that the secured creditor will benefit from, most probably, a security right only in the monies earned before B becomes insolvent. Without such a rule, the monies earned by the activities of the insolvency administration, and at the expense of the insolvency estate, would fall into the hands of the chargee or assignee. That would, for many reasons, be unwelcome. The security right, i.e. charge or security assignment, should, in every case, be communicated to H.[113]

(b) (i) and (ii) The assignment or charge will be valid against the creditors of B only if it was communicated to H prior to the insolvency. Otherwise, the monies would belong to the insolvency estate.

(c) (i) If A's right was communicated to H before B became bankrupt, A would have the normal rights of a chargee or a security assignee to the monies already earned by B but not yet paid to him or her. A could, therefore, collect the monies from H in order to discharge the secured debt, and the claims against H could, if necessary, be sold by A or the insolvency administrator for the satisfaction of A. There would, however, be an inherent risk that the insolvency administrator would be able to avoid the security. This is due to the fact that the security right is, probably, not regarded as properly established until the monies are earned. Such a characterisation, however, will often lead to the conclusion that the security right has not been established without unnecessary delay.[114]

(ii) If H paid the monies to B with knowledge of the assignment or charge, H would still be obliged to pay the monies to A. The payment would not, in other words, discharge the debt. H can, on the other hand, claim the monies paid to B back from the insolvency estate, but he or she would be, in respect of such a claim, an insolvency creditor without any preferential right.

Comparative observations

All systems conclude that B's claims against H can in principle be used as collateral for a loan advanced by A. This is the first and perhaps most surprising result of the comparison. Only the Finnish and Scots reports have expressed some reservations with respect to the feasibility of such a transaction.

---

[113] See s. 31 of the Act on Promissory Notes (*velkakirjalaki/lag om skuldebrev*).
[114] See above, Finnish report, variation to case 11.

CASE 12: BANK LOAN ON THE BASIS OF MONEY CLAIMS (I)   569

For practical purposes, the most important dividing line lies between those jurisdictions which, in order for the security right to be valid as against third parties such as B's insolvency creditors, require the *debitor cessus* to be notified of the security right prior to the commencement of insolvency proceedings and those jurisdictions which do not require such communication or allow it to be replaced by some other, less cumbersome means. The first group consists of France (with respect to assignments under the *Code civil*), Italy, Scotland[115] and the three Nordic countries. The second group comprises Germany, Austria, Greece, France (with respect to assignments under the *Loi Dailly*), Belgium, Portugal, the Netherlands (silent charge), England, Ireland and South Africa. Within the second group, Portuguese law should be regarded as a special case in so far as it does require notification to be made to the *debitor cessus* as a prerequisite for the validity of the assignment or the charge as against third parties, but allows such communication to be made even after the commencement of insolvency proceedings over the assignor's or chargor's estate. With respect to the silent charge which must be registered prior to the chargor's insolvency, Dutch law likewise allows for notification after the commencement of insolvency proceedings, yet this notification does not serve the purpose of rendering the charge valid but it confers upon the chargee the right to claim payment directly from the *debitor cessus*.

The possibilities and prerequisites for a security right in B's claims against H can be examined under the following three headings:[116]

(1) legal form or nature of the security right;
(2) the requirement of notification of the *debitor cessus* or acceptance by him; and
(3) further requirements for the validity of the security right as against third parties.

(i) Legal form or nature of the security right

The security right can take the form of either an assignment (for security purposes) or a charge or both. German and Greek law allow claims to be assigned as security and charged, but do not extend the formal requirements of the charge, especially the need for notification, to security assignment. The same seems to apply in South Africa. In practice,

---

[115] Leaving aside what the Scots report calls 'perhaps the modern position', that *de facto* knowledge is sufficient.
[116] The analysis is better approached by considering these questions, than by considering each individual part of the case (that is, (a), (b) and (c)).

therefore, assignment is preferred in these countries. Other jurisdictions treat both transactions in exactly the same way. This is the case in Austria, Portugal, Italy, Sweden and Finland.[117] A number of countries do not allow claims to be both assigned and charged. In Belgian and Dutch law, on the one hand, claims can only be charged, not assigned for the purpose of granting security. So far as the same requirements as to form and publicity extend to both transactions (see Belgian law), this view can only be explained by tradition. The common law jurisdictions seem to pay little attention to the question of the transaction's 'legal nature'. The English report mixes assignment with charge and mortgage by stating that 'a claim may be assigned by way of a charge or mortgage'.

A number of reports point out that the transaction between A and B may also take the form of a factoring agreement. Especially in Italy, such an arrangement would make the transfer of the claim far less cumbersome. Nevertheless, for the reasons given in the Italian report, this comparative summary will not extend to factoring.

(ii) Notification of or acceptance by the *debitor cessus*

The requirement of making notification to the *debitor cessus*, or of obtaining his acceptance, prior to the assignor's or chargor's insolvency, is crucial for the practicability of the transaction. The *debitor cessus* can only be notified or asked to accept the assignment or charge once his identity is known and even where it is known, as in case 12, notification or acceptance remain cumbersome procedures, especially if they must be performed in a formal way or through a bailiff.

One might argue that there is only a minor difference between those jurisdictions which require notification and those which do not, since under the latter, a *bona fide debitor cessus* can extinguish the claim by validly paying B, thus reducing the security's value to zero. This is illustrated by the answers to parts (b)(ii) and (c)(ii). If H pays B in ignorance of A's rights, the claim is discharged and the monies belong to the insolvency estate. A may only exceptionally maintain a right to the proceeds if they have been kept separate. If, on the other hand, H pays B knowing of the assignment or charge, the debt is not discharged and H runs the risk of having to pay a second time. With respect to these two situations all

---

[117] In Spain, the distinction between charging a claim and assigning it for security purposes is not yet fully developed, nor are the respective requirements fully identified. For an overview see Hellmich, *Kreditsicherungsrechte in der spanischen Mehrrechtsordnung* 111 ff.

jurisdictions reach the same results, the only difference arising, in the context of situation (b)(ii), in the rationale underpinning the discharge of H's indebtedness. In those systems which do not require notification, the rationale is H's belief in B's right to claim payment. In those which do, it is invalidity of the assignment or charge.

However, the practical difference that results from the notification requirement can be seen in situation (b)(i). In those systems that require notification or acceptance prior to B's insolvency, A has no rights to the still existing claim, but under either those which do not require notification at all, or those which allow notification to be performed after the commencement of insolvency proceedings, A will still be able to enforce his right to the claim.

The requirement of formal notification or acceptance for the transfer of a claim to have effect *erga omnes* was developed in France and codified in C.civ., article 1690. Of those jurisdictions which have been heavily influenced by the French *Code civil*, only Italy still adheres strictly to this principle. Portuguese law has watered down the requirement by allowing notification to be performed even after the assignor's insolvency. Since 1994, Belgian law requires an *informal* notification only for the validity of the assignment or charge as against the *debitor cessus* and third parties with vested rights. The new Dutch Civil Code has introduced a silent charge, under which notification is replaced by a registration requirement or the use of a notarial deed. In France and Italy, too, commercial reality has prompted legislative intervention to introduce more practical regimes at least for those business sectors where there is the greatest need to recognise the effectiveness of the assignment of future claims (in particular, for example, in the factoring sector). Also, in Scotland, the strict requirement of notification has been lessened; today mere knowledge on the part of the *debitor cessus* is probably sufficient.

One can therefore identify a general trend which moves away from notification requirements. They are generally thought to hamper the potential for the assignment of claims (that is, their negotiability) without being necessary either for the protection of the *debitor cessus* or of other third parties.

(iii) Further requirements

In England and Ireland, an assignment of claims 'by way of a charge' represents a charge over book debts and must thus be registered in the Companies Register if the assignor is a limited company. The same is true for Scots law, although in Scots legal terminology the expression 'assignation in security' is used rather than 'assignment by way of charge'. According to Austrian law, notification can be replaced by an entry in the books of the assignor and, according to Dutch law, the parties may choose the 'silent' but registrable charge instead of one requiring notification. All three prerequisites may be summarised under the heading of publicity. However, whereas registration under the Companies Acts does in fact serve the purpose of making A's rights public, the same can hardly be said of the Austrian and Dutch regimes, especially considering the *Hoge Raad's* judgment on the admissibility of the registration of so-called master-lists.[118]

---

[118] See *infra*, Dutch report, case 13(a).

Case 13: Bank loan on the basis of money claims (II)

(Security right to a claim against a debtor whose identity is unknown at the time the security right is created – rights of the secured party in execution)

B, an engineer, is a sole trader. He wishes to expand his business. As security for a bank loan from A, he can offer only the claims that will arise against future customers who, at the present time, are unidentified.

Questions

(a) Is there an arrangement by which B can grant to A a security in his claims against future customers? If so, describe its main features and prerequisites. How common are agreements of this kind in business practice?

(b) After concluding the security agreement with A, B acquires a claim against customer D worth 3,000 Euros. A bailiff wishes to execute against that claim on behalf of an unsecured creditor of B. Who has priority, A or the unsecured creditor? On what further circumstances does A's right depend (e.g. communication of the assignment to D, revocation of B's entitlement to collect the claims against his customers)?

(c) B becomes bankrupt, having outstanding claims worth 10,000 Euros against customers C1–C5. Does A have any rights in respect of these claims? On what further circumstances do any rights of A depend (e.g. communication of the assignment to C1–C5, revocation of B's entitlement to collect the claims against his customers)?

(d) If B grants to A a security right in all his claims against his customers, are there any limits as to the value of the collateral in relation to the amount of the secured loan?

Discussions

GERMANY

(a) As has already been explained in the context of proceeds clauses, it is possible under German law to assign future claims for security purposes.[1] 'Future' in this sense includes claims where the obligation from which they will arise does not yet exist. The principle of specificity can be satisfied even by an assignment 'of all claims arising out of contracts concluded within the business of the assignor'.[2] Agreements of this kind (called *Sicherungsglobalzession*) are extremely common.

(b) Because of the anticipatory security assignment, B's claim against D will be transferred to A. As to the procedure by which A can realise his security right to the claim, as against an executing creditor, there remains a divergence of opinion, which has been set out *supra*, case 8(d). In any event, A will take priority over the executing creditor.[3] So long as D does not pay the assignor (B), A's rights against other creditors of B do not depend on a communication of the assignment or the revocation of B's entitlement to collect the claims.

(c) If A and B have concluded a security assignment of future claims, including those against customers C1–C5, A will have a right to preferential payment out of the realisation of these claims.[4] A will have priority over B's insolvency creditors. Again, this solution does not depend on any additional requirements.

(d) A security assignment of all of B's claims against his customers would be valid provided that the clause is adequately drafted. As to the limits of such an arrangement, the rules explained *supra* in the context of security transfer of ownership[5] also apply *mutatis mutandis* to security assignment. A duty to reassign claims to the debtor arises if the nominal value of the collateral exceeds the quantum of the secured debt

---

[1] See *supra*, German report, case 5(c).
[2] BGH 9 June 1960, WM 1960, 838; Lwowski, *Das Recht der Kreditsicherung* n. 759; Reinicke/Tiedtke, *Kreditsicherung* n. 608.
[3] Here, the execution takes place after B's claim against D has come into existence and has been transferred to A. But even if the execution had taken place prior to the conclusion of the contract between B and D, the claim would have been regarded as directly vesting in A: see *supra*, German report, case 12(b).
[4] See in detail *supra*, German report, case 5(c).   [5] See *supra*, German report, case 11(d).

by more than 150 per cent. In contrast to earlier judgments, this duty no longer has to be explicitly stated in the contract; instead, the appropriate terms will be implied into the security agreement, as part of its fiduciary character.

AUSTRIA

(a) Yes: see answer to case 12(a). It does not make any difference whether the claim is not yet due, future or conditional. Such claims can be charged or assigned[6] as security provided the publicity requirement is fulfilled.[7]

(b) If the publicity requirement (entry in the books of B) is fulfilled, A takes priority.

(c) See part (b).

(d) See Austrian report, case 11(d).

GREECE

(a) All the methods discussed in the Greek report to case 12(a) may be used to grant a security right to A. The more interesting question is, however, whether B can assign by way of security all claims against future customers. As to the admissibility of global assignment, it is suggested[8] that in principle it is possible to assign all future claims arising from a concrete legal relationship, profession or enterprise activity. The validity of the assignment depends, however, on the claims in question being capable of identification, at the latest, at the moment they arise by criteria specified in the assignment contract.[9]

Of greater importance is the issue of whether the assignment of all future claims is contrary to public policy (articles 178, 179 A.K.) or to the provision of article 281 A.K. on the abuse of a right. The prevailing view[10]

---

[6] Rummel/Ertl § 1393 ABGB n. 4; OGH SZ 44/108; SZ 61/47.
[7] For details, see Austrian report, case 5(c).
[8] Balis, Enochikon Dikaion, Genikon Meros para. 152 n. 1; Kritikos, in: Georgiadis/Stathopoulos 455 n. 53; Sourlas, ErmAK 455 n. 15.
[9] Georgiadis, Empragmato Dikaio II 258; Kornilakis, I katapisteutiki ekchorisi ton apaitiseon 57; Livanis, Diathesi mellondikou dikaiomatos 141.
[10] Kornilakis, I katapisteutiki ekchorisi ton apaitiseon 83; Livanis, Diathesi mellondikou dikaiomatos 144, 146 ff.

suggests that the question will be answered according to the particular elements of each case: e.g. whether and to what extent the enterprise freedom of the assignor, and regular functioning of his enterprise, are affected by the assignment; whether a disproportionality exists between the value of the assigned claims and the secured debt. In particular circumstances, global assignment may be nullified on the basis that it hampers excessively the debtor's freedom, or because it constitutes an abuse of contractual freedom on the part of the assignee. Global assignment is not known in Greek practice.

(b) B's unsecured creditor seeks to execute against the assigned claim of B against D, the third-party customer of B (articles 982, 1022 KPolD) before notification has been made of the assignment. According to the prevailing view, the validity of the assignment is not conditional on the notification of the *debitor cessus*. The assigned claim is transferred to the assignee by virtue of the agreement of the parties. A notification requirement is, however, imposed by law for the protection of the *debitor cessus* and third parties who are in good faith, so that they know the identity of the creditor of the claim. According to article 460 A.K., for the assignee to acquire the claim as against the *debitor cessus* and third parties, the *debitor cessus* must be notified of the assignment. Unsecured creditors of the debtor are regarded as third parties.[11] If notification is made to D, A takes priority.

(c) See Greek report, case 12.

(d) See Greek report, case 11(d).

FRANCE

(a) In this case, the assignment would be of future prospective claims, the value of which is presently unknown. In the context of a *Dailly* assignment (see French report, case 12), it is possible to assign future claims, the amount of which is not yet known, so long as these claims can be individualised, as they must be listed in the document exchanged by the parties (article 1, para. 3 *Loi Dailly*[12]). A number of particulars must appear in the *bordereau*, such as the name of the debtor, the place of payment, the term of the claim and the amount or prospective

---

[11] Kritikos, in: Georgiadis/Stathopoulos 460 n. 12.   [12] Law No 81-2 of 2 Jan. 1981.

CASE 13: BANK LOAN ON THE BASIS OF MONEY CLAIMS (II)   577

amount.[13] Here, B does not know who his customers will be, let alone the amount of their orders. The *Dailly* assignment could not, therefore, be used in these circumstances. If B had orders on his books, he could assign the orders, under the same conditions as described in case 12. In practice, A would take a security right over B's trading activity. The Law of 17 March 1909 provides for an enterprise charge (*nantissement de fonds de commerce*): see case 11.

(b) For the sake of argument, we shall assume here that B was able to assign to A the claims he had against customers D, C1, C2, C3, C4 and C5, in order to guarantee the loan. The assignment, as described in case 12, is valid against all parties from the date of its creation. From that date, the assignee has title to the claims subject to the assignment and the assignor could not validly assign the same claim (should he do so, the second assignee would have to return payment).[14] If the *debitor cessus* is notified of each assignment, he must pay the assignee whose title is the oldest. In a conflict between the assignee and an unsecured creditor who has an enforceable claim and wants to execute against the assigned claim, because the assignment preceded the execution, there is no doubt that A's right will prevail. Moreover, pursuant to article 44 of the Law of 9 July 1991 on Execution, the *debitor cessus* of the claim which is the object of the execution procedure must immediately inform the bailiff of the previous assignment of the claim, or run the risk to having to pay twice.

(c) See French report, case 12.

(d) No limit is imposed in respect of the value of assigned debts referable to the amount of the secured loan.

BELGIUM

(a) Belgian law offers many possibilities for the assignment or charge of future claims. It is sufficient that the claims can be determined or at least that they are capable of determination.[15] A charge of all claims against existing and future customers will be regarded as sufficiently

---

[13] See Versailles, 2 June 1988, D 1989, Som, 185, obs. Vasseur.
[14] Paris, 4 Jan. 1990, D 1990, Som, 233, obs. Vasseur.
[15] Cass. 9 Apr. 1959, RCJB 1961, 32 note Heenen; Dirix/De Corte, *Zekerheidsrechten* 296, n° 443; Grégoire, RevBanque 1998, 447 (448).

determinable. In practice, since A is a bank, A will ask for an enterprise charge (*gage sur fonds de commerce/pand handelszaak*), which can include all existing and future claims related to B's business (see case 11).

(b) The majority of legal authors hold the view that creditors of the chargor who have executed against the claim cannot be considered to be 'protected' third parties in whose favour the priority contest will be resolved (see case 12). This type of conflict must be dealt with according to the principle of article 2075 s. 1 C.civ., which provides that the chargee obtains his security right as from the moment when the charge agreement is concluded. According to this view, the absence of notification will not endanger the position of the chargee in the case of an execution by other creditors of the chargor. The same solution applies in the event of the insolvency of the chargor. If, however, the bailiff collects the monies before any notification has taken place, it is not possible to challenge the distribution of the proceeds to the execution or insolvency creditors. As D was not notified of the charge, any payment to the bailiff must be considered to have been made in good faith and is, as a consequence of this, valid.

(c) The same solution applies in the event of insolvency. Moreover, notifying the *debitor cessus* after the commencement of the insolvency procedure is superfluous.

(d) There are no limitations regarding the value of the collateral.

PORTUGAL

(a) As stated in case 12(a), Portuguese law does not prohibit the assignment of future claims; such claims may also be charged. It would, therefore, be possible to establish an arrangement according to which B grants to A a security over the claims against his future customers by an assignment (article 577° C.C.) or a charge (article 679° C.C.). There are no special requirements of form or registration applicable to the assignment or charge of claims. It is only necessary to inform the *debitor cessus* of it, in order to make it effective against them and third parties. In fact, according to articles 583° and 669° n°2 C.C., the assignment or charge of claims is effective only after its communication to the *debitor cessus* or after his acceptance of it. An assignment like this is common in factoring activity, but the Portuguese legal system has no experience of using it as a security.

(b) According to article 584° C.C., priority in the case of an assignment or charge of the claim would be determined by the moment that it was communicated to the *debitor cessus*. Therefore, if the *debitor cessus* is notified of the execution against the claim before the communication of the assignment or charge, the unsecured creditor would have priority in payment. Otherwise, A would take priority. Here, D is under a duty to inform the court of the assignment or charge of the claim to A, otherwise he will be forced to pay the claim twice (article 856° CPC).

(c) The solution to this case does not differ from the previous one (case 12). If B goes bankrupt, the insolvency administrator would collect the claims from C1–C5 (article 146° CPEREF). If B goes bankrupt before the assignment or charge in favour of A is communicated to the *debitores cessi*, A would not have any priority to payment. If the communication has already taken place, A would have priority, as he would be regarded as the creditor to whom they owed the claim. However, if the assignment or charge was created within a period of two years prior to the declaration of insolvency, it would be presumed to constitute a *fraus creditorum* (article 158° (d) CPEREF), so it could be avoided by the insolvency administrator by an *actio Pauliana* (article 157° CPEREF).

(d) There are no limits in respect of the value that the collateral may have in relation to the amount of the secured loan. In Portuguese law, there are no restrictions on the securities a creditor may take. It is only possible that, in certain circumstances, a debtor may be able to have set aside a contract under which he has granted too great an extent of security in a state of weakness (usury, article 282° C.C.).

SPAIN

(a) Today, such an agreement would be possible even though the future customers are not yet identified. The contract providing for the assignment of future debts in exchange for a lump sum is not explicitly addressed in the CC, but an agreement along these lines between the parties was admitted in legal literature[16] under the principle of freedom

---

[16] See Sequeira Martín, in: Rafael García Villaverde, El contrato de factoring 309, 311.

of contract (article 38 CE and article 1255 CC) and by analogy with a similar kind of contract, which is the sale for a lump sum of certain specified rights (article 1532 CC), whenever future debtors were current customers of B. Such arrangements are common in financial contracts and they would be plausible within the current legal framework of the factoring contract. Law 1/1999 explicitly recognises the possibility of assigning future debts for a lump sum. Nevertheless, in business reality the financial system does not tend to use this kind of contract.

Other more common financial agreements include the discounting of bills and 'confirming', which consists of the payment and collection from customers that were previously confirmed by the bank. Bank A would have a *tercería de mejor derecho*, which gives it a preferential right over B's insolvency creditors. In the case of a commercial discounting contract, the financial institution buys a claim from a businessman (usually a bill of exchange or a promissory note from one of his debtors). The financial institution then pays to the businessman a sum of money representing the value of the bill minus a deduction reflecting commission for its part in the process. The financial institution does not assume any liability for any default in payment by the *debitor cessus*.[17]

(b) This depends on the security contract with A. If the contract stipulates that the future debts of B against his customer D are to be included within its ambit, the bank, A, would have a *tercería de mejor derecho*, which gives it a preferential right to payment. On the other hand, if such a clause does not exist, then the bailiff, acting on behalf of the unsecured creditor of B, will have priority.

A's right to collect the debt depends on whether D has been notified. If D pays the bailiff, the debt will be released. Also, if D has already paid the bailiff, A is not entitled to claim payment from him (D).

(c) The bank, A, does not have a subrogation claim against C1–C5. If the bank has agreed to a loan in a public deed, as is usually the case, then the bank has a preferential right in B's insolvency estate (article 1924.3 CC). This is a statutory preference, arising by law, which depends on the kind of contract used or on the form by which the agreement is set out. If it has been formalised in an *escritura notarial*, article 1924.3 CC is applicable; but if it is a *póliza mercantil*, then article 913.1, d.4 CCO will be

---

[17] See Vicent Chuliá, *Compendio Crítico de Derecho Mercantil* II 453–458; Cano Rico, *Manual Práctico de Contratación Mercantil* II 246.

applicable. These provisions grant a preferential right to those creditors whose contracts have been formalised in the above-mentioned way; the creditor in this case would be the bank. This statutory right is not only enjoyed by banks, but it is a right that derives from the public form which has been employed and which produces special security effects. Once B is declared bankrupt, only the results of these proceedings will be valid. Any subsequent notifications will no longer be taken into account.

(d) B's autonomy to offer securities over his estate is unrestricted, limited only by creditors' preferences. Therefore, there is no upper limit with regard to the amount of the collateral given as security in relation to the value of the secured claim.

ITALY

(a) Generally speaking, assignments of claims in favour of banks in Italy are governed by the provisions of the Civil Code on the assignment of claims (articles 1260 ff. c.c.), as well as by other rules. For example, quite often banks own factoring companies. Through these companies, banks operate as factors, under the Law 52/1991.[18] This law provides a rather liberal regime for the assignment of claims, though it does not specifically address the topic of the assignment of claims for security purposes.

To be sure, the Civil Code articles on the assignment of claims do not apply to case 13, because they are not designed to effect transfers of claims against future, unidentified debtors. Nevertheless, since 1993, banks should have been able to escape this limitation, by setting up a transaction under the Italian Banking Law of 1993, as amended.[19]

Article 46 of the Banking Law enables a charge (*privilegio*) to be created in favour of banks (and other financial intermediaries) over present and future enterprise assets, which are not registered movables or immovables, including future claims which are generated through the sale of merchandise, etc. This charge secures medium-to long-term loans only. It is created by agreement in writing between the borrower and the lender, whose signatures must be authenticated by a notary. The document in question must specify the amount of the loan and its terms; it must also

---

[18] See above, Italian report, case 12(a), (b).
[19] *Testo unico delle leggi in materia bancaria e creditizia*, d. lgs. n. 385, of 1 Sep. 1993, as amended by d. lgs. n. 342, of 8 Aug. 1999.

accurately describe the assets (whether plants, goods, livestock, claims, including future claims) upon which the debt is secured. The charge is enforceable against unsecured creditors of B from the date of its registration in the register specified by article 1524 c.c.[20] The article 46 Banking Law charge has priority over a number of other charges; it is, however, subordinated to statutory preferences for the administration of justice, wages and commissions of agents, etc. (article 2751 *bis* c.c.).

It is not clear whether transactions of this kind are common in certain sectors of the economy, or for certain types of operation. There are specialised credit institutions which operate in this field, though, as a consequence of the Banking Law of 1993, they no longer enjoy a monopoly over medium-to long-term credit facilities. It is difficult to say, however, whether in Italy B, the engineer, would actually secure the debt through the creation of a charge under article 46 of the Banking Law.

(b) The article 46 charge is enforceable against unsecured creditors of B, provided that their claims arose after the registration of the charge.

(c) Assuming that B created such a charge in A's favour, and that the said charge was duly registered before B's insolvency, A would have priority over B's creditors, as explained above, under parts (a) and (b).

(d) If the debtor secured the debt with excessive collateral, in the face of economic or financial difficulties, the transaction could be considered contrary to the provisions of the Criminal Code against usurious loans (article 644 c.p.; see also l. 7 Mar. 1996, n. 108, *Disposizioni in materia di usura*). There is no legislative or administrative definition of what is 'excessive collateral' in this context. The charge would be void and the lender would have committed a criminal act.

Quite apart from the discussion in parts (a)–(d), it is worth mentioning in this context that article 58 of the Italian Banking Law now allows banks (or other financial institutions) to acquire or to sell claims *en bloc*. In Italy, these forms of global assignment are used by banks to sell claims they have on their books to other financial institutions. The

---

[20] It is also enforceable against secured creditors of A, provided that they are not good faith purchasers of a movable thing (article 46.5 of the banking law; article 1153 c.c.). No provision of the Banking Law explains what happens if the claim over which the debtor created a charge is transferred to a third party, either for security purposes, or for other reasons.

sale usually takes place by auction. The transfer is effective from the date of the publication of the instrument in the Italian Official Gazette. This formality has the same effect as that of communication of the assignment to the *debitor cessus* pursuant to article 1264 of the Italian Civil Code.

THE NETHERLANDS

(a) It is common practice for banks to demand security interests in the future claims of their debtors as part of credit arrangements. However, certain peculiarities must be taken into account. First, as the subject matter of the charge is future claims, parties are only able to create charges 'in advance'. As has been described above, this means that although the parties comply with all the necessary formalities in advance, the charge is not actually created, because B still lacks the power to dispose of the claim. The charge is only created when the claim arises and B acquires the power to dispose.[21]

In principle, both the charge with notification and the charge without notification may be used in respect of future claims. However, notification implies that the identity of the debtor is known. Therefore, this type of charge cannot be used when the future claims will arise against customers whose identity is, at present, unknown.

A charge without notification contains a statutory obstacle: it requires that the debt either exists or arises directly from an existing legal relationship.[22] Possible claims against future and as yet unknown customers evidently fail to meet this criterion. Consequently, such charges can only be created at the time B acquires those claims.

In practice, in particular in cases of long-term credit, credit institutions usually stipulate that their debtors are to provide them with 'lists of claims' on a regular basis. The credit institution is then in a position to create the charge by registering the list, as required by article 3:239 BW.

The use of such lists gives rise to substantial administrative burdens. Not only must each list be registered separately, but also these lists often contain hundreds of claims. In order to ameliorate this burden, it is accepted that banks may use so-called 'master-lists' which only refer to the lists of claims provided by the debtor. The actual lists of claims, containing the detailed information, remain with the bank; only the

[21] See *supra*, Dutch report, case 12.   [22] Article 3:239(1) BW.

master-lists are registered. It must be emphasised that the use of these master-lists is intended solely to reduce administrative burdens. It does not mean that once a master-list has been registered, the credit institution and the debtor are free to modify the list remaining with the credit institution so as to include new claims as they come into existence. For a new claim to come under the charge, a new registration is required. For this purpose banks must register a master-list periodically.[23]

(b) Assuming that the identity of the customer, D, was unknown at the time of the security agreement, A would only acquire a security right in the claim if the charge was communicated to D or registered after the claim arose, but before execution. In practice, the resolution of such cases will often turn on whether the list containing the relevant claim has been registered and, if so, when.

Without notification or registration, A would not have taken an effective security interest in the claim. A would therefore be on an equal footing with the unsecured creditor trying to execute. If, on the other hand, the charge had been perfected by notification or registration, he or she would have the right to resist the execution by the bailiff.[24]

(c) A's position depends on whether the charges were created before the commencement of insolvency proceedings. Once insolvency proceedings have commenced, B loses the right to dispose of his or her property and thus no valid charge can be created.[25]

If a charge has been created, A's position further depends on whether notification of the charge was given or not. If the charge was communicated to C1–C5, A would be able to demand payment from them. A would be granted a statutory charge over the monies paid, against which execution would be possible.[26] If the charge was created by registered or notarised deed without communication to D, A would retain his or her right to notify D even after the commencement of insolvency

---

[23] The *Hoge Raad* approved this use of master-lists in its decision of 14 Oct. 1994, NJ 1995, 447 (*Stichting Spaarbank Rivierenland/Gispen q.q.*); see also Snijders/Rank-Berenschot, *Goederenrecht* n. 546; Pitlo/Reehuis/Heisterkamp, *Het Nederlands burgerlijk recht III* nn. 818–819. In literature, it has recently been argued that reference in the master-lists to the detailed lists with the actual claims is not necessary. It would suffice to refer to *all* existing claims and those that arise from existing relationships. See generally Kortmann/Faber, WPNR 6324 (1998). Against this point of view, Struycken, WPNR 6366 (1999).
[24] See *supra*, case 11.   [25] Articles 23 and 35 Fw.
[26] Article 57 Fw and article 3:246 in conjunction with article 3:255 BW.

proceedings (article 57 Fw). After notification, A would be in the same position as if the charge had been created by means of notification. If, on the other hand, A neglects to communicate the charge to D, the insolvency administrator would be entitled to demand payment from D. A would, however, retain his or her right of priority, though he or she would have to contribute to the administrative costs of the insolvency proceedings.[27]

(d) As has been pointed out in case 11 above, doctrine and case law have barely addressed the issue of proportionality between debt and collateral. Some support can be found for the proposition that the secured creditor in such circumstances is under a duty to take into account the interests of other creditors. Furthermore, the principles of fairness and equity, which apply as between secured creditor and debtor, may also be of relevance.

Moreover, although there is no requirement of 'proportionality', the insolvency administrator does have the right to require the secured creditors to exercise their rights within a reasonable period. If the secured creditor fails so to do, the administrator becomes entitled to execute against those assets him- or herself.[28] Though the secured creditor retains his or her right of priority to the proceeds of the sale, to the extent that the creditor is oversecured, this provision may provide the administrator with some leverage. If the administrator executes, the secured creditor becomes liable to contribute to the general costs of the insolvency administration.

ENGLAND

(a) As the discussion of assignment under case 12 shows, the assignment can be both future and contingent. Therefore, an assignment in respect of future customers' debts is effective, the assignee acquiring a real interest in those debts as and when they come into existence.[29] The transaction is very common indeed. The assignment need not be by way of security. Instead, the debts may be factored to a specialist factor. This means that, instead of using that indebtedness as security to back a loan, the assignor *sells* (i.e., discounts) debts due from future customers for a sum that will reflect the degree of risk of non-payment by those

---

[27] *Hoge Raad* 17 Feb. 1995, NJ 1996, 471 (*Connection Technology BV*).
[28] Article 58 Fw.   [29] See *Tailby v Official Receiver* [1888] 13 App Cas 523.

customers and the accelerated value of the assignor receiving monies now while the assignee will have to wait to collect the debts. This latter item is the discount factor and the size of it will depend on the length of time given by the assignor to the customers to pay.

(b) Once the assignment is complete in favour of A, B's executing creditors cannot obtain priority.

(c) As stated previously, this is a simple matter in English law. The assignment is complete without notification and attaches automatically to debts once they come into existence. The assignee will still take a real interest in those debts even if they fall due during the currency of B's insolvency regime.[30]

(d) As stated above, English law imposes no restrictions on oversecured debt.

IRELAND

(a) There is no fundamental difference in analysis from that in case 12.

(b) It is possible to levy execution against claims but only against claims due, even if unascertained or not presently payable. An execution creditor, however, takes the claims subject to pre-existing equities (various limited real rights) and it is submitted that a prior assignee or a prior fixed chargee prevails over the execution creditor. The issue has been described as at bottom one of appropriation. Have the claims already been appropriated to the assignee or fixed chargee? If so, the latter win in the priority conflict and it is not relevant whether or not the assignment has been communicated to the *debitor cessus* or whether the *assignor's* (B's) entitlement to collect the claims has been revoked.

If A has merely an enterprise charge (*floating charge*) over the claims, then he will lose out in the priority conflict. It is however not possible to take a *floating charge* in this particular case since B is a sole trader. The 'equities' subject to which an execution creditor takes, do not include a *floating charge* which has not crystallised.

---

[30] *Re Lind* [1915] 2 Ch 345.

(c) As explained more fully in relation to case 12(a), A will have security rights with respect to these claims. A's entitlement does not depend on communication of the assignment to the *debitor cessus* nor is revocation of the assignor's authority to collect the debts necessary to validate A's security.

(d) There are no limits with respect to the value the collateral might have in relation to the amount of the secured loan.

SCOTLAND

(a) The law is not wholly certain but it is probable that no security could be granted in these circumstances.[31] The reason is that the law requires intimation (i.e. notification) to be made of assignations (i.e. assignments), and in the present case there is no-one to whom intimation can be given.[32] Of course, there could be assignation, but without intimation a bare assignation can give no priority against other creditors.

One possibility would be for B to hold the future claims in trust for A, but this is likely to be ineffective.[33]

(b) Priority would depend on the dates. If the bailiff[34] executed against the debt[35] before the assignation was intimated, the execution would have priority. If the assignation was intimated before the execution, the assignation would have priority. This is an example of the principle *prior tempore potior iure*.

(c) Once again, it depends on the dates. If the insolvency happens before the intimation of the assignation, the assignation is ineffective. If the assignation is intimated before the insolvency, it should take effect as a security over the claims.

(d) The law does not place any limits on the value of the collateral in relation to the amount of the debt. A security over all claims to secure a debt of £1 would be valid.

---

[31] However, if B were a company, a *floating charge* would be possible.
[32] See Gretton, JR 1993, 23.   [33] See the previous case.
[34] A bailiff is either a '*messenger at arms*' or a '*sheriff officer*', depending on which court is involved. The term 'bailiff' is not used in Scots law.
[35] Execution against a claim is called 'arrestment'.

SOUTH AFRICA

(a) In general, the fact that the claims against future customers are not yet due or contingent has the effect that the enforcement of the security by the bank (A) is postponed until the debt becomes due or has been realised. This is because, although an agreement to cede a future debt is possible, the actual assignment (*cession*) of the debt is only possible once the debt has come into existence. If, however, one accepts that future rights can be transferred by means of a transfer agreement concluded *in anticipando* before the rights have materialised, B's estate would be bound by the transfer of a future right as from the date of assignment. This means that if a so-called *Global cession* was contemplated by the parties, any claims which might accrue to B against future customers would fall in A's rather than B's estate from the date of the *cession*. By contrast, if a *Mantel cession* was contemplated, the assignment (actual *cession*) of the claim would only occur once an enforceable claim came into existence. The assignment of so-called book debts to a factor is very common in South African commercial practice.

(b) Once the claim of B against the customer has arisen, the claim is automatically assigned to A's estate, whether as a direct claim against D (under the out-and-out assignment construction) or as a security right (under the charge construction). On the out-and-out assignment construction, the claim would have been ceded to A and the bailiff would not be able to execute against the claim on behalf of the creditors of B since the claim does not form part of his estate. On the charge construction, the claim would fall into B's estate and could be executed against, but A's security right would give him preference over the unsecured creditor. A's right does not depend on any further circumstances. Communication of the assignment to D is not required for an enforceable *cession*. Revocation of B's entitlement to collect the claims against his customers would strengthen A's position, but would not avoid discharge of the debt by payment to B rather than to A.

(c) If the security assignment is construed as an out-and-out assignment, the outstanding claims would have been transferred automatically to A once they arose. Nothing more would be needed for the validity of the assignment. The claims bypassed the insolvency estate of B; A has a direct claim against customers C1–C5. If it is construed as a charge, the claims

CASE 13: BANK LOAN ON THE BASIS OF MONEY CLAIMS (II)

fall in the insolvency estate of B, but since this right is encumbered with a security right (charge) in favour of A, A has a preferential right to the proceeds of the claims, ranking above the insolvency creditors of B. In both cases, A's right does not depend on any further circumstances.

(d) South African law does not place any limits on the value of the collateral in relation to the amount of the debt.

DENMARK

(a) According to Danish law, a claim can only be given as security if it can be described in such a way as to leave no doubt as to its identity. Furthermore, a security right to a claim is only protected against a third party if the *debitor cessus* has been notified of the security right. Therefore, a future claim cannot be given as security if the identities of the future customers are unknown. (If the identity of a customer is known, it is to some extent recognised that a future claim can be given as security.)

However, claims can be used as security in a factoring agreement where the factoring company gives a loan on the basis of security in the claims, for example up to 80 per cent of the amount of the claim. In this respect, the agreement can stipulate that all the future claims are given as security for the loan. On the other hand, the loan monies should not be paid to the debtor before the claim has arisen and the *debitor cessus* notified, because there would be a risk that the security might be invalidated if the loan debtor was declared bankrupt.

(b) If a bailiff wishes to execute against a claim which has been assigned to A, the assignment is only protected against execution if the *debitor cessus*, D, has been notified of the assignment: cf. section 31 of the Bonds Act. This means that A has priority if D has been notified of the assignment. If not, the execution creditor has priority.

Even if B was entitled to collect the claim, A might yet have priority, if it was agreed that B should settle with A when the claim was collected and A took steps to ensure that B did so.

(c) Under the Bonds Act, section 31 no distinction is drawn between execution and insolvency. The assignment of the claim will be, and is only, protected as against creditors if notification of the assignment has been made to the *debitor cessus*. If the *debitor cessus* has been notified about the security right, A is entitled to the claims; if not, the estate is entitled to the claims.

(d) According to Danish law, there is no limit as to the value of the collateral in relation to the amount of the secured loan. A is, however, only entitled to be repaid the amount of the secured loan out of the proceeds of realisation of the collateral; any surplus must be remitted to the estate.

SWEDEN

(a) B may grant A a security over B's future claims against unidentified customers, provided that the claims are determinable (e.g. 'all claims related to a certain activity'), thereby enabling A to inform the *debitores cessi* of the security when the claim arises and thereby perfecting A's third-party protection. Until the customer is informed, A has no protection against the creditors of B, in respect of his assignment or a charge. However, even if the customers have been identified and notified, A would have no protection against the creditors of B as regards claims that have not been earned when insolvency proceedings commence; earnings during the last three months are also liable to be recovered (see case 12). Alternatively, B may grant to A an enterprise charge, which always includes all claims against customers (see above, cases 10–11). Such a security would require registration, but no notification need be made to the *debitores cessi*. Under this security, A would have priority in respect of claims, provided that they had arisen before B went bankrupt.[36] A third possibility, especially useful when finance is required for a large-scale project and when the future customers are unidentified and therefore cannot be notified, would be to set up a Special Purpose Vehicle. This would be a company, which would borrow the money from A. All claims against customers would be invoiced and collected by the SPV. B would bear all the costs of the operation. B's claim against the SPV would be subordinated to that of A. The only competition that A would have against the assets of the SPV would therefore be the claims of the tax creditor; if A was granted an enterprise charge

---

[36] According to NJA 1982, 900, an enterprise chargee has a preferential right only in collateral that existed on the date of insolvency. If a claim is partially attributable to performance by the estate, the proceeds are apportioned accordingly.

he could even enjoy priority over these. The final effect is even better than, for instance, a German *Globalzession*, as A will have priority also in respect of what is earned by the estate. The model has not been tested in the Swedish courts.[37]

(b) If A has been granted an assignment or a charge, A will take priority over a creditor that seeks execution only if the *debitor cessus* was informed prior to the execution, further provided that the *debitor cessus* was not permitted to pay his debt to B for B's own use. Here, the claims must have been earned; otherwise execution against the claims cannot take place.

(c) The answer is the same as in part (b) with two additions. In insolvency, future claims belong to the estate, and hence the security is ineffective if the claims were not earned when insolvency commenced. It is also possible for other creditors to recover (avoid) the value that has been earned during the three months prior to the commencement of insolvency proceedings pursuant to chapter 4 section 10 of the Bankruptcy Act (see case 11, Variation).

(d) There is no limit as to the value of the collateral in relation to the amount of the secured claim, apart from the fact that A cannot collect more money from the realisation of the collateral than B owes him. See further under case 11(d).

FINLAND

(a) The only practical way to establish a security right over the future claims would be, in the circumstances of this case, by registering an enterprise charge. The enterprise charge comprises almost all the property of an enterprise except the immovables. One of the weaknesses of the enterprise charge is, however, that B could later charge or assign for security purposes the same money claims. In this situation, the charge or assignment would accord to the secured creditor a superior preferential right to that of an enterprise charge. The legislation accords to the enterprise chargee a lower priority because the enterprise charge

---

[37] It could be asked whether such a puppet company should be respected as a separate entity. See critical remarks by Braekhus, *Omsetning og kreditt* 213.76. However, such companies have been accepted by a Norwegian appellate court, RG 1986.905, on the same legislative basis as in the other Nordic countries.

is designed to be a security right in a large, but fluctuating, mass of property.

(b) A bailiff could execute against B's claim against the customer, D. An enterprise charge would not prevent this. An enterprise chargee would be entitled to be paid from the proceeds of execution, if the bailiff considers that the execution would otherwise endanger his or her rights. If the property subjected to execution is not also charged or assigned for security purposes, the enterprise chargee has normally the best preferential right to the proceeds.

(c) The claims would belong to the insolvency estate. The enterprise chargee would have a high preferential right to 50 per cent of the net assets of the estate, except for immovables.

(d) No limits are imposed on the value of the collateral that may be included within the ambit of an enterprise charge. The efficacy of the security is restricted, however, by limiting, in the legislation, the preferential right of the enterprise chargee to 50 per cent of the net assets of the estate.

Comparative observations

Parts (a)–(c)

In contrast to the previous case, case 13 involves what are clearly future claims. Nevertheless, the majority of jurisdictions offer a practical method by which security can be created over such claims, at least by way of a global security right such as an enterprise charge (*floating charge* or *nantissement de fonds de commerce*). Some reports emphasise that the security right can only come into existence once the claim has arisen. This is true for all legal systems. The crucial question is whether the parties to the security agreement can, prior to the point at which the claim arises, do all that is necessary for the security right to come into existence. It is only then that it is practicable to use future claims as the subject matter of a security right.

Notification of the debtor requires that his identity is known. It is not practicable to assign or charge future claims in any system that requires notification for the assignment or charge to be valid in respect of third parties. This applies to France,[38] the Netherlands,[39] Scotland, Denmark, Sweden and Finland. France, Scotland, Sweden and Finland allow instead future debts to be included within the ambit of a global charge over the enterprise[40] (*floating charge* or *nantissement de fonds de commerce*). It should, however, be noted that on the facts of case 13 a *floating charge* could not be established in England, Ireland or Scotland because B is a sole trader, not a company.

The use of future claims as collateral for a security right is practicable in all those jurisdictions either which do not make notification of the *debitor cessus* a prerequisite for the assignment's validity as against third parties in general (Germany, Greece, Belgium, England, Ireland and South Africa) or where it is possible to substitute for notification a procedure that can be given effect to while the identity of the future debtor remains unknown (book entry in Austria, registration of a *privilegio* in favour of a bank according to article 46 of the Italian Banking Act of 1 September 1993).

Part (d)

In the context of security rights in stock-in-trade,[41] we have already seen that the issue of oversecurity is, or rather was, a matter of concern mainly for German courts and legal science, although one can probably consider the Greek discussion as to whether a global security assignment is contrary to article 178, 179 or 281 A.K. to be in the same vein. One might be tempted to think that the liberal attitude German and Greek law take towards security ownership and security assignment lies at the root of this discussion. However, as has become more and more apparent during the course of these cases, there are other European systems that take no less an open view on the admissibility of security rights over claims and movables. Some possible, but less than entirely satisfactory, explanations have already been advanced in the comparative observations to case 11(d). The special route taken by German judge-made law

---

[38] For a *Dailly* assignment, the identity of the *debitor cessus* must be known.
[39] The master-lists described in the Dutch report are only effective with regard to claims existing at the time of registration or arising from relationships existing at that time. For future claims in the strict sense a new registration is necessary. The debate on the validity of the master-lists concerns the specificity requirement, i.e. the charged claims must be sufficiently specified *by* the registered deed which does not mean that they should all be mentioned *in* this deed.
[40] In the future this may also be possible in Greece.   [41] See *supra*, case 11(d).

in the years prior to the BGH's landmark decision of 1997 might also be explained by the fact that in German contract law in general, the judicial control of consumer *and* commercial contracts under the Unfair Contract Terms Act (AGBG), which is in the meantime incorporated into the BGB (§§ 305 ff.), and the insistence that any contract clause found to be unfair (e.g. a clause in a loan contract containing a security agreement) be regarded as wholly nullified (§ 306 BGB), has reached a degree that might from the outside be well regarded as exaggerated.

Case 14: Finance leasing of computers

(Finance leasing – lessor's and lessee's rights in insolvency of the other partner – effects of purchase option)

S is a supplier of computers. B wants a computer. At the request of B, A (a financial institution) buys the computer from S. A then leases the computer to B. The length of the lease corresponds to the expected useful life of the computer. An unsecured creditor of B executes against the computer. Alternatively, B becomes bankrupt. A asserts ownership of, or a security right in, the computer, or at least to preferential payment out of the proceeds of the sale of the computer.

Questions

(a) Does A have any real rights in the computer? Do such rights depend on any further prerequisites?

(b) Is it relevant whether B has an option to buy the computer at the end of the contractual term?

(c) Is this or some other kind of leasing agreement used instead of other types of security, such as retention of title or security transfer of ownership? Is legislative policy or the approach of the courts more favourable to leasing (in respect of the interests of the supplier/the bank) than to security rights?

(d) What would B's legal position be in respect of the computer if not he but A became bankrupt?

Discussions

GERMANY

(a) This case describes a three-party situation which is typical of finance leasing: the lessor (A) purchases goods from the producer (S) and leases them to the customer (B). In Germany, A would usually be a specialised leasing company rather than a general financial institution. Often, the leasing company itself will be financed by a loan from a bank and will assign the claims arising out of the leasing contracts to the bank (security assignment): see also *infra* part (d). The main issues concerning leasing contracts are contractual, not proprietary, in nature. According to German law, the lessor clearly remains owner of the goods until, at the end of the contract, the lessee purchases the goods and acquires ownership of them. The lessor's ownership does not depend on any means of publicity.

In the event that insolvency proceedings are commenced against B, A can vindicate the computer because he owns it (§ 47 InsO).[1] This right presupposes that either A or the insolvency administrator terminates the leasing contract, otherwise B's right to possess the computer would not determine.[2] If the computer is executed against on behalf of B's creditors, A can bring an action to resist the execution (§ 771 ZPO).[3] Upon such an action, the court will order the execution to be stopped and set aside (§§ 775 nr. 2, 776 ZPO), so that A can recover his property.

(b) The question of whether the lessee has an option to buy the computer at the end of the leasing period is irrelevant in so far as A's real rights are concerned, prior to the exercise of such an option. It may, however, be of relevance as to whether the contract is classified as being one of finance leasing, a classification with consequences under tax and consumer credit legislation (see § 3 s. 2 n. 1 *Verbraucherkreditgesetz*, Consumer Credit Act[4]).

(c) Since security transfer of ownership is clearly valid, there is no need to disguise a security arrangement as a leasing contract. The main difference in respect of the rights of the creditor-lessor is that the security owner has only a right to preferential payment out of the realisation of the property, a process conducted by the insolvency administrator, whereas the lessor can vindicate the goods as his property. Under the old Insolvency Code (*Konkursordnung*) the differences between these two

---

[1] Cf. Martinek, *Moderne Vertragstypen I* 215 f.; Leible, *Finanzierungsleasing und 'arrendamiento financiero'* 195 with further references.
[2] See further *supra*, German report, case 10(b).
[3] General opinion, cf. Leible, *Finanzierungsleasing und 'arrendamiento financiero'* 193; Martinek, *Moderne Vertragstypen I* 215; von Westphalen, *Der Leasingvertrag* n. 1451.
[4] See in detail Leible, *Finanzierungsleasing und 'arrendamiento financiero'* 109 ff.

rights were marginal, whereas today, under the new Code, they are more significant. In particular, the security owner has to pay a lump sum of 9 per cent of the proceeds as costs for the assessment and realisation of his right (§ 171 InsO). Also, he has to rely on the insolvency administrator to realise the collateral (§§ 166 ff. InsO). Yet, there has not been a general move away from traditional security transfers of ownership, towards a more frequent use of sale and lease-back arrangements.

(d) Under the new Insolvency Code it is for the administrator to determine whether he wants to continue the contract (§ 103 InsO). If he opts for termination, B will have to surrender the computer to the insolvency estate. This does not, however, apply to leasing contracts when the leasing company and the financing bank are not identical. According to § 108 s. 1 sent. 2 InsO, such leasing contracts survive the insolvency of the leasing company; the administrator is not entitled to refuse to perform. This special rule has been introduced as an amendment to the new Insolvency Code[5] because, in Germany, it is common practice for leasing companies to refinance their purchases through a bank, to which the leasing payments are assigned as security. If the administrator was allowed to terminate such leasing contracts at his discretion, the security rights of the banks would become vulnerable and they would no longer be willing to finance this kind of transaction.[6]

Yet, in the present case, the special circumstances required by § 108 s. 1 sent. 2 InsO are not satisfied, thus B's position will depend on the decision of the insolvency administrator.

AUSTRIA

(a) According to Austrian law, A is the owner of the computer. If B goes bankrupt, A can therefore vindicate the computer.[7] If B's creditors execute against the computer, A can bring an action to resist the execution.

A finance leasing contract (*Leasingvertrag*) is regarded as an atypical contract in Austrian law. It is atypical because it is not provided for in the ABGB. Therein[8] only the lease and the hire contract are provided

---

[5] Act of 19 July 1996, BGBl I 1013.   [6] *Smid*/Smid § 108 InsO nn. 11 ff.
[7] It does not matter whether the deal concerns hardware or software, nor whether, if the latter, the software is bought off-the-shelf or whether it is bespoke in nature.
[8] §§ 1090 ff. ABGB.

for. Austrian doctrine[9] regards the finance lease as a mixed contract, which contains elements of both the lease and the contract of sale.[10] The ownership of A is recognised because the situation is the same as that in the case of a contract of sale with retention of title.

(b) The existence or absence of an option for the lessee to buy the computer at the end of the contractual term is irrelevant.[11]

(c) There is, in respect of the rights of the creditor, no difference of significance between a leasing agreement and a retention of title construction; due to the publicity requirement, a security transfer of ownership would be impracticable.

(d) As A owns the computer, it forms part of the insolvency estate. It may only be reclaimed from B, however, if the leasing contract is terminated. The insolvency of A is not a ground for termination,[12] unless otherwise agreed.[13]

GREECE

(a) In this case A, by purchasing the computer in its own name from the supplier, S, indirectly finances B (finance leasing).[14] B, instead of expending capital to buy the computer from S, prefers to 'lease' it from the leasing company, A, which must be a company specialising in this

---

[9] Fischer-Czermak, *Mobilienleasing, Rechtsnatur, Gewährleistung und Gefahrtragung*; Schwimann/Binder § 1090 ABGB nn. 56 ff. As in Germany, there exist a number of different theories about the nature of the leasing contract.

[10] Depending on the context, either the legal rules governing lease contracts or the legal rules regulating contracts of sale are applied to such contracts. If the lessee is a consumer, and the consumer has the right to purchase the object at the end of the contractual term, the contract is classified as an instalment purchase, regulated by the special provisions of the Consumer Protection Act on instalment sales (cf. Schwimann/Apathy § 17 KSchG n. 2). If real property is leased, such a contract is regarded as a contract of tenancy, regulated by the special provisions of the Tenancy Act (cf. OGH 14 May 1996, 5 Ob 2099/96 *immolex* 1997, 20).

[11] It may be relevant, however, for tax purposes.

[12] According to § 24 (1) KO, a lease contract is not affected by the insolvency of the lessor.

[13] It is argued by Binder (in: *Schwimann* § 1090 ABGB n. 73) that the administrator can cancel the contract in accordance with § 21 KO in so far as B is granted an option to buy the computer at the end of the contractual term. He argues that such an option is typical for a contract of sale to which § 21 KO applies.

[14] For the compound contract of leasing see in general Georgiadis, *Nees morphes symvaseon tis sygchronis oikonomias*. Also Paparseniou, *I symvasi chrimatodotikis misthosis*.

form of business. Law 1665/1986, which regulates finance leasing of movables and immovables, after its modification by L. 2367/1995, provides the lessee with a right to purchase the thing or renew the lease.

B's insolvency entails the termination of the finance leasing contract (article 4 § 3 L. 1665/1986). After the lease expires the lessor, A, can require the return of the leased computer either by virtue of its contractual rights or by exercising its rights of ownership (article 1094 A.K.).

If during the period of the lease the computer is executed against by another creditor of B, A can resist the execution (article 936 KPolD). Even if the lessor does not, however, the highest bidder cannot acquire ownership of the computer, because, according to article 4 § 2 L. 1665/1986, 'third parties cannot acquire ownership or any other right *in rem* over the thing before the expiry of the finance leasing in any way'.

The leasing contract must be concluded in writing and must be recorded on a special register kept at the Athens Court of First Instance. The cost of registration is minimal.

As during the leasing contract third parties cannot acquire ownership of or any other real right in the thing, even if they are in good faith, it makes no difference whether the ownership of the lessor is marked on the goods or not.

(b) If the lessee, B, has been provided with a right to purchase the computer at the end of the contractual term, in the event of his insolvency he will not be entitled to exercise or transfer this option, as it belongs to the insolvency estate (article 2 § 4 L. 635/37). The administrator can exercise and transfer the right with the permission of the *judge rapporteur* (article 576 EmbN).[15]

(c) Other securities, such as fiduciary transfer of ownership and leaseback, serve similar purposes. Nevertheless, the taxation of leasing agreements is more favourable.

(d) If A goes bankrupt, the insolvency administrator is not entitled to bring the contract to an end by a termination notice.[16]

Therefore, B will be able to resist a claim, on the grounds of his own right to possession, by A's creditors to the computer made before the

---

[15] See further, Georgiadis, *Symphonon proaireseos kai dikaioma proaireseos* 265.
[16] Georgiadis, *Nees morphes symvaseon tis sygchronis oikonomias* 96; Kotsiris, *Ptocheutiko Dikaio* 353; N. Rokas *Stoicheia ptocheutikou dikaiou* 52; Mazis, *I chrimatodotiki misthosi – Leasing* 158.

expiry of the finance leasing (article 1095 A.K.). The insolvency administrator has the right to terminate the contract only in the event of B's default in payment.

FRANCE

(a) The leasing contract is especially designed to be used as the basis of this type of agreement, involving machines and industrial equipment (see Law No 66-455 of 2 July 1966, article 1).[17] As seen in case 10, the leasing contract must be registered by the lessor on a register held at the Commercial Court having jurisdiction over the lessor, and the registration is to be renewed every five years. Absence of registration would result in the lessor being unable to enforce his title against third parties, unless he could prove that these third parties had actual knowledge of his title (article 8 of Decree No 72-665 of 4 July 1972).

(b) The inclusion of an option to purchase is a necessary condition for a transaction to be regarded as one of lease. If the contract stipulates that at the end of the rental period, the lessee is to become the owner of the asset automatically, the contract would not be regarded as one of leasing, but possibly one of sale under suspensive condition, which may affect the title of A to the computer.

(c) Under the lease, title remains with the lessor, providing a better protection than that of a security right, such as pledge. In contrast to the special charge on machines and industrial equipment provided by the Law of 18 January 1951,[18] the secured creditor is entitled to apply for the asset to be sold in order to be paid out of the proceeds of sale. The procedure is governed by article L. 521-3 of the Commercial Code on the enforcement of pledges: on the date of payment, the pledgee must notify the pledgor, by registered letter, that payment is due. He must wait eight days before proceeding with the sale of the asset by auction. He will then be paid in priority to the unsecured creditors, but he has no

---

[17] See Duranton, 'Crédit-bail (Leasing)', Encyclopédie Dalloz, vol. Commercial, 1999.
[18] The Act was adopted with a view to encouraging modernisation of and investment in machines and equipment used in business activities. See Ripert, D 1951, Chr, 41. The conditions for the creation of the charge are cumbersome: the contract must be a deed signed before a notary or a contract signed by the parties and subsequently registered on a register held by the Commercial Court. Registration must be done by the creditor-chargee within two weeks of the date of the charge contract (article 3).

right to the machine itself.[19] Clearly, leasing offers the best protection available, that is, ownership. Retention of title will also be effective and, as discussed previously, does not require publication.

(d) If A becomes bankrupt and insolvency proceedings are commenced, the question is whether the insolvency administrator will continue with the leasing contract. The insolvency administrator could, pursuant to article 37, decide to terminate the ongoing contract and claim *rei vindicatio* of the computer, since A has never ceased to be the owner (see case 10(d)).

BELGIUM

(a) The lessor (A) remains the owner of the computer. The lessor can recover the leased objects from the insolvency estate or can resist an execution against the equipment by other creditors. Finance leasing is partially regulated by a Royal Decree of 10 November 1967. According to these provisions, the finance lease is limited to equipment; the duration of the contract must correspond to the estimated working life of the equipment; the instalments must amortise the capital cost; and the lessee must have the option to acquire the equipment at its residual value at the end of the lease. The equipment must be marked with a notice stating that it is subject to a finance lease. All these statutory provisions are however of an administrative nature, in the sense that they have to be observed by financial institutions in order for them to be allowed to offer their services to the public in this capacity. The *Cour de cassation* has ruled that the fact that equipment was not marked by the lessor is irrelevant in so far as the effectiveness of the lessor's rights as against third parties is concerned.[20] Likewise, lower courts have ruled that the question of whether the lessor is an authorised institution under the Royal Decree of 10 November 1967 is irrelevant to the question of whether the contract is valid and whether the ownership of the lessor is effective as against third parties.

---

[19] A clause purporting to allot the machine to the chargee in case of non-payment ('*pacte commissoire*') would be void. However, a court could decide to allot the machine to the chargee if he decides not to pursue the sale of the machine. See Ass plén, 26 Oct. 1984, D 1985, 33, Conc Cabannes, note Derrida; JCP 1985, II, 20342, Rapp Viennois, note P. Corlay.

[20] Cass. 27 Nov. 1981, Pas 1982, I, 434, RW 1981–82, 2141 concl. proc. gen. Dumon.

(b) The option for the lessee to acquire the equipment after expiration of the rental term of the contract is regarded as an essential element of the leasing contract, in order to distinguish it from other contracts, such as hire purchase.

(c) It is said that the courts are rather favourable towards leasing. The right of the lessor under a finance lease to recover the goods in the event of the insolvency of the lessee was recognised at an early point by the *Cour de cassation*, in 1981, notwithstanding the general hostility towards fiduciary transfers and the fact that, at that point, reservation of title was not recognised. A fiduciary transfer of ownership is still not recognised and the external effects of other devices, such as hire purchase or consignment, are uncertain. According to article 103 Bankruptcy Act, the goods given in consignment can be reclaimed by the owner. The court restricts this possibility to 'true' consignments, however: arrangements that can be regarded as normal transactions in the particular branch or trade.

(d) The insolvency of the lessor will not alter the position of the lessee.

PORTUGAL

(a) As the computer was bought by the lessor from a producer to the order of the customer to whom it was then leased, this case would be regarded as a typical case of finance leasing (*locação financeira*). Therefore, during the leasing period, A will be regarded as the owner of the computer. B will not have any real right in the computer, but only a claim against A (article 9°(b) of DL 149/95 of 24 June). As owner of the thing leased, A will be protected should B's creditors execute against it. If B becomes bankrupt, the leasing contract can be terminated by A (article 18°(b) of DL 149/95).

(b) In Portuguese law, the leasing contract must always include an *option* to buy the things leased at a predetermined price (article 1° of DL 149/95). There is already a High Court decision stating that a clause in a leasing contract obliging the lessee to purchase the things is void.[21]

(c) Security transfer of ownership is not allowed in Portuguese law. It is forbidden for a pledgee or chargee to become owner of the things

---

[21] STJ 7 Mar. 1991 (*Afonso De Albuquerque*) BMJ 405 (1991) 465–470.

pledged or charged, without a judicial sale (*pacto comissório*, articles 694° and 678° C.C.). In the case of lease-back, it would therefore be possible to use the leasing agreement as a security. However, the statute governing leasing contracts (DL 149/95, of 24 June) does not contain any rule about lease-back. Only legal writers have referred to it.[22] If a lease-back is used in order to grant a security to a creditor, it is possible that the courts would treat it as a sham pledge or charge and subject it to the rules applying to pledges and charges (article 241° C.C.).

The use of the leasing contract as a substitute for retention of title is not very common, because the protection offered to the creditor under retention of title would not be different.

(d) In this case, by analogy with the rule applicable to contracts of lease (article 170° CPEREF), the insolvency of the lessor cannot affect the rights of the lessee, so he will be able to require the insolvency administrator to perform the contract.

SPAIN

(a) A remains the owner of the computer and may therefore enforce his ownership against the unsecured creditor of B, who is executing against B's goods.

A's right does not depend on any further prerequisites. However, if A either holds a public deed of this transaction or has registered the contract of sale, according to the fill-in form available at the Chattels Registry, then A may execute more expeditiously against the secured goods. If the contract has been legalised in a public deed (article 517.4°–5° LEC) the corresponding procedure will be the executive suit for non-pecuniary goods (articles 699 ff. LEC). If, on the other hand, the contract has been legalised in accordance with the fill-in form which is available at the Registry and has been recorded in the Chattels Registry, then the corresponding procedure will be the summary oral suit (article 250.11° LEC). If B becomes bankrupt, the leased goods will not be included in B's insolvency estate and therefore the goods should be at the lease-holder's disposal, after the contract has been brought before the judge. The insolvency judge will recognise the leaseholder's right and order that the goods be separated from the insolvency estate.[23]

---

[22] See Menezes Cordeiro, *Manual de Direito Bancário* 554 and Romano Martinez, *Contratos em especial* 311.
[23] See Supplementary Provision 5/II LVBMP.

(b) Leasing includes an option to purchase the financed movable. This distinguishes it from renting, which does not incorporate an option to purchase the financed goods. B, on exercising his option to purchase, will become the owner of the computer and the consequences of A's insolvency will not affect him. It goes without saying that, in order to exercise his option, he must have paid all the leasing instalments.

(c) Leasing of movables is not the most common type of security right used in Spain. Reservation of title and the statutory restriction of transfer are more common. From a very general point of view, they all serve a common economic goal. However, a reservation of title clause is usually set out in a contract of sale and provides the seller with a specific guarantee with regard to the goods sold, whereas a leasing operation has basically a financing goal for commercial or industrial establishments. Although the aim may be similar, there are other differences of importance between them: (1) property transfer occurs in the reservation of ownership, whereas in leasing, transfer of property does not happen; (2) a leasing operation enjoys certain tax advantages, which makes it more appealing to potential consumers; (3) leasing is usually carried out between, on the one hand, a financial institution, and, on the other hand, a businessman, a self-employed person or professional, or a firm, but not between private individuals. In sum, both the financing aspects and the tax benefits make the leasing contract very appealing to companies which deal either in consumer goods or in goods the life-span of which is rather short. These are, surely, noteworthy reasons that may help to explain why the leasing of movables is most often used to secure the acquisition of some commodities, for example, computers, machinery, cars, office equipment, etc.

(d) If the financial institution, A, becomes bankrupt, the insolvency administrator may require B to pay the leasing instalments due prior to or at the point of A's insolvency. On the other hand, B could exercise his rights against the insolvency estate to maintain his option to buy the computer. This is the case if a special agreement was reached in the leasing contract which allows the lessee (B) to provide the full payment (leasing payments plus option to purchase) for, and subsequently to acquire, the computer.

The insolvency administrator cannot terminate the leasing contract with B, as long as he (B) keeps up with the agreed payments. In other words, insolvency does not destroy the contractual bonds that exist

CASE 14: FINANCE LEASING OF COMPUTERS   605

between the lessee and the lessor. If the contract of leasing was agreed within the suspect period, the contract would be declared invalid. On the other hand, if the leasing contract was agreed outside the suspect period, the contract is valid and the insolvency administrator must comply with its clauses. The debtor (B) can continue paying the instalments until he has paid off the whole debt. In the end, he will have the right to exercise his option to purchase, if he wishes.

ITALY

(a) The fact pattern of this case is by now extremely common in Italy, though it was almost unknown before 1970.[24] The lessor purchases goods from the seller, which are then leased to the lessee. The lessor, a leasing company, is the owner of the goods during the period when they are used by the lessee. The rent, which is fixed by the leasing contract, reflects the discounted value of the goods, and the finance charges of the operation. At the agreed time, the lessee has the option to purchase the goods, or to return them to the lessor.

The lessor is the owner of the goods that are leased to the lessee. He may therefore claim that the leased goods are not to be subjected to an execution by an unsecured creditor of B, on the ground that the goods in question do not belong to the debtor. Article 619 c.p.c. governs how execution is opposed.[25] Despite the fact that the Civil Code does not establish a requirement of form applicable to leasing contracts, such as that which governs the enforcement of reservation of title clauses against creditors (article 1524 c.c.), the lessor's right will be protected in case of execution only if the lessor establishes the contract of lease by documentary evidence showing the reason why the goods in question are on the business premises of the debtor. That evidence will usually consist of a written document bearing a certain date which precedes attachment to the goods. The judge may, however, relax the requirement of proof if the trade or profession of the debtor, or that of the third party, of itself explains why goods belonging to the third party are found by the executing creditor at the debtor's place of business

[24] Hence there is no Civil Code provision which regulates leasing as such. The UNIDROIT Convention on International Financial Leasing of 1988 entered into force in Italy on 1 May 1995 (l. 14 July 1993, n. 259); however, it is not relevant to the point raised by this case.
[25] For a full discussion of the protection of the lessor's right: Bussani, *Proprietà-garanzia e contratto* 103 ff.

(or in his house). Article 621 c.p.c. establishes these exclusionary rules of evidence by expressly prohibiting witness evidence or presumptive inferences concerning the rights of third parties over assets kept on the debtor's business premises or at his house. Though the Insolvency Act does not contain a similar rule, these exclusionary rules of evidence govern insolvency proceedings as well.[26] Hence the lessor's right to the leased goods will be protected in the case of insolvency only if he can prove it by documentary evidence having a certain date, which precedes the commencement of the insolvency proceedings, or if he is able to persuade the judge that the requirement of proof should be relaxed, because of the trade or profession of the insolvent.

It is debated whether the Civil Code rules on the restitutionary claims following the rescission of sales with retention of title can be applied to leasing contracts if the insolvency administrator of the lessee decides to rescind the leasing contract instead of adopting it.[27]

According to article 1526 c.c., if the sale with retention of title is terminated due to the buyer's non-performance, the seller must return the instalments he has received, subject to his right to fair compensation for the use of the things and for damages. If it was provided that the instalments paid should be retained by the seller as indemnity, the judge may, according to the circumstances, reduce such indemnity. The Civil Code states that the same rule applies if the contract is in the form of a lease (*locazione*), if it is provided that, at the end of the lease, ownership of the thing will pass to the lessee as a result of payment of the agreed rent. This provision was not enacted to deal with leasing contracts such as those with which the present case is concerned. Yet its possible application to the present circumstances must be considered.

The approach to the question differs according to the specific content of the particular agreement in question. In particular, whenever the option price at the end of the leasing period is considerably lower than the residual value of the goods, and there are grounds to infer that the agreement of the parties at the time when the contract was formed was that the goods would eventually be acquired by the lessee, retention of title in favour of the lessor is considered by authors and cases to be the predominant feature of the contract. In this instance, therefore, rules on

---

[26] Bonfatti, in: Ragusa Maggiore/Costa 435.
[27] For a succinct presentation of the various alternatives: Maffei Alberti, *Commentario breve alla legge fallimentare* sub-articles 72–83 VIII, 291–292.

sale with reservation of title (article 1526 c.c.) apply by way of analogy to the leasing contract. Hence, if the lease is rescinded, the lessor will be entitled to recover the leased goods and to equitable compensation for their use by the lessee. However, the lessor will have to pay back to the insolvency administrator the instalments that he received from the bankrupt before the commencement of insolvency proceedings.[28]

On the other hand, if the leasing contract was concluded to finance the use of the object of the lease by the lessee, and a transfer of ownership of the leased goods to the lessee is only a remote possibility, despite the fact that the lessee may exercise an option to purchase at the expiry of the contract, the consequences of the insolvency of the lessee will be different. In this case, the lessor will be entitled to recover the thing that was leased. The lessee is not entitled to restitution of the instalments paid until the commencement of insolvency proceedings, inasmuch as those payments were due as consideration for the use of the object of the lease, by analogy with article 1458 c.c., which provides that the termination of a contract for continuous performance does not have retroactive effects with respect to performance already made.[29]

In this case, A owns the computer, and can therefore enforce his real right against any creditor executing against B.

In the case of B's insolvency, the prevailing opinion is that article 72 of the Insolvency Act is fully applicable. Therefore, the insolvency administrator will be entitled to decide whether to perform the leasing contract or terminate it.

(b) As seen under part (a), an option to purchase in favour of B may be relevant, especially in order to establish a certain interpretation of the will of the parties concerning the transfer of ownership in favour of the lessee at the end of the leasing period.

(c) Whilst leasing contracts are not considered invalid if concluded in the normal course of business, transfer of ownership for security purposes

---

[28] Cass. 22 Mar. 1994, n. 2743, Fallimento, 1994, 1119; Cass. 22 Feb. 1994, n. 1731, Fallimento, 1994, 591; Cass. s.u., 7 Jan. 1993, n. 65, Fallimento, 1993, 521; Cass. 24 Aug. 1993, n. 8919, Fallimento, 1994, 39; Cass. 18 June 1992, n. 7556, Fallimento, 1992, 1118. The *fons* and *origo* of this line of cases is traceable to: Cass. 13 Dec. 1989, n. 5569, 5570, 5571, 5572, 5573, 5574. For in-depth commentary see Bussani, *Proprietà-garanzia e contratto* 76 ff.

[29] See the cases cited in the previous footnote.

is null and void under the current interpretation of article 2744 c.c. on foreclosure agreements (*pactum commissorium*).

(d) See part (d) of case 10.

THE NETHERLANDS

(a) Although, strictly speaking, it is not necessarily the case, in practical terms the lessor will almost always prove to be the owner of the object of the lease.[30] It will therefore be assumed that the lessor is the owner in the discussion of this case.

A contract of lease as such is not a specific contract governed by mandatory rules of Dutch law. However, the agreement may sometimes be classified as either a rental agreement, particularly in the case of an operational lease, or as hire purchase, in particular the finance lease. Both the contracts of rent and hire purchase are subject to specific rules of Dutch law. Care should be taken in the process of classification, however, paying due regard to the particular facts of the case in question.

In most instances of the operational lease, the lessor is a 'normal' owner of the object of lease. Execution against the property by the lessee's creditors, in this case against the computer by B's creditors, would not be possible. The lessee has no real claim to the leased property whatsoever. If B, the lessee, fails to pay because he or she has become bankrupt, the lessor will be able to terminate the contract and rely on *rei vindicatio* to claim back the property.

With regard to finance leases, it is possible that the lessee will have a real claim to the leased property.[31] In particular, this would be the case when the contract of lease is regarded as one of hire purchase. The latter contract requires that ownership is to pass automatically to the buyer under the contract, B, after he or she has made all the periodical payments.[32] It is sometimes said that such contracts concern a situation where both the seller and the buyer have ownership: the lessor under a resolutive condition, the lessee under a suspensive condition.[33]

---

[30] Van Hees, *Leasing* 19–20.
[31] See the study by Van Hees, *Leasing*, in particular chapters 4 and 5, the latter addressing the situation of an unsecured creditor seeking to execute against the property as well as the situation of one of the parties being adjudicated bankrupt. A summary of the dissertation has been translated into English.
[32] Article 7A:1576h BW.
[33] This view is not without controversy; it implies the recognition of an *Anwartschaftsrecht*. See Van Hees, *Leasing* 98 ff.

In practice, most leases do not envisage the automatic transfer of ownership at the end of the term of lease. Usually, the lease is not a conditional transfer of ownership but only grants the lessee an option to buy the property at the end of the lease. This would in principle prevent the agreement from being classified as one of hire purchase.

(b) The Code defines the contract of hire purchase as a contract under which ownership automatically passes to the buyer/lessee at the end of the term of lease upon full payment (article 7A:1576h BW). This would normally imply the use of a retention of title clause and a conditional transfer. An option to buy the property instead of an automatic transfer would thus normally prevent the contract from being subject to the rules applicable to hire purchase. However, parties will not be allowed to circumvent these mandatory rules by agreeing that ownership will not pass automatically but only upon payment of a token price.[34]

(c) Lease agreements in various forms are quite common in practice.

Even though the lessor essentially assumes the position of a fiduciary owner, the lessor is not treated as a holder of a security right (*in rem*). In particular, unlike the holder of a charge or a pledge, the lessor is not obliged to execute against the property by means of a public sale nor is he or she under a duty to return any surplus if he or she was to sell the property. The latter may be different if the contract is regarded as one of hire purchase.[35]

It should be noted in this regard that a security transfer of ownership as such is prohibited by the Code.[36] This prohibition became of particular relevance in a case concerning a 'sale and lease-back' arrangement. The Supreme Court, however, saw no infringement of the Code's prohibition.[37] In the Court's view, the prohibition is essentially confined

---

[34] Pitlo/Reehuis/Heisterkamp, *Het Nederlands burgerlijk recht III* n. 975.
[35] Article 7A:1576A BW.
[36] Article 3:84(3) BW. Before the introduction of the new Civil Code in 1992, fiduciary transfers in combination with a *traditio constitutum possessorium* were the accepted means of creating a non-possessory security right. The fiduciary owner was, however, treated analogously to the holder of a pledge. Thus, he was not allowed to appropriate the property but was bound to execute by public sale and return any surplus realisation. The fiduciary ownership was difficult to reconcile with the closed system of real rights under Dutch law: ownership does not know these restrictions. The Civil Code introduced the silent or non-possessory pledge (and charge) which was to replace the fiduciary transfer. The prohibition underpins the closed system.
[37] *Hoge Raad* 19 May 1995, NJ 1996, 119 (*Sogelease*).

to preventing parties from creating real rights other than those recognised by the Code. As the parties did not intend to restrict the rights of the lessor as owner in any way, it was not regarded as a prohibited transfer.[38]

(d) The effects of the insolvency of the lessor depend on whether the lease concerned a conditional transfer (such as hire purchase or retention of title in general) or not. If it did, B as the lessee would have become the owner under a suspensive condition, whereas A would only have ownership under a resolutive condition. A's insolvency administrator would therefore only function as a conditional owner. A sale by the administrator would result only in the transfer of ownership under the same condition. Consequently, B's position would not be affected.[39]

Where the lease agreement does not involve a conditional transfer, the lessor would be regarded as having retained full title to the property. The lessee's claims would therefore be *in personam* only and B would not have any real right. A's insolvency administrator would therefore take free of any rights and B would in principle be left with a simple claim in insolvency.

It has been argued that the limited scope of ownership, i.e. security for debt, must have consequences for the owner and therefore also for his or her creditors.[40] In particular, third-party acquirers should be bound by the lease agreement. In other words, the lessee's claims should be accorded a degree of *droit de suite*.[41]

ENGLAND

(a) This is a straightforward transaction in English law. As the owner of the computer, A can assert its real rights in B's insolvency. A is not required to register its ownership.

(b) If B has an option to purchase, then the contract will be one of hire purchase. To a degree, English hire-purchase law treats the option as

---

[38] Vriesendorp, AA 1995, 872; Rank-Berenschot, NTBR 1995, 207.
[39] See *Hoge Raad* 25 May 1962, NJ 1962, 256. *Hoge Raad* 28 Apr. 1989, NJ 1990, 252 (*Puinbreker*). Transfer of the lease property by (a creditor of) the lessor will therefore often be combined with the assignment of the remaining payments to be made by the lessee.
[40] The lessor is in fact a fiduciary owner.
[41] See Van Hees, *Leasing* 143–145 and 208 (summary).

an item of property in its own right.⁴² Unless the contract excludes the possibility, B's insolvency administrator may take steps to perform the contract,⁴³ which the administrator will be disposed to do if the value of the computer exceeds the sum of remaining instalments.

The difference in English law between genuine hire purchase (where there is an option to purchase) and conditional sale (where ownership automatically vests at the end of the instalment plan) does not matter for insolvency purposes, but it does matter as regards the disposing power of the hirer/buyer. A hirer will have disposing power in respect only of motor vehicles (Part III Hire Purchase Act 1964), whereas a conditional buyer under a non-consumer transaction (Sale of Goods Act 1979, section 25) has disposing power in respect of all types of goods.⁴⁴

(c) This type of transaction is common: it has certain accountancy advantages. It is neither easier nor more difficult than conventional security, apart from the absence of any registration requirement in the case of lease and hire purchase.

(d) If A goes into *liquidation* (the insolvency proceedings applicable to companies), then, as discussed previously, this does not as such amount to a repudiation of the contract. A's insolvency administrator (*liquidator*) may choose to perform the contract if it is profitable. Otherwise the *liquidator* will disclaim the contract.⁴⁵ The consequence of this is that B will have to prove as an unsecured creditor in A's *liquidation*.

IRELAND

(a) The answers given in relation to case 10 basically apply here. The issue turns on whether there is a genuine lease of the computer and, *prima facie*, the question must be answered in the affirmative notwithstanding the fact that A, the financial institution, does not itself have any immediate economic need for the computer. Finance leasing is quite a common and well-established form of business financing. Neither the nature of the goods as computers nor the fact that the

---

⁴² See *Whiteley v Hilt* [1918] 2 KB 808; *Transag Haulage Ltd v Leyland DAF Finance plc* [1994] BCC 356.
⁴³ Insolvency is not as such a repudiation of the contract entitling the other party to terminate it: *Jennings' Trustee v King* [1952] 2 All ER 608.
⁴⁴ *Forthright Finance Ltd v Carlyle Finance Ltd* [1997] 4 All ER 90.
⁴⁵ S. 178 of the Insolvency Act 1986.

transaction is a three-party one demands a different analysis from that supplied in relation to case 10 above. The aforementioned principles still apply.

(b) The fact that B has an option to purchase the computer at the end of the contractual term does not fundamentally affect the analysis or the 'genuineness' of the transaction. In fact, 'hire purchase' under which consumer goods are rented for a period, at the end of which period the hirer has an option to purchase, has traditionally been the main method of consumer finance in Ireland. Often the option to purchase may be exercised for a trifling sum which is rolled up with the last rental payment. In economic substance, the consumer is paying the 'full' price of the asset over the duration of the contractual hiring period, but legal theory is different.

(c) It is difficult to generalise on this issue, but basically the Irish courts look sympathetically at both transactions of charge and finance leasing. Both forms of transaction are quite common and it is difficult to say that there is a discernible difference in judicial handling of the respective matters. Finance leases and hire-purchase transactions do not have to be registered.

(d) Basically, B can continue the contract in the event of A becoming insolvent. If, however, the contract is unduly onerous from A's point of view, then A's insolvency administrator (*liquidator*) can disclaim it, in which eventuality B would have to submit a claim in the insolvency proceedings applicable to A's estate (*liquidation*). The claim would be as an unsecured creditor for any loss suffered as a result of the discontinuance of the contract. The power to disclaim in the insolvency legislation is designed to facilitate the efficient and speedy administration of an insolvency estate.

SCOTLAND

(a) A is the owner of the computer. There was a valid contract of sale between S, the original owner, and A, and there is nothing to prevent ownership from passing. Delivery is not necessary.

(b) The example given is a straightforward 'finance lease'. In 'hire purchase' the arrangement is similar except that B has the right to acquire ownership from A. In hire-purchase contracts it might be argued that the contract between S and A is not a genuine contract of sale and that therefore ownership cannot pass without delivery. However, it is accepted (perhaps illogically) that in hire purchase the original sale is a valid contract of sale regulated by the Sale of Goods Act 1979. Hire-purchase arrangements do not have to be registered.

(c) Leasing and hire purchase are widely used for the acquisition of movables. If B is a natural person not involved in commerce,[46] then certain protections apply in his favour.[47]

(d) According to the common law, following Roman law, a contract of lease has no real effect. For immovable property the rule was changed by a statute of 1449[48] which provides that a lease of immovable property is a real right. Thus, for an immovable lease the lessee is protected against the insolvency of the owner. But this has never been extended to movables. The common law rule (i.e. the Roman rule) still applies. Thus, if A became bankrupt, A's insolvency administrator would be able to repossess the computer and sell it. That would leave B with a damages claim against the insolvency administrator, but of course that claim would not be paid in full.

SOUTH AFRICA

(a) This case describes a typical finance leasing transaction. The customer (B) selects a computer from the supplier (S) and requests the financing company (A) to buy the computer from the supplier and to transfer possession to him under a lease. The leasing contract can be construed either as a simple contract of lease or as a (disguised) hire-purchase contract. In any event, A remains the owner of the computer. Since finance leasing is not regulated by statute in South Africa, A's right does not depend on any further prerequisites.

(b) If the customer is granted an option to purchase the computer at the end of the contractual term, this is taken to be a strong factor in

---

[46] That is to say, in German, that he is not a *Kaufmann*. But Scots law does not have this concept in a general sense, and so has no word for it, though something like this concept is used in certain statutes.
[47] Currently the Consumer Credit Act 1974.   [48] Leases Act 1449 (still in force).

interpreting the contract as a simple lease rather than a hire-purchase agreement.

(c) As already stated, the finance leasing transaction can also be construed as a hire-purchase agreement between the finance company (A) and the customer (B), with the finance company (A) retaining title to the computer. A strong indication to this effect is if the contract contains a clause transferring ownership of the computer to the customer (B) at the end of the useful life of the computer. Since A retains ownership under both constructions, the courts' approach to leasing and to a security right in the form of retention of ownership is equally favourable to A. The only difference would be that in the case of a hire-purchase agreement, the hire-purchaser's/seller's (A's) ownership of the computer would, according to section 84 of the Insolvency Act, be replaced by a security right (a *tacit hypothec*) in his favour.[49]

(d) Once the computers have been delivered to B, the insolvency of the financial institution (A) will not affect the lease if the insolvency administrator has notified the lessee (B) that he intends to abide by the lease. In general, the insolvency of A has no other effect than to place the insolvency administrator in the shoes of the bankrupt, neither rescinding the obligations of either party, nor imposing new ones, nor anticipating the period of performance on either side. The insolvency administrator will for instance be bound if the lease contains an option for renewal: he will not be able to compel B to return the computer so long as B continues to pay his monthly rental. Since the insolvency administrator has title of the computer, he may sell it to an outsider. Such purchaser, however, steps into the shoes of the administrator and must allow B to remain in possession on the same terms if the administrator has elected to abide by the lease. If the administrator does not elect to abide by the lease and terminates it, notifying the lessee accordingly, the insolvency will take precedence over the lease and the computer can be claimed by the administrator on behalf of the creditors of A. The lessee will then have nothing but a claim for breach of contract against the estate of A.[50]

---

[49] See *supra*, case 3.
[50] See Smith, *The Law of Insolvency* 161–164; Smith/Sharrock, in: *The Law of South Africa XI* para. 175.

DENMARK

(a) According to a normal contract of leasing, A, the lessor, can claim ownership of the goods against the creditors of B, the lessee. The lessor's right does not depend on any further prerequisites other than the contract of leasing. If B is declared bankrupt and the rent is not paid, A can terminate the contract. The termination of the contractual obligations normally gives A a right to the difference between the sum of the remaining rentals to the end of the leasing period discounted up to termination and the value of the asset.

(b) If B has an option to buy the computer at the end of the contractual period, the agreement might be regarded as a contract of sale stipulating a reservation of title clause. But in practice the settlement should not differ from that mentioned in part (a).

(c) In Denmark, finance leasing cannot be said to be used instead of other security rights. It might be said that if a bank granted a loan to finance the purchase of the equipment, the bank would probably take a charge over the equipment or some other assets. But if B wishes to obtain the loan from another source, he would often prefer to have the equipment financed by a leasing company and in this case they would make a finance leasing agreement. Sale with a reservation of title clause in the contract is not very common in commercial relations.

It could not be said that the approach – either of the legislature or of the courts – to leasing is more favourable than their approach to security rights. However, leasing may carry certain tax advantages.

(d) If A is declared bankrupt, the estate has to respect the terms stipulated in the contract. Since the agreement in reality is a sort of loan agreement, the estate has no right to give notice of termination before the end of the contractual period. (Such a right is recognised in respect of some long-term contracts under section 61 of the Bankruptcy Act.)

SWEDEN

(a) The finance company, A, is the owner of the computer, since A has not transferred it to B without a reservation of title or right of rescission. Nor does there seem to be a clause providing that B shall automatically become owner of the computer when all payments are made. In such a case, the transaction would have been one of purchase, but reservation of title would most probably have been implied and A would still have had a real right, unless he had permitted B to dispose of the computer prior to full payment. It does not matter whether or not the lease corresponds to the expected useful life of the computer. Reservation of title is valid, even if the instalment period corresponds to the expected useful life of the goods, provided that the purchaser is not permitted to dispose of the goods prior to full payment. Since the computer never belonged to B, no requirement of publicity applies.[51] As there is no leasing legislation applicable to movables, and no general rules on the subject in the Bankruptcy Act, and no precedents, it is unclear whether a clause providing that the lessor can terminate the contract should the lessee go bankrupt is valid even if the insolvency administrator demands fulfilment.[52]

(b) If B has an option to buy the computer at the end of the contractual term, there is no doubt that A will be regarded as having retained title and will have a right of separation, when the option requires B to make payment immediately on the exercise of the option and prior to obtaining any power to dispose of the computer. Should B be entitled to exercise the option in circumstances where payment is deferred, but the entitlement to dispose is acquired immediately, it could be argued that the policies of the rules on reservation of title demand that A should not have a *ius separationis* (even during the period before the option is exercised). However, as stated previously, a commission principal has a *ius separationis* pursuant to section 53 of the Commission Agency Act even if the agent may buy the goods for himself; the statute is silent on the issues of deferred payment and the intermediate prohibition on disposals (see case 7(c)). Also, in these circumstances, an acquisition by the agent may be the ordinary termination. No Supreme Court case exists, but it may be assumed that the expectations of commercial life and the fact that the goods are not yet assigned will distinguish the case from perfected transfers with a void reservation of

---

[51] As to sale and lease-back, see *supra*, Swedish report, case 10. Tenants of immovable property are protected against the termination of their leases by a bankrupt landlord by legislation.

[52] Concerning leasing in general, see Möller, *Civilrätten vid finansiell leasing*.

title clause. In the preparatory works to the hire-purchase legislation in force, the existence of an option to buy is not (at least not generally) regarded as having the effect of transforming the agreement into one of purchase.[53]

(c) Finance leases, with the finance company standing between the supplier and the user of the goods, are frequently used instead of sale with reservation of title. The explanation is partly to be found in private law because some mandatory rules in the hire-purchase legislation do not apply (at least not directly) to leasing and partly due to tax considerations.

(d) Should the lessor, A, become bankrupt, the traditional point of departure, based on the Commercial Code from 1734, is that the lessee, B, has no protection against the insolvency creditors, resulting in an entitlement of the lessor's insolvency administrator to terminate the contract and leave the lessee with a non-preferential claim for damages. However, there is no Supreme Court precedent confirming this after 1905 (with the exception of a case concerning short-term operational leasing in 1975). In the literature many authors argue that the finance lessee should be protected against termination since the lease may be of great importance to him and because the contract of lease will normally be of the same value to the creditors as the goods that are the subject of it. Reference is also made to recent legislation under which the lease of a patent or a trademark, i.e. a licence, is binding on the lessor's creditors. It is possible that a finance lessee will be protected against termination by a decision of the Supreme Court, but the Court may choose to await a decision of the legislature on a pending committee report addressing this issue.[54] Should the lessee have a call option, there are additional arguments that he should be protected against termination. This situation seems akin to the situation where A has offered to sell some goods to B and has transferred possession of them to B; B then being able to accept the offer with effect also against A's insolvency creditors. Parallels could also be drawn with a binding hire-purchase contract, which the buyer may require to be fulfilled, despite the seller's insolvency.

---

[53] NJA II 1977, 163 and 1978, 6.   [54] SOU 1994:120. Such caution is often exercised.

FINLAND

(a) The lessor who has bought a computer to be leased to his or her client ('indirect leasing') is protected against other creditors of the lessee. The lessor is regarded as the owner of the computer.

(b) The lessor is protected against other creditors even if the lessee has an option to buy the computer. The most important consequence of an option to buy could be that the rules concerning instalment sales could be held to be applicable in some cases, especially when the purchase price at the end of the term would be essentially below the real value of the item.[55] Because the present case involves a lease for the expected useful life of the computer, the Instalment Sales Act *(laki osamaksukaupasta/lag om avbetalningsköp)* would not, most probably, be applicable. Even if this act did apply, A would be protected against B's creditors. B's creditors could execute against the computer, but A would enjoy the best preferential right to the proceeds of sale.[56]

(c) Retention of title is a common alternative to leasing. From the point of view of the supplier or the financier, leasing is a little more favourable than retention of title, because the Instalment Sales Act is not, normally, applicable to the leasing agreements. This act contains mandatory provisions that protect the buyer, especially when he or she breaches the contract. In a similar way, the provisions of the Consumer Protection Act *(kuluttajansuojalaki/konsumentskyddslag)*, protecting the consumer in credit sales, can normally be avoided by using leasing instead of retention of title. In practice, the contractual terms concerning the breach of finance leasing are, however, nowadays usually very similar to the corresponding provisions of the Instalment Sales Act or the Consumer Protection Act.[57]

(d) It has until recently been unclear whether the lessee is protected against the creditors of the lessor. The analogy to instalment sales could form the basis of an argument for the protection of the lessee. On the other hand, there is an ancient norm according to which the sale of a leased item 'breaches' the leasing contract. Some scholars regard this norm as still applicable to the lease of movables, though it ceased to

---

[55] See e.g. Tuomisto, *Omistuksenpidätys* 67 ff. and Wilhelmsson, *Suomen kuluttajansuojajärjestelmä* 233–234.
[56] See Finnish report, case 3(d).   [57] See also above, part (b).

be applied to the lease of immovables a long time ago.[58] The Finnish Supreme Court has quite recently, by a narrow majority, accepted the last-mentioned interpretation.[59]

Comparative observations

Part (a)

In all jurisdictions agreements such as the present one are regarded as perfectly valid leasing contracts and are commonly used for the financing of equipment. According to all legal systems, the lessor principally remains the owner of the computer and will be able to enforce his ownership should the lessee become bankrupt or should another creditor try to execute against the goods.

However, some jurisdictions require more than just a valid agreement between A and B. For example, in Greece and France, the leasing contract must be registered; otherwise the lessor's ownership of the goods will not be enforceable as against third parties. In Greece and France, registration also prevents *bona fide* acquisition of ownership in the goods. In Italy, the rules relating to retention of title are partly extended to leasing contracts. Therefore, the lessor will not be able to claim ownership of the goods as against third parties unless the contract is in writing and bears a 'certain date' (*data certa*) prior to insolvency or execution. Other means of proving that the contract is a leasing contract and that the lessor has remained the owner of the goods will not be admitted by the courts. In Belgium, leasing companies also must observe a number of requirements when establishing and performing leasing contracts, such as, for instance, the marking of the goods. However, non-compliance does not render invalid either the contract or the lessor's rights in the goods. The rules are only of an administrative nature: companies which do not observe them might lose their entitlement to engage in the leasing business.

Part (b)

If finance leasing is regulated by statute, the statute usually contains a provision to the effect that the lessee must be given the option to purchase the goods on the expiration of the lease. This is the case in

[58] See e.g. Kartio, *Esineoikeuden perusteet* 220.   [59] See KKO 1997:6.

Greek, Portuguese, French and Spanish law. If finance leasing is not regulated by statute, it is normal commercial practice to include such an option for the benefit of the lessee (Germany, Italy, South Africa, Sweden).

Often, the question of whether the parties have included a purchase option or whether ownership will automatically vest in the lessee at the end of the rental period will be relevant to the characterisation of the contract. According to Dutch, Swedish and Finnish law, a clause that transfers ownership automatically to the lessee will render the contract a hire-purchase agreement under which both lessor and lessee are somehow regarded as owners; the first under a resolutive condition, the second under a suspensive condition. Other jurisdictions regard a purchase option as an essential element of a leasing contract. This is not only the case under Greek, Portuguese, French and Spanish law, where the purchase option is accorded to the lessee *ex lege*, but it is also true for Belgium and South Africa. On the other hand, there are a number of legal systems which take the opposite view, that an option to buy the goods makes the agreement one of hire purchase (England, Ireland, Scotland) or makes it begin to approximate an instalment sale under retention of title (Italy, Denmark, Sweden, Finland), provided that the price is significantly lower than the expected residual value of the goods. Under the Nordic systems, such a characterisation may lead to difficulties if the lessee is permitted to resell the commodity prior to full payment (see Swedish report and case 4). Otherwise, it does not seem to make any practical difference if the contract is considered to be one of hire purchase (see English, Irish and Scots reports). In some jurisdictions the exact nature of the contract may also have consequences for the applicability of consumer legislation, especially legislation enacting the EU Directive on consumer credit.[60]

Part (c)

Finance leasing, especially sale and lease-back transaction, can evidently perform the same economic function as that served by a secured loan. In jurisdictions which prohibit or limit the use of non-possessory security

---

[60] Council Directive of 22 Dec. 1986 for the approximation of the laws, regulations and administrative provisions of the Member States concerning Consumer Credit 87/102/EEC, O.f. 1987 L 42/48.

rights, or place them under requirements such as registration, questions of consistency within a legal system may arise if the treatment of leasing contracts is more permissive. In Portugal and Italy, for example, where security ownership is regarded as invalid, leasing agreements have to be distinguished from such invalid transactions and may themselves be held invalid if a court finds that what on its face appears as a sale and lease-back transaction is really a security transfer of ownership. Austrian law, on the other hand, seems to see no problem in giving full effect to leasing contracts while regarding security ownership to be invalid. Belgian law has reduced, but not eliminated, its former inconsistencies by fully recognising the validity of retention of title, including in circumstances of the buyer's insolvency. But as the Belgian report states, it continues to regard leasing more favourably than security rights in movables generally. The same is true for Dutch law, which honours sale and lease-back transactions despite the express prohibition of security transfer of ownership. This again demonstrates that Dutch courts do not seem to take this prohibition seriously. In English and Irish law, too, leasing is treated more favourably than the creation of a charge which under certain circumstances requires registration. Nevertheless, there does not seem to be a clear dividing line between the two kinds of transactions.

Part (d)

The majority of jurisdictions (France, Italy, the Netherlands, England, Ireland, Scotland, South Africa, Finland and Germany, the latter subject to certain exceptions) apply the usual rules on contracts that are not yet fully performed: the insolvency administrator can decide whether or not to continue the contract. The decision will be taken in accordance with the interests of the insolvency creditors. The lessee does not enjoy any special protection nor is he given any real right that he could invoke against the administrator. If the administrator terminates the contract, the lessee will have to return the commodity and he will be a mere insolvency creditor with a claim for damages. The other jurisdictions take the opposite view: they do not allow the lessor's insolvency administrator to discontinue the contract, at least for as long as the lessee is not in default of payment. This is the rule in Greece, Austria, Portugal, Belgium, Spain and Denmark. In Sweden, this view predominates in legal literature, but there is no Supreme Court decision to this effect.

It is hard to see any pattern in this division. The distinction cuts across the usual division of jurisdictions into legal families, with Germany on one side and Greece and Austria on the other, France and Italy differing from Portugal, Belgium and Spain, and even Finland adopting a different solution to that of Denmark and the Swedish majority view. Also, the solution does not seem to depend on whether a jurisdiction has set up a special statutory regime for leasing contracts (compare France to Greece or Portugal).

Case 15: Indebted businessman sells business to brother

(Liability of purchaser of a business for pre-existing debts – actio Pauliana)

A operates a business as a sole trader. Bank B lends money to A. The loan is unsecured. On 1 July, A defaults on his loan payments. On 1 September, B executes against the business assets. It transpires that these assets were, in early July, sold to A's brother, C. A continued, however, to run the business. The purchase price was in fact paid and was a fair market price.

Questions

(a) Can B still execute against the business assets?
(b) Can B have the sale between A and C set aside?
(c) Would the answers to parts (a) and (b) change if the price paid was well below a fair market price?

Discussions

GERMANY

(a) According to § 25 HGB, the purchaser of a business is liable for previous debts of that business if the business is continued under the same name. This liability can be excluded by means of an agreement between the parties to the contract of sale. Such an exclusion will be valid as against third parties (i.e. former creditors), provided that either it is entered on the commercial register and published, or the creditors are notified individually of it (§ 25 s. 2 HGB). The crucial requirement for this liability under § 25 HGB to arise is the continued use of the old name of the firm;[1] although minor changes to the name will be ignored for these purposes.

If in the present case, C continues to use the former name of the business, he will, together with A, be jointly liable for all the debts which A has previously incurred for the purposes of this business. This will include the credit advanced by B, if the loan was made for the business. C's liability is not limited to a ceiling determined by the value of the business purchased.[2] B can execute against the assets used in the business as well as against C's other property, provided that he obtains a judgment against C. A judgment against A, which B has acquired before C has purchased A's business, can be altered so as to be enforceable against C under an accelerated procedure (§§ 729 s. 2, 727 ZPO). If, however, C does not continue to use the former name of the business, § 25 HGB does not apply. So far as the applicability of § 25 HGB is concerned, it does not matter whether A or C runs the business. Equally, the amount paid for the business is irrelevant.

(b) In addition to the possibility of purchasers' liability, discussed above, B may also be able to avoid the contract between A and C according to § 3 s. 2 AnfG. According to this provision, a creditor may avoid contracts that the debtor has concluded with a close relative (the relatives in question being enumerated in § 138 InsO) if such a contract is designed directly to prejudice creditors. A contract may not be avoided if it was concluded more than two years before the point at which avoidance is sought or if, at the moment the contract was concluded, the other party to it (C) was ignorant of the debtor's (A's) intention to prejudice his creditors.

C, as A's brother, is a closely related person pursuant to § 3 s. 1 AnfG (see § 138 InsO). Since the contract between A and C was concluded only two months ago, an action will not be time-barred (§ 3 s. 1 AnfG). B need only prove that the contract prejudiced A's creditors. It is for C to establish that he was ignorant of such an intent.

---

[1] BGH 29 Nov. 1956, BGHZ 22, 234 (236); BGH 1 Dec. 1986, NJW 1987, 1633 (note K. Schmidt); BGH 17 Sep. 1991, NJW 1992, 12 (113); Baumbach/Hopt, *Handelsgesetzbuch* § 25 HGB n. 7. For a critical assessment of this criterion see K. Schmidt, *Handelsrecht* § 8 II 1(c).

[2] BGH 29 June 1955, BB 1955, 652; Baumbach/Hopt, *Handelsgesetzbuch* § 25 HGB n. 10; contra: Canaris, *Die Vertrauenshaftung im deutschen Privatrecht* 186.

Whilst an action under § 3 s. 2 AnfG would not be possible if C was not A's close relative, or if more than two years had elapsed, avoidance could still be sought pursuant to § 3 s. 1 AnfG. Here, the limitation period is ten years and, again, A must have acted with the intention to prejudice his creditors. Under this provision, however, it falls to B to prove that the other party to the contract (C) knew of this intent.

(c) An abnormally low price may be of evidential value when seeking to establish that B had the intention of prejudicing other creditors and that the counter-party knew this.

AUSTRIA

(a) C is liable for A's debts on the basis of § 1409 ABGB. According to § 1409 ABGB, the acquirer of a business or of the entirety of a person's assets is liable[3] for the debts of that business or person.[4] This liability includes only those debts that the acquirer knew of, or should have known of,[5] when the business or the assets were handed over to him. This is a personal liability; it is not restricted to the business or the assets. The liability is, however, limited in quantum to the value of the business or the assets acquired.[6] The debtor (i.e. A) remains liable, notwithstanding the possibility of the purchaser's liability.

If C continues to use the former name of the firm, he will also be liable because of § 25 HGB. According to § 25 HGB, the person who takes over control of a business is liable for the debts of the business, if the acquirer continues to use the former name of the business. This liability can be excluded by an agreement between the transferor and transferee, provided this agreement is made public by entry on the Companies Register.

(b) It is possible that the sale of A's business will be regarded as a fraudulent transaction to the disadvantage of his creditors. In such a case, B

---

[3] This liability cannot be excluded by an agreement between the debtor and the acquirer: cf. § 1409 (3) ABGB.

[4] By purchasing the assets C acquires A's business.

[5] This has to be proven by the creditor, unless the person who takes over the business or the assets is a close relative of the debtor: § 1409 (2) ABGB.

[6] The liability is reduced by payments to the creditors made from the purchase monies paid for the business or the assets (cf. OGH, 13 Jan. 1983, SZ 56/6; OGH 20 Dec. 1994, ÖBA 1995, 475).

would be able to avoid the transaction in accordance with § 2 (a) AnfO (*Anfechtungsordnung*), provided that A had the intention to defraud his creditors.[7]

(c) If the price is abnormally low § 2 (b) AnfO could apply.[8]

GREECE

(a) If the assets have been sold and transferred to C, B can execute against the assets which are not owned by the debtor pursuant to article 479 A.K. According to this article, C is liable towards B for A's debts burdening his property or his enterprise to the extent of the value of the assets contractually transferred by A, since they constitute the entirety of A's property or of his enterprise. It is disputed whether the new owner is liable *cum viribus* or *pro viribus*. The provision, which has as its aim the protection of creditors, has been strongly criticised, as it may burden the new owner excessively. In this case of *ex lege* cumulative assumption, it is not a prerequisite that C knew of A's debts. It is sufficient that the acquirer is aware of the fact that the transferred assets constitute the entirety of the transferor's property or of his enterprise.

(b) The transactions could be void as simulated (article 138 A.K.). According to the prevailing view in jurisdiction and amongst scholars,[9] if the recipient of the simulated declaration is not aware of the simulation (mental reservation), the juridical act is valid (see article 139 A.K.). But if C was aware that A's declaration was simulated, the transfer of ownership is void and B can execute against the assets. Alienations may be contested according to articles 939–946 A.K., the *actio Pauliana* of Roman law, if: (1) the alienation caused insolvency of the debtor (that is, his inability to pay his creditors); (2) it was made with an intention of prejudicing the creditors; (3) the transferee was aware of this intention. The action to contest the alienation must be brought within five years of the

---

[7] See Austrian report, case 11 (Variation).
[8] § 28 N 4 KO refers to transactions where the debtor sold goods at dumping prices. Such a transaction can be avoided if it took place within a year before avoidance is sought, provided the buyer had to know that these were transactions by which goods were sold at dumping prices to the disadvantage of the seller's creditors.
[9] AP 262/1967 NoV 15,1038; AP 265/1967 NoV 15,1040; Balis, *Genikai Archai tou Astikou Dikaiou* 40; Simantiras, *Genikes Arches tou Astikou dikaiou* n. 705; Karakatsanis, in: Georgiadis/Stathopoulos 138–139 n. 4; *contra* Papantoniou, *Genikes Arches tou Astikou Dikaiou* 379; Spyridakis, *Genikes Arches* n. 198.

alienation being made. Gratuitous alienations can be contested without knowledge on the part of the transferee (article 942 A.K.). Such knowledge will also be presumed, in the case of an onerous alienation, when the third party is the spouse of the debtor, or a close relative as defined by law (article 941 § 2 A.K.). Since C was A's brother, knowledge will be presumed (a presumption that can be rebutted) for a period of one year from the alienation. The effects of the action to contest are limited to the parties to it. The third party, to whom an item of property has been transferred, is obliged to restore the *status quo ante*. The ambiguity of the provision has given rise to many theoretical disputes as to its meaning. If the alienation is successfully contested, however, C, though a third party, cannot resist the execution against the assets (article 936 § 3 KPolD).

(c) The abnormally low price can simply evidence the simulated nature of the transaction (article 138 A.K.), or the fact that the alienation which caused A's insolvency was carried out with an intention of prejudicing the creditors (article 939 A.K.). The burden of proof will obviously be much easier to discharge when the price paid was abnormally low.[10]

FRANCE

(a) Once the assets have been transferred to a third party, B cannot execute against them unless he manages to have the transfer of the assets set aside in court, on the basis of a specific action, the *actio Pauliana* (*action Paulienne*).

(b) This action is defined in C. civ, article 1167. It provides a means of protection for creditors, against their debtors' deceptive attempts to reduce their estates by transferring assets to third parties. This is the civil remedy parallel to the criminal offence of the fraudulent preparation of insolvency. The *action Paulienne* is brought by a creditor against a third party who has benefited from the fraud of the debtor. The plaintiff must establish that he has suffered personal and direct loss from the transaction. The case law has developed the following requirements:

(1) The plaintiff must show that he attempted to obtain payment of the debt, or performance of the obligation, from the debtor directly, without success.

---

[10] Banakas, in: Georgiadis/Stathopoulos 939 n. 38.

(2) If the debt consists of a payment of money, the amount must be ascertainable and the debt enforceable.
(3) The fraud must have occurred after the debt arose. If the debt is contractual, the agreement must be dated.
(4) The plaintiff must show that his loss results directly from the deceptive transaction. If the transferred assets were already subject to a charge, for instance, no loss arises, since the creditor could not have had recourse to them in any event.
(5) It is not necessary that the debtor intended to prejudice the creditor; it is sufficient that he had actual knowledge of the loss or damage caused by his act, i.e., the diminution of his estate.

Finally, the creditor who brings this action does so on his own behalf. Thus, if he is successful, creditors will not benefit generally. If a court decision sets aside the agreement and orders the retransfer of the assets, they will not pass into the initial debtor's estate, where they could be subjected to execution by other creditors or be comprised within the insolvency estate (if insolvency proceedings have been commenced).[11] The assets will pass directly to the successful creditor, in order to satisfy his claim.

(c) In principle, an *action Paulienne* will succeed only if the deceptive transaction resulted in the diminution of the debtor's estate. This requirement would not appear to be met when a normal price was paid to the debtor. This criterion, however, has been interpreted in a fairly broad way by the courts. Even when the sale price was a market one, the sale could still be declared void if it resulted in the sale of assets and their substitution for assets which are easier to hide and conceal, such as money, provided of course that this was done with the intention to prejudice creditors.[12] Moreover, the third party must have known of the prejudice that the transaction would cause to creditors.

An *action Paulienne* has been upheld in circumstances where the debtor was allotted shares in a company in return for the transfer of assets, which caused prejudice to his creditors.[13] However, the creditor had to prove that the other shareholders knew about the member's insolvency.[14]

In the present case, if B was able to prove that both A and A's brother (C) knew that the sale of assets would cause prejudice to B (this was

---

[11] Com 8 Oct. 1996, JCPédE II 914, note Guyon.
[12] Civ. (1), 18 Feb. 1971, Bull civ I, No 56; D 1972, 53, note Agostini; Civ. (1), 18 July 1995, Bull civ I, No 324; D 1996, 391, note Agostini.
[13] Civ. 14 Feb. 1995, JCPédE Pan, 417.   [14] Paris 8 May 1939, S 1939, 2, 132.

clearly so, since the sale took place shortly after he defaulted), the sale could be declared void by the court and the business assets would be used for the exclusive benefit of B. The fact that the price paid was a fair one would not alter this, so long as B can show that the money paid is no longer in A's hands to repay the loan (that is, it was dissipated).

Naturally, when the price paid was abnormally low, it is easier to establish that there was fraud on the part of the debtor and that the third party knew of it. However, a very low price is not of itself conclusive. A low price could, for example, be justified by the familial relationships of the parties.[15] So long as the transaction is a transfer for consideration, as opposed to a gift, the creditor must prove that the third party knew of the fraud.

BELGIUM

(a) According to the general principle of article 2279 C.civ., creditors may assume that the debtor is the owner of the assets in his possession. Creditors can therefore execute against the goods found in the possession of their debtor without having to prove that the debtor is the owner.[16]

(b) The execution can be challenged by C by means of a *rei vindicatio* (article 1514 Judiciary Code). Whether this action will be successful is questionable. Although the transfer of property is in principle valid as from the agreement between the parties without the need for delivery, third parties with conflicting rights can seek protection under the principle of article 2279 C.civ. when the seller remains in possession of the goods (see Belgian report, case 1). In the given circumstances, the creditors could argue that the principle of the protection of third parties in good faith cannot be challenged by an agreement which is clearly not a normal business transaction. When the purpose of the sale was to infringe the rights of creditors, the contract can also be challenged on the basis of the *actio Pauliana* (see Belgian report, case 11).

(c) The price paid is certainly relevant to the determination of the genuineness of the transaction. The same goes for the reality of the payment. If there is uncertainty about whether payment has actually been made, or if the price paid is below the normal market value, the creditors could

---

[15] Civ. (1), 27 June 1984, Bull civ I, No 211.
[16] Cass. 10 June 1976, Pas 1976, I, 1101, RW 1976–77, 601.

additionally argue that the agreement between A and C is a 'simulated' transaction, which can be set aside by third parties on the basis of article 1321 C.civ. If it can be ascertained that the purpose of the parties was to allow A to escape from his creditors, the sale can be declared void by the *actio Pauliana* (article 1167 C.civ.). Under these circumstances, the amount paid is of no importance.

PORTUGAL

(a) A has transferred his business to his brother, C. B cannot therefore execute against the business, because it will now be regarded as belonging to C. If B executes against the business, C can resist the execution by the *embargos de terceiro* proceedings.

(b) The only ways by which B may seek to set aside the agreement between A and C are a nullity action or an *actio Pauliana*.

In fact, if B establishes that the agreement between A and C is a sham, pursued with the intention to defraud creditors, B will be entitled to a nullity action on the ground that the transaction is a simulated one (article 240° C.C.). This action, if granted by the court, renders the act of transfer from A to C of no effect (article 605° C.C.). However, in order to be successful, B must prove that the sale was a sham and that both parties had the intention of deceiving A's creditors, which could be difficult in the present situation.

Apart from the nullity action, if B establishes that the sale was pursued with intention to defraud creditors, and A has no other assets against which he can execute, he could be entitled to an *actio Pauliana* (article 610° C.C.), on the ground of fraud to creditors (*fraus creditorum*). As stated in the Variation to case 11, this action, if successful, would force C to deliver to the creditor who brought it the assets that he has acquired from the debtor (or their value). It further allows the creditor to execute against these assets in order to enforce this obligation (article 616° C.C.). However, as sale is an onerous transfer, B will have to establish before the court that C was aware of the damage caused to A's creditors (article 612° C.C.). This may be difficult to do in a case such as this.

(c) The fact that the price paid was well below the market price does not change the analysis under part (a). In relation to part (b), the only difference would be that the court would presume, on the facts of this case, that there was an intention by both parties to defraud or deceive A's creditors, which makes it easier for B to establish the actions considered.

SPAIN

(a) B cannot execute against the business assets because C is the new owner.

(b) B may have the sale set aside, but only if he can produce evidence that there was a fraudulent agreement between A and C intended to harm B's rights of collection. According to article 1111 CC and STS of 28 Nov. 1997, the following prerequisites have to be fulfilled: (1) that the debt exists and is legitimate; (2) that the goods have been transferred to C; and (3) that there was an intentional fraud on the part of the seller (A) and the buyer (C). These prerequisites are evaluated by the judge. In the present case, the fact that A still runs the business and that the buyer is his brother may be considered circumstantial evidence in the determination of fraud. Another key element in this determination would be whether A can prove that he used C's payment to pay his debts to creditors other than B, or if in fact he claims no longer to have money from C's payment and thus cannot pay B.[17]

The *acción Pauliana* (or *revocatoria*) is set out in article 1111 CC. The creditors, having tried to execute against the goods of their debtor, and finding them either dissipated or inadequate to meet their claims, can contest any acts which the debtor may have carried out to reduce or dissipate his assets in order to defraud their collecting rights.

The *actio Pauliana* is an action against the person. It is not aimed at a specific asset of the debtor, but rather has the effect, if successful, of revoking acts or contracts of the debtor which reduce his credit standing with regard to his creditors. Such acts on the part of the debtor are regarded as illicit if they have been carried out to defraud the creditors (articles 1297 and 1111 CC). On the one hand, article 1297 CC presumes that contracts are fraudulent if: (1) the debtor disposes of his property without receiving payment; or (2) the debtor, although disposing of his property in exchange for payment, has previously been sentenced by court ruling or if a writ of embargo on the debtor's goods has been issued by the court. On the other hand, article 1292

---

[17] See Rodríguez Vela, in: Consejo General del Poder Judicial 59.

CC sets out that payments made by the debtor during insolvency which cannot be enforced against the debtor at the time of making them are rescindable.

For the creditor to bring the *actio Pauliana*, it is necessary that he proves: (1) that his credit with the debtor arises from an agreement prior to the date on which the fraudulent act or contract was carried out; (2) that it is an act or a contract that is legally valid, complying with the formal and material requirements demanded by law for it to be valid; and (3) that the creditor's debt has fallen due.[18]

The creditor may bring the *actio Pauliana* to rescind any acts (charges, waivers, etc.) or contracts which the debtor may have entered into and which potentially diminish his financial capacity to meet his existing debts. The *actio Pauliana* can give rise to a partial revocation only. It will only operate to rescind to the extent necessary to avoid the losses that the creditor would otherwise suffer as a result of such a debtor's act or contract.[19]

The creditor, his heirs or his succession executors can bring an *actio Pauliana* within the time-span of four years, starting from the day of the fraudulent disposal. A suspension and subsequent extension of that time period is not allowed (article 1299 CC). The creditor has to be affected by the debtor's acts of disposal, that is, there must be a causal relationship between the loss to the creditor and the debtor's acts. It is not necessary, however, for the debtor to be declared insolvent for the *actio Pauliana* to be brought. It is sufficient that the debtor, by carrying out an act or entering into a contract, prejudiced the collecting rights of the creditor in question. This is to be assessed by considering whether it is reasonably foreseeable, as a result of the act or contract, that, at the time the creditor's debt falls due, he will be unable to find sufficient assets in his debtor's estate for its satisfaction.

It is not necessary for the creditor to produce evidence of the debtor's intention to defraud. Since intention is a subjective element and thus difficult to prove, it is enough for the creditor to produce evidence that the debtor knew of the possible loss which he might cause his creditor by his fraudulent conduct. Such knowledge may become more evident from the debtor's acts carried out subsequent to debts which have previously been incurred; but in the case of the debtor having disposed of assets

---

[18] See Díez-Picazo, *Fundamentos de derecho civil patrimonial* II 735.
[19] Garrido de Palma, in: *Diccionario Jurídico Espasa* 15.

in favour of a third party before the emergence of the creditor's right to credit, this creditor can only bring the *actio Pauliana* if he produces clear evidence that the previous disposal of assets was planned beforehand by his debtor with the aim of preventing the future creditor from collecting what would be due to him later.

c) According to the Civil Code, the fact that the price was well below a fair market price would not change the validity of the transaction between A and C, and so this transaction would be upheld. Despite this, that fact could be used as circumstantial evidence in the determination of fraud. The only exception to this would be, according to article 321 CDCC, a case in which the goods constituted real estate (and the sale was not governed by commercial law), when A could request that his contract with C be declared null and void by the judge, if the amount paid by C was less than half the fair market price. Notwithstanding this, article 322 CDCC would not grant to B the right to sue for the rescission of the contract between A and C to be effected, even if the amount paid by C was less than half the fair market price. Nevertheless, the fact that the amount paid by C to A was less than half the fair market price could also be used as circumstantial evidence in determining whether or not there had been fraud.

ITALY

(a) Whether execution can proceed against the assets sold to the buyer, which remain on the business premises of the seller, depends in general on the rules concerning the effects of the transfer of assets *vis-à-vis* creditors. The *data certa* requirement, which was mentioned above in case 3, is just one such rule. Other rules concern claims, registrable movables and immovables. They are all contained in article 2914 of the Civil Code. With reference to movables which are on the debtor's premises, sale is ineffective *vis-à-vis* an executing creditor, unless it is proved by an act which has a certain date antedating execution. The sale of registrable movables and of immovables is effective against creditors only if it is registered on the relevant public register prior to execution. Assignment of claims must be notified to the *debitor cessus*, or accepted by him, by an act that has a certain date prior to execution, except in the case of assignments to factors, or in case of other special laws.

Here, however, we are not dealing with the sale of any single asset that is instrumental to the business activity, but with the entire going concern (*azienda*).[20] In such a case, special rules apply. The sale of an ongoing concern must be evidenced in writing, or be concluded by a notarised act, or by a written document with notarised signatures, if such formalities are prescribed for the sale of assets which are part of the going concern. A notarised act or a document with notarised signatures is required to register the contract on the commercial register within thirty days from its date (article 2556 c.c., as amended by the Law of 12 August 1993, n. 310, article 6). Article 2560 c.c. establishes that the buyer of the going concern shall be liable for claims incurred by the seller before the sale, if such claims are related to the business, provided that they are evidenced by annotations in the books that every entrepreneur is legally obliged to keep. Article 2560 c.c. also provides that the seller shall be jointly liable with the buyer in respect of creditors for the claims incurred before the sale, unless the creditors agree that liability should rest with the buyer alone.

In this case, therefore, B can execute against C's business assets (as well as against other assets belonging to C).

(b) Quite apart from the right to proceed to execution on the basis of article 2560 c.c., B may be able to set aside the sale with the revocatory action of article 2901 c.c., mentioned in the Variation to case 11. If the revocatory action is successful, the sale, though effective as between the parties, will be without effect in respect of the creditor, who may then proceed with execution. In the present case, it is likely that the requirements of the revocatory action are satisfied. The seller is likely to be aware of the prejudice caused by the sale to his creditors' rights, given the timing of the sale. If it is assumed that the debtor's brother is close to him, it can probably also be assumed that he knew that the sale was prejudicial to creditors. That the price of the sale was fair may point to a different conclusion. Yet, court decisions and authors hold that the substitution of assets with monies may be prejudicial to creditors, especially if those monies have been dissipated, or invested by the debtor into assets of no objective value.[21]

---

[20] See the definition of *azienda* in article 2555 c.c.
[21] Cass. 22 Mar. 1990, n. 2400, Fallimento, 1990, 790; Cass. 9 July 1979, n. 3925, Dir. fall., 1979 II, 453; Vassalli, Giur. comm. 1974 I, 289; Lucchini Guastalla, *Danno e frode nella revocatoria ordinaria* 170 ff., 187 ff., 286 ff.

(c) If the sale price is abnormally low, the presumption is that both parties intended to prejudice creditors. Therefore, the revocatory action is more likely to be successful.

THE NETHERLANDS

(a) The basic principle is that creditors only have recourse against the assets of their debtor.[22] Consequently, after the transfer of ownership to the brother, C, the business assets are in principle beyond the reach of A's creditors. The fact that A continues to run the business is, for these purposes, immaterial.

An exception to this principle is that a transaction may be avoided on grounds that it is fraudulent or preferential: *actio Pauliana*. If avoided, the assets are deemed never to have left the ownership of the debtor, allowing A's creditors to execute against them.

(b) The requirements for a successful action for avoidance have been set out above.[23] Assuming that the agreement was entered into by A without an obligation arising from law or contract, the question turns on whether the transaction with the brother, C, resulted in detriment to creditor B and whether A and C knew, or ought to have known, that this would be the result. As to this latter issue, a rebuttable presumption that both the debtor and the transferee were fixed with this knowledge arises in respect of transactions with siblings or any family member up to the third degree.[24] As to the question of detriment, a transaction may result in detriment even when the transaction was for a fair value or price. If the debtor subsequently has placed that value beyond the reach of his or her creditors, it may constitute detriment for the purposes of the *actio Pauliana*.[25]

(c) A transaction at undervalue would directly result in detriment to A's other creditors, in contrast to a transaction under which fair value was given. Furthermore, a transaction at a manifest undervalue raises a presumption of mutual knowledge of detriment on the part of the debtor and transferee. In this particular case, it would however make no difference. The fact that ownership of the business assets was transferred to A's brother (C) results in the same presumption being raised.[26]

[22] Article 3:276 BW. [23] See *supra*, Dutch report, case 11. [24] Article 3:46(1°) BW.
[25] See *Hoge Raad* 22 May 1992, NJ 1992, 526 (*Montana I*).
[26] Article 3:46(1°) and (3°)(a) BW and Article 42(1°) and (3°)(a) Fw.

ENGLAND

(a) The limits on executing against assets not owned by the debtor have already been discussed above.[27] Nothing in this case affects the general rules regarding the exigibility of goods by a bailiff (*sheriff*) when executing judgment.

(b) In English law, there is no good reason to set aside the sale. Unlike the United States and most Canadian common law jurisdictions, English law has never had provisions for invalidating bulk sales, that is, block sales of a trader's stock and other assets out of the ordinary course of business that leave him with more liquid assets (money) and so facilitate evasion of his creditors. The transaction is not a sale at an undervalue.[28] This means also that it cannot be treated as a fraudulent conveyance.[29] Finally, as stated above,[30] there is no principle of reputed ownership that would allow creditors and insolvency officers, in the event of insolvency proceedings, to execute against assets in the possession of the insolvent trader.[31]

(c) If there is an undervalue element, the transaction can be challenged and a (discretionary) order made which can take due account of the purchaser's legitimate interests.[32]

IRELAND

(a) The facts do not state that the bank has taken security over the assets in question. If the bank has no security then its claim is simply a personal claim against A which might be satisfied out of the proceeds generated by a sale of the business. B cannot execute against the business assets because these belong now to C.

---

[27] See English report, case 2.
[28] Ss. 339, 341 of the Insolvency Act 1986. See English report, case 11.
[29] Under s. 423 of the Insolvency Act 1986. See English report, case 11.
[30] See English report, cases 4 and 7.
[31] Before the insolvency legislation of the 1980s, there used to be a provision in the case of *bankruptcy* (but not company *liquidation*) that called for the distribution by the *trustee-in-bankruptcy* of assets that 'at the commencement of the bankruptcy [were] in the possession, order or disposition of the bankrupt, in his trade or business, by the consent and permission of the true owner, under such circumstances that he is the reputed owner thereof' (Bankruptcy Act 1914, s. 38(e)).
[32] Under ss. 342 and 425 of the Insolvency Act 1986.

CASE 15: INDEBTED BUSINESSMAN SELLS TO BROTHER 637

(b) As a general proposition, payments made by a company or individual in the six-month period prior to the commencement of insolvency proceedings (*liquidation* or *bankruptcy*, respectively) may be set aside if the effect of the payment was to give the recipient an advantage over other creditors and there was an intention to prefer. The overall aim of the legislation is to create a level playing field among creditors, and preferential payments have the effect of disrupting the equilibrium. There are three conditions which must be met before a payment can be set aside:

(1) The impugned act must have taken place at a time when the company was unable to pay its debts as they became due from its own monies.
(2) The act must have been done in favour of any creditor of the company with a view to giving such creditor, or any surety or guarantor for the debt due to such creditor, a preference over the other creditors.
(3) The act must have been done voluntarily as distinct from being coerced by pressure.

It is difficult to see, however, how this provision would operate in the context under discussion nor does the transaction appear to be one which A has entered into for the purpose of defeating, hindering or delaying his creditors.

(c) The analysis is generally the same but if the sale is at an abnormally low price it may put C on notice that there is something suspicious about the transaction.

As stated, transactions which have the effect of giving one creditor an advantage over other creditors may be set aside if they take place within a certain period prior to the commencement of insolvency proceedings (the suspect period) and provided also that certain other conditions are fulfilled. More generally, transactions entered into for the purpose of defrauding creditors may be set aside. The court may order a person to return property of a bankrupt which was disposed of in order to perpetrate a fraud on the bankrupt's creditors. The jurisdiction of the court arises where the transferor intended to defeat, hinder or delay his creditors. A transfer will, however, be upheld where it is made upon good consideration and *bona fide* to a person not having knowledge of the transferor's objective. In this particular example, even though the sale was below a fair market price it would still, for the purposes of the law, be regarded as being made for 'good consideration'. The essential question is whether C is acting *bona fides*. The low price may serve to put him on notice that the transaction is not above board and thereby affect his *bona fides*.

SCOTLAND

(a) Probably not. The assets do not now belong to B's debtor. Scots law does not have any general principle whereby a person who purchases a business becomes liable for the business debts of the seller. (In some cases where there is a transfer from a sole trader to a partnership of which the former sole trader is a member, or a transfer from a partnership to another partnership with similar membership, it has been held that there is an assumption of liability. But the law in this area is obscure, and it has never been held that there is an assumption of liability where there is a transfer from one sole trader to another.[33]) Even if C were liable, B would have to obtain a decree against C before execution against C's assets would be competent.

(b) No. Scots law divides the *actio Pauliana* into two parts: see case 11. Under the law of 'gratuitous alienations', a juridical act may be open to attack if it had the effect of diminishing the net value of the debtor's estate (patrimony). That has not happened here, for A's estate has the same value as before; all that has happened is that instead of assets of one kind he has assets of another kind, of the same value. Under the law of 'unfair preferences', certain kinds of acts in favour of a preferred creditor (such as the giving of security for a previously unsecured loan) may be open to attack. But C was not a creditor.

(c) Yes. If this was a sale at undervalue this would be a gratuitous alienation, for A's estate would have been diminished to the extent of the undervalue. A gratuitous alienation can be attacked if made within two years prior to the commencement of insolvency proceedings, or within five years if the beneficiary was an 'associate'.[34] A precondition of challenge is that at the time of the 'alienation' the debtor's debt already exceeded his assets.

In a case of this sort there are difficulties as to the appropriate remedy. In practice, it is likely that C's ownership of the goods would not be

---

[33] For a review of the authorities see Miller, *Law of Partnership in Scotland* chapter 7.
[34] See generally South African report, case 11. A's brother is an 'associate'.

challenged, but that A's insolvency administrator would require him (C) to repay the amount of the undervalue.

SOUTH AFRICA

(a) The bank (B) can only execute against the business assets if it can prove that they belong to A. If it can be proved that the assets in fact belong to A's brother (C), the execution can be set aside. C must then prove that the business has been delivered to him most probably by means of *constitutum possessorium*.[35]

(b) Section 34 of the Insolvency Act[36] covers instances where a trader disposes of his business outside the ordinary course of business. This section provides that if the trader does not publish a notice of such intended disposition in the Government Gazette or in a local newspaper within a period of not less than thirty days and not more than sixty days before the date of disposition, the disposition shall be void as against creditors for a period of six months after such disposition and shall be void against the insolvency administrator of his estate, if he becomes bankrupt at any time within the said period. This section is aimed at traders in financial difficulties who seek to dispose of their businesses to third parties not liable for their business debts. In such circumstances, the seller will be free to dissipate the purchase price and the assets will become part of the property of the buyer, outside the grasp of creditors. The main purpose of the section is to protect all the creditors of the trader concerned. It either affords creditors the opportunity of demanding immediate payment of any liquidated claims against the trader, which are due at some future date, or renders the disposition void under certain circumstances.[37]

The fact that the price is a fair market price might indicate that the business was sold in the ordinary course of business. Nevertheless, the crucial point under section 34 is prejudice to creditors. In view of this, it is immaterial whether the disposition is advantageous or disadvantageous since creditors can be prejudiced even in the case of an advantageous disposition of a business, its goodwill or stock forming a part thereof. This disposition can probably therefore be set aside under section 34 of the Insolvency Act.

[35] Cf. *Vasco Dry Cleaners v Twycross* 1979 1 SA 620 (A).   [36] Act 24 of 1936.
[37] See Smith, *The Law of Insolvency* 143–144; Smith/Sharrock, in: *The Law of South Africa* XI para. 191.

(c) If the price is well below a fair market price, either section 34 of the Insolvency Act or the *actio Pauliana* can be applied to set aside the alienation of the business to the brother. Under the *actio Pauliana*, creditors have the right to attack alienations *in fraudem creditorem*. They must prove: (1) that the alienation caused diminution of the debtor's assets; (2) that the person to whom the asset was alienated did not receive his own property; (3) that there was an intention to defraud; and (4) that the fraud caused the diminution.[38] An intention to defraud is taken to exist if the object of the transaction was to give one creditor an unfair advantage over other creditors on insolvency. Alienations *ex titulo lucrativo* may be revoked to the extent that the alienee has benefited from the fraud. Alienations *ex titulo onerosa* may by contrast be set aside only if it can be shown that the transferor intended to defraud his creditors and that the transferee knew of this intention or was privy to it. Formal insolvency is not a condition precedent for this action; an individual creditor may avail himself of this remedy notwithstanding that the estate of the debtor has not been declared bankrupt. On insolvency the administrator, as the representative of all proved creditors, is obliged to bring this action.[39]

If C was not A's brother but a close friend, this would make no difference. Section 34 applies to the transfer of the business of the trader to *anyone*. If the required notice of the transfer has not been given, the transfer would be void for a period of six months after the disposition. Since the applicability of the *actio Pauliana* is based on an intention to defraud, the fact that C was a close friend could be a factor indicating an intention to defraud on the part of C, but apart from that no special rules apply.

DENMARK

(a) and (b) It is very difficult to give precise answers to these questions. But if the sale of the business was made on normal terms and A thereafter works as an employee, the assets used in the business cannot be executed against by B. If A runs the business on his own account the transaction would probably be seen as an evasion which need not be respected by B. In this case the sale of the business could also be said

---

[38] See *Fernhalls v Ebrahim* 1956 4 SA 723 (D).
[39] See Smith, *The Law of Insolvency* 147–148; De Wet/Van Wyk, *Die Suid-Afrikaanse Kontraktereg en Handelsreg* 482–483.

to be *pro forma*. (The reason for this is almost the same as the reason mentioned in case 10(b). If A runs the business on his own account it could be argued that the purchase price in fact is a loan and it was only intended that B should obtain security for that loan.)

(c) If the price was abnormally low the transaction might be invalidated if A was declared bankrupt. Under section 74 of the Bankruptcy Act, unduly impairing dispositions can be invalidated if the estate is able to prove that the debtor was insolvent and that the other party was aware of this fact. A's sale at an abnormally low price is an example of such a transaction.

The transaction might also be seen as a gift which can be invalidated under section 64 of the Bankruptcy Act.

SWEDEN

(a) In Swedish law there is no general rule that a purchaser of a business, who is continuing under the same firm, is liable for the outstanding debts. However, such rules exist concerning special kinds of debt, namely debts to pay wages[40] and rent.[41] Furthermore, such a liability is often agreed, expressly or impliedly, in relation to customers, with a right for the customers to take action independently (agreement in favour of a third party).

As stated in case 10, a transfer of movables is not binding on the creditors of the seller unless the buyer has taken possession of the goods (a *constitutum possessorium* will not do) or the sale has been registered under the Bills of Sales Act and thirty days have elapsed. Also after thirty days the registered sale will not be binding on creditors with an enterprise charge provided that the enterprise charge was registered prior to the sale or during the thirty-day period. In the present case, this means that even the unsecured creditor B may execute against movables, since the purchase was not registered and A, because he continued to conduct the business, remained in possession of the movables.[42] As stated in case 12, assignments of claims normally have effect in relation to creditors only after notification to the *debitores cessi*. However, when a whole business is transferred, the purchaser is protected already by the agreement.[43] The same goes for transfer of real estate and immaterial rights.

[40] Section 6 b *lagen (1982:80) om anställningsskydd* (Employment Act).
[41] Chapter 12 section 36 *jordabalken* (Land Code).   [42] NJA 1926, 281.
[43] 31 § 3 st *skuldebrevslagen* (Promissory Notes Act).

(b) Although the brother C is protected against the creditors of B as regards claims, immaterial rights and real estate, the transfer could be attacked pursuant to the special rules on avoidance in insolvency. *Note bene*, these rules do not apply in execution. The general rule is to be found in chapter 4 section 5 of the Bankruptcy Act (*konkurslagen*). The prerequisites are: (1) a creditor has been favoured inappropriately, or property has been withheld inappropriately, or net indebtedness has increased inappropriately; (2) the debtor was or became insolvent; and (3) the other party knew, or ought to have known, of the insolvency and the circumstances that made the transaction inappropriate. Persons closely related to the debtor are presumed to have the required knowledge. Regarding such persons there is no time-limit; otherwise the petition for insolvency must have been made within five years of the transaction. By the prerequisite 'inappropriately', it is indicated that it is not enough that a creditor is favoured; a margin must be surpassed. Even if full consideration is rendered, the transaction may be avoided if the other party knew or ought to have known that the debtor intended to withhold the consideration from the creditors.

In the present case, a fair market price has been paid. Therefore, the transaction cannot be avoided unless the compensation has been withheld from the insolvency creditors by A, and C knew or ought to have known of such an intent.

(c) If the price was well below a fair market price, C has – especially as he is A's brother – been inappropriately favoured and the relevant bad faith is presumed. Chapter 4 section 5 thus may be applied. In addition, the transaction may obviously be regarded as a partial gift, which renders section 6 on gifts applicable. Pursuant to this rule, the transaction can be avoided within six months with no further provisos. As C was closely related to A, the partial gift could be avoided within three years unless it is proved that A after the transaction had assets that obviously corresponded to his debts.

FINLAND

(a) If a genuine contract of sale has been concluded between A and C, B cannot, normally, directly execute against the business assets.[44] The

---

[44] The general prerequisites for the purchaser to be protected as against the seller's creditors must, of course, be fulfilled. According to the rules concerning, for instance,

CASE 15: INDEBTED BUSINESSMAN SELLS TO BROTHER   643

bailiff would in this case inform B about A's insolvency and, most probably, also about the suspicious features of the contract between A and C. After that official notice, B could try to rely on the rules concerning the avoidance of transactions in insolvency. These rules can also be applied to execution. If the contract was clearly made only *pro forma*, execution would be possible immediately. The genuineness of the contract could, even in this case, alternatively be decided by the court.

(b) If the contract was not made *pro forma*, and was at a fair market price, which was actually paid, the only avenue open to B would probably be to resort to the general rule of recovery relating to insolvency estates. According to that rule, the legal consequences of any act or omission of the debtor can be avoided, if: (1) that act or omission was disadvantageous towards creditors; (2) the debtor was insolvent or became insolvent wholly or partially because of that act or omission; (3) the other person knew, or should have known, of these facts; and (4) the act or omission took place within the period of five years before the insolvency petition was filed.[45] In this particular case, the conduct of A and C could probably be regarded as inappropriate: for example, if A had dissipated the money and C knew, or should have known, that this was A's intention from the beginning. Because C is A's brother, i.e. A's close relative,[46] he is presumed to be in *mala fides* in respect of A's inappropriate intention and A's economic difficulties. Also, because of the close relationship between A and C, the time-limit of five years would be inapplicable.

(c) If the price paid was well below the fair market price, B could also have claimed recovery according to the provisions concerning gifts and similar dispositions. This would be advantageous to B, because the recovery would not depend on, for example, the inappropriateness of the sale or the *mala fides* of C. On the other hand, the limitation period would, according to these provisions, be three years in respect of persons close to each other, for example, near relatives, such as in this case. Otherwise, the period is one year.

---

tangible goods and real property, such protection is acquired by the purchaser on grounds of a mere contract. Even the purchaser of claims, which are not connected with negotiable documents, is protected *solo consensu* when the claims are sold with all other business assets. The purchaser of shares and bonds must, however, obtain possession of the relevant certificates or make an appropriate book-entry registration. See Finnish report, case 1.

[45] See above, Finnish report, case 11 (Variation).   [46] *Ibid.*

Comparative observations

The Variation to case 11 explored the ways in which a security given to a specific creditor in preference to insolvency creditors might be set aside. The present case also concerns creditors' powers of avoidance, yet not in relation to the creation of a security right but in relation to the transfer of an entire business. Thus, this last case departs from the central subject of the volume and turns to consider the much wider question of determining the legal relationship between a creditor who has recourse on movable assets actually or formerly detained by his debtor and third parties who claim property rights in the same movable assets.[47]

Yet, the present case is also closely related to the subject of security rights: first, because it provides the opportunity to explore further the applicability of what in most jurisdictions is known as the *actio Pauliana* and, secondly, because the rules on a transferee's liability for pre-existing debts provide an opportunity for creditors potentially to execute against assets otherwise not available to them. Such rules are of special interest to unsecured creditors and to creditors in jurisdictions where secured credit is expensive or not easily obtainable or both.

Part (a)

In the majority of jurisdictions under consideration, the answer to part (a) is simply that B cannot execute against the assets which form part of the sold business, because they are now owned by C. This is the solution in France, Belgium, Spain, the Netherlands, Scotland, the two common law jurisdictions and Sweden. The other jurisdictions either provide special legislation (Germany, Austria, Greece, Italy and South Africa) or may regard the sale as 'simulated' (Greece and Portugal) or made '*pro forma*' (Denmark and Finland).

The special provisions which exist in Germany, Austria, Greece, Italy and South Africa merit some further consideration. The basic reason for their existence is pointed out in the South African report: creditors of pre-existing debts should be protected if the debtor alienates either his whole patrimony or a significant part of it, as for example

---

[47] See also Introduction, p. 29 (original topic of the questionnaire: 'Movable assets and general creditors. Enforcement of claims by recourse on movable assets actually or formerly detained by a debtor, but on which third persons claim property rights').

his business. In Germany, where a provision similar to that of Austrian, Greek and Italian law existed until 1 January 1999 (§ 419 BGB), the rule was said additionally to rest on the idea that a patrimony always has to be regarded as a whole, including rights, claims in favour of the patrimony and claims against it. The German provision was severely criticised and finally abolished in the course of the insolvency law reform, although it was weaker in its effect than its counterparts in the other jurisdictions mentioned. In contrast to Austrian, Greek and Italian law, § 419 BGB was only applicable if the whole of the debtor's patrimony was transferred so as to leave merely approximately 10 per cent in the hands of the transferor. The transfer of a business alone could not lead to transferees' liability unless the value of such a business exceeded 90 per cent of the value of the transferor's whole patrimony.

Greek, Austrian and Italian law hold the transferee personally liable for the pre-existing debts incurred in the business, but restrict this liability to the value of the acquired assets. This was also the solution of § 419 BGB before 1999. The South African rule adopts a different solution which comes close to the result of an *actio Pauliana*: the transfer itself is deemed to be invalid as against the creditors of the transferor, thus enabling creditors to execute against the transferred assets. Another difference lies in the time-span during which the acquirer continues to be liable for the transferor's debts: in South Africa the liability only subsists for a period of six months from the transfer. The other reports do not specify the time-span but it will certainly be longer. Finally, the South African rule sets out a practical way for the transferee to escape liability: he must only ensure that the transferor duly publishes the transfer. Such a possibility does not exist under Greek, Austrian and Italian law.

A further basis for the acquirer's (C's) personal liability is provided in Germany and Austria by § 25 HGB. Although the ideas which underlie the rules just presented may also be said to have inspired § 25 HGB, the requirements and the results are quite different. First, the transferees' liability under § 25 HGB is not restricted to the value of the transferred business. Secondly, liability can be excluded by a duly registered agreement between the parties to the transfer. Thirdly, the transferee is only liable if he continues to use the former business name. His liability is said to be founded on the appearance of continuity which is created by such use. The validity of this criterion is more and more questioned in German legal literature; § 25 (German) HGB might be abolished in the future.

Parts (b) and (c)

All jurisdictions in principle provide the possibility to have a transfer of assets set aside if it has been made either fraudulently, with an intention to prejudice creditors, or within a certain 'suspect' period. The basic rules on the *actio Pauliana* have been set out and discussed in the Variation to case 11.

In the present case, three elements, whether alone or taken together, may be considered as potential grounds for setting the transfer aside: (1) the transfer took place when A was no longer able to meet his obligations towards his creditor, B; (2) the business was transferred to a close relative; and (3) A, the transferor, continued to run the business. Of special interest is a fourth factor, namely the price paid by the brother. In part (b), the price paid was a fair market price, whereas in the alternative, part (c), it was well below that level.

There are marked differences in the solutions adopted. In the large majority of jurisdictions, the price paid is but one consideration of many in determining whether the transaction was of a fraudulent character. Such jurisdictions do not regard avoidance as barred in principle by the fact that the price was a fair market price. This group consists of Germany, Austria, Greece, Portugal, France, Spain, Italy, the Netherlands, South Africa, Denmark and Finland. English, Irish, Scots and Swedish law, on the other hand, as a matter of principle deny the possibility of an avoidance if the price was fair. This conclusion rests on the idea that the creditors cannot be prejudiced by a transaction which does not diminish the overall value of the debtor's assets. On the other hand, one may argue that money is always easier to spend or hide and thus of greater fungibility than assets such as a business. This may be the reason why the first-mentioned jurisdictions do not take such a strict view.

Evaluation: a common core? Convergences, subsisting differences and possible ways for harmonisation

EVA-MARIA KIENINGER

Each of the fifteen cases has been concluded with comparative observations trying to take stock of the national solutions and to find reasons for at least some of the differences. The purpose of the present evaluation is neither to present a summary of these comparisons nor to give another overview of the law relating to security rights in the different jurisdictions under consideration. Rather, these final remarks aim at drawing a few more general conclusions in view of the need for some measure of European harmonisation that has been identified in the Introduction. Therefore, I will seek to identify common tendencies as well as subsisting differences both with respect to general principles and in relation to specific security devices. The evaluation will conclude with some suggestions as to possible ways for harmonisation.

A. General tendencies

I. Common developments

1. Evolution of secured transactions law outside the Civil Codes

A first, very general, but nonetheless significant common element lies in the fact that the development of secured transactions law on the Continent largely took place (and continues to take place) outside the national Civil Codes. The legal regime is either entirely based on case law, as for example in Germany, or contained in special, fragmented legislation as, for example, in France, Italy and Spain. Even the text of

---

Thanks are due to Michael Bridge, Eric Dirix, Michele Graziadei and Harry Sigman for their discussion of an outline of this evaluation at the 7th General Meeting of the Common Core Project (12–14 July 2001) and many helpful suggestions.

the Dutch Civil Code of 1992, which certainly made an attempt to regain ground, has already partly lost its significance in light of the case law on leasing[1] and on the use of so-called master-lists for creating a *stil pandrecht* in claims.[2] Overall, one can say that by reading the property law provisions of the respective Civil Codes one will not be able to get a clear picture, and in some cases not even a faint conception, of the reality of the law on secured transactions.

2. No unitary, functional approach to security rights

A second common feature is connected with the fragmentation of the legal sources just mentioned. In contrast to US law[3] and the EBRD Model Law,[4] none of the jurisdictions of the EU Member States has developed a comprehensive, functional approach to security rights in movables.[5] Instead, there exists in each jurisdiction a wide range of security devices, which differ from each other with respect to the character of the secured debt, the collateral that may be used, and the legal concept on which the security rights are based: title-based security rights such as retention of title, security transfer of ownership or leasing exist side by side with the possessory pledge and various devices that are based on the idea of the pledge such as non-possessory registered charges in individualised property or entities of assets.[6]

The lack of a functional approach goes hand in hand with such fragmentation. The economic function of providing security is often either not recognised with respect to title-based security devices such as retention of title or leasing or such recognition remains without legal consequences, the latter alternative being far more frequent. For example, the House of Lords in *Armour v Thyssen* clearly denied the security character of an all-monies retention of title, declaring it to be simply retained ownership within the meaning of section 19 of the Sale of

---

[1] See Dutch report, case 10(b).   [2] See Dutch report, case 13(a).
[3] See Sigman, *supra*, pp. 54 ff.
[4] See Dahan/Simpson, *supra*, pp. 98 ff.; cf. further Röver, *Vergleichende Prinzipien dinglicher Sicherheiten* 183 ff.
[5] The only jurisdiction which may be said to have at least developed a comprehensive security device resting on a single legal concept is Germany which practically knows only retention of title and security ownership or security assignments.
[6] For a short overview of the main divergences, see Introduction, pp. 9 ff.

Goods Act 1979[7] and thus exempting it from the registration requirement for charges over companies' assets. Generally speaking, in none of the European jurisdictions covered in this study is (simple) retention of title subjected to publicity requirements comparable to those existing for non-possessory charges, despite its evident security function. Another – rather extreme – example of the lack of a functional approach is provided by Belgian law which submits charges over claims to exactly the same requirements as assignments, yet treats the charge over a claim as valid but the identical transaction framed as a security assignment as invalid.[8]

3. Enlarging the range of security rights

In most jurisdictions there is a noticeable and continuing tendency to enlarge the range of security rights that are available for the parties, thereby also enlarging the range of possible collateral. Three examples illustrate this point.

The first example relates to security rights in claims. Before 1981, France and Belgium strictly required a formal notification of the *debitor cessus* or an acceptance formally declared by the latter in order for an assignment to become valid as against third parties in general (so-called *signification*, laid down in article 1690 C.civ.).[9] This rule effectively barred any attempt to use claims as collateral. In 1981, France introduced special legislation on the assignment of professional debts to financial institutions (*Loi Dailly*); such professional claims could hitherto be assigned by simply entering them on a document called *'bordereau Dailly'*. A subsequent change to the relevant Act in 1984[10] opened up the possibility to assign future claims, too. Thus, today, at least financial institutions can take security rights in claims, the general mistrust of security transfers never having been extended to security assignments. A similar but slightly different development took place in Belgium. Rather than introducing special legislation in favour of specific claims

---

[7] *Armour and another v Thyssen Edelstahlwerke AG* [1990] 3 All ER 481 (485) G (*per* Lord Keith): 'I am, however, unable to regard a provision reserving title to the seller until payment of all debts due to him by the buyer as amounting to the creation by the buyer of a right of security in favour of the seller.'
[8] See Belgian report, case 5(c) and comparative observations, case 5(c) (ii) and (iii).
[9] For the following see French report, cases 12(a) and 13(a); Belgian report, case 12(a).
[10] L. 84-46 of 24 Jan. 1984, articles 61 ff.

and/or parties to an assignment, Belgium altered its article 1690 C.civ. in 1994. It no longer requires the formal *signification* for the validity of the assignment as against third parties in general; only with respect to the rights of the assignee towards the *debitor cessus* does a formless notification remain necessary. Although, as has already been mentioned under section 2, Belgian law still considers the security assignment of claims to be invalid, it allows a charge over claims to take place under the same prerequisites as an assignment. Thus, parties seeking to establish a security right in claims can make use of the reformed article 1690 C.civ. provided that they frame their transaction as a charge rather than an assignment. In Austrian law, the requirements for a valid charge over a claim are likewise extended to the security assignment of claims. The parties to the assignment can choose between notification of the *debitor cessus* or an entry of the assignment in the books of the assignor. In order to make the security assignment more practicable in business reality, a recent change in the predominant doctrine has opened up the possibility to enter assignments into the assignor's books and thus also to fulfil the publicity requirement before the respective claims have come into existence and even before their individual debtors are known.[11]

The rise of the enterprise charge provides a second example of the overall tendency to enlarge the possible range of available security rights and the range of potential collateral. The English *floating charge*, which enables the creditor to take a security interest in a constantly changing entity of tangible and intangible property, has been exported to various civil law jurisdictions, albeit with differing degrees of similarity to the original. Certainly, the closest proximity exists with the *floating charge* under Scots law which was introduced by legislation in 1961.[12] Sweden introduced the enterprise charge in 1984.[13] However, by contrast to the English *floating charge*, the range of collateral that can be included in a Swedish enterprise charge is more limited. A number of (rather valuable) assets cannot be charged: for example, immovable property, shares and claims against banks. Finland also knows the enterprise charge, yet its commercial significance is lessened by the rule that, in insolvency, the rights of the chargee extend only to 50 per cent of the charged property.[14] The most recent example of the transplantation of the *floating charge* is provided by Greek law which has just

---

[11] Cf. Austrian report, case 5(c).
[12] Cf. Scottish report, case 11.
[13] Cf. Swedish report, case 11.
[14] Cf. Finnish report, case 11(a).

introduced rules on a registered enterprise charge into its Commercial Code.[15]

The development of the German security transfer of ownership and security assignment should also be mentioned in this context. Over the years, the courts have reduced the requirements of the principle of specificity to such an extent that, today, it is clearly possible to include all present and future stock-in-trade and all present and future claims arising out of the enterprise's business connections in these security transfers.[16] The last obstacle to such global security rights (called '*Globalsicherungsübereignung*' and '*Globalzession*'), which stemmed from an unduly narrow interpretation of the AGBG (Act on Unfair Contract Terms), was removed by the BGH in 1997.[17] Today, the courts no longer consider security transfers of ownership or security assignments to be invalid on the grounds of 'oversecurity' but rather read the necessary contractual clauses that avoid oversecurity into the security agreement. Overall, German law seems flexible enough to enable the parties to reach the same results as would be possible under a regime that encompasses an enterprise charge strictly speaking.[18]

The only example of a discordant development is the prohibition of the security transfer of ownership and the security assignment in the Dutch Civil Code of 1992 (article 3:84(3) BW).[19] Yet, since both security rights have been replaced by the so-called silent pledge (*stil pandrecht*) which requires no more than a notarised deed or registration in a register that is – *nota bene* – not accessible by the public, one can hardly say that the overall range of possible security rights has been diminished, especially since the courts have materially facilitated compliance with the registration requirement through acceptance of the use of so-called master-lists.[20] In addition, the *Hoge Raad* has interpreted article 12 Rome

---

[15] Cf. Greek report, case 5(c), also mentioned in case 10(a) (iii) and case 11(a) at the end.
[16] Cf. German report, cases 3(c) (i) and 11(a). It should be mentioned, however, that due to the priority conferred upon sellers under retention of title (with proceeds clauses), claims arising out of sub-sales of goods delivered under retention of title have to be exempted from global security assignments: see e.g. BGH 8 Dec. 1998, JZ 1999, 404 (note Kieninger).
[17] Cf. German report, case 11(d).
[18] As to the possibility to translate or 'transpose' an English *floating charge* into the German *Globalsicherheiten*, see Wenckstern, RabelsZ 56 (1992) 624.
[19] As to its previous admissibility, see Introduction, *supra*, p. 12, and Zwalve, *supra*, p. 51.
[20] See Dutch report, case 13(a).

Convention in a way that enables parties to an international assignment to choose the applicable law even with respect to third parties (including the insolvency administrator) so that these parties can make use of legal regimes which, like German law, are more favourable to security assignments.[21]

4. Limiting the rights of secured creditors in insolvency

Another common tendency, which partly runs counter to and partly supplements the move just mentioned (under section 3), lies in the tendency to diminish the powers of the secured party, especially in insolvency. Various reports have pointed out that insolvency administrators or courts surveying the proceedings can opt for a moratorium during which secured creditors are unable to enforce their rights.[22] Such a stay enables the insolvency administrator to let the business carry on as a going concern while exploring the possibilities for reconstruction or the most efficient way for a liquidation. Another example is the introduction of a contribution to the costs of realising the security in German insolvency law in the course of its 1999 reform.[23]

5. Decline of the significance of possession

A further common tendency on a general level lies in the decline of the significance of possession and the gradual disappearance of the doctrine of ostensible or apparent ownership. This doctrine rests on provisions like article 2279 (French and Belgian) C.civ.: '*En fait de meubles la possession vaut titre.*'[24] The rule is regarded not only as the foundation of the principle governing the acquisition of ownership in good faith from a non-owner but also as the cornerstone of the doctrine according to which third parties are entitled to rely on the fact of possession when trying to evaluate their business-partner's creditworthiness. This consideration lies at the heart of the principle of publicity through (direct) possession

---

[21] *Hoge Raad* 16 May 1997, *Rechtspraak van de Week* 1997, no 126 c. See Struycken, *Lloyd's Maritime and Commercial Law Quarterly* 1998, 345.
[22] See Dutch report, cases 1(a) and 3(a); German report, case 3(a); French report, case 1(a).
[23] See German report, case 6(b).
[24] Translation: 'With respect to movables possession equals title.' See also article 464 C.c. (Spain): '*La posesión de los bienes muebles, adquirida de buena fe, equivale al título.*' ('The possession of movables, acquired in good faith, equals title.') § 1006 (1) BGB: '*Zugunsten des Besitzers einer Sache wird vermutet, daß er Eigentümer der Sache sei.*' ('In favour of the possessor of a thing, it is assumed that he owns it.')

and is thus also the foundation of the requirement that a pledge can only be constituted through a transfer of possession from the pledgor to the pledgee. In France and Belgium, the doctrine of apparent ownership has for a long time been the basis for denial of the validity of (simple) title retention in the buyer's insolvency.[25]

The significance of possession fades away once a jurisdiction admits non-possessory security interests without compensating the lack of a transfer of possession through other, effective means of publicity. Such a development can be seen most prominently in German law. Here, a doctrine of apparent ownership that would have prevented the creation of non-possessory, non-publicised security rights never developed under the BGB. But the decline of the significance of possession is affecting the second function of § 1006 BGB,[26] namely its function to provide a basis for *bona fide* acquisition. With the increasing use of ownership-based, non-possessory security interests (retention of title with various extensions, security transfer of ownership) the question arises of whether purchasers today can still believe that movables which they find in the possession of the seller are in fact owned by the latter. In 1980, the BGH decided that in those business sectors where practically all goods are sold under retention of title, purchasers can no longer trust that the goods which the seller possesses are in fact his property.[27] It should be noted, however, that the BGH has not yet drawn the general conclusion that possession has completely lost its decisiveness for the solution of proprietary conflicts, but decides each case on its merits.[28]

The admission of hidden, non-possessory security rights is not the only reason for the decline of the significance of possession and the doctrine of apparent ownership. Other factors undermine the practicability of inferring creditworthiness from the fact of possession. First, besides non-possessory security rights, there are also contractual relationships

---

[25] See, for France, *infra*, n. 29; for Belgium, Cass. 9 Feb. 1933, Pasicrisie 1933, I, 103.
[26] See *supra*, note 24.
[27] BGH 18 June 1980, BGHZ 77, 274. The BGH held that in the course of economic development, the decisiveness of factual possession, which forms the basis for the statutory provisions on *bona fide* acquisition, had lost its meaning to a considerable extent. This applied to all movables which are normally purchased on credit and therefore delivered under retention of title. According to the BGH, in this area, possession points to ownership only to a very limited extent.
[28] See BGH 9 July 1990, ZIP 1991, 176 (178): 'Although one has to acknowledge the eminent importance of retention of title in today's business, the statutory principle laid down in §§ 932, 935 BGB should not be lost sight of. This principle says that whoever voluntarily gives up possession of his things takes the risk that another acquires ownership in them.'

which allow possession and ownership to be distributed among different persons, such as leasing or hire purchase. In addition and even more importantly, credit in today's business reality is no longer granted because of the physical existence of assets on the debtor's premises. It was for both reasons that in 1980, the French legislature provided for the validity of retention of title in the buyer's insolvency. The draft of the so-called *Loi Dubanchet*, which brought the change, was put rather ironically: '*Il faut ajouter que, du point de vue commercial, le crédit apparent – fondé sur l'aspect des marchandises en magasin –, s'il a peut-être été une réalité du temps de Balzac, n'est absolument plus pris en considération depuis si longtemps qu'aucun commerçant actuel n'a l'idée saugrenue d'aller visiter les magasins d'un collègue en vue de lui faire crédit.*'[29] It was for the same reasons that in 1998 Belgium followed France and introduced the validity of retention of title not only *vis-à-vis* third-party creditors executing against the buyer's assets (which in Belgium, in contrast to France, had been denied before the reform) but also in the latter's insolvency. So even in those two jurisdictions, where the doctrine of apparent ownership had developed and long been upheld, it has today lost much of its original significance.

6. The rise of contractual devices coupled with title-based security rights

A final common tendency lies in the growing use of types of contracts such as leasing, sale under retention of title and factoring which operate, functionally, as security interests through their effects on the location of ownership. It seems to be easier to acknowledge a non-possessory, non-publicised functional security right if it is supplemented by some contractual elements or goals in addition to the pure security function. The prime example is retention of title which will be more closely examined on pp. 658 f. As far as leasing is concerned, the national solutions to case 14 show that, with the exception of Greece and France, the restrictions placed on non-possessory security rights strictly speaking

---

[29] *Proposition de loi présentée par M. F. Dubanchet et plusieurs de ses collègues, Sénat, no. 407* (1977–1978), *Exposé des Motifs*, 5. Translation: 'One must add that – from a commercial point of view – the notion of "crédit apparent" founded upon the actual existence of goods on someone's premises was perhaps a reality at the time of Balzac; but that this is no longer the case since no merchant or businessman today has the absurd idea of going to visit the premises of a colleague before giving him credit.'

are not extended to sale and lease-back arrangements, although this type of leasing contract is extremely similar to the pure security transfer of ownership. The attempts in case law to draw a distinction between these two types of transactions, mentioned by some reporters under part (c) of case 14, remain unconvincing. A number of country reports also mention factoring as a method to overcome the restrictions on security rights over claims.[30]

II. Persisting differences

1. General attitude towards security rights in movables

Despite the common tendencies just mentioned, there still exist a number of areas where substantial differences of principle persist. Taken together, these differences amount to a general dividing line between one group of jurisdictions, e.g. Austria, France, Belgium, Portugal, Italy, Spain, the Netherlands, Scotland and the three Nordic countries, which opt for a rather narrow interpretation of common principles such as publicity, specificity, the mandatory character of property law rules and the prohibition of the *pactum commissorium* and which, as a consequence, adopt a comparatively hostile attitude towards non-possessory security rights, and other jurisdictions (e.g. Germany, Greece, England and Ireland) where such principles are either wholly neglected or interpreted in a more generous way so as to allow for non-possessory security rights that have been developed *praeter legem* by practice. This difference in tendency will be considered in greater detail in the following paragraphs.

2. Significance of the principle of publicity

The principle that proprietary rights must in some way be made public to the outside world because of their enforceability *erga omnes* generally exists in all jurisdictions which have been covered in this volume. For proprietary rights in movables, the traditional means to comply with the principle of publicity is the transfer of possession. Yet, as has just been pointed out (*supra* pp. 652 ff.), the significance of possession in performing the publicity function has gradually declined. Even more

---

[30] See Greek report, case 12(a) (4) and (5); Italian report, case 12(a) and (b); Irish report, case 12(a).

importantly, for the greater part of suitable collateral, a transfer of possession in order to publicise a security right does not represent a practical possibility. However, leaving aside for a moment simple retention of title, the various jurisdictions reacted differently to this common phenomenon. The greater number of jurisdictions either have introduced special non-possessory security rights which are publicised through registration and – as a consequence – deny the validity of non-publicised non-possessory security rights (e.g. France, Belgium) or deny such validity without providing for practical substitutes (e.g. Austria, Spain, Italy). A small minority of EU Member States, namely Germany and Greece, have effectively ceased to adhere to the principle of publicity as far as the various extensions of retention of title and the security transfer of ownership are concerned. A special case in this context is Dutch law: it has abandoned the security transfer of ownership, among other reasons because of its hidden character, but replaced it with the *stil pandrecht*, which is no less hidden since it only requires a notarised deed or an entry into a registry which is not open to inspection by interested members of the public.[31]

In the national reports, the different attitudes towards the principle of publicity can most prominently be observed in the context of retention of title in raw material, coupled with a products clause,[32] retention of title with an all-monies clause[33] and in the cases dealing with the question of creating a non-possessory security interest in equipment (case 10) and stock-in-trade (case 11).

3. Significance of party autonomy in matters of property law

Another principle of property law which most jurisdictions are usually said to adhere to is the mandatory character of property law rules. Again, however, this common principle is enforced to differing degrees. A good example is provided by case 7. There, the question arises of whether the parties can contract around rules on *specificatio* in order to give the seller under retention of title a security right in the newly manufactured products. German and Greek law effectively allow a derogation by the parties from the rules on *specificatio*, the Italian, Scots and South African reporters have expressed some reservations as to such a

---

[31] Dutch report, cases 5(c) and 12(a).   [32] See comparative observations, case 7(c).
[33] See comparative observations, case 9(a) (ii).

possibility, whereas in all other jurisdictions it seems clear that a purported extension of retention of title into products manufactured by the buyer would amount to a hidden charge and thus be unenforceable *vis-à-vis* third parties.

4. Significance of the prohibition of '*pactum commissorium*'

The prohibition of the '*pactum commissorium*' is another principle which is known to all jurisdictions but adhered to differently. The principle is used as an argument against the possibility of the security transfer of ownership, e.g. in France, Portugal and Italy,[34] whereas in German law, where it can likewise be found among the rules on pledges (see § 1229 BGB), it has never been regarded as a reason for not admitting the validity of security ownership.[35]

5. Notification requirements in relation to assignments or charges of claims

Despite the tendencies of convergence with respect to the assignment of claims described on pp. 649 ff., it is still true that a major dividing line exists between those jurisdictions which, in order for the assignment to be valid as against third parties, require the *debitor cessus* to be notified or to obtain a formal acceptance by him (France, with respect to assignments outside the *Loi Dailly*, Italy, Scotland and the three Nordic countries) and those jurisdictions which dispense with such formal requirements or replace them with less cumbersome ones (Germany, Austria, Greece, France, as far as assignments under the *Loi Dailly* are concerned, Belgium, Portugal, the Netherlands, England, Ireland, and South Africa).[36] This difference still stands in the way of making effective use of claims as collateral in international cases, i.e. cases where either the assignment or the claim has an international character.

---

[34] As to Italian law, see, from a comparative perspective, most recently Greving, *Der Treuhandgedanke bei Sicherungsübertragungen im italienischen und deutschen Recht* 64 ff.
[35] See case 10, German, French, Portuguese and Italian reports as well as comparative observations, parts (a) to (c).
[36] See comparative observations, case 12.

B. Convergences and divergences in relation to specific security rights

I. Security rights with strong convergence

1. Simple retention of title

Case 3 has shown that with respect to simple retention of title, a marked convergence has occurred over the last twenty-five years. For most Member States it is sufficient that seller and buyer have mutually agreed that title is to be retained until full payment of the purchase price and that this agreement has been entered into orally prior to the delivery of the goods. A written document is required by French, Belgian and Portuguese law. According to Italian and Spanish law, the agreement to reserve title must, in addition, carry a 'certain date' (*data certa* or *fecha cierta*) to prevent fraudulent antedating. In Italy, this requirement must be complied with in order to render the retention of title enforceable as against third parties such as creditors of the buyer (article 1524 C.c.); in Spain, the question whether, in relation to third parties, the certain date could possibly be substituted through other means of proving that the agreement to retain title has been entered into prior to delivery, is not yet finally settled.[37] Compulsory registration for retention of title exists only in Spain, if the contract is subject to the *Ley sobre venta a plazos de bienes muebles*,[38] and in Portugal and Denmark for certain high-value equipment (motor vehicles, vessels, aircraft).

In all Member States bar Sweden, retention of title gives the seller the right to vindicate the goods as their owner in the event of the buyer's insolvency. In Sweden and South Africa, the seller's rights are also upheld in insolvency, but they are reduced to those of the holder of a security right.

Case 4 has brought out a final difference which concerns retention of title in goods which are meant to be resold by the buyer. If the agreement does not comply with the relatively strict requirements of a credit consignment or commission agreement as set out by the Danish, Swedish

---

[37] See Hellmich, *Kreditsicherungsrechte in der spanischen Mehrrechtsordnung* 166 with references to STS 16 May 1996 (Aranzadi 1996 n. 4348), STS 29 Mar. 1995 (Aranzadi 1995 n. 2333), STS 22 Jan. 1995 (Aranzadi 1995, n. 177): *fecha cierta* no constitutive element of retention of title; but see for the opposite opinion STS 24 Oct. 1995 (Aranzadi n. 7846).

[38] See Hellmich, *Kreditsicherungsrechte in der spanischen Mehrrechtsordnung* 164 f.

and Finnish reporters, the title retention agreement will be considered to be invalid from the beginning, including with respect to goods that are still unsold in the hands of the first buyer.

The reason why all jurisdictions regard simple retention of title more favourably than other non-possessory security rights in movables[39] is threefold: sellers are often forced to extend credit in order to stay in business; they can be said to enhance the assets of the buyer's business; and there usually is no other available, unencumbered collateral apart from the sold goods.

2. Leasing

Next to simple retention of title, sale and lease-back is the second security device which is roughly regarded as valid and enforceable under similar preconditions in the large majority of Member States.[40] Only French and Greek law require public registration of the leasing contract; Italian law extends the preconditions for retention of title to leasing contracts (*data certa* as a requirement for the agreement to be opposable towards third-party creditors). Otherwise, a simple leasing contract will suffice for the lessor to remain the owner of the leased assets and thus be secured in the case of execution or the insolvency of the lessee. Surprisingly, sale and lease-back transactions are treated as valid and enforceable despite their obvious function to provide security even in jurisdictions which would not consider the transaction as valid and opposable if framed as a security transfer of ownership.[41]

---

[39] The French report, case 3(e), calls simple retention of title the 'queen of security'. The favour accorded to retention of title in many of the jurisdictions covered here lies in the fact that the usual requirements for the enforceability of a security interest in movables, such as dispossession, registration or special formalities, are not applied to it. A more favourable treatment may also lie in the fact that the seller under retention of title enjoys priority over other secured creditors contrary to the usual rules on priority. This is the case, for example, in Germany, where sellers under retention of title with products clauses are preferred to assignees (usually banks) under a security assignment even if the security assignment was agreed upon prior to the retention of title (see e.g. BGH 8 Dec. 1998, JZ 1999, 404 (note Kieninger)). Likewise in the US, where retention of title is in principle subjected to the general rules on security rights of Article 9 UCC, it nevertheless enjoys a so-called super-priority: see Sigman, *supra*, chapter 3, pp. 74 f.

[40] See case 14, national reports and comparative observations.

[41] See comparative observations, case 14(c) and especially Dutch report, case 14(c).

II. Security rights where some elements of convergence are present but where significant differences continue to subsist

1. Security rights in entities of property – enterprise charge

Case 11 has shown that more and more jurisdictions provide the possibility to charge the property of an enterprise as a whole or significant parts of it, or at least furnish practicable means to create a charge in entities of assets, such as stock-in-trade. This is the case in England, Ireland and Scotland (*floating charge*), Sweden, Finland and Greece (enterprise charge), Belgium and France (*nantissement de fonds de commerce*), Germany (*Globalsicherungsübereignung* and *Globalzession*) and the Netherlands (*stil pandrecht*). A common feature of such security rights is that the charged property may at least in part be changing without affecting the nature of the charge. However, there are also a number of notable differences concerning the following points: the floating or fixed character of the charge, the extent to which the property may be charged (all assets of an enterprise, only a certain percentage or only certain kinds of assets), the requirements as to formalities and registration and the priorities conferred upon the chargee in the case of the chargor's insolvency.[42]

2. Security assignment of claims or charge over claims (outside retention of title)

Where the claim has already come into existence or where its legal foundation has at least been laid, all jurisdictions conclude that in principle such claims can be used as collateral.[43] Differences subsist mainly in two respects, the first of which is the legal form of the security right. It may take the form either of an assignment or of a charge. More important than this formal distinction is the question whether requirements that exist for a charge over claims, namely the notification of the third-party debtor, are extended to security assignments. This is the case in, for example, Austria, whereas in Germany only the rules on assignment are applied. This leads to the second area of subsisting differences, which relates to the prerequisites for an assignment or a charge to be valid and enforceable as against the third-party debtor and other third parties such as the assignor's or chargor's other creditors. Here, a

---

[42] See in detail comparative observations, case 11(a)–(c).
[43] See for this and the following: comparative observations, case 12.

marked difference exists between those jurisdictions which require no more than a formless agreement between assignor and assignee/chargor and chargee (e.g. Germany), others which do adhere to requirements of registration or notification of/acceptance by the third-party debtor but have developed a practicable method for their fulfilment (e.g. Belgium, the Netherlands, Austria, France as far as assignments under the *Loi Dailly* are concerned) and yet others where the notification or registration requirements are construed in a way that makes security assignments or charges over claims unduly burdensome in commercial reality (e.g. Italy, France outside the scope of application of the *Loi Dailly*).

The diversities are even greater when it comes to assignments of or charges over truly future claims, that is claims where the legal relationship out of which they will arise is not yet existent.[44] Some jurisdictions allow future claims to be included within an enterprise charge (*nantissement de fonds de commerce* in France and Belgium, *floating charge* in England, Scotland and Ireland). Outside the enterprise charge, the possibility to assign or charge a future claim largely depends on the notification or registration requirements. Notification is clearly impossible with claims where the debtor is not yet known. Registration on the other hand is possible; here, it depends on how the legal system organises such registration. Austrian law (book-entry)[45] and Dutch law (periodical registration of master-lists)[46] provide examples where the registration requirement has been adapted in such a way that the charging of future claims is made practicable.

3. Extensions of retention of title

(a) All-sums clauses: Among the various extensions of retention of title, the all-sums clauses perhaps present, relatively speaking, the greatest degree of harmony:[47] most jurisdictions see them as a fruitless attempt to create a non-possessory security right in movable property which does not share the preferential status accorded to simple retention of title.[48] Only English, Scots and Irish law regard the retained title as 'normal' ownership, irrespective of whether the purchase price for the particular

---

[44] See in detail comparative observations, case 13(a)–(c).
[45] See Austrian report, case 5(c).   [46] See Dutch report, case 13(a) and (b).
[47] See for the following: comparative observations, case 9(a) (i) and (ii).
[48] See above, note 39.

goods sold under an all-sums clause has already been paid. In German and Portuguese law, which are the other two jurisdictions where all-sums clauses are held to be effective, the retained title is transformed into security ownership once the purchase price for the goods sold under the particular contract has been paid.

(b) Proceeds clauses: With respect to the question of whether retention of title extends to proceeds arising out of sub-sales, we can find elements of convergence side by side with old and newly developed divergences.[49] It is difficult to detect any common pattern other than perhaps a tendency potentially to extend the security right into proceeds. With the introduction of the opposability of retention of title in insolvency, French and Belgian law also introduced real subrogation: as long as the claim arising out of the sub-sale is still existing, the buyer's rights against his sub-buyer are by operation of statute transferred to the seller. This leads to roughly the same results as an anticipatory security assignment of such claims which is practised in Germany and Greece. The notification requirements which often stand in the way of a security assignment or a charge have been relaxed in Belgium and in Austria, where notification can be replaced by a book entry which can be made before the claims come into existence. In most jurisdictions, however, there are no practicable means to extend retention of title into proceeds, which are typically claims the legal foundation of which does not yet exist at the time of creating the charge or concluding the assignment. Registration and notification requirements are either construed in such a way that they cannot be satisfied in the case of truly future claims or render the operation too costly (e.g. England, Scotland, Ireland, the Netherlands, Italy, Finland).

(c) Products clauses: With respect to products clauses, there are still marked differences between the European jurisdictions.[50] There are systems which allow the parties effectively to derogate from the rules on *specificatio* (Germany, Greece, Scotland and – with reservations – Italy and South Africa), whereas other systems regard such derogation as the creation of a non-possessory charge which is hence invalid as against third parties (France, Belgium and Austria) or subject to registration (England, Ireland and the Netherlands), or require the seller who purports to be

---

[49] See for the following: comparative observations, case 5(c).
[50] See for the following: comparative observations, case 7(c).

the manufacturer effectively to carry the business risk (Austria, France, Italy, Denmark, Sweden and Finland).

4. Non-possessory security rights in individualised property (other than retention of title and leasing)

Most EU Member States only allow non-possessory security rights (other than simple retention of title and leasing) within the framework of special legislation.[51] Usually, such legislation prescribes a system of publicity via asset-based registration, replacing the traditional means of publicity through transfer of possession. Some jurisdictions (e.g. France, Belgium, Italy) have adopted specific pieces of legislation, each for a different kind of collateral, ranging from Parma ham[52] to agricultural equipment[53] or cars.[54] Such legislation is often the product of lobbying by specific branches of trade or industry. The more modern approach is to provide for a single type of non-possessory security interest, which in principle encompasses all kinds of tangible movables (Dutch *stil pandrecht*,[55] Spanish *hipoteca mobiliaria* or *prenda sin desplazamiento*[56]). Currently, only a small minority of Member States (Germany,[57] Greece[58]) allow the security transfer of ownership as a way to contract around the restrictions of the traditional rules on pledge (general prohibition of non-possessory security rights, prohibition of the *pactum commissorium*) and to set up non-possessory security rights that are enforceable as against third parties. A special midway route is followed by English law,[59] which, on the one hand, adheres to the principle of freedom of contract, including within the field of secured transactions, thereby allowing a creditor to take a fixed charge in practically all kinds of collateral, but which, on the other hand, requires such charges to be registered if the debtor is a company, which in the commercially important instances is almost invariably the case.

[51] For the following, see also Introduction, pp. 10 ff.
[52] Law of 24 July 1985, no 401, *Norme sulla costituzione di pegno sui prosciutti a denominazione di origine tutelata.* See Greving, *Der Treuhandgedanke bei Sicherungsübertragungen im italienischen und deutschen Recht* 60 f.
[53] See French report, case 11(a). For Belgium see Kieninger, *Mobiliarsicherheiten im Europäischen Binnenmarkt* 25 f. with further references.
[54] See French report, case 5(c) and Italian report, case 10(a).
[55] See Dutch report, cases 5(c) and 12(a).
[56] Act of 16 Dec. 1954, BOE no 352 of 18 Dec. 1954. See further Hellmich, *Kreditsicherungsrechte in der spanischen Mehrrechtsordnung* 80 ff.
[57] See German report, cases 5(c) (2) and 10(a). [58] See Greek report, case 10(a) (i).
[59] See Bridge, pp. 85 ff.

C. Possible ways towards harmonisation

In the introduction, it has been pointed out that within the EU a pressing need exists for a harmonisation in the field of secured transactions, a need which legitimises some final considerations of possible steps towards this goal. The study has shown that there are only two areas (simple retention of title and leasing) where harmonisation will be comparably easily attainable. Because of the EU's hitherto fruitless attempts,[60] simple retention of title merits some further comments (section I). Beyond retention of title, harmonisation will be a much more complex endeavour. section II will set out the different possibilities.

I. Simple retention of title

Today, all Member States[61] should be able to concur that a retention of title clause, mutually agreed by the parties to the contract of sale prior to the delivery of the goods, is valid and enforceable, not only as between the parties but also as against third parties such as the creditors of the buyer in execution and insolvency. A directive along these lines would only lead to minor changes in some of the Member States' laws: France, Belgium, Luxembourg and Portugal would have to sacrifice the requirement that the agreement be in writing; Italy and Spain would have to abandon the requirement of the certain date which, however, would leave open the possibility to prevent fraudulent antedating by other, less cumbersome means. Spain, in addition, would have to forgo the requirements of registration of the contract of sale in cases which fall under the Act on Instalment Sales (*Ley sobre venta a plazos de bienes muebles*). Finally, the Nordic countries would have to accept the validity and enforceability of simple retention of title in goods destined to be resold or used in a manufacturing process without requiring the contract to be framed as a commission agreement or credit consignment. For the sake of clarity, the directive could further stipulate that retention of title remains valid even if the sold goods are incorporated into other goods, as long as they remain separable without difficulty or damage. Even without any further harmonisation in the field of property law, such as the rules on *bona fide* acquisition, *specificatio* or commingling or

---

[60] Cf. Introduction, *supra*, pp. 22 f.
[61] See, for Luxembourg, which is not included in the present study: *Loi* 31 Mar. 2000, *Mémorial, Journal Officiel du Grand Duché de Luxembourg/Amtsblatt des Großherzogtums Luxembourg* A-N° 32 of 21 Apr. 2000, 814. The new Luxembourg law in this area is practically identical to that of Belgium.

in the field of execution or insolvency law, such a mini-directive would have considerable merits for intra-community trade.

II. Harmonisation or unification beyond simple retention of title

1. Form, scope and context

One of the principal questions discussed with respect to European private law unification in general and to European contract law especially[62] is whether European legislation should be introduced as an additional model for parties to opt for instead of the otherwise applicable autonomous national law or whether such European legislation should replace national law altogether. In the area of secured transactions law, authors have hitherto argued in favour of an additional 'European Security Right' which would supplement but not replace national law.[63] Such a European Security Right was already felt to be an extremely ambitious project the acceptance of which should not be undermined from the outset by the goal of replacing national law.[64] On a theoretical level, one may also argue that the so-called '15 plus 1' model[65] would leave room for 'competition among legal systems' or 'regulatory competition' and that it would restrict the detrimental effects of errors or false compromises in the legislative process. In practice, the issue will probably depend on development in the area of contract law and of European private law as a whole. If the EU institutions seriously started to prepare a regulation on European contract law or even a European Civil Code replacing autonomous national law, there is no reason why the area of secured transactions should be left outside; rather security rights in movables is the field where unification is most desirable. If, on the other

---

[62] See, for example, options IV (a) and (b) on the one hand and IV (c) on the other hand presented by the European Commission in its 'Communication from the Commission to the Council and the European Parliament on European Contract Law' of 11 July 2001, COM (2001) 398 final.

[63] See foremost Kreuzer, in: *Festschrift für von Overbeck*, 613 (637 ff.); Kreuzer, in: Henrich, *Vorschläge und Gutachten zur Reform des deutschen internationalen Sachen- und Immaterialgüterrechts*, 37 (107 ff.); Kreuzer, *Recueil des Cours* 259 (1996) 9 (303 ff.). Cf. also Kieninger, *Mobiliarsicherheiten im Europäischen Binnenmarkt* 240; Seif, *Der Bestandsschutz besitzloser Mobiliarsicherheiten im deutschen und englischen Recht* 310 ff. An overview of the different suggestions can be found in Kaufhold, *Internationales und europäisches Mobiliarsicherungsrecht* 216 ff. and 304 ff.

[64] According to Kreuzer (*Recueil des Cours* 259 (1996) 9 (304)), a uniform security right replacing national law would neither today nor in the near future have any realistic chance of being adopted.

[65] Which from May 2004 should be called '25 plus 1' model, or even, taking account of the autonomy of Scots law, '26 plus 1' model.

hand, the general trend is towards the so-called '15 plus 1' model, it is likely that the EU institutions would rather opt for a European Security Right supplementing existing national law. In that case, the additional question arises whether the supranational legislation should be framed as an opt-in or an opt-out model, that means, whether parties, in case the requirements of an intra-community transaction are satisfied (which would have to be defined in such an instrument), have to declare expressly the applicability of European law (opt-in) or to declare its inapplicability (opt-out). Experiences, especially with the CISG, have shown that an opt-out model is better able to foster acceptance and to provide practice with court decisions in a reasonably short time-span. If an opt-in model is favoured, the parties should be given the option of adopting the European Security Right in cases where the requirements of transnationality are not satisfied. This again would enhance practical experience and acceptance.

The scope of potential European legislation would again depend on its context. If a European Security Right is created within the framework of a European Civil Code, it could be embedded into a unification of the general rules of property law such as the transfer of ownership, the significance of possession, *bona fide* acquisition from a non-owner or *specificatio* and commingling. Such a comprehensive unification would seem to be the most desirable option. However, if such a wide-ranging unification is not attainable in the near future, this would not render a more limited project ineffective. This study has shown that the differences of approach towards security rights do not rest on the different systems regarding the transfer of ownership:[66] English law, which can be said to adhere to the consensus principle, is nearly as open towards security in movables as is German law with its principle of abstraction. On the other hand, Scots law, if one disregards the elements transplanted into it from English law such as the *floating charge* or all-monies clauses, adopts a strict stance towards non-possessory security rights comparable to that of French, Belgian or Italian law, although Scots law is an abstract system whereas Belgium and Italy have taken over the French *solo consensu* rule. This is not to say that the rules on the transfer of ownership do not matter as far as security rights are based on title; yet, the creation of a European Security Right that would not be title-based would not depend on unifying at the same time the rules on the passing of ownership.

---

[66] As to the different systems of transfer of ownership, see comparative observations, case 1(a).

Likewise, the effectiveness of a uniform security regime would not necessarily depend on a simultaneous unification of the rules on *bona fide* acquisition, *specificatio*, commingling, etc., if the uniform security right either automatically extended to whatever is received in respect of the charged movables ('proceeds'[67]) or if it was possible for the parties anticipatorily to agree on a security right in such proceeds (claims, manufactured goods, etc.).[68]

Another reason that is often advanced against the possibility of harmonising or unifying security rights in movables lies in the differences between insolvency law regimes. It is, of course, right that one of the crucial aspects of any regime of security interests is the effect such an interest will have in the event of the debtor's insolvency, or as Roy Goode has stated, 'it is bankruptcy that provides the acid test of the efficacy of real rights in general and security interests in particular'.[69] This study has confirmed the general hypothesis that with respect to the secured creditors' remedies in insolvency, great differences exist between the various jurisdictions, concerning *inter alia* (1) the nature of the remedies (*rei vindicatio*, right of separation or right to preferential payment out of the proceeds), (2) rights of the insolvency administrator to postpone or modify such remedies in the interest of general creditors, (3) priority rules, especially priorities granted to privileged claims such as unpaid wages, taxes, costs of the insolvency administration, debts incurred by the insolvency administrator, etc., and (4) rules relating to the avoidance of fraudulent or gratuitous transactions or transactions within a suspect period prior to insolvency. Any attempt to harmonise this especially sensitive area of national law would almost certainly frustrate the whole endeavour. The question, however, is whether a uniform European Security Right could not be introduced without such an all-embracing unification of insolvency remedies.

One possibility, which has been advanced by Kreuzer, lies in establishing uniform rules only for the creation of a European Security Right but leaving its effects (in- and outside insolvency) to national legislation by providing for its transposition into the already existing national security rights.[70] The Cape Town Convention on International Interests in Mobile Equipment and its supplementing Aircraft Protocol follow a

---

[67] Cf. the definition of 'proceeds' in article 5(j) United Nations Convention on the Assignment of Receivables in International Trade of 12 Dec. 2001: 'Proceeds means whatever is received in respect of the assigned receivable.'
[68] That is, for example, the solution of the EBRD Model Law, article 5.8 and 5.9.
[69] Goode, Unif. L. Rev./Rev. dr. unif. 1998, 453 (456).   [70] See *supra*, note 63.

slightly more ambitious but less clear-cut approach. Article 30(1) of the Convention states as the basic principle the effectiveness of the international interest in insolvency; article 30(3) exempts national rules on preferences and fraudulent transfers as well as powers of the insolvency administrator to limit the enforcement of security rights in the interests of the general body of creditors, for example, in order to facilitate a reorganisation.[71] The Aircraft Protocol, article XI, contains two sets of additional rules on remedies in insolvency, a 'hard' alternative A and a 'softer' alternative B, the latter leaving a broad discretion to the court administering the insolvency to act in accordance with the applicable national law. Upon ratification, states have to declare which of the alternatives they are going to apply (Article XXX(3)). It remains to be seen whether contracting states will be pushed by the interested industries to adopt alternative A in order to get better access to credit.

Within the EU, it should probably be possible to go a step further than the Cape Town Convention and to define the insolvency remedies without granting the Member States any options. However, in the realm of preferences, powers of the administrator to limit the enforcement of security rights in favour of general creditors and priorities of certain preferred unsecured creditors, it appears most unrealistic to impose uniform rules; here, it will still be necessary to apply national insolvency law which would have to be determined, for example, by declaring the European Security Right as equivalent to a certain domestic interest. Nevertheless, it is suggested that such a limited unification will still be of considerable value to intra-community trade. A crucial task in drafting will be to separate with utmost clarity the area where national law applies from that of the uniform rules.

2. Main policy choices concerning the substantive rules

This evaluation is not the place to present in any detail a suggestion for substantive rules on a uniform European Security Right, therefore a few sentences on the main policy choices should suffice. In any event, the European institutions should take a close look at the draft legal guide on secured transactions currently under preparation at UNCITRAL.[72]

---

[71] In this last respect the wording of article 30(3) Cape Town Convention is not very clear, but see the official commentary by Goode (published on the website of UNIDROIT), article 30 para. 2 with illustrations 14 and 15.
[72] The current status of the drafts is published on the official website of UNCITRAL: www.uncitral.org.

It should also be borne in mind that if a European Security Right is going to be introduced as a supranational model and not as a replacement of national law, the European legislature should all the more be able to realise innovative concepts and have to pay less attention to the existing national law, which would be another advantage of this option.

(a) Uniform, functional approach
The present fragmentation of the law on security rights that has been observed in the European jurisdictions has its roots in historical evolution. It is a source of uncertainty and not infrequently gives rise to frictions within the jurisdictions themselves. It is hard to see any substantive merits justifying the retention of the present system. It is therefore suggested that a European Security Right should be introduced as a uniform, functionally defined interest, following the examples of Article 9 UCC and the EBRD Model Law. Such an interest would have to include retention of title and leasing agreements, which would, however, not necessarily mean that purchase-money security interests would be subjected to exactly the same rules as the rest (see *infra*, section (e)).

(b) Range of possible collateral
Limitations as to what kinds of assets can be charged are another feature of the present fragmentation and in some jurisdictions a consequence of the principle of specificity and/or the impossibility of charging future assets (or, in other words, after-acquired property) which in its turn is mostly due to publicity requirements which are ill-equipped to be satisfied before the assets exist. On the other hand, there is a clear tendency to enlarge the range of possible collateral in most EU jurisdictions.[73] This latter approach should be followed and developed further. Following the seventh EBRD core principle[74] and the approach of Article 9 UCC,[75] it should be left to the parties to choose and define the collateral according to their business needs, be it present or future, a number of single, individually definable movables or an entity of constantly changing assets (e.g. stock-in-trade or assets of an enterprise as a whole). The concern that the ability to charge practically every asset of the debtor might lead to injustice towards later creditors seeking a security or unsecured

---

[73] See *supra*, pp. 649 ff.   [74] Cf. Dahan/Simspon, *supra*, chapter 5, p. 103.
[75] Cf. Sigman, *supra*, chapter 3, p. 57.

creditors should be met by the rules on publicity and priority but not by restricting the range of possible collateral from the outset.

(c) Publicity

As to publicity, we can presently find at least five different systems within the EU: a complete denial of publicity, as for example in Germany; reliance on notification as a means of publicity, as for example in France with respect to security assignments; asset-based registries as for example in France, Italy or Spain with respect to certain non-possessory charges in specific assets; debtor-based registries as for example in England with respect to the *floating charge*; and, as a final category, registration systems which instead of providing publicity strictly speaking, aim rather at fixing the date of the transaction in question (e.g. Dutch silent pledge, Spanish and Italian 'certain date'). The German system of hidden security rights, which functions reasonably well within a secluded national credit market, is ill-suited for a Common Market of now twenty-five Member States where personal reliance must be replaced by reliance on institutions. Notification is only possible with claims or other personal rights where someone exists who can be notified; but even then, a register appears to be a more reliable and more readily accessible source of information. Asset-based registries are certainly a reliable source of information, yet for a potential creditor who merely knows his future debtor but not his potentially encumbered assets, it is difficult if not impossible to find the right registries in which to look. If publicity in its strict sense is sought, tax registries and the like which cannot be searched by the interested public are even less equipped than the aforementioned sources to serve the purpose. To conclude, the only viable method seems to be a debtor-based registry. Since the European Security Right should be open to all kinds of parties, it is evident that it cannot be restricted to debtors, which, like companies, are registered anyway. In addition, such a register should reveal as much information on the debtor and the secured transaction as is necessary to alert the interested creditor and to enable him to obtain further particulars. As the filing system under Article 9 UCC shows, it is not necessary to exhibit any business secrets or anything other than the most basic particulars of the debtor and the encumbered assets. Restricting the registered information to an utmost minimum not only serves the legitimate interests of the parties to the secured transaction but – together with the help of modern database systems – also keeps the registry manageable. Compared to an asset-based registry, a debtor-based registry has the additional advantage of creating fewer problems with respect to cross-border situations. In most cases, the interested party will know where the debtor is situated and can search a regionally organised registry (e.g. the registry of a certain Member State) accordingly. In contrast, an asset-based registry for security rights in movables either would have to be organised European-wide or its regime would need additional rules for moving an entry from one national registry to another (including grace periods) in the case where the movable is brought onto the territory of another Member State.

(d) Priority

The priority rules for conflicts between different secured creditors and between secured creditors and general unsecured creditors (i.e. creditors who do not enjoy a preferred status due to social or other public policy considerations) are closely linked to the publicity regime. If, as is suggested here, a debtor-based registry was introduced, the principal rule for conflicts among secured creditors would be that the creditor who registers first will be first in right.[76] The time of registration could also determine priority as between a secured creditor and unsecured creditors in execution or insolvency, the crucial point in time being either the commencement of the seizure or the commencement of insolvency proceedings. As between a secured creditor and a good-faith purchaser, entry of a security right onto a debtor-based register would – in contrast to an asset-based register – provide no reason to deny good faith in an ordinary business situation. Any other solution would unnecessarily burden day-to-day business transactions.

(e) Special rules for purchase-money security interests

If retention of title and leasing are included within a uniform regime, the question arises of whether the suggested basic rules on registration and priority would need some modification in order to accommodate the special needs of creditors of purchase money, such special needs being reflected in the preferential treatment of retention of title and leasing in all European jurisdictions. A modification should be discussed in two respects. One is the requirement of registration for rendering the purchase money security interest enforceable with priority towards

---

[76] Cf. United Nations Convention on the Assignment of Receivables in International Trade of 12 Dec. 2001, Annex, section I article 1. As to the priority rules under Article 9 UCC which basically follow the same approach, see Sigman, *supra*, chapter 3, pp. 71 ff.

unsecured creditors or secured creditors who have registered after the sales contract has been concluded. The EBRD Model Law (article 9)[77] provides that during the six months following the conclusion of a sales contract with retention of title, the so-called unpaid vendor's charge which only secures the purchase price specific to the charged goods need not be registered. After six months it either ceases to exist or must be transformed into a registered charge. In contrast, Article 9 UCC submits the purchase money security interest to the general requirement of filing and only allows for a grace period of twenty days.[78] For the EU Member States, a general exemption from the need to register what has hitherto been known as simple retention of title, be it for six months or a slightly longer or shorter period, seems better to reflect the status of spontaneous harmonisation already reached. The other question is whether a purchase-money security interest should be given a general priority over previously registered security interests, since otherwise sellers will not be able to take any security in the sold goods if those are already included within a security right over after-acquired property. Such priority is granted by Articles 9–324 UCC[79] as well as by the EBRD Model Law (article 17.3.). Under the present European systems, the same result is reached through regarding the seller's right as retained ownership which could never pass to the buyer or his creditors before payment of the purchase price. It seems indisputable that a super-priority along the lines of Article 9 UCC and the EBRD Model Law must be conferred on a purchase-money security interest also within a uniform European Security Rights regime. Another, far more difficult, question is how far this priority should be extended to claims that are not related to the particular goods in question (all-monies clauses) and, even more importantly, to proceeds of the sold goods. Other than in the area of simple retention of title, we have seen that the European jurisdictions are divided on these issues,[80] so that no recommendation can be founded on a common core.

Bibliography

Roy Goode, 'The Protection of Interests in Movables in Transnational Commercial Law', Unif. L. Rev./Rev. dr. unif. 1998, 453 ff.

Jörg Stefan Greving, *Der Treuhandgedanke bei Sicherungsübertragungen im italienischen und deutschen Recht* (2002).

---

[77] See Dahan/Simpson, *supra*, chapter 5, pp. 105 f.
[78] See Sigman, *supra*, chapter 3, p. 72.   [79] *Ibid.*, p. 74.   [80] See *supra*, pp. 661 ff.

Stefanie Hellmich, *Kreditsicherungsrechte in der spanischen Mehrrechtsordnung* (2000).

Sylvia Kaufhold, *Internationales und europäisches Mobiliarsicherungsrecht* (1999).

Eva-Maria Kieninger, *Mobiliarsicherheiten im Europäischen Binnenmarkt* (1996).

Karl Kreuzer, "Europäisches Mobiliarsicherungsrecht oder: Von den Grenzen des Internationalen Privatrechts" in: *Festschrift für von Overbeck* (1990), 613 ff.

"Gutachtliche Stellungnahme zum Referentenentwurf eines Gesetzes zur Ergänzung des Internationalen Privatrechts (Außervertragliche Schuldverhältnisse und Sachen)" in: D. Henrich (ed.), *Vorschläge und Gutachten zur Reform des deutschen internationalen Sachen- und Immaterialgüterrechts*, 37 ff.

"La propriété mobilière en droit international privé", *Recueil des Cours* 259 (1996) 9 ff.

Jan-Hendrik Röver, *Vergleichende Prinzipien dinglicher Sicherheiten* (1999).

Ulrike Seif, *Der Bestandsschutz besitzloser Mobiliarsicherheiten im deutschen und englischen Recht* (1997).

Teun Struycken, "The International Assignment of Debts: the Dutch Hoge Raad applies the Rome Convention, Article 12, to the Proprietary Issues", *Lloyd's Maritime and Commercial Law Quarterly* 1998, 345 ff.

Manfred Wenckstern, "Die englische Floating Charge im deutschen Internationalen Privatrecht", RabelsZ 56 (1992) 624 ff.

Index by country

(Reference should also be made to the Table of Legislation and Table of Cases Cited by Name)

Austria
accession, transfer or ownership/title
and
bona fide acquisition 253
registration of reservation of title 253
all monies/sums retention of title
(framework agreement) 419–420
frequency of use 420, 437
seller's rights in unsold goods,
non-possessory ownership 419, 435
specificity principle: clarity of
drafting, need for 419; risk 419, 436;
validity 419; obligation to store
separately, relevance 419, 437
bona fide acquisition
belief in seller's right to sell 308,
345: in case of cash purchase 309;
negligence and 308; resale of cars
supplied on credit for that purpose
308–309, 343–344
by purchase at public auction
307–308
in case of purchase on credit 309
constructive delivery/*constitutum
possessorium* 308
delivery and 308
execution 232
gratuitous transactions 308
of money and negotiable instruments
308
of object sold by businessman in
ordinary course of business
307–308, 309

of object stolen or lost by original
owner 308
burden of proof, pre-existing debts 625
car fleet as collateral for non-possessory
security right
loan for purchase/reservation of title
in sales contract to creditor 443, 474
publicity/registry requirement, effect
443
sale and lease-back 443–444
charge of money claims
debitor cessus, notice to, relevance
534–535, 650
excess collateral, relevance 534
frequency of use 534
future claim, whether/applicability to
534, 574–575
insolvency 534–535
priority 534–535
security assignment of earnings
compared 534–535
third-party rights 534
commingling/distinguishability of
monies paid to bankrupt, security
assignment of earnings 535
constructive delivery/*constitutum
possessorium* 175–176
anticipated *constitutum possessorium*
12–13, 310–311
bona fide acquisition 308
pledge and 309–310
contract, avoidance
for fraud 232

674

INDEX BY COUNTRY 675

for intention to defraud/prejudice
creditors 625–626
for mistake 178
contract, termination in case of
insolvency proceedings 176–177.
See also insolvency, contract, effect
on *below*
administrator's rights/duty 251–252
automaticity 176–177, 251
default of administrator
(*Masseverwalter*) and 176–177, 251
contract, termination for failure to
pay 177, 251
non-termination, right of 251
parties' agreement and (resolutive
clause) 251
retroactive/*ex tunc* effect 178
as right *in personam* 228
time-limits/grace period 251
corporeal movables, applicability of
non-possessory security rights 444
credit consignment agreement, sale and
lease-back as 443–444
debitor cessus, notice to, relevance
charge of money claims 534–535, 650
entry in books as 534–535, 571–572,
575, 593
identity of debtor, relevance 363–364,
415
security assignment of earnings
534–535
security assignment of future
claims/debts 12–13, 347, 415
delivery, relevance 175, 223
constructive. *See* constructive
delivery/*constitutum possessorium*
above
symbolic 175–176
where object held by third party
(instruction to hold on behalf of
transferee/*Besitzanweisung*) 175–176
where transferee in possession of
property (*traditio brevi manu*) 175–176
excess collateral, relevance
charge of money claims 534
security assignment of earnings 534
security assignment of future
claims/debts 575
execution
against purchaser of business for
pre-existing debt, business assets,
applicability to 625

bona fide acquisition 232
intention to defraud/prejudice other
creditors, effect 487–488
stock-in-trade as collateral for
non-possessory security right 486,
487–488
finance leasing/leasing contract 597–598
applicable law 598 n.10
contractual nature of relationship
597–598
as hire purchase/payment by
instalment 598 n.10
insolvency of creditor, debtor's rights
598
option to acquire, effect on real rights
598
publicity/registry 598
rei vindicatio in case of insolvency 597
reservation of title 598 n.10
security transfer of ownership
compared 598
tax and consumer credit legislation,
applicability 598
termination in case of insolvency
proceedings: administrator's
right/duty 598; automaticity 598
fraud, avoidance of contract for, transfer
of ownership/title, effect on 232,
244
hire purchase/payment by instalment,
finance leasing as 598 n.10
insolvency 176–177
accession and 279
administrator's right/duty to sell,
insolvent's possession of another's
movable property 173
administrator's rights/duties,
avoidance of onerous/
disadvantageous transactions
486–487
charge of money claims 534–535
contract, effect on: fulfilment of
obligations prior to commencement
of proceedings, relevance 177,
251–252; payment at insolvency
creditor rate, limitation to 177
goods in transit, rights over, transfer
of ownership/title as determining
factor 178
gratuitous transactions 487
incongruous/congruous securities: as
attempt to prefer one creditor over

Austria (cont.)
    others 487; in respect of debt or legal act to detriment of creditors 487; when creditor not entitled to claim at that time 487
    intention to defraud/prejudice other creditors, effect 486: critical dates 486–487
    onerous/disadvantageous transactions, dumping 487
    property of debtor: goods in possession of bankrupt 177; loss of right to manage 177; monies paid to bankrupt for goods resold under sale on credit 309; monies paid to bankrupt for resale of cars supplied for that purpose 311
    security assignment of earnings 534–535
    stock-in-trade as collateral for non-possessory security right 486
ius separationis (*Aussonderungsrecht*) 251–252
liability of purchaser of business for pre-existing debt 625–626
    ceiling, whether 625, 645
    continued use of old name, relevance 625, 645: exclusion by duly registered or notified agreement 625, 645
    continuing liability of original debtor 625
    exclusion, possibility of 625
    knowledge/'should have known' requirement 625
    as personal liability 625
    purchase price, relevance 626
mistake, contract, effect on 178
new goods manufactured out of materials supplied (*specificatio*) 369–370
    execution in the absence of proceeds clause: before payment by second buyer 400; following payment by second buyer 400
    insolvency in the absence of proceeds clause 370, 400
    ownership: publicity/registry and 369–370; risk, relevance 370, 397; value of material/value of work, relevance 369–370

    reservation of title 369–370
    specificatio, ownership, creation/termination and 369, 397
    third-party rights 370
'ordinary course of business' rule, resale of cars supplied on credit for that purpose 307–308, 309
possession, as real right (right *ad rem*) 174 n.16
possessory pledge
    completion many months after loan at time of financial difficulty, effect 486–487
    constructive delivery/*constitutum possessorium* 309–310
    excess collateral, relevance/implied waiver 486
    priority 485–486
    publicity/registry 527
    stock-in-trade as collateral for non-possessory security right 485–486: control of stock, need for 485–486; priority 485–486
priority
    charge of money claims 534–535
    equality of creditors/unfair preferences 487
    possessory pledge 485–486
    reservation of title 251, 283
    security assignment of earnings 534–535
    stock-in-trade as collateral for non-possessory security right, possessory pledge 485–486
proceeds clause (extended reservation of title) 309–311, 350, 353–354, 363–364
    new goods manufactured out of materials supplied (*specificatio*) [with products clause], execution, relevance 415
publicity/registry
    book entry 309–310, 350, 363–364, 593, 661, 662
    car fleet as collateral for non-possessory security right 443–444
    finance leasing/leasing contract 598
    possessory pledge 527
    sale and lease-back 443–444
    security assignment of earnings 534

security interests requiring 252–253, 309–310: machinery 253
rei vindicatio in case of insolvency 178, 232
  goods in possession of buyer in case of voided contract 178
  reservation of title, effect 251, 298, 658
  resale of cars supplied on credit for that purpose 307–311
  monies paid to bankrupt, right to 309: commingling/distinguishability of monies, relevance 310–311, 347; payments made after start of insolvency proceedings 353–354
  transfer of ownership/title as result of 307: authorisation to sell, relevance 308–309, 343–344
reservation of title
  authorisation to sell, relevance 250–251, 288
  delivery without receipt of payment (*kurzfristiger Eigentumsvorbehalt*) 176
  formal requirements 252–253
  machinery, publicity/registry and 253
  new goods manufactured out of materials supplied (*specificatio*) 369–370
  as preferred method 443
  priority 251, 283
  process of goods, right to 250–251
  publicity/registry and 252–253, 283: machinery 253
  rei vindicatio in case of insolvency 251, 298, 658
  sale on credit 176, 177, 225
  as [suspensive] condition for payment of purchase price 250–251
  timing of reservation, relevance 250–251, 252, 285–286
  unilateral declaration of, validity 252, 285
rights
  absolute and relative rights distinguished 174 n.16
  real rights (rights *ad rem/dingliche Rechte*) 174 n.16: possession as 174 n.16; right of inheritance as 174 n.16
risk
  all-monies/sums retention of title 419, 436

new goods manufactured out of materials supplied (*specificatio*), ownership, risk, relevance 370, 397
sale and lease-back
  car fleet as collateral for non-possessory security right 443–444
  as credit consignment agreement 443–444
  publicity/registry 443
  as sham credit consignment agreement 443, 474–475
security assignment of earnings 534–535
  charge of money claim as alternative 534–535, 569–570
  commingling/distinguishability of monies paid to bankrupt 535
  debitor cessus, notice to, relevance 534–535: entry in books as 534–535, 571–572; money earned but not paid before insolvency 534, 535; money earned and paid before insolvency 535
  excess collateral, relevance 534
  frequency of use 534
  future claim, whether 534
  insolvency 534–535: money earned and paid before insolvency, *debitor cessus*, notice to, relevance 535; money not yet earned ('future' claim) 535
  priority 534–535
  publicity/registry 534
  third-party rights 534
security assignment of future claims/debts
  anticipated assignment of claims
  debitor cessus, notice to, relevance 12–13, 415: entry in books as 575, 593
  resale of cars supplied on credit for that purpose 309–311
  specificity principle 310, 347, 350
security interest, publicity/registry 309–310
security rights, future claim against unknown debtor, possibilities 575, 650
security transfer of ownership
  exclusion 12–13
  finance leasing compared 598, 620–621

678 INDEX BY COUNTRY

Austria (*cont.*)
specificity principle
ascertainment of goods 205–206, 208–209, 274–275; all-monies/sums retention of title 419
clarity of drafting, need for 419
fungible assets
security assignment of future claims/debts 310, 347, 350
stock-in-trade as collateral for non-possessory security right
excess collateral, relevance 486
execution 486, 487–488
frequency of use 486
future stocks, possessory pledge 485–486
insolvency 486
possessory pledge 485–486: future stock 485–486; priority 485–486
third-party rights
charge of money claims 534
new goods manufactured out of materials supplied (*specificatio*) and 370
security assignment of earnings 534
transfer of ownership/title
agreement that title should pass ('real agreement'/*Einigung*), need for 175, 224: time of conclusion 175
payment of purchase price, relevance 176, 252
time of: conclusion of contract 175; transfer to carrier 175–176. *See also* delivery, relevance *above*
'title' in form of contract, testamentary disposition or legal provision 174–175
unfair terms (*contra bonos mores*) 486

Belgium
actio Pauliana
gratuitous transactions and 494
requirements: detrimental effect 494; intention to defraud/prejudice other creditors, relevance 494, 629–630; knowledge of third party 494
third-party rights 494
all-monies/sums retention of title (framework agreement) 422
fiduciary relationship (beneficial trust) 422

frequency of use 422, 437
seller's rights in unsold goods: limitation to unpaid balance of particular sale 422; non-possessory ownership 422, 435
specificity principle 422, 436–437
validity 422
bona fide acquisition 71–72, 629
debitor cessus, notice to, relevance 543–544
of object sold by businessman in ordinary course of business 315
possession 186–187: sale and lease-back 474
reservation of title 299
car fleet as collateral for non-possessory security right
fiduciary relationship (beneficial trust) 449
sale and lease-back 449, 474
charge of money claims 542–544
debitor cessus, notice to, relevance 346–347, 542–544, 649–650
third-party rights 542–543
contract, annulment of simulated/*pro forma*, price as evidence of simulation 629–630, 644
contract, avoidance
for fraud 234–235
for intention to defraud/prejudice creditors, price as evidence of intention 629–630
third-party rights 234–235
contract, termination in case of insolvency proceedings 189
contract, termination for failure to pay
judicial termination, need for 188, 227
parties' agreement and (resolutive clause) 188–189, 225–226
third-party rights 189, 225–226
time-limits/grace period 226
credit consignment agreement
reservation of title distinguished 299
right of owner to recover 602
debitor cessus, notice to, relevance
bona fide acquisition 543–544
charge 306
charge of money claims 542–544, 649–650
formal requirements 542–543, 649–650
insolvency, notification following 578

modification of requirement 571,
    649–650
nantissement de fonds de commerce 577
delivery, relevance, insolvency 187
excess collateral, relevance, *nantissement
    de fonds de commerce* 494, 529,
    578
execution
    against purchaser of business for
        pre-existing debt, presumption of
        ownership and 629
    nantissement de fonds de commerce 578
fiduciary relationship (beneficial trust)
    all-monies/sums retention of title
        (framework agreement) 422
    avoidance of 543
    car fleet as collateral for
        non-possessory security right 449
    finance leasing/leasing contract
        compared 602
    third-party rights 422, 449
finance leasing/leasing contract
    administrative requirements 601, 619
    debtor's rights in case of insolvency of
        creditor 602
    execution, right to resist 601
    hire purchase/payment by instalment
        compared 602
    lessor's right on termination to return
        of goods, as owner 601, 602
    option to acquire: at price reflecting
        amount paid in rent 601;
        characterization of contract and
        602
    for term equivalent to working life of
        equipment 601
    third-party rights 601
fixed charge, warrant compared 493
form/nomenclature, relevance 58
fraud, avoidance of contract for, transfer
    of ownership/title, effect on
    234–235, 244
future claim against unknown debtor
    577–578, 649–650
*gage sur fonds de commerce/pand
    handelszaak*. See *nantissement de fonds
    de commerce* below
hire purchase/payment by instalment,
    finance leasing/leasing contract
    compared 602
insolvency 187–189

concursus creditorum 29–30, 187, 189,
    259–260, 315–316
contract, effect on, fulfilment of
    obligations before commencement
    of proceedings, relevance 189
debitor cessus, notice to, relevance,
    notification following 578
goods in transit, rights over, stoppage
    189, 229
intention to defraud/prejudice other
    creditors, effect, avoidance of
    fraudulent proceedings 494–495
nantissement de fonds de commerce
    493–494, 577, 578
property of debtor: delivery, relevance
    187; existing assets and assets
    coming into existence during
    proceedings 187; payment of
    purchase price, relevance 187
sale and lease-back 449: debtor's rights
    in case of insolvency of creditor 449
security assignment of earnings
    543–544
stock-in-trade as collateral for
    non-possessory security right
    493–494
suspect period 494–495
legislation, role 55
liability of purchaser of business for
    pre-existing debt 629–630
rei vindicatio and 629
nantissement de fonds de commerce
    applicability: all types of asset 493;
        limitation to 50 per cent of assets
        493–494, 525–526; limitation to
        bank or financial institution 57,
        493
    completion many months after loan
        at time of financial difficulty, effect
        494–495
    debitor cessus, notice to, relevance 577
    excess collateral, relevance 494, 529,
        578
    execution 578
    fluctuating future assets 493, 494, 661
    frequency of use 494
    insolvency 493–494, 577, 578
    inventory collateral, exclusion 57
    'ordinary course of business' rule
        493
    publicity/registry 493, 527

Belgium (cont.)
   as security right to claim against unknown debtor 577–578
   stock-in-trade as collateral for non-possessory security right 493
   third-party rights 493–494
  natural justice, *accessio/specificatio* 374
  new goods manufactured out of materials supplied (*specificatio*)
   commingling, priority 374
   execution in the absence of proceeds clause 374–375: before payment by second buyer 404; following payment by second buyer 404
   insolvency in the absence of proceeds clause 375, 404
   natural justice and 374
   ownership, value of material/value of work, relevance 395
   priority, commingling and 374
   reservation of title 374–375
   specificatio: determination of 374, 662–663; ownership, creation/termination and 374, 397
  'ordinary course of business' rule 186–187, 315
  possession
   bona fide acquisition of real rights in movable property: 186–187; sale and lease-back 474
   presumption of ownership and 317, 629, 652–653
  possessory pledge
   publicity/registry 527
   stock-in-trade as collateral for non-possessory security right, control of stock, need for 493–494
  priority
   delivery, relevance 186–187
   paritas creditorum 187
   retention of asset as security for performance/performance withhold (*droit de retention/retentierecht*) 75
   statutory preferences: carrier 189; seller [on credit] (*privilège du vendeur*) 10, 187, 226
  products clause, exclusion 375
  publicity/registry 59
   nantissement de fonds de commerce 493, 527

  real subrogation (assignment of future claim) 315–316, 349–350, 355–356, 363, 662
  new goods manufactured out of materials supplied (*specificatio*) 404, 415
  third-party rights 187, 189, 315–316, 346, 355–356, 363
  [registered] charge
   debitor cessus, notice to, relevance 316
   limited use of 316, 404, 414–415
  rei vindicatio in case of insolvency
   insolvent's possession of another's movable property 299
   liability of purchaser of business for pre-existing debt and 629
   reservation of title, effect 225–226, 259–260, 283–284, 289, 658
   transfer of ownership in the absence of obligation to deliver 188–189
  remedies, disposal of collateral, need for judicial involvement 79
  resale of cars supplied on credit for that purpose 315–316
   monies paid to bankrupt, right to: commingling/distinguishability of monies, relevance 315–316; payments made after start of insolvency proceedings 355–356
   transfer of ownership/title as result of 315: authorisation to sell, relevance 315, 344, 363
  reservation of title 187–188, 316
   authorisation to sell, relevance 289, 299
   carrier's right 189
   credit consignment agreement distinguished 299
   formal requirements 259–260: general conditions, adequacy 422; signature 260; writing 259–260, 283–284, 658
   insolvency 11
   new goods manufactured out of materials supplied (*specificatio*) 374–375
   publicity/registry and 260, 283
   rei vindicatio in case of insolvency 225–226, 259–260, 283–284, 289, 658: customary law provision 188
   third-party rights 226, 652–653

timing of reservation, relevance 260, 285–286
unilateral declaration of, validity 260, 285: implied consent 260
retention of asset as security for performance/performance withhold (*droit de retention/retentierecht*) 187–188, 226
　carrier's right 189
　rei vindicatio 225–226
sale and lease-back
　applicability, business purposes 449
　bona fide acquisition 474
　car fleet as collateral for non-possessory security right 449, 474
　insolvency 449: debtor's rights in case of insolvency of creditor 449
security assignment of earnings
　debitor cessus, notice to, relevance: money earned but not paid before insolvency 543–544; money earned and paid before insolvency 543–544
　insolvency 543–544
　third-party rights 543
security rights, *concursus creditorum* 187
special registered charge 477–478
　variety 10–11
specificity principle 186, 224
　reservation of title 259–260
　security rights, future claim against unknown debtor 574, 577–578
　stock-in-trade as collateral for non-possessory security right insolvency 493–494
　nantissement de fonds de commerce 493
　warrant 493
third-party rights
　actio Pauliana 494
　assignment of claim to recovery 189
　charge of money claims 542–543
　fiduciary relationship (beneficial trust) 422, 449
　finance leasing/leasing contract 601
　nantissement de fonds de commerce 493–494
　reservation of title 226, 652–653
　security assignment of earnings 543
　termination/avoidance of contract and 189, 225–226: in case of fraud or mistake 234–235

transfer of ownership/title
　obligation to transfer, principle of abstraction, revesting of title on termination of contract and 227–228
　requirements: consent, sufficiency 186, 223, 475; payment of purchase price, relevance 186, 187, 363
warrant
　fixed charge compared 493
　stock-in-trade as collateral for non-possessory security right 493

Denmark
agency, resale of cars supplied on credit for that purpose 337
all-monies/sums retention of title (framework agreement) 431
credit consignment agreement rules, applicability 431
frequency of use 431, 437
insolvency: *ius separationis* 431; part of insolvency estate, whether 431
seller's rights in unsold goods, non-possessory ownership 435
validity, authority to sell before payment of purchase price, relevance 431, 437
bona fide acquisition, reservation of title 336–337
car fleet as collateral for non-possessory security right
　registered vehicle charge 467
　sale and lease-back 467
commission [undisclosed] agency 337, 348–349, 361
　certain date (*data certa*) before execution or commencement of insolvency proceedings, need for 361
contract, annulment of simulated/*pro forma* 640–641, 644
　price as evidence of simulation 641
contract, avoidance
　for fraud 242: transfer of ownership/title, effect on 242, 244
　for intention to defraud/prejudice creditors, price as evidence of intention/knowledge 641, 646
contract, termination in case of insolvency proceedings, administrator's rights/duty 278

Denmark (*cont.*)
  contract, termination for failure to pay
    parties' agreement and (resolutive
      clause) 217
    reservation of title, relevance 278
    reversion of title 216: mistake and 216
  credit consignment agreement
    all-monies/sums retention of title
      (framework agreement) and 431
    commingling/distinguishability,
      relevance 338, 348–349, 361
    conditions for settlement 295,
      337–338, 360–361, 390: payment to
      consignor on resale 295, 431
    ius separationis 431
    new goods manufactured out of
      materials supplied (*specificatio*) 390,
      411–412
    obligation to store separately 431,
      437
    resale of cars supplied on credit for
      that purpose 337–338, 360–361:
      registry, relevance 338
    reservation of title distinguished 295,
      299
    specificity principle 390, 431
    stock-in-trade as collateral for
      non-possessory security right 518
  debitor cessus, notice to, relevance
    identity of debtor, relevance 589
    security assignment of claims/debts
      563, 589
    security assignment of future
      claims/debts 589–590
    excess collateral, relevance, security
      assignment of future claims/debts
      590
  execution
    against purchaser of business for
      pre-existing debt, business assets,
      applicability to 640–641
    [registered] charge 518
    security assignment of claims/debts
      589
  factoring contract
    security assignment of future
      claims/debts 589
    as security for bank loan, loan as
      discounted value of assigned claims
      589
  finance leasing/leasing contract 615
    frequency of use 615
  insolvency of creditor, debtor's rights
    615
  option to acquire: characterization of
    contract and 615; as evidence of sale
    with reservation of title 615
  reservation of title/retention of
    ownership 615
  as sale with reservation of title 615
  termination in case of insolvency
    proceedings: administrator's
    right/duty 615; lessor's right 615
  insolvency
    administrator's rights/duties, sale of
      assets, registered charge 468–469
    goods in transit, rights over:
      enforcement of contract and 217;
      stoppage 217
    property of debtor, assets excluded
      from execution, exclusion 391
    protection of buyer against seller's
      creditors 215–216, 223–224
    protection of seller against buyer's
      creditors 216, 223–224
    recovery of goods handed over by
      mistake 217
    security assignment of future
      claims/debts 589–590
    ius separationis, all-monies/sums
      retention of title (framework
      agreement) 431
  liability of purchaser of business for
    pre-existing debt 640–641
    continued management by original
      owner, relevance 640–641
  new goods manufactured out of
    materials supplied (*specificatio*)
    authority to manufacture before
      payment of purchase price,
      relevance 395–396
    credit consignment agreement 390,
      411–412
    execution in the absence of proceeds
      clause 390: before payment by
      second buyer 411; following
      payment by second buyer 411
    insolvency in the absence of proceeds
      clause 391, 412
    mandate to manufacture and sell 391
    ownership: payment of purchase
      price, relevance 390; risk, relevance
      391, 397
    reservation of title 390–391, 411

security assignment of future
   claims/debts 411–412
possessory pledge
   priority 518
   registry 314–315
   stock-in-trade as collateral for
      non-possessory security right 517:
      control of stock, need for 517
priority
   equality of creditors/unfair
      preferences 518–519
   possessory pledge 518
   [registered] charge 518
   reservation of title 217, 283
   security assignment of claims/debts
      589
proceeds clause (extended reservation of
   title) 300, 361, 363–364
publicity/registry, cars 279, 336–337, 338
[registered] charge
   execution 518
   fixtures/commingling/
      distinguishability of monies paid to
      bankrupt 468
   priority 518
   resale of cars supplied on credit for
      that purpose 338–339
   specificity principle 339, 517
   stock-in-trade as collateral for
      non-possessory security right 517,
      527: long-term storage with
      obligation to settle on sale 517
registered vehicle charge
   car fleet as collateral for
      non-possessory security right 467
   debtor's rights in case of insolvency of
      creditor 468–469
   specificity principle 467
rei vindicatio in case of insolvency,
   reservation of title, effect 278,
   283–284, 658
resale of cars supplied on credit for that
   purpose 336–339
   agency and 337
   credit consignment agreement:
      conditions for settlement and
      337–338; registry, relevance 338
   monies paid to bankrupt, right to 337:
      commingling/distinguishability of
      monies, relevance 338, 348–349,
      361; payments made after start of
      insolvency proceedings 360–361;

reservation of title 337, 349;
   security assignment of future
   claims/debts 338
registry, relevance 336–337, 338
transfer of ownership/title as result of
   336–337: authorisation to sell,
   relevance 337, 344
used car sales, registry 338
reservation of title 216, 217, 223–224
   authorisation to sell, relevance 295,
      299
   bona fide acquisition 336–337
   in case of consumer sales 217
   credit consignment agreement
      distinguished 295, 299, 658–659
   formal requirements 278: fixed price
      278; price threshold 278
   new goods manufactured out of
      materials supplied (*specificatio*)
      390–391, 411
   priority 217, 283
   publicity/registry and 279, 283, 658:
      used cars 337
   rei vindicatio in case of insolvency 278,
      283–284, 658
   resale of cars supplied on credit for
      that purpose 336–337, 360–361: as
      preferred method 349
   sale on credit 217, 336–337: agreement
      to settle at time of resale, need for
      337–338, 360–361
   specificity principle 279
   timing of reservation, relevance 278,
      279, 285–286
   unilateral declaration of, validity 278,
      279, 285
risk, new goods manufactured out of
   materials supplied (*specificatio*),
   ownership, risk, relevance 391, 397
sale and lease-back
   car fleet as collateral for
      non-possessory security right 467
   frequency of use 468
   as sham charge 467–468,
      474–475
security assignment of claims/debts
   563–564
   debitor cessus, notice to, relevance
      563
   execution 589
   frequency of use 563
   priority 589

684 INDEX BY COUNTRY

Denmark (*cont.*)
security assignment of earnings, *debitor cessus*, notice to, relevance, money earned and paid before insolvency 563–564
security assignment of future claims/debts
  debitor cessus, notice to, relevance 589–590
  excess collateral, relevance 590
  factoring contract 589
  insolvency 589–590
  new goods manufactured out of materials supplied (*specificatio*) 411–412
  resale of cars supplied on credit for that purpose 338
security rights
  duration of charge before insolvency, relevance 518–519
  future claim against unknown debtor, possibilities 589–590
security transfer of ownership, completion many months after loan at time of financial difficulty, effect 518–519
special registered charge 468, 477–478
specificity principle 215–216, 223–224
  credit consignment agreement 390, 431
  fungible assets 431
  [registered] charge 339, 517
  registered vehicle charge 467
  reservation of title 279
stock-in-trade as collateral for non-possessory security right
  credit consignment agreement 518
  excess collateral, relevance 518
  frequency of use 518
  obligation to store separately 517
  [registered] charge 517, 527: long-term storage with obligation to settle on sale 517
transfer of ownership/title, requirements, consent, sufficiency 223–224

England
accession, transfer or ownership/title and
reversibility, relevance 382–383
specificatio distinguished 382
agency
  carrier as 207
  resale of cars supplied on credit for that purpose 326
all-monies/sums retention of title (framework agreement) 426–427
  frequency of use 427, 437
  payment of purchase price, relevance 426–427, 435
  seller's rights in sold goods, proceeds clause (extended reservation of title) as parallel 427
  specificity principle 426–427
  validity 426–427, 434–435: excess collateral, relevance 427; publicity/registry 426–427; as reservation of title clause 427, 435, 648–649, 661–662
appropriation, definition 272
bona fide acquisition
  belief in seller's right to sell 343–344
  execution 239, 270
  possession 326–327, 344–345
  reservation of title 270
  sale and lease-back 460–461
  statutory provisions 326
car fleet as collateral for non-possessory security right
  fixed charge 458–459, 476
  floating [enterprise] charge/lien/mortgage 459–460
  possessory pledge 458
  sale and lease-back 460–461
carrier, as agent 207
choice of law, *conflit mobile* 17
constructive delivery/*constitutum possessorium* 46 n.28
contract, avoidance
  for fraud 238–240: transfer of ownership/title, effect on 238–240
  for intention to defraud/prejudice creditors 636: price as evidence of intention/knowledge 636, 646
  for misrepresentation 238–239
contract, termination in case of insolvency proceedings 207
contract, termination for failure to pay parties' agreement and (resolutive clause) 206–207

reversion of title [where seller remains in possession of goods] 206–207: principle of abstraction and 227–228
corporate debtors 85
damages in case of contract avoided for fraud or misrepresentation 238–239
debitor cessus, notice to, relevance, security assignment of claims/debts 556–557, 586
delivery, relevance 206, 223, 271–272
  gift/transactions other than sale 206
equitable/legal ownership distinguished 82, 458–459
excess collateral, relevance
  security assignment of claims/debts 586
  stock-in-trade as collateral for non-possessory security right 509, 528–529
execution
  against purchaser of business for pre-existing debt 636
  bailiff/sheriff's rights/duties 239–240, 636: sale of assets subject to reservation of title, liability 270, 383; timely completion of execution 239–240
  bona fide acquisition 239, 270
  floating [enterprise] charge/lien/ mortgage 383
  nature of right in property under execution 239–240
  procedure 239–240
  security assignment of claims/debts 586
  security assignment of earnings, joinder of parties 556
  stock-in-trade as collateral for non-possessory security right 508
factoring contract
  as security for bank loan 585–586: loan as discounted value of assigned claims 585–586
fiduciary relationship, resale of cars supplied on credit for that purpose 329–330, 347–348
finance leasing/leasing contract 610–611
  frequency of use 611
  insolvency of creditor, debtor's rights 611

lessor's right on termination to return of goods, as owner 610
  option to acquire, characterisation of contract and 610–611
  termination in case of insolvency proceedings, administrator's right/duty 610–611
fixed charge 13
  car fleet as collateral for non-possessory security right 458–459, 476
  equitable nature of real right 458–459
  expansion of coverage 89–90
  priority 459
  publicity/registry 458–459
flexibility of system 87
floating charge
  applicability: corporate debtors, de facto limitation to 57, 508–509, 525: limitations 89–90
  car fleet as collateral for non-possessory security right 459–460
  characteristics 459–460
  completion many months after loan at time of financial difficulty, effect 509
  crystallisation 13, 459–460, 525
  equitable nature of real right 458–459, 508
  execution 383
  fluctuating future assets 87, 458–459, 661: duration of charge before insolvency, relevance 328, 509
  freedom of contract and 85, 663
  insolvency 84–85, 87–89
  priority 459–460, 508
  resale of cars supplied on credit for that purpose 326
  stock-in-trade as collateral for non-possessory security right 508–509, 525
  unlawful preferences 328
fraud, transfer of ownership/title, effect on 326–327
hire purchase/payment by instalment
  as legal fiction 87
  power of disposal 610–611
  [suspensive] condition for payment of purchase price 610–611

686 INDEX BY COUNTRY

England (cont.)
  transfer of title/ownership, as option 610–611
insolvency
  administration by insolvency administrator 206
  corporate insolvency 206
  extension of system, means 60
  floating [enterprise] charge 84–85, 87–89, 239–240
  goods in transit, rights over on completion of transit 207: enforcement of contract and 207; seller's statutory possessory lien and 207; stoppage 206–207, 229
  gratuitous transactions 509
  Insolvency – A Second Chance (2001) 84 n.13
  onerous/disadvantageous transactions, administrator's rights/duty to avoid 461–462
  property of debtor: goods in possession of bankrupt 636; property disposed of after commencement of proceedings 326–327
  Report on Insolvency Law and Practice (Cork Report 1982) 84 n.13, 90, 90
  security assignment of claims/debts 556–557
  stock-in-trade as collateral for non-possessory security right 508
legal fictions 87
  hire purchase 87
liability of purchaser of business for pre-existing debt 636
misrepresentation
  avoidance/rescission of contract for 238–239: *bona fide* acquisition 238–239
  damages for 238–239
  definition 238–239
mortgage, definition 87 n.22
mortgage (chattel)
  civil law right of redemption distinguished 52 n.54
  common law: Bills of Sale Acts 1878 ff, effect 51–52; as *hypotheca* 49–50
  as 'equity of redemption' 52 n.54
  as proprietary interest 52 n.54
new goods manufactured out of materials supplied (*specificatio*)
  accession and 382–383
  execution in the absence of proceeds clause 383: before payment by second buyer 409; following payment by second buyer 409
  insolvency in the absence of proceeds clause 384, 409
  ownership: risk, relevance 382; value of material/value of work, relevance 382, 395
  possessory pledge 384
  proceeds clause (extended reservation of title) 383–384
  [registered] charge 409
  reservation of title 85–86, 382–384
  specificatio: accession distinguished 382; ownership, creation/termination and 382
  tenancy in common rights 384
'ordinary course of business' rule, resale of cars supplied on credit for that purpose 326
perfection, registry of company charge as 92–93
possession
  bona fide acquisition of real rights in movable property 326–327, 344–345
  protection of better right to in the absence of concept of absolute ownership 204, 326
  sale and lease-back 460–461
possessory pledge
  car fleet as collateral for non-possessory security right 458
  new goods manufactured out of materials supplied (*specificatio*), trust receipt/bills of lading and 384
priority
  distributional considerations 84–85
  fixed charge 459
  future advances on existing position ('tacking') 86–87, 90–92, 328: discretionary advances by bank after notice 91, 92–93
  paritas creditorum 84–85, 206
  publicity/registry and. *See* publicity/registry *below*

purchase money security interest 86, 91
rankings, absence of legislative statement or organized collocation 86–87
reservation of title 91–92, 283
statutory preferences 327, 459–460
proceeds clause (extended reservation of title) 329
  limited scope for 13
  new goods manufactured out of materials supplied (*specificatio*) [with products clause] 383–384
publicity/registry 85–86
  all-monies/sums retention of title (framework agreement) 426–427
  constructive notice 91, 92–93
  filing of charge, disadvantages 86–87: notice filing, proposals for 90–91
  future trade creditors and 85–86
  pre-existing unsecured creditors and 85–86
  priority 90–92
  registered charge 458–459
  registration of company charge 92–93, 228, 270–271, 327–328, 556, 663
  registration of individual charge 228, 346–347, 556
  registration of title clauses 90–92
  sale and lease-back 460–461
  security assignment of earnings 556
purchase money security interest, priority 86, 91
reform, proposals for 90–93
  company charges: *Modern Company Law for a Competitive Economy* (June 2001) 90–91, 93; notice filing 90–91; 'registry of Company Charges', Consultation Document (9 October 2000) 90; rejection 90
  Modern Company Law for a Competitive Economy (June 2001) 90–91, 93, 94
  reluctance to pursue, reasons 93
  Report of the Committee on Consumer Credit (Crowther Report 1971) 90
  Report on Insolvency Law and Practice (Cork Report 1982) 84 n.13, 90, 90
  reservation of title 90–92
  A Review of Security Interests in Property (Diamond Report 1989) 90

registered charge. *See also* fixed charge *and* floating charge *above*
  equitable nature of real right 458–459
  filing, complications 86–87
  new goods manufactured out of materials supplied (*specificatio*) and 409
  publicity/registry 458–459, 460–461
  registry of company charge 92–93, 228, 556
  registry of individual charge 228, 346–347
remedies 93–94
  acceleration of payment 94
  appointment of administrator by agreement 93–94
  in tort 204
resale of cars supplied on credit for that purpose 327–329, 347, 359. *See also bona fide* acquisition; hire purchase/payment by instalment *above*
  agency and 326
  fiduciary relationship 329–330, 347–348
  monies paid to bankrupt, right to 326–327, 330: agency relationship and 327; commingling/distinguishability of monies, relevance 328–329; payments made after start of insolvency proceedings 358–359; registered charge 327–329, 347, 359; security assignment of future claims/debts 329, 347
  reservation of title 326–327
  transfer of ownership/title as result of 326–327: authorisation to sell, relevance 326–327, 343–344
rescission 239
reservation of title. *See also* transfer of ownership/title *below*
  administrator in insolvency's rights/duties, effect on 270
  authorisation to sell, relevance 293–294, 298
  bona fide acquisition 270
  charge/security interest distinguished 272

England (cont.)
  formal requirements: fixed price 278; inclusion in delivery note, sufficiency 272; reservation of both legal and beneficial ownership 270–271; writing 272
  new goods manufactured out of materials supplied (*specificatio*) 85–86
  priority 91–92, 283
  publicity/registry and 90–92, 272, 283
  resale of cars supplied on credit for that purpose 326–327
  as [suspensive] condition for payment of purchase price 270, 271–272
  timing of reservation, relevance 271–272, 285–286
  as transfer of ownership/reversion of equitable real interest 270–271, 326–327
  unilateral declaration of, validity 271–272, 285
restitution, contract and 85 n.17
Roman law and 49–50
  pledge/pawn as *pignus* 49
sale and lease-back
  applicability 461
  bona fide acquisition 460–461
  car fleet as collateral for non-possessory security right 460–461
  insolvency, debtor's rights in case of insolvency of creditor 461, 478–479
  possession 460–461
  publicity/registry 460–461
  real/personal nature of lessee's interest 461
  as sham charge 449–450, 460–461, 474–475
  third-party rights 460–461
security assignment of claims/debts 555–557
  by charge 555, 556, 571–572
  by discount 556
  by mortgage 555, 556
  conditional/contingent nature, relevance 555, 585–586
  debitor cessus, notice to, relevance 556–557, 586: money earned but not paid before insolvency 556–557; money earned and paid before insolvency 556–557

  as equitable right 555–557
  excess collateral, relevance 586
  execution 586: joinder of parties 556
  formal requirements 555–556: absolute assignment 556
  frequency of use 555, 585–586
  future debt 555, 585–586
  insolvency 556–557
  publicity/registry 556
  requirements, writing 556
security assignment of earnings, future claim, whether 555
security assignment of future claims/debts, resale of cars supplied on credit for that purpose 329, 347, 349–350
security rights
  completion many months after loan at time of financial difficulty, effect 509
  future claim against unknown debtor, possibilities 585–586
specificity principle 205–206, 224
  ascertainment of goods 205–206
  commodities sold in bulk 205
  fungible assets 426–427
stock-in-trade as collateral for non-possessory security right
  excess collateral, relevance 509, 528–529
  execution 508
  floating [enterprise] charge 508–509, 525
  frequency of use, floating [enterprise] charge/lien/mortgage 508
  insolvency 508
tenancy in common rights, new goods manufactured out of materials supplied (*specificatio*) 384
third-party rights
  Privity of Contract: Contracts for the Benefit of Third Parties 85 n.16
  privity of contract and 85
  sale and lease-back 460–461
  termination/avoidance of contract and, *bona fide* acquisition 238–239
transfer of ownership/title 204–207
  obligation to transfer 271–272: principle of abstraction, revesting of title on termination of contract and 227–228

INDEX BY COUNTRY 689

relevance 82–84
requirements: consent, sufficiency
  271–272; deed, sufficiency 206; *nemo
  plus* principle 326, 345, 358–359;
  payment of purchase price,
  relevance
time of: agreement as determining
  factor 204–205, 223, 228;
  ascertainment of unascertained
  goods 205–206; conclusion of
  contract 205–206; notification that
  goods ready for collection 205–206;
  surrender of possession 205–206;
  transfer to carrier 205–206, 207

Finland
actio Pauliana 524
  burden of proof, family membership
    as evidence of intent 643
  gratuitous transactions 643
  judicial avoidance 524
  limitation period 524, 643
  requirements: detrimental effect 524,
    643; insolvency attributable to
    transaction 524, 643; third-party's
    knowledge/'should have known'
    requirement 524, 643
all-monies/sums retention of title
  (framework agreement) 434
  credit consignment agreement rules,
    applicability 434
  frequency of use 434, 437
  hire purchase/payment by instalments
    434
  insolvency, part of insolvency estate,
    whether 434
  seller's rights in unsold goods,
    non-possessory ownership 435
  specificity principle 434: risk 436, 437
  validity: authority to sell before
    payment of purchase price,
    relevance 437; general
    clauses/framework agreement,
    acceptability; third-party rights 434
assignment of claim to recovery
  as alternative to delivery, *debitor cessus*,
    notice to, relevance 220
  debitor cessus, notice to, relevance 220,
    343
bona fide acquisition
  enterprise charge 471–472, 522–523

gratuitous transactions 643
possession 220–221, 341, 344–345
reservation of title 282, 341
car fleet as collateral for non-possessory
  security right
  enterprise charge 471–472
  registered vehicle charge 471–472
charge of money claims
  debitor cessus, notice to, relevance:
    money earned but not paid before
    insolvency 568; money earned and
    paid before insolvency 568
  future earnings as collateral for bank
    loan 567–568
commingling/distinguishability of
  monies paid to bankrupt
commission [undisclosed] agency 342,
  348–349, 413
risk 436
commission [undisclosed] agency
  commingling/distinguishability of
    monies, relevance 342, 348–349, 413
  credit consignment agreement
    compared 297 n.24
  new goods manufactured out of
    materials supplied (*specificatio*) 394,
    413, 415–416
  resale of cars supplied on credit for
    that purpose 362
  reservation of title distinguished
    299–300
  sale or return arrangement between
    original seller and reseller,
    relevance 299, 342, 364, 413
contract, annulment of simulated/*pro
  forma* 642–643, 644
contract, avoidance
  for fraud 243: transfer of
    ownership/title, effect on 243, 244
contract, termination for failure to pay
  following delivery 221
  parties' agreement and (resolutive
    clause) 221: third-party rights 221
  reversion of title [where seller remains
    in possession of goods], principle of
    abstraction and 227–228
credit consignment agreement
  commission [undisclosed] agency
    compared 297 n.24
  reservation of title distinguished
    299–300, 658–659

Finland (cont.)
  debitor cessus, notice to, relevance
    enterprise charge 343, 346–347
    identity of debtor, relevance 364
    security assignment of future claims/debts 413, 415
  delivery, relevance, priority 221
  enterprise charge 57, 477
    applicability 472: future debts as collateral for bank loan 591–592; limitations 525, 650–651
    bona fide acquisition 471–472, 522–523
    car fleet as collateral for non-possessory security right 471–472: frequency of use 471–472
    excess collateral, relevance 592
    execution 592
    frequency of use 523
    insolvency 592
    limited applicability 343, 650–651
    'ordinary course of business' rule 471–472, 522–523
    priority 414, 523, 525, 591–592
    publicity/registry 522–523
    resale of cars supplied on credit for that purpose, monies paid to bankrupt, right to 343
    stock-in-trade as collateral for non-possessory security right 522–523, 528
  excess collateral, relevance, enterprise charge 592
  execution
    against purchaser of business for pre-existing debt, business assets, applicability to 642–643
    enterprise charge 592
    stock-in-trade as collateral for non-possessory security right 523
  finance leasing/leasing contract 618–619
    frequency of use 618–619
    option to acquire: characterisation of contract and 618; hire purchase/payment by instalment and 617, 618
    reservation of title/retention of ownership 618
    sale with reservation of title compared 618
    for term equivalent to working life of equipment 618
  hire purchase/payment by instalment
    all-monies/sums retention of title (framework agreement) 434
    reservation of title 281
  insolvency 219–222
    administrator's rights/duties: default, effect 281; sale of assets, preservation of assets 220; satisfaction of claims of creditors and return residue to bankrupt 219–220
    contract, effect on, fulfilment of obligations before commencement of proceedings, relevance 221
    corporate insolvency 219–220
    enterprise charge 592
    good faith and, acquisition from insolvent 220–221
    goods in transit, rights over: enforcement of contract and 222; reservation of title, relevance 221–222; stoppage 221–222, 229; transfer of ownership/title, relevance 221–222
    intention to defraud/prejudice other creditors, effect, avoidance of fraudulent proceedings 642–643
    property of debtor: property sold before insolvency 220; shares, bonds and other securities 220
    protection of buyer against seller's creditors 220–221, 223–224
    recovery of property disposed of before insolvency proceedings (*actio Pauliana*) 524
    registered vehicle charge, debtor's rights in case of insolvency of creditor 472–473
    sale and lease-back, insolvency, debtor's rights in case of insolvency of creditor 472–473
    seller's protection against buyer's creditors 223–224
    stock-in-trade as collateral for non-possessory security right 523
  ius separationis 281, 283–284, 299
  liability of purchaser of business for pre-existing debt 642–643
    assets as entirety of debtor's property, relevance 642 n.44

new goods manufactured out of
    materials supplied (*specificatio*)
  authority to manufacture before
    payment of purchase price,
    relevance 393–394, 395–396,
    413
  commission [undisclosed] agency 394,
    413, 415–416
  execution in the absence of proceeds
    clause 393: before payment by
    second buyer 413; following
    payment by second buyer 413
  insolvency in the absence of proceeds
    clause 393, 394, 414
  monies paid to bankrupt, right to,
    commingling/distinguishability of
    monies, relevance 413
  ownership: risk, relevance 394, 397,
    413, 415–416; value of material/value
    of work, relevance 394, 395
  reservation of title 393–394,
    413
  security assignment of future
    claims/debts 413–414
  specificatio, determination of 394
  third-party rights 393–394
'ordinary course of business' rule
  enterprise charge 471–472,
    522–523
  resale of cars supplied on credit for
    that purpose 341, 344, 362
possession, *bona fide* acquisition of real
    rights in movable property 341,
    344–345
possessory pledge
  stock-in-trade as collateral for
    non-possessory security right:
    control of stock, need for 522;
    delivery to third party to hold for
    pledgee, need for 522
priority
  delivery, relevance 221
  enterprise charge 414, 523, 525,
    591–592
  registered vehicle charge 471–472
publicity/registry
  book entry 220, 642 n.44
  cars. *See* registered vehicle charge
    below
  enterprise charge 522–523, 527
  shares, bonds and other securities 220

registered vehicle charge
  car fleet as collateral for
    non-possessory security right
    471–472
  frequency of use 471–472
  insolvency, debtor's rights in case of
    insolvency of creditor 472–473
  priority 471–472
  resale of cars supplied on credit for
    that purpose 343, 347: monies paid
    to bankrupt, right to and 343,
    347
  third-party rights 471–472
resale of cars supplied on credit for that
    purpose 341–343
  dealer arrangements 342–343
  monies paid to bankrupt, right to 341:
    commingling/distinguishability of
    monies, relevance 342, 348–349;
    enterprise charge 343; payments
    made after start of insolvency
    proceedings 362; registered vehicle
    charge 343, 347; reservation of title
    342; security assignment of future
    claims/debts 343
  reseller's obligation to transfer monies
    received to original seller 342
  transfer of ownership/title as result of
    341: authorisation to sell, relevance
    341, 344, 362
reservation of title 221, 223–224
  authorisation to sell, relevance 297,
    299–300
  bona fide acquisition 282, 341
  commission [undisclosed] agency
    distinguished 299–300
  formal requirements 282: general
    conditions, adequacy 282; writing
    282
  goods in transit and 221–222
  machinery, publicity/registry and 282,
    283
  new goods manufactured out of
    materials supplied (*specificatio*)
    393–394, 413
  reasonableness test 393
  resale of cars supplied on credit for
    that purpose 342: payment to
    original seller as prerequisite for
    delivery to final buyer 342
  third-party rights 221, 282, 413

Finland (cont.)
  timing of reservation, relevance 282, 285–286
  unilateral declaration of, validity 281–282, 285
  risk, new goods manufactured out of materials supplied (specificatio), ownership 394, 397, 413, 415–416
  sale and lease-back
    insolvency, debtor's rights in case of insolvency of creditor 472–473
    as sham charge 472, 474–475
    validity 472
  security assignment of claims/debts, conditional/contingent nature, relevance 567–568
  security assignment of earnings 567–568
    charge of money claim as alternative 569–570
    debitor cessus, notice to, relevance
    money earned but not paid before insolvency 568; money earned and paid before insolvency 568
    insolvency, money not yet earned ('future' claim) 567–568
  security assignment of future claims/debts 349–350
    new goods manufactured out of materials supplied (specificatio) 413–414
    resale of cars supplied on credit for that purpose 343
    resale of goods supplied for that purpose 300
  security rights
    completion many months after loan at time of financial difficulty, effect 523–524
    duration of charge before insolvency, relevance 523–524
    future claim against unknown debtor, possibilities 591–592
  special registered charge
    aircraft 472
    applicability 477–478
    patents and industrial/intellectual property rights 472
    publicly traded shares, bonds and securities 472
    vessels 472

  specificity principle 220, 223–224
    all-monies/sums retention of title 434
  stock-in-trade as collateral for non-possessory security right 522–524
    enterprise charge 522–523, 528
    excess collateral, relevance 522, 523, 529
    execution 523
    frequency of use, enterprise charge 523
    insolvency 523
  third-party rights
    all-monies/sums retention of title (framework agreement) 434
    new goods manufactured out of materials supplied (specificatio) 393–394
    parties' agreement to terminate contract (resolutive clause) and 221
    reservation of title 221, 282, 413
  transfer of ownership/title
    obligation to transfer, principle of abstraction, revesting of title on termination of contract and 227–228
    requirements: consent, sufficiency 223–224; payment of purchase price, relevance 341
    time of, as gradual process/reflection of factual system 221 n.146

France
  actio Pauliana
    gratuitous transactions and 629
    requirements: ascertainability of sum owed 628; debtor's knowledge of likely detriment 628; detrimental effect 627; diminution of debtor's capacity to pay debts 627, 628–629, 646; intention to defraud/prejudice other creditors, relevance 628; losses attributable to transaction 628; pre-existing debt 628; prior attempt by creditor to secure settlement 627; third-party's knowledge/'should have known' requirement 628
  agency, resale of cars supplied on credit for that purpose 313–314
  all-monies/sums retention of title (framework agreement) 420–421

frequency of use 421, 437
insolvency: priority 420–421;
   rei vindicatio 420–421, 436
seller's rights in unsold goods,
   non-possessory ownership 435
specificity principle: ascertainment
   of goods 420–421, 436; real
   subrogation 421; risk 436
validity 421
assignment of claim to recovery/future
   claim (*Loi Dailly*)
   against unknown debtor 576–577
   limitation to bank or financial
      institution 538–540
bona fide acquisition
   belief in seller's right to sell, resale of
      cars supplied on credit for that
      purpose 313
   possession 288–289, 344–345
   reservation of title 288–289, 299
car fleet as collateral for non-possessory
   security right 447
   finance leasing/leasing contract
      447–448
   possessory pledge distinguished 447
   registered vehicle charge (*gage sur
      véhicule*) (*Loi Malingre*) 477–478
choice of law, *conflit mobile* 18
commingling/distinguishability of
   monies paid to bankrupt, new goods
   manufactured out of materials
   supplied (*specificatio*) and 373
constructive delivery/*constitutum
   possessorium*. See also hypothec and
   nantissement below
   Code civil 1804 and 47
   gage/bailment resulting from,
      abolition (1804) 47
   Loi Malingre 314–315
contract, avoidance
   for fraud 233: decisive influence on
      other party, need for 233; burden of
      proof 233; judicial avoidance, need
      for 233; transfer of ownership/title,
      effect on 233
   for intention to defraud/prejudice
      creditors, price as evidence of
      intention 625, 627, 646
   retroactive/*ex tunc* effect 233
contract, termination in case of
   insolvency proceedings

administrator's rights/duty 448
suspension of payments, preclusion as
   ground for termination 184
contract, termination for failure to pay
   forced execution as alternative 184
   insolvency proceedings and 184
   judicial termination, need for
      184–185, 227
   parties' agreement and (resolutive
      clause) 184–185, 225–226
   reversion of title [where seller remains
      in possession of goods], principle of
      abstraction and 227–228
credit consignment agreement,
   reservation of title distinguished
   288–289, 299
damages, contract avoided for fraud 233
debitor cessus, notice to, relevance
   modification of requirement 571
nantissement de fonds de commerce
   539–540
security assignment of future
   claims/debts 315, 415, 538–539, 577,
   649
enterprise contract, new goods
   manufactured out of materials
   supplied (*specificatio*) 397
excess collateral, relevance, security
   assignment of future claims/debts
   577
execution
   execution judge, role 234
   nantissement de fonds de commerce 577
   procedure (as amended by Law
      No 91-650 of 9 July and Decree
      No 92-755 of 31 July 1992) 233–234
fiduciary relationship (beneficial trust),
   security assignment of future
   claims/debts 539 n.29
finance leasing/leasing contract 600–601
   applicability, computer 600
   car fleet as collateral for
      non-possessory security right
      447–448
   insolvency 448
   insolvency of creditor, debtor's rights
      601
   as necessary condition 600
   option to acquire: at price reflecting
      amount paid in rent 447–448;
      characterisation of contract and 600

France (cont.)
  possessory pledge compared 600–601
  publicity/registry 448, 475, 600–601, 619
  reservation of title/retention of ownership 600–601
  termination in case of insolvency proceedings: in case of creditor's insolvency 448; debtor's rights in case of insolvency of creditor 448
  third-party rights 448
floating charge, exclusion 490
forfeiture clause (*pactum commissorium*), security transfer of ownership 657
hypothec
  aeroplanes and ships, applicability to 47 n.33
  immovable property, limitation to 47
insolvency
  administrator's rights/duties: notification to secured creditor of intention to sell collateral 448; termination of finance leasing/leasing contract 448, 601
  contract, effect on, fulfilment of obligations before commencement of proceedings, relevance 226
  critical date 183, 403–404
  goods in transit, rights over: carrier's statutory preference 185–186. *See also* retention of asset as security for performance/performance withhold *below*
  priority 183
  security assignment of earnings 540–542
  stock-in-trade as collateral for non-possessory security right 491–492
  suspect period 183, 492–493: security assignment of future claims/debts 540
  suspension of transactions 492–493, 540, 652
legislation, role 55, 647–648
liability of purchaser of business for pre-existing debt 627–629
nantissement, Roman law/French customary law and 47

nantissement de fonds de commerce
  assignment of future claims/debts 539–540, 661
  completion many months after loan at time of financial difficulty, effect 492–493
  debitor cessus, notice to, relevance 539–540
  definition/requirements 491
  excess collateral, relevance 492
  execution 577
  frequency of use 492
  inventory collateral, exclusion 57, 491–492
  judicial enforcement, need for 491–492
  as pledge 491–492
  priority 492
  publicity/registry 491–492
  as security right to future claim against unknown debtor 576–577
  specificity principle 539–540
  stock-in-trade as collateral for non-possessory security right 525–526
new goods manufactured out of materials supplied (*specificatio*)
  commingling/distinguishability of monies paid to bankrupt 373
  execution in the absence of proceeds clause 373
  insolvency in the absence of proceeds clause 374: payment before commencement of insolvency proceedings, relevance 403–404
  monies paid to bankrupt, right to, commingling/distinguishability of monies, relevance 402–403
  ownership: critical date 374; enterprise contract 373–374, 397; value of material/value of work, relevance 372–373
  real subrogation and. *See* real subrogation (assignment of future claim) *below*
  reservation of title 371–374: strict interpretation of *specificatio* requirement 371–373
  specificatio: determination of 371–373; examples 372–373

ownership, creation/termination and 371–372, 397
possession
  bona fide acquisition of real rights in movable property 288–289, 344–345, 652–653
  as evidence of creditworthiness 653–654
  presumption of ownership and 652–653
possessory pledge
  car fleet as collateral for non-possessory security right 447
  constructive delivery/*constitutum possessorium* 314–315
  nantissement de fonds de commerce 491–492
  registry 314–315
  resale of cars supplied on credit for that purpose 314–315, 447
priority
  all-monies/sums retention of title (framework agreement) 420–421
  goods on credit and 182, 226
  insolvency proceedings, effect 183
  nantissement de fonds de commerce 492
  reservation of title, agreement to delay payment and (article 40 debt) 255–257
  security assignment of future claims/debts 577
  statutory possessory liens 75
  statutory preferences, carrier 185–186
publicity/registry 59
  finance leasing/leasing contract 448, 475, 600–601, 619
  nantissement de fonds de commerce 491–492
  possessory pledge 314–315
  warrant 490–491
real subrogation (assignment of future claim) 402, 662
  execution: after payment by second buyer 402–403; before payment by second buyer 403
  new goods manufactured out of materials supplied (*specificatio*) 402, 415
  proceeds clause (extended reservation of title) 402, 662
  specificity principle 421

third-party rights 346, 355, 363: change in nature of goods, relevance 355, 402–403, 415
redemption, right of (*contrat à réméré/faculté de rachat*) 50
  hypothec, abolition and 50
registered vehicle charge (*gage sur véhicule*), (*Loi Malingre*), car fleet as collateral for non-possessory security right 10, 477–478
  resale of cars supplied on credit for that purpose 314–315
rei vindicatio in case of insolvency
  all-monies/sums retention of title (framework agreement) 436
  following distribution of proceeds from sale of assets 234
  insolvent's possession of another's movable property 299, 420–421
  inventory, relevance 255–257
  reservation of title, effect 255–257, 283–284, 658
  specificatio, need for 371–372
  termination of finance leasing/leasing contract 448, 601
  termination of sale before insolvency proceedings, limitation to 184–185
  timing of claim 256, 284
resale of cars supplied on credit for that purpose 313–315
  agency and 313–314
  concession contract and 314
  monies paid to bankrupt, right to: commingling/distinguishability of monies, relevance 313–314; payments made after start of insolvency proceedings 314, 355; security assignment of future claims/debts 315, 349–350
  registered vehicle charge (*gage sur véhicule*) (*Loi Malingre*) 314–315, 349
  reseller's obligation to transfer monies received to original seller 313–314
  transfer of ownership/title as result of 313–315: authorisation to sell, relevance 313, 344, 363
reservation of title
  authorisation to sell, relevance 288–289
  automaticity 285

France (cont.)
  bona fide acquisition 288–289, 299
  credit consignment agreement distinguished 288–289, 299
  formal requirements 257–258, 259: writing 257, 283–284, 658
  insolvency 11
  new goods manufactured out of materials supplied (*specificatio*) 371–374: change in nature of goods, relevance 403
  as preferred method 659 n.39
  process of goods, right to 255–257
  publicity/registry 259, 283: timing, relevance 259
  rei vindicatio in case of insolvency 255–257, 283–284, 658
  specificity principle 255
  as [suspensive] condition for payment of purchase price 255, 282–283
  third-party rights 226, 652–653
  timing of reservation, relevance 258, 285–286
  unilateral declaration of, validity 255, 257–258, 285: conflict between general conditions of sale and general conditions of purchase 258; implied consent 257–258
  retention of asset as security for performance/performance withhold 185–186, 225–226
  resale of cars supplied on credit for that purpose 314–315, 447
  reservation of title/ownership distinguished 185–186
  sale and lease-back
    applicability 448
    finance leasing/leasing contract compared 447, 600
  security assignment of earnings
    debitor cessus, notice to, relevance 538–539, 540–542, 660–661: money earned but not paid before insolvency 540–541, 542; money earned and paid before insolvency 541–542
    insolvency 540–542: suspect period 540
    third-party rights 540–541
  security assignment of future claims/debts

debitor cessus, notice to, relevance 315, 415, 577, 649
excess collateral, relevance 577
fiduciary relationship (beneficial trust) 539 n.29
priority 577
resale of cars supplied on credit for that purpose 315, 349–350
as security for bank loan 538–542
security rights, future claim against unknown debtor 576–577
security transfer of ownership
  finance leasing/leasing contract compared 600–601
  forfeiture clause (*pactum commissorium*) 657
special registered charge 477–478
variety 10–11
specificity principle 181–182, 224
  fungible assets 420–421, 436
  nantissement de fonds de commerce 539–540
  real subrogation (assignment of future claim) 421
  reservation of title 255
stock-in-trade as collateral for non-possessory security right
  insolvency 491–492
  nantissement de fonds de commerce 525–526
  warrant 490–491
third-party rights
  finance leasing/leasing contract 448
  reservation of title 226, 652–653
  security assignment of earnings 540–541
  warrant 490–491
transfer of ownership/title
  obligation to transfer, principle of abstraction, revesting of title on termination of contract and 227–228
  requirements: consent, sufficiency 181, 223, 226–227, 475; *nemo plus* principle 288–289, 313; payment of purchase price, relevance 181, 363
warrant
  car accessories, exclusion 491
  professionals, limitation to 490–491
  publicity/registry 490–491

stock-in-trade as collateral for non-possessory security right 490–491
third-party rights 490–491
types of warrant 10–11, 491

Germany
accession, transfer or ownership/title and, requirements, movable as essential part of immovable 248
agency, possession distinguished 174 n.12
all-monies/sums retention of title (framework agreement) 418–419
  examples: *Kontokorrentvorbehalt* 418–419; *Konzernvorbehalt* 418–419
  insolvency, part of insolvency estate, whether 418, 435
  security transfer of ownership 418, 435, 661–662
  seller's rights in unsold goods, security transfer of ownership 418, 435
  validity 418, 434–435: excess collateral, relevance/implied waiver 418; general clauses/framework agreement, acceptability 418; implied waiver of creditor's rights 418; unfair contract term (*contra bonos mores*), whether 418
assignment of claim to recovery
  as alternative to delivery 174, 302 n.2: *bona fide* acquisition 302
bona fide acquisition
  assignment of claim to recovery 302 n.2
  belief in seller's right to sell 343–344: negligence and 302, 653
  constructive delivery/*constitutum possessorium* 302
  delivery and 302–303
  gratuitous transactions 302
  possession 344–345: hire purchase/payment by instalment 303; involuntary deprivation of possession and 302, 653; money and negotiable instruments 302; security transfer of ownership in stock-in-trade 482–483
  security transfer of ownership 303

stock-in-trade as collateral for non-possessory security right 482–483
unjust enrichment and 302
car fleet as collateral for non-possessory security right
  sale and lease-back 442, 474
  security transfer of ownership 438–443, 473–474
charge of money claims, *debitor cessus*, notice to, relevance 11
choice of law, *conflit mobile* 17–18
commingling/distinguishability, security assignment of earnings 532
commingling/distinguishability of monies paid to bankrupt, security assignment of earnings 532
constructive delivery/*constitutum possessorium*
  anticipated *constitutum possessorium* 481
  bona fide acquisition 302
  as means of creating security right after transfer of ownership/title 249–250
  sale and lease-back 51, 475
  security interest as *causa* 51
  security transfer of ownership 439, 481
contract, avoidance
  for fraud 230–232: principle of abstraction 243–244
  for intention to defraud/prejudice creditors 624–625: burden of proof 624–625; contract between family members 624; limitation period 624–625
contract, termination in case of insolvency proceedings, administrator's rights/duty, termination of contract 247, 442
contract, termination for failure to pay reservation of title, relevance 247
retroactive/*ex tunc* effect 173
reversion of title [where seller remains in possession of goods], principle of abstraction and 227–228
corporeal movables, applicability of non-possessory security rights 442
customary law, security transfer of ownership 440–441

Germany (*cont.*)
debitor cessus, notice to, relevance
  charge of money claims 11
  security assignment of claims/debts 11, 306, 660–661
  security assignment of earnings 532–534, 660–661
  security assignment of future claims/debts 306, 347, 574
delivery, relevance 172, 174, 223
  assignment of claim to recovery as alternative 174, 302
  bona fide acquisition 302–303
  taking of possession and 174
  where transferee in possession of property (*traditio brevi/longa manu*) 249–250, 285, 439
excess collateral, relevance, security assignment of future claims/debts 574–575, 651
execution
  against purchaser of business for pre-existing debt: business assets, applicability to 624; execution judgment, need for 624
  sale and lease-back 442
  security assignment of earnings 533–534
  security assignment of future claims/debts 574
  security transfer of ownership 439–440
fiduciary relationship (beneficial trust)
  forfeiture clause (*pactum commissorium*) 441, 657
  proceeds clause (extended reservation of title) as 352
  security transfer of ownership 439, 441
finance leasing/leasing contract 595–597
  contractual nature of relationship 595–596
  execution, right to resist 596
  frequency of use 596–597
  insolvency of creditor, debtor's rights 597
  option to acquire, effect on real rights 596
  publicity/registry 595–596
  rei vindicatio in case of insolvency 596: termination of contract by insolvency administrator or lessor 596
  security transfer of ownership compared 596–597
  termination in case of insolvency proceedings, administrator's right/duty 596, 597
  transfer of ownership/title on purchase at end of contract 595–596
forfeiture clause (*pactum commissorium*)
fiduciary relationship (beneficial trust) 441
  security transfer of ownership 441
form/nomenclature, relevance 58
global assignment, acceptability/requirements 441–442, 532–533, 651
hire purchase/payment by instalment
  bona fide acquisition 303
  reservation of title 248–249, 303: expectancy (*Anwartschaftsrecht*) 248–249, 250
  as reversion of title 250
hypothec (*Mobiliarhypothek*), abolition 47
  leaseback and 50–51
insolvency 172–173
  administration by insolvency administrator 172–173
  administrator's rights/duties: incongruous/congruous securities 484; notification to secured creditor of intention to sell collateral 368–369; payment of interest for delay in realising assets 368–369; postponement of sale 247–248, 284, 368–369, 441, 442, 652; realisation of bankrupt's assets within statutory time-limits 352–353; reservation of title, relevance 247–248; satisfaction of creditor's contractual claims in case of reservation of title 247; satisfaction of original seller's claims after deduction of administration costs 352, 368–369, 441, 527, 652
  critical date 484
  damages for losses incurred from failure to sell at best price 368–369
  goods in transit, rights over: stoppage 181, 229; transfer of ownership/title as determining factor 174

intention to defraud/prejudice other creditors, effect 484–485: critical date 484
onerous/disadvantageous transactions, administrator's rights/duty to avoid 484–485
property of debtor, monies paid to bankrupt for resale of cars supplied on credit for that purpose 304
'property that belongs to the debtor' 172–173
sale and lease-back 442
security assignment of earnings 532–534
security assignment of future claims/debts 574
security transfer of ownership 439–440: security owner's obligation to pay percentage of costs 596–597
self-administration (*Eigenverwaltung*) 172 n.6
judicial development 55, 58, 60, 476–477
legislation, role 647–648
liability of purchaser of business for pre-existing debt 623–625
    ceiling, whether 624, 645
    continued management by original owner, relevance 624
    continued use of old name, relevance 623, 645: exclusion by duly registered or notified agreement 623–624, 645
    continuing liability of original debtor 624
    loan/credit 624
    purchase price, relevance 624
new goods manufactured out of materials supplied (*specificatio*)
    execution in the absence of proceeds clause 366: before payment by second buyer 399; following payment by second buyer 398–399
    insolvency in the absence of proceeds clause 368–369, 400
    ownership: risk, relevance 366–367: value of material/value of work, relevance 395
    priority, third-party rights, products clause 399–400
    reservation of title 366–369
    specificatio, ownership, creation/termination and 366

possession
    agency distinguished 174 n.12
    possessor as *Besitzdiener* 174 n.12
possessory pledge
    products clause as 368 n.13, 399–400
    security assignment distinguished 306
    security transfer of ownership compared 11, 12, 306, 439–441
priority
    all-monies/sums retention of title (framework agreement) 418, 435
    new goods manufactured out of goods supplied (*specificatio*) 399–400
    proceeds clause (extended reservation of title) 306–307
    reservation of title 247, 302 n.2, 306, 439–440
    security assignment of future claims/debts 574
    security transfer of ownership 302, 306, 439–440
    seller [on credit] 173: negotiated settlement 353
    statutory preferences: carrier 174; seller [on credit] 352–353
proceeds clause (extended reservation of title) 11, 12, 13, 300, 304–307, 350, 352, 363–364, 662
    fiduciary nature of relationship 352
    priority 306–307
products clause
    effect 366–369
    formal requirements 368
    'manufacturer'/'owner', parties' right to determine 367–368, 396
    'manufacturer'/'owner', statutory definition 367–368
    as pledge 368 n.13, 399–400
    priority 368, 400
    publicity/registry 368
    security transfer of ownership 368–369
    third-party rights 366–367, 368
products and proceeds clauses combined
    definition/explanation 399
    execution: before payment by second buyer 399–400; following payment by second buyer 399, 414
    insolvency: before payment by second buyer 400; following payment by second buyer 400

700 INDEX BY COUNTRY

Germany (cont.)
  requirements 399
  rights arising from 399
publicity/registry 59
  finance leasing/leasing contract
    595–596
  products clause 368
  security transfer of ownership
    440–441, 476, 527
  stock-in-trade as collateral for
    non-possessory security right 482,
    527
rei vindicatio in case of insolvency 173
  finance leasing/leasing contract 596
  insolvent's possession of another's
    movable property and (Aussonderung)
    173, 287–288
  insolvent's possession of another's
    security right and (Absonderung) 173
  reservation of title, effect 247,
    283–284, 298, 658
  sale and lease-back 442
  unlawful frustration of right of 304,
    351–352, 363
resale of cars supplied on credit for that
  purpose 302–307
  monies paid to bankrupt, right to 304:
    in the absence of right to resell 304;
    administrator's obligation to satisfy
    original seller's claims after
    deduction of administration costs
    352, 368–369; commingling/
    distinguishability of monies,
    relevance 304, 307, 347, 363;
    payments made after start of
    insolvency proceedings 351–352;
    security assignment of future
    claims/debts 304–307; unlawful
    frustration of rei vindicatio 304,
    351–352, 363
  reseller's obligation to transfer monies
    received to original seller 306–307:
    in personam nature of seller's right
    306–307
  termination of reseller's right to
    collect claims 306–307: insolvency
    proceedings and 304 n.10; notice of
    assignment of claim, relevance
    306–307; on termination of
    payments 304 n.10
  termination of right to resell:
    insolvency proceedings and 304

  n.10; on termination of payments
    304 n.10
  transfer of ownership/title as result of
    302: authorisation to sell, relevance
    302, 351–352, 363
reservation of title
  administrator in insolvency's
    rights/duties, effect on 247–248,
    283–284
  authorisation to sell, relevance
    287–288, 298
  formal requirements 250
  hire purchase/payment by instalment
    248–249, 303
  new goods manufactured out of
    materials supplied (specificatio)
    366–369
  as preferred method 659 n.39
  priority 247, 302 n.2, 306–307, 439–440
  publicity/registry 250, 283
  rei vindicatio in case of insolvency 247,
    283, 298, 658
  stock-in-trade as collateral for
    non-possessory security right
    482–483
  as [suspensive] condition for payment
    of purchase price 246–247
  termination of contract and 247
  timing of reservation, relevance
    249–250, 285–286
  unilateral declaration of, validity
    248–249, 285
risk, new goods manufactured out of
  materials supplied (specificatio),
  ownership 366–367
sale and lease-back
  car fleet as collateral for
    non-possessory security right 442
  constructive delivery/constitutum
    possessorium 51, 475
  execution 442
  frequency of use 442
  insolvency 442
  option/duty to reacquire 50–51
  rei vindicatio in case of insolvency 442
  termination for non-payment 442
security assignment of claims/debts
  debitor cessus, notice to, relevance 11,
    12, 306, 660–661
  possessory pledge compared 11, 12,
    306
  validity 306

security assignment of earnings 532–534
  commingling/distinguishability of monies paid to bankrupt 532
  debitor cessus, notice to, relevance 532–534: money earned but not paid before insolvency 532; money earned and paid before insolvency 532
  execution, money not yet earned ('future' claim) 533–534
  frequency of use 532
  future claim, whether 532–534
  insolvency 532–534: money earned and paid before insolvency 532; money not yet earned ('future' claim) 532–534
  as preferred method 569–570
  as proceeds clause 532
  termination of right to collect claims following failure to make loan payments 532
  unjust enrichment 534
security assignment of future claims/debts 352
  anticipated assignment of claims 304–305, 399, 574
  debitor cessus, notice to, relevance 574
  duration of assignment, relevance 306, 347
  excess collateral, relevance 574–575, 651
  execution 574
  insolvency 574
  priority 574
  specificity principle 305–306, 347
security rights
  future claim against unknown debtor, possibilities 574: specificity principle 574
security transfer of ownership 11, 12
  all-monies/sums retention of title (framework agreement) 418, 435, 661–662
  applicability to corporeal movables 442
  bona fide acquisition 303
  car fleet as collateral for non-possessory security right 438–443, 473–474
  completion many months after loan at time of financial difficulty, effect 484–485

constructive delivery/*constitutum possessorium* 439
  as customary law 440–441
  debtor's rights in case of insolvency of creditor 443, 478–479
  excess collateral, relevance/implied waiver 439, 441–442, 483–484, 651
  execution 439–440
  fiduciary relationship (beneficial trust) 439, 441, 443
  finance leasing/leasing contract compared 596–597
  forfeiture clause (*pactum commissorium*) 441, 657
  future claims/debts 651
  insolvency 439–440: security owner's obligation to pay percentage of costs 596–597
  possessory pledge compared 306, 439–441
  priority 302 n.2, 306–307, 439–440, 306–307, 439–440
  products clause and 368–369
  publicity/registry 440–441, 476, 527
  repossession: non-payment, need for 439; right to sell collateral 439
  sale and resale 474
  security agreement, need for 439
  stock-in-trade as collateral for non-possessory security right 481–484, 526–527: future stocks 481, 526
special registered charge 11, 12
specificity principle
  future claim against unknown debtor 574
  proceeds clause (extended reservation of title) 574
  security assignment of future claims/debts 305–306, 347
  stock-in-trade as collateral for non-possessory security right 481–482, 526–527
stock-in-trade as collateral for non-possessory security right
  bona fide acquisition 482–483
  future stocks: security transfer of ownership 481, 526, 527; specificity principle 481–482, 526–527
  obligation to store separately 481–483, 526–527

702   INDEX BY COUNTRY

Germany (cont.)
  publicity/registry 482
  reservation of title 482–483:
    expectancy (Anwartschaftsrecht)
    528–529
  security transfer of ownership
    481–484: creditor's status 483; excess
    collateral, relevance/implied waiver
    483–484, 528–529; frequency of use
    483; publicity/registry 482, 527
  specificity principle 481–482, 526–527
  third-party rights, products clause and
    366–367, 368
  transfer of ownership/title
    agreement that title should pass
      ('real agreement'/Einigung), need for
      171–172, 224, 481: independence
      from contract of sale, relevance
      246–247; transfer of security
      ownership 481
    obligation to transfer: distinguished
      171–172; principle of abstraction
      172, 212, 227–228, 230–231;
      revesting of title on termination of
      contract and 227–228
    ownership and right to dispose of
      property distinguished 287–288, 399
    requirements: delivery of movable.
      See delivery, relevance above;
      independence from contract of sale,
      relevance 246–247; payment of
      purchase price, relevance 172, 173,
      363
    transfer of security ownership 481
  unjust enrichment
    bona fide acquisition 302
    contract voided for fraud and 230–231
    reversion of title/ownership and 173
    security assignment of earnings 534

Greece
  abuse of rights, security assignment of
    future claims/debts 575–576
  actio Pauliana
    burden of proof 626–627
    gratuitous transactions and 626–627
    limitation period 626–627
    requirements: insolvency attributable
      to transaction 626–627; intention to
      defraud/prejudice other creditors,
      relevance 626–627; third-party's
    knowledge/'should have known'
      requirement 626–627; valid
      transaction 626–627
    third-party rights 626–627
  all-monies/sums retention of title
    (framework agreement) 420
    frequency of use 420, 437
    insolvency, reservation of title as basis
      of entitlement 417–436
    seller's rights in unsold goods,
      co-ownership 420
  bona fide acquisition
    belief in seller's right to sell 343–344:
      negligence and 311
    in case of insolvency 179–180
    constructive delivery/constitutum
      possessorium 311
    execution 232–233
    finance leasing/leasing contract 599
    payment of debtor to insolvent and
      179–180
    possession 180, 344–345
    publicity/registry 311
  car fleet as collateral for non-possessory
    security right
    sale and lease-back 445
    security transfer of ownership
      444–445, 473–474
    special registered charge, tour coaches
      445
  charge of money claims
    certain date (data certa), need for
      535–536
    debitor cessus, notice to, relevance
      535–536, 537–538: money earned
      but not paid before insolvency
      537–538; money earned and paid
      before insolvency 537, 538
    frequency of use 535–536
    insolvency 537
    public [notarial] deed, need for 535–536
    as real right 534
    security assignment of earnings
      compared 535–536
    special charge applicable to
      corporations 536: debitor cessus,
      notice to, relevance 536;
      requirements 536
  commission [undisclosed] agency
    bank loan 536–537
    insolvency 538

INDEX BY COUNTRY 703

maturity factoring 537
writing, need for 536–537
constructive delivery/*constitutum possessorium* 179
    anticipated *constitutum possessorium* 371, 488
    bona fide acquisition 311
    as means of creating security right after transfer of ownership/title 254
    possessory pledge 444–445
    security transfer of ownership 444, 488
contract, annulment of simulated/*pro forma* 626–627, 644
    price as evidence of simulation 627, 646
contract, avoidance
    for fraud 232: principle of abstraction 232, 243–244; transfer of ownership/title, effect on 232
    for intention to defraud/prejudice creditors, price as evidence of intention 627, 646
    principle of abstraction 232
    retroactive/*ex tunc* effect 232–233
contract, termination in case of insolvency proceedings
    administrator's rights/duties 446–447
    default of administrator and 253–254
contract, termination for failure to pay
    parties' agreement and (resolutive clause) 180–181, 253: security transfer of ownership 446
    reversion of title [where seller remains in possession of goods], principle of abstraction and 227–228
    time-limits/grace period and 180–181
    unilateral 180–181
corporeal movables, applicability of non-possessory security rights 446
customary law, security transfer of ownership 444
debitor cessus, notice to, relevance
    charge of money claims 535–536, 537: special charge applicable to money claims 536
    enterprise charge 537
    identity of debtor, relevance 536–537
    security assignment of earnings 536–537

security assignment of future claims/debts 354–355, 401–402
delivery, relevance 179, 223
    as publicity 179
enterprise charge 312, 477, 650–651
    applicability, bank or financial institutions 537
    debitor cessus, notice to, relevance 537
    insolvency 537
    publicity/registry 489, 537
    stock-in-trade as collateral for non-possessory security right 489, 528
excess collateral, relevance, security assignment of earnings 537
execution
    bona fide acquisition 232–233
    finance leasing/leasing contract, right to resist 599–600
    security transfer of ownership 445
factoring contract 654–655
    as security for bank loan 536: loan as discounted value of assigned claims 536
fiduciary relationship (beneficial trust)
    finance leasing/leasing contract compared 599
    new goods manufactured out of materials supplied (*specificatio*) 371
    possessory pledge, assimilation to 354–355
    proceeds clause (extended reservation of title) as 354, 401
    products and proceeds clauses combined as 401
finance leasing/leasing contract
    bona fide acquisition 599
    execution, right to resist 599–600
    fiduciary relationship (beneficial trust) compared 599
    frequency of use 599
    insolvency of creditor, debtor's rights 599–600
    lessor's right on termination to return of goods: contractual basis 599; as owner 599
    option to acquire: effect on real rights 599; right to transfer option 599
    publicity/registry 599, 619

Greece (cont.)
    sale and lease-back compared 599
    tax and consumer credit legislation, applicability 599
    termination in case of insolvency proceedings: administrator's right/duty 599–600; automaticity 599
    termination for failure to pay 599–600
    third-party rights 599
    writing, need for 599
  global assignment, acceptability/requirements 575–576, 593–594
  insolvency
    administration by insolvency administrator 179–180: *rei vindicatio* 179–180
    administrator's rights/duties, sale of assets 446
    charge of money claims 537
    commission [undisclosed] agency 538
    enterprise charge 537
    goods in transit, rights over: stoppage 181, 229; transfer of ownership/title, relevance 181
    invalidity of transactions relating to 179–180
    proceedings, limitation to merchants/businessmen, limitation of proceedings to 179
    property rights of bankrupt person, effect on. *See* administration by insolvency administrator *above*
    reservation of title 13
    sale and lease-back 446–447
    security assignment of earnings 537
    security transfer of ownership 445: debtor's rights in case of insolvency of creditor 478–479
    stock-in-trade as collateral for non-possessory security right 489
  liability of purchaser of business for pre-existing debt 626–627
    assets as entirety of debtor's property, relevance 626
    ceiling, whether 626, 645
    knowledge/'should have known' requirement 626
  new goods manufactured out of materials supplied (*specificatio*)

execution in the absence of proceeds clause: before payment by second buyer 401; following payment by second buyer 401
  fiduciary relationship (beneficial trust) 371
  insolvency in the absence of proceeds clause 371, 401–402
  ownership: payment of purchase price, relevance 371; risk, relevance 370; value of material/value of work, relevance 370, 394–395
  reservation of title 370–371
  third-party rights 370, 371
possession
  bona fide acquisition of real rights in movable and 180, 344–345
  as publicity 180
possessory pledge
  constructive delivery/*constitutum possessorium* 444–445
  fictitious pledges 312–313: priority 312–313
  publicity/registry 311, 312–313
  resale of cars supplied on credit for that purpose 312
  security transfer of ownership compared 444, 446
priority
  fictitious pledge and 312–313
  seller [on credit], fiduciary relationship assimilated to pledge 354–355
proceeds clause (extended reservation of title) 350, 354–355, 363–364, 662
  new goods manufactured out of materials supplied (*specificatio*) [with products clause] 371: execution, relevance 401; insolvency 401–402
  timing, relevance 401–402
  unjust enrichment 401
products clause
  'manufacturer', parties' right to determine 371, 396
  priority 371
  as security transfer of ownership of future products with resolutive condition 371
products and proceeds clauses combined 414

publicity/registry
  delivery as 179
  enterprise charge 489, 537
  finance leasing/leasing contract 599, 619
  pledge registry 311
  possession as 180
  sale and lease-back 445, 475
  security interests requiring 254–255
  security transfer of ownership 444–445, 527
  transfer of ownership of movable, relevance 179, 180, 254–255, 312–313
rei vindicatio in case of insolvency 179–180, 181
  goods in transit 181
  reservation of title, effect 253, 283–284, 298, 658
resale of cars supplied on credit for that purpose
  monies paid to bankrupt, right to 311: in the absence of right to resell 312; commingling/distinguishability of monies, relevance 347; payments made after start of insolvency proceedings 354–355; possessory pledge and 312
  transfer of ownership/title as result of 311: authorisation to sell, relevance 311, 343–344
reservation of title
  authorisation to sell, relevance 288, 298
  formal requirements 254–255
  insolvency 13
  publicity/registry 254–255, 283
  rei vindicatio in case of insolvency 253, 283–284, 298, 658
  stock-in-trade as collateral for non-possessory security right, authorisation to transfer, relevance 489
  as [suspensive] condition for payment of purchase price 253
  timing of reservation, relevance 254, 285–286
  unilateral declaration of, validity 254, 285
sale and lease-back
  applicability 446

car fleet as collateral for non-possessory security right 445
  duration 445: aircraft 446
  finance leasing/leasing contract compared 599
  frequency of use 445
  insolvency 446–447
  publicity/registry 445, 475
  as statutory form of security ownership 445
  third-party rights 445
security assignment of earnings 13, 535–538
  charge of monies as alternative 535–536
  debitor cessus, notice to, relevance 536–537: money earned but not paid before insolvency 537, 538; money earned and paid before insolvency 538
  excess collateral, relevance 537
  frequency of use 536–537
  insolvency 537
  possessory pledge, assimilation to charge of money claims 535–536
  as preferred method 569–570
  as security for bank loan 536–537
  unjust enrichment 537, 538
security assignment of future claims/debts 650–651
  as abuse of right 575–576
  anticipated assignment of claims 347
  frequency of use 575–576
  public policy issues 575–576
  resale of cars supplied on credit for that purpose 312
security rights
  future claim against unknown debtor, possibilities 575–576: specificity principle 575
security transfer of ownership 11, 12, 13, 489
  applicability to corporeal movables 446
  car fleet as collateral for non-possessory security right 444–445, 473–474
  completion many months after loan at time of financial difficulty, effect 490

Greece (cont.)
  constructive delivery/*constitutum possessorium* 444, 488
  as customary law 444
  execution 445
  insolvency 445: debtor's rights in case of insolvency of creditor 446, 478–479
  iusta causa 444–445, 475–476
  possessory pledge compared 444, 446
  publicity/registry 444–445
  stock-in-trade as collateral for non-possessory security right 488–489: future stocks 488–489, 526–527
  special registered charge, car fleet as collateral for non-possessory security right, tour coaches 445
  specificity principle
    future claim against unknown debtor 575
    stock-in-trade as collateral for non-possessory security right 488, 526–527
  stock-in-trade as collateral for non-possessory security right
    enterprise charge 489
    excess collateral, relevance 489
    future stocks, security transfer of ownership 488–489, 526–527
    insolvency 489
    obligation to store separately 488, 526–527
    reservation of title 488: expectancy (*Anwartschaftsrecht*) 488
    security transfer of ownership 488–489: frequency of use 489
    specificity principle 488, 526–527
  third-party rights
    finance leasing/leasing contract 599
    new goods manufactured out of materials supplied (*specificatio*) and 370, 371
    sale and lease-back 445
  transfer of ownership/title
    agreement that title should pass ('real agreement'), need for 179, 224
    obligation to transfer, principle of abstraction, revesting of title on termination of contract and 227–228, 232
    obligation to transfer distinguished 179
    requirements: delivery of movable. *See* delivery, relevance *above*; payment of purchase price, relevance 178–179, 371; public [notarial] deed, relevance 179
    transfer of warrants/bills of lading and 181
  unjust enrichment
    bona fide payment of debt to insolvent and 179–180
    contract voided for fraud and 232
    as *in personam* right 232
    proceeds clause (extended reservation of title) 401
    security assignment of earnings 537, 538

Hungary, publicity/registry 59

Ireland
  all-monies/sums retention of title (framework agreement) 427–429
    clarity of drafting, need for 428–429
    delivery, relevance 422, 429
    frequency of use 429, 437
    insolvency, part of insolvency estate, whether 429
    payment of purchase price, relevance 427–429, 435
    seller's rights in unsold goods, real, whether 429
    validity 427–429, 434–435: general clauses/framework agreement, acceptability 429; incorporation in each contract of sale as safer alternative 429; as reservation of title clause 428, 435, 661–662
  bona fide acquisition
    belief in seller's right to sell 330, 343–344
    possession 330, 344–345
  car fleet as collateral for non-possessory security right, sale and lease-back 461–462
  contract, avoidance
    for fraud 240: transfer of ownership/title, effect on 240, 244
    for intention to defraud/prejudice creditors 637: limitation period 637–638; price as evidence of intention/knowledge 637–638, 646

contract, termination in case of
    insolvency proceedings, seller's
    right 210–211
contract, termination for failure to pay,
    reversion of title 210–211
debitor cessus, notice to, relevance
    fixed charge 558
    floating [enterprise] charge/lien/
        mortgage 558, 586
    security assignment of claims/debts
        557–558, 586, 587
delivery, relevance 207, 223
    all-monies/sums retention of title
        (framework agreement) 422,
        429
excess collateral, relevance
    security assignment of claims/debts
        587
    stock-in-trade as collateral for
        non-possessory security right 511,
        528–529
execution
    against purchaser of business for
        pre-existing debt, business assets,
        applicability to 636
    security assignment of claims/debts
        586
    stock-in-trade as collateral for
        non-possessory security right 511
factoring contract 654–655
    frequency of use 557
    recourse factoring 557
    as security for bank loan 557: loan as
        discounted value of assigned claims
        557
fiduciary relationship, resale of cars
    supplied on credit for that purpose
    330–332
finance leasing/leasing contract
    611–612
    frequency of use 611–612
    insolvency of creditor, debtor's rights
        612
    option to acquire, hire purchase/
        payment by instalment and 612
    publicity/registry 612
    sale and lease-back compared 611–612,
        620–621
fixed charge
    debitor cessus, notice to, relevance 558
    priority 558
floating charge 209, 477

applicability: all types of assets 510;
    corporate debtors, de facto
    limitation to 510–511, 525
characteristics 331–332, 509–510
crystallisation 509–510, 511, 525, 586
debitor cessus, notice to, relevance 558,
    586
equitable nature of real right
    509–510
floating agricultural chattel mortgage
    510–511
fluctuating future assets, duration of
    charge before insolvency, relevance
    511
frequency of use 511
limited applicability 209, 274
new goods manufactured out of
    materials supplied (*specificatio*) and
    386–387, 396–397
'ordinary course of business' rule
    510–511
priority 511, 558, 586
publicity/registry 510–511, 525
resale of cars supplied on credit for
    that purpose 331–332
specificity principle 510
stock-in-trade as collateral for
    non-possessory security right
    509–511, 525
forfeiture clause (*pactum commissorium*),
    sale and lease-back 462–463
'goods' 207
hire purchase/payment by instalment
    210, 273
    frequency of use 612
    as legal fiction 612
    publicity/registry 612
insolvency
    corporate insolvency 209
    goods in transit, rights over: on
        completion of transit 211; stoppage
        211, 229; 'transit' 211
    onerous/disadvantageous transactions,
        administrator's rights/duty to avoid
        612
    real rights, effect on 209–210
    security assignment of claims/debts
        558, 587
    stock-in-trade as collateral for
        non-possessory security right 511
liability of purchaser of business for
    pre-existing debt 636–638

Ireland (cont.)
  misrepresentation, avoidance/rescission of contract for, bona fide acquisition 244–245
  new goods manufactured out of materials supplied (specificatio)
    execution in the absence of proceeds clause 386: before payment by second buyer 409; following payment by second buyer 409
    floating [enterprise] charge/lien/mortgage 386, 396–397
    insolvency in the absence of proceeds clause 388
    manufacture for self, relevance 384–385
    'ordinary course of business' rule 387–388
    ownership: risk, relevance 386; value of material/value of work, relevance 386, 395
    proceeds clause (extended reservation of title) 386, 387–388
    [registered] charge 409
    reservation of title 384–388
    specificatio 384–388: examples 385–386; reversibility, relevance 385
  'ordinary course of business' rule
    floating [enterprise] charge/lien/mortgage 510–511
    new goods manufactured out of materials supplied (specificatio) 387–388
  possession
    bona fide acquisition of real rights in movable property 330, 344–345
    protection of better right to in the absence of concept of absolute ownership (nemo plus principle) 209–210
  priority
    fixed charge 558
    floating [enterprise] charge/lien/mortgage 511, 558, 586
    security assignment of claims/debts 558, 586
    seller [on credit] 210–211
    statutory preferences 511
    tax claims 511
  priority in case of insolvency 209–211
    unascertained bulk commodities 208
  proceeds clause (extended reservation of title) 332–333
  new goods manufactured out of materials supplied (specificatio) [with products clause] 386, 387–388, 409: exclusion 409
  unjust enrichment and 333
  products clause, as security transfer of ownership of future products with resolutive condition 388
  products and proceeds clauses combined, exclusion 409
  publicity/registry
    finance leasing/leasing contract 612
    floating [enterprise] charge/lien/mortgage 510–511, 525
    hire purchase/payment by instalment 210, 612
    registration of company charge 461–462
    registration of individual charge 461–462
    sale and lease-back 461–462
    security assignment of claims/debts 558
    security interests requiring 210, 274
  [registered] charge
    frequency of use 612
    insolvency, debtor's rights in case of insolvency of creditor 463, 478–479
    new goods manufactured out of materials supplied (specificatio) and 409
    resale of cars supplied on credit for that purpose 332–333, 359–360
  resale of cars supplied on credit for that purpose 330–333
    fiduciary relationship 330–332, 347–348
    monies paid to bankrupt, right to: payments made after start of insolvency proceedings 359–360; [registered] charge 332–333, 359–360; reservation of title 330–331; unjust enrichment and 333
    transfer of ownership/title as result of 330: authorisation to sell, relevance 330, 343–344

reservation of title 207, 209–210
  authorisation to sell, relevance 294, 298
  charge/security interest distinguished 274
  formal requirements 273–274, 276: general conditions, adequacy 275; reservation of both legal and beneficial ownership 273–274
  new goods manufactured out of materials supplied (*specificatio*) 384–388
  publicity/registry 209–210, 274, 275, 283, 386–387: reservation of legal and beneficial ownership and 275
  resale of cars supplied on credit for that purpose 330–331
  as [suspensive] condition for payment of purchase price 273
  timing of reservation, relevance 274–275, 285–286
  as transfer of ownership/reversion of equitable real interest 273–274
  unilateral declaration of, validity 276, 285
risk, new goods manufactured out of materials supplied (*specificatio*), ownership, risk, relevance 386
sale and lease-back
  applicability 463
  car fleet as collateral for non-possessory security right 461–462
  finance leasing/leasing contract compared 611–612, 620–621
  forfeiture clause (*pactum commissorium*) 462–463
  insolvency, debtor's rights in case of insolvency of creditor 463, 478–479
  publicity/registry 461–462
  as sham charge 461–462, 474–475
security assignment of claims/debts 557–559, 586–587
  by charge, floating charge 557, 571–572
  by fixed charge 557
  by floating charge 557
  by mortgage 557
  conditional/contingent nature, relevance 557

debitor cessus, notice to, relevance 557–558, 586, 587: money earned but not paid before insolvency 558–559; money earned and paid before insolvency 558–559
  as equitable right 557–558
  excess collateral, relevance 587
  execution 586
  formal requirements: absolute assignment 557–558; writing 557–558
  frequency of use 557
  future debt 557
  insolvency 558, 587
  priority 558, 586
  publicity/registry 558
  statutory assignment 557–558, 587
security rights, future claim against unknown debtor, possibilities 586–587
specificity principle 207–209, 224
  ascertainment of goods 208–209, 274–275
  commodities sold in bulk 208–209
  floating [enterprise] charge/lien/mortgage 510
  priority 208
  stock-in-trade as collateral for non-possessory security right 510
statutory assignment, security assignment of claims/debts 557–558, 587
stock-in-trade as collateral for non-possessory security right
  excess collateral, relevance 511, 528–529
  execution 511
  floating [enterprise] charge/lien/mortgage 509–511, 525
  insolvency 511
  specificity principle 510
transfer of ownership/title
  requirements: *nemo plus* principle 209–210, 330, 345; payment of purchase price, relevance 207, 273, 428–429
  time of: agreement as determining factor 207, 223; ascertainment of unascertained goods 274–275; conclusion of contract 207

Ireland (*cont.*)
  unjust enrichment
    proceeds clause (extended reservation of title) 333
    resale of cars supplied on credit for that purpose 333

Italy
  actio Pauliana 199
    burden of proof, price, relevance 634, 635
    insolvency proceedings 503
    limitation period 501–502
    requirements: debtor's knowledge of likely detriment 634; intention to defraud/prejudice other creditors, relevance 501–502
    third-party rights 501–502, 634
  agency, resale of cars supplied on credit for that purpose 322
  all-monies/sums retention of title (framework agreement) 423–425
    frequency of use 423–424, 437
    insolvency: priority 423; *rei vindicatio* 424–425
    seller's rights in unsold goods, real, whether 423
    specificity principle, *rei vindicatio* in case of insolvency 424–425
    validity: fraudulent evasion of the law, whether 424; general clauses/framework agreement, acceptability 423–424; unfair contract term (*contra bonos mores*), whether 424
  bona fide acquisition
    execution 236–238
    possession 344–345: period of possession, relevance 319–320, 582
    publicity/registry 319–320, 582
  car fleet as collateral for non-possessory security right
    frequency of use 453–454
    registered vehicle charge 453–454
  commingling/distinguishability of monies paid to bankrupt, new goods manufactured out of materials supplied (*specificatio*) 408
  commission [undisclosed] agency
    certain date (*data certa*) before execution or commencement of insolvency proceedings, need for 292–293, 322, 357
    resale of cars supplied on credit for that purpose 348–349, 357: used car sales 322
  contract, avoidance
    for fraud 236–238: judicial avoidance, need for 236
    for incapacity 236
    retroactive/*ex tunc* effect 237
    for usury 501, 582
  contract, termination in case of insolvency proceedings. *See also* insolvency, contract, effect on *below*
    administrator's rights/duty 266
    automaticity 266
  contract, termination for failure to pay 266, 606–607
    judicial termination, relevance 200–201, 227
    parties' agreement and (resolutive clause) 200
    retroactive effect 200
    time-limits/grace period and 200
  credit consignment agreement
    priority 292–293
    reservation of title distinguished 292–293
    third-party rights 292–293
  damages, contract terminated for failure to pay, retention of instalments as 266
  data certa
    execution and 605–606, 633
    finance leasing/leasing contract 605–606, 619, 659
    reservation of title 268, 283, 290–291, 322, 357, 658
  debitor cessus, notice to, relevance
    factoring contract 551–552
    formal requirements 550–551
    identity of debtor, relevance 406–407
    modification of requirement 571
    publicity/registry 575–576
    security assignment of earnings 550–551
    security assignment of future claims/debts 322, 406–407, 415, 550, 633: money earned but not paid before insolvency 551–552

delivery, relevance 198
enterprise charge
  completion many months after loan at time of financial difficulty, effect 501–504
  excess collateral, relevance 501
  execution 501
  fluctuating future assets 425 n.18, 499, 499
  frequency of use 501
  as growing list of exceptions to equality of creditors rule 499–500
  priority 500–501
  publicity/registry 498–499
  specificity principle 499
  stock-in-trade as collateral for non-possessory security right 498–500
  writing, need for 499
excess collateral, fairness 499–500
excess collateral, relevance, registered bank charge 582
execution
  against purchaser of business for pre-existing debt 633–634: business assets, applicability to 633–634
  bona fide acquisition 236–238
  contratto d'appalto 407–408
  data certa and 633
  enterprise charge 501
  finance leasing/leasing contract: evidential requirements 605–606; right to resist 605
  registered bank charge 582
  stock-in-trade as collateral for non-possessory security right 501
  third-party rights, real/personal right as basis for opposition 237
factoring contract
  data certa, need for 551–552
  debitor cessus, notice to, relevance 551–552: money earned but not paid before insolvency 551–552; money earned and paid before insolvency 551–552
  definition/description 551–552
  frequency of use 551–552
  as security for bank loan 551–552, 570
  third-party rights 551–552
finance leasing/leasing contract 605–608
  data certa 605–606, 619
  evidential requirements 605–606

execution, right to resist 605
frequency of use 605
lessor's right on termination to return of goods, leasing nature of contract 607
option to acquire: as evidence of intention to transfer ownership on termination of contract 607; as necessary condition 605; probability of exercise, relevance 607
as rental agreement 607
reservation of title/retention of ownership 606–607
as sale with reservation of title 606–607
termination in case of insolvency proceedings: administrator's right/duty 607; applicable law 606–607; return of money paid 606–607; termination of contract for continuous performance compared 607
transfer of ownership/title on purchase at end of contract 606–607
writing, need for 605–606, 619
forfeiture clause (*pactum commissorium*)
  security assignment of future claims/debts 550
  security transfer of ownership 454, 607–608, 657
global assignment, acceptability/requirements 321, 582–583
hire purchase/payment by instalment
  reservation of title 267, 319: right to retain instalments as damages in case of default 266, 606–607
  specificity principle 319
hypothec, abolition 47
insolvency
  administration by insolvency administrator 199: individual right of action, exclusion 199
  administrator's rights/duties, satisfaction of claims of creditors and return of residue to bankrupt 199
  concorso dei creditori 199
  contract, effect on 200–201, 607: fulfilment of obligations before commencement of proceedings, relevance 200; payment at insolvency creditor rate, limitation to 200

Italy (cont.)
  goods in transit, rights over: enforcement of contract and 201; recovery on payment of transit costs 201; stoppage 201, 229; transfer of ownership/title, relevance 201
  gratuitous transactions 501–502, 503–504
  intention to defraud/prejudice other creditors, effect 501–502: *actio Pauliana*. *See actio Pauliana above*
  onerous/disadvantageous transactions 503: administrator's rights/duty to avoid 503–504
  proceedings, limitation to commercial enterprises 503
  recovery of property disposed of before insolvency proceedings (*actio Pauliana*) 199
  registered bank charge 582
  security assignment of future claims/debts 407, 550–551
  stock-in-trade as collateral for non-possessory security right 497–501
  suspect period 199
  suspension of transactions 199
  liability of purchaser of business for pre-existing debt 633–635
  new goods manufactured out of materials supplied (*specificatio*) authority to manufacture before payment of purchase price, relevance 407–408
  contratto d'appalto 407–408: agency relationship execution 379
  execution in the absence of proceeds clause 379: before payment by second buyer 406; *contratto d'appalto* 407–408
  insolvency in the absence of proceeds clause 379, 408
  monies paid to bankrupt, right to, commingling/distinguishability of monies, relevance 408
  ownership: risk, relevance 379, 397; value of material/value of work, relevance 378
  proceeds clause (extended reservation of title) 378–379

reservation of title 378–379
'ordinary course of business' rule, sale and lease-back 454
personal security including bank guarantees, promissory notes and performance bonds, preference for in case of car sales 320–321, 348–349
possession
  bona fide acquisition of real rights in movable property, period of possession, relevance 319–320, 344–345, 582 n.20
  goods held in safe custody 200
priority
  all-monies/sums retention of title (framework agreement) 423
  credit consignment agreement 292–293
  enterprise charge 500–501
  equality of creditors/unfair preferences 499–500, 503
  reservation of title 283
  statutory possessory liens 199–225, 226, 233: machinery 267–268
  statutory preferences 501, 581–582
privilegi. *See* enterprise charge *above*
proceeds clause (extended reservation of title), new goods manufactured out of materials supplied (*specificatio*) [with products clause] 378–379
products clause, 'manufacturer'/'owner', parties' right to determine 378–379, 396
publicity/registry
  cars (*pubblico registro automobilistico*), delay in 319
  enterprise charge 498–499
  as notification to *debitor cessus* 575–576
  registered bank charge 498–499, 581–582
  security interests requiring: bank loans 581–582; machinery 267–268
  transfer of ownership of movable, relevance 633
registered bank charge 498–499, 581–582
  excess collateral, relevance 582
  execution 582
  frequency of use 582
  insolvency 582
  priority 581–582

public [notarial] deed, need for
    581–582
publicity/registry 498–499,
    581–582
specificity principle 581–582
registered vehicle charge (*privilegio
    sull'autoveicolo*) 10, 477–478
  car fleet as collateral for
    non-possessory security right
    453–454, 478
  cars (*pubblico registro automobilistica*)
    453–454
  resale of cars supplied on credit for
    that purpose 357–358
rei vindicatio in case of insolvency
  all-monies/sums retention of title
    (framework agreement) 424–425
  goods owed by third party to original
    seller's agent 321–322
  reservation of title, effect 266,
    283–284, 298, 658
  specificity principle 424–425
  termination of sale before insolvency
    proceedings 200
  timing of claim 236
remedies
  disposal of collateral, need for
    judicial involvement 199–226, 233,
    500–501
  recovery of goods 198–199
rental agreement, finance leasing/
    leasing contract as 607
resale of cars supplied on credit for that
    purpose 318–323
  agency and 322
  commission [undisclosed] agency and
    321–322, 348–349: certain date (*data
    certa*) before execution or
    commencement of insolvency
    proceedings, need for 322, 357; used
    car sales 322
  monies paid to bankrupt, right to:
    commingling/distinguishability of
    monies, relevance 323, 348–349;
    payments made after start of
    insolvency proceedings 357–358;
    security assignment of future
    claims/debts 322–323
  registered vehicle charge (*privilegio
    sull'autoveicolo*) 357–358
  reservation of title 318–319

transfer of ownership/title as result
    of 318–320
reservation of title
  authorisation to sell, relevance
    290–293, 298
  credit consignment agreement
    distinguished 292–293
  formal requirements 265–266: certain
    date (*data certa*) before execution or
    commencement of insolvency
    proceedings, need for 268, 283,
    290–291, 322, 357, 658; express
    provision in contract of sale 266–267;
    general conditions, adequacy
    266–267; writing 267–268, 283–284
  machinery, right to prevent sale 266
  new goods manufactured out of
    materials supplied (*specificatio*)
    378–379
  priority 283
  publicity/registry 283: machinery 268
  rei vindicatio in case of insolvency 266,
    283–284, 298, 658
  resale of cars supplied on credit for
    that purpose 318–319
  sale on credit 200
  third-party rights 226, 268
  timing of reservation, relevance
    265–266, 268, 285–286
risk, new goods manufactured out of
    materials supplied (*specificatio*) 379,
    397
sale of business, public [notarial] deed,
    need for 633–634
sale and lease-back
  applicability 455
  car fleet as collateral for
    non-possessory security right,
    imported luxury cars 454–455
  frequency of use 454–455
  insolvency, debtor's rights in case of
    insolvency of creditor 455–456
  option/duty to reacquire, insolvency
    455–456
  'ordinary course of business' rule 454
  termination in case of insolvency
    proceedings, debtor's rights in case
    of insolvency of creditor 455–456
  third-party rights 454
  validity, consent of parties as
    determining factor 454, 475

INDEX BY COUNTRY

Italy (cont.)
  security assignment of earnings
    charge of money claim as alternative 569–570
    debitor cessus, notice to, relevance 550–551
  security assignment of future claims/debts
    certain date (data certa), need for 322
    consideration, need for 550
    debitor cessus, notice to, relevance 322, 406–407, 550, 633: money earned but not paid before insolvency 551–552; money earned and paid before insolvency 552
    forfeiture clause (pactum commissorium) 550
    insolvency 550–551: assignment following 407
    resale of cars supplied on credit for that purpose 322–323, 357
    as security for bank loan 550–551, 581
    specificity principle 322–323, 406–407
    third-party rights 550–551
  security rights, future claim against unknown debtor, possibilities 581–583
  security transfer of ownership, forfeiture clause (pactum commissorium) 454, 607–608, 620–621
  special registered charge
    machinery 10, 267–268
    variety 10–11
  specificity principle 198, 200
    enterprise charge 581–582
    fungible assets 424–425
    hire purchase/payment by instalment 319
    [registered] charge (privilegio speciale) 499
    rei vindicatio in case of insolvency 424–425
    security assignment of future claims/debts 322–323
  stock-in-trade as collateral for non-possessory security right
    enterprise charge 498–500
    excess collateral, relevance 501
    execution 501
    frequency of use, enterprise charge 501
  insolvency 497–501
  third-party rights
    actio Pauliana 501–502, 634
    credit consignment agreement 292–293
    execution, real/personal right as basis for opposition 237
    factoring contract 551–552
    reservation of title 226, 268
    sale and lease-back 454
    security assignment of future claims/debts 550–551
    termination/avoidance of contract and: bona fide acquisition 236–237; in case of fraud or mistake 236–238
  transfer of ownership/title
    obligation to transfer, principle of abstraction, revesting of title on termination of contract and 227–228
    original acquisition: commixtio 197–198, 378; specificatio 197–198, 378
    ownership and right to dispose of property distinguished 291–292
    requirements: consent, sufficiency 198, 223, 236, 475; payment of purchase price, relevance 198, 267, 321–322; 'title' in form of contract, testamentary disposition or legal provision 198
  usury 501, 582

Netherlands
  accession, transfer or ownership/title and, stock-in-trade as collateral for non-possessory security right 504 n.61
  actio Pauliana 506–507
    burden of proof 507: price, relevance 635
    execution, effect on 635
    insolvency proceedings 506–507
    limitation period 507
    requirements: debtor's knowledge of likely detriment 635; detrimental effect 507, 635; intention to defraud/prejudice other creditors, relevance 507, 635; third-party's knowledge/'should have known' 507
  all-monies/sums retention of title (framework agreement) 425–426

frequency of use 426, 437
insolvency, part of insolvency estate, whether 425
payment of purchase price, relevance 426
seller's rights in sold goods 426
seller's rights in unsold goods, non-possessory ownership 12, 425, 435
specificity principle, ascertainment of goods 426
validity 425: general clauses/framework agreement, acceptability 425–426, 436–437
bona fide acquisition 202 n.100
belief in seller's right to sell: reasonable doubt 323–324; resale of cars supplied on credit for that purpose 323–324, 343–344
execution 238
pledge (silent) 504
car fleet as collateral for non-possessory security right
pledge (silent) 456
sale and lease-back 456–457, 474
charge of money claims 552–555
conditional/contingent nature, relevance 553
debitor cessus, notice to, relevance 584–585: money earned but not paid before insolvency 554–555; money earned and paid before insolvency 553–554, 555
delayed power of disposal/'act of creation' 552–553, 583
excess collateral, relevance 585
execution 584
existing legal relationship, need for 583–584
future claim, whether/applicability to: future claims as basis of bank loan 583; future earnings as collateral for bank loan 553
insolvency 584–585: creation of charge following 584
priority 584
publicity/registry 584: master-list of claims 583–584, 651–652
with/without notification (*openbar/stil pandrecht*) 552–553, 583–584. *See also* pledge (silent) *and* [registered] charge *below*
choice of law, Rome Convention on the Law Applicable to Contractual Obligations (1980) 651–652
commingling/distinguishability of monies paid to bankrupt, stock-in-trade as collateral for non-possessory security right 505
constructive delivery/*constitutum possessorium*
sale and lease-back 51, 475
security interest as *causa* 51
contract, avoidance
for fraud 238: transfer of ownership/title, effect on 238
for intention to defraud/prejudice creditors 635: family members and 635; price as evidence of intention 635, 646; price as evidence of intention/knowledge 635, 646
for misrepresentation 238
for mistake 238
contract, termination in case of insolvency proceedings 202–203
default of administrator and 268–269
seller's right 202–203
contract, termination for failure to pay
insolvency proceedings, effect 268–269
non-termination, right of 268–269
parties' agreement and (resolutive clause) 203–204
as right *in personam* 203–221, 228
seller's right of recovery (*recht van reclame*) 202–203, 226
time-limits/grace period and 202–203, 226, 268–269
debitor cessus, notice to, relevance
charge of money claims 555, 584–585
charge over future claims 324–325, 569
identity of debtor, relevance 324–325
insolvency, notification following 578, 584–585
modification of requirement 571
money earned and paid before insolvency 553–554, 555
pledge (silent) 553–554
[registered] charge 324–325, 553
delivery, relevance 201, 223
pledge (silent) 456, 504

Netherlands (cont.)
  where transferee in possession of property (*traditio brevi/longa manu*) 201
  excess collateral, relevance
    charge of money claims 585
    fairness 506, 585
    stock-in-trade as collateral for non-possessory security right 506
  execution
    actio Pauliana, effect 635
    against purchaser of business for pre-existing debt, business assets, applicability to 635
    bona fide acquisition 238
    charge of money claims 584
    stock-in-trade as collateral for non-possessory security right 505–506
    third-party rights, property on debtor's premises 269 n.79, 425, 425
  fairness, excess collateral 506, 585
  fiducia [cum creditore], *causa traditionis*, whether 456–457
  fiduciary relationship (beneficial trust)
    pledge (silent) as replacement for 609 n.36
    sale and lease-back distinguished 456–457
  finance leasing/leasing contract 608–610
    fiduciary relationship (beneficial trust) compared 609–610
    frequency of use 609–610
    hire purchase/payment by instalment compared 608–609
    insolvency of creditor, debtor's rights 610
    option to acquire: characterisation of contract and 609; hire purchase/payment by instalment and 609–610; as option not to acquire 608
    rei vindicatio in case of insolvency 608
    as rental agreement 608
    reservation of title/retention of ownership 608
    security transfer of ownership compared 609–610
    termination in case of insolvency proceedings, lessor's right 608
    transfer of ownership/title on purchase at end of contract 608
    form/nomenclature, relevance 58
    hire purchase/payment by instalment
      finance leasing/leasing contract compared 608–609
      resolutive clause 608, 609–610
      [suspensive] condition for payment of purchase price 608, 609–610
      transfer of title/ownership, automaticity 608, 609–610
  hypothec
    abolition 47: leaseback and 50–51
  insolvency
    administrator's rights/duties: notification to secured creditor of intention to sell collateral 505; postponement of sale/execution 505, 652
    avoidance of fraudulent proceedings. *See actio Pauliana above*
    charge of money claims 584–585
    debitor cessus, notice to, relevance, notification following 578, 584–585
    goods in transit, rights over: stoppage 181, 229; transfer of ownership/title, relevance 204
    gratuitous transactions 507
    intention to defraud/prejudice other creditors, effect: avoidance of fraudulent proceedings 202; failure to take interests of other creditors into account 506
    pledge (silent), debtor's rights in case of insolvency of creditor 457–458
    proceedings, effect 202–204, 382
    sale and lease-back, debtor's rights in case of insolvency of creditor 458
    stock-in-trade as collateral for non-possessory security right 505
    suspension of transactions 202, 268–269, 382
  legislation, role 647–648
  liability of purchaser of business for pre-existing debt 635
    continued management by original owner, relevance 635
  new goods manufactured out of materials supplied (*specificatio*)
    Breda/St Antonius 379–381
    execution in the absence of proceeds clause 381: before payment by

second buyer 408; following payment by second buyer 406, 408
insolvency in the absence of proceeds clause 382: after payment by second buyer 408; before payment by second buyer 408
manufacture for self, relevance 379–381, 382
ownership: risk, relevance 380, 382, 395; value of material/value of work, relevance 369–370, 372–373, 375, 376, 378, 381, 395
pledge (silent) 381–382, 396–397
[registered] charge 408
reservation of title 379–382
specificatio: determination of 379–380; ownership, creation/termination and 379–380, 408
'ordinary course of business' rule
resale of cars supplied on credit for that purpose 323
stock-in-trade as collateral for non-possessory security right 504
pledge (silent) 14. *See also* charge of money claims *above*
bona fide acquisition 504
debitor cessus, notice to, relevance 553–554
delayed power of disposal/'act of creation' 12, 456, 504, 552–553: charge of money claims 552–553, 583; new goods manufactured out of materials supplied (*specificatio*) 381–382, 396–397; stock-in-trade as collateral for non-possessory security right 504
delivery, relevance 456, 504
existing legal relationship at time of creation of charge, need for 553, 583–584
fiduciary relationship (beneficial trust) and 609 n.36
frequency of use 506
insolvency 554: debtor's rights in case of insolvency of creditor 457–458
new goods manufactured out of materials supplied (*specificatio*), delayed power of disposal/'act of creation' 381–382, 396–397

notarial/registered deed (in non-public registry), need for 14, 456, 515, 527, 651–652, 656
priority 505, 527: tax authorities 505
public pledge: conversion to 505; distinguished 325, 346–347, 456, 478, 504–506, 552–553
as real right 504
specificity principle 504, 526–527
stock-in-trade as collateral for non-possessory security right 504–506, 526–527, 660: future stock acquired after commencement of insolvency proceedings 505
priority
charge of money claims 584
pledge (silent) 505
reservation of title 283, 325
statutory possessory liens 325
tax claims 505
proceeds clause (extended reservation of title), exclusion 12, 358, 364, 381
products clause, exclusion 381, 396–397
publicity/registry
charge of money claims 584
as critical date for effectiveness of transaction 78
public [notarial] deed distinguished 324, 456
security interests requiring 324, 346–347
[registered] charge
debitor cessus, notice to, relevance 324–325, 346–347, 553
fluctuating future assets 325, 346–347, 349–350, 364: limited applicability 324–325
future claims as basis of bank loan 583
future earnings as collateral for bank loan 553
new goods manufactured out of materials supplied (*specificatio*) and 408
resale of cars supplied on credit for that purpose 324
with/without notification (*openbar/stil pandrecht*) 325, 346–347, 456, 478, 504–506, 552–553. *See also* pledge (silent) *above*

Netherlands (*cont.*)
  rei vindicatio in case of insolvency
    finance leasing/leasing contract 608
    reservation of title, effect 268–269, 283–284, 298, 658
  remedies, recovery of sale price 202
  rental agreement
    finance leasing/leasing contract as 608
    sale and lease-back distinguished 458
  resale of cars supplied on credit for that purpose
    monies paid to bankrupt, right to 324: payments made after start of insolvency proceedings 358; public [notarial] deed, relevance 324; [registered] charge 325
    reservation of title 325
    transfer of ownership/title as result of 323: authorisation to sell, relevance 323
  reservation of title
    authorisation to sell, relevance 293, 298: as resolutive condition 293, 504
    formal requirements: certain date (*data certa*) before execution or commencement of insolvency proceedings, need for 270, 283–284; general conditions, adequacy 270; writing 269, 270, 283–284
    new goods manufactured out of materials supplied (*specificatio*) 379–382
    priority 283, 325
    publicity/registry 270, 283
    rei vindicatio in case of insolvency 268–269, 283–284, 293, 658
    resale of cars supplied on credit for that purpose 325
    stock-in-trade as collateral for non-possessory security right, authorisation to sell, relevance 504
    as [suspensive] condition for payment of purchase price 268, 293: hire purchase/payment by instalment 608, 609–610; implied authorisation to sell and 293, 298
    third-party rights 12, 226
    timing of reservation, relevance 269, 285–286
    unilateral declaration of, validity 269, 285
  resolutive clause, hire purchase/payment by instalment and 608
  risk
    new goods manufactured out of materials supplied (*specificatio*) 395
    sale and lease-back 457
  sale and lease-back
    applicability, know-how 457
    car fleet as collateral for non-possessory security right 456–457, 474
    constructive delivery/*constitutum possessorium* 51, 475
    fiduciary relationship (beneficial trust) distinguished 456–457: as sham 457
    hire purchase/payment by instalment distinguished 458
    insolvency, debtor's rights in case of insolvency of creditor 458
    rental agreement distinguished 458
    risk 457
    validity 456–457
  security assignment of earnings, frequency of use 552
  security assignment of future claims/debts
    exclusion 552–555
    as security for bank loan 552–555
  security rights
    completion many months after loan at time of financial difficulty, effect 506–507
    future claim against unknown debtor, possibilities 583–585
  security transfer of ownership 11, 12, 489
    exclusion 12, 58, 396–397, 456, 609–610
    finance leasing/leasing contract compared 609–610
    sale and resale 474, 609–610
  specificity principle 65–66
    fungible assets 426
    pledge (silent) 504, 526–527
  stock-in-trade as collateral for non-possessory security right
    accession, transfer of ownership/title and 504 n.61
    excess collateral, relevance 506
    execution 505–506
    frequency of use 506
    insolvency 505

obligation to store separately 504, 526–527: commingling/ distinguishability of monies paid to bankrupt 505
'ordinary course of business' rule 504
pledge (silent) 504–506: future stock acquired after commencement of insolvency proceedings 505
third-party rights
  execution, property on debtor's premises 269 n.79, 425, 425
  fraudulent dealings and 202, 507
  reservation of title 12, 226
  termination of contract and, *bona fide* faith acquisition 202 n.100
  termination/avoidance of contract and 238
transfer of ownership/title
  agreement that title should pass ('real agreement'), need for 201, 224
  obligation to transfer 269
  requirements: *causa traditionis (titel)* 201, 238, 456, 504, 552–553; *nemo plus* principle 201

Norway, publicity/registry 59

Portugal
actio Pauliana
  gratuitous transactions and 496
  insolvency proceedings 579
  requirements: debtor's knowledge of likely detriment 630; intention to defraud/prejudice other creditors, relevance 496, 630
  reservation of title as modification to contract and 262
all-monies/sums retention, delivery, relevance 422
all-monies/sums retention of title (framework agreement) 422–423
  frequency of use 423, 437
  payment of purchase price, relevance 422, 435
  security transfer of ownership 661–662
  validity 422, 434–435: as reservation of title clause 422, 435
bona fide acquisition, exclusion 289, 298–299
  of object sold by businessman in ordinary course of business 289

car fleet as collateral for non-possessory security right
finance leasing/leasing contract 449–450
  sale and lease-back 449–450
  special registered charge 449
charge of money claims 545
  debitor cessus, notice to, relevance 544–545, 569: money earned but not paid before insolvency 544–545; money earned and paid before insolvency 545
  execution 579
  frequency of use 544
  future claim, whether/applicability to 544, 578–579: unknown debtor 578–579
  ius separationis 545
  priority 579
  publicity/registry 544
  retroactive application 544
  unjust enrichment 545
contract, annulment of simulated/*pro forma* 630, 644
  intention to defraud/prejudice other creditors, need for 630
contract, avoidance
  for fraud 235: transfer of ownership/title, effect on 235; sufficiency of contract to transfer title and 235, 244
  for intention to defraud/prejudice creditors 630: price as evidence of intention 630–631, 646
  for usury 496, 579
contract, termination in case of insolvency proceedings 190
  alternatives 191
contract, termination for failure to pay, parties' agreement and (resolutive clause) 190
debitor cessus, notice to, relevance
  charge of money claims 544–545, 569
  modification of requirement 571
  security assignment of earnings 544–545
  security assignment of future claims/debts 578–579
delivery, relevance
  all-monies/sums retention 422

Portugal (cont.)
   floating [enterprise] charge/lien/
      mortgage, symbolic delivery 495
   money and 404
   possessory pledge 495: in case of
      banks 495
   excess collateral, relevance, security
      rights 579
   execution
      actio Pauliana, effect 496
      against purchaser of business for
         pre-existing debt, right to resist 630
      charge of money claims 579
      possessory pledge 495–496
      priority, as means of securing 405
      security assignment of future
         claims/debts 579
      subrogation action 404–405
   factoring contract, as security for bank
      loan 578–579
   finance leasing/leasing contract
      602–603
      frequency of use 602–603
      insolvency of creditor, debtor's rights
         603
      lessor's right on termination to return
         of goods, as owner 602
      option to acquire: at predetermined
         price 602; as necessary condition
         602
      security transfer of ownership
         compared 602–603
      termination in case of insolvency
         proceedings, administrator's
         right/duty 602
   floating [enterprise] charge/lien/
      mortgage
      applicability, all types of asset 495,
         496
      delivery, relevance, symbolic delivery
         495
   forfeiture clause (*pactum commissorium*)
      security transfer of ownership 602–603
      special registered charge 449–450
   insolvency
      administrator's right/duty to sell,
         assets already executed against 190
      contract, effect on 190: payment at
         insolvency creditor rate, limitation
         to 191
      goods in transit, rights over, recovery
         on payment of transit costs 191

      gratuitous transactions 496
      intention to defraud/prejudice other
         creditors, effect, avoidance of
         fraudulent proceedings 194, 496
      possessory pledge 495–496
      property rights of bankrupt person,
         effect on 190
      security assignment of earnings
         544–545
      security assignment of future
         claims/debts 579
      special registered charge, debtor's
         rights in case of insolvency of
         creditor 450, 478–479
      stock-in-trade as collateral for
         non-possessory security right
         495–496
      suspect period 194
   ius separationis
      charge of money claims 545
      security assignment of earnings 545
   liability of purchaser of business for
      pre-existing debt 630–631
   new goods manufactured out of
      materials supplied (*specificatio*)
      execution in the absence of proceeds
         clause 375: before payment by
         second buyer 404–405; following
         payment by second buyer 404
      insolvency in the absence of proceeds
         clause 376, 405
      mandate to manufacture and sell
         375–376
      ownership: risk, relevance 375; value
         of material/value of work, relevance
         375, 394–395
      reservation of title 375–376
      third-party rights 375
   possessory pledge
      completion many months after loan
         at time of financial difficulty, effect
         496
      delivery, relevance 495
      disposal without authority as criminal
         offence 495
      execution 495–496
      insolvency 495–496
      specificity principle 495
      stock-in-trade as collateral for
         non-possessory security right 495:
         future stock 495
      writing, need for 495

priority
  charge of money claims 579–580
  execution as means of securing 405
  special registered charge 449
  subrogation action 404–405
publicity/registry
  charge of money claims 544
  security assignment of earnings 544
  security interests requiring 261
  transfer of ownership of movable, relevance 189–190: resale of cars supplied on credit for that purpose 316, 344
rei vindicatio in case of insolvency
  insolvent's possession of another's movable property 289
  reservation of title, effect 298–299, 658
  timing of claim 235
resale of cars supplied on credit for that purpose 316
  monies paid to bankrupt, right to 316: payments made after start of insolvency proceedings 356
  transfer of ownership/title as result of, registration of original seller's claim, relevance 316, 344
reservation of title
  authorisation to sell, relevance 289, 298–299: resale as sale of future goods (expectancy) 289, 298–299
  formal requirements 261: signature 262, 289, 376, 422; writing 283–284, 658
  machinery, publicity/registry 261, 262
  as modification to contract, *actio Pauliana* 262
  new goods manufactured out of materials supplied (*specificatio*) 375–376
  as preferred method 261, 317, 349
  publicity/registry 283, 658: machinery 261, 262; notification to other party, need for 262; timing, relevance 262
  rei vindicatio in case of insolvency 298–299, 658
  resale of cars supplied on credit for that purpose 356, 363: as preferred method 317, 349
  as [suspensive] condition for payment of purchase price 261

  timing of reservation, relevance 262, 285–286, 289
sale and lease-back
  car fleet as collateral for non-possessory security right 449–450
  as sham charge 449–450, 474–475, 602–603
  validity, consent of parties as determining factor 449–450
security assignment of earnings 545
  charge of money claim as alternative 569–570
  debitor cessus, notice to, relevance 544–545, 569: money earned but not paid before insolvency 544–545
  frequency of use 544
  insolvency 544–545
  ius separationis 545
  publicity/registry 544
  retroactive application 544
  unjust enrichment 545
security assignment of future claims/debts
  debitor cessus, notice to, relevance 578–579
  duration of assignment, relevance 579
  execution 579–580
  frequency of use 544
  insolvency 579–580
security rights
  duration of charge before insolvency, relevance 579
  excess collateral, relevance 579
  future claim against unknown debtor, possibilities 578–579
security transfer of ownership
  all-monies/sums retention of title (framework agreement) 661–662
  exclusion 602–603, 620–621
  finance leasing/leasing contract compared 602–603
  forfeiture clause (*pactum commissorium*) 602–603
  special registered charge 477–478
  car fleet as collateral for non-possessory security right 449
  cars, ships and aircraft 450
  forfeiture clause (*pactum commissorium*) 449–450

722   INDEX BY COUNTRY

Portugal (cont.)
  insolvency, debtor's rights in case of insolvency of creditor 450, 478–479, 603
  judicial sale and 449–450, 602–603
  priority 449
specificity principle, possessory pledge 495
stock-in-trade as collateral for non-possessory security right
  excess collateral, relevance 496
  frequency of use 496
  future stocks, possessory pledge 495
  insolvency 495–496
  possessory pledge 495: over shares 496
third-party rights
  new goods manufactured out of materials supplied (*specificatio*) 375
  termination of contract and 190: registration of acquisition before termination, need for 235
transfer of ownership/title
  obligation to transfer, validity, relevance 189–190
  requirements: consent, sufficiency 189–190, 223, 235, 261; payment of purchase price, relevance 189–190, 289, 344, 356; title 189–190
  time of, conclusion of contract 189–190, 261
unjust enrichment
  charge of money claims 545
  security assignment of earnings 545
usury 496, 579

Scotland
actio Pauliana 513–514
  gratuitous transactions 514, 638–639
  judicial avoidance (reduction), retroactive/*ex tunc* effect 513
  limitation period 513, 638–639
  requirements: debtor's inability to meet commitments at time of transaction 638–639; diminution of debtor's capacity to pay debts 514, 638, 646; intention to defraud/prejudice other creditors, relevance 513; pre-existing debt 513; technical insolvency at time of transaction 513

all-monies/sums retention of title (framework agreement) 430
  frequency of use 430, 437
  insolvency, part of insolvency estate, whether 430
  payment of purchase price, relevance 430, 435
  validity 430, 434–435: consent of parties as determining factor 430; as reservation of title clause 430, 435, 661–662
assignation of incorporeals. *See* security assignment of claims/debts *below*
bona fide acquisition
  belief in seller's right to sell 343–344
  cars bought by private person 333–334
  stock-in-trade as collateral for non-possessory security right 513–514
car fleet as collateral for non-possessory security right
  floating [enterprise] charge/lien/mortgage 463, 464
  sale and lease-back 463
carrier, as agent 213
constructive delivery/*constitutum possessorium* 45–46, 211, 212–213
  sale and lease-back 463–464
  traditio ficta 45–46
contract, avoidance
  for fraud 240–241: principle of abstraction 243–244; transfer of ownership/title, effect on 240–241
contract, termination in case of insolvency proceedings, as right *in personam* 211–212, 213
contract, termination for failure to pay
  judicial termination, need for 211–212
  parties' agreement and (resolutive clause) 213
reversion of title [where seller remains in possession of goods] 211–212: principle of abstraction and 227–228
debitor cessus, notice to, relevance
  modification of requirement 571
  security assignment of claims/debts 559–560, 587
  security assignment of future claims/debts 360, 415

INDEX BY COUNTRY 723

delivery, relevance 211, 223, 275–276, 612
  avoidance of contract for fraud 241
  gift/transactions other than sale
    212–213
  insolvency, buyer's duty to refuse in
    case of inability to pay 212
  reversion of ownership 276–277
  reversion of ownership following
    termination of contract 211–212
excess collateral, relevance
  security assignment of claims/debts
    587
  stock-in-trade as collateral for
    non-possessory security right 513,
    528–529
execution
  against purchaser of business for
    pre-existing debt, business assets,
    applicability to 638
  security assignment of claims/debts
    587
factoring contract
  definition/description 559–560
  frequency of use 559–560
fiduciary relationship (beneficial trust)
  resale of cars supplied on credit for
    that purpose 334, 360
  security assignment of claims/debts
    560, 587
finance leasing/leasing contract 612–613
  frequency of use 613
  hire purchase/payment by instalment
    compared 612–613
  insolvency of creditor, debtor's rights
    613
floating charge 477, 526
  applicability: all types of asset 512,
    525; corporate debtors 512, 525,
    587; future debts as collateral for
    bank loan 587; whole or part of
    patrimony 512, 513, 525
  car fleet as collateral for
    non-possessory security right 463,
    464
  crystallisation 512, 525, 526
  equitable nature of real right 512
  fluctuating future assets 512–513,
    650–651, 661
  insolvency: insolvency of creditor 464;
    suspect period 514
  priority 513

publicity/registry 512, 525
receivership/liquidation 512
Scottish/English systems distinguished
  512, 526
statutory nature 512
stock-in-trade as collateral for
  non-possessory security right
  512–513, 525
third-party rights 512–513
hire purchase/payment by instalment
  finance leasing/leasing contract
    compared 612–613
  frequency of use 613
  as legal fiction 87, 612–613
  publicity/registry 612–613
insolvency
  avoidance of fraudulent proceedings
    212: retroactive/*ex tunc* effect 514
  floating [enterprise] charge/lien/
    mortgage, insolvency of creditor
    464
  goods in transit, rights over, stoppage
    213
  onerous/disadvantageous transactions,
    administrator's rights/duty to avoid
    513
  security assignment of claims/debts
    587
  suspect period, floating [enterprise]
    charge/lien/mortgage 514
intimation. *See debitor cessus*, notification
  to, relevance *above*
liability of purchaser of business for
  pre-existing debt 638–639
new goods manufactured out of
  materials supplied (*specificatio*)
  execution in the absence of proceeds
    clause 389: before payment by
    second buyer 410; following
    payment by second buyer 410
  insolvency in the absence of proceeds
    clause 389, 410: following payment
    by second buyer 410
  ownership, value of material/value of
    work, relevance 388, 395
  reservation of title 388–389
  specificatio: determination of 388,
    656–657, 662–663; ownership,
    creation/termination and 388
  third-party rights, refusal of sums due
    to bankrupt 410

Scotland (*cont.*)
  possession
    presumption of ownership 277
    sale and lease-back 463–464
  priority
    equality of creditors/unfair preferences 513–514, 638
    statutory preferences 513
    tax claims 513
  proceeds clause (extended reservation of title), new goods manufactured out of materials supplied (*specificatio*) [with products clause], exclusion 410
  products clause, 'manufacturer'/'owner', parties' right to determine 389, 396
  publicity/registry
    floating [enterprise] charge/lien/mortgage 512, 525
    hire purchase/payment by instalment 612–613
    registration of company charge 559
    security assignment of claims/debts 559
  resale of cars supplied on credit for that purpose 333–334
    monies paid to bankrupt, right to 334: payments made after start of insolvency proceedings 360
    transfer of ownership/title as result of 333–334: authorisation to sell, relevance 333, 343–344
  reservation of title 211
    authorisation to sell, relevance 294, 298
    formal requirements 277: certain date (*data certa*) before execution or commencement of insolvency proceedings, need for 277, 283; general conditions, adequacy 277; writing 277
    new goods manufactured out of materials supplied (*specificatio*) 388–389
    timing of reservation, relevance 276–277, 285–286
  risk, new goods manufactured out of materials supplied (*specificatio*), ownership, risk, relevance 388
  Roman law and, *specificatio* 388

  Roman–Dutch law and 45–46
  sale and lease-back
    applicability 464
    car fleet as collateral for non-possessory security right 463
    constructive delivery/*constitutum possessorium* 463–464
    possession 463–464
    as sham charge 463–464, 474–475
  security assignment of claims/debts 559–560
    by charge 571–572
    debitor cessus, notice to, relevance 559–560, 587: money earned but not paid before insolvency 560; money earned and paid before insolvency 560
    excess collateral, relevance 587
    execution 587
    as fiduciary relationship (beneficial trust) 560, 587
    future debt 559
    insolvency 587
    publicity/registry 559
  security assignment of future claims/debts, resale of cars supplied on credit for that purpose 360, 364
  security rights
    completion many months after loan at time of financial difficulty, effect 513–514
    future claim against unknown debtor, possibilities 587
  stock-in-trade as collateral for non-possessory security right
    bona fide acquisition 513–514
    excess collateral, relevance 513, 528–529
    floating [enterprise] charge/lien/mortgage 512–513, 525
    third-party rights, floating [enterprise] charge/lien/mortgage 512–513
  transfer of ownership/title
    burden of proof 277
    obligation to transfer: principle of abstraction 211–212, 227–228; revesting of title on termination of contract and 227–228
    requirements: intention to acquire (*animus accipiendi dominii*) 275–276; intention to transfer (*animus*

transferendi dominii) 275–276; *nemo plus* principle 333–334, 345
time of: agreement as determining factor 211, 276; conclusion of contract 46; transfer to carrier 213
Voet, Johannes and 45–46

South Africa
accession, transfer or ownership/title and, reservation of title 390
actio Pauliana
burden of proof, family membership as evidence of intent 640
gratuitous transactions 640
requirements: diminution of debtor's capacity to pay debts 640; insolvency at time of transaction, relevance 640; intention to defraud/prejudice other creditors, relevance 640; third-party's knowledge/'should have known' requirement 640
agency
carrier as 215
resale of cars supplied on credit for that purpose, monies paid to bankrupt, right to 336
all-monies/sums retention of title (framework agreement) 430–431
insolvency, part of insolvency estate, whether 430
payment of purchase price, relevance 430
seller's rights in unsold goods: non-possessory ownership 435; real, whether 430
specificity principle 430: risk 436
validity: car industry 430; general clauses/framework agreement, acceptability, incorporation in each contract of sale, need for 430
car fleet as collateral for non-possessory security right
possessory pledge 465
reservation of title 465–466, 474
security transfer of ownership, sale and resale 465–466, 474
charge of money claims
debitor cessus, notice to, relevance: money earned but not paid before insolvency 562, 563; money earned and paid before insolvency 562, 563
security assignment of earnings compared 560–561
commingling/distinguishability of monies paid to bankrupt
all-monies/sums retention of title 430, 436
exclusion, scope for 431
new goods manufactured out of materials supplied (*specificatio*) 410
commission [undisclosed] agency 336
constructive delivery/*constitutum possessorium*
fiducia [cum creditore] 464–465
as means of setting aside execution 639
security transfer of ownership 514–515
traditio ficta 45–46, 464–465
contract, avoidance
for fraud 241–242: resale of cars supplied on credit for that purpose, principle of abstraction 241–242, 243–244; unjust enrichment and 241–242
for intention to defraud/prejudice creditors 639
contract, termination in case of insolvency proceedings
in case of creditor's insolvency 466–467
as right *in personam* 215, 466–467
contract, termination for failure to pay
parties' agreement and (resolutive clause) 215
reversion of title [where seller remains in possession of goods], principle of abstraction and 227–228
damages, wrongful manufacture of goods supplied 389
debitor cessus, notice to, relevance, security assignment of claims/debts 562
delivery, need for 223
delivery, relevance, possessory pledge 465
estoppel
as basis of *rei vindicatio* 294–295, 299, 335
as defence 335, 346

South Africa (*cont.*)
  requirements: detriment to person raising estoppel 335; fault on part of person making representation 335; reliance as proximate cause of detriment 335; reliance on representation 335; representation by owner of entitlement to dispose of property 294–295, 335, 336
  security assignment of claims/debts 562
 excess collateral, relevance, security assignment of claims/debts 589
 execution
  against purchaser of business for pre-existing debt, business assets, applicability to 639
  security assignment of claims/debts 588
  stock-in-trade as collateral for non-possessory security right 515–516
 fiducia [cum creditore]
  causa traditionis, whether 464–465, 475–476
  constructive delivery/*constitutum possessorium* 464–465
  finance leasing/leasing contract 613–614
  hire purchase/payment by instalment compared 613
  insolvency of creditor, debtor's rights 614
  option to acquire: characterisation of contract and 613; hire purchase/payment by instalment and 613
  as rental agreement 613
  reservation of title/retention of ownership 613, 614
  termination in case of insolvency proceedings, debtor's rights in case of insolvency of creditor 614
 global assignment, acceptability/requirements 561–562, 588
 hire purchase/payment by instalment 224
  finance leasing/leasing contract compared 613
  insolvency, debtor's rights in case of insolvency of creditor 466–467
  sale and lease-back distinguished 465–466
  time-limits/grace period 294 n.15
  transfer of title/ownership, automaticity 614
 insolvency
  administration by insolvency administrator 214
  administrator's rights/duties: sale of assets, preservation of assets 214; satisfaction of claims of creditors and return of residue to bankrupt 214, 466–467
  contract, effect on, transfer of seller's ownership to administrator 277, 283–284
  goods in transit, rights over, stoppage 215, 229
  property of debtor, transfer of title to insolvency administration 214
  security assignment of claims/debts 588–589
  stock-in-trade as collateral for non-possessory security right 515–516
 liability of purchaser of business for pre-existing debt 639–640
  exclusion, possibility of 645
  limitation period 645
 new goods manufactured out of materials supplied (*specificatio*)
  as delict 389
  execution in the absence of proceeds clause 389: before payment by second buyer 410; following payment by second buyer 410
  insolvency in the absence of proceeds clause 390, 411
  monies paid to bankrupt, right to, commingling/distinguishability of monies, relevance 410
  ownership: payment of purchase price, relevance 390; risk, relevance 389; value of material/value of work, relevance 389, 395
  [registered] charge 410, 414–415
  reservation of title 389–390
  specificatio: ownership, creation/termination and 389; reversibility, relevance 389

INDEX BY COUNTRY 727

third-party rights, refusal of sums due to bankrupt 410
unjustified enrichment and 389
'ordinary course of business' rule
  resale of cars supplied on credit for that purpose 335
  sale of business 639
possessory pledge
  car fleet as collateral for non-possessory security right 465
  delivery, relevance 465
  notarial/registered deed, need for 465, 515
  priority 515–516
  security transfer of ownership compared 514–515
  specificity principle 465
  stock-in-trade as collateral for non-possessory security right 515
priority
  equality of creditors/unfair preferences 516–517
  insolvency 214–215
  paritas creditorum 214–215
  possessory pledge 515–516
  privileged rights 214–215
publicity/registry, sale of business 639, 640
[registered] charge
  new goods manufactured out of materials supplied (*specificatio*) and 410, 414–415
  resale of cars supplied on credit for that purpose 327–329, 332–333, 336
rei vindicatio in case of insolvency
  estoppel and 294–295, 335
  reservation of title, effect 294–295, 658
rental agreement, finance leasing/leasing contract as 613
resale of cars supplied on credit for that purpose 335–336
  monies paid to bankrupt, right to: agency relationship and 336; payments made after start of insolvency proceedings 360; [registered] charge 336; reservation of title 336, 349, 363
  transfer of ownership/title as result of 335: authorisation to sell, relevance 336
  unjust enrichment 475–476

reservation of title
  accession, transfer or ownership/title and 390
  authorisation to sell, relevance 294–295, 299
  car fleet as collateral for non-possessory security right 465–466, 474
  formal requirements 277, 278: general conditions, adequacy 278; writing 278
  rei vindicatio in case of insolvency 294–295, 658
  resale of cars supplied on credit for that purpose 336: as preferred method 349
  third-party rights 278
  timing of reservation, relevance 278, 285–286
  unilateral declaration of, validity 278, 285: implied consent 278
risk, new goods manufactured out of materials supplied (*specificatio*), ownership, risk, relevance 389
Roman–Dutch law and 44
sale of business
  ordinary course of business rule 639
  publicity/registry 639, 640
sale and lease-back
  applicability 466
  hire purchase/payment by instalment distinguished 465–466
  insolvency, debtor's rights in case of insolvency of creditor 466–467
security assignment of claims/debts 560–563, 588–589
  by charge 560–561, 588–589
  conditional/contingent nature, relevance 588
  debitor cessus, notice to, relevance 562: money earned but not paid before insolvency 562, 563; money earned and paid before insolvency 562, 563
  excess collateral, relevance 589
  execution 588
  formal requirements: estoppel in case of breach 562
  future debt 561–562, 588
  insolvency 588–589
security assignment of earnings, as preferred method 569–570

728   INDEX BY COUNTRY

South Africa (cont.)
  security right (tacit hypothec) 360
    concursus creditorum 214–215
      resulting from commencement of
        insolvency proceedings 277,
        283–284, 614
  security rights
    completion many months after loan
      at time of financial difficulty, effect
      516–517
    future claim against unknown debtor,
      possibilities 588–589
  security transfer of ownership
    constructive delivery/constitutum
      possessorium 514–515
    excess collateral, relevance 516
    framework agreement 516
    possessory pledge compared 514–515:
      as sham pledge 514–515, 516
    sale and resale 465–466, 474
    stock-in-trade as collateral for
      non-possessory security right
      514–515
  specificity principle
    fungible assets 430
    possessory pledge 465, 515
  stock-in-trade as collateral for
    non-possessory security right
    514–517
    excess collateral, relevance 516
    execution 515–516
    pledge with notarial bond 515
    security transfer of ownership
    514–515
  third-party rights, reservation of
    title 278
  transfer of ownership/title
    agreement that title should pass
      ('real agreement'), need for 224:
      anticipatory agreement 561–562,
      588; assignment of debts 561–562
    obligation to transfer: principle of
      abstraction 213–214, 227–228;
      revesting of title on termination of
      contract and 227–228
    requirements, payment of purchase
      price, relevance 224
    time of: delivery 213–214, 215; transfer
      to carrier 215
  unjust enrichment
    contract voided for fraud and 241–242

  new goods manufactured out of
    materials supplied (specificatio) and
    389
  resale of cars supplied on credit for
    that purpose 475–476

Spain
  actio Pauliana
    as action of last resort 498, 631
    burden of proof 632–633: statutory
      presumptions 631–632
    limitation period 632
    partial revocation 632
    as personal action 631
    requirements: detrimental effect 632;
      due debt 626–627; intention to
      defraud/prejudice other creditors
      498; pre-existing debt 632; valid
      transaction 632
    third-party rights 498
  after-acquired collateral, priority 195
  all monies/sums retention of title
    (framework agreement) 423
    examples 423
    frequency of use 423, 437
    insolvency, priority 423
    validity 423, 434–435
  bona fide acquisition 263
    execution 236
    possession 317, 344–345, 652–653
    precautionary measures 236
    reservation of title 263
    stock-in-trade as collateral for
      non-possessory security right 498
  car fleet as collateral for non-possessory
    security right
    [registered] charge 451
    sale and lease-back 450–451
    security transfer of ownership
    451–453, 473–474
  Catalan, security transfer of ownership
    452–453
  constructive delivery/constitutum
    possessorium 191–192
    traditio ficta 191–192
  contract
    formal requirements 192–193
    freedom of contract, restraint of sale
      and 194
  contract, avoidance
    for absence of consent 235–236

for defect of form 235–236
for fraud 194: judicial avoidance, need for 235–236; requirements 235–236; transfer of ownership/title, effect on 244
for intention to defraud/prejudice creditors 631: family members and 631; price as evidence of intention 633, 646
for mistake 235–236
contract, termination for failure to pay
non-termination, right of 264–265
parties' agreement and (resolutive clause) 195–196
precautionary measures 262–263
as right *in personam* 228, 262–263
customary law, security transfer of ownership 451–452
damages
contract avoided for fraud or misrepresentation 498
contract terminated for failure to pay 264–265
debitor cessus, notice to, relevance
discounting of bills as means of providing loan 580
factoring contract 546–547, 580
delivery, relevance 191–192, 223
where transferee in possession of property (*traditio brevi manu*) 191–192
discounting of bills as means of providing loan 546–547, 580
debitor cessus, liability for payment by 546–547, 580
debitor cessus, notice to, relevance 580
priority 580
excess collateral, relevance, security rights 581
execution
against purchaser of business for pre-existing debt 631
bona fide acquisition 236
security right against unknown debtor 580–581
factoring contract
assignment of future claims/debts 546–547
debitor cessus, notice to, relevance 546–547: money earned but not paid before insolvency 548–549;

money earned and paid before insolvency 548, 549
definition/description 545–546
frequency of use 546, 579–580
insolvency 548–549
public [notarial] deed, need for 548
publicity/registry 546
as security for bank loan 545–546, 579–580
writing, need for 546
fiduciary relationship (beneficial trust), security transfer of ownership 452–453
finance leasing/leasing contract 603–605
banks and financial institutions, role 604
contractual nature of relationship 604–605
frequency of use 604
insolvency of creditor, debtor's rights 604–605
option to acquire: characterisation of contract and 604; as necessary condition 604
public [notarial] deed, relevance 603
publicity/registry 603
reservation of title/retention of ownership 604
suspect period 604–605
forfeiture clause (*pactum commissorium*), security transfer of ownership 452
hire purchase/payment by instalment
formal requirements 192
registration 193–194, 196
reservation of title 194, 318
sale and lease-back distinguished 451
insolvency
administration by insolvency administrator, individual right of action, exclusion 193, 194–195
administrator's right/duty to sell, preservation of assets 193
avoidance of fraudulent proceedings (*retroacción de la quiebra*) 194, 235–236
concurso de acreedores 193–196
factoring contract 548–549
goods in transit, rights over: stoppage 181, 229; transfer of ownership/title, relevance 197

Spain (cont.)
  intention to defraud/prejudice other creditors, effect 498: *actio Pauliana*. See *actio Pauliana* above
  proceedings, limitation to merchants/businessmen 193
  property of debtor, loss of right to manage 190
  recovery of property disposed of before insolvency proceedings (*actio Pauliana*) 498
  restraint of sale and 194
  sale and lease-back 450–451
  security assignment of future claims/debts 406
  stock-in-trade as collateral for non-possessory security right 497–501
  suspect period 235–236, 290: finance leasing/leasing contract 604–605
  suspension of transactions 193
legislation, role 647–648
liability of purchaser of business for pre-existing debt 631–633
  continued management by original owner, relevance 631
Navarre, security transfer of ownership 452–453
new goods manufactured out of materials supplied (*specificatio*)
  execution in the absence of proceeds clause 376: before payment by second buyer 405; following payment by second buyer 405
  insolvency in the absence of proceeds clause 377–378: before payment by second buyer 405
  ownership, value
    of material/value of work, relevance 376, 394–395
  possessory pledge 377
  public [notarial] deed conferring special security 377
  [registered] charge (*hipoteca mobiliaria*) 377, 396–397
  rei vindicatio in case of insolvency 377–378
  reservation of title 376–378
  security assignment of future claims/debts 405

third-party rights 376
personal security including bank guarantees, promissory notes and performance bonds 317, 318
  as means of providing loan 547
possession
  bona fide acquisition of real rights in movable property 317, 344–345, 652–653
  presumption of ownership 317, 652–653
possessory pledge, new goods manufactured out of materials supplied (*specificatio*), raw materials/commodities 377
precautionary measures
  bona fide acquisition, prevention of 236
  termination of contract for failure to pay and 262–263
priority
  after-acquired collateral 195
  all-monies/sums retention of title (framework agreement) 423
  bilateral regulation, exclusion 196
  classification of rights: *ius separationis* 195–196; privileged rights 194–195; rights giving rise to separate execution 195–196
  date of contract and 196
  discounting of bills as means of providing loan 580
  non-possessory pledge and 195–196
  paritas creditorum 195–196, 290
  [registered] charge (*hipoteca mobiliaria*) 195–196, 497
  reservation of title 283, 290, 317
  sale and lease-back 450–451
  secured lender, public [notarial] deed conferring special security 580–581
  security rights, parties' intention as determining factor 580
  seller [on credit], public [notarial] deed conferring special security 356–357
publicity/registry
  absence of provision for 193–194
  factoring contract 546
  hire purchase/payment by instalment 193–194
  priority 196

public [notarial] deed distinguished 603
sale and lease-back 451
security interests requiring, machinery 263
[registered] charge (*hipoteca mobiliaria*) 10
car fleet as collateral for non-possessory security right 450, 451
frequency of use 496–497
judicial sale and 452 n.62
limited use of/restrictions on 196 n.81
new goods manufactured out of materials supplied (*specificatio*) 377, 396–397
priority 195–196, 497
public [notarial] deed, need for 451, 496–497
resale of cars supplied on credit for that purpose 318
specificity principle 450, 496–497
stock-in-trade as collateral for non-possessory security right 496–497
rei vindicatio in case of insolvency
all-monies/sums retention of title (framework agreement) 423
insolvent's possession of another's movable property 290
new goods manufactured out of materials supplied (*specificatio*) 377–378
reservation of title, effect 262–263, 264–265, 283, 290, 658
remedies
procedure 192–193
recovery and sale of goods 192–193
resale of cars supplied on credit for that purpose 317–318
monies paid to bankrupt, right to 317: payments made after start of insolvency proceedings 356–357; public [notarial] deed, need for 317
reseller's obligation to transfer monies received to original seller, *in personam* nature of original seller's right 317
reservation of title 317
transfer of ownership/title, authorisation to sell as result of, relevance 317, 344
reservation of title 195–196

authorisation to sell, relevance 289–290
formal requirements 263–264: certain date (*data certa*) before execution or commencement of insolvency proceedings, need for 283; general conditions, adequacy 264; public [notarial] deed, need for 263–264; writing 263–264, 269, 283–284
hire purchase/payment by instalment 194, 318
new goods manufactured out of materials supplied (*specificatio*) 376–378
priority 283, 290, 317
publicity/registry 284–285: machinery 263, 658; notification to other party, need for 264; registration in Chattels Registry 263, 265 n.69, 356
rei vindicatio in case of insolvency 262–263, 264–265, 283, 658
resale of cars supplied on credit for that purpose 317
sale and lease-back 451
specificity principle 263–264: machinery 263
third-party rights 226
timing of reservation, relevance 263–264, 285–286
unilateral declaration of, validity 263, 285
restraint of sale
insolvency 194
prohibition on 194
sale and lease-back
applicability 450–451
car fleet as collateral for non-possessory security right 450–451
expedited public deed 450–451
frequency of use 451, 453
hire purchase/payment by instalment distinguished 451
insolvency 450–451: debtor's rights in case of insolvency of creditor 453
option/duty to reacquire 451, 453: on repayment of original debt with interest 452–453
priority 450–451
publicity/registry 451: registration in Chattels Registry 451–452, 453
reservation of title, relevance 451
sale under guarantee as 452–453

Spain *(cont.)*
  specificity principle 453
  third-party rights 451, 453
  security assignment of claims/debts,
    possessory pledge distinguished
    547–549
  security assignment of earnings
    applicability to business or
      professional activities 547–548
    debitor cessus, notice to, relevance:
      limitation to claims arising within
      one year in absence of 547–548;
      money earned but not paid before
      insolvency 549
    frequency of use 548
    future claim, whether 547–548
    public [notarial] deed, need for 548
    specificity principle 547
  security assignment of future
    claims/debts
    insolvency, assignment following 406
    new goods manufactured out of
      materials supplied (*specificatio*) 405,
      415
    specificity principle 405
  security rights
    against unknown debtor, possibilities
      579–581
    completion many months after loan
      at time of financial difficulty, effect
      497–498
    excess collateral, relevance 581
    future claim against unknown debtor,
      possibilities, execution 580–581
    priority, parties' intention as
      determining factor 580
  security transfer of ownership
    car fleet as collateral for
      non-possessory security right
      451–453, 473–474
    Catalan 452–453
    as customary law 451–452
    fiduciary relationship (beneficial trust)
      452–453
    forfeiture clause (*pactum commissorium*)
      452
    iusta causa 475–476
    judicial sale and 452
    Navarre 452–453
    option/duty to reacquire, payment of
      repurchase price by instalment
      452–453

special registered charge, variety 10–11
  specificity principle
    public [notarial] deed conferring
      special security 356–357, 377
    [registered] charge (*hipoteca mobiliaria*)
      450
    reservation of title 263–264
    sale and lease-back 453
    security assignment of earnings 547
  stock-in-trade as collateral for
    non-possessory security right 497
  stock-in-trade as collateral for
    non-possessory security right
    bona fide acquisition 498
    excess collateral, relevance 497
    frequency of use 497
    insolvency 497–501
    [registered] charge 496–497
    specificity principle 497
  third-party rights
    actio Pauliana 498
    fraudulent dealings and 194
    new goods manufactured out of
      materials supplied (*specificatio*) 376
    precautionary measures and 236
    reservation of title 226
    sale and lease-back 451, 453
  transfer of ownership/title
    payment of purchase price, relevance,
      due date 290
    purchase contract distinguished 191
    purchase in shop open to public,
      relevance 356
    requirements: public [notarial] deed,
      relevance 191–192, 264, 356–357,
      377; *titulo y modo* 191–192, 223

Sweden
  actio Pauliana, limitation period
    521–522
  after-acquired collateral 521–522, 566
    n.103, 591
  agency
    commingling/distinguishability of
      monies, relevance 340, 348–349
    resale of cars supplied on credit for
      that purpose, monies paid to
      bankrupt, right to 340
    specificity principle 340
  all-monies/sums retention of title
    (framework agreement) 431–433
    frequency of use 433, 437

insolvency, *ius separationis* 432–433
seller's rights in unsold goods:
  co-ownership 432–433;
  non-possessory ownership 435
specificity principle 432–433: risk 436, 437
validity: authority to sell before payment of purchase price, relevance 431–432, 437; general clauses/framework agreement, acceptability 432; incorporation in each contract of sale, need for/as safer alternative 433
bona fide acquisition
  belief in seller's right to sell, resale of cars supplied on credit for that purpose 339
  enterprise charge 469
  possession 344–345: involuntary deprivation of possession and 339
car fleet as collateral for non-possessory security right
  constructive delivery/*constitutum possessorium* 470–471
  enterprise charge 469, 470–471
  registered sale 469–470, 473–474
  sale and lease-back 470–471
charge of money claims
  authority to receive money for own use 566, 591
  commingling/distinguishability of monies paid to bankrupt 566, 567
  debitor cessus, notice to, relevance 564–567: money earned but not paid before insolvency 566; money earned and paid before insolvency 566, 567
  frequency of use 565–566
  future earnings as collateral for bank loan 564–567
commingling/distinguishability of monies paid to bankrupt
  all-monies/sums retention of title 432–433
  charge of money claims 566, 567
  money paid to bankrupt, resale of cars supplied on credit for that purpose, monies paid to bankrupt, right to 340, 348–349
  security assignment of earnings 566

commission [undisclosed] agency 340, 361–362
  ius separationis 296–297, 392–393, 616–617
  new goods manufactured out of materials supplied (*specificatio*) 392–393, 412–413
  reservation of title distinguished 296–297, 299–300, 412
  sale or return arrangement between original seller and reseller, relevance 296–297, 299, 361–362, 364
constructive delivery/*constitutum possessorium* 219, 224
car fleet as collateral for non-possessory security right 470–471
enterprise charge 469, 470–471, 641
finance leasing/leasing contract 564–565
new goods manufactured out of materials supplied (*specificatio*) 393, 412
reversion of title and 280–281
contract, avoidance
  for fraud 242–243: transfer of ownership/title, effect on 242–243, 244
  for intention to defraud/prejudice creditors 642: family members and 642; insolvency, relevance 642; limitation period 642; price as evidence of intention/knowledge 642, 646; requirements 642
contract, termination in case of insolvency proceedings, administrator's rights/duty 471
contract, termination for failure to pay 217–218
  parties' agreement and (resolutive clause) 218, 219, 223–224, 228
  reservation of title, relevance 218, 228
  reversion of title [where seller remains in possession of goods] 210–212, 216, 227–228, 280–281: constructive delivery/*constitutum possessorium* 280–281
credit consignment agreement
  ius separationis 296–297
  reservation of title distinguished 296–297, 299–300, 658–659

Sweden (cont.)
  sale or return arrangement between original seller and reseller, relevance 296–297, 299
  debitor cessus, notice to, relevance
    assignment of future earnings 564–567
    charge of money claims 564–567
    enterprise charge 590, 591
    identity of debtor, relevance 364
    security assignment of future claims/debts 340, 590, 591, 641
  delivery, relevance, enterprise charge 469, 470–471
  enterprise charge 57, 477
    after-acquired collateral 591
    applicability 471: all types of asset 520; future claims as collateral for bank loan 590; future earnings as collateral for bank loan 566; limitations 525, 650–651
    bona fide acquisition 469
    car fleet as collateral for non-possessory security right 469, 470–471
    constructive delivery/*constitutum possessorium* 469, 470–471, 641
    crystallisation 520
    debitor cessus, notice to, relevance 590, 591
    delivery, relevance 469, 470–471
    as factoring contract 566
    fluctuating future assets 471, 520, 650–651, 661: duration of charge before insolvency, relevance 340, 521–522, 591
    forfeiture clause (*pactum commissorium*) 470–471
    frequency of use 520
    insolvency of creditor 471
    ius separationis 469, 470–471
    priority 525, 590
    publicity/registry 469, 641
    resale of cars supplied on credit for that purpose 340
    specificity principle 471
    stock-in-trade as collateral for non-possessory security right 519–520, 525, 528
    third-party rights 519–520
  excess collateral, relevance
    enterprise charge 591
    security assignment of future claims/debts 591
    stock-in-trade as collateral for non-possessory security right 521
  execution
    against purchaser of business for pre-existing debt 641
    security assignment of claims/debts 565–567
    security assignment of future claims/debts 591
  factoring contract, floating [enterprise] charge/lien/mortgage as 566
  fiduciary relationship (beneficial trust)
    debitor cessus, notice to, relevance, money earned but not paid before insolvency 566
    security assignment of claims/debts 564
    stock-in-trade as collateral for non-possessory security right 519
  finance leasing/leasing contract 615–617
    constructive delivery/*constitutum possessorium* 564–565
    frequency of use 617
    insolvency, debtor's rights in case of insolvency of creditor 471, 617
    option to acquire, *ius separationis* 616–617
    publicity/registry 475, 615–616
    reservation of title/retention of ownership 615–616
    sale with reservation of title compared 617
    for term equivalent to working life of equipment 615–616
    termination in case of insolvency proceedings, lessor's right 615–616
    transfer of ownership/title, on purchase at end of contract 615–616
  forfeiture clause (*pactum commissorium*), enterprise charge 470–471
  insolvency
    enterprise charge, insolvency of creditor 471
    goods in transit, rights over: bill of lading, retention and 218; on completion of transit 218; sale on credit and 218; stoppage 218

gratuitous transactions 642
'property that belongs to the debtor' 218
protection of buyer against seller's creditors 218–219, 223–224
protection of seller against buyer's creditors 217–218, 223–224, 279
security assignment of claims/debts 565–567
ius separationis 218–219, 242, 279, 283–284, 299
  accession and 279
  all-monies/sums retention of title (framework agreement) 432–433
  authorisation to sell/dispose of, relevance 242, 616–617, 620
  enterprise charge 469, 470–471
  finance leasing/leasing contract, option to acquire 616–617
liability of purchaser of business for pre-existing debt 641–642
  assets as entirety of debtor's property relevance 641
  third-party rights, agreement on 641
new goods manufactured out of materials supplied (*specificatio*)
  authority to manufacture before payment of purchase price, relevance 391–392, 395–396, 412
  commission [undisclosed] agency 392–393, 412–413
  constructive delivery/*constitutum possessorium* 393, 412
  execution in the absence of proceeds clause 392: before payment by second buyer 412
  insolvency in the absence of proceeds clause 393, 413
  manufacture for self, relevance 392
  ownership: payment of purchase price, relevance 391–392; risk, relevance 392, 397, 412–413; value of material/value of work, relevance 392, 395
  possessory pledge 393
  [registered] charge 393
  reservation of title 391–393, 412
  third-party rights 392: refusal of sums due to bankrupt 412

'ordinary course of business' rule
  resale of cars supplied on credit for that purpose 339
  security of assignment of earnings 565–566
possession
  bona fide acquisition of real rights in movable property 339, 344–345
  as real right (right *ad rem*) 219
possessory pledge
  fictitious pledges 340
  new goods manufactured out of materials supplied (*specificatio*) 393
  publicity/registry 527
  resale of cars supplied on credit for that purpose 340
  specificity principle 519
  stock-in-trade as collateral for non-possessory security right, delivery to third party to hold for pledgee, need for 519
priority
  enterprise charge 525, 590
  ius separationis, rights giving rise to 218–219
  tax claims 520
products and proceeds clauses
  combined, execution, following payment by second buyer 412
publicity/registry
  enterprise charge 469, 641
  finance leasing/leasing contract 475, 615–616
  possessory pledge 527
  priority, critical date 469–470, 566
  sale and lease-back 470–471, 475
  sale for security purposes 469–470
  as source of real rights 219, 223–224
[registered] charge, new goods manufactured out of materials supplied (*specificatio*) and 393
registered sale, car fleet as collateral for non-possessory security right 469–470, 473–474
remedies, recovery [and sale] of goods 217–218
resale of cars supplied on credit for that purpose 339–341
  commission [undisclosed] agency and 340–341, 348–349

Sweden (cont.)
  credit consignment agreement
    340–341, 348–349
  monies paid to bankrupt, right to:
    agency relationship and 340;
    payments made after start of
    insolvency proceedings 361–362;
    pledge and 340; reservation of title
    340; security assignment of future
    claims/debts 340
  reseller's obligation to transfer monies
    received to original seller, holding
    account/advance payments
    340–341
  transfer of ownership/title as result of
    339: authorisation to sell, relevance
    339, 361–362
  reservation of title 217–218
    authorisation to sell, relevance 280,
      295–297, 299–300: obligation to pass
      on reservation to next buyer and
      295
    charge/security interest distinguished
      279
    commission [undisclosed] agency
      distinguished 296–297, 299–300,
      412
    formal requirements, general
      conditions, adequacy 280, 281
    new goods manufactured out of
      materials supplied (*specificatio*)
      391–393, 412
    resale of cars supplied on credit for
      that purpose 340
    reservation of right to terminate
      distinguished 218, 219, 223–224,
      228, 280, 283
    timing of reservation, relevance
      280–281, 285–286
    unilateral declaration of, validity 280,
      285: implied consent 280
  risk, new goods manufactured
    out of materials supplied
    (*specificatio*), ownership 392, 397,
    412–413
  sale and lease-back
    car fleet as collateral for
      non-possessory security right
      470–471
    frequency of use 470–471
    publicity/registry 470–471, 475

security assignment of claims/debts
  debitor cessus, notice to, relevance
    564–567
  execution 565–567
  frequency of use 565–566
  insolvency 565–567
  suspension of assignor's rights to
    dispose of collateral 564–565
security assignment of earnings 564–567
  authority to receive money for own
    use 566, 567, 591
  charge of money claim as alternative
    569–570
  commingling/distinguishability of
    monies paid to bankrupt 566, 567
  debitor cessus, notice to, relevance:
    money earned but not paid before
    insolvency 566; money earned and
    paid before insolvency 566, 567
  execution, money not yet earned
    ('future' claim) 565–566, 590
  as fiduciary relationship (beneficial
    trust) 564, 566
  insolvency, money not yet earned
    ('future' claim) 565–566, 590
  'ordinary course of business' rule
    565–566
security assignment of future
  claims/debts
  after-acquired collateral 591
  debitor cessus, notice to, relevance 340,
    590, 591
  duration of assignment, relevance
    565–566
  execution 591
  resale of cars supplied on credit for
    that purpose 340
  resale of goods supplied for that
    purpose 300
security rights, future claim against
  unknown debtor, possibilities
  590–591
security transfer of ownership,
  completion many months after loan
  at time of financial difficulty, effect
  521–522
Special Purpose Vehicle (SPV) 590–591
special registered charge 477–478
specificity principle 219, 223–224
  agency and 340
  enterprise charge 471

fungible assets 432–433, 519
money 519
possessory pledge 519
stock-in-trade as collateral for non-possessory security right 519–522
  enterprise charge 520, 525, 528
  excess collateral, relevance 521
  fiduciary relationship (beneficial trust) 519
  frequency of use, enterprise charge 520
  possessory pledge, delivery to third party to hold for pledgee, need for 519
third-party rights
  enterprise charge 520

new goods manufactured out of materials supplied (*specificatio*) 392
termination/avoidance of contract and: *bona fide* acquisition 242–243; legal policy and 243
transfer of ownership/title 218–219
  agreement that title should pass ('real agreement'), need for 219, 224
  overlapping ownership 219
  requirements, payment of purchase price, relevance 219
  time of, as gradual process/reflection of factual system 218–219
  transfer of warrants/bills of lading and 218

Index by subject

(Reference should also be made to the Index by Country)

9 UCC
  applicability
    accounts/conditional sales 67
    all creditors including sellers on secured credit 56
    consignments 67
    consumer transactions subject to specific protective rules 56
    exclusions 67
    finance leasing/leasing contract 84, 110
    future/present property as collateral 56, 57
    instrument evidencing obligation to pay 64–65
    inventory. *See* inventory collateral *below*
    monies subject to a trust 84
    personal property including intellectual property and rights against third-party rights 56
    primacy of rule of law establishing different rule for consumers 67
    proceeds including checks and rights to payment on open account 64–65
    secured party in possession or control of the collateral 67
    transfers of rights to payments not made for security purposes 67
  attachment, enforceability 65
    after-acquired collateral 66, 71
    critical date 71
    value/consideration, need for 65
  attachment, requirements
    authenticated security agreement or collateral in secured party's possession or control 65
    debtor's rights in collateral 65
    'indirectly held' securities and 66
    rights in supporting obligation and 66
  choice of law (filing system) 68–69
    deemed location in District of Columbia in case of unacceptability of law of debtor's jurisdiction 68
    foreign bank branches and agencies 68
    jurisdiction of organisation (registered organisation) 68
    motor vehicles 70
    perfection: effect of change of governing law 69; local law of securities intermediary's jurisdiction 68–69
    place of business (organisation) 68
    principal residence (individual) 68
    priority 68–69
    registered organisations under federal law 68
    state or federal law other than 9 UCC 70
  co-existence and scope for creation of variety of security rights 58
  control
    as means of perfecting 70
    possession distinguished 70
    priority 75

INDEX BY SUBJECT 739

definitions/defined terms
  'account debtor' 75–76
  'authenticate' 65
  'broker' 69
  'chattel paper' 64–65
  'consignment' 67
  'control' 65
  'electronic chattel paper' 70
  'fixtures' 67
  'general intangible'
    importance 55
  'instrument' 64–65
  'letter-of-credit right' 66
  'lien, creditor' 71
  'ordinary course of business' 58–59, 71–72
  'organization' 68
  'payment intangibles' 67
  'perfection' 69
  'possession' 65
  'proceeds' 64–65
  'promissory notes' 67
  'pursuant to commitment' 66
  'record' 65
  'registered organization' 68
  'securities' 66, 272
  'securities account' 66
  'security agreement' 64
  'security entitlements' 66
  'signing' 65
  'value' 65
description of collateral (specificity principle) 65–66
English system compared 81–85
  equitable/legal ownership distinction 82
European Security Right and 669
facilitative nature 54–55
filing system. See also choice of law (filing system) above; publicity/registry below
  authorisation/authentication, need for 77
  duration/continuation statement 77
  electronic filing 76, 78
  limited nature of available information 76–77
  as model for European Security Right 670–671
  priority 73–74
  registry distinguished 78

required information 76, 77–78
  simplicity/cheapness 76–78
floating lien 57, 66. See also inventory collateral below
  priority 74–75
form/nomenclature, relevance 58, 81–85
  attachment. See attachment, requirements above
  authenticated agreement 65
  creation of security interest 64–65
influence outside US 54
inventory collateral 57, 64–65, 71–72
  priority 74
judicial development, limitation on 55, 75
knowledge, relevance 73
market orientation 54–55
modification by parties 67–68
perfection
  automatic 69–70
  buyer/lessee without consideration and delivery, relevance to 72
  choice of law 68–69
  choice of method, relevance 70
  secured interests co-existing in the same collateral and 73–74
  'securities intermediary' 69
  techniques in case of non-automaticity 70–71. See also attachment, requirements; control and filing system above; possession and priority below
personal guaranty
  as personal right 56–57
  as supporting obligation 56–57
policy goals 58–59
  distributional considerations 84–85
possession
  as means of perfecting 70–71
  tangible collateral, limitation to 70–71
priority 58–59, 71–75. See also filing system above; third-party rights below
  after-acquired collateral 75, 87
  choice of law 68–69
  conflicting interests in instruments and chattel paper 75
  control over deposit accounts, investment property or letter-of-credit rights 75

9 UCC (*cont.*)
   definitions/defined terms 72–73
   filing and 59, 73
   'first to file or perfect' rule 73–74
   fixtures/accession (commingling) 75
   grace period to allow prompt delivery of goods sold on credit 72
   inventory collateral 74
   merger of debtor and successor entity 75
   perfection and. *See* perfection *above*
   purchase money security interest 74–75, 671–672
   purchaser 72–73
   secured interests co-existing in the same collateral 73–74
   secured party/buyer of collateral 71–73
   secured party/lien, creditor 71
   statutory possessory liens 75
   publicity/registry 59, 73, 76–78. *See also* filing system *above*
   consignments and 67
   purpose 54, 74
   remedies 78–79
     acceptance of collateral in full or partial satisfaction 79
     independence of legal designation of security right 82
     unilateral disposal in good faith 59–60, 79
   reservation of title as preferred method 659 n.39
   revisions (2000) 62–64, 78
     consultation process 62–63, 75
   risk, *bona fide* acquirer rule distinguished 71–72
   security interest
     as real right 56–57
     third-party guarantees distinguished 56–57
   stay of proceedings
     bankruptcy proceedings 79
     priority 79
   technological developments and 63–64, 76, 78
   third-party rights 75–76. *See also* priority *above*
     anti-assignment clauses, override 75–76
     enforceability of agreement not to assert claim or defence against assignee 75–76
   title, relevance 57–58, 82–84
   as unitary system 56–58
     realism and 81–85
     single regime covering tangibles and rights to payment 56
     uncertainties/complications relating to operation 82–84
   waiver of debtor protection 78–79

abstraction principle. *See* transfer of ownership/title, obligation to transfer
abuse of rights. *See also* fairness; unfair terms (*contra bonos mores*)
   security assignment of future claims/debts 575–576
accession, transfer or ownership/title and. *See also* new goods manufactured out of materials supplied (*specificatio*), accession and
   bona fide acquisition 253
   ius separationis 279
   registration of reservation of title 253
   requirements, movable as essential part of immovable 248
   reservation of title 390
   reversibility, relevance 382–383
   specificatio distinguished 382
   stock-in-trade as collateral for non-possessory security right 504 n.61
actio Pauliana 199
   as action of last resort 498, 631
   burden of proof 507, 626–627, 632–633
     family membership as evidence of intent 640, 643, 646
     price, relevance 635
     statutory presumptions 631–632
   convergence/divergence of practice 644–646
   execution, effect on 496, 635
   gratuitous transactions 494, 496, 514–515, 626–627, 629, 640, 643
   insolvency proceedings 503, 507, 529–530, 579
   judicial avoidance 513, 524

limitation period 501–502, 507, 513, 521–522, 524, 626–627, 632, 638–639, 643
  partial revocation 632
  as personal action 631
  requirements
    ascertainability of sum owed 628
    debtor's inability to meet commitments at time of transaction 638–639, 646. *See also* insolvency at time of transaction, relevance *below*
    debtor's knowledge of likely detriment 628, 630, 634, 635
    detrimental effect 494, 507, 524, 627, 632, 635, 643. *See also* insolvency attributable to transaction *below*
    diminution of debtor's capacity to pay debts 514, 627, 628–629, 632, 638, 640, 646
    due debt 626–627
    insolvency at time of transaction, relevance 513, 640. *See also* debtor's inability to meet commitments at time of transaction *above*
    insolvency attributable to transaction 524, 626–627, 643. *See also* detrimental effect *above*
    intention to defraud/prejudice other creditors, relevance 494, 496, 498, 501–502, 507, 513, 626–627, 628, 630, 640
    losses attributable to transaction 628
    pre-existing debt 513, 628, 632
    prior attempt by creditor to secure settlement 627
    third-party's knowledge/'should have known' requirement 494, 507, 524, 626–627, 640, 643
    valid transaction, relevance 626–627, 632, 635
  reservation of title as modification to contract and 262
  third-party rights 494, 498, 502–503, 626–627, 628, 634
after-acquired collateral 521–522, 566 n.103, 591
  execution 66, 71
  priority 75, 195
agency
  carrier as 207, 213, 215

  commission [undisclosed] agency. *See* commission [undisclosed] agency
  possession distinguished 174 n.12
  resale of cars supplied on credit for that purpose 313–314, 322, 326, 337
    monies paid to bankrupt, right to 327, 336, 340
  specificity principle 340
all-monies/sums retention of title (framework agreement). *See also* proceeds clause (extended reservation of title); reservation of title
  clarity of drafting, need for 419
  convergence/divergence of practice 434–437, 661–662
  credit consignment agreement rules, applicability 431, 434
  delivery, relevance 422, 429
  examples 418–419, 423
  fiduciary relationship (beneficial trust) 422
  frequency of use 418–419, 420, 422, 423–424, 426, 427, 429, 430, 431, 433, 434, 437
  hire purchase/payment by instalment 434
  insolvency
    ius separationis 431, 432–433
    part of insolvency estate, whether 417–436
    priority 418, 421, 423, 435
    rei vindicatio 420, 423, 424–425, 436
    payment of purchase price, relevance 422, 426–429, 430, 435
  publicity/registry 656
  security transfer of ownership 418, 435, 661–662
  seller's rights in sold goods 426
    proceeds clause (extended reservation of title) as parallel 427
  seller's rights in unsold goods
    co-ownership 420, 432–433
    limitation to unpaid balance of particular sale 422
    non-possessory ownership 12, 419, 422, 425, 435
    real, whether 423, 429, 430
    security transfer of ownership 418, 435

all-monies/sums retention of title (framework agreement) *(cont.)*
  specificity principle 422, 426–427, 430, 432–433, 436–437
    ascertainment of goods 420–421, 426
    real subrogation 421
    rei vindicatio in case of insolvency 436–437
    risk 436–437
  validity 418, 419, 421, 422, 423, 425, 427–429, 430, 434–435
    authority to sell before payment of purchase price, relevance 431–432, 437
    car industry 430
    consent of parties as determining factor 430
    excess collateral, relevance/implied waiver 418, 427
    fraudulent evasion of the law, whether 424
    general clauses/framework agreement, acceptability 418, 423–424, 425–426, 429, 432, 436–437: incorporation in each contract of sale, need for/as safer alternative 429, 430, 433
    implied waiver of creditor's rights 418
    obligation to store separately, relevance 419, 431, 436, 437
    publicity/registry 426–427
    as reservation of title clause 422, 427, 428, 430, 435, 648–649, 661–662
    third-party rights 434
    unfair contract term, whether 418, 424
applicable law. *See* choice of law
assignment of claim to recovery. *See also* charge of money claims; proceeds clause (extended reservation of title); real subrogation (assignment of future claim); [registered] charge; security assignment of claims/debts; security assignment of earnings; security assignment of future claims/debts
  as alternative to delivery 174, 302 n.2
  bona fide acquisition 302 n.2
    third-party rights 189; anti-assignment clauses, override 75–76

limitation to bank or financial institution 538–539

bailiff. *See* execution
bank charge. *See* registered bank charge
banker's reference/promissory note as security. *See* personal security including bank guarantees, promissory notes and performance bonds
bankruptcy. *See* insolvency
Bell, G. J. 46
***bona fide* acquisition**
  accession and 253
  assignment of claim to recovery 302 n.2
  belief in seller's right to sell 308, 330
    in case of cash purchase 309
    in case of insolvency 179–180
    negligence and 302, 308, 311, 653
    reasonable doubt 323–324
    resale of cars supplied on credit for that purpose 308–309, 313, 323–324, 339, 343–345
  by purchase at public auction 307–308
  cars bought by private person 333–334
  constructive delivery/*constitutum possessorium* 302, 308, 311
  convergence/divergence of practice 343–345, 346
  debitor cessus, notice to, relevance 543–544
  delivery and 302–303, 308, 311, 653
  execution 232–233, 236–237, 239, 270
  finance leasing/leasing contract 599
  floating [enterprise] charge/lien/ mortgage 469, 471–472, 522–523
  from insolvent 179–180, 220–221
  gratuitous transactions 302, 308, 643
  misrepresentation 238–239, 244–245
  of money and negotiable instruments 302, 308
  non-possessory security right 14
  of object sold by businessman in ordinary course of business 289, 307–308, 309, 315, 344–345
  of object stolen or lost by original owner 308
  payment of debtor to insolvent and 179–180

possession 180, 186–187, 220–221,
    288–289, 317, 326–327, 330, 341,
    344–345, 652–653
  hire purchase/payment by instalment
    303
  involuntary deprivation of possession
    and 302, 339, 653
  period of possession, relevance
    319–320, 582 n.20
  security transfer of ownership in
    stock-in-trade 482–483
  possessory pledge 504–505
  precautionary measures 236
  publicity/registry and 311, 319–320,
    582 n.20
  reservation of title 263, 270, 282,
    288–289, 336–337, 341
  risk allocation and 71–72
  sale and lease-back 460–461
  security assignment of future
    claims/debts 302 n.2
  security ownership and 33
  statutory provisions 326
  stock-in-trade as collateral for
    non-possessory security right
    482–483, 498, 514
  unjust enrichment and 302
bona fide disposal of collateral 59–60
book entry 220–221, 309–310, 347, 350,
    363–364, 593, 642 n.44, 661,
    662
Bulgaria, publicity/registry 59
burden of proof
  actio Pauliana 507, 626–627, 635
  decisive influence 233
  intention to defraud/prejudice creditors
    624–625
  pre-existing debts 625
  transfer of ownership/title 277
Bynkershoek, Cornelis van 45

Cape Town Convention. *See* UNIDROIT
    Conventions, International Interests
    in Mobile Equipment (2001)
**car fleet as collateral for non-possessory
    security right**
  constructive delivery/*constitutum
    possessorium* 470–471
  fiduciary relationship (beneficial trust)
    449

finance leasing/leasing contract 447–448,
    449–450, 475
  fixed charge 458–459, 476
  floating [enterprise] charge/lien/
    mortgage 459–460, 463, 464, 469,
    471–472, 476
  frequency of use 453–454
  loan for purchase/reservation of title in
    sales contract, to creditor 443
  possessory pledge 447, 456, 465
  publicity/registry 279, 336–337, 338,
    357–358, 443
  [registered] charge 451, 471–472
  registered sale 469–470, 473–474
  registered vehicle charge 453–454, 467,
    471–472, 477–478
  reservation of title 443, 465–466, 474
  sale and lease-back 443–444, 445,
    447–448, 449–451, 456–457, 463, 467,
    470–471, 474
  security transfer of ownership 438–443,
    444–445, 451–453, 473–474
  sale and resale 465–466, 474
  special registered charge 449
  tour coaches 445
carrier
  as agent 207, 213, 215
  statutory preference 174, 185–186, 189
charge of money claims. *See also* floating
    [enterprise] charge/lien/mortgage;
    possessory pledge; [registered]
    charge; security assignment of
    earnings; security assignment of
    future claims/debts
  authority to receive money for own use
    566, 591
  certain date (*data certa*), need for
    535–536
  commingling/distinguishability of
    monies paid to bankrupt 566, 567
  conditional/contingent nature, relevance
    553
  convergence/divergence of practice 364,
    660–661
  debitor cessus, notice to, relevance 11, 415,
    534–535, 537, 542–545, 564–567,
    584–585, 649–650, 660–661
  money earned but not paid before
    insolvency 537–538, 544–545,
    554–555, 568, 571

INDEX BY SUBJECT

charge of money claims (*cont.*)
   money earned and paid before insolvency 538, 553–554, 555, 562, 563, 566, 567, 568, 570–571
   EBRD Model Law on Secured Transactions 112
   excess collateral, relevance 534, 585
   execution 579, 584
   existing legal relationship, need for 583–584
   frequency of use 534, 535–536, 544
   future claim, whether/applicability to 534, 544, 574–575, 578–579, 661
     future earnings as collateral for bank loan 553
     unknown debtor 578–579
   insolvency 534–535, 537, 584–585
     creation of charge following 584
   ius separationis 545
   priority 534–535, 579, 584
   public [notarial] deed, need for 535–536
   publicity/registry 544, 584
     master-list of claims 583–584, 651–652
   retroactive application 544
   security assignment of earnings compared 112, 534–536, 560–561, 660–661
   as security for bank loan 552–555, 564–567
   special charge applicable to corporations 536
     debitor cessus, notice to, relevance 536
     requirements 536
   third-party rights 534, 542–543
   unjust enrichment 545
choice of law
   9 UCC 68–69
   conflit mobile 17–18
   Hague Convention on Securities held with an Intermediary (2002 draft) 68–69
   lex situs 16–18
   Rome Convention on the Law Applicable to Contractual Obligations (1980) 16, 17, 18–20, 651–652
commingling/distinguishability of monies paid to bankrupt. *See also* specificity principle
   all-monies/sums retention of title 417–436. *See also* all-monies/sums retention of title (framework agreement), specificity principle
   charge of money claims 566, 567
   commission [undisclosed] agency 340, 342, 348–349, 413
   convergence/divergence of practice 434–437
   exclusion, scope for 431
   new goods manufactured out of materials supplied (*specificatio*) 373, 374, 402–403, 408, 410
   resale of cars supplied on credit for that purpose 304, 307, 310–311, 313–314, 315–316, 323, 338, 340, 342, 347, 348–349, 350, 361, 363
   risk 436–437
   security assignment of earnings 532, 535, 566
   stock-in-trade as collateral for non-possessory security right 505–506
commission [undisclosed] agency. *See also* credit consignment agreement
   bank loan 536–537, 538
   certain date (*data certa*) before execution or commencement of insolvency proceedings, need for 292–293, 322, 357, 361
   commingling/distinguishability of monies, relevance 340, 342, 413
   convergence/divergence of practice 364
   credit consignment agreement compared 297 n.24
   insolvency 538
   ius separationis 296–297, 392–393, 616–617
   maturity factoring 537
   new goods manufactured out of materials supplied (*specificatio*) 392–393, 394, 412–413, 415–416
   resale of cars supplied on credit for that purpose 336, 337, 340, 348–349, 357, 361–362
   used car sales 322, 348–349
   reservation of title distinguished 296–297, 299–300, 412
   sale or return arrangement between original seller and reseller, relevance 296–297, 299, 342, 361–362, 364, 413
   writing, need for 536–537
concursus creditorum (Belgium) 29–30, 187, 189, 315–316

confusio. See commingling/
distinguishability of monies paid to
bankrupt; specificity principle
**constructive delivery/*constitutum
possessorium*** 45–46, 46 n.28 179,
191–192, 211, 212–213, 219, 224. *See
also* delivery, relevance; *hypotecha;
mobilia non habent sequelam*
anticipated *constitutum possessorium*
12–13, 310–311, 481, 488
bona fide acquisition 302, 308, 311
car fleet as collateral for non-possessory
security right 470–471
fiducia [cum creditore] 464–465
finance leasing/leasing contract
564–565
floating [enterprise] charge/lien/
mortgage 469, 470–471, 641
gage/bailment resulting from, abolition
(1804) 47
as means of creating security right after
transfer of ownership/title 249–250,
254, 439
as means of setting aside execution 639
new goods manufactured out of
materials supplied (*specificatio*) 393,
412
possessory pledge 444–445
reversion of title and 280–281
Roman law (*Corpus Iuris Civilis*) 42
Roman-Dutch law 45
sale and lease-back 51, 463–464, 475
security interest as *causa* 51
security transfer of ownership 439, 444,
481, 488
traditio ficta 45–46, 191–192, 464–465
contract. *See also* finance leasing/leasing
contract; retention of asset as
security for performance/
performance withhold
formal requirements 192–193
freedom of contract
floating [enterprise] charge/lien and 85
restraint of sale and 194
third-party rights. *See* third-party rights,
termination/avoidance of contract
and
**contract, annulment of simulated/*pro
forma*** 626–627, 630, 640–641,
642–643, 644
intention to defraud/prejudice other
creditors, need for 630

price as evidence of simulation 627,
629–630, 641, 646
contract, avoidance
for absence of consent 235–236
for defect of form 235–236
for fraud 194, 230–244, 326–327. *See also*
for intention to defraud/prejudice
creditors *below; actio Pauliana*
decisive influence on other party,
need for 233: burden of proof
233
judicial avoidance, need for 233,
235–236
principle of abstraction 232, 241–242,
243–244
requirements 235–236
resale of cars supplied on credit for
that purpose, transfer of
title/ownership, effect on 326–327
transfer of ownership/title, effect on
230–244, 326–327: sufficiency of
contract to transfer title and 235
unjust enrichment and 230–231, 232,
241–242
for incapacity 236 n.31
for intention to defraud/prejudice
creditors 624–626, 630, 631, 635,
636, 637, 639, 642. *See also actio
Pauliana*
burden of proof 624–625
convergence/divergence 529–530
family members and 624, 631, 635,
642, 646
insolvency, relevance 642
limitation period 624–625, 637–638
price as evidence of intention/
knowledge 625, 627, 629–631, 633,
635, 636, 637–638, 641, 642
requirements 637, 642
for misrepresentation 238–239
for mistake 178, 235–236, 238, 245
principle of abstraction 232, 241–242,
243–244
retroactive/*ex tunc* effect 232–233,
237
for usury 496, 579, 582
**contract, termination in case of
insolvency proceedings** 176–177,
184, 188, 200–201, 207, 448, 601,
607. *See also* finance leasing/leasing
contract; insolvency, contract, effect
on

contract, termination in case of
  insolvency proceedings (cont.)
  administrator's right/duty 247, 251–252,
    266, 278, 284, 442 n.29, 446–447,
    448, 455–456, 471
  alternatives 191
  automaticity 251, 266
  in case of creditor's insolvency 448,
    466–467
  default of administrator and 176–177,
    251, 253–254, 268–269
  as right in personam 203–212, 213,
    215, 221, 224–225, 228–229,
    466–467
  seller's right 202–203, 210–211
  suspension of payments, preclusion as
    ground for termination 184
contract, termination for failure to pay
    217–218, 227–229, 253–254, 266,
    606–607
  convergence/divergence of practice
    227–229
  following delivery 221
  forced execution as alternative 184
  insolvency proceedings, effect 268–269
  judicial termination, need for 184–185,
    188, 200–201, 211–212, 227
  non-termination, right of 191, 251,
    264–265, 268–269
  parties' agreement and (resolutive
    clause) 180–181, 184–185, 188–189,
    190, 195–196, 200, 203–204, 213, 215,
    217, 218, 219, 221, 223–224, 225–226,
    228, 251, 253
    security transfer of ownership 446
    third-party rights 221, 228–229, 251
  precautionary measures 262–263
  reservation of title, relevance 218, 219,
    223–224, 228, 247, 255–257, 278
  retroactive/ex tunc effect 173, 178
  reversion of title [where seller remains
    in possession of goods] 210–212, 216,
    227–228, 280–281
    constructive delivery/constitutum
      possessorium 280–281
    mistake and 216
    principle of abstraction and 227–228
  as right in personam 262–263
  sale and lease-back. See sale and
    lease-back, termination for
    non-payment

  seller's right of recovery (recht van
    reclame) 202–203, 226. See also rei
    vindicatio in case of insolvency
  third-party rights 188, 189, 225–226
  time-limits/grace period and 180–181,
    184–185, 200, 202–203, 226, 268–269
  unilateral 180–181
control
  9 UCC 70
  possession distinguished 70
  possessory pledge 485–486, 493
copyright 72
corporate debtors, England 85
corporeal movables, applicability of
  non-possessory security rights 442,
  444, 446
credit consignment agreement. See also
  commission [undisclosed] agency
  all-monies/sums retention of title
    (framework agreement) and 431
  commingling/distinguishability,
    relevance 348–349
  commission [undisclosed] agency
    compared 297 n.24
  conditions for settlement 295, 337–338,
    348–349, 360–361, 390
    payment to consignor on resale 295,
    431
  ius separationis 296–297, 431
  new goods manufactured out of
    materials supplied (specificatio) 390,
    411–412
  obligation to store separately 431, 437
  priority 292–293
  registry, relevance 338
  resale of cars supplied on credit for that
    purpose, conditions for settlement
    and 337–338, 348–349, 360–361
  reservation of title distinguished
    288–289, 292–293, 295, 296–297
  right of owner to recover 602
  sale and lease-back as 443–444
  sale or return arrangement between
    original seller and reseller,
    relevance 296–297, 299
  specificity principle 390, 431
  stock-in-trade as collateral for
    non-possessory security right 518
  third-party rights 292–293
criminal law, relevance, Roman law
  (Corpus Iuris Civilis) 43

cross-border transactions
    reservation of title 105–106
    transposition doctrine 16–18
customary law, security transfer of
    ownership 440–441, 444, 451–452

damages
    contract avoided for fraud or
        misrepresentation 233, 238–239, 498
    contract terminated for failure to pay
        264–265
        retention of instalments as 266
    for losses incurred from insolvency
        administrator's failure to sell at best
        price 368–369
    wrongful manufacture of goods
        supplied 389
data certa
    commission [undisclosed] agency
        292–293, 322, 357, 361
    definition 265 n.71
    EU Directive 2000/35/EC 268 n.77
    execution and 605–606, 633
    factoring contract 551–552
    finance leasing/leasing contract 605–606,
        619, 659
    reservation of title 268, 270, 277, 283,
        290–291, 322, 357, 658
debitor cessus, notice to, relevance
        9 UCC 75–76
    bona fide acquisition 543–544
    charge of money claims 11, 346–347, 415,
        534–535, 537–538, 542–545, 553–554,
        555, 564–567, 584–585, 649–650,
        660–661. See also charge of money
        claims, debitor cessus, notice to,
        relevance
        special charge applicable to money
            claims 536
    convergence/divergence of practice
        568–569, 570–571
    discounting of bills as means of
        providing loan 580
    divided practice 657
    entry in books as 534–535, 571–572, 575,
        593
    factoring contract 546, 580
    fixed charge 558
    floating [enterprise]
        charge/lien/mortgage 324–325, 343,
        415, 537, 558, 586, 590, 591

    formal requirements 542–543, 550–551,
        559, 649–650
    identity of debtor, relevance 12–13,
        309–310, 324–325, 406–407, 415,
        536–537, 589, 592–593
    insolvency, notification following 578,
        584–585
    modification of requirement 571
    nantissement de fonds de commerce
        539–540, 577
    possessory pledge 553–554
    publicity/registry 575–576
    [registered] charge 306, 309–310, 316,
        324–325, 346–347, 415, 553
    security assignment of claims/debts 11,
        306, 556–558, 563, 564–567, 586,
        587, 589, 660–661
    security assignment of earnings
        544–545, 550–551, 564–567, 660–661.
        See also security assignment of
        earnings, debitor cessus, notice to,
        relevance
    security assignment of future
        claims/debts 12–13, 306, 309–310,
        315, 322, 340, 347, 354–355, 360,
        363–364, 401–402, 406–407, 413, 415,
        574, 589–590, 591, 593, 633, 641
    variety of approaches 568–569, 570–571
delivery, relevance 172, 174, 179,
        186–187, 191–192, 198, 201, 206, 207,
        211, 223, 271–272, 612. See also
        constructive delivery/constitutum
        possessorium
    all-monies/sums retention of title
        (framework agreement) 422,
        429
    assignment of claim to recovery as
        alternative 174, 302 n.2
    avoidance of contract for fraud 241
    bona fide acquisition 302–303, 653
    convergence/divergence of practice
        285–286, 475
    floating [enterprise] charge/lien/
        mortgage 469
    symbolic delivery 495
    gift/transactions other than sale 206,
        212–213
    insolvency 187
        buyer's duty to refuse in case of
            inability to pay 212
    money and 404

748   INDEX BY SUBJECT

delivery, relevance (cont.)
  where object held by third party
    (instruction to hold on behalf of
    transferee/Besitzanweisung)
    175–176
  possessory pledge 456, 465, 495, 504,
    652–653
    in case of banks 495
  priority 186–187, 221
  reversion of ownership 276–277
    following termination of contract
    211–212
  taking of possession and 174
  where transferee in possession of
    property (traditio brevi/longa manu)
    175–176, 191–192, 201, 249–250, 285,
    439
discounting of bills as means of
  providing loan 546–547, 580.
  See also charge of money claims;
  factoring contract; personal security
  including bank guarantees,
  promissory notes and performance
  bonds; security assignment of
  claims/debts; security assignment of
  earnings
  debitor cessus, liability for payment by
    546–547, 580
  debitor cessus, notification to, relevance
    580
  priority 580

EBRD Model Law on Secured
  Transactions
  9 UCC and 54
  charge of money claims 112
  class charge 108–110
  Core Principles 101–104
    adaptability by parties 103
    cheapness 103
    coverage of all types of assets, debts
      and persons 103
    effective publicity 103
    effectiveness after insolvency 102
    efficient security without depriving of
      use of assets 102
    priority rules 103
    prompt realisation at market value
      102
    realisation of assets/priority in case of
      non-payment 102
    reduction of risk 102
  enterprise charge 57
  fluctuating future assets 108–110
  European Security Right and 669
  execution 106–107
  finance leasing/leasing contract 110
  new goods manufactured out of
    materials supplied (specificatio) and
    108
    [registered] charge as additional
    security 108
  purchase money security interest,
    priority 671–672
  [registered] charge 110–111
  security assignment of claims/debts
    111–112
  security assignment of future
    claims/debts 112
  statutory possessory liens 112
  as tool for support of legal reform in
    Eastern Europe 26, 112–113
    check list for legislation 99
    guidance to expectations of
      international investors and bankers
      100
    illustration of components of rules for
      secured transactions 99
    promotion of harmonisation 100–101
  unpaid vendor's charge 112
    automaticity 105–106, 107
    insolvency 107
    [registered] charge as additional
    security 108
    as replacement for reservation of title
    105–106
    resale of goods supplied for that
    purpose 107–108
economic reasons for security rights 7–9,
  27, 60, 63–64, 99, 113, 440–441, 471,
  499–500. See also risk
  asymmetric information 7–8
  interest rate, relevance 7–9
  possessory pledge, limitations 9–10
  third-party rights 8–9
Eigentumsvorbehalt. See reservation of
  title
enterprise charge/mortgage. See EBRD
  Model Law on Secured Transactions,
  enterprise charge; floating
  [enterprise] charge/lien/mortgage;
  [registered] charge

INDEX BY SUBJECT 749

enterprise contract, new goods manufactured out of materials supplied (*specificatio*) 397
estoppel
  as basis of *rei vindicatio* 294–295, 299, 335
  as defence 335, 346
  requirements
    detriment to person raising estoppel 335
    fault on part of person making representation 335
    reliance as proximate cause of detriment 335
    reliance on representation 335
    representation by owner of entitlement to dispose of property 294–295, 335, 336
  security assignment of claims/debts 562
EU Convention on International Insolvency (2000) 22
EU Directives
  93/13/EEC (unfair contract terms) 418
  2000/35/EC (late payment in commercial transactions) 21–22, 268 n.77
  data certa 268 n.77
EU harmonisation, need for 20–22.
  See also security rights, harmonisation, possibilities/arguments for attempts at 22–24
EU Regulations, 1475/95 (long-term dealer arrangements) 320 n.77
European Security Right 665–672
  9 UCC as model 669, 670–671
  collateral, options 669–670
  EBRD Model Law on Secured Transactions as model 669
  extension of right to 'proceeds' as basis 666–667
  insolvency, diversity of rules and 667
  national law, relationship with 665–666
    incorporation/choice of means 667–668: UNIDROIT Convention on International Interests in Mobile Equipment (2001) 667–668; within the EU 668
  as part of European Civil Code 666
  priority 671
  publicity/registry 670–671
    debtor register, advantages

  purchase money security interest, priority 671–672
  transfer of ownership/title, diversity of rules and 666
  UNCITRAL draft legal guide on secured transactions (2002) as basis 668–669
excess collateral, relevance
  all-monies/sums retention of title (framework agreement) 418, 427
  charge of money claims 534, 585
  convergence/divergence of practice 528–529, 593–594
  fairness 506–507, 585
  floating [enterprise] charge/lien/mortgage 494, 501–502, 591, 592
  nantissement de fonds de commerce 492, 494, 528–529, 578
  non-possessory security right 14
  possessory pledge 486
  registered bank charge 582
  security assignment of claims/debts 586, 587, 589
  security assignment of earnings 534, 537
  security assignment of future claims/debts 577, 590, 591, 593–594, 651
  security rights 579, 581
  security transfer of ownership 439, 441–442, 483–484, 489, 516
  stock-in-trade as collateral for non-possessory security right 483–484, 486, 489, 496, 497, 501, 506, 509, 511, 513, 516, 518, 521, 522, 523, 528–529
execution. See also liability of purchaser of business for pre-existing debt
  actio Pauliana, effect 496, 635
  after-acquired collateral 66, 71
  against purchaser of business for pre-existing debt 631, 633–634, 636, 641, 644. See also *actio Pauliana*
  business assets, applicability to 624, 625, 633–634, 635, 636, 638, 639, 640–641, 642–643
  execution judgment, need for 624
  presumption of ownership and 629
  right to resist 630
  bailiff/sheriff's rights/duties 239–240, 636

execution (cont.)
  sale of assets subject to reservation of title, liability 270, 383
  timely completion of execution 239–240
  bona fide acquisition 232–233, 236–237, 239, 270
  charge of money claims 579
  contratto d'appalto 407–408
  data certa and 633
  EBRD Model Law on Secured Transactions 106–107
  execution judge, role 234
  finance leasing/leasing contract
    evidential requirements 605–606
    right to resist 596, 599–600, 601, 605
  floating [enterprise] charge/lien/mortgage 383, 592
  intention to defraud/prejudice other creditors, effect 487–488
  nantissement de fonds de commerce 577, 578
  nature of right in property under execution 239–240
  new goods manufactured out of materials supplied (specificatio). See new goods manufactured out of materials supplied (specificatio), execution in the absence of proceeds clause
  possessory pledge 495–496
  priority, as means of securing 405
  procedure 233–234
  registered bank charge 582
  [registered] charge 518
  sale and lease-back 442
  security assignment of claims/debts 565–567, 586, 587, 588, 589
    joinder of parties 556
  security assignment of earnings 533–534
  security assignment of future claims/debts 574, 579, 591
  security transfer of ownership 439–440, 445
  stock-in-trade as collateral for non-possessory security right 486, 487–488, 501, 505–506, 508, 511, 523
  subrogation action 404–405

third-party rights
  property on debtor's premises 269 n.79, 425, 425
  real/personal right as basis for opposition 237

factoring contract 654–655; See also charge of money claims; discounting of bills as means of providing loan; registered bank charge; security assignment of claims/debts; security assignment of earnings; security assignment of future claims/debts
  data certa, need for 551–552
  debitor cessus, notice to, relevance 546–547, 551–552
    money earned but not paid before insolvency 548–549, 571
    money earned and paid before insolvency 551–552, 570–571
  definition/description 545–546, 551–552, 559–560
  floating [enterprise] charge/lien/mortgage as 566
  frequency of use 546, 551–552, 557, 559–560, 579–580
  insolvency 548–549
  public [notarial] deed, need for 548
  publicity/registry 546–547
  recourse factoring 557
  security assignment of future claims/debts 546–547, 589
    as security for bank loan 536, 545–546, 557, 570, 578–580, 585–586
    loan as discounted value of assigned claims 536, 557, 585–586, 589
  third-party rights 551–552
  writing, need for 546–547
fairness. See also unfair terms (contra bonos mores)
  equality of creditors 487, 499–500, 503, 513–514
  excess collateral 499–500, 506, 585
fiducia [cum creditore]
  causa traditionis, whether 456–457, 464–465, 475–476
  constructive delivery/constitutum possessorium 464–465
  reintroduction into civil law systems 51–52

INDEX BY SUBJECT 751

Roman law (*Corpus Iuris Civilis*) 38, 39
fiduciary relationship (beneficial trust)
  all-monies/sums retention of title (framework agreement) 422
  avoidance of 543
  car fleet as collateral for non-possessory security right 449
  debitor cessus, notice to, relevance, money earned but not paid before insolvency 566
  finance leasing/leasing contract compared 599, 602, 609 n.36 609–610
  forfeiture clause (*pactum commissorium*) 441, 475–476
  new goods manufactured out of materials supplied (*specificatio*) 371, 384–388
  pledge (silent) as replacement for 609 n.36
  possessory pledge, assimilation to 354–355
  proceeds clause (extended reservation of title) as 352, 354, 401
  products and proceeds clauses combined as 401
  resale of cars supplied on credit for that purpose 329–330, 334, 347–348, 360
  sale and lease-back distinguished 456–457
  security assignment of claims/debts 560, 564, 587
  security assignment of future claims/debts 539 n.29
  security transfer of ownership 439, 441, 443, 452–453
  stock-in-trade as collateral for non-possessory security right 519
  third-party rights 422, 449
finance leasing/leasing contract. *See also* hire purchase/payment by instalment; sale and lease-back
  9 UCC 84, 110
  administrative requirements 601, 619
  applicable law 598 n.10
  banks and financial institutions, role 604
  bona fide acquisition 599
  car fleet as collateral for non-possessory security right 447–448
  charge compared 111, 620–621
  computers 595–619
  constructive delivery/*constitutum possessorium* 564–565
  contractual nature of relationship 595–596, 597–598, 604–605
  convergence/divergence of practice 619–622, 659
  data certa 605–606, 619, 659
  EBRD Model Law on Secured Transactions 110
  evidential requirements 605–606
  execution, right to resist 596, 599–600, 601, 605
  fiduciary relationship (beneficial trust) compared 602, 609–610
  frequency of use 599, 602–603, 605, 609–610, 617, 618
  hire purchase/payment by instalment compared 598 n.10, 602, 612–613
  insolvency of creditor, debtor's rights 471, 597, 598, 599–600, 601, 602, 603, 604–605, 610, 611, 612, 613, 614, 615, 617, 618–619
  lessor's right on termination to return of goods 607
    contractual basis 599
    leasing nature of contract 607
    as owner 599, 601, 602, 610
  option to acquire
    at predetermined price 602
    at price reflecting amount paid in rent 447–448, 601
    characterisation of contract and 600, 602, 604, 609, 610–611, 613, 615, 618, 619–620
    effect on real rights 596, 598, 599
    as evidence of intention to transfer ownership on termination of contract 607
    as evidence of sale with reservation of title 615
    hire purchase/payment by instalment and 609–611, 612, 613, 617, 618, 619–620
    ius separationis 616–617
    as necessary condition 600, 602, 604, 605, 619–620
    as option not to acquire 608
    probability of exercise, relevance 607
    right to transfer option 599
  possessory pledge compared 600–601

finance leasing/leasing contract (*cont.*)
  public [notarial] deed, relevance 603
  publicity/registry 448, 595–596, 598, 599, 600, 603, 612, 615–616, 619, 649, 659
  rei vindicatio in case of insolvency 596, 597, 608
    termination of contract by insolvency administrator or lessor 448, 596, 601
  as rental agreement 607, 608, 613
  reservation of title/retention of ownership 598 n.10, 600–601, 606–607, 608, 613, 614, 615–616, 618, 619
    right to retain instalments as damages in case of default 606–607
  sale and lease-back compared 447, 599, 611–612, 620–621
  sale with reservation of title compared 606–607, 615, 618. *See also* reservation of title/retention of ownership *above*
  security transfer of ownership compared 598, 602–603, 609–610, 620–621
  suspect period 604–605
  tax and consumer credit legislation, applicability 596, 598, 599
  for term equivalent to working life of equipment 601, 615–616, 618
  termination in case of insolvency proceedings. *See also rei vindicatio* in case of insolvency *above*
    administrator's right/duty 448, 596, 597, 598, 599–600, 601, 602, 607, 610–611, 615
    applicable law 606–607
    automaticity 598, 599
    debtor's rights in case of insolvency of creditor. *See* insolvency of creditor, debtor's rights *above*
    lessor's right 608, 615–616
    return of money paid 606–607: termination of contract for continuous performance compared 607
  termination for failure to pay 599–600
  third-party rights 448, 599, 600, 601
  transfer of ownership/title, on purchase at end of contract 595–596, 606–607, 608, 615–616
  UNIDROIT International Financial Leasing Convention (1988) 605 n.24
  writing, need for 599, 605–606, 619
fixed charge 13
  car fleet as collateral for non-possessory security right 458–459, 476
  debitor cessus, notice to, relevance 558
  equitable nature of real right 458–459
  priority 459, 558
  publicity/registry 458–459, 476
  security assignment of claims/debts 557
floating [enterprise] charge/lien/mortgage 312, 477
  after-acquired collateral 591
  applicability 468, 471, 498–499
    all types of asset 493, 495, 496, 510, 512, 520, 525
    banks and financial institutions 493, 537. *See also* registered bank charge
    corporate debtors 512, 525, 587: de facto limitation to 57, 508–509, 510–511
    future debts as collateral for bank loan 587, 591–593
    future earnings as collateral for bank loan 566
    limitations 89–90, 209, 274, 342–343, 525–526, 650–651: 50 per cent of assets 493–494
    whole or part of patrimony 512, 513, 525
  bona fide acquisition 469, 471–472, 522–523
  car fleet as collateral for non-possessory security right 459–460, 463, 464, 469, 471–472, 476
    frequency of use 471–472
  characteristics 459–460, 509–510
  completion many months after loan at time of financial difficulty, effect 494–495, 501–504, 509, 523–524
  convergence/divergence of practice 364, 525–526, 528, 660
  crystallisation 13, 459–460, 509–510, 511, 512, 520, 525, 526, 586
  debitor cessus, notice to, relevance 537, 558, 586, 590, 591
  delivery, relevance 469
    symbolic delivery 495
  equitable nature of real right 458–459, 508, 509–510, 512, 526
  European/US examples 57
  excess collateral, relevance 494, 501, 592

execution 383, 501, 592
fairness 499–500
floating agricultural chattel mortgage 510–511
fluctuating future assets 87, 458–459, 493, 494, 499, 512–513, 519–520, 650–651, 661
  class charge (EBRD) and 108–110
  duration of charge before insolvency, relevance 328, 340, 509, 511, 521–522
  forfeiture clause (*pactum commissorium*) 470–471
  freedom of contract and 85, 663
  frequency of use 494, 501, 511, 520, 523
  as growing list of exceptions to equality of creditors rule 499–500
  insolvency 84–85, 87–89, 209, 239–240, 493–494, 537, 592
    insolvency of creditor 464, 471
    suspect period 514
  inventory collateral, applicability to, USA 57, 66, 71–72
  ius separationis 469, 470–471
  new goods manufactured out of materials supplied (*specificatio*) and 386, 414
  'ordinary course of business' rule 459–460, 471–472, 493, 510–511, 522–523
  priority 74–75, 414, 459–460, 500–501, 508, 511, 513, 520, 523, 525, 558, 586, 590, 591–592
  publicity/registry 469, 476, 489, 493, 510–511, 512, 519–520, 522–523, 525, 537, 641
  receivership/liquidation 512
  resale of cars supplied on credit for that purpose 324–325, 326, 331–332, 340, 343
  Scottish/English systems distinguished 512, 526
  security assignment of claims/debts 557
  specificity principle 15–16, 471, 477, 510
  statutory nature 512
  stock-in-trade as collateral for non-possessory security right 489, 493, 498–500, 508–511, 520, 522–523, 525, 528
  third-party rights 493–494, 512–513, 520
  unlawful preferences 328

forfeiture clause (*pactum commissorium*)
  convergence/divergence of practice 475–476
  fiduciary relationship (beneficial trust) 441
  floating [enterprise] charge/lien/ mortgage 470–471
  sale and lease-back 462–463
  security assignment of future claims/debts 550
  security transfer of ownership 441, 452, 454, 475–476, 491, 602–603, 607–608
  special registered charge 449–450
form/nomenclature, relevance 58, 81–85
fraud. *See* contract, avoidance

general/special interests, priority 42–43
global assignment, acceptability/ requirements 321, 441–442, 532–534, 561–562, 582–583, 588, 592–594, 651
good faith. *See bona fide* acquisition; *bona fide* disposal of collateral
governing law. *See* choice of law
Grotius, Hugo 44–45

Hague Convention on Securities held with an Intermediary (2002 draft) 62
  choice of law 68–69
hire purchase/payment by instalment 14–15, 87, 192–194, 210, 224. *See also* finance leasing/leasing contract; sale and lease-back
  finance leasing/leasing contract compared 598 n.10, 602, 608–609, 612–613
  formal requirements 192
  frequency of use 612, 613
  insolvency, debtor's rights in case of insolvency of creditor 466–467
  as legal fiction 87, 612–613
  power of disposal 610–611
  publicity/registry 193–194, 196, 612–613
  reservation of title 176, 177, 194, 224, 225, 248–249, 267, 281, 303, 318, 319
    expectancy (*Anwartschaftsrecht*) 248–249, 250

hire purchase/payment by
  instalment (cont.)
  right to retain instalments as
    damages in case of default 266,
    606–607
  resolutive clause 608
  as reversion of title 250
  sale and lease-back distinguished 451,
    465–466
  specificity principle 319
  [suspensive] condition for payment of
    purchase price 608, 610–611
  time-limits/grace period 294 n.15
  transfer of title/ownership
    automaticity 608, 609–610, 614
    as option 610–611
hypotecha. *See also* constructive
  delivery/*constitutum possessorium*;
  possessory pledge; [registered]
  charge; Roman law (*Corpus Iuris
  Civilis*), *pignus*/*hypotheca*
  abolition
    alternatives to *hypotheca*: charge on
      warrants/bills of lading 48; personal
      guarantees as preferred alternative
      48; redemption, right of (*contrat à
      réméré/faculté de rachat*) and 50; sale
      and lease-back 50–51
    disadvantages 47–48
    changes to in the *ius commune* 44–46
    sale and lease-back and 50–51

ICC Uniform Customs and Practices 62
immovable/movable property, distinction,
  Roman law (*Corpus Iuris Civilis*) 40
insolvency. *See also* execution
  actio Pauliana 503, 506–507, 529–530, 579
  administration by insolvency
    administrator 172–173, 179, 199,
    206, 214
    individual right of action, exclusion
      193, 194–195, 199
  administrator's rights/duties
    avoidance of onerous/
      disadvantageous transactions. *See*
      onerous/disadvantageous
      transactions *below*
    default, effect 176–177, 253–254, 251,
      268–269, 281
    notification to secured creditor of
      intention to sell collateral 368–369,
      448, 505

payment of interest for delay in
  realising assets 368–369
postponement of sale/execution
  247–248, 284, 368–369, 441 n.19,
  442 n.29, 505, 652
realisation of bankrupt's assets within
  statutory time-limits 352–353
reservation of title, relevance 247–248
sale of assets: assets already executed
  against 190; insolvent's possession
  of another's movable property 173;
  preservation of assets 193, 214, 220;
  registered charge 468–469; security
  transfer of ownership 446
satisfaction of claims of creditors and
  return of residue to bankrupt 199,
  214, 219–220, 466–467
satisfaction of creditor's contractual
  claims in case of reservation of title
  247
satisfaction of original seller's claims
  after deduction of administration
  costs 352, 368–369, 441 n.19, 527,
  652
termination of contract. *See* contract,
  termination in case of insolvency
  proceedings
termination of finance leasing/leasing
  contract 448, 601
all-monies/sums clauses. *See* all-monies/
  sums retention of title (framework
  agreement), insolvency
avoidance of fraudulent proceedings,
  administrator's rights/duties. *See*
  intention to defraud/prejudice other
  creditors, effect *below*
charge of money claims 534–535, 537,
  584–585
commission [undisclosed] agency 538
concorso dei creditori (Italy) 199
concurso de acreedores (Spain) 193–196
concursus creditorum (Belgium) 29–30, 187,
  189, 315–316
contract, effect on. *See also* contract,
  termination in case of insolvency
  proceedings
fulfilment of obligations before
  commencement of proceedings,
  relevance 177, 188, 200, 221, 226,
  251–252
payment at insolvency creditor rate,
  limitation to 177, 191, 200

INDEX BY SUBJECT 755

transfer of seller's ownership to administrator 283–284
corporate insolvency 206, 209, 219–220. *See also* proceedings, limitation to merchants/businessmen/commercial enterprises *below*
  critical date 183, 403–404
  intention to defraud/prejudice other creditors, effect 486–487
  damages for losses incurred from failure to sell at best price 368–369
  debitor cessus, notice to, relevance, notification following 578, 584–585
  diversity of practice as impediment to European Security Right 667
  factoring contract 548–549
  finance leasing/leasing contract. *See* finance leasing/leasing contract, insolvency of creditor, debtor's rights
  floating [enterprise] charge/lien/mortgage 84–85, 209, 239–240, 493–494, 537, 592
    insolvency of creditor 464, 471
  good faith and. *See bona fide* acquisition
  goods in transit, rights over. *See also* priority, statutory preferences, carrier
    bill of lading, retention and 218
    carrier's statutory preference 185–186
    on completion of transit 207, 211, 218, 229
    enforcement of contract and 201, 207, 217, 222
    recovery on payment of transit costs 191, 201
    reservation of title, relevance 221–222
    sale on credit and 218
    seller's statutory possessory lien and 224–227
    stoppage 181, 211, 213, 217, 218, 221–222, 229
    transfer of ownership/title, relevance 181, 197, 201, 204, 229: as determining factor 178
    'transit' 211
  gratuitous transactions 487, 496, 501–502, 503–504, 507, 509, 514, 529–530, 642
  incongruous/congruous securities 484
    as attempt to prefer one creditor over others 487
    in respect of debt or legal act to detriment of creditors 487
    when creditor not entitled to claim at that time 487
  intention to defraud/prejudice other creditors, effect 484–485, 498, 501–502, 529–530. *See also* contract, avoidance, for intention to defraud/prejudice creditors
    actio Pauliana. *See actio Pauliana*
    avoidance of fraudulent proceedings 194, 202, 212, 235–236, 494–495, 496, 642–643: retroactive/*ex tunc* effect 514
    critical dates 484, 486–487
    failure to take interests of other creditors into account 506
    UNIDROIT Convention on International Interests in Mobile Equipment (2001) 529–530
  ius separationis. *See ius separationis*
  limiting the rights of the secured creditor 652
  nantissement de fonds de commerce 493–494, 577
  new goods manufactured out of materials supplied (*specificatio*) and. *See* new goods manufactured out of materials supplied (*specificatio*), insolvency in the absence of proceeds clause; proceeds clause (extended reservation of title); products and proceeds clauses combined
  onerous/disadvantageous transactions 503. *See also* gratuitous transactions *above*
    administrator's rights/duty to avoid 461–462, 484–485, 486–487, 503–504, 513, 612
    dumping 487
  possessory pledge 495–496
  priority. *See* priority
  proceedings
    effect 202–204, 382
    limitation to commercial enterprises 503
    limitation to merchants/businessmen/commercial enterprises 179, 193, 503. *See also* corporate insolvency *above*

756 INDEX BY SUBJECT

insolvency (cont.)
  property of debtor. See also
      administration by insolvency
      administrator above
    assets excluded from execution 391
    delivery, relevance 187
    existing assets and assets coming into
      existence during proceedings 187
    goods in possession of bankrupt 177,
      636
    loss of right to manage 177, 190
    monies paid to bankrupt for resale of
      cars supplied on credit for that
      purpose 304, 309, 311, 316
    payment of purchase price, relevance
      187
    property disposed of after
      commencement of proceedings
      326–327
    property sold before insolvency
      220–221
    'property that belongs to the debtor'
      172–173, 218, 220–221
    shares, bonds and other securities
      220–221
    transfer of title to insolvency
      administration 214
  protection of buyer against seller's
    creditors 215–216, 218–219, 220–221,
      223–224
  protection of seller against buyer's
    creditors 216, 217–218, 223–224,
      279
  real rights, effect on 209–210
  recovery of property disposed of before
    insolvency proceedings (actio
    Pauliana), 199, 498, 524. See also
    intention to defraud/prejudice other
    creditors, effect above
  registered bank charge 582
  [registered] charge, debtor's rights in
    case of insolvency of creditor
    457–458
  rei vindicatio. See rei vindicatio in case of
    insolvency
  resale of cars supplied on credit
    for that purpose, effect on
    304 n.10
  reservation of title 13
  restraint of sale and 194
  sale and lease-back 446–447, 449,
    450–451
  debtor's rights in case of insolvency
    of creditor 449, 458, 472–473,
    478–479
  security assignment of claims/debts
    556–557, 558, 565–567, 587,
    588–589
  security assignment of earnings
    532–535, 537, 540–542, 543–545
  security assignment of future
    claims/debts 406, 407, 550–551, 579,
    589–590
  security transfer of ownership 439–440,
    445
    debtor's rights in case of insolvency of
      creditor 443, 446
    security owner's obligation to pay
      percentage of costs 596–597
  self-administration 172 n.6
  special registered charge, debtor's rights
    in case of insolvency of creditor 450,
    463, 468–469, 472–473, 478–479,
    603
  stock-in-trade as collateral for
    non-possessory security right 486,
    489, 491–492, 493–494, 495–496,
    497–501, 505, 511, 515–516, 523
  suspect period 183, 194, 199, 235–236,
    290, 492–493, 494–495
    finance leasing/leasing contract
      604–605
    floating [enterprise] charge/lien/
      mortgage 514
    security assignment of future
      claims/debts 540
  suspension of transactions 193, 199, 202,
    268–269, 382, 492–493, 540, 652
  unpaid vendor's charge (EBRD) and 107
instalment, payment by. See hire
  purchase/payment by instalment
International Sale of Goods Convention
  (CISG) 280
inventory collateral
  9 UCC 57, 64–65, 71–72
  priority 74
ius commune. See also Roman law (Corpus
  Iuris Civilis)
  Corpus Iuris Civilis, role 38
  mobilia non habent sequelam. See mobilia
    non habent sequelam
  priority, general/special interests 42–43
  publicity/registry, deficiencies of Roman
    law system and 43–44

INDEX BY SUBJECT 757

Roman–Dutch law and 44. *See also* Roman–Dutch law
  as subsidiary source of law 44
Voet, Johannes (1647–1713) and. *See* Voet, Johannes (1647–1713)
ius separationis 195–196, 218–219, 242, 251–252, 279, 281, 283–284, 299
  accession and 279
  all-monies/sums retention of title (framework agreement) 431, 432–433
  authorisation to sell/dispose of, relevance 242, 616–617, 620
  charge of money claims 545
  commission [undisclosed] agency 296–297, 392–393, 616–617
  finance leasing/leasing contract 616–617
  floating [enterprise] charge/lien/mortgage 469, 470–471

judicial development. *See also Table of Cases Cited by Name*
  Germany 55, 58, 60, 476–477
  USA 55, 75

legal fictions, England 87
legislation, role 647–648
  Belgium 55
  England 51–52
  France 55, 647–648
  Germany 647–648
  Netherlands 647–648
  parties' right to derogate from 656–657, 662–663
  Scotland 46
  Spain 647–648
liability of purchaser of business for pre-existing debt. *See also* contract, avoidance, for intention to defraud/prejudice creditors; execution, against purchaser of business for pre-existing debt
  assets as entirety of debtor's property, relevance 626, 641, 642 n.44
  ceiling, whether 624, 625, 626, 645
  continued management by original owner, relevance 624, 631, 635, 640–641, 646
  continued use of old name, relevance 623, 625, 645
    exclusion by duly registered or notified agreement 623–624, 625, 645

  continuing liability of original debtor 624, 625
  exclusion, possibility of 625, 645
  knowledge/'should have known' requirement 625, 626
  limitation period 645
  loan/credit 624
  as personal liability 625
  purchase price, relevance 624, 626
  rei vindicatio and 629
  third-party rights, agreement on 641
Luxembourg, special registered charge, variety 10–11

machinery
  publicity/registry, need for 253, 261, 263, 267–268
  statutory possessory lien 267–268
misrepresentation
  avoidance of contract for 238–239
  damages for 233, 238–239
  definition 238–239
mistake
  contract, effect on 178, 235–236, 238
  third-party rights 245
mobilia non habent sequelam 44–46
  applicability under *ius commune* 44 n.20
  in Normandy 45 n.21

nantissement de fonds de commerce.
    See also floating [enterprise] charge/lien/mortgage; [registered] charge
  applicability
    all types of asset 493
    bank or financial institution 57, 493, 539–540
    limitation to, 50 per cent of assets 493–494, 525–526
  assignment of future claims/debts 539–540, 661
  completion many months after loan at time of financial difficulty, effect 492–493, 494–495
  debitor cessus, notice to, relevance 539–540, 577
  definition/requirements 491
  excess collateral, relevance 492, 494, 528–529, 578
  execution 577, 578
  fluctuating future assets 493, 494
  frequency of use 492, 494
  insolvency 493–494, 577, 578

nantissement de fonds de commerce (cont.)
  inventory collateral, exclusion 57, 491–492
  judicial enforcement, need for 491–492
  'ordinary course of business' rule 493
  as pledge 491–492
  priority 492
  publicity/registry 491–492, 493, 527–528
  as security right to claim against unknown debtor 576–578, 592–593
  specificity principle 539–540
  stock-in-trade as collateral for non-possessory security right 493, 525–526
  third-party rights 493–494
natural justice, *accessio/specificatio* 374
new goods manufactured out of materials supplied (specificatio). *See also* products and proceeds clauses combined
  accession and 382–383
  authority to manufacture before payment of purchase price, relevance 391–392, 393–394, 395–396, 407–409, 412, 413
  commingling and 373, 374
    priority 374
  commission [undisclosed] agency 392–393, 394, 412–413, 415–416
  constructive delivery/*constitutum possessorium* 393, 412
  contratto d'appalto 379. *See also* manufacture for self, relevance *below*
    agency relationship 407–408
    execution 407–408
  credit consignment agreement 390, 411–412
  as delict 389
  execution in the absence of proceeds clause 366, 373, 374–375, 376, 379, 381, 383, 386, 389, 390, 392, 393, 396. *See also* proceeds clause (extended reservation of title); products clause; products and proceeds clauses combined; real subrogation (assignment of future claim)
    before payment by second buyer 399, 400, 401, 404–405, 406, 408, 409, 410, 411, 412, 413, 414

  contratto d'appalto 407–409
    following payment by second buyer 398–399, 400, 401, 404, 405, 406, 408, 409, 410, 411, 413, 414
  fiduciary relationship (beneficial trust) 371
  floating [enterprise] charge/lien/mortgage 386, 396–397, 414
  insolvency in the absence of proceeds clause 368–369, 370, 371, 374, 375, 376, 377–378, 379, 382, 384, 388, 389, 390, 394, 397, 400, 401–402, 404, 408, 409, 410, 411, 412, 413, 414
    after payment by second buyer 408
    before payment by second buyer 405, 408
    following payment by second buyer 410
    payment before commencement of insolvency proceedings, relevance 403–404
  mandate to manufacture and sell 375–376, 391
  manufacture for self, relevance 379–381, 382, 384–385, 392. *See also contratto d'appalto above*
  monies paid to bankrupt, right to, commingling/distinguishability of monies, relevance 402–403, 408, 410, 413
  natural justice and 374
  'ordinary course of business' rule 387–388
  ownership
    critical date 374
    enterprise contract 373–374, 397
    payment of purchase price, relevance 371, 390, 391–392
    publicity/registry 369–370, 372–373
    risk, relevance 366–367, 370, 372–373, 375, 379, 380, 382, 385, 389, 391, 392, 394, 397, 412–413, 415–416
    value of material/value of work, relevance 369–370, 372–373, 375, 376, 378, 381, 382, 385–386, 388, 389, 392, 394
  possessory pledge 377, 381–382, 384, 393, 396–397
  products clause as 368 n.13
  priority, commingling and 374
  proceeds clause (extended reservation of title) 378–379, 381, 383–384, 386

real subrogation (assignment of future claim) and. *See* real subrogation (assignment of future claim)
[registered] charge 108, 377, 393, 396–397, 408, 409, 410, 414–415
rei vindicatio in case of insolvency 377–378
reservation of title 365–393, 411, 412, 413
security assignment of future claims/debts 405, 406–407, 411–412, 413–414
specificatio
  accession distinguished 382
  determination of 374, 379–380, 388, 389, 394, 656–657
  examples 372–373, 385–386
  ownership, creation/termination and 366, 369, 371–372, 374, 379–380, 388, 389, 397, 408
  reversibility, relevance 385, 389
  strict 371–373
tenancy in common rights 384
third-party rights 370, 371, 372–373, 375, 376, 392. *See also* products clause
refusal of sums due to bankrupt 410
unjustified enrichment and 389
non-possessory security rights: *See also* assignment of claim to recovery; car fleet as collateral for non-possessory security right; factoring contract; finance leasing/leasing contract; floating [enterprise] charge/lien/mortgage [registered] charge; reservation of title; security assignment of future claims/debts; special registered charge
bona fide acquisition 14
convergence/divergence of practice 663
divided attitudes towards 655
excess collateral, relevance 14
growth in 654–655
publicity/registry 476–477, 656, 663
retention of non-possessory elements 14
right to retake possession of collateral 14
specificity principle 477

OAS Model Inter-American Law on Secured Transactions, 9 UCC and 54
'ordinary course of business' rule 58–59, 71–72, 186–187

floating [enterprise] charge/lien/mortgage 459–460, 471–472, 493, 511, 522–523
new goods manufactured out of materials supplied (*specificatio*) 387–388
resale of cars supplied on credit for that purpose 307–308, 309, 315, 323, 326, 335, 339, 341, 344, 362
sale of business 639
sale and lease-back 454
security assignment of earnings 565–566
stock-in-trade as collateral for non-possessory security right 504
ownership/title. *See* transfer of ownership/title

pactum commissorium. *See* forfeiture clause (*pactum commissorium*)
Pandectist movement 44
Pauw, Willem 45, 48
performance withhold. *See* retention of asset as security for performance/performance withhold
personal security including bank guarantees, promissory notes and performance bonds. *See also* discounting of bills as means of providing loan
  as means of providing loan 547
  as personal right 56–57
  preference for in case of car sales 317, 318, 348–349
  as supporting obligation 56–57
pledge. *See* possessory pledge
Poland, publicity/registry 59
possession. *See also mobilia non habent sequelam*
  agency distinguished 174 n.12
  bona fide acquisition of real rights in movable property 180, 186–187, 220–221, 288–289, 317, 319–320, 326, 330, 339, 341, 344–345, 582 n.20, 652–653
  sale and lease-back 474
  decline in importance 652–654
  as evidence of creditworthiness 652–654
  as fact 174 n.12
  goods held in safe custody 200
  presumption of ownership 186–187, 277, 317, 629, 652–653

possession (*cont.*)
   protection of better right to in the absence of concept of absolute ownership 204, 326
   as publicity 180, 652–654, 655–656
   as real right (right *ad rem*) 174 n.16, 219, 219
   sale and lease-back 460–461, 463–464, 474
   tangible collateral, limitation to 70–71
possessory pledge
   car fleet as collateral for non-possessory security right 447, 456, 458, 465
   completion many months after loan at time of financial difficulty, effect 486–487, 496
   constructive delivery/*constitutum possessorium* 309–310, 314–315, 444–445
   control 485–486, 493
   debitor cessus, notice to, relevance 553–554
   delivery, relevance 11, 12, 456, 465, 495, 504, 652–653
   disposal without authority as criminal offence 495
   economic reasons for security rights and 9–10
   excess collateral, relevance/implied waiver 486
   execution 485–486
   fictitious pledges 312–313, 340
      priority 312–313
   new goods manufactured out of materials supplied (*specificatio*) 393, 396–397
      delayed power of disposal 381–382
      manufactured goods 377
      raw materials/commodities 377
      trust receipt/bills of lading and 384
   notarial/registered deed, need for 456, 465, 515, 527, 651–652
   pignus 40–41
      pledge/pawn in England and 49
   priority 485–486, 515–516, 518, 527
   products clause as 368 n.13
   publicity/registry 311, 312–313, 314–315, 458, 476, 477–478, 527, 652–653
   as real right 504
   resale of cars supplied on credit for that purpose 312, 314–315, 340, 447
   security assignment distinguished 306

security transfer of ownership compared 306, 439–441, 444, 446, 514–515
special registered charge as alternative 10–11, 477–478. *See also* special registered charge
specificity principle 465, 495, 504, 515, 519, 526–527
stock-in-trade as collateral for non-possessory security right 456, 478, 485–486, 495, 504–506, 515, 517, 526–527
   control of stock, need for 485–486, 493, 517, 522
   delivery to third party to hold for pledgee, need for 519, 522
   execution 485–486
   frequency of use 506
   future stock 485–486, 495, 504, 505
   priority 485–486
   writing, need for 495
Pothier, R. J. 45 n.21, 47 n.32
precautionary measures
   bona fide acquisition, prevention of 236
   termination of contract for failure to pay and 262–263
priority. *See also* third-party rights
   9 UCC 58–59, 71–75
   after-acquired collateral 75, 195
   all-monies/sums retention of title (framework agreement) 418, 420–421, 423, 435
   bilateral regulation, exclusion 196
   charge of money claims 534–535, 579, 584
   classification of rights
      ius separationis 195–196
      ius separationis, rights giving rise to 195–196, 218–219, 279
      privileged rights 194–195, 214–215
   co-existing rights in same collateral 73–74
   conflicting interests in instruments and chattel paper 75
   control over deposit accounts 75
   convergence/divergence of practice 671
   credit consignment agreement 292–293
   date of contract and 196
   delivery, relevance 186–187, 221
   discounting of bills as means of providing loan 580
   distributional considerations 85

EBRD Model Law on Secured
    Transactions 103
equality of creditors/unfair preferences
    487, 499–500, 503, 513–514, 516–517,
    518–519, 638
execution as means of securing 405
fictitious pledge and 312–313
fixed charge 459, 558
fixtures/commingling/distinguishability
    of monies paid to bankrupt 75
floating [enterprise] charge/lien/
    mortgage 74–75, 414, 459–460,
    500–501, 508, 511, 520, 523, 525,
    558, 586, 590, 591–592
future advances on existing position
    ('tacking') 86–87, 90–92, 328
general/special interests 42–43
insolvency 187
    unascertained bulk commodities 208
insolvency proceedings, effect 183,
    209–211, 214–215
inventory collateral 74
Ireland 210–211
merger of debtor and successor
    entity 75
nantissement de fonds de commerce 492
non-possessory pledge and 195–196
paritas creditorum 187, 195–196, 206, 290
possessory pledge 485–486, 515–516, 518
proceeds clause (extended reservation of
    title) 306–307
products clause. See products clause,
    priority
publicity/registry. See publicity/registry,
    priority
purchase money security interest 74–75,
    86
registered bank charge 581–582
[registered] charge 195–196, 497, 518
registered vehicle charge 471–472
reservation of title 91–92, 217, 247, 251,
    283, 302 n.2, 317, 325
    agreement to delay payment and
        255–257
Roman law (*Corpus Iuris Civilis*) 42–43
sale and lease-back 450–451
secured lender, public [notarial] deed
    conferring special security 580–581
secured party/buyer of collateral 71–73
secured party/lien, creditor 71, 182
security assignment of claims/debts 558,
    586, 589

security assignment of earnings 534–535
security assignment of future
    claims/debts 577
security rights, parties' intention as
    determining factor 580
security transfer of ownership 302 n.2,
    306–307, 439–440
seller [on credit] 173, 182, 187, 206,
    210–211, 226
    fiduciary relationship assimilated to
        pledge 354–355
    negotiated settlement 353
    public [notarial] deed conferring
        special security 356–357, 376–377
    special registered charge 449
    statutory possessory liens 75, 199–225,
        226, 233
    machinery 267–268
statutory preferences 327, 459–460, 508,
    511, 513
    carrier 174, 185–186, 189
    seller [on credit] 10, 187, 225–227,
        352–353: reasons for differences
        between European systems
        226–227
stay of proceedings and 79
stock-in-trade as collateral for
    non-possessory security right,
    possessory pledge 485–486
subrogation action 404–405
tax claims 505, 511, 513, 520
third-party rights, products clause
    366–367, 368, 371, 399–400
**proceeds clause (extended reservation of
    title)** 11, 12, 13, 300, 304–307,
    309–311, 312, 329, 350, 352,
    353–355, 361, 363–364. See also real
    subrogation (assignment of future
    claim); security assignment of
    future claims/debts, anticipated
    assignment of claims
convergence/divergence of practice
    363–364, 662
exclusion 12, 358, 364, 381
fiduciary nature of relationship 352,
    354, 401
limited scope for 13
new goods manufactured out of
    materials supplied (*specificatio*) [with
    products clause] 371, 378–379, 381,
    383–384, 386, 387–388
    exclusion 409, 410

proceeds clause (*cont.*)
    execution, relevance 401, 415
    insolvency, relevance 401–402
    priority 306–307
    timing, relevance 401–402
    unjust enrichment 333, 401
products clause
    convergence/divergence of practice 394–397, 662–663
    effect 366–369
    exclusion 375, 381, 396–397
    formal requirements 368
    'manufacturer'
        parties' right to determine 367–368, 371, 378–379, 389, 396
        statutory definition 367–368
    as pledge 368 n.13, 399–400
    priority 368, 371, 400
    publicity/registry 368, 656
    security transfer of ownership 368–369
    as security transfer of ownership of future products with resolutive condition 371, 388
    third-party rights 366–367, 368, 371, 399–400
products and proceeds clauses combined
    convergence/divergence of practice 414–416
    definition/explanation 399
    exclusion 409
    execution
        before payment by second buyer 399–400
        following payment by second buyer 399, 412, 414
    insolvency
        before payment by second buyer 400
        following payment by second buyer 400
    requirements 399
    rights arising from 399
proportionality. *See* excess collateral, relevance
provisional measures. *See* precautionary measures; stay of proceedings
public policy issues, security assignment of future claims/debts 575–576
publicity/registry. *See also debitor cessus*, notice to, relevance
    9 UCC (filing system) 59, 73, 76–78, 670–671

absence of provision for 193–194
all-monies/sums retention of title (framework agreement) 656
book entry 220–221, 309–310, 347, 350, 363–364, 593, 642 n.44, 661, 662
car fleet as collateral for non-possessory security right 443–444
cars 279, 336–337, 338, 357–358, 453–454, 471–472
    delay in 319
charge of money claims 544, 584
constructive notice 91, 92–93
convergence/divergence of practice 15, 284–285, 670–671
    publicity/registry 670–671
criminal law, relevance in the absence of provision for 43
critical date for effectiveness of transaction 78
debtor register, advantages 670–671
delivery as 179
distinction 78
divided attitudes towards 655–656
EBRD Model Law on Secured Transactions 103
electronic filing 76
European Security Right 670–671
finance leasing/leasing contract 448, 475, 595–596, 598, 599, 600–601, 603, 612, 615–616, 619, 649, 659
floating [enterprise] charge/lien/mortgage 469, 476, 489, 493, 512, 522–523, 537
future trade creditors and 85–86
hire purchase/payment by instalment 193–194, 196, 210, 612–613
liability of purchaser of company for pre-existing debts 623–624, 625, 645
nantissement de fonds de commerce 491–492, 493, 527
new goods manufactured out of materials supplied (*specificatio*) 108, 368, 369–370, 372–373, 393, 396–397, 408, 409, 410, 414–415
non-possessory security right 14, 476–477, 656
as notification to *debitor cessus* 575–576
possession as 180, 652–654, 655–656
possessory pledge 311, 312–313, 314–315, 458, 476, 477–478

pre-existing unsecured creditors and 85–86
priority 59, 73, 90–92, 193–194, 196, 671
 critical date 469–470, 566
 Roman law (*Corpus Iuris Civilis*) 42
products clause 368, 656
public [notarial] deed distinguished 324, 456, 603
registered bank charge 498–499, 581–582
[registered] charge 460–461
registration of company charge 92–93, 228, 270–271, 346–347, 556, 559, 663
registration of individual charge 228, 346–347, 461–462, 556
required information 76, 77–78
reservation of title. *See* reservation of title, publicity/registry
Roman Law (*Corpus Iuris Civilis*) 42
sale of business 639, 640
sale and lease-back 443, 445, 451, 460–461, 470–471, 659
sale for security purposes 469–470
security assignment of claims/debts 556, 558, 559
security assignment of earnings 534, 544
security interests requiring 210, 252–253, 254–255, 261, 309–310, 324, 346–347
 bank loans 581–582
 machinery 253, 261, 263, 267–268
security transfer of ownership 440–441, 444–445, 476, 527
shares, bonds and other securities 220–221
as source of real rights 78, 180, 219, 223–224
stock-in-trade as collateral for non-possessory security right 482, 527, 656
transfer of ownership of movable, relevance 179, 180, 189–190, 254–255, 312–313, 633
 resale of cars supplied on credit for that purpose 316–317, 338, 344
UNIDROIT Convention on International Interests in Mobile Equipment (2001) 59
variety of practice 9–16
warrant 490–491
purchase money security interest, priority
 9 UCC 74–75, 83, 671–672

convergence/divergence of practice 671–672
EBRD Model Law on Secured Transactions 671–672
England 86, 91
European Security Right 671–672

real subrogation (assignment of future claim) 315–316, 402
 execution
  after payment by second buyer 402–403
  before payment by second buyer 403
 new goods manufactured out of materials supplied (*specificatio*) 402, 404, 415
 proceeds clause (extended reservation of title) 402
 specificity principle 421
 third-party rights 187, 189, 315–316, 363
  change in nature of goods, relevance 355, 402–403, 415
redemption, right of. *See also* sale and lease-back
 chattel mortgage (England) and civil law transfer of title with right/duty to redeem distinguished 52 n.54
 'equity of redemption' 52 n.54
 France 50
 as proprietary interest 52 n.54
registered bank charge
 excess collateral, relevance 582
 execution 582
 frequency of use 582
 insolvency 582
 priority 581–582
 public [notarial] deed, need for 581–582
 publicity/registry 498–499, 581–582
[registered] charge. *See also* fixed charge; floating [enterprise] charge/lien/mortgage; *nantissement de fonds de commerce*; possessory pledge; registered bank charge; registered vehicle charge; special registered charge
 car fleet as collateral for non-possessory security right 450, 451
 debitor cessus, notice to, relevance 306, 309–310, 316, 324–325, 346–347, 415, 553

[registered] charge (cont.)
  debtor's rights in case of insolvency of creditor 450, 463, 478–479
  EBRD Model Law on Secured Transactions 110–111
  equitable nature of real right 458–459
  execution 518
  finance leasing/leasing contract compared 111, 620–621
  fixtures/commingling/distinguishability of monies paid to bankrupt 468
  fluctuating future assets 87, 325, 346–347, 349–350, 425 n.18
  frequency of use 496–497, 612
  future claims as basis of bank loan 583
  future earnings as collateral for bank loan 553
  insolvency, debtor's rights in case of insolvency of creditor 457–458
  limited use of/restrictions on 196 n.81, 316, 404, 414–415
  new goods manufactured out of materials supplied (*specificatio*) 108, 377, 393, 396–397, 408, 409, 410, 414–415
  priority 195–196, 449, 497, 518
  public [notarial] deed, need for 451, 496–497
  publicity/registry 458–459
  resale of cars supplied on credit for that purpose 318
    monies paid to bankrupt, right to and 327–329, 332–333, 338–339, 343, 346–347, 357–358, 359–360, 364
  specificity principle 339, 467, 496–497, 517
  stock-in-trade as collateral for non-possessory security right 496–497, 517
    long-term storage with obligation to settle on sale 517
  unpaid vendor's charge (EBRD) and 108
  writing, need for 499
registered sale, car fleet as collateral for non-possessory security right 469–470, 473–474
registered vehicle charge
  applicability 477–478
  car fleet as collateral for non-possessory security right 10, 453–454, 467, 471–472, 477–478

cars (*pubblico registro automobilistica*) 453–454
debtor's rights in case of insolvency of creditor 468–469, 472–473
frequency of use 471–472
insolvency, debtor's rights in case of insolvency of creditor 472–473
priority 471–472
resale of cars supplied on credit for that purpose 314–315, 343, 347, 357–358
specificity principle 467
third-party rights 471–472
registry. *See* publicity/registry
***rei vindicatio* in case of insolvency**
  all-monies/sums retention of title (framework agreement) 420, 423, 424–425, 436
  estoppel and 294–295, 335. *See also* estoppel
  finance leasing/leasing contract 596, 608
  following distribution of proceeds from sale of assets 234
  goods handed over by mistake 217
  goods owed by third party to original seller's agent 321–322
  goods in possession of buyer in case of voided contract 178
  goods in transit 181
  insolvent's possession of another's movable property 173, 287–288, 289, 290, 298. *See also* all-monies/sums retention of title (framework agreement) *and* finance leasing/leasing contract *above*
  judicial determination, need for 290
  insolvent's possession of another's security right 173
  insolvent's transfer of ownership to third party 179–180
  inventory, relevance 255–257
  liability of purchaser of business for pre-existing debt and 629
  new goods manufactured out of materials supplied (*specificatio*) 377–378
  reservation of title, effect 247, 251, 255–257, 259–260, 262–263, 264–265, 266, 268–269, 278, 283–284, 289, 293, 294–295, 298–299, 658
  sale and lease-back 442

specificatio, need for 371–372
specificity principle 424–425
termination of finance leasing/leasing contract 448, 601
termination of sale before insolvency proceedings 184–185, 200
timing of claim 235, 236, 256, 284
transfer of ownership in the absence of obligation to deliver 188–189, 225–226. *See also* retention of asset as security for performance/performance withhold
unlawful frustration of right of 304, 351–352, 363
remedies. *See also actio Pauliana*; damages; *rei vindicatio* in case of insolvency; unjust enrichment
9 UCC 78–79
acceleration of payment 94
acceptance of collateral in full or partial satisfaction 79
appointment of administrator by agreement 93–94
disposal of collateral, need for judicial involvement 79, 199–226, 233, 500–501
independence of legal designation of security right 82
procedure 192–193
recovery [and sale] of goods 192–193, 198–199, 217–218
 delivered after commencement of insolvency proceedings 222
recovery of sale price 202
reduction (Scotland), definition 513
in tort 204
unilateral disposal in good faith 59–60, 79
US/European systems distinguished 79
rental agreement. *See also* finance leasing/leasing contract; hire purchase/payment by instalment; sale and lease-back
finance leasing/leasing contract as 607, 608, 613
sale and lease-back distinguished 458
resale of cars supplied on credit for that purpose. *See also bona fide* acquisition; credit consignment agreement; hire purchase/payment by instalment

agency and 313–314, 322, 326, 337
commission [undisclosed] agency and 314, 321–322, 340–341, 348–349, 357, 361
certain date (*data certa*) before execution or commencement of insolvency proceedings, need for 322, 357, 361
concession contract and, used car sales 322
credit consignment agreement 340–341, 348–349
 conditions for settlement and 337–338, 348–349
 registry, relevance 338, 348–349
dealer arrangements 342–343
fiduciary relationship 329–330, 347–348
monies paid to bankrupt, right to 304, 309, 311, 316, 317, 324, 334, 337, 341, 345. *See also* priority, seller [on credit]
 in the absence of right to resell 304, 312
 administrator's obligation to satisfy original seller's claims after deduction of administration costs 352
agency relationship and 327, 336, 340
commingling/distinguishability of monies, relevance. *See* commingling/distinguishability of monies paid to bankrupt
floating [enterprise] charge/lien/mortgage and 325, 343
payments made after start of insolvency proceedings 314, 345, 351–364
possessory pledge and 312, 340
public [notarial] deed, relevance 317, 324
[registered] charge 327–329, 332–333, 336, 338–339, 343, 346–347, 357–358, 359–360
reservation of title 317, 318–319, 325, 326–327, 330–331, 336, 337, 340, 342, 356
security assignment of future claims/debts 304–307, 309–311, 312, 315, 322–323, 329, 338, 340, 343, 360, 364
unjust enrichment and 333

resale of cars supplied on credit for that purpose (*cont.*)
  unlawful frustration of *rei vindicatio* 304, 351–352, 363
  registry, relevance 338
  reseller's obligation to transfer monies received to original seller 306–307, 313–314, 342
    holding account/advance payments 340–341
    in personam nature of original seller's right 306–307, 317
    termination of reseller's right to collect claims 306–307
      insolvency proceedings and 304 n.10
      notice of assignment, relevance 306–307
      on termination of payments 304 n.10
    termination of right to resell
      insolvency proceedings and 304 n.10
      on termination of payments 304 n.10
    transfer of ownership/title as result of 302, 307, 311, 316, 318–320, 323, 326–327, 330, 333–334, 335, 339, 341, 343–345
      authorisation to sell, relevance 302, 308–309, 311, 315, 317, 323, 326–327, 330, 333, 336, 337, 339, 341, 344–345, 351–352, 363
      registration of original seller's claim, relevance 344
  unjust enrichment 475–476
  used car sales
    concession contract and 322
    registry 337, 338
resale of goods supplied on credit for that purpose, unpaid vendor's charge (EBRD) 107–108
reservation of title. *See also* all-monies/sums retention of title (framework agreement); retention of asset as security for performance/performance withhold; transfer of ownership/title
  accession, transfer of ownership/title and 390
  administrator in insolvency's rights/duties, effect on 247–248, 270, 283–284
  authorisation to sell, relevance 250–251, 280, 289, 293

  obligation to pass on reservation to next buyer and 295
  resale as sale of future goods (expectancy) 289, 298–299
  as resolutive condition 293, 504
  stock-in-trade as collateral for non-possessory security right 489, 504
  automaticity 285
  bona fide acquisition 263, 270, 282, 288–289, 299, 336–337, 341
  car fleet as collateral for non-possessory security right 443, 465–466, 474
  in case of consumer sales 217
  charge/security interest distinguished 272, 274, 279
  commission [undisclosed] agency distinguished 296–297, 299–300, 412
  contractual nature. *See* unilateral declaration of, validity *below*
  convergence/divergence of practice 282–286, 658–659
    sale and resale 474
  credit consignment agreement distinguished 288–289, 295, 299
  cross-border transactions 105–106
  finance leasing/leasing contract. *See* finance leasing/leasing contract, reservation of title/retention of ownership
  formal requirements 250, 252–253, 254–255, 257–258, 259–260, 261, 263–264, 265–266, 273–274, 276, 277, 278, 282. *See also* publicity/registry *below*
    certain date (*data certa*) before execution or commencement of insolvency proceedings, need for 268, 270, 277, 283, 290–291, 322, 357, 658
    express provision in contract of sale 266–267
    fixed price 278
    general conditions, adequacy 264, 266–267, 270, 275, 277, 278, 280, 281, 282, 422
    inclusion in delivery note, sufficiency 272
    price threshold 278
    public [notarial] deed, need for 263–264

INDEX BY SUBJECT 767

reservation of both legal and
  beneficial ownership 270–271,
  273–274
signature 260, 262, 289, 376, 422
writing 257, 259–260, 263–264,
  267–268, 269, 270, 272, 277, 278,
  282, 283, 658
goods in transit and 221–222
harmonization, possibilities for 664–665
insolvency 11, 13
machinery
  publicity/registry 253, 261, 263, 268
  right to prevent sale 266
as modification to contract, *actio
  Pauliana* 262
new goods manufactured out of
  materials supplied (*specificatio*)
  365–393, 411, 412, 413
  change in nature of goods, relevance
    403
as preferred method 261, 317, 349, 443
priority 91–92, 217, 247, 251, 283, 290,
  302 n.2, 317, 325
process of goods, right to 250–251,
  255–257
publicity/registry 90–92, 209–210, 250,
  252–253, 254–255, 259, 260, 262,
  270, 272, 274, 275, 282, 283,
  386–387, 658
  machinery 253, 261, 263
  notification to other party, need for
    262, 264
  registry in Chattels Registry 263, 356
  reservation of legal and beneficial
    ownership and 275
  timing, relevance 259, 262
  used cars 337
reasonableness test 393
rei vindicatio in case of insolvency 247,
  251, 255–257, 259–260, 262–263,
  264–265, 266, 278, 283, 289, 290,
  293, 294–295, 298–299, 658
resale of cars supplied on credit for that
  purpose 317, 318–319, 325, 326–327,
  330–331, 336, 340, 342, 356,
  360–361, 363
  convergence/divergence of practice
    363–364
  payment to original seller as
    prerequisite for delivery to final
    buyer 342

as preferred method 317, 349
reservation of right to terminate
  distinguished 218, 219, 223–224,
  228, 280, 283
sale on credit 176, 177, 200, 217, 225,
  248–249
  agreement to settle at time of resale,
    need for 337–338, 360–361
  delivery without receipt of payment
    (*kurzfristiger Eigentumsvorbehalt*) 176
  hire purchase/payment by instalment
    176, 177, 194, 224, 225, 248–249,
    250, 267, 281, 303, 318, 319
sale and lease-back 451
specificity principle 255, 259–260,
  263–264, 279
stock-in-trade as collateral for
  non-possessory security right
  482–483
  authorisation to sell, relevance 489,
    504–505
as [suspensive] condition for payment of
  purchase price 246–247, 250–251,
  253, 255, 261, 268, 271–272,
  282–283, 293, 298
  hire purchase/payment by instalment
    608, 609–610
  implied authorisation to sell and
    293
termination of contract and 218, 219,
  223–224, 228, 247, 255–257
third-party rights 221, 226, 268, 278,
  282, 413, 652–653
timing of reservation, relevance
  249–251, 252, 254, 258, 260, 262,
  263–264, 265–266, 268, 269, 276–277,
  278, 282, 285–286, 289
as transfer of ownership/reversion of
  equitable real interest 270–271,
  273–274, 326–327
unilateral declaration of, validity
  248–249, 252, 254, 255, 257–258,
  260, 263, 271–272, 276, 278, 279,
  280, 281–282
  conflict between general conditions of
    sale and general conditions of
    purchase 258
  implied consent 257–258, 260, 278,
    280
unpaid vendor's charge (EBRD) as
  replacement for 105–106

resolutive clause. *See also* contract, termination for failure to pay, parties' agreement and (resolutive clause); products clause
  hire purchase/payment by instalment and 608, 609–610
restitution, contract and 85 n.17
restraint of sale
  insolvency 194
  prohibition on 194
retention of asset as security for performance/performance withhold 185–186, 187–188, 226
  carrier's right 189
  possessory lien, compared 75
  Principles of European Contract Law (1998) 225 n.159
  rei vindicatio 225–226
    customary law provision 188
  resale of motor vehicles supplied on credit for that purpose 314–315
  reservation of title/ownership distinguished 185–186, 259
retention of title. *See* reservation of title
risk. *See also* economic reasons for security rights
  all-monies/sums retention of title 436–437
  commingling and 436–437
  new goods manufactured out of materials supplied (*specificatio*), ownership 366–367, 370, 375, 379, 380, 382, 385, 386, 388, 389, 391, 392, 394, 395, 397, 412–413, 415–416
  sale and lease-back 457
Roman law (*Corpus Iuris Civilis*). *See also ius commune*
  actio Serviana 39–40
    rei vindicatio distinguished 39–40
  constitutum possessorium 42
  curator bonorum, priority over chargee 40
  fiducia [cum creditore]
    exclusion 38
    as transfer of ownership/title 39
  Gaius 40
  Leo I, priority (decree of 472)
  Marcianus 41
  modern law and 38, 40–41, 42
    England 49–50, 51–52
    Scotland 388

  movable/immovable property, irrelevance of distinction 40
  Papinianus 42–43
  pignus
    pledge in modern law distinguished 40–41, 42
    possessory/non-possessory alternatives 41–42: *constitutum possessorium* 42
    traditio 40–41
    transfer to chargor, effect 41–42
  pignus/hypotheca 39–43. *See also hypotheca*
    chargee's rights. *See also* priority *below*: enforcement. *See actio Serviana above*; non-secured creditors and 39–40; priority of security of interest against later interest 39–40; as right *in rem* 39–40
    chargor's rights: charge property to secure another debt 39; as possessor 40–41; to dispose of property 39; transfer title to third party 39
    contract between chargor and chargee restricting, third-party rights 39
    equity in property 40
    as *iura in re aliena* 39–41
    mode of creation as distinguishing feature 40–42
  Pomponius 40
  priority
    decree of Leo I, effect 42
    general/special interests 42–43
    prior tempore, potior iure 42
    publicity and 42
  publicity
    absence of system 42: criminal law (*stellionatus*) as remedy 43; response of *ius commune* 43–44
    priority 42
  stellionatus 43
  traditio 40–41
  Ulpian 42
Roman–Dutch law. *See also* hire purchase/payment by instalment
  constitutum possessorium 45
  as exemplar of *usus modernus* 44
    Pandectist movement, effect 44
  mobilia non habent sequelam 44–46
  Scotland and 45–46
  in South Africa 44

INDEX BY SUBJECT 769

specificity principle, *mobilia non habent sequelam* 44–46
Rome Convention on the Law Applicable to Contractual Obligations (1980) 16, 17, 18–20, 651–652

sale of business
 'ordinary course of business' rule 639
 public [notarial] deed, need for 633–634
 publicity/registry 639, 640
sale and lease-back. *See also* finance leasing/leasing contract
 applicability 446, 448, 455, 461, 463, 464, 466
  business purposes 449
  know-how 457
 bona fide acquisition 460–461, 474
 car fleet as collateral for non-possessory security right 442, 443–444, 445, 447–448, 449–450, 456–457, 460–461, 463, 467, 470–471, 474
  imported luxury cars 454–455
 constructive delivery/*constitutum possessorium* 463–464, 475
 convergence/divergence of practice 474–475, 659
 as credit consignment agreement 443–444
 duration 445
  aircraft 446
 execution 442
 expedited public deed 450–451
 fiduciary relationship (beneficial trust) distinguished 456–457
  as sham 457
 finance leasing/leasing contract compared 447, 599, 600, 611–612. *See also* finance leasing/leasing contract
 forfeiture clause (*pactum commissorium*) 462–463
 frequency of use 442, 445, 451, 453, 454–455, 468, 470–471
 hire purchase/payment by instalment distinguished 451, 458, 465–466
 hypotecha 50–51
 insolvency 442, 446–447, 449
  debtor's rights in case of insolvency of creditor 449, 453, 455–456, 458, 461, 463, 466–467, 472–473
 option/duty to reacquire 50–51, 451, 453
 insolvency 455–456

 on repayment of original debt with interest 452–453
 possession 460–461, 463–464
 publicity/registry 443–444, 445, 451, 460–461, 470–471, 659
  registration in Chattels Registry 451, 453
 real/personal nature of lessee's interest 461
 rei vindicatio in case of insolvency 442
 reservation of title, relevance 451
 risk 457
 sale under guarantee as 452–453
 as sham charge 449–450, 460–461, 463–464, 467–468, 472, 474–475, 602–603
 as sham credit consignment agreement 443–444, 474–475
 specificity principle 453
 as statutory form of security ownership 445
 termination for non-payment 442
 third-party rights 445, 451, 453, 454, 460–461
 validity 456–457, 472, 659
  consent of parties as determining factor 449–450, 454, 475
security assignment of claims/debts. *See also* charge of money claims; discounting of bills as means of providing loan; factoring contract; security assignment of earnings; security assignment of future claims/debts
 authority to receive money for own use 566, 567
 by charge 555, 556, 560–561, 571–572, 588–589
  fixed charge 557
  floating charge 557
 by discount 556
 by mortgage 555, 556, 557
 conditional/contingent nature, relevance 555, 557, 567–568, 585–586, 588
 convergence/divergence of practice 568–572
 debitor cessus, notice to, relevance 11, 306, 556–558, 563, 564–567, 586, 587, 589, 660–661
  divergence/convergence of practice 568–569

security assignment of claims/debts (*cont.*)
  money earned but not paid before insolvency 551–552, 556–557, 560, 562, 563, 566, 571
  money earned and paid before insolvency 556–557, 560, 562, 563, 570–571
  EBRD Model Law on Secured Transactions 112
  economic reasons for. *See* economic reasons for security rights
  as equitable right 555–558
  excess collateral, relevance 586, 587, 589
  execution 565–567, 586, 587, 588, 589
  joinder of parties 556
  as fiduciary relationship (beneficial trust) 560, 564, 587
  formal requirements 555–556, 562
    absolute assignment 556, 557–558. *See also* factoring contract
    estoppel in case of breach 562
    writing 556, 557–558
  frequency of use 555, 557, 563, 565–566, 585–586
  insolvency 556–557, 558, 565–567, 587, 588–589
  possessory pledge compared 11, 306
  priority 558, 589
  publicity/registry 556, 558, 559
  statutory assignment 555–556, 557–558
  suspension of assignor's rights to dispose of collateral 564–565
  validity 306
security assignment of earnings 13, 531–537, 538–542, 545, 547–549, 572 n.118. *See also* charge of money claims; discounting of bills as means of providing loan; factoring contract; security assignment of claims/debts; security assignment of future claims/debts
  applicability to business or professional activities 547–548
  authority to receive money for own use 566, 567
  charge of money claims as alternative 112, 534–535, 569–570, 660–661
  commingling/distinguishability of monies paid to bankrupt 532, 535, 566, 567
  debitor cessus, notice to, relevance 534–535, 536–537, 544–545, 550–551
    entry in books as 534–535, 571–572
    limitation to claims arising within one year in absence of 547–548
  money earned but not paid before insolvency 532, 534, 535, 537, 540–541, 542, 544–545, 548–549, 563–564, 568, 571
  money earned and paid before insolvency 532, 535, 537, 541–542, 543–544, 563–564, 566, 567, 568, 570–571
  excess collateral, relevance 534, 537
  execution, money not yet earned ('future' claim) 533–534, 565–566
  frequency of use 532, 534, 536–537, 544, 548, 552
  future claim, whether 532, 534, 555
    limitation to claims arising within one year 547–548
  insolvency 532–535, 537, 540–542, 544–545. *See also debitor cessus*, notice to, relevance *above*
  money not yet earned ('future' claim) 535, 538, 544, 565–566, 567–568, 590
  ius separationis 545
  'ordinary course of business' rule 565–566
  possessory pledge, assimilation to charge in case of claims 535–536
  as preferred method 569–570
  priority 534–535
  as proceeds clause 532
  publicity/registry 534, 544
  retroactive application 544
  specificity principle 547
  termination of right to collect claims following failure to make loan payments 532
  third-party rights 534, 540–541, 543
  unjust enrichment 534, 537, 538, 545
security assignment of future claims/debts 555, 557, 559, 561–562, 585–586, 588. *See also* charge of money claims; discounting of bills as means of providing loan; factoring contract; real subrogation (assignment of future claim);

security assignment of claims/debts;
security assignment of earnings
after-acquired collateral 66, 71, 75, 195,
    521–522, 566 n.103, 591
anticipated assignment of claims
    304–305, 347, 399, 574. *See also*
    proceeds clause (extended
    reservation of title)
certain date (*data certa*), need for 322
consideration, need for 550
convergence/divergence of practice 364,
    592–593, 661
debitor cessus, notice to, relevance 12–13,
    220–221, 306, 309–310, 315, 322,
    340, 343, 347, 354–355, 360,
    363–364, 401–402, 406–407, 413, 415,
    550, 574, 589–590, 591, 593, 633
  entry in books as 575, 593
  money earned but not paid before
    insolvency 551–552, 571
  money earned and paid before
    insolvency 552, 570–571
duration of assignment, relevance 306,
    346, 565–566, 579
earnings, limitations in respect of 551
EBRD Model Law on Secured
    Transactions 112
excess collateral, relevance 577, 590, 591,
    593–594, 651
exclusion 552–555
execution 574, 579, 591
factoring contract 546–547, 589
fiduciary relationship (beneficial trust)
    539 n.29
forfeiture clause (*pactum commissorium*)
    550
frequency of use 544, 575–576
insolvency 550–551, 574, 579, 589–590
  assignment following 406, 407
  suspect period 540
new goods manufactured out of
    materials supplied (*specificatio*) 405,
    406–407, 411–412, 413–414
priority 577
public policy issues 575–576
resale of cars supplied on credit for that
    purpose 315, 329, 338, 340, 343,
    352, 357, 360

as security for bank loan 550–551,
    581
specificity principle 310, 322–323, 350,
    405, 406–407, 571–572
third-party rights 550–551
security rights[1] 360. *See also*
    non-possessory security rights
  completion many months after loan at
    time of financial difficulty, effect
    484–485, 486–487, 490, 497–498,
    506–507, 509, 513–514, 516–517,
    523–524
  concursus creditorum 187, 214–215
  convergence/divergence of practice 9–16.
    See also harmonisation,
    possibilities/arguments for *below*
  abstract/causal systems 243–244,
    475–476
  actio Pauliana 644–646
  all-monies/sums retention of title
    (framework agreement) 434–437,
    661–662
  autonomy of parties 16, 656–657,
    662–663
  bona fide acquisition 343–345, 346
  charge of money claims 364, 660–661
  collateral, options 669–670
  commingling/distinguishability of
    monies paid to bankrupt 434–437
  commission [undisclosed] agency 364
  debitor cessus, notice to 568–569,
    570–571
  delivery, relevance 285–286, 475
  excess collateral, relevance 528–529,
    593–594
  finance leasing/leasing contract
    619–622, 659
  floating [enterprise] charge/lien/
    mortgage 364, 525–526, 528, 660
  forfeiture clause (*pactum
    commissorium*) 475–476
  intention to defraud/prejudice
    creditors, avoidance for 529–530
  non-possessory security rights 663
  priority 671
  proceeds clause (extended reservation
    of title) 363–364, 662
  products clause 394–397, 662–663

---

[1] Entries under this heading are limited to material which cannot be attributed to a specific security right.

772   INDEX BY SUBJECT

security rights (cont.)
  products and proceeds clauses
    combined 414–416
  publicity/registry 15, 284–285, 670–671
  purchase money security interest,
    priority 671–672
  real right, definition 15–16
  reservation of title 282–286, 658–659:
    and resale 474
  sale and lease-back 474–475
  security assignment of claims/debts
    568–572
  security assignment of future
    claims/debts 364, 592–593, 661
  security transfer of ownership
    473–477
  special registered charge 10–11
  specificity principle 15–16
  stock-in-trade as collateral for
    non-possessory security right
    525–530
  termination of contract for failure to
    pay 227–229
  third-party rights 244–245
  transfer of ownership/title 11–13,
    222–224: time of
  unpaid vendor's rights 225–227
  duration of charge before insolvency,
    relevance 518–519, 523–524
  enlarging the range 649–652
    Austria 650
    Belgium 649–650
    France 649
    Germany 651
  excess collateral, relevance 579, 581
  future claim against unknown
    debtor, possibilities 573–593, 649,
    650
  execution 580–581
  specificity principle 574, 575
  harmonisation, possibilities/arguments
    for 20–24, 664–672. See also EBRD
    Model Law on Secured Transactions;
    UNIDROIT Conventions
  economic benefits 7–8
  European Security Right. See European
    Security Right
  reservation of title 664–665
  UNCITRAL 24–25
  within EU 20–21
  inconsistencies 648–649
  insolvency 667

  increasing limitation of the rights of
    secured creditors 652
  leasing 659
  non-possessory rights, growth in 654–655
  priority, parties' intention as
    determining factor 580
  resulting from commencement of
    insolvency proceedings 283–284,
    614
  variety, co-existence and scope for in
    US/European systems 58, 647–648
security transfer of ownership 11, 12, 13,
    489
  all-monies/sums retention of title
    (framework agreement) 418, 435,
    661–662
  applicability to corporeal movables
    212–213, 442, 446
  bona fide acquisition 303
  car fleet as collateral for non-possessory
    security right 438–443, 444–445,
    473–474
  completion many months after loan at
    time of financial difficulty, effect
    484–485, 490, 518–519, 521–522,
    529–530
  constructive delivery/constitutum
    possessorium 439, 444, 481, 488,
    514–515
  convergence/divergence of practice
    473–477
  as customary law 440–441, 444, 451–452
  excess collateral, relevance/implied
    waiver 439, 441–442, 483–484, 489,
    516, 651
  exclusion 58, 396–397, 456, 602–603,
    609–610
  execution 439–440, 445
  fiduciary relationship (beneficial trust)
    439, 441, 443, 452–453
  finance leasing/leasing contract
    compared 596–597, 598, 600–601,
    602–603, 609–610
  floating future assets 481, 488–489,
    526–527
  forfeiture clause (pactum commissorium)
    441, 452, 454, 475–476, 491,
    602–603, 607–608, 620–621, 657
  framework agreement 516
  insolvency 439–440, 445, 527
    debtor's rights in case of insolvency of
      creditor 443, 478–479

security owner's obligation to pay percentage of costs
iusta causa 444–445, 475–476
judicial sale and 452, 602–603
option/duty to reacquire, payment of repurchase price by instalment 452–453
payment of repurchase price by instalment 452–453
possessory pledge compared 306, 439–441, 446
as sham pledge 14–15, 514–515, 516
priority 302 n.2, 306–307, 439–440, 439–440
products clause and 368–369, 371, 388
publicity/registry 440–441, 444–445, 476, 527
repossession
non-payment, need for 439
right to sell collateral 439
sale and resale 465–466, 474
stock-in-trade as collateral for non-possessory security right 481–484, 488–489, 514–515
future stocks 481, 488–489
sheriff. *See* execution
simulated transaction. *See* contract, annulment of simulated/*pro forma*
Special Purpose Vehicle (SPV) 590–591
special registered charge 15, 468, 477–478, 663. *See also* floating [enterprise] charge/lien/mortgage; registered bank charge; registered vehicle charge
agricultural inventory 11, 12, 491, 663
aircraft 11, 12, 472
car fleet as collateral for non-possessory security right 449
tour coaches 445
cars 314–315, 453–454, 471–472, 477–478, 491, 663
cars, ships and aircraft 450, 477–478
convergence/divergence of practice 10–11
forfeiture clause (*pactum commissorium*) 449–450
judicial sale and 449–450, 452 n.62
machinery 10, 267–268
patents and industrial/intellectual property rights 472
priority 449
publicly traded shares, bonds and securities 472

variety 10–11
vessels 11, 472
specificatio. See new goods manufactured out of materials supplied (*specificatio*)
specificity principle 65–66, 219, 223–224
9 UCC (description of collateral) 65–66
agency and 340
ascertainment of goods 205–206, 208–209, 274–275, 420–421, 426
all-monies/sums retention of title 419, 426–427, 434
clarity of drafting, need for 419
class charge (EBRD) and 108–110
commodities sold in bulk 205, 208–209
convergence/divergence of practice 15–16
credit consignment agreement 390, 431
floating [enterprise] charge/lien/ mortgage 15–16, 471, 477, 510
fungible assets 420–421, 424–425, 426, 430, 431, 432–433, 436, 519
hire purchase/payment by instalment 319
mobilia non habent sequelam 44–46
money 519–520
nantissement de fonds de commerce 539–540
possessory pledge 465, 495, 504, 515, 519, 526–527
priority 208
proceeds clause (extended reservation of title) 574
public [notarial] deed conferring special security 356–357, 376–377
real subrogation (assignment of future claim) 421
registered bank charge 581–582
[registered] charge 339, 499, 517
registered vehicle charge 467
rei vindicatio in case of insolvency 424–425
reservation of title 255, 259–260, 263–264, 279
sale and lease-back 453
security assignment of earnings 547
security assignment of future claims/debts 305–306, 310, 322–323, 347, 350, 406–407
security rights, future claim against unknown debtor 574, 577–578
stock-in-trade as collateral for non-possessory security right 481–482, 488, 497, 510, 526–527

Stair, Lord J. Dalrymple 46
statutory possessory liens
  EBRD Model Law on Secured Transactions 112
  goods in transit and 207
  priority 75, 199–225, 226, 233
  machinery 267–268
statutory preferences. *See* priority, statutory preferences
stay of proceedings
  bankruptcy proceedings 79
  priority 79
stock-in-trade as collateral for non-possessory security right 480–530
  accession, transfer or ownership/title and 504 n.61
  bona fide acquisition 498, 513–514
  convergence/divergence of practice 524–530
  credit consignment agreement 518
  excess collateral, relevance 483–484, 486, 489, 496, 497, 501, 506, 509, 511, 513, 516, 518, 521, 522, 523, 528–529
  execution 486, 487–488, 501, 505–506, 508, 511, 515–516, 523
  fiduciary relationship (beneficial trust) 519
  floating [enterprise] charge/lien/ mortgage 489, 493, 498–500, 508–511, 512–513, 520, 522–523, 528
  frequency of use 483, 486, 496, 497, 506, 518
    floating [enterprise] charge/lien/ mortgage 501, 508, 520, 523
  future stocks
    possessory pledge 485–486, 495
    security transfer of ownership 481, 488–489
    specificity principle 481–482, 526–527
  insolvency 486, 489, 491–492, 493–494, 495–496, 497–501, 505, 511, 515–516, 523
  nantissement de fonds de commerce 493, 526
  obligation to store separately 481–482, 488, 504, 517, 526–527
    commingling/distinguishability of monies paid to bankrupt 505–506
    'ordinary course of business' rule 504–505

possessory pledge 456, 478, 485–486, 495, 504–506, 515, 517, 526–527
  delivery to third party to hold for pledgee, need for 519
  future stock 485–486, 495, 504–506: acquired after commencement of insolvency proceedings 505
  notarial bond 515
  over shares 496
proceeds clause (extended reservation of title) 482–483
publicity/registry 482, 527, 656
[registered] charge 496–497, 517
  long-term storage with obligation to settle on sale 517
reservation of title 488
  expectancy (*Anwartschaftsrecht*) 488, 528–529
security transfer of ownership 481–484, 488–489, 514–515, 526–527
  creditor's status 483
  frequency of use 489
  publicity/registry 482, 527
  specificity principle 481–482, 488, 497, 510, 526–527
warrant 490–491, 493
suspect period. *See* insolvency, suspect period
Switzerland, Private International Law Act 1989 16 n.57

tax claims, priority 505, 511, 513, 520, 525
technological developments, relevance 63–64
  electronic filing 76, 78
tenancy in common rights, new goods manufactured out of materials supplied (*specificatio*) 384
third-party rights. *See also* priority; products clause
  9 UCC 75–76
  actio Pauliana 494, 498, 501–502, 626–627, 628, 634
  all-monies/sums retention of title (framework agreement) 434
  anti-assignment clauses, override 75–76
  charge of money claims 534, 542–543
  convergence/divergence of practice 244–245
  credit consignment agreement 292–293

economic reasons for security rights 8–9
enforceability of agreement not to assert claim or defence against assignee 75–76
England 85–86
execution
  property on debtor's premises 269 n.79, 425, 425
  real/personal right as basis for opposition 237
factoring contract 551–552
fiduciary relationship (beneficial trust) 422, 449
finance leasing/leasing contract 448, 599, 600, 601
floating [enterprise] charge/lien/mortgage 493–494, 512–513, 520
fraudulent dealings and 194, 202, 507
new goods manufactured out of materials supplied (*specificatio*) 370, 371, 375, 376, 392
parties' agreement to terminate contract (resolutive clause) and 221, 228–229
precautionary measures and 236
privity of contract and 85
real subrogation (assignment of future claim) and. *See* real subrogation (assignment of future claim)
registered vehicle charge 471–472
reservation of title 12, 221, 226, 268, 278, 282, 413, 652–653
Roman law (*Corpus Iuris Civilis*) 39
sale and lease-back 445, 451, 453, 454, 460–461
security assignment of earnings 534, 540–541, 543
security assignment of future claims/debts 550–551
termination/avoidance of contract and 188, 189, 190, 225–226, 238
  bona fide acquisition 202 n.100, 236–237, 238–239, 242–243, 244–245
  in case of fraud or mistake 234–235, 245
  legal policy and 243
  registration of acquisition before termination, need for 235
warrant 490–491
title. *See* transfer of ownership/title

transfer of ownership/title. *See also bona fide* acquisition; contract, avoidance, for fraud, transfer of ownership/title, effect on; *mobilia non habent sequelam*; possession; resale of cars supplied on credit for that purpose; reservation of title
accession and. *See* accession, transfer or ownership/title and
agreement that title should pass ('real agreement'), need for 171–172, 175, 179, 201, 219, 481
  anticipatory agreement 174, 561–562, 588
  assignment of debts 561–562
  independence from contract of sale, relevance 246–247
  transfer of security ownership 481
burden of proof 277
convergence/divergence of practice 11–13, 222–224
European Security Right and 666
European systems compared 222–224
fiducia [cum creditore] 39
finance leasing. *See* finance leasing/leasing contract, transfer of ownership/title
obligation to transfer 269
  distinguished 171–172, 179
  principle of abstraction 172, 189–190, 211–212, 212 n.121 224, 227–228, 230–231, 475–476: convergence/divergence of practice 243–244, 475–476; revesting of title on termination of contract and 227–228, 232
original acquisition
  commixtio 197–198, 378
  specificatio 197–198, 378
overlapping ownership 219
ownership and right to dispose of property distinguished 287–288, 399
pignus/hypotheca 39–43. *See also* Roman law (*Corpus Iuris Civilis*), *pignus/hypotheca*
purchase contract distinguished 191
purchase in shop open to public, relevance 356
requirements. *See also* agreement that title should pass ('real agreement'), need for *above*

transfer of ownership/title (cont.)
  causa traditionis (titel) 201, 238, 456, 504, 552–553
  consent, sufficiency 181, 186, 189–190, 198, 223–224, 226–227, 235, 236, 261, 271–272, 475
  delivery of movable. See delivery, relevance
  intention to acquire (animus accipiendi dominii) 275–276
  intention to transfer (animus transferendi dominii) 275–276
  nemo plus principle 201, 209–210, 288–289, 313, 326, 330, 333–334, 345, 358–359
  payment of purchase price, relevance 172, 173, 176, 181, 186, 189–190, 198, 207, 219, 224, 252, 267, 289, 316, 321–322, 341, 356, 363: due date
  public [notarial] deed, relevance 179, 191–192, 206, 264, 356–357, 376–377
  registration. See publicity/registry
  'title' in form of contract, testamentary disposition or legal provision (causa traditionis) 174–175, 189–190, 191–192, 198, 201
  titulo y modo 191–192, 223
time of. See also delivery, relevance
  agreement as determining factor 207, 211, 223, 228, 276
  ascertainment of unascertained goods 205–206, 274–275
  conclusion of contract 46, 175–176, 189–190, 205–206, 207, 261
  convergence/divergence of practice
  delivery 215
  as gradual process/reflection of factual system 218–219, 221 n.146
  notification that goods ready for collection 205–206
  surrender of possession 205–206
  transfer to carrier 175–176, 178, 205–206, 207, 213
  transfer of warrants/bills of lading and 48, 181, 218
  US/European systems distinguished 57–58, 82–84
transposition doctrine 16–18
trust, monies subject to as collateral, 9 UCC 84

UN Convention on the Assignment of Receivables in International Trade (2001) 24–25, 667 n.66
  9 UCC and 54
UNCITRAL draft legal guide on secured transactions (2002) 24–25, 668–669
unfair terms (contra bonos mores), 418, 424, 486, 593–594. See also abuse of rights; fairness
UNIDROIT Conventions
  International Factoring (1988) 25–26, 551 n.55
  International Financial Leasing (1988) 25–26, 605 n.24
  International Interests in Mobile Equipment (2001) 25–26, 529–530
    9 UCC and 54
    incorporation/choice of means 667–668
    intention to defraud/prejudice other creditors, effect 529–530
    international registry 59
    Protocol on Matters Specific to Aircraft Equipment (2001) 25–26
United States of America (USA)
  federal/state responsibilities 60
  Restatement of the Law of Suretyship and Guaranty 56–57
  UCC
    9 UCC. See 9 UCC
    enactment by states, need for 60, 62, 63
    history and context: revision of articles other than Article 9 60–61, 62
    structure and coverage 61–62
unjust enrichment
  bona fide acquisition 302
  bona fide payment of debt to insolvent and 179–180
  charge of money claims 545
  contract voided for fraud and 230–231, 232, 241–242
  as in personam right 232
  new goods manufactured out of materials supplied (specificatio) and 389
  proceeds clause (extended reservation of title) 333, 401

resale of cars supplied on credit for that purpose 333, 475–476
reversion of title/ownership and 173
security assignment of earnings 534, 537, 538, 545
usury 496, 501, 579, 582

Verlängerter Eigentumsvorbehalt. *See* proceeds clause (extended reservation of title)
vindication. *See rei vindicatio*
Voet, Johannes (1647–1713) 43–44
  Scottish law and 45–46

waiver of debtor protection, 9 UCC 78–79
warrant
  car accessories, exclusion 491
  fixed charge compared 493
  professionals, limitation to 490–491
  publicity/registry 490–491
  stock-in-trade as collateral for non-possessory security right 490–491, 493
  third-party rights 490–491
  types of warrant 10–11, 490–491
warrant (bill of lading), charge on as non-possessory security 48

For EU product safety concerns, contact us at Calle de José Abascal, 56–1°, 28003 Madrid, Spain or eugpsr@cambridge.org.